Lecture Notes in Computer Science 16903

The series Lecture Notes in Computer Science (LNCS), including its subseries Lecture Notes in Artificial Intelligence (LNAI) and Lecture Notes in Bioinformatics (LNBI), has established itself as a medium for the publication of new developments in computer science and information technology research, teaching, and education.

LNCS enjoys close cooperation with the computer science R & D community, the series counts many renowned academics among its volume editors and paper authors, and collaborates with prestigious societies. Its mission is to serve this international community by providing an invaluable service, mainly focused on the publication of conference and workshop proceedings and postproceedings. LNCS commenced publication in 1973.

Peter Kieseberg · Florian Skopik · Buse Atli ·
Mikael Asplund
Editors

Availability, Reliability and Security

ARES 2026 EU Projects Symposium Workshops

Linköping, Sweden, August 24–27, 2026
Proceedings

Springer

Editors
Peter Kieseberg
St. Pölten University of Applied Sciences
St. Pölten, Austria

Florian Skopik
Austrian Institute of Technology
Vienna, Austria

Buse Atli
Linköping University
Linköping, Sweden

Mikael Asplund
Linköping University
Linköping, Sweden

ISSN 0302-9743 ISSN 1611-3349 (electronic)
Lecture Notes in Computer Science
ISBN 978-3-032-37217-8 ISBN 978-3-032-37218-5 (eBook)
https://doi.org/10.1007/978-3-032-37218-5

This Springer imprint is published by the registered company Springer Nature Switzerland AG
The registered company address is: Gewerbestrasse 11, 6330 Cham, Switzerland

ARES EU Projects Symposium Workshops 2026 Foreword

Alongside the main track of the 21st International Conference on Availability, Reliability and Security (ARES), the EU Projects Symposium again provided an outlet for academic research, organized and thematically shaped by European Projects. This year, the symposium hosted a total of six workshops, spanning a large diversity of topics and fields in the area of IT Security. These workshops collectively received 111 paper submissions, of which 38 were accepted for publication and presentation at ARES 2026, resulting in an acceptance rate below 34%. All submissions that were not desk-rejected underwent a rigorous double-blind peer-review process, with each receiving a minimum of three independent reviews by members of the respective technical program committees (TPCs). In cases where conflicts of interests with the workshop organizers arose, the ARES organizing committee took responsibility for assigning alternative reviewers and managing the final decision process to ensure impartiality and fairness.

As the chairs of the EU Symposium workshops, we are pleased to see how these workshops have been shaped into vibrant platforms for focused discussion and dynamic exchange, reflecting the breadth and depth of ongoing research in numerous EU-funded projects. The diversity of topics and the engagement of participants contribute meaningfully to the overarching goals of the ARES conference and highlight the importance of continued collaboration across disciplines and institutions.

We would like to take this opportunity to express our sincere gratitude to all the workshop organizers for their dedication and commitment, from initial proposal submission through review coordination and to final session delivery. Organizing a workshop is no small task, and your efforts have been essential to the success of this year's program. A special word of appreciation goes to the TPC members, who, often under significant time pressure, provided thoughtful, thorough, and constructive reviews. Your contributions, regardless of whether a paper was ultimately accepted or not, helped authors improve their work and ensured that the proceedings uphold the high standards that the ARES community expects. Your efforts play a crucial role in maintaining the academic rigor and vitality of both the workshops and the wider ARES conference community

August 2026

Peter Kieseberg
Florian Skopik

ARES EU Projects Symposium Workshops 2026 Organization

General Chair

Mikael Asplund	Linköping University, Sweden

EU Projects Symposium Workshop Chairs

Peter Kieseberg	St. Pölten University of Applied Sciences, Austria
Florian Skopik	Austrian Institute of Technology AIT, Austria
Buse Atli	Linköping University, Sweden

Workshop Chairs

Aida Akbarzadeh	Norwegian University of Science and Technology, Norway
Giuseppe Bianchi	Consorzio Nazionale Interuniversitario per le Telecomunicazioni, Italy
Pascal Bisson	Thales, France
Krzysztof Cabaj	Warsaw University of Technology, Poland
Valentina Casola	University of Naples Federico II, Italy
Aristeidis Farao	InQbit Innovations SRL, Romania
Jan Hajny	Brno University of Technology, Czech Republic
Sebastian Heil	Chemnitz University of Technology, Germany
Georgios Kavallieratos	Norwegian University of Science and Technology, Norway
Pavel Loutocky	Masaryk University, Czech Republic
Lukas Malina	Brno University of Technology, Czech Republic
Wissam Mallouli	Montimage, France
Raimundas Matulevičius	University of Tartu, Estonia
Wojciech Mazurczyk	Warsaw University of Technology, Poland/FernUniversität in Hagen, Germany
Rocco De Nicola	IMT School for Advanced Studies Lucca, Italy
Edgardo Montes de Oca	Montimage, France
Sara Ricci	Brno University of Technology, Czech Republic

Georgios Spathoulas	Norwegian University of Science and Technology, Norway
Christos Xenakis	University of Piraeus, Greece
Ilsun You	Kookmin University, South Korea
Apostolis Zarras	Foundation for Research Technology – Hellas, Greece

IWAPS 2026 Preface

The 6th International Workshop on Advances on Security and Privacy Technologies and Solutions (IWAPS 2026) aimed to advance secure, privacy-preserving, and trustworthy AI systems by fostering research and practical solutions for next-generation cyber-resilient architectures. The workshop addressed a broad spectrum of topics including advanced cyber-defense strategies, large-scale data analytics and fusion platforms, secure protocols and services, adversarial robustness, federated learning, confidential computation, differential privacy, trustworthy model deployment, and privacy-enhancing technologies for IoT and cyber-physical systems. It also explicitly encouraged multi-disciplinary work at the intersection of technology, policy, regulation, ethics, human-centered security, and societal impact in order to shape the future roadmap for secure and trustworthy AI systems.

August 2026

Christos Xenakis
Aristeidis Farao
Apostolis Zarras

IWAPS 2026 Organization

Workshop Chairs

Christos Xenakis	University of Piraeus, Greece
Aristeidis Farao	InQbit Innovations SRL, Romania
Apostolis Zarras	University of Piraeus & Foundation for Research & Technology – Hellas, Greece

Program Committee

Vaios Bolgouras	UniSystems, Greece
Ioannis Stylianou	University of Piraeus, Greece
Anastassios Voudouris	University of Piraeus, Greece
Michail Bampatsikos	University of Piraeus, Greece
Ioannis Chouchoulis	InQbit Innovations SRL, Romania
Panagiotis Bountakas	Sphynx Technology Solutions AG, Greece
Ioannis Makropodis	InQbit Innovations SRL, Romania
Kostas Giapantzis	InQbit Innovations SRL, Romania
Cristina Alcaraz	University of Malaga, Spain
Iman Hasnaouia Meskini	University of Malaga, Spain
Panagiotis Radoglou-Grammatikis	University of Western Macedonia, Greece, K3Y Ltd, Bulgaria

ENS 2026 Preface

It is our great pleasure to introduce research papers presented at the 9th International Workshop on Emerging Network Security (ENS 2026), co-located with the 21st International Conference on Availability, Reliability and Security (ARES 2026). The conference was held in Linköping, Sweden from August 24 to August 27, 2026.

The ENS 2026 workshop focused on presenting recent scientific and industry developments in tools and methodologies for threat detection, vulnerability assessment, and incident response across all types of emerging networks. Grounded in the philosophy of security-by-design, the workshop aimed to explore resilient systems engineering from the hardware level (e.g., RISC-V and FPGA) up to the software and cloud layers. A central theme of this edition was the role of Artificial Intelligence and Machine Learning as a double-edged sword: both as powerful tools for predictive analytics and anomaly detection, and as a source of novel, automated threats. ENS 2026 served as an interdisciplinary forum for researchers and practitioners to share innovative methods for protecting digital infrastructures, including energy, telecommunications, and research networks, explore Explainable AI (XAI) and trustworthy ML models that allow human analysts to interpret and validate automated security decisions, bridge the gap between academia, industry, and security operations centers (SOCs) to foster a secure and trustworthy digital society, and address the evolving landscape of privacy, ethics, and regulatory frameworks, such as EU technological sovereignty and cybersecurity standards.

This year ENS received 10 submissions, of which 50% were accepted. Each paper was peer-reviewed by our experts from the Technical Program Committee (TPC) and, each received three reviews. This year, our TPC consisted of eleven experts from four countries (France, Italy, Poland, and the UK). The whole review process was conducted using double-blind methodology and assisted by five Workshop Chairs.

August 2026

Pascal Bisson
Krzysztof Cabaj
Wojciech Mazurczyk
Edgaro Montes de Oca
Ilsun You

ENS 2026 Organization

Workshop Chairs

Pascal Bisson	Thales, France
Krzysztof Cabaj	Warsaw University of Technology, Poland
Wojciech Mazurczyk	Warsaw University of Technology, Poland
Edgaro Montes de Oca	Montimage, France
Ilsun You	Kookmin University, South Korea

Program Committee

Grzegorz Blinowski	Warsaw University of Technology, Poland
Daniele Bringhenti	Politecnico di Torino, Italy
Luca Caviglione	IMATI CNR, Italy
Michał Choraś	ITTI Ltd., Poland
Gilles Guett	IMT Atlantique, France
Zbigniew Kotulski	Warsaw University of Technology, Poland
Rafał Kozik	Bydgoszcz University of Science and Technology, Poland
Marek Pawlicki	Bydgoszcz University of Science and Technology, Poland
Paweł Rajba	University of Wrocław, Poland
Leonardo Regano	Università degli Studi di Cagliari, Italy
Stavros Shiaeles	University of Portsmouth, UK

ETACS/STRAI 2026 Preface

This volume contains the proceedings of the International Workshop on Education, Training, and Awareness in Cybersecurity & Secure, Trustworthy, and Robust AI (ETACS/STRAI), held in conjunction with the 21st International Conference on Availability, Reliability and Security (ARES 2026) in Linköping, Sweden, on August 24–27, 2026. ETACS/STRAI 2026 combined the 6th Workshop on Education, Training and Awareness in Cybersecurity (ETACS) and the 2nd International Workshop on Secure, Trustworthy, and Robust AI (STRAI), bringing together researchers, practitioners, industry, government, and EU agencies to discuss current challenges and solutions in cybersecurity education, training, awareness, and trustworthy artificial intelligence.

ETACS seeks novel submissions from academia, government, as well as industry contributing to cybersecurity education, training and awareness. The focus is on practical research into higher-education cybersecurity curricula, professional training, building of cyber ranges and their coalitions across Europe, methods to assess and raise awareness in cybersecurity, the implementation of systems, and lessons learned. Furthermore, the EU-wide agreement on the identification of skills necessary for cybersecurity work roles is one of the main interests of the workshop.

The increasing use of AI systems creates concerns about security, privacy, and trust. The security risks for AI systems, the privacy implications stemming from their use, and the requirements for human-to-machine and machine-to-machine trust establishment and management are highly critical topics requiring concrete methodologies and solutions. The wide adoption of AI systems necessitates urgent advancements in AI security, trustworthiness, and robustness. STRAI provides a forum for researchers, engineers, and governmental actors to discuss these challenges and present novel approaches to secure, trustworthy, and robust AI.

The ETACS papers included in this volume were selected through a double-blind peer-review process. Each submission was reviewed by at least three reviewers, with a total of 19 reviewers participating in the evaluation process. Chairs and Program Committee members with conflicts of interest were excluded from reviewer assignment, reviews, and decisions. Six papers were submitted to ETACS 2026, of which three were accepted. STRAI 2026 attracted five high-quality submissions, each assigned to three independent reviewers. Following the review process, two papers were accepted for presentation and publication in these proceedings. Chairs and Program Committee members had no involvement with or visibility of the review process for submissions authored or co-authored by them.

ETACS was supported by the European Union under Grant Agreement No. 101087529 CHESS and by the European Commission under Grant Agreement No. 101120657, while STRAI was supported by European Lighthouse to Manifest Trustworthy and Green AI (ENFIELD). Views and opinions expressed are, however, those of the authors only and do not necessarily reflect those of the European Union, the European Research Executive Agency, or the European Commission. Neither the European Union nor the granting authorities can be held responsible for them.

We would like to thank all authors for submitting their work, the members of the Program Committees for their timely and rigorous reviews, and the ARES Workshop Chairs and Organizers for their continuous support. Their contributions made it possible to assemble an interesting and high-quality workshop program and these proceedings.

August 2026

Jan Hajny
Georgios Spathoulas
Georgios Kavallieratos
Aida Akbarzadeh
Sebastian Heil

ETACS/STRAI 2026 Organization

Workshop Chairs

Jan Hajny	Brno University of Technology
Pavel Loutocky	Masaryk University, Czech Republic
Giuseppe Bianchi	Consorzio Nazionale Interuniversitario per le Teleco-municazioni, Italy
Rocco De Nicola	IMT School for Advanced Studies Lucca, Italy
Sara Ricci	Brno University of Technology, Czech Republic
Aida Akbarzadeh	Norwegian University of Science and Technology, Norway
Georgios Kavallieratos	Norwegian University of Science and Technology, Norway
Georgios Spathoulas	Norwegian University of Science and Technology, Norway
Sebastian Heil	Chemnitz University of Technology, Germany

Program Committee

Pedro Adao	University of Lisbon, Portugal
Rémi Badonnel	University of Lorraine, France
Yianna Danidou	European University Cyprus, Cyprus
Petr Dzurenda	Brno University of Technology, Czechia
Letterio Galletta	IMT Lucca, Italy
Magdalena Glas	University of Regensburg, Germany
František Kasl	Masaryk University, Czechia
Imre Lendak	University of Novi Sad, Serbia Eövös Loránd University, Hungary
Olivier Levillain	Télécom SudParis, France
Raimundas Matulevičius	University of Tartu, Estonia
Marc Ohm	University of Bonn & Fraunhofer FKIE, Germany
Edmundas Piesarskas	Lithuanian Cybercrime Center of Excellence for Training, Research & Education, Lithuania
Paolo Prinetto	CINI - Cybersecurity National Lab, Italy
Joseph Squillance	Penn State University, USA
Tanja Zseby	Vienna University of Technology, Austria

Aida Akbarzadeh	Norwegian University of Science and Technology, Norway
Abubaker Gaber	Chemnitz University of Technology, Germany
Sebastian Heil	Chemnitz University of Technology, Germany
Sandeep Pirbhulal	Norwegian Computing Center, Norway
Sokratis Katsikas	Norwegian University of Science and Technology, Norway
Georgios Spathoulas	Norwegian University of Science and Technology, Norway
Georgios Kavallieratos	Norwegian University of Science and Technology, Norway

Additional Reviewers

Nektaria Kaloudi
Sushma Venkatesh
Chhagan Lal
Athanasia Kollarou
Vyron Kampourakis
Abdoul Aziz Maiga

SP2I 2026 Preface

Recent years have seen the proliferation of Intelligent Infrastructures (IIs) in domains such as the internet of vehicles, industrial IoT, cyber manifacturing, e-healthcare, smart city services, smart grids, smart home applications. Intelligent Infrastructure services consist of layers that capture, exchange and analyse data as well as invoke autonomic responses, sometimes supported by emerging Artificial Intelligence (AI) systems. The goal of IIs is a higher level of convenience for mankind, but with those promises have come privacy and security issues and concerns. Therefore, increasing security and privacy by designing new efficient solutions is an important research direction. Moreover, quantum-resistant security and the connection of privacy to the law are also important research topics nowadays.

The 6th International Workshop on Security and Privacy in Intelligent Infrastructures (SP2I 2026) was organised in conjunction with the ARES conference, to be held on 24–27 August 2026. The SP2I 2026 workshop aimed to gather the most relevant ongoing research on privacy and security in Intelligent Infrastructures. The second goal of the workshop was to report on interdisciplinary research connecting privacy to law, formal modelling, policy and data privacy management. SP2I 2026 also served as a forum for relevant research projects to disseminate privacy- and security-related results and boost future cooperation.

The workshop attracted 13 submissions. After an in-depth review and discussion, 5 papers were accepted for publication in the workshop proceedings. Each submission was reviewed by 3 reviewers and further assessed by the workshop chairs. The workshop's reviewing process was double-blind. All chairs and program committee members with conflicts of interest were excluded from the review process, including reviewer assignments, reviews and decisions. All accepted papers had non-negative weighted-average scores, suggesting acceptance by the review process. The workshop program also included an invited talk given by Simon Hacks.

We wish to thank all those who contributed to making SP2I 2026 a success: the authors who submitted papers, the members of the Program Committee who carefully reviewed and discussed the submissions, and the speakers who presented their work at the workshop. We also express our gratitude to the ARES 2026 organisers for their support in preparing the workshop.

The workshop was supported by the European Union under Grant Agreement No. 101087529 CHESS. Views and opinions expressed are, however, those of the author(s) only and do not necessarily reflect those of the European Union or European Research Executive Agency. Neither the European Union nor the granting authority can be held responsible for them.

August 2026

Lukas Malina
Raimundas Matulevičius

SP2I 2026 Organization

Workshop Chairs

Lukas Malina	Brno University of Technology, Czech Republic
Raimundas Matulevičius	University of Tartu, Estonia

Program Committee

Jakub Breier	TTControl GmbH, Austria
Gabriele Costa	CINI, Italy
Lukaš Daubner	University of Tartu, Estonia
George Drosatos	Athena Research and Innovation Centre, Greece
Petr Dzurenda	Brno University of Technology, Czech Republic
Alireza Esfahani	University of West London, UK
Lothar Fritsch	Oslo Metropolitan University, Norway
Simon Hacks	Stockholm University, Sweden
Jan Hajny	Brno University of Technology, Czech Republic
Xiaolu Hou	Slovak University of Technology, Slovakia
Mubashar Iqbal	University of Tartu, Estonia
Alireza Jolfaei	Flinders University, Australia
Liina Kamm	Cybernetica, Estonia
Maryline Laurent	Institut Mines-Télécom, France
Pavel Loutocky	Masaryk University, Czech Republic
Zdenek Martinasek	Brno University of Technology, Czech Republic
Jakub Misek	Masaryk University, Czech Republic
Aleksandr Ometov	Tampere University, Finland
Sara Ricci	Brno University of Technology, Czech Republic
Branka Stojanovic	Joanneum Research, Austria
Aimilia Tasidou	CESI LINEACT, France
Luca Verderame	University of Genoa, Italy

Additional Reviewers

Sedat Akleylek
Patrik Dobias
Adelen Festin
Willi Lazarov
Kubra Seyhan
Jelizaveta Vakarjuk

STAM 2026 Preface

The 6th International Workshop on Security Testing and Monitoring (STAM 2026) was held in conjunction with the 21st International Conference on Availability, Reliability and Security (ARES 2026). STAM provides an international forum for researchers, practitioners, and industry experts to present and discuss the latest advances in security testing, security monitoring, vulnerability assessment, penetration testing, cyber threat detection, AI-driven cybersecurity, and security evaluation methodologies for emerging computing systems and critical infrastructures.

The workshop aimed to foster collaboration between academia and industry by bringing together novel research contributions, practical experiences, and innovative tools addressing the challenges of securing modern digital ecosystems, including cloud and edge computing, IoT, cyber-physical systems, software-defined infrastructures, and AI-enabled applications.

This year, STAM received 18 paper submissions from researchers across the world. Each submission underwent a rigorous peer-review process involving at least three expert reviewers from the Technical Program Committee. Following careful evaluation based on originality, technical quality, relevance, significance, and presentation, 9 papers were accepted for publication in the workshop proceedings, resulting in an acceptance rate of 50%.

The accepted papers cover a broad spectrum of topics including AI-assisted penetration testing, firmware security, DevSecOps, healthcare cybersecurity, attack emulation, moving target defense, security auditing, and cybersecurity for critical infrastructures.

The workshop chairs would like to express their sincere gratitude to all authors for submitting their work, to the members of the Program Committee for their valuable reviews and constructive feedback, and to the ARES 2026 Organizing Committee for their continuous support in organizing the workshop.

August 2026

Valentina Casola
Wissam Mallouli

STAM 2026 Organization

Workshop Chairs

Valentina Casola	University of Naples Federico II, Italy
Wissam Mallouli	Montimage, France

Program Committee

Andrey Sadovykh	Softeam, France
Umberto Villano	University of Sannio, Italy
Edgardo Montes de Oca	Montimage, France
Nicolas Ferry	Université Côte d'Azur, France
Umberto Barbato	University of Campania "L. Vanvitelli", Italy
Daniele Iorio	University of Naples Federico II, Italy
Ana Rosa Cavalli	Institut Polytechnique de Paris/Télécom SudParis, France
Francesco Grimaldi	Università degli Studi di Napoli Federico II, Italy
Erkuden Rios	Tecnalia, Spain
Francesco Vitale	Università degli Studi di Napoli Federico II, Italy
Felice Moretta	University of Campania "L. Vanvitelli", Italy
Kitty Kioskli	trustilio BV, Netherlands
Eider Iturbe	Tecnalia, Spain
Martin Schneider	Fraunhofer FOKUS, Germany
Massimiliano Rak	University of Naples Federico II, Italy
Charalambos Klitis	EBOS Technologies Ltd, Cyprus
Alessandra Bagnato	Softeam, France
Alessandra De Benedictis	University of Naples Federico II, Italy
Gürkan Gür	Zurich University of Applied Sciences, Switzerland
Flora Amato	University of Naples Federico II, Italy
Mario Barbareschi	University of Naples Federico II, Italy

Contents

Proceedings of the Sixth International Workshop on Advances on Security and Privacy Technologies and Solutions (IWAPS 2026)

Physics-Informed Generative AI-Framework for Secure Anomaly Detection in Class-Imbalanced Industrial Control Systems

Veysel Alevcan[1,4], Urvashi Chaudhary[1], Yakubu Tsado[2], Zehra Civan[3], Mohammad Furqan Ali[1(✉)], and Luís Miguel Campos[1,4]

[1] INSEC INOV-Lab, Lusófona University, 1000-029 Lisbon, Portugal
{a22300943,a22408492}@alunos.ulht.pt,
{p8243,luis.miguel.campos}@ulusofona.pt

[2] Manchester Metropolitan University, Manchester, UK
y.tsado@mmu.ac.uk

[3] Fenerbahçe University, Istanbul, Turkey
zehra.civan@fbu.edu.tr

[4] PDMFC SA Project Development and Consulting, Lisbon, Portugal
{veysel.alevcan,luis.campos}@pdmfc.com

Abstract. Anomaly detection in Industrial Control Systems (ICS) is critically undermined by severe class imbalance as in SWaT and HAI, normal samples outnumber attacks by ratios exceeding 100:1, collapsing standard models toward the majority class and producing dangerously low attack recall. This imbalance is compounded by physical ICS telemetry constraints, including hydraulic dependencies, temporal correlations, and bounded operational ranges, that generic oversampling methods such as SMOTE cannot faithfully reproduce. We present a physics-aware data augmentation framework based on Wasserstein GAN with Gradient Penalty (WGAN-GP), evaluated on two ICS benchmarks: SWaT (water treatment) and HAI (power grid). The generator enforces physical plausibility through bounded `tanh` activations and max-norm weight regularization. An autoencoder-based anomaly detector is trained under three controlled configurations (real data only, real augmented with WGAN-GP synthetic samples, and synthetic only), isolating the augmentation contribution with recall as the primary safety metric. A secondary contribution is an IQR-based adaptive thresholding mechanism that self-calibrates to false-positive feedback, eliminating manual tuning across heterogeneous industrial environments. On SWaT, WGAN-GP augmentation raises attack recall from 19.6% to 77.5% and accuracy from 78.3% to 91.1%. On HAI, all metrics exceed 92%. These results confirm that physics-aware generative augmentation is a principled, deployable solution to class imbalance in safety-critical ICS environments.

Keywords: Anomaly detection · Class imbalance · Data augmentation · Industrial control systems · WGAN-GP

P. Kieseberg et al. (Eds.): ARES 2026 Workshops, LNCS 16903, pp. 3–14, 2027.
https://doi.org/10.1007/978-3-032-37218-5_1

1 Introduction

Industrial Control Systems (ICS), including water treatment plants, power grid controllers, and manufacturing automation, represent some of the most security-critical infrastructure in modern society. The convergence of Operational Technology (OT) with IP-connected networks has expanded the attack surface of these systems dramatically, making anomaly detection a fundamental defensive mechanism [1]. Yet effective anomaly detection for ICS is systematically constrained by a data-level problem: *severe class imbalance*. In the SWaT water treatment dataset fewer than 1% of records are attacks; in HAI the figure is approximately 3.2%. A model trained on such distributions will, by construction, optimize for the majority class, producing high accuracy while catastrophically failing to detect attacks. Standard remedies (cost-sensitive learning, threshold adjustment, and Synthetic Minority Over-sampling (SMOTE) and its variants) transfer poorly to ICS and IIoT telemetry because sensor readings are not independently distributed. A water treatment plant's flow rate, pressure, and valve state at time t are causally linked to readings at $t-1, \ldots, t-k$ through hydraulic dynamics. SMOTE-interpolated samples may be individually plausible but jointly violate physical process constraints [2]. Standard GANs trained on imbalanced ICS data suffer from two failure modes: training instability under sparse minority classes and mode collapse that further reduces attack pattern diversity.

Wasserstein GAN with Gradient Penalty (WGAN-GP) addresses both by replacing the Jensen-Shannon divergence with the Wasserstein-1 distance, providing non-vanishing gradients even when distributions have minimal overlap [3]. The gradient penalty enforces Lipschitz continuity without weight clipping, and bounded `tanh` output activation together with max-norm weight regularization keeps synthetic samples within the physical operational envelope. This is necessary to maintain the validity of ICS telemetry because random interpolation used in standard oversampling often leads to physically impossible results. Through embedding the generative procedure within these physical laws, WGAN-GP could generate minority class instances which are both statistically varied and practically relevant. Apart from the issue of data scarcity, there is another problem related to practical anomaly detection which is due to the sensitivity of threshold values. In fact, most approaches rely on a fixed value for T determined via a training phase carried out in a controlled environment. But the actual environment of ICS undergoes sensor drifts, seasonal changes, and mode shifts, which create false alarm fatigue in operators. Therefore, we propose a novel adaptive threshold approach based on Inter-quartile range (IQR).

The system self-regulates based on the information obtained from false positive ratios, making sure that the threshold between normal and abnormal behaviors can be adjusted accordingly to maintain high accuracy without requiring continuous human supervision. The validity of the proposed solution is proven through the experiment that consists of three configurations, which allows us to understand the effect of data augmentation on the results. We compare three sets of models: one model trained only using real data, another model trained using real data and synthetic data, and another model using only synthetic data. Physics-informed WGAN-GP synthetic data plays an important role in helping the models become more effective. Our approach is tested using two datasets: the Secure Water Treatment (SWaT) and HIL-based Augmented ICS (HAI).

This work investigates to what extent WGAN-GP augmentation improves anomaly detection on physically constrained, class-imbalanced ICS datasets. We evaluate three configurations on SWaT and HAI: real only (Config. A), real + WGAN-GP (Config. B), and synthetic only (Config. C), deliberately excluding general-purpose datasets where sensor interdependencies do not constrain generation quality.

The main contributions of this study are:

1. **Physics-constrained WGAN-GP augmentation** via bounded output activations and max-norm regularization.
2. **Controlled three-configuration evaluation** isolating the augmentation contribution with recall as the primary safety metric.
3. **Interquartile range (IQR)-based adaptive thresholding** that self-calibrates to false-positive feedback, enabling cross-environment deployment.

The remainder of this paper is organised as follows. Section 2 reviews related work on ICS anomaly detection and GAN-based data augmentation, identifying the gap this study addresses. Section 3 describes the proposed methodology, covering data preprocessing, the WGAN-GP architecture with physical constraint enforcement, the autoencoder-based anomaly detector, and the IQR-based adaptive thresholding mechanism. Section 4 defines the three-configuration experimental protocol and evaluation metrics. Section 5 presents and discusses the results on SWaT and HAI. Section 6 concludes the paper and outlines directions for future work.

2 Related Work

Autoencoder-based reconstruction-error methods have demonstrated strong performance on physically constrained ICS benchmarks, establishing reconstruction loss as the dominant unsupervised scoring signal for tabular sensor telemetry. The efficacy of the AE framework in ICS systems is based on its ability to learn an efficient representation of normal states. Through minimizing the reconstruction error with respect to benign telemetry, the AE models construct a threshold that can distinguish any deviations caused by cyber physical attacks [5]. This reconstruction error represents a key unsupervised metric for tabular sensor telemetry [6]. Additionally, the class imbalance becomes highly significant in domains where attacks form a very limited set in the entire data set available. Traditional learning techniques such as KNN and SVM show poor detection capabilities on imbalanced data sets [7]. The Generative Adversarial Network (GAN) is an improvement because it models the distribution from which the data is generated [10]. Specifically, the WGAN-GP can be used successfully to analyze multivariate time-series data. The use of the Wasserstein distance in such a model allows maintaining a stable gradient even if the real and generated distributions are far apart and hence solving issues associated with training instability and mode collapse [11]. As a result, WGAN-GP showed its potential in generating highly realistic data that was previously inaccessible due to limitations related to anomaly data. WGAN-GP was able to convert the limited amount of data into the one that could be used in training a classifier of high accuracy [8]. Recently, the efficiency of WGAN-GP was tested in comparison with vanilla GAN objectives [9].

There are few prior studies provide a focused, reproducible evaluation of WGAN-GP augmentation on *physically constrained* ICS datasets with explicit class-imbalance analysis. Existing WGAN studies evaluate on generic benchmarks or single-dataset scenarios without isolating the augmentation contribution. The present work fills this gap directly by providing the first controlled, three-configuration evaluation of WGAN-GP augmentation on two physically constrained ICS benchmarks, isolating the contribution of generative augmentation to recall improvement under severe class imbalance, and introducing an IQR-based adaptive threshold that removes the need for manual calibration across heterogeneous industrial environments.

3 The Proposed WGAN-GP Methodology

The framework contains the four sequential phases as follows; 1) Data preprocessing, 2) WGAN-GP synthetic data generation, 3) Autoencoder-based anomaly detection and 4) Adaptive thresholding. The whole proposed end-to-end pipeline is depicted by Fig. 1.

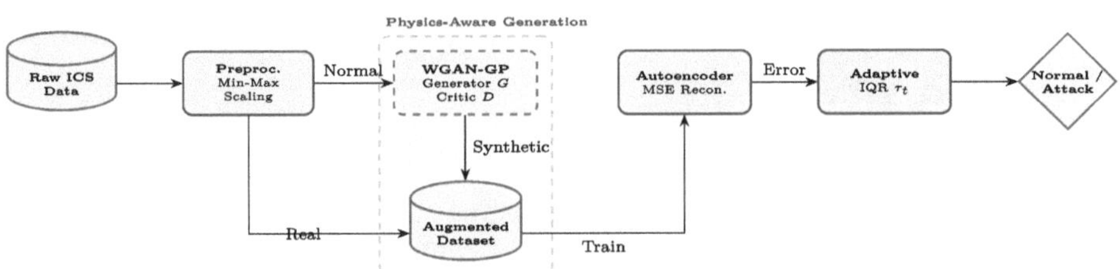

Fig. 1. WGAN-GP augmentation pipeline. Imbalanced ICS telemetry is normalized; WGAN-GP synthesizes physics-constrained attack samples; the augmented dataset trains an autoencoder classified by an adaptive IQR threshold.

3.1 Data Preprocessing

The two ICS benchmarks used in this study are summarized in Table 1. SWaT [12]: ≈495,000 normal and 4,230 attack records from a water treatment testbed with strong inter-sensor hydraulic dependencies (attack ratio <1%).

HAI [13]: ≈530,200 normal and 17,520 attack records from a power grid testbed with temporally correlated false data injection attacks (attack ratio ≈3.2%).

Timestamps were decomposed into cyclic components (day, hour, minute, second); near-zero-variance features (threshold $< 10^{-9}$) were removed; all features were Min-Max normalized to $[-1, 1]$. The scaler was fitted exclusively on the training split. The original train-test splits defined by the respective benchmark providers were preserved throughout all experiments.

Table 1. Dataset characteristics.

Dataset	Normal	Attack	Atk.%	Context
SWaT	495,000	4,230	<1%	Water treatment
HAI	530,200	17,520	3.2%	Power grid

3.2 WGAN-GP for Physics-Constrained Synthetic Generation

Wasserstein Distance and Gradient Penalty. WGAN-GP replaces the Jensen-Shannon divergence with the Wasserstein-1 distance [3]:

$$W(p_r, p_g) = \sup_{\|f\|_L \leq 1} \mathbb{E}_{x \sim p_r}[f(x)] - \mathbb{E}_{\tilde{x} \sim p_g}[f(\tilde{x})], \quad (1)$$

providing non-vanishing gradients when distributions have minimal overlap. The gradient penalty [4] enforces Lipschitz continuity without weight clipping:

$$\mathcal{L}_{\text{WGAN-GP}} = \underbrace{\mathbb{E}[D(x)] - \mathbb{E}[D(G(z))]}_{\text{Wasserstein estimate}} + \underbrace{\lambda\,\mathbb{E}_{\hat{x}}\left[(\|\nabla_{\hat{x}} D(\hat{x})\|_2 - 1)^2\right]}_{\text{Gradient penalty}}, \quad (2)$$

where $\hat{x} = \alpha x + (1-\alpha)G(z)$, $\alpha \sim \mathcal{U}(0,1)$, $\lambda = 10$, and a stabilizer $\epsilon = 10^{-10}$ prevents division-by-zero.

Generator with Physical Constraint Enforcement. The generator G maps $z \in \mathbb{R}^{100}$ from $\mathcal{N}(0, I)$ to $\tilde{x} \in \mathbb{R}^d$ through a feedforward network ($128 \to 256 \to 512$) with ReLU activations and He normal initialization. Two design choices enforce physical plausibility: (i) **Bounded** tanh **output** constrains synthetic sensor values to $[-1, 1]$, matching the Min-Max normalized range; (ii) **Max-norm regularization** (bound 0.5) promotes smooth latent-to-observation mappings, supporting temporal coherence. The critic uses a symmetric $512 \to 256 \to 1$ structure with a linear (unbounded) output. Full hyperparameters are given in Table 2.

Table 2. WGAN-GP architecture and hyperparameters.

Parameter	Value
Latent dimension z	100
Generator layers	$128 \to 256 \to 512 \to d_{\text{out}}$
Critic layers	$512 \to 256 \to 1$
Activation (hidden / output G)	ReLU / `tanh`
Weight init.	He Normal (hidden), Glorot (output)
Max-norm constraint	0.5
Gradient penalty λ	10
Critic updates n_{critic}	5
Optimizer / learning rate	Adam / 5×10^{-5}
β_1, β_2	0.5, 0.9
Gradient clip norm / batch size	1.0 / 32
Training epochs (active / total)	500 / 800

3.3 Autoencoder-Based Anomaly Detector

WGAN-GP synthetic samples augment the minority class, yielding $\mathcal{D}_{\text{aug}} = \mathcal{D}_{\text{normal}} \cup \tilde{\mathcal{D}}_{\text{synthetic}}$. An autoencoder ($d_{\text{in}} \to 64 \to 32 \to 64 \to d_{\text{in}}$) with ReLU hidden activations and a linear output is trained on normal data only (Adam, MSE loss). At inference, the anomaly score is the per-sample reconstruction error:

$$s(x) = \|x - \hat{x}\|_2^2. \tag{3}$$

Attack samples deviate from the learned normal manifold, producing disproportionately high scores.

3.4 IQR-Based Adaptive Anomaly Detection Threshold

The adaptive threshold at step t is:

$$\tau_t = Q_3 + 1.5 \cdot \text{IQR} \cdot \left(1 + \frac{1 - S_t}{S_t}\right), \qquad S_t = 0.9 - 0.1 \cdot \frac{FP_t}{FP_t + TN_t}, \tag{4}$$

where Q_3 and $\text{IQR} = Q_3 - Q_1$ are computed on normal validation reconstruction errors, and FP_t, TN_t denote false positives and true negatives at step t. The base term $Q_3 + 1.5 \cdot \text{IQR}$ is the classical Tukey outer fence; in an approximately normal distribution this boundary encapsulates roughly 99.3% of data variance, systematically filtering benign hydraulic noise and minor sensor fluctuations without domain-specific tuning. As FP_t increases, S_t falls below 0.9, raising τ_t and suppressing spurious alarms. At $t = 1$, τ is initialized at the 95th percentile of normal validation errors. The decision mechanism functions as a binary classifier: samples with $s(x) > \tau_t$ are flagged as *Attack*; otherwise classified as *Normal*.

4 Experimental Setup

Three configurations isolate the augmentation contribution:

Config. A (Real Only): Autoencoder trained on real normal data.
Config. B (Real+WGAN-GP): Autoencoder trained on real data augmented with WGAN-GP synthetic samples. Proposed method.
Config. C (Synthetic Only): Autoencoder trained exclusively on WGAN-GP-generated samples; no real training data.

All configurations share the identical autoencoder, preprocessing, and adaptive threshold; only training data composition differs. Two classical unsupervised baselines are included: Isolation Forest, an ensemble method that scores anomalies by average path length in random partition trees, and One-Class SVM, a kernel method that constructs a maximum-margin hyperplane separating normal instances from the origin in a reproducing kernel Hilbert space. Together they cover the two dominant inductive biases in unsupervised anomaly detection, providing a broad and representative comparison against the proposed augmentation-based approach. Primary metric: Recall (missed attacks cause physical harm); secondary metrics: Accuracy, Precision, F1-Score, ROC-AUC. To ensure reproducibility, all experiments were conducted with a fixed random seed (seed = 42); results are reported as final-epoch values over a single run, consistent with the deterministic evaluation protocol of the benchmark datasets.

5 Results and Discussion

5.1 WGAN-GP Training Stability

Figure 2 shows the training loss progression on SWaT across 800 epochs. Two distinct phases are visible. In the early phase (epochs 0–150), the critic loss drops sharply from approximately 6 to near zero, while the generator loss exhibits large oscillations as the adversarial game stabilises. This rapid critic convergence reflects the Wasserstein-1 objective's ability to provide informative gradients even when the generated and real distributions have minimal overlap, the typical condition under severe class imbalance. After epoch 150, both losses enter a controlled oscillatory regime: the critic maintains near-zero values and the generator oscillates within a narrow band, confirming stable minimax equilibrium with no mode collapse. The absence of divergence throughout training validates the gradient penalty ($\lambda = 10$) as an effective Lipschitz constraint, ensuring the critic remains a well-behaved Wasserstein estimator for the full 500 active training epochs.

5.2 Anomaly Detection Performance

Table 3 presents the full comparison. Figure 3 visualizes augmentation impact on the three primary metrics.

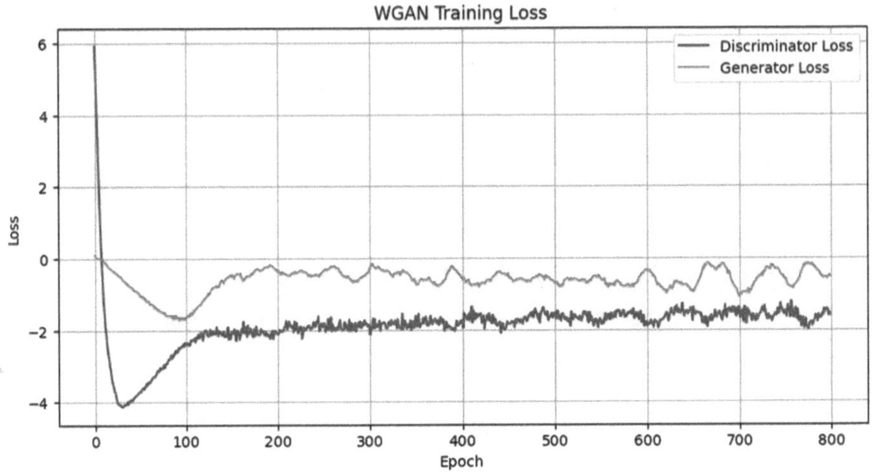

Fig. 2. WGAN-GP training loss on SWaT over 800 epochs. The critic loss drops rapidly to near zero in the early phase, then stabilises; the generator loss enters a narrow oscillatory regime confirming stable adversarial equilibrium and absence of mode collapse.

Table 3. Performance evaluation on SWaT and HAI. Config. B (proposed) rows are **bold**.

Dataset	Method / Config.	Acc.	Prec.	Recall	F1	AUC
SWaT	Isolation Forest	0.892	0.763	0.821	0.791	0.872
	One-Class SVM	0.868	0.746	0.802	0.773	0.853
	Config. A: Real	0.783	0.527	0.196	0.286	0.781
	Config. C: Synth.	0.836	0.712	0.434	0.539	0.814
	Config. B: Real+WGAN-GP	**0.911**	**0.815**	**0.775**	**0.794**	**0.876**
HAI	Isolation Forest	0.683	0.948	0.683	0.785	0.805
	One-Class SVM	0.673	0.935	0.673	0.781	0.833
	Config. A: Real	0.924	0.939	0.924	0.932	0.932
	Config. C: Synth.	0.922	0.938	0.922	0.930	0.930
	Config. B: Real+WGAN-GP	**0.927**	**0.942**	**0.927**	**0.934**	**0.934**

SWaT Analysis: Without augmentation, Config. A misses four out of every five attacks despite 78.3% accuracy, a direct consequence of the model collapsing toward the majority class under 100:1 imbalance. Config. B closes this gap, reaching 77.5% recall and 91.1% accuracy after WGAN-GP augmentation. Precision rises from 52.7% to 81.5% in parallel, indicating a genuine improvement in detection quality rather than a recall-precision trade-off. Config. C still achieves 83.6% accuracy and 43.4% recall, suggesting the generator has captured enough of the data structure to be useful even without real training samples. Isolation Forest reports higher recall (82.1% vs. 77.5%), yet Config. B leads on accuracy

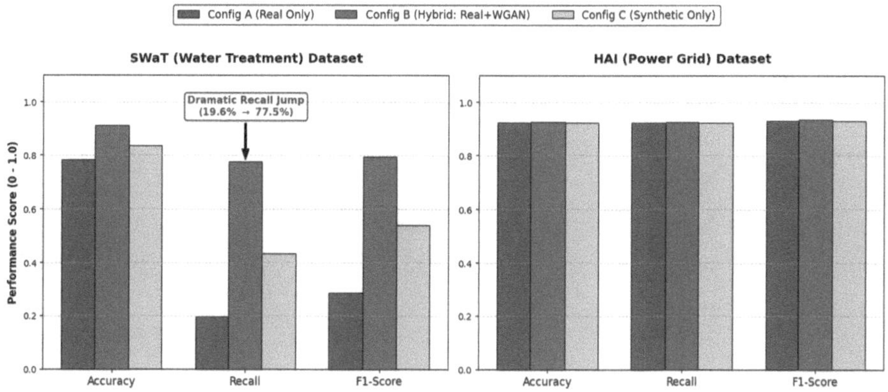

Fig. 3. Performance across the three configurations on SWaT (left) and HAI (right). On SWaT, Config. B raises recall from 19.6% to 77.5%, recovering the autoencoder to a level competitive with classical baselines.

and ROC-AUC with near-identical F1 scores (79.4% vs. 79.1%). The more relevant comparison is against Config. A: augmentation moves the autoencoder from operationally unacceptable recall to a level competitive with established baselines.

HAI Analysis: HAI's lower imbalance (3.2%) means all three configurations outperform centralized baselines by a large margin (best centralized F1 = 78.5% vs. Config. A F1 = 93.2%). Config. B leads on all metrics (Accuracy: 92.7%, F1: 93.4%, AUC: 93.4%); the marginal gain over Config. A (ΔF1 = +0.2% points) reflects lower augmentation need when the minority class is less sparse. Config. B nevertheless consistently leads, confirming it is a safe default across imbalance regimes.

5.3 Adaptive Threshold Behavior

The Fig. 4 illustrates the self-calibrating behavior under a simulated false-positive spike. When FP_t rises (for example, due to distribution shift at a new industrial site), S_t decreases, raising τ_t and suppressing alarms automatically, without operator intervention.

5.4 Augmentation Impact Summary

Table 4 quantifies Config. B vs. Config. A gains. This contrast confirms that WGAN-GP augmentation provides greatest benefit precisely where imbalance is most severe: SWaT (ratio >100:1) benefits greatly, while HAI (ratio ≈30:1) sees only marginal gains.

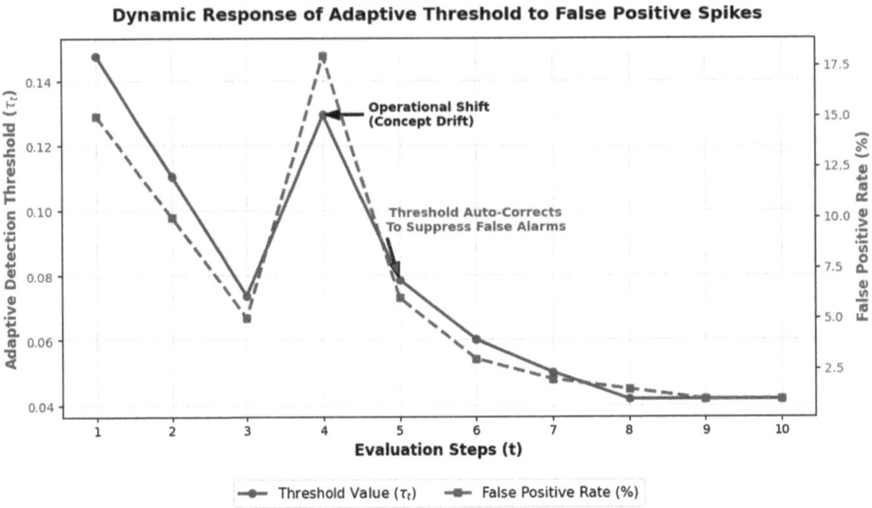

Fig. 4. Adaptive threshold response to a false-positive spike. τ_t rises automatically when FP_t increases (Eq. 4), self-calibrating without manual tuning.

Table 4. Config. B vs. Config. A: augmentation impact. pp = percentage points.

Dataset	ΔAcc.	ΔRecall	ΔF1	ΔAUC
SWaT	+16.4%	+57.9 pp	+50.9 pp	+9.4 pp
HAI	+0.3%	+0.3 pp	+0.2 pp	+0.2 pp

6 Conclusion

We presented a physics-aware WGAN-GP data augmentation framework for anomaly detection in class-imbalanced ICS environments. By replacing the Jensen-Shannon divergence with the Wasserstein-1 distance and enforcing Lipschitz continuity through gradient penalty, WGAN-GP provides stable training even when minority-class samples are extremely sparse; bounded `tanh` activations and max-norm regularization further ensure synthetic samples remain within the physical operational envelope, addressing the fundamental inadequacy of generic oversampling in process-constrained environments. Experiments on SWaT and HAI confirm that Config. B delivers transformative recall improvements (+57.9 percentage points on SWaT), while the synthetic-only Config. C reaching 83.6% accuracy confirms the generator faithfully learns the physical manifold, and the IQR-based adaptive threshold eliminates manual calibration across heterogeneous ICS environments. Evaluation is currently restricted to two laboratory-grade testbeds and the three-configuration protocol does not isolate WGAN-GP architecture choices independently of the augmentation ratio, leaving production validation and architectural ablation as immediate open problems. The physics constraints applied here operate at the data boundary level via bounded activations and weight regularization; deeper integration of domain-specific hydraulic or electrical process models remains a direction for future work. Future work will compare WGAN-GP against VAEs and diffusion models under equivalent ICS physical constraints, extend evaluation to WADI and integrate explainability mechanisms to support operator-facing detection justifications in agentic ICS defense deployments.

Acknowledgments. This work was funded by the European Union under Grant Agreements No. 101131292 (AIAS), 101183162 (ANTIDOTE), 101145872 (NITRO), 101086387 (REMARKABLE) and 101168490 (RECITALS). The NITRO and RECITALS projects are supported and managed by the European Cybersecurity Competence Centre (ECCC).

Disclosure of Interests. The authors have no competing interests to declare that are relevant to the content of this article.

References

1. Dehlaghi-Ghadim, A., Moghadam, M.H., Balador, A., Hansson, H.: Anomaly detection dataset for industrial control systems. IEEE Access **11**, 107982–107996 (2023)
2. Li, Y., Yang, Y., Song, P., Duan, L., Ren, R.: An improved SMOTE algorithm for enhanced imbalanced data classification by expanding sample generation space. Sci. Rep. **15**(1), 23521 (2025)
3. Arjovsky, M., Chintala, S., Bottou, L.: Wasserstein generative adversarial networks. In: Proceedings of the 34th International Conference on Machine Learning, PMLR, vol. 70, pp. 214–223 (2017)
4. Gulrajani, I., Ahmed, F., Arjovsky, M., Dumoulin, V., Courville, A.: Improved training of Wasserstein GANs. In: Advances in Neural Information Processing Systems (NeurIPS), vol. 30 (2017)
5. Ponomarev, S., Atkison, T.: Industrial control system network intrusion detection by telemetry analysis. IEEE Trans. Dependable Secure Comput. **13**(2), 252–260 (2015)
6. Nankya, M., Chataut, R., Akl, R.: Securing industrial control systems: components, cyber threats, and machine learning-driven defense strategies. Sensors **23**(21), 8840 (2023)
7. Silva, P., Schukat, M.: On the use of K-NN in intrusion detection for industrial control systems. In: Proceedings of The IT&T 13th International Conference on Information Technology and Telecommunication, Dublin, Ireland, pp. 103–106 (2014)
8. Zhang, C., Yang, T.: Anomaly detection for wind turbines using long short-term memory-based variational autoencoder Wasserstein generation adversarial network under semi-supervised training. Energies **16**(19), 7008 (2023)
9. Pu, Z., Cabrera, D., Li, C., de Oliveira, J.V.: Sliced Wasserstein cycle consistency generative adversarial networks for fault data augmentation of an industrial robot. Exp. Syst. Appl. **222**, 119754 (2023)
10. Alabugin, S.K., Sokolov, A.N.: Applying of generative adversarial networks for anomaly detection in industrial control systems. In: 2020 Global Smart Industry Conference (GloSIC), pp. 199–203. IEEE (2020)

11. Zhou, C., Xiao, W., Wang, Q., Feng, Z.: Research on an improved Wasserstein generative adversarial network early fault warning method for rotating machinery. IEEE Access **12**, 109109–109127 (2024)
12. iTrust, Centre for Research in Cyber Security: Secure water treatment (SWaT) dataset. Singapore University of Technology and Design (2016). https://itrust.sutd.edu.sg/itrust-labs_datasets/dataset_info/
13. Kim, K.D., et al.: A practical security testbed for industrial control systems. IEEE Access **8**, 114630–114641 (2020). https://doi.org/10.1109/ACCESS.2020.3003010

Empirical Evaluation of Confidentiality-Protecting Technologies for Industrial Data Collaboration

Andy Izaber-Ludwig[1,2(✉)], Miriam Fehn[2], and Alexander Giehl[2]

[1] School of Computation, Information and Technology, Technical University of Munich, Munich, Germany
[2] Department of Product Protection and Industrial Security, Fraunhofer AISEC, Garching near Munich, Germany
andy.izaber-ludwig@aisec.fraunhofer.de

Abstract. Machine learning applications, such as predictive maintenance and tool condition monitoring, can enhance the productivity of manufacturing companies. The performance of these models depends on the quantity and quality of training data. Small and medium-sized companies are often unable to meet these requirements, therefore, industrial data collaboration can offer a solution. By sharing data, companies can jointly benefit from improved models to optimize their processes. However, concerns about intellectual property contained in training data and the potential loss of competitive advantage often hinder data sharing. This study presents a single-source case study on confidentiality-protecting technologies (CPTs) in a real-world milling scenario. Thirteen potential techniques derived from privacy-enhancing technologies were applied to original manufacturing data. These techniques fall into the categories of noise masking, information reduction, affine transformation, and time-series permutation. We examined their impact on a tool condition monitoring model and divided them into promising CPTs and pseudo-protection techniques. Furthermore, we demonstrated that point-wise distortion metrics, such as the mean square error, are not suitable for quantifying confidentiality. While motivated by cross-company industrial data collaboration, our empirical findings provide a first step towards understanding confidentiality–utility trade-offs in such settings.

Keywords: Intellectual Property Protection · Confidentiality-Protecting Technologies · Industrial Collaboration · Operational Technology

1 Introduction

Modern production environments generate a multitude of data as a byproduct of digitalized manufacturing and increased sensor deployment on the shopfloor. This data offers great potential for data-driven services such as predictive maintenance, process optimization and Tool Condition Monitoring (TCM). In TCM,

P. Kieseberg et al. (Eds.): ARES 2026 Workshops, LNCS 16903, pp. 15–32, 2027.
https://doi.org/10.1007/978-3-032-37218-5_2

sensor signals are used to determine the current tool wear and to predict its Remaining Useful Life (RUL). Reliable TCM models can reduce unplanned downtime and stabilize product quality. However, these benefits can only be realized if the underlying machine learning models are trained on datasets that are both sufficiently large and heterogeneous in capturing a wide variety of tools, machines, and operating conditions to generalize beyond a single production line. Small and medium-sized enterprises (SMEs) often lack access to such comprehensive datasets. One promising approach is cross-company data collaboration, whereby several organizations contribute production data to a shared server-side data lake for joint model training [24].

At the same time, sharing shop-floor data is associated with confidentiality risks. Machine signals and process parameters can contain sensitive information about production strategies, machine configurations, and geometries of produced workpieces. For many companies, this information is marked as intellectual property (IP) and forms the basis of their competitive advantage. As a result, organizations are often reluctant to provide raw machine data to external partners or centralized platforms, even if they would benefit from the resulting models. Herein lies the challenge for secure industrial data collaboration, as only jointly aggregated, high-quality data allows companies to fully leverage the potential of industrial machine learning, yet sharing this data is perceived as a threat to intellectual property.

The MINERVA research project addresses this challenge by designing a secure and transparent architecture for collaborative model training in industrial environments [24]. The proposed system follows a defense-in-depth strategy and emphasizes local control over data protection. Before any data leaves the company network, it is transformed by Confidentiality-Protecting Technologies (CPTs), which are derived from concepts known from Privacy-Enhancing Technologies (PETs) [11]. In this architecture, CPTs are applied directly at the data source on the shopfloor, as illustrated in Fig. 1. This allows each participant to decide which part of their data is considered IP-critical and how strongly this part should be protected. Domain experts can tailor the choice and configuration of CPTs to their specific processes and risk assessments while retaining full control over their raw data.

However, applying CPTs, such as noise masking, alters the properties of the original data. From a confidentiality perspective, stronger transformations are desirable, as they make it more difficult to reconstruct IP. From a machine learning perspective, these transformations may degrade the predictive performance of models trained on the protected data. This results in a trade-off between confidentiality and utility that must be carefully managed. Despite its practical relevance, there is limited empirical evidence on how concrete CPTs affect both real industrial time-series data and the performance of TCM models.

In this initial empirical study, we collected multi-sensor time-series data from a milling machine, where 14 tools were operated until they were worn. We focus on a controlled single-source setting with data from one milling machine and one company. This allows us to isolate the impact of local CPTs on model

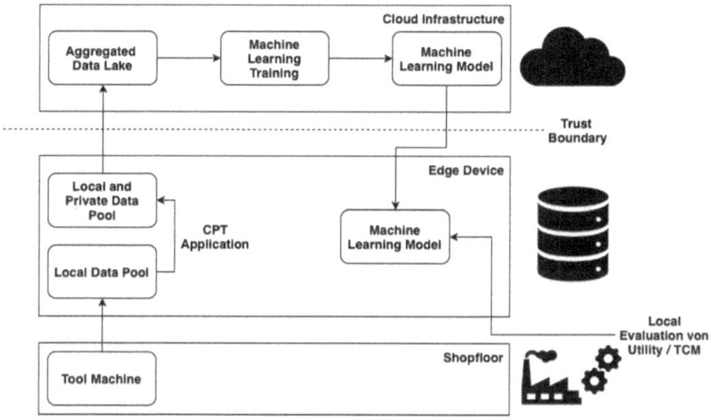

Fig. 1. Scheme for local CPT application

utility. As a reference, we first trained a Long Short-Term Memory (LSTM) model on the unprotected data to establish a baseline TCM performance. We then applied 13 potential CPTs, organized into four groups—noise masking, information reduction, affine transformations, and time series permutation—to the dataset. For each protected variant, we retrained and evaluated the LSTM model and compared its performance to the baseline. In parallel, we quantified the distortion introduced by each approach using the Root Mean Squared Error (RMSE) between the original and the transformed time series. This dual perspective allowed us to study how different classes of CPTs simultaneously affect data characteristics and model utility.

To summarize, our main contributions of this work are:

- We categorized and implemented 13 CPTs for real-world industrial time-series data into four groups—noise masking, information reduction, affine transformations, and time series permutation.
- We quantified the impact of each CPT on the dataset by measuring the distortion from the original time series using RMSE.
- We systematically analyzed how the different CPTs influence the performance of an LSTM-based TCM model.

2 Background and Related Work

The growing availability of personal and operational data raises significant privacy concerns. Privacy-Enhancing Technologies (PETs) have been developed to enable analysis of sensitive data while limiting disclosure of identities or behavior [11,14,22]. Typical PETs perturb, aggregate or otherwise transform data, and should be selected according to the type and properties of the protected data [22].

PETs are particularly relevant for IoT applications in domains such as automotive, healthcare, and smart housing, where services rely on continuous streams of personal or behavior-related data [4]. Similar requirements arise in industrial environments, where predictive maintenance and TCM process machine signals and process parameters that encode valuable IP. We therefore adapt PET-inspired mechanisms to protect IP in industrial collaboration scenarios while retaining sufficient utility for machine learning.

2.1 Confidentiality-Protecting Technologies

To protect IP in industrial data, PET concepts have been adapted into Confidentiality-Protecting Technologies (CPTs) that are applied locally before data leaves the company network [18,24]. In this work we focus on local transformations and group the considered CPTs by their main protection mechanism.

Noise Masking methods perturb individual values by adding or multiplying random noise drawn from different distributions, such as uniform, Gaussian, Cauchy or Laplace [9,20]. Differential privacy further adjusts the noise based on sensitivity in order to conceal individual data points while preserving the aggregated statistics [10].

Information Reduction techniques remove or aggregate information instead of adding stochastic variation. Examples include recoding to coarser categories, microaggregation that replaces groups of records by a representative, and suppression combined with interpolation between remaining points to smooth local fluctuations while retaining overall trends [6,12,17,22].

The third group contains *Affine Transformations*, that modify the geometric representation of the data by scaling, rotating, translating, or shearing feature vectors. These geometric perturbations generally preserve the overall shape or structure of the underlying object, even though individual coordinates change [5]. As such, they can give the impression of protection while still maintaining much of the original geometric information.

Time Series Permutation methods change the temporal order of observations without modifying individual values. Besides classical swapping, which exchanges attribute values between records [22], we consider permutations of complete time series and local sliding-window permutations that disrupt fine-grained sequential patterns while preserving some temporal locality.

2.2 Protecting Intellectual Property in Machine Learning

A variety of approaches have been proposed to protect sensitive or proprietary data used for training machine learning models. Liu et al. introduce membership fingerprint authentication to detect whether a given model exhibits the same prediction behavior as a model trained on IP-bearing data [23]. Their approach targets subsequently detection of IP violations at the model level, whereas our work aims at preventing such violations by transforming the data locally before it is used for training. Differential privacy is widely used to mitigate information leakage in machine learning. Differential privacy has been combined with federated learning and edge computing in industrial settings to balance privacy and utility [15,19,30]. These approaches mainly modify training architectures and update protocols, whereas we treat noise addition inspired by differential privacy as one local CPT.

Another area of work secures the training and inference pipeline using cryptographic and hardware-based mechanisms. Trusted Execution Environments (TEEs) can protect model execution at the edge [8], while schemes based on homomorphic encryption enable inference or even training on encrypted data without revealing the inputs [3,27]. These techniques keep raw data conceptually unaltered and rely on secure computation. In contrast, we change the time-series data themselves through simple local CPTs before they enter a centralized pipeline.

In industrial scenarios, Giehl et al. discussed how PET-inspired techniques can be integrated into manufacturing ecosystems to protect IP while enabling data-driven services [13]. Pimenta et al. study the effect of anonymized training data on model performance using PPM-Anon and focus on feature-selection aspects [26]. Our work complements these efforts by evaluating multiple local CPTs on a real-world dataset and quantifying their impact on TCM regression task.

Several surveys highlight the broader landscape of privacy threats and defenses in machine learning and call for more empirical evaluations on real-world data [7,29]. We contribute to this from an industrial perspective by systematically assessing how different CPT categories affect both data distortion and the performance of TCM models trained on real manufacturing time series.

2.3 Tool Condition Monitoring

Tool Condition Monitoring (TCM) estimates the state of cutting tools and predicts their remaining useful life during machining. Since tool wear directly affects surface quality, dimensional accuracy and process stability, reliable TCM helps to avoid unexpected failures and reduce scrap [28]. Modern TCM systems use sensor signals such as forces, vibration, acoustic emission, spindle currents and tool positions, which are processed into features or fed directly into models that map machine behaviour to tool wear [28]. With growing sensor availability and computational power, machine-learning-based approaches, such as LSTM models, have become a central basis for TCM because they can process multivariate time series and capture temporal dependencies in the data [2,21,25].

3 Methods

To protect machine data locally before sharing it with other parties, different CPTs can be applied. Depending on the CPT category, the underlying mechanism and thus the impact on the data differ. In addition, the strength of each individual CPT can be controlled via parameters. In this section, we first introduce the considered CPTs and their parameterizations, grouped by their protection mechanism. We then describe how we quantify their impact on the time-series data and on the performance of the LSTM-based TCM model.

3.1 Protecting Manufacturing Data

We defined four categories of CPTs according to their impact on the original time-series data: noise masking, information reduction, affine transformation, and time series permutation (cf. Table 1). Each technique was parameterized by a small, discrete set of values, and all parameterizations are applied independently to each sensor signal. The parameter values were chosen to cover a wide range of impact. All statistics required by the methods (standard deviation, minimum, maximum) were computed per feature and per machining tool. Unless stated otherwise, transformations were applied only to the sensor values and not to the time stamp. Labels, like the Tool-IDs and Part-IDs, are not affected by the CPTs. The Tool-IDs are only used to split dataset into meaningful sections of training-, validation-, and test-datasets. The validation and test data is not altered with CPTs, but scaled like the training data.

Table 1. Overview of CPT-groups and their respective techniques

Group	CPT	Parameters
Noise masking	Random noise	x, mode
	Gaussian scaled noise	α, mode
	Additive Cauchy noise	γ, mode
	Laplace noise using differential privacy	ϵ
Information reduction	Rounding (Recoding)	base
	Microaggregation	w, mode
	Sliding window interpolation	window size w
Affine transformation	Scaling	scale factor s
	Rotating	angle α
	Translating	distance d
	Shearing	shear factor m
Time series permutation	Swapping	/
	Sliding window permutation	window size w

Noise Masking. The first category comprises perturbative techniques that modify the original values by adding or multiplying random noise. The noise is drawn from different probability distributions, with the overall magnitude controlled by the empirical variability of the data.

Random noise was drawn from a continuous uniform distribution and either added to or multiplied with the original value. For each feature, we computed its standard deviation σ. The noise range was defined as $[-x \cdot \sigma, x \cdot \sigma]$, so that the amplitude of the perturbation scales with the feature's variability. We did not enforce preservation of any particular global statistic (e.g., mean or variance) of the original dataset. We evaluated the parameter $x \in \{0.1, 1.0, 10\}$ and, in addition, we fixed $x = 1$ for one configuration in which the noise was applied multiplicatively instead of additively (mode parameter in Table 1).

Gaussian scaled noise uses a normal distribution with a scale parameter derived from the feature-wise standard deviation. For each feature with standard deviation σ, we defined a scaling factor *scale* that depends on the selected mode: $scale = \alpha + \sigma$ and $scale = \alpha \cdot \sigma$ in multiplicative mode. Noise was drawn from a zero-mean normal distribution. Again, σ was computed per feature and machining tool. We evaluated $\alpha \in \{0.1, 1.0, 10\}$, and additionally fix $\alpha = 0.1$ for one multiplicative configuration.

To introduce heavy-tailed perturbations, we draw noise from a Cauchy distribution, which allows for larger deviations and extreme values. In contrast to the previous methods, we did not bound the resulting noise interval. For each feature, we estimated a scale parameter from its empirical range: $scale = \gamma * (max - min)$, where max and min denoted the maximum and minimum of a feature for a given machining tool. The sampled Cauchy noise was multiplied by this scale and added to the original value. We evaluated $\gamma \in \{0.01, 0.1, 1\}$, and additionally fix $\gamma = 0.01$ for one multiplicative configuration.

The last noise masking technique adopts the differential privacy mechanism using Laplace distribution. In our setting, the primary goal was to protect Intellectual Property (IP) rather than individual data subjects, and we therefore did not claim formal ϵ-differential-privacy guarantees. Instead, we reused the functional form of the Laplace mechanism to systematically control the perturbation magnitude. For each feature, we computed a local sensitivity $sens = max - min$, where max and min were taken over all samples of that feature for one machining tool. We evaluated $\epsilon \in \{30, 15, 5\}$, with smaller ϵ corresponding to stronger perturbation. Noise masking methods were never applied to the time stamp, they affected only the sensor values.

Information Reduction. The second category comprises techniques that do not add noise but reduce the granularity of the data. These methods aim to remove fine-grained details while preserving the overall structure and length of the time series. Rounding maps each value to a coarser representation by rounding to the nearest multiple of a base b. Formally, each value v is transformed to $v' = round(v/b) \cdot b$. The parameter b controls the amount of information loss: larger bases merge more distinct values into the same rounded result. We evaluated $base \in \{1, 10, 100\}$.

Microaggregation aggregates local neighborhoods in the time series per feature. Given a window of size w, we compute a representative value for all samples within the window and replace each of them with this representative. The total length of the series remains unchanged, but local variability is reduced. We considered three aggregation modes, which define the representative: the centroid of the window, the minimum and the maximum value within the window. For the mean, we evaluated $w = \{3, 10, 30\}$ and for $w = 10$, also minimum and maximum were evaluated.

Sliding window interpolation replaces the detailed shape within a window by a linear trend between its endpoints. For a window of size w, the first and last values are kept, and all intermediate values in the window are replaced by linearly interpolated values between these endpoints. This preserves the global length and approximate trend of the series while discarding higher-frequency fluctuations within each window. We evaluated $w = \{5, 20, 250\}$.

Affine Transformation. The third category includes operations that apply affine transformations to the data. These techniques preserve the relative relationships between data points. We therefore refer to them as pseudo-protection techniques, as they do not inherently destroy the underlying structure of the original data. For a feature vector x_t at time t, an affine transformation is defined as $x'_t = Ax_t + b$, where A is a linear transformation (scaling, rotating, shearing) and b is a translation. Each technique uses a single parameter:

- Scaling: all values are multiplied by a constant scale factor s. We used $s = 3$.
- Rotation: feature vectors are rotated in the feature space by a fixed angle α. We set $\alpha = 60$.
- Translation: a constant offset d is added to all values. We used $d = 250$.
- Shearing: a shear transformation with factor m is applied, distorting the feature space. We used $m = 0.6$.

Each affine transformation was applied consistently to the geometry of the dataset, so that relative distances and temporal ordering are preserved. As we did not consider chained techniques in this study, each affine operation is evaluated in isolation.

Time Series Permutation. The final category modifies the temporal order of the data while leaving the individual values unchanged. These techniques aim to obscure temporal patterns, machine behavior, or process states encoded in the sequencing of observations. In the swapping configuration, the complete time series is randomly permuted. All samples of a time series are shuffled using a random permutation of their indices. No additional parameters are required. This transformation completely breaks the original temporal order.

Sliding window permutation restricts the permutation to local neighborhoods. For each window of size w, the samples within the window are randomly permuted, while the windows themselves remain in their original order. This preserves some local temporal proximity while still obfuscating fine-grained patterns. We evaluated $w \in \{5, 20\}$. In both permutation techniques, the sensor values themselves were left unchanged, only their temporal ordering was modified.

3.2 Assessing the Data Impact of CPTs

Each approach has a different influence on the original data. To assess a CPT's impact, the Root Mean Square Error (RMSE) is calculated between the original dataset and the corresponding protected one:

$$RMSE = \sqrt{\frac{1}{n}\sum_{i=1}^{n}(x_{o,i} - x_{p,i})^2} \quad (1)$$

The result quantifies the difference between the time series. We use RMSE purely as a quantitative measure of point-wise distortion between original and protected time series. From an IP protection perspective, this distortion measurement alone is not sufficient to guarantee confidentiality, as our results in Sect. 4 demonstrate.

3.3 Assessing the Utility of Protected Machine Data

To assess the utility of the protected datasets for TCM model training, we trained a LSTM model to predict flank wear from the multivariate time series. LSTM models are well suited for this task because they can capture long-range temporal dependencies in sensor data [16]. The model was implemented in Python using the PyTorch `nn.LSTM module` with three hidden layers, a hidden size of 16, and a final linear layer mapping the last hidden state to the wear value. We used the `optim.Adam` with a learning rate of 0.0001 and mean squared error (MSE) as loss function. A dropout layer with probability 0.2 after the LSTM model mitigated overfitting, and all models were trained for 250 epochs using a batch size of 64. Before training, all features were standardized to zero mean and unit variance using sklearn's `StandardScaler()` to stabilize optimization and ensure comparable scaling across inputs.

3.4 Attacker Model

The attacker model reflects the socio-technical complexity of collaborative machine learning in industrial settings. It combines the Dolev–Yao (DY) network attacker model with aspects of Byzantine Fault Tolerance (BFT) to account for both intercepted communication and malicious or colluding authenticated participants. In addition, attackers are assumed to be rational in the sense of the BAR (Byzantine, Altruistic, Rational) model [1], deviating from protocols only if the expected benefit outweighs the risk of detection. We assume that the adversary—either colluding companies or a compromised cloud provider—has legitimate access to the aggregated data lake at or beyond the trust boundary. Their primary goal is to compromise data confidentiality by extracting IP-relevant information, but they deliberately avoid disruptive actions such as Denial-of-Service, since the availability and reliability of the ML pipeline are prerequisites for successful data exfiltration. The attacker has white-box knowledge of which CPT category was applied to the data, but does not know the specific techniques and parameters. The overall objective is to approximate or invert the applied CPTs, reconstruct the original machine data, and derive process know-how and workpiece geometries.

4 Experimental Evaluation

For evaluation, a real world manufacturing dataset was used[1]. We first describe the recorded milling data and the TCM setup, and then report, for each CPT and parameter configuration, the distortion of the sensor time series (RMSE) and the resulting LSTM-based wear prediction performance (MSE).

4.1 Evaluation Setup

A milling machine was used to manufacture the workpiece as shown in Fig. 2a. During this process, the production relevant time series was recorded with 2 Hz. The shape of the workpiece is one of the most sensitive information in the dataset and is therefore used in this evaluation to visualize the impact of the CPTs. The original recorded shape without any protection techniques is shown in Fig. 2b. An overview of all recorded features is given in Table 2.

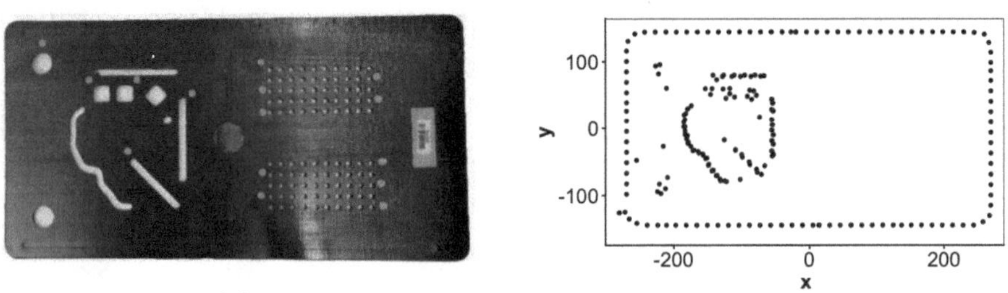

(a) (b)

Fig. 2. (a) The manufactured workpiece of a milling machine; (b) The recording with 2 Hz of the manufactured workpiece.

Fourteen tools have been used to produce these workpieces until they were worn. During this process, the wear mark was assessed multiple times with a microscope. This discrete assessment was used to calculate a continuous wear mark by interpolating for the remaining time steps.

[1] Machined by Hufschmied Zerspanungssysteme GmbH.

Table 2. Data recorded from milling process

Attribute	Description
{x, y, z}_pos	Absolute position of the tool along the X, Y, Z-axis
{x, y, z}_feed_rate	Tool movement speed along the X, Y, Z-axis
s_pos_abs	Absolute position of the spindle
s_feed_rate	Spindle feed rate
analytical_features_{1, 2, 3, 4}	Vibration data from external sensors
timestamp	Timestamp for each recorded entry
part_id	ID of the produced workpiece
tool_id	ID of the actual tool
avg_wear	Interpolated wear for each timestamp

For all experiments, we treat each tool, producing several workpieces until it is worn, as one multivariate time series consisting of the signals listed in Table 2. In total, the dataset contains 14 different tools, resulting in 24010 recorded time steps - 1715 per tool.

To evaluate the impact of the different CPTs on TCM performance in a controlled manner, we split the dataset on the tool level in order to avoid information leakage between training and test sets. Out of the 14 tools, 12 tools are used for training, one tool for validation, and one tool is held out exclusively for testing. The splitted dataset is kept fixed across all CPT configurations and the unprotected baseline, so that any change in model performance can be attributed solely to the applied protection technique.

4.2 Results and Discussion

For model performance, we used the MSE on flank wear, and for data distortion we use the RMSE between original and protected sensor values in the original scale. Results are based on a single training run per configuration. As IP-critical representatives, we focus on the x- and y-positions in result tables, the remaining features show comparable trends. The baseline LSTM model trained on unprotected data achieves an MSE of 0.0004245. We assume the best performance possible with the original dataset. Table 3 summarizes the impact of all CPTs from the noise masking category.

Noise masking (Table 3) shows the expected behavior: increasing the magnitude of random, Gaussian or Cauchy noise monotonically increases RMSE and degrades TCM performance. Among these, Cauchy noise yields the largest deviations and worst MSE, especially in multiplicative mode. Laplace noise configured in a differential-privacy-inspired manner allows precise control of the perturbation magnitude via ϵ, but for comparable RMSE it results in lower utility than uniform or Gaussian noise. Overall, strong noise masking effectively destroys the usefulness of the data for TCM.

Table 3. Noise masking impact on data and TCM model. RMSE between the original and the protected machine data. Each value is averaged over all twelve tools used for training (M). The relative standard deviation in percentage (SD) in brackets. The performance of the TCM model is quantified via MSE.

CPT	Parameter	x_pos M (SD)	y_pos M (SD)	Loss TCM
Random Noise	$x = 0.1$, mode = add	9.42 (1.00)	5.71 (0.83)	0.00049
	$x = 1.0$, mode = add	94.22 (1.00)	57.15 (0.83)	0.00553
	$x = 10$, mode = add	942.17 (1.00)	571.50 (0.83)	0.62912
	$x = 1.0$, mode = mul	1664.94 (2.00)	570.52 (1.40)	4.01275
Gaussian Scaled Noise	$\alpha = 0.1$, mode = add	16.28 (0.99)	9.93 (1.47)	0.00152
	$\alpha = 1.0$, mode = add	162.81 (0.99)	99.30 (1.47)	0.00768
	$\alpha = 10$, mode = add	1628.06 (0.99)	993.04 (1.47)	0.80945
	$\alpha = 0.1$, mode = mul	2836.83 (1.96)	973.17 (3.07)	0.52844
Additive Cauchy Noise	$\gamma = 0.01$, mode = add	986.08 (103)	316.56 (161)	0.10381
	$\gamma = 0.1$, mode = add	9860.82 (102.62)	3165.64 (160.69)	3.87287
	$\gamma = 1.0$, mode = add	98608.25 (102.62)	31656.41 (160.69)	2.48671
	$\gamma = 0.01$, mode = mul	158190.65 (108.59)	31986.02 (126.47)	7.57351
Laplace Noise using Diff. Privacy	$\epsilon = 30$	25.38 (0.11)	13.21 (0.00)	0.00382
	$\epsilon = 15$	50.75 (0.21)	26.41 (0.00)	0.01574
	$\epsilon = 5$	152.26 (0.64)	79.24 (0.00)	0.10950

In comparison, the next group containing rounding, microaggregation and sliding window interpolation alters the original data by reducing the information content. Table 4 summarizes the impact of this category.

Information reduction techniques (Table 4) behave differently. Rounding already causes a notable loss in TCM performance, even though the RMSE—especially for base = 1—is the lowest across all CPTs. In contrast, microaggregation and sliding window interpolation induce substantially larger point-wise deviations but achieve near-baseline MSE for suitable window sizes. Using the mean as representative yields better performance and lower RMSE than using minimum or maximum values. These findings suggest that carefully parameterized information reduction can provide a favorable confidentiality–utility trade-off.

The affine transformation alters the data by preserving dimension and affine subspaces. As these operations alters the geometry of the workpiece, only the x and y positions as feature were impacted by these operations. Table 5 summarizes the impact of all CPTs from the affine transformation category.

This category differs from the previous ones, because the data is not manipulated by adding distribution based values or reducing details in the data, but by performing geometric operations on the original data. Obviously, these operations do not enhance the protection of the sensitive geometry as the outcome is close to the input. Assuming our attacker model, these operations do not pre-

Table 4. Information reduction impact on data and TCM model. RMSE between the original and the protected machine data. Each value is averaged over all twelve tools used for training (M). The relative standard deviation in percentage (SD) in brackets. The performance of the TCM model is quantified via MSE.

CPT	Parameter	x_pos M (SD)	y_pos M (SD)	Loss TCM
Rounding	base = 1	0.33 (0.63)	0.36 (0.43)	0.01535
	base = 10	2.82 (0.83)	3.40 (0.77)	0.05291
	base = 100	30.37 (0.37)	35.47 (0.39)	0.10166
Microaggregation	$w = 3$, mode = center	9.91 (20.86)	15.48 (20.88)	0.00071
	$w = 10$, mode = center	28.15 (20.66)	32.04 (14.92)	0.00065
	$w = 30$, mode = center	72.84 (21.75)	54.34 (16.09)	0.00162
	$w = 10$, mode = min	52.07 (20.55)	57.45 (15.51)	0.00189
	$w = 10$, mode = max	51.28 (21.15)	54.73 (14.93)	0.00298
Sliding Window Interpolation	$w = 5$	6.96 (23.64)	15.14 (26.51)	0.00083
	$w = 20$	25.80 (22.59)	43.09 (15.29)	0.00132
	$w = 250$	233.38 (2.23)	106.04 (10.58)	0.00285

Table 5. Affine transformation impact on data and TCM model. RMSE between the original and the protected machine data. Each value is averaged over all twelve tools used for training (M). The relative standard deviation in percentage (SD) in brackets. The performance of the TCM model is quantified via MSE.

CPT	Parameter	x_pos M (SD)	y_pos M (SD)	Loss TCM
Scaling	$s = 3$	349.46 (0.40)	196.94 (0.60)	0.00068
Rotating	$\alpha = 60$	122.62 (0.57)	158.72 (0.51)	0.00107
Translating	$d = 250$	250.00 (0.0)	250.00 (0.0)	0.00224
Shearing	$m = 0.6$	59.08 (0.60)	104.84 (0.40)	0.00093

vent the reconstruction of IP. Following this argumentation, the RMSE is not a sufficient measure to quantify the level of protection: the values suggest a high difference between both versions, but the proximity of the resulting shape to the original one is not considered. For example, the translation factor of $d = 250$ itself is the result of the RMSE, as this value is added to each data point. The best performance delivers scaling, while introducing the largest RMSE. In general, all techniques deliver good TCM model performances, thus worse than the original dataset. Summarizing, those techniques can be called pseudo-protection techniques, as no real protection of sensitive information is added.

Finally, the remaining group does not affect the values of the features, but the order of the time series. Table 6 summarizes the impact of all CPTs from the Time Series Permutation category.

Table 6. Time series permutation impact on data and TCM model. RMSE between the original and the protected machine data. Each value is averaged over all twelve tools used for training (M). The relative standard deviation in percentage (SD) in brackets. The performance of the TCM model is quantified via MSE.

CPT	Parameter	x_pos M (SD)	y_pos M (SD)	Loss TCM
Swapping	/	229.53 (1.69)	139.29 (1.13)	1.03123
Window Permutation	$w = 5$	21.81 (21.01)	30.96 (16.82)	0.00043
	$w = 20$	73.85 (22.73)	60.42 (11.90)	0.00160

Swapping has no parameters to set and is besides the added Cauchy noise the lowest-performing technique of all compared. The TCM loss of around one is significantly above the baseline. This technique results in randomly permuted time steps, causing the original order to be lost and leading to a non-functional model. In contrast, window permutation does not shuffle the data across the complete dataset. Using the window size, the shuffled entries of the time series can stay closer to the original position. This is the reason for the significant better results in sliding window permutation, especially if smaller window sizes are used. This leads to results just above the baseline. The downside of this small TCM model loss is the similarity to the original dataset. All of these approaches maintain the original geometry and therefore no IP in the shape is protected. The RMSE is not applicable in these cases, as the shapes are easily accessible in shuffled datasets. Values larger than zero are produced by comparing different entries.

Across all CPT categories, there is no simple monotonic relationship between point-wise distortion and model performance. Strongly perturbative techniques such as heavy-tailed noise or global permutations simultaneously yield high RMSE and poor TCM utility. Affine transformations and local permutations can exhibit large RMSE while leaking most geometric and temporal structure. Information reduction methods, particularly microaggregation and sliding window interpolation, offer the most promising trade-off in our setting. Figure 3 summarizes the relationship between RMSE for the x-coordinate and the TCM MSE across all CPTs.

From the perspective of our attacker model, the experimental results reveal that point-wise distortion measurement by RMSE is not a sufficient indicator of effective confidentiality protection. A rational adversary with white-box knowledge of the CPT category and legitimate access to the protected data lake is

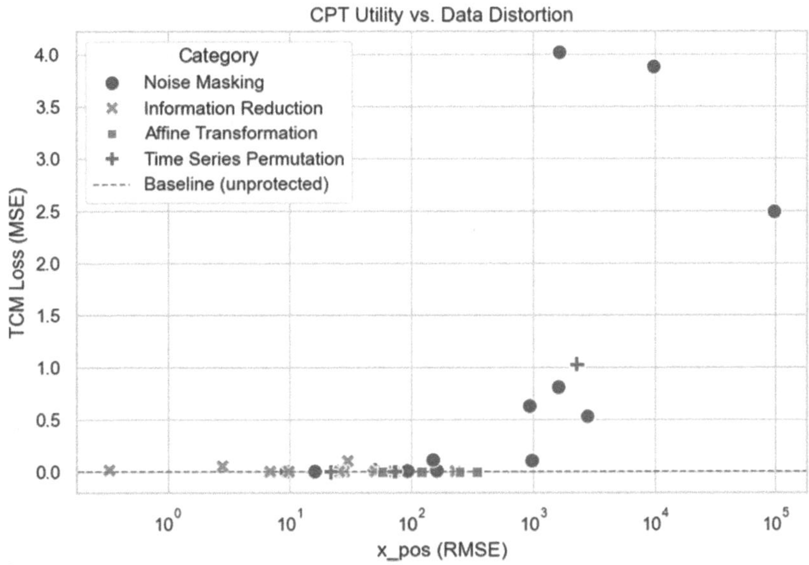

Fig. 3. Relation between the RMSE of the x coordinates and the MSE in TCM model performance. Each CPT category is visualized, but there is no differentiation between the actual techniques. The baseline performance is specified.

primarily interested in reconstructing process know-how and workpiece geometry. Overall, the results demonstrate a systematic mismatch between RMSE and confidentiality under our attacker model and underline the need for IP-aware evaluation metrics that explicitly account for geometric and temporal invariances rather than relying solely on point-wise numerical differences.

5 Limitations and Future Work

This work provides an initial empirical view on confidentiality–utility trade-offs for CPTs in an industrial TCM scenario, but some limitations constrain the generalizability of our results. First, our experiments assume a homogeneous single-source setting where all time series stem from one machine and CPT parameters are computed per tool. In real cross-company collaborations, machines, sensors and feature distributions differ and each participant may choose different CPT parameters. We do not study how such heterogeneous local transformations interact in the shared data lake, nor how global vs. local parameter alignment strategies affect utility. We consider this an important direction for future work.

Second, data impact is primarily quantified via RMSE between original and protected time series. Although we assume an informed, rational attacker with access to the protected data lake and knowledge of the CPT categories, we do not implement concrete reconstruction or inference attacks. Instead, confidentiality assessments are based on distortion measures and visual inspection. Future work should include explicit attack-based evaluations like trained models to invert CPTs or to reconstruct workpiece geometries.

Third, we apply only single CPTs in isolation. Combinations or chained techniques, such as microaggregation or sliding window interpolation followed by low-amplitude noise, may offer more favorable trade-offs between reconstruction resistance and model utility. Exploring such compositions and adaptive parameterizations remains an important direction.

Finally, we concentrate on a centralized setting where each participant applies a single, static CPT configuration locally. We do not study system-level aspects such as federated learning, heterogeneous CPT choices across organizations, or dynamic adaptation during operation. Additionally, we limit our analysis to local data transformations that alter the time series prior to training. Cryptographic methods, such as homomorphic encryption and secure multi-party computation, leave the data in its original form and protect it at the system or protocol level. Their impact on the model's performance is therefore unrelated to the CPTs examined here.

6 Conclusion

In this initial empirical study, we investigated how 13 potential Confidentiality-Protecting Technologies (CPTs), organized into four categories, affect both industrial time-series data and the performance of an LSTM-based TCM model. Using real milling data from 14 tools, we applied each technique with several parameter configurations, quantified the distortion with RMSE, and evaluated the impact on wear prediction.

Our results reveal distinct category-specific behaviors. Strong perturbative methods, especially heavy-tailed Cauchy noise and global time-series swapping, effectively destroy data utility. In contrast, moderate information reduction techniques such as microaggregation and sliding window interpolation achieve near-baseline TCM performance while inducing substantial data distortion. Simple rounding, despite minimal point-wise deviation, already causes notable performance degradation. Affine transformations and local permutations emerge as pseudo-protection techniques as they preserve geometric and temporal structure and therefore do not sufficiently conceal IP under our attacker model.

A key finding is that RMSE is not a reliable proxy for confidentiality protection. Affine transformations yield large RMSE values while preserving the essential workpiece geometry, whereas rounding introduces small deviations but degrades utility substantially. This systematic mismatch underlines the need for IP-aware evaluation metrics that account for geometric and temporal invariances.

Acknowledgments. This work was supported by the German Federal Ministry of Research, Technology and Space under grant number 16KIS1803K.

Disclosure of Interests. The authors have no competing interests to declare that are relevant to the content of this article.

References

1. Aiyer, A.S., Alvisi, L., Clement, A., Dahlin, M., Martin, J.P., Porth, C.: Bar fault tolerance for cooperative services. In: Proceedings of the Twentieth ACM Symposium on Operating Systems Principles, pp. 45–58 (2005)
2. Ambhore, N., Kamble, D., Chinchanikar, S., Wayal, V.: Tool condition monitoring system: a review. In: 4th International Conference on Materials Processing and Characterization (2015)
3. Balaban, B., et al.: Privacy-preserving machine learning (PPML) inference for clinically actionable models. IEEE Access **13**, 37431–37456 (2025)
4. Cha, S., Hsu, T., Xiang, Y., Yeh, K.: Privacy enhancing technologies in the internet of things: perspectives and challenges. IEEE Internet Things J. **6**(2), 2159–2187 (2019)
5. Chen, K., Liu, L.: Geometric data perturbation for privacy preserving outsourced data mining. Knowl. Inf. Syst. **29**(3), 657–695 (2011)
6. Daberdaku, S., Tavazzi, E., Camillo, B.D.: A combined interpolation and weighted k-nearest neighbours approach for the imputation of longitudinal ICU laboratory data. J. Healthc. Inf. Res. **4**(2), 174–188 (2020)
7. De Cristofaro, E.: A critical overview of privacy in machine learning. IEEE Secur. Privacy **19**(4), 19–27 (2021)
8. Ding, R., Xu, T., Ding, A.A., Fei, Y.: Graph in the vault: protecting edge GNN inference with trusted execution environment. In: 2025 62nd ACM/IEEE Design Automation Conference (DAC), pp. 1–7 (2025)
9. Domingo-Ferrer, J., Sebe, F., Castella-Roca, J.: On the security of noise addition for privacy in statistical databases (2004)
10. Dwork, C., Roth, A.: The algorithmic foundations of differential privacy. Found. Trends Theor. Comput. Sci. **9**, 211–407 (2014)
11. Fischer-Hübner, S. (ed.): IT-Security and Privacy. LNCS, vol. 1958. Springer, Heidelberg (2001). https://doi.org/10.1007/3-540-45150-1
12. Fischetti, M., González, J.: Models and algorithms for optimizing cell suppression in tabular data with linear constraints. J. Am. Stat. Assoc. **95**, 916–928 (2000)
13. Giehl, A., Schneider, P., Busch, M., Schnoes, F., Kleinwort, R., Zaeh, M.F.: Edge-computing enhanced privacy protection for industrial ecosystems in the context of SMEs (2019)
14. Heurix, J., Zimmermann, P., Neubauer, T., Fenz, S.: A taxonomy for privacy enhancing technologies (2015)
15. Hou, J., et al.: Low-cohesion differential privacy protection for industrial Internet. J. Supercomput. **76**, 8450–8472 (2020)
16. Houdt, G., Mosquera, C., Nápoles, G.: A review on the long short-term memory model. Artif. Intell. Rev. **53**, 5929–5955 (2020)
17. Hundepool, A., et al.: Statistical Disclosure Control. Wiley Series in Survey Methodology. John Wiley & Sons, New York, NY (2012)
18. Izaber-Ludwig, A., Giehl, A., Myhsok, F.: Group signatures for secure and reliable industrial data collaboration. In: Availability, Reliability and Security: ARES 2025 EU Projects Symposium Workshops, Ghent, Belgium, 11–14 August 2025, Proceedings, Part I, pp. 110–127. Springer, Heidelberg (2025). https://doi.org/10.1007/978-3-032-00642-4_7
19. Jiang, B., Li, J., Wang, H., Song, H.: Privacy-preserving federated learning for industrial edge computing via hybrid differential privacy and adaptive compression. IEEE Trans. Industr. Inf. **19**, 1136–1144 (2023)

20. Jung, M.: A variational image denoising model under mixed Cauchy and gaussian noise. AIMS Math. **7**, 19696–19726 (2022)
21. Kothuru, A., Nooka, S.P., Liu, R.: Application of deep visualization in CNN-based tool condition monitoring for end milling. In: 47th SME North American Manufacturing Research Conference, Penn State Behrend Erie, Pennsylvania, USA (2019)
22. Kunz, I., Banse, C., Stephanow, P.: Selecting privacy enhancing technologies for IoT-based services. In: Security and Privacy in Communication Networks (Securecomm2020), pt II, vol. 336, pp. 455–474 (2020)
23. Liu, G., Xu, T., Ma, X., Wang, C.: Your model trains on my data? Protecting intellectual property of training data via membership fingerprint authentication. IEEE Trans. Inf. Forensics Secur. **17**, 1024–1037 (2022)
24. Ludwig, A., Heinl, M.P., Giehl, A.: MINERVA: secure collaborative machine tool data utilization leveraging confidentiality-protecting technologies. In: OpenIdentity Summit2024, Lecture Notes in Informatics, Gesellschaft für Informatik, Bonn (2024)
25. Niu, M., Liu, K., Wang, Y.: A semi-supervised learning method combining tool wear laws for machining tool wear states monitoring. Mech. Syst. Signal Process. **224**, 112032 (2025). https://doi.org/10.1016/j.ymssp.2024.112032
26. Pimenta, I., Silva, D., Moura, E., Silveira, M., Gomes, R.L.: Impact of data anonymization in machine learning models. In: 13th Latin-American Symposium on Dependable and Secure Computing, LDAC 2024, pp. 188–191 (2024)
27. Tang, W., Qin, B., Zhao, S., Zhao, B., Xue, Y., Chen, H.: Privacy preserving machine learning with limited information leakage. In: Liu, J.K., Huang, X. (eds.) Network and System Security, pp. 352–370. Springer International Publishing (2019)
28. Wang, S., Li, S., Lin, X., Shi, Y., Zhu, K.: Mechanism-driven data model for tool condition monitoring. Mech. Syst. Signal Process. **237**, 113042 (2025). https://doi.org/10.1016/j.ymssp.2025.113042
29. Xie, H., Wei, L., Fang, F.: Research on privacy protection based on machine learning. In: 2021 International Wireless Communications and Mobile Computing (IWCMC), pp. 1003–1006 (2021)
30. Zhao, H., Pan, C., Liu, M., Jiao, D., Zhu, H.: Adaptive noise trap of layered differential privacy against privacy leakage for large-scale industrial federated learning. IEEE Trans. Netw. Sci. Engineer. **12**(5), 4044–4059 (2025)

Optimized DYST-Like Amplification Covert Channel
Short Paper

Carina Heßeling[1], Jörg Keller[1(✉)], and Steffen Wendzel[2]

[1] FernUniversität in Hagen, Hagen, Germany
carina.hesseling@fernuni-hagen.de,
joerg.keller@fernuni-hagen.de
[2] Universität Ulm, Ulm, Germany
steffen.wendzel@uni-ulm.de
https://www.fernuni-hagen.de/pv/en/ , https://www.uni-ulm.de/en/in/omi/

Abstract. Covert channels are tailored to enable a stealthy communication of secret data. Methods to establish covert channels have been optimized for several decades. Recently, *covert channel amplification* was proposed, which allows to signal more data to a receiver than are embedded by a sender. However, an in-depth analysis of optimal configurations for covert channel amplification is still missing. To this end, we formulate an *amplification channel optimization problem* and investigate optimal configurations for such covert channel amplifications.

Keywords: Steganography · Amplification Channel · Network Optimization · Information Hiding · Network Security

1 Introduction

Covert channels represent policy-breaking and stealthy communication channels [8] that have been studied for several decades. While they are often used by malware, they can also be employed for censorship circumvention and other legitimate use-cases. Despite their long-lasting analysis since the 1970s, recent work revealed a new design paradigm called *covert channel amplification* [14] with a prototype implementation called DYST (*Did you see that?*). Covert channel amplification allows to increase the size of a secret message that is transferred through a covert channel by referring to third-party data. While a preliminary analysis of the optimization of covert channel amplification is given in [14], the present work investigates where optimal configurations of such types of covert channels can be found. The key contributions of our paper are the following:

1. We present amplification channels in a formal way which enables us to formulate the amplification channel optimization problem (ACOP).

All authors contributed equally to this research.

P. Kieseberg et al. (Eds.): ARES 2026 Workshops, LNCS 16903, pp. 33–44, 2027.
https://doi.org/10.1007/978-3-032-37218-5_3

2. We present lower and upper bounds to the number of observed carrier objects needed to transmit a secret message and we present an average case analysis for common scenarios.
3. We show that the common wisdom to randomize the secret message and the carrier-extracted data to minimize the average number of observed carrier objects can be wrong in corner cases due to imperfections of coding.

The remainder of this article is structured as follows. In Sect. 2, we summarize background information and discuss related work. In Sect. 3, we present an abstract description and threat model and we formulate the amplification channel optimization problem (ACOP). Section 4 provides analytic results with examples while Sect. 5 presents conclusions and an outlook to future work.

2 Background and Related Work

Covert Channels enable hidden communication by transmitting secret information through mechanisms not intended for information exchange, thereby circumventing system security policies. The concept was first formalized by Lampson [6] and later systematized for network environments in [15], where covert data is embedded into observable properties of a *carrier*, such as packet timings, header fields, or traffic volume. Thus, covert communication is inherently detectable if it introduces statistical or structural deviations from legitimate carrier behavior.

In general, the stealthiness of covert communication is also linked to the amount of data that is transferred through such a channel [2]: the more data is transferred, the more traces are left, making the channel easier to detect and block by an adversary. For this reason, one aim of network covert channels is to minimize the amount of data that is transmitted. Therefore, complementary to distribution-aware encoding, prior work has explored reducing the transmitted data volume itself. Early protocol-level techniques (e.g., *Compressed Serial Line Interface Protocol* (CSLIP) [4] and the *Building Automation Control Networks* (BACnet) [10]) encode information implicitly through compact signaling.

From a statistical perspective, the carrier's observable behavior induces characteristic patterns that can be described in terms of probability distributions over features such as symbols, packet sizes, or timing characteristics. While these distributions are typically not known a priori, they implicitly define a baseline against which deviations may be detected. Stealthiness therefore aims to reduce the statistical distinguishability between legitimate and modified carrier traffic, for example in terms of divergence measures [1].

Entropy, introduced by Shannon, quantifies the uncertainty of such statistical descriptions and establishes the fundamental limit of lossless compression [12]. If symbols i from a finite alphabet Σ appear randomly and independently with a distribution p_i, where $0 < p_i < 1$ and $\sum_{i \in \Sigma} p_i = 1$, then the Shannon entropy of this symbol source is defined as

$$H(p) = \sum_{i \in \Sigma} -p_i \cdot \log_2 p_i \ . \tag{1}$$

The entropy is maximized to $H_{max} = \log_2 |\Sigma|$ for equi-distribution. Thus, the relative entropy is defined as $H_r(p) = H(p)/H_{max}$ with range $[0; 1]$.

Accordingly, no encoding scheme can achieve an average code length below the entropy without loss of information. Lossless compression exploits redundancy in the secret message to reduce its size up to a factor of H_r, thereby lowering the amount of data that must be embedded into the carrier and thus the potential observable footprint. Classical methods such as Huffman coding [3] approach this limit by assigning shorter representations to more probable symbols. Prefix-free codes guarantee instantaneous and unambiguous decoding and are constrained by the Kraft–McMillan inequality [9]. However, compression alone does not ensure stealthiness, as it does not control the statistical characteristics of the resulting carrier observations.

To address this limitation, the encoding process should take the observable (or at least estimable) statistics of the carrier into account. Distribution matching provides a way to do this by mapping input data to sequences whose empirical distribution follows a desired target. As a result, the transmitted symbols can better resemble the statistical behavior of legitimate carrier traffic. Practical approaches such as constant composition distribution matching enable this kind of control over the output distribution [11]. In the context of covert channels, this enables encoding the hidden message such that it limits observable deviations in the carrier.

History Covert Channels and Amplification. In a recent approach [14], a covert channel named "DYST" and the concept of covert channel *amplification* are introduced: by sending a *small* pointer through a covert channel that refers to channel-*external* data *larger* than the pointer, the size of the transmitted message is effectively amplified (see Fig. 1). For example, the sender can refer to previously seen network packets or their hash values [14]. When the pointer refers to already seen packets (or other types of previously recorded data), such a channel is called a *history covert channel.*

The original transmission rate of DYST was slow (with at most a few bits per second). To address this issue, Weißenborn and Wendzel [13] introduced a DYST-variant called the *Silent History Protocol* (SHP). By pointing to meta characteristics of network transmissions, such as the current number of packets of an ongoing flow, SHP is able to lift the transmission rate of DYST by a factor of more than hundred. Existing research thus points to two optimization paths: minimizing payload volume and shaping symbol statistics. This work investigates the latter, as no clear optimization strategy has been formulated so far.

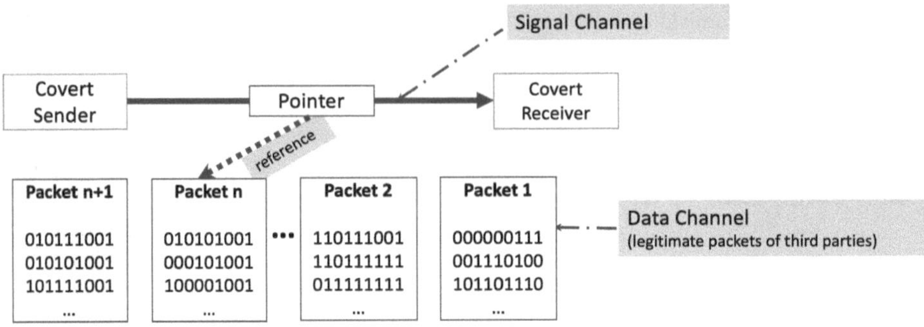

Fig. 1. Concept of a History Covert Channel (derived from [14]).

3 Optimization Problem Definition

Threat Model. We assume a scenario in which a covert sender (CS) aims to stealthily transfer secret data to a covert receiver (CR). To this end, CS and CR use a shared medium, such as a local network, to exchange messages. CS and CR assume that their exchanges are monitored by an adversary capable of *observing and recording all packets* within the network for an arbitrary duration. The adversary can run any desired covert channel detection algorithm on that traffic, either on-the-fly (live traffic) or during an ex-post processing. Since covertness increases with a decreasing fraction of a covert channel's capacity being used [2], CS and CR aim to minimize that fraction (amount of traffic) via covert channel amplification [14]. Both, CS and CR, are able to concurrently access the shared network. This allows to reference third-party traffic through pointers in a history covert channel. While not focus of our study, CS and CR could employ a control protocol [8, Ch. 4] to ensure synchronization and robustness.

Generalized Covert Channel Amplification. We provide an abstract and generalized version of the scenario in which DYST is applied [14]. The covert sender wants to send a secret message of N symbols that come from a secret message alphabet Σ_s. We assume that the symbols in the message are independent and random with probabilities r_j, where $\sum_{j\in\Sigma_s} r_j = 1$ and $0 < r_j < 1$. We distinguish *two scenarios*: either, the complete message is present at the beginning of the transmission, or the symbols of the message appear by and by, possibly only just in time to be transmitted, yet their distribution is known.

In either scenario, the secret message can be source encoded, e.g., via a Huffman code, but also via a $\log_2 |\Sigma_s|$-bit binary encoding of the symbol indices. This reduces the length of the message if r is not equi-distributed, with $N \cdot H(r)$ bits being a lower bound, which however normally is not reached in practice. The distribution of the bits (or bytes) of the encoded message also might be closer to equi-distribution than the distribution of a fixed-length encoding of the message, yet equi-distribution is often not reached (cf. Sect. 4). We denote the target alphabet of the encoding, which normally is $\{0, 1\}^*$, by Σ_c.

Furthermore, after source encoding the message can be encrypted via a symmetric block or stream cipher. The latter possibility is especially useful for the second scenario, where symbols arrive by and by. We assume that encryption does not change the length of the message, i.e., we ignore a possible padding. After encryption, the bits and bytes of the encrypted message are equi-distributed.

Finally, the message could undergo a lossless compression in the first scenario. The lower bound is $N \cdot H(r)$ bits, similar to source encoding, yet also here this bound is often not reached in practice and the distribution will not necessarily be equi-distribution nor will the values appear independent, i.e., a compressed source is not random [5]. In the following, we will treat lossless compression implicitly by considering it similar to source encoding for the reasons given above. As a consequence, we need not distinguish between the two scenarios as both source encoding and encryption is possible in both scenarios. We denote the encoding (and possibly encryption) procedure of a secret message by `encode`.

CS and the covert receiver (CR) observe the packets of a shared carrier with an `extract` function that produces symbols from the packets (observed through the data channel in Fig. 1). Using the extract function, CS and CR learn the carrier alphabet Σ_c and the probabilities p_i of the carrier symbols, where $\sum_{i \in \Sigma_c} p_i = 1$ and $0 < p_i \leq p_{i-1} < 1$ for $i > 0$ (to have numeric indices, we identify Σ_c with $\{0, \ldots, |\Sigma_c| - 1\}$ and define a suitable total order on the elements from a descending order of their probabilities).

For example, the `extract` function could be a hash function (as in DYST) with h-bit values on a number of packet header fields (possibly including some sequence number or counter `cnt`), so that we assume that all $p_i = 1/|\Sigma_c|$, i.e., the carrier symbols are independent and equi-distributed. As another example, the `extract` function could just return the contents of a particular header field such as ToS, h-bit values with $h = 8$ and a highly skewed p_i distribution.

From Σ_s, r_j, Σ_c and p_i, CS (and CR) derive a code $c : \Sigma_s \to \Sigma_c^*$ which must be uniquely decodable or prefix-free so that CS and CR can extend the code in straight-forward manner to Σ_s^* by symbol-wise encoding to a function `encode` that results in a sequence of $N' = N\bar{L}$ carrier symbols, where $\bar{L}$ is the average codeword length and q_i is the expected carrier symbol distribution in the encoded message, given a probability distribution r_j on the secret message symbols. CR in addition also creates a `decode` function that undoes the encoding. The existence of the decoding is guaranteed by the code properties. We note that $\bar{L}$ and q_i depend on c, i.e., they also possibly depend on r_j and p_i.

In DYST for example, also the encoded secret message is split into chunks of h-bit values, i.e., $\Sigma_c = \Sigma_s$ and the encoding function is identity, so that $\bar{L} = 1$ and $q_i = r_i$, where the r_i are independent and equi-distributed in case of an encrypted secret message. As another example, the secret message symbols could be bytes with an uneven distribution (such as ASCII text) and the code into typical packet header field values (e.g., IP ToS) could be complex to derive.

Now the actual transmission starts. The secret message is encoded and split into chunks of h bit each, i.e., into symbols of Σ_c. We denote the next chunk to be transmitted by `next`. In case of scenario 2, where secret message symbols arrive by and by, we assume an encoding buffer where codewords of arriving secret message symbols are appended at the end and transmitted chunks are removed from the head of the buffer. By appearing "just in time" (cf. scenario 2 description), we mean that the encoding buffer always contains at least h bits. When the next chunk to be transmitted is $i = \texttt{next}(msg)$ with $i \in \Sigma_c$, CS waits until a matching packet pk with $\texttt{extract}(pk) = i$ appears, then it sends a signal (the "pointer" in Fig. 1) to CR. The procedure is visualized in Fig. 2.

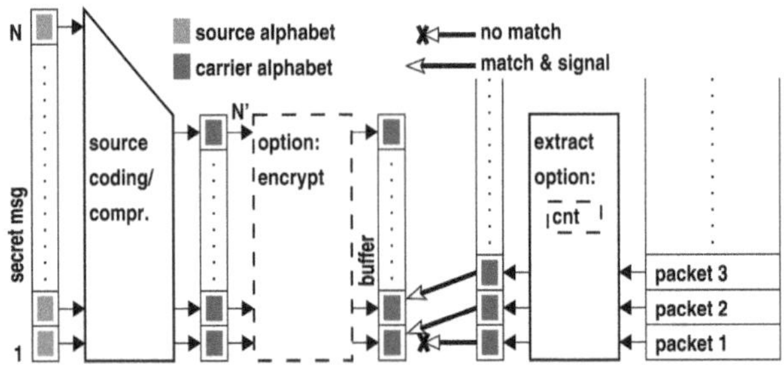

Fig. 2. Encoding secret message into alphabet Σ_c, extracting symbols from packets and matching & signalling. Only second extracted symbol matches first chunk.

Upon receipt of a signal, CR extracts the actual carrier packet into carrier symbol i. When CR has received all N' carrier symbols, i.e., the complete encoded message, then CR applies the `decode` function and obtains the secret message as the result. Please note that we leave out details that are merely technical, e.g., how N' is transmitted to CR and how the robustness, i.e., exact sync between receipt of signal and packet on the side of CR, is achieved. Regarding N', the message could be encoded in a self-delimiting way or N' could be agreed upon in advance between CS and CR (especially if $N' = N$). For robustness, see [14] for details.

The problem to be solved, denoted as *amplification channel optimization problem (ACOP)*, is:

> *Given Σ_s, r_j, Σ_c, and p_j, design a code c that minimizes the average number of packets to wait until the next symbol of the encoded secret message can be signaled.*

Naturally, we are also interested in the numeric value of this minimum.

4 Analytic Results

Match Probabilities. When CS waits for carrier symbol i to appear, the match probability is p_i for each packet, so that the expected number of packets up to a match is $1/p_i$. As symbol i appears with frequency q_i in the encoded secret message, the expected number of packets for a single encoded symbol is $\sum_{i \in \Sigma_c} q_i/p_i$ and the total number of packets needed on average will be

$$N' \cdot \sum_{i \in \Sigma_c} q_i/p_i \ . \tag{2}$$

As N secret message symbols have been transported, the expected number of packets needed to transmit a *single* encoded secret message symbol is

$$\bar{L} \cdot \sum_{i \in \Sigma_c} q_i/p_i \ . \tag{3}$$

We will first discuss cases where Eq. (3) can be simplified, before treating lower and upper bounds and the general case. Special cases appear when one of the distributions q_i or p_i is equi-distribution or both distributions are equal.

Special Case 1: Equi-Distributed Encoded Message. If the q_i are equi-distributed, e.g., because the message is encrypted, then Eq. (3) simplifies to

$$\frac{\bar{L}}{|\Sigma_c|} \sum_{i \in \Sigma_c} 1/p_i \ , \tag{4}$$

where

$$\bar{L} = \lceil \log_{|\Sigma_c|}(|\Sigma_s|) \rceil \ , \tag{5}$$

as a fixed-length encoding is most appropriate for equi-distributed symbols.

The last term of Eq. (4) is minimized when all p_i are equal, which is always possible by hashing carrier contents with a counter, cf. Sect. 3. Thus, this special case can always be transformed into one of the other special cases.

Special Case 2: Equi-Distributed Carrier Symbols. If the p_i are equi-distributed, Eq. (3) simplifies to

$$\bar{L}|\Sigma_c| \ , \tag{6}$$

independent of q_i, where $\bar{L} = \lceil \log_{|\Sigma_c|}(|\Sigma_s|) \rceil$ if no source encoding is applied.

Hence, in this case, an entropy source encoding should be applied if possible as it will reduce the number of symbols that must be transmitted. This case is described in DYST as all packet hash values have equal probability $p_i = 1/2^h$. As $\Sigma_s = \Sigma_c$ of size 2^h, $\bar{L} = 1$ and the average number of packets until a match occurs amounts to 2^h.

Special Case 3: Distributions of Message and Carrier Symbols Match. If $q_i = p_i$, Eq. (3) simplifies to Eq. 6, yet $\bar{L}$ may be higher than in Eq. (5).

Lower and Upper Bound. A lower bound would be achieved if the secret message could be optimally compressed into $N \cdot H(r)$ bits. In this case, the bits (or bytes) of the encoded secret message will be random and equi-distributed and thus the first special case applies which is optimized by choosing equi-distributed carrier symbols, cf. special case 1. In this case, each of the h-bit chunks would be transmitted after $|\Sigma_c| = 2^h$ packets on average. The result of this argument is the following Lemma 1.

Lemma 1. *To transmit a secret message with N symbols of distribution r via a carrier with extract alphabet $\Sigma_c = \{0,1\}^h$ and equi-distribution p, at least*

$$\frac{N \cdot H(r)}{h} \cdot |\Sigma_c| = \frac{N \cdot H(r) \cdot 2^h}{h} \tag{7}$$

packets must be observed on average.

If $\Sigma_s = \{0,1\}$ and r is equi-distributed, i.e., $H(r) = 1$, we achieve the result of [14], where the bandwidth per observed packet is $h/2^h$ bits. In this sense, the DYST prototype achieves optimal bandwidth, only to be improved by pointing to larger external data [16] or artificially computed (flow) metadata [13].

As the second special case (equi-distributed carrier symbols) can always be achieved (see above), it can serve as an upper bound on the optimum. Thus, we obtain the following Lemma 2.

Lemma 2. *The optimal transmission of a secret message via a DYST-like channel will not need more than $\bar{L}|\Sigma_c|$ observed packets per encoded message symbol.*

General Case. The bound of $|\Sigma_c|$ in the second factor of Eq. (3) can only be reduced if the p_i are not equi-distributed *and* the q_i are not distributed like p_i.

Proposition 1. *In the general case, $\sum_{i\in\Sigma_c} q_i/p_i$ can be smaller than $|\Sigma_c|$.*

Proof. For symbol i, we choose $q_i = p_i + \varepsilon < 1$ and for symbol j with $j > i$, we choose $q_j = p_j - \varepsilon > 0$ for some ε with $0 < \varepsilon < 1$, which will always be possible. If all other i' with $i' \neq i, j$ have $q_{i'} = p_{i'}$, then still $\sum_i q_i = 1$. We get

$$q_i/p_i = 1 + \varepsilon/p_i \qquad q_j/p_j = 1 - \varepsilon/p_j$$

and as $j > i$, we have $p_j \leq p_i$ and thus $1/p_j \geq 1/p_i$, so that we get

$$q_i/p_i + q_j/p_j = 2 - \varepsilon \cdot \underbrace{\left(\frac{1}{p_j} - \frac{1}{p_i}\right)}_{\geq 0} < 2 \tag{8}$$

As all other terms $q_{i'}/p_{i'} = 1$ for $i' \in \Sigma_c$ with $i' \neq i, j$, we have proven that there are situations where

$$\sum_{i\in\Sigma_c} \frac{q_i}{p_i} < |\Sigma_c| \, . \tag{9}$$

□

The general case seems to lead to quite skewed probability distributions so that encoding would lead to quite long codewords, i.e., large $\bar{L}$ that "eats" away the advantage gained in the second factor of Eq. (3). Yet, we illustrate with the following example that already the imperfection of entropy-based encoding can lead to distributions where the expected number of observed packets is between the lower bound and the number achievable by one of the special cases.

Example. Let us assume that the secret message is based on an alphabet Σ_s of size 4 with a probability distribution $r_j = [0.4, 0.3, 0.2, 0.1]$. The entropy of the source is $H(r) \approx 1.846$, while a Huffman encoding leads to a tree as in Fig. 3(left), resulting in an average codeword length of 1.9, which is close to the entropy but not identical. Also, we note that both entropy and average codeword length are close to the maximum possible entropy 2 for an alphabet with 4 symbols, so the distribution is not very skewed.

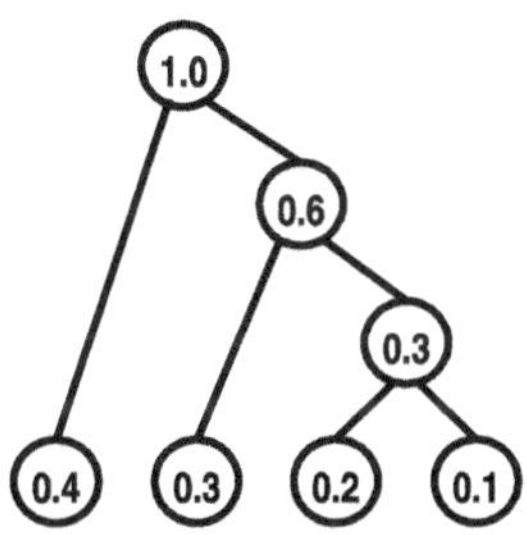

code	$c_i(s_0)$	$c_i(s_1)$	$c_i(s_2)$	$c_i(s_3)$
c_1	0	10	110	111
c_2	0	11	100	101
c_3	0	10	111	110
c_4	0	11	101	100
c_5	1	01	001	000
c_6	1	00	011	010
c_7	1	01	000	001
c_8	1	00	010	011

Fig. 3. Left: Huffman tree for four symbols with probabilities $[0.4, 0.3, 0.2, 0.1]$. Right: Different codes resulting from this tree with different edge marks. In the last four codes, the codewords are the inverse of the codewords of the first four codes.

However, this tree is not unique, as in each of the three inner nodes we can choose whether to mark the left or the right outgoing edge with 0 (and the other edge with 1), cf. Fig. 3(right). While this has no influence on the average codeword length, it influences the average relative frequencies of 0 s and 1 s, i.e., the distribution q_i in a codeword sequence. Let o_i be the number of 1 s in the codeword of symbol i. Then the average relative frequency of 1 s is given by

$$\frac{\sum_i r_i \cdot o_i}{\sum_i r_i \cdot |c(i)|}, \tag{10}$$

where $c(i)$ is the codeword for symbol i. In our example, the possible relative frequencies are 0.421, 0.474, 0.523 and 0.579 (rounded to 3 decimal digits). We choose the last, i.e., $q_0 = 0.421$ and $q_1 = 0.579$.

For a carrier with alphabet $\Sigma_c = \{0, 1\}$, the lower bound according to Eq. (7) is $1000 \cdot 1.846 \cdot 2 = 3692$ observed packets on average until the secret message is transmitted. If we choose the Huffman coding of the secret message together with an equi-distribution $p_i = [0.5, 0.5]$ on the carrier symbols, then we need $1000 \cdot 1.9 \cdot 2 = 3800$ observed packets on average.

However, if the carrier symbols are distributed with $p_i = [0.54, 0.46]$, which is not too unrealistic, we achieve an average number of packets according to Eq. (3) of $1.9875 \cdot 1.9 = 3.776$, i.e., 3776 packets in total, which indeed is between the lower bound and the special case of equi-distributed carrier symbols. We have found this most advantageous symbol distribution on the carrier by plotting the average number of observed packets for p_1 between 0.5 and 0.6, cf. Fig. 4.

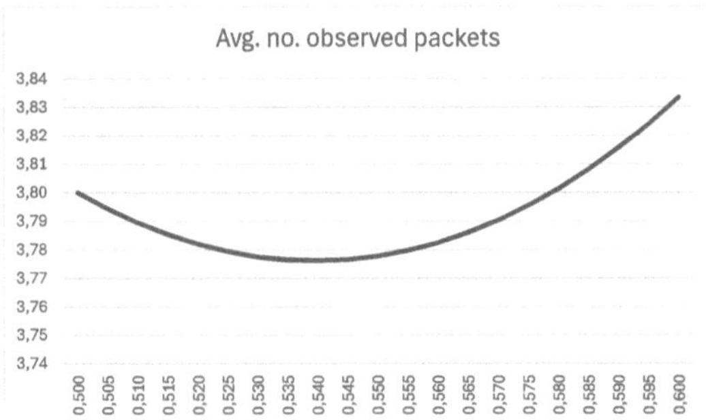

Fig. 4. Average number of observed packets for different carrier symbol distributions.

As a realistic example, we consider a text message comprised from 40 symbols (26 letters, 10 digits, blank space, full stop, comma and questionmark) with a Zipf distribution, i.e., $r_j = c/j$ where c is the inverse of the 40th harmonic number. Entropy is 4.38 bit/symbol. A near-Huffman encoding encodes the 8 most frequent symbols in 4-bit codewords 0xxx and the other 32 symbols get 6-bit codes 1yyyyy, all grouped into 2-bit symbols as we extract 4 carrier symbols. Average codeword length is 2.36. Frequencies q_i are 0.42, 0.22, 0.21, 0.15.

From IPv4 packets on the carrier, we extract 2nd to 5th most frequent values of the ToS field with relative frequencies p_i 0.31, 0.29, 0.21, 0.19, from the MAWI dataset trace of 2024-07-01 [7]. For stealthiness, we do not use the most frequent ToS value 0x00 as it occurs in more than 90% of the packets. The lower bound is 8.76 packets per message symbol on average, while the upper bound (achieved with equi-distributed extraction) is 9.46. With our encoding and carrier distribution, we achieve 9.23 packets per message symbol. More information on the example can be found at https://github.com/cdpxe/ACOP/.

5 Conclusions

We described DYST-like covert channels, i.e., history channels as a form of amplification channels, in a formal way and thus were able to formulate the amplification channel optimization problem. We showed that the entropy of the secret message source puts a lower bound on the number of observed packets necessary to transmit the secret message. In general, a source encoding of the secret message with an entropy encoder and hashing the carrier information with a counter—to achieve equi-distribution of values extracted from observed packets—leads to a number of observed packets for transmitting the message that is close to the entropy bound. However, we also demonstrated that there are corner cases where other solutions could even get closer to the lower bound.

In future work, we would like to investigate whether allowing varying width of values extracted from carrier information could further improve the situation. Also, the relation of this problem to distribution matching and the performance of distribution matching relative to the information-theoretic approach presented here might deserve further attention. Finally, we would like to implement our scheme for a real network carrier.

Disclosure of Interests. J. Keller is supported by project PERUN funded by EU's Horizon Europe Research and Innovation programme under Grant Agreement No. 101225653.

References

1. Cachin, C.: An information-theoretic model for steganography. In: Aucsmith, D. (ed.) IH 1998. LNCS, vol. 1525, pp. 306–318. Springer, Heidelberg (1998). https://doi.org/10.1007/3-540-49380-8_21
2. Giani, A., Berk, V.H., Cybenko, G.V.: Data exfiltration and covert channels. In: Sensors, and Command, Control, Communications, and Intelligence (C3I) Technologies for Homeland Security and Homeland Defense, vol. 6201, p. 620103. SPIE (2006). https://doi.org/10.1117/12.670123
3. Huffman, D.A.: A method for the construction of minimum-redundancy codes. Proc. IRE **40**(9), 1098–1101 (1952). https://doi.org/10.1109/JRPROC.1952.273898
4. Jacobson, V.: Compressing TCP/IP headers for low-speed serial links (1990). https://www.rfc-editor.org/rfc/rfc1144.html. RFC 1144
5. Klein, S.T., Shapira, D.: On the randomness of compressed data. Inf. **11**(4), 196 (2020). https://doi.org/10.3390/INFO11040196
6. Lampson, B.W.: A note on the confinement problem. Commun. ACM **16**(10), 613–615 (1973). https://doi.org/10.1145/362375.362389
7. MAWI, Working Group Traffic Archive: Packet traces from WIDE backbone (2025). https://mawi.wide.ad.jp/mawi/. Accessed 10 May 2025
8. Mazurczyk, W., Wendzel, S., Zander, S., Houmansadr, A., Szczypiorski, K.: Information Hiding in Communication Networks: Fundamentals, Mechanisms, and Applications. Wiley-IEEE Press (2016). https://doi.org/10.1002/9781119081715
9. McMillan, B.: Two inequalities implied by unique decipherability. IRE Trans. Inf. Theory **2**(4), 115–116 (1956). https://doi.org/10.1109/TIT.1956.1056818
10. Merz, H., Hansemann, T., Hübner, C.: Building Automation. Springer (2009)
11. Schulte, P., Böcherer, G.: Constant composition distribution matching. Trans. Inform. Theory **62**(1), 430–434 (2016). https://doi.org/10.1109/TIT.2015.2499181
12. Shannon, C.E.: A mathematical theory of communication. Bell Syst. Tech. J. **27**, 379–423 (1948). https://doi.org/10.1002/j.1538-7305.1948.tb01338.x

13. Weißenborn, C., Wendzel, S.: History covert channels with relative timing pointers: design, error resilience, and detectability. J. Inf. Secur. Appl. **99**, 104431 (2026). https://doi.org/10.1016/j.jisa.2026.104431
14. Wendzel, S., Schmidbauer, T., Zillien, S., Keller, J.: DYST (did you see that?): an amplified covert channel that points to previously seen data. IEEE Trans. Dependable Secure Comput. (TDSC) **22**(1), 614–631 (2025). https://doi.org/10.1109/TDSC.2024.3410679
15. Zander, S., Armitage, G., Branch, P.: A survey of covert channels and countermeasures in computer network protocols. IEEE Commun. Surv. Tutorials **9**(3), 44–57 (2007). https://doi.org/10.1109/COMST.2007.4317620
16. Zillien, S., Schmidbauer, T., Kubek, M., Keller, J., Wendzel, S.: Look what's there! Utilizing the internet's existing data for censorship circumvention with OPPRESSION. In: Proceedings 19th ACM Asia Conference on Computer and Communications Security, ASIA CCS 2024. ACM (2024). https://doi.org/10.1145/3634737.3637676

LDPKiT: Superimposing Remote Queries for Privacy-Preserving Distillation

Kexin Li[1(✉)], Aastha Mehta[2], and David Lie[1]

[1] University of Toronto, Toronto, ON, Canada
cassiekx.li@mail.utoronto.ca

[2] The University of British Columbia, Vancouver, BC, Canada

Abstract. To protect privacy in regulated domains such as healthcare and finance, model owners may allow only remote API access while keeping both the training data and model parameters private. However, model users performing inference on such remotely hosted models may be required to transmit potentially sensitive inputs, raising privacy concerns. In this work, we present LDPKiT, a framework for non-adversarial, privacy-preserving model distillation that leverages a user's private in-distribution data while bounding privacy leakage. LDPKiT introduces a novel superimposition technique that generates approximately in-distribution samples, enabling effective knowledge transfer under local differential privacy (LDP). Experiments on Fashion-MNIST, SVHN, and PathMNIST demonstrate that LDPKiT consistently improves utility while maintaining privacy, with benefits that become more pronounced at stronger noise levels. For example, on SVHN, LDPKiT achieves nearly the same inference accuracy at $\epsilon = 1.25$ as at $\epsilon = 2.0$, yielding stronger privacy guarantees with less than a 2% accuracy reduction. We further conduct sensitivity analyses to examine the effect of dataset size on performance and provide a systematic analysis of latent space representations, offering intuitive and empirical insights into the accuracy gains of LDPKiT.

Keywords: Local differential privacy · Inference data privacy protection · Privacy-preserving knowledge distillation · Data augmentation

1 Introduction

A machine learning (ML) model, trained on a dataset, is a representation of the data that can be used to make predictions and offer insights on other data that is of a similar distribution to the original training set. As a result, even in cases where the training data itself cannot be shared due to privacy restrictions, there is still a strong incentive to share access to the ML model. Moreover, techniques such as PATE [27] and federated learning [42] have been proposed to enable training such models while limiting the privacy impact on the training

P. Kieseberg et al. (Eds.): ARES 2026 Workshops, LNCS 16903, pp. 45–62, 2027.
https://doi.org/10.1007/978-3-032-37218-5_4

set. The privacy protection such techniques confer is maximized when offering only black-box access (*i.e.* keeping the weights private) to such models, so that the intermediate activations computed during inference remain hidden [30].

Sensitive data is sometimes shared for socially beneficial reasons, particularly in regulated sectors where organizations must disclose privacy-sensitive information to protect public welfare. For example, hospitals may be required to share patient information during disease outbreaks, and financial institutions may need to report accounts suspected of money laundering. ML could enable similar benefits while reducing the need to share sensitive datasets directly: organizations with large proprietary datasets could train predictive models using privacy-protective techniques [27,42] and provide controlled access to entities without comparable data. For instance, a healthcare network could offer smaller clinics access to a model that predicts disease risk, while a large financial institution could provide local banks with a model for detecting money laundering.

However, while black-box models trained using privacy-preserving methods protect the training set, inference in the black-box setting still requires the model user to transmit potentially sensitive inputs. While various methods for protecting privacy during inference have been proposed, none satisfy the requirements of efficiency and ease of adoption. For instance, homomorphic encryption [14] can impose severe overheads and typically targets an honest-but-curious adversary model, while hardware-enforced trusted execution environments [32] require specialized hardware that is currently not broadly available.

The strongest privacy guarantee available to a model user is to obtain the trained model weights and perform inference locally, so that the user's data never leaves their control. However, this would open up the original model to white-box attacks. To address this, we propose a privacy-preserving distillation of black-box models while bounding the privacy leakage of query inputs, which we call LDPKiT (*Local Differentially-Private and Utility-Preserving Inference via Knowledge Transfer*). Effective distillation requires users' queries to be representative of the model's training data distribution, so ideally, they should use real data. However, in regulated privacy-sensitive domains, users typically possess only small amounts of such data, *e.g.* smaller clinics may have far fewer patients. LDPKiT addresses the privacy and data-shortage challenges by applying local differential privacy (LDP) to bound the privacy leakage of each query while introducing a data augmentation technique that superimposes pairs of noised inputs to generate additional in-distribution queries. This combination enables users to distill useful knowledge from remote models while ensuring protection of sensitive query data.

Our analysis is guided by the following research questions:

RQ1. Does LDPKiT recover the utility impacted by LDP noise? (Sect. 4.1)
RQ2. Why does superimposition work in LDPKiT? (Sect. 4.2)
RQ3. How do the size of the private dataset and the number of queries impact LDPKiT? (Sect. 4.3)

Contributions. LDPKiT enables privacy-preserving distillation from remote black-box models by generating augmented inference datasets from users' ϵ-

LDP-protected private samples. Across three image-classification datasets and two models, LDPKiT recovers much of the utility lost to LDP noise. We further study the impact of private-dataset size and number of queries, and conduct latent-space analysis to uncover factors contributing to LDPKiT's effectiveness.

2 Overview

Motivation. Our scenario considers privacy-sensitive ML services used to label privacy-sensitive data. Effective distillation for privacy requires realistic in-distribution data, which may itself be sensitive and unavailable publicly. Using out-of-distribution data is ineffective. For instance, distilling a ResNet-18 trained on Fashion-MNIST with SVHN samples, or vice versa, yields approximately random-guessing accuracy (*i.e.* 10%) for these 10-class datasets. By contrast, noisy in-distribution samples perform better: models distilled using ϵ-LDP data with $\epsilon = 2.0$ achieve roughly 21% accuracy on SVHN and 28% on Fashion-MNIST.

Preliminaries and General Setup. Our scenario involves two parties: a model provider hosting a remote model, $\mathcal{M}_{\text{R}}$, and a user with a small, unlabelled, sensitive dataset, $\mathcal{D}_{\text{priv}}$, who distills a local model, $\mathcal{M}_{\text{L}}$. The user may be an organization or individual with black-box access to $\mathcal{M}_{\text{R}}$. To protect $\mathcal{D}_{\text{priv}}$, the user applies ϵ-LDP noise to each sample, producing $\mathcal{D}_{\text{protected}}$, where $|\mathcal{D}_{\text{priv}}| = |\mathcal{D}_{\text{protected}}|$. Since $|\mathcal{D}_{\text{priv}}|$ is typically small, we augment $\mathcal{D}_{\text{protected}}$ to form an expanded inference dataset, $\mathcal{D}_{\text{infer}}$. Its size, $|\mathcal{D}_{\text{infer}}|$, is determined by the user's query budget for $\mathcal{M}_{\text{R}}$, allowing the user to select some or all augmented samples. These samples are labelled by $\mathcal{M}_{\text{R}}$ and used to train $\mathcal{M}_{\text{L}}$. We compare against *SIDP*, a baseline in which the user directly queries $\mathcal{M}_{\text{R}}$ with $\mathcal{D}_{\text{protected}}$ and accepts the returned predictions, despite errors caused by LDP noise. To improve accuracy on $\mathcal{D}_{\text{priv}}$, LDPKiT distills $\mathcal{M}_{\text{L}}$ using samples from $\mathcal{D}_{\text{infer}}$ generated by two augmentation methods, *LDPKiT-Rand* and *LDPKiT-Sup*.

Threat Model. The user's goal is to label samples in $\mathcal{D}_{\text{priv}}$ with reasonable accuracy when interacting with an ML service in a privacy-preserving way. We only assume that $\mathcal{M}_{\text{R}}$ provides faithful responses so that the user can obtain faithful predictions on inputs. Furthermore, the service provider has complete control of the model implementation and, as a result, has full access to the inference inputs. We note that the assumption of faithful responses is not required for LDPKiT's privacy guarantees, only for the utility of the $\mathcal{M}_{\text{L}}$. To mitigate the threat of exposing sensitive data, the user applies ϵ-LDP to their data before querying $\mathcal{M}_{\text{R}}$, limiting the amount of information that can be inferred from individual samples. Our privacy goal is to protect the user's inference inputs from the remote model provider; LDPKiT does not aim to protect the provider's proprietary model beyond the provider's existing black-box access policy.

Privacy Guarantee. LDPKiT ensures the privacy of $\mathcal{D}_{\text{priv}}$ during inference by applying LDP noise to each data sample. Intuitively, ϵ-LDP ensures that after observing a protected query, the provider cannot confidently distinguish which raw private input produced it; a smaller ϵ makes inputs harder to distinguish.

Definition 1. ***ϵ-Local Differential Privacy (LDP).*** *We define ϵ-LDP as follows [7]: A randomized algorithm $\mathcal{A}$ satisfies ϵ-LDP if for all pairs of values and all sets $\mathcal{S}$ of possible outputs, where $\mathcal{S} \subseteq Range(\mathcal{A})$,*

$$\Pr[\mathcal{A}(v_1) \in \mathcal{S}] \leq e^{\epsilon} \Pr[\mathcal{A}(v_2) \in \mathcal{S}] \tag{1}$$

A lower ϵ indicates a tighter bound in the inequality and a stronger privacy guarantee. We choose ϵ values primarily based on common industry standards [2, 25] and empirically verify that protected data is resilient to data reconstruction attacks [29]. We apply Laplace noise to satisfy the ϵ-LDP privacy guarantee.

Definition 2. ***Laplace Mechanism.*** *For $x \in \mathcal{X}$, let $\Delta_1 = \max_{x,x' \in \mathcal{X}} \|x - x'\|_1$ denote the ℓ_1 sensitivity under the chosen neighboring relation. The mechanism releases $\tilde{x} = x + \eta$, where each coordinate $\eta_k \sim \mathrm{Lap}(0, \lambda)$ independently and $\lambda = \Delta_1/\epsilon$. This calibration satisfies ϵ-LDP for each protected sample. For a scalar variable t, the probability density function of the Laplace distribution is*

$$p_\eta(t; \lambda) = \frac{1}{2\lambda} \exp\left(-\frac{|t|}{\lambda}\right). \tag{2}$$

For constructing the inference dataset $\mathcal{D}_{\text{infer}}$, we use LDP's post-processing property: any processing of an ϵ-LDP output remains ϵ-LDP [8]. This allows LDPKiT to improve utility through augmentation without weakening privacy [36].

Definition 3. ***Post-Processing Property in ϵ-LDP.*** *The post-processing property of LDP [8] states that if a randomized algorithm $\mathcal{A}$ satisfies ϵ-LDP, then for any deterministic or randomized function g independent from the original input values, the composed mechanism $g(\mathcal{A}(\cdot))$ also satisfies ϵ-LDP. Specifically, for all v_1, v_2 (i.e. all values in the domain) and for all subsets $\mathcal{T} \subseteq Range(g(\mathcal{A}))$:*

$$\Pr[g(\mathcal{A}(v_1)) \in \mathcal{T}] \leq e^{\epsilon} \Pr[g(\mathcal{A}(v_2)) \in \mathcal{T}]. \tag{3}$$

3 Design

Figure 1 summarizes SIDP and LDPKiT. Since $|\mathcal{D}_{\text{protected}}| < |\mathcal{D}_{\text{infer}}|$, SIDP has a lower query cost than LDPKiT, but at the cost of utility. SIDP directly queries $\mathcal{M}_{\text{R}}$ with $\mathcal{D}_{\text{protected}}$ and accepts the returned labels, while LDPKiT post-processes $\mathcal{D}_{\text{protected}}$ into a larger $\mathcal{D}_{\text{infer}}$, queries $\mathcal{M}_{\text{R}}$ for labels, and trains $\mathcal{M}_{\text{L}}$ for local inference on $\mathcal{D}_{\text{priv}}$. Thus, SIDP has lower query cost, whereas LDPKiT uses additional post-processed queries to recover utility.

Preliminary Experiments. Distillation with OOD public data is ineffective (Sect. 2); hence, users must query $\mathcal{M}_{\text{R}}$ with in-distribution samples from $\mathcal{D}_{\text{priv}}$.

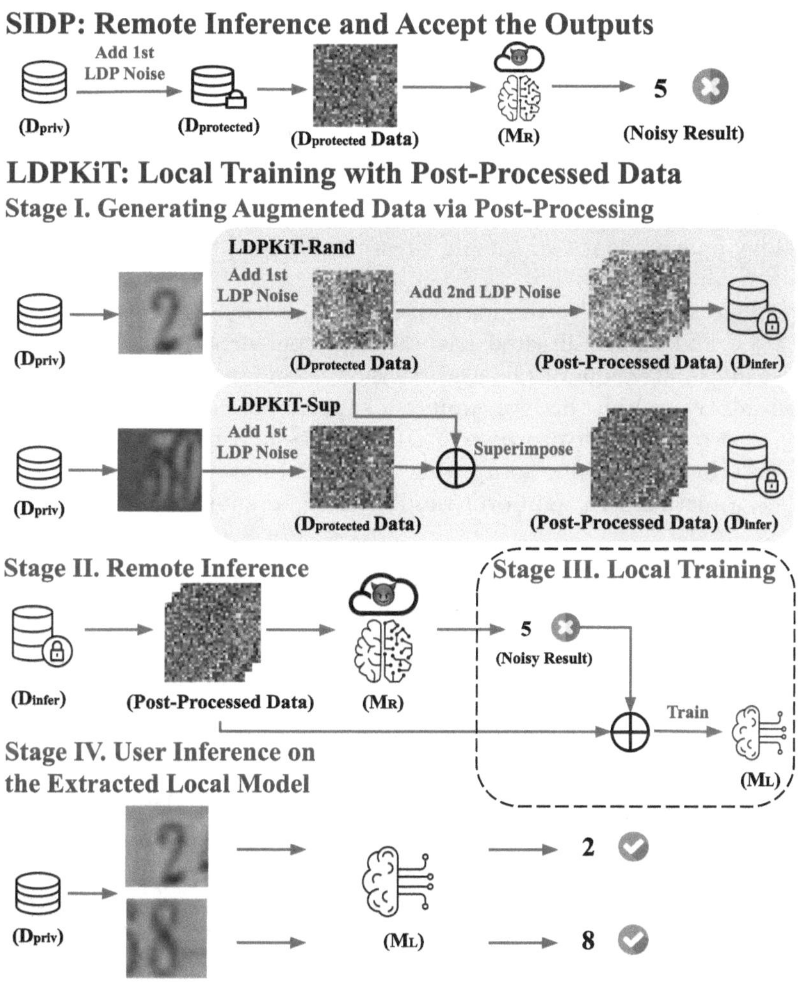

Fig. 1. LDPKiT system overview.

To protect these samples, LDPKiT applies an ϵ-LDP mechanism to obtain $\mathcal{D}_{\text{protected}}$. However, $\mathcal{D}_{\text{priv}}$ is often small, and LDP noise degrades utility. LDPKiT therefore augments $\mathcal{D}_{\text{protected}}$ into a larger inference dataset, $\mathcal{D}_{\text{infer}}$, while preserving privacy through LDP's post-processing property. $\mathcal{D}_{\text{protected}}$ retains sufficient distributional information for distillation, yielding 2–3× higher utility than OOD data (Sect. 2). A natural augmentation strategy is to generate n perturbed variants of each protected sample, producing $|\mathcal{D}_{\text{infer}}| = n \times |\mathcal{D}_{\text{protected}}|$. Since augmentation operates only on $\mathcal{D}_{\text{protected}}$, the ϵ-LDP guarantee is preserved.

We validate this idea on SVHN using 500 randomly selected private samples, ResNet-152 as $\mathcal{M}_{\text{R}}$, and ResNet-18 as $\mathcal{M}_{\text{L}}$. Results are averaged over three runs and three dataset splits. With $\epsilon = 1.5$, SIDP achieves only 14.16% inference accuracy, indicating that $\mathcal{M}_{\text{R}}$ provides limited but nontrivial information under privacy protection. We then add a layer of random noise 499 times to each protected sample, yielding $|\mathcal{D}_{\text{infer}}| = 249{,}500$ augmented queries. Distillation on $\mathcal{D}_{\text{infer}}$ improves $\mathcal{M}_{\text{L}}$ accuracy to 34.07%, whereas distillation using only the 500 samples in $\mathcal{D}_{\text{protected}}$ yields near-random accuracy (*i.e.* 10%). Compared with SIDP, this gives a 20% absolute accuracy improvement without additional privacy loss; a dependent two-sample t-test confirms statistical significance ($p < 0.05$).

Nevertheless, this naïve random-noise augmentation is limited by the small size of $\mathcal{D}_{\text{priv}}$ and the undirected nature of the perturbations. We hypothesize that more informative queries lie near decision boundaries in the latent data distribution. Motivated by this, we explore a superimposition-based augmentation strategy that refines post-processed LDP samples and better captures decision boundaries. Under the same setup, this approach improves ResNet-18 accuracy to 45.69%, a further 10% gain over random-noise augmentation.

3.1 LDPKiT's Data Augmentation Mechanism

LDPKiT first applies the ϵ-LDP mechanism [7] to each private sample in $\mathcal{D}_{\text{priv}}$ once, producing $\mathcal{D}_{\text{protected}}$. All subsequent augmentation operates only on $\mathcal{D}_{\text{protected}}$ and data-independent randomness. We consider two post-processing strategies: LDPKiT-Rand, which adds additional random perturbations to protected samples, and LDPKiT-Sup, which averages pairs of protected samples.

Mechanism-level Privacy Guarantee. Let $\mathcal{M}(\mathcal{D}_{\text{priv}})$ denote the complete user-side procedure. Each private sample $d_{\text{priv}_i} \in \mathcal{D}_{\text{priv}}$ is randomized once by an ϵ-LDP mechanism $\mathcal{A}_\epsilon$ to produce $d_{\text{protected}_i} = \mathcal{A}_\epsilon(d_{\text{priv}_i})$, using the Laplace mechanism in Definition 2. The augmented query set $\mathcal{D}_{\text{infer}}$ is then constructed only from $\{d_{\text{protected}_i}\}$ using data-independent post-processing, including additional random perturbation (LDPKiT-Rand) or pairwise averaging (LDPKiT-Sup).

For any two private datasets D and D' that differ in one record, all protected records except the changed one have the same distribution, while the changed record is protected by $\mathcal{A}_\epsilon$. Since the construction of $\mathcal{D}_{\text{infer}}$ and the selection of any query set are post-processing of protected records, for any event T over query sets, $\Pr[\mathcal{M}(D) \in T] \leq e^\epsilon \Pr[\mathcal{M}(D') \in T]$. Thus, the query set $\mathcal{D}_{\text{infer}}$ preserves record-level ϵ-LDP, assuming each private record is randomized once and later augmentations access only protected records and data-independent randomness.

LDPKiT-Rand. We formally describe the augmentation technique: for each $d_{\text{priv}_i} \in \mathcal{D}_{\text{priv}}$, we construct an augmented dataset of the form: $d_{\text{infer}_i} \in \mathcal{D}_{\text{infer}} = d_{\text{priv}_i} + \mathcal{L}_i + \mathcal{L}_j$, where $\mathcal{L}_i$ and $\mathcal{L}_j$ are Laplace noise samples drawn independently with the same scale. The first noise layer, $\mathcal{L}_i$, is used to generate the initial privacy-protected dataset: $d_{\text{protected}_i} = d_{\text{priv}_i} + \mathcal{L}_i$, where $i = 1, 2, \ldots, |\mathcal{D}_{\text{protected}}|$. We then apply the second noise layer, $\mathcal{L}_j$, where $j = 1, 2, \ldots, |\mathcal{D}_{\text{protected}}| - 1$, as post-processing to create an expanded augmented dataset for querying. While it is theoretically possible to generate an infinite number of such noisy variants per data point, we cap the size of the maximum possible augmented dataset $\mathcal{D}_{\text{infer}}$ to $|\mathcal{D}_{\text{protected}}| \cdot (|\mathcal{D}_{\text{protected}}| - 1)$ to make it comparable to LDPKiT-Sup below.

LDPKiT-Sup. LDPKiT-Rand introduces unrelated noise that may cause the resulting data to deviate further from the distribution of $\mathcal{D}_{\text{priv}}$. LDPKiT-Sup is thus proposed as an alternative to better preserve the characteristics of $\mathcal{D}_{\text{priv}}$. After applying the first layer of ϵ-LDP random noise to each data point in $\mathcal{D}_{\text{priv}}$ to produce $\mathcal{D}_{\text{protected}}$, we combine pairwise samples of $\mathcal{D}_{\text{protected}}$ for all pairs by averaging corresponding pixel values. Each augmented inference data point $d_{\text{infer}_i} \in \mathcal{D}_{\text{infer}}$ is computed as $d_{\text{infer}_i} = avg(d_{\text{protected}_i}, d_{\text{protected}_j})$ where $i, j = 1, 2, \ldots, |\mathcal{D}_{\text{protected}}|, i \neq j$. This process results in at most $|\mathcal{D}_{\text{protected}}| \cdot (|\mathcal{D}_{\text{protected}}| - 1)$ permutations in $\mathcal{D}_{\text{infer}}$. Since averaging is symmetric, pairs (i, j) and (j, i) are identical; in our implementation, we retain these ordered samples to match the experimental query budget of LDPKiT-Rand, but deduplication could reduce the query count without changing the set of unique superimposed images.

The mechanism-level guarantee above also covers structure-aware providers that know the LDPKiT-Sup construction. In particular, when sufficiently many pairwise averages are observed, a provider may recover protected records algebraically: $d_{\text{protected}_i} = \text{avg}(d_{\text{protected}_i}, d_{\text{protected}_j}) + \text{avg}(d_{\text{protected}_i}, d_{\text{protected}_k}) - \text{avg}(d_{\text{protected}_j}, d_{\text{protected}_k})$. Such recovery does not violate the formal guarantee: the recovered $d_{\text{protected}_i} \in \mathcal{D}_{\text{protected}}$ is already the output of $\mathcal{A}_\epsilon$, and the attack does not recover the private sample d_{priv_i} or break the ϵ-LDP privacy guarantee.

4 Evaluation

In this section, we present the evaluation results and address our research questions in Sect. 1 with empirical analysis.

Experimental Setup. We run our experiments on two machines. One has two GPUs, NVIDIA GeForce RTX 3090 and 4090, with 24 GB of dedicated memory, and an Intel 12th Gen i7-12700 CPU with 12 cores and 64 GB of RAM. The other has two NVIDIA GeForce RTX 4090 GPUs and an AMD Ryzen Threadripper PRO 5955WX CPU with 16 cores and 64 GB of RAM. The underlying operating systems are 64-bit Ubuntu 22.04.3 LTS and Ubuntu 24.04 LTS, respectively. We use Python 3.9.7 and PyTorch v2.1.2 with CUDA 12.1.

We evaluate LDPKiT on three diverse datasets: SVHN [22], Fashion-MNIST [37], and PathMNIST from MedMNIST2D [39] for medical imaging in pathology. For ML models, we use ResNet-152 as $\mathcal{M}_{\text{R}}$, and ResNet-18 and MobileNetV2 as $\mathcal{M}_{\text{L}}$. The $\mathcal{M}_{\text{L}}$ models are initialized with random weights.

To construct $\mathcal{D}_{\text{priv}}$, we train each $\mathcal{M}_{\text{R}}$ on a subset of the original data rather than the default training split: 35k samples for Fashion-MNIST, 48,257 for SVHN, and 89,996 for PathMNIST. The remaining data is divided into a candidate pool for $\mathcal{D}_{\text{priv}}$ and a holdout set, $\mathcal{D}_{\text{val}}$, used to evaluate $\mathcal{M}_{\text{L}}$'s generalizability. The candidate pools contain 25k, 25k, and 10,004 samples for

Fashion-MNIST, SVHN, and PathMNIST, respectively, while $\mathcal{D}_{\text{val}}$ contains 10k, 26,032, and 7,180 samples. To model users with limited private data, we set $|\mathcal{D}_{\text{priv}}| = 1{,}500$ in Sect. 4.1, sampled uniformly across classes from the candidate pool. We study the effect of varying $|\mathcal{D}_{\text{infer}}|$ and $|\mathcal{D}_{\text{priv}}|$ in Sect. 4.3. All experiments are repeated over three random seeds and subset splits; dependent two-sample t-tests confirm that all reported improvements are statistically significant ($p < 0.05$).

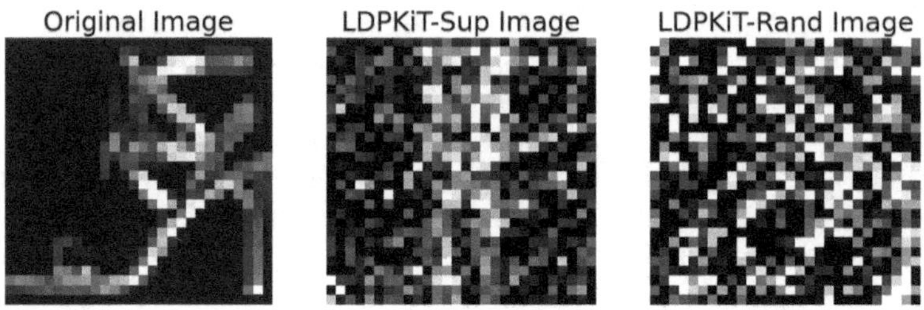

Fig. 2. Example of a Fashion-MNIST sample with label 5 (sandal) and $\epsilon = 1.5$.

We report SIDP accuracy using $\mathcal{M}_{\text{R}}$'s labels on $\mathcal{D}_{\text{protected}}$, while LDPKiT accuracy is measured on $\mathcal{D}_{\text{priv}}$ using $\mathcal{M}_{\text{L}}$ trained with $\mathcal{M}_{\text{R}}$'s labels on $\mathcal{D}_{\text{infer}}$. Following industry practice [2,25], we choose ϵ values so that SIDP achieves 1.5–3× random-guessing accuracy, giving $\mathcal{M}_{\text{R}}$ minimal but useful signal while maintaining robustness to reconstruction attacks (Sect. 4.4). We use $\epsilon \in 2.0, 1.5, 1.25$ for SVHN, $2.0, 1.5$ for Fashion-MNIST, and $10.0, 7.0$ for PathMNIST, consistently across SIDP, LDPKiT-Rand, and LDPKiT-Sup. Figure 2 shows Fashion-MNIST samples in $\mathcal{D}_{\text{infer}}$ generated by LDPKiT-Rand and LDPKiT-Sup.

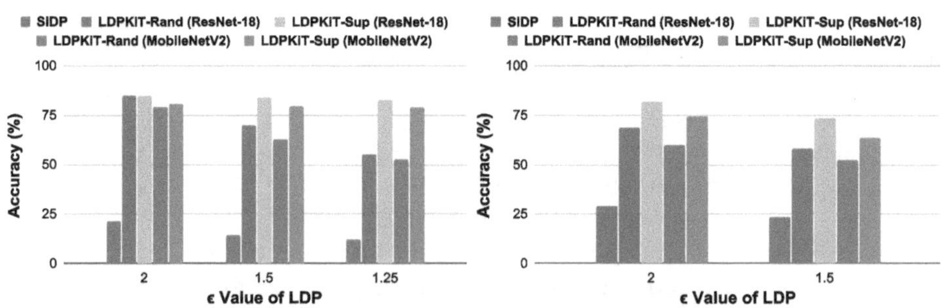

(a) SVHN (b) Fashion-MNIST

Fig. 3. Inference accuracy on $\mathcal{D}_{\text{priv}}$ for SVHN and Fashion-MNIST under different ϵ values, comparing SIDP using $\mathcal{M}_{\text{R}}$ with LDPKiT-Rand and LDPKiT-Sup distillation using $\mathcal{M}_{\text{L}}$. See Fig. 6a for PathMNIST results.

4.1 RQ1: LDPKiT's Utility Recovery on $\mathcal{D}_{\text{priv}}$

In this section, we evaluate whether LDPKiT improves prediction accuracy on $\mathcal{D}_{\text{priv}}$ compared to directly using $\mathcal{M}_{\text{R}}$'s returned labels on $\mathcal{D}_{\text{protected}}$ (*i.e.* SIDP). To simulate a realistic scenario, we set $|\mathcal{D}_{\text{priv}}|$ to 1,500, representing a practical amount of private data available to a user. For variable control, we use the full $\mathcal{D}_{\text{infer}}$, of size $|\mathcal{D}_{\text{protected}}| \cdot (|\mathcal{D}_{\text{protected}}| - 1)$ for querying $\mathcal{M}_{\text{R}}$ and training $\mathcal{M}_{\text{L}}$ to minimize variations from random subset splits.

Without privacy protection, $\mathcal{M}_{\text{R}}$'s average accuracies on noise-free $\mathcal{D}_{\text{priv}}$ of Fashion-MNIST, SVHN, and PathMNIST are 93.33%, 94.73%, and 86.2%, respectively. The accuracies on $\mathcal{D}_{\text{val}}$ are 93.22%, 96.30% and 81.24%, respectively.

To answer RQ1, we compare the last-epoch accuracies of $\mathcal{M}_{\text{L}}$ on $\mathcal{D}_{\text{priv}}$ with $\mathcal{M}_{\text{R}}$'s SIDP accuracies on $\mathcal{D}_{\text{protected}}$ in Fig. 3 and Fig. 6a. Overall, LDPKiT consistently improves accuracy over SIDP. For example, when $\epsilon = 2.0$ on SVHN, ResNet-152's SIDP accuracy is only 21.07%, while both LDPKiT-Rand and LDPKiT-Sup recover ResNet-18 accuracy to about 85%. However, LDPKiT-Rand provides limited gains in some cases. On Fashion-MNIST, ResNet-18 reaches only 68.52% and 58.07% accuracy at $\epsilon = 2.0$ and $\epsilon = 1.5$, respectively, while MobileNetV2 remains below 60%. On PathMNIST, ResNet-18 also performs poorly, and MobileNetV2 with LDPKiT-Rand can even underperform SIDP. These results suggest that adding arbitrary random noise does not generate sufficiently representative training data. By contrast, LDPKiT-Sup consistently outperforms LDPKiT-Rand. Superimposing noised $\mathcal{D}_{\text{priv}}$ samples produces more useful $\mathcal{D}_{\text{infer}}$ than applying random noise. For instance, on Fashion-MNIST with $\epsilon = 2.0$, LDPKiT-Sup raises ResNet-18 accuracy to 81.78%, compared with 28.69% for SIDP and 68.52% for LDPKiT-Rand. On PathMNIST with $\epsilon = 10.0$, LDPKiT-Sup reaches 82.11%, far above SIDP at 28.74% and LDPKiT-Rand at 43.90%. On SVHN, despite SIDP accuracies of only 11.87%–21.07%, LDPKiT-Sup consistently achieves over 80% accuracy with both ResNet-18 and MobileNetV2. These results show that LDPKiT, especially LDPKiT-Sup, effectively recovers much of the utility lost to ϵ-LDP noise while maintaining the same per-sample ϵ-LDP protection.

Table 1. Euclidean distances between centroids of clusters in Fig. 4. $d(C_{\text{N}}, C_X)$ is the Euclidean distance between the Noisy and Class X cluster centroids.

Figure	Strategy	Class(es)	$d(C_{\text{N}}, C_0)$	$d(C_{\text{N}}, C_2)$	$d(C_{\text{N}}, C_9)$
4a	Sup	(0,0)	**1.9835**	2.5191	3.2017
	Rand	0	**2.1195**	2.4666	2.9169
4b	Sup	(9,2)	3.1652	**2.3538**	**2.0524**
	Rand	9	3.0937	2.5595	**1.9333**
4c	Sup	(2,2)	2.9662	**1.7351**	2.9171
	Rand	2	2.7084	**1.9433**	2.7115

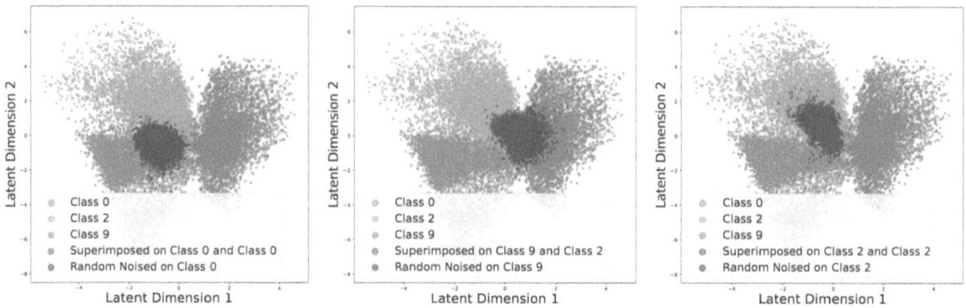

(a) (0,0) (b) (9,2) (c) (2,2)

Fig. 4. Latent space plots of Fashion-MNIST class triplets (C0-T-shirt/top, C2-pullover, C9-ankle boot) and privacy-protected noisy data clusters generated with LDPKiT-Rand and LDPKiT-Sup ($\epsilon = 2.0$).

4.2 RQ2: Latent Space Analysis

Section 4.1 shows that LDPKiT improves accuracy on $\mathcal{D}_{\text{priv}}$ over SIDP, with LDPKiT-Sup consistently outperforming LDPKiT-Rand. We hypothesize that LDPKiT-Sup is more effective because superimposition produces augmented samples that better preserve the target-class structure, yielding more informative data for knowledge transfer. To examine this, we analyze the latent space of $\mathcal{D}_{\text{infer}}$ by training a VAE on ϵ-LDP-noised samples from three randomly selected classes, using $\epsilon = 2.0$ for Fashion-MNIST and SVHN and $\epsilon = 7.0$ for PathMNIST. To obtain separable class clusters, we replace the conventional reconstruction loss with the triplet margin loss. With the trained VAE, we visualize two additional noisy clusters: one generated by LDPKiT-Sup from two target classes and one generated by LDPKiT-Rand from a single class. We then compute the Euclidean distances between these noisy clusters and the original clusters to assess whether LDPKiT-Sup provides a latent-space learning advantage over LDPKiT-Rand.

Figure 4 visualizes the Fashion-MNIST latent space for Classes 0, 2, and 9. The LDPKiT-Sup clusters are generated by superimposing noisy samples from target-class pairs, whereas the LDPKiT-Rand clusters are generated by applying additional random noise to samples from a single class. The plots show that LDPKiT-Sup generally produces samples closer to the target-class regions than LDPKiT-Rand. For example, in Figs. 4a and 4c, the LDPKiT-Sup clusters lie closer to their corresponding target-class clusters than the LDPKiT-Rand clusters. Similarly, in Fig. 4b, the LDPKiT-Sup cluster overlaps more with Classes 2 and 9, while the LDPKiT-Rand cluster is less representative, positioned between the clusters of Classes 0, 2, and 9.

Table 1 reports Euclidean distances between cluster centroids and supports the visual trends. We note, however, that the Euclidean distance between centroids is not always an ideal measure of similarity between clusters. For example, in Fig. 4b, LDPKiT-Sup visually overlaps more with Class 9, but because it combines samples from both Classes 2 and 9, its distribution is more dispersed; consequently, the LDPKiT-Rand centroid can appear slightly closer to the Class 9 centroid despite being less representative overall.

To better understand the latent-space representations, we compute Kullback-Leibler (KL) divergence [15]. Let C_T denote the target triplet cluster, C_S the LDPKiT-Sup cluster generated from superimposed target-class pairs, and C_R the LDPKiT-Rand cluster generated from noisy samples of the same triplet classes, with C_S and C_R matched in size. We define the *Divergence Ratio (DR)* as

$$\mathrm{DR}(\bar{C}_R, \bar{C}_S) = \frac{D_{\mathrm{KL}}(\bar{C}_T \parallel \bar{C}_R)}{D_{\mathrm{KL}}(\bar{C}_T \parallel \bar{C}_S)},$$

where $\bar{C}_T$, $\bar{C}_S$, and $\bar{C}_R$ are normalized distributions. DR > 1 indicates that LDPKiT-Sup is closer to the target triplet distribution than LDPKiT-Rand.

Across 130 triplets from SVHN, Fashion-MNIST, and PathMNIST, LDPKiT-Sup achieves lower KL divergence than LDPKiT-Rand in 68.56% of cases. This supports our hypothesis that LDPKiT-Sup more often preserves the target latent distribution, consistent with its stronger accuracy in Sect. 4.1. However, KL divergence does not fully explain accuracy gains, and a more complete statistical characterization remains future work.

Table 2. Impact of $|\mathcal{D}_{\text{priv}}|$ and $|\mathcal{D}_{\text{infer}}|$, with ResNet-18 ($\mathcal{M}_{\text{L}}$).

Dataset	ϵ	LDPKiT	Accuracy on $\mathcal{D}_{\text{priv}}$ (%)													
	$\lvert\mathcal{D}_{\text{priv}}\rvert$		125	250		500			1k				1.5k			
	$\lvert\mathcal{D}_{\text{infer}}\rvert$		15.5k	15.5k	62.3k	15.5k	62.3k	250k	15.5k	62.3k	250k	500k	15.5k	62.3k	250k	500k
Fashion-MNIST	2.0	Rand	14.8	18.4	36.4	17.7	32.5	52.9	18.1	34.5	57.9	63.4	14.8	34.7	57.2	64.7
		Sup	25.9	28.9	31.4	24.2	37.6	53.0	25.1	47.2	66.5	73.7	25.1	45.1	69.0	74.4
SVHN	1.5	Rand	8.8	11.4	6.9	9.4	6.9	34.1	10.5	9.9	35.3	51.3	10.4	10.0	32.8	48.6
		Sup	9.1	9.7	12.7	10.1	15.3	45.7	10.2	20.0	60.1	69.1	10.1	14.3	62.1	76.9
Path-MNIST	10	Rand	24.4	24.8	29.9	22.9	32.8	44.4	24.5	30.8	50.4	43.4	23.6	29.0	43.7	54.4
		Sup	41.1	41.4	47.5	44.0	55.0	69.9	40.9	48.5	73.3	77.0	43.0	57.2	74.1	76.8

4.3 RQ3: Impact of $|\mathcal{D}_{\text{infer}}|$ and $|\mathcal{D}_{\text{priv}}|$

We analyze the trade-off among privacy exposure ($|\mathcal{D}_{\text{priv}}|$), query cost ($|\mathcal{D}_{\text{infer}}|$), and accuracy by varying the number of private samples used for augmentation and the number of generated queries used to train $\mathcal{M}_{\text{L}}$. As shown in Table 2, we construct multiple $\mathcal{D}_{\text{infer}}$ datasets from $\mathcal{D}_{\text{priv}}$ at different scales. For example, when $|\mathcal{D}_{\text{priv}}| = 125$, the maximum $|\mathcal{D}_{\text{infer}}|$ is 15,500, computed as $|\mathcal{D}_{\text{protected}}| \cdot (|\mathcal{D}_{\text{protected}}| - 1)$. When $|\mathcal{D}_{\text{priv}}| = 250$, $|\mathcal{D}_{\text{infer}}|$ can either remain 15,500 through random selection or increase to a maximum of 62,250. To isolate the effect of $|\mathcal{D}_{\text{priv}}|$, we fix $|\mathcal{D}_{\text{infer}}|$ and compare different $|\mathcal{D}_{\text{priv}}|$ values; to isolate the effect of $|\mathcal{D}_{\text{infer}}|$, we fix $|\mathcal{D}_{\text{priv}}|$ and vary $|\mathcal{D}_{\text{infer}}|$. We exhaustively evaluate these settings for $|\mathcal{D}_{\text{priv}}|$ from 125 to 1.5k and report ResNet-18 ($\mathcal{M}_{\text{L}}$) accuracies.

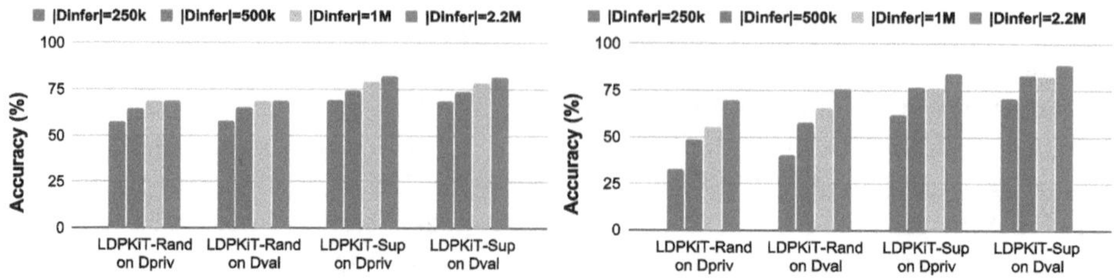

(a) Fashion-MNIST ($\epsilon = 2.0$) (b) SVHN ($\epsilon = 1.5$)

Fig. 5. Impact of $|\mathcal{D}_{\text{infer}}|$ on ResNet-18 $\mathcal{M}_{\text{L}}$ accuracy for Fashion-MNIST and SVHN, with $|\mathcal{D}_{\text{priv}}| = 1.5k$. See Fig. 6b for PathMNIST results.

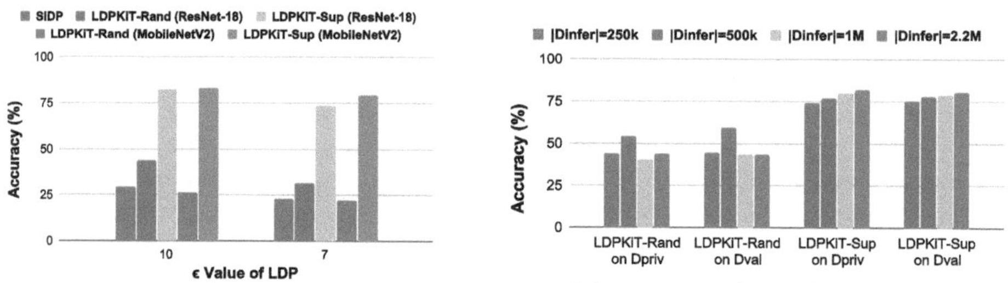

(a) Inference accuracy (b) Impact of $|\mathcal{D}_{\text{infer}}|$ ($\epsilon = 10.0$)

Fig. 6. PathMNIST results: inference accuracy and impact of $|\mathcal{D}_{\text{infer}}|$, evaluated with ResNet-18 $\mathcal{M}_{\text{L}}$ and $|\mathcal{D}_{\text{priv}}| = 1.5k$. Complemantary to Figs. 3 and 5.

The results show that LDPKiT is relatively insensitive to $|\mathcal{D}_{\text{priv}}|$, indicating that users can achieve similar utility with fewer private samples and therefore lower privacy exposure. For example, on Fashion-MNIST with $\epsilon = 2.0$, when $|\mathcal{D}_{\text{infer}}| = 15{,}500$, the maximum accuracy gap across different $|\mathcal{D}_{\text{priv}}|$ settings is below 5%; when $|\mathcal{D}_{\text{infer}}| = 500k$, the gap is only about 0.69%. Thus, with a reasonable $|\mathcal{D}_{\text{infer}}|$, users can generate effective queries from a smaller $\mathcal{D}_{\text{priv}}$. One exception occurs when $|\mathcal{D}_{\text{infer}}| = 250k$, where increasing $|\mathcal{D}_{\text{priv}}|$ improves accuracy, likely because more private samples increase the chance of generating representative and diverse training data.

In contrast, $|\mathcal{D}_{\text{infer}}|$ has a stronger impact on accuracy because it directly determines the amount of training data and query cost. Although $|\mathcal{D}_{\text{priv}}|$ constrains the maximum feasible $|\mathcal{D}_{\text{infer}}|$, sufficient $\mathcal{D}_{\text{infer}}$ is crucial for effective training. For example, on PathMNIST with $\epsilon = 10.0$ and $|\mathcal{D}_{\text{priv}}| = 1.5k$, LDPKiT-Rand improves from 23.56% accuracy at $|\mathcal{D}_{\text{infer}}| = 15{,}500$ to 54.39% at $|\mathcal{D}_{\text{infer}}| = 500k$, while LDPKiT-Sup improves from 42.99% to 76.79%. Conversely, on SVHN, $\mathcal{M}_{\text{L}}$ remains near 10% accuracy when $|\mathcal{D}_{\text{infer}}| = 15{,}500$, regardless of $|\mathcal{D}_{\text{priv}}|$.

Figure 5 and Fig. 6b further illustrate the effect of $|\mathcal{D}_{\text{infer}}|$ under a fixed $|\mathcal{D}_{\text{priv}}| = 1.5k$. LDPKiT-Sup requires a sufficiently large $\mathcal{D}_{\text{infer}}$ to achieve adequate accuracy, such as 250k for PathMNIST and 500k for Fashion-MNIST and

SVHN. Increasing $|\mathcal{D}_{\text{infer}}|$ improves accuracy, but the gains diminish beyond 500k. For instance, on Fashion-MNIST with $\epsilon = 2.0$, ResNet-18 achieves 74.35%, 78.88%, and 81.78% accuracy when $|\mathcal{D}_{\text{infer}}|$ is 500k, 1M, and 2.2M, respectively. Thus, querying all possible $\mathcal{D}_{\text{infer}}$ points is unnecessary; LDPKiT-Sup can achieve satisfactory accuracy using only about 20% of $\mathcal{D}_{\text{infer}}$.

To estimate the API query cost, we use OpenAI's listed GPT-5 nano pricing as of May 2026 ($0.05 per 1M input tokens and $0.40 per 1M output tokens) [23] and OpenAI's image-token accounting rules for patch-based image inputs (2.46 input tokens per image) [24]. Assuming a one-token class-label output, each query costs about 5.23×10^{-7} USD, so 2.2M queries cost about $1.15 under a lower-bound estimate, or $3.35 with a minimal 20-token text prompt. Rate limits, latency, batching, and API policies remain practical constraints.

Finally, the $\mathcal{D}_{\text{infer}}$ subsets used in these experiments are randomly selected, and there is currently no universal lower bound on $|\mathcal{D}_{\text{priv}}|$ that guarantees reliable performance because the required size depends on the task, $\mathcal{M}_{\text{R}}$ complexity, LDP noise level, and the diversity of $\mathcal{D}_{\text{priv}}$. In practice, users can perform small-scale pilot runs by gradually increasing $|\mathcal{D}_{\text{infer}}|$ and monitoring accuracy trends, while systematic estimation of practical $|\mathcal{D}_{\text{priv}}|$ thresholds remains future work.

Table 3. Classification accuracy and image similarity under various ϵ settings. Similarity is measured against the original images before and after denoising.

Dataset	ϵ	Recon.	Acc. (%)↑	MSE ↓	SSIM ↑	LPIPS ↓
SVHN	2.0	Before	16.80	0.0681	0.1210	0.7591
		After	14.20	0.1524	0.0825	0.7183
	1.5	Before	15.30	0.0929	0.0850	0.7747
		After	14.40	0.1436	0.0829	0.7301
	1.25	Before	12.50	0.1098	0.0681	0.7826
		After	13.00	0.1382	0.0810	0.7347
Fashion-MNIST	2.0	Before	16.10	0.0942	0.3869	0.5568
		After	16.70	0.1257	0.3180	0.4492
	1.5	Before	14.80	0.1123	0.3406	0.5928
		After	16.30	0.1395	0.2953	0.5044
Path-MNIST	10.0	Before	22.78	0.0132	0.4823	0.2237
		After	23.89	0.0853	0.3870	0.2593
	7.0	Before	17.56	0.0155	0.3936	0.2507
		After	21.89	0.1012	0.3110	0.2805

4.4 Evaluation of Data Reconstruction Risks

To rigorously evaluate whether the amount of LDP noise added to each private image is sufficient, we audit the privacy guarantees of LDPKiT following the methodology of [29]. Specifically, we conduct data reconstruction attacks using a DDPM trained to model the image prior (*i.e.* trained on the original images). Our experiment spans three datasets: SVHN, Fashion-MNIST, and PathMNIST. For each dataset, we randomly select a subset of 1,000 images (900 for PathMNIST) processed with LDPKiT-Sup, and quantitatively measure reconstruction success with standard image-similarity metrics: MSE, VGG-based LPIPS, and SSIM. We report results in Table 3. Our measurements show that the reconstructed images are generally more dissimilar from the original images after reconstruction (*i.e.* lower SSIM and higher MSE). We did not observe successful reconstructions under our evaluated attack setting. We also show that a fully trained classifier (ResNet-152) shows near-random accuracy on the reconstructed images.

5 Related Work

Knowledge Transfer Techniques. Knowledge distillation is a knowledge transfer technique that distills a large teacher model into a smaller student model while preserving model performance [11,12]. The conventional use case is model compression, enabling deployment in a resource-restricted environment. Knowledge can be transferred in different forms [11], and such techniques can also be used adversarially. Model extraction is an adversarial setting in which the attacker reproduces a model stealthily by stealing its parameters, decision boundaries, or functionalities. It demonstrates that an iterative query-based knowledge transfer process from a high-performance model can be performed via a prediction query interface [17,31,40]. Model extraction can be challenging without knowledge of the victim model's training data distribution [33]. Successful model extractions with partial or zero knowledge of the victim model and training data [26,33] may require more information than hard labels. Related defenses [5,9,20] are in active research. Rather than model compression or adversarial extraction for the purpose of theft, we adopt query-based knowledge transfer techniques in a non-adversarial setting to recover the utility loss introduced by LDP noise while protecting users' private data.

Noise Injection and Differential Privacy (DP). DP can be applied either globally [1,27] or locally [10], both offering provable privacy guarantees. Global DP relies on a trusted curator who accesses raw sensitive data before adding noise to aggregate statistics. To avoid this trust assumption, LDPKiT adopts local DP, where the user perturbs each query before sending it to the ML service. This gives users direct control over privacy protection, but typically reduces utility compared with global DP at the same privacy level [6]. Unlike training-time methods such as DP-SGD [1], LDPKiT protects inputs at inference time. Related split-computation schemes inject noise into intermediate DNN representations [35], but they assume white-box access to a partitioned model.

Federated Learning (FL). FL has emerged as a popular approach to address privacy concerns by enabling collaborative model training without directly sharing users' raw data with a central server [34,38]. However, FL primarily protects users' training data, which is an orthogonal concern to our setting, and it does not mitigate privacy risks during inference. Moreover, FL is vulnerable to gradient inversion attacks that reconstruct local training data from gradient updates, which necessitates extra privacy protection [41]. Finally, FL assumes that users possess labelled local datasets, which is not applicable in our case, where the objective is to annotate unlabelled data. Concerns regarding potential data reconstruction attacks and the integrity of the server imply that relying solely on using shared models from service providers like FL is insufficiently secure and privacy-preserving; therefore, FL is not an ideal solution in our scenario.

Others. Another approach is encrypted inference using homomorphic encryption, but such methods incur high computational overhead [14]. On SVHN, LDPKiT becomes more efficient once the query set reaches roughly 800 samples: full knowledge transfer on 800 samples takes 20.73 s, compared with 22.984 s for a single Lancelot inference [13] and 484.184 s for OpenFHE [3]. Moreover, LDPKiT performs knowledge transfer once, after which inference on data from the same distribution runs locally with negligible overhead. However, encryption-based schemes continue to incur remote per-query costs, leading to higher cumulative overhead for labelling larger datasets. The alternative is hardware-assisted inference using Trusted Execution Environments (TEEs). Slalom protects remote inference by executing computation inside a TEE [32]. However, TEEs still access the original data and remain vulnerable to side-channel attacks [19]. LDPKiT avoids this threat model because it never transmits raw data; any privacy leakage is instead bounded by the LDP mechanism.

6 Limitations

Our per-record ϵ-LDP guarantee is distribution-free and does not rely on an i.i.d. assumption. However, correlations among records may still allow inferences about related records or users and can weaken privacy due to mutual information leakage, so the semantic privacy interpretation is strongest when samples are approximately independent. In practice, many applications use de-duplication to maintain or approximate independence. For example, workflows built on Amazon S3 Inventory, Athena, AWS Lambda, and S3 Batch Operations can identify and remove duplicate objects to reduce storage costs [18]. Similarly, generative AI pipelines commonly de-duplicate LLM training data to improve efficiency and performance while reducing privacy leakage from redundant content [4,16,21].

Currently, LDPKiT only supports the image modality, where superimposition intuitively translates to pixel-level operations. Although textual data does not have a direct counterpart to superimposition, several conceptual approaches can be explored. These include embedding-level averaging, in which two textual embeddings are blended; token-level mixing, which involves interleaving tokens from two samples; and semantic-level merging, such as combining two sentences into a coherent paraphrased summary. Each interpretation may require a distinct adaptation of the LDP scheme. We leave the exploration of these textual superimposition methods as a direction for future research.

We also extended the evaluation of LDPKiT to the ImageNet1K dataset. For reference, the official torchvision ResNet-18 model reports a top-1 accuracy of 69.758% on ImageNet1K [28]. In our evaluation, a randomly selected subset of 15 classes was used. LDPKiT-Sup with ResNet-18 ($\mathcal{M}_{\mathrm{L}}$) achieved 63% top-1 accuracy with 15,000 $\mathcal{D}_{\text{priv}}$ samples at $\epsilon = 5$, whereas the baseline SIDP attained only 19% accuracy under identical conditions. Further enhancing the performance of LDPKiT on larger datasets is left for future work.

7 Conclusion

LDPKiT introduces a privacy-preserving inference framework for protecting sensitive user data when interacting with remote ML model providers. By injecting LDP noise into inference queries, LDPKiT protects user privacy even when queries are logged, retained, or exposed through later infrastructure compromise. The key contribution of LDPKiT is its integration of LDP with a two-layer augmentation mechanism, LDPKiT-Rand and LDPKiT-Sup, which leverages LDP's post-processing property to improve utility without weakening privacy. The first layer provides baseline LDP protection, while the second layer generates an augmented dataset for local model distillation. In particular, LDPKiT-Sup uses superimposition-based augmentation to produce samples that better approximate the private data distribution than LDPKiT-Rand's random-noise strategy. Evaluation results show that LDPKiT-Sup effectively recovers prediction accuracy while preserving privacy, with larger gains under stronger noise levels corresponding to stronger privacy guarantees. Overall, LDPKiT offers a privacy-preserving design aligned with responsible data-use and privacy-by-design principles.

Acknowledgments. Support for this research was provided in part by DND-IDEaS Contract MN3-01, NSERC Discovery Grant RGPIN-2026-07548 and NSERC-CSE Grant ALLRP 588144-23. David Lie is supported in part by Tier 1 Canada Research Chair CRC-2019-00242 and Kexin Li was supported by an SRI Fellowship. Researchers funded through the NSERC-CSE Research Communities Grants do not represent the Communications Security Establishment Canada or the Government of Canada. Any part research, opinions or positions they produce as part of this initiative do not represent the official views of the Government of Canada.

Disclosure of Interests. The authors have no competing interests to declare.

References

1. Abadi, M., et al.: Deep learning with differential privacy (2016). https://doi.org/10.1145/2976749.2978318
2. Apple: Differential Privacy (n.d.). https://www.apple.com/privacy/docs/Differential_Privacy_Overview.pdf
3. Badawi, A.A., et al.: OpenFHE: open-source fully homomorphic encryption library. Cryptology ePrint Archive, Paper 2022/915 (2022). https://eprint.iacr.org/2022/915

4. Carlini, N., et al.: Extracting training data from large language models (2021). https://arxiv.org/abs/2012.07805
5. Chen, H., Rohani, B.D., Koushanfar, F.: DeepMarks: a digital fingerprinting framework for deep neural networks (2018). https://arxiv.org/abs/1804.03648
6. Cormode, G., Jha, S., Kulkarni, T., Li, N., Srivastava, D., Wang, T.: Privacy at scale: local differential privacy in practice. In: Proceedings of the 2018 International Conference on Management of Data, SIGMOD 2018, pp. 1655–1658. Association for Computing Machinery, New York, NY, USA (2018). https://doi.org/10.1145/3183713.3197390
7. Dwork, C., McSherry, F., Nissim, K., Smith, A.: Calibrating noise to sensitivity in private data analysis (2006)
8. Dwork, C., Roth, A.: The Algorithmic Foundations of Differential Privacy. Found. Trends Theor. Comput. Sci. **9**(3–4), 211–407 (2014). https://doi.org/10.1561/0400000042
9. Dziedzic, A., Kaleem, M.A., Lu, Y.S., Papernot, N.: Increasing the Cost of Model Extraction with Calibrated Proof of Work (2022)
10. Erlingsson, U., Pihur, V., Korolova, A.: RAPPOR: randomized aggregatable privacy-preserving ordinal response. In: Proceedings of the 2014 ACM SIGSAC Conference on Computer and Communications Security, CCS 2014, pp. 1054–1067. Association for Computing Machinery, New York, NY, USA (2014). https://doi.org/10.1145/2660267.2660348
11. Gou, J., Yu, B., Maybank, S.J., Tao, D.: Knowledge distillation: a survey. Int. J. Comput. Vision **129**(6), 1789–1819 (2021). https://doi.org/10.1007/s11263-021-01453-z
12. Hinton, G., Vinyals, O., Dean, J.: Distilling the knowledge in a neural network (2015)
13. Jiang, S., Yang, H., Xie, Q., Ma, C., Wang, S., Xing, G.: Lancelot: towards efficient and privacy-preserving Byzantine-robust federated learning within fully homomorphic encryption (2024). https://arxiv.org/abs/2408.06197
14. Juvekar, C., Vaikuntanathan, V., Chandrakasan, A.: GAZELLE: a low latency framework for secure neural network inference (2018). https://doi.org/10.48550/ARXIV.1801.05507
15. Kullback, S., Leibler, R.A.: On information and sufficiency. Ann. Math. Stat. **22**(1), 79–86 (1951). https://doi.org/10.1214/aoms/1177729694
16. Lee, K., et al.: Deduplicating training data makes language models better (2022). https://arxiv.org/abs/2107.06499
17. Lee, S., Lee, G., Kim, J.W., Shin, J., Lee, M.K.: HETAL: efficient privacy-preserving transfer learning with homomorphic encryption (2024). https://arxiv.org/abs/2403.14111
18. Lim, T.: Managing duplicate objects in Amazon S3 (2024). https://aws.amazon.com/blogs/storage/managing-duplicate-objects-in-amazon-s3/
19. Lipp, M., et al.: Meltdown: reading kernel memory from user space. Commun. ACM **63**(6), 46–56 (2020)
20. Liu, Y., et al.: Provenance of training without training data: towards privacy-preserving DNN model ownership verification. In: Proceedings of the ACM Web Conference 2023, WWW 2023, pp. 1980–1990. Association for Computing Machinery, New York, NY, USA (2023). https://doi.org/10.1145/3543507.3583198
21. Maini, P., Jia, H., Papernot, N., Dziedzic, A.: LLM dataset inference: did you train on my dataset? (2024). https://arxiv.org/abs/2406.06443

22. Netzer, Y., Wang, T., Coates, A., Bissacco, A., Wu, B., Ng, A.Y.: Reading digits in natural images with unsupervised feature learning. In: NIPS Workshop on Deep Learning and Unsupervised Feature Learning (2011). http://ufldl.stanford.edu/housenumbers
23. OpenAI: GPT-5 nano Model (2026). https://developers.openai.com/api/docs/models/gpt-5-nano. Accessed 16 May 2026
24. OpenAI: Images and Vision: Calculating Costs (2026). https://developers.openai.com/api/docs/guides/images-vision. Accessed 16 May 2026
25. Orr, A.: Google's differential privacy may be better than Apple's (2017). https://www.macobserver.com/analysis/google-apple-differential-privacy/
26. Papernot, N., McDaniel, P., Goodfellow, I., Jha, S., Celik, Z.B., Swami, A.: Practical black-box attacks against machine learning (2017). https://arxiv.org/abs/1602.02697
27. Papernot, N., Song, S., Mironov, I., Raghunathan, A., Talwar, K., Erlingsson, Ú.: Scalable private learning with PATE (2018)
28. PyTorch Contributors: ResNet18 — Torchvision models documentation. PyTorch (2025)
29. Schwethelm, K., Kaiser, J., Knolle, M., Lockfisch, S., Rueckert, D., Ziller, A.: Visual privacy auditing with diffusion models (2025). https://arxiv.org/abs/2403.07588
30. Shokri, R., Strobel, M., Zick, Y.: On the privacy risks of model explanations (2021). https://arxiv.org/abs/1907.00164
31. Tramèr, F., Zhang, F., Juels, A., Reiter, M.K., Ristenpart, T.: Stealing machine learning models via prediction APIs (2016)
32. Tramèr, F., Boneh, D.: Slalom: fast, verifiable and private execution of neural networks in trusted hardware (2019)
33. Truong, J.B., Maini, P., Walls, R.J., Papernot, N.: Data-free model extraction (2021). https://arxiv.org/abs/2011.14779
34. Truong, N., Sun, K., Wang, S., Guitton, F., Guo, Y.: Privacy preservation in federated learning: an insightful survey from the GDPR perspective. Comput. Stan. Interfaces **78**, 103518 (2021)
35. Wang, J., Zhang, J., Bao, W., Zhu, X., Cao, B., Yu, P.S.: Not just privacy: improving performance of private deep learning in mobile cloud (2018). https://doi.org/10.48550/ARXIV.1809.03428
36. Wang, Z., Reiter, J.P.: Post-processing differentially private counts to satisfy additive constraints. Trans. Data Priv. **14**, 65–77 (2021). https://api.semanticscholar.org/CorpusID:237521561
37. Xiao, H., Rasul, K., Vollgraf, R.: Fashion-MNIST: a novel image dataset for benchmarking machine learning algorithms (2017). https://arxiv.org/abs/1708.07747
38. Xu, S., et al.: Privacy-preserving federated learning via dataset distillation (2024). https://arxiv.org/abs/2410.19548
39. Yang, J., et al.: MedMNIST V2 - a large-scale lightweight benchmark for 2D and 3D biomedical image classification. Sci. Data **10**(1), (2023). https://doi.org/10.1038/s41597-022-01721-8
40. Zhang, J., Chen, C., Lyu, L.: IDEAL: query-efficient data-free learning from black-box models (2022)
41. Zhang, R., Guo, S., Wang, J., Xie, X., Tao, D.: A survey on gradient inversion: attacks, defenses and future directions (2022). https://arxiv.org/abs/2206.07284
42. Zhao, Y., Wang, J., Li, X., Wang, W., Wang, Y.: A comprehensive survey of privacy-preserving federated learning. ACM Comput. Surv. (CSUR) **54**(6), 1–36 (2021)

Cryptokinetics

Hadrien Barral[4], David Naccache[1,2](✉), and Aleksa Veličković[1,3]

[1] DI ENS, École Normale Supérieure, PSL University, CNRS, Paris, France
[2] Fakultet inženjerskih nauka Univerzitet u Kragujevcu, Kragujevac, Serbia
david.naccache@ens.fr
[3] Be-YS Trusted Solutions, Paris, France
[4] Université Gustave Eiffel (UGE), CNRS, LIGM, Paris, France

Abstract. Cryptographic operations are momentary. Typically, the verification of a digital signature validates the signer's intervention at a specific moment in the past whereas a successful Σ-protocol round validates a prover's present existence. While cryptography handles very well the notions of "before" and "after" (typically in the blockchain), it remains blind to *physical time*. In many practical situations it is important to assess the probability that the legitimate user is still present as time elapses. The situation is even more complex when the system needs to provide an assessment based on both cryptographic and non-cryptographic (e.g. biometric) inputs. This paper draws an analogy between Continuous User Authentication (CUA) and pharmacokinetics, a branch of pharmacology that studies how drugs interact with the body over time using differential equations. We introduce mathematical models blending data from heterogeneous security inputs (that we call "sensors") to estimate the overall level of trust at any time. The models take into account the presence of the legitimate user, attackers and the absence of incoming information.

1 Introduction

Continuous User Authentication (CUA) is a dynamic security mechanism employed in computer systems to continuously verify the identity of users throughout their entire session, rather than relying solely on a single authentication event at login. Unlike traditional methods that authenticate users only at the beginning of a session or at some chosen points in time, CUA continuously monitors cryptographic events, user behavior, interactions and biometric traits to ensure that the user remains authenticated and authorized to access a resource.

1.1 Previous Work

Continuous User Authentication has evolved significantly since its early conceptualization. Early CUA systems focused on single-modality approaches.

P. Kieseberg et al. (Eds.): ARES 2026 Workshops, LNCS 16903, pp. 63–80, 2027.
https://doi.org/10.1007/978-3-032-37218-5_5

Naturally, single-modality motivated research into multi-modality with the advent of modern smartphones. Smartphones provide rich sensor arrays enabling simultaneous monitoring of multiple security events [4][1], [15][2].

[22] surveys multi-modal authentication and also explains how different sensors are combined. While effective in practice, most listed approaches are AI/ML-based and lack principled methods for combining heterogeneous evidence. Prior work essentially lists three approaches:

1. *Machine learning:* Neural networks [7], reinforcement learning [2], random forests [8][3], and support vector machines [17] have been applied to learn mapping functions from sensor readings to trust scores. [2] employ reinforcement learning to dynamically adapt authentication policies. While achieving good empirical performance, these works do not provide the level of interpretability that we desire, a critical concern in security systems where understanding failure modes is essential [21].
2. *Statistical fusion:* Bayesian approaches [1,18] model sensor outputs as conditional probabilities and apply Bayes' rule for fusion. [19] achieves fusion using likelihood ratio tests (notably Neyman–Pearson). However, these methods require careful specification of prior distributions and evidence combination rules, which are often chosen *ad hoc*. Informative general methods are given in [10,14].
3. *Rule-based systems:* Simple voting schemes [12], weighted averages [20], and threshold-based logic [23] provide some interpretability but are incomplete in terms of probabilistic theoretical grounding.

1.2 Our Contribution

The main motivation of this work is the will to avoid empirical or hardly explainable trust aggregation methods, typically AI-based. Hence, we model the problem using differential equations governing the decay of trust and explore them via simulation.

While the practical calibration of model parameters remains an empirical question, we argue that an analyzable, explainable model provides a better foundation for security-critical systems than black-box alternatives.

The aim of this work is to model the interplay between four factors encountered in practice: multi-modality[4] (ℓ), the effect of time (t), prior assumptions ($\mathbf{b}$) and application-dependent priorities μ.

This paper explores CUA by drawing inspiration from the field of pharmacokinetics [13]. Pharmacokinetics, a discipline within pharmacology, studies how substances are absorbed, distributed, metabolized, and eliminated within the

[1] Bi-modal.

[2] For aggregation ("fusing" cf. Section 7).

[3] The approach of [8] is not a random forest *per se* but conceptually close. Interestingly [8] takes into account trust decay, a point to which we will come back later on.

[4] Including sensor correlation Σ.

body. This is achieved by modeling drug concentrations using ordinary differential equations. Despite its roots in life sciences, pharmacokinetics provides a powerful framework for modeling dynamic processes over time. By analogizing the trust levels in a user-system interaction to the concentration of a drug within the body, this paper proposes a method for modeling and evaluating trust in CUA systems. The absorption, distribution, metabolism, and elimination (ADME) phases of a substance can be paralleled with the trust-building and decay processes in user authentication, where trust rises through consistent behavior and diminishes (slowly) with inactivity or (quickly) with anomalies.

We focus on soundly *aggregating* CUA data collected from heterogeneous security sensors using an analyzable theoretical model. In typical scenarios, user presence is assessed by monitoring and aggregating system events. Sensor readings may present conflicting outputs and differ in attributes such as False Acceptance Rate (FAR), False Rejection Rate (FRR), response time, activation costs, etc. Our goal is to blend such data streams to estimate an overall trust level at any point in time as soundly as we can. To do so, we borrow only the elementary first-order injection and infusion equations from pharmacokinetics. These equations are recalled for completeness in Appendix A; the rest of the paper uses them directly as trust-evolution primitives.

2 Roadmap

The target system is equipped with sensors that continuously send probabilities $\{p_i(t), q_i(t)\}$ about the presence of the user $p_i(t)$ and the attacker $q_i(t)$; from which the "nobody" probability $n_i(t) = 1 - p_i(t) - q_i(t)$ is implicitly derived. $\{p_i(t), q_i(t)\}$ are aggregated into two global 2D time-series $P(t), Q(t)$ using hyper-parameters Γ. Based on $P(t), Q(t)$ a decision is reached and an action on the target system is potentially taken.

A typical example is the determination of the trust level during mobile phone operation. The various security sensors present in the phone can either send information bursts when triggered by a user action (e.g. password entry) or send a continuous flow of information (e.g. monitoring of the user's geolocation via GPS).

To keep the presentation linear, the paper separates three layers of the model. First, Sects. 3–4 define the local time evolution of individual sensor beliefs, using injection and infusion dynamics. Second, Sect. 5 aggregates these local beliefs into a global point $(P(t), Q(t), N(t))$ on the probability simplex and derives a decision rule. Third, Appendix A provides the pharmacokinetic background, simulation details and orders of magnitude used to instantiate the model. All simulation figures are therefore intended as illustrations of the preceding equations rather than as separate definitions of the model.

3 Adversarial Model

We call a *scenario* $U \in \{\mathbf{Q}, \mathbf{N}, \mathbf{P}\}^t$ an experiment where at times $1, 2, \ldots, t$ each sensor i is either facing the user ($\mathbf{P}$), an attacker using a *stochastically observ-*

able attack against the sensor ($\mathbf{Q}$) or nobody at all ($\mathbf{N}$). We call *stochastically observable attacks* any attack whose discovery success chances are known to the defender given the sensors at hand.

The symbol $\mathbf{Q}$ can represent diverse adversarial goals, typically those listed at Table 1.

Table 1. Example: Some adversarial goals

	the actual situation is:	the attacker tries to convince the sensor that:
$\mathbf{Q}_{\mathbf{P}\to\mathbf{N}}$ (denial of service)	the user faces the sensor	nobody faces the sensor
$\mathbf{Q}_{\mathbf{N}\to\mathbf{P}}$ (spoofing)	nobody faces the sensor	the user faces the sensor
$\mathbf{Q}_{\mathbf{Q}\to\mathbf{P}}$ (impersonation)	the attacker faces the sensor	the user faces the sensor
$\mathbf{Q}_{\mathbf{Q}\to\mathbf{N}}$ (concealment)	the attacker faces the sensor	nobody faces the sensor

We simply "bury" the adversarial goal in the sensor. In other words, the sensor is "tailored" to sense a given stochastically observable attack and provide a $p_i(t), q_i(t)$ data flow expressing the likelihood that *this* stochastically observable attack is currently underway.

4 The Analogy Between Pharmacokinetics and CUA

We now instantiate the pharmacokinetic analogy at the level of individual sensors. The analogy is used only in a narrow mathematical sense: authentication evidence is treated as a quantity that can be supplied instantaneously, supplied continuously, and then decay when no new information is received.

Thus, discrete authentication events such as password entry, fingerprint verification or a digital signature are modeled as *injections*. Continuous or repeated evidence sources such as face monitoring, geolocation, a live video call, or repeated Σ-protocol rounds are modeled as *infusions*. The basic differential equations underlying these two cases are recalled in Appendix A; the present section uses them to define the evolution of sensor-level trust.

For sensor i, the output at time t is denoted by $0 \le p_i(t) \le 1$ and $0 \le q_i(t) \le 1$, with $p_i(t) + q_i(t) \le 1$. The remaining probability $n_i(t) = 1 - p_i(t) - q_i(t)$ corresponds to the hypothesis that nobody is present. We consider ℓ sensors.

A $p_i(t) = 1$ at some point in time t reflects the fact that sensor i is *absolutely certain* that the user is present. Similarly, a $q_i(t) = 1$ at some point in time t reflects the fact that sensor i is *absolutely certain* that the attacker is present.

Injection Examples: A typical injection method is password-based login. The password's verification is (virtually) instantaneous and boosts trust up. Fingerprint authentication has the same properties, as does the use of a secret key to sign a random challenge using a digital signature algorithm.

Infusion Examples: A camera monitoring the user's face continuously during a session $[t_0, t_e]$ acts as an infuser. As long as the user is in the camera's field, trust climbs up (it is assumed that each face identification takes a negligible time). A geolocation (GPS, IP or image-based) can be considered as an infusion if coordinates are measured quickly and repeatedly; otherwise, it can be viewed as a succession of injections. A chat (e.g. WhatsApp or SMS exchange) with a trusted party (e.g. the user's parents) is an infusion with a longer ascent[5], a plateau that lasts until the conversation ends and a decay after t_e. A video conversation with a trusted party can also be approximately regarded as an infusion.

Note that different authentication methods may feature different k values.

A worked-out example (for one-bit Fiat-Shamir) is given in the full ePrint version of this paper [3].

4.1 Multiple Readings of a Same Sensor in the Injection and Infusion Cases

Unlike pharmacokinetics, we intentionally replace additive dosing by a max-operator to reflect trust dominance rather than accumulation. This follows intuition: if the entity behind the keyboard used a digital signature key yesterday and is still using the same key today there is no point in taking into account past *redundant* knowledge. And if the entity successfully used yesterday a 4096-bit RSA key and is successfully using today a 1024-bit key, there is no valid reason to invalidate the past information *unless the decaying* 4096-*bit session is now below the* 1024 *one* (hence the max). This confirms intuition as the attacker has no advantage to replace an old higher level of trust by a lower newly created one.

Assume that an injection has just occurred. As seen in Sect. A.2 this boosts the trust level to some constant C_0. Just before this occurs the system was at some trust level denoted $C_{\text{old}}(t_0)$.

A new injection at time t_0 makes the past obsolete. Hence as this injection succeeds (or fails) we reset the trust level at t_0 to the maximum of $C_{\text{old}}(t_0)$ and C_0. Formally:

$$C_{\text{new}}(t) := \begin{cases} C_{\text{old}}(t) & \text{if } t < t_0 \\ \max\left(C_{\text{old}}\left(t_0\right), C_0\right) & \text{if } t = t_0 \\ C_{\text{new}}(t_0)e^{-k(t-t_0)} & \text{if } t > t_0 \end{cases}$$

The effect of such multiple injections is illustrated in Fig. 1.

However, in the case of multiple infusions, we logically resume ascent from the previous trust level. Formally:

---

[5] While it is easy to impersonate a person for a few seconds by answering banalities, it quickly becomes harder and harder to sustain a credible chat as a conversation goes on.

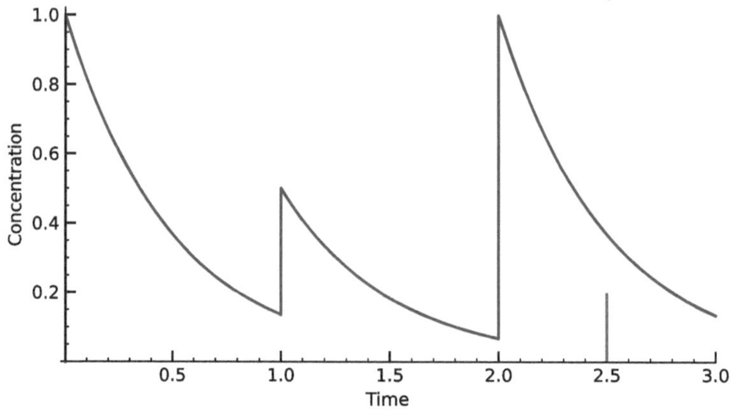

Fig. 1. Illustration of multiple injections for the same sensor. The following drug parameters were used: $(C_0, k) = (1, 2)$. The first injection event occurs at $t = 0$ with $C_0 = 1.0$, the second at $t = 1$ with $C_0 = 0.5$, the third at $t = 2$ with $C_0 = 1.0$ and the last at $t = 2.5$ with $C_0 = 0.2$. Note that the last red one has no effect, as trust level is still higher than 0.2. (Color figure online)

$$C_{\text{new}}(t) := \begin{cases} C_{\text{old}}(t) & \text{if } t \leq t_0 \\ \frac{R}{k}\left(1 - \left(1 - \frac{k}{R}C_{\text{old}}(t_0)\right) e^{-k(t-t_0)}\right) & \text{if } t_0 < t \leq t_e \\ C_{\text{new}}(t_e)e^{-k(t-t_e)} & \text{if } t > t_e \end{cases}$$

The intuitive explanation of this "resuming from past value" is clarified by the example of a user starting and interrupting successive video-calls to a parent. The decaying trust from the past, yet not very distant, strengthens the system's belief in the user's presence. The effect of such multiple infusions is illustrated in Fig. 2.

Note the intuitive correspondences: The "D" in ADME (drug distribution) echoes the propagation of trust across different functions, services or devices within the same "security body" or application. The "M" part (metabolism) is the transformation of raw sensor data into a *trust score*, to which we will return later.

5 Trust Aggregation

As we shall see, there are different ways to aggregate inputs from different sensors.

We model the situation as a discrete random variable X taking values in a sample space $\Omega = \{\mathbf{P}, \mathbf{Q}, \mathbf{N}\}$, where:

- **P**: The legitimate user is facing the sensor.
- **Q**: The attacker is facing the sensor.
- **N**: Nobody is facing the sensor.

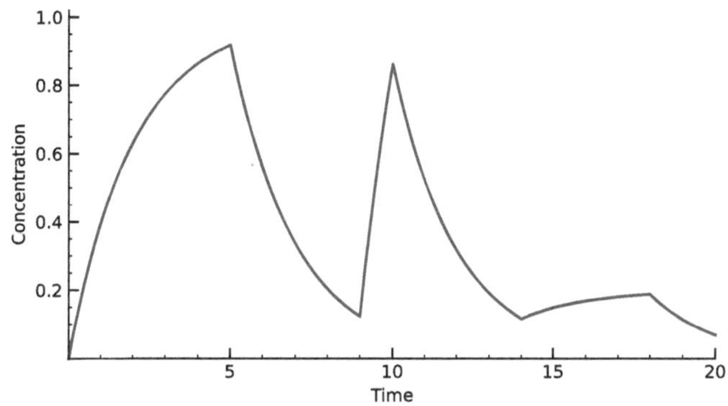

Fig. 2. Illustration of multiple infusions for the same sensor, with $k = 0.5$. The first infusion event occurs in interval $[0, 5]$ with $R = 0.5$, the second in interval $[9, 10]$ with $R = 1$, and the last one in interval $[14, 18]$ with $R = 0.1$.

The set of all possible probability distributions per sensor over Ω is the 2-simplex, denoted by Δ^2:

$$\Delta^2 = \{(p_i, q_i, n_i) \in \mathbb{R}^3 \mid p_i + q_i + n_i = 1, \text{ and } p_i, q_i, n_i \geq 0\}$$

Consider a group of ℓ independent sensors. Each sensor $i \in \{1, \ldots, \ell\}$ provides a probability distribution vector $\mathbf{v}_i \in \Delta^2$:

$$\mathbf{v}_i = \begin{pmatrix} p_i \\ q_i \\ n_i \end{pmatrix}$$

where p_i is the probability assigned to state $\mathbf{P}$, q_i to state $\mathbf{Q}$, and $n_i = 1 - p_i - q_i$ to state $\mathbf{N}$.

To reflect the decision-maker's subjective priorities, we define a global preference vector μ. The role of μ is to favor (i.e. amplify) any of the sensors' readings. μ is application-dependent but we treat it formally.

$$\mu = \begin{pmatrix} \mu_1 \\ \mu_2 \\ \mu_3 \end{pmatrix}, \quad \text{subject to } \sum_{j=1}^{3} \mu_j = 1 \text{ and } \mu_1, \mu_2, \mu_3 > 0$$

We now define the transformation ("metabolism") step: The input of each sensor is transformed into a biased vector $\mathbf{v}'_i$ by element-wise scaling followed by normalization to project the result back onto Δ^2:

$$\mathbf{v}'_i = \phi(\mathbf{v}_i, \mu) = \frac{\mathbf{v}_i \odot \mu}{\mathbf{1}^T(\mathbf{v}_i \odot \mu)} = \begin{pmatrix} p'_i \\ q'_i \\ n'_i \end{pmatrix}$$

The explicit components for sensor i are:

$$p'_i = \frac{\mu_1 p_i}{\mu_1 p_i + \mu_2 q_i + \mu_3 n_i}, \quad q'_i = \frac{\mu_2 q_i}{\mu_1 p_i + \mu_2 q_i + \mu_3 n_i}, \quad n'_i = \frac{\mu_3 n_i}{\mu_1 p_i + \mu_2 q_i + \mu_3 n_i}.$$

The global probabilities P, Q, and N are obtained by calculating the arithmetic mean of the ℓ biased vectors. This represents the mass center centroid of the sensors' opinions in the simplex:

$$\mathbf{V} = \begin{pmatrix} P \\ Q \\ N \end{pmatrix} = \frac{1}{\ell} \sum_{i=1}^{\ell} \mathbf{v}'_i$$

The final decision coordinates are thus:

$$P = \frac{1}{\ell} \sum_{i=1}^{\ell} \frac{\mu_1 p_i}{\mu_1 p_i + \mu_2 q_i + \mu_3 n_i}, \quad Q = \frac{1}{\ell} \sum_{i=1}^{\ell} \frac{\mu_2 q_i}{\mu_1 p_i + \mu_2 q_i + \mu_3 n_i}, \quad N = 1 - P - Q.$$

In other words, we can model the situation as a point in the unit cube's simplex, given the constraint $P + Q + N = 1$.

This representation enables a geometric interpretation of the system state by monitoring the trajectory of the point $\{P(t), Q(t), N(t)\}$ on the simplex that we divide into three Voronoi sectors corresponding to the user, the attacker and nobody as shown in Fig. 3.

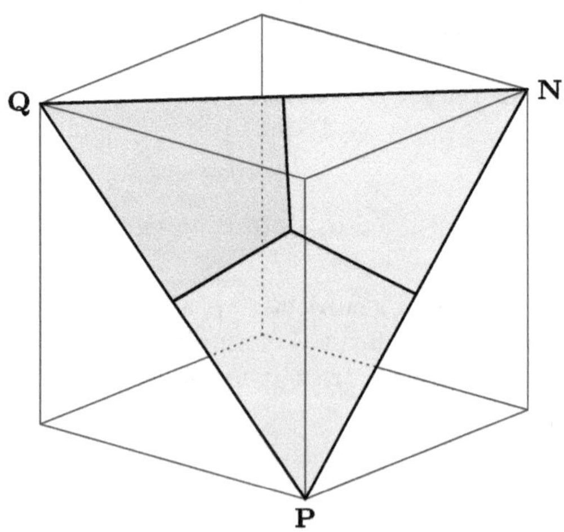

Fig. 3. The simplex and its three Voronoi sectors. The green sector corresponds to the user (P), the red sector to the attacker (Q), and the grey sector to nobody (N). Each colored region contains the points closest to its respective vertex; the instantaneous state (P, Q, N) falls into one of these sectors, which determines the nominal decision (confidence increases toward the corresponding vertex). (Color figure online)

Now, the maximal distance between the three corners and the orthocenter is $\frac{\sqrt{6}}{3}$. We can hence motivate a decision process as in Table 2.

Table 2. Voronoi sector decision and score using $\eta = P^2 + (P+Q)(Q-1)$.

(P, Q, N) is in...	Decision	Criterion	Score$\in [0,1]$
S_P	user	$P > \max(Q, 1-P-Q)$	$1-\sqrt{3(\eta+1-P)}$
S_Q	attacker	$Q > \max(P, 1-P-Q)$	$1-\sqrt{3(\eta+1-Q)}$
S_N	nobody	$1-P-Q > \max(P, Q)$	$1-\sqrt{3(\eta+P+Q)}$

5.1 How to Initialize the System?

The previous sections assumed that in the absence of incoming information, the system re-converges towards a "nobody present" state.

In all generality, during the interval separating reset from the first event, the system may occupy a state $\mathbf{V}_0 = \phi(\mathbf{b}, \mu)$, where $\mathbf{b} = [P_0, Q_0, N_0]^T \neq [0, 0, 1]^T$. $\mathbf{b}$ is the application-dependent initial condition (priors).

For lack of space we cannot provide here the full treatment of this question and refer the reader to the full paper [3].

6 Non-independent (Correlated) Sensors

The centroid aggregation of Sect. 5 implicitly treats sensors as equally informative. This is appropriate when sensors provide independent evidence, but it over-counts redundant sources. For example, GPS and IP geolocation, or two face-recognition models trained on similar data, should not contribute as two fully independent witnesses. Otherwise an attacker who spoofs one underlying physical feature may obtain an artificial confidence gain by affecting several correlated sensors at once.

A simple correction is to replace the arithmetic mean by a precision-weighted mean. Let $\Sigma \in \mathbb{R}^{\ell \times \ell}$ be the sensor covariance matrix, where

$$\Sigma_{ij} = \rho_{ij}\sigma_i\sigma_j.$$

Here ρ_{ij} is the correlation coefficient between sensors i and j, and σ_i^2 models the uncertainty of sensor i. Assuming Σ is positive definite, define

$$W = \frac{\Sigma^{-1}\mathbf{1}}{\mathbf{1}^T\Sigma^{-1}\mathbf{1}}, \qquad W = (w_1, \ldots, w_\ell)^T.$$

The global state is then

$$P(t) = \sum_{i=1}^{\ell} w_i p_i(t), \qquad Q(t) = \sum_{i=1}^{\ell} w_i q_i(t), \qquad N(t) = 1 - P(t) - Q(t).$$

This formula has the expected limiting behavior. If the sensors are independent and have equal variance, then $\Sigma = \sigma^2 I$ and $w_i = 1/\ell$, recovering the centroid rule. If two sensors become highly correlated, the inverse covariance reduces their combined effective weight: they behave more like one virtual sensor than two independent ones. Thus correlation does not change the subsequent Voronoi decision rule; it only changes the location of the aggregated point on the simplex.

In practice, Σ can be estimated during enrollment or during supervised operation from labeled sensor traces.

7 Further Research

A first interesting extension would take into account non-stationary k (in a way similar to the advection term in Navier-Stokes equations where speed increases due to the very movement to a given coordinate[6]). The current model assumes constant decay rates k for each sensor. However, the rate at which trust should decay depends on context, e.g. trust in a password entered at home should decay slower than one entered in a crowded coffee shop.

Moreover, at this stage, the framework is a theoretical blueprint evaluated through synthetic simulations. A natural next step is to collect real interaction traces from instrumented devices, estimate k, C_0, R, $\mathbf{b}$ and μ from these traces, and then replace constant parameters by context-dependent ones such as $k(t, \chi(t))$, where $\chi(t)$ captures location, device state, recent activity density or application risk.

Disclosure of Interests. The authors have no competing interests to declare that are relevant to the content of this article.

A Pharmacokinetics

Pharmacokinetics is a branch of pharmacology that studies the fate of a drug within the body after its administration. It examines how drugs are **a**bsorbed, **d**istributed, **m**etabolized and **e**liminated (ADME) by the body. This discipline is essential to understand how a drug interacts with the body and how its effects manifest over time (t).

Absorption is the process by which a drug enters the bloodstream from its site of administration, whether it be orally, intravenously, transdermally, or via other routes. The speed and the extent of absorption depend on various factors, including the drug formulation, the presence of food in the stomach and the patient's physiological state.

Once in the bloodstream, the drug is distributed to different tissues and organs throughout the body.

---

[6] In this analogy, the "trust equation" would have on its left side a material derivative counting for the prior, an advective term due to context changes and a viscosity term (friction) due to decay, while the right hand represents the "external forces", i.e. the defender and attacker events detected by the sensors.

Distribution depends on factors such as cell membrane permeability, binding to plasma proteins and tissue perfusion.

After distribution, the drug is often *metabolized* in the liver and other organs, where it is transformed into metabolites that may be active, inactive, or toxic.

Finally, the drug and its metabolites are *eliminated* from the body mainly by the kidneys in the form of urine, but also through other routes such as bile, sweat and respiration. The elimination process determines the duration of action of the drug and influences the dosage and frequency of administration.

Denoting by $C(t)$ the concentration of drug in the bloodstream, the mainstream model used in pharmacokinetics is the exponential decay:

$$\frac{dC}{dt} = -kC$$

where k is the elimination rate constant. k is determined by factors such as drug metabolism, renal excretion and tissue distribution. Understanding this equation aids in predicting drug concentrations over time, optimizing dosing regimens and ensuring therapeutic efficacy while minimizing the risk of toxicity in clinical settings.

Integration of $\frac{dC}{dt} = -kC$ with respect to t gives:

$$C(t) = C_0 e^{-kt}$$

where C_0 is the initial concentration of the drug.

A number of administration modes are considered in pharmacokinetics. The most important of those, which will be mirrored by security events, are *injection* and *infusion* that we will briefly overview in the coming subsections.

A.1 Injection

Injections involve administering medication directly into the body through various routes such as intravenous (IV), intramuscular (IM), subcutaneous (SC), or intradermal (ID). In this mode, the drug bypasses the digestive system and enters the bloodstream rapidly, resulting in a quick onset of action. The equation governing drug elimination in the blood after injection is described by first-order kinetics, represented by the previously-mentioned ODE:

$$\frac{dC}{dt} = -kC \Rightarrow C(t) = C_0 e^{-kt}$$

The effect of injection is illustrated in Fig. 4.

A.2 Infusion

Intravenous (IV) infusion involves administering medication directly into a vein over a specific period, typically through a drip system. This mode allows for precise control over the infusion rate and can be used for continuous drug administration. The equation governing drug elimination in the blood during intravenous infusion also follows first-order kinetics, similar to injection. However, it also incorporates an *infusion rate* R:

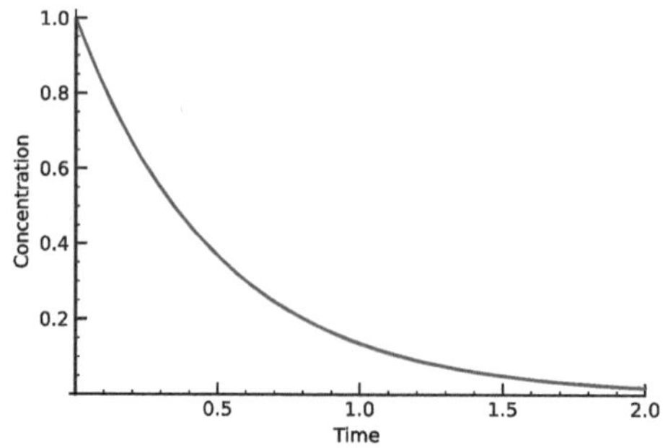

Fig. 4. Illustration of elimination under a single injection at $t = 0$. The following drug parameters were used: $(C_0, k) = (1, 2)$. The mathematical model for successive injections is detailed in Sect. 4.1.

$$\frac{dC}{dt} = R - kC \Rightarrow C(t) = \frac{R}{k}\left(1 - (1 - C_0)e^{-kt}\right)$$

The term $\frac{R}{k}$ represents the steady state concentration reached during continuous infusion, where the drug input rate is equal to the elimination rate.

The function is generalized by adding the parameter t_e ("time of exit") at which the infusion ends to give the overall function:

$$C(t) = \begin{cases} 0 & \text{if } t \leq 0 \\ \frac{R}{k}(1 - e^{-k \cdot t}) & \text{if } 0 \leq t \leq t_e \\ C(t_e)e^{-k(t-t_e)} = \frac{R}{k}(1 - e^{-k \cdot t_e})e^{-k(t-t_e)} = \frac{R(e^{kt_e}-1)}{k}e^{-kt} & \text{if } t > t_e \end{cases}$$

The effect of infusion is illustrated in Fig. 5.

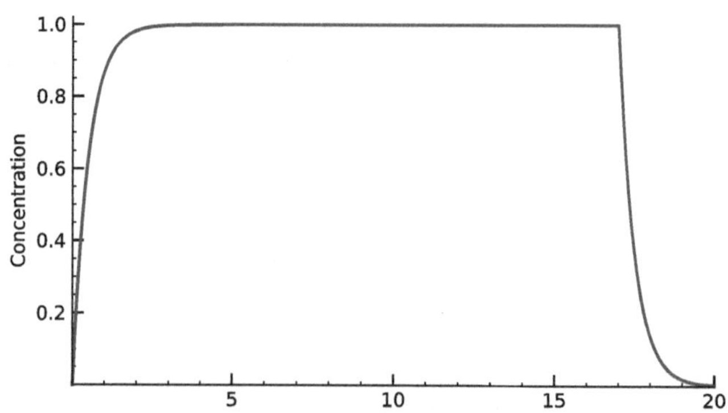

Fig. 5. Infusion administered during $0 \leq t \leq 17$. The following drug parameters were used: $(R, k, t_e) = (2, 2, 17)$.

A.3 Combined Administration

When the same medication is taken via ℓ different channels, functions add-up as shown in Fig. 6 to provide a total concentration : $S(t) = \sum_{i=1}^{\ell} C_i(t)$.

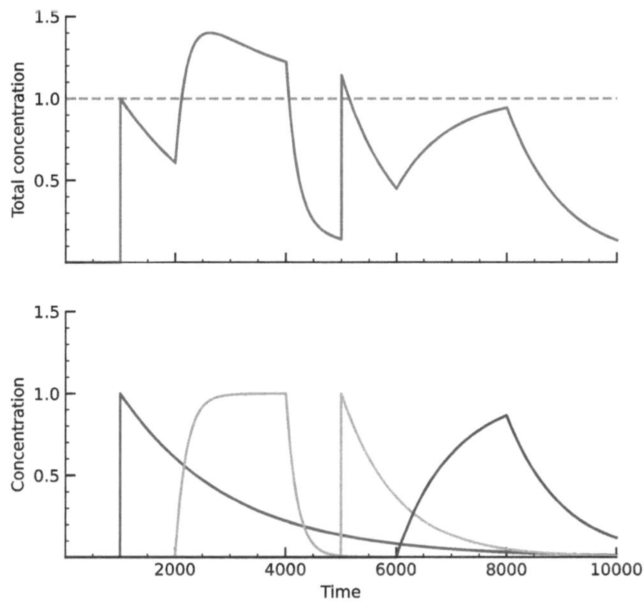

Fig. 6. An injection followed by an infusion, a second injection and a second infusion. The total concentration is plotted in red. Note that at times the concentration in blood exceeds 1 units. The drug parameters are as follows: - first injection $(t, c_0, k) = (1000, 1, 0.0005)$ - first infusion $(t, t_e, R, k) = (2000, 4000, 0.005, 0.005)$ - second injection $(t, c_0, k) = (5000, 1, 0.001)$ - second infusion $(t, t_e, R, k) = (6000, 8000, 0.001, 0.001)$ (Color figure online)

B Simulations

B.1 P, Q, N and Score Derivation

We implemented an interactive interface demonstrating the proposed logic[7]. The model has two sensors, an infusion and an injection. The interface allows selecting the signal's origin which can be either the defender (legitimate user) or the attacker. To reduce the number of cursors a general cursor-selectable k controls all decays. We fixed $\mathbf{b} = [0, 0, 1]^T$. A pair of cursors controls μ. The individual parameters of each event (t_0, C_0 or t_0, R, t_e) are also cursor-definable.

[7] Available on https://github.com/enssec/Cryptokinetics-Simulation-Suite.

The software stacks $P(t)$, $Q(t)$ and $N(t)$ above the events. An upper multi-color line shows the Voronoi sector (S_P, S_Q or S_N) of the point $(P(t), Q(t), N(t))$.

A key feature of the implementation is the introduction of "recoil events": Assume that a legitimate user injection C_0 occurred at t_0. The provided model perfectly defines $p_i(t)$ but what's about $q_i(t)$ and $n_i(t)$?

Because $p_i(t) + q_i(t) + n_i(t) = 1$ the question boils-down to understanding what is $q_i(t)$ or how to simulate it.

Even a successful injection generates a complementary probability mass assigned to competing hypotheses $q_i(t), n_i(t)$. We refer to this induced component as the "recoil" or the "mirror event". The recoil has the same t_0 as the generating (inducing) event but its amplitude, denoted $\bar{C}_0 = m(1 - C_0)$ is computed from the initial event's C_0[8] where $0 \leq m \leq 1$ represents the "opposite magnitude proportion". We hence share the room left free by the event between $q_i(t)$ and $n_i(t)$ at an $m/(1-m)$ proportion. This also applies to attacker events (that generate recoil defender events). The recoil is a fully-fledged defender/attacker event *by its own right* (Fig. 7).

The "linear" split of the "remaining room" is used only for illustration. In all generality, the recoil's parameters are some function[9] H of the system's state and the incoming event's parameters (C_0 or R).

The $1 - \sqrt{3(\eta + \bullet)}$ score, shown in yellow measures the degree of "loneliness" of $P(t), Q(t), N(t)$. As expected, when one of the three is "alone" or "relatively alone" during a time interval, the score surges. This confirms intuition.

B.2 Simplex Trajectory to Priors

The software shown in Fig. 8 illustrates the re-convergence to the prior. The user defines the p_i, q_i, n_i values of five sensors as well as μ and $\mathbf{b}$. The code interactively plots the aggregated $[P, Q, N]^T$ and its convergence to the prior.

The green point in the plot represents the initial state $\mathbf{V}(0)$, which is the centroid of the biased "high-energy" starting points. The curvature of the black trajectory is a result of the differing elimination rates k_i. As time increases, sensors with higher values of k_i relax toward $\mathbf{b}$ more rapidly, shifting the global centroid towards the vectors of slower-decaying sensors.

Since $\lim_{t\to\infty} \mathbf{v}_i(t) = \mathbf{b}$ for all i, the global state converges to:

$$\lim_{t\to\infty} \mathbf{V}(t) = \phi(\mathbf{b}, \mu)$$

This limit corresponds to the red point (the μ-biased prior) displayed in the simplex, i.e. the stable system equilibrium in the absence of information.

To visualize the speed of convergence in a static plot, we added a sequence of blue temporal tick marks (perpendicular bars) along the trajectory. These bars are placed at fixed time intervals (every unit of time). Because the relaxation follows an exponential decay, the bars are widely spaced at the beginning (high

[8] In the case of infusion, the recoil's $\bar{R}$ is similarly defined by $\bar{R} = m(k - R)$.

[9] That we do not aim to characterize in this work.

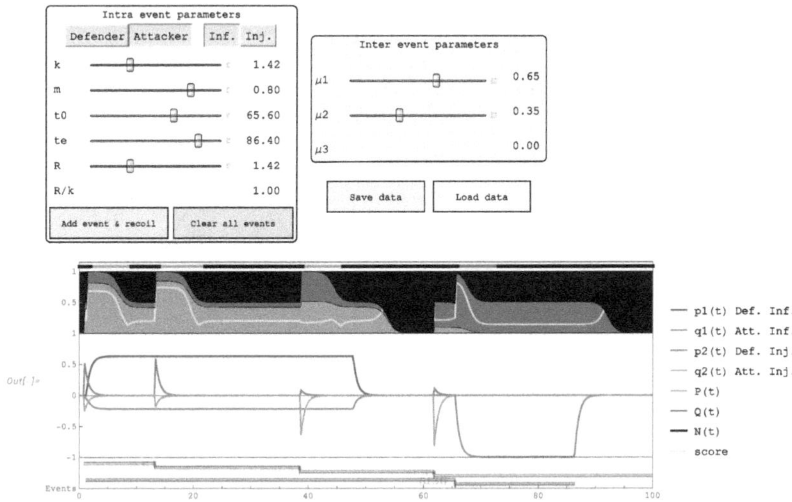

Events Table:

ID	Type	Origin	t0	te	R	C0	Next	X
1	Inj.	Defender	0.90	N/A	N/A	0.62	3	x
2	Inj. (recoil)	Attacker	0.90	N/A	N/A	0.30	4	x
3	Inj.	Defender	13.30	N/A	N/A	0.72	6	x
4	Inj. (recoil)	Attacker	13.30	N/A	N/A	0.22	5	x
5	Inj.	Attacker	38.60	N/A	N/A	0.86	7	x
6	Inj. (recoil)	Defender	38.60	N/A	N/A	0.11	8	x
7	Inj.	Attacker	61.90	N/A	N/A	0.86	None	x
8	Inj. (recoil)	Defender	61.90	N/A	N/A	0.11	None	x
9	Inf.	Attacker	1.30	47.80	0.31	N/A	11	x
10	Inf. (recoil)	Defender	1.30	47.80	0.89	N/A	12	x
11	Inf.	Attacker	65.60	86.40	1.42	N/A	None	x
12	Inf. (recoil)	Defender	65.60	86.40	0.00	N/A	None	x

Fig. 7. Illustrations from the aggregation software. Top: Controls to set global bias parameters (μ_1, μ_2, μ_3) and to add new events (attacker/defender $\times$ injection/infusion). Middle: Time series of per-sensor posteriors $p_1(t), q_1(t), p_2(t), q_2(t)$ and aggregated posteriors $P(t), Q(t), N(t)$, score. Bottom: Table of current events with their parameters.

velocity) and become increasingly crowded as the trajectory approaches the red arrival point (asymptotic slow-down).

C Real-Life Orders of Magnitude

An experimental study by Carolus et al. [6] found that, on average, users touch their mobile phone every 44 seconds. Assuming that phone touches follow a Poisson process with rate $\lambda = \frac{1}{44}$ touches per second.

The probability of observing α events in time t is hence:

$$P(t;\alpha) = \frac{(\lambda t)^\alpha}{\alpha!} e^{-\lambda t}.$$

We are interested in the probability that no touch occurs during t seconds, i.e. $\alpha = 0$: $P(t;0) = e^{-t/44} \Rightarrow k = \frac{1}{44}$.

This gives a rough idea about the "real-life" k for decay.

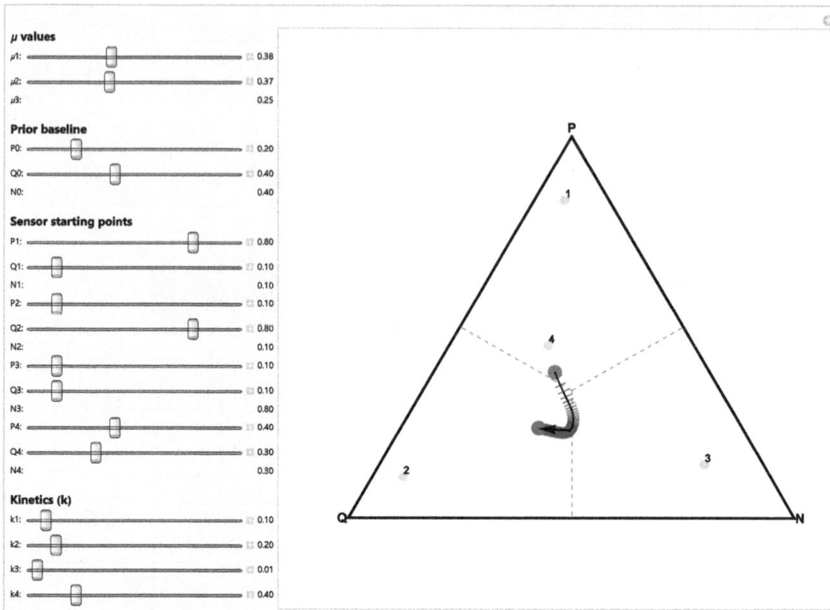

Fig. 8. Convergence to an application-specific prior. Example. This figure is interesting as it shows that the system can "naturally" venture into a Voronoi sector other than the departure and arrival ones during decay. (Color figure online)

For a video-call infusion we may consider that the ascent to the plateau has $k_a = \infty$ if the system performs a caller face recognition before allowing an incoming call to reach the receiver. The descent after t_e will, again, use a $k = \frac{1}{44}$.

The C_0 resulting from a correct password entry or a correct digital signature is hard to estimate as keys can be stolen via different means (e.g. guessing, data breaches, key loggers, etc.) but some statistics [16] provide rough estimates of the order of magnitude. There are about $6 \cdot 10^9$ Internet users and it is known that $\simeq 3.2 \cdot 10^9$ passwords are stolen yearly. If we estimate[10] that each user creates 15 new passwords per year and that only 25% of stolen passwords are still valid when a data breach occurs, we get a "Drake equation"[11] [9] of:

$$a_1 = 1 - \frac{3.2 \cdot 10^9}{4 \times 15 \times 6 \cdot 10^9} \simeq 0.9911$$

However [16], $a_2 = 83\%$ of passwords can allegedly be cracked in under a day. The overall confidence that one can have in a password is, more or less:

[10] This figure is a modeling assumption rather than an empirically sourced estimate. It is stated explicitly so that readers may revise it under alternative assumptions about password-creation behavior.

[11] Interestingly the 25% plays the role of Drake's L, i.e. the lifetime of an alien civilization wherein it communicates its signals into space.

$$1 - ((1 - a_1) + a_2 - (1 - a_1)a_2) \simeq 16.8\% \simeq \frac{1}{6}$$

In other words, roughly 1 in 6 passwords survives the year uncompromised or resistant to compromise. We hence recommend to use $C_0 \simeq \frac{1}{6}$ for password entry.

As key theft is conceivably harder we recommend to use $C_0 = 0.95$ for digital signature injection, without any justification other than the fact that key compromises are usually "rare" [5,11].

References

1. Altinok, A., Turk, M.: Temporal integration for continuous multimodal biometrics. In: Proceedings of the Workshop on Multimodal User Authentication (MMUA) (2003)
2. Bansal, P., Ouda, A.: Continuous authentication in the digital age: An analysis of reinforcement learning and behavioral biometrics. Computers **13**(4) (2024). https://doi.org/10.3390/computers13040103, https://www.mdpi.com/2073-431X/13/4/103
3. Barral, H., Naccache, D., Veličković, A.: Cryptokinetics. Cryptology ePrint Archive, Paper 2026/323 (2026), https://eprint.iacr.org/2026/323
4. Buriro, A., Crispo, B., Votis, K., Tzovaras, D.: Hold and sign: a novel behavioral biometrics for continuous authentication. IEEE Trans. Inf. Forensics Secur. **11**(8), 1681–1693 (2016)
5. Bäumer, F., Brinkmann, M., Radoy, M., Schwenk, J., Somorovsky, J.: On the security of SSH client signatures. In: Proceedings of the 2025 ACM SIGSAC Conference on Computer and Communications Security, CCS 2025, pp. 4619–4633. ACM (2025). https://doi.org/10.1145/3719027.3765079
6. Carolus, A., Schwab, F., Münch, R., Schmidt, C., Schneider, F., Binder, J.: Digital companions. Research report for Kasperski Labs, Julius-Maximilians-University Würzburg and Nottingham Trent University, Würzburg, Germany and Nottingham, United Kingdom (2016)
7. Centeno, M., Marin, I., Pardo, J.M., Hernandez-Encinas, L.: Mobile continuous authentication using touch dynamics. Sensors **18**(8), 2562 (2018)
8. Crawford, H., Renaud, K., Furnell, S.: A survey of linguistic profiling for author identification and verification. Secur. Commun. Networks **6**(1), 44–59 (2013)
9. Drake, F., Sobel, D.: Is Anyone out there?: The Scientific Search for Extraterrestrial Intelligence. Delacorte Press, New York (1992)
10. Fridman, A., Stolerman, A., Acharya, S., Brennan, P., Juola, P., Greenstadt, R., Kam, M.: Decision fusion for multimodal active authentication. IT Professional **17**(1), 13–20 (2015)
11. Heninger, N., Durumeric, Z., Wustrow, E., Halderman, J.A.: Mining your *p*s and *q*s: detection of widespread weak keys in network devices. In: Proceedings of the 21st USENIX Conference on Security Symposium, p. 35. Security'12, USENIX Association,, USA (2012)
12. Jain, A., Nandakumar, K., Ross, A.: Score normalization in multimodal biometric systems. Pattern Recogn. **38**(12), 2270–2285 (2005)
13. Jambhekar, S.S., Breen, P.J.: Basic Pharmacokinetics, 2nd edn. Pharmaceutical Press, London, UK (2012)

14. Li, Y., Zou, B., Deng, S., Zhou, G.: Using feature fusion strategies in continuous authentication on smartphones. IEEE Internet Comput. **24**(2), 47–56 (2020)
15. Mahfouz, A., Mahmoud, Y., Abu-Naser, A.M.: A survey on behavioral biometric authentication on smartphones. J. Inf. Secur. **8**(4), 307–322 (2017)
16. Mitchell, S.: Password hacking statistics: Market data report 2026. https://gitnux.org/password-hacking-statistics/ (2026). https://gitnux.org/password-hacking-statistics/. Accessed 16 Feb 2026
17. Pelto, B., Vanamala, M., Dave, R.: Your identity is your behavior: continuous user authentication based on machine learning and touch dynamics. In: IEEE Conference Publication (2023)
18. Poh, N., Kittler, J., Bourlai, T.: Quality-based score normalisation with device qualitative information for multimodal biometric fusion. In: Proceedings of the IEEE International Conference on Biometrics (ICB), pp. 462–471 (2009)
19. Prabhakar, S., Jain, A.K.: Decision-level fusion in fingerprint verification. Pattern Recogn. **35**(4), 861–874 (2002)
20. Ross, A., Jain, A.: Information fusion in biometrics. Pattern Recogn. Lett. **24**(13), 2115–2125 (2003)
21. Rudin, C.: Stop explaining black box machine learning models for high stakes decisions and use interpretable models instead. Nat. Mach. Intell. **1**, 206–215 (2019)
22. Ryu, R., Yeom, S., Kim, S.H., Herbert, D.: Continuous multimodal biometric authentication schemes: a systematic review. IEEE Access **9**, 34541–34561 (2021)
23. Shi, E., Niu, Y., Jakobsson, M., Chow, R.: Implicit authentication through learning user behavior. In: Proceedings of the 7th International Conference on Information Security and Cryptology (Inscrypt), pp. 99–113 (2011)

Improving the Utility, Privacy, and Human Acceptance of Differentially Private Rewritten Texts

Stephen Meisenbacher(✉), Endrit Jashari, Alexandra Klymenko, and Florian Matthes

School of Computation, Information and Technology, Technical University of Munich, Garching, Germany
{stephen.meisenbacher,endrit.jashari,alexandra.klymenko,matthes}@tum.de

Abstract. Although *differentially private text rewriting* has gained traction as a theoretically viable, yet straightforward way of enacting local Differential Privacy (DP) in the privatization of sensitive texts, it has struggled with usability and practicality. In particular, the ability to produce coherent, yet privacy-preserving rewritten outputs, while also maintaining positive privacy-utility trade-offs, remains elusive. Leveraging the post-processing property of DP, we propose a simple method for LLM-based post-processing of DP rewritten texts, grounded in the use of structured text features to guide a realignment of DP texts. Our evaluations show significant improvements in text quality and coherence, while also demonstrating strong privacy preservation and positive trade-offs. A survey with 252 human participants showcases the higher human acceptance of post-processed texts, as opposed to nearly non-existent acceptance of pure DP outputs. Our work highlights the strong need for increased usability in DP-based text privatization, for which we show that post-processing is a potential solution.

Keywords: Differential Privacy · Text Privatization · Private Text Rewriting · Data Privacy · Natural Language Processing · User Study

1 Introduction

Differentially private text rewriting [15] leverages the promise of Differential Privacy (DP) [8] in protecting privacy when sharing textual data [21], as a response to growing concerns of adversarial threats and misuse of data [43]. At its core, DP text rewriting transforms sensitive input documents locally into rewritten outputs, which ideally both semantically resemble the input while masking sensitive or personal traces. Despite many works showing that local DP text rewriting is theoretically possible [14], the practical feasibility has been called into question over struggles to find an acceptable balance of privacy and utility [9,16,25,31].

The root of the challenge lies in the necessity under DP to add *noise* to textual data representations, in order to achieve a certain level of indistinguishability between output texts from a given input [21]. This addition of noise, which

P. Kieseberg et al. (Eds.): ARES 2026 Workshops, LNCS 16903, pp. 81–98, 2027.
https://doi.org/10.1007/978-3-032-37218-5_6

is calibrated according to a defined privacy budget (ε), often leads to likewise noisy, incoherent, and unnatural rewritten texts, particularly when using stricter (lower) ε values. Thus, the design of DP text rewriting mechanisms may seem to be at odds with the preservation of natural language, and recent works have explored the challenging impact that achieving DP in text carries [16,26,40].

As a potential solution, one recent work [30] shifts the rectification of the privacy-utility trade-off to *after* DP text rewriting has been performed. This is possible by leveraging the *post-processing* property of DP [8], which states that DP guarantees do not degrade if post-processing is conducted on DP outputs. Guided by this notion, Meisenbacher et al. [30] designed a simple technique using encoder-decoder models to "doubly rewrite" DP outputs, that is, to rewrite the DP rewritten texts once again using fine-tuned LMs. In doing this, they demonstrate that post-processing can effectively correct some of the harms induced by text noisification during DP rewriting, while improving coherence and utility.

We identify three remaining gaps. Firstly, this method requires a *setup* stage with expensive fine-tuning processes, which also assumes prior knowledge of the DP rewriting mechanism. Secondly, the method relies on older encoder-decoder models and does not explore the capabilities of modern LLMs; moreover, testing is only performed on DP texts privatized with high privacy budgets. Finally, the method does not implement a mechanism to ensure that the rewritten outputs adhere to the meta-characteristics of the original texts, such as tone or text length. Therefore, we hypothesize that while the method of Meisenbacher and Matthes [30] can regain semantic meaning, it falls short in creating post-processed outputs that stay true to the intent of the original author.

We are guided by the question: *How can LLMs be used with structured text features to post-process DP rewritten texts such that they preserve privacy and utility, and are more human-acceptable?* In addition to focusing on preserving privacy and utility, our work places a particular emphasis on *human acceptability*, given the importance of gaining user trust and acceptance for what is inherently a complex privacy-preserving technology (i.e., DP). We also solely use open-source, locally runnable LLMs for post-processing, mirroring sensitive scenarios in which no texts should be sent to third parties until privatized (and post-processed).

To evaluate our method for LLM post-processing of DP rewritten texts, we conduct a series of experiments to compare the utility- and privacy-preserving capabilities of our texts versus those rewritten with the method of Meisenbacher and Matthes [30]. The results show that feature-assisted LLM post-processing successfully boosts the utility and coherence of DP rewritten texts, while also maintaining empirical privacy protections. In addition, we conduct a user survey with 252 participants from around the world, showcasing the significantly higher preference of humans towards our post-processed texts, but also highlighting remaining challenges in reaching practical usability for DP text rewriting. Our work advances DP text rewriting towards usability with three contributions:

1. We propose an improved method for LLM-based and structured text feature-supported post-processing of DP rewritten texts, which shows superior performance across a range of privacy and utility evaluations.

2. We focus on *human acceptance*, conducting a survey with 252 participants to demonstrate a clear preference for post-processed outputs from our method.
3. We release our code at https://github.com/sjmeis/PPDPTR and discuss critical paths forward for the practical feasibility of DP text rewriting.

2 Foundations and Related Work

DP Text Rewriting. A DP rewriting mechanism takes as input a text, and it outputs a "privatized" text with DP guarantees. Intuitively, a DP rewriting mechanism grants plausible deniability as to what the original input was to the mechanism, given the private, rewritten output [21]. Included in these protections are not only the masking of explicit identifiers, but also the obfuscation of indirect identifiers and protected attributes (such as authorship) [3,36]. In line with the original notion of DP, the degree to which this indistinguishability must be ensured can be scaled based on the privacy parameter (budget), or ε.

Most DP text rewriting approaches leverage the *local* notion of DP [18], which enforces a stricter guarantee, in that a rewritten text must be indistinguishable, to a degree, from all other texts in the range of "texts". This is a highly limiting constraint, and recent works have addressed this by operating on smaller syntactic units such as the word or token [1,10,27], or by leveraging (large) language models for private text generation [16,39]. As noted by Igamberdiev and Habernal [16], rewriting entire documents under local DP quite often necessitates a large ε for coherent outputs, which weakens theoretical privacy guarantees.

DP and Post-processing. The *post-processing* property of DP states that any arbitrary computations performed on DP outputs will still be DP under the original guarantees. Formally, if $\mathcal{F}(x)$ is ε-DP, $g(\mathcal{F}(x))$ is also ε-DP, for any g. Although this was originally envisioned by Dwork [8] as an assurance against adversarial attempts to accurately infer original information, post-processing is also a useful tool for reducing the degrading effects of DP noise, and has been leveraged in various applications outside of the realm of natural language [2,19].

In transferring the usefulness of post-processing as a noise corrector post-DP rewriting, Meisenbacher and Matthes [30] propose an intuitive double rewriting scheme, in which DP rewritten texts are run again through a specialized, fine-tuned encoder-decoder model. They found that doubly-rewritten DP texts generally exhibit higher utility and coherence, while maintaining comparable privacy levels. We build upon this with an improved method (Sect. 3).

Human Perceptions of DP (Text Rewriting). In recent years, a strong effort has been put forward by the research community to investigate human perceptions of DP, with the goal of fusing privacy research with a usability focus. Studies have found that explaining DP to end users is challenging [7,17,32]. Despite this, Xiong et al. [42] find that local DP is more understandable to laypersons, and is more conducive to incentivizing user data sharing. Recent works have begun to investigate human perspectives towards DP in the context of natural language [41]. Meisenbacher et al. [28] uncover challenges in human acceptance

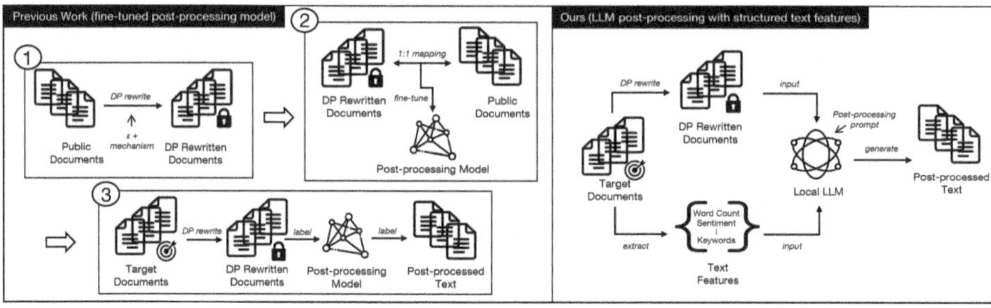

Fig. 1. A comparative illustration of previous work in post-processing DP rewritten texts (left) and our proposed method (right), which is lightweight and does not require fine-tuning or a priori knowledge of the DP rewriting process.

of DP text rewriting, largely due to poor text coherence and perceived low utility despite privacy protection. We continue this human focus, measuring how post-processing can improve acceptance of DP text rewriting.

3 A Post-processing Method Using Structured Text Features with LLMs

We design a simple method that leverages characteristic features extracted from text inputs to DP rewriting mechanisms, which are then inserted into an LLM prompt to post-process the DP outputs. With this, our goal is to propose a lightweight, yet capable post-processing technique that requires no fine-tuning and no prior knowledge of the DP rewriting mechanism or dataset domain.

3.1 Learning from Previous Work

Strengths. As shown in the original work, the post-processing method on the left of Fig. 1 is effective in improving the coherence of DP text rewriting outputs, while also supporting higher utility in downstream tasks at minimal loss to empirical privacy. This ultimately leads to superior trade-offs, making a case for the usefulness of post-processing. The method is grounded in the notion that language models can be fine-tuned to "translate" DP texts into more coherent and acceptable forms. This is accomplished by using DP rewriting methods to create 1:1 original-private text mappings, and then fine-tuning encoder-decoder models (i.e., FLAN-T5 [6]) to learn the "reverse" mapping, that is, generating coherent texts reminiscent of the originals from the DP texts as input.

Limitations. While the abovementioned method is intuitive, it makes a number of assumptions that lead to limitations in its practical applicability. Firstly, the method as described in the original work is *mechanism-specific*, meaning that the fine-tuned language models are specific to a particular DP text rewriting technique. In a second, more advanced version that achieves superior results in evaluation, the method becomes even more use-case-specific, in that the encoder-decoder models are aligned specifically to a dataset or domain, which further limits generalizability. In our work, we seek to create a significantly more generalizable method, which also leverages more capable, autoregressive LLMs.

Relatedly, the implementation by Meisenbacher and Matthes [30] fine-tunes the post-processing models with DP rewritten texts that were privatized at very high ε levels, implying the need for higher-quality 1:1 mappings to achieve sensible results for post-processing. We test this hypothesis, specifically by implementing this method (and comparing it to ours) at strict, lower ε budgets.

We propose a method that is not only more generalizable, but also removes the need for expensive data preparation (i.e., via DP text rewriting) and fine-tuning. We do so by creating a method that requires minimal pre-processing, leveraging LLMs comparable in size to the previously used FLAN-T5 models.

3.2 Text Features for Post-Processing

The basis of our post-processing method is one-shot prompting with small, local LLMs, guided by a set of text features (characteristics) to enable the LLM to align the DP rewritten text back to a text that resembles the original. It is important to note that these base features are *meta-characteristics* of the original texts, and as such, they do not directly leak information about the words or context of the texts. We outline below the collection of features we extract for our method, as well as introduce the post-processing prompt itself.

Text Features (Base). We collect six types of characteristics from the original texts before DP rewriting, comprising our base feature set for post-processing.

Sentiment (Polarity). We calculate the polarity score of a text using Textblob (https://textblob.readthedocs.io/), as *very negative* [–1.0, –0.6), *negative* [–0.6, -0.2), *neutral* [–0.2, 0.2), *positive* [0.2, 0.6), or *very positive* [0.6, 1.0].

Sentiment (Subjectivity). We also calculate the subjectivity score of a text using Textblob: *very objective* [0, 0.25), *objective* [0.25, 0.5), *subjective* [0.5, 0.75), or *very subjective* [0.75, 1.0].

Formality. Using Heylighen and Dewaele's Formality Formula [12], we measure the formality of a given text. This weighs the relative count of "formal" versus "informal" words, represented by their part-of-speech tags. The score is on the scale of 0 to 100, and we bin the results into *very informal* [0, 25), *informal* [25, 45), *neutral* [45, 55), *formal* [55, 75), and *very formal* [75, 100].

Word and Sentence Count. We calculate the simple count of words and sentences in a given text, as tokenized by Textblob.

Readability. We use the Flesch-Kincaid Grade Level assessment [20] to measure the readability of a text, binned into grade levels. We utilize the implementation of Textstat (https://textstat.org/) to retrieve the associated reading grade level. This is categorized into *very easy* (5 and below), *easy* (6–7), *standard* (8–9), *medium difficult* (10–12), *difficult* (college), and *very difficult* (post-grad).

Table 1. A summary of the key characteristics of our four evaluation datasets.

Dataset	Spooky Authors	Topic10	Trustpilot Reviews	Yelp Reviews
Description	Text excerpts from three famous horror genre authors.	Blog posts from Blog Authorship Corpus (top-10 topics only).	User reviews from the Trustpilot platform (English only).	User reviews from the Yelp platform.
Utility Task	–	–	Sentiment Analysis	Sentiment Analysis
Protected Attribute	Authorship (3 IDs)	Author Gender	Author Gender	Authorship (10 IDs)
Dataset Size	19579	16255	29490	17295

Text Features (Advanced). In addition to the above base features, we evaluate a more advanced variant, which leverages two additional extracted features.

Keyword Extraction. We use YAKE [5], a lightweight unsupervised keyword extraction algorithm, to select the most important words from an input text. We limit the extraction to single words and a maximum of five keywords per text.

Topic Modeling. We perform topic clustering using Latent Dirichlet Allocation (LDA) [4], with the GENSIM implementation [34]. We run LDA with three topics, and we take the keywords from the top (first) topic. We then combine the extracted keywords from YAKE and the LDA topic words to form a unified "keywords/topics" feature for post-processing.

3.3 Post-processing Procedure

With the collection of text features extracted from an input text, we craft a one-shot LLM prompt with the task of editing a "noisy text" given the structured text features as a guideline. We drafted a prompt by choosing a DP rewritten text (from the Yelp dataset) using DP-BART [16] with $\varepsilon = 1200$, and then refined the prompt, aiming for clarity and conciseness.

The final prompt is found in our code repository. The inputs are a DP rewritten text and the set of structured text features extracted from the original text, which we call "correction rules", in line with the persona of the "text editor".

4 Experimental Setup and Results

We conduct evaluations that measure the utility and privacy preservation capabilities of post-processed DP texts, compared to the raw DP rewritten texts.

4.1 DP Text Rewriting

We use three DP text rewriting mechanisms and four public datasets of user-written texts to create a plausible test case for text privatization.

Datasets. We use four datasets: *Spooky Authors*[1], *Topic10* [37], *Trustpilot Reviews* [13], and *Yelp Reviews* [44]. These datasets are described in Table 1. We note that for Topic10, we used the subset prepared by Meisenbacher and Matthes [31], and for Yelp, we use the subset prepared by Utpala et al. [39].

Rewriting Mechanisms. We choose three local DP text rewriting mechanisms for our evaluations.

DP-BART [16]. A DP rewriting mechanism based on the BART encoder-decoder model [22]. A text document is written with a single document-level ε budget. We use the DP-BART-CLV variant.

Table 2. Document-level budgets calculated from base ε values scaled by the average words per text in a dataset.

		Document Budget (ε)		
Dataset	Avg. Words	0.1	0.5	1.0
Spooky	26.69	3	14	27
Topic10	86.24	9	43	86
Trustpilot	51.86	5	26	52
Yelp	181.61	18	91	182

DP-Prompt [39]. A DP text rewriting technique that uses zero-shot paraphrasing prompts as a proxy for rewriting, adding noise and providing DP guarantees at the token level. In line with Meisenbacher and Matthes [30], we use a FLAN-T5-LARGE model [6].

DP-MLM [27]. A method that performs token-level DP replacements using Masked Language Models. We use the original open-source implementation, which leverages ROBERTA-BASE [46].

Rewriting Procedure. To ensure consistency and comparability in evaluation, we fix document-level privacy budgets (ε) to be uniform across all three mechanisms, i.e., for all three, an input text is privatized with the same ε value.

To accomplish this, we first choose strict privacy budgets based on the *base* $\varepsilon \in \{0.1, 0.5, 1\}$. For each of the four datasets, these base values are scaled by the average number of words per text in the dataset (calculated from simple whitespace splitting). These resulting three values are used in dataset-specific, document-level privacy budgets, for all rewriting methods (Table 2). With these, we used DP-BART as is, as it operates on the document level. For DP-PROMPT and DP-MLM, we divide the document budget evenly into the token length of a document to be rewritten, i.e., if a target document has n tokens, we use these two mechanisms with $\varepsilon = \text{document\_budget}/n$. For DP-Prompt, we restrict generation to n tokens to ensure comparability.

Following this process across the four datasets and three mechanisms, each with three ε budgets, we created **36** DP rewritten dataset variants.

4.2 Post-processing

We test four post-processing variants, two based on Meisenbacher and Matthes [30] and two of our proposed methods, based on LLM post-processing with structured text features, for a total of **144** post-processed datasets (36 $\times$ 4 methods).

[1] https://www.kaggle.com/c/spooky-author-identification/.

Fine-tuning FLAN-T5. To replicate Meisenbacher and Matthes, we create two variants of their post-processing method, based on fine-tuning a FLAN-T5-LARGE model on 1:1 DP rewritten to original text mappings. For this, we use training datasets of 10k randomly sampled texts from our four datasets, for a total of 40k data points. Note that these 40k texts are not used in our evaluations.

PP-FLAN-MECH. In the first variant, we fine-tune three separate models, each specific to one of our selected DP rewriting mechanisms. Each of the rewriting methods is used to privatize all 40k texts in our training set, at three different ε values. We choose higher ε for this process in order to provide higher quality (less perturbed) data for fine-tuning. Thus, based on the values in the original works, we choose for DP-BART $\varepsilon \in \{600, 1000, 1400\}$ (per text), and for DP-MLM and DP-PROMPT $\varepsilon \in \{35, 80, 140\}$ (per token). Each mechanism-specific post-processing model was fine-tuned for three epochs on the 120k data points.

PP-FLAN-FULL. We train a mechanism-agnostic post-processing model by combining all 360k data points from the above-described process, and fine-tuning a FLAN-T5-LARGE model for one epoch.

Post-processing with Features. Our proposed method comprises two variants, one with the previously introduced *base* features (PP-FEATURES-BASE), and one that also includes extracted keywords and topics (PP-FEATURES-ADVANCED). For both, we use a LLAMA-3.2-3B-INSTRUCT model.

4.3 Privacy Experiments

In addition to providing theoretical guarantees, a DP rewritten text should ideally also provide *empirical* protections against real-world threats [25,27,39]. In the context of text data sharing, this can be interpreted as the masking of direct and indirect identifiers, as well as other sensitive information or attributes, such as authorship or gender. Thus, we conduct two tests, one based on modeling adversaries and one with LLM-as-a-Judge for privacy evaluation.

Defense Against Attribute Inference. A strong DP rewriting mechanism should provide protection for attributes such as authorship or gender, such that they are not accurately discernible given a capable adversary. We model two types of adversaries, who use publicly available texts and possess knowledge of DP rewriting procedures to infer sensitive attributes from shared privatized texts.

The former, which is coined the *static* attacker, trains an adversarial classification model on original, non-privatized plain texts, in order to infer protected attributes from released DP rewritten texts. The *adaptive* attacker is able to replicate the DP rewriting process in order to train on DP texts, ideally matching more closely the distribution of the target texts from which to infer attributes.

To model these adversaries, we split each of our 180 total datasets into 90/10 train/test splits, and train a DEBERTA-V3-BASE model [11] for one epoch, where the static attacker trains on the original train split, and the adaptive attacker trains on the rewritten (or post-processed) train split. In both cases, we evaluate these adversaries on the 10% test split, and provide the resulting F1 score (attacker inference success, or empirical privacy), denoted *EP (S)* and *EP (A)*.

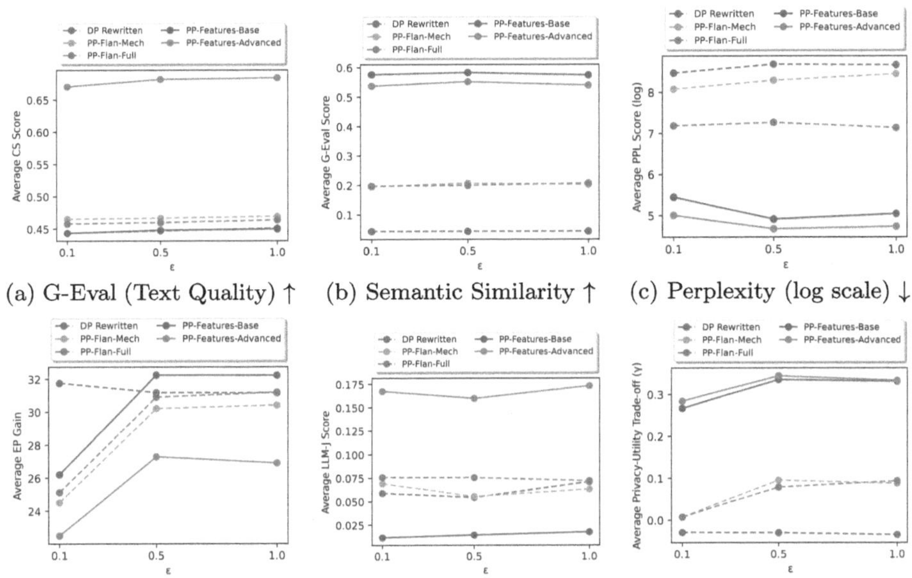

(a) G-Eval (Text Quality) ↑ (b) Semantic Similarity ↑ (c) Perplexity (log scale) ↓

(d) Emp. Privacy Gain ↑ (e) LLM-J Privacy Eval. ↓ (f) Trade-off (γ) ↑

Fig. 2. A graphical overview of the experiment results, shown for each of the base $\varepsilon \in \{0.1, 0.5, 1.0\}$ values, averaged over all three DP rewriting mechanisms and four evaluation datasets. We note that *PPL* is displayed on the natural logarithm scale, and that for *EP*, we average the static (S) and adaptive (A) results, and furthermore, display the *privacy gain*, or the absolute difference between *EP* score and the baseline adversarial performance.

LLM-as-a-Judge Evaluation. We use *LLM-as-a-Judge* [29,45] to measure the degree to which direct and indirect identifiers have been removed from input texts. We design a prompt for GPT-4O-MINI to compare the original and privatized texts, and to provide a binary decision whether any sensitive information from the former is still present in the latter. This prompt can be found in our code repository. We run this process (*LLM-J*) on a randomly sampled 100 texts from each of the 180 dataset variants, and calculate the average results (0–1, 0 is the best). We do not use *LLM-J* for Spooky Authors, as the texts are fictitious.

4.4 Utility Experiments

Along with the essential aspect of privacy preservation, an effective DP text rewriting mechanism should ideally preserve downstream utility, semantic similarity, and general coherence, so as to maintain data usability while also protecting privacy. We run five evaluations that capture these critical aspects.

Downstream Utility. For the two datasets (Trustpilot and Yelp) that have associated downstream tasks (binary sentiment analysis), we measure the ability of each of our 180 private dataset variants to retain downstream task utility. For each of the datasets, we take a 90/10 train/test split, fine-tune a DEBERTA-V3-BASE, and evaluate the model on the test split. The micro-F1 score for the sentiment analysis task is reported as the *Util* score.

Semantic Similarity. We also measure the average semantic (cosine) similarity between all rewritten-original text pairs, to estimate how semantically reminiscent the private texts are of their corresponding originals. We take the mean score between three Sentence Transformer embedding models: ALL-MPNET-BASE-V2 [35], GTE-LARGE [23], and JINA-EMBEDDINGS-V3 [38]. These scores are averaged over each dataset for the final *CS* score.

Perplexity. We calculate perplexity as a proxy for text naturalness, measuring how plausible a text is to a language model. We use GPT-2 [33], and we report the mean perplexity (*PPL*) score for the first 128 tokens of all texts in a dataset.

Text Quality. We use G-EVAL [24] to evaluate five text quality criteria: *clarity, conciseness, consistency, fluency*, and *repetitiveness*. We use the Deepeval framework[2] with GPT-4O-MINI to run the evaluations, which are each on a scale of 0 (worst) to 1 (best). We average the five scores for each text, and take the mean of all averages over a dataset to reach the final *G-Eval* (μ) score.

Trade-offs. We also calculate a privacy-utility trade-off score (γ), which weighs *relative gains* in privacy against losses in utility, as compared to the non-private baselines. The γ score is calculated as $\left(\frac{1}{3}\sum_i 1 - P_i^r/P_i^b\right) - \left(\frac{1}{3}\sum_j 1 - U_j^r/U_j^b\right)$, for $i \in \{EP(S), EP(A), LLM\text{-}J\}$ and $j \in \{Util, CS, G\text{-}Eval\}$, where b denotes baseline and r denotes rewritten. A positive score, therefore, implies that privacy gains outweigh utility losses, and vice versa. Note that *Util* is not included in Spooky Authors and Topic10, as these datasets do not have associated downstream utility tasks. *PPL* is not included in trade-off calculations, due to unbounded and potentially large values.

Results. The aggregate experiment results are visualized in Fig. 2, which represents the averages over all datasets and mechanisms.

A Note on Training Procedures. Where the fine-tuning of a language model was involved (i.e., *Util* and *EP (A)*), we reported the average of three runs, each with a different random shuffle of the training dataset. This is to account for variability in model optimization. All DP rewriting was run using a single Nvidia V100 16GB GPU, and all evaluations with CUDA acceleration were run on an Nvidia RTX A6000 48GB GPU, which was also used for LLM post-processing. For all required random sampling, we used a random seed of 42.

5 Ablation Study

To build upon the experiment results, we conduct an ablation study to measure the importance of key aspects in our post-processing method, namely the impact of (1) *individual text features* and (2) *LLM model size.*

[2] https://www.confident-ai.com/.

Ablation 1: Text Features. In the first ablation, we measure the individual impact of each structured text feature we utilize in the *base* version of our post-processing method. We sequentially disable each of the six base text features, i.e., remove them from the post-processing prompt. Then, we run the same experiments and capture the corresponding metrics as in the previous section. However, to illustrate the impact of disabling each feature, we report the *relative* performance as compared to the baseline (all features enabled). We focus on the *Yelp* dataset, privatized with DP-MLM (for all three privacy budgets). The results are shown in Table 3.

Ablation 2: Model Size. As our primary experiments leverage only one LLM as the underlying post-processing model (LLAMA-3.2-3B-INSTRUCT), we run an ablation to measure the impact of using larger LLMs. We control for model family by using only LLAMA-3.1-8B-INSTRUCT and LLAMA-3.3-70B-INSTRUCT. As previously, we run post-processing on the *Yelp* dataset, privatized with DP-MLM using three ε budgets. The results are found in Table 4.

Table 3. Results of Ablation 1 (*Text Features*). *w/o* denotes which feature was ablated from the post-processing prompt. **Note**: the provided scores represent the percent change compared to the full (non-ablated) results. The highest γ improvements are **bolded**.

		DP-MLM		
		0.1	0.5	1
w/o Polarity	Util. (F1) ↑	+0.00%	+0.00%	+0.00%
	CS ↑	+1.76%	+1.57%	+0.97%
	PPL ↓	-10.11%	-8.98%	-2.86%
	G-Eval (μ) ↑	+3.07%	+2.06%	+1.04%
	EP (S) ↓	-24.68%	-18.07%	-9.86%
	EP (A) ↓	-1.60%	+1.59%	+3.29%
	LLM-J ↓	+45.45%	-27.27%	+8.33%
	γ ↑	+48.10%	+48.39%	+50.16%
w/o Subjectivity	Util. (F1) ↑	+0.00%	+0.00%	+0.00%
	CS ↑	+3.53%	+3.73%	+2.72%
	PPL ↓	-16.21%	-2.14%	+7.95%
	G-Eval (μ) ↑	+6.74%	+6.93%	+2.94%
	EP (S) ↓	-15.58%	-18.67%	-6.34%
	EP (A) ↓	+1.45%	+8.26%	-4.93%
	LLM-J ↓	+36.36%	-18.18%	+0.00%
	γ ↑	+49.85%	+50.34%	+54.94%
w/o Formality	Util. (F1) ↑	+0.00%	+0.00%	+0.00%
	CS ↑	+6.08%	+6.27%	+5.45%
	PPL ↓	-16.72%	-0.41%	+8.09%
	G-Eval (μ) ↑	+10.69%	+9.69%	+6.97%
	EP (S) ↓	-10.39%	-21.08%	-11.27%
	EP (A) ↓	-5.96%	-1.59%	+0.45%
	LLM-J ↓	+9.09%	-36.36%	-25.00%
	γ ↑	+56.81%	+58.34%	+61.13%
w/o Word Count	Util. (F1) ↑	+0.00%	+0.00%	+0.00%
	CS ↑	+0.78%	+0.78%	+0.19%
	PPL ↓	+40.05%	+47.41%	+53.09%
	G-Eval (μ) ↑	-6.04%	-7.38%	-10.84%
	EP (S) ↓	+3.25%	-7.23%	+6.34%
	EP (A) ↓	+2.03%	+12.03%	+8.52%
	LLM-J ↓	-9.09%	+18.18%	+0.00%
	γ ↑	+39.44%	+31.84%	+37.20%
w/o Sent. Count	Util. (F1) ↑	+0.00%	+0.00%	+0.00%
	CS ↑	+5.10%	+5.10%	+4.28%
	PPL ↓	+5.17%	+11.53%	+16.23%
	G-Eval (μ) ↑	+5.87%	+0.84%	+2.41%
	EP (S) ↓	-9.09%	-14.46%	+0.70%
	EP (A) ↓	+7.56%	+7.83%	+8.07%
	LLM-J ↓	+27.27%	+45.45%	+33.33%
	γ ↑	+47.72%	+39.93%	+46.80%
w/o Readability	Util. (F1) ↑	+0.00%	+0.00%	+0.00%
	CS ↑	+0.20%	+0.00%	-0.97%
	PPL ↓	-12.16%	-9.54%	+2.32%
	G-Eval (μ) ↑	+12.44%	+13.19%	+12.64%
	EP (S) ↓	-48.05%	-43.37%	-40.14%
	EP (A) ↓	-30.38%	-42.03%	-28.10%
	LLM-J ↓	+0.00%	+27.27%	+8.33%
	γ ↑	**+69.22%**	**+65.99%**	**+72.56%**

6 Human Acceptance of DP Text Rewriting

The final stage of our evaluation measures *human acceptance*, which we define as the degree to which humans perceive DP rewritten outputs to be acceptable for both utility and privacy preservation.

We conducted an online survey using Google Forms. Firstly, we chose a random text from each of our four datasets, as well as all DP rewritten and post-processed counterparts from DP-BART

Table 4. Results for Ablation 2 (*Model Size*). The best resulting trade-offs (γ) per tested ε are **bolded**.

		Baseline	Llama-3.2-3B-Instruct			Llama-3.1-8B-Instruct			Llama-3.3-70B-Instruct		
			0.1	0.5	1	0.1	0.5	1	0.1	0.5	1
PP-Features-Base	Util. (F1) ↑	94.98	$92.74_{0.0}$	$92.74_{0.0}$	$92.74_{0.0}$	$92.74_{0.0}$	$92.74_{0.0}$	$92.74_{0.0}$	$92.74_{0.0}$	$92.74_{0.0}$	$92.51_{0.3}$
	CS ↑	–	0.51	0.51	0.51	0.52	0.52	0.52	0.51	0.51	0.51
	PPL ↓	57	106	100	93	39	40	38	21	22	22
	G-Eval (μ) ↑	0.63	0.57	0.57	0.56	0.60	0.57	0.56	0.57	0.57	0.59
	EP (S) ↓	92.05	21.10	22.74	19.45	17.67	23.70	21.64	21.64	23.15	20.41
	EP (A) ↓	92.05	$31.42_{1.0}$	$31.51_{1.5}$	$30.55_{0.3}$	$38.04_{0.34}$	$38.26_{0.47}$	$38.36_{0.11}$	$38.31_{0.96}$	$39.95_{0.56}$	$40.32_{1.21}$
	LLM-J ↓	–	0.11	0.11	0.12	0.16	0.17	0.15	0.12	0.11	0.09
	γ ↑	–	**0.58**	**0.57**	**0.58**	0.57	0.53	0.53	0.55	0.54	0.57

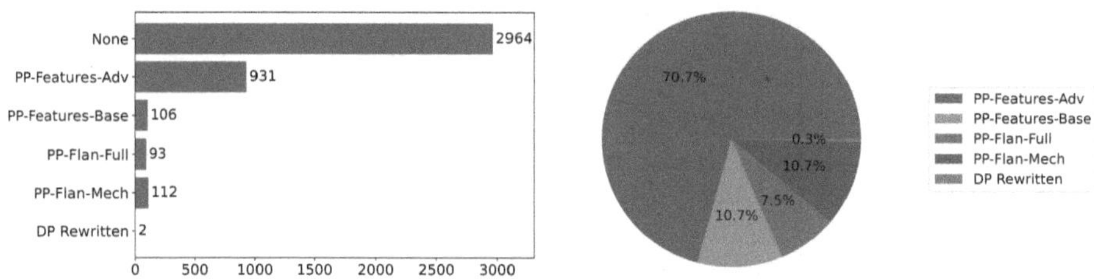

(a) Part One: *Acceptable* Candidates (b) Part Two: *Best* Candidate

Fig. 3. Survey results. (a) shows the raw selections for *acceptable* rewritten candidates, if any. (b) shows the distribution of choices for the *best* candidate.

and DP-MLM[3], for the base ε values of 0.5 and 1.0. This resulted in 16 selected texts and their rewritten counterparts (4 texts $\times$ 2 mechanisms $\times$ 2 ε). This number of questions was selected to be a reasonable amount for each participant to answer, such that all participants received the same question set. The answer options were randomized, however.

We presented the original texts with five response options (DP rewritten and four post-processed texts). For each, we asked participants which, if any, of the outputs are *acceptable* replacements for the original text; otherwise, "none" could be chosen. In a second question, we asked which of the five variants was the *best*.

We pilot tested the survey with two close colleagues to spot ambiguities and correct errors. We then recruited participants using Prolific, first with a batch of 10 participants to gauge survey completion time. The median time was calculated to be 13 min, and the following 240 participants were recruited for £1.95, for an hourly rate of £9.00. In total, **252** participants completed our survey.

Our participants included 138 females and 114 males, from 28 countries on six continents. The participants spanned the ages from 20 to 79, with the largest groups between 40–50 (n=64) and 30–40 (n=63). We recruited from the Pro-

[3] We observed that DP-Prompt outputs were generally too long and incoherent to be readable in a survey.

lific "AI taskers" group – those skilled at comparative reasoning. We required fluency in English, at least a 99% approval rate, and at least 50 prior successful submissions. The majority of our participants completed a higher education degree (115 undergraduate, 69 masters, and 21 doctorate), as well as 47 other participants who held a high school, community college, or secondary degree.

The aggregated survey results are found in Fig. 3, which shows the raw counts of chosen acceptable replacements and the proportion of *best* selections.

7 Discussion

We reflect on the findings of our work, leading to lessons learned and implications for future work on DP text rewriting.

Main Findings. From the results, one can see the potential benefits of post-processing DP rewritten texts. Across the board, at least one of our proposed post-processing variants tests higher than all other compared baselines, and in all cases besides *EP*, the difference is significant. An interesting case comes with the *advanced* version of our method, which achieves the worst *EP* and *LLM-J* privacy results (albeit still at comparable levels), whereas the *base* version achieves the best in these two metrics (withholding *EP* at $\varepsilon = 0.1$). The flip side of this observation is made clear in the *G-Eval* results, where *advanced* outputs boast clearly higher text quality. Overall, though, the benefits of our proposed techniques are demonstrated in the trade-offs (γ), which are very positive as compared to the minimal trade-offs of the approach by Meisenbacher and Matthes [30], and those of the original DP rewritten texts, which are never positive.

These results are important in finding a more reasonable balance between privacy and utility in DP text rewriting, where slight empirical privacy protections can be sacrificed (in some cases) for ultimately more favorable trade-offs, boosted by higher text quality, coherence, and semantic meaningfulness. This, of course, depends on which evaluation aspects are most important to a particular use case, as showcased between the *base* and *advanced* results.

The ablation study unveils further insights. Ablation 1 (Table 3) reveals that the original combination of text features may not be optimal, and that in many cases, removing a feature (e.g., readability) will lead to overall more positive privacy-utility trade-offs in the end. The trade-off, however, is not the only metric to consider here, and one must consider that more positive trade-offs can mask worse empirical privacy protections. Ablation 2 (Table 4) teaches an important lesson that LLM model size plays an insignificant role; in fact, the smallest used model (3B) results in the best trade-offs.

A Way Forward for Local DP Text Rewriting. These insights are supported by an abundantly clear signal arising from the survey results, in that DP rewritten texts in their raw form, particularly at lower ε, are not usable or acceptable. Out of the 4208 total choices deemed to be acceptable by our 252 participants, just **2** of these were DP rewritten texts without post-processing! The PP-FLAN texts represent a larger portion, but those derived from our method were chosen 1037 times, a far greater prospect for acceptability. One cannot miss, however, that in nearly 75% of the cases, *none* was chosen, suggesting that even with post-processing, DP text rewriting has a long journey ahead to practicality.

Nevertheless, we highlight the fact that such results were achieved with texts rewritten at considerably low ε values, which, without post-processing, score very poorly on all utility metrics (Fig. 2). This leads to the important discussion in general DP text privatization regarding the impact and feasibility of maintaining reasonably low privacy guarantees (governed by ε), without the need for any post-processing that could potentially degrade these guarantees empirically. Importantly, although the *base* version of our post-processing method does not leak direct information about the unit of protection in the utilized DP rewriting mechanisms (i.e., words/tokens or documents), the text features could be considered auxiliary information. In the *advanced* version, we do input such words (i.e., a maximum of five keywords) into the LLM post-processing *prompt*. Despite this, we note that this post-processing occurs locally, and including such words in the *prompt* does not necessitate leakage. Thus, this opens an interesting question, namely the effect of such post-processing on the *theoretical guarantees* offered by DP text rewriting, as well as a clearer definition of acceptable post-processing of DP rewritten texts without degrading the original guarantees.

Such questions, combined with the promise of post-processing DP-rewritten texts, make a strong case for further exploration into the matter. With greater advances in post-processing and related alignment techniques, we envision that producing usable, privacy-preserving, *and* acceptable outputs may be feasible, presenting a clear way forward for future research on DP text rewriting.

Limitations. We acknowledge limitations of our post-processing method, namely that our selected text features were not grounded in a comprehensive search for characterizing textual data, but are rather the result of collective brainstorming and prior experience of our research team members.

As discussed, a potential limitation is our interpretation of the post-processing property of DP. As we extract only *meta-characteristics* from the original texts and fuse these into the LLM post-processing prompt, we do not view such information as directly leaking original (semantic) information from the texts, i.e., with respect to exact word choice. Nevertheless, this highlights the need for a better understanding of the confines of post-processing in DP text privatization.

We are also limited by the extent of the insights that can be drawn from our survey, as we selected a small representative sample of texts from our entire collection of rewritten/post-processed datasets. We do not account for confounding factors such as the effects of text content, domain, or length, which could reasonably bias the perception of *acceptability*. This comes in addition to the general difficulty in explaining the purpose and degrading effects of local DP text rewriting, which could be perceived negatively by laypersons.

8 Conclusion

We introduce an improved, LLM-based method for post-processing DP rewritten texts, which contributes to outputs that are superior in utility, comparable or better in empirical privacy protections, and significantly higher in human acceptance. We show that by incorporating key characteristics of the original text into the post-processing stage, aided by capable LLMs, effective post-processing can be performed without the need for expensive fine-tuning. We discuss the implications of our results, which, above all, highlight the possibility of operating local DP text rewriting at lower privacy budgets, as well as the need for further work on addressing the crucial usability challenge in this field.
Outlook and Future Work. We envision a number of paths for future work, including (1) further research into optimal techniques for post-processing DP rewritten texts, (2) empirical and theoretical testing of the impact of post-processing on privacy protections, and (3) the promotion of human acceptance as a key metric in evaluating the effectiveness of (DP) text privatization.

Disclosure of Interests. The authors have no competing interests to declare that are relevant to the content of this article.

References

1. Awon, A.M., Lu, Y., Potka, S., Thomo, A.: CluSanT: differentially private and semantically coherent text sanitization. In: Chiruzzo, L., Ritter, A., Wang, L. (eds.) Proceedings of the 2025 Conference of the Nations of the Americas Chapter of the Association for Computational Linguistics: Human Language Technologies (Volume 1: Long Papers), pp. 3676–3693. ACL, Albuquerque, New Mexico (2025)
2. Balle, B., Wang, Y.X.: Improving the Gaussian mechanism for differential privacy: analytical calibration and optimal denoising. In: Dy, J., Krause, A. (eds.) Proceedings of the 35th International Conference on Machine Learning. Proceedings of Machine Learning Research, vol. 80, pp. 394–403. PMLR, 10–15 July 2018
3. Baroud, I., Raithel, L., Möller, S., Roller, R.: Beyond de-identification: a structured approach for defining and detecting indirect identifiers in medical texts. In: Habernal, I., Ghanavati, S., Jain, V., Igamberdiev, T., Wilson, S. (eds.) Proceedings of the Sixth Workshop on Privacy in Natural Language Processing, pp. 75–85. ACL, Albuquerque, New Mexico (2025)
4. Blei, D.M., Ng, A.Y., Jordan, M.I.: Latent dirichlet allocation. J. Mach. Learn. Res. **3**, 993–1022 (2003)
5. Campos, R., Mangaravite, V., Pasquali, A., Jorge, A.M., Nunes, C., Jatowt, A.: Yake! collection-independent automatic keyword extractor. In: European Conference on Information Retrieval, pp. 806–810. Springer (2018)
6. Chung, H.W., et al.: Scaling instruction-finetuned language models (2022)
7. Cummings, R., Kaptchuk, G., Redmiles, E.M.: I need a better description: an investigation into user expectations for differential privacy. In: Proceedings of the 2021 ACM SIGSAC Conference on Computer and Communications Security, CCS 2021, pp. 3037–3052. ACM, New York, NY, USA (2021)

8. Dwork, C.: Differential privacy. In: International Colloquium on Automata, Languages, and Programming, pp. 1–12. Springer (2006)
9. Feyisetan, O., Aggarwal, A., Xu, Z., Teissier, N.: Research challenges in designing differentially private text generation mechanisms. In: The International FLAIRS Conference Proceedings, vol. 34 (2021)
10. Feyisetan, O., Balle, B., Drake, T., Diethe, T.: Privacy- and utility-preserving textual analysis via calibrated multivariate perturbations. In: Proceedings of the 13th International Conference on Web Search and Data Mining, WSDM 2020, pp. 178–186. ACM, New York, NY, USA (2020)
11. He, P., Liu, X., Gao, J., Chen, W.: Deberta: decoding-enhanced bert with disentangled attention (2021)
12. Heylighen, F., Dewaele, J.M.: Formality of language: definition, measurement and behavioral determinants. Interner Bericht, Center "Leo Apostel", Vrije Universiteit Brüssel **4**(1) (1999)
13. Hovy, D., Johannsen, A., Søgaard, A.: User review sites as a resource for large-scale sociolinguistic studies. In: Proceedings of the 24th International Conference on World Wide Web, WWW 2015, pp. 452–461. International World Wide Web Conferences Steering Committee, Republic and Canton of Geneva, CHE (2015)
14. Hu, L., Habernal, I., Shen, L., Wang, D.: Differentially private natural language models: recent advances and future directions. In: Graham, Y., Purver, M. (eds.) Findings of the Association for Computational Linguistics: EACL 2024, pp. 478–499. ACL, St. Julian's, Malta (2024)
15. Igamberdiev, T., Arnold, T., Habernal, I.: DP-rewrite: towards reproducibility and transparency in differentially private text rewriting. In: Calzolari, N., et al. (eds.) Proceedings of the 29th International Conference on Computational Linguistics, pp. 2927–2933. International Committee on Computational Linguistics, Gyeongju, Republic of Korea (2022)
16. Igamberdiev, T., Habernal, I.: DP-BART for privatized text rewriting under local differential privacy. In: Rogers, A., Boyd-Graber, J., Okazaki, N. (eds.) Findings of the Association for Computational Linguistics: ACL 2023, pp. 13914–13934. ACL, Toronto, Canada (2023)
17. Karegar, F., Alaqra, A.S., Fischer-Hübner, S.: Exploring user-suitable metaphors for differentially private data analyses. In: Eighteenth Symposium on Usable Privacy and Security (SOUPS 2022), pp. 175–193. USENIX Association, Boston, MA (2022)
18. Kasiviswanathan, S.P., Lee, H.K., Nissim, K., Raskhodnikova, S., Smith, A.: What can we learn privately? In: 49th Annual IEEE Symposium on Foundations of Computer Science, pp. 531–540 (2008)
19. Kenny, C.T., Kuriwaki, S., McCartan, C., Rosenman, E.T.R., Simko, T., Imai, K.: The use of differential privacy for census data and its impact on redistricting: the case of the 2020 u.s. census. Sci. Adv. **7**(41), eabk3283 (2021)
20. Kincaid, J.P., Fishburne Jr, R.P., Rogers, R.L., Chissom, B.S.: Derivation of new readability formulas (automated readability index, fog count and flesch reading ease formula) for navy enlisted personnel. Technical Report (1975)
21. Klymenko, O., et al.: Differential privacy in natural language processing: The story so far. In: Mireshghallah, F. (ed.) Proceedings of the Fourth Workshop on Privacy in Natural Language Processing, pp. 1–11. ACL, Seattle, United States (2022)
22. Lewis, M., et al.: BART: denoising sequence-to-sequence pre-training for natural language generation, translation, and comprehension. In: Jurafsky, D., Chai, J., Schluter, N., Tetreault, J. (eds.) Proceedings of the 58th Annual Meeting of the Association for Computational Linguistics, pp. 7871–7880. ACL (2020)

23. Li, Z., Zhang, X., Zhang, Y., Long, D., Xie, P., Zhang, M.: Towards general text embeddings with multi-stage contrastive learning (2023)
24. Liu, Y., Iter, D., Xu, Y., Wang, S., Xu, R., Zhu, C.: G-eval: NLG evaluation using gpt-4 with better human alignment. In: Bouamor, H., Pino, J., Bali, K. (eds.) Proceedings of the 2023 Conference on Empirical Methods in Natural Language Processing, pp. 2511–2522. ACL, Singapore (2023)
25. Mattern, J., Weggenmann, B., Kerschbaum, F.: The limits of word level differential privacy. In: Carpuat, M., de Marneffe, M.C., Meza Ruiz, I.V. (eds.) Findings of the Association for Computational Linguistics: NAACL 2022, pp. 867–881. ACL, Seattle, United States (2022)
26. Meisenbacher, S., Chevli, M., Matthes, F.: On the impact of noise in differentially private text rewriting. In: Chiruzzo, L., Ritter, A., Wang, L. (eds.) Findings of the Association for Computational Linguistics: NAACL 2025, pp. 514–532. Association for Computational Linguistics, Albuquerque, New Mexico (2025)
27. Meisenbacher, S., Chevli, M., Vladika, J., Matthes, F.: DP-MLM: differentially private text rewriting using masked language models. In: Ku, L.W., Martins, A., Srikumar, V. (eds.) Findings of the Association for Computational Linguistics: ACL 2024, pp. 9314–9328. Association for Computational Linguistics, Bangkok, Thailand (2024)
28. Meisenbacher, S., et al.: Investigating user perspectives on differentially private text privatization. In: Wilson, S. (ed.) Proceedings of the Sixth Workshop on Privacy in Natural Language Processing, pp. 86–105. ACL, Albuquerque, New Mexico (2025)
29. Meisenbacher, S., Klymenko, A., Matthes, F.: Llm-as-a-judge for privacy evaluation? exploring the alignment of human and llm perceptions of privacy in textual data. In: Proceedings of the 2025 Workshop on Human-Centered AI Privacy and Security, HAIPS 2025, pp. 126–138. ACM, New York, NY, USA (2025)
30. Meisenbacher, S., Matthes, F.: Just rewrite it again: a post-processing method for enhanced semantic similarity and privacy preservation of differentially private rewritten text. In: Proceedings of the 19th International Conference on Availability, Reliability and Security. ARES 2024, ACM, New York, NY, USA (2024)
31. Meisenbacher, S., Matthes, F.: Thinking outside of the differential privacy box: a case study in text privatization with language model prompting. In: Al-Onaizan, Y., Bansal, M., Chen, Y.N. (eds.) Proceedings of the 2024 Conference on Empirical Methods in Natural Language Processing, pp. 5656–5665. ACL, Miami, Florida, USA (2024)
32. Nanayakkara, P., Smart, M.A., Cummings, R., Kaptchuk, G., Redmiles, E.M.: What are the chances? explaining the epsilon parameter in differential privacy. In: Proceedings of the 32nd USENIX Conference on Security Symposium, SEC 2023, USENIX Association, USA (2023)
33. Radford, A., Wu, J., Child, R., Luan, D., Amodei, D., Sutskever, I.: Language models are unsupervised multitask learners. OpenAI (2019)
34. Řehůřek, R., Sojka, P.: Software framework for topic modelling with large corpora. In: Proceedings of the LREC 2010 Workshop on New Challenges for NLP Frameworks, pp. 45–50. ELRA, Valletta, Malta (2010)
35. Reimers, N., Gurevych, I.: Sentence-BERT: sentence embeddings using Siamese BERT-networks. In: Inui, K., Jiang, J., Ng, V., Wan, X. (eds.) Proceedings of the 2019 Conference on Empirical Methods in Natural Language Processing and the 9th International Joint Conference on Natural Language Processing (EMNLPIJC-NLP), pp. 3982–3992. ACL, Hong Kong, China (2019)

36. Ren, Y., Ramesh, K., Yao, Y., Field, A.: How do we measure privacy in text? a survey of text anonymization metrics. In: Inui, K., Sakti, S., Wang, H., Wong, D.F., Bhattacharyya, P., Banerjee, B., Ekbal, A., Chakraborty, T., Singh, D.P. (eds.) Proceedings of the 14th International Joint Conference on Natural Language Processing and the 4th Conference of the Asia-Pacific Chapter of the Association for Computational Linguistics. pp. 1532–1544. The Asian Federation of Natural Language Processing and The Association for Computational Linguistics, Mumbai, India (2025)
37. Schler, J., Koppel, M., Argamon, S.: Effects of age and gender on blogging. In: AAAI Spring Symposium: Computational Approaches to Analyzing Weblogs, vol. 6, pp. 199–205 (2006)
38. Sturua, S., et al.: jina-embeddings-v3: multilingual embeddings with task lora (2024)
39. Utpala, S., Hooker, S., Chen, P.Y.: Locally differentially private document generation using zero shot prompting. In: Bouamor, H., Pino, J., Bali, K. (eds.) Findings of the Association for Computational Linguistics: EMNLP 2023, pp. 8442–8457. Association for Computational Linguistics, Singapore (2023)
40. Vu, D.N.L., Igamberdiev, T., Habernal, I.: Granularity is crucial when applying differential privacy to text: an investigation for neural machine translation. In: Al-Onaizan, Y., Bansal, M., Chen, Y.N. (eds.) Findings of the Association for Computational Linguistics: EMNLP 2024, pp. 507–527. Association for Computational Linguistics, Miami, Florida, USA (2024)
41. Weiss, C., Kreuter, F., Habernal, I.: To share or not to share: what risks would laypeople accept to give sensitive data to differentially-private NLP systems? In: Calzolari, N., Kan, M.Y., Hoste, V., Lenci, A., Sakti, S., Xue, N. (eds.) Proceedings of the 2024 Joint International Conference on Computational Linguistics, Language Resources and Evaluation (LREC-COLING 2024), pp. 16331–16342. ELRA and ICCL, Torino, Italia (2024)
42. Xiong, A., Wang, T., Li, N., Jha, S.: Towards effective differential privacy communication for users' data sharing decision and comprehension. In: 2020 IEEE Symposium on Security and Privacy (SP), pp. 392–410. IEEE (2020)
43. Yan, B., et al.: On protecting the data privacy of large language models (llms) and llm agents: a literature review. High-Confidence Comput. **5**(2), 100300 (2025)
44. Zhang, X., Zhao, J., LeCun, Y.: Character-level convolutional networks for text classification. In: Proceedings of the 29th International Conference on Neural Information Processing Systems, NIPS 2015, vol. 1, pp. 649–657. MIT Press, Cambridge, MA, USA (2015)
45. Zheng, L., et al.: Judging llm-as-a-judge with mt-bench and chatbot arena. In: Proceedings of the 37th International Conference on Neural Information Processing Systems. NIPS 2023, Curran Associates Inc., Red Hook, NY, USA (2023)
46. Zhuang, L., Wayne, L., Ya, S., Jun, Z.: A robustly optimized BERT pre-training approach with post-training. In: Li, S., et al. (eds.) Proceedings of the 20th Chinese National Conference on Computational Linguistics, pp. 1218–1227. Chinese Information Processing Society of China, Huhhot, China (2021)

Asymmetric Resource Constrained Decoding for Lightweight Linguistic Steganography in Causal LLMs

Paweł Moszczyński[1], Szymon Tokarski[2(✉)], Jakub Nowakowski[4], and Wojciech Mazurczyk[2,3]

[1] Military University of Technology, Warsaw, Poland
[2] Warsaw University of Technology, Warsaw, Poland
szymontokarski98@gmail.com
[3] IDEAS Research Institute, Warsaw, Poland
[4] Warsaw, Poland

Abstract. This paper presents ARCDStego, a lightweight linguistic steganography framework for causal large language models that embeds hidden information directly into token generation using two-universal hash-based token masking. Unlike many existing neural steganography methods, ARCDStego does not require access to the original language model, logits, or token probability distributions during decoding. Instead, hidden messages can be recovered using only a shared secret key, the tokenizer, and the embedding matrix, making the method practical for black-box communication settings. Experiments with the Qwen1.5–0.5B model show that ARCDStego effectively hides information while maintaining plausible text generation. The results demonstrate a trade-off between embedding rate and perplexity, where higher payload capacity leads to stronger distributional deviations. The evaluation also highlights the importance of context selection for improving statistical plausibility and generation quality. Overall, the proposed method demonstrates that practical, lightweight LLM-based linguistic steganography is possible without requiring access to the model internals during message extraction.

Keywords: Linguistic Steganography · Causal Large Language Models · Constrained Beam Search · Information Hiding · Token Masking Steganography

1 Introduction

Large Language Models (LLMs) have become deeply integrated into online communication ecosystems, significantly increasing the proportion of machine-generated content on social media platforms [18]. The boundary between human-generated and AI-generated content is becoming increasingly blurred, both in

P. Kieseberg et al. (Eds.): ARES 2026 Workshops, LNCS 16903, pp. 99–116, 2027.
https://doi.org/10.1007/978-3-032-37218-5_7

public interactions and in autonomous communication between bots. Information exchange between conversational agents is no longer merely an experimental construct but an emerging, increasingly common phenomenon, often indistinguishable from human dialogue in terms of style, coherence, and pragmatic function. Consequently, systems such as Moltbook[1] were developed, which facilitate interaction among artificial intelligence agents, enabling them to generate posts and comments in an online environment. As a result, natural language is no longer used exclusively for human communication but also serves as an interface for interactions between automated systems.

The increasing use of large language models in natural language generation has opened new opportunities to embed additional information directly into generated text. In particular, the multiplicity of valid continuations in autoregressive language models enables constrained decoding approaches that encode additional information while preserving fluent and coherent text generation. Existing LLM-based methods for information embedding often require access to model logits or probability distributions during decoding, which limits their applicability in lightweight or black-box settings. Unlike classical steganographic approaches that rely on low-level signal manipulation (e.g., digital image or audio) [14,15], linguistic steganography leverages the inherent redundancy and expressiveness of natural language to encode hidden messages within semantically valid and contextually coherent text [27]. This makes generation quality and distributional consistency central challenges in constrained decoding. Large language models further amplify these challenges and opportunities due to their probabilistic decoding process and the large number of valid surface realizations for a given semantic intent.

In this work, we focus on the trade-off between semantic coherence and payload capacity under strict decoding-resource constraints. In particular, we investigate lightweight asymmetric decoding for linguistic steganography in causal LLMs. We propose ARCDStego, a constrained generation framework that embeds hidden information directly into token generation via embedding-space token masking using two-universal hash functions.

Unlike prior approaches in neural linguistic steganography [6,30,31], ARCDStego does not require access to the original language model during message extraction, nor to the model's internal logits or generation probabilities during decoding. Message extraction requires only the shared steganographic key, the tokenizer, and the embedding matrix, making the proposed framework more practical and easier to deploy in real-world communication scenarios.

We evaluate standard and constrained generation using perplexity-based metrics. In addition, we analyze the trade-off between embedding capacity and generation quality induced by token-selection constraints derived from two-universal hash-based masking.

Empirical evaluation against statistical and neural steganalysis methods is outside the scope of this work. Instead, the present study focuses on practical constrained decoding under asymmetric resource assumptions and investi-

[1] https://www.moltbook.com.

gates the trade-off between payload capacity and generation plausibility using perplexity-based analysis.

Considering the above, the main contributions of this work can be summarized as follows:

- We propose ARCDStego, a lightweight, constrained-decoding framework for causal large language models that embeds hidden messages directly during token generation via embedding-space token masking with two-universal hash functions.
- We introduce an asymmetric decoding procedure that enables deterministic payload recovery without requiring access to the original language model, token logits, or probability distributions during decoding. In particular, decoding relies only on a shared secret key, the tokenizer, and the embedding matrix associated with the encoding model.
- We show that context selection plays a critical role in constrained linguistic generation. In particular, we demonstrate that selecting contexts that satisfy the embedding constraints substantially reduces perplexity and mitigates distributional degradation compared with existing constrained decoding approaches.
- We provide an empirical analysis of the trade-off between payload capacity and generation plausibility under constrained decoding using perplexity-based evaluation on real-world Moltbook contexts.

2 Related Work

Steganography enables *plausible deniability* [2] by concealing the existence of hidden communication within seemingly innocuous data. Unlike cryptography, which protects the *content* of a message, steganography aims to hide the *existence* of the message itself [10].

Classical steganographic methods primarily focused on digital media such as images, audio, video, or network traffic, where hidden information is embedded by modifying redundant signal components [7,10,19]. Techniques such as least significant bit (LSB) and transform-domain embedding exploit signal redundancy while preserving perceptual quality [8,19,21]. A central challenge in steganography is balancing embedding capacity, robustness, and undetectability [8,10]. However, these signal-based approaches are not directly applicable to natural language due to its low redundancy and strict syntactic and semantic constraints.

2.1 Linguistic Steganography

Linguistic steganography focuses on embedding hidden information in natural language text [1,27]. Unlike steganography in images or audio, it operates on discrete symbolic sequences with limited redundancy and strong syntactic and semantic constraints. Consequently, the primary challenge is to preserve grammatical correctness, semantic coherence, and stylistic naturalness while keeping the generated text indistinguishable from human-written language [5]. In modern LLM-based settings, robustness against paraphrasing, rewriting, and adversarial transformations has also become an important concern [30].

Neural linguistic steganography extends generative linguistic steganography by embedding hidden information directly during text generation [9]. Recent advances in LLMs have significantly improved the fluency, coherence, and diversity of generated stegotexts [31], enabling more practical and secure generation-based methods. Lightweight decoding approaches [9,30] further advance applicability in constrained or black-box environments by avoiding direct access to the original language model during extraction. However, stricter token selection constraints may still reduce text quality and naturalness [20,28,30].

2.2 Distributionally Indistinguishable and Coverless Steganography in LLM Text Generation

Recent advances in large language models (LLMs) have enabled highly effective steganographic communication via AI-generated text, embedding secret information while preserving indistinguishability from standard model outputs [26]. A central challenge in this domain is balancing two competing objectives: maintaining the statistical properties of the original language model distribution and efficiently embedding hidden information [23,26]. Many earlier approaches introduce detectable distortions to token probability distributions, which may accumulate over long sequences and increase the risk of steganalysis [27].

Coverless steganography addresses this issue by generating new text samples rather than modifying existing carriers. Hidden information is implicitly encoded in the linguistic or statistical properties of the generated output, thereby avoiding explicit perturbations, such as synonym substitution or syntactic manipulation, that are common in traditional linguistic steganography [25,26]. As modern steganalysis increasingly relies on deep learning and large-scale language models, minimizing detectable deviations from natural text has become particularly important [29].

Recent methods such as OD-Stega formulate steganographic generation as an optimization problem under divergence constraints—typically minimizing KL–divergence between modified and original token distributions—to ensure that generated text remains aligned with the model's natural generative process [12]. By guiding token selection with secret bits while enforcing distributional consistency, these approaches produce fluent, coherent, and statistically indistinguishable text that can carry hidden messages [3,26].

The ARCDStego method proposed in this work is closely related to constraint-based decoding approaches [6,30], as it encodes information by restricting the set of admissible tokens during generation. However, unlike prior methods that rely on probabilistic mappings or require access to model logits during message extraction [31], ARCDStego operates directly in the token embedding space using masking based on a family of 2-universal hash functions.

Consequently, message extraction does not depend on the model's probability distributions and can be performed using only a shared steganographic key, a tokenizer, and the encoding model's embedding matrix.

In addition, ARCDStego is designed for communication between agents rather than for isolated language model sampling. The proposed context-selection mechanism reflects how practical AI agents construct responses by drawing on conversation history, retrieved knowledge, auxiliary tools, and task-specific prompts. Accordingly, statistical deviation from the base model distribution should not be viewed as the only relevant evaluation criterion in agentic communication settings. In this work, we use perplexity as a local proxy for distributional plausibility, while a broader evaluation of agent-level plausibility, including contextual relevance, grounding, and task appropriateness, is left for future work.

3 Proposed Approach

This section describes the proposed ARCDStego framework. Subsection 3.1 introduces the considered communication setting, while Subsects. 3.2 and 3.3 describe the assumptions and design objectives adopted in this work. Subsection 3.4 presents the token masking mechanism based on two-universal hash functions. Subsection 3.5 describes the constrained beam search algorithm used during constrained text generation, and Subsect. 3.6 introduces the encoding and decoding procedures of ARCDStego. Finally, Subsect. 3.7 presents the context selection strategy designed to improve compatibility between embedding constraints and the underlying language model distribution.

3.1 Communication Scenario

We consider a linguistic steganographic communication scenario involving a covert sender and one or more covert receivers, communicating via natural-language text generated by a causal large language model. The sender may generate text either with an embedded hidden payload or as ordinary cover text without a payload. The resulting generated text (stegotext) is transmitted through a public communication channel.

Communication may occur in either a one-to-one or a one-to-many setting, where multiple authorized receivers who possess the required shared information can independently recover the hidden message. The sender is assumed to have access to the underlying language model used for stegotext generation. The receiver does not require direct access to the language model during transmission, but must possess the same tokenizer, embedding representation, and secret parameters required for deterministic message recovery.

Figure 1 illustrates the considered communication setting and the interaction between the covert sender and the covert receivers.

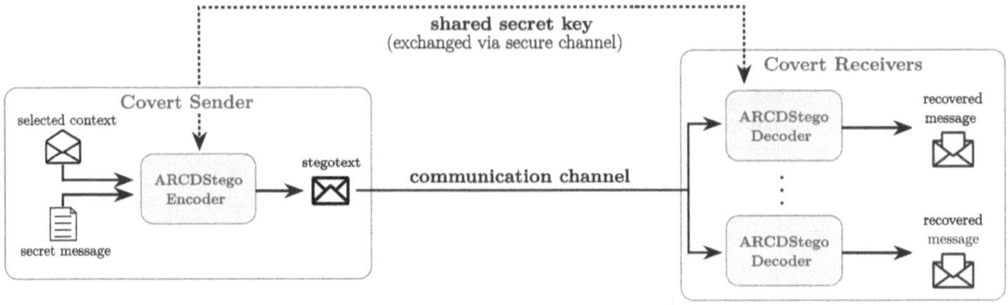

Fig. 1. Communication Scenario

3.2 Communication Assumptions

The proposed ARCDStego method assumes that the communicating parties share a secret key k that is exchanged via a secure external channel prior to communication. The shared key is used to initialize the pseudorandom masking procedure employed during constrained token selection and payload recovery (see Figs. 2 and 3). We additionally assume that all authorized communicating parties use the same tokenizer, vocabulary, and embedding matrix associated with the underlying language model. Consistency among these components is required to ensure identical token masking during both constrained generation and message extraction. The communication channel is assumed to preserve the transmitted text at the lexical and tokenization levels; paraphrasing, normalization, and other tokenization-changing transformations are outside the considered communication model.

3.3 Design Objectives

The primary objective of ARCDStego is to enable lightweight and deterministic payload recovery without requiring access to the original language model during decoding. In particular, the proposed framework is designed for asymmetric settings in which constrained generation is performed by the sender, while receivers operate under reduced computational and model-access requirements.

A secondary objective is to preserve the plausibility of generations under token-selection constraints introduced by message embedding. To analyze this effect, we evaluate the statistical behavior of generated text using perplexity-based distributional analysis.

3.4 Two-Universal Based Token Masking

In this work, we use a family of two-universal hash functions introduced by Carter and Wegman [4] to construct a deterministic yet pseudorandom token masking mechanism for the ARCDStego method. The goal is to ensure that both the encoding and decoding procedures can reproduce identical masking decisions using a shared secret key k. As illustrated in Fig. 2 and Fig. 3, the token masking mechanism is applied in both pipelines as a preprocessing step that determines the set of admissible tokens.

Let $E \in \mathbb{R}^{|\mathcal{V}| \times d}$ denote the embedding matrix of the language model, where $|\mathcal{V}|$ is the vocabulary size and d is the embedding dimension. For each token t, the corresponding embedding vector $\mathbf{e}_t \in \mathbb{R}^d$ is extracted from E. To construct a scalar function of the token, a subset I_t of embedding positions is selected. The parameter $l = |I_t|$ determines the number of embedding positions participating in the hashing procedure. The selected embedding positions are quantized into 16-bit integer representations and aggregated into a scalar value:

$$x_t = \sum_{j \in I_t} \text{quantized}(e_t^{(j)}).$$

We now consider a family of two-universal hash functions

$$\mathcal{H}_1 = \{h_{a,b} : \mathcal{V} \to \{0, \ldots, 2^y - 1\} \mid a \in \{1, \ldots, 65536\},\ b \in \{0, \ldots, 65536\}\},$$

where $\mathcal{V}$ denotes a vocabulary space. For a token value $t \in \mathcal{V}$, the scalar value x_t is used as an input to a two-universal hash function $h_{a,b} \in \mathcal{H}_1$, parameterized by a pair (a, b), and defined as

$$h_{a,b}(x_t) = ((a \cdot x_t + \text{ b}) \bmod 65537) \bmod 2^y,$$

where 65537 is a prime number satisfying $65537 > 2^{16}$, so that the modulus exceeds the range of 16-bit quantized input values.

This process does not fix a single deterministic hash function, but instead induces a random selection of a function $h_{a,b}$ from the family $\mathcal{H}_1$. The two-universality property holds at the level of the family $\mathcal{H}_1$, i.e., when the function $h_{a,b}$ is sampled uniformly at random from $\mathcal{H}_1$. In particular, for any two distinct tokens $x_1 \neq x_2$, it holds that

$$\Pr_{h_{a,b} \sim \mathcal{H}_1} \left[h_{a,b}(x_1) = h_{a,b}(x_2)\right] \leq 2^{-y}.$$

The parameters $a \in \{1, \ldots, 65536\}$, and $b \in \{0, \ldots, 65536\}$ are generated using the same pseudorandom generator initialized with the shared key k. The parameter y defines the number of bits encoded per token.

3.5 Constrained Beam Search

The constrained beam search algorithm [22] aims to maximize the likelihood of generated text while simultaneously satisfying the steganographic embedding constraints. In contrast to classical beam search [16], the proposed variant restricts the search space to tokens satisfying the steganographic constraint at each generation step (Fig. 2). Token masking may force the generation process to select tokens with relatively low probability under the original language model distribution. To mitigate this effect, the constrained beam search algorithm evaluates multiple alternative continuations and selects those that maximize the overall sequence score. For a token sequence $s = (s_1, \ldots, s_N)$, we define the score function as $\text{score}(s) = \sum_{i=1}^{N} \log p(s_i \mid s_1, \ldots, s_{i-1})$, where $p(\cdot)$ denotes the probability distribution induced by the language model. The score is accumulated incrementally during beam expansion.

Algorithm 1: Constrained Beam Search

Input:

$\mathcal{M}$: autoregressive language model
$E \in \mathbb{R}^{|\mathcal{V}| \times d}$: embedding matrix of $\mathcal{M}$
$\mathbf{c}$: prompt tokens
$\mathbf{m} = (m_1, \ldots, m_N)$: message symbols, where $m_i \in \{0, \ldots, 2^y - 1\}$
k: secret key

Parameters:

D: lookahead depth
B: beam width
l: number of selected embedding dimensions
y: number of bits encoded per token

Output:

$\mathbf{s}$: generated token sequence

```
s ← c
σ_s = 0
m̃ = (m_1, ..., m_N, 0, ..., 0) padded to length N + D
g ← PRNG(k)
h ← (hash_{l,y}(E, g), ..., hash_{l,y}(E, g))
for i ← 1 to N do
    𝓑 ← {(0, s)}
    for d ← 0 to D − 1 do
        b ← m̃_{i+d}
        𝓒 ← ∅
        foreach (σ_b, s_b) ∈ 𝓑 do
            z ← 𝓜(s_b)
            p(· | s_b) ← softmax(z)
            𝓣 ← {t ∈ V : h_{i+d}[t] = b}
            if 𝓣 = ∅ then
                return ⊥, −∞
            foreach t ∈ 𝓣 do
                s'_b ← s_b || t
                σ'_b ← σ_b + log p(t | s_b)
                𝓒 ← 𝓒 ∪ (σ'_b, s'_b)
        𝓑 ← Top-B(𝓒)
    (σ*, s*) = arg max_{(σ,s)∈𝓑} σ
    t* = s*_{|s|+1}
    s ← s || t*
    σ_s = σ*
return s, σ_s
```

At each generation step, the algorithm performs a lookahead beam search of depth D. Starting from the current prefix, the algorithm expands candidate sequences by considering all admissible tokens satisfying the constraint. For each candidate, only the score is retained, and the top B candidates are retained after each expansion step.

The algorithm follows a model predictive control scheme: although a depth-D rollout is performed to evaluate future trajectories, only the first token of the highest-scoring sequence is appended to the output. The procedure is repeated autoregressively from the updated prefix. This lookahead strategy allows the algorithm to compensate for locally suboptimal token choices introduced by the masking constraint by considering their long-term impact on sequence likelihood. The constrained beam search pseudocode is presented in Algorithm 1.

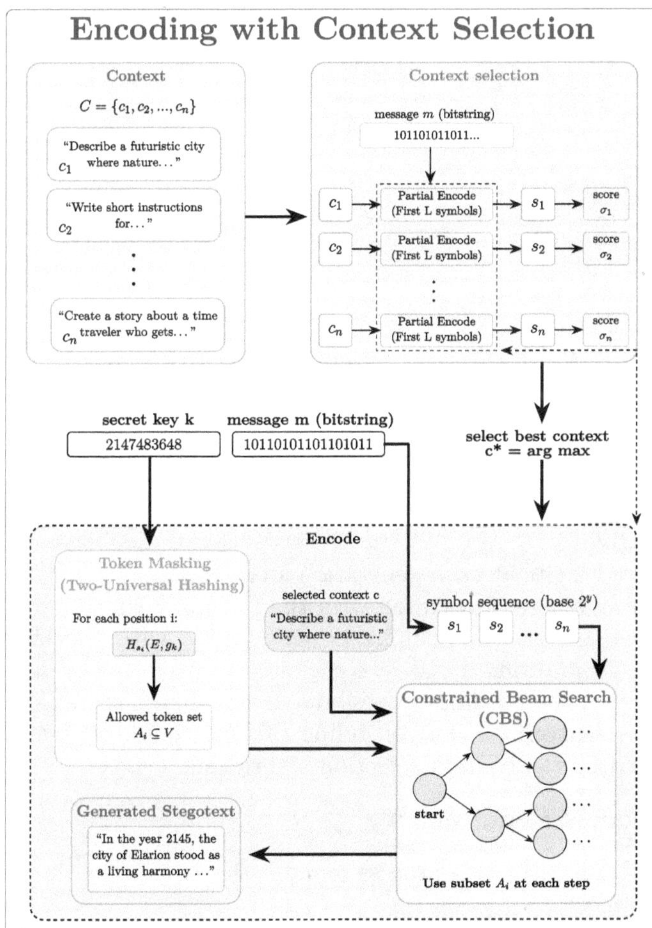

Fig. 2. ARCDStego Visualization - Encoding

3.6 Encoding and Decoding

An overview of the encoding and decoding pipelines is illustrated in Fig. 2 and Fig. 3. The ARCDStego method assumes asymmetric computational requirements between the encoding and decoding procedures. Encoding requires access to the language model and performs computationally intensive constrained generation, whereas decoding reconstructs the hidden message using only the generated token sequence, the embedding matrix, and the shared secret key. In the following, we define the requirements for both procedures.

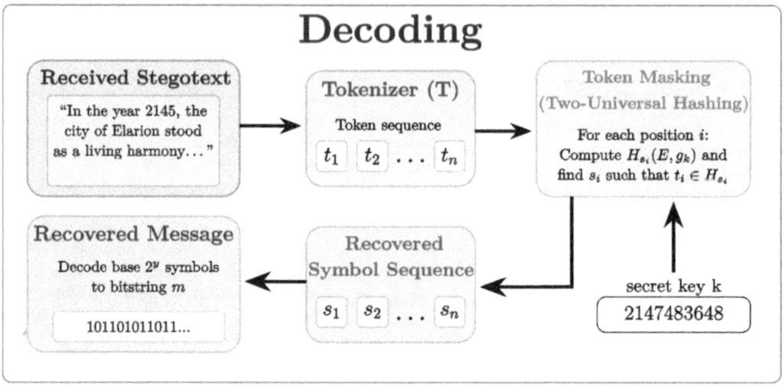

Fig. 3. ARCDStego Visualization - Decoding

Encoding Process Requirements

1. **Language model** – The encoding procedure requires an autoregressive LLM with access to:
   (a) token-level logits at each generation step,
   (b) embedding matrix associated with the tokenizer vocabulary.
2. **Tokenizer** – The tokenizer must be compatible with the language model used during generation.
3. **Secret key** – The encoding process requires a shared secret key.
4. **Candidate contexts** – The encoding process requires a set of candidate contexts used by the context selection algorithm.

Decoding Process Requirements

1. **Tokenizer** – The decoding process requires the same tokenizer that was used during encoding.
2. **Embedding matrix** – The decoding algorithm requires access only to the embedding matrix corresponding to the tokenizer vocabulary.
3. **Secret key** – The decoding process requires the same shared secret key that was used during encoding.

Algorithm 2: Decode

Input:
s: generated text containing the hidden message
$\mathcal{T}$: tokenizer used during encoding procedure
E: embedding matrix of model $\mathcal{M}$
k: secret key

Parameters:
l: number of selected embedding positions
y: number of bits encoded per token

Output:
$\mathbf{m}^*$: recovered bit sequence

$\mathbf{t} \leftarrow \mathcal{T}(s)$
$\mathbf{m}^* \leftarrow ()$
$g \leftarrow \text{PRNG}(k)$

for $i \leftarrow 1$ **to** $|\mathbf{t}|$ **do**
  $\mathbf{h} \leftarrow \text{hash}_{l,y}(E, g)$
  $m_b \leftarrow \mathbf{h}[t_i]$
  $\mathbf{m}^* \leftarrow \mathbf{m}^* \parallel m_b$
return $\mathbf{m}^*$

Algorithm 3: Encode

Input:
$\mathcal{M}$: autoregressive language model
$\mathcal{T}$: tokenizer associated with $\mathcal{M}$
c: context (string)
m: hidden message (bitstring)
k: secret key

Parameters:
B: beam width
D: lookahead depth
l: number of selected embedding positions
y: number of bits encoded per token

Output:
s: generated text containing the hidden message

$\mathbf{x} \leftarrow \mathcal{T}(c)$
$\mathbf{b} \leftarrow \text{symbols}_y(m)$

$\mathbf{y}, \sigma \leftarrow \text{CBS}_{l,y,D,B}(\mathcal{M}, \mathbf{x}, \mathbf{b}, k)$ (see Alg. 1)
if $\mathbf{y} = \perp$ **then**
  return $\perp, -\infty$
$\mathbf{y}' = \mathbf{y}_{|\mathbf{x}|+1:}$
$s \leftarrow \mathcal{T}^{-1}(\mathbf{y}')$
return s, σ

Encode Algorithm. Before describing the encoding procedure, we briefly clarify the role of the input context c in ARCDStego. The context serves as the prompt prefix from which the language model starts constrained generation. Its choice is important because the token masking procedure may exclude some high-probability tokens from the admissible token set, forcing the model toward less likely continuations. Therefore, ARCDStego assumes that the encoder is provided with one or more candidate contexts and may select a context that is compatible with both the hidden message and the base model distribution. In practice, such candidate contexts may come from ongoing conversations, social-media comments, manually prepared prompts, or auxiliary prompt-generation agents. In Moltbook-like environments, such an agent may also be connected to an external knowledge base through retrieval-augmented generation, so that candidate prompts can be grounded in both the current thread and retrieved evidence [11,17,24]. Low-perplexity contexts are preferred as a practical heuristic, since perplexity is closely related to cross-entropy and reflects predictive uncertainty during token generation; however, it is used here only as an indicator of model confidence, not as a standalone measure of factual correctness or text quality [13]. We define $\text{symbols}_y(m)$ as a deterministic mapping from bitstring to base-2^y symbols induced by the binary expansion of the UTF-8 encoding of message m, followed by chunking into y-bit blocks. The encoding procedure defines a partial function, where infeasible constraint configurations result in rejection of the encoding attempt, denoted by $\perp$.

The pseudocode for the encoding process is presented in Algorithm 3, while the pseudocode for the decoding procedure is enclosed as Algorithm 2.

3.7 Context Selection

The constrained beam search (CBS) algorithm described in Subsect. 3.5 is designed to prevent the selection of extremely low-probability tokens during generation. However, the masking procedure may exclude highly probable tokens from the feasible token set. To address this limitation, we propose a context-selection algorithm that chooses the best context for embedding the hidden message. As illustrated in Fig. 2, the context-selection procedure operates on top of the encoding pipeline and evaluates multiple candidate contexts by performing partial executions of the encoding procedure.

For each candidate context c_i from a set of candidate contexts $C = c_1, c_2, \dots, c_n$, a partial execution of the encoding procedure is performed using the initial segment of the hidden message m_p. The resulting generated sequence s_i is evaluated using the same score function as in the beam search algorithm 1. Higher scores indicate stronger compatibility between the embedding constraints and the language model distribution under the given context. The context with the highest score is selected as the final context c^*.

This procedure aims to select a context in which the embedding constraints are better aligned with the language model probability distribution. In practice, the set of candidate contexts may come from a variety of sources, such as social media comments or synthetically generated data. The ARCDStego algorithm is flexible in its choice of contexts.

Algorithm 4: Context Selection

Input:
- $\mathcal{M}$: autoregressive language model
- $\mathcal{T}$: tokenizer associated with $\mathcal{M}$
- $C = \{c_1, \ldots, c_n\}$: set of candidate contexts
- m_p: part of hidden message (bitstring)
- k: secret key

Parameters:
- B: beam width
- D: lookahead depth
- l: number of selected embedding positions
- y: number of bits encoded per token

Output:
- c^*: selected context

```
σ* ← −∞
c* ← ⊥

foreach c_i ∈ C do
    s_i, σ_i ← Encode_{l,y,B,D}(c_i, m_p, k, M, T)
    if s_i = ⊥ then
        continue
    if σ_i > σ* then
        σ* ← σ_i
        c* ← c_i

return c*
```

3.8 Perplexity-Based Analysis

In realistic AI-agent communication settings, generated responses are rarely produced by a language model in an isolated environment. Practical agents typically rely on additional mechanisms, such as retrieval-augmented generation (RAG), external knowledge bases, conversation memory, context selection, intent recognition, and tool use. These components help construct grounded and semantically stable prompts, while increasing the likelihood of coherent, high-confidence continuations.

In ARCDStego, such context construction directly supports constrained generation. A well-selected context can better align the hidden message and token-selection constraints with the model distribution, reducing the risk of incoherent, hallucinated, or off-distribution text. To quantify this effect, we use perplexity (PPL) as a proxy for distributional plausibility, rather than as a complete security measurement. For a generated sequence $s = (s_1, \ldots, s_N)$, perplexity is defined as

$$\mathrm{PPL}(s) = \exp\left(-\frac{1}{N}\sum_{i=1}^{N} \log p(s_i \mid s_1, \ldots, s_{i-1})\right),$$

where $p(s_i \mid s_1, \ldots, s_{i-1})$ denotes the probability assigned by the base model to token s_i given the preceding context. Lower PPL indicates that the sequence is more probable under the model distribution, whereas higher PPL suggests that the sequence deviates from typical model behavior.

A complete distributional analysis must also account for the variability induced by different embedded messages. Since different messages constrain the decoding process in different ways, they may lead to outputs with substantially different likelihoods under the base model. For instance, in one observed case using an English context with the DISCOP method [6] based on the Qwen1.5-0.5B model, embedding a specific message caused the model to shift to Chinese-language generation. Although such hallucinations or linguistic shifts are part of AI models' known behavior and do not necessarily constitute a compromise in the same sense as a failure in human-mimicking steganography, they nevertheless reflect statistical deviations, as evidenced by increased PPL.

4 Perplexity Analysis on Moltbook Contexts

A key challenge in constrained generation-based information embedding is the sensitivity of output distribution to the choice of input context. When the prompt context is poorly aligned with embedding constraints, decoding may force the model into low-probability regions of the token space, leading to distributional drift and degraded linguistic quality. This effect becomes particularly noticeable in methods that do not explicitly control for context–constraint alignment. The purpose of this evaluation is to determine whether ARCDStego can generate text that remains a plausible output of the underlying language model under constrained decoding. This requirement follows from the observation that encoding performance depends not only on the message, but also on whether the generated sequence remains within high-probability regions of the base model distribution under a given prompt.

In this section, we evaluate the performance of the ARCDStego framework. We analyze the statistical impact of steganographic constraints on the generated text using perplexity. All experiments were conducted using the Qwen1.5-0.5B model as the base generator. We compare two variants of the method: ARCDStego-1, which embeds one bit per token, and ARCDStego-2, which embeds two bits per token. In addition, we compare ARCDStego against DISCOP [6], a reference method, to assess whether the proposed embedding-space constraint mechanism preserves distributional plausibility and linguistic quality relative to an existing steganographic generation approach.

We use a set of 50 real-world contexts that were collected from publicly available Moltbook posts[2]. Each prompt is constructed in the following form: *"Reply to the following post. Title: [title]. Post: [post]."*. For each context, we generate steganographic text of fixed length of 100 tokens. This setup enables controlled comparison across methods and allows us to analyze how embedding constraints influence perplexity behavior over longer generations.

[2] https://www.moltbook.com.

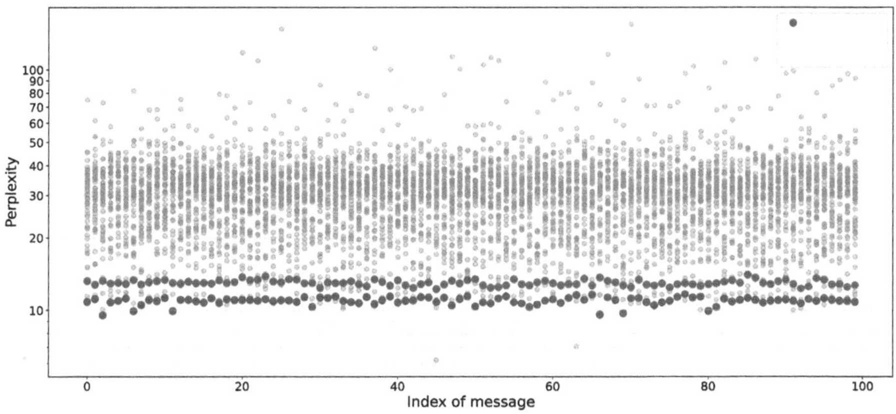

Fig. 4. Perplexity values obtained for different Moltbook contexts for each message-key pair using ARCDStego-1, ARCDStego-2, and DISCOP.

The gray points in Fig. 4 correspond to DISCOP. In contrast to both ARCD-Stego variants, DISCOP exhibits a much wider dispersion of perplexity values and a substantially higher overall perplexity. Most DISCOP samples are concentrated in the range 15–50, with an average perplexity of approximately 33.97, and several outliers exceed 100. This behavior indicates a strong dependence on the previously agreed context and on the embedded message. In particular, if the shared context is selected without knowledge of the message to be embedded, the resulting generation may be poorly aligned with the language model's distribution, leading to very high perplexity values. By comparison, in ARCDStego, the final context is selected from a set of 50 candidate contexts as the one yielding the lowest perplexity for the constrained generation attempt. As a result, ARCDStego-1 achieves a substantially lower average perplexity of 10.91, while ARCDStego-2 obtains an average perplexity of 13.00. Thus, although ARCDStego-2 increases the embedding rate relative to ARCDStego-1, both proposed variants remain considerably closer to the high-probability region of the base model than DISCOP. The results, therefore, suggest that the proposed embedding-space constraint mechanism, combined with context selection, better preserves statistical plausibility, whereas DISCOP is more sensitive to context–message mismatch and introduces stronger distributional deviations.

Figure 5 shows the effect of the number of available candidate contexts on the perplexity of the generated stegotext. The results confirm that perplexity increases as the context pool becomes smaller. This effect is expected when fewer candidate contexts are available, the encoder has fewer opportunities to find a prompt that is well aligned with the hidden message, the secret key, and the constraints imposed during token selection. The comparison between ARCDStego-1 and ARCDStego-2 shows that the context pool size substantially affects statistical plausibility. ARCDStego-1 consistently achieves lower perplexity than ARCDStego-2 for the same number of candidate contexts, since it embeds only

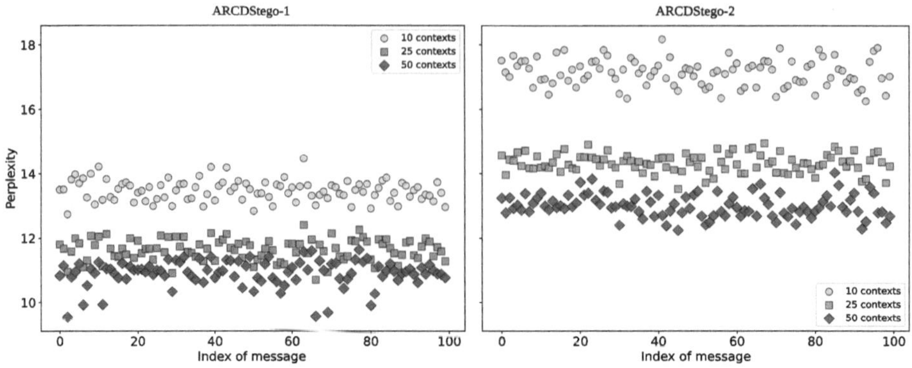

Fig. 5. Perplexity values obtained for different sizes of the Moltbook context set for each message-key pair using ARCDStego-1, ARCDStego-2.

one bit per token and therefore imposes weaker constraints on generation. However, an interesting observation is that ARCDStego-2 with 50 candidate contexts achieves perplexity values comparable to ARCDStego-1, with only 10 candidate contexts. This indicates that a larger context pool can partially compensate for the stronger token-selection constraints introduced by the higher embedding rate.

Overall, the results demonstrate that context selection plays a central role in mitigating distributional degradation in constrained encoding and that it interacts directly with embedding capacity in determining generation plausibility.

5 Conclusion

This paper introduces ARCDStego, a lightweight constrained decoding framework for causal large language models that embeds messages via structured modulo-based masking in the token-embedding space. The proposed method enables deterministic payload recovery without requiring access to internal logits or probability distributions during decoding, relying only on a shared secret key, the tokenizer, and the embedding matrix. Experimental results showed that context selection plays a central role in stabilizing constrained encoding under embedding constraints. In particular, larger context pools substantially improve generation plausibility, while increasing the embedding rate introduces stronger distributional deviations and higher perplexity. These results indicate that embedding practical information into LLM-generated text is feasible under asymmetric decoding-resource assumptions, without requiring access to the model internals during extraction. In particular, the experiments demonstrate that the availability of context must be balanced against payload capacity and plausibility of generation, especially in environments such as Moltbook, where autonomous agents continuously generate text.

Future work will expand the evaluations to include larger context pools, longer horizons, and empirical evaluation against statistical and neural steganalysis methods. Additionally, for better adaptation to the communities of AI agents, future research should investigate behavioral and stylistic statistics such as posting frequency, topic variability, as well as discourse styles and levels of discussion complexity.

Disclosure of Interests. The authors have no competing interests to declare that are relevant to the content of this article.

References

1. Agarwal, M.: Text steganographic approaches: a comparison. Int. J. Netw. Secur. Appl. **5**, 91–106 (2013)
2. Anderson, R., Needham, R., Shamir, A.: The Steganographic File System, pp. 73–82 (1998)
3. Bai, M., Yang, J., Pang, K., Huang, Y., Gao, Y.: Shifting-merging: secure, high-capacity and efficient steganography via large language models (2025)
4. Carter, J., Wegman, M.N.: Universal classes of hash functions. J. Comput. Syst. Sci. **18**, 143–154 (1979)
5. Chaudhary, S., Dave, M., Sanghi, A.: Review of linguistic text steganographic methods. Int. J. Recent Innov. Trends Comput. Commun. **4**, 377–381 (2016)
6. Ding, J., Chen, K., Wang, Y., Zhao, N., Zhang, W., Yu, N.: Discop: provably secure steganography in practice based on "distribution copies". In: 2023 IEEE Symposium on Security and Privacy (SP), vol. 2023, pp. 2238–2255 (2023)
7. Driss, M., Berriche, L., Atitallah, S.B., Rekik, S.: Steganography in IoT: a comprehensive survey on approaches, challenges, and future directions. IEEE Access **13**, 74844–74875 (2025)
8. Evsutin, O., Melman, A., Meshcheryakov, R.: Digital steganography and watermarking for digital images: a review of current research directions. IEEE Access **8**, 166589–166611 (2020)
9. Fang, T., Jaggi, M., Argyraki, K.: Generating steganographic text with LSTMs. In: Ettinger, A., Gella, S., Labeau, M., Alm, C.O., Carpuat, M., Dredze, M. (eds.) Proceedings of ACL 2017, Student Research Workshop, pp. 100–106 (2017)
10. Fridrich, J.: Steganography in Digital Media: Principles, Algorithms, and Applications, 1st edn. Cambridge University Press, New York (2009)
11. Gao, Y.: Retrieval-augmented generation for large language models: a survey. arXiv preprint arXiv:2312.10997 (2024)
12. Huang, Y.S., et al.: OD-Stega: LLM-based relatively secure steganography via optimized distributions. In: Proceedings of the 19th Conference of the European Chapter of the Association for Computational Linguistics, vol. 1, pp. 827–851 (2026)
13. Jurafsky, D., Martin, J.H.: Speech and language processing: an introduction to natural language processing, computational linguistics, and speech recognition with language models. 3rd edn. (2026). https://web.stanford.edu/~jurafsky/slp3/
14. Kombrink, M.H., Geradts, Z.J.M.H., Worring, M.: Image steganography approaches and their detection strategies: a survey. ACM Comp. Surv. **57**(2), (2024)

15. Kose, J., et al.: Review and test of steganography techniques. ArXiv **abs/2012.08460** (2020). https://api.semanticscholar.org/CorpusID:229181214
16. Leblond, R., et al.: Machine translation decoding beyond beam search (2021)
17. Lewis, P.: Retrieval-augmented generation for knowledge-intensive NLP tasks. In: Advances in Neural Information Processing Systems, vol. 33, pp. 9459–9474 (2020)
18. Møller, A.G., Romero, D.M., Jurgens, D., Aiello, L.M.: The impact of generative AI on social media: an experimental study. Sci. Rep. **16**, 9376 (2026)
19. Provos, N., Honeyman, P.: Hide and seek: an introduction to steganography. IEEE Secur. Priv. **1**, 32–44 (2003)
20. Qin, Z., et al.: ADLM-Stega: a universal adaptive token selection algorithm for improving steganographic text quality via information entropy (2024). http://arxiv.org/abs/2410.20825
21. Shamsi, Z., et al.: Advances in steganography systems for image and audio data: a survey on techniques, limitations, and future prospects. SN Comput. Sci. **7**, 325 (2026)
22. Shati, P., Cohen, E., McIlraith, S.: Neural sequence generation with constraints via beam search with cuts: a case study on VRP. In: Proceedings of the International Symposium on Combinatorial Search, vol. 17, pp. 118–126 (2024)
23. Shen, J., Ji, H., Han, J.: Near-imperceptible neural linguistic steganography via self-adjusting arithmetic coding. In: Webber, B. (ed.) Proceedings of the Conference on Empirical Methods in Natural Language Processing (EMNLP), pp. 303–313 (2020)
24. Singh, A., Ehtesham, A., Kumar, S., Khoei, T.T., Vasilakos, A.V.: Agentic retrieval-augmented generation: a survey on agentic RAG (2026)
25. Wang, K., Gao, Q.: A coverless plain text steganography based on character features. IEEE Access **7**, 95665–95676 (2019)
26. Woźniak, K., Ogiela, M.R., Ogiela, L.: Multi-criteria linguistic optimization for covert communication in secure LLM-based steganography. Appl. Soft Comput. **185**, 113960 (2025)
27. Yan, R., Chu, C., Yang, Z., Murawaki, Y.: A comprehensive survey on linguistic steganography: methods, countermeasures, evaluation, and challenges (2025). https://doi.org/10.13140/RG.2.2.36031.98727
28. Yang, B., Peng, W., Xue, Y., Zhong, P.: A generation-based text steganography by maintaining consistency of probability distribution. KSII Trans. Internet Inf. Syst. **15**(11), 4065–4083 (2021)
29. Yang, Z., Wei, N., Sheng, J., Huang, Y., Zhang, Y.J.: TS-CNN: text steganalysis from semantic space based on convolutional neural network (2018). https://arxiv.org/abs/1810.08136
30. Zhang, S., Yang, Z., Yang, J., Huang, Y.: Provably secure generative linguistic steganography. In: Zong, C., Xia, F., Li, W., Navigli, R. (eds.) Findings of the Association for Computational Linguistics: ACL-IJCNLP 2021, pp. 3046–3055 (2021)
31. Ziegler, Z., Deng, Y., Rush, A.: Neural linguistic steganography. In: Inui, K. (ed.) Proceedings of the EMNLP-IJCNLP 2019, pp. 1210–1215 (2019)

Defence Framework For The Holistic Protection Of AI Applications

Salvador Cuñat(✉), Evangelos Floros, Evangelos Loutsetis, Alessandro Finocchi, Giuseppe Marseglia, Aikaterini Psychogyiou, Stamatios Kostopoulos, Vassilis Prevelakis, Evangelos K. Markakis, Rafael Vaño, and Ignacio Lacalle

Escuela Técnica Superior de Ingeniería de Telecomunicaciones, Camí de Vera, s/n, 46022 Valencia, Spain
salcuane@upv.es

Abstract. The work reflects on the importance of security layers in the context of AI applications and operations. The paper explores the cybersecurity challenges in designing a defence framework for protecting AI systems against malicious actions and adversarial AI attacks, understanding the figures and mechanisms that govern the process. The authors link those reflections to the direct transfer into a research project, cPAID, that faces such challenges head on as a leading Horizon Europe project. By integrating cutting-edge AI-assisted technologies in Intrusion Detection Systems, using novel unsupervised and XAI methods in conjunction with traditional SIEMs and AI-assisted penetration testing for AI, cPAID provides an adaptive security framework that thoroughly assesses the robustness and resiliency of Machine and Deep Learning algorithms against attacks.

Keywords: Cybersecurity Research Domains · Artificial intelligence · Security · Intrusion Detection System · Security Information and Event Management

1 Introduction

The explosion of global data and massive leaps in computing power have accelerated the integration of Artificial Intelligence (AI) into industrial operations and vital infrastructure. From the management of smart cities to the navigation of autonomous vessels, 5G drones, and advanced medical hardware, the success of these innovations depends greatly on Machine Learning (ML) and Deep Learning (DL) algorithms [1]. These models digest vast datasets to perform critical decision-making tasks; for example, autonomous ships rely on AI to interpret sensor data and adjust movements in real-time. As a consequence, these systems often function in high-stakes environments where even minor algorithmic errors can lead to catastrophic failures, including the potential loss of life [5].

However, the rapid transition from legacy methods to AI-centric solutions has left organizations and industries exposed to profound risks. These threats range

P. Kieseberg et al. (Eds.): ARES 2026 Workshops, LNCS 16903, pp. 117–134, 2027.
https://doi.org/10.1007/978-3-032-37218-5_8

from 0-day vulnerabilities and model theft to data integrity breaches, largely due to a lack of mature tactical tools for securing AI infrastructure [8]. As AI adoption grows, so does the sophistication of the threat landscape. A new attack surface known as adversarial AI attacks has emerged, where threat actors exploit the inherent vulnerabilities of ML and DL models. These techniques include evasion attacks, which introduce deceptive inputs during the model testing phase, and poisoning attacks, which corrupt the training data itself to compromise the system's foundational logic [6].

This work specializes in the cybersecurity aspect of protecting against malicious actions and adversarial attacks. In the last twenty years, after the rise of adversarial attacks, the number of incidents in AI-involved training of ML and DL models has continued to grow [3] and many industry members are not suited for dealing with these sort of incidents [7]. In this work the topic is addressed in three steps: (i) a Risk Management for AI to contextualize and prioritize threats to the system, (ii) an Adversarial Intrusion Detection System responsible for the detection of attacks directed towards a target ML model and (iii) a Security Information and Event Management system to focus on the attack-handling workflow.

2 Context and Background

2.1 Related Work in Adversarial Artificial Intelligences

Research on Adversarial Artificial Intelligence has produced a rich ecosystem of tools and frameworks. There exists a multitude of adversarial AI studies that resulted in developing an entire landscape of tooling and frameworks dedicated to discovering, assessing, and addressing the vulnerabilities of ML systems. While the early research in this field revolved around creating adversarial samples to showcase the susceptibility of neural nets, more recent works started to include other threats to the safety and security of models such as poisoning of training datasets, model extraction, privacy breaches, and various forms of abuse in AI systems. Nevertheless, these tools do not address the problem of continuous management and justification of robustness and security measures. cPAID introduces a new approach to achieving assurance by focusing on the processes of continuous assessment and communication of robustness measures. This section is intended to place some notable adversarial AI tools within the context of cPAID.

Recent Literature: According to recent research Sotiris Pelekis et al. (2025) [13], in his paper, presents a comprehensive survey of adversarial machine learning (AML), focusing on both robustness and privacy of modern AI systems. The research systematically categorizes adversarial attacks and defenses, reviews leading benchmarks and open-source tools, and analyzes how AML threats and mitigation strategies manifest in four critical domains and in particular autonomous vehicles, healthcare, electrical power and energy systems, and large language model (based NLP), highlighting current limitations, trade-offs, and future research directions.

The lack of robustness in modern AI systems remains a primary obstacle to real-world trust and widespread adoption. In this survey, Qingzhe Tang et al. (2026) [16] how the "black-box" design of these models reduces stability and transparency, especially in complex or adversarial environments. The survey systematically examines robustness evaluation methods, lifecycle-based enhancement strategies, and the relationships between robustness and other trustworthy AI principles, with special focus on hallucinations and robustness issues in large language models. It concludes by outlining key open challenges and future research directions for building more robust and trustworthy AI.

Yan Qiao et al. (2026) [14] in his paper outlines the rise of adversarial machine learning as a critical response to the growing deployment of machine learning systems in high-stakes, real-world applications. Despite strong performance, modern ML models—especially deep neural networks—are highly vulnerable to adversarial manipulation due to their statistical foundations, high-dimensional input spaces, and inherent accuracy–robustness trade-offs. Adversarial threats now span the entire ML lifecycle, including evasion, data poisoning, backdoors, privacy attacks, and model extraction, and are amplified by defender–attacker asymmetry and increasing model complexity. The survey addresses these challenges by systematically reviewing attack surfaces, defense mechanisms, and domain-specific considerations, drawing on recent foundational work to highlight both current limitations and promising directions toward more robust, secure, and theoretically grounded ML systems.

Another comprehensive overview from Hubert Baniecki et al. (2024) [2] provides how adversarial methods can manipulate or undermine explainable AI (XAI) systems, as well as the techniques developed to detect and defend against such threats. This paper reviews attack strategies targeting explanations (rather than predictions alone), categorizes existing defense mechanisms, and discusses their implications for trust, robustness, and reliability of XAI in high-stakes applications, while also highlighting open challenges and future research directions.

Tomas Bueno Momcilovic et al. (2024) [10] states that Large language models (LLMs) deliver strong generative performance but are increasingly vulnerable to adversarial misuse during training, prompting, and deployment, creating risks to privacy, safety, and fundamental rights—especially in high-stakes applications such as healthcare, autonomous systems, and robotics. The authors propose a framework based on ontologies, assurance cases, and factsheets to help engineers and legal stakeholders systematically assess, document, and maintain the security, safety, and regulatory compliance of LLM-based systems.

Existing Frameworks: IBM Adversarial Robustness Toolbox (ART) [17] is an open-source framework designed to help developers evaluate, defend, and monitor machine-learning models against adversarial threats across the entire ML lifecycle. It provides practical tools for generating adversarial attacks, measuring robustness, applying defenses such as adversarial training, preprocessing, and detection, and assessing privacy risks like model extraction and membership inference. ART is therefore an operational toolkit, focused on implementing and testing concrete robustness mechanisms. On the other hand, ART does not orchestrate how these defenses are deployed, maintained, and justified throughout the system's lifecycle.

Microsoft Counterfit [9], serves a much narrower but complementary role in the AI robustness and security landscape. Counterfit is primarily an offensive testing and assessment tool, focused on adversarially probing machine-learning models to uncover vulnerabilities such as evasion, poisoning, or misuse prior to deployment. Its strength lies in simulating attacker behaviour and exposing failure modes, but it does not manage how discovered risks are mitigated, tracked, or governed over time.

Focused on developing, benchmarking, and reproducing adversarial examples against machine-learning models, CleverHans [12] is primarily a research-oriented adversarial attack library. It provides canonical implementations of attacks such as FGSM, PGD, and CW, and is widely used to study model vulnerabilities and evaluate robustness in controlled experimental settings, particularly in academia. However, CleverHans does not address how identified vulnerabilities are managed, mitigated, or tracked over time, nor does it support operational processes such as continuous monitoring, remediation cycles, or compliance documentation.

Foolbox [15], is a lightweight adversarial attack benchmarking library focused on evaluating the robustness of machine-learning models through standardized, framework-agnostic adversarial attacks. It emphasizes usability and reproducibility, enabling practitioners to quickly apply a wide range of gradient-based and decision-based attacks across different model architectures and libraries to quantify vulnerability. However, Foolbox is limited to point-in-time robustness measurement and does not provide mechanisms for defense orchestration, continuous monitoring, mitigation tracking, or governance.

To create and assess attacks against Natural Language Processing (NLP) models, TextAttack [11] is an adversarial testing framework tailored to tasks and modalities. In order to evaluate the robustness, fairness, and dependability of models across classification, generation, and other NLP tasks, it focuses on text-based perturbation techniques, such as synonym substitution, character-level modifications, and paraphrasing. TextAttack does not offer mechanisms for ongoing risk management, remediation lifecycle tracking, or governance-oriented oversight procedures, despite being very successful at identifying linguistic vulnerabilities and benchmarking NLP model robustness at particular stages.

Academic Positioning of cPAID: Existing work typically addresses adversarial AI from isolated perspectives, such as attack taxonomies, robustness evaluation, explainability, compliance, or runtime monitoring. However, few approaches provide an integrated, platform-agnostic, cloud-based framework combining adversarial defense, AI lifecycle protection, explainability, privacy-preserving mechanisms, threat intelligence, context awareness, and certification-oriented trustworthy AI governance. cPAID aims to bridge this gap through a holistic operational defense architecture for secure and trustworthy AI systems.

2.2 Horizon Europe - cPAID

The cPAID framework proposes an integrated methodology for enhancing the security and resilience of AI systems against adversarial threats. Its underlying premise is that robustness cannot be achieved through isolated mitigation techniques alone; rather, it emerges from the continuous interaction of secure engineering practices, runtime protection mechanisms, risk governance processes, and operational awareness. While many existing approaches focus on specific aspects of adversarial machine learning, such as attack generation, detection, or robustness evaluation, cPAID adopts a system-level perspective that spans the entire AI lifecycle, from design and development to deployment, monitoring, and continuous adaptation.

The methodology is structured around a cloud-native and platform-agnostic architecture that enables the orchestration of multiple defensive, assurance, and governance components as interoperable services. The framework is implemented through containerised modules that can be deployed across heterogeneous environments, thereby supporting both edge-based and cloud-based AI applications. This architectural approach enhances scalability, portability, and the continuous integration of adversarial intelligence across distributed deployments. Its main functional components include intrusion detection and prevention capabilities, Security Information and Event Management (SIEM), explainable AI services, risk management modules, cyber range support, and a unified data fabric for secure and structured information exchange.

In addition to secure development practices, cPAID incorporates generative and analytical mechanisms for the production and evaluation of adversarial intelligence. Generative Adversarial AI is used to synthesise realistic adversarial datasets covering poisoning, evasion, inference, and extraction attacks. These synthetic attack vectors support both pre-deployment robustness testing and continuous stress-testing of deployed AI systems. This capability is further complemented by intrusion detection and prevention mechanisms operating at the network and system levels. These mechanisms employ deep learning, ensemble learning, and reinforcement learning techniques to identify, prioritise, and mitigate adversarial activity in near real time.

To provide operational visibility and support coordinated response, the framework integrates a meta-SIEM layer that aggregates and correlates security-relevant events across all system components. This layer supports incident prioritisation, explainable alert generation, automated response orchestration and analysis of adversarial behaviour patterns. In parallel, a dedicated risk management subsystem enables the structured assessment of AI-specific threats, including data poisoning, model extraction, evasion attacks, and privacy leakage. Risk representation is formalised through an ontology-based model aligned with established frameworks and regulatory instruments, including the NIST AI

Risk Management Framework, the EU AI Act, and the OWASP Machine Learning Security guidelines. This alignment enables continuous, interpretable, and lifecycle-oriented risk evaluation.

The methodology also includes supporting mechanisms for validation, training, and empirical assessment. A dedicated adversarial AI cyber range is used as a controlled environment for selected attack simulations and defensive exercises, complementing the framework's broader validation activities. Real-world validation is conducted across heterogeneous application domains, including autonomous systems, energy infrastructures, environmental monitoring, and medical AI applications. These validation activities allow the framework to be assessed in terms of robustness, scalability, transferability, and operational applicability.

cPAID contributes to the development of resilient, explainable, and certifiable AI systems, while addressing the practical need for security mechanisms that are scalable, interoperable, and adaptable to evolving threat landscapes.

3 AI Driven Adversarial Attack Detection and Risk Management

The proposed cPAID operational workflow is deployed within a unified AI security architecture that integrates infrastructure-level monitoring, adversarial machine learning protection, and risk-aware orchestration into a single analytical pipeline. As illustrated in Fig. 1, the system combines Wazuh-based telemetry collection at the infrastructure layer, the AIPS adversarial intrusion detection component at the model layer, the RIMA risk assessment framework for contextual threat interpretation, and the mSIEM as the central correlation and incident management layer. This multi-layered configuration enables the joint interpretation of heterogeneous security evidence, allowing model-level and infrastructure-level signals to be analysed within a consistent operational and risk-aware context.

Within this setting, Generative Adversarial AI (GenAAI) is used as a supporting mechanism to model and simulate adversarial behaviours relevant to machine learning security. In particular, it enables the generation of inference-time evasion and input-manipulation patterns that approximate realistic attacker strategies against deployed AI models. These synthesized behaviours are used to establish the initial threat assumptions underlying the scenario described in this section.

In the considered scenario, an adversary targets an AI-enabled service deployed within the monitored pilot environment by performing an inference-time evasion attack against the machine learning model while simultaneously exhibiting probing and interaction patterns at the infrastructure layer. At the model layer, carefully crafted inputs are submitted to induce misclassification while remaining close to benign distributions. At the same time, the surrounding infrastructure may exhibit suspicious activity such as repeated API requests, abnormal authentication patterns, or anomalous system-level behaviour. The combination of these signals is treated as a potential cross-layer incident and is further detailed in Sect. 3.1, where the full interaction flow and system-level response are formally described.

3.1 Attack Scenario

The proposed scenario considers an adversarial attack against an AI-enabled service deployed within a monitored pilot environment. The objective of the scenario is to illustrate how the cPAID components cooperate during the detection, contextualisation, correlation, explanation, and handling of an attack that affects both the infrastructure layer and the AI/model layer. A diagram of the workflow can be found in Fig 1 and a brief description of each component can be seen in 1. In this scenario, the mSIEM acts as the operational fusion layer, AIPS provides runtime adversarial AI detection, and the Risk Assessment component of RIMA provides the contextual risk information required to prioritise and interpret the incident.

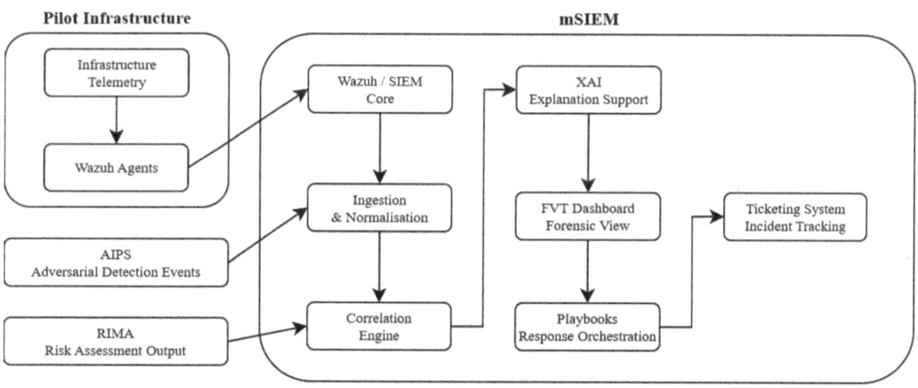

Fig. 1. Workflow of the attack resolution.

The attack starts at the infrastructure layer, where the adversary interacts with the environment hosting the AI-enabled service. This activity may include abnormal authentication attempts, unexpected process execution, unusual network connections, file-integrity changes, repeated API-level probing, or other suspicious behaviours affecting the host or service environment. These observations are generated within the pilot infrastructure. Wazuh agents deployed on the monitored hosts collect the relevant telemetry and forward logs, events, and security alerts to the Wazuh/SIEM component of the mSIEM.

In parallel, the adversary attempts to manipulate the behaviour of the deployed machine-learning model. In this part of the scenario, the attacker submits crafted inputs designed to trigger an incorrect prediction while remaining difficult to distinguish from legitimate input data. This corresponds to an

Table 1. Component roles in the proposed attack scenario workflow

Component	Role
Pilot Infrastructure	External environment hosting the monitored AI-enabled service and generating operational telemetry.
Wazuh Agents	Deployed in the pilot infrastructure to collect logs and security events and forward them to the mSIEM.
AIPS	cPAID component providing runtime adversarial AI detection events.
RIMA Risk Assessment	cPAID component providing asset criticality, risk level, impact, and mitigation priority.
mSIEM	Central operational and analytical layer that ingests pilot telemetry, AIPS adversarial detection events, and RIMA risk assessment outputs, and transforms them into correlated, explainable, and actionable incidents.
Wazuh/SIEM Core	Internal mSIEM subcomponent receiving and structuring telemetry from Wazuh agents.
Correlation Engine	Internal mSIEM function correlating infrastructure alerts, adversarial detections, and risk assessment outputs.
XAI	Internal mSIEM subcomponent providing interpretable reasoning for correlated incidents.
FVT Dashboard	Internal mSIEM subcomponent providing the analyst-facing forensic and operational view.
Playbooks	Internal mSIEM subcomponent supporting predefined response procedures.
Ticketing System	Internal mSIEM subcomponent supporting incident tracking, auditability, and remediation management.

inference-time evasion attempt. AIPS monitors the AI/model layer and detects indicators of adversarial behaviour, such as suspicious input patterns, abnormal model-state behaviour, or deviations that suggest possible adversarial manipulation. Once such behaviour is detected, AIPS generates an adversarial detection event and forwards it to the mSIEM through the platform communication layer.

At the same time, the Risk Assessment component of RIMA provides contextual information about the affected AI asset. This information may include the criticality of the service, the current risk level, the estimated operational impact, and the mitigation priority associated with the affected asset or system. In this workflow, RIMA does not act as the runtime attack detector. Instead, it provides the risk context required for the mSIEM to evaluate the operational relevance and severity of the incoming alerts.

The mSIEM receives the infrastructure alert collected through Wazuh, the adversarial detection event generated by AIPS, and the risk assessment output provided by RIMA. Each event is normalised and enriched with metadata, including timestamp, source component, affected asset, severity, confidence, event type, evidence references, and provenance. The mSIEM then correlates the events using shared asset identifiers, temporal proximity, event type, severity, confidence level, and risk context. If the Wazuh alert and the AIPS detection refer to the same AI-enabled service or hosting environment, and the RIMA Risk

Assessment output indicates elevated risk or high asset criticality, the mSIEM treats the case as a cross-layer adversarial security incident rather than as a set of isolated alerts.

Following correlation, the mSIEM creates a consolidated incident representation. The XAI subcomponent then enriches the incident with interpretable reasoning, helping the analyst understand why the event was considered anomalous and which indicators contributed to the final prioritisation. The incident is presented through the Forensics Visualization Toolkit (FVT), where the analyst can inspect the timeline, review the Wazuh telemetry, examine the AIPS detection, observe the associated RIMA risk context, and follow the correlation chain produced by the mSIEM.

Finally, the incident can trigger controlled response actions through the mSIEM playbook and ticketing mechanisms. Depending on the correlated severity and risk context, the response may include notifying operators, escalating the incident, increasing monitoring of the affected asset, isolating a suspicious endpoint, opening a ticket for manual investigation, or initiating a model review process. The Ticketing System preserves the full incident context, including source alerts, affected assets, risk level, explanation outputs, response actions, and remediation status. This ensures that the adversarial attack is handled as an auditable cybersecurity incident that connects model-level manipulation, infrastructure-level evidence, and risk-aware operational prioritisation.

3.2 RIMA-Based Risk Contextualisation and Prioritisation

In the proposed attack scenario, the Risk Management for AI (RIMA) module provides the risk-aware contextualisation and prioritisation layer of the cPAID workflow. The AI-based Harmonisation (AIH) submodule is the analytical component of RIMA responsible for harmonising heterogeneous evidence, mapping it to AI assets and threats, estimating risk levels, and supporting the selection of mitigation controls. While AIPS detects adversarial behaviour at the AI/model layer and Wazuh collects infrastructure-level telemetry, RIMA evaluates the operational significance of the detected activity and provides the risk context required for incident interpretation.

RIMA is not considered the primary runtime detector in this scenario. Its role is to determine whether the observed activity represents an isolated technical anomaly or a risk-relevant adversarial incident affecting an AI-enabled service. This is particularly important because the scenario combines two complementary layers of evidence: model-level adversarial behaviour and infrastructure-level suspicious activity. Through AIH, these signals are interpreted in relation to the affected AI asset, its criticality, its exposure, and the possible consequences of incorrect model behaviour.

The scenario is represented in RIMA as an inference-time evasion and input-manipulation incident affecting a deployed AI model and its supporting runtime environment. The attacker is assumed to interact with the AI-enabled service through its operational interface by submitting crafted inputs designed to mislead the model while remaining difficult to distinguish from legitimate input data. At the same time, the surrounding infrastructure may show suspicious activity, such as abnormal authentication attempts, unexpected process execution, unusual network connections, file-integrity changes, or repeated API-level probing. These observations strengthen the interpretation of the model-level anomaly as part of a broader cross-layer incident.

The RIMA threat pool is not used as a generic checklist. Instead, AIH selects only the threats that are directly supported by the observed attack evidence. The primary threat is **T2.4, Evasion attacks**, since the attacker submits crafted inputs at inference time to bypass detection or induce incorrect model behaviour. This is also connected to **T2.1, Adversarial attacks**, which represents the broader category of intentional manipulation of AI systems through adversarial inputs. Since the attack is carried out through manipulated input submitted to the deployed model, it is also linked to **T1.1, Input manipulation**. The operational consequence is represented by **T4.4, Specific failure cases**, because the model may fail under crafted or edge-case conditions. Finally, the infrastructure-level evidence is mapped to **T6.1, Technical deficiencies**, because abnormal authentication attempts, exposed interfaces, unusual connections, or API probing may indicate weaknesses in the environment supporting the AI service (Table 2).

Table 2. RIMA threat mapping for the proposed attack scenario

Threat ID	Threat	Relevance to the scenario
T2.4	Evasion attacks	Primary threat. The attacker crafts inputs at inference time to bypass detection or induce incorrect model behaviour.
T2.1	Adversarial attacks	Broader adversarial machine-learning category covering intentional manipulation of the model through adversarial inputs.
T1.1	Input manipulation	The attack is performed through manipulated input data submitted to the deployed AI model.
T4.4	Specific failure cases	The crafted input may trigger incorrect behaviour under specific adversarial or edge-case conditions.
T6.1	Technical deficiencies	Infrastructure-level activity may indicate exposed services, weak authentication, misconfiguration, or other weaknesses in the AI service environment.

Threats such as poisoning attacks, model extraction, membership inference, and model theft are not considered primary in this scenario. The attacker is not assumed to compromise the training dataset, retrain the model, extract model parameters, or reconstruct the model. These threats may become relevant in an extended scenario, but they remain outside the core scope of the present workflow.

The affected AI-enabled service is represented in RIMA through the assets that are directly involved in inference-time operation, monitoring, deployment, and incident reconstruction. The primary affected asset is **A2.2, Models**, because the attacker attempts to manipulate the behaviour of the deployed machine-learning model. The runtime execution of the model is represented by **A6.6, Inference engines**, while the deployment and operational environment are represented by **A6.2, ML platforms**. The observation of abnormal model behaviour is linked to **A5.8, Model monitoring**, and the reconstruction and correlation of the incident depend on **A1.5, Log data** (Fig. 3).

Table 3. RIMA assets directly involved in the proposed attack scenario

Asset ID	Asset	Relevance to the scenario
A2.2	Models	The deployed machine-learning model is directly targeted by the inference-time evasion attempt.
A6.6	Inference engines	The attack occurs during runtime execution of the trained model in production.
A6.2	ML platforms	The AI-enabled service is deployed and operated through an ML platform or equivalent runtime environment.
A5.8	Model monitoring	Runtime monitoring is directly involved, since adversarial indicators are observed and reported during model operation.
A1.5	Log data	Logs, alerts, events, predictions, and operational records are required for correlation and forensic reconstruction.

This asset mapping allows AIH to evaluate the incident as a concrete set of asset-threat pairs. For example, the evasion attempt is represented as T2.4 affecting A2.2, while the suspicious infrastructure behaviour is represented as T6.1 affecting A6.2 and A6.6. The monitoring and forensic dimensions of the scenario are captured through A5.8 and A1.5 respectively.

AIH performs risk assessment by combining the observed evidence with the criticality of the affected assets and the relevance of the mapped threats. In this scenario, the risk level increases when model-level adversarial indicators are accompanied by infrastructure-level suspicious activity, such as repeated probing, abnormal authentication attempts, or unusual service behaviour. The assessment also considers the importance of the affected AI service, the role of the deployed model in the pilot environment, and the possible consequences of an incorrect prediction. The result is expressed as a qualitative risk level, such as Minimal, Limited, High, or Critical, together with a mitigation priority. This allows RIMA to support the mSIEM in deciding whether the event should remain under observation, be escalated for investigation, or trigger a response workflow. In this way, AIH does not only classify the incident technically, but evaluates its operational relevance for the affected AI-enabled service.

After identifying the relevant threats and affected assets, AIH links the resulting asset-threat pairs with appropriate controls from the RIMA control catalogue. For this scenario, only the controls that directly address inference-time adversarial manipulation, production access control, runtime monitoring, telemetry logging, and infrastructure protection are selected. At the model layer, controls C4, C11, C16, C47, and C48 address adversarial input manipulation, model robustness, input validation, and runtime anomaly detection. At the service and infrastructure layer, controls C5, C20, and C52 support query restriction, authenticated access, and secure deployment of the AI-enabled service. Control C24 provides the telemetry needed to preserve the incident context and support forensic review (Fig. 4).

Table 4. Selected RIMA controls for the proposed attack scenario

Control ID	Control	Relevance to the scenario	Control type
C4	Model Hardening	Increases the robustness of the deployed model against adversarial inputs, for example through adversarial training or similar hardening techniques.	Preventive/Corrective
C5	Restrict Number of ML Model Queries	Limits repeated or automated querying of the model, reducing the effectiveness of probing and iterative adversarial input generation.	Preventive
C11	Input Restoration	Preprocesses inference-time inputs to reduce or reverse potential adversarial perturbations before they reach the model.	Preventive/Corrective
C16	Adversarial Input Detection	Detects and blocks adversarial inputs or atypical queries that deviate from known benign behaviour.	Preventive/Detective
C20	Control Access to ML Models and Data in Production	Requires authentication for production model access and supports monitoring of API usage to prevent misuse.	Preventive
C24	AI Telemetry Logging	Logs model inputs, outputs, and operational events, supporting detection, correlation, forensic analysis, and incident reconstruction.	Preventive/Detective
C47	Continuous Model Monitoring	Provides real-time surveillance of model performance, anomalies, drift, and possible adversarial behaviour.	Detective
C48	Secure Input Validation	Applies strict validation techniques to prevent adversarial or malformed inputs from compromising the AI model.	Detective
C52	Secure AI Infrastructure	Ensures end-to-end protection of the software, hardware, and cloud environment supporting the AI-enabled service.	Detective/Preventive

The output of RIMA/AIH includes the affected asset identifier, the asset category, the mapped threat category, the probability level, the impact level, the composite risk score, the qualitative risk level, the mitigation priority, the recommended controls, and provenance information. These outputs allow the incident to be enriched with risk semantics and support prioritisation, escalation, and analyst interpretation.

In the proposed workflow, an incident is treated as cross-layer when infrastructure-level evidence and model-level adversarial evidence refer to the same AI-enabled service, the same runtime environment, or temporally related activity affecting the same operational workflow. The correlation is strengthened when AIH reports high asset criticality, elevated probability, or high potential impact for the relevant asset-threat pairs. The resulting incident representation includes the original infrastructure alert, the adversarial detection event, the

RIMA asset-threat mapping, the probability and impact values, the computed risk score, the recommended controls, and the response actions initiated through the operational workflow.

Overall, RIMA contributes the risk-management semantics required to assess the severity and relevance of the adversarial incident. Its role is to connect observed evidence with AI-specific assets, threats, impacts, and controls, thereby transforming technical observations into a structured and prioritised risk assessment for the affected AI-enabled service.

3.3 Runtime Adversarial Evasion Detection Using AIPS Adversarial IDS

The Adversarial Intrusion Detection System is the sub-component of the AI-assisted Adversarial Intrusion Detection and Prevention system (AIPS) responsible for the detection of evasion attacks directed towards a target ML model.

Unlike traditional detection mechanism that track network or host-level anomalies, the Adversarial IDS operates independently by directly monitoring the inputs and the internal state of the ML models being protected, to identify subtle, well crafted perturbations tailored to force model misclassification at runtime, de facto by acting as a binary detector that assigns a label `real` or `adversarial`.

This requirement arises from the increased frequency of ML models being used to make safety-critical decisions. Specifically, evasion attacks are among the most practical methods an attacker can use to bypass the control enforced by an ML model.

To ensure robust threat recognition, the adversarial IDS can employ a dual inspection architecture, comprising an Input-based detector and an Activation-based detector.

The Input-based detector serves as the initial line of defence, evaluating the raw input feature vectors fed into the monitored model. Following methodologies that evaluate raw input feature vectors to intercept malicious perturbations [4], its goal is to assess whether the data exhibits signs of adversarial tampering.

The Activation-based detector, on the other hand, monitors the internal state of the target ML model. In particular, it tracks the activations values across hidden layers, looking for specific, abnormal stimulations of the network's neurons, which are triggered by malicious perturbations to the input.

While input-level detection is crucial, adversarial perturbations specifically aim to be almost imperceptible. But, as the adversarial input vector passes through the non-linear transformations of the neural network layers, the initial error is amplified. As a result, by the time the signal reaches the mid-to-late layers, the activation patterns for an adversarial input can deviate significantly from normal. Furthermore, the input space can be massive (e.g. images domains), making internal layers monitoring a potentially more compact and computationally efficient approach to anomaly detection.

Eventually, combining these two form of detection provides a complete view of all the factors involved in the context of the attack.

In the event that an attacker to a ML model is detected during its operational time, the framework issues precise alerts to the mSIEM component, detailing the presence of an adversarial manipulation attack taking place.

The alert is comprehensive of all the data which the mSIEM needs to infer as much information as possible about what is happening to the system at a given time of the operational timeline, such as the event timestamp, the actual detector responsible for the detection, and the information about the target model like its version and input, useful to successfully trace the history of threats, and inference impact that the attack had, highlighting the prediction that was inferred to the target model.

In addition, the AIPS synergizes with the mSIEM XAI component to resolve the intrinsic opacity of deep neural network monitoring. Following the ingestion of AIPS telemetry within the XAI service, comprehensive explainability profiles are constructed to differentiate standard operational noise and environmental drift from sophisticated adversarial intent or environmental anomalies. This structured interpretability facilitates profound forensic analysis, accurately steering analysts toward the root-cause evidence validating each diagnostic deduction or conclusion.

While RIMA is architected to be an offline, proactive framework engineered to assess risk across the entire lifecycle of AI systems, the Adversarial IDS is a specialized sub-module dedicated strictly to inference-time detection.

RIMA, and in particular its AIVAS sub-component for model vulnerability analysis, it's capable to examine the AI and ML models prior to operational deployment. Consequently, its temporal horizon is proactive, focused on vulnerability discovery before live exposure occurs.

Conversely, the Adversarial IDS functions strictly online, it is designed for continuous inspection in order to safeguard against runtime bypass attempts, showcasing a localized and reactive role.

Although RIMA framework provides a valuable and necessary quantified baseline for assessing and understanding the static risk exposure of a system, its inherent limitations become apparent when considering the dynamic nature of threats, particularly at runtime. RIMA's analysis is fundamentally based on pre-existing knowledge and trained data, which means it is inherently insufficient for the interception and mitigation of attacks that manifest during operational execution. Specifically, adversarial evasion attacks pose a significant problem: imperceptible perturbations to new input instances —those the model was not trained on— could be capable to bypass model decisions. These new, unconsidered points in the problem space highlight a failure that RIMA cannot address, making a runtime operational shield critically important.

By working together, the two component can establish a synergistic, bidirectional feedback that enhances the overall system security.

3.4 Risk-Aware Event Correlation and Incident Handling Through the cPAID mSIEM

The following subsection focuses on the role of the mSIEM in the proposed attack-handling workflow. While AIPS and the Risk Assessment component of RIMA act as external input providers, the mSIEM provides the operational layer that correlates their outputs with infrastructure telemetry collected from the pilot environment.

The cPAID Meta-Security Information and Event Management system (mSIEM) acts as the central operational and analytical layer of the proposed attack-handling workflow. Its role is to transform heterogeneous security evidence into a unified, explainable, and actionable incident representation. In the context of the proposed scenario, the mSIEM does not operate as an isolated SIEM instance, but as a cross-layer correlation mechanism that combines infrastructure-level telemetry, AI/model-level adversarial indicators, and risk assessment outputs. This allows adversarial AI events to be handled not only as isolated model anomalies, but as risk-aware cybersecurity incidents linked to the operational state and criticality of the affected AI-enabled service.

The mSIEM receives three main categories of input. First, infrastructure-level telemetry is generated within the pilot environment and collected by Wazuh agents deployed on monitored hosts, services, or systems. These agents operate outside the mSIEM boundary, as part of the pilot infrastructure, and forward logs, file-integrity events, authentication anomalies, process activity, network-related observations, and other security-relevant alerts to the Wazuh/SIEM component of the mSIEM. Second, AIPS provides adversarial AI detection events related to the protected machine-learning model, such as suspicious inference-time inputs, abnormal model-state behaviour, or indicators of evasion attempts. Third, the Risk Assessment component of RIMA provides contextual risk information for the affected AI asset, including its criticality, current risk level, estimated operational impact, and mitigation priority.

Within the mSIEM, these inputs are ingested, normalised, and enriched with metadata such as timestamp, source component, affected asset, severity, confidence, event type, evidence references, and provenance. The purpose of this common representation is to allow heterogeneous events to be analysed within a single operational context. For example, a Wazuh alert indicating suspicious activity on the host running an AI-enabled service can be correlated with an AIPS event indicating possible adversarial manipulation of the model input. When the same asset is associated with an elevated risk level according to the RIMA Risk Assessment output, the mSIEM increases the priority of the incident and treats it as a cross-layer adversarial security event rather than as a set of unrelated alerts.

The correlation engine of the mSIEM is responsible for linking these signals into a coherent incident narrative. A single attack may appear as several weak or partial indicators when observed independently: an unusual process execution, a sequence of failed authentication attempts, a spike in model inference requests, a deviation in input characteristics, or an elevated risk score for the affected AI asset. By correlating these signals through shared asset identifiers, temporal proximity, event type, severity, confidence, and risk context, the mSIEM produces a consolidated view of the attack. This risk-aware correlation supports more accurate prioritisation and reduces the likelihood that adversarial AI behaviour is treated as a low-level technical anomaly without operational significance.

Once an incident is correlated, the XAI subcomponent enriches the detection with interpretable reasoning. This step supports analyst understanding by exposing the features, behaviours, or event relationships that contributed to the anomaly or to the final prioritisation decision. In this way, XAI helps distinguish between benign operational drift, conventional infrastructure issues, and behaviour that is more likely to indicate adversarial intent. The resulting explanations are then exposed through the Forensics Visualization Toolkit (FVT), which provides the analyst-facing interface of the mSIEM. Through FVT, operators can inspect the incident timeline, review the originating Wazuh telemetry, examine the AIPS adversarial detection event, observe the associated RIMA risk context, and follow the correlation chain that led to the final incident classification.

The final stage of the mSIEM workflow concerns response and incident management. Based on the correlated severity and the risk context provided by RIMA, the mSIEM can trigger predefined playbooks or escalate the incident to the Ticketing System. Playbooks define structured and repeatable response actions, such as notifying responsible operators, increasing monitoring of the affected asset, isolating a suspicious endpoint, requesting manual validation of model behaviour, or initiating a controlled model review process. When coordination or human validation is required, the Ticketing System records the full incident context, including source alerts, affected assets, risk level, explanation outputs, response actions, and remediation status. This creates an auditable chain from detection to analysis and response.

In this workflow, the mSIEM operationalises the interaction between AIPS and the RIMA Risk Assessment component. AIPS provides runtime adversarial detection, while RIMA provides the risk context required to interpret and prioritise the incident. The mSIEM combines these inputs with telemetry originating from the pilot infrastructure and transforms them into explainable and actionable incidents. As a result, cPAID supports a continuous operational loop in which infrastructure monitoring, adversarial AI detection, risk assessment, explanation, visualisation, and response are handled within a unified incident-management process.

4 Conclusions

This paper presented the cPAID framework, an integrated approach for securing AI-enabled systems against adversarial and infrastructure-level threats. The proposed methodology combines secure AI engineering practices, runtime adversarial detection, risk-aware assessment, and explainable incident handling into a unified operational ecosystem for trustworthy and resilient AI deployments.

The presented attack-handling workflow demonstrated how cPAID correlates infrastructure telemetry, adversarial AI detection events, and contextual risk information to transform fragmented observations into explainable and actionable cybersecurity incidents. Within this process, AIPS provides runtime detection of adversarial manipulation attempts against machine-learning models, while RIMA contributes contextual risk evaluation and prioritisation. These inputs are implemented through the mSIEM, which supports cross-layer correlation, forensic analysis, explainability, and response orchestration.

In addition to runtime protection, the framework features MLprivSecOps principles and generative adversarial testing methods, as well as cyber-range validation environments, all geared toward continuous assurance throughout the AI lifecycle. Ontology-based risk modelling and interoperability mechanisms are implemented in parallel to ensure alignment with new regulatory and governance needs, such as EU AI Act and existing AI security frameworks.

In summary, cPAID takes the state of the art in the area of resilient, explainable, and risk-aware AI security further by embedding adversarial AI protection, operational monitoring and governance components in the same framework. Further validation of the technology at scale across diverse environments, as well as enhanced adaptive detection and further automation of incident response and risk management processes, are future priorities.

Acknowledgments. The project funded under Grant Agreement No. 101168407 is supported by the European Cybersecurity Competence Centre. Views and opinions expressed are however those of the author(s) only and do not necessarily reflect those of the European Union or European Cybersecurity Competence Centre. Neither the European Union nor the granting authority can be held responsible for them.

Funded by the European Union

ECCC EUROPEAN CYBERSECURITY COMPETENCE CENTRE

Disclosure of Interests. The authors have no competing interests to declare that are relevant to the content of this article.

References

1. Alfred, R.: The rise of machine learning for big data analytics. In: 2016 2nd International Conference on Science in Information Technology (ICSITech), vol. 26, pp. 2016–2027. IEEE (2016)
2. Baniecki, H., Biecek, P.: Adversarial attacks and defenses in explainable artificial intelligence: a survey. Inf. Fusion **107**, 102303 (2024). https://doi.org/10.1016/j.inffus.2024.102303

3. Biggio, B., Roli, F.: Wild patterns: Ten years after the rise of adversarial machine learning. In: Proceedings of the 2018 ACM SIGSAC Conference on Computer and Communications Security, pp. 2154–2156 (2018)
4. Finocchi, Marseglia, C.R.R.B.: Toward a combined view of intrusion and evasion: an adversary-aware ids (2026)
5. Hendrycks, D., Mazeika, M., Woodside, T.: An overview of catastrophic ai risks. arXiv preprint arXiv:2306.12001 (2023)
6. Huang, L., Joseph, A.D., Nelson, B., Rubinstein, B.I., Tygar, J.D.: Adversarial machine learning. In: Proceedings of the 4th ACM Workshop on Security and Artificial Intelligence, pp. 43–58 (2011)
7. Kumar, R.S.S., et al.: Adversarial machine learning-industry perspectives. In: 2020 IEEE Security and Privacy Workshops (SPW), pp. 69–75. IEEE (2020)
8. Kurakin, A., Goodfellow, I., Bengio, S.: Adversarial machine learning at scale. arXiv preprint arXiv:1611.01236 (2016)
9. Azure, M.: Counterfit: an automation layer for assessing the security of machine learning systems (2021)
10. Momcilovic, T.B., Buesser, B., Zizzo, G., Purcell, M., Balta, D.: Towards assuring eu ai act compliance and adversarial robustness of llms (2024). https://arxiv.org/abs/2410.05306
11. Morris, J.X., Lifland, E., Yoo, J.Y., Grigsby, J., Jin, D., Qi, Y.: TextAttack: a framework for adversarial attacks, data augmentation, and adversarial training in NLP. In: Proceedings of the 2020 Conference on Empirical Methods in Natural Language Processing: System Demonstrations, pp. 119–126. ACL (2020). https://doi.org/10.18653/v1/2020.emnlp-demos.16, https://aclweb.org
12. Papernot, N., et al.: Technical report on the CleverHans v2.1.0 library for adversarial machine learning. arXiv preprint arXiv:1610.00768 (2018), https://arxiv.org
13. Pelekis, S., et al.: Adversarial machine learning: a review of methods, tools, and critical industry sectors. Artif. Intell. Rev. **58**(226), (2025). https://doi.org/10.1007/s10462-025-11147-4
14. Qiao, Y., Sathyanarayana, N.B., Shi, C., He, Z., Wang, T., Hou, T.: A survey on adversarial machine learning: attacks, defenses, real-world applications, and future research directions. Neurocomputing **671**, 132670 (2026). https://doi.org/10.1016/j.neucom.2026.132670
15. Rauber, J., Zimmermann, R., Bethge, M., Brendel, W.: Foolbox native: fast adversarial attacks to benchmark the robustness of machine learning models in PyTorch, TensorFlow, and JAX. J. Open Source Softw. **5**(53), 2607 (2020). https://doi.org/10.21105/joss.02607
16. Tang, Q., Qian, J., Du, X., Wang, S., Liu, H.: Advancing adversarial and LLM robustness in trustworthy AI: a comprehensive survey. Artif. Intell. Rev. (2026). https://doi.org/10.1007/s10462-026-11558-x, published online: 07 April 2026
17. The Linux Foundation AI & Data Foundation: Adversarial robustness toolbox (art). https://github.com/trusted-ai/adversarial-robustness-toolbox (2025), originally developed by IBM Research. Accessed 12 May 2026

Privacy by Design in AI-Assisted Cybersecurity Policy Generation: Benchmarking Private RAG Against Frontier AI Models

Davide Carboni and Marcello Verona(✉)

The Lisbon Council, Brussels, Belgium
marcello.verona@lisboncouncil.net

Abstract. The NIS 2 Directive and GDPR impose on regulated EU organisations a growing policy compliance gap: the obligation to produce context-specific cybersecurity policy artefacts has outpaced internal capacity to create them. Large language models offer scalable assistance, but effective policy generation requires routing sensitive organisational data through an inference pipeline. Under GDPR Arts. 28, 32, and 44–49, this creates a structural tension: the data required to generate a useful policy is precisely the data that cannot be processed without adequate legal safeguards.

We present a controlled empirical benchmark comparing six AI configurations spanning the design space from unaugmented frontier chat to privacy-by-design private RAG. Sixty policy artefacts were generated across two regulated contexts—a fictitious Italian public hospital and a fictitious NATO detachment, constructed as representative synthetic profiles with no connection to real entities—and five policy types, then evaluated by an LLM-as-judge pipeline using a seven-criterion rubric derived from the Anthropic agent evaluation framework and extended with three cybersecurity compliance dimensions.

The best frontier configuration (gpt-5.5 + web search) achieves a mean score of 4.60/5; the private RAG configuration (Kimi K2.5 on EU-resident infrastructure under a DPA) scores 4.15/5—a 9 % gap. The OpenAI Assistants RAG configuration falls below the no-RAG baseline (3.70 vs. 3.83), suggesting that cloud-hosted RAG does not automatically improve output quality. A backbone ablation (10/0 pairwise comparisons, Kimi K2.5 over DeepSeek V3.2) isolates normative citation discipline as the decisive differentiator. Under the EC Cloud Sovereignty Framework, the private RAG architecture classifies at SEAL-2; frontier configurations qualify at SEAL-0. The 9 % quality gap is identified as the operational cost of regulatory-grade data sovereignty.

Keywords: cybersecurity policy generation · large language models · retrieval-augmented generation · data sovereignty · privacy-preserving AI · LLM evaluation

P. Kieseberg et al. (Eds.): ARES 2026 Workshops, LNCS 16903, pp. 135–148, 2027.
https://doi.org/10.1007/978-3-032-37218-5_9

1 Introduction

The NIS2 Directive [7] extends mandatory cybersecurity obligations to over 160,000 organisations across the EU—healthcare, energy, transport, public administration, defence supply chains—many of which previously operated without formal information security policies. Combined with GDPR [6] and the AI Act [8], regulated organisations now face a growing policy compliance gap: the legal requirement to produce, maintain, and audit cybersecurity policy artefacts has outpaced the internal capacity to create them. The burden falls hardest on resource-constrained organisations—a regional hospital with a single IT manager, a small NATO support unit without a dedicated CISO—for which producing context-specific, regulation-aligned policies from scratch represents a prohibitive cost in both expertise and time.

Frontier AI models offer a compelling response: scalable, on-demand access to expertise that would otherwise require external consultants. The effectiveness of AI-assisted policy generation has begun to be validated [10,13]. Yet effective policy generation is not a one-shot task. A policy that does not reflect the organisation's actual asset inventory, threat model, regulatory regime, and operational constraints is at best a template and at worst a compliance artefact that conveys false assurance. Context-elicitation—a structured dialogue that gathers organisational specifics before drafting—is therefore essential to output quality.

Here lies a fundamental tension. The data required to generate a useful policy is by definition sensitive: organisational structure, known vulnerabilities, gap analyses, incident history, cloud footprint. Under GDPR Arts 28, 32, and 44–49 [6], organisations in regulated sectors cannot route this data through processors without an adequate Data Processing Agreement (DPA), let alone across extra-EU boundaries without a transfer mechanism. A healthcare provider generating its data protection policy through a consumer-tier frontier assistant is, structurally, already in violation of the regime the policy is meant to implement. The industry has responded with two patterns: cloud RAG on proprietary providers (OpenAI Assistants, Azure OpenAI)—which improves grounding but does not address EU data residency, open-weight portability, or DPA; and private RAG on EU-resident open-weight models—which addresses all three. Yet no prior study evaluates output quality and privacy compliance of the underlying inference architecture simultaneously under the same evaluation rubric. Figure 1 illustrates the three architectural patterns and their respective EU data perimeters.

Research Question: *Does a well-architected private RAG system (EU-region + DPA + open-weight) produce cybersecurity policies of comparable or superior quality to frontier AI models, while remaining consistent with GDPR data-processing obligations by design?*

We address this question by contributing: (i) an empirical benchmark comparing six AI configurations on 60 policy generation tasks in two regulated contexts; (ii) a controlled pairwise ablation for backbone selection within the same

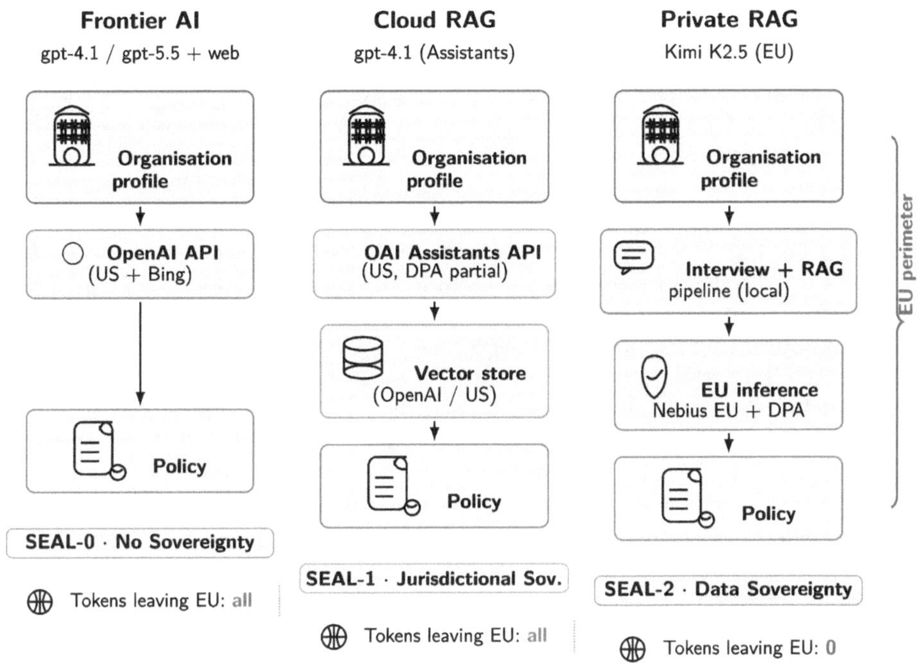

Fig. 1. The three architectural patterns benchmarked in this study. The green bracket in the Private RAG column indicates that no data leaves the EU perimeter. SEAL levels follow the EC Cloud Sovereignty Framework [5] (Color figure online).

RAG architecture; and (iii) a joint quality-and-privacy evaluation framework applicable to regulated deployment contexts.

2 Related Work

LLM-based cybersecurity policy generation is an emerging area. McIntosh et al. [13] demonstrated that GPT-4 can generate GRC policies that outperform human-written ones in certain ransomware mitigation contexts; the study relies on human moderation and legal expert oversight throughout—an implicit acknowledgement that data handling risks are unresolved. Jawhar et al. [10] similarly demonstrate AI effectiveness for security policy and procedure drafting without addressing GDPR or data residency constraints. In both cases, quality is assessed informally without a replicable evaluation rubric, and no privacy-compliant architecture is tested.

LLM-as-judge methodology provides the evaluation backbone for our study [1]. Zheng et al. [16] demonstrate that GPT-4 as a judge reaches over 80% agreement with human experts on instruction-following tasks; positional and verbosity biases can be partially mitigated by swapping answer positions and using chain-of-thought prompting. Liu et al. [12] introduce G-Eval, a form-filling framework with probability-weighted scoring that correlates more strongly with human judgement than string-overlap metrics. Human calibration of automated rubrics is typically quantified via Cohen's κ; Dubois et al. [3] provide a methodological baseline for this calibration step in the context of preference evaluation.

The deployment of AI for cybersecurity policy generation in regulated organisations raises privacy constraints that go beyond GDPR surface compliance. Two distinct properties must be distinguished: *data residency*—the physical location of storage and processing, including logs, backups, and telemetry—and *data sovereignty*—the legal jurisdiction governing the provider and its sub-processor chain [2,6]. A provider incorporated outside the EU may retain legal exposure even when operating EU-located servers: the US Clarifying Lawful Overseas Use of Data Act (CLOUD Act) [15] permits US authorities to compel disclosure of data held by US-incorporated entities regardless of physical location. An additional risk vector is the sub-processor chain: a provider with EU legal domicile may add an extra-EU sub-processor unilaterally, extending the exposure perimeter without customer notification [6]. Existing benchmarks of AI-assisted cybersecurity policy generation [10,13] evaluate output quality in isolation; to our knowledge, no prior work simultaneously evaluates output quality and the privacy compliance of the underlying inference architecture within a unified framework.

3 Methodology

3.1 Experimental Design

The study adopts a two-phase design. In the first phase, a backbone selection experiment compares two open-weight models running on an identical private RAG architecture, in order to select the stronger candidate before the full benchmark. In the second phase, the selected private RAG configuration is benchmarked against four frontier AI configurations spanning the design space from unaugmented chat to cloud-hosted RAG.

All policy artefacts are generated from synthetic organisational profiles designed to represent typical regulated-sector environments (see Sect. 4). The use of synthetic data allows full control over the experimental conditions and avoids any real data privacy concern in the evaluation pipeline itself.

3.2 Policy Generation

Each artefact is produced through a single prompt containing the full organisational profile, eliciting the policy in one response (*rapid-policy* mode). The online deployment of PolicyCoach gathers the same profile through a 6–8-turn adaptive interview before generating the policy; for the benchmark, the interview output is rendered once per context from a structured YAML, equalising the input across all six configurations and isolating the policy-generation step as the single variable under test. The private RAG configurations augment this generation with retrieval from a curated knowledge base of 837 chunks drawn from NIST CSF 2.0, ISO/IEC 27001:2022, GDPR, NIS2, the AI Act, and sector-specific guidance for healthcare and defence. Frontier configurations either use no augmentation or rely on live web search.

3.3 Evaluation Framework

Each artefact is evaluated by an LLM-as-judge pipeline using Claude Opus 4.7 as the scoring model, following the structured grader blueprint described in [1]. The judge receives three inputs: the generated policy, the synthetic organisational profile used during generation, and a detailed scoring rubric. It returns a score from 1 to 5 on each of seven quality dimensions (see Sect. 4.3), accompanied by a brief scoring rationale.

The judge is invoked once per (artefact, criterion) pair with temperature 0.0, scoring one dimension at a time to prevent cross-criterion anchoring. The judge receives no configuration label or model identifier, eliminating self-preference and provenance-based bias in scoring. Following the Anthropic "escape valve" principle [1], the judge returns *insufficient_evidence* (null) rather than guess when a criterion has no observable signal in the policy; null scores are excluded from per-configuration means. In our benchmark this occurred 5 times across 350 artefact–criterion evaluations (1.4 %), predominantly on the *Resource consideration* dimension.

The rubric combines objective checks—for example, presence of specific regulatory citations or mandatory policy clauses—with holistic LLM-scored assessments of coherence and contextual fit. This two-layer structure reduces sensitivity to surface variation while preserving sensitivity to substantive quality differences. To validate the rubric, two rounds of human calibration were conducted. The first round was carried out by experts with ISO/IEC 27001 knowledge, scoring Password Policy artefacts representing opposite ends of the quality spectrum (judge mean 4.71/5 vs. 2.43/5) on all seven criteria, yielding Cohen's weighted $\kappa_w = 0.65$ (*substantial agreement*, Landis and Koch [11]). A second, post-submission round extended the calibration with three external raters from two COcyber Advisory Board organisations (GuardedBox, ES; Universidad Internacional de La Rioja, ES), scoring two policy pairs (Password and Incident Response) drawn from the same calibration bundles. Pooled across the 37 criterion–artefact pairs with non-missing human scores, the extended calibration yields $\kappa_w = 0.28$ (*fair agreement*). Rank ordering was fully preserved across all three rater–bundle combinations (binary rank-ordering $\kappa = 1.0$): every rater assigned a higher mean score to the frontier-model output than to the private-RAG output. A noteworthy pattern emerged on C4 (*Implementability*) and C7 (*Resource consideration*), where one rater panel assigned higher scores to the private-RAG output, attributing this to the frontier model's verbosity being potentially excessive for a non-specialised hospital manager—a practically relevant dimension that the LLM judge does not fully capture. The lower κ_w in the extended round, compared with the initial calibration, reflects the broader diversity of rater backgrounds and calibration lenses (compliance expertise vs.

operational practitioner perspective); the rank-ordering result confirms that the judge's core comparative signal is robust.

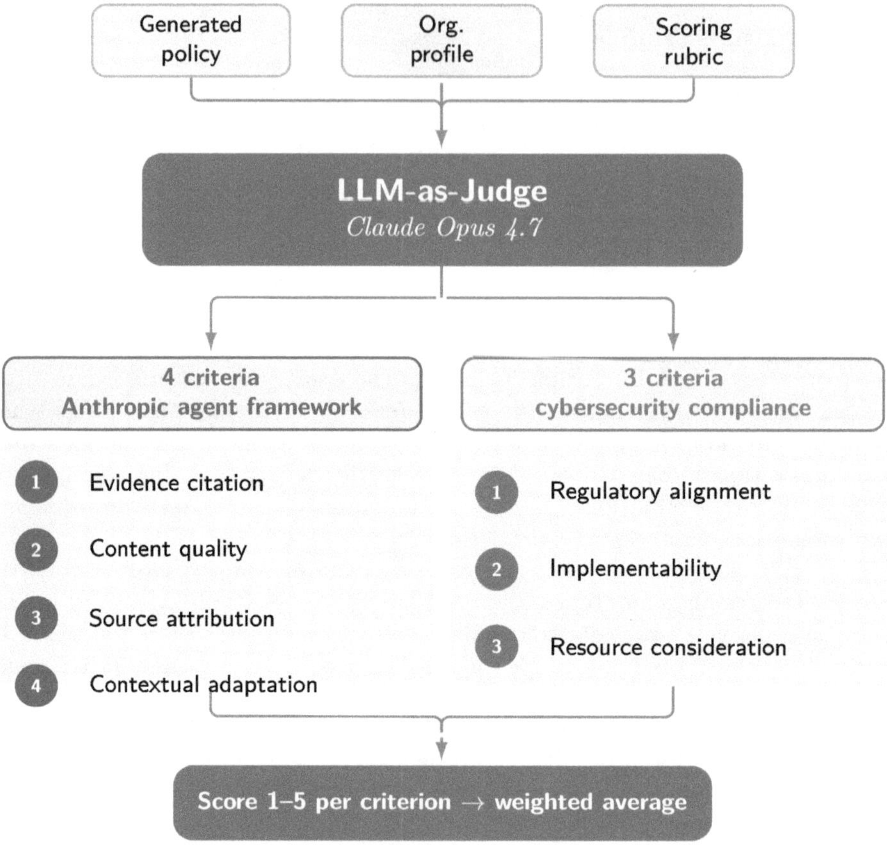

Fig. 2. LLM-as-judge evaluation pipeline. Four criteria are mapped from the Anthropic research agent grading framework [1]; three are added for the cybersecurity compliance domain.

Rubric Design Rationale. The seven dimensions were derived in two steps. First, we mapped the grading dimensions proposed by Anthropic for research agents [1]—groundedness of claims against sources, coverage of key facts, source quality, and coherence of synthesis—onto the policy generation task, yielding *Evidence citation*, *Content quality*, *Source attribution*, and *Contextual adaptation* respectively. Second, we extended the rubric with three dimensions specific to the cybersecurity compliance domain: *Regulatory alignment* (coverage of applicable regulatory obligations, absent in generic agent evals); *Implementability* (actionability under real operational constraints); and *Resource consideration* (fitness for SME and public-sector organisations where budget and staffing are primary constraints). The extended rubric is publicly available with the evaluation code. Figure 2 summarises the evaluation pipeline and the derivation of the seven criteria.

4 Experimental Setup

4.1 Configurations

We compared six configurations spanning the design space from consumer-tier AI chat to privacy-compliant private RAG (Table 1).

Table 1. Experimental configurations. GDPR compliance denotes the ability to operate under GDPR Art. 28 (DPA), Art. 32 (security measures), and Art. 44–49 (third-country transfers) as assessed from available provider documentation. † OpenAI Assistants API provides a DPA for API customers but does not guarantee EU data residency; data may be processed under SCCs outside the EU. ‡ SEAL-2 per-objective assessment: Table 3.

Model	Knowledge Base	Web	Provider	GDPR
gpt-4.1	–	–	OpenAI consumer	×
gpt-4.1 + web search	–	✔	OpenAI + Bing	×
gpt-5.5 + web search	–	✔	OpenAI + Bing	×
gpt-4.1 (OpenAI Assistants RAG)	✔	–	OpenAI Assistants	partial†
Kimi K2.5 (private RAG)	✔	–	Nebius EU + DPA	✔‡
DeepSeek V3.2 (private RAG)	✔	–	Nebius EU + DPA	✔

The first four configurations offer no EU data residency guarantee. The private RAG configurations (Kimi K2.5 and DeepSeek V3.2) are privacy-by-design: all inference runs within a Nebius EU region under a DPA, using open-weight models whose weights can be independently audited.

4.2 Backbone Selection

Before the full benchmark, we compared Kimi K2.5 and DeepSeek V3.2 under strictly identical conditions—same curated KB, identical system prompt, same EU-region provider (Nebius), and no model-specific prompt tuning. This controlled ablation isolates the backbone model as the sole variable, ruling out architecture or prompt design as confounds.

4.3 Evaluation Contexts and Policy Types

Each configuration was tested across two regulated contexts: **ctx-H** (a small Italian public hospital, ≈200 staff, subject to Italian healthcare regulations, NIS2, and GDPR) and **ctx-M** (a NATO detachment in Romania, subject to NATO information security policy). Both are *fictitious* organisational profiles constructed to be representative of their respective sectors; no data from real entities was used at any stage of the study. Five policy types were generated per context: Password Policy, Data Protection Policy, Access Control Policy, Incident Response Policy, and General Cybersecurity Policy, yielding 60 artefacts in total.

Each artefact was evaluated on seven quality dimensions (Sect. 3.3) with 1–5 Likert anchors:

1. **Content quality:** accuracy and completeness of cybersecurity controls
2. **Contextual adaptation:** fit to the specific organisational context
3. **Evidence citation:** grounding in standards and regulatory sources
4. **Implementability:** actionability and practical feasibility
5. **Regulatory alignment:** coverage of applicable compliance requirements
6. **Source attribution:** traceable references to cited sources
7. **Resource consideration:** acknowledgement of organisational resource constraints

5 Results

5.1 Backbone Selection: Kimi K2.5 vs. DeepSeek V3.2

The pairwise judge returned 10/10 comparisons in favour of Kimi K2.5 over DeepSeek V3.2. Both models ran on the same private RAG architecture with identical system prompt and KB; the result is attributable solely to the models' differential ability to follow structured citation directives. The gap is concentrated on normative traceability: source attribution (4.10 vs. 2.30, $\Delta = 1.80$) and regulatory alignment (4.20 vs. 2.90, $\Delta = 1.30$). Implementability is the sole dimension where the models converge ($\Delta = 0.60$, 3 ties). Kimi K2.5 was selected as the private RAG backbone for the full benchmark.

The pairwise outcome is consistent with the full-benchmark scoring: across the same matched set of ten artefacts per configuration, DeepSeek V3.2 averaged 3.12/5 versus Kimi K2.5's 4.15/5—a 1.03-point gap, larger than the 0.45-point gap between Kimi K2.5 and the best frontier configuration (gpt-5.5 + web; cf. Table 2). The backbone-selection step is therefore methodologically necessary: the choice of open-weight backbone contributes more to output quality than the choice between the selected private RAG and the best frontier system. The gap reflects two distinct mechanisms. The first is the systematic deficit in normative traceability already reported above. The second is a generation-robustness failure observed on one DeepSeek artefact, in which a token-repetition loop iterated the string "Govern" throughout the NIST CSF compliance section, rendering that portion of the policy unusable; Kimi K2.5 produced no comparable failures across the matched set. Generation robustness under structured policy prompts is itself a legitimate selection criterion for a production private RAG backbone and is reported here alongside the quality gap.

5.2 Quality Scores Across Configurations

Table 2 reports mean scores across all ten artefacts per configuration (two contexts × five policy types), with per-configuration standard deviation in the row below. gpt-5.5 + web search achieves the highest average (4.60, SD 0.82), followed by Kimi K2.5 private RAG (4.15, SD 0.94) and gpt-4.1 + web search (3.90, SD 0.89). The OpenAI Assistants RAG configuration falls below the no-RAG gpt-4.1 baseline on the overall average (Fig. 3).

Table 2. Mean quality scores by configuration (1–5 Likert scale). Bold: highest value per row. DeepSeek V3.2 was eliminated after backbone selection (Section 5.1) and is not included here. Cost estimates based on average token counts from generation logs and API list prices (May 2026). Latency: median wall-clock time, client-side. * gpt-5.5 cost reflects token usage at OpenAI short-context list prices ($5.00 / $30.00 per 1M input/output) and does not include web_search_preview tool fees, which add an estimated $0.30 per query (12.4 calls per query at typical tool pricing) bringing the all-in cost to ~$1.08 per query. Kimi K2.5 cost computed from Nebius list prices ($0.50 / $2.50 per 1M input/output) and average token usage of 25.5K input and 6.5K output per query.

Dimension	gpt-4.1	gpt-4.1+web	**gpt-5.5**+web	gpt-4.1(Asst.)	**Kimi** K2.5
Content quality	4.10	4.00	**5.00**	4.00	4.60
Contextual adaptation	4.60	4.40	**5.00**	4.50	**5.00**
Evidence citation	3.60	4.00	**5.00**	3.80	4.10
Implementability	4.20	4.50	**4.60**	4.10	4.20
Regulatory alignment	3.90	3.90	**4.90**	4.10	4.20
Source attribution	4.20	4.50	**4.50**	3.80	4.10
Resource consideration	2.00	2.00	**3.20**	1.60	**2.50**
Average	3.83	3.90	**4.60**	3.70	**4.15**
Std. dev.	0.91	0.89	0.82	1.01	0.94
Cost / query (USD)	~0.02	~0.03	~0.77*	~0.07	~0.03
Latency (s)	33	30	278	41	36
Tokens leaving EU	all	all	all	all	**0**

6 Discussion

6.1 Backbone Selection Within the Same RAG Architecture

The 10/0 pairwise result and the per-dimension gap analysis establish that, under equal conditions, Kimi K2.5 substantially outperforms DeepSeek V3.2

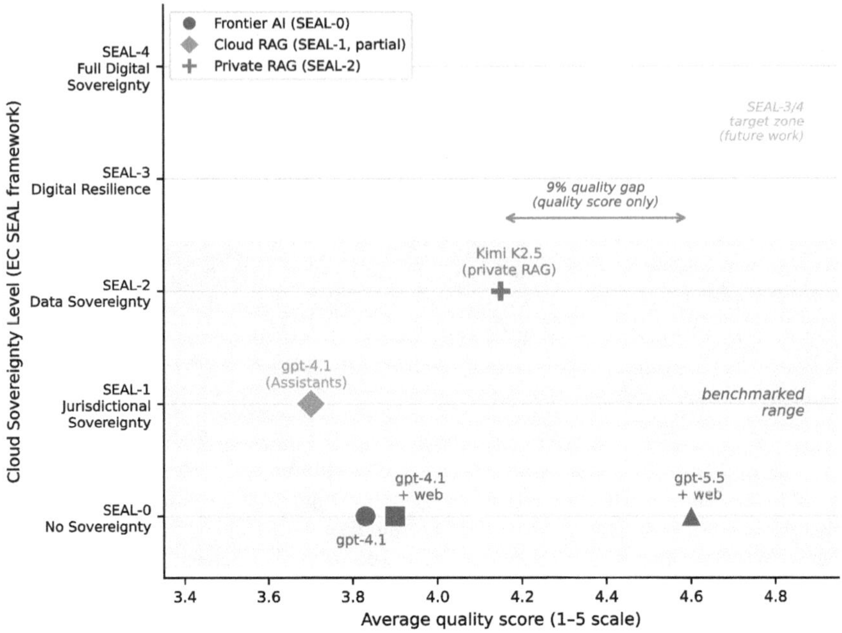

Fig. 3. Quality vs. privacy posture for the five benchmarked configurations. The 9% quality gap between the best frontier configuration (gpt-5.5 + web, avg. 4.60) and the private RAG configuration (Kimi K2.5, avg. 4.15) corresponds to a jump from SEAL-0 to SEAL-2 compliance.

on dimensions requiring normative traceability. The concentration of the gap on source attribution ($\Delta = 1.80$) and regulatory alignment ($\Delta = 1.30$) suggests that the two models differ in their ability to follow structured citation directives—a finding that is independent of prompt design, since both models received identical instructions. Implementability ($\Delta = 0.60$, 3 ties) is the sole dimension where the models converge, suggesting that general instruction-following is comparable but domain-specific citation discipline is not.

A natural question is why the backbone selection did not include Mistral Large, the most capable EU-origin open-weight model at the time of the experiments. Mistral was considered as a third candidate: preliminary pilot scoring on the 7-criterion rubric placed it below both Kimi K2.5 and DeepSeek V3.2, and it was therefore not advanced to the full benchmark. We report this transparently: the choice of benchmarking the best-performing open-weight backbone available, rather than the most sovereignty-compliant one, leaves the EU-origin sovereignty–quality trade-off (the SEAL-3 path discussed in Sect. 4 and Sect. 7) empirically uncharacterised. Sovereignty and quality are orthogonal dimensions; the paper quantifies both separately, and the path from SEAL-2 to SEAL-3 via a Mistral-based backbone is identified as future work precisely because it carries a quality cost that has not yet been measured under the present rubric.

6.2 Frontier Benchmark Interpretation

The 9% quality gap between the best frontier configuration (gpt-5.5 + web search, avg. 4.60) and the private RAG configuration (Kimi K2.5, avg. 4.15) is concentrated in ctx-H, where the Italian regulatory web corpus is rich and live web search provides substantive grounding. The gap halves in ctx-M (NATO classified), precisely the context where privacy posture matters most and where web search offers the least domain-specific value.

The apparent advantage of gpt-5.5 + web search must be discounted by three caveats: two processors without DPA (OpenAI and Bing), more than 25× higher cost (token-only; ~35× including web search tool fees), 7× higher latency, and citations drawn from blogs and vendor whitepapers rather than institutional sources. The audit trail of a private RAG with a curated KB is deterministic and reproducible; the audit trail of a frontier model with live web search is neither.

7 Conclusion

For regulated organisations the question is not "which model writes the best policy" but "which architecture produces adequate policies under the constraint that no data shall leave the perimeter." A private RAG on EU-resident open-weight models is today a technically competitive option: it achieves 90% of frontier quality at one-tenth the cost, with full GDPR compliance and a deterministic audit trail. The marginal quality gain offered by frontier AI models does not justify the privacy cost they impose.

A further open question concerns the relative weight of two distinct privacy properties: *legal domicile* of the provider versus *physical residency* of the data. A provider legally incorporated in the EU but operating sub-processors outside the EU may, in practice, offer weaker GDPR protection than an EU-domiciled provider with a clean sub-processor chain, even if the latter is less well-known. Conversely, a non-EU provider (e.g., subject to the US CLOUD Act) that operates servers exclusively in an EU region may offer strong data residency guarantees while remaining legally exposed to extra-EU compelled disclosure. Our experimental setup treats GDPR compliance as a binary dimension assessed from published provider documentation; a more nuanced analysis should evaluate the full sub-processor chain and the legal jurisdiction of each entity in the inference path. We leave this as a direction for future work.

These considerations are acquiring regulatory urgency. In April 2026 the European Commission awarded its first procurement contract under the Cloud Sovereignty Framework [5], which defines five Sovereignty Effectiveness Assurance Levels (SEAL-0 to SEAL-4) and sets SEAL-2 as the minimum threshold for EU institutional procurement. Under this framework, frontier AI providers incorporated outside the EU qualify at SEAL-0 at best, regardless of server location; all four winning consortia are EU-incorporated. The private RAG architecture evaluated in this paper—EU-resident open-weight models under a DPA with an EU-incorporated provider—aligns structurally with SEAL-2 requirements, making the 9% quality gap relative to the best frontier configuration the operational cost of regulatory-grade sovereignty. The adequacy basis underpinning US transfers, the EU–US Data Privacy Framework [4], meanwhile faces continued uncertainty: the General Court upheld it in September 2025 [9], but the case is on appeal before the CJEU, and the temporary loss of quorum of the Privacy and Civil Liberties Oversight Board—a structural redress pillar of the framework—illustrates the fragility of building long-term GDPR compliance on executive-dependent mechanisms. The GDPR and the CLOUD Act are therefore in structural, not episodic, conflict [2,15]: two sovereign legal orders asserting concurrent jurisdiction over the same data. The Cloud Sovereignty Framework [5] represents the first objective metric for distinguishing verifiable legal sovereignty from superficial geographic residency claims. For AI-assisted policy generation in regulated EU contexts, a provider's SEAL level is a criterion complementary to, and arguably more discriminating than, ISO/IEC 27001 certification or server location alone. Table 3 disaggregates this claim by sovereignty objective, providing per-dimension evidence for the SEAL-2 alignment assessment of the private RAG configuration evaluated in this paper.

Table 3. Per-objective sovereignty assessment for the private RAG configuration (Kimi K2.5 on Nebius EU). Objectives and SEAL levels follow the EC Cloud Sovereignty Framework v1.2.1 [5].

SOV	Dimension	Assessment	SEAL
SOV-1	Strategic	EU-based AI infrastructure (NL), NASDAQ-listed; partial EU ecosystem anchoring	SEAL-2
SOV-2	Legal/Juris.	EU-incorporated provider; no CLOUD Act exposure; Moonshot AI (CN) raises Chinese Cybersecurity Law question at model layer	SEAL-2
SOV-3	Data & AI	Data confined to EU; open-weight model auditable; training origin outside EU (Moonshot AI)	SEAL-2
SOV-4	Operational	Open-weight portability enables EU-operated self-hosting; residual Nebius API dependency	SEAL-2/3
SOV-5	Supply Chain	NVIDIA hardware (US); Kimi K2.5 weights (CN); material non-EU supply chain	SEAL-1/2
SOV-6	Technology	Open-weight licence; auditable weights; standard APIs	SEAL-2/3
SOV-7	Security	GDPR Art. 28 DPA; NIS2-aligned; EU certification status of Nebius unverified	SEAL-2
SOV-8	Environmental	Out of scope for this study	—

Across assessed dimensions, the configuration demonstrates SEAL-2 alignment consistently, in line with the framework definition: *EU law applicable and enforceable, with material non-EU dependencies remaining* [5]. The principal non-EU dependencies are the model supply chain (Moonshot AI, CN) and hardware (NVIDIA, US); both qualify as material rather than marginal, precluding SEAL-3 under the current architecture.

Several limitations bound the scope of this study. First, the benchmark covers only two synthetic organisational contexts (Italian public hospital and NATO detachment) and five policy types; broader coverage across sectors, jurisdictions, and real-world organisations is needed before general conclusions can be drawn. Second, evaluation relies on a single LLM judge (Claude Opus 4.7); no formal significance testing was performed, and results constitute descriptive comparative evidence rather than statistically warranted claims. Cross-validation against a second judge model is left as future work. Third, human calibration yields $\kappa_w = 0.65$ in the initial round and $\kappa_w = 0.28$ in the extended external round; the lower value in the extended round reflects diverse rater backgrounds rather than judge unreliability, as rank ordering was fully preserved ($\kappa = 1.0$). No validation by operational CISOs or legal experts was performed; such practitioner review would strengthen the practical validity of the conclusions. Fourth, sovereignty and GDPR conclusions are assessed from provider-published documentation and contractual commitments, not from independent technical audit of sub-processor chains or legal jurisdiction—a more rigorous evaluation should verify the full legal exposure of each entity in the inference path. Fifth, cost estimates for gpt-5.5 + web search are preliminary pending stable API pricing.

A natural next step is to characterise the path from the current SEAL-2 private RAG architecture to SEAL-3. The binding constraint is the model backbone: Kimi K2.5 is developed by Moonshot AI (China) and its weights depend on an entity subject to the Chinese National Intelligence Law, creating a residual non-EU supply-chain dependency. A SEAL-3 configuration would require replacing the backbone with an EU-origin model—Mistral being the most mature candidate—deployed on SEAL-3-certified infrastructure (OVHcloud, STACKIT, or Scaleway), together with a locally hosted embedding model to remove the remaining Nebius API call from the retrieval pipeline. Notably, this requirement is not satisfied by Mistral's primary commercial channels: API access via Microsoft Azure—Mistral's strategic distribution partner since 2024 [14]—is subject to CLOUD Act extraterritorial reach, whilst Mistral's own managed platform (la.plateforme.ai) does not carry explicit SEAL-3 certification under the EC Cloud Sovereignty Framework [5]. EU-origin model selection and SEAL-3-certified deployment infrastructure are therefore orthogonal requirements that must both be satisfied independently. Whether this full architectural upgrade preserves the observed quality level relative to frontier systems is an open empirical question.

Experimental code and generated policy artefacts are available at https://github.com/lisboncouncil/cocyber-policycoach to support reproducibility.

Acknowledgements. This work has been carried out within the COcyber project (*Coordination Between the Cybersecurity Civilian and Defence Spheres*), which has received funding from the European Union's Digital Europe Programme (DIGITAL) under Grant Agreement No. 101158606 (Call DIGITAL-ECCC-2023-DEPLOY-CYBER-04).

Views and opinions expressed are however those of the author(s) only and do not necessarily reflect those of the European Union or the European Cybersecurity Competence Centre (ECCC). Neither the European Union nor the granting authority can be held responsible for them.

Disclosure of Interests. The authors have no competing interests to declare that are relevant to the content of this article.

References

1. Anthropic: Demystifying evals for AI agents. Anthropic Engineering Blog (2024). https://www.anthropic.com/engineering/demystifying-evals-for-ai-agents. Accessed May 2026
2. Court of Justice of the European Union: Data Protection Commissioner v. Facebook Ireland Ltd and Maximillian Schrems. Case C-311/18, ECLI:EU:C:2020:559 (2020)
3. Dubois, Y., et al.: AlpacaFarm: a simulation framework for methods that learn from human feedback. In: Advances in Neural Information Processing Systems. vol. 36 (2023)
4. European Commission: Commission implementing decision (EU) 2023/1795 on the adequate level of protection of personal data under the EU-US data privacy framework. Off. J. Eur. Union (2023). L 231/118
5. European Commission: Cloud sovereignty framework (SEAL): Commission advances cloud sovereignty through strategic procurement. Press release, 17 April 2026 (2026). https://commission.europa.eu/news-and-media/news/commission-advances-cloud-sovereignty-through-strategic-procurement-2026-04-17_en
6. European Parliament and Council of the European Union: Regulation (EU) 2016/679 on the protection of natural persons with regard to the processing of personal data (GDPR). Regulation. Off. J. Eur. Union, (2016)
7. European Parliament and Council of the European Union: Directive (EU) 2022/2555 on measures for a high common level of cybersecurity across the union (NIS2). Directive. Off. J. Eur. Union (2022)
8. European Parliament and Council of the European Union: Regulation (EU) 2024/1689 laying down harmonised rules on artificial intelligence (AI act). Regulation, Official Journal of the European Union (2024)
9. General Court of the European Union: Latombe v. Commission, Case T-553/23. Judgment of 3 September 2025 (2025). appeal pending before the CJEU
10. Jawhar, S., Miller, J.R., Bitar, Z.: AI-based cybersecurity policies and procedures. In: Proceedings of 3rd IEEE International Conference on AI in Cybersecurity (ICAIC), Houston, TX, USA (2024). https://doi.org/10.1109/ICAIC60265.2024.10433845
11. Landis, J.R., Koch, G.G.: The measurement of observer agreement for categorical data. Biometrics **33**(1), 159–174 (1977)
12. Liu, Y., Iter, D., Xu, Y., Wang, S., Xu, R., Zhu, C.: G-Eval: NLG evaluation using GPT-4 with better human alignment. In: Proceedings of 2023 Conference on Empirical Methods in Natural Language Processing (EMNLP) (2023)
13. McIntosh, T.R., et al.: Harnessing GPT-4 for generation of cybersecurity GRC policies: a focus on ransomware attack mitigation. Comput. Secur. **134**, 103424 (2023). https://doi.org/10.1016/j.cose.2023.103424
14. Microsoft: Microsoft and Mistral AI announce new partnership to accelerate AI innovation and introduce Mistral Large, first on Azure. Microsoft Azure Blog, 26 February 2024 (2024)
15. United States Congress: Clarifying lawful overseas use of data act (CLOUD act). Pub. L. 115-141, Title VII (2018)
16. Zheng, L., et al.: Judging LLM-as-a-Judge with MT-Bench and Chatbot Arena. In: Advances in Neural Information Processing Systems. vol. 36 (2023)

A Post-quantum Security Framework for European Digital Identities

José Manuel Merlos Espín[1(✉)], Jesús García-Rodríguez[1], Antonio Skarmeta[1], Stefan More[2], Sakshyam Panda[3], Iakovos Pittaras[4], and Vasilios A. Siris[4]

[1] University of Murcia, Murcia, Spain
josemanuel.merlose@um.es, jesus.garcia15@um.es, skarmeta@um.es
[2] Graz University of Technology, Graz, Austria
stefan.more@tugraz.at
[3] Cylo Labs, Guildford, UK
s.panda@cylolabs.com
[4] Athens University of Economics and Business, Athens, Greece
pittaras@aueb.gr, vsiris@aueb.gr

Abstract. Quantum computing threatens the foundations of current cryptography, posing critical risks to digital identity systems. This paper presents a modular framework to support the transition of European digital identities toward post-quantum cryptography (PQC). Developed within the context of the POSEIDON project, the framework considers both Self-Sovereign Identity (SSI) principles and the European Digital Identity (EUDI) Wallet ecosystem.

Our framework centers on crypto-agile abstraction layers and decouples identity components from underlying cryptographic primitives, enabling the adoption of classical, hybrid, and post-quantum algorithms. The framework supports user-centric credential management, qualified signatures, and resource-constrained IoT environments through interoperable building blocks and lightweight components. Additionally, we complement our framework with the Quantum Risk Assessment Toolkit, a lifecycle-aware recommendation platform that rounds out the framework's capabilities for achieving an agile PQC transition across different deployment scenarios.

Keywords: Post-Quantum Cryptography (PQC) · Digital Identity · European Digital Identity (EUDI) Wallet · Self-Sovereign Identity (SSI) · Cryptographic Agility

1 Introduction

The rapid evolution of quantum computing has significant implications for the security of today's digital systems. Current cryptography relies on mathematical assumptions that have been shown to be vulnerable to quantum computers.

P. Kieseberg et al. (Eds.): ARES 2026 Workshops, LNCS 16903, pp. 149–165, 2027.
https://doi.org/10.1007/978-3-032-37218-5_10

Ensuring that critical infrastructures and services remain secure in the post-quantum landscape must therefore become a key objective in the coming years.

In response, the transition to Post-Quantum Cryptography (PQC) has been identified as a strategic priority. This priority is reflected in initiatives such as the European Commission Recommendation C(2024) 2393 [1], which prompted the coordinated European implementation roadmap for the transition to PQC [10].

These initiatives highlight the need to progressively migrate existing systems and infrastructures toward quantum-resistant cryptographic mechanisms, and they show how this transition presents several challenges. Existing digital infrastructures rely on complex and heterogeneous cryptographic deployments. This makes large-scale transitions difficult without disrupting current services. Ensuring interoperability with established identity protocols, maintaining performance, and supporting cryptographic agility are key technical challenges in this process. Additionally, adopting hybrid approaches that combine classical and post-quantum cryptography requires careful integration to ensure a smooth transition toward long-term security while maintaining compatibility with current systems.

These challenges are particularly relevant in the context of emerging European digital identity initiatives, such as the European Digital Identity (EUDI) Wallet under the revised eIDAS 2 regulation [2], where ensuring strong security, privacy, and trust is essential for widespread adoption. Addressing these issues requires new technological solutions and methodologies capable of enabling a secure and gradual transition toward post-quantum-ready digital identity infrastructures.

Contributions: This paper presents a detailed identity framework that tackles the challenges associated with transitioning to PQC. The framework addresses these challenges through the definition of Self-Sovereign Identity (SSI) building blocks, which modularize and abstract the complexity of managing diverse credential formats and their lifecycles. These building blocks distinguish between those oriented toward user identity (e.g., wallets and credential management) and those designed for IoT deployments in constrained environments. Furthermore, we propose an abstraction layer between these components and the underlying cryptographic implementations, rendering them agnostic to low-level primitives and their secure implementations. This provides a clear blueprint for supporting different post-quantum and hybrid schemes in identity management ecosystems, enabling the transition to PQC in such critical infrastructures.

POSEIDON: This work is being conducted within the context of the POSEIDON project, funded by the European Union under the Horizon Europe Programme. The project started in October 2025 and will run for three years. Its primary objective is to design and develop technological capabilities that enable digital identity management systems to securely transition to post-quantum cryptography, supporting hybrid cryptographic approaches and ensuring crypto-agility so that identity infrastructures can adapt to emerging quantum threats.

To achieve this objective, POSEIDON develops and integrates a set of interoperable components that enable post-quantum-secure identity management and evaluates them through realistic pilot scenarios across multiple application domains. Through these activities, the project aims to contribute to the secure evolution of European digital identity and support the broader transition toward post-quantum-resilient digital systems.

Outline: Section 2 overviews some background and works related to the paper's context. In Sect. 3, we present the blueprint of our framework. Section 4 provides an overview of demonstration scenarios that contextualize the design and validation of our framework, and Sect. 5 discusses the main characteristics of the framework design and their relationship to the PQC transition challenges in identity. In Sect. 6, we conclude the paper.

2 Background

User-centric digital identity systems allow users to obtain, store, and present attested attributes to service providers. Wallet-based approaches typically involve issuers, holders, and verifiers: issuers create credentials, holders manage them in their wallets, and verifiers check presented claims. These attested attributes are commonly represented as Verifiable Credentials (VCs) [13], which bind claims to a holder and can later be presented to a verifier. Self-Sovereign Identity (SSI) emphasizes user control and decentralized trust, while the European Digital Identity (EUDI) Wallet follows a related model within the regulated eIDAS 2 ecosystem [2,3]. Depending on the trust model, public verification material can be obtained through Decentralized Identifiers (DIDs) and Verifiable Data Registries (VDRs). In the EUDI ecosystem, trust is established through mechanisms such as PKI-based trust lists and trusted issuer registries.

Wallet systems depend on cryptography for credential signatures and trust establishment. Traditional public-key cryptography relies mainly on the hardness of integer factorization and discrete logarithms. RSA depends on factoring large composite integers, while Diffie-Hellman, DSA, and elliptic-curve schemes rely on the hardness of discrete logarithms in finite fields or elliptic-curve groups. A sufficiently large quantum computer running Shor's algorithm can solve these problems in polynomial time.[1] This would allow an attacker to recover private keys, and thus forge digital signatures, or decrypt key exchanges. Post-quantum cryptography addresses this problem by replacing these assumptions with problems for which no efficient classical or quantum algorithms are known. Examples of such mathematical problems are lattice problems, code-based decoding, multivariate equations, hash-based constructions, or symmetric-key-based signatures. PQC thus provides cryptographic primitives whose security is designed to withstand known quantum attacks.

[1] A so-called cryptographically relevant quantum computer (CRQC).

The transition to PQC therefore affects not only individual signatures, but also credential formats, trust chains, revocation and status mechanisms, secure key storage, and protocol flows such as credential issuance and presentation. Since these infrastructures are long-lived and heterogeneous, practical migration requires crypto-agility and hybrid schemes. These schemes combine different cryptographic approaches while preserving interoperability with existing systems.

2.1 Related Work

The broader challenge of transitioning existing systems and protocols to PQC has also received attention in the literature. Aramide [14] provides a general overview of the quantum threat to identity management systems, identifying key integration challenges such as key size overhead, legacy system compatibility, and performance trade-offs, and advocates for hybrid and decentralized approaches to enable a secure migration. Schardong et al. [15] illustrate the practical complexity of this transition by examining the specific challenges of adapting widely deployed identity protocols, namely OpenID Connect and OAuth 2.0, to the post-quantum era. Aydeger et al. [16] take a broader cybersecurity perspective, presenting a comprehensive transition strategy across multiple domains and deriving recommendations from early adopters to guide efforts toward a quantum-resilient digital landscape. Our framework aims to provide a broad ecosystem for digital identity scenarios and will be piloted in relevant environments to generate insights and recommendations for a wider transition to PQC.

Specifically, the intersection of PQC and verifiable credentials has received growing attention as quantum threats have become more concrete.

Wood et al. [11] analyze the PQC migration landscape for VC systems and conclude that, while standardized post-quantum algorithms provide viable drop-in replacements for signature-based credentials, more privacy-preserving schemes currently lack mature post-quantum constructions, making the transition inherently gradual and use-case-dependent. Crucially, they recommend the adoption of crypto-agile approaches defining standard cryptographic APIs that allow algorithms to be swapped in and out as the field evolves and new attacks or standards emerge. Our framework directly operationalizes this recommendation through the Crypto API and the modular SSI building blocks, which together provide crypto-agility at both the cryptographic and identity protocol levels.

Arakawa [12] benchmarks a comprehensive set of classical and post-quantum signature algorithms in realistic VC scenarios and concludes that there is no single optimal solution for PQC migration and appropriate algorithm selection is inherently use-case-dependent, with different algorithms presenting fundamentally different trade-offs across performance, credential size, and security guarantees. This finding directly motivates the crypto-agile design of our framework: rather than committing to a specific algorithm, the Crypto API abstraction layer allows each deployment to select and swap the primitive that best fits its operational constraints, whether that is a high-throughput credential issuance service, a size-constrained IoT device, or a long-lived qualified signature requiring maximum security guarantees.

3 The Framework Blueprint

To strengthen the PQ-readiness of the European digital identity ecosystem, we propose a modular framework. Figure 1 provides a high-level view of our framework's components, roles, and interactions of the digital identity management scenarios.

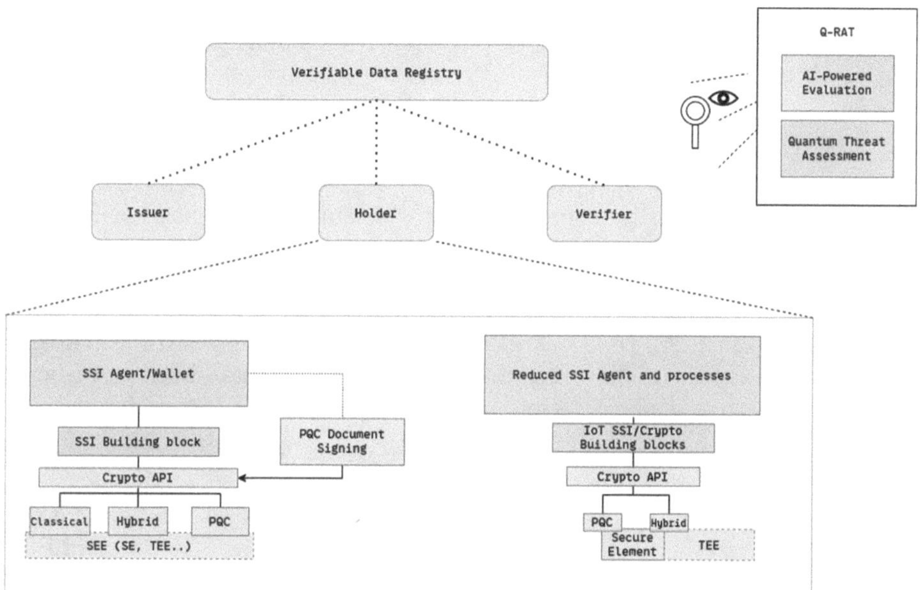

Fig. 1. The identity management framework blueprint

3.1 Overall Design

Entities: At the core of our framework are the roles typically involved in identity management systems. An Issuer is responsible for issuing credentials after appropriate authentication procedures. A Holder obtains and stores these credentials in their wallet. The holder later presents these credentials when required during authentication or authorization processes. A Verifier (or relying party, RP) validates the claims provided by holders according to defined policies. Supporting these interactions, a Verifiable Data Registry (VDR) provides trusted public information such as public keys, schemas, or trusted issuer lists, enabling the establishment of trust across the ecosystem.

Components: To support these roles, our framework introduces a layered toolset composed of interoperable components. The general toolset targets environments such as servers, personal computers, and mobile devices. The framework includes a cryptographic abstraction layer (Crypto API) that allows applications to access cryptographic operations independently of the underlying implementation. Beneath this abstraction layer, various implementations of classical, hybrid, and post-quantum cryptographic algorithms provide the core cryptographic functionality.

Secure execution environments such as trusted execution environments, secure elements, or hardware security modules may be used to protect sensitive operations and key material. On top of these cryptographic layers, SSI building blocks integrate the cryptographic capabilities into identity protocols and standards, enabling functionalities such as credential management within digital identity wallets or agents.

Supported Platforms: Our framework supports common identity management platforms, i.e., mobile-phone-based wallets and server-based issuers and verifiers. Additionally, the framework also supports resource-constrained devices, such as IoT systems. For these scenarios, a specialized toolset provides lightweight implementations of the cryptographic primitives, secure key storage mechanisms (e.g., trusted execution environments or delegation to secure hardware), and simplified SSI components adapted to limited computational capabilities. These components allow devices to securely participate in identity-based interactions, such as authentication, domain enrollment, or secure communication.

Risk Assessment: Finally, our framework is complemented by the Quantum Risk Assessment Toolkit (Q-RAT) and AI-driven evaluations of hybrid and PQC schemes [17]. These components analyze trade-offs between security, performance, and energy, alongside modules for quantum threat modeling, continuous risk assessment, and anomaly detection, to deliver a dynamic security view.
Q-RAT functions as a lifecycle-aware decision-support platform, enabling organizations to prioritize and plan PQC transitions in line with EU timelines and regulatory requirements. By combining asset discovery, risk scoring, compliance mapping (NIS2, CRA), and actionable mitigation guidance, it supports deployment across diverse scenarios, for example, long-lived digital identity systems such as educational credentials or resource-constrained and highly distributed environments such as IoT and edge ecosystems. This allows deployments to adapt to varying operational constraints while ensuring robust, future-ready, secure systems.

3.2 PQC Wallet Architecture

Our framework is designed around both Self-Sovereign Identity (SSI) principles and the emerging European Digital Identity (EUDI) Wallet ecosystem.

Both models build on the same user-centric model (issuer-holder-verifier) and rely on user-controlled wallets for identity data management. While the models share many technical standards, their governance differs. SSI emphasizes user-controlled, decentralized identity free from institutional intermediaries. The EUDI Wallet introduces a regulated framework that places governance and interoperability requirements at the center. While both models are distributed, SSI also aims for full decentralization, relying on Decentralized Identifiers (DIDs) and distributed-ledger-based VDRs. EUDI, on the other hand, naturally builds on government-issued identities and a more centrally controlled ecosystem, relying on hierarchical trust status lists and PKI.

The project navigates this dichotomy by adopting modular components that honor SSI's core credential lifecycle: issuance, storage, and verification, while remaining aligned with the compliance and interoperability demands of the EUDI landscape. This flexibility is enabled by the project's modularity and Crypto API (Sect. 3.4 below). Beyond these user-focused models, the project further extends the framework by introducing adaptations for constrained IoT environments and integrating post-quantum and hybrid cryptographic mechanisms to future-proof identity operations across both paradigms.

PQC Wallet Components. Our architecture is built upon established specifications such as the W3C Verifiable Credentials (VC) Data Model. These components ensure interoperability with frameworks such as the eIDAS 2 Regulation [2] and the European Blockchain Services Infrastructure.

This architecture enables the full lifecycle of verifiable credentials, including issuance, presentation, and verification. Users manage their credentials through a wallet, an application that allows secure storage and selective disclosure when interacting with relying parties. Credential issuance and verification functionalities are supported by backend components implementing issuer and verifier roles. These capabilities follow standards such as OpenID for Verifiable Credential Issuance (OID4VCI) or OpenID for Verifiable Presentations (OID4VP). Additionally, our architecture enables post-quantum security for the entire EUDI trust layer, namely trust status lists and PKI.

Wallet Building Blocks for Constrained Environments. In addition to the full-featured architecture, our proposed framework defines a reduced set of SSI building blocks and processes tailored for constrained environments such as IoT devices. This reduced approach focuses on minimizing computational and storage requirements while preserving essential identity functionalities. It follows existing data models where possible but prioritizes simplicity and agility in implementation. This includes, for example, lightweight credential handling and a primitive form of DID management through lightweight DID methods. Advanced features such as full credential lifecycle management, complex cryptographic operations, or extensive interoperability layers are omitted or simplified.

Additionally, the framework considers alternative approaches for managing device authentication and authorization that are common in IoT environments, such as simple authenticated TLS channels for MQTT deployments. This design enables deployment in resource-constrained environments while maintaining post-quantum security and compatibility with the broader wallet ecosystems.

3.3 Document Signing and Timestamping

The PQC Document Signing and Timestamping component provides the capability to create qualified signatures for digital documents, such as PDFs. Qualified signatures following the eIDAS regulation provide the same legal value as handwritten signatures. These functions are particularly relevant in digital processes where legally binding or auditable records are required. By integrating PQC into the qualified signature stack, we future-proof the integrity, authenticity, and long-term verifiability of PDFs.

Within our framework, this component is linked to the identity management capabilities provided by the wallet ecosystem. Users authenticate through their wallet-based identity, allowing the signing operation to be associated with a verifiable digital identity. Additionally, this component relies on the Crypto API abstraction (see below) to provide agile cryptographic mechanisms while considering the strict legal requirements applicable to secure hardware used for qualified signatures.

3.4 Unified Crypto API

Our framework defines a common Cryptographic Application Programming Interface (Crypto API) as a unified abstraction layer for accessing cryptographic services across different hardware platforms. Its main objective is to decouple higher-level identity and security components from the specific characteristics of the underlying algorithms and their implementations, whether software-based or relying on secure hardware such as Trusted Execution Environments (TEEs), Secure Elements (SEs), or Hardware Security Modules (HSMs). Through this abstraction, all SSI building blocks, wallets, agents, and credential management services interact with cryptographic services in a consistent manner, remaining portable and interoperable across a wide range of devices and secure infrastructures.

To provide flexibility for different development contexts, the Crypto API defines a specification covering aspects such as method signatures and parameters, error codes, and session handling, establishing a consistent behavioral contract that concrete implementations must follow. For example, a signing operation is uniformly expressed as: `pca_sign(key_handle, raw_data, algo, *signature)`, where `key_handle` is a logical key identifier rather than the key material itself, with the actual key management and storage being fully abstracted by the API, and `algo` is drawn from a standardized set of algorithm identifiers defined by the specification itself, covering classical, hybrid, or post-quantum primitives. This allows language-specific instantiations to be developed independently while guaranteeing interoperability and uniform semantics across the ecosystem, for example, as a header file in C or an interface in Java. Currently, the framework provides instantiations in these languages as well as in Kotlin, targeting environments ranging from constrained IoT devices to higher-level application integration.

The design of the Crypto API was informed by existing cryptographic interface standards, most notably PKCS#11 and the Java Cryptography Extension (JCE). Rather than designing a new interface from scratch, the methodology focuses on taking inspiration from these already established but heterogeneous specifications and unifying them under a common abstraction. The Crypto API defines a common set of names and codes that all implementations must adhere to, ensuring a consistent interface surface regardless of the underlying backend or programming language. This homogenization is the central design objective: by grounding the Crypto API in conventions already present in widely deployed standards, the aim is to reduce adoption friction and facilitate integration across environments that may rely on PKCS#11-compliant hardware or JCE-based implementations, while the precise degree of interoperability with each will be refined as the framework matures. The extension toward post-quantum and hybrid primitives follows the same philosophy. New algorithm identifiers and operation types are introduced within the unified naming scheme, ensuring that PQC support integrates naturally rather than appearing as a bolted-on addition.

The Crypto API supports classical, hybrid, and post-quantum cryptographic mechanisms, with definitions for quantum-resistant primitives aligned with emerging PQC standards. This means that classical and post-quantum algorithms can coexist and be combined transparently beneath a stable interface, without requiring changes to higher-level identity logic.

Concretely, a hybrid scheme that combines a classical algorithm such as ECDSA with a post-quantum primitive such as ML-DSA is exposed to higher-level components as a single, opaque cryptographic operation. The SSI building blocks, wallets, and credential managers invoking the Crypto API remain fully agnostic to whether the underlying implementation is a standalone classical algorithm, a standalone post-quantum algorithm, or a hybrid version, such as a composite signature [18]. This design is aligned with ongoing standardization efforts by ETSI on hybrid cryptographic schemes [9], which advocate treating hybrid combinations as first-class primitives that can be swapped in transparently without requiring protocol-level changes above them.

The interface is also designed for extensibility: as new algorithms or standards emerge, it can incorporate additional primitives such as those supporting anonymous credentials while maintaining backward compatibility. A concrete example of this evolution in supporting infrastructure is PKCS#11 V3.2 [8], which extends the widely deployed token interface

standard to natively support post-quantum primitives.

Cryptographic Algorithms. Our framework is designed to accommodate a diverse set of cryptographic algorithms with the objective of supporting the secure transition to post-quantum-resilient digital identities. The framework supports algorithms covering several design paradigms, including ML-DSA [5], FAEST [6], and FALCON [4]. The realization of privacy-enhancing technologies (PETs) with post-quantum cryptography is also considered. This includes exploring quantum-resistant primitives for anonymous credentials or pseudonyms, aiming to preserve privacy and compliance with regulatory requirements while ensuring long-term cryptographic security. These algorithms are encapsulated behind the Crypto API, so that higher-level components and the rest of the infrastructure can transparently adopt them.

Secure Execution Environment. To enhance the protection of sensitive cryptographic operations and key material, algorithms must be deployed within secure execution environments, such as Trusted Execution Environments (TEEs), Secure Elements (SEs), or (remote) Hardware Security Modules (HSMs). These mechanisms provide an additional layer of security against physical attacks and software-level compromise.

The concrete instantiation of cryptographic algorithms within these secure environments is abstracted by the Crypto API. Components in the framework can then remain fully agnostic to the specifics of the secure execution environment being used, allowing deployments to adapt to the available hardware capabilities and security requirements while maintaining uniform access to cryptographic services.

3.5 Verifiable Data Registry

The Verifiable Data Registry (VDR) provides a reliable mechanism for publishing and retrieving publicly verifiable information. It acts as a shared trust anchor where entities can register and access information necessary to establish trust relationships within the ecosystem.

In the context of SSI, the VDR is used to store or reference public data such as cryptographic keys associated with Decentralized Identifiers, trusted issuer lists, credential schemas, and other metadata required for credential verification. Thus, the registry enables participants to validate identities and credentials, potentially without relying on centralized authorities by using technologies such as distributed ledgers.

Additionally, our architecture is designed to be compatible with other trust models, including those promoted by the EUDI framework. This flexibility allows the system to adopt different mechanisms for trust establishment, such as trusted lists or federation-based approaches, depending on regulatory, technical, or deployment requirements, without impacting the overall design.

4 Pilot Scenarios

To validate the framework, POSEIDON defines a set of pilot scenarios that will drive and contextualize implementation. As the project is in its early stages, these scenarios currently serve as design anchors that shape architectural decisions rather than deployment environments for quantitative evaluation. Here, we give a brief overview of how the proposed framework maps to one such scenario.

The **eID Education Credentials** pilot explores the deployment of a post-quantum-secure identity management service within research and education institutions. The pilot enables users to manage their academic certificates and micro-credentials using user-centric identity technologies while ensuring long-term security. The system supports scenarios such as student enrollment in courses and the submission of credentials for grant applications, with evaluations conducted across multiple universities.

The overall approach aligns with the EUDI Wallet paradigm, aiming to provide a transparent user experience. At a high level, this involves integrating with existing identity flows while adapting data models, credential formats, and cryptographic algorithms to the specific requirements of educational certificates, which differ in structure, trust, and lifecycle constraints. To support this adaptation, the pilot leverages the internal design of credential issuance and presentation flows, as illustrated in the User Registration Flow (Fig. 2). This figure depicts a high-level view of the issuance process for educational certificates, relying on OID4VCI [7]. In the use case, we consider both "pre-authorized" flows, where an offline process, such as an in-person registration, authorizes the issuance of the user credential, and "authorized" flows, where the user must additionally present information using their wallet, such as their personal identification credentials. The integration of OID4VCI is handled in a manner transparent to the user, abstracting protocol complexity while maintaining interoperability. This design enables flexibility in modifying the type of Verifiable Credential (VC) and the underlying cryptographic mechanisms in a simple and modular way.

While the external operations occur in an interoperable manner using OID4VCI, a more detailed perspective on how the framework components provide the necessary functionality is provided in the Signing Flow (Fig. 3). In particular, the figure shows how the framework's different layers operate together to produce and sign the Verifiable Credential.

As a first step, the Issuer initiates the signing process and provides the VC manager with the unsigned VC data, along with the algorithm and key to be used. The VC manager then parses the data according to the requirements of the data model (e.g., creating the necessary digest of the credential for signing) and calls the Crypto API, supplying the raw data to be signed and a key identifier. The Crypto API instantiation translates the request to the underlying architecture (such as PKCS#11 on a Java Card) and returns the signed data, which is then used to construct the final signed VC.

Two additional pilot scenarios will help demonstrate the feasibility, interoperability, and performance of the proposed solutions across different domains. The **Smart Spaces pilot** addresses IoT environments by integrating post-quantum cryptographic mechanisms into smart building infrastructures. In this scenario, lightweight IoT and edge devices used for monitoring and controlling systems require authentication and communication mechanisms that have traditionally employed lightweight cryptography. The pilot aims to address challenges arising

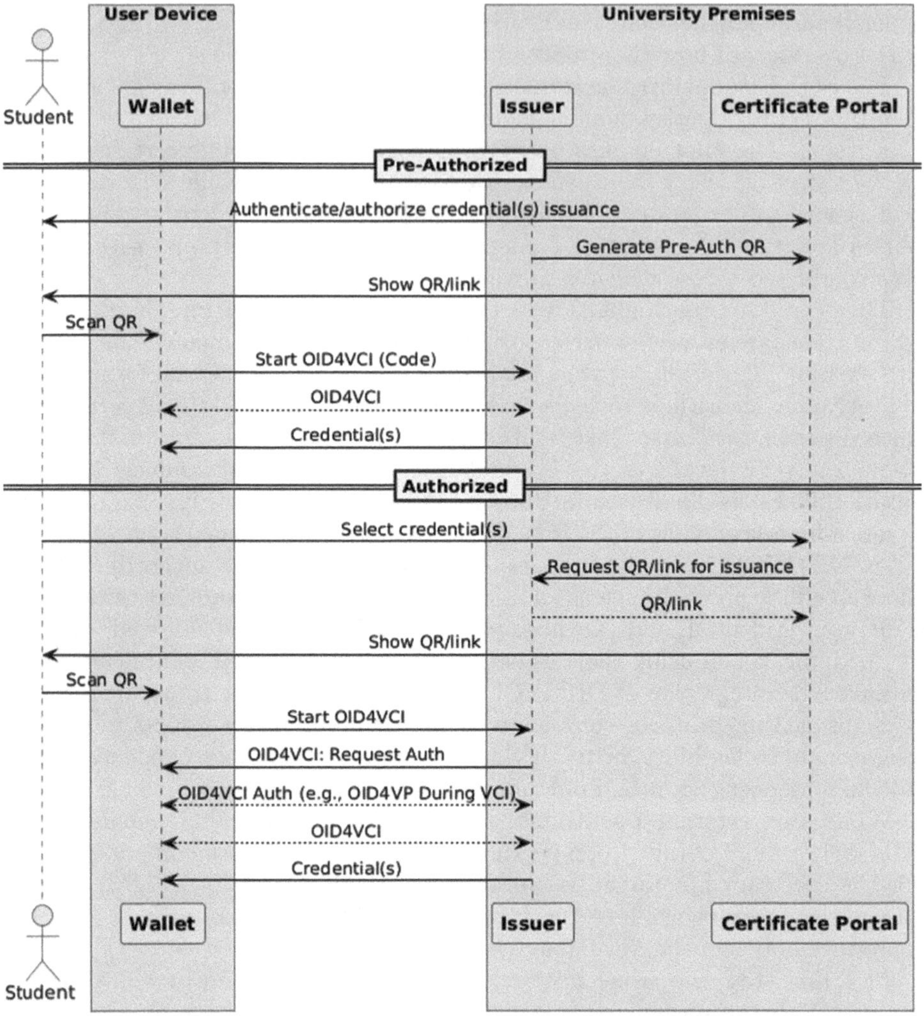

Fig. 2. Educational pilot user registration flow

from hardware resource constraints and heterogeneity. The **Secure and Trustworthy Insurance pilot** demonstrates the use of a digital wallet for data exchange and document signing in insurance-related processes. This pilot provides a core use case for digitally signed insurance applications, where qualified post-quantum signatures will be necessary for long-term contracts.

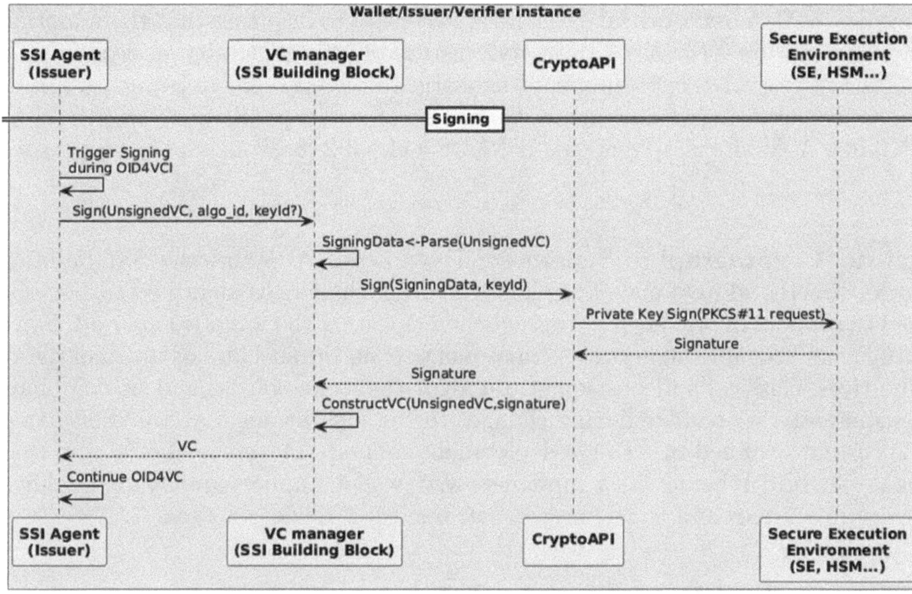

Fig. 3. Signing flow within the framework's components

5 Discussion

The presented framework addresses post-quantum transition challenges with a multidimensional approach. Here, we discuss key aspects that emerge from the design.

Interoperability with Established Standards: This is a foundational design principle of the framework. By aligning with widely adopted specifications such as OID4VCI, OID4VP, and the W3C Verifiable Credentials Data Model, the framework ensures that integration into existing identity ecosystems requires minimal disruption. As illustrated in the educational pilot, the adoption of post-quantum mechanisms remains fully transparent at the user level; interactions follow the same flows as today, with interactions compatible with the EUDI Wallet and credential exchanges proceeding as expected, while the underlying cryptographic layer evolves independently beneath the abstraction boundaries.

Flexibility in Higher-Level Identity Processes: The SSI building blocks can be adapted or replaced to support different credential formats (such as SD-JWT, JSON-LD, or plain JWT) as well as diverse management approaches, including privacy-enhancing technologies or alternative signing mechanisms. This flexibility, analogous to that provided by the Crypto API at the cryptographic layer, ensures that the system can accommodate emerging standards and heterogeneous ecosystems without requiring architectural changes.

Crypto API Abstraction: This layer is central to ensuring that the adoption of post-quantum primitives does not disrupt existing identity ecosystems. It makes the rest of the components agnostic to the specific implementation of algorithms, allowing for incremental adoption of new capabilities as they become available. A good example of this is PKCS#11 V3.2 [8], which adds support for PQC.

Hybrid Cryptographic Schemes: The Crypto API and the SSI building blocks directly address one of the key transition challenges identified earlier: the need to support hybrid cryptographic schemes during the migration period. Since both layers decouple higher-level components from the specifics of the underlying primitives, classical and post-quantum algorithms can coexist and be combined transparently, without requiring changes to the identity logic above. This capability is not confined to a single deployment context. The same abstraction that enables hybrid schemes in a human-centric wallet applies equally to qualified signature services and to resource-constrained IoT devices.

Different Identity Paradigms: The framework addresses two identity paradigms with substantially different requirements. On the one hand, the framework provides SSI components aligned with the EUDI Wallet that target human-centric use cases where regulatory alignment and user experience are primary concerns. Moreover, beyond credential management, we specifically address the use of qualified signature services. The framework maintains these services but establishes a link to the overall identity management solution through the authentication mechanism. This offers significant operational advantages for the initial stages of the transition: it allows qualified signature ecosystems to keep working with minimal changes while fulfilling the strong regulatory requirements that are difficult to satisfy in wallet systems, particularly due to constraints on secure hardware availability.

EUDI Wallet Integration: A natural evolution path leads toward tighter integration with the EUDI Wallet as the ecosystem matures. The qualified signing functionality could be progressively absorbed into the wallet itself as an additional native capability, allowing users to sign or timestamp documents directly within their identity management environment. The pace of this evolution is largely contingent on how quickly the EUDI Wallet ecosystem and secure hardware technologies advance. This is precisely the kind of evolution that the modular, crypto-agile architecture is designed to support: the component boundary exists today as a pragmatic seam, and it can be restructured as the surrounding landscape evolves without disrupting the rest of the framework.

IoT Environments: Resource-constrained settings present a fundamentally different set of challenges that preclude the deployment of full-featured SSI stacks. Devices in these environments are often limited in processing power, memory, and energy budget, making it impractical to run credential management logic or complex cryptographic schemes. Despite operating with reduced capabilities, IoT components in our framework expose the same consistent Crypto API surface as the human-centric stack. This design decision ensures that cryptographic operations retain their semantic coherence across both paradigms. This layer also accommodates the heterogeneity among IoT devices: while some may have TPMs or SEs directly connected, in other cases operations may have to be delegated to edge devices. This consistency simplifies integration with broader identity ecosystems and audit processes, and ensures that the transition to post-quantum primitives can be managed uniformly across the full deployment landscape.

Risk Assessment and Evaluation: At the core of the framework are performance evaluation, attack detection, and quantum risk assessment capabilities, which analyze cryptographic inventories and configurations to generate prioritized and actionable risk mitigation, compliance management, and transition recommendations.

6 Conclusion

The transition to PQC is becoming critical in scenarios where hardware or software artifacts are expected to have long lifetimes. For different reasons, such scenarios are common in digital identity management. In this paper, we present a framework blueprint designed to provide identity management capabilities in a flexible and agile way to facilitate the transition to PQC. This framework has been designed in the context of the POSEIDON project and its pilots, covering educational credentials, qualified document signatures, and management of IoT identities. Thus, the framework is aligned with SSI principles, the eIDAS 2 regulation, and specific IoT needs for authentication and authorization.

A key aspect of the framework design is the establishment of two levels of abstraction for the management of identity material: the Crypto API for cryptographic algorithm implementations and the SSI building blocks for higher-level concepts, namely the widespread Verifiable Credentials. The former allows cryptographic applications to flexibly choose between algorithms and underlying implementations, hiding specifics such as which secure execution environment is used. The latter enables the construction of identity applications such as wallets or issuers with agile mechanisms for managing cryptographic validation, including whether hybrid or standalone schemes are used. In both cases, we address not only the transition to PQC but also the need for a fully flexible and agile ecosystem that will remain useful in the long term.

The proposed framework thus not only addresses the immediate need for a secure transition to post-quantum cryptography but also introduces a forward-looking approach to identity management that emphasizes modularity, interoperability, and long-term adaptability. Moreover, aligning the framework with Self-Sovereign Identity principles and emerging European regulatory efforts ensures that security enhancements do not come at the expense of usability, privacy, or user control. This holistic perspective is particularly relevant for diverse application domains, ranging from human-centric digital identities to large-scale IoT ecosystems, where flexibility and scalability are essential. Ultimately, the framework contributes to establishing a resilient and future-proof foundation for trusted digital interactions in a post-quantum era.

Future work will focus on refining the instantiation of the framework's components, implementing them in practice, and fully validating the framework in real-world scenarios with quantitative evaluation of performance, interoperability, and security trade-offs across the defined pilot environments. These activities will improve its applicability across various domains and use cases and will use the results to create recommendations for the transition to PQC not only in identity management but also in other domains.

Acknowledgments. This work has been funded by the European Union as part of the Horizon Europe Framework Programme under grant agreement 101225797 (POSEIDON).

Disclosure of Interests. The authors have no competing interests to declare that are relevant to the content of this article.

References

1. Commission Recommendation of 11, European Commission (2024). 4.2024 on a Coordinated Implementation Roadmap for the transition to Post-Quantum Cryptography
2. Regulation (EU) 2024/1183 of the European Parliament and of the Council of 11 April 2024 amending Regulation (EU) No 910/2014 as regards establishing the European Digital Identity Framework. European Commission. https://eur-lex.europa.eu/legal-content/EN/TXT/?uri=OJ:L_202401183
3. European Commission. EU Digital Identity Wallet Home. EU Digital Identity Wallet. Retrieved May 15, 2026, from (2026). https://ec.europa.eu/digital-building-blocks/sites/spaces/EUDIGITALIDENTITYWALLET/pages/694487738/EU+Digital+Identity+Wallet+Home
4. Fouque, P., Prest, T.: FALCON: Fast-Fourier Lattice-based Compact Signatures over NTRU. In: Post-Quantum Cryptography Standardization Project. National Institute of Standards and Technology (NIST). Retrieved March 20, 2026 (2025). https://falcon-sign.info/
5. National Institute of Standards and Technology (NIST). Module-Lattice-Based Digital Signature Standard (ML-DSA). Federal Information Processing Standards Publication (FIPS) 204. Retrieved March 20, 2026 (2024). https://csrc.nist.gov/pubs/fips/204/final
6. Baum, C., Beullens, W., et al.: FAEST v2: Algorithm Specifications. Retrieved May 05, 2026 (2025). https://faest.info/faest-spec-v2.0.pdf
7. OpenID Foundation. OpenID for Verifiable Credential Issuance (OID4VCI). OpenID Foundation. Retrieved March 23, 2026 (2025). https://openid.net/specs/openid-4-verifiable-credential-issuance-1_0.html

8. OASIS Open. PKCS #11 Cryptographic Token Interface Base Specification Version 3.2. OASIS Committee Specification Draft 01. Retrieved March 23, 2026. (2025) https://docs.oasis-open.org/pkcs11/pkcs11-spec/v3.2/csd01/pkcs11-spec-v3.2-csd01.html
9. ETSI. Draft ETSI TS 119 312: Cryptographic Suites V1.5.5 (2026-05) European Telecommunications Standards Institute (2026)
10. NIS. A Coordinated Implementation Roadmap for the Transition to Post-Quantum Cryptography", Part 1, Version: 1.1 NIS Cooperation Group. Retrieved from (2025). https://digital-strategy.ec.europa.eu/en/library/coordinated-implementation-roadmap-transition-post-quantum-cryptography
11. Wood, T., Thomas, K., Dean, M., Kannan, S., Learney, R.: Towards post-quantum verifiable credentials. In: Proceedings of 19th International Conference on Availability, Reliability and Security (ARES) (2024). https://doi.org/10.1145/3664476.3669932
12. Arakawa, M.: Post-Quantum Cryptography for Verifiable Credentials: Comprehensive Performance Evaluation Including Selective Disclosure. TechRxiv (preprint) (2025). https://doi.org/10.36227/techrxiv.176118722.22701360/v1
13. Sporny, M., Longley, D., Chadwick, D., Steele, O.: Verifiable credentials data model v2.0. W3C, W3C Recommendation (2024)
14. Aramide, O.O.: Post-quantum cryptography (PQC) for identity management. ADHYAYAN J. Manag. Sci. **12**(2), 59–67 (2023). https://doi.org/10.21567/adhyayan.v12i2.11
15. Schardong, F., Giron, A.A., Müller, F.L., Custódio, R.: Post-quantum electronic identity: adapting OpenID connect and OAuth 2.0 to the post-quantum era. In: Proceedings of International Conference on Cryptology and Network Security (CANS) (2022). https://doi.org/10.1007/978-3-031-20974-1_20
16. Aydeger, A., Zeydan, E., Yadav, A.K., Hemachandra, K.T., Liyanage, M.: Towards a quantum-resilient future: strategies for transitioning to post-quantum cryptography. In: Proceedings of 15th International Conference on Network of the Future (NoF) (2024). https://doi.org/10.1109/NoF62948.2024.10741441
17. Panda, S., et al.: A data lifecycle-aware risk assessment framework for post-quantum cryptography [Pre-print]. In: 2025 IEEE Symposium on Computers and Communications (ISCC), IEEE (2026). pre-print. https://sakshyampanda.com/publication/panda2026data/
18. Ounsworth, M., Gray, J., Pala, M., Klaußner, J.: Composite signatures for use in internet PKI. Internet-Draft draft-ietf-lamps-pq-composite-sigs-00, Internet Engineering Task Force, Work in Progress (2024). https://datatracker.ietf.org/doc/draft-ietf-lamps-pq-composite-sigs/00/

Federated Learning for Electric Vehicle Energy Demand Prediction Across Distributed Users

Vasilis Perifanis[1(✉)], Foteini Nikolaidou[1], Panagiotis Thomakos[1], Nikolaos Pavlidis[1], Andreas Sendros[1], Ignacio Lacalle Úbeda[2], Felix Mondl[3], and Michael Glensvig[4]

[1] Indigma Innovations, Komotini, Greece
{vasilis,f.nikolaidou,p.thomakos,nikos,andreas}@indigma.eu
[2] Universitat Politècnica de València, Valencia, Spain
iglaub@upv.es
[3] Österreichische Post AG, Vienna, Austria
felix.mondl@post.at
[4] AVL List GmbH, Graz, Austria
Michael.Glensvig@avl.com

Abstract. Accurate prediction of daily electric vehicle (EV) energy demand supports charging planning across home users, commercial fleets, depots, and charging service providers. We study this problem as a supervised regression task under centralized and Federated Learning (FL) settings, using heterogeneous EV data sources that include two public datasets and a private commercial dataset from a postal service. Raw EV records are transformed into vehicle-day samples through a unified preprocessing pipeline based on a common schema of vehicle identifier, date, time, state of charge (SOC), and odometer readings. Daily travelled distance and energy demand are derived from these records, and the prediction target is estimated from discharge segments between charging events. The input features also combine calendar, historical demand, and weather descriptors. We evaluate local, centralized, cross-device, and cross-silo FL across three deep learning architectures, and implement a buffered asynchronous FL orchestration pipeline on a Raspberry Pi testbed to assess practical deployment. The results show that distributed EV energy demand models can approach centralized performance while preserving data locality, and that buffered asynchronous FL is practical for heterogeneous EV deployments.

Keywords: Electric Vehicles · Energy Demand Prediction · Federated Learning · Buffered Asynchronous FL · Privacy-Preserving AI

1 Introduction

The increasing adoption of electric vehicles (EVs) is reshaping energy demand planning at the user, fleet, and infrastructure levels [25]. In all these settings,

P. Kieseberg et al. (Eds.): ARES 2026 Workshops, LNCS 16903, pp. 166–184, 2027.
https://doi.org/10.1007/978-3-032-37218-5_11

knowing how much energy an EV is expected to require over a future day supports better charging decisions, reduces operational uncertainty, and enables more informed use of available charging capacity [10].

A practical forecasting task in this context is the prediction of EV energy demand from expected daily mobility. In this setting, the goal is to estimate the total energy an EV will require over a given day from planning-level information, such as the anticipated distance to be travelled. This formulation is directly aligned with real-world planning: a home user may know the approximate distance to be travelled the next day, or a fleet or depot operator may have access to route plans or vehicle schedules. If the corresponding energy requirement can be estimated in advance, charging can be planned earlier and more effectively.

This prediction supports multiple use cases. For home users, daily energy demand estimates help determine whether overnight charging is sufficient, whether charging should be delayed to lower-cost periods, or whether locally generated energy can cover part of the expected need. For fleet operators, the same prediction supports charger allocation, depot readiness, and operational continuity. For charging service providers and aggregators, daily demand estimates contribute to short-term load planning. In the longer term, such predictions may be combined with photovoltaic generation forecasts, local storage, electricity prices, and charger constraints to enable energy-aware charging schedules [1].

Learning reliable EV energy demand models is challenging because EV data are naturally distributed. Different EVs, users, and fleets exhibit different usage patterns, sampling characteristics, and operating conditions. Public EV datasets provide reproducible benchmarks but typically cover a limited number of vehicles or operating scenarios [16,23]. Private EV datasets offer valuable real-world coverage but are often restricted by privacy, governance, or commercial confidentiality constraints. These limitations make centralized model training difficult in settings where collaboration across users or organizations would be beneficial.

Several challenges arise in this setting. EV data are non-IID and often imbalanced across vehicles or organizations, telemetry may include missing values, SOC noise, odometer resets, and irregular sampling, and deployment must account for privacy, governance, intermittent availability, and edge-resource constraints [22]. These challenges motivate a Federated Learning (FL) formulation for heterogeneous data ownership and uneven client data sizes.

FL offers a natural solution to this problem [11]. In FL, participating clients train models locally and share only model updates with a coordinator server, without transmitting raw data. This allows a shared model to be learned across distributed sources while preserving data locality. For EV energy demand prediction, each client may correspond to a vehicle, user, household, depot, or fleet, making FL well suited to the broader EV charging scenarios where data ownership and privacy are important [14].

In this work, we study EV energy demand prediction as a supervised task under centralized and FL settings. Each sample corresponds to one vehicle-day. Raw EV records are transformed into daily driving events using a common schema, from which daily travelled distance and energy demand are derived. The learning objective is to estimate the required daily energy from the expected distance, calendar features, weather descriptors, and historical demand summaries.

We evaluate the proposed formulation using two public EV datasets [16,23] and a private commercial dataset from a postal service. We compare local, centralized, cross-device, and cross-silo FL across three deep learning (DL) architectures. Beyond predictive accuracy, we also consider the practical deployment of FL, since real systems must address communication cost, latency, client availability, and update synchronization [22]. To this end, we implement a buffered asynchronous FL orchestration pipeline on a Raspberry Pi testbed, where the server aggregates received updates once a predefined buffer condition is satisfied [13]. This design is well suited to EV settings, where vehicles or fleets may differ in local data size, computational capacity, and communication delay.

The main contributions of this work are summarized as follows:

1. We formulate daily EV energy demand prediction as a planning-level regression task over vehicle-day samples using expected distance, calendar, weather, and historical demand features.
2. We build a unified preprocessing pipeline that maps heterogeneous public and private EV records to a common schema and derives daily energy-demand targets.
3. We compare centralized, cross-device, and cross-silo FL across three model architectures, showing that FL can approach centralized performance while preserving data locality.
4. We deploy buffered asynchronous FL on a Raspberry Pi testbed and report accuracy together with communication, latency, update-delay, and convergence metrics.

This work is developed in the context of the O-CEI project[1], where FL is considered as an enabling mechanism for cross-domain collaboration without centralizing raw data. The O-CEI marketplace[2] provides a potential deployment channel for sharing trained models, generated datasets, or updated model weights; however, the scientific focus of this paper is the EV energy-demand formulation, preprocessing pipeline, FL evaluation, and edge deployment.

The remainder of this paper is organized as follows. Section 2 reviews related work on EV energy demand prediction and FL Sect. 3 describes the dataset construction, feature engineering, and learning formulation. Section 4 presents the experimental settings and results. Section 5 concludes the paper.

2 Related Work

EV energy prediction has been studied from several complementary perspectives, including vehicle energy consumption modelling, remaining range estimation, charging load forecasting, and privacy-preserving distributed learning. Recent

[1] https://o-cei.eu/.

[2] https://marketplace.pre.o-cei.eu/.

reviews the growing role of machine learning (ML) and DL methods, but also show that most formulations focus on trip-level consumption, range prediction, SOC management, or charging infrastructure integration [2,18,25].

Recent studies have advanced EV energy consumption prediction using real-world operating, temporal, environmental, and driver-specific factors. Hussain et al. [7] study real-world EV energy consumption prediction, Wang et al. [21] propose a transformer-based model for trip-level battery EV consumption under inconsistent feature spaces, and Rachavelpula and Cha [17] combine map-derived context, driver-specific velocity prediction, and physics-based modelling for personalized energy estimation. Public datasets such as Dynamic BEV [23] and ESOGU-ML5EV [16] support reproducible benchmarking, but remain limited in vehicle coverage or operating contexts, motivating approaches that can combine public and private data without centralizing raw records.

A second line of work focuses on charging demand and station-level load forecasting, where the target is commonly aggregate station load, regional demand, or charging behaviour. Van Etten et al. [5] study large-scale charging demand forecasting using time-series models and evaluate generalization to unseen stations. Gowda et al. [12] apply transfer learning and model-agnostic meta-learning for charging load forecasting. Tian et al. [19] combine temporal convolutional networks and LSTM for short-term charging load prediction, while Chen et al. [4] examine charging station demand under climatic influence. Cavus et al. [3] forecast EV charging demand in smart city settings using behavioural, spatial, and demographic data. These studies address grid operation and infrastructure planning, but their targets are aggregated charging load or station-level usage rather than the daily energy required by a specific EV given expected mobility.

FL has recently gained visibility in EV charging and energy analytics, as EV and charging records are naturally distributed across users, vehicles, stations, fleets, and organizations. Yin and Ji [24] propose a horizontal FL framework for EV charging load prediction using VMD-LSTM models. Han and Li [6] study vertical FL for charging station load prediction in coupled transportation and power distribution systems. Jin and Liu [8] propose a blockchain-based federated transfer learning framework for privacy-aware probabilistic EV load forecasting. Marlin et al. [9] introduce a hierarchical FL framework for spatio-temporal EV charge prediction with secure aggregation. Perifanis et al. [15] study FL for early prediction of EV charging demand, where the total session energy is estimated using information available at plug-in time and during the first minutes of charging. Tritsarolis et al. [20] examine the effect of FL on EV energy demand forecasting across distributed users. While these works demonstrate the applicability of FL to EV and charging analytics, most existing formulations remain station-oriented, grid-facing, session-level, or next-charge oriented. In contrast, the present work studies planning-level daily EV energy demand prediction from vehicle-day samples derived from telemetry and SOC trajectories, and evaluates buffered asynchronous FL on a real edge hardware testbed.

3 Dataset Construction and Learning Formulation

3.1 Problem Definition

We formulate daily EV energy demand prediction as a supervised regression task. Let v denote an EV and d a calendar day. Each vehicle-day pair defines one sample with input vector $\mathbf{x}_{v,d}$ and target $y_{v,d}$, corresponding to the energy required by vehicle v at day d, expressed in kWh. The learning objective is to estimate $f : \mathbf{x}_{v,d} \mapsto y_{v,d}$. The input vector combines planning, temporal, historical, and weather features, with EV embeddings included as a learned branch. The main planning variable is the expected daily distance, which in offline experiments is approximated from the realized distance through binning, and in deployment can be replaced by a user-provided estimate, or a schedule.

We evaluate four learning settings. In the *local* setting, one model is trained independently per dataset group. In the *centralized* setting, all training samples are pooled. In the *cross-device* FL setting, each EV acts as one client. In the *cross-silo* FL setting, each dataset group acts as one client, representing collaboration across data owners with heterogeneous operational contexts.

3.2 Preprocessing Pipeline

The original datasets differ in structure and naming conventions. All sources are first mapped to a common minimal schema $\{\texttt{EV id}, \texttt{date}, \texttt{time}, \texttt{SOC}, \texttt{odometer}\}$. For energy estimation, we use dataset-specific nominal battery capacities. The two Dynamic BEV vehicles [23] use 60.5 kWh and 78.8 kWh, respectively, the ESOGU [16] EV uses 15.5 kWh, and the private postal-operation EVs use 50.0 kWh. Weather information is associated with each dataset group according to its location. Table 1 summarizes the configuration.

Table 1. Dataset-specific battery capacities and weather sources.

Dataset group	Vehicles	Battery capacity (kWh)	Weather source
Dynamic BEV 1 [23]	1	60.5	Genk, Belgium
Dynamic BEV 2 [23]	1	78.8	Genk, Belgium
ESOGU [16]	1	15.5	Eskişehir, Turkey
Private postal operations	10	50.0	Local weather data

After schema harmonization, records are ordered by EV identifier and timestamp. The odometer signal is repaired before distance computation, since real telemetry may include backward jumps or reset artifacts. To avoid negative travelled distances, the odometer is forced to be non-decreasing within each vehicle trajectory via a cumulative maximum. The SOC signal is cleaned by treating values outside $[0, 100]$ as invalid and smoothing isolated one-step bounces where the previous and next values are equal and the middle value differs only slightly.

Interval-level differences are then computed between consecutive records. Let $\Delta O_{v,t}$ denote the odometer difference and B_v the nominal battery capacity of vehicle v. The battery energy at timestamp t is approximated as:

$$E_{v,t} = \frac{\mathrm{SOC}_{v,t}}{100} B_v, \tag{1}$$

and positive discharge between consecutive records is defined as:

$$\Delta E_{v,t}^{\mathrm{dis}} = \max\left(E_{v,t-1} - E_{v,t}, 0\right). \tag{2}$$

When $\Delta O_{v,t} > 0$, an interval-level consumption estimate is computed as:

$$c_{v,t} = \frac{\Delta E_{v,t}^{\mathrm{dis}}}{\Delta O_{v,t}}. \tag{3}$$

Cleaned interval-level data are aggregated into a vehicle-day table. For each vehicle-day, we compute the total travelled distance, starting, minimum and ending SOC, and summary statistics of interval-level consumption.

The daily energy target is estimated using discharge segments between charging events. A charging event is detected as a contiguous run of positive SOC increments with limited odometer movement, retained when the SOC gain is at least 3 percentage points and the odometer gain is at most 1 km. This captures parked charging events and avoids treating driving-related SOC fluctuations as charging. Daily discharged energy is estimated by summing SOC drops between charging runs, with each segment's contribution computed from the difference between the segment peak SOC and the following valley SOC, multiplied by the nominal battery capacity. The resulting target is:

$$y_{v,d} = \{\texttt{day energy kwh}\}_{v,d}. \tag{4}$$

The expected daily distance is represented through a coarse planning proxy. The realized daily distance $D_{v,d}$ is rounded down to the nearest 10 km bin:

$$\{\mathrm{expectedkm}\}_{v,d} = 10 \left\lfloor \frac{\max(D_{v,d}, 0)}{10} \right\rfloor, \tag{5}$$

preserving the planning-level nature of the task while avoiding the use of exact realized distance as a direct predictor. Calendar variables (month, ISO week, weekday, and a weekend indicator) are extracted and encoded with sine and cosine transformations to capture periodic structure.

Weather records are aggregated at the daily level. Temperature features include daily mean, minimum, maximum, and standard deviation, together with morning and typical driving-hour summaries, as well as heating and cooling degree indicators relative to base temperatures of 18°C and 22°C. Precipitation features include total daily precipitation, maximum and mean hourly precipitation, precipitation during typical driving hours, total precipitation duration, and binary indicators for rainy, heavy-rain, morning-rain, and afternoon-rain days.

Same-day weather variables are used as forecast inputs; in a production setting, these values would be obtained from day-ahead or intra-day weather forecasts, whereas in offline experiments historical observations are used as proxy forecasts. Access to weather information is assumed to be feasible for all clients, since EVs can obtain area-level weather data either through onboard sensing systems or via network connectivity when visiting a depot [7].

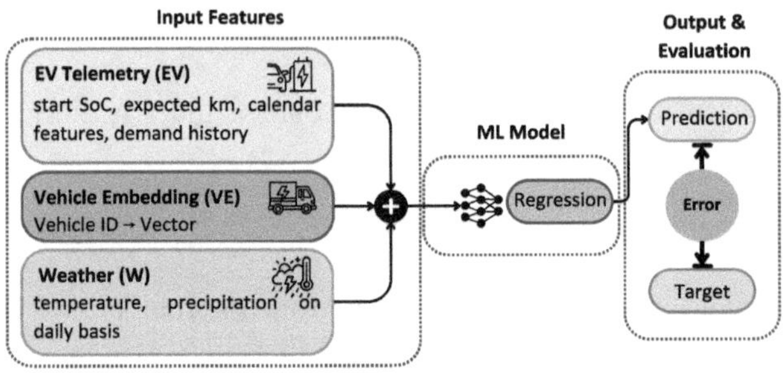

Fig. 1. Pipeline for daily EV energy demand prediction. EV telemetry provides the core daily input. Learned EV embeddings and weather descriptors are fused with the telemetry representation and processed by a deep tabular model.

After daily aggregation and weather merging, each sample has the form $(\mathbf{x}_{v,d}, y_{v,d})$, where $y_{v,d}$ is the daily energy demand. The base feature set is:

$$\mathbf{x}_{v,d}^{\text{base}} = \{\texttt{start SOC}, \texttt{expected km}, \texttt{month sin}, \texttt{month cos}, \texttt{week sin}, \texttt{week cos}, \texttt{weekday sin}, \texttt{weekday cos}, \texttt{is weekend}\}. \tag{6}$$

To capture recent EV-specific usage patterns, we include historical energy demand features computed from past days of the same vehicle. The first is the previous day's energy demand, $y_{v,d-1}$, and the second is the average energy demand over the previous three available days, $\bar{y}_{v,d}^{(3)} = \frac{1}{m_{v,d}} \sum_{j=1}^{m_{v,d}} y_{v,d-j}$, where $m_{v,d} = \min(3, N_{v,d}^{\text{past}})$ and $N_{v,d}^{\text{past}}$ denotes how many past observations are available for vehicle v before day d. Weather features are appended to complete the input vector. Rows with missing predictors or targets are removed before training. The dataset is split into training, validation, and test subsets within each vehicle, with feature and target scaling estimated on the training split. Figure 1 illustrates the pipeline. Vehicle telemetry provides the mandatory daily signal. Learned vehicle embeddings and weather descriptors are fused with the telemetry representation before the regression head predicts the daily energy target.

3.3 Federated Learning Settings

We evaluate FL under two partitioning schemes (Fig. 2). In the *cross-device* setting, each EV is one client, yielding 13 clients in total (two Dynamic BEV, one

ESOGU EV, and 10 private EVs). In the *cross-silo* setting, each dataset group is one client, yielding three clients. The clients correspond to heterogeneous groups collected in different locations and operational contexts.

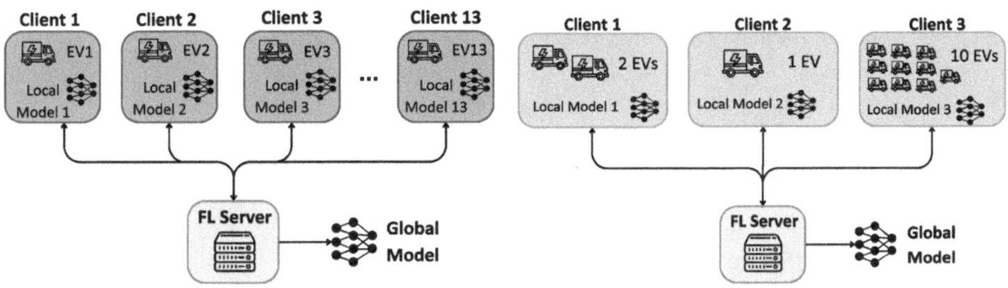

(a) Cross-device FL: one client per EV (13 clients total).

(b) Cross-silo FL: one client per dataset group (3 clients total).

Fig. 2. Federated partitioning schemes. In both cases, the FL server exchanges only model parameters with clients. Cross-device FL captures vehicle-level heterogeneity; cross-silo FL models collaboration across data silos.

The global FL objective is:

$$F(w) = \sum_{k=1}^{K} \frac{n_k}{n} F_k(w), \tag{7}$$

where $n = \sum_{k=1}^{K} n_k$ and the objective for client k with dataset $\mathcal{D}_k$ of size n_k is:

$$F_k(w) = \frac{1}{n_k} \sum_{(\mathbf{x}_i, y_i) \in \mathcal{D}_k} \ell(f_w(\mathbf{x}_i), y_i), \tag{8}$$

and $\ell(\cdot)$ is the regression loss.

To support heterogeneous and intermittently available clients, we adopt buffered asynchronous FedAvg [13]. Unlike synchronous FL, the server does not wait for all selected clients before aggregating. Instead, client updates are stored as they arrive and the global model is updated once the buffer reaches a predefined size. This setting reduces idle waiting time and is well suited to EV deployments where vehicles, users, or organizational silos may differ in data volume, connectivity, and computational capacity. The procedure is detailed in Algorithm 1.

Algorithm 1 Buffered Asynchronous FedAvg

Require: Initial model w^0, clients $\mathcal{K} = \{1, \ldots, K\}$, maximum server updates T, local epochs E, learning rate η, buffer size B, staleness limit $\tau_{\max}$

Initialize server update index $t \leftarrow 0$ and buffer $\mathcal{B} \leftarrow \emptyset$
while $t < T$ **do**
Client polling and local training
  for all available clients k that poll the server **do**
    Server returns the current task (w^t, t) to client k
    Client k sets $w_k \leftarrow w^t$ and $t_k \leftarrow t$
    for $e = 1, \ldots, E$ **do**
      Client k updates w_k on local data $\mathcal{D}_k$ using learning rate η
    end for
    Client k submits update (w_k, n_k, t_k) to the server
  end for
Server-side buffering
  for all submitted updates (w_k, n_k, t_k) **do**
    if $t - t_k \leq \tau_{\max}$ **then**
      $\mathcal{B} \leftarrow \mathcal{B} \cup \{(w_k, n_k, t_k)\}$
    end if
  end for
Buffered aggregation
  if $|\mathcal{B}| \geq B$ **then**
    Select a batch $\mathcal{U}^t \subseteq \mathcal{B}$ with $|\mathcal{U}^t| = B$
    $n_{\mathcal{U}} \leftarrow \sum_{(w_k, n_k, t_k) \in \mathcal{U}^t} n_k$
    $w^{t+1} \leftarrow \sum_{(w_k, n_k, t_k) \in \mathcal{U}^t} \frac{n_k}{n_{\mathcal{U}}} w_k$
    $\mathcal{B} \leftarrow \mathcal{B} \setminus \mathcal{U}^t$
    $t \leftarrow t + 1$
  end if
end while
return w^T

4 Experiments

4.1 Dataset

The experiments use the final vehicle-day dataset produced by the preprocessing pipeline described in Sect. 3. The dataset contains 3247 samples, split randomly within each vehicle into 2271 training, 488 validation, and 488 test samples. Table 2 reports the resulting counts and shows the client definitions used in the centralized, cross-device, and cross-silo settings. The data are highly imbalanced across sources. The private postal operation group contributes 2864 samples (88.2% of the full dataset), Dynamic BEV contributes 379 samples, and ESOGU contributes 4 valid vehicle-day samples after preprocessing. At the vehicle level, the postal EVs contain between 247 and 312 samples each, while the public vehicles range from 4 samples to 256. The cross-silo setting therefore represents collaboration across data owners with substantially different data sizes.

Figure 3 summarizes the distribution of daily consumption (kWh/km). The private EVs exhibit the widest spread and several high-consumption outliers,

Table 2. Train/validation/test counts per vehicle and dataset group. Vehicle identifiers define cross-device clients, dataset groups define cross-silo and local clients, and the final row corresponds to centralized learning.

Identifier	Train	Val	Test	Total	
PostVan EV1	207	44	45	296	Cross-device FL
PostVan EV2	195	42	42	279	
PostVan EV3	218	47	47	312	
PostVan EV4	209	45	45	299	
PostVan EV5	204	44	43	291	
PostVan EV6	190	41	40	271	
PostVan EV7	197	42	43	282	
PostVan EV8	173	37	37	247	
PostVan EV9	203	44	43	290	
PostVan EV10	208	45	44	297	
BEV-D1	86	18	19	123	
BEV-D2	179	38	39	256	
ESOGU	2	1	1	4	
Postal	2004	431	429	2864	Cross-silo FL local
Dynamic BEV	265	56	58	379	
ESOGU	2	1	1	4	
all	2271	488	488	3247	Centralized learning

while Dynamic BEV and ESOGU show lower medians and narrower interquartile ranges. Despite overlapping consumption ranges, individual EVs display distinct density profiles, confirming the heterogeneous nature of the FL setting. Figure 4 shows the temporal variation of daily consumption, with a seasonal increase toward winter months followed by a decrease toward spring, consistent with heating demand and reduced battery efficiency in cold conditions.

4.2 Learning Settings

All models predict three quantiles of the daily energy demand distribution, $\tau \in \{0.1, 0.5, 0.9\}$, corresponding to lower, median, and upper demand estimates. This formulation is suitable for planning tasks where uncertainty awareness is important. The median represents the typical expected demand, while the upper quantile captures high-demand scenarios relevant to capacity reservation. Training minimizes the summed pinball loss across quantiles:

$$\mathcal{L}(w) = \frac{1}{|\mathcal{B}|} \sum_{i \in \mathcal{B}} \sum_{j=1}^{3} \rho_{\tau_j} \left(y_i - \hat{y}_{\tau_j,i} \right), \tag{9}$$

where $\rho_\tau(u) = u(\tau - \mathbf{1}[u < 0])$ and $\mathcal{B}$ denotes a mini-batch.

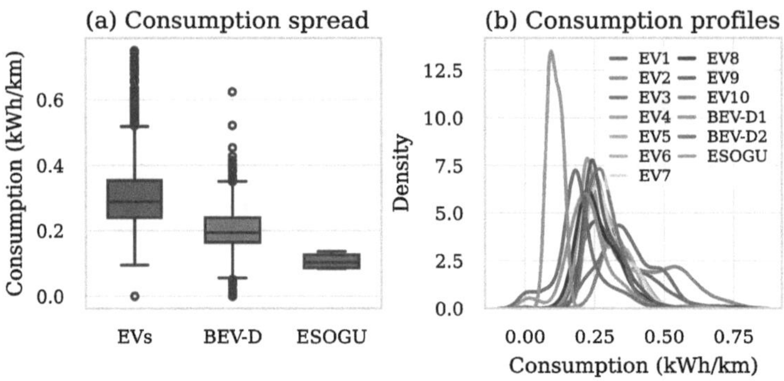

Fig. 3. Consumption distribution. Panel (a) compares the consumption spread across dataset groups. Panel (b) shows per-vehicle consumption density profiles.

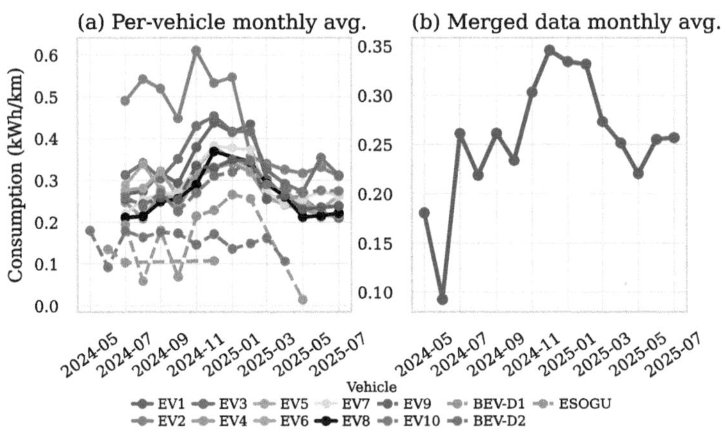

Fig. 4. Monthly average daily consumption. Panel (a) reports per-vehicle monthly averages. Panel (b) reports the merged monthly average across all vehicle-day samples.

We evaluate three neural tabular architectures.

MLP. A shared trunk with two hidden layers of sizes $(128, 64)$, ReLU activations, batch normalization, and dropout ($p = 0.15$). Separate quantile heads of hidden dimension 32 are applied after the shared representation.

TabNet. Two attentive feature-selection steps, each computing a soft feature mask and processing the masked input through a shared feature block of hidden size 128. A complementary prior discourages repeated feature selection across steps. Step outputs are summed and passed to a linear quantile head.

Transformer. Each input feature is treated as a token, projected to a hidden dimension of 128 and combined with learnable feature embeddings. A Transformer encoder with 2 layers, 4 attention heads, and feedforward dimension 512 processes the tokens. Representations are mean-pooled before the quantile head.

All models are trained for up to 80 epochs, or 80 server aggregation rounds in FL, using Adam with mini-batch size 128 and early stopping with patience 8. The checkpoint with the lowest validation MAE is used for test evaluation. In centralized and local training, standard supervised optimization is used. In FL, each selected client trains locally for up to 3 epochs. For cross-device FL, 4 clients are sampled per round from the 13 vehicle clients, with buffer size $B = 4$. For cross-silo FL, all 3 dataset-group clients participate in each round, with buffer size $B = 3$. Server-side aggregation follows Algorithm 1.

Models are evaluated using Mean Absolute Error (MAE) and Root Mean Squared Error (RMSE), reported in kWh. For the FL experiments, we additionally report orchestration-level metrics (e.g., communication ingress, egress, and latency) to assess practical deployability under heterogeneous client conditions.

4.3 Results

All results are means over five random seeds with standard deviations in parentheses. The full feature configuration, i.e., *base* (Eq. 6), vehicle embeddings (*VE*) and *weather* information is used throughout unless stated otherwise.

Table 3. Test MAE and RMSE (kWh) for the full feature set across learning settings and architectures. Results are means over five seeds (std in parentheses). CD = cross-device; CS = cross-silo. **Bold** marks the best result per metric column.

	Centralized		CD Global		CD FT		CS Global		CS FT	
Model	MAE	RMSE	MAE	RMSE	MAE	RMSE	MAE	RMSE	MAE	RMSE
MLP	2.695	3.764	3.069	4.010	2.345	3.247	4.098	5.155	2.894	3.890
(std)	(0.288)	(0.305)	(0.202)	(0.199)	(0.049)	(0.065)	(0.496)	(0.497)	(0.578)	(0.603)
TabNet	2.444	3.471	2.585	3.535	**2.124**	**2.967**	**2.027**	**3.088**	**1.839**	**2.924**
(std)	(0.133)	(0.271)	(0.030)	(0.040)	(0.038)	(0.054)	(0.052)	(0.055)	(0.102)	(0.102)
Transformer	**2.433**	**3.417**	2.698	3.635	2.538	3.507	2.844	3.994	2.033	3.373
(std)	(0.170)	(0.308)	(0.157)	(0.132)	(0.165)	(0.184)	(0.851)	(0.864)	(0.592)	(0.674)

Centralized Versus Federated Learning. Table 3 reports the test MAE and RMSE across all learning settings and architectures. Under centralized training, the Transformer achieves the lowest MAE and RMSE (2.433 kWh and 3.417 kWh, respectively), with TabNet close behind (2.444 kWh MAE, 3.471 kWh RMSE) and MLP trailing (2.695 kWh MAE, 3.764 kWh RMSE).

In the cross-device (CD) setting, the global model trained across the 13 vehicle clients degrades modestly relative to centralized, with TabNet reaching 2.585 kWh MAE (+0.141 kWh over centralized TabNet) and the Transformer reaching 2.698 kWh MAE (+0.265 kWh). Cross-device fine-tuning (CD FT), in which the global model is further fine-tuned on each client's local data after federated training, recovers this gap. TabNet CD FT achieves 2.124 kWh MAE and 2.967 kWh RMSE, which is 0.320 kWh below the centralized TabNet baseline, demonstrating that personalization through fine-tuning can improve upon the centralized model. MLP CD FT similarly improves to 2.345 kWh MAE, reducing the global CD error by 0.724 kWh. The Transformer CD FT, however, shows only modest improvement over its global counterpart (2.538 vs. 2.698 kWh MAE), suggesting that the higher-capacity architecture is less amenable to local adaptation, possibly due to the limited amount of client-specific data available during fine-tuning. Transformer-based models typically require larger training corpora to fully exploit their representational capacity and to avoid unstable parameter adaptation under low-sample regimes, which is consistent with the relatively small number of vehicle-day samples available per client in the cross-device setting.

The cross-silo (CS) setting represents collaboration across three heterogeneous dataset groups with highly uneven sample sizes. TabNet is again the strongest model, with CS global TabNet reaching 2.027 kWh MAE, while CS, FT TabNet achieves the best aggregate result, with 1.839 kWh MAE and 2.924 kWh RMSE. This indicates that silo-level fine-tuning is beneficial in the evaluated setting, where each silo represents a distinct operational distribution. However, because the test set is dominated by postal-operation samples and ESOGU is extremely small, this result should not be interpreted as a general claim that cross-silo FL always outperforms centralized training. MLP and Transformer also benefit from fine-tuning, although the Transformer shows higher variance under cross-silo training.

Across all settings, TabNet is the strongest architecture as it achieves the best fine-tuned result in both FL partitioning schemes and is competitive with the Transformer under centralized training despite being a lighter model.

Table 4. Feature ablation under centralized training (all architectures), cross-device FT TabNet, and cross-silo FT TabNet. **Bold** marks the best MAE per setting.

	Cent. MLP		Cent. TabNet		Cent. Transf.		CD FT TabNet		CS FT TabNet	
Features	MAE	RMSE	MAE	RMSE	MAE	RMSE	MAE	RMSE	MAE	RMSE
EV only	2.898	4.015	2.806	3.889	2.955	4.099	2.569	3.797	3.685	4.510
EV + VE	2.677	3.701	2.485	3.382	2.772	3.822	2.483	3.684	2.378	3.251
EV + W	2.968	4.119	2.862	3.908	2.897	4.019	2.127	2.986	1.934	2.976
EV + VE + W	**2.695**	**3.764**	**2.444**	**3.471**	**2.433**	**3.417**	**2.124**	**2.967**	**1.839**	**2.924**

Feature Ablation. Table 4 reports the effect of progressively adding feature groups to the base EV telemetry signal under centralized training and for the two best fine-tuned FL configurations (CD FT and CS FT TabNet). Starting from the base configuration, adding vehicle embeddings consistently reduces error across all model and setting combinations. For centralized TabNet, the addition of vehicle embeddings reduces MAE from 2.806 to 2.485 kWh (−0.321 kWh), and for centralized MLP from 2.898 to 2.677 kWh (−0.221 kWh). This improvement confirms that learned embeddings capture EV-specific consumption characteristics that are not explained by the shared input features alone.

Adding weather data to the base feature set without EV embeddings improves performance in the FL fine-tuned settings more markedly than under centralized training. For CD FT TabNet, it achieves 2.127 kWh MAE, which is already below the centralized TabNet baseline, while for CS FT TabNet it reaches 1.934 kWh MAE. By contrast, under centralized training, the weather data slightly degrades performance relative to the base features for MLP and Transformer.

The full feature set achieves the lowest MAE and RMSE in every model and setting. For centralized TabNet the full configuration reduces MAE from 2.806 to 2.444 kWh; for CS FT TabNet the reduction is from 3.685 to 1.839 kWh, a decrease of 1.846 kWh. The consistent superiority of the full feature set across architectures and learning regimes confirms that vehicle embeddings and weather descriptors are complementary, i.e., embeddings capture inter-vehicle heterogeneity while weather features account for environmental variability that affects both energy consumption and battery efficiency.

Table 5. Test MAE and RMSE (kWh) for the local setting using TabNet. Each model is trained on one dataset group and evaluated on all test groups. Results are means over five seeds (std in parentheses).

	Test on EVs		Test on BEV		Test on ESOGU		Overall	
Train on	MAE	RMSE	MAE	RMSE	MAE	RMSE	MAE	RMSE
BEV	8.835	10.181	**4.511**	8.515	6.444	6.444	7.986	9.637
(std)	(0.399)	(0.476)	(0.230)	(0.482)	(1.761)	(1.761)	(0.397)	(0.507)
ESOGU	34.842	38.103	19.593	28.328	**1.418**	**1.418**	29.925	33.778
(std)	(37.161)	(41.549)	(19.959)	(26.315)	(1.011)	(1.011)	(31.616)	(35.969)
EVs	**2.229**	**2.940**	6.280	**8.276**	8.679	8.679	**3.349**	**4.203**
(std)	(0.070)	(0.094)	(1.450)	(1.405)	(4.529)	(4.529)	(0.265)	(0.216)

Local Training and Cross-Dataset Transfer. Table 5 evaluates TabNet models trained on a single dataset group and tested on all three groups, to assess how well locally trained models generalize and to provide a lower bound on collaborative learning. When trained on the postal EVs and tested within the same group, the local model achieves 2.229 kWh MAE and 2.940 kWh RMSE, the strongest within-group result of the three local models. However, generalizing this model to the Dynamic BEV vehicles degrades accuracy substantially (6.280 kWh MAE), and to ESOGU (8.679 kWh MAE), reflecting the large operating differences between commercial postal vans and the public benchmark vehicles.

Training locally on BEV yields 4.511 kWh MAE within group, but predicting on the postal EVs is highly inaccurate (8.835 kWh MAE), with the overall MAE being 7.986 kWh. The ESOGU-trained model is practically unusable outside its own group, with MAE of 34.842 kWh on the postal EVs and 19.593 kWh on Dynamic BEV. This is expected given that the ESOGU group contributes only 4 valid vehicle-day samples after preprocessing, making local training unreliable.

These results highlight the limitations of purely local training under data scarcity and cross-dataset shift. The best local model reaches 3.349 kWh overall MAE, compared with 1.839 kWh for CS, FT TabNet. Thus, FL with fine-tuning provides a meaningful aggregate gain in this heterogeneous setting. However, ESOGU has only one test sample, so its local and transfer metrics are diagnostic rather than statistically robust.

4.4 Raspberry Pi Deployment

To evaluate the practical feasibility of the proposed FL pipeline, we deployed the cross-silo setting on a four-node Raspberry Pi testbed. One device acts as the FL server and the remaining three act as clients corresponding to the three dataset groups. This setup is the closest to the intended real-world deployment, where each data owner keeps raw records locally and exchanges model parameters.

The deployed system follows the same buffered asynchronous protocol used in simulation. Each client polls the server, receives the current global model, performs local training, and submits the updated model together with local metrics. The server aggregates received updates when the buffer condition is satisfied. Predictive accuracy is computed from the same MAE and RMSE metrics used in simulation, and the Raspberry Pi execution produced the same ranking and no substantial accuracy degradation compared to simulation mode, confirming that deployment affects mainly the runtime and communication behavior.

Communication cost is measured directly based on the HTTP communication. For every request-response exchange, we record the request payload size, response payload size, and endpoint latency. Round-level ingress and egress are computed as the total bytes received and sent by the server per round, converted to MB. The communication overhead ratio is defined as:

$$r_{\text{comm}} = \frac{\text{total protocol bytes}}{\text{serialized model-state bytes}}, \tag{10}$$

where a value close to 1 indicates that communication volume is dominated by model parameters with limited additional protocol overhead.

Figure 5 reports model-level profiling on the largest client, corresponding to the private postal-operation silo. The Transformer has the largest parameter

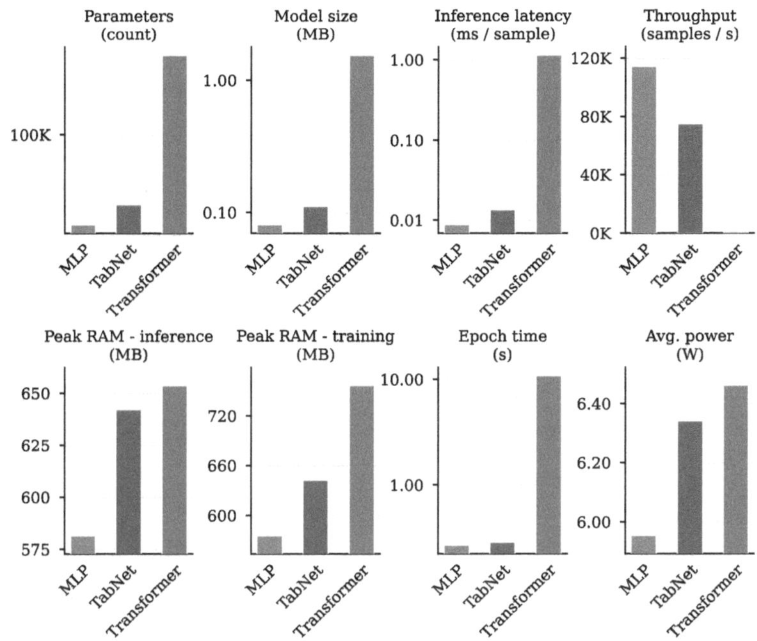

Fig. 5. Raspberry Pi profiling results for the three model architectures, measured on the client with the largest local dataset (private postal-operation silo). Metrics include inference latency, epoch time, throughput, peak RAM, and average power draw.

count, which directly translates into higher inference latency, longer epoch time, and lower throughput. The MLP is the smallest and fastest model, with the lowest inference latency and highest throughput. TabNet lies between the two: more expensive than the MLP but substantially lighter than the Transformer. Peak RAM remains within budget for all architectures, although the Transformer requires the most memory during both inference and training. Average power differs only moderately across models, suggesting that the primary practical cost of larger architectures is runtime rather than instantaneous power draw.

Figure 6 summarizes communication and orchestration metrics. The MLP and TabNet require less than 0.5 MB of ingress and egress per round, while the Transformer requires ≈ 6.17 MB in each direction, directly reflecting its larger serialized model state. Similarly, MLP and TabNet complete task assignment, submission, and aggregation with low latency, whereas the Transformer introduces substantially higher submission and aggregation delays, most visibly in participation time. MLP and TabNet complete several rounds per minute on the testbed, while the Transformer is considerably slower. The communication overhead ratio is close to 1 for all models, confirming that communication volume is dominated by model parameters rather than HTTP or metadata overhead.

Overall, the deployment confirms that buffered asynchronous FL is feasible on low-cost edge hardware. However, architecture choice has a strong effect on

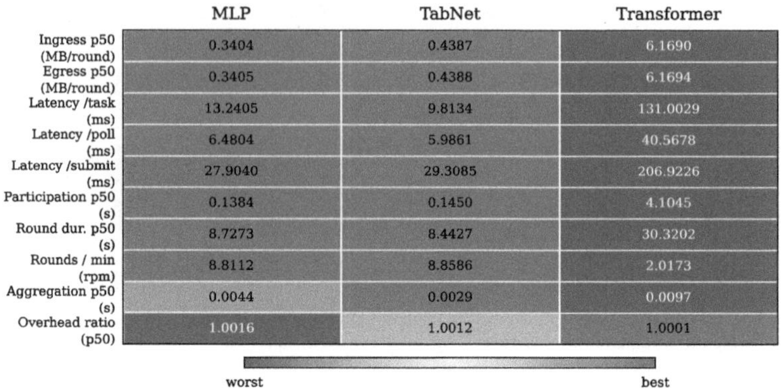

Fig. 6. Communication and orchestration metrics in the Raspberry Pi deployment. Green indicates better values and red indicates worse values. (Color figure online)

communication volume and round latency, with lightweight models offering an attractive balance between predictive quality and deployability.

5 Conclusion

In this paper, we presented a framework for daily EV energy demand prediction under centralized, cross-device, and cross-silo FL settings. A unified preprocessing pipeline transforms heterogeneous public and private EV records into vehicle-day samples, while the final model combines telemetry, vehicle embeddings, and weather descriptors. Results show that FL can approach centralized performance while preserving data locality, and the Raspberry Pi deployment confirms the feasibility of buffered asynchronous FL on resource-constrained hardware.

Future work will consider richer planning signals, simpler non-DL baselines, alternative FL algorithms, more balanced datasets, repeated splits, and sensitivity to noisy expected-distance estimates. Although FL preserves raw data locality, stronger privacy guarantees also require secure aggregation, differential privacy, and evaluation against inference or adversarial client attacks.

Acknowledgments. This work is supported by the European Commission under Grant No 101189589 through the Horizon EU program for the project "Open Cloud-EdgeIoT Platform Uptake in Large Scale Pilots (O-CEI)".

Disclosure of Interests. The authors have no competing interests to declare that are relevant to the content of this article.

References

1. Akshay, K., Grace, G.H., Gunasekaran, K., Samikannu, R.: Power consumption prediction for electric vehicle charging stations and forecasting income. Sci. Rep. **14**(1), 6497 (2024)
2. Amin, A., Amin, M.S., Park, H., Lee, D.: Electric vehicle range prediction models: a systematic review of machine learning, mathematical, and simulation approaches. World Electric Veh. J. **16**(11), 607 (2025). https://doi.org/10.3390/wevj16110607
3. Cavus, M., Ayan, H., Dissanayake, D., Sharma, A., Deb, S., Bell, M.C.: Forecasting electric vehicle charging demand in smart cities using hybrid deep learning of regional spatial behaviours. Energies **18**(13), 3425 (2025). https://doi.org/10.3390/en18133425
4. Chen, P., Qin, J., et al.: Electric vehicle charging demand forecasting at charging stations under climate influence for electricity dispatching. IET Power Electron. (2025). https://doi.org/10.1049/pel2.12833
5. van Etten, T., Degeler, V., Luo, D.: Large-scale forecasting of electric vehicle charging demand using global time series modeling. In: Proceedings of the 10th International Conference on Vehicle Technology and Intelligent Transport Systems (VEHITS), pp. 40–51 (2024). https://doi.org/10.5220/0012555400003702
6. Han, Q., Li, X.: A vertical federated learning method for electric vehicle charging station load prediction in coupled transportation and power distribution systems. Processes **13**(2), 468 (2025). https://doi.org/10.3390/pr13020468
7. Hussain, I., Ching, K.B., Uttraphan, C., Tay, K.G., Noor, A., Memon, S.A.: Optimizing electric vehicle energy consumption prediction through machine learning and ensemble approaches. Scientific Reports (2025). https://www.nature.com/articles/s41598-025-14129-2
8. Jin, R., Liu, H.: Privacy-aware electric vehicle load forecasting via blockchain-based federated transfer learning. Complex Intell. Syst. (2025). https://doi.org/10.1007/s40747-025-02002-8
9. Marlin, R., Jurdak, R., Abuadbba, A.: H-FLTN: A privacy-preserving hierarchical framework for electric vehicle spatio-temporal charge prediction (2025). https://arxiv.org/abs/2502.18697
10. Marzbani, F., Osman, A.H., Hassan, M.S.: Electric vehicle energy demand prediction techniques: an in-depth and critical systematic review. IEEE Access **11**, 96242–96255 (2023)
11. McMahan, B., Moore, E., Ramage, D., Hampson, S., y Arcas, B.A.: Communication-efficient learning of deep networks from decentralized data. In: Artificial Intelligence and Statistics, pp. 1273–1282. PMLR (2017)
12. Narayana Gowda, S., et al.: Short-term aggregate electric vehicle charging load forecasting in diverse conditions with minimal data using transfer and meta-learning. Energy Syst. (2024). https://doi.org/10.1007/s12667-024-00682-8
13. Nguyen, J., et al.: Federated learning with buffered asynchronous aggregation. In: International Conference on Artificial Intelligence and Statistics, pp. 3581–3607. PMLR (2022)
14. Perifanis, V., et al.: Towards energy-aware federated traffic prediction for cellular networks. In: 2023 Eighth International Conference on Fog and Mobile Edge Computing (FMEC), pp. 93–100. IEEE (2023)
15. Perifanis, V., Nikolaidou, F., Pavlidis, N., Thomakos, P., Sendros, A.: Federated learning for early prediction of EV charging demand (2026). https://arxiv.org/abs/2605.04993

16. Polat, A.A., Keser, S.B., Sarıçiçek, İ, Erdoğmuş, A.K., Kafall, A., Yazıcı, A.: A dataset for state of charge and range estimation of an l5 type electric vehicle that is used for urban logistic. Data Brief 111933 (2025)
17. Rachavelpula, S.V.R., Cha, S.: Personalized electric vehicle energy consumption estimation framework that integrates driver behavior with map data (2026). https://arxiv.org/abs/2604.20764
18. Szumska, E.M., et al.: Machine learning applications in energy consumption forecasting and management for electric vehicles: a systematic review. Energies **18**(20), 5420 (2025). https://doi.org/10.3390/en18205420
19. Tian, J., Liu, H., Gan, W., et al.: Short-term electric vehicle charging load forecasting based on TCN-LSTM network with comprehensive similar day identification. Appl. Energy **381**, 125174 (2025). https://doi.org/10.1016/j.apenergy.2024.125174
20. Tritsarolis, A., Sampaio, G., Pelekis, N., Theodoridis, Y.: On electric vehicle energy demand forecasting and the effect of federated learning. arXiv preprint arXiv:2602.20782 (2026)
21. Wang, Y., Huang, H., et al.: Prediction of battery electric vehicle energy consumption via pre-trained model under inconsistent feature spaces. Technologies **13**(11), 493 (2025). https://doi.org/10.3390/technologies13110493
22. Wen, J., Zhang, Z., Lan, Y., Cui, Z., Cai, J., Zhang, W.: A survey on federated learning: challenges and applications. Int. J. Mach. Learn. Cybern. **14**(2), 513–535 (2023)
23. Yasko, M., Moussa Issaka, A., Tian, F., Kazmi, H., Driesen, J., Martinez, W.: Unveiling energy dynamics of battery electric vehicle using high-resolution data. Sci. Data **12**(1), 1878 (2025)
24. Yin, W., Ji, J.: Prediction of EV charging load based on federated learning. Energy **316**, 134559 (2025). https://doi.org/10.1016/j.energy.2025.134559
25. Zhang, X., Zhang, Z., Liu, Y.: A review of machine learning approaches for electric vehicle energy consumption modelling in urban transportation. Renewable Energy **234**, 121243 (2024). https://doi.org/10.1016/j.renene.2024.121243

A Benchmark for Multi-dimensional Evaluation of Location Privacy Protection Mechanisms

Toon Dehaene(✉), Michiel Willocx, Bert Lagaisse, and Vincent Naessens

DistriNet, KU Leuven, Leuven, Belgium

Abstract. A multitude of Location Privacy Protection Mechanisms (LPPMs) are presented in recent years. They aim to balance two competing objectives, namely preserving utility for downstream analytics while limiting sensitive information that can be inferred from traces. A fair comparison of existing work is currently hard as different studies rely on heterogeneous datasets, attacker models, privacy notions, and utility tasks for assessing their effectiveness. This paper presents a benchmarking framework for evaluating and comparing LPPMs with respect to utility and privacy. Our framework is equipped with a repository of representative concrete components, including LPPMs used in real deployments, attacks from prior work and realistic crowd-sensing utility tasks. Multi-dimensional evaluation across diverse real-world mobility datasets reveals a nuanced privacy-utility picture that remains hidden under single-metric analyses. Our results demonstrate the added value of multi-view benchmarking and showcase the framework as an extensible foundation for future research on location privacy.

Keywords: Location Privacy · LPPM · Utility

1 Introduction

Over the past decade, location data has become an increasingly valuable asset in modern digital services. It enables crowd insights such as travel-time estimation, hotspot detection, and urban-planning support. Businesses employ aggregated mobility information for site selection and demand modeling [31], while governments rely on it for traffic management and infrastructure planning. During public-health crises, large-scale mobility indicators have informed population-level decision-making [20,56]. While accurate location traces enable substantial benefits, they simultaneously expose individuals to significant risks [17,18,57]. They reveal habits, identities, social relationships, and sensitive places, and can be misused for profiling, targeted coercion, extortion, or discrimination.

These risks arise from how location data is collected in practice. Many mobile applications embed third-party software libraries as a monetization strategy [15,30]. The libraries continuously collect and send accurate location traces

P. Kieseberg et al. (Eds.): ARES 2026 Workshops, LNCS 16903, pp. 185–203, 2027.
https://doi.org/10.1007/978-3-032-37218-5_12

of the users to data brokers. These location traces contain an accurate GPS location, a timestamp, and a persistent pseudonym for long-term tracking. Most users remain unaware of these data collection practices. Data brokers make the collected accurate location traces commercially accessible on a large-scale, meaning that both legitimate analytics firms and malicious actors can obtain such data with limited oversight.

Privacy Enhancing Techniques (PETs)–and, in the context of location data, Location Privacy Protection Mechanisms (LPPMs)–seek to mitigate the privacy risks involved with sharing and processing large-scale location trace datasets by transforming data in a way that preserves sufficient utility for legitimate crowd-based analytics while limiting what can be inferred about specific individuals. However, designing and evaluating LPPMs is fundamentally tied to utility: without a reference to some downstream use, the ideal privacy strategy would be to share no data at all. Meaningful comparisons between Privacy-Enhancing Technologies require privacy metrics that apply consistently across mechanisms. In the tabular-data setting, well-established notions such as k-anonymity, ℓ-diversity, and (ε, δ)-differential privacy enable comparisons. Directly transferring these ideas to location data has proven problematic. Accurate mobility traces exhibit strong spatio-temporal correlations and highly characteristic movement patterns, rendering most trajectories effectively unique [33].

A different strategy is to define privacy with respect to specific personal information. In practice, however, when high-frequency location traces themselves are treated as sensitive, existing models are unable to achieve acceptable privacy-utility trade-offs [2,47,52]. This motivates an alternative perspective on sensitive information in location privacy. Rather than focusing on re-identification or full-trajectory protection, researchers evaluate privacy through what we refer to as privacy dimensions. These inference targets represent the personal information an adversary seeks to derive from location traces. Under this view, even if a user is effectively unique in a dataset, it does not necessarily imply that sensitive properties (such as home-work labels, visits to particular places, or demographic attributes) are leaked from the dataset [33,47].

To assess data quality after applying an LPPM, many works evaluate performance based on a selection of one or multiple privacy and utility dimensions. Privacy dimensions are defined through the specification of attacker models, capturing the adversary's prior knowledge and inference capabilities. Utility dimensions measure performance in downstream tasks such as travel-time estimation, hotspot detection, or crowd-level mobility analysis. In addition, evaluations rely on specific datasets, which may differ substantially from one study to another. While these design choices are typically well-motivated in isolation, together they create a heterogeneous evaluation landscape with many degrees of freedom. As a result, LPPMs are assessed under context-specific and often incomparable assumptions. Mechanisms are optimized for one combination of a privacy objective, a utility task, a threat model, and a dataset, and cannot be directly contrasted with those developed under different conditions. The frequent absence of publicly released implementations further hampers reproducibility and systematic comparison. This paper addresses this fragmentation by proposing a benchmark for the structured and reproducible evaluation of LPPMs.

Our Contribution. This work presents a benchmarking framework for the systematic evaluation of LPPMs, providing a controlled environment for assessing privacy-utility trade-offs and enables fair and transparent comparisons. The benchmark adopts a modular architecture with well-defined interfaces that explicitly separate datasets, LPPMs, and *Privacy Scorer* and *Utility Scorer*. This decoupling facilitates experimentation across a wide range of LPPM techniques, supports large-scale parameter sweeps, and allows researchers to substitute individual components – such as alternative privacy dimensions, utility dimensions, attacker models, or datasets – without redesigning the evaluation pipeline. We validate the benchmark through an extensive experimental study on multiple datasets, demonstrating its effectiveness in enabling structured analysis, meaningful comparison, and actionable insights for location-data analytics. A fully documented implementation of the benchmark, together with an initial suite of reusable components is publicly released, providing a practical foundation for subsequent research.

The remainder of this paper is structured as follows. Section 2 reviews prior work and motivates the need for a multi-dimensional benchmark. Section 3 introduces the framework design and component implementations. Section 4 presents experiments across datasets, LPPMs, and evaluation dimensions. Section 5 discusses the unique insights the framework provides, Sect. 6 concludes.

2 Related Work

The design and evaluation of LPPMs has been a central focus of privacy research for over a decade. This section identifies gaps in existing methodologies and highlights the fragmented nature of current evaluation practices. First, we categorize broad classes of LPPMs to assess their compatibility with a benchmarking framework. Second, recent literature is analyzed to show that evaluations rarely cover the full spectrum of relevant experimental components. Finally, existing comparative frameworks are examined, revealing critical gaps in modularity, scale, and utility integration.

2.1 Categorization of LPPMs

Table 1 summarizes the main categories of LPPMs, based on the work of Primault et al. [44]. The table lists representative works for each category and indicates the number of outgoing location reports generated per original input report. Note that Primault et al. also identify protocol-based LPPMs as a distinct category. These mechanisms rely on cryptographic techniques such as homomorphic encryption or secure multi-party computation. Unlike the other categories, which produce a *dataset* of privacy-enhanced location reports suitable for sharing and downstream use (e.g., ML model building), protocol-based LPPMs compute only an *aggregate result*–a yes/no proximity answer or a route–without releasing individual records. Their privacy stems from cryptographic security assumptions rather than tunable noise, and they are evaluated via formal security proofs rather than empirical attacks. As Primault et al. [44] argue, their narrow use-case tailoring, lack of interoperability with existing LBSs, and high computational cost further hinder practical deployability–detecting nearby friends [37,39] and outsourced navigation [9] being representative examples. The remaining categories share a common output model suitable for joint evaluation, while fundamental differences place protocol-based LPPMs out of scope.

Table 1. Classification of LPPMs and their outputs

LPPM Type	Example Works	Output Type
Mix-Zones	[24,26,36,45]	Single location per report
Generalization-Based	[1,4,13,14,28,34,40,51,54]	Single location per report
Dummies-Based	[5,29,32,46]	Multiple locations per report
Perturbation-Based	[2,3,6,11,12,27,35,42,43,53,55]	Single location per report
Rule-Based	[10,23,38]	Implementation-dependent
Protocol-Based	[9,25,37,39]	No direct location sharing

Mix-zones define areas where users are not tracked, and their identities are shuffled to prevent adversaries from linking entry and exit points. These mechanisms rely on a trusted communication channel to manage pseudonyms and typically require a critical mass of users to achieve meaningful anonymity. Generalization-based LPPMs obfuscate precise locations by replacing them with cloaking regions such as city blocks or grid cells. These often enforce k-anonymity, ensuring a user's location remains indistinguishable from at least $k-1$ other users in the same region. Dummies-based LPPMs generate synthetic locations or trajectories to conceal a user's true location among fake data. Perturbation-based LPPMs add noise to location data to obscure a user's true whereabouts. Techniques such as Planar Laplace apply differential privacy principles to location data, ensuring that nearby locations produce similar protected outputs. Finally, Rule-based LPPMs combine multiple protection strategies and dynamically select the most appropriate one based on contextual rules, for example by switching between generalization and perturbation depending on the sensitivity of the location.

The output of Perturbation and Generalization-based mechanisms makes them particularly suitable for the continuous reporting pipelines this work emphasizes, as they operate directly on the mandatory location fields–latitude and longitude–while preserving the dataset's tabular structure, identifiers, and timestamps. Furthermore, their parameterized nature–e.g., noise levels or grid sizes–enables the systematic exploration of privacy-utility trade-offs. Rule-based mechanisms, while lacking a uniform behavior, are also suitable provided they encapsulate their logic within a standard transformation interface that maps input traces to protected output traces.

In contrast, other categories face architectural or structural mismatches. Mix-zones, while technically suitable for continuous reporting pipelines, rely on strong assumptions about infrastructure that limit their applicability in the context of this work. Specifically, they assume that third-party libraries and data brokers do not leak persistent identifiers or track users outside the mix-zones. Dummies-based approaches, while operating on standard data formats, present a challenge. By injecting multiple simultaneous reports for a single user ID, they disrupt utility metrics designed for single-trajectory analysis. Assessing them within the context of continuous reporting pipelines therefore requires specialized utility dimensions capable of filtering or tolerating synthetic traffic.

2.2 Fragmented Evaluation Approaches

As previously established, privacy and utility are multi-faceted concepts that cannot be captured by a single metric, necessitating a framework that enables experimental exploration across variable datasets, LPPMs, and privacy-utility dimensions. Analysis of related work reveals that existing evaluations typically vary only a limited subset of these components. For instance, several works explore multiple LPPM configurations and datasets but employ fixed privacy metrics [12,42], while others focus on novel utility or privacy metrics with limited LPPM comparison [8,38,50]. Some recent contributions even speculate about LPPM effects without implementing them [17]. This fragmented experimental scope expresses a demand for a unified framework where all component types can be systematically varied and combined, enabling comprehensive utility-privacy trade-off analysis that prior work achieves only partially.

Table 2. Papers that propose a framework for comparing LPPMs and what aspects can be explored in their API, showing a lack of works that unify all aspects.

Work	Year	Dataset	LPPM	Privacy Metric	Utility Metric	Trade-off Insights	Exploration API
[48,49]	'11, '12	◐	◐	●	○	○	◐
[42]	'17	◐	●	●	○	◐	○
[7]	'19	◐	●	●	●	◐	○
[22]	'20	○	●	○	○	○	○
This Work	*'26*	●	●	●	●	●	●

Table 2 categorizes existing frameworks by the components they support, highlighting the scarcity of solutions that unify all aspects of LPPM benchmarking. While foundational works like Shokri et al. [49] provided an exploration API, they focused primarily on adversarial correctness without explicit metrics for downstream utility tasks. Conversely, later studies by Oya et al. [42] and Boukoros et al. [7] developed methodologies for privacy-utility trade-offs but did not release an extensible API required to expand their experiments. Toolkits such as Geopriv4j [22] offer a wide range implementations of LPPMs but lack the evaluation harness for datasets and metrics.

3 Design of the Benchmarking Framework

To enable fair and systematic comparisons of LPPMs, this section designs a benchmarking framework that provides an environment that standardizes component interactions, ensures consistent data formats, and supports experimental workflows with large-scale parameter sweeps. By decoupling core functionalities into interchangeable components, the framework enables researchers to compare mechanisms fairly, explore varied configurations, and derive actionable insights while keeping the evaluation pipeline consistent.

The framework consists of six core components: *Data Loader*, *LPPM*, *Personal Feature Extractor*, *Privacy Scorer*, *Population Feature Extractor*, and *Utility Scorer*. Each component defines a specific interface, allowing for substitution of implementations to explore different configurations. This modular architecture supports parameterization (e.g., privacy budgets, grid sizes) for systematic exploration of both algorithmic variations and parametric effects. The framework produces standardized reports of privacy-utility trade-offs, which facilitates comparative analysis across mechanisms, datasets, and evaluation metrics. The rest of this section introduces the architecture of the benchmarking framework for evaluating *LPPMs*.

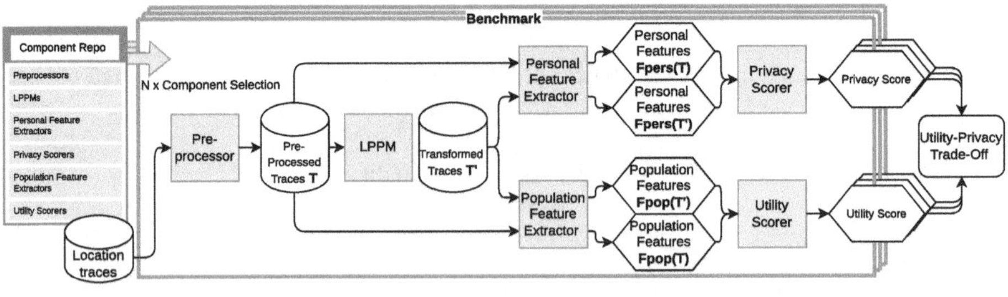

Fig. 1. Multiple sets of components are selected, each set producing both a privacy score and utility score. Subsequently a report is generated, visualizing the privacy-utility trade-offs for all component selections.

3.1 Composing a Benchmark

Figure 1 depicts a single benchmark instance in orange, representing one fully specified evaluation flow. The process starts with the *Data Loader*, which ingests a user-defined dataset and produces a preprocessed tabular representation containing the mandatory columns. The *LPPM* then applies privacy-preserving transformations to the location and time fields. Next, the *Personal Feature Extractor* computes a sensitive information-related prediction on both the original and transformed data, after which the *Privacy Scorer* compares the predictions to yield a scalar privacy score. In parallel, the *Population Feature Extractor* and *Utility Scorer* compute a downstream utility-related prediction on both versions of the data, and the *Utility Scorer* compares these to produce a scalar utility score. Together, these steps constitute the smallest complete evaluation supported by the framework, producing exactly one privacy-utility score pair for the chosen configuration.

A concrete benchmark is constructed by selecting a single implementation from the framework's repository for each of the six components. Using diverse combinations of component implementations, multiple benchmark runs are executed, each producing a pair of scalar outcomes in the form of a privacy score and a utility score. After all runs have completed, the resulting pairs are aggregated into a report that visualizes privacy-utility trade-offs across the user-defined exploration space.

The framework maintains a repository containing concrete implementations of components. Each adheres to the interface of its type and is therefore interchangeable. A component instance optionally depends on tunable parameters that modify its internal logic, such as thresholds, privacy budgets, radii, or temporal filters. When composing multiple benchmarks, two implementations with different parameter settings are treated as distinct instances, enabling systematic exploration of algorithmic variations and parametric effects on the same level.

3.2 Components and Their Interfaces

The *Data Loader* takes a user-defined dataset and produces a canonical tabular representation suitable for downstream processing. This preprocessing step includes type conversion, bounds checking, handling of missing or invalid values, and normalization. The resulting table contains mandatory columns with specific types: `user_id` (unsigned 64-bit integer), `epoch` (signed 32-bit integer), `longitude` (64-bit float), and `latitude` (64-bit float), along with any auxiliary fields from the original dataset. This standardized representation serves as the original input for both privacy and utility scores within the benchmarking framework.

The *LPPM* then applies privacy-preserving transformations to the location and time fields. Commonly, implementations expose parameters such as privacy budgets, radii, or grid sizes that influence the strength of transformation. The *LPPM* is restricted to modifying only the mandatory columns `user_id`, `epoch`, `longitude`, and `latitude`, and must preserve all auxiliary fields to ensure compatibility with downstream utility analyses. The output of the *LPPM* is a table with the same schema and types as the input but containing privacy-transformed values for the location and, where permitted, temporal fields.

Next, the *Personal Feature Extractor* computes a privacy-related prediction on both the original and transformed data. It evaluates specific privacy dimensions using attack models, typically inference attacks, producing two predictions passed to the *Privacy Scorer*, one on the transformed data, one on the original. Depending on the chosen privacy dimension, the resulting measurement may be an (enhanced) prediction of raw locations, or the outcome of an inference attack–such as POI prediction or social link reconstruction–scored against baseline labels. Its configuration may rely on task definitions, feature choices, model hyperparameters, or temporal aggregation settings.

The *Privacy Scorer* compares these predictions to yield a scalar privacy score. Its behavior may be influenced by normalization choices, aggregation methods, or emphasis on worst-case versus average-case outcomes. The result is a single numerical value summarizing how much privacy improvement the applied *LPPM* provides for the assessed privacy dimension.

In parallel, the *Population Feature Extractor* computes a non-sensitive, utility prediction on both data versions. It focuses on specific utility dimensions, such as the accuracy of downstream prediction tasks or the stability of aggregate statistics, producing two predictions forwarded to the *Utility Scorer*. Each outcome reflects how well the two versions of the dataset support the intended predictive purpose. Equivalent to the *Personal Feature Extractor*, its configuration may involve task definitions, feature choices, model hyperparameters, ...

The *Utility Scorer* compares the outcomes to produce a scalar utility score. It handles normalization and unit heterogeneity based on the evaluated utility dimension. The result is a single value summarizing the degradation in utility caused by the applied *LPPM*. The utility and privacy scores produced by one or more benchmarks are collected into a table, supporting various analytics.

3.3 Component Implementations

The repository[1] includes a set of implemented components for all six types.

Table 3. Location Traces Dataset Statistics

Metric	D_BE	D_NL	Geolife	RadioCells
Total Reports	450,319,679	2,336,240,479	17,662,984	36,311,606
Distinct Users	121,391	330,632	10,336	187,506*
Collection Period (Days)	91	91	6	19,619
Median Reports per User	555	5,023	1,399	162
Mean Time Between Reports (s)	981.32	700.94	296.98	158.92
Median Time Between Reports (s)	288.0	150.0	163.0	0.0
Additional Labels	×	×	✓	✓

[1] https://gitlab.kuleuven.be/u0161628/lppmbench.

Datasets. The framework supports multiple real-world mobility datasets spanning different collection practices and geographic regions. These include the large, covertly-collected D_BE and D_NL datasets [17], the research-participant-based GeoLife GPS trajectories [58], and the crowdsourced RadioCells radio tower measurements [41]. Datasets D_BE and D_NL were collected without informed consent and can therefore not be shared. Together they provide wide coverage in terms of temporal sparsity, reporting frequency, and auxiliary labels. Table 3 provides a summary.

LPPMs. Three *LPPMs* are implemented: Planar Laplace [2], which provides geo-indistinguishability by adding calibrated planar Laplacian noise; DSO [19], designed for continuous release with persistent privacy zones; and Location-Fudger [21], a grid-snapping mechanism from Android's Approximate Location.

Personal Feature Extractors. Two inference attacks are implemented: POI extraction [17] applies ST-DBSCAN clustering to identify sensitive locations; and Social Linkage detection [17] identifies user co-location patterns.

Privacy Scorers. Metrics include Haversine Distortion for spatial displacement, F1-score and Error Rate for binary classification attacks, and Jaccard Distance for graph-structured predictions such as Social Linkage.

Population Feature Extractors. Three utility-focused components are included: Transportation Mode Detection [16] trains a model to predict transport labels for location trajectories; RadioCells averaging [7] for radio tower localization; and TimeCurves for temporal busyness estimation on unlabeled data.

Utility Scorers. Utility is assessed through Total Variation Distance for distribution comparison, ML Test Accuracy and Inference Accuracy for supervised learning tasks.

4 Experiments and Results

This section illustrates benchmark construction and interpretation through representative experiments. The orchestration patterns that generate runs are introduced first, followed by subsections examining privacy from multiple perspectives, utility across different downstream tasks, and joint analysis of both dimensions. All plots are reproducible via the documentation[2], which includes instructions for extending the benchmark with custom components.

4.1 Experimental Setup

The API supports a high degree of freedom for composing benchmarks. In practice, most users will follow more structured workflows, and for this reason the implementation provides two orchestration patterns.

The first orchestration takes as input one *Data Loader* and three collections:

[2] https://u0161628.pages.gitlab.kuleuven.be/lppmbench/.

- $N\times$ `LPPMs`,
- $K\times$ `(Personal Feature Extractor, Privacy Scorer)` pairs,
- $J\times$ `(Population Feature Extractor, Utility Scorer)` pairs.

It evaluates all $N \times K \times J$ combinations. *Population Feature Extractors* typically assume dataset-specific labels, producing `NULL` on incompatible inputs, and cross-dataset composition is therefore kept as a manual step.

The second orchestration targets benchmarks involving Machine Learning-based *Population Feature Extractors.* To avoid inflating performance estimates through train-test leakage, this orchestration evaluates accuracy directly on K-fold inference results rather than comparing original versus transformed data–since accuracy is already on a normalized, comparable scale. For reference, an identity *LPPM* (a zero-operation transformation) is also evaluated: in utility scoring it yields the highest accuracy, while in privacy scoring it produces the lowest attainable privacy score. This baseline appears as a separate "*LPPM*" in the final report, serving as a useful reference for interpreting the other results.

All results are stored in a single dataframe. Each row records the score type (privacy/utility), the Feature Extractor, *LPPM*, and *Data Loader* with their parameters. After concatenation, rows with `NULL` or invalid outputs are filtered. The dashboard then visualizes all remaining utility–privacy dimension pairs.

The result dataframe is the canonical output of the framework. While the dashboard described below serves as a reference visualization, alternative visualizations or analytical interpreters can be built directly on the same result dataframe.

4.2 Interpreting the Privacy-Utility Reports

The reference dashboard visualizes results in a matrix layout, with columns representing privacy dimensions and rows representing utility dimensions. Each marker corresponds to one *LPPM* configuration, positioned according to its privacy and utility scores. Visual encoding supports rapid identification of viable configurations: a blue dashed vertical line marks the privacy threshold and red dashed horizontal lines indicate utility thresholds, with configurations failing to meet either requirement shown with reduced opacity. When multiple *LPPMs* are benchmarked, distinct colors distinguish mechanisms. Clicking a single marker will invert its color, show full details of that particular benchmark, as well as highlighting markers in all other subplots that correspond to the same *LPPM* configuration with the same inverted color.

Utility Scorer and *Privacy Scorer* units are designed such that a higher value indicates higher privacy/utility. For prediction-based privacy attacks, this usually means attacker confidence is subtracted from a base value of 1.0; a strong adversary will score near 0.0 on the privacy axis.

4.3 Experimenting with Multiple Views on Privacy

Figure 2 illustrates the utility-privacy trade-off across a range of *LPPM* parameter configurations. The D_BE dataset is transformed using AndroidLocationFudger under a space-radius sweep $[8, 16, \ldots, 1024]$ meters and time-interval sweep $[4, 8, \ldots, 64]$ seconds. Each marker represents one configuration, with faded markers indicating those that fall below at least one of the chosen privacy thresholds, shown as blue dashed lines. The Haversine Distortion threshold is a minimum of 800 m mean distance between original and reported locations after *LPPM* processing. For Sensitive POI, we set a threshold of 0.7 Prediction Error–meaning the attacker can be at most 30% confident in identifying a user's POI–and the 0.6 threshold for Sensitive Social Contacts correspondingly caps attacker confidence at 40%. These values reflect a realistic use case with a privacy-aware user group. The *Privacy Scorer* for Sensitive Social Contacts uses an F1-Score on time-spent-together detection, while utility is scored via Total Variation Distance on predicted busyness distributions (see Sect. 3.3).

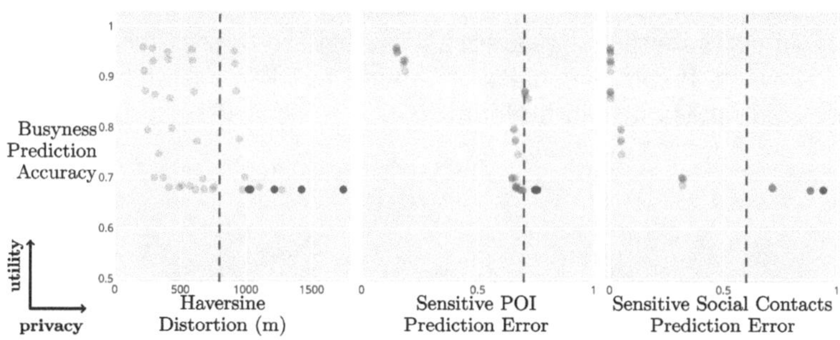

Fig. 2. D_BE dataset is transformed by `AndroidLocationFudger`, 40 LPPM parameters. It is measured by one utility dimension and three privacy dimensions.

In the leftmost panel, the broad spread of Haversine Distortion scores is driven by the wide space-radius sweep, not the time-interval sweep: increasing space-radius substantially raises distortion, whereas lengthening the time-interval leaves scores largely unchanged. An analyst optimizing solely for this dimension can therefore preserve substantially more utility by prioritizing larger space-radius values over longer time-intervals. In the middle panel, the privacy-utility spread is narrower than in the leftmost: both space-radius and time-interval affect the Sensitive POI score. Beyond a modest privacy floor of 0.2, utility saturates at 0.88. Around the stricter threshold of 0.7, however, configuration choice matters substantially–the right *LPPM* parameters can yield over 20% more utility than poorly chosen ones. The rightmost panel is similarly tight. Here as well, configuration choice heavily influences the privacy axis: at comparable utility levels, privacy scores diverge widely, meaning the analyst can gain substantially stronger protection with negligible utility sacrifice.

Considered in isolation, each panel offers useful guidance; taken together, they reveal the framework's strength. Critically, each of the three subplots in Fig. 2 contains markers that pass the local threshold yet are faded–meaning they fail at least one of the other two. *A single privacy threshold would not provide the same discriminatory power as their conjunction*, underscoring the need for multi-dimensional trade-off analysis. It ensures that optimizing for one privacy threat does not inadvertently expose vulnerabilities in another.

4.4 Experimenting with Multiple Views on Utility

Figure 3 illustrates the output of a multi-metric orchestration with one privacy dimension evaluated across three utility dimensions. Location data is collected, but not always for a singular downstream utility task. This experiment explores how well *LPPMs* can target a range of utility dimensions. The same configurations are used as in Sect. 4.3. One interesting insight is that both Radio Tower Prediction and Train Station Busyness, whose core logic relies mainly on averaging out reports in space or time, are only slightly impacted for high privacy gains. Meanwhile the Machine Learning-based Transportation Mode Prediction introduces an accuracy penalty of about 4% relative to the 70% baseline, which is marked in black. If such a penalty of about 4 to 8% is within thresholds, many acceptable configurations can be found.

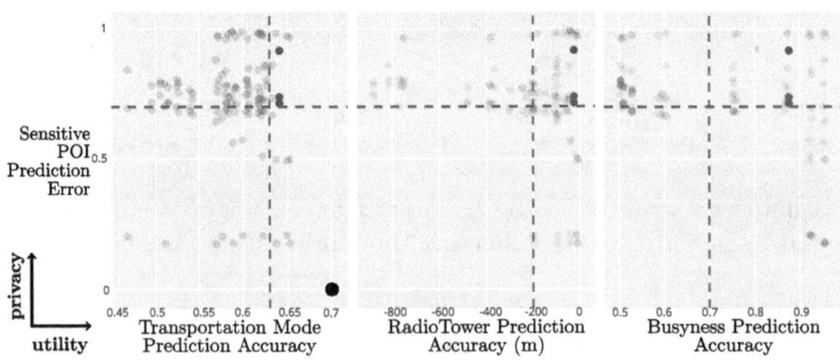

Fig. 3. `D_NL`, `RadioCells` and `Geolife` datasets are transformed by `Android-Obfuscator`. 40 LPPM parameters are evaluated in three utility dimensions. Axes are flipped compared to default output.

4.5 Exploring Utility and Privacy Jointly

Figure 4 presents an extensive benchmarking experiment that varies all component types. For Planar Laplace, we examine a privacy budget ranging from 0.1 up to 100,000. Both AndroidLocationFudger and DSO use a space radius parameter spanning 8 to 4096. All three *LPPMs* consider a time interval parameter between 4 and 256 s. Certain $(Extractor, dataset)$ pairs were excluded for compatibility reasons. Transportation Mode Detection and Radio Tower Prediction are executed only on their respective compatible dataset. We omit POI and Social Linkage attacks on RadioCells because of its unreliable user labels. For similar reasons–namely low user count and strong social correlation–we do not apply Social Linkage on GeoLife. *D_BE* serves as the only dataset applicable to all privacy dimensions and Busyness Prediction.

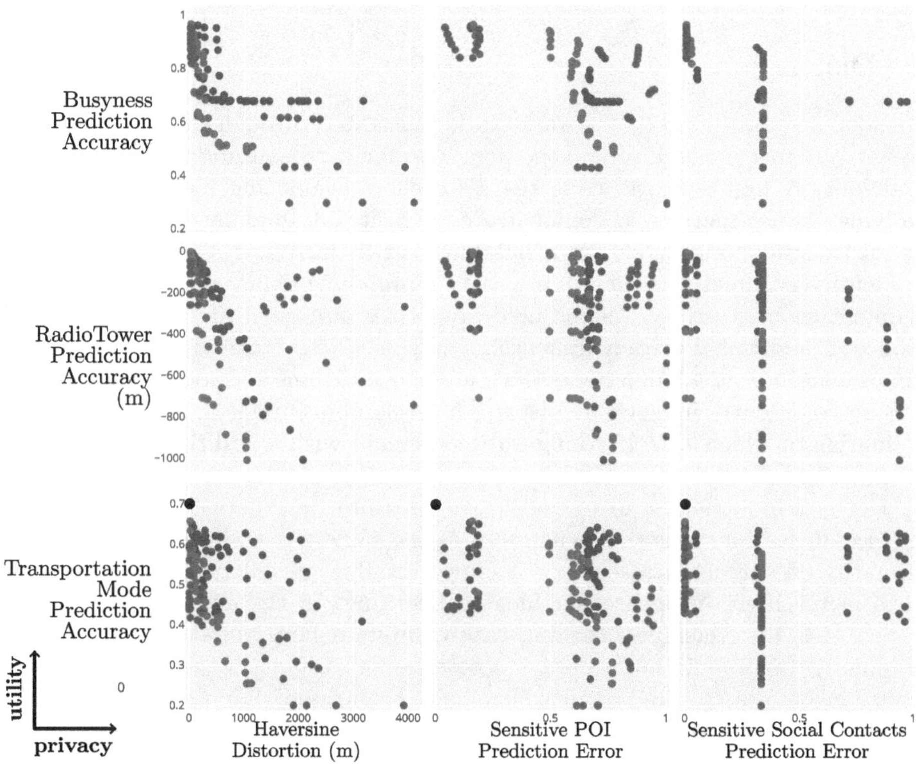

Fig. 4. Three LPPMs, applied on three datasets, evaluated under three privacy and three utility dimensions. `AndroidLocationFudger` in blue, `DSO` in red, and `Planar Laplace` in green. No-op LPPM for reference in black. (Color figure online)

Across this evaluation matrix, several consistent patterns emerge. Most plots show no distinct separation or cluster forming among *LPPM* tactics. Instead, each *LPPM* attains a wide range of scores depending on its parameter settings, suggesting that selecting a tactic is often less decisive than properly tuning its parameters. An exception arises with Sensitive Social Contact Prediction Error, where only AndroidLocationFudger obtains privacy scores above 35%. This is due to Android's *LPPM* employing a global grid shared across all users, which readily introduces artificial social connections–in contrast to DSO, where users construct Privacy Zones dynamically, producing a personalized grid with fewer false positive social connections. Planar Laplace, which does not apply grid mapping, typically ranks mid-range across dimensions. On the RadioCells utility case, however, it significantly outperforms the other *LPPMs* at higher privacy scores. This may stem from Planar Laplace's predictable, zero-mean noise, which preserves expected distances under aggregation–well-suited to RadioCells' average-distance utility metric. Within all its configurations, DSO is seldom the better choice, even in the Sensitive POI dimension for which it was specifically designed.

5 Discussion

The analytics produced by the framework, illustrated through the experiments in Sect. 4, support a range of stakeholders who must reason about privacy-utility trade-offs. A first scenario concerns researchers evaluating mechanisms under evolving privacy metrics, as demonstrated in Sect. 4.3. In many research settings, an initial study might rely on a baseline metric such as Haversine Distortion to identify parameter ranges that satisfy minimum privacy requirements while maintaining high utility. As the field progresses and new inference attacks are proposed, additional privacy dimensions may need to be taken into account. The experiment in Sect. 4.3 illustrates that sensitive locations and social contacts may still be confidently inferred at distortion levels above 1000 m, prompting a re-evaluation of which *LPPM* configurations remain within additional constraints.

A second scenario considers location data brokers who must limit the accuracy of collected data–due to legislative pressure or otherwise–while preserving usefulness for diverse downstream tasks. Whereas traditional clients rely primarily on classic data science for crowd-insights, recent commercial applications increasingly make use of Machine Learning. In the experimental setting of Sect. 4.4, the Machine Learning task exhibits a largely flat utility response of roughly 64% prediction accuracy across configurations. If this level of performance meets the required quality threshold, then many different *LPPM* configurations remain acceptable, effectively turning the Machine Learning criterion into a near-binary check rather than a finely discriminative utility dimension. It remains to be seen if this combination of an inherent penalty and flat response generalizes to other Machine Learning models.

A third scenario involves exploring broader patterns in privacy-utility behavior across multiple *LPPMs*, as in Sect. 4.5. This allows analysts to study how mechanisms behave across heterogeneous conditions and to identify structural trade-off patterns. One such pattern from early results is that no single *LPPM* dominates across all conditions; instead, tuning an *LPPM* to specific utility and privacy requirements often has greater impact than choosing among different tactics. For researchers developing new *LPPMs*, this is a central use case: newly proposed mechanisms can be inserted into the benchmark and immediately compared against existing *LPPMs* under identical conditions, ensuring fair and reproducible evaluation. The same applies when new inference attacks on location traces appear – their impact is assessed by implementing them as additional Feature Extractors and reusing existing benchmarks without modifying the remainder of the pipeline. Thanks to the modular benchmark design, new attacks only require implementation as additional *Personal Feature Extractors*, after which existing benchmarks can be extended without modifying the pipeline. Similarly, new utility tasks can be added as *Population Feature Extractors* and evaluated with minimal effort.

When an analyst includes multiple utility dimensions, *Population Feature Extractors* that rely on auxiliary labels often cannot be applied to the same dataset. In such cases, the benchmark produces a separate privacy score for each dataset. By default, all scores are reported. Alternatively, the report can retain only the worst privacy score, providing a conservative lower bound. The appropriate way to combine these scores must be determined by the analyst.

The framework supports varying only the Scorers while keeping the same Feature Extractors, enabling comparisons such as best-case against worst-case privacy. Consider a benchmark comparing two *LPPMs* using a *Personal Feature Extractor* that predicts monthly income per user. A *Privacy Scorer* reporting average accuracy may indicate that mechanism A outperforms B. Closer inspection might reveal that mechanism A performs either extremely well or produces zero-information outputs, thereby skewing the mean. Implementing an alternative Scorer–such as one incorporating conditional entropy, following the arguments of Oya et al. [42]–allows the analyst to capture uncertainty more faithfully. This logic extends symmetrically to *Utility Scorers*: the same *Population Feature Extractor* can be scored by accuracy, top-k recall, or log-loss, each potentially reordering which *LPPM* appears most suitable. The experiments in Sect. 4 primarily vary (Feature Extractor, Scorer) as preconfigured pairs; a natural next step is to systematically re-score the same attack outputs under alternative scoring strategies to test whether observed trade-off patterns are robust to the choice of scorer. Ultimately, the scorer is where the analyst encodes what "privacy" and "utility" mean in operational terms–whether as a population average, a worst-case guarantee, or an information-theoretic bound.

6 Conclusion

This work introduced a benchmarking framework for evaluating Location Privacy Protection Mechanisms under realistic continuous-reporting conditions. It is built around six well-defined, interchangeable component types. By separating *Data Loaders*, *LPPMs*, *Personal* and *Population Feature Extractors*, and *Privacy* and *Utility Scorers*, the framework enables fair comparison, large-scale exploration, and reproducible evaluation of privacy-utility trade-offs.

The framework provides a sizable repository of implemented components and supports conducting large-scale experiments. The current implementation contains more than twenty component implementations, including three *LPPMs*, three *Personal Feature Extractors*, and three *Population Feature Extractors*. The experimental study explores more than two hundred *LPPM* configurations across several real-world mobility datasets, combining three privacy dimensions with three utility dimensions. Results indicate that relying on a single metric or privacy dimension can yield a distorted picture. Privacy that appears strong under one specific adversary model may still break down when evaluated against other sensitive inference attacks. The multi-view analytics counter this by revealing where privacy and utility measures align or diverge.

The design of the framework supports systematic extensions to the component repository. Researchers can add new *LPPMs*, introduce additional privacy or utility dimensions, or incorporate alternative scoring strategies, all without modifying the underlying architecture. Through iterative use, current and future *LPPM* tactics can be extensively evaluated and tuned.

Acknowledgement. The authors have no competing interests to declare that are relevant to the content of this article.

References

1. Agir, B., Papaioannou, T.G., Narendula, R., Aberer, K., Hubaux, J.P.: User-side adaptive protection of location privacy in participatory sensing. GeoInformatica **18**(1), 165–191 (2014)
2. Andrés, M.E., Bordenabe, N.E., Chatzikokolakis, K., Palamidessi, C.: Geo-indistinguishability: differential privacy for location-based systems. In: Proceedings of the 2013 ACM SIGSAC Conference on Computer & Communications Security, pp. 901–914 (2013)
3. Assam, R., Seidl, T.: Preserving privacy of moving objects via temporal clustering of spatio-temporal data streams. In: Proceedings of the 4th ACM SIGSPATIAL International Workshop on Security and Privacy in GIS and LBS, pp. 9–16 (2011)
4. Bamba, B., Liu, L., Pesti, P., Wang, T.: Supporting anonymous location queries in mobile environments with privacy grid. In: Proceedings of the 17th International Conference on World Wide Web, pp. 237–246 (2008)
5. Bindschaedler, V.E.A.: Synthesizing plausible privacy-preserving location traces. In: 2016 IEEE Symposium on Security and Privacy, pp. 546–563. IEEE (2016)
6. Bordenabe, N.E.E.A.: Optimal geo-indistinguishable mechanisms for location privacy. In: Proceedings of the 2014 ACM SIGSAC Conference on Computer and Communications Security, pp. 251–262 (2014)
7. Boukoros, S., Humbert, M., Katzenbeisser, S., Troncoso, C.: On (the lack of) location privacy in crowdsourcing applications. In: 28th USENIX Security Symposium (USENIX Security 19), pp. 1859–1876 (2019)
8. Brickell, J., Shmatikov, V.: The cost of privacy: destruction of data-mining utility in anonymized data publishing. In: Proceedings of the 14th ACM SIGKDD International Conference on Knowledge Discovery and Data Mining, pp. 70–78 (2008)
9. Carter, H., Mood, B., Traynor, P., Butler, K.: Secure outsourced garbled circuit evaluation for mobile devices. J. Comput. Secur. **24**(2), 137–180 (2016)
10. Chakraborty, S.e.a.: {ipShield}: A framework for enforcing {Context-Aware} privacy. In: 11th USENIX Symposium on Networked Systems Design and Implementation (NSDI 14), pp. 143–156 (2014)
11. Chatzikokolakis, K., Palamidessi, C., Stronati, M.: A predictive differentially-private mechanism for mobility traces. In: International Symposium on Privacy Enhancing Technologies Symposium, pp. 21–41. Springer (2014). https://doi.org/10.1007/978-3-319-08506-7_2

12. Chatzikokolakis, K., Palamidessi, C., Stronati, M.: Constructing elastic distinguishability metrics for location privacy. arXiv preprint arXiv:1503.00756 (2015)
13. Chow, C.Y., Mokbel, M.F., Aref, W.G.: Casper* query processing for location services without compromising privacy. ACM Trans. Database Syst. (TODS) **34**(4), 1–48 (2009)
14. Chow, C.Y., Mokbel, M.F., Liu, X.: A peer-to-peer spatial cloaking algorithm for anonymous location-based service. In: Proceedings of the 14th Annual ACM International Symposium on Advances in GIS, pp. 171–178 (2006)
15. Cox, J.: Candy Crush, Tinder, MyFitnessPal: see the thousands of apps hijacked to spy on your location — wired.com. https://www.wired.com/story/gravy-location-data-app-leak-rtb/ (2025). Accessed 11 Feb 2026
16. Dabiri, S., Heaslip, K.: Inferring transportation modes from GPS trajectories using a convolutional neural network. Transp. Res. Part C: Emerging Technol. **86**, 360–371 (2018)
17. Boeck, D., Verdonck, K., J.: Big broker is tracking you! a privacy assessment of large-scale location trace datasets. In: 2025 Annual Computer Security Applications Conference (ACSAC) (2025)
18. De Montjoye, Y.A., Hidalgo, C.A., Verleysen, M., Blondel, V.D.: Unique in the crowd: the privacy bounds of human mobility. Sci. Rep. **3**(1), 1376 (2013)
19. Dehaene, T., Willocx, M., Lagaisse, B., Naessens, V.: Masking location streams in the presence of colluding service providers. In: 2023 IEEE European Symposium on Security and Privacy Workshops (EuroS&PW), pp. 405–414. IEEE (2023)
20. DePhillipo, N.N., Chahla, J., Busler, M., LaPrade, R.F.: Mobile phone GPS data and prevalence of covid-19 infections: quantifying parameters of social distancing in the us. Arch. Bone Joint Surgery **9**(2), 217 (2021)
21. Developers, A.: Android LocationFudger source code. https://cs.android.com/android/platform/superproject/main/+/main:frameworks/base/services/core/java/com/android/server/location/fudger/LocationFudger.java (2026). Accessed 23 Feb 2026
22. Fan, L., Gunja, S.Y.: Geopriv4j: an open source repository for practical location privacy. In: Proceedings of the Sixth International ACM SIGMOD Workshop on Managing and Mining Enriched Geo-Spatial Data, pp. 1–6 (2020)
23. Fawaz, K., Shin, K.G.: Location privacy protection for smartphone users. In: Proceedings of the 2014 ACM SIGSAC Conference on Computer and Communications Security, pp. 239–250 (2014)
24. Freudiger, J., Shokri, R., Hubaux, J.P.: On the optimal placement of mix zones. In: Goldberg, I., Atallah, M.J. (eds) International Symposium on Privacy Enhancing Technologies Symposium, pp. 216–234. Springer, Berlin, Heidelberg (2009). https://doi.org/10.1007/978-3-642-03168-7_13
25. Ghinita, G., Kalnis, P., Skiadopoulos, S.: Prive: anonymous location-based queries in distributed mobile systems. In: Proceedings of the 16th International Conference on World Wide Web, pp. 371–380 (2007)
26. Gong, X., Chen, X., Xing, K., Shin, D.H., Zhang, M., Zhang, J.: From social group utility maximization to personalized location privacy in mobile networks. IEEE/ACM Trans. Networking **25**(3), 1703–1716 (2017)
27. Hoh, B., Gruteser, M., Xiong, H., Alrabady, A.: Preserving privacy in GPS traces via uncertainty-aware path cloaking. In: Proceedings of the 14th ACM Conference on Computer and Communications Security, pp. 161–171 (2007)
28. Huguenin, K., et al.: A predictive model for user motivation and utility implications of privacy-protection mechanisms in location check-ins. IEEE Trans. Mob. Comput. **17**(4), 760–774 (2017)

29. Kato, R.E.A.: A dummy-based anonymization method based on user trajectory with pauses. In: Proceedings of the 20th International Conference on Advances in Geographic Information Systems, pp. 249–258 (2012)
30. Keegan, J., Ng, A.: There's a multibillion-dollar market for your phone's location data. The Markup, p. 30 (2021)
31. King, K.: Location (data) is everything for retailers opening stores. The Wall Street J. (2024). https://www.wsj.com/real-estate/commercial/location-data-is-everything-for-retailers-opening-stores-545c3442
32. Krumm, J.: Realistic driving trips for location privacy. In: Tokuda, H., Beigl, M., Friday, A., Brush, A.J.B., Tobe, Y. (eds) International Conference on Pervasive Computing, pp. 25–41. Springer, Berlin, Heidelberg (2009). https://doi.org/10.1007/978-3-642-01516-8_4
33. Krumm, J.: A survey of computational location privacy. Pers. Ubiquit. Comput. **13**(6), 391–399 (2009)
34. Li, C., Palanisamy, B.: ReverseCloak: protecting multi-level location privacy over road networks. In: Proceedings of the 24th ACM International on Conference On Information and Knowledge Management, pp. 673–682 (2015)
35. Li, Y., Zhu, Y., Fei, J., Wu, W.: Diverse metrics for robust LBS privacy: distance, semantics, and temporal factors. Sensors **24**(4), 1314 (2024)
36. Liu, X., Zhao, H., Pan, M., Yue, H., Li, X., Fang, Y.: Traffic-aware multiple mix zone placement for protecting location privacy. In: Proceedings IEEE INFOCOM, pp. 972–980. IEEE (2012)
37. Mascetti, S., Freni, D., Bettini, C., Wang, X.S., Jajodia, S.: Privacy in geo-social networks: proximity notification with untrusted service providers and curious buddies. VLDB J. **20**(4), 541–566 (2011)
38. Micinski, K.K., Phelps, P., Foster, J.S.: An empirical study of location truncation on Android. In: Proceedings of Mobile Security Technologies (MoST'13). San Francisco, CA, USA (May 2013). https://www.cs.tufts.edu/~jfoster/papers/most13.pdf, workshop co-located with IEEE Symposium on Security and Privacy
39. Narayanan, A., Thiagarajan, N., Lakhani, M., Hamburg, M., Boneh, D.: Location privacy via private proximity testing. In: NDSS, vol. 11 (2011)
40. Ngo, H.E.A.: Location privacy via differential private perturbation of cloaking area. In: IEEE 28th Computer Security Foundations Symposium, pp. 63–74. IEEE (2015)
41. openBmap Project: openbmap: open source radio cell database and community map. Internet Archive (2017). https://archive.org/details/openbmap, Accessed 11 Feb 2026. Data archived for long-term accessibility
42. Oya, S., Troncoso, C., Pérez-González, F.: Back to the drawing board: revisiting the design of optimal location privacy-preserving mechanisms. In: Proceedings of the 2017 ACM SIGSAC Conference on Computer and Communications Security, pp. 1959–1972 (2017)
43. Pingley, A., Yu, W., Zhang, N., Fu, X., Zhao, W.: CAP: a context-aware privacy protection system for location-based services. In: 29th IEEE International Conference on Distributed Computing systems, pp. 49–57. IEEE (2009)
44. Primault, V., Boutet, A., Mokhtar, S.B., Brunie, L.: The long road to computational location privacy: a survey. IEEE Commun. Surv. Tutorials **21**(3), 2772–2793 (2018)
45. Quercia, D.E.A.: SpotMe if you can: Randomized responses for location obfuscation on mobile phones. In: 2011 31st International Conference on Distributed Computing Systems, pp. 363–372. IEEE (2011)

46. Shankar, P., Ganapathy, V., Iftode, L.: Privately querying location-based services with sybilquery. In: Proceedings of the 11th International Conference on Ubiquitous Computing, pp. 31–40 (2009)
47. Shokri, R., Freudiger, J., Hubaux, J.P.: A unified framework for location privacy. In: 3rd Hot Topics in Privacy Enhancing Technologies (HotPETs), p. 71 (2010)
48. Shokri, R., Theodorakopoulos, G.E.A.: Protecting location privacy: optimal strategy against localization attacks. In: Proceedings of the 2012 ACM Conference on Computer and Communications Security, pp. 617–627 (2012)
49. Shokri, R.E.A.: Quantifying location privacy. In: 2011 IEEE Symposium on Security and Privacy, pp. 247–262. IEEE (2011)
50. Theodorakopoulos, G., Panaousis, E., Liang, K., Loukas, G.: On-the-fly privacy for location histograms. IEEE Trans. Dependable Secure Comput. **19**(1), 566–578 (2020)
51. Verdonck, J.E.A.: A clustering approach to anonymize locations during dataset de-identification. In: Proceedings of the 16th International Conference on Availability, Reliability and Security, pp. 1–10 (2021)
52. Wagner, I., Eckhoff, D.: Technical privacy metrics: a systematic survey. ACM Comput. Surv. (CSur) **51**(3), 1–38 (2018)
53. Xiao, Y.E.A.: LocLok: location cloaking with differential privacy via hidden markov model. Proc. VLDB Endowment **10**(12), 1901–1904 (2017)
54. Xu, T., Cai, Y.: Feeling-based location privacy protection for location-based services. In: Proceedings of the 16th ACM Conference on Computer and Communications Security, pp. 348–357 (2009)
55. Yu, L., Liu, L., Pu, C.: Dynamic differential location privacy with personalized error bounds. NDSS **17**, 1–15 (2017)
56. Yu, W.E.A.: Analyzing spatial community pattern of network traffic flow and its variations across time based on taxi GPS trajectories. Appl. Sci. **9**(10), 2054 (2019)
57. Zang, H., Bolot, J.: Anonymization of location data does not work: a large-scale measurement study. In: Proceedings of the 17th Annual International Conference on Mobile Computing and Networking, pp. 145–156 (2011)
58. Zheng, Y., Li, Q., Chen, Y., Xie, X., Ma, W.Y.: Understanding mobility based on GPS data. In: Proceedings of the 10th International Conference on Ubiquitous Computing, pp. 312–321 (2008)

A Multimodal Digital Twin Framework for CBAM-Oriented Maritime Trade Integrity

Muhammad Faisal[1], Amna Shifa[2,3](✉), and Zina Jerjees[1]

[1] University of Hull, Cottingham Rd, Hull HU6 7RX, UK
{m.faisal-2025,z.jerjees}@hull.ac.uk

[2] The Islamia University of Bahawalpur, Bahawalpur 63100, Punjab, Pakistan
amna.shifa@iub.edu.pk

[3] Data Science Institute, University of Galway, Galway, Ireland

Abstract. As maritime trade becomes increasingly digitised, the effectiveness of Carbon Border Adjustment Mechanism (CBAM) enforcement depends on the integrity of digital declarations that remain only weakly linked to the physical cargo they describe. Existing Digital Twin (DT) systems in logistics primarily focus on operational visibility and efficiency, while offering limited mechanisms for adversarial verification, provenance assurance, or compliance-oriented anomaly detection. This creates significant risks in CBAM-regulated trade environments, including manifest manipulation, route spoofing, origin fraud, and falsified emissions declarations. This paper proposes a Multimodal DT Framework for CBAM-oriented maritime trade integrity. The framework integrates customs profiling, multimodal sensor fusion, and DT synchronisation to support continuous cross-verification between declared shipment data and independently observable physical evidence. The proposed architecture combines visual inspection, weight-based verification, and vessel-tracking intelligence within a provenance-aware enforcement layer capable of detecting inconsistencies between declared and observed cargo states. To demonstrate the feasibility of the approach, a synthetic proof-of-concept simulation was developed using density-based anomaly detection aligned with HS-code cargo profiles. The results illustrate how discrepancy detection mechanisms can identify one class of manifest divergence under controlled conditions. The framework further introduces a trust-oriented DT model incorporating multimodal validation, integrity risk scoring, and closed-loop synchronisation between sensor events and customs verification systems. The study argues that future DT infrastructures for maritime logistics should evolve beyond passive visibility platforms toward enforcement-oriented compliance systems capable of supporting secure, transparent, and low-carbon maritime trade within CBAM-regulated supply chains.

Keywords: Maritime security · Digital Twin · Customs enforcement · Multimodal data integrity · Carbon Border Adjustment Mechanism (CBAM) · Data provenance · Supply chain security

P. Kieseberg et al. (Eds.): ARES 2026 Workshops, LNCS 16903, pp. 204–221, 2027.
https://doi.org/10.1007/978-3-032-37218-5_13

1 Introduction

The Carbon Border Adjustment Mechanism (CBAM), entering its definitive implementation phase in 2026 under the European Union Green Deal framework, introduces a new compliance landscape in which imported goods are financially accountable for their embedded carbon emissions [1]. Closely linked to the European Union Emissions Trading System (EU ETS), CBAM aims to reduce carbon leakage by ensuring that imported carbon-intensive goods are subject to equivalent carbon pricing mechanisms [2]. As carbon reporting transitions from voluntary sustainability disclosure toward legally enforceable trade compliance, the integrity of emissions declarations and customs documentation becomes increasingly critical for both regulatory enforcement and international supply chain governance.

Despite ongoing digitalisation across maritime logistics, a fundamental enforcement problem remains unresolved: digital trade declarations are still only weakly connected to independently verifiable physical cargo states [3]. Maritime supply chains involve complex transshipments operations, multiple custodians, fragmented data ownership, and heterogeneous information systems, creating opportunities for manifest manipulation, origin spoofing, route obfuscation, and falsified certification records. Existing customs verification procedures continue to rely heavily on documentary checks, periodic audits, and selective inspection workflows, which improve administrative visibility but offer limited capacity for continuous physical verification under adversarial conditions.

Digital Twin (DT) technologies have emerged as a promising approach for synchronising digital representations of physical logistics operations with real-time operational data. In maritime and logistics environments, DTs are increasingly applied for vessel monitoring, predictive maintenance, port optimisation, and supply chain visibility [6, 7]. However, most current DT implementations are designed primarily for operational efficiency and assume that upstream data streams are trustworthy. As a result, these systems often reproduce the same integrity vulnerabilities embedded within the underlying data infrastructure. In compliance-sensitive environments such as CBAM-regulated trade, visibility without provenance assurance creates a critical enforcement limitation.

To address this challenge, this paper proposes a Multimodal DT Framework for secure and compliance-oriented maritime trade verification. The framework combines customs profiling with multimodal sensor fusion, including weight-based measurements, visual inspection systems, and vessel-tracking intelligence, to continuously compare declared shipment information against independently observable physical evidence. Unlike conventional visibility-centric DT architectures, the proposed framework adopts an enforcement-oriented approach in which all digital declarations are treated as provisional until corroborated through multimodal verification and provenance-aware synchronisation mechanisms.

The remainder of this paper is structured as follows. Section 2 reviews related work on CBAM enforcement, DT technologies, maritime customs security, and multimodal data fusion. Section 3 presents the CBAM-oriented threat model and identifies the primary integrity risks in digitally mediated maritime trade. Section 4 introduces the proposed Secure Green Corridor (SGC) framework and its multimodal DT architecture. Section 5 presents the synthetic proof-of-concept and anomaly detection methodology. Section 6 discusses the implications and limitations of the framework, while Sect. 7 concludes the paper and outlines directions for future research [21].

2 Related Work and Research Context

Recent advances in DT technologies, maritime logistics digitalisation, and multimodal sensing have accelerated the development of intelligent trade and transport infrastructures. At the same time, emerging carbon-regulation frameworks such as the CBAM are transforming emissions reporting into a compliance-critical process requiring higher levels of data integrity, traceability, and verification. While significant research has explored Digital Twins, customs modernisation, multimodal analytics, and smart port systems independently, limited attention has been given to enforcement-oriented architectures capable of continuously validating the correspondence between digital declarations and physical cargo states. This section reviews the existing literature across these domains and identifies the research gap addressed by this study.

2.1 CBAM Enforcement Landscape and Emerging Risks

The CBAM, formally adopted under Regulation (EU) 2023/956, represents a major regulatory extension of the European Union Emissions Trading System (EU ETS) into international trade [1]. CBAM aims to address carbon leakage by ensuring that imported carbon-intensive goods are subjected to carbon pricing mechanisms equivalent to those in the EU ETS. According to the International Carbon Action Partnership (ICAP), carbon pricing systems are rapidly expanding globally, increasing the importance of reliable emissions accounting and verifiable trade declarations within cross-border supply chains [2]. As a result, emissions reporting is evolving from a sustainability-oriented disclosure practice into a legally enforceable compliance requirement with direct financial implications for importers, exporters, and customs authorities.

Current CBAM enforcement mechanisms rely heavily on self-reported emissions declarations, third-party certification, documentary validation, and periodic audit procedures. Although these mechanisms improve reporting transparency, they provide limited capability to independently verify that declared shipment attributes accurately correspond to the physical cargo being transported. This limitation becomes particularly significant in maritime logistics environments characterised by transshipment operations, fragmented custodianship, and heterogeneous digital infrastructures. Under such conditions, opportunities emerge for origin manipulation, route obfuscation, manifest falsification, and emissions-reporting fraud, thereby creating enforcement vulnerabilities within digitally mediated trade systems [10].

Several recent studies have highlighted the growing cybersecurity and trust challenges associated with digital trade infrastructures, particularly in environments involving automated customs processing and cross-border electronic documentation. However, most current compliance architectures remain document-centric and assume the trustworthiness of upstream digital submissions. Consequently, the enforcement problem extends beyond data availability toward the broader challenge of establishing a verifiable link between digital declarations and observable physical cargo conditions in real time.

2.2 Digital Twin Technology and Synchromodality in Logistics

Digital Twin (DT) technology enables the creation of dynamic virtual representations of physical systems through continuous synchronisation between operational assets and digital models using real-time data streams. Within logistics and maritime domains, DT systems have been increasingly applied for predictive maintenance, vessel monitoring, terminal optimisation, fleet management, and supply chain visibility [7]. Recent advances in Industry 4.0 technologies, including Internet of Things (IoT) sensing, edge computing, cloud analytics, and artificial intelligence, have further accelerated the deployment of DT-driven logistics infrastructures across smart ports and transport networks.

DT adoption, synchromodality has emerged as a logistics coordination paradigm that enables flexible and real-time switching between transport modes through integrated information exchange across logistics actors. Similarly, PCS facilitate digital coordination between shipping companies, customs authorities, terminal operators, and regulatory agencies. Collectively, these systems enhance operational efficiency, transport visibility, and supply chain responsiveness by enabling synchronised decision-making across distributed maritime environments [5, 7]. Despite these advances, existing DT and synchromodal systems provide limited capability for verifying whether digital shipment records accurately reflect physical cargo states. As a result, discrepancies arising from manipulated declarations, falsified compliance documentation, or compromised telemetry streams may remain undetected. This limitation becomes particularly critical in CBAM-regulated environments, where the reliability of emissions-related declarations carries direct regulatory and financial implications [18].

2.3 Maritime Security and Customs Enforcement

Maritime supply chains are inherently complex due to long-distance routing, transshipment operations, and multi-actor custodianship. These conditions increase exposure to concealment, misclassification, and fraudulent manipulation of cargo data. International organisations such as the World Customs Organisation (WCO) and the United Nations Office on Drugs and Crime (UNODC) promote intelligence-led and risk-based inspection frameworks, notably through initiatives such as the Container Control Programme (CCP) [4] and the SAFE Framework of Standards [5].

These enforcement mechanisms rely heavily on the analysis of Goods Declarations (GD) and electronic manifests to identify high-risk consignments. However, such documents remain vulnerable to manipulation, including misdeclaration of cargo type, weight, or composition. Industry reports highlight persistent manifest physical divergences, where declared attributes do not align with measurable physical properties. Traditional inspection approaches such as manual sampling, scanning, or static imaging are resource-intensive and difficult to scale in high-throughput port environments. As a result, while digitalisation has improved the speed and efficiency of customs processes, it has not fundamentally resolved the challenge of verifiability, leaving a persistent enforcement gap between digital records and physical cargo reality [25].

Recent customs modernisation initiatives increasingly emphasise intelligence-led enforcement, risk-based cargo profiling, and integrated information sharing across international trade systems. Existing customs risk assessment workflows continue to rely predominantly on documentary analysis and historical shipment patterns rather than on continuous multimodal verification of cargo states. As trade ecosystems become increasingly digitised, the challenge is no longer limited to detecting suspicious declarations but rather to establishing trustworthy correspondence between digital records and independently verifiable physical evidence throughout the cargo lifecycle.

2.4 Multimodal Data Fusion and Integrity Challenges

Multimodal data fusion integrates heterogeneous information sources, including IoT telemetry, container weight measurements, vessel-tracking signals, visual inspection systems, and customs transaction records into a unified analytical environment capable of comparing declared shipment attributes with independently observable physical evidence. In maritime logistics, this integration is essential, as no single data source provides sufficient assurance of cargo authenticity under adversarial conditions.

Recent advances in sensing technologies and artificial intelligence have strengthened cross-verification capabilities. Computer vision systems can validate container identifiers and seal integrity through Optical Character Recognition (OCR) and image analysis, while IoT-enabled weight and volumetric sensors can detect inconsistencies between declared and observed cargo characteristics. In parallel, AIS and satellite-based vessel monitoring systems support spatial and temporal verification of shipping routes and transshipment activity.

These complementary sensing modalities introduce redundancy, enabling the identification of anomalies through cross-modal consistency analysis [11, 12, 14]. However, multimodal architectures also introduce integrity challenges related to provenance, synchronisation, and data trustworthiness. Maritime cyber-physical systems remain exposed to risks such as AIS spoofing, GNSS manipulation, sensor tampering, and falsified digital certificates. These vulnerabilities can compromise individual data streams and affect the reliability of integrated analytical outputs [13, 14, 24].

These limitations indicate that multimodal integration alone is insufficient without mechanisms to ensure traceability, temporal alignment, and evidentiary integrity across data sources. Effective Digital Twin systems therefore require provenance-aware architectures capable of validating data origin, consistency, and synchronisation throughout the supply-chain lifecycle [15, 16]. Accordingly, this study adopts a zero-trust verification approach in which digital declarations are continuously corroborated against independently observable physical evidence. This principle underpins the SGC framework introduced in Sect. 4.

2.5 Limitations of Existing Digital Twin Systems

Although DT technologies have enhanced operational visibility and efficiency in maritime logistics, several limitations constrain their applicability in compliance-sensitive trade environments. Current implementations provide limited assurance that digital representations consistently correspond to physical cargo conditions, particularly in contexts involving manipulated declarations or compromised data inputs. While multimodal sensing technologies are increasingly integrated into logistics systems, they are often not deployed within continuous cross-verification frameworks capable of systematically identifying inconsistencies between declared and observed shipment attributes.

In addition, existing architectures offer only partial support for data provenance, traceability, and auditability, which are essential for evidentiary validation in regulatory contexts. Mechanisms for comprehensive discrepancy detection, integrity risk scoring, and structured alert escalation are also typically underdeveloped in logistics-oriented DT systems [19]. Taken together, these limitations indicate that current DT implementations are not yet equipped to support continuous, evidence-based compliance verification in adversarial maritime trade environments. Addressing this gap requires the integration of multimodal validation, provenance-aware synchronisation, and real-time anomaly detection within a unified, enforcement-oriented framework.

2.6 Research Gap

Despite rapid advancements in DT systems, customs digitalisation, and multimodal analytics, these domains have largely evolved in isolation. Existing DT frameworks focus on operational visibility and process optimisation; customs enforcement systems are document-centric, and multimodal analytics research emphasizes detection in controlled environments rather than adversarial trade conditions. A critical gap exists in the lack of an enforcement-oriented architecture that continuously links digital trade declarations with verifiable physical cargo states in real time.

Current systems do not fully close the verification loop between reported shipment information and observable physical evidence, particularly under conditions involving manipulated declarations, spoofed routing data, or compromised sensor inputs. This limitation is especially significant in CBAM-regulated maritime trade, where compliance depends on accurate emissions reporting and verifiable alignment between declared and actual embedded carbon throughout the supply chain. Addressing this challenge requires a transition from visibility-centric DT infrastructures to provenance-aware, enforcement-oriented verification architectures.

To address this research gap, this paper proposes a Multimodal DT Framework integrating customs profiling, multimodal sensor verification, discrepancy detection, and provenance-aware synchronisation mechanisms. Unlike conventional logistics Digital Twins that primarily support operational visibility, predictive maintenance, or transport optimisation, the proposed framework explicitly incorporates compliance verification, integrity-risk scoring, and adversarial cross-validation between digital declarations and independently observable physical evidence. This enforcement-oriented design distinguishes the framework from existing visibility-centric DT architectures and maritime monitoring platforms. The framework is designed to support real-time anomaly detection and compliance-oriented cargo verification within secure and low-carbon maritime trade environments [17].

3 CBAM Data Integrity Threat Model

To design an effective enforcement architecture for CBAM-regulated maritime supply chains, it is essential to first characterise the adversarial strategies that exploit existing digital compliance workflows. Moving beyond traditional security frameworks that assume the validity of upstream electronic data, this section defines an enforcement-oriented threat model. This model systematically captures how multimodal trade data streams can be intentionally manipulated, intercepted, or falsified by economic actors attempting to evade carbon liabilities, exploit regulatory arbitrage, or mask illegal transshipments. The proposed taxonomy identifies three primary threat vectors (T1, T2, and T3). Each represents a distinct category of data–physical divergence where digitally declared compliance states do not correspond to the actual physical reality of the underlying cargo.

3.1 Taxonomy of Fraudulent Vectors

This section categorises the primary threat mechanisms observed in CBAM-regulated maritime trade.

T1: Origin and Route Spoofing: An operator intentionally misdeclares the country of origin of carbon-intensive goods by routing the vessel through intermediate jurisdictions with lower regulatory scrutiny or specific CBAM exemptions. During transshipment or mid-voyage handovers, digital manifests, Bills of Lading, and Port Community System (PCS) entries are altered to obscure the high-emission source country, particularly for sensitive primary commodities like steel (e.g., HS Code 7208) or aluminium.

Systemic Vulnerability: Current logistics DTs and port monitoring systems rely almost exclusively on public Automatic Identification System (AIS) data for maritime spatial tracking. Because AIS transponders can be intentionally deactivated ("going dark"), spoofed using software-defined radio (SDR) arrays, or manipulated via proxy vessels, discontinuities in route visibility remain common. Without continuous cross-verification against satellite synthetic aperture radar (SAR) or terrestrial port sensors, digital transit trails can be completely falsified [13].

T2: Density–Manifest Divergence: High-density, carbon-heavy materials (e.g., primary steel bars, aluminum ingots) are physically combined, interleaved, or layered inside containers alongside low-density, "green" or bio-based materials (e.g., recycled plastics or mycelium-based bio-composites). The entire consignment is then declared under the lower-emission category to bypass emissions reporting thresholds or secure lower tariff rates.

Systemic Vulnerability: Standard document-based risk profiling tools and simple optical container scanning methods cannot evaluate the interior density profiles of tightly packed containers. Because traditional customs risk frameworks do not execute real-time physical cross-correlation between a commodity's declared Harmonized System (HS) code, its volumetric footprint, and its actual dynamic kinetic weight during crane operations, mixed-density smuggling passes completely undetected [11].

T3: Fraudulent Certification and Data Injection: Malicious actors introduce forged, cloned, or illegally altered carbon compliance certificates into electronic customs filing portals. These "ghost" credentials fake the actual production-level emissions metrics (Scope 3 analytics), making high-emission factory outputs appear compliant with strict EU/UK standards.

Systemic Vulnerability: Port Community Systems (PCS) and digital customs gateways check electronic filings primarily for syntax, formatting compliance, and valid cryptographic signatures from authorised declarants. However, they lack end-to-end data provenance tracking. Because there is no verifiable cryptographic link connecting shopfloor IoT energy monitoring systems at the manufacturing plant directly to the downstream maritime shipping manifests, falsified data packages can be cleanly injected at any point in the logistical custody chain [17].

3.2 Summary of Threat Vectors

The identified threat vectors are summarised in Table 1, highlighting the relationship between physical manipulation strategies and their corresponding data integrity impacts.

Table 1. CBAM Data Integrity Threat Taxonomy

Threat ID	Threat Category	Physical Mechanism	Data Integrity Impact
T1	Origin and Route Spoofing	Transshipment substitution	Falsified country of origin and routing history
T2	Density–Manifest Divergence	Mixed-density cargo composition	Underreported embedded carbon emissions
T3	Certification Fraud	Forged compliance credentials	Invalid or unverifiable carbon declarations

3.3 Implications for CBAM Enforcement

These threat vectors highlight a fundamental challenge in current green supply-chain initiatives: verifying documents does not necessarily verify physical reality. When financial liabilities are linked directly to digital declarations, those declarations become attractive targets for manipulation. To strengthen CBAM enforcement, digital trade infrastructures should incorporate:

- Multi-source physical data provenance to confirm that telemetry originates from authenticated sensors.
- Automated edge-to-cloud cross-validation to identify structural inconsistencies before cargo enters a jurisdiction.
- Socio-technical exception handling mechanisms that route system-generated alerts to customs officials for targeted inspection and investigation.

Together, these capabilities support a transition from document-centric compliance verification toward evidence-based validation grounded in independently observable physical data.

4 Proposed Framework: Secure Green Corridor

To mitigate the CBAM data integrity threats identified in Sect. 3, this paper introduces the SGC framework illustrated in Fig. 1. The SGC transforms the conventional DT from a passive visibility platform into an active, enforcement-oriented verification engine. Rather than accepting digital trade submissions as inherently reliable, the framework adopts a verification-first paradigm in which electronic manifests, shipping declarations, and compliance certificates are treated as provisional claims. These claims are continuously evaluated against independent physical, spatial, and visual sensor observations before being considered valid.

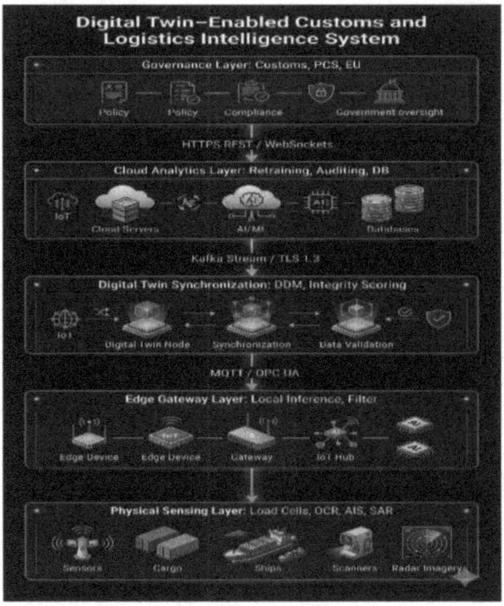

Fig. 1. AI-Driven Customs Digital Twin Architecture.

4.1 Layered Data Pipeline Architecture

The SGC architecture is structured into five functional layers to ingest, securely process, and validate heterogeneous data streams in real time.

The **Multimodal Sensor Layer** provides real-time, independent measurements of cargo characteristics, forming the physical basis for verification. It integrates three complementary data channels:

1. **Visual Integrity (CCTV/OCR):** Computer vision systems deployed at port entry and exit points capture container identifiers (ISO codes), seal conditions (e.g., smart seals), and surface-level anomalies. Optical Character Recognition (OCR) enables automated comparison between observed identifiers and declared shipment records.

2.**Kinetic Integrity (Weight-in-Motion):** High-precision load-cell systems integrated into ship-to-shore cranes and port handling equipment measure container mass during loading and unloading operations. These measurements support continuous validation of declared weight and facilitate detection of anomalies linked to density–manifest divergence (T2).
3.**Spatial Integrity (AIS/Satellite Tracking):** Vessel movements are monitored using Automatic Identification System (AIS) data, supplemented by satellite tracking to ensure continuity. This allows identification of route deviations, signal suppression ("dark periods"), and irregular routing patterns associated with origin and route spoofing (T1).

Collectively, these sensing modalities provide a redundant and cross-verifiable representation of cargo state, reducing dependence on self-reported digital inputs. To operate reliably in high-throughput port environments, initial data filtering occurs at the network edge. Port-side edge computing units process high-frequency raw sensor data (e.g., 100 Hz crane load signals) via Modbus TCP or OPC-UA protocols to remove background dynamic noise prior to transmission. Filtered parameter vectors are streamed asynchronously from edge gateways to the core cloud infrastructure using lightweight MQTT or Apache Kafka pipelines secured with TLS 1.3 encryption. External regulatory platforms access validated analytical outputs via authenticated HTTPS REST APIs and live WebSocket interfaces [19, 20].

Storage Architecture and Trust Provenance Model.

The system's data repository separates operational state tracking from evidentiary provenance:

- Time-Series Database: Stores raw sensor telemetry logs chronologically for detailed auditing.
- DT State Repository: Maintains a live key-value representation of each active container's current state.
- Provenance Cryptographic Store: Each sensor event is tagged at source with timestamp, device identity, and geospatial metadata, and cryptographically signed at the edge to ensure integrity and prevent downstream data injection (T3).

At the core of the framework, the Discrepancy Detection Module (DDM) compares declared shipment attributes with sensor-derived observations across three dimensions: 1) Mass-declaration alignment, 2) Route continuity and 3) Visual identity consistency. This enables detection of inconsistencies such as weight mismatches, anomalous routing behaviour, and discrepancies in container identification.

A key component of the DDM is the **Density-to-HS Code Correlation Logic**, which maps expected physical properties (e.g., density ranges) to declared commodity classifications. For example, a shipment declared as low-density insulation material that exhibits weight characteristics consistent with high-density metals would be flagged as anomalous.

Each shipment is assigned an **Integrity Risk Score (IRS)**, representing the likelihood of divergence between reported and observed cargo states. When predefined thresholds are exceeded, an Integrity Breach Alert is generated and transmitted to the Port Community System (PCS) and relevant Customs authorities for further inspection. This ensures that automated detection is complemented by human oversight in compliance-critical decisions. The IRS is computed as a weighted aggregation of discrepancies across validation dimensions:

$$\mathrm{IRS} = \mathrm{W}_1\mathrm{D}_\mathrm{k} + \mathrm{W}_2\mathrm{D}_\mathrm{s} + \mathrm{W}_3\mathrm{D}_\mathrm{v} \tag{1}$$

where D_k, D_s, and D_v represent normalized discrepancy scores derived from kinetic, spatial, and visual data streams, w_1, w_2, w_3 are tunable weights reflecting their relative significance [14].

4.2 Digital Twin Enforcement Layer

Within the SGC, the DT functions as a synchronisation and audit layer rather than a passive operational mirror. Each sensor event is time-stamped and linked to the corresponding shipment record, creating a traceable relationship between physical observations and declared data. This design enables continuous validation workflows in which digital records are dynamically checked against evolving physical evidence. Rather than relying on static document verification, the system maintains a persistent linkage between data origin, transformation, and observation, supporting auditable decision-making.

The enforcement layer is designed to support three core functions:

- End-to-end data provenance
- Real-time anomaly detection
- Compliance verification

Through this integration, the DT serves as a control mechanism to identify inconsistencies, support enforcement actions, and detect certification fraud.

4.3 System Integration and Data Flow

The interaction between system components is illustrated in Fig. 2. The framework operates as a closed-loop system. Sensor data are collected, transmitted to the DT, evaluated by the DDM, and compared against records in the Port Community System and CBAM registry. When inconsistencies are detected, the system generates an integrity alert and routes it to the appropriate enforcement authority. This closed-loop design supports continuous verification rather than periodic inspection, reducing reliance on manual document review by introducing automated cross-validation between physical measurements and digital declarations.

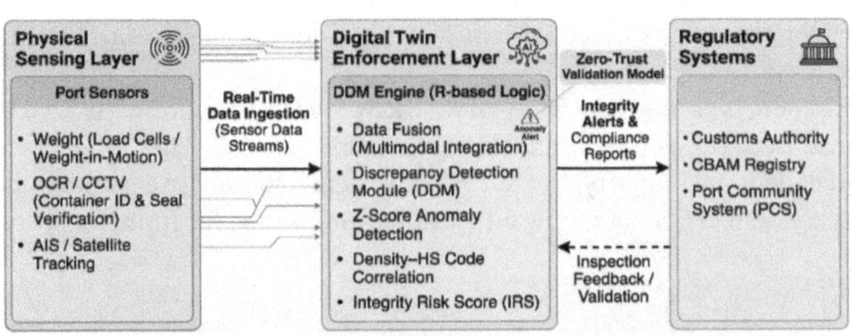

Fig. 2. Multimodal Data Integrity Framework Architecture for Secure Trade.

4.4 Design Implications

The SGC directly addresses the three threat vectors identified in Sect. 3. Route spoofing is mitigated through spatial verification, density–manifest divergence through weight-based and multimodal consistency checks, and certification fraud through provenance-aware validation mechanisms. Instead of treating declarations as authoritative inputs, the framework evaluates their consistency against independent observational data throughout the cargo lifecycle. This approach enables discrepancies to be detected early, before they propagate through downstream compliance processes. By integrating multimodal sensing, provenance-aware data handling, and continuous verification workflows, the proposed framework establishes a scalable architecture for CBAM-oriented compliance enforcement.

5 Anomaly Detection Proof of Concept (PoC)

This section demonstrates how the multimodal data-integrity concept underlying the SGC can operationalize threat vector T2 (Density-Manifest Divergence) using a measurable discrepancy between declared and physically observed cargo characteristics. The proof-of-concept evaluates only a single discrepancy-detection mechanism associated with threat vector T2 and should not be interpreted as a comprehensive validation of the complete SGC architecture. The proof-of-concept focuses on density-consistency verification as an illustrative decision mechanism while remaining conceptually aligned with the DDM and the SGC closed-loop enforcement architecture.

The proof-of-concept relies on a synthetic dataset comprising 100 simulated shipments and is intended solely to demonstrate the feasibility of the discrepancy-detection principle within the SGC architecture. It is not designed to provide a comprehensive assessment of operational performance, scalability, or detection effectiveness in real-world maritime environments. Consequently, the results should be interpreted as an illustrative validation of the detection concept rather than evidence of operational performance.

5.1 Simulation Methodology

To illustrate the potential feasibility of the SGC DDM under controlled adversarial conditions, a synthetic dataset representing 100 maritime shipments was generated to emulate port-centric measurement conditions. The simulation instantiates T2 by assigning shipments a declared HS classification associated with an expected physical density profile, while the observed physical state is modelled as either consistent (benign) or materially inconsistent (fraudulent).

For the purposes of this PoC, the simulation assumes a fixed container volume of 33.2 m^3. In a live operational environment, however, the DDM would integrate LiDAR or other volumetric sensing technologies to estimate actual cargo volume, including partially filled containers, thereby improving the accuracy of the density ratio calculation. The dataset comprises two classes:

- **Compliant Shipments (n = 95):** Physical cargo density is generated to match the reference density associated with the declared HS code (e.g., lightweight composite-like goods), representing ordinary low-risk cargo traffic.
- **Fraudulent Shipments (n = 5):** The digital paperwork remains consistent with a low-density declaration, while the simulated physical cargo state contains a higher-density commodity, such as steel (HS 7208), concealed within the declared low-density category.

Although synthetic, the simulation reflects the core SGC premise: the DDM does not accept declarations at face value but instead evaluates whether declared commodity profiles are physically plausible based on available kinetic and volumetric evidence.

5.2 Framework-Aligned Anomaly Detection Logic (DDM)

Within the SGC, the DDM produces an enforcement-oriented assessment by quantifying divergence between declared expectations and observed sensor evidence. In this PoC, divergence is represented through a density-consistency test using a Density Ratio (DR) derived from physical measurements. The z-score mechanism should be interpreted as a simplified analytical proxy used solely to demonstrate the discrepancy-detection principle. The SGC architecture does not constrain the DDM to a specific statistical technique. In operational deployments, the DDM may incorporate machine learning, graph-based anomaly detection, multimodal fusion models, or adaptive risk-scoring algorithms capable of identifying more complex adversarial behaviours.

$$\mathrm{DR} = \frac{Weight_{Physical}}{Volume_{Con\,tainer}} \tag{2}$$

The declared HS code defines a statistical baseline for expected density behavior. For each HS category, the PoC models a historical density distribution and computes a standardized discrepancy score using a z-score formulation:

$$\mathrm{Z} = \frac{x - \mu}{\sigma} \tag{3}$$

where x represents the observed Density Ratio derived from physical measurement proxies, μ is the declared category mean density baseline, and σ is the standard deviation of that baseline. A shipment is flagged as a potential high-risk integrity breach when its discrepancy exceeds a predefined threshold. In this PoC, the decision rule is implemented through a z-score thresholding mechanism:

- If $Z > 2.5$, classify as ALERT: FRAUD (density–manifest divergence consistent with T2).
- Otherwise, classify as VERIFIED.

This reflects the SGC principle that the DDM converts multimodal evidence into an integrity decision signal, which would feed into the DT enforcement layer to generate an alert and evidence trace for Customs and Port Community System workflows. The DDM was implemented using the R script to automate cross-verification between declared HS codes and physically observed shipment data [20]. The discrepancy-detection logic presented in this proof of concept is intentionally simplified to demonstrate the operational feasibility of linking physical cargo measurements to compliance-verification workflows. The SGC framework does not prescribe a specific detection algorithm; rather, it provides an architectural foundation within which more advanced statistical, machine-learning, graph-analytic, or multimodal anomaly-detection techniques may be deployed according to operational requirements and threat models.

5.3 Results and Findings

The PoC demonstrates that the DDM's density-consistency verification can identify T2-style fraud within the simulated environment. In the synthetic 100-shipment dataset, the simulation correctly identified all five fraudulent shipments. Importantly, detection occurs even when the digital paperwork is internally consistent, because the decision process is driven by physical plausibility under the declared HS density baseline. As shown in Table 2, shipment SH-90 is flagged because its measured density proxy yields a z-score of 4.12, which substantially exceeds the declared category's expected statistical range. This renders the declared low-density classification inconsistent with the observed kinetic and volumetric state.

Table 2. Z-Score Based Anomaly Detection Results (Simulation Output)

Shipment ID	Declared HS Code	Measured Weight (kg)	Z-Score	Integrity Status
SH-088	3921 (Composite)	4150	0.22	Verified
SH-089	3921 (Composite)	4280	0.41	Verified
SH-90	**3921 (Composite)**	**19400**	**4.12**	**ALERT: FRAUD**

Overall, the PoC supports the SGC proposition that integrity enforcement can be strengthened through quantitatively grounded discrepancy detection. When declared HS attributes imply density characteristics that conflict with sensor-derived physical evidence, the framework generates an integrity-breach signal suitable for downstream verification within the DDM → DT → PCS/Customs workflow [23, 24]. These results should be interpreted as an illustrative validation of the density-consistency concept rather than evidence of operational readiness. Additional evaluation using large-scale maritime datasets, live sensor feeds, AIS streams, and customs records would be required to assess robustness, scalability, and detection accuracy under real-world conditions. This proof-of-concept is a feasibility demonstration, not a performance evaluation. The synthetic dataset was deliberately constructed to illustrate how multimodal discrepancy detection can operationalise density–manifest divergence within the SGC architecture.

6 Discussion

6.1 Operational Integration and Scalability

Embedding the proposed SGC framework within existing PCS introduces a new approach to maritime border management. Rather than relying exclusively on post-arrival document checks, customs authorities can leverage continuous stream processing to support predictive risk profiling. Dynamically generating an IRS for each container before vessel arrival, the framework enables more targeted inspection decisions. Compliant supply chains may benefit from expedited "Green Lane" routing, reducing terminal dwell times. Conversely, containers exhibiting significant data–physical divergence can be directed to non-intrusive inspection (NII) facilities or manual examination lanes. This risk-based allocation of inspection resources improves operational efficiency while maintaining enforcement capability in high-throughput port environments [5, 22].

6.2 Socio-Technical Exception Handling

A core strength of the SGC architecture is its socio-technical trust layer. The system is explicitly designed as a decision-support mechanism rather than a fully autonomous execution tool. While the DDM handles the high-volume computation of parsing mechatronic and spatial data streams, the final decision to block a shipment or penalise an importer remains under human oversight. When an *Integrity Breach Alert* is triggered, the DT compiles an immutable cryptographic evidence package (the data provenance trail). This allows customs officers to exercise professional discretionary judgment backed by verifiable physical metrics, ensuring legal defensibility and reducing false-positive friction.

6.3 Limitations and Future Work

While the synthetic proof-of-concept demonstrates structural feasibility, several operational limitations must be addressed prior to real-world deployment:

- **Mechatronic Sensor Noise:** In active maritime environments, physical sensors are subjected to harsh environmental variables. Ship-to-shore crane load cells experience severe dynamic vibrations, wind vectors, and spray calibration drift, which can distort raw mass readings. Future work must integrate advanced Kalman filtering and edge-computing to isolate environmental noise from true structural fraud.
- **Heterogeneous Data Latency:** Merging instantaneous visual OCR data with intermittent satellite tracking feeds and low-frequency custom document filings creates a data alignment problem. Future iterations should incorporate adaptive temporal windowing algorithms to prevent asynchronous data arrivals from generating false anomaly spikes.
- **Absence of Operational Data Validation:** This study does not evaluate the framework using real-world maritime sensor feeds, AIS streams, customs declarations, or live port community data. Future research should focus on pilot deployments and industry partnerships that enable validation under operational conditions, including assessment of scalability, false positives, and integration complexity.

- **False Positive Management:** Because compliance decisions can have significant operational and financial consequences, minimising false positives is essential. Sensor noise, temporary communication failures, asynchronous data, and cargo variability may produce signals that do not indicate fraud. Future research should evaluate precision, recall, false-positive rates, and alert-calibration strategies using operational datasets to ensure proportionate and sustainable enforcement actions.
- **Adversarial Adaptation:** Sophisticated smuggling syndicates may adapt to basic z-score thresholding by executing "micro-leakage" tactics, hiding precisely calculated, sub-threshold masses of high-carbon materials across hundreds of compliant containers. This necessitates upgrading the DDM from static thresholds to multi-variate deep learning models that detect distributed fraud over time. The current proof-of-concept is a foundation for developing more advanced detection models, not final resilience against sophisticated threats.
- **Adversarial Sensor and Data Manipulation:** While the framework incorporates provenance-aware logging and multimodal cross-validation, the present study does not provide a formal security evaluation against coordinated adversarial campaigns involving AIS spoofing, sensor tampering, GNSS manipulation, collusive data injection, or compromised edge devices. Future work should incorporate red-team testing, attack-tree analysis, and adversarial simulation environments to quantify framework resilience under sophisticated cyber-physical attack scenarios.
- **Operational Validation and Scalability:** The present study does not evaluate the framework using operational maritime datasets or high-volume trade environments. Future research should investigate scalability, detection performance, false-positive rates, and computational requirements using real-world sensor networks, AIS data streams, customs records, and Port Community System integrations.
- **Comparative Evaluation Against Existing Frameworks:** The present study does not include a quantitative comparison against existing maritime anomaly-detection systems or DT platforms. This is primarily because the proposed SGC framework is introduced as a compliance-oriented architectural model rather than a standalone detection algorithm. Future research should evaluate the framework against established maritime monitoring and anomaly-detection approaches using common datasets and operational performance metrics to quantify detection effectiveness, scalability, and resilience under adversarial conditions.
- **Future validation:** This should incorporate operational port datasets, larger shipment populations, and longitudinal deployment studies to assess detection performance under real-world conditions.

7 Conclusion

This paper has presented an enforcement-oriented Multimodal Data Integrity Framework for securing digitised maritime trade against emerging carbon fraud and supply-chain manipulation. The primary contribution of this work is the proposed SGC architecture, which integrates multimodal sensing, DT synchronisation, provenance-aware validation, and discrepancy detection within a unified compliance-verification framework. While the proof-of-concept demonstrates the feasibility of detecting one representative threat vector through density-consistency analysis, the broader framework should be regarded as a conceptual architecture that requires further validation using operational maritime datasets and real-world deployment scenarios. Integrating empirical field insights from global customs enforcement with mechatronic data fusion pipelines, the architecture establishes a zero-trust verification model where digital declarations are continuously validated against physical ground truths. As global trade vectors increasingly tie financial liabilities to digitised emissions metrics, architectures enforcing cryptographic data provenance and multi-sensor cross-validation will become foundational to ensuring the security, transparency, and fiscal integrity of next-generation green supply chains.

Disclosure of Interests.. The authors have no competing interests to declare that are relevant to the content of this article.

References

1. Commission, E.: Regulation (EU) 2023/956 of the European Parliament and of the Council of 10 May 2023 establishing a carbon border adjustment mechanism. Official Journal of the European Union, L **130**, 52–104 (2023)
2. International Carbon Action Partnership (ICAP): Emissions Trading Worldwide: 2024 ICAP Status Report. Berlin: ICAP (2024)
3. World Customs Organization: SAFE Framework of Standards to Secure and Facilitate Global Trade. WCO Publications, Brussels (2021)
4. United Nations Office on Drugs and Crime (UNODC): Container Control Programme: Annual Progress Report. UNODC, Vienna (2022)
5. Zuidwijk, R.: Synchromodal Logistics. In: Lee, C.Y., Meng, Q. (eds.) Handbook of Ocean Container Transport Logistics. International Series in Operations Research & Management Science, vol. 220, pp. 235–251. Springer, Cham (2015)
6. Grieves, M., Vickers, J.: Digital twin: mitigating unpredictable, unsustainable, and unsafe outcomes. In: Transdisciplinary Perspectives on Complex Systems, pp. 85–113. Springer, Cham (2017)
7. Ivanov, D.: Digital twin" in supply chain management: a conceptual framework for resilient, sustainable, and agile operations. Int J Log Res Appl **26**(11), 1435–1455 (2023)
8. Giusti, R., Catena, M., Di Francesco, M.: Synchromodality in Logistics: an overview of capabilities, risks, and security imperatives. Int. J. Prod. Econ. **245**, 108390 (2022)
9. World Economic Forum: Shareable Data Ocean: Securing Maritime Trade Corridors Through Trusted Multimodal Exchange. WEF White Paper, Geneva (2023)
10. Marra, M., Hoang, T., van Sinderen, M.: Architectural gaps in port community systems: vulnerabilities to manifest manipulation and arbitrage. Maritime Econom. Logist. **24**(3), 412–436 (2022)
11. Zhang, J., Dong, Y., Wang, S.: IoT-enabled load cell systems for dynamic crane weight validation in high-throughput terminals. IEEE Trans. Industr. Inf. **19**(4), 5512–5521 (2023)
12. Nguyen, S., Turnca, O., Harris, I.: Computer vision applications in maritime customs gates: container identification and smart seal verification. Comput. Ind. **142**, 103730 (2022)
13. Katsikas, S., Gkioulos, V.: Cyber-physical security threats in maritime logistics: a taxonomy of spoofing and interception vectors. J. Mar. Sci. Eng. **11**(2), 294 (2023)
14. Belles-Sampera, J., Guillen, M., Santolino, M.: Anomaly scoring models for risk mitigation in multimodal port-centric ingestion pipelines. Reliab. Eng. Syst. Saf. **218**, 108115 (2022)

15. IBM Security: Security and Provenance in Next-Generation Electronic Customs Environments: A Zero-Trust Approach. IBM Whitepaper Series on Global Trade Security (2023)
16. National Institute of Standards and Technology (NIST): Secure Data Provenance for Multi-Source Industrial IoT Telemetry Networks. NIST Special Publication 800–213 (2022)
17. Choi, T.M., Feng, L.: Blockchain-enabled or twin-driven? Choosing the right provenance ledger for carbon footprint tracking in supply chains. Prod. Oper. Manag. **32**(6), 1845–1862 (2023)
18. Heilig, L., Voß, S.: Port community systems: a structured review of information ingestion, data integrity, and inter-organizational trust. Inf. Syst. Front. **25**(1), 115–139 (2023)
19. Wang, L., Lin, Y., Wang, K.: Edge-to-cloud distributed digital twins for high-velocity industrial systems. J. Manuf. Syst. **62**, 894–907 (2022)
20. Apache Software Foundation: Architecture and Benchmarking of High-Throughput Stream Ingestion Engines using Kafka and MQTT in Maritime Gateways. Apache Tech Report (2024)
21. United Kingdom Department for Business and Trade: Guidance on UK-EU Carbon Border Adjustment Compliance and Cross-Border Scope 3 Reporting. HMSO, London (2025)
22. Lee, P.T.W., Lin, C.W.: Green shipping corridors: data integrity infrastructure and environmental law enforcement gaps. Transp. Res. Part D: Transp. Environ. **115**, 103590 (2023)
23. Huber, M., Wimmer, M.: Z-score threshold optimization techniques for non-intrusive cargo inspection in dynamic terminal environments. Int. J. Disast. Risk Reduct. **86**, 103541 (2023)
24. Sharma, R., Singh, S.: Zero-trust industrial data architectures: protecting ingestion layers against adversarial spoofing and falsified injections. Comput. Secur. **129**, 103210 (2023)
25. World Bank: Digitization of Customs Administrations: Enhancing Fiscal Collections and Verifying Green Supply Chains. World Bank Group Flagship Report, Washington DC (2024)

Hybrid Hierarchical Runtime Verification for Edge-IoT Security: Combining MonPoly and RTLola

Nikolaos Kekatos[1(✉)], Marinelio Chintri[2], Panagiotis Katsaros[3], Alexios Lekidis[4], Tom Nianios[1], Ioannis Seitoglou[2], Anastasios Temperekidis[1], and Stylianos Basagiannis[2]

[1] Clone Systems, Larnaca, Cyprus
nkekatos@clone-systems.com, tnianios@clone-systems.com, atemperekidis@clone-systems.com

[2] International Hellenic University, Serres, Greece
marchint@ihu.gr, ioaseito@ihu.gr, basagiannis@ihu.gr

[3] Aristotle University of Thessaloniki, Thessaloniki, Greece
katsaros@csd.auth.gr

[4] University of Thessaly, Larissa, Greece
alekidis@uth.gr

Abstract. Security monitoring of edge-IoT fleets faces three structural challenges. (i) A per-node monitor is cheap but cannot see attacks that coordinate across devices. (ii) A cloud monitor sees the full fleet but pays for that view in bandwidth. (iii) Even at the cloud, a monitor built on a single RV engine can be fooled by an attacker who compromises a device, raises one malicious request, and then goes silent: once the events stop, an event-triggered monitor has nothing left to evaluate. We propose a three-layer hierarchical runtime-verification framework that addresses all three. The edge layer classifies events as they happen, the gateway layer aggregates short windows of per-device behaviour, and the cloud layer runs two complementary RV engines. MonPoly handles first-order temporal correlation over the merged alert stream: coordinated overflow (which genuinely quantifies across devices) plus per-device multi-vector APT, escalation, and persistent-campaign patterns. RTLola handles a time-triggered silent-node property that an event-triggered engine cannot detect within a bounded delay under fleet silence. We evaluate the framework on a 15-actor Docker testbed covering eight attack profiles plus a silent-bypass scenario. In the controlled labelled testbed, every device-attributable incident the framework raises names an attacker-labelled device, and the RTLola tier catches silent-bypass attempts the event-triggered tier misses. Per-event monitoring stays in the microsecond range at the edge and gateway, with low end-to-end alert-to-incident latency at the cloud.

Keywords: Hierarchical runtime verification · Edge-IoT security · Hybrid MFOTL/stream RV · MonPoly · RTLola · Silent-bypass detection · Coordinated APT

P. Kieseberg et al. (Eds.): ARES 2026 Workshops, LNCS 16903, pp. 222–240, 2027.
https://doi.org/10.1007/978-3-032-37218-5_14

1 Introduction

Security-critical decisions in edge-IoT deployments are pushed ever closer to the device [9], but doing everything at the edge has a structural cost in visibility. A per-node monitor sees only its own device, so an attack that coordinates across devices [24] is invisible to it. Pushing every event to a central cloud monitor restores the fleet-wide view, but pays for it in bandwidth and detection latency. And even a well-resourced cloud monitor built on a single RV engine keeps one blind spot: silence. An attacker who compromises the on-device monitor, issues a single malicious request, and then goes quiet leaves an event-triggered monitor [8] with nothing left to evaluate.

Each of these choices fixes one weakness only to expose another, so neither a single tier nor a single engine suffices. To cover all three at once, this paper proposes a three-layer hierarchical runtime-verification framework built on formal RV methods [14,18] that assigns each tier the checks it can afford and reserves for the cloud the checks no lower tier can express. The edge layer (L1) is a per-event canonicaliser that classifies buffer overflows, time spoofing, fuzzing, and safe transactions. The gateway layer (L2) aggregates short windows per device, covering repeated overflows, spam and pulsing DoS, and immediate fuzz or time-anomaly alerts. The cloud layer (L3) is where the paper makes its central design choice: rather than pick one RV engine, we run two side by side. The first RV engine is MonPoly [6]; its expressive first-order temporal specification language handles four past-time correlation properties over the merged alert stream. One of them, coordinated overflow, genuinely quantifies across devices and is provably inexpressible at any single-device tier (Theorem 1); the other three (multi-vector APT, escalation, persistent campaign) are per-device patterns ($\forall d$) that we consolidate at the cloud by choice. The second is RTLola [15], which handles a single time-triggered property, silent-node anomaly, whose verdict must be emitted at a fixed deadline rather than on input. When fed the merged multi-device stream, an event-triggered engine like MonPoly stalls only under *total* fleet silence – exactly the silent-bypass case – which RTLola's time-triggered semantics bounds natively. The result is that fast, deterministic decisions stay at the edge; per-device temporal aggregation stays at the gateway; cross-device correlation and absence-of-event detection live at the cloud.

We evaluate the framework on a 15-actor Docker testbed spanning eight attack profiles (normal, overflow, time-spoof, spam/DoS, low-and-slow overflow, fuzz, pulsing DoS, mixed APT). Single-node attacks are caught by the edge and gateway tiers; multi-vector APT, persistent campaigns, and silent-bypass require the hybrid cloud tier.

Why Three Layers. Edge-only stream-based RV [11,15,21] offers rich per-trace semantics but cannot correlate behaviour across N devices. A gateway tier that counts events over short windows brings repeated overflow and spam into reach. But it still misses attacks that mix *different* vectors across *different* devices in one window. That is exactly the pattern multi-vector APT and coordinated campaigns follow, as in ICS incidents like the 2015 Ukrainian power-grid attack [24]. MonPoly's specification language [6] supplies the quantifiers this class of property needs, but running it on every raw packet from N devices is too costly in bandwidth and compute. That is why correlation sits at the cloud tier.

Hierarchical CPS-RV literature [5,20] establishes the decomposition pattern; we refine it on four axes. First, we prove a layer non-collapse theorem (Theorem 1, Sect. 3.3): under the single-device gateway abstraction we adopt, no per-device rule can decide a property that quantifies over two distinct devices, so detecting a coordinated cross-device attack is provably impossible below the cloud under that abstraction. The cloud tier therefore fills a gap the lower tiers cannot, by construction, fill.

Second, we identify a gap less often discussed: event-triggered monitors like MonPoly report a missing event only once a later-timestamped event arrives, with no bound on detection latency. Time-triggered stream monitors like RTLola, by contrast, emit a verdict at the deadline regardless of input but express cross-device joins less naturally. Running both engines side by side covers both gaps without pushing either outside the properties it handles well. Third, we contribute an executable artefact that turns the per-tier specifications into an end-to-end audit trail, tracing every cloud incident back to the gateway alerts and edge events that produced it. Fourth, we report measured per-event monitoring cost at each tier and end-to-end alert-to-incident latency at the cloud (Sect. 5.5), making these deployment choices quantifiable.

Cost Asymmetry and Adversary Model. The framework forces an attacker to pay coordination cost across at least three devices, while the defender pays only a bounded per-event canonicaliser at the edge (mean $\sim$57 μs) and a sliding-window update at the gateway (mean $\sim$710 μs, Sect. 5.5), with constant-size witness sets per alert. On our workload the gateway-to-cloud alert stream is roughly 7$\times$ smaller than the edge input; we do not claim a larger reduction, as that would assume a raw-packet upstream our testbed does not measure. End-to-end cloud latency stays around 1.7 s, with the silent-node detector adding a fixed five-second window.

We assume an adversary who compromises one or more edge monitors and knows the framework's thresholds and the cloud property catalogue. "Success" for the adversary means causing exfiltration or disruption without raising any cloud-level MonPoly or RTLola incident. Supply-chain compromise of the edge or gateway binaries (assumed handled by attestation), gateway-timestamp tampering, and direct interference with the edge sidecar are out of scope.

Contributions. The paper makes four contributions. We give a three-layer formal specification with thirteen properties (P1.1–P1.4 at the edge, P2.1–P2.4 at the gateway, and P3.1–P3.5 at the cloud) that together cover eight attack classes plus a silent-bypass scenario. We describe a hybrid reference architecture in which the cloud tier runs four MonPoly processes alongside one RTLola time-triggered process. We instantiate the architecture on a 15-actor Docker testbed, and we evaluate it by reporting per-property incident counts, per-tier monitoring cost, alert-to-incident latency, and a replay of real IoT-23 data.

2 Attack-Type Catalogue

The framework is evaluated on eight IoT attack profiles drawn from the attack-surface taxonomy in edge-IoT-security surveys [9]. Each profile is realised as a Python device emulator with controlled parameters (Table 1). The eight profiles are deployed across 15 containers via `docker-compose`: five clean baselines (NODE-1–NODE-5) and ten attackers (NODE-6–NODE-15), one of each non-clean profile plus a mix of mixed-APT actors; ground-truth labels are recorded at the generator.

Table 1. The eight attack profiles emulated by the testbed (A1–A8) plus the silent-bypass scenario (AS1), with the detecting tier/property. AS1 is not a separate node: it arises as a behaviour of existing attackers.

ID	Profile	Parameters	Detected by
A1	Normal traffic	$[10, 30]$ B, interval $U(0.1, 4.0)$ s	(baseline)
A2	Buffer overflow	$[35, 60]$ B; 80% vulnerable_send	L1 / P1.1
A3	Time spoof	turn offset $\pm 300/600$ s	L1 / P1.2; L2 / P2.3
A4	Spam DoS	interval $U(0.005, 0.05)$ s, safe_send	L2 / P2.2
A5	Low-and-slow ovfl	31–32 B payloads, 10% rate	L1 / P1.1; L2 / P2.1
A6	Fuzz	malformed content*	L1 / P1.3; L2 / P2.4
A7	Pulsing DoS	20-event bursts every 20–30 s	L2 / P2.2
A8	Mixed APT	40% mix of overflow / spoof	L3 / P3.1, P3.2
AS1	Silent bypass	overflow then silence (≥ 5 s)	L3 / P3.5

* Fuzz payloads are non-printable or structurally invalid.

The attack profiles partition cleanly by the kind of quantification needed to detect them: single-event classes (A2, A3, A6) by an L1 per-event predicate; time-windowed classes (A4, A5, A7) by L2 sliding counts; the multi-vector class (A8) by L3's parametric quantification – a logical necessity for the cross-device form P3.2 under the single-device gateway abstraction (Theorem 1), and an engineering choice for the per-device properties P3.1, P3.3, P3.4 – and the silent-bypass scenario (AS1) by the time-triggered P3.5. Empirical distributions appear in Tables 4 and 5.

3 Three-Layer Specification

The framework is given as a triple of formal specifications $\Phi = \langle \varphi_{L1}, \varphi_{L2}, \varphi_{L3} \rangle$, each scoped to its tier's data granularity: L1 is per-event, L2 is per-window-per-device, L3 is multi-device past-time. We write all specifications in standard temporal logic for engine-independence; the reference implementation (Sect. 4) realises them as Python stream processors at L1 and L2 and as MonPoly [6] metric first-order temporal logic (MFOTL) formulas at L3.

3.1 Event Schema

Four event types flow through the pipeline. A raw device event $e_i = \langle \mathsf{turn}, \mathsf{actor}, \mathsf{tool}, \mathsf{args} \rangle$ has a tool field over {safe, vulnerable, time-spoof, fuzz} sends and an args record of attempted-size, actual-sent, buffer-limit and content. L1 emits one canonical event per input event (buffer-overflow, time-anomaly, logic-fuzz, or safe-tx). L2 emits one of three alert types (repeated-overflow, dos, immediate) and forwards safe-tx to L3. L3 emits one of five incidents (apt-indicator, coordinated-attack, escalation-pattern, persistent-threat, silent-node-anomaly) with a severity label. We write Σ_{raw}, Σ_{canon}, and Σ_{alert} for the sets of raw events, canonical events, and alerts, respectively. For example, a raw vulnerable_send whose 48 B payload exceeds the 30 B buffer limit (Σ_{raw}) becomes the canonical event buffer_overflow(node-6, 48) (Σ_{canon}), and three such within 30 s raise the alert overflow(node-6) (Σ_{alert}).

3.2 Per-Layer Property Specifications

L1: Per-event Properties (canonicaliser). The L1 monitor enforces four memoryless boolean predicates over the current raw event e (no inter-event state), each emitting a single canonical event when its body holds:

- **P1.1** (buffer overflow): $e.\mathsf{tool} = \mathsf{vulnerable\_send} \wedge e.\mathsf{actual\_sent} > e.\mathsf{buffer\_limit}$.
- **P1.2** (time spoofing): $|current\_time - e.\mathsf{turn}| > \tau_{ts}$ (τ_{ts}=15 s).
- **P1.3** (input fuzzing): $e.\mathsf{tool} = \mathsf{fuzz\_send} \wedge \neg\,\mathsf{wellformed}(e.\mathsf{content})$, where $\mathsf{wellformed}(c)$ holds iff c conforms to the expected payload contract (a printable-ASCII string within the valid length domain). Oversized payloads ($e.\mathsf{actual\_sent} > e.\mathsf{buffer\_limit}$) are by construction the buffer-overflow class (P1.1); fuzzing here is value/content well-formedness, so the fuzz and overflow domains are disjoint.
- **P1.4** (safe_tx, residual): $\neg$P1.1 $\wedge$ $\neg$P1.2 $\wedge$ $\neg$P1.3.

The four predicates are mutually exclusive and exhaustive: every raw event emits exactly one canonical event, with arguments ($e.\mathsf{actor}$, x) where x is either the violating actual_sent (P1.1, P1.3, P1.4) or the suspect turn (P1.2). *Semantic note.* P1.4 is a *residual* predicate (the event did not match P1.1–P1.3), not a positive "verified-safe" assertion. Downstream properties built on safe_tx (notably P3.3 escalation) therefore detect transitions from *not-one-of-these-three-anomalies* to overflow plus time-spoof; they are signature-style temporal patterns, not general threat-progression detectors.

L2: Time-Bounded Temporal Properties (Gateway Monitor). L2 maintains short-window per-device counters and evaluates four temporal predicates over sliding windows (W_{ovf}=30 s for repeated overflow, W_{spam}=5 s for spam/pulsing, stateless for the immediate alerts). Let $\#_W(\pi, d)$ denote the count of events $\pi(d, \cdot)$ in the past W seconds for device d.

- **P2.1** (repeated buffer overflow):

$$\square(\#_{[30\,s]}(\mathsf{buffer\_overflow}, d) \geq N_{ovf} \rightarrow \mathsf{overflow}(d)),$$

with $N_{ovf} = 3$ over a 30 s window; this is the gateway rule that catches sustained-overflow attack patterns, including the low-and-slow overflow profile (A5).
- **P2.2** (spam / pulsing DoS):

$$\square(\#_{[5\,s]}(\mathsf{safe\_tx}, d) \geq N_{spam} \rightarrow \mathsf{dos\_attack\_alert}(d)),$$

with $N_{spam} = 30$ for sustained spam and a tighter $N_{pulse} = 15$ over $W_{pulse} = 2$ s for pulsing bursts.
- **P2.3** / **P2.4** (immediate alerts): any time_anomaly or fuzz event triggers an immediate alert. These are deliberately stateless: a single event suffices because neither has a plausible benign-traffic baseline.

L3: Cross-Device Correlation Properties (MFOTL). L3 consumes the L2 alert stream and evaluates *five* properties: four event-triggered MFOTL formulas (P3.1–P3.4) executed by MonPoly and one time-triggered stream property (P3.5) executed by RTLola. Let $\mathsf{evt}_i \in \{\mathsf{overflow}, \mathsf{timespoof}, \mathsf{fuzzing}\}$ range over the L2 alert predicates.

$$\begin{aligned}
&\textbf{P3.1}: \forall d.\,\square\big(\exists t_1{<}t_2,\ t_2{-}t_1{\leq}60,\ \mathsf{evt}_1(d,t_1) \wedge \mathsf{evt}_2(d,t_2),\\
&\qquad\qquad \mathsf{evt}_1{\neq}\mathsf{evt}_2 \rightarrow \mathsf{apt_indicator}(d)\big)\\
&\textbf{P3.2}: \square\big(\Diamond_{[0,30\mathrm{s}]}\mathsf{overflow}(d) \wedge cnt = \#\{d' \mid \Diamond_{[0,30\mathrm{s}]}\ \mathsf{overflow}(d')\} \wedge cnt \geq 3\\
&\qquad\qquad \rightarrow \mathsf{coordinated_attack}(d, cnt)\big)\\
&\textbf{P3.3}: \forall d.\,\square\big(\Diamond_{[10,60\mathrm{s}]}\mathsf{safe_tx}(d) \wedge \Diamond_{[0,50\mathrm{s}]}\mathsf{overflow}(d) \wedge\\
&\qquad\qquad \Diamond_{[0,50\mathrm{s}]}\ \mathsf{timespoof}(d) \rightarrow \mathsf{escalation_pattern}(d)\big)\\
&\textbf{P3.4}: \forall d.\,\square\big(\#_{[1\mathrm{h}]}(\mathsf{overflow}, d) \geq 5 \rightarrow \mathsf{persistent_threat}(d)\big)\\
&\textbf{P3.5}: \forall d.\,\square\big(\mathsf{overflow}(d, t_0) \wedge \neg\,\Diamond_{[t_0, t_0+5\mathrm{s}]}\ \mathsf{safe_tx}(d)\\
&\qquad\qquad \rightarrow \mathsf{silent_node_anomaly}(d)\big)
\end{aligned}$$

P3.1–P3.4 are MFOTL formulas executed by MonPoly; P3.5 is the silent-node anomaly. MFOTL can express it as a bounded-response formula and MonPoly supports bounded-future operators; however, an event-triggered monitor advances its clock only with the timestamps of incoming events. Because MonPoly is fed the merged multi-device stream, any device's alert advances its clock, so its detection latency is unbounded only under *total* fleet silence – precisely the silent-bypass case. Injecting synthetic clock-ticks into MonPoly would bound the delay, but only via a timer outside the specification driven by an external scheduler. RTLola's time-triggered semantics instead emits the verdict at the 5 s window closure without input, bounding detection at the window length natively. Table 2 summarises the thirteen properties.

Table 2. The thirteen formal properties across the three monitoring tiers. $\square$ denotes always; $\diamond_{[a,b]}$ a bounded-past existential and future-bounded for P3.5; $\#_W$ a sliding count. P3.1–P3.4 use MonPoly (event-triggered); P3.5 uses RTLola (time-triggered).

ID	Layer	Engine	Type	Targets
P1.1	L1	Python	Per-event	buffer overflow
P1.2	L1	Python	Per-event	time spoofing
P1.3	L1	Python	Per-event	fuzzing
P1.4	L1	Python	Per-event	safe transactions
P2.1	L2	Python	Temporal (30 s)	repeated overflow
P2.2	L2	Python	Temporal (5 s)	spam / pulsing DoS
P2.3	L2	Python	Immediate	time anomaly
P2.4	L2	Python	Immediate	fuzz events
P3.1	L3	MonPoly	MFOTL (60 s)	multi-vector APT
P3.2	L3	MonPoly	MFOTL count & witness (30 s)	coordinated attack
P3.3	L3	MonPoly	MFOTL (10–60 s)	escalation pattern
P3.4	L3	MonPoly	MFOTL count (1 h)	persistent campaign
P3.5	L3	RTLola	Time-triggered (5 s)	silent-node anomaly

3.3 Hierarchical Composition

The three layers form a strict containment hierarchy by data locality: L1 sees one event at a time; L2 sees one device's events over a few seconds; L3 sees alert summaries across all devices over minutes-to-hours. Composition is operationally a streaming pipeline: L1 emits canonical events forwarded to L2; L2 emits alert events forwarded to L3; L3 emits incident events to the audit log. Each layer attaches a witness sub-trace (layer, device, predicate, timestamp) to every output, so an L3 incident is mechanically traceable back through the contributing L2 alerts and the contributing L1 canonical events. In particular, P3.2 incidents carry the full contributing device set as a runtime witness emitted directly from MonPoly's satisfying assignments. L1 alone classifies the four per-event categories (three single-event attack classes plus the residual safe_tx); L2 adds temporal patterns invisible at the per-event level; L3 adds the cross-device correlations that no single-device monitor can express, a claim Theorem 1 below makes precise. The split is asymmetric in deployment cost: per-event work stays on the edge, per-device temporal aggregation at the gateway, parametric MFOTL only at the cloud correlator.

Layer Abstractions. Let an L1 monitor be a total memoryless map (function) $\mu_1 : \Sigma_{raw} \to \Sigma_{canon}$ (P1.1–P1.4 are exhaustive, so every raw event yields exactly one canonical event), and an L2 *single-device* monitor a map $\mu_2 : (\Sigma_{canon})^*_d \to 2^{\Sigma_{alert}}$, where $(\Sigma_{canon})^*_d$ is the set of finite canonical-event sequences of a single fixed device d (with finite sliding-window counters) and $2^{\Sigma_{alert}}$ the sets of alerts; μ_2's domain contains no device variable. Let $\mathcal{F}_{single}$ denote the class decidable by any such μ_2.

Theorem 1. (P3.2 requires cross-device quantification). *Property P3.2 quantifies existentially over distinct devices; even its two-device core ($\exists d_1 \neq d_2.\ \mathsf{overflow}(d_1) \wedge \Diamond_{[0,30\,s]}\mathsf{overflow}(d_2)$) is not expressible in $\mathcal{F}_{single}$.*
Proof. Suppose for contradiction that $\psi \in \mathcal{F}_{single}$ decides P3.2. Consider a two-device trace $T = T_{d_1} \sqcup T_{d_2}$ where T_{d_1} has $\mathsf{overflow}(d_1)$ at t_1 and T_{d_2} has $\mathsf{overflow}(d_2)$ at t_2, $|t_2 - t_1| \leq 30\,\mathrm{s}$. By construction of $\mathcal{F}_{single}$, $\psi(T)$ is determined by $\psi(T_{d_1})$ and $\psi(T_{d_2})$ separately: neither call sees the other device. Each single-device projection lacks the second-device witness P3.2 needs, so both return false, contradicting the assumption. □

Note that the abstraction restricts the L2 *rule class*, not the gateway's physical visibility: the gateway observes all devices, but each rule's state and verdict involve exactly one device, matching the per-device deques of the implementation.
Scope. A hypothetical multi-device gateway μ_2^{multi} that saw all devices' streams could express P3.2 (with $O(N)$ per-gateway state vs. $O(1)$-per-device for μ_2); P3.1, P3.3, P3.4 lie also outside the *chosen* L2 fragment (5–30 s windows, no joint vector predicates, no hour-scale counts), but not outside every conceivable L2-shaped monitor: their placement at L3 is an engineering choice, not a logical necessity. The layering claim is therefore threefold: (i) formal necessity of cross-device quantification for P3.2 under $\mathcal{F}_{single}$; (ii) the choice of the single-device abstraction itself, motivated by O(1)-per-device gateway state and (iii) measured cost separation (Sect. 5.5).

4 Runtime Architecture

We instantiate Sect. 3 in a Docker testbed: one process per IoT device, a *monitor* container hosting the L1→L2 pipeline as a Unix pipe between Python stream processors, and a separate *correlator* container hosting the L3 MonPoly and RTLola subprocesses (Fig. 1). The co-located reference layout maps directly to a physical deployment, with L1 on each edge device, L2 on a local gateway, L3 in a regional cloud / SOC. Inter-tier traffic on the measured workload is dominated by forwarded safe_tx events required by P3.3 and P3.5; only the security-alert subset (941 of 6861 L2 outputs) is genuinely smaller than the L1 input.

L1 – Edge Canonicaliser. The L1 monitor is a short Python stream processor that reads JSON-encoded raw events and emits one canonical event per input event as a MonPoly-friendly record `@T predicate("device", arg)`. The four predicates P1.1–P1.4 are evaluated in priority order.

L2 – Gateway Temporal Monitor. The L2 monitor maintains three per-device sliding-window deques (spam, pulsing, overflow) and evaluates P2.1–P2.4 incrementally; P2.2 is structurally identical to P2.1 with a safe_tx queue and a higher threshold, while P2.3 / P2.4 fire on the first matching event. Every L2 output is JSON-serialised to L3.

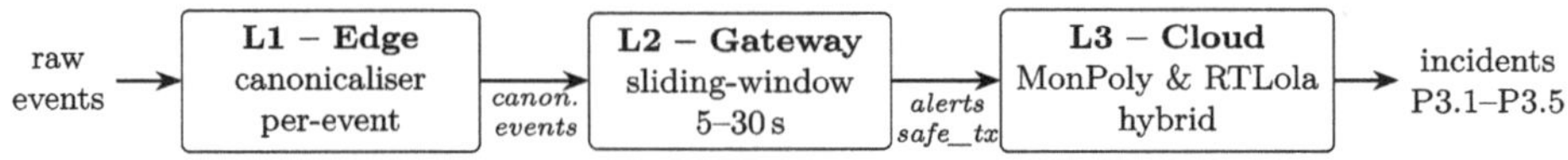

Fig. 1. Three-layer runtime architecture. L1 (edge) classifies each raw event into a canonical event in constant time. L2 (gateway, 5–30 s windows) aggregates canonical events into repeated-overflow or DoS alerts and forwards both alerts and safe-transaction events to L3. L3 (cloud) hosts four persistent MonPoly MFOTL monitors and one RTLola time-triggered monitor that consume the L2 stream incrementally and emit multi-device security incidents (P3.1–P3.5) tagged with severity. All three layers run as cooperating processes inside a *monitor* container hosting L1 and L2 as a Unix pipe, and a separate *correlator* container hosting L3 in the reference implementation; the boundaries map directly to a physical edge / gateway / cloud deployment.

L3 – Hybrid MonPoly & RTLola Correlator. L3 hosts five persistent subprocesses: four MonPoly MFOTL processes (P3.1–P3.4) fed the full L2 alert stream, and one online RTLola process hosting P3.5, fed only the safe_tx and overflow predicates it references. Reader threads parse each subprocess's output, deduplicate by ($prop$, $device$, $\lfloor t/W \rfloor$), and append to an incident log tagged with the producing engine and severity (CRITICAL for P3.1/P3.2/P3.5, HIGH otherwise).

Orchestrator Generalisation. The orchestrator (per-engine event filtering, format translation, subprocess management, verdict aggregation) generalises to additional RV engines: a third engine needs only its predicate subset, input encoding, and output regex.

5 Evaluation

We describe the methodology in sufficient detail to support independent reproduction on the 15-actor Docker testbed packaged in the accompanying artefact. All experiments were run on a single MacBook Pro with an Apple M1 SoC (8-core CPU) and 8 GB unified memory. The stack executed under Docker Desktop 29.4.3, whose Linux VM was allocated 8 CPUs and ~3.8 GB RAM.

5.1 Dataset

All traces are generated on the Docker-based testbed: fifteen device emulators (one per actor, configured via per-device identity and profile environment variables), one *monitor* container hosting the L1→L2 pipeline, and one *correlator* container hosting the L3 MonPoly and RTLola subprocesses. Each node appends JSON-line tool_call events with fields turn (device-reported Unix seconds, spoofable), actor, tool ∈ {safe_send, vulnerable_send, time_spoof_send, fuzz_send}, and args = ⟨attempted_size, actual_sent, buffer_limit=30⟩. The 17 containers share a host-bind-mounted volume for the log files; logs are append-only JSON lines, re-analysable offline. Because `shared_data` is a host bind mount, ingest and inter-tier I/O traverse the Docker Desktop file-sharing layer, which accounts for the occasional millisecond-scale contention spikes in Table 7.

Per-actor configuration. Table 3 summarises the fifteen actors: five clean baselines and ten attackers spanning the eight profiles, with payload distribution, inter-arrival (*iat*), and resulting event rate per node. Every profile additionally inserts a $U(0.5, 1.5)$ s idle gap on 15% of iterations and a $U(1.0, 5.0)$ s startup delay.

Table 3. Device profiles used in the testbed. Buffer limit = 30 B.

Nodes	Profile	Payload & tool	*iat* (s)	evt/min
node-1..5-clean	normal	[10, 30] B, safe_send	$U(0.1, 4.0)$	29
node-6-overflow	overflow	[35, 60] B vulnerable_send	$U(4.0, 10.0)$	9
node-7-timespoof	timespoof	time_spoof_send*	$U(2.0, 6.0)$	15
node-8-spammer	spam	legal payloads	$U(0.005, 0.05)$	2200
node-9-lowslow	low-slow	10% borderline 31–32 B	$U(0.5, 3.0)$	34
node-10-fuzzer	fuzzer	60% malformed content	$U(0.5, 2.0)$	48
node-11-pulsing	pulsing	20-safe bursts every 20–30 s	burst, 50 ms	48
node-12..15-mixed	mixed	weighted send mix†	$U(0.2, 3.5)$	32

* Timestamp offset $\Delta = \pm 300/600$ s.
† Send weights (0.6, 0.2, 0.2) over {safe, ovfl, spoof}.

The *monitor* container runs the L1 canonicaliser (tailing the shared events log) and the L2 monitor (consuming canonical events and writing alerts); a separate *correlator* container tails the alert stream and drives the MonPoly and RTLola subprocesses, writing incidents.

Protocol. An orchestration script brings the stack up, sleeps T_{run}=600 s for the primary run, tears down, and runs metric-collection over the three log files. Reported metrics: alert and incident counts, per-property device-attributable rate, and alert-to-incident latency.

5.2 Aggregate Workload

Table 4 summarises the 600 s primary run. Of the 6872 raw events, 72 (1.0%) are lost at the shared-log→L1 ingest boundary (partial-line reads) *before* canonicalisation; L1 then processes the 6800 it receives and emits 6800 canonical events, one per input, consistent with the totality of μ_1. L2 consumes all 6800 (no L1→L2 loss) and produces 6861 output records, of which 941 are *security alerts* and 5920 are forwarded safe_tx events required by P3.3 and P3.5. L3 emits 137 incidents. A framed message bus with a start-of-stream barrier would close the ingest gap, and we list it as the top engineering follow-up.

Table 4. Aggregate workload over a 600 s 15-actor run. "L2 sec. alerts" excludes forwarded safe_tx.

Tier / metric	Count	L2 break-down	Count
Total raw events (L1)	6872	L2 sec. alerts (total)	941
L2 outputs (to L3)	6861	time_anomaly	371
of which forwarded safe_tx	5920	dos_spam	219
L3 incidents	137	fuzzing	258
Total / attacker devices	15 / 10	overflow	93

5.3 L3 Incident Detection

Table 5 reports per-property L3 incident counts on the same run, together with the unique attacker devices each property identifies. We report raw incident counts rather than normalising by a fixed denominator because each MFOTL property fires once per matching past-window, so a single attacker device can emit several incidents in one run.

Table 5. Per-property L3 incident emission, 600 s 15-actor primary run. *Inc.* is the total incidents fired; *Dev.* is the number of unique attacker devices that triggered the property; *Win.* is the temporal/window bound.

ID	Incident type	Engine	Inc.	Dev.	Win.
P3.1	apt_indicator	MonPoly	41	4	60 s
P3.2	coordinated_attack	MonPoly	19	6	30 s
P3.3	escalation_pattern	MonPoly	41	4	10–60 s
P3.4	persistent_threat	MonPoly	6	6	1 h
P3.5	silent_node_anomaly	RTLola	30	5	5 s*

* Measured from the triggering overflow alert.

P3.1 fires on the four mixed-APT nodes (NODE-12–NODE-15); P3.4 fires once for each of six attackers that accumulate at least five overflow alerts within its 1 h window during the 600 s run. **P3.5 fires 30 times** across five devices, once per overflow that is followed by $\geq$ 5 s of silence; per-incident latency 4.99–5.01 s by RTLola construction. The count is dominated by NODE-6 (20 of 30), whose bursty overflow profile produces many overflow-then-silence episodes; the number of *unique* silent devices is five.

Incident Accounting and P3.2 Witnesses. Table 6 sorts the 137 incidents into: attributable-true, -mixed, -false-positive, and unattributed. In this controlled labelled run, all 137 attributable incidents (P3.1–P3.5) correspond to attacker-labelled devices. Each P3.2 incident has $\geq$ 3 attacker contributors and no clean contributor, checked directly against the incident log. We report *witness completeness ratio* WCR = 137/137 = 100% as a first-class metric.

Table 6. Four-bucket accounting of the 137 L3 incidents on the 600 s primary run. *Attr. true*: attributed to genuine attacker device(s) only; *Attr. mixed*: attacker and clean devices both contribute; *Attr. FP*: attributed to a clean device (false positive); *Unattr.*: no device attribution.

Property	Attr. true	Attr. mixed	Attr. FP	Unattr.	Total
P3.1	41	0	0	0	41
P3.2	19	0	0	0	19
P3.3	41	0	0	0	41
P3.4	6	0	0	0	6
P3.5	30	0	0	0	30
Total	**137**	**0**	**0**	**0**	**137**

End-to-End Witness Example. One P3.3 incident on NODE-12-MIXED traces cleanly back to L1: four safe_sends, a back-jumped time_spoof_send (a time_anomaly/P2.3 alert), and a vulnerable_send over the buffer limit (a buffer_overflow/overflow) together fire escalation_pattern(NODE-12-MIXED); the witness is the six L2 alerts within 60 s and the six raw L1 events behind them.

5.4 Ablation: Contribution of Each Layer

Theorem 1 covers P3.2 (logically inexpressible below L3); P3.1/P3.3/P3.4 are placed at L3 by design. Operationally on the 600 s primary run: the per-event L1 tier classifies events but expresses no temporal pattern; *L1+L2* yields 941 attack alerts (371 time-anomaly, 219 dos-spam, 258 fuzzing, 93 overflow) that name the device but no cross-device pattern; *L1+L2+L3(MonPoly)* adds 107 multi-event/multi-device incidents (P3.1–P3.4) that lie outside the lower tiers;

L1+L2+L3(MonPoly & RTLola) adds a further 30 P3.5 silent-node anomalies that no MonPoly-only configuration can detect within a bounded delay, since an event-triggered engine emits the verdict only when a later-timestamped input arrives.

In the controlled labelled run, all 137 device-attributable incidents correspond to attacker-labelled devices. Removing L3(MonPoly) loses 41 P3.1 + 19 P3.2 + 41 P3.3 + 6 P3.4; removing L3(RTLola) loses the 30 P3.5 detections.

5.5 Computational Cost

Across the 118 incidents carrying a single triggering alert (all but the 19 coordinated P3.2 incidents, which aggregate over a device set), alert-to-incident latency is 1.71 s mean (min 0, max 5.0 s); the 30 P3.5 incidents each carry RTLola's fixed 5 s window by construction and dominate the mean, while every MonPoly incident is resolved within that same 5 s bound.

L1's $\sim$33 μs median reflects JSON parsing, three Boolean checks, and the content well-formedness scan; L2 is an order of magnitude higher (605 μs median)

Table 7. Per-event wall-clock cost at L1 and L2, measured inside the monitor container during the 600 s primary run.

Tier	N events	mean (μs)	p50 (μs)	p95 (μs)	p99 (μs)	max (μs)
L1	6800	56.6	32.8	253.0	329.6	679.1
L2	6800	710.6	604.8	1494.8	1860.2	15066.6

because each event triggers up to three deque updates plus per-alert file writes. The L2 p99 of 1.86 ms leaves ample headroom under a sub-second budget; the 15.1 ms max is a one-off shared-volume contention spike. L1's ~12× gap between mean (56.6 μs) and max (679 μs) is dominated by occasional GIL releases and Python GC pauses; p99 (330 μs) is a tighter steady-state bound. Measurements were taken on the host described in Sect. 5.1; absolute μs figures are hardware-dependent and should be read as orders of magnitude rather than portable constants.

Accumulation Over Time. Figure 2 plots cumulative incidents per property over elapsed time. Rather than saturating, all five properties accumulate steadily as the attackers persist through the run, so absolute counts scale with run length (P3.4, on a 1 h window, grows most slowly); this is the run-length bound discussed next.

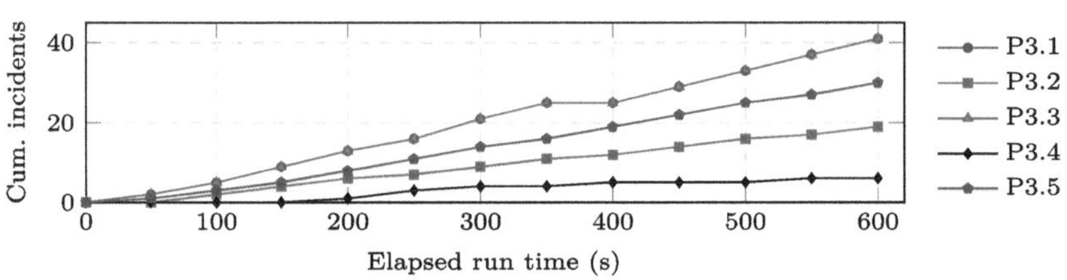

Fig. 2. Cumulative L3 incidents vs. elapsed time (600 s primary run, 50 s sampling); incidents accumulate roughly linearly as attackers persist.

Bounding Factors. Counts are bounded by run length (short T_{run} truncates the 1 h P3.4 window) and by the mixed-APT vector weights $(0.6, 0.2, 0.2)$, which make joint vector pairs rare per 60 s window; both raise P3.1 monotonically without changing the spec.

5.6 Coverage, Evasion, and Threats to Validity

Per-device Coverage (False-Negative Analysis). P3.1 covers all four mixed-APT nodes; no gap is due to mis-specification: every formula is satisfied iff the run is long enough to accumulate the required evidence. Specifically, P3.1 and P3.3 each fire on all four mixed-APT nodes (NODE-12–NODE-15, ~10× each), P3.4 once on each of six attackers, and P3.5 mostly on NODE-6 (20 of 30); P3.2 draws on a contributing set of six (NODE-6, NODE-9, NODE-12–NODE-15), every incident with ≥ 3 contributors and none clean. *Evasion under known thresholds.* An adversary knowing the L1/L2 thresholds has three evasion options, each with a quantifiable cost. *(i) Throttle below a threshold:* to keep below N_{ovf}=3-in-30 s the attacker must drop to ≤ 2 overflow events per 30 s, a $\sim 6\times$ slowdown over an unconstrained attacker (mean inter-arrival $\approx$ 3 s in the `overflow` profile); the analogous argument applies for spam vs. N_{spam}=30. *(ii) Stay within a single L3 window:* single-vector attacks on one device evade P3.1–P3.3 by construction, but the throttling cost of (i) still applies at L1/L2. *(iii) Coordinate across one device only:* P3.2 requires overflow alerts on ≥ 3 distinct devices within 30 s, so a single-device adversary cannot trigger the predicate but also cannot mount the multi-device threat the predicate targets. The framework therefore converts single-device evasion into a constraint on attack *breadth* ($\geq$3 devices) and per-device *slowdown* $\lceil$(nominal-rate)/(threshold-rate)$\rceil$, supporting the cost-asymmetry claim of Sect. 1.

Real-Data Replay (IoT-23). We replay one capture of the IoT-23 dataset [16] (a Zeek log from a Mirai-infected device, ≈23 k connections) as a compatibility/stress test, not a detection-accuracy validation: its per-connection Benign/Malicious labels do not align with our event-level catalogue. A coarse adapter maps each connection to our schema (source IP as device, IP-byte count as payload, Ethernet-MTU as buffer limit; failed half-open connections trip the fuzz predicate; time-spoof disabled for historical timestamps). The L2 alert stream names a single source IP, the capture's ground-truth-malicious device (source-IP precision 1/1); integrating a new dataset is a dataset-specific adapter that emits the Sect. 3.1 event schema, with L1/L2 unmodified.

Threats to Validity. The dataset is synthetic and the eight attack classes are a closed set; physical-hardware deployment is a follow-up (Sect. 7). Single-host containers compress network jitter and clock skew present on a real multi-gateway deployment. *Absence of a Synchronisation Layer.* A Python supervisor over a shared log file dispatches events between tiers; there is no dedicated synchronisation layer. Four limitations follow: (i) the shared-log dataflow is the source of the L1→L2 event-loss gap above; (ii) one-second timestamp resolution means two devices emitting in the same second can reach the log out of true order, which MonPoly's monotone-timestamp assumption tolerates only at low event rates; (iii) the RTLola subprocess runs on the system clock, so P3.5 deadlines fire even with no further input; however, events are timestamped on arrival rather than with their upstream timestamps, so pipeline latency shifts the 5 s window and incident times are reconstructed as overflow-time + 5 s; (iv) writes to the five L3 subprocesses are sequential and unflow-controlled. A proper event-bus design (at-least-once delivery, per-consumer offsets, periodic clock-tick) closes all four. *Threshold calibration, sensitivity, and benign bursts.* The L1/L2 thresholds (N_{ovf}=3, N_{spam}=30, τ_{ts}=15 s, W_{ovf}=30 s, W_{spam}=5 s) are tuned to the testbed and not claimed to generalise. A quantitative sweep over N_{ovf}, N_{spam}, τ_{ts}, and W_{L2}, reporting detection, FP, and latency at each operating point, is queued as follow-up; Theorem 1 itself is parameter-independent, but precision/recall numbers are not. Real workloads also exhibit *benign* bursts (firmware updates, post-reconnect catch-up) whose statistics can resemble attack patterns: our `pulsing` profile is benign-shaped yet trips P2.2 at current thresholds, so deployment-time calibration of $N_{spam}, N_{pulse}, W_{spam}$ against the actual workload is a prerequisite.

6 Related Work

Hierarchical CPS-RV and Runtime Assurance. STREL [5] and SaSTL [20] formalise hierarchical spatio-temporal monitoring; we reuse the decomposition but replace propositional spatial operators with parametric MFOTL for cross-node correlation. SOTER [12] and safe-RL shielding [3] pair monitors with controller fallback. Temperekidis et al. [27] embed RV in FMI-based co-simulation, a design-time analogue to our deployment-time edge tier.

Comparison of RV Engines for L3. The cloud tier needs two capabilities at once: cross-device first-order quantification (to even write properties like "three different devices overflow within 30 s") and the ability to flag a silent attacker when no event has arrived. MonPoly [6] and the Isabelle-verified VeriMon [26] cover the first natively but are event-triggered, detecting absence only when a later event arrives, without a delay bound; RTLola [15] is time-triggered and handles the silent-node case but expresses parametric joins less ergonomically. TeSSLa [11,17]'s static parametrization scales poorly to runtime-varying fleet sizes, and Copilot [21] targets single-device embedded instrumentation. Pairing MonPoly with RTLola is the minimal combination covering both capabilities with mature, online-capable engines.

Runtime Verification in Digital Twins. A complementary line integrates RV with digital-twin (DT) executions: Temperekidis et al. [28] sketch a DT architecture with formal analysis for learning-enabled autonomous systems [7,13], instantiated for traffic-sign recognition [2] and depth-of-anesthesia control [1]. These share the per-tier formal-spec design at *design* time over a DT trace; our framework moves the same discipline to *deployment* time over a fleet of edge devices.

IoT Security Monitoring and Layered Architectures. Cavalli et al. [9] survey three-, four-, and five-layer IoT monitoring reference models, arguing no single-layer monitor suffices. We differ on three axes: (i) we give each tier a formal specification in a chosen logic (boolean / past-MTL / MFOTL), making Theorem 1 provable from the logical fragment of each tier; (ii) we instantiate each attack class on a 15-actor Docker testbed; (iii) our composition tags every L3 incident with the contributing L1/L2 sub-trace, giving the audit record required by NIST SP 800-160 Vol. 2 and DORA.

IDS, Resiliency Frameworks, and Audit Alignment. Signature- and ML-classifier IDS [25] and uncertainty-aware classifier monitoring [19] are complementary to L1: a learned classifier could populate the canonical-event stream without changing L2 or L3, though deploying such CNN detectors on edge hardware carries its own performance trade-offs [10]. Cyber-resiliency catalogues such as NIST SP 800-160 Vol. 2 [23] and NIST Zero-Trust [22] enumerate techniques but stop short of numerical cost models; our framework instantiates one such technique with measured costs.

7 Discussion

Limitations. The 15-actor dataset is synthetic and the eight attack classes are a closed set; real-world traffic mixes are heavier-tailed and would require additional L1 predicates or threshold tuning. Drift on the underlying packet distribution may degrade the L1 thresholds over time and is not yet modelled. Sub-second event timestamps would remove a class of near-coincident-event false positives observed on coarse-grained testbed logs.

Partial Compromise of L1. If an attacker bypasses the L1 canonicaliser on device d and emits raw events directly to the gateway log, L2's sliding counts (P2.1, P2.2) and L3's properties (P3.1–P3.3) still apply, since both consume the *observed* stream, not the L1 verdict. The residual risk is silent-bypass (dropping events entirely); an L2 heartbeat predicate ("d emitted ≥ 1 event in the past 30 s") is a planned mitigation.

Artefact and Reproducibility. The artefact bundles the three monitor programs, the four MonPoly specs and the RTLola P3.5 spec, the device emulator, and the 15-actor Docker Compose topology. A single shell command rebuilds the image, runs the stack, and emits JSON metrics and analysis files.

Future Directions. (i) Hardware deployment on Raspberry-Pi-class devices to replicate L1 timing off the container host. (ii) Live-deployment, closed-loop evaluation measuring throughput and operator workload under gateway-side APT alerts. (iii) Multi-gateway aggregation for fleets larger than one gateway's capacity. (iv) Replacing the shared-log supervisor with an acknowledged event bus (at-least-once delivery, ordering barrier, periodic clock ticks), closing the synchronisation limitations of Sect. 5. (v) Automated property-catalogue synthesis from natural-language procedural manuals (cf. [4]).

8 Conclusion

We have presented a three-layer hierarchical security-monitoring framework for edge-IoT, with a hybrid cloud tier that pairs MonPoly with RTLola. The pairing is what allows the framework to close two gaps that show up together in practice and that no single RV engine handles cleanly: cross-device quantification, which becomes logically necessary once the gateway is restricted to single-device state, and absence-of-event detection, which becomes necessary as soon as an attacker can compromise an edge monitor and go quiet. On the controlled labelled 15-actor Docker testbed, every cloud incident the framework attributes to a device names an attacker-labelled device, the RTLola tier catches silent-bypass attempts that the MFOTL tier cannot detect within a bounded delay, and per-tier monitoring cost stays well below typical real-time budgets.

Acknowledgements. This work has received funding from the European Union's Digital Europe Programme under grant agreement No 101190251 (CYBERGUARD).

Disclosure of Interests. The authors have no competing interests to declare that are relevant to the content of this article.

References

1. AbdElSalam, M., et al.: Digital twin for the formal analysis of a depth-of-anesthesia controller. SIMULATION **101**(3), 341–360 (2025). https://doi.org/10.1177/00375497241311617
2. AbdElSalam, M., et al.: A digital twin prototype for traffic sign recognition of a learning-enabled autonomous vehicle. In: Companion Proceedings of the PoEM 2023. CEUR Workshop Proceedings, vol. 3645. CEUR-WS.org (2024). https://doi.org/10.48550/arXiv.2402.09097
3. Alshiekh, M., Bloem, R., Ehlers, R., Könighofer, B., Niekum, S., Topcu, U.: Safe reinforcement learning via shielding. In: AAAI Conference on Artificial Intelligence (2018). https://doi.org/10.1609/aaai.v32i1.11797
4. Anand, A., Chatzi, I., Raha, R., Schmuck, A.K.: MANTRA: synthesizing SMT-validated compliance benchmarks for tool-using LLM agents. arXiv preprint arXiv:2605.06334 (2026)
5. Bartocci, E., Bortolussi, L., Loreti, M., Nenzi, L.: Monitoring mobile and spatially distributed cyber-physical systems. In: ACM-IEEE International Conference on Formal Methods and Models for System Design (MEMOCODE) (2017). https://doi.org/10.1145/3127041.3127050
6. Basin, D., Klaedtke, F., Müller, S., Zălinescu, E.: MonPoly: monitoring usage-control policies. In: Runtime Verification (RV 2011). LNCS, vol. 7186, Springer (2012). https://doi.org/10.1007/978-3-642-29860-8_27
7. Bensalem, S., Katsaros, P., Ničković, D., Liao, B.H.C., Ruiz Nolasco, R., et al.: Continuous engineering for trustworthy learning-enabled autonomous systems. In: Bridging the Gap Between AI and Reality (AISoLA 2023). LNCS, vol. 14380, pp. 256–278. Springer, Cham (2024). https://doi.org/10.1007/978-3-031-46002-9_15
8. Bonakdarpour, B., Navabpour, S., Fischmeister, S.: Time-triggered runtime verification. Formal Methods Syst. Design **43**(1), 29–60 (2013). https://doi.org/10.1007/s10703-012-0182-0
9. Cavalli, A.R., Mallouli, W., Montes de Oca, E., Rivera, D.: IoT security monitoring tools and models. In: Ziegler, S., Radócz, R., Quesada Rodriguez, A., Matheu Garcia, S.N. (eds.) Springer Handbook of Internet of Things, pp. 289–315. Springer Handbooks, Springer Nature Switzerland, Cham (2024). https://doi.org/10.1007/978-3-031-39650-2_13
10. Chintri, M., Seitoglou, I., Efthymiou, V., Kekatos, N., Petridou, S.G., Basagiannis, S.: Edge-oriented evaluation of CNN-based vehicle detection on embedded V2X platforms. In: Conference on Innovation in Clouds, Internet and Networks (ICIN), pp. 1–5. IEEE, Athens, Greece (2026). https://doi.org/10.1109/ICIN69025.2026.11481844
11. Convent, L., Hungar, S., Leucker, M., Scheffel, T., Schmitz, M., Thoma, D.: TeSSLa: Temporal stream-based specification language. In: Brazilian Symposium on Formal Methods (SBMF) (2018). https://doi.org/10.1007/978-3-030-03044-5_10

12. Desai, A., Ghosh, S., Seshia, S.A., Shankar, N., Tiwari, A.: SOTER: a runtime assurance framework for programming safe robotics systems. In: IEEE/IFIP Internatinal Conference on Dependable Systems and Networks (DSN) (2019). https://doi.org/10.1109/DSN.2019.00027
13. Eleftheriadis, C., Kekatos, N., Katsaros, P., Tripakis, S.: On neural network equivalence checking using SMT solvers. In: Formal Modeling and Analysis of Timed Systems (FORMATS) (2022). https://doi.org/10.1007/978-3-031-15839-1_14
14. Falcone, Y., Krstić, S., Reger, G., Traytel, D.: A taxonomy for classifying runtime verification tools. Int. J. Software Tools Technol. Transfer (STTT) **23**(2), 255–284 (2021). https://doi.org/10.1007/s10009-021-00609-z
15. Faymonville, P., et al.: StreamLAB: stream-based monitoring of cyber-physical systems. In: Computer Aided Verification (CAV) (2019). https://doi.org/10.1007/978-3-030-25540-4_24
16. Garcia, S., Parmisano, A., Erquiaga, M.J.: IoT-23: a labeled dataset of malicious and benign IoT network traffic (version 1.0.0). https://www.stratosphereips.org/datasets-iot23 (2020), capture `CTU-IoT-Malware-Capture-34-1`
17. Kallwies, H., Leucker, M., Schmitz, M., Schulz, M., Thoma, D., Weiss, A.: TeSSLa: an ecosystem for runtime verification. In: Dang, T., Stolz, V. (eds) Runtime Verification (RV 2022). LNCS, vol. 13498, Springer, Cham (2022). https://doi.org/10.1007/978-3-031-17196-3_20
18. Leucker, M., Schallhart, C.: A brief account of runtime verification. J. Logic Algebraic Program. **78**(5), 293–303 (2009). https://doi.org/10.1016/j.jlap.2008.08.004
19. Lukina, A., Schilling, C., Henzinger, T.A.: Into the unknown: active monitoring of neural networks. In: Runtime Verification (RV) (2021). https://doi.org/10.1007/978-3-030-88494-9_3
20. Ma, M., Bartocci, E., Lifland, E., Stankovic, J.A., Feng, L.: SaSTL: spatial aggregation signal temporal logic for runtime monitoring in smart cities. In: ACM/IEEE International Conference on Cyber-Physical Systems (ICCPS) (2020). https://doi.org/10.1109/ICCPS48487.2020.00013
21. Pike, L., Goodloe, A., Morisset, R., Niller, S.: Copilot: a hard real-time runtime monitor. In: Barringer, H., et al. Runtime Verification (RV 2010). LNCS, vol. 6418, Springer, Berlin, Heidelberg (2010). https://doi.org/10.1007/978-3-642-16612-9_26
22. Rose, S., Borchert, O., Mitchell, S., Connelly, S.: Zero trust architecture. In: National Institute of Standards and Technology (NIST) Special Publication, pp. 800–207 (2020). https://doi.org/10.6028/NIST.SP.800-207
23. Ross, R., Pillitteri, V., Graubart, R., Bodeau, D., McQuaid, R.: Developing cyber-resilient systems: a systems security engineering approach. In: NIST Special Publication 800-160, vol. 2 Rev. 1, National Institute of Standards and Technology (2021). https://doi.org/10.6028/NIST.SP.800-160v2r1
24. E-ISAC: Analysis of the cyber attack on the Ukrainian power grid: defense use case. In: SANS Industrial Control Systems and Electricity Information Sharing and Analysis Center (2016). Tech. rep SANS ICS / E-ISAC
25. Kumar, S., Selvi, S.V.N., Kannan, M., A.: A comprehensive survey on machine learning-based intrusion detection systems for secure communication in the internet of things. Comput. Intell. Neurosci. **2023**, 8981988 (2023). https://doi.org/10.1155/2023/8981988
26. Schneider, J., Basin, D., Krstić, S., Traytel, D.: VeriMon: Verifying MFOTL monitors. In: Computer Aided Verification (CAV). LNCS, Springer (2021)

27. Temperekidis, A., Kekatos, N., Katsaros, P.: Runtime verification for FMI-based co-simulation. In: Dang, T., Stolz, V. (eds.) RV 2022. LNCS, vol. 13498, pp. 304–313. Springer, Cham (2022). https://doi.org/10.1007/978-3-031-17196-3_19
28. Temperekidis, A., Kekatos, N., Katsaros, P.: Towards a digital twin architecture with formal analysis capabilities for learning-enabled autonomous systems. In: Mazal, J., et al. MESAS 2022. LNCS, vol. 13866, pp. 163–181. Springer, Cham (2023). https://doi.org/10.1007/978-3-031-31268-7_10

Proceedings of the Ninth International Workshop on Emerging Network Security (ENS 2026)

Disrupting LoRaWAN IoT Deployments: Analysis of Join DoS Attacks in Practical Scenarios

Taregh Khanjari[1], Amirhossein Noshadi[1,2], Matteo Repetto[3], Luca Caviglione[3], and Enrico Cambiaso[1(✉)]

[1] Computer and Telecommunication Engineering Consiglio Nazionale delle Ricerche (CNR-IEIIT), Institute of Electronics, Genova, Italy
{tareghkhanjari,amirhosseinnoshadi,enrico.cambiaso}@cnr.it, amirhossein.noshadi@edu.unige.it

[2] Department of Naval, Electrical, Electronic, and Telecommunications Engineering, Università degli Studi di Genova, Genova, Italy

[3] Consiglio Nazionale delle Ricerche (CNR-IMATI), Institute for Applied Mathematics and Information Technologies, Genova, Italy
{matteo.repetto,luca.caviglione}@ge.imati.cnr.it

Abstract. The massive deployment of resource-constrained IoT ecosystems has been made possible owing to efficient transmission technologies. To this aim, the LoRaWAN standard is gaining momentum, especially since it supports long-range transmission capabilities with a reduced energy consumption. Despite its security model is becoming well understood, issues of the process used by nodes to join the network have been only partially assessed, especially in real-world scenarios. Therefore, this paper investigates practical aspects of the *Join DoS attack*, i.e., a novel threat that can prevent nodes to join a LoRaWAN network. To assess its impact, we conducted tests in both simulated and real network conditions. Results demonstrated the effectiveness of the attack and allowed us to elaborate some prime mitigation techniques, especially in the view of supporting the deployment of LoRaWAN in softwarized environments.

Keywords: LoRaWAN · Cybersecurity · Join procedure · Denial of Service · Internet of Things

1 Introduction

Modern Internet of Things (IoT) deployments are characterized by increasing complexity and heterogeneity, for instance to cover large urban areas or to capture a wide-array of data and environmental information. To support scalability and mitigate costs, the majority of sensors are resource-constrained or progressively endowed with softwarized components. This paradigm offers several benefits, such as the ability of partitioning IoT devices or enforcing fine-grained access rules. Nodes handling sensitive information can be isolated from the rest of the network and the overall attack surface can be better outlined or controlled [2].

P. Kieseberg et al. (Eds.): ARES 2026 Workshops, LNCS 16903, pp. 243–256, 2027.
https://doi.org/10.1007/978-3-032-37218-5_15

In general, the most demanding IoT scenarios require simple but effective communication protocols to avoid the quick depletion of energy or complex maintenance operations [5]. To meet such constraints, the LoRaWAN protocol has emerged as a key technological driver for the creation of massive IoT applications. First, it provides very-long transmission range capabilities with a small power footprint [17]. Second, it can support ubiquitous AI-intensive frameworks, such as those based on federated paradigms [31]. Unfortunately, guaranteeing a suitable degree of security is not trivial, especially since softwarization of large-scale IoT ecosystems requires to orchestrate a multitude of functionalities, ranging from access control to data privacy [23]. At the same time, the LoRaWAN protocol is characterized by many security and privacy vulnerabilities, which can disrupt the service, account for tampered IoT nodes, or allow to gather confidential information [27]. Therefore, increasing the security of LoRaWAN is vital to pursue the vision of mobile and cost-effective nodes supporting sophisticated applications (e.g., urban digital twins [25]) and softwarized data collection endpoints, edge services, and IoT brokers. However, mitigation is not always possible and requires to address issues at every stages of the life-cycle of an IoT node endowed with LoRaWAN interfaces [15]. Among the possible attacks that can be launched, malicious operations performed by nodes when joining the network could be extremely effective [15,23]. In fact, preventing a node to join the network may disrupt the service or allow a threat actor to substitute endpoints for pivoting operations. The diffusion of LoRaWAN in IT/OT scenarios requires also to consider emerging offensive templates, which can exploit covert communications or generative AI [20].

This paper advances the security of LoRaWAN deployments by investigating the impact of DoS attacks against the join process of end nodes, especially the one that has been named as *Join DoS attack* in the rest of this work. Specifically, it considers malicious join requests that can prevent nodes from communicating over a LoRaWAN network. Even if this attack template has been already sketched in the literature, its feasibility and impact have never been assessed in real scenarios. For instance, [27] introduces a potential threat targeting the LoRaWAN join procedure, but it does not cover its practical evaluation. Considering the increasing deployment of LoRaWAN sensors in real scenarios, such as smart cities or industrial control systems, our work opens to a novel landscape of threats for disrupting communications with reduced effort. Therefore, the contribution of this work is twofold: it demonstrates a major weakness of the LoRaWAN protocol architecture via a proof-of-concept implementation, and it elaborates on possible countermeasures.

The rest of the paper is structured as follows. Section 2 reviews past works addressing security issues of LoRaWAN, whereas Sect. 3 provides basic information on main protocol operations. Section 4 introduces the considered threat model and its implementation, Sect. 5 showcases numerical results, and Sect. 6 discusses possible mitigation strategies. Finally, Sect. 7 concludes the paper and outlines future research directions.

2 Related Work

Owing to its rapid diffusion to support a vast array of IoT applications, advancing the security posture of LoRaWAN deployments is a prime research goal [27]. In this perspective, a very recent survey work on LoRaWAN security highlighted the need of focusing on advanced countermeasures, possibly without causing major overheads in terms of energy consumptions. At the same time, the increasing complexity of attacks requires to consider "preventive" mechanisms for anticipating threats [30]. Being able to model new attacks is then of paramount importance, especially to prepare suitable indicators or datasets to train emerging AI-based countermeasures.

For the specific case of LoRaWAN security, the standard offers several entry points to an attacker and their mitigation has already been proposed, possibly through the early detection of malicious nodes [17]. Despite the efforts, a major concern is still rooted in the join process of the LoRaWAN protocol, which can be exploited to implement many offensive templates [15]. In more detail, join request messages exchanged during the Over-The-Air Activation (OTAA) phase are not encrypted, resulting in an attack surface difficult to control [26]. For instance, [27] highlights vulnerabilities of both OTAA and Activation By Personalization (ABP) methods caused by the use of static keys. This attack template is particularly subtle as it can be also exploited in wide area networks relying upon satellite connectivity [9]. A malicious actor can also capture unencrypted join request messages and exploit them for overwhelming the network through a replay attack, see, e.g., [26]. Possible workarounds rely upon the adoption of XOR masking mechanisms combined with a session key to ensure unique join requests and prevent duplicates [26] or the use of the received signal strength indicator to early detect possible replay attacks [29].

The LoRaWAN protocol also exhibits several vulnerabilities at the physical layer, which can be exploited to implement various side-channel threats. As an example, [3] discusses malicious jamming mechanisms, where attackers deliberately disrupt legitimate communications with a minimal footprint in terms of additional noise. Instead, [34] demonstrates a practical side-channel attack based on the collection of electromagnetic firms of devices/nodes that are further processed via deep learning algorithms to recover AES-128 encryption keys. A similar attack scenario is evaluated in [13]: in this case, the work emphasizes the importance of pursuing a secure hardware design to mitigate risks arising by the "imperfect isolation" of the LoRaWAN link. Techniques to secure LoRaWAN-capable IoT nodes are discussed in detail in [24], especially to not endanger advanced manufactoring deployments. Additional vulnerabilities are caused by the random number generation process (DevNonce). As an example, predictable or reused DevNonces can be collected to perform a DoS campaign against IoT nodes or supporting servers [27].

More recently, the security of LoRaWAN protocol has been also investigated in terms of susceptibility to offensive schemes leveraging covert communication mechanisms. To this aim, the chirp spread spectrum technique used to modulate the LoRa symbols can be forced to encode arbitrary data, allowing an external node to infer information [21]. A more advanced hiding scheme is proposed in [16] and it exploits the amplitude of LoRa chirps without altering the transmission frequency. Moreover, [18] showcases a mechanism to adjust transmission power to improve the robustness of the covert communication while not impacting its undetectability.

Similarly to other previous research works, we also target the join process of the LoRaWAN protocol, see, e.g., references [15,17,27]. However, we focus on the definition of the attack template for invalidating the join procedure of a legitimate node, rather than possible threat-dependent or protocol-specific countermeasures, which may address a similar case but on a by product manner [9]. Compared to other offensive templates devoted to impair a LoRaWAN network, we propose to generate valid join requests and disrupt the process at an exact timing point. Thus, the *Join DoS attack* differs from other similar research works, especially [26], which focuses on replay attacks using previously captured join requests. Additionally, while [8] examines randomness interference via jamming approaches, our scenario represents a more targeted attack based on crafting valid join requests to disrupt uplink communication requiring a less invasive approach.

3 Background

As discussed, the LoRaWAN protocol standard has been engineered for building a power-efficient communication channel over long distances. To this aim, it defines how the end nodes exchange information with a Network Server. In between, gateways are responsible for "bridging" the LoRa wireless link to common Internet protocols. The gateway is totally transparent to end nodes and it encapsulates wireless frames directly into raw UDP datagrams or other high-level message buses, such as MQTT. The LoRaWAN specification covers all the phases needed by end nodes and the network to operate, e.g., disconnections, negotiations of parameters, and data transmission. However, for the sake of brevity, this work only focuses on the portion devoted to define and rule the join process. Reference [4] provides a detailed discussion including a vis-à-vis comparison with other similar transmission mechanisms.

In essence, end nodes can join a LoRaWAN network by using both OTAA or ABP mechanisms. While the OTAA implements a join procedure where devices dynamically generate session keys to secure communication, ABP relies on pre-configured static security keys, permanently stored in the device. Because of this, ABP does not require a join procedure to complete [27]. As a consequence, the *Join DoS attack* affects only OTAA-based environments. Figure 1 depicts the complete join procedure required to enter a LoRaWAN network. For the sake of readability, encryption and decryption operations have not been reported, but only specified throughout the text. To join the network, a device must know in advance the value of the application key, which is shared with the Network Server. The node then initiates the process by sending a *join request* message, composed of the device identifier `dev_id`, the application unique identifier `app_eui`, a random nonce `dev_nonce` (which has to be unique for each session, to prevent discarding of packets [29]), and a `mic_request` used for integrity check and computed through the shared application key [11]. With such information, a device can authenticate on the network and join a specific application on the server. As a response, the Network Server generates the network session key (`NwkSKey`) and the application session key (`AppSKey`), which are valid only for the current session.

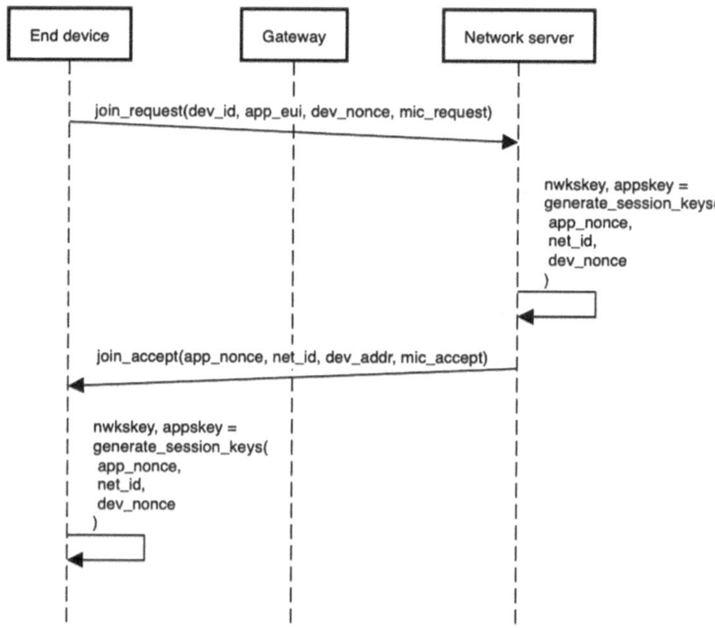

Fig. 1. Temporal evolution of the operations used by the LoRaWAN standard protocol to implement the join process.

The Network Server then responds with a *join accept* message, which is encrypted with the application key. The message also includes information such as a temporary application nonce `app_nonce`, the network identifier (`net_id`), and the physical address of the device (`dev_addr`). Similar to the previous case, also the *join accept* leverages a MIC (`mic_accept`) for integrity check, which is computed by using the shared application key. Upon receiving this message, the end device is able to compute the `NwkSKey` and the `AppSKey` required to securely communicate on the network.

As a last remark, we point out that when the join is done via the OTAA mechanism, the various session keys are never directly exchanged between the end device and the Network Server.

4 Threat Model

As hinted, we consider an attacker targeting an end device to disrupt its communications with the LoRaWAN Network Server. In more detail, we assume that the attacker is able to generate LoRaWAN traffic within the network and directly communicate at least with one gateway node, by exploiting the `dev_id` and `app_eui` values used by the victim. Since join request frames are not encrypted, an attacker could easily retrieve the `dev_id` by passively monitoring the radio channel. However, this is not sufficient, since the `app_eui` remains protected through encryption. In this case, the attacker could follow two possible paths: *i*) to break the encryption, which should be considered unfeasible, or *ii*) to have some proximity with the target during the reconnaissance phase, since off-the-shelf hardware may directly report `app_eui` data. We also point out that our threat model does not require that the attacker and the end device are served by the same gateway. Therefore, the *Join DoS attack* can also be launched remotely, i.e., by a device not in the proximity of the victim. The aim of the attacker is to invalidate the session keys of the victim, preventing the normal data exchange by triggering a new join procedure. To this aim, the attacker sends a "fraudulent" join request impersonating the end device of the victim. This prevents the Network Server to decode its uplink data, while traffic from other nodes is still correctly received.

Figure 2 depicts the temporal evolution of the *Join DoS attack* against an end device part of a LoRaWAN network. For the sake of readability, the gateway node has been omitted. As shown, a malicious join request (depicted in red) is sent with the proper `dev_id` and `app_eui` values to impersonate the end device of the victim. This triggers a reset of the session keys used by the Network Server. As a result, the previously-generated keys are rendered invalid and further uplink messages of the targeted end device would be discarded by the Network Server.

However, the targeted device may initiate a new join procedure to re-connect to the LoRaWAN network. To avoid such possibility, the malicious node should remain in an "offensive" state in a permanent manner, i.e., he/she must send additional crafted join requests to prevent that the connectivity of the victim is restored. To be effective, bogus requests have to be sent during the time that occurs between a legitimate join request and the next (valid) uplink message. Alas, estimating the proper time to send a malicious join request is not trivial: while specific use cases may require sending data at constant intervals [12], other scenarios may need to generate messages at an unpredictable way (e.g., when an IoT sensor asynchronously communicates the outcome of an actuator).

If a malicious node acts in proximity of the end device and monitors the radio channel, it can capture join request messages. In this case, the malicious join request can be sent immediately. Otherwise, if the attacker acts remotely from the victim, there is the need of estimating the average update time [19] or resorting to a flood-like approach. While the use of flooding may be successful, it could result less effective, since the resulting network activity can be easily detected [15] or impact over the duty cycle of end nodes [1].

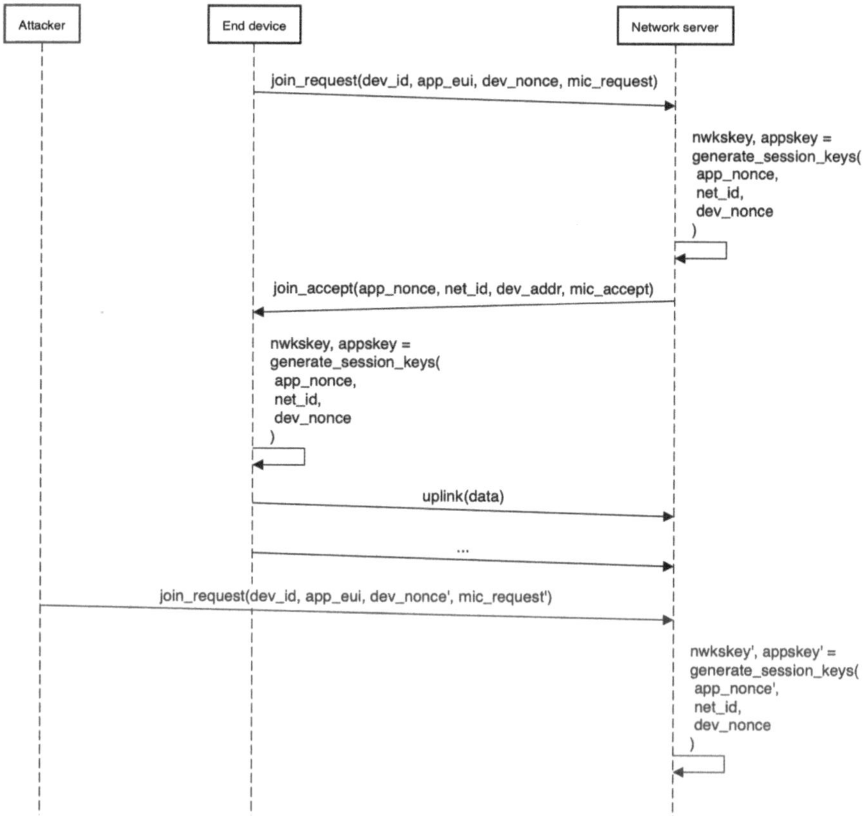

Fig. 2. Initiating the Join DoS attack against a registered end device.

5 Numerical Results

To demonstrate the effectiveness of the *Join DoS attack*, we performed a set of tests to quantify the optimal transmission rates at which malicious join request messages should be generated to make the attack successful. Such values depend on the configuration of the legitimate/targeted node(s).

In our implementation, at the beginning of the attack, the node needs to join the Network Server. To hinder the transmission of legitimate data, the attacker should send the malicious join request between each legitimate join request and the first uplink message. Such attack window is denoted in the following as T_j. In our tests, we analyzed how the effectiveness of the attack varies in function of the time between one malicious join request and the next one, denoted as T_a. We also consider a node periodically sending data without joining the Network Server multiple times. In this case, the node sends subsequent uplink messages every T_i seconds. We point out that, for correctly capturing how the attacker should behave, we introduced the two timing variables T_i and T_j. However, for the sake of simplicity, in the following we considered a threat actor launching the *Join DoS attack* under the $T_i = T_j$ condition. Investigating more complex behaviors is part of our ongoing research. The effectiveness of the *Join DoS attack* has been measured by considering two performance indicators. The T_n considers the time between the initial join request and the first successful uplink message. The P_n considers the percentage of successful uplink messages over the total attempts. For our tests, we have considered $T_i \in [5, 10, 15]$, while T_a values range from 5 to 35. Since each test has been replicated 12 times, the attack performance has been reported in terms of mean and standard deviation values.

To assess the *Join DoS attack*, we considered a simulated wireless link and a real deployment. In both scenarios, we used the real Network Server from ChirpStack [14]. For the *simulated* environment, we implemented a malicious node in Python that directly sends LoRaWAN packets to the Network Server. To emulate all the radio entities, i.e., the node and the gateway, we used the LWN-simulator [28]. For the *real* environment, we used the Arduino Uno R3 hardware to implement both the legitimate and malicious end devices. All the nodes have been placed ∼10 meters away from the gateway to model an urban deployment scenario, e.g., a traffic light feeding a digital twin. To implement the gateway, we used the RAK7248C embedding a Raspberry Pi and running ChirpStack. All the nodes operates over the EU868 frequency band. Each legitimate uplink payload consisted of a 8-byte long fixed-size data frame, representative of IoT telemetry data.

Section 5.1 reports results collected in the simulated environment, whereas Sect. 5.2 focuses on the real testbed.

5.1 Simulated Scenario

In our simulated scenario, we perpetrated a set of *Join DoS attacks* by sending malicious join request messages every $0 < T_a \leq 35$ seconds.

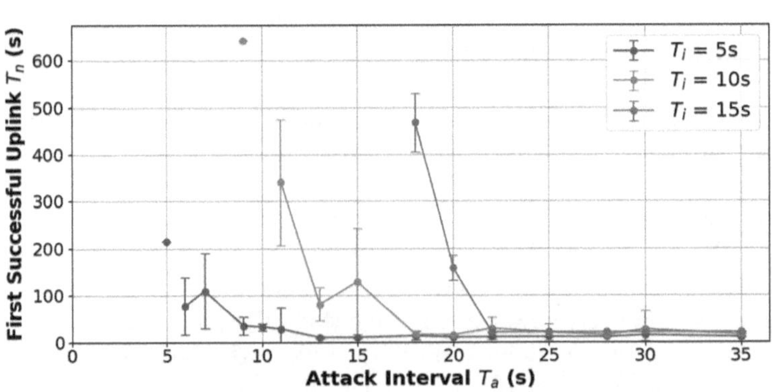

Fig. 3. Impact on the uplink messages reception monitored on the Network Server (T_n) for different values of T_a and T_i for the simulated test.

Table 1. Time of first successful uplink (T_n) and percentage of successful uplinks (P_n) for different attacker intervals T_a and simulator intervals T_i. Values in bold are relative to unexpected unsuccessful attacks.

T_a	(T_n) For $T_i = 5$			(T_n) For $T_i = 10$			(T_n) For $T_i = 15$			(P_n) For $T_i = 5$		(P_n) For $T_i = 10$		(P_n) For $T_i = 15$	
	#	Mean	Std. Dev.	#	Mean	Std. Dev.	#	Mean	Std. Dev.	Mean	Std. Dev.	Mean	Std. Dev.	Mean	Std. Dev.
5	1	**214.0000**	–	0	–	–	0	–	–	0.0339	–	0.0000	–	0.0000	–
6	11	76.5455	61.4091	0	–	–	0	–	–	0.2394	0.2272	0.0000	–	0.0000	–
7	12	109.3333	80.0322	0	–	–	0	–	–	0.1574	0.1007	0.0000	–	0.0000	–
9	12	34.5833	18.8412	1	**642.0000**	–	0	–	–	0.4311	0.3178	0.7500	–	0.0000	–
10	12	32.2500	7.4970	0	–	–	0	–	–	0.3991	0.0387	0.0000	–	0.0000	–
11	12	27.5833	45.5142	9	340.5556	134.0691	0	–	–	0.3364	0.0816	0.1233	0.1955	0.0000	–
13	12	9.6667	1.4975	11	80.5455	35.5875	0	–	–	0.4293	0.0443	0.2488	0.0617	0.0000	–
15	12	9.5833	1.5050	5	128.6000	113.6499	0	–	–	0.5039	0.0678	0.1653	0.1607	0.0000	–
18	12	12.7500	8.9150	12	15.3333	0.6513	4	467.2500	62.0074	0.6677	0.0191	0.4114	0.0850	0.0632	0.0183
20	12	9.9167	0.2887	12	14.8333	1.6422	12	157.8333	26.0588	0.6772	0.0650	0.6032	0.1274	0.4180	0.0382
22	12	10.0833	0.2887	12	28.0833	24.2016	12	20.0833	0.2887	0.4724	0.0718	0.5264	0.1086	0.1968	0.0595
25	12	10.0833	0.2887	12	19.8333	17.4868	12	20.0000	0.0000	0.4486	0.0784	0.5635	0.1406	0.2995	0.0961
28	12	10.0000	0.0000	12	14.1667	2.2088	12	20.0000	0.0000	0.5539	0.0759	0.4017	0.0646	0.4595	0.1168
30	12	13.7500	13.3084	12	25.8333	40.4111	12	20.0833	0.2887	0.5527	0.0627	0.1916	0.2650	0.5042	0.0159
35	12	9.9167	0.2887	12	15.0833	0.2887	12	19.9167	0.2887	0.6650	0.0368	0.3281	0.0196	0.3549	0.0035

Figure 3 and Table 1 showcase the collected results. As it can be noticed, the attack always succeeds whenever $T_a \leq T_j$, except in case of $T_a = 5$, $T_i = 5$ and $T_a = 9$, $T_i = 10$. Such results have been reported in bold in Table 1. This behavior was unexpected, since the rate at which malicious frames are sent is higher than the rate of legitimate ones, i.e., $T_a \leq T_j$. However, we found that a single test was leading to a successful uplink, although obtained T_n samples assume relatively high values. Such evolution is also visible in Fig. 3, depicted as blue and orange dots. Based on the test results, for $T_a > T_j$, the Network Server almost always receives the (legitimate) uplink. Such a result is expected, as the probability to send legitimate data increases with the increase of T_a. On the same concept, it is expected that T_n decreases with the increase of T_a, where we measured a stabilization for $T_a > 22$ values. Conversely, as shown in Table 1, for $T_a \leq T_j$ legitimate uplink messages are never received, thus making the DoS successful.

Therefore, we can observe that an attacker generating malicious frames by using a T_a value lower or equal to T_i always leads to a successful DoS. The only notable exception is for very specific cases in the order of $\frac{1}{12 \cdot T_i}$, where the legitimate node experiences a significant delay in sending uplink data.

5.2 Real Scenario

To validate the effectiveness of the *Join DoS attack*, we also conduct tests on real nodes communicating over LoRa. This aspect is of paramount importance, as simulated environments may not efficiently capture corner cases or implementation-specific issues, which can be exploited by threat actor acting in-the-wild. Furthermore, using real hardware allowed to evaluate whether low-cost and resource-constrained devices can successful launch the attack. To reflect such constraints, we performed tests considering a threat actor launching the *Join DoS attack* every $0 < T_a \leq 25$ seconds.

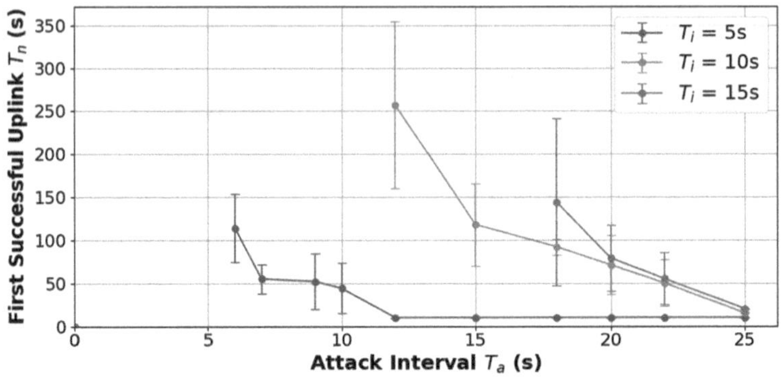

Fig. 4. Impact on the uplink messages reception monitored on the Network Server (T_n) for different values of T_a and T_i for the real experimental test.

Figure 4 depicts the collected results. In more detail, we can observe that when $T_a \leq T_i$, no successful uplinks occur, hence making the attack successful. Therefore, during our tests, we measured that, for $T_a \leq T_i$, the real scenario always leads a DoS on the targeted node, without exceptions. Differently, for higher values of T_a, T_n tends to assume a high value, then decreasing and eventually stabilizing, similarly to what found on the simulated scenario.

Based on the real tests, we can state that choosing a T_a value lower or equal to T_i always leads to a successful DoS. Among these values, choosing $T_a = T_i$ could be the preferred choice for the attacker. Indeed, in such a case, the frequency of frames sent by the malicious node would be very similar to the frequency of legitimate frames from the targeted device. In addition, adopting such a value would lead to the same success rate for the *Join DoS attack* observed for configurations with lower T_a values. This characteristic can be leveraged by a threat actor to launch an attack against an IoT node while reducing the required power consumption. For instance, this can be used to implement the *Join DoS attack* on resource-constrained hardware or even mobile nodes operated via batteries.

6 Detection and Mitigation of the Attack

A major outcome of the performance evaluation campaign is the assessment of the inflated delays experienced by nodes targeted by the *Join DoS attack*. As an example, the resulting timing behavior can serve as a condensed indicator for computing suitable signatures for network intrusion detection frameworks or AI-based countermeasures [32]. Another possible indicator concerns the ability of spotting anomalous battery drains of IoT devices or resource-constrained nodes. Alas, developing energy-aware countermeasures could be very hard in realistic scenarios as the attacker can reduce the number of malicious frames, thus making deviations from typical sleep/wake cycles almost negligible [22]. Another mitigation mechanism leverages more standard approaches, such as those based on traffic analysis. Alas, the literature showcased that detecting DoS attacks in LoRaWAN scenarios should be considered a hard problem, mainly due to the involved simple medium access control layer and limitations in the duty cycles enforced by the protocol. In this perspective, an effective strategy exploits the occupation of the downlink [7] but require to have suitable visibility both over the stack of devices and the whole network. For instance, this can be achieved via efficient programmable data gathering frameworks especially if edge nodes are available, since they could not run over simple devices or end nodes [6].

If direct inspection of the LoRaWAN network is not feasible, another effective approach can leverage data available to the Network Server. This behavior can be used to design suitable signatures for the early detection of the threat. Specifically, anomalous patterns of join request messages (and related UDP datagrams) could be inferred through a software process monitoring the volume of syscalls (e.g., `socket()`) or the network traffic. However, this requires to meet proper visibility constraints, but many tools like the extended Berkely Packet Filter demonstrated to be efficient in gathering both network-dependent and -agnostic indicators (see, e.g., [37] and the references therein). Despite server-class devices are expected to have a more resources than simple IoT nodes, gathering information for protecting LoRaWAN ecosystems from *Join DoS attack* require to consider several tradeoffs [6]. For instance, a suitable balance in terms of accuracy of the inspection and overheads should be searched, mainly to not causing additional bottlenecks or introducing new entry points for DoS/DDoS attacks.

Mitigating the *Join DoS attack* can also take advantage of the constant softwarization of many core network functionalities. In fact LoRaWAN deployments are expected to be partially absorbed within cloud computing continuums envisioned for supporting future massive IoT scenarios [35]. For instance, the anomalous churning of nodes may increase the resources needed by Network Server(s) to implement core functionalities, e.g., to handle the join procedure or generate the *network session key*. The deployment of probes for monitoring functions granting access to LoRaWAN networks could support the creation of high-level indicators based on energy drains or depletion of computing resources [33].

Another important aspect concerns that both real and emulated scenarios led to very similar results. This allows to take advantage of real hardware and devices for implementing fuzz or pseudo-fuzz testing campaigns [36], which can capture corner cases difficult to achieve through simulations. This knowledge can be then ported to fully softwarized environments for implementing digital twins of the security posture of LoRaWAN deployments [10].

Lastly, threat models based on the *Join DoS attack* templates could be dramatically reduced by introducing some form of encryption. For instance, [9] discusses the security improvements introduced by the encryption of join request messages. Unfortunately, this type of mitigation may require a major rework of both hardware and software used in the wild.

7 Conclusions and Future Work

This paper investigated security implications of the *Join DoS attack*, i.e., an offensive template disrupting the connection process of LoRaWAN deployments. Obtained results demonstrated its effectiveness when launched against both real and simulated conditions. Specifically, the normal behavior of the network is impaired under a load of join requests, e.g., its data rate is reduced or delays become unbound.

The security implications of this class of attacks are different, especially in the perspective of deploying LoRaWAN in emerging network scenarios, such as those based on massive and softwarized IoT paradigms. To this aim, a relevant part of our research is devoted to extend the validation of the *Join DoS attack* to production-quality environments. Additionally, future work aims at improving the security of LoRaWAN, for instance by enforcing a dynamic adjustment of join requests. Finally, we are working towards mechanisms to detect malicious load of requests, e.g., via AI techniques operating in resource-constrained conditions.

Acknowledgments. This research was partially supported by Project FOLLOWME – Flying drOnes to Locate cyber-attackers in LOraWan Metropolitan nEtworks and by Project PERUN (101225653) – Protecting Sensitive Cyber Ecosystems from Upcoming Next Generation and AI-generated Malware Threats under the Horizon Europe Program. This research was also partially supported by Project STRIVE/URAN – Advanced Approaches for Transitions in Urban Environments.

Disclosure of Interests. The authors have no competing interests to declare that are relevant to the content of this article.

References

1. Adelantado, F., Vilajosana, X., Tuset-Peiro, P., Martinez, B., Melia-Segui, J., Watteyne, T.: Understanding the limits of LoRaWAN. IEEE Commun. Mag. **55**(9), 34–40 (2017)
2. Alam, I., et al.: A survey of network virtualization techniques for internet of things using SDN and NFV. ACM Comput. Surv. **53**(2), 1–40 (2020)
3. Aras, E., Small, N., Ramachandran, G., Delbruel, S., Joosen, W., Hughes, D.: Selective jamming of LoRaWAN using commodity hardware. In: Proceedings of the 14th EAI International Conference on Mobile and Ubiquitous Systems: Computing, Networking and Services, pp. 363–372. Melbourne, Australia (2017)
4. Ayoub, W., Samhat, A.E., Nouvel, F., Mroue, M., Prévotet, J.C.: Internet of mobile things: overview of LoRaWAN, DASH7, and NB-IoT in LPWANs standards and supported mobility. IEEE Commun. Surv. Tutorials **21**(2), 1561–1581 (2018)
5. Bagwari, S., Gehlot, A., Singh, R., Priyadarshi, N., Khan, B.: Low-cost sensor-based and LoRaWAN opportunities for landslide monitoring systems on IoT platform: a review. IEEE Access **10**, 7107–7127 (2021)
6. Carrega, A., Caviglione, L., Repetto, M., Zuppelli, M.: Programmable data gathering for detecting Stegomalware. In: 2020 6th IEEE Conference on Network Softwarization, pp. 422–429. IEEE (2020)

7. Chen, M., Ben-Othman, J., Mokdad, L., Yang, X.: A countermeasure for DoS attack on MAC layer in massive LoRaWAN. IEEE Network **39**(4), 312–320 (2025)
8. Danish, S.M., Nasir, A., Qureshi, H.K., Ashfaq, A.B., Mumtaz, S., Rodriguez, J.: Network intrusion detection system for jamming attack in LoRaWAN join procedure. In: Proceedings of the International Conference on Industrial Electronics and Applications. IEEE, New York, NY, USA (2018)
9. Dave, J., Choudhury, N.: Security enhancement of OTAA based joining procedure in LoRaWAN for satellite communication. In: 2024 IEEE 99th Vehicular Technology Conference, pp. 1–5 (2024)
10. Eckhart, M., Ekelhart, A.: Digital twins for cyber-physical systems security: state of the art and outlook. In: Security and Quality in Cyber-Physical Systems Engineering, pp. 383–412. Springer, Cham (2019). https://doi.org/10.1007/978-3-030-25312-7_14
11. Fan, C.I., Zhuang, E.S., Karati, A., Su, C.H.: A multiple end-devices authentication scheme for LoRaWAN. Electronics **11**(5), 797 (2022)
12. Finochietto, M., Santos, R., Ochoa, S.F., Meseguer, R.: Reducing operational expenses of LoRaWAN-based internet of remote things applications. Sensors **22**(20), 7778 (2022)
13. Fukushima, K., Marion, D., Nakano, Y., Facon, A., Kiyomoto, S., Guilley, S.: Experiment on side-channel key-recovery using a real LPWA end-device. In: Proceedings of the 5th International Conference on Information Systems Security and Privacy, pp. 67–74 (2019)
14. Hernandez, C.F., Iova, O., Valois, F.: Downlink scheduling in LoRaWAN: ChirpStack vs the things stack. In: 2024 IEEE Latin-American Conference on Communications, pp. 1–6. IEEE (2024)
15. Hessel, F., Almon, L., Hollick, M.: LoRaWAN security: an evolvable survey on vulnerabilities, attacks and their systematic mitigation. ACM Trans. Sensor Netw. **18**(4), 1–55 (2023)
16. Hou, N., Xia, X., Zheng, Y.: CloakLoRa: a covert channel over LoRa PHY. IEEE/ACM Trans. Networking **31**(3), 1159–1172 (2022)
17. Jouhari, M., Saeed, N., Alouini, M.S., Amhoud, E.M.: A survey on scalable LoRaWAN for massive IoT: recent advances, potentials, and challenges. IEEE Commun. Surv. Tutorials **25**(3), 1841–1876 (2023)
18. Liu, B., Gu, C., He, S., Chen, J.: LoPhy: a resilient and fast covert channel over LoRa PHY. In: Proceedings of the 22nd International Conference on Information Processing in Sensor Networks, IPSN '23, pp. 1–13. Association for Computing Machinery, New York, NY, USA (2023)
19. Magrin, D., Capuzzo, M., Zanella, A.: A thorough study of LoRaWAN performance under different parameter settings. IEEE Internet Things J. **7**(1), 116–127 (2019)
20. Mantravadi, S., Schnyder, R., Møller, C., Brunoe, T.D.: Securing IT/OT links for low power IIoT devices: design considerations for industry 4.0. IEEE Access **8**, 200305–200321 (2020)
21. Maurya, P., Daksha, L., Kahar, V., Kherani, A.A.: Performance analysis of CoLoRa: covert channel over LoRa PHY. In: 2024 National Conference on Communications, pp. 1–6. IEEE (2024)
22. Merlo, A., Migliardi, M., Caviglione, L.: A survey on energy-aware security mechanisms. Pervasive Mob. Comput. **24**, 77–90 (2015)
23. Molina Zarca, A., Bernal Bernabe, J., Farris, I., Khettab, Y., Taleb, T., Skarmeta, A.: Enhancing IoT security through network softwarization and virtual security appliances. Int. J. Network Manage **28**(5), e2038 (2018)

24. Monjur, M., Calzadillas, J., Yu, Q.: Hardware security risks and threat analyses in advanced manufacturing industry. ACM Trans. Des. Autom. Electron. Syst. **28**(5), 1–22 (2023)
25. Motlagh, N.H., et al.: Digital twins for smart spaces-beyond IoT analytics. IEEE Internet Things J. **11**(1), 573–583 (2023)
26. Na, S., Hwang, D., Shin, W., Kim, K.H.: Scenario and countermeasure for replay attack using join request messages in LoRaWAN. In: 2017 International Conference on Information Networking, pp. 718–720. IEEE (2017)
27. Noura, H., Hatoum, T., Salman, O., Yaacoub, J.P., Chehab, A.: LoRaWAN security survey: issues, threats and possible mitigation techniques. Internet of Things **12**, 100303 (2020)
28. Santoro, C., Santoro, F.F.: LWN simulator - A LoRaWAN network simulator. In: International Conference on Enabling Technologies: Infrastructure for Collaborative Enterprises, pp. 1–6. IEEE (2023)
29. Sung, W.J., Ahn, H.G., Kim, J.B., Choi, S.G.: Protecting end-device from replay attack on LoRaWAN. In: International Conference on Advanced Communication Technology, pp. 167–171. IEEE (2018)
30. Toe, E., Jaafar, F., Charles André Ferrier, L.: Securing LoRaWAN in the AIoT era: a systematic mapping study and an MITRE-based threat matrix. IEEE Internet Things J. **13**(3), 3827–3849 (2026)
31. Triantafyllou, A., et al.: Resource efficient federated LoRaWAN architecture for far-edge IoT applications. IEEE Access (2025)
32. Trilles, S., Hammad, S.S., Iskandaryan, D.: Anomaly detection based on artificial intelligence of things: a systematic literature mapping. Internet of Things **25**, 101063 (2024)
33. Verginadis, Y.: A review of monitoring probes for cloud computing continuum. In: Barolli, L. (eds.) International Conference on Advanced Information Networking and Applications, pp. 631–643. Springer, Cham (2023). https://doi.org/10.1007/978-3-031-28694-0_59
34. Xu, J., Tang, Y., Wang, Y., Wang, X.: A practical side-channel attack of a LoRaWAN module using deep learning. In: International Conference on Anti-counterfeiting. Security, and Identification, pp. 17–21. IEEE, Xiamen, China (2019)
35. Yi, B., Wang, X., Li, K., Huang, M., et al.: A comprehensive survey of Network Function Virtualization. Comput. Netw. **133**, 212–262 (2018)
36. Zhu, X., Wen, S., Camtepe, S., Xiang, Y.: Fuzzing: a survey for roadmap. ACM Comput. Surv. **54**(11s), 1–36 (2022)
37. Zuppelli, M., Repetto, M., Schaffhauser, A., Mazurczyk, W., Caviglione, L.: Code layering for the detection of network covert channels in agentless systems. IEEE Trans. Netw. Serv. Manage. **19**(3), 2282–2294 (2022)

Comparing Global vs. Local Large Language Models in Task of Understanding Disinformation: A Real Case Study of the Eastern Border Migration Crisis

Gracjan Kątek[1(✉)], Rafał Kozik[1,2(✉)], Marta Gackowska-Kątek[1], Marek Pawlicki[1,2], and Michał Choraś[1,2]

[1] Bydgoszcz University of Science and Technology, Bydgoszcz, Poland
{gracjan.katek,rafal.kozik}@pbs.edu.pl
[2] IDEAS Research Institute, Warsaw, Poland

Abstract. Weakly supervised and few-shot Large Language Models (LLMs) show great promise in handling complex text analysis without the need for extensive retraining or finetuning. In this paper, we assess practical capabilities of LLMs in disinformation analysis during the eastern border migration crisis. In particular, we evaluated and compared four specific models: Llama 3.1, Qra, Bielik, and PLLuM. Each model was tasked with labeling news articles based on credibility, disinformation types, and thematic categories. By using Cohen's Kappa coefficient, we measured how much these models actually agree with each other. Our results show a major sensitivity gap. Particularly, while global models like Llama often view reports as neutral, the Polish-centric models flagged significantly more content as propaganda. In this paper, we investigate the origins of this phenomenon and provide details of the conducted experiments.

Keywords: Large Language Models · Automatic Annotation · Disinformation

1 Introduction

With more and more information appearing online, disinformation has become a major challenge. The rise of LLMs and generative AI has made this problem even more complex. Until recently, disinformation created with the use of generative AI models was straightforward and easy to detect. Currently, more advanced LLMs understand much better national context, local languages and societal aspects creating more challenges for detection techniques.

In the literature, there are different ways to automatically counter disinformation. As shown by Jaleite-Pastel [12], we can divide these methods into three

P. Kieseberg et al. (Eds.): ARES 2026 Workshops, LNCS 16903, pp. 257–273, 2027.
https://doi.org/10.1007/978-3-032-37218-5_16

groups: pure supervised learning, weak supervision, and LLM-based techniques. The first group (supervised learning) can produce excellent results on specific topics [19]. However, its effectiveness drops quickly when moving to new topics. These models also need high-quality datasets labeled by humans. To solve these issues weak supervision was proposed. At first, it relied on simple features like word counts or the number of reposts. Later, researchers added more complex features [11], such as checking for a "lack of evidence" or "calls to action". However, these (at some level of complexity) again require specialized models, which are trained on human-labeled data. As a result, the original problems reappear again. Because of this, LLMs with zero-shot and few-shot capabilities are expected to close those gaps. These models already perform well on many tasks without specific training. This means that they can find complex disinformation indicators in text without the need for constant fine-tuning [12].

While most studies focus on general accuracy, our work provides an analysis of how different AI models behave in specific cases. Our main contributions are:

- Analysis of capabilities – we evaluate how four different LLMs (Llama 3.1, Qra, Bielik, and PLLuM) handle complex tasks like labeling disinformation and identifying propaganda during the Eastern Border Migration Crisis.
- Identification of the "sensitivity gap" – we identify differences in how different models perceive the same information. We show that a model's training background and "geographical focus" (Polish-centric vs. Global) can lead to different results.
- Reliability measurement – by using Cohen's Kappa coefficient, we provide a mathematical measure of how much these models actually agree (or disagree) when analyzing the same controversial content.

The remainder of this paper is structured as follows: in Sect. 2 related works are shortly over-viewed. The proposed approach to evaluate LLMs in the eastern border migration crisis is detailed in Sect. 3. The created dataset is presented in Sect. 4, while annotation results are described in Sect. 5. Section 6 details the comparison of the used and evaluated LLMs, while conclusions are given thereafter.

2 Related Works

While global AI models offer strong performance across various NLP tasks, they often lack the local cultural and political context needed for specific regions. In this section, we provide an overview of observations made in previous research studies on the topic.

As Prier [9] points out, social media enable the rapid amplification of desired narratives. This is thanks to various trending mechanisms, bots, and coordinated networks of accounts. This leads to the situation where the effectiveness of an information depends not on its quality but on its continuous presence in the digital space [17].

Moreover, as Schafer [15] observed, modern conflicts increasingly use information to influence how opponents think, feel, and make decisions. In this context, Dzhendzhero et al. [6] argue that in the war in Ukraine, disinformation acts as a 'force multiplier'. As a result, it makes hybrid warfare more effective and helps to achieve political and psychological goals.

Also the previous research by Dov Bachmann et al. [5] shows that disinformation campaigns constituted an integral part of both the preparation and the conduct of military operations. These campaigns were used, among other purposes, to promote narratives about the alleged "Nazification" of Ukraine and to undermine the credibility of the West. The authors emphasize that such activities are intended to generate information chaos and weaken international cohesion.

As disinformation grows, detecting fake content is a major challenge for modern information systems [16]. Khan et al. [10] study this problem in armed conflicts. They emphasize that digital verification tools are essential. Techniques like geolocation, metadata analysis, and archiving make verification much more effective. However, the authors note that these tools require high expertise, well-trained human operators and better technology to work well.

D'Ulizia et al. [7] study how AI can detect disinformation using special datasets. The authors reviewed current datasets and found several problems. Many lack specific topics or have poor labeling. The article also points out ethical risks. For example, AI can pick up and repeat human biases from the data. The authors conclude that we need better AI tools and high-quality data to fight disinformation effectively.

3 Proposed Approach to Evaluate LLMs in Understanding the Eastern Border Migration Crisis

3.1 General Remarks

In this research, we looked back (from the end of 2025 perspective) at the eastern EU border crisis, which escalated in 2021. The problem has been widely studied from a geopolitical standpoint, and many works discuss origins, context of the propaganda and disinformation campaigns that took place during that period [18].

For our analysis, we collected historical data using several crawling techniques described in the next section. The dataset focuses in particular on key crisis moments and incidents that repeatedly intensified and then subsided during the 2021–2024 period. In this study, we did not limit ourselves to Polish or Western information sources. We also included news published by Russian, Belarusian, and Ukrainian entities. The analysis was based solely on textual data gathered from publicly available sources.

3.2 Data Corpus Collection Process

To ensure the reliability and representativeness of the data corpus, in the first stage, a dedicated methodology for systematic data acquisition was developed.

As shown in Fig. 1, the data was collected using a two-step crawling approach.

First, we analyzed Google RSS feeds by searching them with selected keywords. These keywords were prepared in several languages, including Polish, English, and Russian. Then, RSS feed addresses were automatically identified and gathered. Based on these feeds, an automated extraction process retrieved links that led directly to the original information sources. In the next step, data from the collected sources was extracted and organized as JSON object according to the predefined schema. Content in languages other than Polish was automatically translated, and the data was then cleaned and normalized by removing redundant or irrelevant information.

In order to complement the RSS-based collection, in parallel, a second data acquisition path was used based on queries sent to the Google Search API. Automatically generated keyword-based queries were used to identify potential information sources from the returned search results. The content of these pages was then downloaded, filtered, and processed using the same data model and schema as in the RSS-based path.

Finally, both data streams were merged at the content acquisition stage, and their structure was unified according to the adopted ontology. This made it possible to process all data within a single analytical pipeline and to prepare the corpus for annotation with LLMs.

In our opinion, the combination of RSS-based collection and Google Search API queries increased the completeness of the dataset, as these two acquisition paths captured partly overlapping but also complementary sets of sources.

3.3 Data Cleaning and Normalization

A challenging step in the whole procedure was transforming the raw data into a structured JSON format and handling anomalies resulting from the specific nature of the collected content. However, this allowed for full interoperability between various aggregation channels (RSS, Wikipedia, Google Search API). The document structure was designed to support multilingualism and the metadata necessary for disinformation analysis.

Moreover, due to the variety of sources (news portals, Wikipedia, search results), the data cleaning process included the following steps:

1. Removing information noise – Website interface elements, advertisements and scripts have been removed from the content of articles, leaving only the text itself.
2. Handling missing data – In cases where the author was not specified, the system automatically assigned the publisher name to the author field, which allowed for maintaining database continuity.
3. Distribution analysis and outlier handling – Statistical analysis of text length across all corpuses revealed a strong right-skewed bias. Although the median length ranged from several hundred to 2,500 words, a few records with extreme lengths (exceeding 15,000–20,000 words) were identified. These texts were retained in the corpus due to their substantive value (e.g., extensive Wikipedia

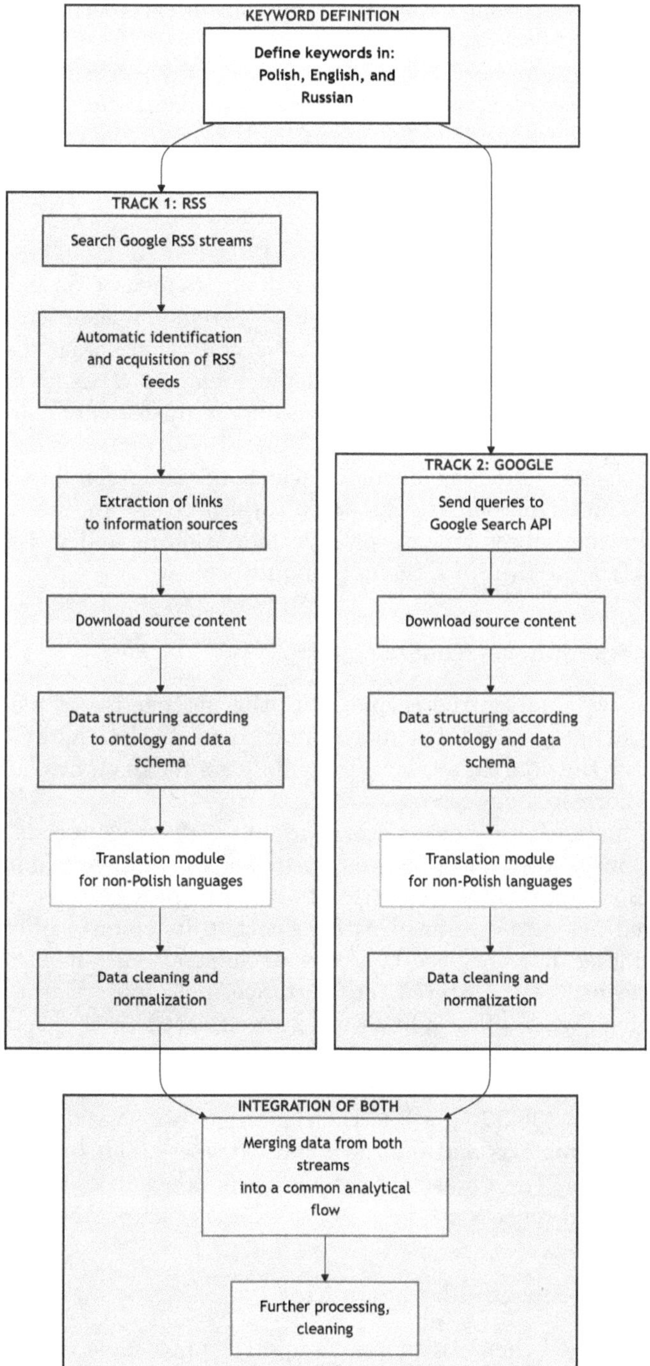

Fig. 1. The proposed process of the data crawling and processing.

articles), but their presence was taken into account when calibrating the tokenizers in the LLM models.
4. Publish date extraction—This process relied mainly on metadata embedded in HTML headers to extract publication dates accurately. When such metadata was missing, we applied additional heuristics and manual verification.

4 Dataset Overview

This dataset contains news headlines and media texts focused on the Belarus and Poland border crisis as well as broader view on regional security, and broader geopolitical tensions in Eastern Europe. The collection spans themes related to migration, border violence, military deployments, NATO-related risks, the war in Ukraine, Belarusian domestic repression, and historical memory conflicts. Although the dataset is centered on the Polish–Belarusian border, it also captures a wider narrative environment in which migration, military escalation, hybrid threats, and symbolic attacks on cultural heritage are interconnected.

In the following subsection, we provide more details and insights into how the corpus is structured from a thematic point of view.

4.1 Document Source Analysis

In this section, we analyze the corpus from the perspective of its origin. Each news item in the dataset contains information about its URL address. From each URL, we extract the domain to identify the data source (e.g., https://www.nato.int/.../...html corresponds to www.nato.int).

Using this method, we identified around 300 distinct sources in the dataset. The distribution is relatively balanced, with no source clearly dominating the corpus. The most frequent source accounts for only 2% of all documents.

Each source was also examined with respect to its country of origin. In this case, we considered not only the language of publication, but also the country in which the website is registered. For instance, polskiobserwator.de publishes content in Polish, while often addressing issues related to the German context (Fig. 2).

As it is shown in Fig. 3 polish sources account for slightly more than one-third of the dataset (36.36%), while the remaining observations originate from a range of other countries and international categories. This percentage distribution suggests that the dataset is not narrowly concentrated in one national context, but instead reflects a broad and diversified perspective.

4.2 Embedding-Based Thematic Map

The embedding-based thematic map is intended to provide a compact and intuitive overview of the main topics present in the corpus. By projecting semantically similar texts into nearby regions, it highlights both thematic groups and the relationships between them.

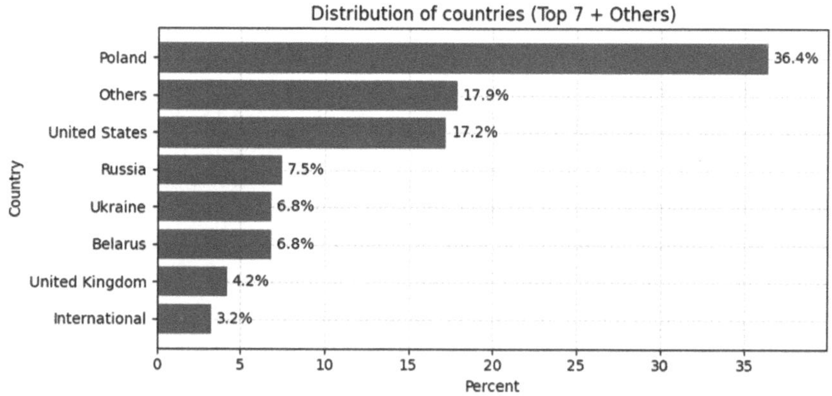

Fig. 2. Percentage distribution of sources by country.

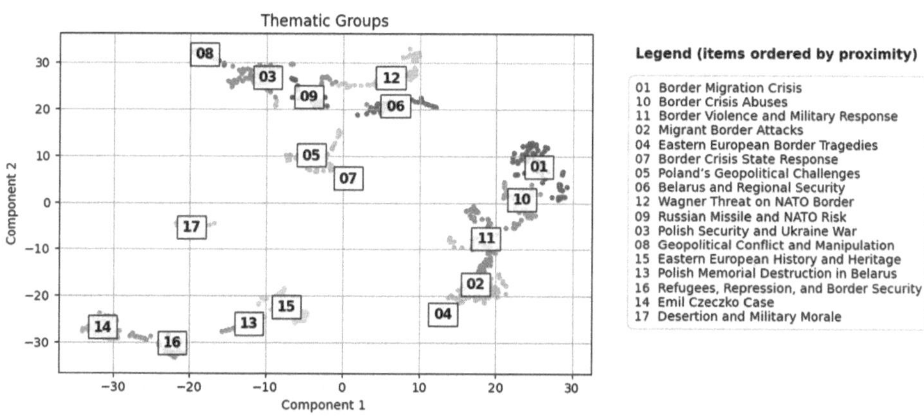

Fig. 3. Thematic groups identified in the dataset.

The embedding-based thematic map for the considered dataset (Fig. 3) reveals that semantically related topics form clear local structures, with cluster centroids positioned close to one another when they share vocabulary, actors, and narrative framing. The arrangement of centroids suggests that the dataset is not composed of isolated themes, but rather of several larger narrative blocks.

The first major thematic block is formed by clusters 1, 2, 4, 10, and 11, which collectively represent the Belarus–Poland border crisis. These clusters are tightly connected because they revolve around migration pressure, border incidents, violence, humanitarian controversies, state intervention, and reactions from the military and public authorities. While each cluster emphasizes a slightly different angle, together they describe one broader discourse centered on the operational, political, and human dimensions of the border crisis.

Another connected area includes clusters 5, 6, 12, 9, and 3, which can be interpreted as a security and geopolitical escalation block. These topics focus on

Poland's strategic position, Belarus–Russia relations, NATO risks, missile incidents, the Wagner Group presence, and the consequences of the war in Ukraine. In contrast to the border-crisis clusters, this part of the map is more strongly oriented toward military risk, deterrence, and interstate tensions.

The more distant clusters, such as 14 and 17, represent more specific narratives related to desertion, military morale, and the fugitive named Emil Czeczko case [8]. Their relative separation indicates that these topics are thematically related to the broader crisis environment, but they rely on a more specialized vocabulary and narrower event framing.

5 Data Annotation Using LLM

The collected dataset was annotated using the LLM models. The annotation process was implemented using LLM language models such as Bielik [14], Qra [1], Llama [13], and PLLuM [2]. At this stage, a formal specification of annotation fields was developed, ensuring a high level of consistency and comparability of results generated by all the models used.

Each model independently assessed the same pool of documents, which made it possible to compare their annotations, identify discrepancies between them, and analyze these differences in detail.

The annotation process focused on several levels of document content, namely:

- **Information credibility** – An assessment of the credibility of the information contained in the text, indicating the level of trust in the source and the consistency of the content with verified facts.
- **Disinformation type** – A classification of the type of disinformation present in the text (e.g., fake news, propaganda, manipulation, conspiracy theory, or no signs of disinformation).
- **Thematic category** – The thematic category assigned to the article's content (e.g., geopolitics, military equipment, security, etc.).

In the following subsections, each model is analyzed separately, with particular attention paid to its responses and the most relevant insights they provide.

5.1 LLama-Based Annotations

Based on the established prompt structure, the Llama model was used to analyze the corpus across several dimensions described in the previous section. The results provide a detailed view of the information landscape, especially in terms of credibility and topic distribution.

The distribution of these labels shows the overall nature of the analyzed data:

- Information Credibility (78.1%): Most of the articles were classified as highly credible. This suggests that the majority of the collected data followed standard journalistic practices.

- Disinformation Types (94.4%): The model indicated that nearly 95% of the content did not contain identifiable disinformation. This provides an important baseline and helps distinguish the remaining 5.6% of cases in which specific disinformation techniques were detected.
- Tone of Expression (95.2%): The clearly dominant neutral tone suggests that the corpus was interpreted mainly as informative and report-based.

The annotation process also included the identification of key military and geopolitical entities. This allowed for a quantitative assessment of the actors most frequently associated with the research scenarios:

- Primary Actors: Russia (143 mentions) and Poland (121 mentions) emerged as the central figures in the discourse, followed by Ukraine (106) and NATO (95).
- Regional Focus: Belarus (81 mentions) maintained a high frequency, reflecting its critical role in the border-related narratives.

At this stage, the model identified USA and United States as two separate terms, with 20 mentions each. To ensure comparability across models, these results were treated as referring to the same country, giving a total of 40 mentions for the United States.

The final layer of the annotation involved assigning each article to one of the predefined thematic categories (Table 1). The distribution reflects the model's ability to categorize complex security narratives:

Table 1. Thematic Classification Results - Llama Model

Category	Share (%)	Contextual Relevance
Other	28.3	General news and multi-topic reports.
Geopolitics	16.7	International relations and strategic security.
NATO	15.6	Alliance activities and collective defense.
Ukraine	13.4	War-related updates and regional impact.
Russia	12.3	Threat analysis and military movements.
Polish Military	11.2	National defense and modernization.
Belarus	1.1	Specific border-related incidents.

The thematic alignment (with over 45% of the articles falling into Geopolitics, NATO, and Ukraine) validates the effectiveness of the dedicated prompt in guiding the Llama model toward the research objectives.

5.2 PLLuM-Based Annotations

The same methodology was applied using the PLLuM - large-scale Polish language model. The results obtained from this model reveal significant differences in data interpretation compared to international models, particularly in the assessment of source reliability and thematic precision.

The analysis of information quality by PLLuM showed a more cautious approach to assessing credibility:

- Information Credibility (56.2%): More than half of the articles were categorized as having "unknown credibility", with an additional 26.0% classified as "medium credibility". This differs substantially from the Llama model, suggesting that PLLuM applies more conservative or different criteria for evaluating journalistic reliability.
- Disinformation Types (92.0%): Similar to Llama model, the vast majority of articles were found to be free of disinformation. However, the remaining 8.0% were specifically identified as propaganda, indicating the model's focus on identifying state-sponsored or biased narratives.
- Tone of Expression (93.3%): Consistent with the overall corpus characteristics, PLLuM identified a neutral tone in the vast majority of analyzed texts.

PLLuM identified military entities mainly related to the Central and Eastern European security axis (Ukraine–Russia–NATO), which shows a strong regional focus in the analyzed discourse:

- Primary Entities: The distribution is highly balanced, with Ukraine (43 mentions) leading the ranking, followed by Russia (40), NATO (37), Poland (34), and Belarus (32).
- Geopolitical Context: This distribution reinforces the model's alignment with the regional security scenario, accurately identifying the key actors involved in the border crisis and the ongoing conflict.

The thematic labeling performed by PLLuM (Table 2) highlighted certain technical challenges related to the model's adherence to the provided instructions:

Table 2. Thematic Classification Results - PLLuM Model

Category	Share (%)	Analytical Observations
Other	55.8	Dominant category, significantly higher than in other models.
Polish Military (Wojsko PL)	12.7	High focus on domestic defense topics.
NATO	10.5	Consistent identification of alliance-related content.
Ukraine	5.2	Lower share compared to Llama, despite high entity frequency.

An important observation at this stage was the presence of model hallucinations. Although the prompt included a formal specification, PLLuM produced more thematic labels than expected. This suggests that the model followed the output format less strictly, which led to a more fragmented classification and a large share of articles being placed in the 'Other' category.

5.3 Bielik-Based Annotations

The third stage of the comparative annotation was performed with the Bielik model. Its results show a distinct profile, with high confidence in source reliability and a stronger sensitivity to propaganda.

However, Bielik's assessment differs clearly from the patterns observed in both Llama and PLLuM:

- Information Credibility (69.3%): In contrast to PLLuM, which was more cautious, Bielik classified nearly 70% of the articles as credible. At the same time, 27.3% of the content was marked as having unknown credibility.
- Disinformation and Propaganda (55.2% vs. 34.3%): This is the most notable result for Bielik. While 55.2% of the articles were classified as free from disinformation, as many as 34.3% were labeled as propaganda. This suggests that Bielik is more sensitive than the other tested models to persuasive or politically charged language.
- Tone of Expression (97.0%): Despite the relatively high number of propaganda labels, the model identified the tone as neutral in almost all cases. This suggests that Bielik often recognized propaganda in content that still appeared formal and factual in style.

Bielik's analysis of military entities shows a strong focus on national and regional actors, with a high number of mentions in the five most frequent categories:

- Primary Focus: Poland was mentioned most often (85 occurrences), followed by Russia (78) and Ukraine (75).
- Security Structures: NATO (74 mentions) was also one of the central entities, with a frequency similar to that of the main national actors.
- Regional Context: Belarus (45 mentions) appeared regularly, although much less often than the four most frequently mentioned entities listed above.

The thematic distribution generated by Bielik shows the strongest thematic concentration among all tested models (Table 3):

Table 3. Thematic Classification Results - Bielik Model

Category	Share (%)	Analytical Observations
Polish Military (Wojsko PL)	66.8	Strongest focus on national defense among all models.
Other	33.2	Remaining content not fitting the primary military category.

The model's classification is clearly polarized, with 66.8% of the corpus assigned to the Polish Military category. This strong concentration suggests that Bielik places much more emphasis on national defense topics than the other models, giving a more specific view of the security narratives than Llama, while PLLuM produced a more fragmented classification.

5.4 Qra-Based Annotations

The final stage of the comparative study was carried out using the Qra model. The results show that Qra produced a stable and consistent annotation profile, with high confidence in source reliability and a balanced identification of geopolitical entities. Qra's evaluation of corpus quality was close to the results obtained by the other models, while also showing a consistent interpretation of the data:

- Information Credibility (78.1%): The model classified more than three-quarters of the dataset as credible, which is similar to the result obtained by Llama. Only 15.2% of the articles were marked as having unknown credibility.
- Disinformation and Propaganda (94.0%): Qra labeled 94% of the content as free from disinformation or propaganda. This suggests that the model was effective in recognizing standard news content and separating it from clearly deceptive material.
- Tone of Expression (94.8%): Almost all analyzed texts were classified as neutral in tone, which confirms that the collected material was mainly informative in nature.

Qra's analysis of military entities shows a clear hierarchy of actors shaping the current regional security discourse:

- Dominant Entities: Russia (143 mentions) and Poland (121 mentions) were the most frequently identified entities.
- Regional Security Axis: Ukraine (108 mentions) and NATO (95 mentions) were also among the main elements of the military context, while Belarus (84 mentions) provided an important geopolitical background.
- Transatlantic Context: The model identified 'United States' and 'USA' with a combined total of 37 mentions, which further highlights the international dimension of the analyzed events.

The thematic distribution generated by Qra (Table 4) shows a structured approach to content labeling, although it is broader and less specialized than the distribution produced by Bielik.

The Qra model provides a strong reference point, combining the identification of regional actors with a broader understanding of thematic categories. As a result, it forms a consistent final layer of the multi-model annotation process.

6 Study of the Selected LLM Models in the Context of Automatic Annotation

Automatic annotation of the selected corpora resulted in four JSON files, one for each model. It is worth noting that the models used in the annotation process were not trained. The goal of this stage was to analyze the capabilities and

Table 4. Thematic Classification Results - QRA Model

Category	Share (%)	Contextual Relevance
Other	28.3	General news and multi-topic reports not fitting primary categories.
Geopolitics	16.0	International relations and global strategic security balance.
NATO	15.2	Alliance activities, cooperation, and collective defense.
Polish Military	13.0	National defense potential and domestic military affairs.
Ukraine	12.6	War-related updates and regional impact of the conflict.
Russia	12.3	Threat analysis, military movements, and hostile actions.

usefulness of large language models for automatic data annotation, particularly in the context of military issues.

Cohen's Kappa coefficient [4] was used to assess the level of agreement between pairs of annotating models with respect to content classification, including information credibility, disinformation type, and topic categories. This coefficient is used to reliably assess the degree of agreement between two classification systems, while correcting for random effects [3].

$$\kappa = \frac{P_o - P_e}{1 - P_e} \tag{1}$$

where:

- P_o is the relative observed agreement among raters (empirical probability of agreement),
- P_e is the hypothetical probability of chance agreement (expected agreement when raters assign labels randomly).

It is estimated using empirical prior data for individual annotators with respect to class labels. The following model pairs were used for the analysis:

- 'llama3.1:70b', 'emsi/qra-13b'
- 'llama3.1:70b', 'mwiewior/bielik'
- 'llama3.1:70b', 'PRIHLOP/PLLuM'
- 'emsi/qra-13b', 'mwiewior/bielik'
- 'emsi/qra-13b', 'PRIHLOP/PLLuM'
- 'mwiewior/bielik', 'PRIHLOP/PLLuM'

Figure 4 presents the matrix of average Cohen's Kappa values for the model pairs used. In the literature, it is assumed that for $\kappa = 1$, there is complete agreement between the models, while $\kappa \approx 0$ indicates no agreement above chance, and negative values indicate inconsistent estimates.

Table 5 shows clear differences in agreement between the analyzed models across all annotation categories. The strongest consistency was observed for the Llama–Qra pair, which achieved very high Cohen's Kappa values in every dimension, including credibility (0.939), disinformation type (0.966), topic category (0.946), and tone (0.923). This indicates that these two models followed very similar interpretation patterns and produced highly comparable annotations.

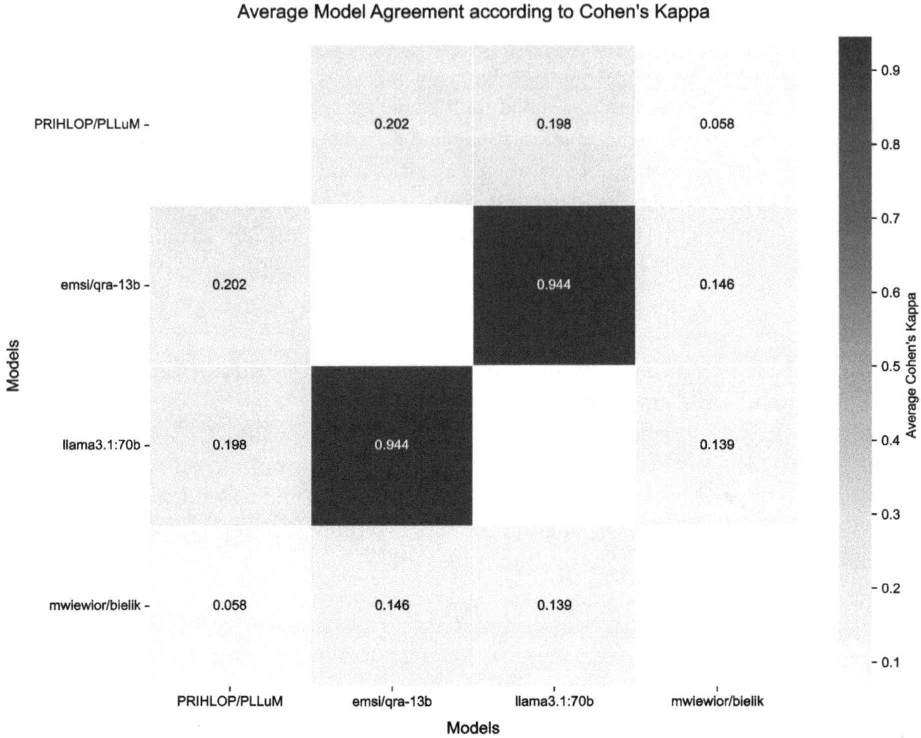

Fig. 4. Average Model Agreement according to Cohen's Kappa

The second, clearly weaker level of agreement can be seen for pairs involving Bielik and either Llama or Qra. In both cases, agreement was moderate only for credibility assessment (0.418 and 0.435, respectively), while the remaining categories showed very low or no agreement. This suggests that Bielik applied a substantially different interpretative strategy, particularly in identifying disinformation, topic categories, and tone.

Pairs involving PLLuM showed generally low agreement, although slightly higher consistency appeared for disinformation type and topic category. The Llama–PLLuM and Qra–PLLuM pairs reached Kappa values of around 0.24–0.27 in these two dimensions, but remained very weak in credibility and tone. This indicates partial overlap in broader thematic judgments, combined with considerable divergence in more fine-grained assessments.

The lowest agreement was observed for the Bielik–PLLuM pair, where all Kappa values remained close to zero. This points to an almost complete lack of consistency between these two models and confirms that they represented the most divergent annotation profiles in the study.

Table 5. Cohen's Kappa coefficients for pairwise agreement between models across annotation categories

Model pair	Credibility	Disinfo type	Topic category	Tone
Llama – Qra	0.939	0.966	0.946	0.923
Llama – Bielik	0.418	0.018	0.145	-0.024
Llama – PLLuM	0.073	0.244	0.269	0.206
Qra – Bielik	0.435	0.029	0.146	-0.027
Qra – PLLuM	0.077	0.264	0.268	0.199
Bielik – PLLuM	0.043	0.033	0.081	0.074

Overall, the results reveal three main patterns:

- a very strong convergence between Llama and Qra
- a partially shared but clearly distinct profile for Bielik
- a generally inconsistent profile for PLLuM, which showed only weak agreement with the other models.

These differences confirm that, although all models annotated the same document set under the same formal specification, their interpretations of credibility, disinformation, thematic structure, and tone varied substantially.

7 Conclusions

In this paper, we tested several LLMs including Llama 3.1, Qra, Bielik, and PLLuM for automatic disinformation understanding related to the eastern border migration crisis. The results show that a model's origin and training data affect how it understands documents' content.

Our experiments reveal that difference between global models and Polish-focused models. Llama 3.1 and Qra gave very similar results and usually treated the texts as neutral or credible. In contrast, the Polish-focused models, especially Bielik, were more sensitive to subjective and propaganda-like language. Bielik marked more than 34% of the texts as propaganda, while Llama marked less than 6%.

The study also shows differences in reliability. Llama and Qra gave stable and consistent topic classifications. PLLuM, however, produced more hallucinations and followed the required output format less accurately.

Overall, there is no single best model for all cases. Global models work well as a general baseline, but local models are more useful for finding region-specific propaganda signals. In the future, the best solution may be to use hybrid ensembles of LLM models that combine the stability of global models with the local sensitivity of regional ones.

Disclosure of Interests. The authors have no competing interests to declare that are relevant to the content of this article.

References

1. OPI-PG/Qra-13b · hugging face. https://huggingface.co/OPI-PG/Qra-13b. Accessed 21 Mar 2026
2. PLLuM - polish large language model. https://pllum.org.pl/. Accessed 21 Mar 2026
3. Artstein, R., Poesio, M.: Inter-coder agreement for computational linguistics. Comput. Linguist. Assoc. Comput. Linguist. **34**(4), 555–596 (2008)
4. Cohen, J.: A coefficient of agreement for nominal scales. Educ. Psychol. Meas. **20**(1), 37–46 (1960)
5. Dov Bachmann, S.D., Putter, D., Duczynski, G.: Hybrid warfare and disinformation: a Ukraine war perspective. Global Pol. **14**(5), 858–869 (2023). https://doi.org/10.1111/1758-5899.13257
6. Dzhendzhero, D., Nakonechnyi, V., Poberezhnyi, A.: Methodological approaches to identifying the features of false information within the information security system of the defense forces of Ukraine. Honor Law **95**(4), 43–48 (2025). https://doi.org/10.33405/2078-7480/2025/95/4/353274, https://chiz.nangu.edu.ua/article/view/353274
7. D'Ulizia, A., D'Andrea, A., Pirrone, M.: Fighting disinformation with AI tools: datasets for detecting fake news on climate change and the Russian invasion of Ukraine. Data Technol. Appl., 1–20 (2026). https://doi.org/10.1108/dta-06-2025-0489
8. Info Warfare: Emil czeczko – Russian and Belarusian disinformation (Dec 2023). https://infowarfare.pl/2023/12/06/emil-czeczko-russian-and-belarusian-disinformation/. Accessed 01 Apr 2026
9. Jarred, P.: Commanding the trend: social media as information warfare. JSTOR Strategic Stud. Q. **11**(4) (2017). http://www.jstor.org/stable/26271634
10. Khan, S.A., et al.: Debunking war information disorder: a case study in assessing the use of multimedia verification tools. J. Am. Soc. Inf. Sci. **76**(5), 752–769 (2025). https://doi.org/10.1002/asi.24970
11. Ksieniewicz, P., Zyblewski, P., Choraś, M., Kozik, R., Gielczyk, A., Woźniak, M.: Fake news detection from data streams. In: 2020 International Joint Conference on Neural Networks (IJCNN), pp. 1–8 (2020). https://doi.org/10.1109/IJCNN48605.2020.9207498
12. Leite, J.A., Razuvayevskaya, O., Bontcheva, K., Scarton, C.: Weakly supervised veracity classification with LLM-predicted credibility signals. EPJ Data Sci. **14**(1), 16 (2025). https://doi.org/10.1140/epjds/s13688-025-00534-0
13. Meta, A.I.: The llama 3 herd of models (2024)
14. Prejzner, J.: Bielik-Q2-Sharp: a comparative study of extreme 2-bit quantization methods for a polish 11B language model (2026)

15. Schäfer, P.J.: Reconfiguring international security - the strategic evolution of modern warfare. Zeitschrift für Außen- und Sicherheitspolitik (2025). https://doi.org/10.1007/s12399-025-01018-9
16. Shu, K., Sliva, A., Wang, S., Tang, J., Liu, H.: Fake news detection on social media: a data mining perspective (2017). http://arxiv.org/abs/1708.01967
17. Vosoughi, S., Roy, D., Aral, S.: The spread of true and false news online. Science (New York, N.Y.) **359**(6380), 1146–1151 (2018). https://doi.org/10.1126/science.aap9559
18. Wikipedia contributors: Belarus - European union border crisis. https://en.wikipedia.org/w/index.php?title=Belarus%E2%80%93European_Union_border_crisis&oldid=1345608612 (2026). Accessed 21 Mar 2026
19. Zhou, X., Zafarani, R.: A survey of fake news: fundamental theories, detection methods, and opportunities. ACM Comput. Surv. **53**(5) (2020). https://doi.org/10.1145/3395046

Evaluation of Machine Learning Approaches for Intrusion Detection in UAV Networks

Sebastian Szelest[1], Marek Pawlicki[1,2](✉), Rafał Kozik[1,2], and Michał Choraś[1,2]

[1] ITTI Sp. z o.o, Poznań, Poland
marek.pawlicki@itti.com.pl
[2] Bydgoszcz University of Science and Technology, Bydgoszcz, Poland

Abstract. Unmanned aerial vehicles are more and more often being deployed in both civilian and military contexts. One of the pressing issues of the technology is their resilience to network intrusions. This paper addresses issues related to the growing problem of cyberattacks on unmanned aerial vehicles (UAV).

This paper presents an empirical evaluation of a novel benchmark dataset, UAVIDS-2025, and its suitability for training machine learning-based network intrusion detection systems. The authors used this dataset to train three different artificial intelligence models: Random Forest, XGBoost, and Deep Neural Network, trained with minimal processing and default hyperparameters. All three models achieve strong classification performance without any additional feature engineering. The findings confirm initial machine learning viability for detection of cyberattacks targeting UAV.

Keywords: UAV Security · Intrusion Detection · Machine Learning

1 Introduction

Nowadays, as technology advances, security measures for new technologies often fail to keep up. This creates significant risks that can be felt in real life [27]. Unmanned aerial vehicles (UAVs) are one such technology. Their development over the past few years has been astonishing. What was initially a subject of interest for enthusiasts has turned into a tool used in many different aspects of everyday life. This technology is currently being used for civilian applications, such as filmmaking or parcel delivery, as well as destructive applications in the context of armed conflicts.

An important aspect is that it can become a target for malicious actors. To prevent this, the technology must be resilient against possible external cyberattacks.

In recent years, due to geopolitical pressures, with the wide range of applications for UAVs, on multiple instances, these devices have been subjected to cyberattacks.

P. Kieseberg et al. (Eds.): ARES 2026 Workshops, LNCS 16903, pp. 274–288, 2027.
https://doi.org/10.1007/978-3-032-37218-5_17

One such incident was the Iranian military's seizure of the American RQ-170 Sentinel stealth drone. This was accomplished by combining satellite link jamming with GPS spoofing. The drone was forced into autopilot mode and then redirected to false GPS coordinates. As a result, instead of landing at its base in Afghanistan, it landed intact on Iranian territory [21].

Another example of UAV hacking involves attacks by drug cartels on the U.S. border patrol drones. According to the U.S. Department of Homeland Security and Customs and Border Protection, drug cartels used GPS spoofing and jamming against drones monitoring the border. The attacker falsified the GPS signal, causing the drones to become disoriented, lose their position, and disrupt their patrol missions [6].

Many UAV-related incidents are also currently occurring during the Russia-Ukraine war [19]. One such incident involved GPS spoofing on reconnaissance drones, where Russian EW systems took control of the navigation, causing deviations from the planned route and loss of operational control.

Another incident involving GPS spoofing was a massive attack on Ukraine in November 2024. By employing this type of attack against enemy drones, 151 drones entered Belarusian airspace, and many others crashed or were redirected to less critical targets [10]. Due to all these incidents, Ukraine has implemented its own system called Pokrova, which replaces satellite signals with a false navigation field. This directly affects the autopilots of Russian drones, often causing them to fail to reach their targets [14].

Developing novel security measures based on artificial intelligence (AI) may prove to be an essential factor in the cybersecurity arms race for the protection of UAVs. However, the use of AI necessitates sufficient and appropriate data [29]. Thus, this work seeks to answer the following research questions:

RQ1 Is machine learning (ML) suitable for detecting attacks on UAV infrastructure?
RQ2 Is the UAVIDS-2025 dataset suitable for training ML models?
RQ3 What are the detection metrics of different ML algorithms achieved on the benchmark dataset.

This work is structured as follows: Sect. 2 describes current issues related to attacks on UAVs and presents various perspectives on the topic. Section 3 describes the data and ML models selected. Section 4 describes the environment in which this work was conducted and presents the results achieved by each model. Section 5 provides the analysis and the description of the results. Conclusions are given thereafter.

2 Related Works

While the topic of UAV cybersecurity has recently gained prominence due to the geopolitical events, there are already numerous publications on the subject.

In intrusion detection literature overall, signature-based detection proves highly efficient against well-documented threats, provided the "fingerprint" is already captured [24]. Similarly, neural networks and ML approaches emerge as a compelling solution for handling network intrusion detection (NIDS) [25]. A survey of various flow formats, flow capture utilities, and flow exporters is presented in [43]. A systematic examination of existing IDS datasets, conducted in [8], identifies two overarching categories of problems encountered in IDS research. The first pertains to broader research-level challenges, most notably the scarcity of authentic, real-world network traffic datasets. The second encompasses a series of technical issues inherent to the collected data itself. Such data is frequently noisy, certain attack categories suffer from insufficient labeled samples, and even when adequate data volume is attained, severe class imbalance can influence model reliability. The scale of the data to be processed further compounds these difficulties. In one of the recent surveys [5], the authors analyzed the security ecosystem of UAV systems. The emphasis of this work is on the rapid growth in the use of the technology in both personal and military applications, which has not been adequately balanced by the development of security measures for such systems. This results in a situation where an increasingly widespread technology faces growing security challenges, which can lead to real-world consequences. The survey describes five key UAV subsystems: control, navigation and timing, identification, sensors, and communication. It is noted that each of these elements can constitute a potential attack surface. The authors also conducted a review of the tools and datasets available to UAV researchers. However, despite the recency of the review itself, the UAVIDS-2025 dataset, which is the subject of this research, was not included.

Over the years, multiple studies have highlighted issues related to UAV resilience against cyberattacks. In [40] from 2012, the authors presented the results of tests involving the spoofing of civilian GPS signals under controlled conditions. These tests were conducted at the White Sands Missile Range (WSMR) on two systems using civilian GPS. The tests conducted on a civilian device demonstrated that UAVs can be hijacked by spoofing the GPS signal. The paper also discusses the consequences associated with such attacks.

Another example comes from [15], which describes the case of Iran's takeover of an American drone. Based on this incident and the global trends at the time of publishing, the authors predict that UAVs will become an increasingly important part of our lives, both in the private and public spheres. They primarily highlight the volume of critical information that UAVs will need to carry in order to operate autonomously. For these reasons, they proposed in their work a risk assessment method specific to UAVs, which takes into account factors such as: exposure, communication systems, data carriers, sensor systems, and error handling mechanisms.

The authors of [39] show that despite previously documented problems with attacks on UAVs, security measures are still not effective enough to minimize the scope of these attacks. The research aimed to describe the attack methods and UAV vulnerabilities relevant at the time to raise basic and general awareness of issues related to UAV cybersecurity.

Another study [38] focused on describing UAV security issues in the Internet of Things (IoT) industry. The authors point to a gap in research on this topic and to the risks arising from the lack of features in current solutions that would allow for the incorporation of security principles, which could be useful in assessing UAV vulnerability with greater accuracy. The authors propose their own method to fill this gap. It is based on a Petri net model that not only evaluates drone behaviour but also analyses it for potential vulnerabilities by applying security principles.

Recent studies, such as [1] continue to highlight the same issues that appeared in the previously cited studies. Here, however, the authors concluded that UAVs require an adaptive intrusion detection system (IDS) that would help identify intruders and ensure the UAVs safe return to base. The authors proposed such a system consisting of a combination of Self-Training learning (STL) and a Support Vector Machine (SVM), utilizing AI capabilities to enhance UAV resilience.

On the other hand, the authors of [44] analyse the current state of drone security and present a set of vulnerabilities in drones equipped with Wi-Fi. They identified 5 different types of attacks, which they then exploited on devices to test their resilience.

In the latest literature, there is a strong emphasis on UAV-based research in the IoT. For example, in [20] the authors describe growing issues related to IoT security, while highlighting the need for ethical hacking of these devices for educational purposes and the potential detection of security vulnerabilities. The article is based on the implementation of ethical hacking of a drone by taking control of it and, based on this, drawing conclusions regarding possible countermeasures for the drones.

According to the authors of the paper [41], another potential vulnerability could be the sensors on UAVs. The authors describe how taking over a single sensor using spoofing can lead to taking control of the entire UAV. Additionally, they provided information on what an unauthorized person can gain by compromising a given sensor. Furthermore, the authors conclude that current security standards implemented in UAVs are insufficient and contain serious vulnerabilities.

There are also issues related to the storage of sensitive information by UAVs. Due to this fact, the authors of [37] research aimed at obtaining results indicating critical network parameters that should be taken into account when developing security policies regarding UAV communication.

Given the extensive literature review presented in the Table 1 on cyberattacks against UAVs, it can be concluded that although these problems have been known for many years, there are still no sufficiently effective solutions. For this reason, the evaluation of novel datasets that could support the development of ML models for detecting attacks on UAVs is all the more important.

Table 1. Summary of related works

Paper Title	Short Description
Detection and Mitigation of Cyber Attacks on UAV Networks	Survey about security ecosystem of the UAV systems
Evaluation of smart grid and civilian UAV vulnerability to GPS spoofing attacks	Study about spoofing of civilian GPS signals
The vulnerability of UAVs to cyber attacks-An approach to the risk assessment	Study about Iran's takeover of an American drone
Analysis of vulnerabilities in modern unmanned aircraft systems	Study indicating that security issues with UAVs persists
Behavior and vulnerability assessment of drones-enabled industrial internet of things (iiot)	Study about UAV security problems in IoT
Detecting signal spoofing and jamming attacks in UAV networks using a lightweight IDS	Study highlighting the need to integrate the IDS with UAVs
Drone hacking with raspberry-pi 3 and wifi pineapple: Security and privacy threats for the internet-of-things	Study about vulnerabilities in drones equipped with Wi-Fi
Security of Internet of Things devices: Ethical hacking a drone and its mitigation strategies	Study highlighting the need for ethical hacking of UAVs
Assessing UAV sensor spoofing: More than a GNSS problem	Study about new attack surface for UAVs
Investigating Patterns of UAV Attacks for Building Secure UAV Network	Study about storage of sensitive information by UAVs

3 Materials and Methods

The following section describes the methods and materials used in this work. Specifically, it focuses on the dataset, processing steps, and the artificial intelligence models used.

3.1 Random Forest Model

The Random Forest (RF) Classifier was selected on account of its well-documented performance in classification tasks within the domain of NIDS [22], where it is also valued for its fast execution time [28]. RF, introduced by [4] and [16], is an ensemble approach that extends the Decision Tree approach [4] with the aim of enhancing predictive accuracy while mitigating the risk of overfitting. The algorithm constructs an array of individual decision trees [4], each grown from an independently and randomly resampled subset of the training data, a strategy known as bootstrap aggregation [2]. Within each tree, a randomly selected subset of inputs is evaluated at every node, and partitions are determined so as to minimize information entropy or Gini Index. The individual trees are grown to their full depth following the Classification and Regression Tree (CART) methodology [3] and are subsequently left unpruned. Final decisions are obtained by aggregating the outputs of all trees, typically via a majority vote [4]. The generalization performance of the ensemble is dependent on the predictive strength of each individual tree and the degree of diversity across the ensemble. As noted by Breiman, the generalization error of a forest is fundamentally dependent on the interplay between these two quantities. Despite the apparent simplicity of its underlying mechanism, this combination of properties has led RF to be widely regarded as one of the most capable and reliable supervised learning algorithms available [36].

3.2 Extreme Gradient Boosting Model

Extreme Gradient Boosting (XGBoost) is an efficient, scalable and regularized implementation of the gradient boosting algorithm, proposed by Chen and Guestrin [7]. This method has been optimised for both classification performance and computational efficiency in decision tree-based models. As a member of the broader family of boosting algorithms, XGBoost operates on the ensemble principle of sequentially constructing a collection of weak learners, typically shallow decision trees, where each successive model is tasked with correcting the residual errors of its predecessor by approximating the gradient of the loss function [11]. The distinction from classical gradient boosting is in XGBoost's substitution of standard gradient descent with a Newton-Raphson update scheme and the incorporation of both L1 [42] and L2 [17] regularisation terms directly into the objective function. This penalises model complexity, reducing the risk of overfitting. The algorithm also leverages a parallelised tree construction procedure alongside optimised processor cache utilisation, resulting in considerable gains in training speed.

This model is highly resistant to overfitting and is designed to operate on large datasets.

3.3 Deep Neural Network

A deep neural network (DNN) is a type of artificial neural network, composed of multiple hidden layers, which allow the model to learn complex relationships within the data [23,35]. The versatility of DNNs has been demonstrated across a vast array of domains. From their foundational architectures to subsequent advancements such as CNNs and RNNs [13], these models have found wide applications in fields including Biometrics, Natural Language Processing, Shape Recognition, Face Recognition, Intrusion Detection [34], and a multitude of others. DNNs have cemented their status as an indispensable instrument. The foundational premise underlying DNNs draws, to a degree, upon the operational principles observed in biological neural systems [26]. The aptitude of DNNs for uncovering recurring and meaningful patterns within data stems from the manner in they adapt to the training examples. DNNs acquire knowledge about the underlying data through the iterative adjustment of weights and biases. This is achieved by cycling through batches of training samples and refining the parameters so as to minimize the discrepancy between the predicted output and the ground truth, commonly referred to as the supervisory signal [32].

The TensorFlow library can be used to build such a network. It allows one to create both simple and advanced DNNs using the Sequential model.

3.4 UAVIDS-2025

At present, the many of proposed ML-based NIDS favor flow-based data over packet-based alternatives, owing to the richer perspective it affords on network activity [12,33]. Several flow-based standards have emerged in this space, among them NetFlow, IP Flow Information eXport (IPFIX), sFlow, and OpenFlow. The term 'Flow' itself denotes an aggregation of IP packets traversing a designated capture point within a network over a defined time interval, wherein the constituent packets share a common set of properties [9]. As outlined in [18], flow-based data carries a number of advantages, as it is well-suited to high-speed network environments and benefits from already broad real-world deployment.

UAVIDS-2025 [45,46] is a benchmark dataset compiled to evaluate intrusion detection systems (IDS) in swarm networks of UAV. This dataset was generated based on simulations using the NS-3.24 network simulation. Realistic UAV mobility was ensured here through the use of an extended BOID [45] algorithm. The entire dataset contains over 120 000 records across five different categories of network traffic. These include traffic types such as: normal flow, blackhole, flooding, sybil, and wormhole attacks. Each traffic sample contains 22 features, which are grouped by connections, traffic intensity, and performance metrics.

3.5 Standard Scaler

The Standard Scaler [31] operates by subtracting the feature mean from each data point, thereby centering the distribution around zero, followed by division by the standard deviation to yield unit variance [30]. This transformation is formally expressed in Eq. 1, where X_{scaled} denotes the resulting standardized value, X represents the original observation, μ corresponds to the mean of the respective feature, and σ denotes its standard deviation.

$$X_{\text{scaled}} = \frac{X - \mu}{\sigma} \tag{1}$$

4 Experimental Setup

This section presents the employed framework, including the pipeline, the environment, the applied preprocessing and the ML models.

4.1 Research Pipeline

The procedure followed in the study is illustrated in Fig. 1. The process starts by loading the data from the UAVIDS-2025 files, processing them by removing duplicate records, removing rows with missing and NaN values, removing malformed entries such as infinite values, dropping constant-value features, label encoding categorical features, standard-scaling the features, undersampling the majority benign class, and stratified splitting into train/test sets, and then training the three ML models. In the final stage, the performance of the models was evaluated using the standard IDS detection metrics.

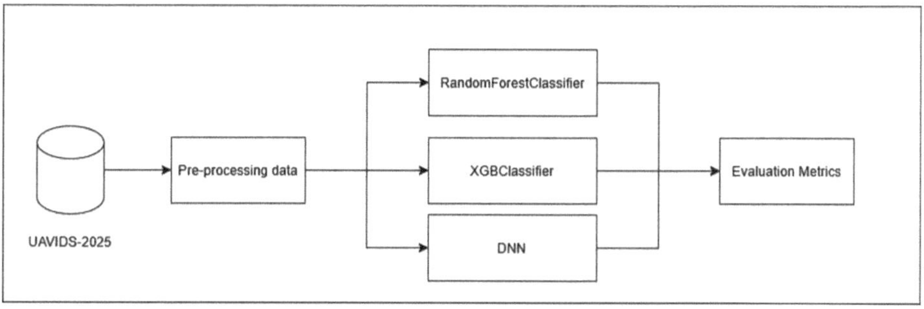

Fig. 1. The Research Pipeline

4.2 Environment

All experiments were performed on Windows version 10.0.26200, build 26200. The implementation was carried out using Python version 3.10 and the following libraries: pandas v2.3.3, scikit-learn v.1.7.2, xgboost v3.2.0, numpy v2.2.6, and tensorflow v2.21.0. The computer specifications were as follows: i7-12650H processor, 64GB RAM, RTX 4070 Laptop GPU.

4.3 Data Preprocessing

Apart from the preprocessing steps described earlier, feature selection was performed.

The FlowID, SrcAddr, DstAddr, and Protocol columns were discarded. The dataset was split in an 80/20 ratio into training and test data.

5 Results

The three different models were trained and tested with the same splits of the dataset. The first was the RandomForestClassifier, which was trained using the

Table 2. Classification results for individual traffic types and attacks for the RandomForestClassifier model

Class	Precision	Recall	F1-score
Blackhole Attack	0.92	0.87	0.90
Flooding Attack	1.00	0.99	0.99
Normal Traffic	0.99	0.99	0.99
Sybil Attack	0.99	1.00	1.00
Wormhole Attack	0.87	0.92	0.89
Accuracy			0.95
Macro avg	0.95	0.95	0.95
Weighted avg	0.95	0.95	0.95

Table 3. Classification results for individual traffic types and attacks for the XGB-Classifier model

Class	Precision	Recall	F1-score
Blackhole Attack	0.95	0.86	0.91
Flooding Attack	0.99	0.99	0.99
Normal Traffic	0.99	0.99	0.99
Sybil Attack	0.99	1.00	1.00
Wormhole Attack	0.87	0.95	0.90
Accuracy			0.96
Macro avg	0.96	0.96	0.96
Weighted avg	0.96	0.96	0.96

Table 4. Hyperparameters of the DNN model

Hyperparameter	Value
Architecture	Fully-connected DNN
Number of layers	3 (1 input + 1 hidden + 1 output)
Input Layer	32 neurons, ReLU, input shape (18,)
Hidden Layer 1	16 neurons, ReLU
Output Layer	5 neurons, Softmax
Optimizer	Adam
Learning rate	0.001
Loss function	Sparse categorical cross-entropy
Batch size	32
Epochs	10

default parameters for this model, except for the 'random_state' parameter, which was set to 42 to ensure reproducibility of the results. The model training result are presented in Table 2.

The second model was XGBClassifier, which, like the previous model, was trained using default parameters, except for the 'random_state' parameter, which was again set to 42 for the same reasons. The training results for this model are presented in Table 3.

The final model was a simple DNN. It consisted of 3 layers. The hyperparameter setup is disclosed in Table 4

The Adam optimizer was used for its training. The results of this model are presented in Table 5.

The classification results presented in Tables 2, 3, and 5 showcase that the evaluated models achieve strong performance on the UAVIDS-2025 dataset. The reported results are obtained with default hyperparameters and without substantial feature engineering, establishing that both ML is a suitable approach

Table 5. Classification results for individual traffic types and attacks for the DNN model

Class	Precision	Recall	F1-score
Blackhole Attack	0.92	0.85	0.88
Flooding Attack	0.95	0.93	0.94
Normal Traffic	0.98	0.97	0.98
Sybil Attack	0.95	0.95	0.95
Wormhole Attack	0.82	0.91	0.86
Accuracy			0.92
Macro avg	0.93	0.92	0.92
Weighted avg	0.92	0.92	0.92

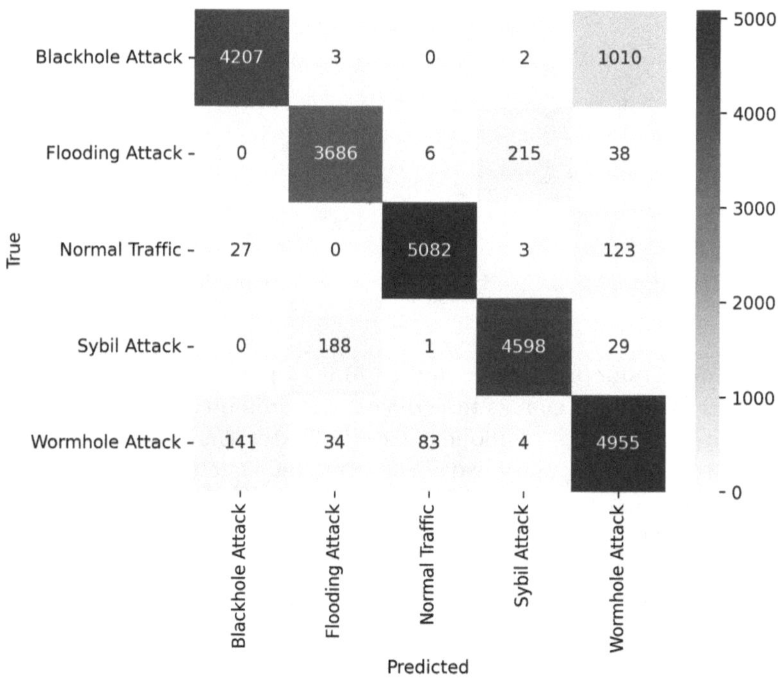

Fig. 2. Confusion Matrix for DNN model

for detecting attacks on UAV infrastructure and that the dataset is suitable for training ML models, answering **RQ1** and **RQ2**. The top performing model was XGBoost, as seen in Table 3, outperforming RF (Table 2). The DNN model came in third, as seen in Table 5. This is consistent with prior findings from NIDS literature, where tree-based ensembles tend to outperform DNNs on tabular flow-level features [30]. The pattern emerging from the results contained in Tables 2, 3, and 5 is consistent across the three models, pointing to Sybil, Flood-

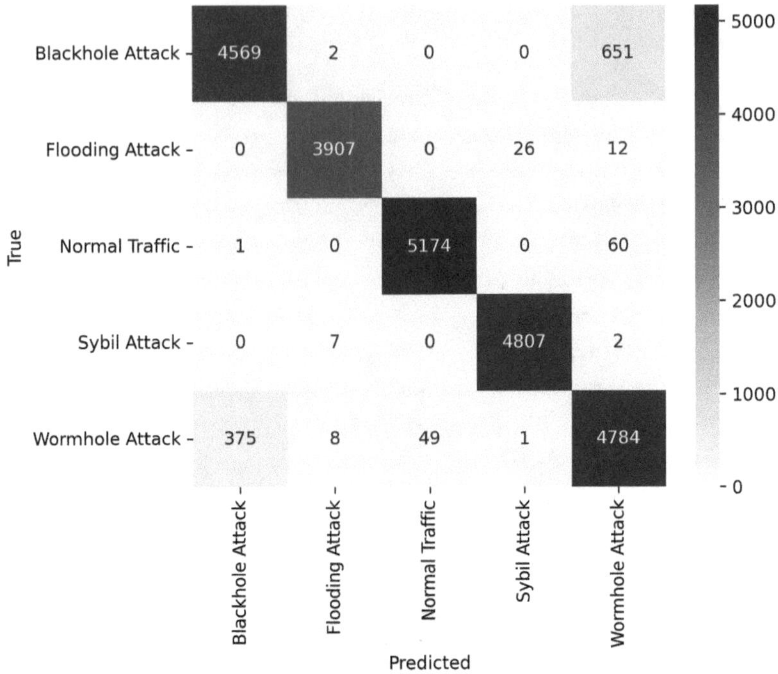

Fig. 3. Confusion Matrix for RF model

ing and Normal Traffic being detected at almost perfect performance, whereas Blackhole and Wormhole classes introduce some difficulty, with F1-scores in the 0.86–0.91 range regardless of model. This indicates that the limitation is not attributable to model capacity, rather to the fact that the current feature set does not allow to clearly distinguish between the classes. The confusion matrices in Figs. 3, 4, and 2 confirm and quantify this interpretation. Across all three classifiers, Blackhole instances were classified as Wormhole and the other way round. Together, these two off-diagonal cells account for the overwhelming majority of all misclassifications. This also explains the recall deficit on the Blackhole class and the precision deficit on the Wormhole class observed in Tables 2 and 3. With respect to**RQ3**, the detection metrics reported in Tables 2 to 5 establish a quantitative baseline for the dataset, the Blackhole/Wormhole separation remains an open challenge that will likely require enriched feature representations.

It can be concluded that the dataset used contains the appropriate features for the accurate identification of many attacks on UAVs.

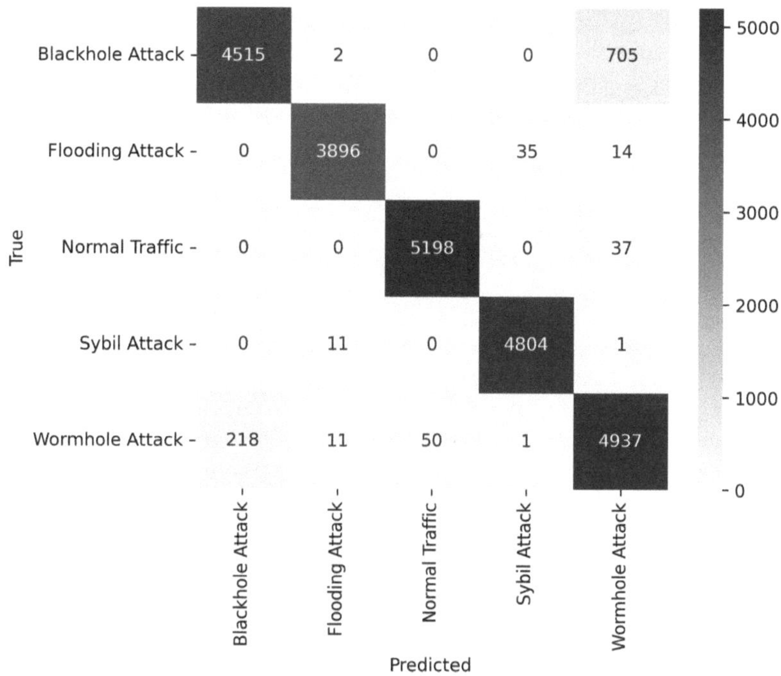

Fig. 4. Confusion Matrix for XGB model

6 Discussion and Conclusions

In today's world, where UAVs are playing an increasingly significant role both on the battlefield and in people's daily lives, it is important to emphasise the need to adequately protect these devices from cyberattacks. Due to the novelty of this challenge, the amount of available data from such devices is limited for researchers. This work has presented an empirical evaluation of UAVIDS-2025, a recently published flow-level benchmark for intrusion detection in UAV swarm networks. The three classifiers examined, XGBoost, RF and DNN, were trained with default hyperparameters and evaluated on a stratified hold-out split of the dataset. The findings support affirmative answers to **RQ1** and **RQ2**, and the reported metrics constitute an answer to **RQ3**.

Acknowledgement. This research is funded under the HARPIA-DEFENCE Project, which has received funding from the EUROPEAN DEFENCE FUND (EDF) under Grant Agreement No. 101224172.

Competing Interests. The authors have no competing interests to declare that are relevant to the content of this article.

References

1. Arthur, M.P.: Detecting signal spoofing and jamming attacks in UAV networks using a lightweight ids. In: 2019 International Conference on Computer, Information and Telecommunication Systems (CITS), pp. 1–5. IEEE (2019)
2. Biau, G.: Analysis of a random forests model. J. Mach. Learn. Res. **13**(null), 1063–1095 (2012)
3. Breiman, L., Friedman, J., Stone, C., Olshen, R.: Classification and Regression Trees. Taylor & Francis (1984). https://books.google.pl/books?id=JwQx-WOmSyQC
4. Breiman, L.: Random forests. Mach. Learn. **45**(1), 5–32 (2001)
5. Burbank, J., Caleb, T., Andam, E., Kaabouch, N.: Detection and mitigation of cyber attacks on UAV networks. Electronics **15**(2) (2026). https://doi.org/10.3390/electronics15020317, https://www.mdpi.com/2079-9292/15/2/317
6. Business Insider: drug traffickers are hacking us border drones (2015). https://www.businessinsider.com/drug-traffickers-are-hacking-us-border-drones-2015-12
7. Chen, T., Guestrin, C.: XGBoost: a scalable tree boosting system. In: Proceedings of the 22nd ACM SIGKDD International Conference on Knowledge Discovery and Data Mining, pp. 785–794 (2016)
8. Chou, D., Jiang, M.: Data-driven network intrusion detection: a taxonomy of challenges and methods (2020). arXiv preprint arXiv:2009.07352
9. Claise, B., Bryant, S.: Specification of the IP flow information export (IPFIX) protocol for the exchange of IP traffic flow information. RFC 5101. Tech. rep (2008)
10. Euronews: lost and spoofed: how Ukraine redirects Russian drones to belarus (2024). https://www.euronews.com/my-europe/2024/12/04/lost-and-spoofed-how-ukraine-redirects-russian-drones-to-belarus
11. Friedman, J.H.: Greedy function approximation: a gradient boosting machine. Ann. Stat., 1189–1232 (2001)
12. Ghafir, I., Prenosil, V., Svoboda, J., Hammoudeh, M.: A survey on network security monitoring systems. In: IEEE 4th International Conference on Future Internet of Things and Cloud Workshops (FiCloudW), pp. 77–82 (2016)
13. Goller, C., Kuchler, A.: Learning task-dependent distributed representations by backpropagation through structure. In: Proceedings of International Conference on Neural Networks (ICNN'96), vol. 1, pp. 347–352 (1996)
14. Hambling, D.: Ukraine's pokrova spoofing system tells shaheds to get lost (2024). https://www.forbes.com/sites/davidhambling/2024/02/12/ukraines-pokrova-spoofing-system-tells-shaheds-to-get-lost/
15. Hartmann, K., Steup, C.: The vulnerability of UAVs to cyber attacks-an approach to the risk assessment. In: 2013 5th International Conference on Cyber Conflict (CYCON 2013), pp. 1–23. IEEE (2013)
16. Ho, T.K.: Random decision forests. In: Proceedings of 3rd International Conference on Document Analysis and Recognition, vol. 1, pp. 278–282. IEEE (1995)
17. Hoerl, A.E., Kennard, R.W.: Ridge regression: Biased estimation for nonorthogonal problems. Technometrics **12**(1), 55–67 (1970)
18. Hofstede, R., et al.: Flow monitoring explained: from packet capture to data analysis with NetFlow and IPFIX. IEEE Commun. Surv. Tutorials **16**, 2037–2064 (2014)
19. Jhanjhi, N.U.A., et al.: The rise of GPS spoofing attacks on drones in the Russia-Ukraine war. Authorea Preprints (2025)

20. Karmakar, G., Petty, M., Ahmed, H., Das, R., Kamruzzaman, J.: Security of internet of things devices: ethical hacking a drone and its mitigation strategies. In: 2022 IEEE Asia-Pacific Conference on Computer Science and Data Engineering (CSDE), pp. 1–5. IEEE (2022)
21. Keller, J.: Iran–U.S. RQ-170 incident has defense industry saying 'never again' to unmanned vehicle hacking (2016). https://tinyurl.com/4eyyn66u
22. Komisarek, M., Pawlicki, M., Kozik, R., Choras, M.: Machine learning based approach to anomaly and cyberattack detection in streamed network traffic data. J. Wirel. Mob. Networks Ubiquitous Comput. Dependable Appl **12**(1), 3–19 (2021)
23. LeCun, Y., Bengio, Y., Hinton, G.: Deep learning. Nature **521**(7553), 436–444 (2015)
24. Magán-Carrión, R., Urda, D., Díaz-Cano, I., Dorronsoro, B.: Towards a reliable comparison and evaluation of network intrusion detection systems based on machine learning approaches. Appl. Sci. **10**(5), 1775 (2020)
25. Mahfouz, A.M., Venugopal, D., Shiva, S.G.: Comparative analysis of ml classifiers for network intrusion detection. In: Fourth International Congress on Information and Communication Technology, pp. 193–207. Springer, Singapore (2020). https://doi.org/10.1007/978-981-32-9343-4_16
26. Maimon, O., Rokach, L.: Data Mining and Knowledge Discovery Handbook, 2nd ed.(2010)
27. Pawlicka, A., Choraś, M., Pawlicki, M.: Cyberspace threats: not only hackers and criminals. raising the awareness of selected unusual cyberspace actors-cybersecurity researchers' perspective. In: Proceedings of the 15th International Conference on Availability, Reliability and Security, pp. 1–11 (2020)
28. Pawlicki, M., Choraś, M., Kozik, R., Hołubowicz, W.: On the impact of network data balancing in cybersecurity applications. In: Computational Science–ICCS 2020: 20th International Conference, Amsterdam, The Netherlands, June 3–5, 2020, Proceedings, Part IV 20, pp. 196–210. Springer, Cham (2020). https://doi.org/10.1007/978-3-030-50423-6_15
29. Pawlicki, M., Kozik, R., Choraś, M.: Artificial neural network hyperparameter optimisation for network intrusion detection. In: International Conference on Intelligent Computing, pp. 749–760. Springer, Cham (2019). https://doi.org/10.1007/978-3-030-26763-6_72
30. Pawlicki, M., Kozik, R., Choraś, M.: The impact of data scaling approaches on deep learning, random forest and nearest neighbour-based network intrusion detection systems for dos detection in IoT networks. In: International Conference on Mobile Internet Security, pp. 197–208. Springer, Singapore (2023). https://doi.org/10.1007/978-981-97-4465-7_14
31. Pedregosa, F., et al.: Scikit-Learn: machine learning in Python. J. Mach. Learn. Res. **12**, 2825–2830 (2011)
32. da Silva, I.N., Hernane Spatti, D., Andrade Flauzino, R., Liboni, L.H.B., dos Reis Alves, S.F.: Artificial Neural Networks. Springer, Cham (2017). https://doi.org/10.1007/978-3-319-43162-8
33. Ring, M., Wunderlich, S., Scheuring, D., Landes, D., Hotho, A.: A survey of network-based intrusion detection data sets. Comput. Secur. **86**, 147–167 (2019)
34. Ryan, J., Lin, M.J., Miikkulainen, R.: Intrusion detection with neural networks. In: Advances in Neural Information Processing Systems, pp. 943–949 (1998)
35. Schmidhuber, J.: Deep learning in neural networks: an overview. Neural Netw. **61**, 85–117 (2015)

36. Schonlau, M., Zou, R.Y.: The random forest algorithm for statistical learning. Stand Genomic Sci. **20**(1), 3–29 (2020). https://doi.org/10.1177/1536867X20909688
37. Sharma, I., Kaushik, K., Chhabra, G.: Investigating patterns of UAV attacks for building secure UAV network. In: 2023 6th International Conference on Contemporary Computing and Informatics (IC3I), vol. 6, pp. 136–141. IEEE (2023)
38. Sharma, V., Choudhary, G., Ko, Y., You, I.: Behavior and vulnerability assessment of drones-enabled industrial internet of things (IIoT). IEEE Access **6**, 43368–43383 (2018)
39. Shashok, N.: Analysis of Vulnerabilities in Modern Unmanned Aircraft Systems, pp. 1–10. Tuft University (2017)
40. Shepard, D.P., Bhatti, J.A., Humphreys, T.E., Fansler, A.A.: Evaluation of smart grid and civilian UAV vulnerability to GPS spoofing attacks. In: Proceedings of the 25th International Technical Meeting of the Satellite Division of the Institute of Navigation, pp. 3591–3605. (2012) ION GNSS 2012
41. Srimoungchanh, B., Morris, J.G., Davidson, D.: Assessing UAV sensor spoofing: more than a GNSS problem. In: 2024 Annual Computer Security Applications Conference (ACSAC), pp. 1032–1046. IEEE (2024)
42. Tibshirani, R.: Regression shrinkage and selection via the lasso. J. R. Stat. Soc. Ser. B Stat Methodol. **58**(1), 267–288 (1996)
43. Vormayr, G., Fabini, J., Zseby, T.: Why are my flows different? A tutorial on flow exporters. IEEE Commun. Surv. Tutorials **22**, 2064–2103 (2020)
44. Westerlund, O., Asif, R.: Drone hacking with raspberry-pi 3 and WiFi pineapple: security and privacy threats for the internet-of-things. In: 2019 1st International Conference on Unmanned Vehicle Systems-Oman (UVS), pp. 1–10. IEEE (2019)
45. Zeng, Q., Bashir, A., Nait-Abdesselam, F.: Uavids-2025: a benchmark dataset for intrusion detection in UAV networks using machine learning techniques. In: 2025 IEEE Conference on Communications and Network Security (CNS), pp. 1–9. IEEE (2025)
46. Zeng, Q., Fu, Y., Nait-Abdesselam, F.: FedGraph-id: a federated graph learning framework for intrusion detection in UAV networks under adversarial settings. In: IEEE INFOCOM 2026-IEEE Conference on Computer Communications, IEEE (2026)

Experimental Analysis of Authentication-Based Privacy Leakage in 5G SA

Hamza Ahmed Farah[1(✉)], Azza H. Ahmed[1,2(✉)], and Thomas Dreibholz[2]

[1] Oslo Metropolitan University, Oslo, Norway
hamza.a.m.farah@gmail.com
[2] Simula Metropolitan Centre for Digital Engineering, Oslo, Norway
azzahass@oslomet.no dreibh@simula.no

Abstract. 5G Standalone (SA) networks introduce the Subscriber Concealed Identifier (SUCI) and the 5G Authentication and Key Agreement (5G-AKA) protocol to eliminate the plaintext identity exposure of earlier generations. However, privacy leakage can persist through observable protocol behaviour rather than exposed identifiers. This paper presents an experimental evaluation of two such attack classes—the *SUCI-catcher* and the *SQN inference attack*—implemented as a transparent N2-interface proxy on a fully virtualised, 3GPP Release 16-compliant testbed built on OpenAirInterface, UERANSIM, and a custom NGAP proxy. The SUCI-catcher exploits the binary outcome of the 5G-AKA challenge-response exchange as a presence oracle, successfully recording SUCIs from six subscribers and confirming target presence without recovering any keying material, weakening location privacy and unlinkability in a controlled virtualised environment. The SQN inference attack recovers subscriber sequence-number bits through controlled synchronisation failures, accurately inferring 8 bits of *SQN* verified against ground-truth core network state, and demonstrating that SQN changes between observations track subscriber activity, weakening undetectability in a controlled virtualised environment. Both attacks share a structural dependency on abusing core-network authentication-vector generation. Operator-level rate-limiting and anomaly detection are identified as near-term mitigations; long-term protection requires protocol-level changes to 5G-AKA.

Keywords: 5G Networks · Privacy Attacks · Authentication Security · Subscriber Tracking · Protocol Vulnerability · Experimental Security Analysis

1 Introduction

Fifth-generation mobile networks have become critical infrastructure for mobile broadband, IoT, and industrial services worldwide [16,17]. Because these networks carry sensitive subscriber data, privacy is a fundamental requirement

P. Kieseberg et al. (Eds.): ARES 2026 Workshops, LNCS 16903, pp. 289–307, 2027.
https://doi.org/10.1007/978-3-032-37218-5_18

addressed in 3GPP Release 15 [11]. Earlier generations exposed the permanent *International Mobile Subscriber Identity* (IMSI) in plaintext, enabling IMSI-catcher attacks [10]. 5G Stand-Alone (SA) addresses this with the *Subscriber Concealed Identifier* (SUCI), which encrypts the permanent identifier, and the improved *5G Authentication and Key Agreement* (5G-AKA) protocol [4,11,14].

Despite these protections, privacy in 5G depends not only on cryptographic strength but also on protocol behaviour. Observable message exchanges—registration requests, authentication challenges, and synchronisation failures—can expose subscriber information without revealing the permanent identifier. Two attack classes exploit this property.

The *SUCI-catcher* [3,6,8] conventionally operates as a rogue base station. In this work we implement an equivalent capability via an N2-interface proxy—a transparent man-in-the-middle between a legitimate gNB and the Access and Mobility Management Function (AMF)—achieving the same SUCI substitution without radio hardware, making the implementation faster and more reproducible. A known SUCI is injected into a live Registration Request; the UE's binary response (Authentication Response or MAC Failure) confirms or denies subscriber presence, weakening location privacy and unlinkability.

The *SQN inference attack* [5,7] recovers bits of SQN_{UE} by XOR-cancelling the anonymity key across two AUTS resynchronisation responses collected under the same RAND. Because the SQN encodes cumulative authentication events, inferred SQN changes between observations reveal subscriber activity, weakening undetectability. This attack was theorised for 5G SA [5] but had not been experimentally validated prior to this work.

Both attacks have been individually studied [5,8,13], but no prior work provides a joint evaluation within the same 5G SA testbed [3,9]. This paper addresses that gap using a fully virtualised, 3GPP Release 16-based environment: OpenAirInterface (OAI) core network, UERANSIM, and a custom N2 proxy.

Our contributions.

- *First experimental validation* of the SQN inference attack in a 5G SA environment, with ground-truth verification against the OAI core.
- Experimental confirmation of the SUCI-catcher covering SUCI recording, presence confirmation, and multi-subscriber probing.
- Comparative analysis of both attacks against the 5G privacy model—unlinkability, undetectability, and behavioural privacy.
- Identification of practical operator-level and protocol-level mitigations.

Paper organization. First, Sects. 2–4 cover background, related work, and the threat model. In the following, Sect. 5 describes the testbed and implementation. After that, Sect. 6 presents results. Finally, Sects. 7–8 discuss countermeasures, limitations, and conclude.

2 Background

This section introduces the 5G Standalone architecture, the subscriber identity mechanisms, and the 5G-AKA authentication protocol to the extent required to understand the two attacks evaluated in this paper.

2.1 5G Standalone Architecture

5G is defined by the 3GPP under the ITU IMT-2020 framework, with the first New Radio (NR) specification completed in Release 15 (2019) [17]. Early deployments operate as *Non-Standalone* (NSA), anchoring the 5G radio to existing 4G LTE infrastructure. The focus of this paper is *5G Standalone* (SA), in which a native 5G Core (5GC) independently manages both the control plane and the user plane alongside 5G NR.

The 5GC adopts a *Service-Based Architecture* (SBA) in which modular *Network Functions* (NFs) communicate via REST APIs over HTTP/2, as standardised in the Common API Framework (CAPIF) [11]. Control- and user-plane traffic are separated (CUPS): the *User Plane Function* (UPF) forwards data packets, while the control plane is handled by the following NFs relevant to authentication:

- **AMF** (Access and Mobility Management Function)—terminates Non-Access Stratum (NAS) signalling from the UE and initiates authentication procedures.
- **AUSF** (Authentication Server Function)—validates UE credentials, derives serving-network anchor keys, and interfaces with the home network.
- **UDM/ARPF** (Unified Data Management / Authentication Credential Repository and Processing Function)—holds the home-network private key for SUCI decryption and stores long-term subscriber credentials mirrored on the USIM.
- **SEAF** (Security Anchor Function)—acts as the security-context holder during authentication; holds the root anchor key for visited networks.

The radio access side is provided by the *next-generation base station* (gNB), which splits into a *Centralised Unit* (CU) handling non-real-time protocols and a *Distributed Unit* (DU) for physical-layer and real-time functions. *User Equipment* (UE) consists of *Mobile Equipment* (ME) and a tamper-proof *Universal Subscriber Identity Module* (USIM) stored on a *Universal Integrated Circuit Card* (UICC). The USIM stores the long-term secret key and performs authentication functions, acting as the ultimate trust anchor for the subscriber.

2.2 Subscriber Identity and SUCI

Every 5G subscriber is identified by a *Subscriber Unique Permanent Identifier* (SUPI), equivalent to the legacy IMSI. To prevent the plaintext-IMSI exposure that plagued earlier generations, the USIM conceals the SUPI before any over-the-air transmission, using the *Subscriber Concealed Identifier* (SUCI) [11].

The SUCI is a structured field composed of: *SUPI Type*, *Home Network ID* consisting of Mobile Country Code (MCC) and Mobile Network Code (MNC), *Routing Indicator*, *Protection Scheme ID*, *Home Network Public Key ID*, and a *Scheme Output*. When a non-null protection scheme is active, the scheme output is produced using the *Elliptic Curve Integrated Encryption Scheme* (ECIES): the UE generates an ephemeral key pair, encrypts the MSIN (the subscriber-specific portion of the SUPI) with the home network's public key, and appends a MAC tag. Only the home network's UDM can reverse this using its private key via the *Subscription Identifier De-concealment Function* (SIDF).

The SUCI therefore changes with every registration—providing pseudonymity—but its static fields (Home Network ID, Routing Indicator) remain constant across registrations. Although the scheme outputs are unique, the decrypted content remains identical, a property exploited by the SUCI-catcher attack described in Subsect. 5.3.

2.3 5G-AKA Authentication Protocol

The gNB connects to the AMF via the *N2 interface*, carrying NGAP (Next-Generation Application Protocol) signalling using the Stream Control Transmission Protocol (SCTP) over IP [18]. Key N2 messages include the *Initial UE Message* (delivers the NAS Registration Request, containing the SUCI, from the UE to the AMF) and *Downlink / Uplink NAS Transport* (carries subsequent NAS exchanges). NAS itself is divided into 5G Mobility Management (5GMM), which handles authentication and registration, and 5G Session Management (5GSM).

3GPP defines three UE authentication methods: 5G-AKA, EAP-AKA′, and EAP-TLS [11]. This paper focuses on 5G-AKA, the primary method for 5G SA, which involves four entities: the UE, the SEAF, the AUSF, and the UDM/ARPF. The protocol, illustrated in Fig. 1, proceeds as follows:

1. **HE AV Generation.** The UDM/ARPF generates a 5G Home Environment Authentication Vector (HE AV) comprising a random challenge ($RAND$), an authentication token ($AUTN$), an expected response ($XRES^*$), and a home-network anchor key (K_{AUSF}).
2. **SUCI Decoding.** The SIDF at the UDM decrypts the SUCI, revealing the SUPI, which is included in the response to the AUSF.
3. **5G AV Derivation.** The AUSF transforms the HE AV into a Serving-network AV by deriving K_{SEAF} from K_{AUSF} and $HXRES^*$ from $XRES^*$.
4. **Authentication Request.** The SEAF forwards $RAND$ and $AUTN$ to the UE inside a NAS Authentication Request message.
5. **UE Challenge Response.** The USIM verifies the freshness of $AUTN$. If valid, it computes a response (RES) and the ME derives RES^*, K_{SEAF}, and K_{AUSF} locally. The UE returns RES^* in an Authentication Response.
6. **Verification.** The SEAF hashes RES^* and compares it with $HXRES^*$; the AUSF compares RES^* with $XRES^*$. Agreement indicates successful mutual authentication.

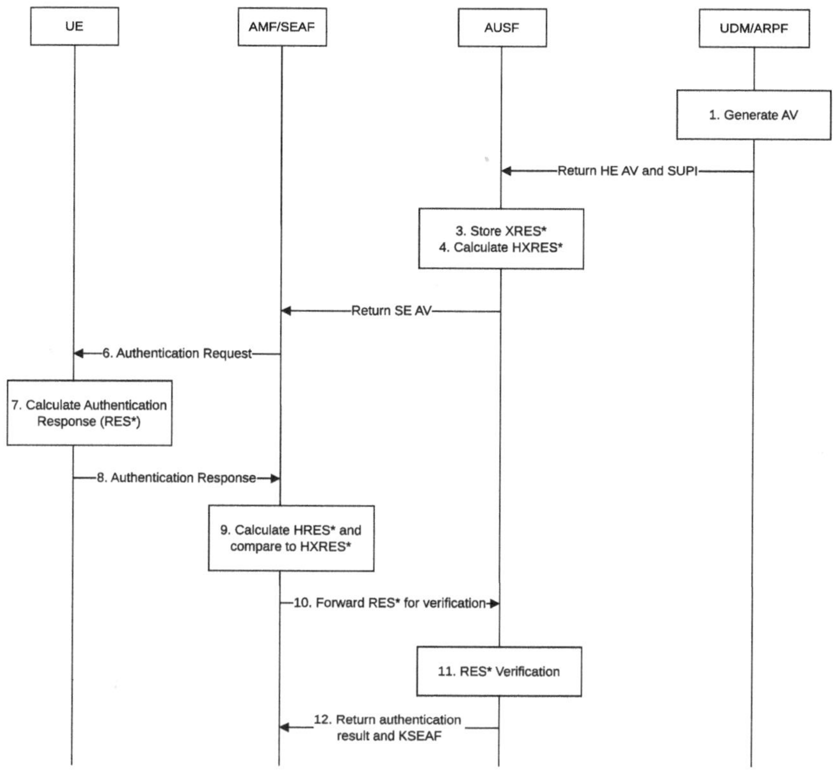

Fig. 1. 5G-AKA protocol overview (based on 3GPP TS 33.501 [11]).

7. **Activation.** The AUSF delivers K_{SEAF} to the SEAF, which derives K_{AMF}. The AMF initiates a NAS Security Mode Command, establishing an encrypted and integrity-protected NAS channel.

If the AUSF or SEAF verification of RES^* fails, the SEAF either rejects the authentication or requests a fresh SUCI via an Identity Request. If the USIM's verification of $AUTN$ fails, the UE sends an *Authentication Failure* whose cause distinguishes two cases relevant to the attacks in this paper: a *MAC failure* (challenge bound to a different subscriber, no AUTS parameter) and a *Synchronization Failure* (stale SQN, accompanied by the AUTS resynchronization parameter described below).

2.4 Sequence Number Mechanism

The AKA *Sequence Number* (SQN) is a 48-bit counter used for replay protection [5]. It comprises a 43-bit sequence counter (*SEQ*) and a 5-bit serving-network index (*IND*). The home network maintains SQN_{HN} and increments it after each successful authentication; the UE maintains SQN_{UE}, updated to match SQN_{HN} upon every successful challenge response.

The SQN is not transmitted in plaintext. Instead, $AUTN$ includes a concealed value:

$$CONC = SQN_{HN} \oplus AK, \tag{1}$$

where the *Anonymity Key* $AK = f_5(R, K_{\text{IMSI}})$ is derived from the challenge random value R and the subscriber's long-term shared key. Upon receiving $AUTN$, the UE recomputes AK from the same R and recovers $SQN_{HN} = CONC \oplus AK$.

The UE then checks freshness: authentication proceeds only if $SQN_{HN} > SQN_{UE}$ and $SQN_{HN} \leq SQN_{UE} + \Delta$, where Δ is an operator-configured acceptance window. If this check fails, the UE sends an Authentication Failure with cause `Sync Failure`, including an $AUTS$ resynchronization parameter:

$$AUTS = \langle\, SQN_{UE} \oplus AK,\ MAC^* \,\rangle, \tag{2}$$

which allows the home network to re-synchronise SQN_{HN} to SQN_{UE}.

The critical observation for the SQN inference attack is that, when the same R is reused in two replayed challenges, the anonymity key AK is identical in both AUTS responses. XOR-ing the two $CONC$ values therefore cancels AK:

$$CONC_1 \oplus CONC_2 = (SQN_{UE} \oplus AK) \oplus (SQN'_{UE} \oplus AK) = SQN_{UE} \oplus SQN'_{UE}, \tag{3}$$

leaking the difference between two SQN states and enabling bit-by-bit inference of SQN_{UE}, as detailed in Sect. 3.

3 Related Work

The *IMSI-catcher* is a well-documented attack spanning 2G, 3G, and 4G networks [10]. The attack deploys a rogue base station that attracts nearby UEs by broadcasting a stronger signal than the legitimate network. Once the UE associates with the rogue station, the attacker sends an Identity Request or awaits a Registration Request; because earlier generations transmit the IMSI in plaintext, the UE transmits with the IMSI directly. This enables persistent tracking and linkability of a Person of Interest (POI) without any cryptographic capability on the attacker's side.

Hussain et al. [12] demonstrated a systematic, model-based approach to uncovering pre-authentication vulnerabilities in 4G LTE with LTEInspector, identifying several protocol-level weaknesses that persist even with partial encryption. 5G SA was designed to close the IMSI exposure vector by replacing plaintext IMSI transmission with SUCI concealment, motivating the evolution to the SUCI-catcher class of attacks described below.

The SUCI-catcher exploits a logical vulnerability in 5G-AKA: initial NAS signalling messages are transmitted before the NAS Security Mode Command establishes encryption and integrity protection. Although SUCI prevents direct SUPI exposure, it does not prevent an adversary from *linking* a SUCI to a specific subscriber through the authentication protocol's response behaviour [8].

The attack operates in two phases. During the *discovery phase*, the adversary obtains a SUCI associated with the target subscriber, either by passively sniffing a prior Registration Request or by computing a SUCI from a known SUPI using the home network's public key. During the *attack phase*, the adversary operates a rogue gNB or an N2 proxy, intercepts a live Registration Request, replaces the SUCI with the previously recorded one, and forwards it to the core network. The network issues an authentication challenge bound to the target subscriber. The UE's response reveals its identity: an *Authentication Response* confirms that the UE owns the injected SUCI; an *Authentication Failure* with MAC cause indicates it does not.

Chlosta et al. [8] introduced the foundational SUCI-catcher, proving experimentally that SUCI concealment alone does not guarantee unlinkability, anonymity, or undetectability. The paper also characterises the *Reset & Sync* mechanism and evaluates a multi-POI probing scenario in a lab environment. Cabrera and Gallego [6] extended the attack to commercial deployments in Germany, the UK, and Spain via the SUCI-Cracker variant, which leverages a 4G discovery phase to obtain subscriber-specific authentication material for use in the 5G probing phase. Barraud et al. [3] implemented the attack in an open-source 5G testbed and shifted focus to *detection*, proposing rule-based detection of registration-request spikes and ML-based anomaly classification. A complementary protocol fix, 5G-AKA′, was proposed by Wang et al. [20]: it applies ECIES to encrypt portions of the authentication challenge, rendering replayed challenges indistinguishable to the UE and removing the observable response difference the SUCI-catcher relies upon.

Collectively, the existing literature shows that SUCI-catcher attacks are technically feasible and applicable to commercial 5G SA deployments. However, prior work focuses primarily on the attack mechanism, protocol behaviour, and detection; less attention has been paid to systematically evaluating which 5G privacy properties are violated in a controlled experimental environment.

The SQN inference attack exploits the synchronization-failure mechanism to recover bits of the subscriber's sequence counter. When the same RAND is reused across two replayed challenges, AK is identical in both AUTS responses; XOR-ing the two concealed values cancels AK, exposing the XOR of two SQN states (Eq. 3).

Borgaonkar et al. [5] introduced and cryptographically analysed this vulnerability, validated it on a 4G environment, and noted that the attack is theoretically applicable to 5G SA under 3GPP Release 16 but did not provide experimental validation in 5G SA, leaving a gap between standard-level analysis and practical confirmation. Cheng and Shen [7] presented a concrete tracking scenario in an srsLTE testbed, demonstrating that inferred SQN changes can reveal subscriber presence and behaviour patterns, and proposed a countermeasure requiring the UE to generate a fresh RAND in the AUTS. Whereas the SUCI-catcher has been validated in real 5G SA deployments, the SQN inference attack has not been experimentally confirmed in a 5G SA environment prior to this work.

Several works analyse 5G-AKA through formal methods. Basin et al. [4] performed the first comprehensive formal verification using the Tamarin prover, confirming stronger identity-privacy guarantees than 4G-AKA while revealing that certain privacy properties depend on assumptions not stated in the standard. Koutsos [14] formally analysed unlinkability and anonymity, showing that residual linkability remains possible when an adversary can trigger observable protocol-state differences—precisely the mechanism exploited by both attacks in this paper. Hussain et al. [13] uncovered eleven design-level weaknesses in 5G control-plane protocols with 5GReasoner, several of which expose privacy-relevant information through side-channel responses akin to the synchronization-failure leakage studied here. Most recently, Eleftherakis et al. [9] systematised knowledge across all known 5G-Advanced privacy and security attacks, confirming that authentication-layer behavioural leakage remains an open problem in Release 18 and beyond.

Three gaps motivate this paper:

1. The SQN inference attack has been theorised but never experimentally validated in a 3GPP-compliant 5G SA environment.
2. No prior work provides a *joint* experimental evaluation of the SUCI-catcher and SQN inference attack in the same 5G SA testbed, preventing a direct comparison of preconditions, scalability, and privacy impact.
3. Existing implementations provide limited engineering detail on translating attack descriptions into working prototypes against standards-compliant 5G components, reducing reproducibility.

This paper addresses all three gaps through controlled experimentation in a fully virtualised 5G SA testbed, as described in Sect. 5.

4 Threat Model

4.1 Attacker Position

We consider an adversary positioned on the *N2 interface* between the gNB and the AMF, implemented as a transparent NGAP proxy. Figure 2 illustrates the architecture: The gNB is configured to direct its N2 connection to the proxy, which forwards all traffic to the legitimate AMF. The proxy operates exclusively on the N2 interface; all other core-network interfaces (N11, N4) and the user-plane interface (N3) remain unmodified.

This proxy position is equivalent to a *man-in-the-middle* on the N2 interface and is representative of a scenario in which an adversary has compromised the backhaul link between the base station and the core network [4,13]. Notably, the attacker does *not* require physical radio access or a rogue base station: the N2 proxy intercepts and manipulates NGAP signalling at the software level, making the attack more accessible than a rogue-gNB deployment.

4.2 Attacker Capabilities

The attacker is an *active* adversary with the following capabilities on the N2 interface:

- **Intercept**—read all NGAP messages, including NAS payloads encapsulated in Initial UE Message and Downlink/Uplink NAS Transport messages.
- **Modify**—alter NAS content before forwarding; specifically, replace the SUCI field in a Registration Request.
- **Replay**—retransmit captured NGAP messages, including Authentication Requests, to induce controlled UE responses (Authentication Response or Sync Failure). Also replay of Initial UE Message to collect Authentication Request for both attacks.
- **Delay**—hold messages temporarily to serialise or coordinate attack steps.

The attacker does *not* possess the subscriber's SUPI or long-term key, the home network's private key, or the ability to decrypt NAS traffic (which is protected only after the Security Mode Command—but all exploitable signals occur before this point). For the SUCI-catcher discovery phase, the attacker requires a previously captured SUCI or knowledge of the target's SUPI and the public home-network key. For the SQN inference attack, the attacker requires the ability to trigger repeated authentication interactions with the same UE.

4.3 Privacy Assets at Risk

3GPP TS 33.501 [11] defines five subscriber privacy properties that 5G SA is designed to enforce. Table 1 maps these properties to the two attacks.

Table 1. 5G privacy properties violated by each attack. ✓ = violated; – = not violated.

Privacy Property	SUCI-Catcher	SQN Inference
Identity privacy	–	–
Location privacy	✓	✓
Unlinkability	✓	✓
Undetectability	✓	✓
Behavioural privacy	–	✓

Identity privacy is not violated: neither attack recovers the SUPI. **Location privacy** is violated by both: confirming a subscriber is active at a gNB reveals cell-level location. **Unlinkability** is violated by both: the SUCI-catcher links a known SUCI to an active session; SQN tracking correlates successive observations. **Undetectability** is the primary goal of both attacks. **Behavioural privacy** is additionally broken by SQN inference: the SQN increments on each authentication event, so the inferred value between two observations reveals subscriber activity volume.

5 Testbed and Attack Implementation

5.1 Testbed Architecture

Figure 2 illustrates our testbed setup: The OpenAirInterface[1] (OAI) 5G-SA core is instantiated as containers in a virtual machine setup within a data centre. The components of the core basically use the upstream OAI implementation, with some debugging, monitoring, and maintenance tools added into the containers. A detailed description of this setup, including Git repository links of the implementation, is provided in [2]. Since the 5G-SA core is left unmodified, to mimic a "normal" 5G network provider, and just works as defined in the standard, we omit a detailed description here.

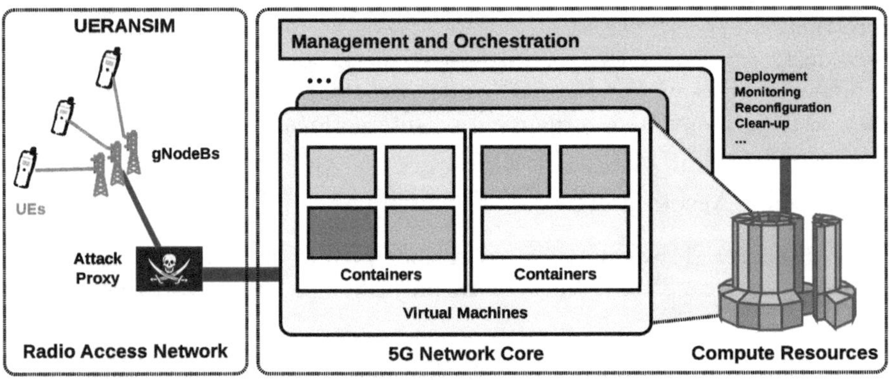

Fig. 2. The 5G testbed setup used for the attack evaluation.

Connected to the core is the RAN simulation setup using RANSIM. Since we do not need the actual RAN communication, the RAN part is also fully virtualised as container in another virtual machine. Particularly, the NGAP communication session between simulated gNB and 5G-SA core over SCTP is intercepted by the attack proxy.

5.2 N2 Proxy Design

The proxy runs on a `Python:3.11-slim` container, using mainly the library `pycrate` [15] with SCTP to read and send NGAP messages. This is based on architecture presented in related work, but no implementation could be found. The proxy maintains two concurrent SCTP associations—one towards the gNB and one towards the AMF—and decodes all NGAP PDUs before forwarding. Core capabilities include:

- **NGAP parsing**—full decoding to extract NAS-PDUs from Initial UE Message and NAS Transport containers.

[1] OpenAirInterface (OAI): https://openairinterface.org.

- **NAS field access**—extraction and replacement of individual NAS information elements, including the Mobile Identity field carrying the SUCI.
- **Message injection and replay**—holding, duplicating, or re-injecting captured NGAP messages in a controlled sequence.
- **Session state tracking**—per-UE context (SUCI, AMF-UE-NGAP-ID, RAN-UE-NGAP-ID) to correctly route modified messages.

A key implementation constraints are the NAS *T3560 timer* and UE fail attempt counter: consecutive invalid authentication challenges or timeout to complete registration cause the UE to stop responding [1]. Both attacks are required to stay within the time window given by the timeout setting. The SUCI-catcher therefore implements a *Reset & Sync* step—injecting one valid Authentication Request between rounds—to maintain the UE session.

5.3 SUCI-Catcher Implementation

Phase 1: Discovery. The proxy passively monitors uplink N2 traffic. Each Initial UE Message carries a NAS-PDU whose Mobile Identity field contains the SUCI. The proxy extracts and stores each observed SUCI with a timestamp and session identifiers, requiring no active interference.

Phase 2: Attack. When a new UE registers, the proxy intercepts the Initial UE Message, replaces the Mobile Identity with a stored target SUCI, re-encodes the NGAP PDU, and forwards it to the AMF. The AMF generates an Authentication Request bound to the target subscriber and sends it to the UE. The outcome is binary:

- **Authentication Response**—the challenge was valid for this UE; the target subscriber is present.
- **Authentication Failure (MAC cause)**—the challenge was not directed at this UE; the injected SUCI belongs to a different subscriber.

After each probe, a valid Authentication Request is injected to resynchronise the UE before the next round.

5.4 SQN Inference Implementation

The attack recovers the j-th bit of SQN_{UE} through XOR-cancellation of two controlled Sync Failure responses:

1. **Vector collection.** Trigger 2^j Registration Requests; the CN increments SQN_{HN} by 1 per round, producing 2^j fresh Authentication Requests.
2. **First valid exchange.** Forward $(RAND_0, AUTN_0)$ to the UE. The UE accepts and updates SQN_{UE} to SQN_{HN}.
3. **Forced failure.** Inject an Authentication Request with a fabricated RAND. The UE rejects it naturally via MAC failure, resetting its stored authentication state.

4. **Baseline Sync Failure.** Replay $(RAND_0, AUTN_0)$. The UE returns:

$$AUTS_0 = \langle\, SQN_{UE} \oplus AK_0,\ MAC_0^* \,\rangle$$

5. **Offset exchange.** Forward the stored Auth. Request with $SQN_{HN} + 2^j$; the UE accepts and updates SQN_{UE} to $SQN_{HN} + 2^j$.
6. **Forced failure.** Re-trigger authentication failure to prevent UE from accepting old data.
7. **Second Sync Failure.** Replay $(RAND_0, AUTN_0)$ again:

$$AUTS_1 = \langle\, (SQN_{UE} + 2^j) \oplus AK_0,\ MAC_1^* \,\rangle$$

8. **Bit recovery.** XOR the two $CONC^*$ values; AK_0 cancels, yielding:

$$CONC_0^* \oplus CONC_1^* = SQN_{UE} \oplus (SQN_{UE} + 2^j) \tag{4}$$

Carry propagation reveals whether bit j is 0 or 1.

Recovery cost grows as 2^n+ Authentication Requests for the first n bits, scaling exponentially with bit depth and bounded in practice by NAS timers and CN rate limits.

5.5 Experimental Scenarios

Scenarios 0–3 cover the SUCI-catcher, from passive recording through multi-target probing. Scenarios 4–5 cover the SQN inference attack, from bit recovery through activity tracking. Scenario 6 characterises the practical boundaries of both attacks under NAS timer and CN rate-limiting constraints. A summary of the scenarios is provided in Table 2.

Table 2. Experimental scenarios and their attack mapping.

No.	Scenario	Attack	Goal
0	Baseline Authentication	None	Verify testbed compliance
1	SUCI Recording	SUCI-catcher	Discovery feasibility
2	Single SUCI Replacement	SUCI-catcher	Presence confirmation
3	Multi-SUCI Probing	SUCI-catcher	Probing scalability
4	SQN Inference Attack	SQN inference	LSB recovery
5	Activity Tracking via SQN	SQN inference	Behavioural leakage
6	Scalability and Limits	Both	Attack boundaries

6 Experimental Results

All seven scenarios executed successfully on the testbed described in Subsect. 5.5. Table 3 summarises each scenario's primary outcome and privacy finding; the subsections below detail the key evidence.

Table 3. Summary of scenario outcomes.

No.	Primary outcome	Privacy finding
0	Baseline confirmed	5G-AKA / SUCI compliant
1	6/6 SUCIs recorded	Discovery phase feasible
2	Presence confirmed	Location privacy broken
3	POI found (probe 3)	Unlinkability broken
4	SEQ = 172 recovered	SQN inference feasible
5	ΔSEQ = 3 observed	Behavioural leakage confirmed
6	Incomplete at 11 bits	Bounded by NAS timers

6.1 Baseline Compliance and SUCI Recording (Scenarios 0–1)

Scenario 0. Without proxy interference, the complete 5G-AKA message sequence was observed in Wireshark, shown in Fig. 3. The Registration Request carried a correctly formed SUCI using ECIES scheme profile A (scheme 1), with the MSIN concealed under an ephemeral elliptic-curve key. The Authentication Request appeared in plaintext. UERANSIM confirmed the initial SQN as `0x40` (decimal 64) and a PDU session was established successfully.

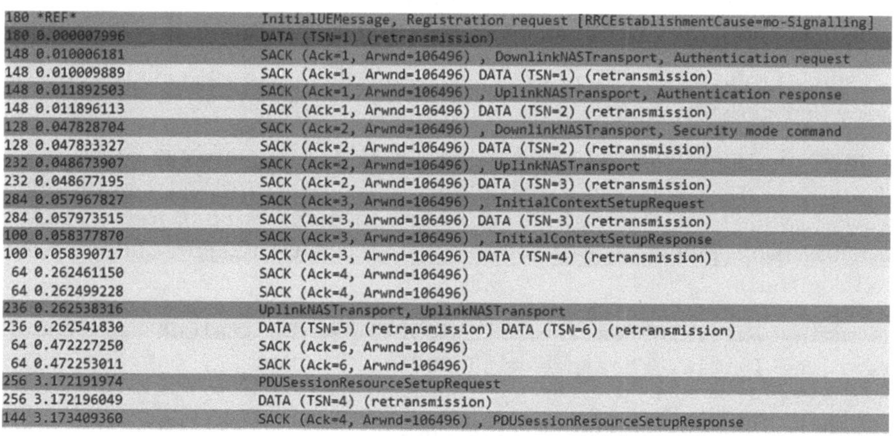

Fig. 3. Wireshark screenshot of UE registration and authentication

Scenario 1. With the proxy in passive recording mode, six UEs registered sequentially, each with a distinct SUPI. The proxy extracted every SUCI from the corresponding *InitialUEMessage* and stored it in JSON format without modifying any message or disrupting any authentication exchange. All six UEs authenticated and established PDU sessions identically to Scenario 0. Table 4 shows the recorded SUCI structure; the ECC ephemeral key, ciphertext, and MAC differ per registration, confirming ECIES freshness.

Table 4. SUCI components recorded in Scenario 1 (all: PLMN = 20895, routing = 0210, scheme = 1).

UE	ECCEphemPK (prefix)	CipherText	MAC (prefix)
031	676130f3...	588798faae	21652595...
032	26cb957d...	04d3034d74	6324e035...
033	a196dc1d...	8c9d3eded9	f45a4f41...
034	6c916921...	2c1780887c	917ec4f0...
035	1e2e9d16...	7c22404638	3418a2d7...
036	d76c3d1b...	9b0139fd5c	78aaa1ed...

6.2 SUCI-Catcher Attack (Scenarios 2–3)

Scenario 2. A single stored SUCI (UE 031, index 0) was injected into a live Registration Request while the genuine UE was present. The AMF generated an Authentication Request for the target subscriber, and the UE responded with a valid *Authentication Response*, confirming its presence. Proxy log:

```
Forwarding InitialUEMessage with SUCI 0
Replaced SUCI with: {...}
Authentication Response - RAN-UE-NGAP-ID: 1
UE successfully found 0
```

A single probe was sufficient to confirm subscriber presence, violating location privacy and undetectability.

Scenario 3. Six SUCIs were probed sequentially; the matching SUCI was at index 4. Each non-matching SUCI produced an *Authentication Failure* (`MAC_-FAILURE`), while the matching SUCI produced an *Authentication Response*. After two consecutive failures the Reset & Sync step was triggered automatically. Proxy log trace:

```
Forwarding InitialUEMessage with SUCI 0  -> MAC FAILURE
Forwarding InitialUEMessage with SUCI 1  -> MAC FAILURE
Reset &Sync
Forwarding InitialUEMessage with SUCI 2  -> MAC FAILURE
Forwarding InitialUEMessage with SUCI 3  -> MAC FAILURE
Reset &Sync
Forwarding InitialUEMessage with SUCI 4  -> AUTH RESPONSE
UE successfully found 4
```

The UE eventually deregistered due to NAS timer T3510 expiry, but the subscriber match was recorded beforehand. The UE remained connected through modified session and the subscriber match was recorded. The binary SUCI-probing oracle is reliable: non-matching and matching SUCIs produce unambiguously different protocol responses, and unlinkability is broken because a connection attempt can be tied to a known stored SUCI.

6.3 SQN Inference Attack (Scenarios 4–6)

Scenario 4. The OAI core was pre-loaded with SQN = 0x2B00, SEQ = 172 (the number of past AKA sessions). The proxy replayed 257 Registration Requests to obtain 257 authentication vectors, then executed the AUTS-based bit-recovery procedure (Subsect. 5.4). Nine AUTS values were collected—one baseline plus one per bit position ($j = 0, \ldots, 7$, targeting SQN bits 6–13)—and XOR-cancellation yielded the delta values in Table 5.

Table 5. SQN bit-inference results (Scenario 4).

Probe j	Bit pos.	Delta ($CONC_0^* \oplus CONC_j^*$)	Bit
0	6	0x000000000040	0
1	7	0x000000000080	0
2	8	0x000000000700	1
3	9	0x000000000600	1
4	10	0x000000000400	0
5	11	0x000000001800	1
6	12	0x000000001000	0
7	13	0x000000006000	1

The recovered bit string `00110101` (bits 6–13) corresponds to an inferred SEQ of 172 and can be extend to a SQN value of 0x2B00 with the IND, matching the ground-truth OAI database value exactly:

```
Inference results
Bit string: 00110101
Inferred SEQ: 172 (amount of past AKA sessions)
Inferred SQN_HN: 11008  (0x000000002b00)
```

After bit inferrence, the UE recovered and completed registration. Later *Authentication Reject* messages from leftover registration attempts were blocked by the proxy and did not reach the UE.

Scenario 5. Two SQN measurements were taken around three legitimate authentication sessions. The first inference yielded SEQ = 1; after the four sessions the inference was repeated:

```
Bit string: 10000000   Inferred SEQ: 1
     [3 legitimate authentication events]
Bit string: 10100000   Inferred SEQ: 5
```

The inferred SEQ increased by 4 (one more than the three explicitly simulated sessions; the extra increment stems from an additional Authentication Request at the end of the first inference round needed to connect UE). The change in inferred

SEQ directly reflects UE activity, demonstrating that an adversary can estimate the number of authentication events a subscriber performs between observations without recovering the absolute SQN value—a violation of behavioural privacy and undetectability.

Scenario 6. Extending inference to 11 bits requires 2049 authentication vectors. The collection phase took significantly longer, and the NAS timer T3510 expired before the baseline challenge could be delivered. Multiple spontaneous UE re-registrations interspersed themselves during collection, injecting new NGAP sessions that disrupted the controlled message sequence and caused the collection counter to reset:

```
Setup: collected auth vector 2048/2049
Initial UE Message - RAN-UE-NGAP-ID: 2
Setup: collected auth vector 2008/2049
```

In some runs, a short sequence of replayed Registration Requests were rejected with `ILLEGAL_UE`, terminating the UE's connection to the network. This appears to stem from unexpected CN behavior, with the likelihood increasing as the number of Authentication Requests grows.

Bit recovery did not complete reliably, confirming that the practical limit is approximately 8 bits under 3GPP NAS timer constraints. The exponential cost ($2^{n+1} - 2$ vectors for n bits) eventually exhausts the session window, establishing a measurable boundary on the attack's reach without protocol-level changes.

7 Discussion

7.1 Privacy Impact

The experimental results confirm that, within the controlled testbed environment, residual privacy leakage in 5G SA arises from observable differences in protocol behaviour rather than failures of SUCI concealment itself; their applicability to operational deployments is subject to the limitations discussed in Subsect. 7.3.

The SUCI-catcher exploits the binary outcome of the 5G-AKA exchange as: the UE's distinguishable response to a correctly or incorrectly targeted challenge was shown to reveal whether the subscriber is present in the cell, violating location privacy and unlinkability without recovering the SUPI.

The SQN inference attack exploits the AUTS resynchronisation mechanism. XOR-cancellation of two AUTS values collected under the same RAND recovers individual bits of SQN_{UE}, demonstrating the feasibility of behavioural tracking—changes in the inferred SQN between observations reveal the subscriber's authentication activity—and cross-session linkability via a distinctive SQN fingerprint. This violates undetectability and unlinkability (Table 1).

The two attacks differ in network footprint. SUCI probing scales linearly with the candidate population and produces low, inconspicuous traffic. SQN inference requires $2^n + 2$ requests per n bits, generating an anomalous burst detectable by the core network [19], and is practically bounded at $\approx$8 bits by NAS timer constraints in this implementation.

7.2 Countermeasures

The observed attack behaviour suggests both near-term operational mitigations and longer-term protocol-level remedies.

Rate Limiting Authentication-Vector Generation. Both attacks depend on the core network servicing a large number of authentication requests from the same gNB or for the same SUCI. Operators can enforce per-gNB and per-SUCI rate limits on AUSF/UDM vector generation to cap the number of vectors an attacker can collect within a session window, directly constraining the SQN inference bit depth and slowing SUCI probing.

Anomaly Detection on Authentication Patterns. The SQN inference attack produces a distinctive trace: hundreds of Registration Requests replayed with the same SUCI, followed by alternating Authentication Responses and Synchronisation Failures. Core-network intrusion detection can flag repeated Sync Failures for a single subscriber or abnormally high registration rates from a single gNB, consistent with the detection approach of Tucker et al. [19].

Binding SUCI Freshness to SQN State. The SUCI-catcher succeeds because a recorded SUCI remains valid across multiple authentication rounds. Incorporating a UE-side freshness indicator—such as a counter derived from SQN_{UE}—into the SUCI construction, and verifying it at the home network, would invalidate replayed SUCIs. This is consistent with the direction proposed by Wang et al. [20], whose privacy-preserving AKA protocol addresses linkability in the authentication exchange.

Randomised AUTS Concealment. Replacing the deterministic f_5 anonymity-key derivation with a randomised function would prevent XOR-cancellation across AUTS values, blocking SQN inference [5].

7.3 Limitations

The evaluation is conducted on a software-simulated testbed and is subject to several limitations. First, the testbed models a single-cell environment; real deployments involve inter-cell mobility and multiple AMF instances, which may affect attack timing and session stability. Second, UERANSIM initially required a modification to suppress AUTN verification for the SQN inference attack; a hardware USIM would enforce this check and may behave differently under out-of-range challenges. The fabricated RAND forced-failure step described in Subsect. 5.4 removes this dependency with negligible impact on timing and traffic overhead; however, the results presented are based on the modified UERANSIM. Third, the observed NAS timer constraints represent UERANSIM's default configuration. Operator deployments may use different timer values that expand or shrink the practical attack window. Fourth, the N2 proxy design already assumes a privileged placement, and operator-side rate limiting on authentication vector generation would further constrain practical attack reach.

7.4 Ethical Considerations

All experiments were conducted in a fully isolated, software-defined testbed with no connection to any live operator network. No real subscriber credentials, SIM cards, or user data were used at any point. The SUCI and SQN values processed are synthetic, generated by UERANSIM against a locally-deployed OAI core. The attacks described pose no risk to real subscribers or network infrastructure.

8 Conclusion

This paper experimentally evaluated two residual privacy attacks against 5G Standalone authentication: the SUCI-catcher and the SQN inference attack. Using a transparent N2-interface proxy on a 3GPP-compliant open-source testbed, the study showed that SUCI concealment prevents direct identity disclosure but does not eliminate indirect privacy leakage through observable authentication behaviour.

The SUCI-catcher enables subscriber presence confirmation through the binary outcome of the 5G-AKA challenge-response exchange, while the SQN inference attack can recover up to 8 bits of the subscriber sequence number through controlled replay and AUTS collection. The results show that SUCI probing is scalable and stealthy, whereas SQN inference is practically limited by NAS timer constraints.

Overall, the findings demonstrate that identity protection and unlinkability are distinct privacy goals in 5G SA. Stronger unlinkability requires protocol-level improvements, such as SUCI freshness binding and randomised AUTS concealment.

Acknowledgments. The authors have no competing interests to declare that are relevant to the content of this article.

References

1. 3GPP: 5G; Non-Access-Stratum (NAS) Protocol for 5G System (5GS); Stage 3. Technical Specification TS 124 501 V15.1.0, ETSI (2018). https://www.etsi.org/deliver/etsi_ts/124500_124599/124501/15.01.00_60/ts_124501v150100p.pdf
2. Ahmed, A.H., Dreibholz, T., Michelinakis, F.I., Čičić, T.: Open 5G Testbed: a cyber range platform for security research. In: 2025 Annual Computer Security Applications Conference Workshops (ACSAC Workshops), pp. 579–586. IEEE (2025)
3. Barraud, L., et al.: 5G SUCI Catcher: attack and detection. In: 2023 IEEE International Conference on Cloud Computing Technology and Science (CloudCom), pp. 285–290. IEEE (2023). https://doi.org/10.1109/CloudCom59040.2023.00053
4. Basin, D., Dreier, J., Hirschi, L., Radomirović, S., Sasse, R., Stettler, V.: A formal analysis of 5G authentication. In: Proceedings of the 25th ACM Conference on Computer and Communications Security (CCS 2018), pp. 1383–1396. ACM (2018). https://doi.org/10.1145/3243734.3243846

5. Borgaonkar, R., Hirschi, L., Park, S., Shaik, A.: New privacy threat on 3G, 4G, and upcoming 5G AKA protocols. Proc. Priv. Enhancing Technol. (PoPETs) **2019**(3), 108–127 (2019). https://doi.org/10.2478/popets-2019-0039
6. Cabrera, P., Gallego, M.: 5G SUCI Probing in the Wild (2024)
7. Cheng, Y.C., Shen, C.A.: A new tracking-attack scenario based on the vulnerability and privacy violation of 5G AKA protocol. IEEE Access **10**, 77679–77687 (2022). https://doi.org/10.1109/ACCESS.2022.3193372
8. Chlosta, M., Rupprecht, D., Pöpper, C., Holz, T.: 5G SUCI-Catchers: still catching them all? In: Proceedings of the 14th ACM Conference on Security and Privacy in Wireless and Mobile Networks (WiSec 2021), pp. 359–364. ACM (2021)
9. Eleftherakis, S., Giustiniano, D., Kourtellis, N.: SoK: evaluating 5G-advanced protocols against legacy and emerging privacy and security attacks. In: Proceedings of the 18th ACM Conference on Security and Privacy in Wireless and Mobile Networks (WiSec 2025), pp. 196–210. ACM (2025). https://doi.org/10.1145/3734477.3734716
10. Eleftherakis, S., Otim, T., Santaromita, G., Zayas, A.D., Giustiniano, D., Kourtellis, N.: Demystifying privacy in 5G stand alone networks. In: Proceedings of the 30th Annual International Conference on Mobile Computing and Networking (MobiCom 2024), pp. 1330–1345. ACM (2024)
11. ETSI: ETSI TS 133 501 V17.11.0 — Technical Specification: 5G System; security architecture and procedures for 5G system. Technical Specification TS 133 501 V17.11.0, ETSI (2023). https://www.etsi.org/deliver/etsi_ts/133500_133599/133501/17.11.01_60/ts_133501v171101p.pdf
12. Hussain, S.R., Chowdhury, O., Mehnaz, S., Bertino, E.: LTEInspector: a systematic approach for adversarial testing of 4G LTE. In: Proceedings of the 25th Annual Network and Distributed System Security Symposium (NDSS 2018). Internet Society (2018). https://www.ndss-symposium.org/wp-content/uploads/2018/02/ndss2018_02A-3_Hussain_paper.pdf
13. Hussain, S.R., Echeverria, M., Karim, I., Chowdhury, O., Bertino, E.: 5GReasoner: a property-directed security and privacy analysis framework for 5G cellular network protocol. In: Proceedings of the 26th ACM Conference on Computer and Communications Security (CCS 2019), pp. 669–684. ACM (2019). https://doi.org/10.1145/3319535.3354263
14. Koutsos, A.: The 5G-AKA authentication protocol privacy. In: 2019 IEEE European Symposium on Security and Privacy (EuroS&P), pp. 464–479. IEEE (2019)
15. Michau, B.: PyCrate (2026). https://github.com/pycrate-org/pycrate
16. Mishra, S., et al.: Characterizing 5g adoption and its impact on network traffic and mobile service consumption. In: IEEE INFOCOM 2024-IEEE Conference on Computer Communications, pp. 1531–1540. IEEE (2024)
17. Nair, P.: Securing 5G and Evolving Architectures, Addison-Wesley Professional (2021)
18. Silveira, L.B.D., Resende, H.C.D., Both, C.B., Marquez-Barja, J.M., Silvestre, B., Cardoso, K.V.: Tutorial on communication between access networks and the 5G core. Comput. Netw. **216**, 109301 (2022)
19. Tucker, T., Brotman, A., Bhattacharya, A., Kloti, R., Noubir, G.: Detecting IMSI-catchers by characterizing identity exposing messages in cellular traffic. In: Proceedings of the 2025 Network and Distributed System Security Symposium (NDSS 2025). Internet Society (2025). https://doi.org/10.14722/ndss.2025.241115
20. Wang, Y., Zhang, Z., Xie, Y.: Privacy-preserving and standard-compatible AKA protocol for 5G. In: Proceedings of the 30th USENIX Security Symposium (USENIX Security 2021), pp. 3595–3612. USENIX Association (2021)

Unified Incident Monitoring and Response in Softwarized Networks with OpenC2

Hani Zeid[1], Daniele Canavese[2(✉)], and Matteo Repetto[2]

[1] Politecnico di Torino, Turin, Italy
s322821@studenti.polito.it
[2] CNR-IMATI, Genoa, Italy
{daniele.canavese,matteo.repetto}@cnr.it

Abstract. Security operations in software-defined and virtualized networks often require coordinating heterogeneous tools for monitoring, evidence collection, and response. However, these tools expose different configuration models, APIs, and execution semantics, which complicates automation and incident response workflows. This paper presents an OpenC2-based orchestration layer that extends command-level cyber-defense coordination beyond classical enforcement actions. We introduce three actuator profiles for network-flow monitoring, file/log collection, and constrained remote command execution, and implement them using nProbe, Packetbeat, Filebeat, and Linux-based actuators. The resulting prototype provides a uniform command interface for activating monitoring functions, collecting operational evidence, and executing controlled response actions. We validate the approach through schema-conformance tests, positive and negative command cases, safety checks, and latency measurements in representative orchestration workflows.

1 Introduction

Modern cyber defense environments are assembled from many specialized components, including flow probes, log collectors, packet filters, endpoint agents, cloud controls, and legacy command-line tools. Each component usually exposes its own API (Application Programming Interface), configuration language, and operational workflow. As infrastructure becomes more virtualized and distributed, this heterogeneity poses a practical obstacle: security teams must coordinate disparate tools under time pressure, yet the orchestration logic is often forced to encode vendor-specific assumptions. The result is brittle automation, limited portability, and slower incident response.

OpenC2 (Open Command and Control) was introduced to address this interoperability problem precisely by defining a nonproprietary language for machine-to-machine command and control of cyber defense functions [1,4]. In OpenC2, a profile specifies the language and syntax for a given operational domain (e.g., packet filtering), while an actuator is the entity that interprets and executes commands on the target system (e.g., iptables). OpenC2 uses a producer-consumer

P. Kieseberg et al. (Eds.): ARES 2026 Workshops, LNCS 16903, pp. 308–324, 2027.
https://doi.org/10.1007/978-3-032-37218-5_19

model to provide a clean abstraction for describing actions independently from the underlying product. In practice, however, the availability of mature OpenC2 implementations remains uneven, and broad operational coverage across monitoring, telemetry collection, and many other security tasks is still incomplete.

This paper explores how OpenC2 can be extended to cover three relevant classes of security functions that frequently appear in softwarized environments. The first is network flow monitoring, where administrators may need to control heterogeneous probes that expose different parameters and output models. The second is log collection, where telemetry may originate from files, URIs, or sockets and must be normalized for centralized processing. The third is remote command-line management, which is still required for legacy tools or instruments that still lack a dedicated OpenC2 interface and can be used for a variety of purposes such as incident response or monitoring.

A key design choice in our work is to treat monitoring and operational control as first-class citizens of the command plane. In many production settings, the orchestration stack is already capable of deciding *what* should be observed or executed, but it still struggles with *how* to express that decision to heterogeneous tools. This gap appears in simple tasks such as starting a temporary flow probe for a suspicious subnet, enabling collection from a newly discovered log source, or activating a packet-filtering or containment action only after a monitoring workflow has confirmed. In all these cases, operators need a robust command model that survives changes in the underlying implementation.

This work does not propose a new OpenC2 language semantics or a new theoretical security model. Its contribution is practical: the design, implementation, and validation of deployable OpenC2 actuator profiles for monitoring, evidence collection, and constrained response in softwarized environments. In particular, the contributions of our paper are therefore threefold:

- We design and implemented three OpenC2 actuator profiles for monitoring-to-response workflows by defining how OpenC2 commands can coordinate runtime monitoring, evidence collection, and constrained response actions across heterogeneous security functions. In particular, we specify profiles (e.g., interfaces) for network-flow monitoring, file/log collection, and restricted command-line execution, with explicit command structures, validation rules, and actuator semantics.
- We provide practical actuator implementations that translate profile-level commands into the native control logic of concrete backends while preserving a uniform response model. We support Packetbeat, Filebeat, and nprobe as flow collectors, Filebeat for log monitoring, and the Linux shell for arbitrary remote commands.
- We evaluate schema compliance, positive and negative command cases, safety checks, and end-to-end orchestration latency in representative incident-response workflows.

The full source code of our implementation is freely available online[1].

[1] https://github.com/mattereppe/otupy.

Our approach demonstrates that OpenC2 can serve not only as a language for enforcement-oriented controls, but also as a unifying control plane for monitoring and operational security functions. For instance, we can consider an incident-response scenario in a softwarized edge network where heterogeneous security functions must be coordinated after the detection of suspicious traffic. In this scenario, a trusted security orchestrator issues OpenC2 commands to dynamically activate network-flow monitoring on the affected segment, collect host and application logs from selected nodes, and, when required, execute a constrained remediation action through a supervised command-line actuator. The workflow follows a detect–investigate–respond pattern: an initial alert triggers targeted observability, the collected evidence supports operator or automated decision-making, and the response action is executed only if it satisfies the authorization and validation constraints enforced by the actuator.

This paper is structured as follows. In Sect. 2 we introduce the basic concepts of OpenC2. Sections 3 and 4 discuss the core of our work and respectively describe our solution and its validation. Finally, Sects. 5 and 6 conclude this article and present some related works and our final remarks.

2 OpenC2 Primer

OpenC2 is a concise and extensible language for the command and control of cyber defense components, agnostic to products, technologies, and communication mechanisms [1]. In addition to defining the abstract syntax and semantics of commands and responses, OpenC2 relies on explicit transfer and serialization mechanisms. From a communication perspective, the standard is transport-agnostic, and OpenC2 messages can be conveyed via several protocols such as HTTP, HTTPS, and MQTT. At the representation level, OpenC2 messages cann be serialized using different formats such as JSON, XML, and CBOR. This separation between language semantics, transport protocol, and message encoding is a key enabler of interoperability, as it allows the same command model to be applied consistently across heterogeneous security components and deployment environments.

Figure 1 reports the general architecture of an OpenC2-based infrastructure.

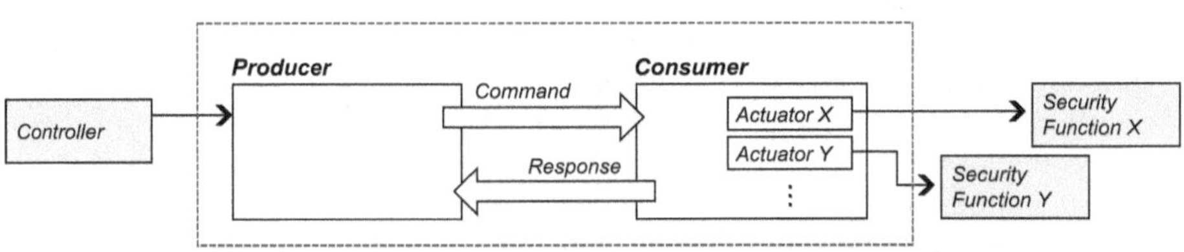

Fig. 1. Architecture of a generic OpenC2 scenario.

At the architectural level, OpenC2 organizes communication around a *producer*, which issues commands, and one or more *consumers*, which execute them and return responses. The consumer forwards a command to an appropriate *actuator*, which translates the command into concrete requests for a specific tool, such as iptables. *Actuator profiles* constitute the standardized interface through which the generic OpenC2 command language is mapped onto the capabilities and constraints of a particular actuator; thus, they define the supported commands and syntax for a specific domain.

An OpenC2 *command* is organized around two core elements: an *action*, which specifies the operation to be performed (e.g., block traffic), and a *target*, which identifies the object to which that operation applies (e.g., a source IP address). In addition, a command may include optional arguments that further qualify the requested operation, as well as *actuator specifiers* that indicate the intended actuator chosen to run the command. The corresponding response communicates the outcome of command processing by reporting status information and, where applicable, returning result data produced during the execution.

The OpenC2 language is intentionally limited. It does not attempt to represent the entire detection, decision, and policy workflow of cyber defense. Instead, it focuses on the action phase, assuming that the need to act has already been determined and that authorization, authentication, and transport security are provided by the surrounding system. This design keeps the core language compact, but also makes actuator profiles essential. All consumers must implement at least the command with the `query` action with the `features` target, which primarily supports capability discovery and interoperability between producers and consumers. More specifically, it allows a producer to request information about the capabilities implemented by a consumer, including the supported OpenC2 versions, actuator profiles, and valid action-target pairs for the supported commands.

From a deployment perspective, OpenC2 also provides a disciplined boundary between decision and execution logic. A detector, an orchestration platform, or a policy engine may remain completely separate from the actuator implementation. This decoupling is one reason why OpenC2 is attractive for software-defined infrastructures. New backends can be added without forcing the producer to learn backend-specific grammars, and existing actions can be logged, authorized, and audited at a uniform semantic level.

3 Design

This section presents the actuator profiles we designed in our OpenC2-based framework and describes how they specialize the abstract command language into concrete interfaces. We outline the structure of the supported commands and responses, and discuss how the proposed profiles enable consistent interaction with monitoring and control actuators.

3.1 Remote Command-Line Interface Profile

The *Remote Command-Line Interface* (RCLI) actuator profile aims to enable remote configuration and control of security functions via command-line interfaces. It is primarily conceived as a fallback mechanism for security components that do not natively implement any specific OpenC2 actuator profile, or for which a dedicated profile has not yet been defined. By providing a standardized method for issuing remote commands, the RCLI profile enables interaction with a wide range of security tools, enabling consistent incident management and control of both legacy and modern systems through a common command-line interface.

Table 1 shows the actions supported by our RCLI profile.

Table 1. Supported actions by our RCLI profile.

ACTION	PURPOSE
`copy`	upload file
`delete`	cleanup files
`query`	discover capabilities, inspect file or process
`start`	launch command
`stop`	terminate execution

The `start` and `stop` actions are respectively used to launch and terminate a remote command, while the `copy` action is used to upload a file required by the command (e.g., a configuration file). When an uploaded file is no longer necessary, it can be removed from the remote server via the `delete` action. Finally, the `query` action is used both to discover supported capabilities through the `features` target or to monitor the status of one or more running security processes.

Figure 2 shows a typical operational workflow for an RCLI session:

1. the producer inspects the supported capabilities by an RCLI consumer issuing the `query` action;
2. the producer uploads one or more files (e.g., configuration files) to the server with a `copy` command;
3. optionally, `query` command can be used to get some additional information (e.g., the remote file path, its MD5 hash) about an uploaded file
4. the producer starts one or more security processes with the `start` command;
5. periodically, and if necessary, the producer can check the status of a running security process with the `query` command;
6. when a process needs to be terminated, the producer can send a `stop` command to do so;
7. finally the producer can issue a `delete` command to remove the leftover files.

We have implemented an actuator that is able to launch command-line applications and manage processes in a Linux environment. Since launching and managing remote processes is a highly critical operation, which if left unchecked can lead to severe security issues, we have implemented a series of security checks which includes:

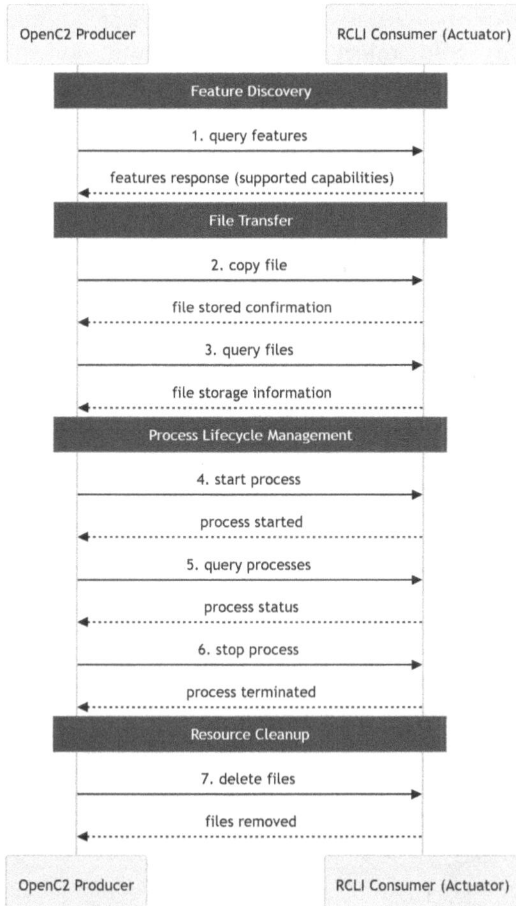

Fig. 2. Operational workflow for an RCLI consumer.

- *Command validation.* Only commands explicitly defined in the actuator's command whitelist may be executed. This approach prevents arbitrary shell instruction execution and ensures that remote control is restricted to a carefully curated subset of approved utilities.
- *Flag validation.* The actuator verifies that only explicitly permitted flags and options are accepted for each whitelisted command.
- *Short flag expansion.* The implementation expands compact short-form flags into their individual components before validation (e.g., the combined flag `-la` will be expanded into `-l -a`). This measure is important because grouped short options may otherwise be used to evade the flag validation checks. By normalizing flags prior to inspection, the actuator ensures that all options are evaluated consistently against the flag whitelist.

- *Rejection of dangerous substrings.* The validator applies several pattern checks to identify and reject inputs containing known dangerous substrings or suspicious constructs (e.g., if a command contains the substring `:(){\s*:|:&\s};`, it is rejected since it can launch a fork bomb[2]).
- *Validation of paths.* Operands such as file paths are subject to explicit validation and are accepted only when the relevant command definition allows them.
- *Ownership-based authorization checks.* Any operation that references an existing process, such as `query` or `stop`, is checked against a run-time local database to ensure that the requesting producer is the same producer that originally created the process. This prevents one producer from interfering with processes initiated by another one and enforces an isolation model across tenants.
- *Forced termination.* When a graceful termination is not sufficient with a `stop` command, the actuator escalates to a forceful termination through a `SIGKILL` signal after a defined timeout. This guarantees deterministic cleanup and prevents long-lived or unresponsive processes from persisting indefinitely after a stop request.

3.2 Network Flow Monitor Profile

The *Network Flow Monitor* (NFM) actuator profile defines a standardized OpenC2 interface for remotely controlling network flow monitoring functions.

Table 2 shows the actions supported by our NFM profile.

Table 2. Supported actions by our NFM profile.

ACTION	PURPOSE
`query`	discover capabilities
`start`	launch monitoring session
`stop`	terminate monitoring session

The `query` action, required by the OpenC2 standard, requests the capabilities exposed by the actuator. The `start` and `stop` actions initiate or terminate a monitoring session on the specified target network interfaces, with optional filtering parameters.

Figure 3 illustrates the traditional life-cycle of a monitoring session, from capability discovery and session establishment to status retrieval and eventual termination:

1. a producer issues a `query` command for discovering the supported capabilities of a NFM actuator;

[2] https://resources.cs.rutgers.edu/docs/preventing-fork-bomb-on-linux/.

2. the producer starts a traffic monitoring session with the `start` command;
3. when monitoring is no longer necessary, the producer can force its termination with a `stop` command.

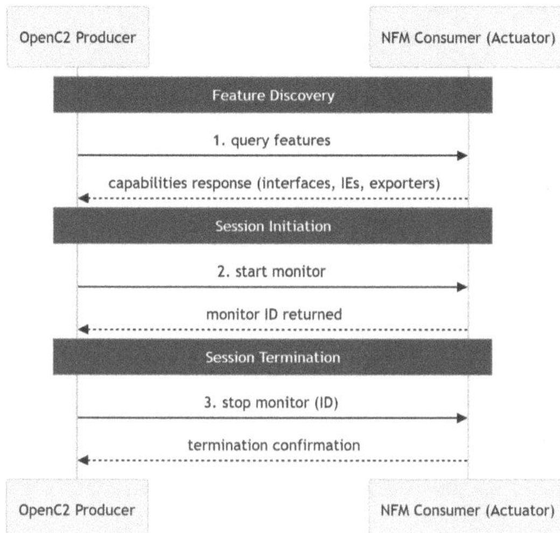

Fig. 3. Operational workflow for an NFM consumer.

We implemented two NFM actuators that manage two different monitoring tools: nProbe[3] and Packetbeat[4]. Based on the tool and its available options, it is possible to configure the output format, such as NetFlow v5 or v7, define where the analysis results should be sent or stored (e.g., a NetFlow collector, a file, Logstash[5]), restrict the traffic sniffing only on specific network interfaces, and adding filters using the BPF (Berkeley Packet Filter) syntax. Furthermore, at the start of a monitoring session, our actuators enforce a 3-second delay before checking the status of the processes. This precaution provides the system with a brief stabilization period to avoid a premature check.

Since traffic sniffing and analysis are critical operations, we implemented a range of security controls to ensure that data is collected, processed, and handled securely and under control. These measures include:

- *Producer-bound isolation.* Each monitoring session is explicitly associated with the producer that initiated it. This design ensures that a producer is only authorized to inspect, manage, or terminate the sessions it created, thereby preventing unauthorized access to monitoring activities established by other entities.

[3] https://www.ntop.org/guides/nprobe/.
[4] https://www.elastic.co/beats/packetbeat.
[5] https://www.elastic.co/logstash.

- *Restriction of interfaces.* The profile limits monitoring activities to a predefined set of authorized network interfaces. Enforcing such restrictions reduces the possibility of unauthorized packet capture on sensitive interfaces.
- *Safe filter construction.* Packet filtering expressions are generated from structured OpenC2 filter objects rather than being directly assembled from arbitrary user-provided strings. This approach improves robustness and significantly reduces the likelihood of malformed expressions, unsafe parsing behavior, or injection-like manipulation of filter definitions.
- *Shell-injection prevention.* The monitoring tools are invoked through structured argument lists rather than through shell-interpreted command strings. This implementation choice prevents untrusted input from being interpreted as shell syntax, thereby mitigating the risk of command-injection attacks during process creation.
- *Controlled output handling.* The profile uses controlled mechanisms to collect and manage process outputs, with particular attention to limiting excessive verbosity and preventing uncontrolled data exposure. Such handling reduces the risk of sensitive information leakage, prevents log flooding, and contributes to more stable, predictable operational behavior.

3.3 FCLM

The File Collection Log Monitoring (FCLM) actuator profile extends the OpenC2 language to provide a unified and interoperable framework for remote control of log collection activities. Its main objective is to standardize how log collection agents are configured and managed across heterogeneous platforms. This profile defines a file-monitoring framework for configuring log collection, either locally or in a centralized location. It allows the coordination of multiple log sources—such as files, URIs, or sockets—through a single, technology-agnostic interface, ensuring that producers can manage diverse collection processes uniformly. This profile provides a common model for specifying what log sources to monitor, how data should be gathered, and where collected logs should be exported.

Table 3 shows the actions supported by this profile.

Table 3. Supported actions by our FCLM profile.

ACTION	PURPOSE
`query`	discover capabilities
`start`	launch monitoring session
`stop`	terminate monitoring session

Analogously to the NFM profile, the FCLM actuator profile supports the `query` action to request an actuator's capabilities, and the `start` and `stop` actions to initiate or terminate a monitoring session.

Figure 4 illustrates the lifecycle of an FCLM monitoring session, from capability discovery to the monitoring session management.

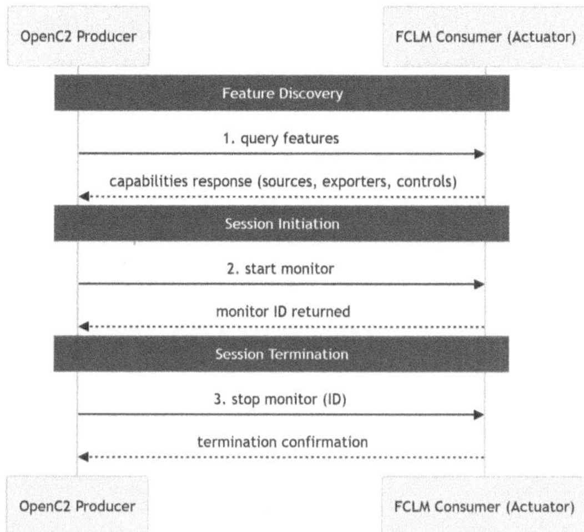

Fig. 4. Operational workflow for an FCLM consumer.

The FCLM operation workflow consists of three phases, as the NFM profile:

1. a producer issues a `query` command for discovering the supported capabilities of a FCLM actuator;
2. the producer starts a log monitoring session with the `start` command;
3. when monitoring is no longer necessary, the producer can force its termination with a `stop` command.

We have implemented an FCLM actuator for the Filebeat[6] tool, a light but powerful log monitoring tool. The actuator, via the profile, allows the definition of the input sources (e.g., log files, URIs), and several other options, such as the scanning frequency.

Since log collection constitutes a critical operation, we introduced a set of security checks to ensure tighter control over the entire process and to prevent misuse or unintended interference. These checks include:

- *Producer-bound isolation.* As in the NFM actuators, each active monitoring process is associated with the producer that initiated it. This ownership binding ensures that only the originating producer can manage the corresponding monitoring session.

[6] https://www.elastic.co/beats/filebeat.

- *Shell-injection prevention.* The FCLM actuator launches the monitoring processes through `subprocess.Popen(shell=False)`, thereby avoiding shell interpretation of user-supplied input. This design choice significantly reduces the attack surface associated with command injection.
- *Early input validation.* The actuator relies on typed OpenC2 Python objects to internally represent critical command parameters. Inputs that do not conform to the expected structure or type are rejected before any operational logic is executed. This early validation step improves robustness and prevents malformed or semantically invalid requests.
- *Controlled export-field resolution.* Exported log flags are not accepted as arbitrary free-form values, but are resolved through predefined mappings maintained by the actuator. Unknown or unsupported fields are ignored. This mechanism reduces the risk of unsafe configuration injection and ensures that only recognized export parameters are propagated to the monitoring backend.

4 Validation

We have implemented our approach in Python and `otupy`[7], an open-source OpenC2 package. We will detail how we tested the correctness of our tool and discuss its performance.

4.1 Functional Correctness

To assess the functional correctness of our implementation, we adopted an automated validation framework based on YAML and JSON fixtures, structured around both positive test cases, expected to succeed, and negative test cases, deliberately designed to trigger validation failures. This methodology allowed us to evaluate not only whether valid commands and responses were correctly accepted and processed, but also whether malformed inputs were consistently rejected.

Data Types Validation. This validation phase assesses whether the implementation strictly enforces the right OpenC2 data types by constructing the Python objects directly and ensuring that invalid values are appropriately rejected by raising an exception. Table 4 reports the number of tests we executed. Our NFM and FCLM profiles passed all the tests, while the RCLI profile failed in one positive and one negative test case. These tests failed due to bugs in the underlying `otupy` library, related to hash-length handling (e.g., MD5 validation behavior) and to overly permissive acceptance of nullable hash fields (e.g., `sha1: null`) in a path.

[7] https://github.com/mattereppe/otupy.

Table 4. Data type validation tests.

	POSITIVE TESTS		NEGATIVE TESTS	
PROFILE	TOTAL	PASSED	TOTAL	PASSED
RCLI	42	41	44	43
NFM	109	109	74	74
FCLM	92	92	95	95

Schema Interoperability. The second phase of validation assesses the strict adherence to the OpenC2 JSON schemas and ensures interoperability over HTTP. Again, we developed several positive and negative test suites to verify the compatibility of multiple commands and responses with the OpenC2 JSON schema. To evaluate robustness, malformed JSON commands are injected to confirm that the actuator gracefully returns HTTP error codes (e.g., `400 Bad Request`) rather than crashing the system. Table 5 recaps the number of tests and shows that our proof-of-concept achieved a 100% success rate.

Table 5. Schema interoperability tests.

	POSITIVE TESTS		NEGATIVE TESTS	
PROFILE	TOTAL	PASSED	TOTAL	PASSED
RCLI	33	33	20	20
NFM	39	39	34	34
FCLM	33	33	20	20

4.2 Performance

We performed a variety of tests to assess the latency in managing commands and running security processes with our actuators. We report the average test results computed on 100 iterations on both the producer and consumer sides for completeness. In the following tables, the column ENC+DEC represents the time to encode/decode an OpenC2 transmission in JSON, while SEND+RECV is the producer-time to send and receive a message, and PROCESS is the consumer-side time to actually execute a command (e.g., to launch `nprobe`).

We performed all our tests locally on a single PC to avoid the variability of a real network scenario and increase the consistency of the results. Our test platform was equipped with an Intel Core i7-11800 CPU and 16 GiB of RAM, and it was running Ubuntu 24.02.2, Python 3.12.3, Packetbeat 8.17.4, Filebeat 8.18.0, and nProbe v.10.7.250402. Note also that the reported START command latency includes a deliberately inserted 3-second stabilization delay used before checking whether Packetbeat, nProbe, or Filebeat has started correctly. Therefore, these values should not be interpreted as pure OpenC2 orchestration overhead.

RCLI Profile Latency. Tables 6 and 7 show the performance results from the perspectives of the producer and consumer. The results show a negligible latency except for the `copy` command. This longer delay, however, is entirely due to local disk I/O and file writing, not to the OpenC2 protocol overhead.

Table 6. RCLI producer-side latency in seconds.

COMMAND	ENC+DEC	SEND+RECV	TOTAL
`start`	0.0020	0.0068	0.0088
`stop`	0.0022	0.0093	0.0115
`delete`	0.0021	0.0110	0.0131
`query features`	0.0030	0.0072	0.0102
`copy`	0.0043	1.3760	1.3803

Table 7. RCLI consumer-side latency in seconds.

COMMAND	ENC+DEC	PROCESS	TOTAL
`start`	0.0008	0.0014	0.0022
`stop`	0.0008	0.0041	0.0049
`delete`	0.0009	0.0054	0.0063
`query features`	0.0010	0.0014	0.0024
`copy`	0.9158	0.4540	1.3698

NFM Latency. Tables 8 and 9 report our results for the NFM profile and its nProbe and Packetbeat actuators. Note that the producer-side time for sending and receiving the command and its response, and the consumer-side processing times for starting the flow monitors are higher than 3 s. These times are deliberately set to include the stabilization delay (see Sect. 3.2). Excluding this delay confirms that the actual processing overhead remains in the millisecond range.

FCLM Latency. Tables 10 and 11 report the timings for our FCLM profile and its Filebeat actuator. As in the NFM profile tests, the send/receive and processing time takes into account the additional 3 s stabilization delay.

Table 8. NFM producer-side latency in seconds.

COMMAND	ENC+DEC	SEND+RECV	TOTAL
`start` nProbe	0.0028	3.0227	3.0255
`start` Packetbeat	0.0026	3.0378	3.0404
`stop`	0.0049	0.0102	0.0151
`query features`	0.0055	0.0204	0.0259

Table 9. NFM consumer-side latency in seconds.

COMMAND	ENC+DEC	PROCESS	TOTAL
`start` nProbe	0.0019	3.0147	3.0166
`start` Packetbeat	0.0023	3.0301	3.0324
`stop`	0.0012	0.0031	0.0043
`query features`	0.0015	0.0130	0.0145

Table 10. FCLM producer-side latency in seconds.

COMMAND	ENC+DEC	SEND+RECV	TOTAL
`start` Filebeat	0.0027	3.0320	3.0347
`stop`	0.0019	0.0058	0.0077
`query features`	0.0054	0.0081	0.0135

Table 11. FCLM consumer-side latency in seconds.

COMMAND	ENC+DEC	PROCESS	TOTAL
`start` Filebeat	0.0014	3.0249	3.0263
`stop`	0.0008	0.0011	0.0019
`query features`	0.0016	0.0014	0.0030

5 Related Works

Recent work on OpenC2 has begun to clarify the practical requirements for its adoption in real systems, though the current literature on this topic remains scarce.

Repetto [6] presents otupy, the framework representing the basis of our approach. Otupy is a flexible and extensible framework for the remote control of security functions based on OpenC2. The main contribution of the work is an API that abstracts message creation, parsing, serialization, and transport, allowing developers to focus on security-function logic rather than protocol-specific details.

Tanzarella et al. propose an OpenC2-based system that extends the language toward context discovery in digital service chains [8]. The paper proposes a protocol that enables OpenC2 consumers to recursively expose contextual information about services, relations, and cybersecurity functions, enabling the construction of a service context graph spanning multiple infrastructures and administrative domains. The approach is validated in OpenStack and Kubernetes environments within a software-defined 5G testbed, demonstrating that OpenC2 profiles can be used not only to issue commands but also to support a richer operational view of the managed environment.

Beyond OpenC2, some works have explored alternative abstract languages for configuring security controls across heterogeneous platforms. These approaches generally begin with higher-level policies, or intents, or capability descriptions, then refine them into technology-specific configurations.

Lingga et al. [2] propose a security policy translator for network security functions in cloud-based security services. Grounded in the I2NSF language [3], their approach translates high-level security policies into corresponding low-level policies required by concrete network security functions. Its main contribution is therefore a structured policy-refinement pipeline that bridges user-facing policy specifications and device-level configurations.

Ribeiro et al. [7] address the inverse problem of intent-based networking by proposing a deterministic, bottom-up approach to extract high-level security intents from existing low-level network configurations. Their work is motivated by the practical difficulty of understanding and evolving deployed security policies when configurations are scattered across heterogeneous devices and expressed in vendor-specific languages. To bridge this gap, the authors develop a prototype called SCRIBE that parses security configurations from various network devices and translates them into an extended version of the Nile intent language.

BASTION [5] by Murcia et al. is closely related to our approach because it addresses automated service and security orchestration in next-generation networks through a ZSM (Zero-touch network and Service Management) aligned and policy-driven meta-orchestration framework. Its objective is to determine how service and security policies should be enforced across heterogeneous B5G infrastructures, including the selection of orchestration strategies and the deployment of security functions. In contrast, our work focuses on the command-execution layer beneath such orchestration logic. Rather than defining policies, placement decisions, or meta-orchestration algorithms, we define OpenC2 actuators and profiles that expose monitoring, file/log collection, and constrained command execution through uniform cyber-defense commands. This distinction makes the proposed framework complementary to policy-driven orchestrators: high-level systems can decide which security action is required, while our proposed OpenC2 profiles provide standardized command semantics for invoking concrete tools and actuators.

6 Conclusions

This paper extends the OpenC2 framework to support security operations beyond traditional enforcement by introducing actuator profiles for remote command-line execution, network flow monitoring, and file and log collection, enabling evidence collection, incident monitoring, and response. The proposed approach enables heterogeneous security capabilities to be managed through a common interoperable command model. Experimental results, including schema-compliance, interoperability, and performance tests, show that the solution is feasible, efficient, and introduces limited overhead, confirming OpenC2 as a promising foundation for orchestrating security functions in virtualized and software-defined environments.

Future work will extend the profiles to additional actuator classes, such as fProbe and eBPF-based monitoring tools, and strengthen the security of remote command execution, particularly in terms of authorization and provenance. We also plan to integrate fine-grained AAA (Authentication, Authorization, and Accounting) mechanisms to support secure, user-aware control of OpenC2 commands.

Acknowledgment. This project has received funding from the European Union's Horizon Europe Research and Innovation Programme under grant agreement No. 101168144. The views and opinions expressed are those of the authors only and do not necessarily reflect those of the European Union or the European Cybersecurity Competence Centre. Neither the European Union nor the granting authority can be held responsible.

Disclosure of Interests. The authors have no competing interests to declare that are relevant to the content of this article.

References

1. Open command and control (openc2) language specification version 1.0. Committee Specification 02, OASIS Open (2019). https://docs.oasis-open.org/openc2/oc2ls/v1.0/cs02/oc2ls-v1.0-cs02.html, 24 Nov 2019
2. Lingga, P., Jeong, J., Yang, J., Kim, J.: SPT: security policy translator for network security functions in cloud-based security services. IEEE Trans. Depend. Secure Comput. **21**(6), 5156–5169 (2024). https://doi.org/10.1109/TDSC.2024.3371788
3. Lopez, D.R., Lopez, E., Dunbar, L., Strassner, J., Kumar, R.: Framework for interface to network security functions (i2nsf). RFC 8329 (2018). https://doi.org/10.17487/RFC8329
4. Mavroeidis, V., Brule, J.: A nonproprietary language for the command and control of cyber defenses - openc2. Comput. Secur. **97**, 101999 (2020)
5. Murcia, J.M.B., Zarca, A.M., Skármeta, A.: Bastion: beyond automated service and security orchestration for next-generation networks. Comput. Netw. **267**, 111352 (2025)
6. Repetto, M.: Otupy: a flexible, portable, and extensible framework for remote control of security functions. Comput. Secur. **158**(C) (2025). https://doi.org/10.1016/j.cose.2025.104597

7. Ribeiro, R.H., et al.: A deterministic approach for extracting network security intents. Comput. Netw. **214**, 109109 (2022)
8. Tanzarella, S., Repetto, M.: Context discovery for digital service chain with openc2. In: 2025 IEEE 11th International Conference on Network Softwarization (NetSoft), pp. 579–584 (2025). https://doi.org/10.1109/NetSoft64993.2025.11080629

Proceedings of the Sixth International Workshop on Education, Training and Awareness in Cybersecurity & the Second Secure, Trustworthy, and Robust AI (ETACS/STRAI 2026)

Systematic Design of Competency-Based HPC and AI Education for Transport Systems

Carmel Somers[1](✉) and Horacio González–Vélez[2]

[1] Digital Technology Skills, Dublin, Ireland
carmel.somers@ictskillnet.ie
[2] Cloud Competency Centre, National College of Ireland, Dublin, Ireland
horacio.gonzalez-velez@ncirl.ie

Abstract. High Performance Computing (HPC) and Artificial Intelligence (AI) are increasingly shaping transport and mobility systems through digitalisation, modelling, optimisation, and data-intensive decision-making. However, postgraduate provision in these areas often remains anchored in traditional computer science pathways, creating misalignment with the applied and interdisciplinary capabilities now required across transport-sector roles. This paper presents a mixed-methods needs analysis developed within the GreenShift project to identify the capabilities required for advanced digital education in the European transport and mobility sector. The study integrates three complementary methods: LLM-assisted desk research in the EU27, a stakeholder survey with 58 valid responses, and nine semi-structured qualitative interviews with transport and mobility stakeholders. Throughout the desk research process, 156 potentially relevant sources were initially identified and 103 were retained after structured manual validation, resulting in a consolidated evidence base on emerging transport-related roles and associated skills. Rather than treating AI, sustainability, governance, and HPC as isolated specialist domains, the analysis shows that these operate as cross-cutting capability layers embedded across four curriculum-oriented Role Families: Transport Data Analytics; Modelling, Simulation and Digital Twin; Systems Integration and Platform; and Digital Innovation Leadership (Transport-specific). The paper argues that curriculum design for non-computer-science learners should be grounded in validated role-capability patterns and translated into flexible, interdisciplinary programme structures aligned with organisational readiness and labour market demand.

Keywords: Curriculum Design · Skills Needs Analysis · Digital Twins · Sustainability · Role-based Learning · High Performance Computing

P. Kieseberg et al. (Eds.): ARES 2026 Workshops, LNCS 16903, pp. 327–344, 2027.
https://doi.org/10.1007/978-3-032-37218-5_20

1 Introduction

Digitalisation, automation, and data-driven operational decision-making are reshaping the European transport and mobility sector, increasing demand for advanced capabilities in AI, modelling, optimisation, simulation, digital infrastructure, and sustainability-oriented systems thinking [16]. Ideally complemented by HPC, these capabilities are no longer confined to specialist computing roles, but are increasingly embedded in smart cities, transport planning, operations, governance, systems integration, and innovation functions across public and private organisations [3,27].

This creates an educational challenge for postgraduate programme design. Traditional HPC and AI curricula remain strongly oriented toward computer science and engineering pathways, whereas many emerging transport roles require applied computational understanding without assuming deep prior expertise in low-level parallel programming or algorithm engineering [12,19,24].

As a multi-million Euro ground-breaking initiative with 16 academic, industry and government partners located throughout Europe, the GreenShift project has identified the requirement for HPC and AI skills in the European transport industry for the eventual development of a postgraduate higher education curriculum.

This paper outlines GreenShift's *Needs Analysis*, an evidence-based academic account of how role-capability analysis can inform curriculum design for advanced digital education in transport and mobility. As a mixed-methods assessment of current and emerging skills needs within the European transport ecosystem, it provides a detailed account of source selection, inclusion criteria, validation, and coding procedures. It *i*) summarises the transition from analytically derived role families to curriculum-oriented role clusters; *ii*) integrates cross-method synthesis across desk research, survey, and interviews; *iii*) and makes explicit the translation from labour market evidence to capability areas, topic domains, and programme architecture.

1.1 Research Question and Contribution

The paper is guided by the following overarching research question: *how can curriculum-relevant HPC, AI, and advanced digital capabilities be systematically identified and translated into an academically robust, curriculum-oriented framework for transport and mobility education using mixed methods?*. Four subquestions structure its analysis:

- How can transport-sector roles and associated capability requirements be extracted from heterogeneous public sources in a traceable and methodologically defensible way?
- How can LLM-assisted extraction be incorporated into educational and labour market research without compromising evidential rigour?
- What do the results of the survey and interviews reveal about capability gaps, organisational barriers, and future training needs in the sector?

- How can validated role-capability findings be translated into curriculum architecture suitable for interdisciplinary and non-computer-science learner cohorts?

The paper contributes a fully articulated methodology for role-anchored curriculum design in an emerging digital-green domain. Its contribution lies not only in the identification of transport-relevant digital capabilities, but also in the demonstration of a transparent workflow that links evidence extraction, validation, synthesis, capability clustering, and curriculum design [22].

Beyond the transport domain, the study contributes a transferable methodology for competency discovery and curriculum development in emerging technology-intensive sectors [17]. The combination of bounded LLM-assisted extraction, structured human validation, multi-source triangulation, and curriculum traceability provides a replicable workflow that can be applied wherever role profiles, skills requirements, and curricular structures need to be kept aligned over time, including cybersecurity, energy, manufacturing, and health.

For ETACS and neighbouring cybersecurity education initiatives, the contribution lies in an end-to-end, role-anchored workflow that starts from documented work roles, incorporates competency frameworks such as the ENISA European Cybersecurity Skills Framework (ECSF) [15], and produces curriculum-ready capability structures with an explicit evidence trail for different skills frameworks [4]. In this sense, the methodological approach is particularly relevant to ETACS, because it offers a concrete model to systematically translate evolving cybersecurity workforce requirements into evidence-based educational design, rather than relying solely on technology-centred or expert-only syllabus updates.

2 Literature Review

The study is located within the literature on HPC education, competency-based learning, workforce-informed curriculum design, and just transition. Its central premise is that advanced digital education for transport systems cannot be designed by transferring conventional computer science curricula to a new application area. Instead, curriculum design must account for the roles, organisational settings, and applied decisions through which HPC, AI, modelling, simulation, digital twins, data governance, and sustainability are now being used in transport and mobility.

HPC education has historically been grounded in Parallel and Distributed Computing (PDC), with emphasis on concurrency, parallel architectures, programming models, performance optimisation, and algorithmic scalability [24]. This disciplinary foundation remains necessary for specialist computing education, but it does not fully address the needs of professionals who engage with HPC through applied modelling, simulation, optimisation, digital twins, or AI-enabled decision-support environments. Therefore, recent work on HPC education points towards domain-driven and competency-based learning models, where learners acquire sufficient computational understanding to reason about scale, data movement, model behaviour, infrastructure constraints, and performance implications in applied contexts rather than necessarily becoming specialist parallel programmers [9,12,31].

This distinction is important for transport and mobility education. Transport professionals may need to understand when large-scale simulation, GPU-accelerated analytics, data-intensive optimisation, or distributed digital-twin infrastructures are appropriate, reliable, sustainable, and governable. Their educational requirements are therefore different from those of conventional computer science cohorts. The curriculum problem is not simply to transfer existing HPC modules into transport programmes, but to identify which computational concepts should be retained, reframed, scaffolded, and connected to transport-sector decisions. This supports a role-first approach in which HPC and AI are treated as enabling capabilities embedded within operational, analytical, governance, and innovation roles [1,10].

The literature also indicates that the integration of AI and HPC into non-computing domains requires curriculum structures that combine technical fluency with contextual judgement. Domain professionals must interpret model outputs, assess data quality, understand uncertainty, evaluate sustainability implications, and collaborate across organisational boundaries. For this reason, advanced digital education should avoid a narrow separation between technical modules and contextual modules. Instead, it should organise learning around capability integration: data, modelling, AI, HPC, digital infrastructure, governance, sustainability, and cybersecurity should be presented as mutually dependent elements of digitally transformed systems [14,19,20].

Transport systems provide a clear example of this integration problem. Digitalisation, automation, and data-driven decision-making are increasingly embedded in infrastructure management, logistics, public transport, mobility services, urban planning, and policy-oriented functions [16]. In these settings, AI and HPC are not isolated technologies but part of wider socio-technical systems affected by legacy infrastructure, fragmented data environments, interoperability constraints, sustainability pressures, and uneven digital maturity [2,3,21]. Green and digital transition agendas also require education to address environmental performance, organisational readiness, and social distribution of capabilities, rather than treating technical development as a narrow software-training problem [23].

2.1 Existing Approaches to Workforce-Informed Curriculum Design

The alignment of educational provision with evolving workforce requirements has been a longstanding concern within professional and vocational education. Traditional approaches to curriculum design have relied on occupational standards, competency frameworks, expert panels, and structured job analysis methods such as Developing A Curriculum (DACUM) [28] and task-based competency modelling [29]. These approaches provide valuable mechanisms for identifying role requirements, but are often resource-intensive, periodic in nature, and limited in their ability to respond rapidly to emerging technological change.

Competency-based education provides a useful foundation because it directs attention to what learners must be able to understand and do in context, but it still requires a defensible process to identify which capabilities matter in a changing domain [22].

More recently, advances in labour market intelligence have enabled the use of skills analytics, occupational databases, job advertisement mining, and sectoral forecasting to identify emerging workforce trends. European frameworks such as the European e-Competence Framework (e-CF), ESCO, DigComp, GreenComp, and the European Cybersecurity Skills Framework (ECSF) provide structured reference models for competency identification and curriculum alignment [7]. These frameworks offer important guidance, but are not designed to identify emerging sector-specific capability requirements in rapidly evolving domains such as AI-enabled transport systems, digital twins, advanced simulation, or HPC-supported optimisation. They also do not automatically explain how a capability should be translated into learning outcomes, assessments, and modular programme structures.

The growing availability of Large Language Models (LLMs) has also led to increased interest in automated approaches to competency extraction and skills intelligence. Recent studies have explored AI-assisted analysis of job advertisements, occupational descriptions, and policy documents to identify skill demands and trends in the workforce. However, concerns remain about transparency, reproducibility, source fidelity, and the risk of generating inferred or unsupported findings. Consequently, AI-assisted approaches require robust validation mechanisms and should complement rather than replace human expertise and judgment [5,8,18].

Workforce-informed curriculum design therefore faces a double translation problem. First, heterogeneous evidence from the labour-market must be converted into stable role and capability patterns. Second, these patterns must be converted into curriculum structures that are teachable, assessable, and accessible to heterogeneous cohorts of learners. Existing curriculum design methodologies frequently address only one side of this problem. Workforce studies often identify emerging skills but provide limited guidance on programme structure, while educational frameworks can define learning outcomes without a transparent evidence trail linking them to labour market requirements. This creates challenges in demonstrating curriculum relevance in interdisciplinary fields where technological, organisational, sustainability, and governance considerations intersect.

The proposed methodology seeks to address this gap through an integrated workflow that combines evidence extraction assisted by bounded LLM, structured human validation, stakeholder consultation, framework mapping, and curriculum traceability. Rather than relying on AI-generated interpretation, the approach constrains LLMs to the identification of explicitly evidenced roles and skills from publicly available sources. The extracted outputs are subsequently validated, normalised, triangulated through survey and interview data, and mapped to recognised competency frameworks before informing curriculum design decisions.

The novelty of the approach lies not in the use of LLMs alone, but in the systematic integration of AI-assisted extraction, expert validation, multi-method triangulation, and curriculum translation within a single methodological framework. This provides a transparent and replicable process for transforming diverse evidence from the labour market into curriculum-relevant capability structures. Although developed within the transport and mobility sector, the methodology has potential applicability in other domains facing rapid digital transformation, including cybersecurity, energy, manufacturing, and healthcare.

3 Methodology

Similarly to previous needs analyses to generate competence-based curricula in computing [30], the GreenShift Needs Analysis has adopted an exploratory mixed-methods design to generate an evidence-based and curriculum-oriented understanding of skills needs in European transport and mobility. Three methods were integrated: desk research, survey research, and qualitative interviews, with triangulation used to strengthen reliability and practical relevance.

The desk research systematically examined transport-related roles and associated skills related to AI, HPC, advanced digital technologies, and sustainability in the EU27. A standardised prompt framework was used to identify only explicitly stated roles and associated skills from verifiable public sources, including policy documents, occupational profiles, industry reports, and labour market analyses [5,8]. The searches were conducted primarily in English, while relevant sources in the national-language were included where they could be reliably interpreted and validated. In the EU27, 156 potentially relevant sources were initially identified and manually screened for accessibility, relevance, and evidential quality. After validation, 103 sources were retained, while 53 were excluded due to inaccessibility, duplication, insufficient role–skill evidence, or lack of verifiability. This explicit inclusion and exclusion logic strengthens the academic robustness of the methodology.

3.1 LLM-Assisted Extraction and Validation

LLMs have been used to support scalable extraction of transport roles and associated skills from public sources, but their use was strictly limited to retrieval and structured extraction rather than interpretation or synthesis. The extraction process was carried out using OpenAI's ChatGPT platform between December 2025 and January 2026 with web search enabled, and outputs were captured in standardised Excel templates containing role title, associated skills, source reference, and country. The prompt is presented in Appendix A.

Several platforms, including ChatGPT, Perplexity Pro, and Microsoft Copilot, were tested for adherence to detailed extraction rules, source fidelity, and Excel-compatible structured output. ChatGPT was retained because it showed the strongest adherence to prompt constraints and the most consistent structured outputs, while systems that produced more inferred or less controllable outputs were excluded from the final methodology [8].

Because transport-sector sources frequently contained evidence relating to more than one capability domain, extraction was conducted separately for each predefined skill category, including AI, HPC, cybersecurity, governance, sustainability, data, and systems integration. Skill categories were treated as controlled analytical lenses rather than mutually exclusive properties of a source. The same source could therefore be processed more than once using category-specific prompts where it contained explicit evidence for multiple capability areas. This design avoided forcing a single dominant label onto multi-capability roles and directly addressed the risk that AI-enabled optimisation, HPC-supported simulation, digital twins, data governance, or cybersecurity governance could otherwise be collapsed into a single technical category.

Each extraction pass used a conservative zero-row rule: if the source did not explicitly evidence both a role and an associated skill within the specified category, no record was created. This rule was particularly important for areas that overlapped, where plausible inference could otherwise be introduced too easily. Following extraction, outputs from different categories were merged, and duplicate role entries were reviewed manually. Cross-domain entries were retained only where the underlying source supported the association. During validation, records were classified as single-category evidence, multi-category evidence, or rejected inference. This allowed overlaps to be analysed as validated cross-cutting capability themes rather than as artefacts of prompt design.

Validation was multi-layered. All extracted entries were manually reviewed by a domain-aware researcher using a structured checklist to verify source accessibility, transport relevance, evidential alignment between roles and skills, and compliance with coding rules. Ambiguous entries were removed rather than rewritten, and a second reviewer examined the methodology, validation approach, and consolidated findings as part of quality assurance.

To support methodological transparency and future replication, the project maintained standardised prompt templates, coding structures, validation checklists, controlled vocabularies, inclusion and exclusion rules, and examples of accepted and rejected extraction records. Subject to consortium approval and project dissemination requirements, these materials will be made available through a public repository following completion of the project.

Data Structuring and Synthesis. An Excel-based coding framework was developed to organise and analyse the extracted evidence. Key fields included country, source title, source type, source URL, role title, role category, skill category, associated skills, maturity level, sector or mode, organisation type, relevance, validation status, and analytic comments. This coding structure supported transparency, auditability, and aggregation across countries. Following validation, 28 distinct transport-related roles were identified in the dataset, with frequencies ranging from one to sixteen occurrences across country-level records. To support robust consolidation, only roles appearing five or more times were retained for detailed clustering, while lower-frequency roles were excluded from role-family analysis but still informed broader capability and topic mapping. This refinement supports methodological clarity and explains how role evidence was translated into stable curriculum-relevant patterns.

Survey and Interview Methods. The stakeholder survey was designed as a structured quantitative instrument aligned to the GreenShift analytical framework, covering digital maturity, AI and digital twin adoption, infrastructure readiness, barriers to adoption, sustainability capability needs, and programme preferences. It was administered online using Microsoft Forms between 3 March 2026 and 27 March 2026, distributed through consortium networks and open dissemination channels such as LinkedIn, and generated 58 valid responses for analysis. The survey sample is exploratory and not statistically representative of the full EU27 sector. Nine semi-structured interviews were also conducted with purposively selected stakeholders from industry, research, public sector, and technology contexts. Interviews were analysed using a hybrid thematic approach and used to validate and deepen understanding of organisational practices, implementation barriers, and future capability requirements.

4 Results

Our results indicate that the European transport and mobility sector is undergoing uneven but accelerating digital transformation, with foundational capabilities more established than advanced data-intensive, simulation, or integrated decision-support practices [23].

The identified four Role Families are:

1. **Transport Data Analytics**
2. **Modelling, Simulation and Digital Twin**
3. **Systems Integration and Platform**
4. **Digital Innovation Leadership (Transport-specific)**

These role families are designed as pedagogically actionable structures rather than as narrow occupational categories. AI capability, sustainability, governance, cybersecurity, systems thinking, and HPC should be treated as cross-cutting capability layers embedded across multiple role families rather than as isolated

Table 1. Role-Family Alignment with Competence Frameworks and Curriculum Implications

Role family	Primary capability focus	Relevant framework alignment	Curriculum implication
Transport Data Analytics	Transport data pipelines, analytics, visualisation, and evidence-based decision support	ESCO data and transport occupations; e-CF data and analysis competences; DigComp information and data literacy; GreenComp sustainability data interpretation	Include transport data management, data quality, applied analytics, visualisation, and interpretation of operational and sustainability indicators.
Modelling Simulation, and Digital Twin	Scenario modelling, simulation, optimisation, digital-twin reasoning, and HPC-enabled analysis	e-CF architecture and solution development competences; ESCO modelling and engineering roles; Green-Comp systems thinking and futures literacy	Develop learning outcomes on simulation design, model assumptions, validation, uncertainty, computational scale, and interpretation of digital-twin outputs.
Systems Integration and Platform	Interoperability, infrastructure integration, data platforms, operational systems, and AI/HPC deployment contexts	e-CF systems architecture, integration, and service delivery competences; ECSF-adjacent architecture, implementation, and risk-management profiles; ESCO ICT and infrastructure roles	Embed systems architecture, interoperability, platform governance, operational resilience, and secure-by-design integration tasks into practical assessments.
Digital Innovation Leadership	Digital transformation, governance, procurement awareness, sustainability strategy, organisational change, and accountability	GreenComp sustainability competences; e-CF governance and strategy competences; ECSF-adjacent policy, compliance, and risk-management profiles; ESCO management and policy roles	Include governance, sustainability, risk, cybersecurity awareness, organisational readiness, and strategic roadmap assessments for AI- and HPC-enabled transport.

standalone domains [26]. This better reflects the convergence of technical, operational, sustainability, and governance demands in real transport systems.

Table 1 consolidates the role-family interpretation against external competence frameworks. The table is intentionally role-family based rather than role-title based. This avoids overfitting the curriculum to unstable job titles and shows how the evidence can be connected to recognised European reference frameworks while retaining sector-specific transport meaning.

Current Capabilities and Skills Gaps. The analysis identifies a baseline of existing digital and operational capability across much of the sector, but also highlights major gaps in data integration, advanced analytics deployment, modelling and optimisation, systems integration, and digitally enabled systems management. Advanced capabilities such as large-scale simulation, intelligent decision support, digital twins, and HPC-supported optimisation remain concentrated in larger organisations and specialised teams.

The analysis places a strong emphasis on the uneven diffusion of AI and HPC. The survey respondents recognised the importance of HPC for future use cases, such as optimisation and simulation, but the current deployment remained limited outside of research-intensive or large infrastructure settings. Similarly, the demand for AI capabilities exceeded the organisational readiness, with implementation often fragmented into pilots rather than embedded operational systems. Cross-cutting gaps also emerged in transversal skills. These include systems thinking, interdisciplinary collaboration, governance awareness, and the ability to connect technical tools to domain-specific operational and strategic decisions. These are not secondary soft skills, but central requirements for effective digital transformation in transport contexts.

Organisational Barriers and Enabling Conditions. Major barriers include siloed structures, legacy systems, limited internal training pathways, resource constraints, fragmented data environments, and challenges in moving from innovation activity to operational deployment. SMEs appear particularly constrained by lower access to specialist expertise, compute infrastructure, and internal digital capability development [6,11]. At the same time, the evidence points to important enablers. Stakeholders consistently emphasised the value of practical, flexible, and industry-relevant learning pathways, including modular study, micro-credentials, applied projects, and work-integrated approaches [13,25]. This finding directly supports a curriculum design model that balances conceptual depth with accessibility for learners entering from varied disciplinary and professional backgrounds.

Cross-Method Synthesis. The cross-method synthesis shows convergence across desk research, survey, and interviews. AI-related capability demand was widely evidenced in role documentation, but survey and interview data showed low implementation maturity and fragmented organisational uptake. Data integration emerged across all three methods as a foundational and cross-cutting challenge, while sustainability appeared as both a strategic priority and an operational capability gap. These differences are analytically important rather than problematic. The desk research revealed structural role and capability patterns, the survey provided directional evidence on adoption and barriers, and the interviews revealed the practical realities of implementation, including organisational silos, cultural barriers, and uneven readiness. Together, the three methods produce a richer basis for curriculum design than any source could provide alone.

The synthesis shows a consistent pattern: capability demand is outpacing organisational readiness. Although AI-, HPC-, and data-related roles are widely recognised, surveys and interviews indicate that adoption is constrained by organisational, infrastructural, and workforce factors. These shortages therefore reflect broader transformation challenges, not only technical skills gaps. Educational interventions must address both technological competencies and adoption capacity.

5 Discussion

The analysis strengthens the case for moving from technology-centred to capability-based and role-anchored curriculum design. Existing approaches frequently separate workforce analysis from curriculum development, creating limited traceability between identified skills needs and educational provision. Our methodology addresses this challenge by establishing an explicit evidence trail linking role identification, capability analysis, stakeholder validation, and curriculum design. In this model, curriculum is not derived from abstract disciplinary content alone, but from validated evidence about what professionals in digitally transforming transport systems need to understand and do.

5.1 From Labour Market Evidence to Curriculum Architecture

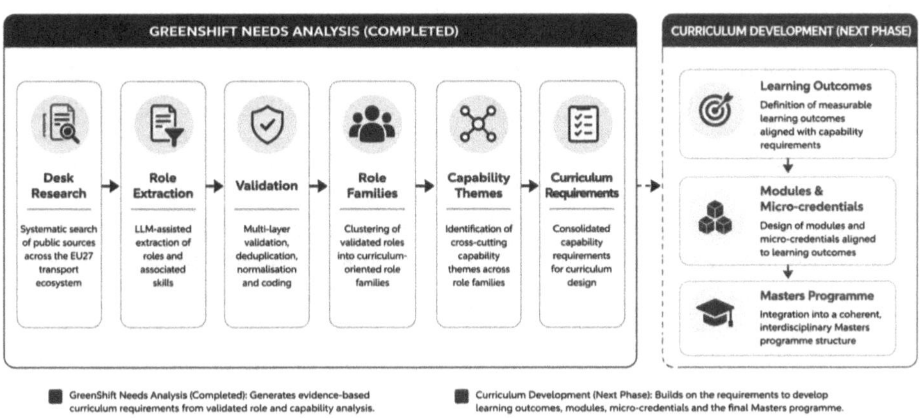

Fig. 1. Evidence-to-curriculum traceability framework. The GreenShift Needs Analysis establishes a pathway from desk research and validated role extraction to role families, capability themes, and curriculum requirements. The next phase translates these requirements into learning outcomes, modules, micro-credentials, and the Master's programme architecture.

A central contribution of the study is the curriculum traceability framework linking desk research roles to role families, capability themes, and curriculum requirements. The framework provides a structured pathway from labour market evidence to subsequent curriculum development activities, including learning outcome definition, module design, and programme architecture.

Figure 1 illustrates the curriculum traceability process developed within GreenShift. The framework provides an explicit link between labour market evidence and curriculum architecture, ensuring that programme design decisions can be traced back to validated role and capability requirements identified through desk research, stakeholder surveys, and interviews. This approach increases transparency, supports curriculum relevance, and provides a reproducible methodology for workforce-aligned educational design.

The role-family analysis should be read as an intermediate artefact in curriculum design, rather than as a final occupational taxonomy. Its purpose is to make role-evidence pedagogically usable. The desk research produced heterogeneous role titles across countries and organisations, but direct translation of these titles into modules would have produced an unstable and overly fragmented curriculum. The synthesis therefore moved from individual role titles to role families, and from role families to capability clusters. This enables curriculum design to respond to recurring work requirements without becoming dependent on the exact vocabulary of particular employers or national labour markets.

The four role families support different curriculum emphases. Transport Data Analytics roles require data acquisition, data management, transport analytics, visualisation, and evidence-based decision support. Modelling, Simulation and Digital Twin roles require understanding of simulation methods, scenario analysis, validation, model limitations, and the computational implications of large-scale modelling. Systems Integration and Platform roles require attention to interoperability, architecture, data platforms, infrastructure integration, and the operational embedding of AI- and HPC-enabled tools. Digital Innovation Leadership roles require governance, sustainability, risk, procurement awareness, cross-organisational coordination, and the ability to translate digital capabilities into organisational change.

These role families imply six curriculum topic groups. First, learners require a foundation in transport systems and domain context, including infrastructure, mobility systems, operations, planning, and sustainability pressures. Second, they require data management and analytics for transport, including transport data types, data pipelines, quality, integration, and analytical interpretation. Third, they require modelling, simulation, and HPC-enabled analysis, including scenario modelling, optimisation, computational scale, and interpretation of model outputs. Fourth, they require digital twins and advanced transport modelling, with emphasis on integrating data, models, simulations, and operational feedback loops. Fifth, they require systems architecture and integration for AI and HPC in transport, including interoperability, platforms, infrastructure, and links between analytical systems and operational environments. Sixth, they require decision support, strategy, and governance in AI-enabled transport, including accountability, risk, sustainability, cybersecurity, and organisational adoption.

This translation provides a concrete response to the curriculum-design problem. The expected next step is not merely to list skills, but to transform validated role-capability evidence into learning outcomes, module specifications, micro-credentials, assessment patterns, and learner pathways. For example, evidence of digital-twin and simulation roles can inform learning outcomes concerned with model interpretation, scenario design, computational constraints, and validation. Evidence of systems-integration roles can inform assessment through architecture design tasks or interoperability case studies. Evidence of digital innovation leadership roles can inform governance-oriented assessments, such as digital transformation roadmaps, sustainability impact analyses, or risk-aware deployment plans (Table 2).

Table 2. Examples of Translation from Evidence to Curriculum Requirements

Evidence Source	Key Finding	Curriculum Requirement
Desk Research	Emerging transport roles increasingly require an understanding of transport systems alongside AI, HPC, digital twins, data analytics, and sustainability concepts. Many prospective learners are expected to enter from non-transport and non-computing backgrounds.	Introduce a foundational Transport Systems and Digital Transformation module providing an overview of the transport sector and its relationship with AI, HPC, sustainability, modelling, simulation, and digital transformation.
Survey	Respondents identified low organisational maturity in AI adoption despite recognising its future importance.	Include introductory AI and data-driven decision-making content to support learners entering with limited prior AI experience.
Interviews	Stakeholders consistently highlighted systems integration, interoperability, and cross-domain collaboration challenges.	Embed systems thinking, interoperability, and interdisciplinary problem-solving concepts across curriculum topics and practical activities.

The analysis also identifies a structured topic development process involving capability mapping, cross-family integration, learning architecture development, and strategic alignment with GreenShift priorities in AI, HPC, sustainability, and transport systems transformation. This supports a curriculum model that is both evidence-based and sufficiently flexible to accommodate future changes in technology and workforce demand.

The role families developed through the needs analysis provide the foundation for subsequent curriculum design activities within GreenShift. The next phase involves translating capability clusters into learning outcomes, module specifications, micro-credentials, assessment strategies, and learner pathways. Particular emphasis is placed on flexible entry routes for non-computer-science learners and on integrating AI, HPC, sustainability, governance, and cybersecurity as cross-cutting themes across the curriculum rather than as isolated specialist topics. This process has already informed the initial identification of curriculum topics, capability areas, and programme design considerations, demonstrating a direct pathway from workforce evidence to educational planning. While this paper focuses on the evidence-to-curriculum requirements phase, subsequent GreenShift work is now translating these requirements into detailed programme structures and pilot learning activities.

Implications for Non-computer-science Learners. Our results reinforce the importance of designing for heterogeneous learner populations. Many prospective learners are likely to engage with HPC, AI, modelling, and digital infrastructure through applied contexts such as simulation, optimisation, emissions analysis, and data-driven decision support rather than through specialist software engineering roles.

This implies that curriculum should provide a strong foundation in transport systems and domain context while offering multiple access points into advanced digital concepts. It also suggests the need for modularity, scaffolded learning, practical cases, and programme structures that support both full Master's participation and shorter upskilling pathways.

Educational and Labour Market Implications. The analysis indicates growing demand for hybrid digital-green professionals who can interpret systems, integrate data, understand governance and sustainability constraints, and apply computational tools to operational transport challenges.

This has implications not only for GreenShift, but for advanced digital education more broadly. It suggests that AI and HPC education in application domains should be organised around capability integration, contextual use, and interdisciplinary problem solving rather than around purely technical specialisation. The same role-anchored, evidence-to-curriculum workflow can be adopted to organise cybersecurity education around validated role profiles and evolving capability requirements, providing a structured alternative to static, technology-centred syllabi.

Although developed in the context of transport systems, the methodological approach has direct relevance for cybersecurity education. The challenge of rapidly evolving role requirements, fragmented competency definitions, and emerging technology adoption is equally visible across cybersecurity domains. The GreenShift workflow therefore offers a potential model for identifying and validating curriculum requirements in distinct computing contexts.

6 Conclusion

This study contributes both substantive findings on HPC and AI capability requirements in transport systems and a transferable methodology for the design of evidence-based curriculum. The principal contribution lies in demonstrating how bounded LLM-assisted extraction, human validation, framework mapping, stakeholder engagement, and curriculum traceability can be integrated into a coherent and academically defensible workflow.

Our results show that the digital transformation of the transport and mobility sectors is real but uneven and that capability development has become a critical condition to translate AI, HPC, and advanced digital technologies into operational and strategic value [23]. The study also demonstrates that curriculum design in such contexts should be grounded in validated role-capability evidence, organised through curriculum-oriented role clusters, and delivered through flexible, interdisciplinary learning architectures that are accessible to non-traditional and non-computer-science learner cohorts.

Some limitations should be acknowledged. First, the study is exploratory and does not claim statistical representativeness across the entire European transport ecosystem. Second, desk research was dependent on publicly available sources whose quality and coverage varied considerably between countries. Third, although LLM outputs were manually validated, extraction quality remains partially dependent on source accessibility and prompt design. Fourth, the rapid evolution of AI, HPC, and transport technologies means that identified capability requirements should be regarded as indicative rather than permanent. Finally, while the methodology was developed within the transport domain, further validation would be required before generalising results to other sectors.

In summary, the GreenShift methodology provides a transferable model for curriculum design in sectors undergoing rapid technological change. The approach demonstrates how role identification, competency analysis, framework mapping, stakeholder validation, and curriculum development can be integrated within a transparent and reproducible workflow. This contribution is potentially applicable to domains such as cybersecurity, energy, manufacturing, and healthcare, where emerging technologies are reshaping workforce requirements faster than traditional curriculum design processes can respond.

Acknowledgements. This work is developed as part of "GreenShift: EU MSc in AI & HPC for Green Digital Innovation in Transport", a project funded by the European Commission, grant no. 101226222; https://www.thegreenshift.eu/.

The authors thank the following individuals who collected and validated results: D. Boyle, M. Castelli, M. Danelutto, D. Harrison, D. Janetzko, I. Kovačević Vukas, C. Landolfo, B. Lu, G. Meijer, G. Mencagli, G. O'Grady, and R. Talevska.

Conflicts of Interest. The authors declare that they have no competing interests.

A Appendix A Representative LLM Extraction Prompt

Listing 1.1. Representative category-specific LLM prompt for evidence extraction

```
A. HPC - High Performance Computing

Search string:
"[Country] high performance computing transport"

LLM Search Request:
Identify explicitly evidenced roles and skills related to the use of High Performance
     Computing (HPC) in the transport sector in [COUNTRY].

Search government policy, national HPC centres, transport authorities, academic research, and
      sector bodies where transport use cases of HPC are clearly stated. Relevant use cases
     include large-scale simulation, transport modelling, infrastructure optimisation,
     traffic systems, logistics modelling, digital twins, and scenario analysis.

Extraction rules:
- Extract only roles and skills explicitly mentioned in the source.
- Do not infer a role from a technology description.
- Do not infer a skill from a project description unless the skill is explicitly stated.
- Use approved role dropdowns only.
- Record skills exactly as evidenced.
- Assign maturity level only where the source provides sufficient evidence.
- Assign SME or MNC relevance only where the source provides sufficient evidence.
- Exclude generic computing strategies, marketing content, and non-transport HPC use cases.
- Exclude inaccessible sources and sources without stable bibliographic or organisational
     information.
- Output Sheet-02-ready records with accessible URLs only.

Skill Category:
HPC - High Performance Computing only.

Zero-row rule:
If the source does not explicitly evidence both a transport-related role and an associated
     HPC skill, return zero rows. Do not create a plausible or inferred entry.

Output fields:
Country | Source title | Source type | Source URL | Role title | Role category | Skill
     category | Associated skill(s) | Transport mode or sector | Organisation type |
     Evidence note | Validation status

Additional searches using the same rules:
1. "[Country] HPC simulation infrastructure"
2. "[Country] national HPC centre transport"
3. "[Country] large-scale simulation transport modelling"
4. "[Country] digital twin transport HPC"
```

The listing shows the controlled prompt structure used for category-specific extraction. The prompt illustrates the conservative extraction logic rather than the complete prompt library.

Sources containing evidence for more than one category were processed through repeated category-specific passes. Records were retained only where the source explicitly evidenced both the role and the associated skill. The same pattern was used for AI, HPC, cybersecurity, governance, sustainability, data, modelling, systems integration, innovation, production, business, leadership, and related capability categories.

References

1. Aggarwal, D., Bokshi, A., Lad, D.: A hands-on approach for scalable parallel applications development: from testbed to Petascale. In: HiPC'22, pp. 36–43. Bengaluru (2022)

2. Aljohani, N.R., Aslam, A., Khadidos, A.O., Hassan, S.U.: Bridging the skill gap between the acquired university curriculum and the requirements of the job market: a data-driven analysis of scientific literature. J. Innovation Knowl. **7**(3), 100190 (2022)
3. Allam, Z., Dhunny, Z.A.: On big data, artificial intelligence and smart cities. Cities **89**, 80–91 (2019)
4. Almeida, F.: Comparative analysis of EU-based cybersecurity skills frameworks. Comput. Secur. **151**, 104329 (2025)
5. Amershi, S.: Guidelines for Human-AI interaction. In: CHI '19, pp. 1–13. ACM, Glasgow (2019)
6. Autor, D.H.: Why are there still so many jobs? The history and future of workplace automation. J. Econ. Perspect. **29**(3), 3–30 (2015)
7. Bacigalupo, M., Binasco, A.: Teaching different key competences at once. EUR Scientific and Technical Research Report JRC136734, Publications Office of the European Union, Luxembourg (2024). https://doi.org/10.2760/013612
8. Bender, E.M., Gebru, T., McMillan-Major, A., Shmitchell, S.: On the dangers of stochastic parrots: can language models be too big? In: FAccT '21, pp. 610–623. ACM, Virtual Event, Canada (2021)
9. Bouvry, P., et al.: The European master for HPC curriculum. J. Parallel Distrib. Comput. **201**, 105081 (2025)
10. Carneiro Neto, J.A., Alves Neto, A.J., Moreno, E.D.: A systematic review on teaching parallel programming. In: EATIS '22. ACM, Aveiro (2022)
11. CEDEFOP: European Centre for the Development of Vocational Training: Skills in transitions – the way to 2035. Tech. Rep. 4213, Publications Office of the European Union, Luxembourg (2023). https://doi.org/10.2801/438491
12. Chen, J., Ghafoor, S., Impagliazzo, J.: Producing competent HPC graduates. Commun. ACM **65**(12), 56–65 (2022)
13. Council of the European Union: Council recommendation of 16 June 2022 on a European approach to micro-credentials for lifelong learning and employability. Official J. Eur. Union **C**(243), 10–25 (2022)
14. Danelutto, M.: HPC master design: experience from Pisa. In: PDP 2025, pp. 357–363. IEEE, Torino (2025)
15. ENISA: European Cybersecurity Skills Framework (ECSF). CC-BY 4.0 report, European Union Agency for Cybersecurity (ENISA) (2022). https://doi.org/10.2824/859537
16. Fetting, C.: The European Green Deal. Report, European Sustainable Development Network (ESDN), Vienna (2020). https://www.esdn.eu/fileadmin/ESDN_Reports/ESDN_Report_2_2020.pdf
17. González-Vélez, H., et al.: Digital4Business: Mastering advanced digital skills for European business transformation. In: WorldCIST 2025. LNNS, vol. 1583, pp. 377–390. Springer, Florianopolis (2025)
18. Kasneci, E., et al.: ChatGPT for good? On opportunities and challenges of large language models for education. Learn. Individ. Differ. **103**, 102274 (2023)
19. Kiesler, N.: Approaching the concept of competency. In: Modeling Programming Competency, chap. 1, pp. 17–36. Springer, Cham (2024)
20. Li, C., Guo, X., Yang, W., Chen, J.: Interdisciplinary practice for HPC competency cultivation. In: CSE 2025, pp. 1–8. IEEE, Guiyang (2025)
21. Mhaske, P., Bhattacharjee, B., Haldar, N., Upadhyay, P., Mandal, A.: Bridging digital skill gaps in the global workforce: a synthesis and conceptual framework building. Research in Globalization, p. 100311 (2025)

22. Mulder, M. (ed.): Competence-based Vocational and Professional Education: Bridging the Worlds of Work and Education, Technical and Vocational Education and Training: Issues, Concerns and Prospects, vol. 23. Springer, Cham, 1 edn. (2017)
23. OECD: OECD employment outlook 2025: Can we get through the demographic crunch? Tech. rep., OECD Publishing, Paris (2025). https://doi.org/10.1787/194a947b-en
24. Raj, R.K.: High performance computing education: Current challenges and future directions. In: ITiCSE-WGR '20, pp. 51–74. ACM, Trondheim (2020)
25. Ricci, S., Dzurenda, P., Somers, C., González-Vélez, H., Moravek, L.J.: Cybersecurity micro-credentials and career path design: The Digital4Security good practices. In: ARES 2025, EU Projects Symposium Workshops. LNCS, vol. 15999, pp. 77–95. Springer, Ghent (2025)
26. Righi, R., et al.: Academic offer of advanced digital skills in 2019-20. international comparison. focus on Artificial Intelligence, High Performance Computing, Cybersecurity and Data Science. JRC Research Reports JRC121680, Joint Research Centre (2020). https://ideas.repec.org/p/ipt/iptwpa/jrc121680.html
27. Silva, B.N., Khan, M., Han, K.: Towards sustainable smart cities: a review of trends, architectures, components, and open challenges in smart cities. Sustain. Cities Soc. **38**, 697–713 (2018)
28. Sinnett, W.E.: The application of DACUM in retraining and post-secondary curriculum development. Tech. Rep. ED119013, Education Resources Information Center (1976). https://eric.ed.gov/?id=ED119013, Revised Second Edition
29. Soderquist, K.E., Papalexandris, A., Ioannou, G., Prastacos, G.: From task-based to competency-based: a typology and process supporting a critical HRM transition. Pers. Rev. **39**(3), 325–346 (2010)
30. Somers, C., et al.: Systematic needs analysis of advanced digital skills for postgraduate computing education: The DIGITAL4Business case. In: AIED 2024. CCIS, vol. 2150, pp. 179–191. Springer, Recife (2024)
31. Stevens, C., Anderson, S., Carlson, A.: Integrating high performance computing into higher education and the pedagogy of cluster computing. In: PEARC '24, ACM, Providence (2024)

A Structured Method for Designing Capture-the-Flag Challenges in Higher Education

Holger Schmidt(✉), Sven Jörges, and Anthony Brunner

Department of Computer Science, Dortmund University of Applied Sciences and Arts, Dortmund, Germany
{holger.schmidt004,sven.joerges,anthony.brunner004}@fh-dortmund.de

Abstract. *Capture-the-Flag (CTF) challenges* are widely used in computer science education to support hands-on learning, problem-solving, and student engagement. However, the design of educational CTF challenges is often experience-driven and lacks systematic methodological support, particularly in higher education contexts with heterogeneous student cohorts and varying prerequisite knowledge.

This paper proposes a *structured method* for designing CTF challenges in higher education. The approach supports the alignment of challenges with prerequisite knowledge from different computer science domains and introduces a systematic approach for calibrating and controlling *challenge difficulty* in heterogeneous student cohorts. The proposed method aims to facilitate curriculum-aligned and pedagogically grounded *challenge-based learning (CBL)* experiences.

Keywords: higher education · cybersecurity education · capture-the-flag · challenge-based learning · challenge design · challenge difficulty

1 Introduction

In computer science education, developing practical and technical competencies is essential. Beyond understanding theoretical concepts taught in classical lectures, students must acquire programming abilities, become proficient in using tools, and strengthen their problem-solving skills. These competencies are primarily developed through repeated hands-on practice and therefore require sustained effort over time. A key challenge for educators is thus to foster and maintain student motivation throughout this learning process. Approaches such as project-based learning [18] and gamification [12] have been proposed to address this issue.

In *challenge-based learning (CBL)* [9,20], *Capture-the-Flag (CTF)* competitions represent a gamification approach consisting of discrete tasks, called *challenges*, which participants solve to find hidden *flags*. Several studies have

P. Kieseberg et al. (Eds.): ARES 2026 Workshops, LNCS 16903, pp. 345–363, 2027.
https://doi.org/10.1007/978-3-032-37218-5_21

demonstrated the educational potential of CTFs in computer science education [5,11,14,21], highlighting their effectiveness in supporting active learning and skill development.

This work focuses on the design of CTF challenges for higher education. Although the proposed approach is also applicable to dedicated information security degree programs, it primarily targets study programs in which security topics are covered in only one or a few modules within a broader computer science curriculum (e.g., computer science, information systems, or media informatics).

A key characteristic of this context is the high heterogeneity of student cohorts. Students differ substantially in their prior knowledge, study progress, and educational background, while security itself is a cross-cutting topic that builds on competencies from other domains such as web technologies, databases, or software engineering. As a result, the design of CTF challenges requires careful alignment with both the curriculum and the expected prerequisites.

However, existing off-the-shelf CTF challenges (e.g., those from Hack The Box[1]) rarely account for the heterogeneity of students' prior knowledge and skill levels. They are typically designed without explicit consideration of specific curricular contexts or varying competencies, which can result in challenges that are too difficult for students encountering them for the first time, leading to frustration and disengagement. Stronger students tend to dominate participation, while those who might benefit most from guided practice are more likely to drop out early. In addition, many challenges are not aligned with the specific learning objectives of individual courses, which limits their contribution to intended learning outcomes and reduces the overall effectiveness of CBL.

This paper addresses these limitations by proposing a structured method for designing CTF challenges in higher education, including (i) guidance for incorporating and aligning prerequisite knowledge from different computer science domains in challenge design, and (ii) an approach for supporting challenge difficulty calibration in heterogeneous student cohorts.

The remainder of this paper is structured as follows. Section 2 introduces the CTF approach in more detail. Section 3 discusses pedagogical foundations and related work on the use of CTFs and challenge-based learning in higher education. Section 4 presents the proposed structured method for designing CTF challenges. Section 5 addresses the calibration of challenge difficulty in heterogeneous student cohorts. Section 6 discusses the applicability and limitations of the approach. Finally, Sect. 7 concludes the paper and outlines directions for future work.

2 CTF Basics

CTF events, originating from cybersecurity practice and education [4], are widely regarded as an engaging and effective method for teaching technical concepts in a fun, non-traditional learning environment, providing a promising approach to foster active learning [10].

[1] https://www.hackthebox.com/.

Typically, CTF events are organized as competitions designed to simulate real-world attacks, providing participants with hands-on experience in identifying and exploiting vulnerabilities in practical settings [10,15].

In a typical jeopardy-style CTF, participants solve challenges to retrieve a hidden string, called a flag. For example, the web-based challenge shown in Fig. 1 requires participants to locate a flag concealed within a file system by exploiting a directory enumeration vulnerability. The flag `ctf_n0t_v3ry_smart` serves as proof of successful task completion.

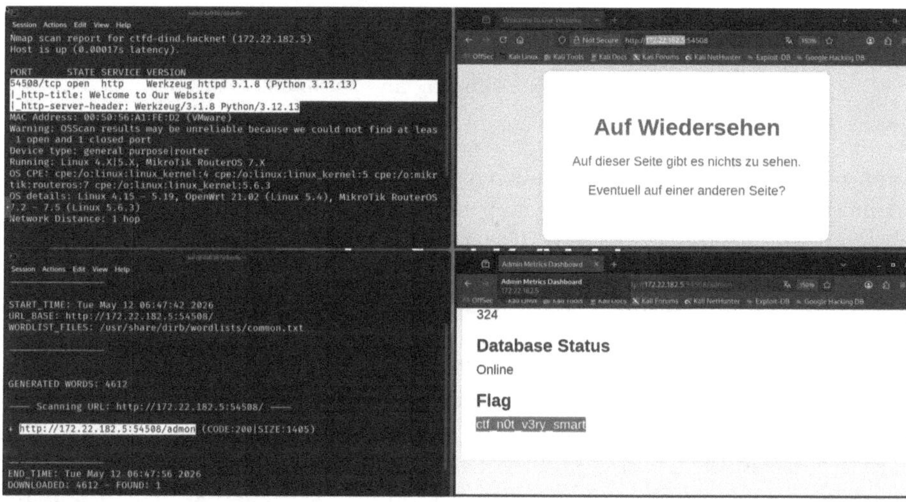

Fig. 1. Example CTF challenge: "Lost in the System"

Figure 2 illustrates the corresponding challenge interface in *CTFd*[2], an open-source (Apache-2.0) platform commonly used to host CTF competitions. The platform provides core functionality such as user and team management, challenge administration, and a live scoreboard. Each challenge is defined by a title, description, and score, supports flag submission, may offer optional hints with associated costs, and displays solve statistics. In the example shown in Fig. 2, the challenge "Lost in the System" has a score of 2, provides no hints, and has been solved once.

3 Background and Related Work

The systematic integration of CTFs into computer science courses requires course designs that are both motivating and accessible. Prior work emphasizes the use of *gamification* and *storytelling* to increase student engagement [15,16]. A central

[2] https://ctfd.io.

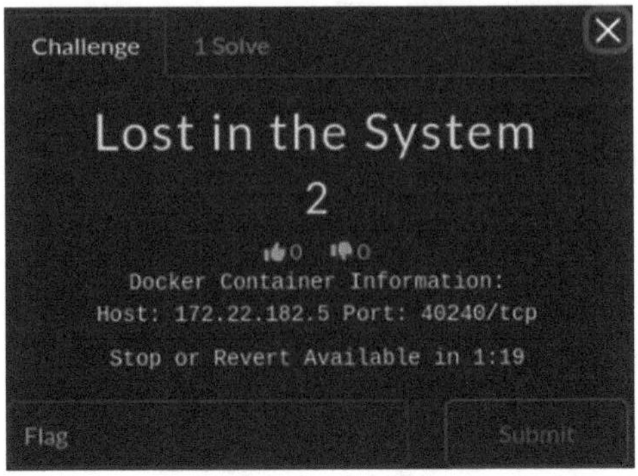

Fig. 2. CTFd interface showing an example challenge

design principle is *scaffolding*: challenges should build on fundamental concepts and increase in difficulty step by step to accommodate different levels of prior competencies [11,16]. CTFs are discussed as a tool for *formative assessment* that can complement classical exams and written assignments to provide a more reliable evaluation of student performance [21].

We present theoretical foundations with respect to the pedagogical considerations such as *instructional design* and *learning taxonomies* in the corresponding Subsect. 4.1 for challenge design and Subsect. 5.1 for quantifying challenge difficulty. Therefore, a detailed theoretical discussion is omitted here.

In [19], the authors address a target group similar to ours, namely undergraduate students. They present a structured approach based on modularization and progressive difficulty to address the issue that off-the-shelf challenges are often too difficult for novices. The "Learn-Practice-Test" approach [23] and the work by Quweider and Khan [20] - though the latter is not exclusively focused on cybersecurity - support the alignment of challenges with the curricular context. Similarly, MetaCTF [11] integrates CTF challenges with course material and supports an incremental learning process through scaffolding. Furthermore, [24] focuses on designing challenges with specific coordination and interaction aids.

While the aforementioned approaches address specific aspects of educational CTF design, such as novice accessibility [19], curricular integration [20,23], or scaffolding and learner support [11,24], they do not provide a unified methodology that systematically links prerequisite knowledge analysis, challenge design, and difficulty estimation. The method proposed in this paper seeks to integrate these aspects within a single instructional design process and complements it with a structured approach for estimating challenge difficulty.

4 CTF Structured Instructional Design Method

This section introduces the *CTF Structured Instructional Design Method (CTF-SIDM)*, a systematic approach for designing CTF challenges in higher education.

CTF-SIDM extends usual instructional design approaches by explicitly addressing the dual nature of CTF challenges as both technical artifacts and assessment instruments. In this context, successful exploitation is not merely a functional outcome, but serves as an operationalization of learning outcome achievement. Hence, CTF-SIDM realizes a tight coupling between vulnerabilities, exploitation via solution paths, and measurable learning objectives.

The following Subsect. 4.1 outlines the theoretical foundations of CTF-SIDM. Then, Subsect. 4.2 details each phase of the method, including their respective inputs, outputs, activities, and validation criteria. Subsequently, Subsect. 4.3 demonstrates the application of the CTF-SIDM by developing a concrete SQL injection challenge.

4.1 Theoretical Foundations

The CTF-SIDM is grounded in *task-based instructional design* [7], which provides a basis for creating effective educational CTF challenges. The method also draws from principles of *inquiry-based learning* [6] and *constructive alignment* [2], with a focus on *backward design* [22], ensuring that challenges foster critical thinking while aligning learning outcomes with assessment mechanisms.

The *systems approach model* [7] comprises the following ten steps for instructional design:

1. **Identify Instructional Goal(s)**: Determining the knowledge and skills learners should acquire upon completing the instruction.
2. **Conduct Instructional Analysis**: Decomposing the instructional goal into its constituent skills and identifying prerequisite (entry) skills required for successful learning.
3. **Analyze Learners and Contexts**: Examining learners' prior knowledge, characteristics, and the contexts in which learning and application take place.
4. **Write Performance Objectives**: Formulating specific, measurable objectives that define expected learner performance, conditions, and success criteria.
5. **Develop Assessment Instruments**: Designing assessments aligned with the objectives to measure learners' achievement of the intended outcomes.
6. **Develop Instructional Strategy**: Defining a theory-informed strategy for instruction, including content presentation, learner engagement, practice, and feedback.
7. **Develop and Select Instructional Materials**: Creating or selecting instructional materials and resources that support the defined strategy and objectives.
8. **Design and Conduct Formative Evaluation**: Evaluating the instruction during development to identify issues and opportunities for improvement.
9. **Revise Instruction**: Refining the instruction iteratively based on insights from formative evaluation across all design components.
10. **Design and Conduct Summative Evaluation**: Assessing the overall effectiveness of the instruction after implementation.

These steps guide the instructional design process in CTF-SIDM to ensure that pedagogical and technical components are appropriately aligned and that the resulting design is effectively tailored to learners' needs. The adaptation of these steps to the context of creating CTF challenges is described in the next Subsect. 4.2.

4.2 Method Overview

The CTF-SIDM organizes the design process into three iterative phases: (1) *Goal Definition*, (2) *Analysis*, and (3) *Development & Prototyping*. These phases aggregate the steps of the systems approach model [7] presented in the previous Subsect. 4.1 into a coherent structure tailored to CTF-based learning scenarios.

Unlike linear instructional models, CTF-SIDM emphasizes iterative refinement cycles, as unintended solution paths or misalignment between task and assessment frequently emerge during implementation. Figure 3 illustrates that workflow, including embedded validation steps and feedback loops.

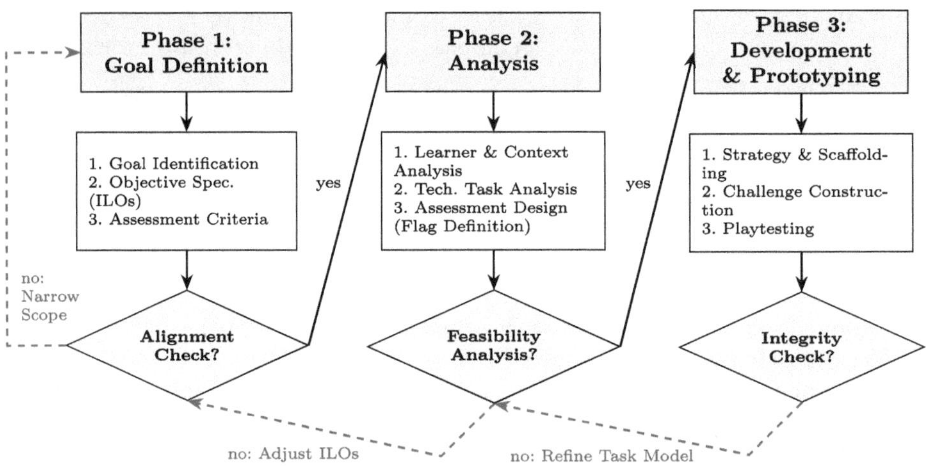

Fig. 3. Iterative workflow of the CTF-SIDM (Validation nodes represent decision points. Dashed red arrows indicate structured feedback loops between phases.) (Color figure online)

Phase 1: Goal Definition

Input: Topic domain and curricular context

Activities (see Fig. 3):

1. *Instructional Goal Identification:* Defining the overarching purpose of the challenge based on the topic domain and the curriculum.
2. *Objective Specification:* Translating goals into measurable *intended learning outcomes* (ILOs).

3. *Assessment Criteria:* Establishing the criteria for success and how the achievement of goals will be measured.

Output: A set of precise and measurable ILOs.

Validation: *Alignment Check* (see Fig. 3)

- Are the ILOs consistent with the topic domain and curricular context?
- Are the ILOs formulated according to the SMART criteria [8]?
- Do the ILOs use action verbs aligned with Bloom's taxonomy [3]?
- Can each ILO be directly assessed through the proposed assessment mechanisms?

This phase operationalizes backward design [22] by shifting the focus from content delivery to demonstrable outcomes. This approach directly supports constructive alignment [2] by linking the goals to assessment criteria (steps 1 & 4 in the systems approach model [7]). In the context of CTFs, this requires anticipating how technical interaction (e.g., exploitation of a vulnerability) can serve as evidence of learning. The explicit definition of flag conditions establishes the basis for subsequent task design and ensures consistency with constructive alignment.

Iteration: If the ILOs cannot be reliably measured through a CTF interaction (e.g., due to ambiguous or unverifiable solution paths), the scope must be refined (see *no: Narrow Scope* in Fig. 3) before proceeding. This ensures pedagogical integrity before technical resources are committed.

Phase 2: Analysis
Input: ILOs and curricular context
Activities (see Fig. 3):

1. *Learner and Context Analysis:* Analyzing prior knowledge, skill levels, and constraints based on the curricular context (educational setting).
2. *Technical Task Analysis:* Translating the targeted vulnerability into a structured sequence of exploitative actions required to solve the challenge. Each action is mapped to the cognitive processes necessary to achieve the ILOs. This includes identifying required knowledge (e.g., SQL syntax), reasoning steps (e.g., interpreting query behavior), and procedural skills (e.g., constructing payloads).
3. *Assessment Design (Flag Definition):* Formalizing the flag logic such that its retrieval is contingent upon successful completion of the intended exploit path. This includes minimizing unintended solution paths and ensuring that alternative approaches do not invalidate the measurement of learning outcomes.

Output: A structured task model, learner profile, and formally specified assessment mechanism.

Validation: *Feasibility Analysis* (see Fig. 3)

- Is the challenge feasible for the target learner group given their assumed prior knowledge and skill level?
- Do the exploit steps operationalize the competencies specified in the ILOs?
- Does the flag mechanism validly measure successful completion of the intended learning process?
- Are unintended solution paths minimized to preserve assessment validity?

This phase focuses on instructional analysis and assessment instrument development (steps 2, 3 & 5 in the systems approach model [7]). By structuring exploit steps and aligning them with ILOs, the method ensures that solving the challenge requires the intended competencies rather than incidental trial-and-error. The precise definition of the flag mechanism ensures that the technical "proof of work" corresponds to the ILOs and delimits the problem space in which learners engage in inquiry-based exploration [6].

Iteration: If the analysis reveals a mismatch between task complexity and learner capabilities, or if the exploit path does not adequately reflect the ILOs (see *no: Adjust ILOs* in Fig. 3), the learning outcomes or the task structure must be refined to restore constructive alignment.

Phase 3: Development & Prototyping
Input: Task model and learner profile
Activities (see Fig. 3):

1. *Strategy and Scaffolding:* Designing the instructional path, including hints, feedback mechanisms, and progressive disclosure of information to support inquiry-based learning.
2. *Challenge Construction:* Implementing the technical environment, including vulnerable code, data structures, and interaction interfaces.
3. *Formative Evaluation (Playtesting):* Conducting systematic testing to identify technical issues, unintended solution paths, and misalignment between task execution and assessment outcomes.

Output: A fully specified and executable CTF challenge.
Validation: *Technical & Didactic Integrity Check* (see Fig. 3)

- Does the challenge function technically as intended?
- Does successful flag retrieval require completion of the intended exploit and reasoning process?
- Do the interactions elicit the intended learning and problem-solving processes?

In this phase, the previously defined task model and instructional strategy are translated into a concrete technical artifact (steps 6–10 in the systems approach model [7]). Particular attention is given to the exclusivity of the solution path, as unintended shortcuts may invalidate the assessment logic. Scaffolding mechanisms are used to guide learners without removing the need for exploration and hypothesis testing, consistent with inquiry-based learning [6].

Iteration: Findings from playtesting often reveal unintended solution paths. This necessitates a return to *Phase 2* (see *no: Refine Task Model* in Fig. 3). The scaffolding is specifically refined here to support the student's process of experimentation and hypothesis testing [6].

CTF-SIDM provides a structured approach to designing CTF challenges in which technical exploitation serves as a valid and aligned measure of learning outcome achievement. A demonstration of this approach is provided in the following Subsect. 4.3.

4.3 Application

To illustrate the practical applicability of the CTF-SIDM, this subsection presents the systematic design of an SQL injection challenge for the course "Information Security" at Dortmund University of Applied Sciences and Arts. The course is attended by students from various bachelor's programs, including Computer Science, Medical Informatics, and Business Informatics, and spans multiple semesters (2nd to 5th). Consequently, the learner cohort is heterogeneous with respect to prior knowledge in computer networks, web technology, databases and SQL.

The design process follows the three phases of the CTF-SIDM as presented in the previous Subsect. 4.2, where only a high-level overview is provided here.

Phase 1: Goal Definition
Input: Topic domain (web security, databases, SQL injection) and heterogeneous learner cohort as described above
Activities:

1. *Instructional Goal Identification:* Understanding the security implications of unsanitized user input in database queries.
2. *Objective Specification:* The resulting ILO is: *"Students can construct an SQL injection payload that manipulates a query to return multiple database entries and explain the underlying mechanism."*
3. *Assessment Criteria:* Success is defined as retrieving a flag that is conditionally exposed only when the manipulated query produces a multi-row result set.

Output: ILO aligned with success criteria as defined above
Validation: *Alignment Check* ensuring that

- the ILO is consistent with the topic domain (SQL injection and database security),
- the ILO is measurable and action-oriented,
- the verbs "construct" and "explain" correspond to cognitive processes in Bloom's taxonomy [3],
- and the flag condition (multi-row result triggered by injection) directly reflects achievement of the ILO.

Iteration: If the ILO cannot be reliably measured through the defined flag condition (e.g., due to error-based leakage enabling an unintended solution path), the scope must be refined before proceeding.

Phase 2: Analysis
Input: Defined ILO
Activities:

1. *Learner and Context Analysis:* The target group possesses at most basic knowledge of SQL (e.g., simple queries), while some learners may have no prior experience with SQL at all, and only limited familiarity with security vulnerabilities. The heterogeneity of the cohort motivates explicit scaffolding and transparent system feedback.
2. *Technical Task Analysis:* The vulnerability (unsanitized user input embedded in an SQL query) is translated into a structured sequence of exploitative actions:
   (a) Identifying the injection point through input manipulation.
   (b) Observing system feedback and interpreting query behavior.
   (c) Constructing a logical condition (e.g., `' OR '1'='1`) to alter query semantics.
   (d) Triggering a multi-row result set from the `users` table.
   These steps require learners to apply and analyze SQL logic, linking procedural actions to conceptual understanding.
3. *Assessment Design (Flag Definition):* The flag `ctf_sql_injection_success` is returned only if (i) the executed query yields multiple rows and (ii) the input exhibits characteristics of an injection attack (e.g., the use of a tautology such as `' OR 1=1 --` or similar query-altering payloads). This ensures that successful flag retrieval operationalizes the intended learning outcome.

Output: A structured task model, learner profile, and formally specified flag logic

Validation: *Feasibility Analysis* ensuring that

- the exploit steps are achievable for the target learner group,
- the task sequence operationalizes the competencies specified in the ILO,
- successful flag retrieval requires completion of the intended reasoning and exploitation process,
- and unintended solution paths are constrained to preserve assessment validity.

Iteration: If the task complexity exceeds the learner profile or if alternative solution paths undermine the alignment between exploit and ILOs, the task model must be refined to restore constructive alignment.

Phase 3: Development & Prototyping
Input: Task model and learner profile
Activities:

1. *Strategy and Scaffolding:* The challenge provides structured guidance through (i) visibility of the database schema (table `users`), (ii) explicit system feedback for invalid inputs, and (iii) progressive hints encouraging logical query manipulation.
2. *Challenge Construction:* The challenge is implemented as a containerized web application using a Python (Flask) backend, an SQLite database, and a minimal HTML interface. User input is directly embedded into an SQL query without sanitization, intentionally introducing the vulnerability. The database contains multiple user entries, and the application returns a flag only when the defined multi-row condition is satisfied.
3. *Formative Evaluation (Playtesting):* During testing, an unintended solution path was identified that allowed participants to obtain the flag without performing the intended tautology-based SQL injection, requiring a revision of the challenge implementation.

Output: A fully functional CTF challenge with integrated scaffolding and controlled flag logic

Validation: *Technical & Didactic Integrity Check* ensuring that

- the challenge functions technically as intended,
- successful flag retrieval requires completion of the intended exploit and reasoning process,
- and the interactions elicit the intended learning and problem-solving processes.

Iteration: The unintended solution path required a return to phase 2 to refine the task model and strengthen the flag condition. This ensured that flag retrieval consistently indicates successful exploitation, thereby preserving constructive alignment.

This section presented the CTF-SIDM, a structured method for designing CTF challenges in higher education. The method also provides the basis for the challenge difficulty estimation approach described in Subsect. 5.

5 Quantifying Challenge Difficulty

This section establishes a quantitative approach for assessing challenge difficulty by grounding it in the revised Bloom's Taxonomy as described in Subsect. 5.1, extending it with a taxonomy matrix as a classification tool in Subsect. 5.2, and introducing a multidimensional scoring formula to support structured difficulty estimation during challenge design in Subsect. 5.3. Subsection 5.4 demonstrates the application of the formula using the same SQL injection challenge presented in Subsect. 4.3.

5.1 Theoretical Foundation

The *revised Bloom's Taxonomy* [17] describes the taxonomy of educational objectives (originally proposed in [3]) as a globally established model for classifying cognitive learning goals. It serves as a common language in educational planning and supports the alignment of learning objectives, instruction, and assessments. The taxonomy divides cognitive skills into six hierarchically structured levels as shown in Table 1.

Table 1. Revised Bloom's Traxonomy adapted to an SQL injection context

Level	Description	Example
1. Remembering	Retrieving relevant knowledge from long-term memory	Naming basic SQL syntax
2. Understanding	Determining the meaning of instructional messages	Describing query flow
3. Applying	Using a procedure in a given situation	Using a basic bypass payload
4. Analyzing	Breaking material into parts and detecting relationships	Identifying column counts
5. Evaluating	Making judgments based on criteria and standards	Comparing bypass payloads
6. Creating	Putting elements together to form a novel whole	Constructing a custom payload

5.2 The Taxonomy Matrix as a Classification Tool

To address the diversity of learning activities, [17] introduced the *knowledge dimension* (see Table 2), which categorizes the type of knowledge a learner interacts with into four categories.

Table 2. Knowledge dimensions according to [17]

Category	Description
A. Factual	Knowledge of discrete content elements and basic terminology
B. Conceptual	Knowledge of classifications, principles, theories, and models
C. Procedural	Knowledge of how to do something (skills, algorithms, methods)
D. Metacognitive	Knowledge about cognitive tasks and one's own strategic thinking

By intersecting the cognitive process dimension (Table 1) with the knowledge dimension (Table 2), a taxonomy matrix is obtained (an instance of such a taxonomy matrix is presented for the SQL injection challenge in Table 5). By counting the marked cells in each column, the variable k_i used in the calculation as presented in the next Subsect. 5.3 is obtained.

5.3 Difficulty Calculation

Challenge difficulty is not solely a property of the challenge itself, but emerges from the interaction between challenge requirements and the competencies of the target learner group. Educational research has shown that prior knowledge significantly influences learning performance and the effort required to solve new tasks [1]. Consequently, the same challenge may be perceived very differently depending on the knowledge and experience of the target cohort.

Following this perspective, the proposed difficulty model conceptualizes challenge difficulty as a combination of three dimensions:

1. **Cognitive complexity**, represented by the cognitive process dimension of the revised Bloom Taxonomy [17].
2. **Knowledge breadth**, represented by the number of knowledge dimensions involved in solving the challenge.
3. **Prior knowledge assumptions**, reflecting the extent to which the required competencies can reasonably be assumed within the target learner cohort.

The proposed formula should not be interpreted as a precise measurement of challenge difficulty, but as a structured mechanism for documenting and comparing difficulty estimates during the design process. Further empirical studies are required to investigate its relationship with learner performance and perceived difficulty.

The cognitive process dimension is weighted because higher levels of Bloom's taxonomy generally require increasingly complex cognitive operations [17]. As an initial operationalization, a linear weighting

$$w_i = i$$

is used, assigning increasing importance to higher cognitive levels while preserving interpretability. Alternative weighting schemes are possible and represent an avenue for future refinement.

The difficulty score is defined by Eq. 1:

$$S = \left\lfloor \frac{\sum_{i=1}^{6} w_i \cdot k_i}{S_{max}} \cdot PK \cdot S_{scale,max} + 0.5 \right\rfloor \tag{1}$$

where

- w_i denotes the weighting of cognitive level i,
- k_i denotes the number of marked cells in column i of the taxonomy matrix,
- PK denotes the prior knowledge factor,
- $S_{scale,max}$ denotes the upper bound of the difficulty scale, and
- S_{max} denotes the theoretical maximum weighted score obtainable within the taxonomy matrix.

The variable k_i represents the density of knowledge requirements within a particular cognitive level. Higher values indicate that more knowledge dimensions are involved at that level and therefore contribute to a higher estimated challenge difficulty.

As discussed above, prior knowledge strongly influences perceived difficulty [1]. The factor PK adjusts the estimated difficulty according to the expected familiarity of the learner cohort with the required concepts.

The normalization factor S_{max} represents the theoretical maximum weighted score obtainable within the taxonomy matrix. Since the matrix contains four knowledge dimensions and six cognitive levels, the maximum number of marked cells per cognitive level is four. Consequently,

$$S_{max} = \sum_{i=1}^{6} w_i \cdot 4.$$

For the linear weighting scheme $w_i = i$, this yields

$$S_{max} = 4 \cdot (1 + 2 + 3 + 4 + 5 + 6) = 84.$$

This normalization ensures that difficulty estimates remain independent of the absolute number of matrix entries and can therefore be compared across challenges.

Table 3 summarizes the prior knowledge adjustment factors used in the model.

Table 3. Prior knowledge (PK) factors for difficulty adjustment

Level	Description	Factor (PK)
1	No prior knowledge available	1.5
2	Conceptually derivable	1.25
3	Topic area generally known	1.0
4	In-depth prior knowledge	0.75
5	Previously taught or not required	0.5

If S exceeds $S_{scale,max}$, the resulting score should be interpreted as a design warning that the challenge may place demands beyond those assumed for the target learner group. Designers should therefore reconsider the challenge scope, prerequisite knowledge assumptions, or the decomposition into smaller learning units.

5.4 Application

To derive a structured difficulty estimate, the SQL injection challenge introduced in Subsect. 4.3 is mapped onto the taxonomy matrix defined in Subsect. 5.2.

To improve traceability and reduce classification subjectivity, the taxonomy matrix is derived directly from the exploit analysis performed during Phase 2 of the CTF-SIDM. Table 4 illustrates the mapping process.

Table 4. Mapping exploit steps to taxonomy dimensions

Exploit Step	Cognitive Process	Knowledge Dimension
Recall the basic structure of SQL queries	Remembering	Factual
Interpret system feedback	Understanding	Conceptual
Construct tautology payload	Applying	Procedural
Trigger multi-row result	Analyzing	Conceptual, Procedural

Based on this mapping, the taxonomy matrix shown in Table 5 is obtained.

Table 5. Taxonomy matrix mapping for the SQL injection challenge

Knowledge Dim.	1. Rem.	2. Und.	3. App.	4. Ana.	5. Eva.	6. Cre.
A. Factual	X					
B. Conceptual		X		X		
C. Procedural			X	X		
D. Metacognitive						
Sum (k_i)	1	1	1	2	0	0

Using the linear weighting scheme $w_i = i$, the weighted sum becomes

$$(1 \cdot 1) + (2 \cdot 1) + (3 \cdot 1) + (4 \cdot 2) = 14.$$

For this example, a prior knowledge level of "conceptually derivable" ($PK = 1.25$) is assumed. This reflects the educational setting in which students are expected to possess basic knowledge of SQL and relational databases from previous coursework, while the specific SQL injection technique has not been taught explicitly.

Using a normalized maximum score of $S_{max} = 84$ and a difficulty scale with $S_{scale,max} = 10$, the resulting difficulty estimate is

$$S = \left\lfloor \frac{14}{84} \cdot 1.25 \cdot 10 + 0.5 \right\rfloor = 2.$$

The resulting score should be interpreted as a relative difficulty estimate rather than an objective measurement. In practice, such estimates can support challenge design decisions by providing a transparent basis for comparing alternative challenge designs and reflecting on prerequisite knowledge assumptions.

6 Discussion

The proposed CTF-SIDM was initially applied in a preliminary form to the design of 15 CTF challenges for the summer semester 2025 practical training of the course "Information Security" at Dortmund University of Applied Sciences and Arts (as already introduced at the beginning of Subsect. 4.3). These challenges were subsequently deployed with approximately 180 students across heterogeneous study programs. An empirical evaluation of this first deployment is provided in [13], which especially investigates perceived challenge difficulty and required prior knowledge. The evaluation results revealed a slight but systematic misalignment between instructor-estimated difficulty and learner-reported experience. Several challenges were perceived as either overly trivial or disproportionately difficult relative to their intended cognitive level. This indicates that, while the initial CTF-SIDM supports structural alignment between learning objectives and technical implementation, it does not by itself ensure consistent calibration of cognitive demand across challenges. This finding highlights a fundamental limitation of purely qualitative instructional design approaches in CTF-based learning environments: even when learning objectives and assessment mechanisms are aligned, difficulty remains an under-specified construct unless explicitly operationalized.

In response to this limitation, a first difficulty estimation approach based on the revised Bloom's Taxonomy was developed. The approach establishes a structured mapping between cognitive processes, knowledge dimensions, and prior knowledge assumptions, thereby supporting a more systematic and transparent estimation of challenge difficulty during the design process. An initial version was prototyped within a student project and applied to a set of firewall-related challenges. The version presented in this paper in Sect. 5 is the result of subsequent refinement based on these experiences.

A central motivation for combining CTF-SIDM with the difficulty estimation approach is the challenge of addressing heterogeneous learner cohorts. Rather than treating the student body as a single cohort, learners are grouped into sub-cohorts with comparable prior knowledge and curricular backgrounds. Challenges can then be designed and evaluated relative to these sub-cohorts, enabling prerequisite knowledge assumptions and estimated difficulty to be aligned with the intended learner group.

In preparation for the summer semester 2026, the refined difficulty estimation approach was applied to the original set of 15 challenges together with CTF-SIDM. The resulting refinements are reflected in the CTF-SIDM presented in Sect. 4 and the difficulty estimation approach introduced in Sect. 5. For the revised set, estimated difficulty broadly matched learner-reported difficulty. However, systematic empirical validation remains an open research task.

From a methodological perspective, this iterative development process highlights two key implications. First, CTF-SIDM provides a structured approach for aligning rather technical CTF challenge design with pedagogical objectives, but requires complementary mechanisms to ensure comparability across challenges. Second, the difficulty formula provides a structured approach for documenting and comparing cognitive demands in CTF environments, but its validity depends on further empirical calibration against observed learner performance.

Overall, the proposed approach supports more systematic and reproducible CTF-based learning design while highlighting the need for empirical validation.

7 Conclusions and Future Work

This paper presented the CTF-SIDM, a structured method for designing CTF challenges in higher education. The method extends established instructional design principles by explicitly modeling the relationship between learning objectives, technical challenge design, and assessment mechanisms within CTF environments. In contrast to ad-hoc challenge creation, CTF-SIDM enables a systematic and iterative design process that ensures alignment between intended learning outcomes and observable learner performance through exploit-based task completion. The method is complemented by a challenge difficulty estimation approach based on revised Bloom's Taxonomy and a multidimensional scoring model incorporating cognitive processes, knowledge dimensions, and prior knowledge assumptions. The approach, operationalized through the formula, supports a more systematic and transparent estimation of challenge difficulty during the design process.

Future work includes empirical validation of both the CTF-SIDM and the challenge difficulty estimation approach in authentic educational settings. Additionally, extending both to non-security domains within computer science represents a promising direction. Finally, applying the method to challenge campaigns, i.e., sequences of interconnected tasks with controlled difficulty progression, is expected to further improve its applicability in course design.

Use of AI Tools. ChatGPT was used during manuscript preparation for language improvement, text reformulation, structuring, and limited translation support. Scopus AI was used to support the literature search. All AI-assisted outputs were critically reviewed by the authors, who take full responsibility for the scientific content and conclusions of this work.

Disclosure of Interests. The authors have no competing interests to declare that are relevant to the content of this article.

References

1. Ambrose, S.A., Bridges, M.W., DiPietro, M., Lovett, M.C., Norman, M.K.: How Learning Works: Seven Research-Based Principles for Smart Teaching. Jossey-Bass, San Francisco, CA (2010)
2. Biggs, J., Tang, C.: Teaching for Quality Learning at University, 5th edn. Open University Press, Maidenhead (2022)
3. Bloom, B.S., Engelhart, M.D., Furst, E.J., Hill, W.H., Krathwohl, D.R.: Taxonomy of Educational Objectives: The Classification of Educational Goals. Cognitive Domain. David McKay Company Inc, New York, Handbook I (1956)

4. Chung, K., Cohen, J.: Learning obstacles in the capture the flag model. In: 2014 USENIX Summit on Gaming, Games, and Gamification in Security Education (3GSE 14). USENIX Association, San Diego, CA (2014). https://www.usenix.org/conference/3gse14/summit-program/presentation/chung
5. Cole, S.V.: Impact of capture the flag (CTF)-style vs. traditional exercises in an introductory computer security class. In: Proceedings of the ACM Conference on Innovation and Technology in Computer Science Education, Vol. 1 (ITiCSE), pp. 470–476. Association for Computing Machinery, New York, NY, USA (2022). https://doi.org/10.1145/3502718.3524806
6. Dewey, J.: Experience and Education. Macmillan, New York (1938)
7. Dick, W., Carey, L., Carey, J.O.: The Systematic Design of Instruction, 9th edn. Pearson, Boston (2022)
8. Doran, G.T.: There's a S.M.A.R.T. way to write management's goals and objectives. Manage. Rev. **70**(11), 35–36 (1981)
9. Doulougeri, K., Vermunt, J.D., Bombaerts, G., Bots, M.: Challenge-based learning implementation in engineering education: a systematic literature review. J. Eng. Educ. **113**(4), 1076–1106 (2024). https://doi.org/10.1002/jee.20588
10. Egamberganova, A., Abdalov, U., Latipova, S., Ataev, S., Ismatova, D., Ubaydullayeva, N.: Teaching cybersecurity with CTF: new pedagogical methods and strategies. In: Proceedings of the International Conference of Young Specialists on Micro/Nanotechnologies and Electron Devices (EDM), pp. 2170–2175. IEEE (2025). https://doi.org/10.1109/EDM65517.2025.11096633
11. Feng, W.: A scaffolded, metamorphic CTF for reverse engineering. In: Proceedings of the USENIX Summit on Gaming, Games, and Gamification in Security Education (3GSE). USENIX Association, (2015)
12. Hou, H.T. (ed.): Game-Based Learning and Gamification for Education. MDPI - Multidisciplinary Digital Publishing Institute, Basel (2023)
13. Jörges, S., Schmidt, H., Bredebach, S., Kettmann, C.: Leveraging different "capture the flag" formats for computer science education: Lessons from two case studies. In: Symposium on Computing Education & Learning Technologies (CELT) at IEEE 50th Annual Computer Software and Applications Conference (COMPSAC). IEEE Computer Society (to be published in 2026)
14. Kaplan, Z., Zhang, N., Cole, S.V.: A capture the flag (CTF) platform and exercises for an intro to computer security class. In: Proceedings of the ACM Conference on Innovation and Technology in Computer Science Education, Vol. 2 (ITiCSE), pp. 597–598. Association for Computing Machinery, New York, NY, USA (2022). https://doi.org/10.1145/3502717.3532153
15. Karagiannis, S., Magkos, E.: Adapting CTF challenges into virtual cybersecurity learning environments. Inf. Comput. Secur. **29**(1), 105–132 (2020). https://doi.org/10.1108/ICS-04-2019-0050
16. Kornegay, M.A., Arafin, M.T., Kornegay, K.: Engaging underrepresented students in cybersecurity using capture-the-flag (CTF) competitions (experience). In: Proceedings of the ASEE Annual Conference and Exposition. American Society for Engineering Education (2021)
17. Krathwohl, D.R.: A revision of bloom's taxonomy: an overview. Theory Into Pract. **41**(4), 212–218 (2002). https://doi.org/10.1207/s15430421tip4104_2
18. Lavado-Anguera, S., Velasco-Quintana, P., Terrón-López, M.: Project-based learning (PBL) as an experiential pedagogical methodology in engineering education: a review of the literature. Educ. Sci. **14**(6), 617 (2024). https://doi.org/10.3390/educsci14060617

19. Nelson, C., Shoshitaishvili, Y.: PWN the learning curve: education-first CTF challenges. In: Proceedings of the 55th ACM Technical Symposium on Computer Science Education. vol. 1, pp. 937–943. Association for Computing Machinery, New York, NY, USA (2024). https://doi.org/10.1145/3626252.3630912
20. Quweider, M.K., Khan, F.: Implementing a challenge-based approach to teaching selected courses in cs and computational sciences. In: ASEE Annual Conference & Exposition. ASEE Conferences, New Orleans, Louisiana (2016). https://doi.org/10.18260/p.25589, https://peer.asee.org/25589
21. Vykopal, J., Švábenský, V., Chang, E.C.: Benefits and pitfalls of using capture the flag games in university courses. In: Proceedings of the 51st ACM Technical Symposium on Computer Science Education, pp. 752–758. SIGCSE '20, Association for Computing Machinery, New York, NY, USA (2020). https://doi.org/10.1145/3328778.3366893
22. Wiggins, G., McTighe, J.: Understanding by Design. Association for Supervision and Curriculum Development (ASCD), Alexandria, VA, expanded 2nd edn. (2005)
23. Xu, F., Xie, P., Wang, Y., Liu, Q., Fu, S., Shi, J.: "Learn, practice, test" integrated dynamic generation method for software security course experiments. Exp. Technol. Manag. **42**(11), 217–222 (2025). https://doi.org/10.16791/j.cnki.sjg.2025.11.026
24. Zhang, K., Wuthier, S., Yoon, K., Chang, S.: Designing and using capture the flag for coordination and interaction in engineering education. In: Proceedings of the IEEE Global Engineering Education Conference (EDUCON), pp. 1555–1560. IEEE (2022). https://doi.org/10.1109/EDUCON52537.2022.9766724

Data-Driven Cybersecurity Job Market Analysis

Paulina Espejo(✉) and Imre Lendák

Data Science and Engineering Department, Faculty of Informatics, Eötvös Loránd University, Budapest, Hungary

pdespejo18@gmail.com, lendak@staff.elte.hu

Abstract. Cybersecurity professionals are in great demand in the job market both in the European Union and in the World. Unfortunately, there is a widely recognized skills gap between the available training options, existing workforce and the roles available in the field. The goal of this research is to understand Europe's cybersecurity job market by exploring relationships and possible discrepancies between market demand and standardised competency definitions, mainly the European Cybersecurity Skills Framework published by the ENISA in 2022. Our analysis started with extensive data collection, during which $\sim 250,000$ cybersecurity job postings were collected from LinkedIn. Our approach analyses semantic similarity between job-market skills and ECSF job position descriptions, relying on Sentence-BERT embeddings to capture conceptual relationships beyond lexical matching. This enabled a systematic mapping between real-world skill demand and framework-defined competencies, allowing the degree of alignment to be quantitatively and qualitatively assessed. In addition, the study includes a skills demand analysis, based on the frequency distribution of cybersecurity job-market skills. Our results indicate that the alignment between job-market skills needs and ECSF descriptions is limited. Confident alignment is observed at the technical side of demanded skills, where core cyber security concepts are well-defined and standardized; however, most of the transversal non-technical skills are not covered in the ECSF, and these are in high demand on the job market. The presented approach is reproducible, scalable, and allows researchers and professionals to study the cybersecurity labour market in the EU by providing insights that may help align higher education curricula, policy frameworks, and industry demands.

Keywords: Cybersecurity · Semantic similarity · Skills gap · S-BERT

1 Introduction

Europe is facing a shortage of cybersecurity professionals, which is also reflected globally. Studies consistently highlight a persistent gap between available professionals and industry demand [5]. Based on the latest estimate offered by the European Union Agency for Cybersecurity (ENISA) [8], ~299,000 specialists in the European Union (EU), and more than 340,000 cybersecurity experts were

P. Kieseberg et al. (Eds.): ARES 2026 Workshops, LNCS 16903, pp. 364–382, 2027.
https://doi.org/10.1007/978-3-032-37218-5_22

missing across the continent in 2024. This suggests that the gap may be further widened, representing an important imbalance in the cybersecurity ecosystem.

That estimate is a signal of a structural problem: a mismatch between supply and demand between academic institutions and employers. Budde et al. [3] argue that the majority of university curricula continue to emphasise cybersecurity basics and core topics, even though employers are looking for skills that are barely taught in these courses. This suggests that the skills gap is also due to the lack of clarity and alignment in professional profiles in cybersecurity.

Simultaneously, emerging technologies such as security automation, machine learning, and artificial intelligence are not only relatively new concepts, but also change the nature of standard workflow in the cybersecurity field [4]. With the impact of emerging technologies on the cybersecurity workforce, the skill gap tends to be more dynamic, thus expanding the scope and complexity of new cybersecurity roles waiting to be filled, while training remains traditional.

The EU developed the European Cybersecurity Framework (ECSF) through ENISA, providing a standardised taxonomy of cybersecurity roles, tasks, and competencies, which aims to harmonise professional profiles in this field across the Member States [7], and supports cybersecurity curriculum design and job profiling. While this framework represents a step toward standardisation, the extent to which its defined competency structure reflects the cybersecurity labour market demand remains insufficiently examined.

Despite the considerable research conducted to explore the cybersecurity workforce, several limitations persist. Many studies focus on a single country or region, analyse a limited range of study programs, use a small representation of the job market, rely on synthetic or outdated datasets, or apply survey-based methodologies. Other studies have demonstrated the value of text mining techniques for analysing the cybersecurity labour market. However, up-to-date analyses across the EU and systematically connections with the ECSF are missing.

This research aims to gain a deep understanding of how the cybersecurity job market is currently structured and to examine how the skills demanded by the EU cybersecurity job market correspond to the standards present in the ECSF, to identify connections and potential gaps. To achieve this, a comprehensive dataset of cybersecurity job postings collected from LinkedIn across the EU countries in 2025–2026 is analysed by implementing a data-driven approach. This study contributes to the literature in three main ways, by providing:

- A data-driven analysis to measure the alignment of the current cybersecurity job market expectations in the EU in relation to the ECSF standards.
- An organised summary of the cybersecurity skills that are currently demanded throughout the EU states, explaining its structure in general, and highlighting variations between regions.
- Qualitative analyses that support the alignment of ongoing academic education and institutional frameworks with the dynamic requirements of the cybersecurity employment landscape.

The proposed solution responds to the limitations found in the literature and provides evidence on the cybersecurity area in the EU. Thus, informed decisions can be made in the field, relying on a data-driven method and employing a reproducible data science process designed for this specific domain.

2 Related Work

The shortage of qualified cybersecurity professionals is a subject of study and an important challenge across the EU. Several reports and academic research highlight a persistent misalignment between the labour market demand and the available skilled workforce. Existing studies analyse the situation through different approaches, finding key facts in the area, where the most prevalent are the impact of emerging technologies, the growing importance of soft skills, the limitations of traditional training, and the challenging dynamic landscape. Research in the EU revealed that the lack of skills is the major problem hindering progress. ENISA [9] lists governance and risk related positions among the most challenging to be filled in cybersecurity, thus implying that the gap is not limited to purely technical positions only. Likewise, Budde et al. [3] show that the skills shortage is not evenly spread across specialisations but focused on areas that combine technical expertise with strategic and regulatory understanding. In his paper, Blažič [2] contends that the shortage of personnel affects not only specialists in technical areas, but also the management and leadership levels, with a greater impact on small organisations.

To understand the current labour market dynamics in cybersecurity, some researchers have adopted data-driven approaches based on data collected from study programs, existing frameworks, and job postings. Text mining and natural language processing (NLP) techniques have proven valuable contributions to identifying emerging skills, competency clusters, role evolution, and more. Jumaan et al. [16] collected cybersecurity job postings and used fuzzy matching techniques, finding that risk management and governance related skills are highly demanded but not well covered in university curricula and shows that the problem is not limited to the EU. Other approaches, such as frequency-based analysis, as used by Ramezan [17], show that demand varies significantly across cybersecurity subfields, with differences between areas such as governance, offensive security, and infrastructure protection. This represents a valuable insight; but they rely on predefined categorisations and do not capture semantic similarity between skill expressions. Moving forward to modern approaches, Benchaaboune et al. [1] used BERT to classify cybersecurity job postings, revealing a structural mismatch between academic focus and real market needs, specifically in certifications, soft skills, and specialised tools. Goupil et al. [15] investigated how cybersecurity job postings compare to university curricula using manual taxonomies and automatic topic modeling techniques. Their findings indicate a large lack of supply in topics such as software security, governance, compliance, and emerging ones. These papers show how methodological NLP approaches can be applied to systematically capture labour market expectations and related analyses.

Another perspective in the literature examines the supply side of the skills problem, focusing on how adequate educational training and university programs prepare professionals for today's cybersecurity workforce. Dawson and Tompson [10] state that in addition to technical competencies, cybersecurity performance also depends on cognitive and behavioural skills such as decision-making, problem-solving, and situational awareness. This introduces the importance and complexity of categorising cybersecurity skills, as job postings often include both technical and non-technical competencies. Besides, in recent years, soft skills have been increasingly recognised as an integral part of the skill set required for a cybersecurity professional. Goupil et al. [15] revealed a trend: recruiters attach great importance to soft skills such as communication, collaboration, and teamwork, which, however, are rarely part of cybersecurity curriculums. This discovery matches general workforce reports [18], which show that adaptability, critical thinking, and interdisciplinary skills are turning out to be crucial factors in hiring decisions. In general, the literature suggests that educational systems struggle adapting to the evolving cybersecurity labour market demands, in terms of emerging technical areas and transversal competencies.

In their research in Central and Eastern European countries, Zivanovic et al. [21] proposed a dynamic optimisation methodology that modernises university curricula, relying on keyword extraction and text mining techniques. Their case study maps curricula against real cybersecurity job postings and the ECSF to find out the requirements of employers, and then adjusts the courses accordingly. Their approach increased the relevance of programs to the labour market by more than 30%. In addition, it exposes the feasibility of data-driven alignment between educational training, labour market demand, and EU frameworks. The disconnection of normative standardisation from the empirical labour market setting indicates the necessity of conducting a thorough comparison between the competency structures derived from the framework and the actual cybersecurity job market data.

3 Methodology

3.1 Problem Definition

Given a set of cybersecurity job postings J, determine the demanded skills in the job market and assess their correspondence with ECSF standards.

Input. Consider $J = \{J_1, J_2, \ldots, J_n\}$ a set of job postings. Each job posting J_i is represented by a tuple containing various features, including a set of skills.

Let S represent the set of all skills extracted from cybersecurity job postings.

Let $E = \{e_1, e_2, \ldots, e_p\}$ denote the set of standards defined in the ECSF, where $e_j \in E$ represents a description comparable to job-skills with $j \in \{1, \ldots, p\}$.

Output. A mapping function $f : S \rightarrow E$ that maps each extracted job-skill $s \in S$ to one or more ECSF standard $e_j \in E$, along with a semantic alignment score measuring the degree of correspondence between market-demanded skills and ECSF definitions, and a skill frequency distribution $F(s)$ representing the demand of each $s \in S$.

Similarity and Mapping. Each market-demanded skill $s \in S$ and ECSF standard $e \in E$ is represented as an embedding vector in a semantic space. To measure the semantic similarity between a job-market skill and an ECSF standard, the cosine similarity is computed using the Formula 1:

$$\mathrm{sim}(v(s_i), v(e_j)) = \frac{v(s_i) \cdot v(e_j)}{\|v(s_i)\| \, \|v(e_j)\|} \tag{1}$$

A mapping between a job-skill and an ECSF standard is considered valid if:

$$\mathrm{sim}(v(s_i), v(e_j)) \geq \tau \tag{2}$$

where τ is a predefined similarity threshold.

For each job-skill s_i, its best equivalent among the ECSF definitions is:

$$f(s_i) = \arg\max_{e_j \in E} \mathrm{sim}(v(s_i), v(e_j)) \tag{3}$$

3.2 Proposed Approach

This research follows a data-driven methodology, shown in Fig. 1, designed to explore how real-world cybersecurity demands align with the ECSF.

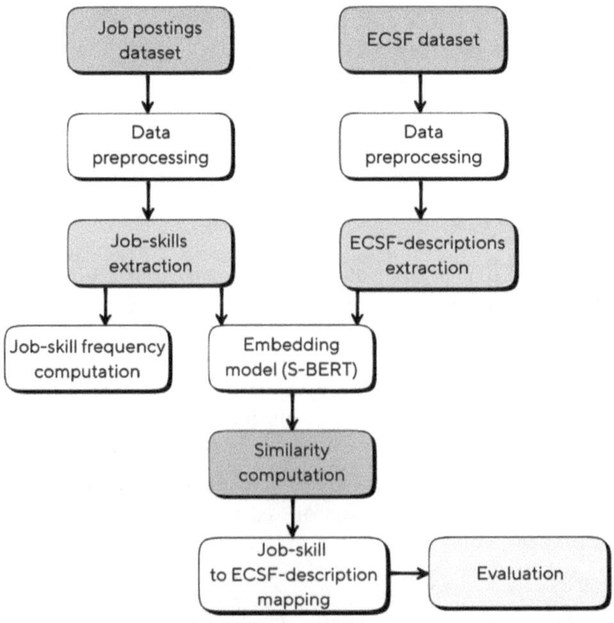

Fig. 1. Overview of the proposed approach

First, the cybersecurity job postings dataset and the ECSF dataset are preprocessed. Relevant and valid skills from job postings were extracted, as well as a subset of descriptions of the ECSF standards. Both extracted job-skills and ECSF definitions are then transformed into vector forms using the Sentence-BERT (S-BERT), used as a pretrained embedding model to generate semantic vector representations. Subsequently, semantic similarity is calculated to find the most appropriate ECSF description for each job market skill together with k mapping candidates. The similarity scores obtained serve as a basis for mapping the job-skills demanded to ECSF standards. Finally, this method is evaluated to find the extent of labour market demand aligned with the ECSF standards. Moreover, a skill frequency demand distribution is computed, and additional exploratory analysis and visualisations are created to reveal patterns in the cybersecurity job market across the entire job postings dataset.

Intuition. Job postings specify the skills that professionals should have to apply for open roles. Therefore, a cybersecurity job postings dataset is a valuable source of information to understand the real job market demand. But these data are expressed in natural language, meaning that they can be written in various manners, using different terms, phrases, or spellings. Representing this information in a semantic embedding space makes it possible to find conceptually similar skills, even though there may be linguistic variations.

Novelty. This study proposes a systematic semantic mapping approach to align cybersecurity job market skills in the EU with standards defined in the ECSF. Unlike many existing job market analyses that rely on traditional methods, this work uses contextual sentence embeddings to capture semantic relationships. Using a large-scale, up-to-date dataset composed of real job postings related to cybersecurity in the EU enables this research to be credible, and results will reflect an approximation to the reality of the cybersecurity job market.

Justification. The embeddings generated by S-BERT are a convenient resource for preserving the contextual meaning of skills and competency descriptions without decreasing accuracy, enabling large-scale semantic clustering and retrieval through cosine similarity, which is commonly used in modern embedding-based approaches to measure semantic similarity [14]. Having cosine similarity as a metric permitsa reliable semantic textual analysis. Finding pair elements from two different sources using a predefined threshold enables interpretability and reduces false positives as well as semantically irrelevant matches.

3.3 Evaluation Methods

The main scientific method of this research relies on the similarity between two different sources. The evaluation methods chosen are defined below.

Semantic Similarity Mean (μ). This metric calculates the average cosine similarity between every extracted job-market skill vector $v(s)$ and its assigned ECSF description vector $v(f(s))$. It is computed as the following formula shows:

$$\mu = \frac{1}{|S|} \sum_{s \in S} \mathrm{sim}(v(s), v(f(s))) \tag{4}$$

Coverage @τ Since semantic embedding models may produce moderately high similarity scores for broadly related concepts, the similarity mean is interpreted with the coverage metric and qualitative analysis to ensure a clear understanding of the mappings. The coverage metric measures the proportion of skills demanded in the job market that could be mapped with a good level of certainty to ECSF standards, at a similarity threshold τ, using the following formula:

$$\mathrm{Coverage@}\tau = \frac{|\{s \in S \mid \max(\mathrm{sim}(s)) \geq \tau\}|}{|S|} \tag{5}$$

Qualitative Analysis. Qualitative analysis enables contextual validation of the results. Domain knowledge is crucial to evaluate the results given the findings; therefore, it is possible to decide whether semantic associations are meaningful and consistent in the cybersecurity field.

4 Experiments and Results

This section describes the implementation of the methodology introduced earlier and describes how each conceptual step was performed.

4.1 Cybersecurity Job Postings Dataset

The cybersecurity labour market consists of multiple online job boards and various recruitment methods. Therefore, it is challenging to have an exact representation of how the cybersecurity job market is currently shaped. To address this limitation, a dataset containing job postings was constructed by web scraping LinkedIn job postings as part of a previous research project [11].

Data Source and Data Collection. The job postings were retrieved from LinkedIn by filtering through the "cybersecurity" keyword in European Union countries [13], plus the United Kingdom (UK) and Switzerland, which were included because of their strong relationship with the EU and their relevance in the labour market in the region. Besides the mentioned locations, these searches retrieved some records from other non-EU countries, such as Serbia, Albania, and Ukraine, due to their proximity to EU Member States. These records were retained in the dataset to preserve the representativeness of the broader EU cybersecurity labour market. Technical details about the implementation are available in the following repository [11]. The dataset used in this study comprises job postings collected between March 2025 and March 2026. It can be accessed through the following link [6] before requesting the corresponding author. This dataset is used exclusively for academic research purposes. All data were collected from publicly available job postings and processed in accordance with the platform's data usage policies. Although LinkedIn is a popular job seeking platform, it does not fully represent the entire cybersecurity job market. Several roles are filled through internal hiring, job boards, and other platforms or channels. Nevertheless, this dataset is still an important resource and becomes useful to help understand how a part of the job market is nowadays shaped.

Dataset Structure. Initially, the dataset contained 250,973 records. Every record in this dataset contains a set of fields including job title, job description, company information, location, associated skills, posting metadata, scraping details, and hiring manager details in text form. For the purposes of this research, a subset of relevant attributes were used, these are summarised in Table 1.

Table 1. Structure of the job postings dataset

Field	Description
Title	Title of the job posting.
Description	Description of the job posting, usually containing responsibilities, requirements, skills and other details of the role.
Primary Description	Minimal description of the job posting's details. It includes the name of the hiring company, its location and work modality.
Location	Geographic location of the job posting (area, city and/or country).
Skill	Skills associated with the job posting.
Created At	Date when the job posting was originally published.
Scraped At	Date when the job posting was scraped.

Preprocessing Pipeline. The preprocessing pipeline was designed according to the EDA findings and consists of the following steps:

Data Cleaning. Unneeded features were dropped to construct a clean schema. Feature selection resulted in the fields described above, see Table 1. Invalid content was removed, noise was striped, and white-spaces and punctuation were normalised for a smooth analysis.

Language Normalisation. Although most of the dataset is in English, some fields were found in different European languages. Therefore, a detection of language and translation to English was performed in required fields.

Feature Engineering. A country attribute was extracted from existing features, as well as the work modality and the hiring company.

Data Filtering. This last step drops rows when all critical fields are invalid, keeping just useful records for this study.

After this preprocessing pipeline, the dataset resulted in 250,852 records, which will be used for analysis and modeling. Unlike classic NLP, in this preprocessing approach it is not required to remove stop words, perform stemming, nor conduct lemmatisation, because S-BERT uses subword tokenisation and contextual embeddings.

4.2 European Cybersecurity Skills Framework Dataset

For these research purposes, a public resource in a Github repository was used [19], as it provides a summarised JSON document based on the official framework [7].

Dataset Structure. The ECSF dataset contains three top level elements corresponding to work roles, tasks, and relationships. This shape is interpreted as two logical base entities representing work roles and main tasks with their details, and one logical entity representing the relationship between the base entities.

Preprocessing Pipeline. ECSF competency descriptions were already provided in structured textual form. Therefore, minimal preprocessing is applied, consisting of basic normalisation of unicode characters found in the text for standardisation and feature selection before generating the corresponding embeddings using S-BERT. The ECSF competency elements were represented in three categories: knowledge, skills, and tasks. In this study, only knowledge and skill description records from the ECSF are used for semantic matching, as these are more comparable to skill expressions. Therefore, tasks description elements and their relationships were excluded due to the nature of their definitions, which are more elaborated than the skills from the jobs dataset and might introduce additional semantic complexity.

4.3 Experimental Setup

Python 3.11 was used as the main programming language, *sentence-transformers* for S-BERT embeddings, PyTorch for the backend, NumPy and pandas to compute array operations and data handling. The pre-trained model *all-MiniLM-L6-v2* was used due to its strong performance in generating semantically meaningful sentence embeddings [20]. PostgreSQL served for persistent storage of data.

Since no ground truth was available for validation, the selection of similarity thresholds was guided by an empirical evaluation strategy. Therefore, multiple threshold values ($\tau = 0.55$, $\tau = 0.65$, and $\tau = 0.75$) were considered to analyse their impact on mapping quality and coverage. Code source, raw data and further technical details are documented in the Github repository [12] for validation and reproduction purposes.

4.4 Implemented Approach

The implementation of the approach proposed follows a sequential pipeline executed over a PostgreSQL database to support data persistence, performance, and reproducibility. Each stage of the pipeline corresponds to essential operations in which textual data is progressively converted into structured representations suitable for semantic comparison and evaluation. The following subsections describe the implementation of each stage in detail.

Job-Skills Extraction and Normalisation. The skill extraction process uses data from job postings, where the skills separated by commas are allocated in the Skill feature. Although it is assumed that this feature represents the skills required for each role, they may be incomplete or inconsistently populated.

After obtaining 245,901 valid records from Skill, representing 493,141 individual skills, the following normalisation techniques were applied on the text: splitting by commas, ASCII folding, punctuation stripping, token replacements, alias mapping, and noise reduction to obtain a consistent skill vocabulary. 7,803 split, unique, and normalised skills fit to embed were derived from this operation. This step supports ensuring that semantically equivalent skills are mapped consistently and improves the reliability of embedding-based similarity.

ECSF-Descriptions Extraction. The ECSF descriptions were extracted from the preprocessed dataset and a simple rearranging was conducted. This resulted in 150 records that contain the descriptions of skills and knowledge required by the different cybersecurity roles defined by the ECSF.

Embedding Generation. Sentence embeddings were generated for normalised job skills and ECSF descriptions using S-BERT, and were L2-normalised during the encoding process. The bi-encoder contained in S-BERT computes embeddings independently for each text, and similarity is computed with a matrix multiplication. This representation enables the transformation of heterogeneous textual inputs into a shared semantic space, allowing meaningful comparison between job-market skills and ECSF descriptions despite differences in wording.

Similarity Computation. Cosine similarity was computed by multiplying in batches the normalised job skill embedding matrix by the embedding matrix of the ECSF descriptions transposed, corresponding to Eq. 1. A minimum similarity threshold $\tau = 0.55$ was applied to avoid weak matches using Eq. 2. For each skill, the top-k most similar ECSF description candidates are retained. In this experimentation, k=3, which allows capturing multiple semantic matches for each skill while maintaining interpretability. This provides flexibility for analysis and inspection, as some skills may correspond to more than one ECSF description. Reference thresholds $\tau = 0.55$, $\tau = 0.65$ and $\tau = 0.75$ were used for reporting and interpretation purposes. The minimum similarity threshold is applied after computing all pairwise similarities to ensure that candidate matches are ranked globally, and only then filtered based on confidence.

This operation resulted in 1,133 candidate mappings, and similarity scores materialised as records later exposed through a SQL view, allowing easy interpretability. In this step, the semantic proximity between vector representations is used as the core mechanism to align real-world demanded skill from cybersecurity job postings with the ECSF standards.

Evaluation Metrics. A mapping was considered valid if it exists in the similarity mapping table, which means that it belongs to the top-k candidates for a specific skill and satisfies the minimum similarity requirement. For each skill, the maximum similarity score among its retained candidates is selected, according to Formula 3, and the mean is calculated over this subset. Therefore, the semantic similarity mean was computed as the average of the best similarity score per skill, considering only skills with at least one valid mapping, see Formula 4. Hence, the mean similarity reflects the strength of alignment for successfully matched skills, rather than the entire skill set. Coverage at a threshold τ was calculated as the proportion of skills whose best similarity score exceeds the predefined threshold, as defined in the Formula 5, where S represents the set of all normalised skills. In this formulation, skills without any valid mapping are implicitly counted as not covered. Together, these metrics provide a quantitative approximation of the alignment between job-market skills and the ECSF standards.

Skill Demand Analysis. To analyse the skill demand in the cybersecurity job market, a frequency-based distribution was computed over the extracted and normalised skills from the job postings dataset. This represents the proportion of job postings that require a given skill, allowing for a comparison across the dataset. Further analysis is performed based on this resource by filtering through countries where skill demand patterns are revealed.

4.5 Results

The outputs generated from the implementation conducted served as a basis for this final stage of the pipeline. The results are composed of a quantitative evaluation of the proposed method, representative examples of job-skill to ECSF-description semantic matches in different similarity ranges followed by a brief qualitative analysis to help understand the mappings produced by the model, and visualisations that complement the interpretation of the current demand of cybersecurity professionals in the region.

Evaluation Metrics Results. The evaluation strategy was conducted over top-1 ranked job-skill to ECSF-description mappings. Results are shown in Table 2.

Table 2. Evaluation metrics results of semantic mapping

Evaluation metric	Value	Number of unique job-skills
Mean similarity (μ)	0.6376	666
Coverage @0.55	0.0854	666
Coverage @0.65	0.0290	226
Coverage @0.75	0.0072	56

The average semantic similarity among the valid job-skill mapped pairs to ECSF-description was 0.6376. This metric was calculated considering the 666 job-skills that met the minimum similarity. This indicates that there is a moderate/medium semantic alignment between job-skills and ECSF descriptions. Table 2 shows how the coverage decreases as the similarity threshold increases, with 8.5% of demanded job-skills reaching a minimum threshold of 0.55, 2.9% reaching 0.65 and only 0.7% reaching 0.75. These results are based on a proportion of the extracted job-skills that could be semantically mapped to ECSF standards through their descriptions. The evaluation metrics results highlight the existing trade-off between mapping strictness and coverage. In this case, the overall alignment remains limited when strict similarity thresholds are applied.

Job-Skill to ECSF-Description Similarity Mappings. To analyse the effect of different similarity thresholds on job-skills to ECSF-description mappings and their quality, representative examples are presented in increasing order of similarity. Similarity levels are defined by the thresholds selected for this study. For reporting purposes, mappings are grouped into three different ranges. Low-similarity mappings fall within the range [0.55, 0.65), medium-similarity mappings within [0.65, 0.75), and high-similarity mappings within [0.75, 1].

Low Similarity Mappings. Representative examples of low-similarity demanded job-skill to ECSF-description mappings are presented below in Table 3. The method resulted in 802 demanded job-skill to ECSF-description mappings that correspond to a low-similarity, these often involve generic or non-cybersecurity skills, highlighting the job postings dataset heterogeneity in the skills definition and some limitations of embedding-based similarity in capturing precise conceptual relationships when a low threshold is applied.

Medium Similarity Mappings. Representative examples of medium-similarity demanded job-skill to ECSF-description mappings are presented in

Table 3. Job-skill to ECSF-description low-similarity mappings [0.55, 0.65)

Job-skill	ECSF-description match	Similarity	Rank
Security systems	Computer networks security	0.644	2
Cloud platforms	Work on operating systems, servers, clouds and relevant infrastructures	0.613	1
Threat modeling	Model threats, actors and TTPs	0.618	2
Stakeholder management	Communicate, coordinate and cooperate with internal and external stakeholders	0.644	1
Information security	Computer networks security	0.604	2
Application development	Develop code, scripts and programmes	0.556	1
Cyber insurance	Cybersecurity policies	0.599	1
Computer literacy	Computer programming	0.552	1

Table 4. Job-skill to ECSF-description medium-similarity mappings [0.65–0.75)

Job-skill	ECSF-description match	Similarity	Rank
Security operations center	Secure Operation Centres (SOCs) operation	0.695	1
Linux security	Operating systems security	0.708	1
Application security architecture	Security architecture reference models	0.710	1
Information security policy	Cybersecurity policies	0.716	1
Security systems integration	Coordinate the integration of security solutions	0.728	1
Threat management	Threat actors Tactics, Techniques and Procedures (TTPs)	0.731	1
Cybersecurity tools	Cybersecurity controls and solutions	0.732	1
Testing tools	Testing procedures	0.747	1

Table 5. Job-skill to ECSF-description high-similarity mappings [0.75–1]

Job-skill	ECSF Match	Similarity	Rank
Computer programming	Computer programming	1.000	1
Risk management tools	Risk management tools	1.000	1
Ethical hacking	Conduct ethical hacking	0.964	1
Test procedures	Testing procedures	0.962	1
Penetration testing	Penetration testing procedures	0.926	1
Social engineering	Perform social engineering	0.906	1
Malware analysis	Malware analysis tools	0.879	1
Network security	Computer networks security	0.881	1

Table 4. Within the implemented approach, 261 demanded job-skill to ECSF-description medium-similarity cases were mapped, and they reflect a qualified alignment where ECSF descriptions capture the general domain, although sometimes lacks specificity. Nevertheless, the results show that the demanded job-skills correspond, in general, to the ECSF description to which they were mapped.

High Similarity Mappings. Representative examples of high-similarity demanded job-skill to ECSF-description mappings are presented in Table 5. From the experimental implementation, 70 mappings were retrieved from the demanded job-skill to ECSF-description high-similarity comparison, and these correspond to well-defined cybersecurity concepts with direct semantic equivalence, in line with reality. In general, these examples support the idea that the embedding-based approach performs best when job market demanded skills are clearly defined in a specific way and closely aligned with ECSF terminology.

Distribution of Demand for Cybersecurity Skills. Visual resources alongside qualitative analyses are presented below for further interpretation.

Demanded Skills in Cybersecurity. The distribution of the most demanded skills in cybersecurity within the EU and the included neighboring countries is shown below in Fig. 2, with a bar chart that includes the number of occurrences per skill in the job postings dataset. Technical and transversal skills are among the most demanded competencies, which highlights the hybrid nature of cybersecurity roles nowadays, where domain expertise is significantly demanded, accompanied by analytical thinking, communication, and other soft skills.

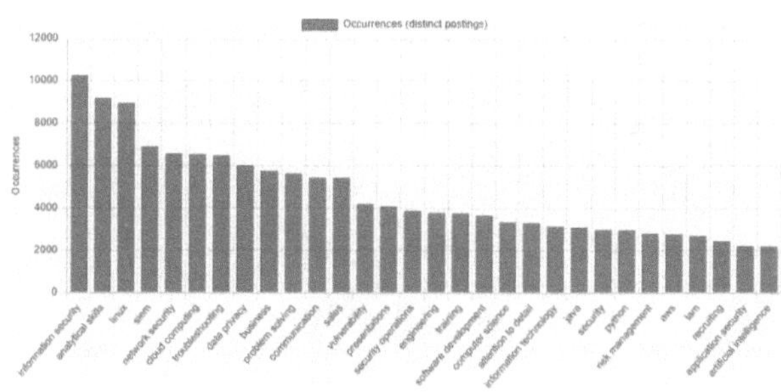

Fig. 2. Bar chart: Top 30 demanded skills in cybersecurity job postings

On another note, skills such as sales, business, recruiting, and training; are not very specific and represent ambiguous expressions for this kind of role requirements. These are considered noise. This confirms that the skills defined by job posters are frequently heterogeneous and justifies the low coverage obtained in the evaluation metrics. These findings partially explain the limited alignment between the cybersecurity job market demand and the ECSF. An important portion of demanded skills consists of transversal, generic, or non-domain-specific competencies, which are not explicitly represented in the framework.

Geographical Distribution of Demand. A choropleth map highlighting the European States included in this research, together with the number of cybersecurity job postings per country is presented in Fig. 3, revealing a highly concentrated cybersecurity labour market.

A relatively small number of countries are dominating the demand for cybersecurity professionals in the region: Germany, UK, France, Italy, and Spain are the ones with the highest number of job postings in the field. This indicates structural differences in the level of sophistication of the cybersecurity job market in the EU and the included neighboring countries, which may influence the degree of alignment with the ECSF.

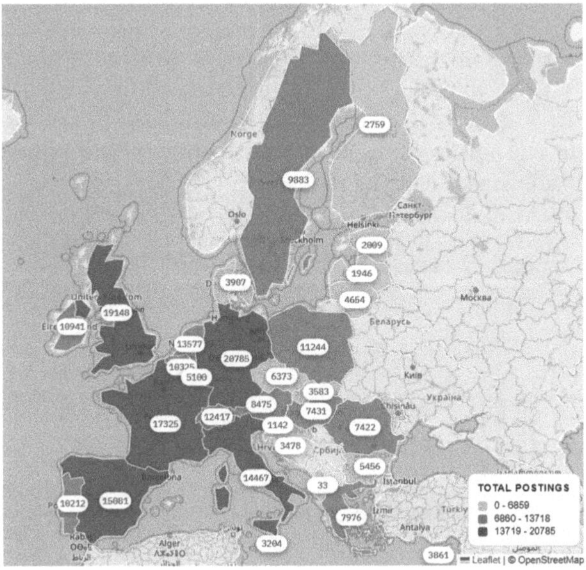

Fig. 3. Choropleth map: Geographic distribution of cybersecurity job postings

Regional Variation in Cybersecurity Skill Demand. Variations and patterns were revealed when analysing skills demanded by countries in Table 6.

In the distribution of cybersecurity skill demand presented in Fig. 2, some countries contribute more than others due to the significant size of their cybersecurity job market. The skills demanded by countries indicate that large labour markets tend to require specialised cybersecurity skills due to the sophistication of their ecosystem, while markets with a lower size exhibit prevalence of transversal and soft skills, suggesting less specialisation and broader role definitions.

Table 6. Top 3 demanded skills by European labour markets

Country	Jobs (#)	Top 3 demanded skills and occurrence (%)
Germany	20,785	Information security (8%), Data privacy (5%), Linux (4%)
UK	19,148	Attention to detail (6%), Communication (6%), Analytical skills (5%)
France	17,325	Interpersonal communication (6%), Linux (4%), Interpersonal skills (4%)
Spain	15,081	Information security (8%), Linux (5%), SIEM (4%)
Italy	14,467	Troubleshooting (6%), Network security (5%), Linux (5%)
Netherlands	13,577	Information security (9%), Analytical skills (5%), Operations management (4%)
Switzerland	12,417	Information security (4%), Cloud computing (4%), Information technology (3%)
Poland	11,244	Analytical skills (5%), Information security (4%), SIEM (4%)
Ireland	10,941	Analytical skills (4%), Cloud computing (4%), Data privacy (4%)
Belgium	10,325	Information security (4%), Analytical skills (4%), Network security (3%)
Portugal	10,212	Linux (4%), Analytical skills (3%), Information security (3%)
Sweden	9,883	Information security (7%), Operations management (4%), Analytical skills (4%)
Austria	8,475	Information security (7%), Cloud computing (4%), Business (4%)
Greece	7,976	Linux (4%), Troubleshooting (4%), Analytical skills (4%)
Hungary	7,431	Analytical skills (5%), Troubleshooting (4%), Linux (4%)
Romania	7,422	Linux (4%), Analytical skills (4%), Information security (4%)
Czechia	6,373	Analytical skills (6%), Linux (4%), Business (4%)
Bulgaria	5,456	Linux (4%), Analytical skills (4%), Troubleshooting (4%)
Luxembourg	5,100	Business (5%), Communication (5%), Analytical skills (4%)
Lithuania	4,654	Analytical skills (5%), Linux (4%), Problem solving (4%)
Denmark	3,907	Sales (7%), Analytical skills (5%), Operations management (4%)
Cyprus	3,861	Sales (4%), Analytical skills (3%), Business (3%)
Slovakia	3,583	Linux (6%), Analytical skills (5%), Business (4%)
Croatia	3,478	Sales (4%), Analytical skills (4%), Linux (4%)
Finland	2,759	Linux (5%), Sales (4%), Software development (3%)
Estonia	2,009	Linux (9%), Analytical skills (5%), Engineering (4%)
Latvia	1,946	Linux (5%), Sales (4%), Analytical skills (4%)
Slovenia	1,142	Linux (9%), Purchase orders (6%), Troubleshooting (4%)

5 Conclusion

The purpose of this research was to analyse the cybersecurity job market in the EU by measuring to what extent the skills currently demanded in the field are aligned with the European Cybersecurity Skills Framework (ECSF) standards, by applying a large-scale data-driven method.

The findings support the literature that describes the cybersecurity skills shortage as a structural problem caused by discrepancies between standardised frameworks, educational programs, and industry requirements. This research shows that a policy-oriented framework like the ECSF is not able to fully represent the dynamic character of the cybersecurity job market.

In general, the results indicate that the alignment of cybersecurity job-market skills and ECSF standards is limited. Even when a relatively low similarity threshold was set for the semantic method, a small portion of the extracted job-skills could be successfully mapped to ECSF descriptions. When stricter thresholds were applied, the number of valid mappings decreased significantly, meaning that a strong semantic alignment is only achieved for a compact subset of the entire skill set. It can be concluded that while the ECSF covers some of the skills in the cybersecurity domain, it does not completely represent the variety of skills that are currently required in the field.

A detailed analysis of the mappings suggests important qualitative patterns. High-similarity matches are largely associated with thoroughly defined and standardised cybersecurity concepts, especially in fundamental technical areas. At the same time, medium and low similarity mappings reveal differences in granularity, where ECSF descriptions represent competencies conceptually and at a standard level, while job postings articulate skills in a more operational and context-dependent manner.

The prominence of transversal and non-technical skills in the cybersecurity job postings studied is a significant discovery. Skills such as communication, analytical thinking, and business understanding often occur in the job postings dataset, but are not reflected in the ECSF. This emphasises the hybrid aspect of current cybersecurity roles and reflects how the role of cybersecurity professionals is constantly changing.

Besides, studying the demand for skills across different European countries revealed patterns and variations. Bigger and well-established markets usually focus on highly technical and specialised skills, whereas smaller or emerging markets more frequently have general and transversal skills. This variety shows that a single standardised framework may be inherently challenged to completely reflect labour market dynamics that are specific to the markedly diverse job markets of EU countries.

From a methodological perspective, the use of embedding-based semantic similarity was a suitable technique to find relations between different textual descriptions of skills. Nevertheless, the findings highlight the drawbacks of this method, as semantic similarity alone is not a sufficient basis for conceptual equivalence, especially when the terms used are ambiguous or general. This reinforces the importance of complementing quantitative similarity measures with qualitative assessment.

Several limitations are acknowledged. The study relies on job postings from one platform, which does not completely reflect the cybersecurity labour market in the region. Besides, the selection of the embedding model and similarity thresholds has an impact on the mapping results, and the lack of ground truth data limits the method from formally verifying the correctness of the generated mappings. However, this research provides a replicable and scalable approach to examine the alignment between labour market demand and standardised competency frameworks.

Future research can rely on the present study by developing sophisticated skill normalisation methods, utilising domain-specific embedding models, and incorporating additional competency frameworks for comparative analyses.

Disclosure of Interests. The authors have no competing interests to declare that are relevant to the content of this article.

References

1. Benchaaboune, A., El Mahdi, M., Beni-Hssane, A.: Analyzing cybersecurity job market needs using BERT-based natural language processing. In: Proceedings of the IEEE Global Engineering Education Conference (EDUCON). IEEE (2024). https://doi.org/10.1109/EDUCON60312.2024.10578703
2. Blažič, B.J.: The cybersecurity labour shortage in Europe: moving to a new concept for education and training. Technol. Soc. **67**, 101769 (2021). https://doi.org/10.1016/j.techsoc.2021.101769
3. Budde, C.E., Karinsalo, A., Vidor, S., Salonen, J., Massacci, F.: Consolidating cybersecurity in Europe: a case study on job profiles assessment. Comput. Secur. **127**, 103082 (2023). https://doi.org/10.1016/j.cose.2022.103082
4. Cusack, B.: Impact of emerging technologies on cybersecurity education (2023)
5. Crumpler, W., Lewis, J.A.: The cybersecurity workforce gap. Technical report, Center for Strategic and International Studies (CSIS) (2019). https://csis-website-prod.s3.amazonaws.com/s3fs-public/publication/190129_Crumpler_Cybersecurity_FINAL.pdf
6. Cybersecurity job postings dataset. Google Drive repository (2025). https://drive.google.com/drive/folders/1urAJnf09u8cNFBN0kFm_UZH3Lhh8oBRa
7. European Union Agency for Cybersecurity (ENISA): European Cybersecurity Skills Framework (ECSF). ENISA (2022). https://doi.org/10.2824/859537
8. European Union Agency for Cybersecurity (ENISA): NIS Investments 2025 Report. ENISA (2025)
9. European Union Agency for Cybersecurity (ENISA), Nurse, J.R., Adamos, K., Grammatopoulos, A., Di Franco, F.: Addressing the EU cybersecurity skills shortage and gap through higher education. Technical report, ENISA (2021). https://doi.org/10.2824/033355
10. Dawson, J., Thomson, R.: The future cybersecurity workforce: going beyond technical skills for successful cyber performance. Front. Psychol. **9**, 744 (2018). https://doi.org/10.3389/fpsyg.2018.00744
11. Espejo, P.: ds-lab-pr. GitHub repository (2025). https://github.com/paulinaeb/ds-lab-pr
12. Espejo, P.: euro-cyber-data. GitHub repository (2026). https://github.com/paulinaeb/euro-cyber-data.git
13. European Union: EU member countries (2024). https://european-union.europa.eu/principles-countries-history/country-profiles_en
14. Géron, A.: Hands-On Machine Learning with Scikit-Learn, Keras, and TensorFlow. O'Reilly (2022)
15. Goupil, F., Laskov, P., Pekaric, I., Felderer, M., Dürr, A., Thiesse, F.: Towards understanding the skill gap in cybersecurity, pp. 7–14 (2022). https://arxiv.org/abs/2204.13793
16. Jumaan, S., Kuzminykh, I., Xiao, H., Ghita, B.V.: Understanding the skills gap between higher education and industry in cybersecurity (2025). https://www.researchgate.net/publication/395473023
17. Ramezan, C.A.: Examining the cyber skills gap: an analysis of cybersecurity positions by sub-field. J. Inf. Syst. Educ. **34**(1), 94–105 (2023). https://aisel.aisnet.org/jise/vol34/iss1/8

18. ISACA: State of Cybersecurity 2025. ISACA (2025)
19. Opliyal, O.: ENISA-ECSF-Dataset. GitHub repository. https://github.com/opliyal3/ENISA-ECSF-Dataset
20. Reimers, N., Gurevych, I.: Pretrained models – Sentence Transformers documentation (2024). https://www.sbert.net/docs/sentence_transformer/pretrained_models.html
21. Zivanovic, M., Lendák, I., Popovic, R.: Tackling the cybersecurity workforce gap with tailored cybersecurity study programs in Central and Eastern Europe. In: Proceedings of the 19th International Conference on Availability, Reliability and Security, pp. 1–8 (2024). https://doi.org/10.1145/3664476.3670468

A Multi-stakeholder Framework for Traceable and Auditable High-Risk AI Systems Under the EU AI Act

Ignacio Miguel Rodríguez(✉), Jordi Castellà Roca, and Alexandre Viejo

Universitat Rovira i Virgili, 43007 Tarragona, Catalonia, Spain
{ignacio.miguel,jordi.castella,alex.viejo}@urv.cat

Abstract. Generative AI has rapidly reshaped products and services across multiple sectors, introducing significant risks including embedded bias, unlawful processing of personal data, and potential erosion of fundamental rights. In response, the European Union has established a complex regulatory ecosystem comprising the AIA, the DA, the DGA, and the GDPR, whose combined operationalization presents considerable challenges for stakeholders such as providers, deployers, auditors, and end-users. This paper proposes a multi-stakeholder framework that provides the structure, tooling, and secure information registration mechanisms to facilitate regulatory adherence and auditability for high-risk AI systems under the EU AI Act. The framework coordinates multiple actors through structured roles and responsibilities, automatically recording all relevant actions and decisions in a tamper-evident and verifiable manner, so that all necessary evidence is readily available in case a compliance assessment or audit is required. This is supported through smart-contract-based mechanisms for model registration, licensing, expert oversight, and decision-level traceability. Each AI prediction generates a Decision Output Object enriched with explainability metrics and optional expert validation, reinforcing transparency and human-in-the-loop supervision. Sensitive components are protected via a digital-envelope encryption scheme enabling fine-grained, role-based access control, while long-term integrity is ensured by anchoring critical artifacts on the blockchain and distributing metadata through IPFS.

Keywords: AI Act · Regulatory Adherence · Auditability · Explainability · Multi-stakeholder · Blockchain

1 Introduction

Recent advances in artificial intelligence (AI) are transforming industries and society by enabling automation, improving productivity, and supporting data-driven decision-making. In healthcare, AI-driven diagnostic systems assist clinicians in detecting diseases earlier and with greater accuracy, improving patient

P. Kieseberg et al. (Eds.): ARES 2026 Workshops, LNCS 16903, pp. 383–400, 2027.
https://doi.org/10.1007/978-3-032-37218-5_23

outcomes and reducing operational costs [5]. In finance, in addition to higher efficiency, machine-learning algorithms support fraud detection, algorithmic trading, and personalized financial services [17]. Meanwhile, in manufacturing, AI-powered systems reduce downtime and optimize energy consumption [2].

Yet the same features that make AI transformative also give rise to substantial risks, disrupting labor markets and introducing new social and ethical challenges. At the center of this transformation lies data, the fundamental resource from which AI systems are built. Data fuels algorithms, shapes predictions, and ultimately influences decisions that affect individuals and organizations. Ensuring trustworthy AI therefore begins with the data itself. High-quality and balanced datasets help prevent biases in model behavior, while an ethical approach to data handling is essential to protecting individuals' rights [12]. These risks illustrate the need for rigorous oversight mechanisms to ensure that technological progress does not compromise fundamental rights, safety, or social welfare.

In response to these growing concerns, governments worldwide have begun introducing regulatory frameworks that establish clear obligations for organizations working with AI. The European Union has led this effort through the Artificial Intelligence Act (AIA) [9], alongside existing data protection laws such as the General Data Protection Regulation (GDPR) [10], the Data Act (DA) [8], and the Data Governance Act (DGA) [11]. Similar initiatives have emerged globally, including the U.S. AI Bill of Rights [25], or China's Generative AI Regulation [3]. Nevertheless, ensuring compliance remains a significant challenge, particularly for small and medium-sized enterprises (SMEs) [6], underscoring the need for a framework that makes regulatory implementation practical, easy, accessible, and as automated as possible for both businesses and end-users.

1.1 Regulatory Background: the EU AI Act

The AIA, adopted by the EU in 2024 [9], establishes a legal framework to protect fundamental rights while promoting responsible AI innovation. Central to its approach is a risk-based classification system, which categorizes AI applications according to the level of risk they pose to individuals and society:

- **Unacceptable risk (Art. 5)**: AI systems that pose a clear threat to safety, fundamental rights, or human lives are strictly banned. Examples include social scoring mechanisms, manipulative technologies, and emotion recognition in sensitive contexts such as workplaces or educational institutions.
- **High risk (Annex III)**: These systems require rigorous compliance and continuous monitoring throughout their lifecycle due to their significant impact on safety and fundamental rights. Examples include AI applications in recruitment, education, and biometric identification.
- **Limited risk (Art. 50)**: These systems are subject primarily to transparency obligations. For instance, users must be informed when interacting with a conversational agent or when content has been artificially generated.
- **Minimal risk**: These AI applications are not subject to specific regulatory requirements and represent the majority of systems deployed within the EU. Common examples include spam filters and AI in video games.

For general-purpose AI (GPAI) systems such as large language models, the AIA introduces specific provisions under Chapter V (Articles 51–56). Certain GPAI models that exceed defined computational thresholds or exhibit systemic impact are subject to stricter requirements, including comprehensive risk assessments, evaluation of systemic impacts, detailed technical documentation, and robust cybersecurity measures.

The obligations imposed on high-risk AI systems are defined across Articles 9–27 of the AIA and span the entire system lifecycle, from design to post-market monitoring. The most relevant to our framework are the following:

1. **Data and data governance** (Art. 10): Training, validation, and testing datasets must meet quality standards and adhere to data governance practices. This includes defining the purpose of data collection, assessing biases, and ensuring that datasets are representative and free from errors.
2. **Technical documentation** (Art. 11): Providers must prepare and maintain comprehensive technical documentation demonstrating compliance with the AIA before placing the system on the market, and keep it updated throughout the system lifecycle.
3. **Record-keeping and logging** (Art. 12, 19): High-risk AI systems must be designed to automatically generate logs of their operation to the extent technically feasible. These logs must enable monitoring of system operation, detection of risks, and post-market surveillance. Deployers are responsible for retaining such logs for the periods specified under applicable law.
4. **Transparency and information to deployers** (Art. 13): Systems must operate transparently, providing deployers with sufficient information to interpret outputs and use the system appropriately. This includes instructions for use, system capabilities and limitations, and performance metrics.
5. **Human oversight** (Art. 14): Systems must be designed to allow effective human oversight during use. Deployers must implement appropriate human oversight measures to detect and correct anomalies, avoid over-reliance on system outputs, and retain the ability to override or disregard decisions.
6. **Accuracy, robustness, and cybersecurity** (Art. 15): Systems must achieve appropriate levels of accuracy and be resilient to errors, faults, and adversarial attacks, including data poisoning and model manipulation.
7. **Post-market monitoring** (Art. 72): Providers must establish and maintain a post-market monitoring plan to systematically collect and analyze data on system performance in real-world conditions throughout the system lifecycle.

1.2 Contribution

In this paper, we introduce a multi-stakeholder framework designed to facilitate regulatory adherence and auditability for high-risk AI systems under the EU AI Act. The specific focus on high-risk AI systems lies in the regulatory obligations imposed on this category under the EU AI Act. Such systems are required to satisfy extensive requirements related to documentation, traceability, transparency, human oversight, and auditability throughout their entire lifecycle.

These requirements create a compliance burden for the stakeholders involved, encouraging the appearance of mechanisms that support evidence collection, verification, and governance. Conversely, AI systems classified as lower risk (e.g., limited-risk systems) are subject to considerably less stringent requirements, making the proposed framework less necessary in those contexts. Consequently, high-risk AI systems represent the domain where the benefits of the framework are most relevant and impactful.

The system provides the structure, tooling, and secure information registration mechanisms that make demonstrating adherence to AIA requirements significantly easier for all stakeholders involved. In particular, it coordinates providers, deployers, auditors, and end-users (refer to Sect. 4.2 for a definition of these actors) through structured roles and responsibilities aligned with AIA requirements. As the system operates, all relevant actions and decisions are automatically recorded on the blockchain and stored in IPFS in a secure, tamper-evident, and verifiable manner. This continuous registration of information means that, should a compliance assessment or audit be required, necessary evidence is already available and independently verifiable without reliance on external auditing infrastructure.

In addition, the framework embeds explainability mechanisms into every prediction, includes an optional expert-in-the-loop component to review model behavior, and enforces fine-grained access control to ensure that each stakeholder can access only the information they are authorized to see. Together, these capabilities ensure that compliance-relevant information is captured by design throughout the system lifecycle, reducing the burden on stakeholders when demonstrating adherence to regulators or auditors.

1.2.1 Organization of the Paper. The remainder of the paper is organized as follows. Section 2 reviews the state of the art. Section 3 defines the requirements of the proposal. Section 4 presents the framework, describing the relevant entities, objects, and protocol stages. Section 5 evaluates the proposal's adherence to the defined requirements. Finally, Sect. 6 presents concluding remarks, limitations of the proposal, and discusses avenues for future work.

2 Related Work

The EU AIA requires that high-risk AI systems produce interpretable outputs, motivating a growing set of domain-specific explainability approaches in areas such as justice, medicine, and finance [4,15,18,19,23,24]. These contributions primarily aim to increase transparency in sector-specific deployments. Yet current methods focus on interpreting model decisions, without offering systematic ways to assess whether model outputs are consistent with expert judgment.

In parallel, early efforts are exploring how to reduce the compliance burden on organizations by operationalizing and automating certain AIA requirements. However, work in this direction is still incipient, and implementable system-level frameworks remain underdeveloped.

Within this landscape, ComplAI [14] provides a technical interpretation of the AIA and an open benchmarking suite focused on LLMs, covering aspects like robustness, privacy, bias, interpretability, and toxicity. Despite its relevance, it is limited to LLMs and still lacks appropriate benchmarks addressing explainability. The remainder of this section reviews the most relevant initiatives addressing AIA-related requirements, grouped by the actors involved in each proposal.

2.1 Contributions Involving Provider and Auditor

Floridi et al. [13] propose *capAI*, a theoretical framework supporting conformity assessments aligned with the AIA across five lifecycle phases. It comprises three components: (1) an Internal Review Protocol for risk management, (2) a Summary Datasheet for EU database registration, and (3) an External Scorecard for public transparency. While valuable from a governance perspective, *capAI* is not fully automated and focuses primarily on the Provider and Auditor, with limited attention to cybersecurity.

Wang et al. [26] propose *AI-Auditor*, a data auditing framework that verifies model integrity in cloud environments through a cryptographic challenge-response mechanism based on provable data possession (PDP). Although effective at ensuring model integrity and trustworthiness, it does not target regulatory compliance such as the AIA, and lacks explainability and broader cybersecurity components.

The framework proposed in [21] addresses four core AIA requirements for high-risk systems: data governance, human oversight, accuracy and robustness, and transparency. The solution uses open source Python libraries such as *FiftyOne*[1] and *AIF360* [1], producing a comprehensive compliance report as output. However, it omits cybersecurity requirements, involves significant manual steps, and provides limited treatment of human oversight.

2.2 Contributions Involving Provider, Auditor, and End-User

Parlak [7] introduces *BAXDT* (*Blockchain-Assisted Explainable Decision Traces*), a framework enhancing transparency and accountability in AI systems through a Decision Output Object that encapsulates decision details alongside explainability metrics such as *SHAP* and a novel density-based metric EDM_{SHAP}. Immutability is ensured by anchoring the object's hash on a blockchain. While BAXDT represents a significant step toward AIA explainability and transparency requirements, it overlooks cybersecurity, since storing the decision object locally as plaintext introduces risks in the event of device compromise or failure.

As discussed, existing approaches to AIA compliance are fragmented, domain-specific, or limited to GPAI systems such as LLMs. Even the most comprehensive proposals lack end-to-end automation, require substantial manual intervention, and fail to reflect the distributed responsibilities inherent across

[1] FiftyOne documentation: https://docs.voxel51.com/.

the AI lifecycle. No existing framework unifies AIA compliance requirements with robust cybersecurity measures and explainability mechanisms while adequately addressing the diverse roles involved throughout development, deployment, and oversight. This gap underscores the need for an integrated, automated, and auditable solution capable of supporting trustworthy AI deployment under regulatory regimes such as the AIA.

3 Requirements

The requirement derivation followed a two-step process. First, we analyzed the literature reviewed in Sect. 2 to identify recurring limitations in existing approaches, including insufficient auditability, limited support for human oversight, fragmented stakeholder coordination, and weak cybersecurity guarantees. Second, we conducted a systematic analysis of the AIA to identify the obligations applicable to high-risk AI systems (Sect. 1.1) and mapped the relevant regulatory provisions to technical system requirements. The final set of requirements was obtained by consolidating the limitations identified in the literature with the obligations established by the AIA. For clarity, the resulting requirements are organized into functional and non-functional categories.

3.1 Functional Requirements

FR1. **Evidence registration/Auditability** (Art. 12, 19, 72): The system shall automatically record every relevant action and event (including model registrations, licensing agreements, predictions, and expert interventions) to ensure full traceability and support post-market monitoring.

FR2. **Transparency and Explainability** (Art. 13): The system shall provide mechanisms that make AI predictions and decision-making processes understandable and interpretable to deployers and end-users, including feature-level attribution or equivalent explainability outputs for each prediction.

FR3. **Human oversight** (Art. 14): The system shall support configurable expert intervention, allowing domain experts to review, supervise, and validate AI-assisted decisions. This mechanism shall be activated by default at the deployer level or on a per-decision basis by the end-user.

FR4. **Multi-stakeholder coordination** (Art. 25): The system shall define structured roles and interaction protocols for all relevant actors (provider, deployer, expert, end-user, and auditor), ensuring that each actor can fulfill their regulatory obligations.

3.2 Non-functional Requirements

NFR1. **Generality**: The framework shall be model- and domain-agnostic, applicable to any high-risk AI system as defined in Annex III of the AIA without modification to its core architecture.

NFR2. **Access control** (Art. 10, 15): The system shall enforce role-based access control ensuring that each actor can access only the data and functions they are authorized to use.

NFR3. **Integrity** (Art. 10, 12, 15): All recorded data shall be protected against unauthorized modification, ensuring that audit records remain trustworthy throughout the system lifecycle.

NFR4. **Confidentiality** (Art. 10, 15): The system shall prevent disclosure of sensitive or personally identifiable information to unauthorized parties, including other actors within the framework.

NFR5. **Availability and resilience** (Art. 15): The system shall ensure that records and services remain available to authorized actors and resilient to failures.

4 Proposed Framework

4.1 Design Rationale: Blockchain and IPFS

The multiple stakeholders involved in the framework may have distinct and sometimes competing interests, making it unsuitable to rely on a single trusted party for record-keeping. While centralized audit logs and secure logging infrastructures provide traceability in single-organization environments, they require trust in the entity managing the logs.

Blockchain addresses this limitation through a decentralized, fault-tolerant ledger, in which committed records are computationally infeasible to alter retroactively without controlling a majority of the network. This satisfies the framework requirements for evidence registration and auditability (FR1), integrity (NFR3), and availability and resilience (NFR5). In addition, smart contracts enable licensing conditions, access-control policies, and expert validation procedures to be enforced automatically and transparently without relying on an intermediary.

The framework also manages large data artifacts, such as licensing terms and model hyperparameters, for which on-chain storage is impractical. Therefore, the data are stored in IPFS, and only their references are anchored on-chain [16]. As a distributed storage system, IPFS improves availability and eliminates single points of failure.

Together, the combination of blockchain as an immutable, decentralized ledger and IPFS as a distributed storage system provides the trust-minimized infrastructure required by the multi-stakeholder nature of our framework.

4.2 Entities

The design of a generic solution requires the inclusion of the entities introduced above. In the following section, we present these entities according to their definitions in the AIA, describe their respective roles, and explain how they interact within the compliance workflow.

- **Provider**: The *Provider* is the entity that develops an AI system (Art. 3, paragraph 3). This includes responsibilities for design, training, and ensuring compliance with applicable regulations.
- **Deployer**: The *Deployer* is the entity that uses an AI system under its authority, excepting personal non-professional activities (Art. 3, paragraph 4). The *Deployer* is responsible for the proper integration, configuration, and operation of the AI system within a specific context of use, and for ensuring that such use complies with applicable legal and ethical obligations.
- **End-user**: Although the AI Act does not impose obligations on individuals using AI systems for personal, non-professional purposes, this role is included to acknowledge and empower the person directly interacting with the system and whose data is being used. The *End-user* is the individual who engages with the AI system to accomplish a specific task or goal.
- **Expert**: The *Expert* is linked to the *Deployer* and is responsible for approving/rejecting the AI model's decisions and providing comments. This role is not explicitly defined in the AIA, although it is necessary to provide better explainability and human oversight.
- **Auditor**: An independent entity responsible for evaluating the AI system's compliance, transparency, and accountability. The *Auditor* assesses risks related to fairness, security, and privacy and verifies adherence to applicable regulations. Under the AI Act, this role is typically carried out by the *Market Surveillance Authority*, the national body empowered to inspect, test, and audit high-risk AI systems (Art. 3, paragraph 26).

4.3 Framework Interaction Overview

To meet the outlined requirements, we propose a framework that encompasses the entities defined in the AIA, such as the *Provider*, *Deployer*, and *Auditor*, as well as two complementary actors: the *End-user* and the *Expert*. These entities interact through smart contracts that follow the protocol defined in Sect. 4.5.

These interactions give rise to the workflow shown in Fig. 1. In this system, the *Provider* first trains the AI model and registers its metadata on the blockchain. Once the model is available, any *Deployer* can request a license from the *Provider* to gain access to the model and begin offering it as a service. After the model is exposed to *End-users* through an access point, they may submit requests, providing their data as input to obtain a prediction. When the model generates a prediction, the *Deployer* creates a Decision Output Object, which includes the prediction itself along with relevant explainability information.

When expert intervention is active (either upon user request or as a default setting within the `PDSC`), an *Expert* reviews the model's decision, adds comments, and indicates whether they agree or disagree with the output. It is important to note that *Experts* are granted access to all relevant information recorded in the Decision Output Object, including the prediction, explainability metrics, and any contextual data required to make an informed assessment. All of this information is then recorded on the ledger by the *Deployer*.

Finally, both the *End-user* (who can track decisions made using their data) and the *Auditor* (who has access to the relevant records) can retrieve the decision from the ledger and distributed storage.

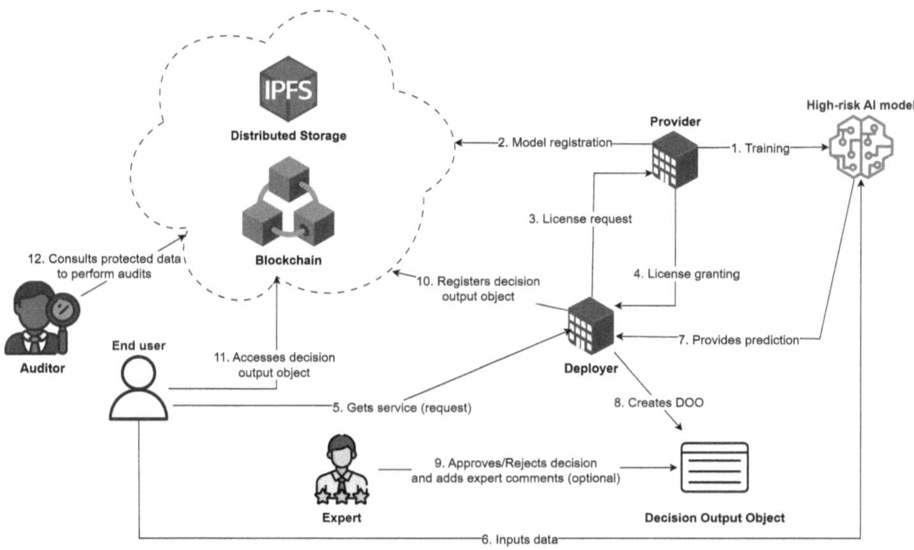

Fig. 1. Overview of the proposed framework.

4.4 Objects

Several components of the framework maintain an internal state that evolves throughout the protocol. Since this behavior cannot be adequately captured through simple transactions, these components are implemented as smart contracts (SCs). This section presents the SCs and objects defined by the framework, along with their main attributes and methods.

4.4.1 EncapsulatedDataSC The `EncapsulatedDataSC` smart contract enforces access control over sensitive data through a dynamic and fine-grained authorization mechanism. It stores references to the encrypted payload and owner-specific key material in IPFS, together with an access control list mapping authorized entities to the information required to decrypt the protected data. Other smart contracts reference instances of this contract for each sensitive attribute they manage, ensuring that encryption and access permissions are consistently applied across the system.

Methods:

`requestAccess()` This method is triggered when an entity seeks permission to access the data. The requester submits a signed transaction that includes its public key. The data owner then decides whether to grant access. If access is approved, the owner updates the access list by calling `addAccess()`.

`addAccess()` This method can only be executed by the data owner. It registers a new *public-key-to-CID* mapping, where the public key of the newly authorized entity serves as the mapping key, and the corresponding CIDs (where the information to recover the encryption keys is stored) serve as the value.

`getAccess()` This method is invoked by an entity that has been granted access. It retrieves the information required for the entity to reconstruct the encryption key and decrypt the protected data.

For instance, a *Provider* may store encrypted model hyperparameters in IPFS, with the corresponding CID referenced by an instance of `EncapsulatedDataSC`. Authorized entities, such as the *Deployer* and *Auditor*, can retrieve the information required to access the protected data, as illustrated in Fig. 2.

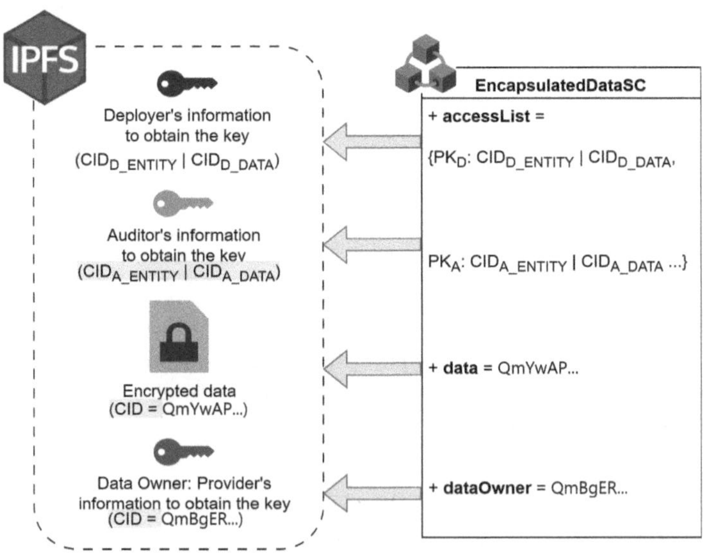

Fig. 2. Structure and workflow of the `EncapsulatedDataSC`. The contract stores a CID referencing the encrypted payload (`data`), an owner-specific CID (`dataOwner`) for key recovery, and an access list mapping each authorized entity's public key to a CID tuple containing the encrypted key material required to decrypt the protected data.

4.4.2 Model Smart Contract (ModelSC) The `ModelSC` stores key information about a model developed by the *Provider*, including its name, identifier, and version, alongside performance metadata such as accuracy, training date, and train-test split ratio. Sensitive assets, including training datasets and hyperparameters, are referenced via `EncapsulatedDataSC` instances. A link to the model's usage guidelines is kept in compliance with AIA's Art. 13. This contract serves as a verifiable registry, ensuring that all relevant information is readily available for auditors or competent authorities to evaluate the model's compliance with regulations. *Deployers* can request a servicing license, and the contract maintains a list of references to all `PDSC` instances deploying it, enabling the *Provider* to track active deployments.

Methods:

`getContract()` This method is invoked by a *Deployer* to request authorization to use the *Provider*'s model. Upon execution, it creates a new instance of the `Provider-Deployer Smart Contract` (`PDSC`), embedding all associated service conditions and linking them to the `ModelSC`.

`cancelContract()` This method can be called by either the *Provider* or the *Deployer*. When executed, it marks the corresponding PDSC as *inactive*, thereby terminating the agreement and stopping any further servicing.

4.4.3 Provider-Deployer Smart Contract (PDSC) This smart contract defines the licensing terms between the *Provider* and the *Deployer*. It stores two types of conditions: the servicing and maintenance terms governing the *Provider-Deployer* relationship, as an `EncapsulatedDataSC` instance, and the general conditions of usage applied to end-users. To support traceability and compliance, it maintains references to the associated `ModelSC`, authorized experts, the assigned auditor, and all `RequestSC` instances generated under the deployment. It also specifies whether expert validation is enabled by default and includes an `active` flag indicating if the contract remains valid.

The `PDSC` also tracks expert evaluations of the model's decisions by recording the cumulative number of approvals and rejections across all reviewed requests. Based on these values, the Expert Model Agreement (EMA) is calculated as:

$$EMA = \frac{\#approvals}{\#approvals + \#rejections} \in [0, 1]$$

Unlike conventional accuracy metrics, EMA provides a human-centered assessment of model behavior in real deployment conditions. Rather than replacing accuracy metrics, it complements them with continuous expert feedback. Since EMA is updated after each evaluation, it reflects the collective judgment of all experts involved in a deployment, rather than that of any single individual. To support informed assessments, the reviewing expert has full access to the end-user's input data, the model's output, and the explainability metrics included in the Decision Output Object (DOO). Values close to 1 indicate strong alignment between model outputs and expert judgments, whereas values near 0 indicate persistent disagreement and may warrant further investigation.

Methods:

`updateStatus()` Called by the *Expert* with an approval or rejection as a parameter. This method updates the total number of approvals and rejections and triggers the `updateEMA()` function to recalculate the EMA metric.

`updateEMA()` Recalculates the EMA whenever the number of approvals or rejections changes.

`getService()` Invoked by the *End-user* to request a prediction on their input data. Each invocation generates a new instance of `RequestSC`, which records all data associated with that specific decision.

`getConditionsWithUser()` Returns the set of conditions that the *End-user* must accept prior to calling `getService()` and accessing the service. This ensures compliance with usage policies and consent requirements.

4.4.4 RequestSC This contract is created every time an *End-user* wants to obtain a prediction from their data using the service provided by the *Deployer*. Each instance is identified by a `decisionID` and stores the `userID` of the requesting *End-user*. The input data provided for prediction, the resulting decision output object, and the user's consent and agreement to service terms are all referenced via `EncapsulatedDataSC` instances, ensuring they remain encrypted and access-controlled. The contract also maintains a reference to the `PDSC` handling the request. If expert review is requested, the status of the decision (e.g., approved, or rejected) and the public key of the reviewing expert are also recorded.

Methods:

`setDecisionObject()` Method called by the *Deployer* after the *Expert* has provided their comments (if requested to). It links the request to its DOO.

`setStatus()` Function called by the *Expert* with the approval/rejection. Its invocation triggers the `updateStatus()` of the corresponding `PDSC`.

4.4.5 Decision Output Object (DOO) The DOO captures the model's prediction (predicted class, class index, and probability distribution), together with a unique decision identifier and prediction timestamps. It also includes explainability outputs such as SHAP [20], LIME [22], and EDM_{SHAP}, as well as optional expert comments when human review is requested. Its structure follows Parlak's BAXDT framework [7]. The DOO is stored as an encrypted JSON in IPFS and referenced through an `EncapsulatedDataSC` linked to the corresponding `RequestSC`.

4.5 Protocol Stages

The protocol consists of eight main stages: setup, licensing, deployment, user interaction, decision and validation, storage, access granting, and auditing. Next, we develop on each of these stages, providing a step-by-step explanation.

4.5.1 Setup Initial stage of the protocol performed by the *Provider*. It involves the model preparation and anchoring to the blockchain. The *Provider*:

1. Trains the model.
2. Uploads the data of the model to the blockchain via the `ModelSC`.

4.5.2 Licensing In this stage, the *Deployer* and the *Provider* negotiate a license that allows the *Deployer* to operate the model as a service. The *Deployer*:

1. Calls `getContract()` to sign and create a contract with the *Provider* stating the conditions of use and subservicing of the model. This operation outputs a new instance of the `PDSC`.

4.5.3 Deployment In this stage, the *Deployer*, having obtained the right to offer the AI system as a service, puts the model into operation. The *Deployer*:

1. Makes the system available to *End-users* under the agreed conditions through the `PDSC`. In practice, the *Deployer* typically exposes the model via an access interface such as a webpage, mobile application, or API endpoint.

4.5.4 User Interaction In this stage, the *End-user* engages with the model (offered by the *Deployer*) by inputting some data to obtain a prediction. The *End-user*:

1. Before requesting the service, calls `getConditionsWithUser()` to retrieve the system's terms of use.
2. Requests the *Deployer*'s service by calling `getService()`. This interaction triggers the creation of a new `RequestSC`.
3. Provides the required input data and explicitly consents to the purpose, retention period, and authorized recipients of their data. Users also indicate whether human oversight is requested and complete the necessary payment. All this information is automatically recorded in the `RequestSC`.

4.5.5 Decision and Validation In this stage, the model makes a prediction based on the input data. The *Expert* may optionally review the prediction and provide comments. Finally, the *End-user* will be able to access the decision made based on their data.

1. Upon request submission, the model processes the user's input and generates a prediction.
2. The *Deployer* generates the decision object based on the model's prediction.
3. If the *End-user*'s preferences require human expert review, or if enabled in the `PDSC`, the *Expert*:
   3.1. Either accepts or rejects the proposed decision, updating the status of acceptance in both `RequestSC` and `PDSC` by calling `setStatus()` (triggering the update of the EMA metric in the `PDSC`).

3.2. May append comments or annotations to the decision object.
4. Otherwise: the decision is processed automatically without human intervention.
5. The *Deployer* references the final Decision Output Object in the `RequestSC` by calling `setDecisionObject()`, ensuring that the *End-user* (and other authorized entities) can access it at any time.

4.5.6 Storage Whenever a step in the protocol involves sensitive attributes, the protocol implicitly triggers the creation of an `EncapsulatedDataSC`. The data owner:

1. Generates a symmetric session key K using its public key PK through a key encapsulation mechanism. This produces C_1, which contains the information needed to recover K using the corresponding secret key SK.
2. Symmetrically encrypts the sensitive data with the key K, obtaining C_2.
3. Stores C_1 in the IPFS obtaining CID_{DATA_OWNER}.
4. Stores C_2 in the IPFS obtaining CID_{DATA}.
5. Deploys a new instance of `EncapsulatedDataSC`, uploading the information in CID_{DATA_OWNER} and CID_{DATA}.

4.5.7 Access Granting to Entity *B* This stage is performed by any entity B that wants access to a specific piece of sensitive data.

1. Entity B requests access to the data by calling `requestAccess()`, sharing its public key PK_B.
2. If the owner decides to grant access:
   2.1. Obtains CID_{DATA_OWNER} by calling `getDataOwner()`, therefore getting C_1.
   2.2. Uses its secret key SK to decapsulate the session key K from C_1.
   2.3. Uses PK_B to generate a session key K_B through a key encapsulation mechanism. This produces C_{B_1}.
   2.4. Symmetrically encrypts the data encryption key K obtaining C_{B_2}.
   2.5. Uploads C_{B_1} and C_{B_2} to the IPFS, obtaining CID_{ENTITY} and CID_{DATA}, respectively.
   2.6. Updates the `EncapsulatedSC` linked to the data appending the key-value pair $\langle PK_B : CID_{ENTITY} \mid CID_{DATA} \rangle$ to the access list, by calling `addAccess()`.
3. Otherwise, the owner ignores the request.

4.5.8 Auditing The auditing phase encompasses not only the verification performed by the auditor to ensure compliance with requirements, but also the formal procedures that any entity (other than the data owner) must follow to obtain access to sensitive data. Therefore, entity B:

1. Calls `getAccess()` with its public key PK_B, obtaining the tuple (CID_{ENTITY} ,CID_{DATA}) that contains the cryptograms (C_{B_1}, C_{B_2}).
2. Uses C_{B_1} to decapsulate the session key K_B.
3. Uses K_B to decipher C_{B_2} and obtain the data encryption key K.
4. Obtains CID_{DATA} by calling `getData()` and decrypts the content using K.

5 Requirements Coverage Analysis

This section assesses the fulfillment of the requirements stated in Sect. 3.

5.1 Functional Requirements

FR1. **Evidence registration/Auditability**. Every significant action in the system (ranging from model registration and contract creation to user requests, decision generation, expert validation, and audit access) is recorded in a blockchain transaction, ensuring immutable, tamper-evident logging by design. Because smart contracts store timestamps, identifiers, and status updates, the framework provides full traceability and supports both internal logging requirements and post-market auditing.

FR2. **Transparency and Explainability**. Each prediction generates a Decision Output Object that includes explainability measures such as SHAP and LIME, aligned with the structure defined in Parlak's BAXDT framework [7]. These metrics are input-focused, describing the contribution of each feature to the final decision. This design ensures that every model output remains transparent and interpretable to both deployers and end-users, independently of the underlying model architecture.

FR3. **Human oversight**. Expert intervention is optional and can be enabled by default through the `PDSC` or explicitly requested by the end-user. When active, expert assessments and comments are securely stored in IPFS and anchored on the blockchain via the corresponding `RequestSC`, supporting the human-in-the-loop mechanisms required by Art. 14. Additionally, the `PDSC` tracks expert-model agreement through the EMA metric, which is recalculated after each expert assessment to produce a dynamic, real-time signal of consistency or divergence between model outputs and human expertise.

FR4. **Multi-stakeholder coordination**. The architecture supports the roles defined in the AIA: provider, deployer, and auditor. Additionally, it incorporates the end-user and expert roles, empowering end-users to have control over decisions derived from their personal data and to obtain expert validation. Interactions are managed through dedicated smart contracts, enforcing separation of responsibilities, least-privilege access, and accountability while enabling each actor to fulfill their regulatory obligations independently.

5.2 Non-functional Requirements

NFR1. **Generality**. The framework is model- and domain-agnostic, operating on abstract metadata rather than task-specific structures. Consequently, it can be applied across different high-risk sectors. For example, in healthcare, the deployer corresponds to the hospital, the expert to the physician, and the end-user to the patient. The configurable expert-review mechanism further supports domains such as credit scoring and recruitment, where the frequency and urgency of human oversight may differ.

NFR2. **Access control**. Access control is enforced at two levels. At the data level, `EncapsulatedDataSC` binds authorized entities to their public keys, ensuring that only permitted parties can access the key material needed to decrypt protected data. At the operational level, smart contracts enforce method-level authorization: transactions must be signed by the caller, and execution is denied if the signature is invalid or unauthorized for the requested method.

NFR3. **Integrity**. Sensitive data (including model metadata, decision logs, and licensing conditions) is encrypted and stored in IPFS. By anchoring its content identifier (CID) on the blockchain, the information becomes immutable and tamper-evident, ensuring full integrity throughout the system lifecycle.

NFR4. **Confidentiality**. Neither the blockchain nor IPFS ever store plaintext sensitive data. All sensitive attributes are encrypted before being stored off-chain, and the digital envelope mechanism ensures that even if the underlying storage is compromised, the encrypted content remains unintelligible to unauthorized parties, including other actors within the framework.

NFR5. **Availability and resilience**. Blockchain and IPFS operate in distributed environments, eliminating single points of failure and ensuring data availability even during node failures. This is particularly beneficial in cases of device loss, as users do not need to store DOOs locally.

6 Conclusions and Future Work

In this work, we proposed a multi-stakeholder framework designed to guide the development and deployment of high-risk AI systems in alignment with the EU AI Act. The framework structures the roles and responsibilities of all relevant actors, and embeds the mechanisms necessary for traceability, explainability, and accountability directly into the system. By combining blockchain-based auditability, secure information registration, and explainable decision outputs, the framework facilitates post-market monitoring and independent compliance assessments without relying on external auditing infrastructures.

A current limitation of this work is the lack of a real-world implementation, preventing quantitative evaluation of efficiency, scalability, usability, and costs. Future work will focus on implementing and evaluating the framework across different blockchain platforms and governance models to assess its technical and economic viability. In addition, we intend to extend the traceability layer with data-provenance mechanisms, explore blockchain events to reduce on-chain costs, and refine the EMA metric through weighted expert assessments and domain-specific expertise categorization.

Acknowledgments. This work is supported by Project HERMES (EU NextGeneration EU/PRTR via INCIBE), MCIN/AEI projects PID2021-125962OB-C32 "SECUR-

ING/DATA" and PID2024-156914OB-C42 "SAFE/DATA", and AGAUR Grant SGR2021-00115 (Generalitat de Catalunya). Ignacio Miguel Rodríguez is supported by a FI-STEP fellowship (Generalitat de Catalunya, ref. 2025 STEP 00378).

Disclosure of Interests. The authors have no competing interests to declare that are relevant to the content of this article.

References

1. Bellamy, R.K.E., et al.: AI Fairness 360: an extensible toolkit for detecting, understanding, and mitigating unwanted algorithmic bias (2018). https://arxiv.org/abs/1810.01943
2. Biswas, P., et al.: AI-driven approaches for optimizing power consumption: a comprehensive survey. Discover Artif. Intell. **4**(1), 116 (2024). https://doi.org/10.1007/s44163-024-00211-7
3. Cyberspace Administration of China: Interim Measures for the Management of Generative Artificial Intelligence Services (2023). Available at: https://www.cac.gov.cn/2023-07/13/c_1690898327029107.htm (Chinese)
4. Demertzis, K., Rantos, K., Magafas, L., Skianis, C., Iliadis, L.: A secure and privacy-preserving blockchain-based XAI-justice system. Information **14**(9), 477 (2023). https://doi.org/10.3390/info14090477
5. Devi, K.J., Alghamdi, W., N, D., Alkhayyat, A., Sayyora, A., Sathish, T.: Artificial intelligence in healthcare: diagnosis, treatment, and prediction. E3S Web Conf. **399**, 04043 (2023). https://doi.org/10.1051/e3sconf/202339904043
6. Dey, D., Bhaumik, D.: APPRAISE: a governance framework for innovation with artificial intelligence systems. In: Proceedings of the AAAI/ACM Conference on AI, Ethics, and Society, vol. 7, pp. 328–340 (2024). https://doi.org/10.1609/aies.v7i1.31640
7. Parlak, İ. E.: Blockchain-assisted explainable decision traces (BAXDT): an approach for transparency and accountability in artificial intelligence systems. Knowl.-Based Syst. **329**, 114402 (2025). https://doi.org/10.1016/j.knosys.2025.114402
8. European Parliament and Council of the European Union: Regulation (EU) 2023/2854 of the European Parliament and of the Council of 13 December 2023 on harmonised rules on fair access to and use of data and amending Regulation (EU) 2017/2394 and Directive (EU) 2020/1828 (Data Act). Official Journal of the European Union (2023). available at https://eur-lex.europa.eu/eli/reg/2023/2854/oj/eng
9. European Parliament and Council of the European Union: Regulation (EU) 2024/1689 of the European Parliament and of the Council of 13 June 2024 laying down harmonised rules on artificial intelligence (Artificial Intelligence Act). Official Journal of the European Union, L 2024/1689, 12 July 2024 (2024). available at https://eur-lex.europa.eu/eli/reg/2024/1689/oj/eng
10. European Parliament and the Council of the European Union: Regulation (EU) 2016/679 of the European Parliament and of the Council of 27 April 2016 on the protection of natural persons with regard to the processing of personal data and on the free movement of such data (General Data Protection Regulation) (2016). available at: https://eur-lex.europa.eu/eli/reg/2016/679/oj/eng

11. European Parliament and the Council of the European Union: Regulation (EU) 2022/868 of the European Parliament and of the Council of 30 May 2022 on European data governance and amending Regulation (EU) 2018/1724 (Data Governance Act) (2022). available at https://eur-lex.europa.eu/eli/reg/2022/868/oj/eng
12. European Union Agency for Fundamental Rights: Data Quality and Artificial Intelligence – Mitigating Bias and Error to Protect Fundamental Rights. Fra focus, European Union Agency for Fundamental Rights (FRA) (2019). https://doi.org/10.2811/546219
13. Floridi, L., Holweg, M., Taddeo, M., Amaya, J., Mökander, J., Wen, Y.: capAI - a procedure for conducting conformity assessment of AI systems in line with the EU artificial intelligence act. SSRN Electron. J. (2022). https://doi.org/10.2139/ssrn.4064091
14. Guldimann, P., et al.: COMPL-AI Framework: a technical interpretation and LLM benchmarking suite for the EU artificial intelligence act (2025). https://arxiv.org/abs/2410.07959
15. Hasan, R., Dattana, V., Mahmood, S., Hussain, S.: Towards transparent diabetes prediction: combining AutoML and explainable AI for improved clinical insights. Information **16**(1), 7 (2025). https://doi.org/10.3390/info16010007
16. Hepp, T., Sharinghousen, M., Ehret, P., Schoenhals, A., Gipp, B.: On-chain vs. off-chain storage for supply- and blockchain integration. It - Info. Technol. **60**(5-6), 283–291 (2018). https://doi.org/10.1515/itit-2018-0019
17. Iqbal, S.: Ascendancy of artificial intelligence (AI) in finance: How are financial institutions leveraging AI for competitive advantages. J. Bus. Develop. Stud. **3**(1), 77–101 (2024)
18. Jovanovic, Z., Hou, Z., Biswas, K., Muthukkumarasamy, V.: Robust integration of blockchain and explainable federated learning for automated credit scoring. Comput. Netw. **243**, 110303 (2024). https://doi.org/10.1016/j.comnet.2024.110303
19. Kumar, P., Javeed, D., Kumar, R., Islam, A.: Blockchain and explainable AI for enhanced decision making in cyber threat detection. Softw.: Pract. Exper. **54**(8), 1337–1360 (2024). https://doi.org/10.1002/spe.3319
20. Lundberg, S., Lee, S.I.: A unified approach to interpreting model predictions (2017). https://arxiv.org/abs/1705.07874
21. Obradov, A., Pavković, B.: Ensuring compliance of high-risk AI systems with the EU AI act using open source libraries. In: 2025 IEEE Zooming Innovation in Consumer Technologies Conference (ZINC), pp. 54–59 (2025). https://doi.org/10.1109/ZINC65316.2025.11103517
22. Ribeiro, M.T., Singh, S., Guestrin, C.: "Why Should i trust you?": explaining the predictions of any classifier (2016). https://arxiv.org/abs/1602.04938
23. Sachan, S., Liu (Lisa), X.: Blockchain-based auditing of legal decisions supported by explainable AI and generative AI tools. Eng. Appl. Artif. Intell. **129**, 107666 (2024). https://doi.org/10.1016/j.engappai.2023.107666
24. Santos-Silva, M.A., Sousa, N., Sousa, J.C.: Artificial intelligence in routine blood tests. Front. Med. Eng. **2** (2024). https://doi.org/10.3389/fmede.2024.1369265
25. Science and Technology Police Office: Blueprint for an AI Bill of Rights: Making Automated Systems Work for the American People (2022). Available at: https://www.govinfo.gov/app/details/GOVPUB-PREX23-PURL-gpo193638
26. Wang, L., Hu, M., Yang, L.T., Sun, X., Chen, Z.: AI-auditor: a data auditing framework for enhancing the trustworthiness of AI models. IEEE Trans. Industr. Inf. **21**(12), 9208–9216 (2025). https://doi.org/10.1109/TII.2025.3593981

A Security-Oriented Lifecycle Model for Large Language Model Systems

Eleftherios Batzolis[1,2](✉), George Drosatos[2], Vassilis Katsouros[2], and Konstantinos Rantos[1]

[1] Department of Informatics, Democritus University of Thrace, Kavala, Greece
{ebatzoli,krantos}@cs.duth.gr, e.batzolis@athenarc.gr
[2] Institute for Language and Speech Processing, Athena Research Center, Xanthi, Greece
{gdrosato,vsk}@athenarc.gr

Abstract. Large language models are being integrated into critical infrastructure and enterprise workflows at unprecedented scale, yet the lifecycle frameworks governing their development and operations were designed for operational efficiency rather than security analysis. As a result, security-relevant activities such as data provenance verification, artifact signing, agentic permission control, and decommissioning are often left implicit or assumed to receive due care. Governance frameworks, in turn, organise requirements around risk levels or management processes without clearly linking them to the lifecycle stages where they apply. This paper addresses both deficiencies. We propose a lifecycle model for LLM systems that supports security analysis by structuring it around security-relevant boundaries rather than workflow optimisation. The model comprises 32 stages across four core pipeline layers (Data, Model, Distribution, Application), supported by a 12-stage LLMOps pillar and a 9-category governance pillar. Thirteen stages are introduced here as separate units because they expose distinct security concerns that existing frameworks do not clearly distinguish. A governance mapping synthesising the NIST AI RMF, the EU AI Act, and ISO/IEC 42001 reveals a structural property of the current regulatory landscape: governance evidence concentrates at deployment-facing stages, where systems are visible to regulators, while the most consequential decisions, data selection, alignment strategy, and capability boundaries, are made at development-facing stages, where regulatory visibility is lowest.

Keywords: LLM security · AI lifecycle · AI governance · attack surface · supply chain security · LLMOps

1 Introduction

Large Language Models (LLMs) have evolved from research artifacts into foundational components of critical infrastructures and enterprise workflows [49]. Their development spans multi-stage chains that include data sourcing and curation,

P. Kieseberg et al. (Eds.): ARES 2026 Workshops, LNCS 16903, pp. 401–419, 2027.
https://doi.org/10.1007/978-3-032-37218-5_24

alignment via Reinforcement Learning from Human Feedback (RLHF) [4], post-training optimisation, distribution through public model hubs [39], and deployment within orchestrated stacks incorporating Retrieval-Augmented Generation (RAG), autonomous agents, and multi-model architectures [16]. Each stage introduces distinct artifacts, access models, threat actors, and attack vectors, making the LLM lifecycle a substantially broader attack surface than that of conventional software systems.

The security research community has responded by cataloguing threat categories such as data poisoning [6], prompt injection [15], and model extraction and privacy leakage [18], and by developing industry frameworks including the OWASP Top 10 for LLM Applications [31] and MITRE ATLAS [24]. In parallel, governance instruments such as the NIST AI RMF [25] and ISO/IEC 42001 [20] have established organisational controls intended to fortify AI deployments against malicious activity. What remains absent, however, is a lifecycle structure that connects these perspectives: a model that decomposes the LLM lifecycle at the boundaries where security-relevant distinctions arise, thereby enabling systematic analysis of threats, governance provisions, and operational requirements at appropriate granularity.

Existing lifecycle and governance frameworks, surveyed in Sect. 2, exhibit a consistent pattern: stage boundaries are defined by engineering workflow or by regulatory logic, neither of which aligns cleanly with security-relevant distinctions. The result is a four-fold gap. First, a *granularity gap*: activities associated with different threat profiles are merged under broader categories, hiding important security differences. Second, a *security-specificity gap*: security-relevant activities such as model signing, red teaming, and input validation are not clearly mapped to distinct lifecycle stages. Third, an *architectural completeness gap*: no existing framework combines end-to-end lifecycle coverage with cross-cutting governance and operational support. Fourth, a *governance mapping gap*: governance frameworks are not sufficiently linked to specific lifecycle stages.

We argue that existing LLM lifecycle and governance frameworks are structurally misaligned for security analysis, and that a security-oriented lifecycle model, decomposed along attack-surface boundaries and mapped to governance provisions, makes that misalignment analysable. We address the four gaps with the following contributions:

1. An *LLM lifecycle model that supports security analysis*, comprising 32 stages across four core pipeline layers. Thirteen are identified here as separate lifecycle stages because they expose distinct security concerns not clearly distinguished in existing frameworks. Several of the underlying activities, such as red teaming and synthetic data generation, are already recognised in practice; what is new here is their treatment as separate analytical units for security analysis.
2. A *12-stage LLMOps operational pillar* synthesised from three academic sources [7,32,36] and elevated from a single lifecycle step to a cross-cutting support layer.

3. A *9-category governance pillar* synthesising the NIST AI RMF [25], the EU AI Act [12], and ISO/IEC 42001 [20], that maps governance concerns to lifecycle stages and identifies three governance handoffs at layer boundaries.

The remainder of this paper is organized as follows. Section 2 reviews related work. Section 3 describes the methodology. Section 4 presents the core pipeline. Sections 5 and 6 detail the LLMOps and governance pillars, respectively. Section 7 discusses differentiation and limitations, and Sect. 8 concludes.

2 Related Work

Existing lifecycle models exhibit a consistent pattern: stage boundaries are typically defined by engineering workflow, which limits their utility for security analysis because activities with different threat profiles are grouped together. MLOps frameworks [22] provide a general pipeline structure but lack granularity for LLM-specific activities such as alignment or prompt engineering. LLMOps definitions [7,32,36] address LLM-specific concerns but merge activities with distinct security profiles, treating alignment and fine-tuning as one stage despite different threat actors and poisoning vectors, and combining packaging and distribution across different trust boundaries. Enterprise blueprints [5] provide operational context but not the stage decomposition needed for per-stage security assessment. These frameworks address the *granularity gap* and *security-specificity gap* only partially.

Security-oriented framings partially address these gaps. Wang et al. [45] provide the broadest empirical coverage (529 CVEs, 13 stages) but merge distinct threat profiles and lack governance mapping. NIST AI 100-2e2025 [42] compresses the upstream pipeline into a single training phase, precluding distinction among annotation, alignment, and distribution stages. ENISA [10] and ETSI EN 304 223 [11] include decommissioning and apply Confidentiality, Integrity, and Availability (CIA) assessment, validating our design choices, but restrict security analysis to high-level policy guidance without per-stage decomposition. MITRE ATLAS [24] provides indispensable threat intelligence but its kill-chain orientation serves threat hunting rather than lifecycle governance mapping. Google's SAIF [14] organises security around component-risk mappings and distinguishes Model Creator from Model Consumer roles; its 2.0 release adds agentic concerns that corroborate the need for our Stage 4.11, but its structure remains risk-oriented rather than lifecycle-oriented and does not map to external governance instruments. Supply-chain studies [44] validate the four-layer structure as a recurring pattern but predate LLM-specific concerns or provide research agendas without per-stage decomposition. Developer-centric studies [27] corroborate the security significance of stages our framework foregrounds but organize findings by developer themes rather than lifecycle stages. These works address the *architectural completeness gap* only partially: ENISA and ETSI achieve end-to-end coverage including decommissioning, but none combines this with cross-cutting operational and governance pillars.

On governance, the three dominant frameworks, NIST AI RMF [25] (functional axis), the EU AI Act [12] (risk-and-role axis), and ISO/IEC 42001 [20] (management-cycle axis), embody structurally distinct logics, none of which maps onto the operational stages of LLM development. Organisations must navigate all three, yet none indicates how its requirements relate to specific lifecycle stages, leaving the *governance mapping gap* unaddressed.

The present work responds to these four gaps by proposing a lifecycle model that combines a core pipeline structured around security-relevant boundaries with cross-cutting LLMOps and governance pillars. Table 1 summarises the comparison across key dimensions, and the differentiation can be articulated concretely along four axes. On *lifecycle granularity*, the proposed model decomposes the LLM lifecycle into four layers and 32 stages, exceeding the resolution of prior treatments that adopt three architectural layers [44], thirteen stages without end-to-end coverage [45], or two phases that collapse the upstream pipeline [42]. On *security-specific decomposition*, the model identifies thirteen stages as separate lifecycle units on the basis of distinct threat actors, exposed artifacts, and access models; prior frameworks treat these activities either implicitly within broader stages or as risk categories rather than lifecycle units, with the partial exception of ENISA [10] and ETSI [11], which include decommissioning but stop short of per-stage decomposition. On *end-to-end coverage*, the model spans data sourcing through decommissioning, matching ENISA and ETSI in scope while exceeding them in granularity; most other frameworks, including SAIF [14] and MITRE ATLAS [24], omit decommissioning entirely. On *governance linkage*, the model provides an explicit provision-to-stage mapping synthesising the NIST AI RMF, the EU AI Act, and ISO/IEC 42001, which no prior framework in Table 1 offers; ENISA and ETSI achieve partial governance linkage but do not map provisions to stages at the resolution required for per-stage accountability analysis.

3 Methodology

The proposed framework is analytically derived rather than empirically measured: it is constructed through structured synthesis of prior lifecycle, security, and governance literature, and provides a scaffold against which empirical security data can subsequently be organised rather than reporting new empirical findings.

The lifecycle model was constructed through analytical synthesis of three source categories: (i) existing lifecycle frameworks (Sect. 2), which provided the baseline stage inventory; (ii) the supply-chain and security literature [13,44,45] [6,15,18], which documented threats at stages existing frameworks omit; and (iii) governance instruments [12,20,25,26], whose requirements imply lifecycle stages that operational frameworks do not make explicit.

The organising principle is *attack surface exposure*, characterised along three dimensions: the threat actors with access to a stage, the artifacts exposed at that stage, and the access model governing how those artifacts are reached. Stage boundaries are placed where one or more of these dimensions change in

Table 1. Comparison of LLM/AI Lifecycle and Security Frameworks Against the Four Identified Gaps

Source	Lifecycle Granularity	Security-Specific Stages	Evidence Base	Gov. Linkage	End-to-End Coverage
Wang et al. [44]	3 layers (infra, model, app)	No	Theoretical	None	No (no decommissioning stage)
Steidl et al. [40]	4 stages (general AI)	No	Mixed	None	No (no decommissioning stage)
Wang et al. [45]	13 stages, 3 layers	Partial	Empirical	None	No (no decommissioning stage)
NIST AI 100-2e2025 [42]	2 phases	No	Theoretical	None	No (no decommissioning stage)
Patel et al. [33]	3 attack families	No	Mixed	None	No
Huang et al. [19]	Stakeholder view	No	Mixed	None	No
Nguyen et al. [27]	Developer themes	No	Empirical	None	No
Jiang et al. [21]	Issue categories	No	Empirical	None	No
ENISA [10]	Concept to decom.	Partial	Theoretical	Partial	Yes
ETSI EN 304 223 [11]	5 phases, 13 princ.	Partial	Theoretical	Partial	Yes
MITRE ATLAS [24]	Kill chain tactics	Partial	Mixed	None	No
Google SAIF [14]	Risk-oriented (15 risks)	Partial	Mixed	None	No (no decommissioning stage)
This work	**4 layers, 32 stages**	**Yes (13 stages)**	**Mixed**	**Explicit**	**Yes**

Columns map to the four gaps from Sect. 1: Lifecycle Granularity, Security-Specific Stages, End-to-End Coverage, and Governance Linkage. Evidence Base indicates each work's empirical grounding.

a way that materially alters the security concerns applicable to the activity in question. We distinguish four threat actor classes along this principle. *External adversaries* (e.g., data poisoners, supply-chain attackers) operate without legitimate access, acting through indirect channels such as publicly scraped data or compromised upstream dependencies. *Insiders* (e.g., compromised annotators, preference evaluators) hold privileged access to internal development artifacts and corrupt training or alignment signals at their point of creation. *Supply-chain intermediaries*, further divided into infrastructure operators (e.g., model hub platforms) and dependency maintainers (e.g., library authors), control artifacts in transit between development and deployment. *End users* (e.g., prompt injectors, agent manipulators) hold legitimate credentials and operate within sanctioned interfaces but may abuse those interfaces in ways that external adversaries cannot, because end users interact with the system after deployment-time controls have already been applied; the mitigations applicable to this class (input validation, output filtering, permission control) are correspondingly distinct from those applicable to external adversaries (perimeter and supply-chain controls). The *access model*, namely the type of artifact exposed, the level of privilege available, and the authentication boundary in place, is the third dimension of attack surface exposure and the dimension along which threat actor classes are distinguished in practice. Lifecycle operations on data, models, or deployed systems are grouped into the same stage when they share similar threat actors, exposed artifacts, and access patterns; they are separated when these characteristics differ enough to warrant independent security analysis. This principle operates as a guiding heuristic rather than a formal decision procedure.

As a worked example, the separation of Supervised Fine-Tuning (SFT, Stage 2.3) from Alignment (Stage 2.4), here understood as preference-based fine-tuning that shapes model behaviour toward human preferences and safety constraints [4], follows directly from this principle. SFT poisoning is mounted by data curators against instruction-response pairs through instruction injection, whereas alignment poisoning is mounted by preference evaluators and reward-model trainers against preference rankings and reward models, through label corruption [23] and reward-model backdoors [43]. The three dimensions of attack surface exposure thus differ across the two activities, warranting separate treatment. The same reasoning, applied across the lifecycle, separates other commonly merged pairs (data sourcing from annotation, packaging from signing) and underlies the introduction of thirteen stages whose security concerns are not represented as separate units in existing lifecycle models.

The governance pillar synthesizes provisions from the NIST AI RMF [25] (including AI 600–1 [26]), the EU AI Act [12], and ISO/IEC 42001 [20], selected because they represent three complementary approaches: voluntary guidance, prescriptive regulation, and certifiable standardization. Provisions were inventoried, assigned to the lifecycle stage(s) where they are most relevant, and aggregated into nine categories (defined in Sect. 6.1). Governance handoffs, that is, transfers of responsibility and accountability, were identified at points where responsibility shifts, where specific evidence must be passed between roles, or where decisions affect later stages of the lifecycle. The structural asymmetry was identified by classifying each provision as either evidence-producing (e.g., documentation, logging, reporting) or decision-shaping (e.g., data selection, alignment strategy, capability boundaries). This classification revealed that evidence-producing provisions concentrate at Layers 3–4, while decision-shaping provisions concentrate at Layers 1–2.

The LLMOps pillar was derived through three-phase synthesis of three primary sources [7,32,36]: consensus identification (seven sub-stages appearing as named functions in at least two sources), elevation of implicitly treated concerns to named stages (Guardrails and Content Safety, Security and Compliance Automation), and gap closure (three sub-stages absent from the initial inventory). The twelve stages were cross-referenced against practitioner sources [5]; Table 2 shows the derivation provenance.

4 Core Pipeline: Data, Model, Distribution, Application

The lifecycle model comprises four core layers arranged as a sequential pipeline: Data, Model, Distribution, and Application, comprising 32 stages in total, and is supported by two cross-cutting pillars: the LLMOps pillar (Sect. 5) and the Governance pillar (Sect. 6). A continuous feedback loop connects the Application layer back to the Data layer; this loop has security implications, as adversarial feedback collected at Layer 4 can be reintroduced into training data at Layer 1, propagating issues across iterations. Figure 1 presents the complete model. The subsections below define each layer, focusing on the 13 additional stages; stages that refine existing categories are summarised in Fig. 1. Each stage is exposed to different types of threats, and representative examples are provided to illustrate these differences.

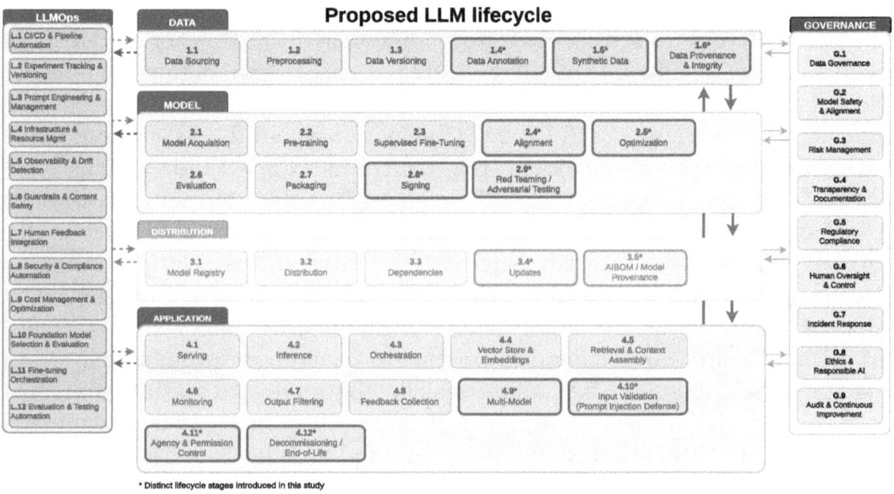

Fig. 1. LLM Lifecycle: four core pipeline layers (Data, Model, Distribution, Application), the LLMOps operational pillar (left), the Governance pillar (right), and the continuous feedback loop.

4.1 Layer 1: Data (Stages 1.1–1.6)

The Data layer produces, curates, and governs the corpora from which an LLM acquires its capabilities; a compromise at any stage of this layer propagates through every subsequent layer [6]. We decompose the Data layer into six stages, two more than typical MLOps frameworks [22] and three more than NIST's monolithic training-data category [42], reflecting differences in security-relevant concerns. Stages 1.1–1.3 (Data Sourcing, Preprocessing, Versioning) refine existing categories. Three additional stages address gaps: *Data Annotation* (1.4) introduces a human-in-the-loop attack surface (label manipulation [1], annotator data exposure, platform injection [34]) materially distinct from automated stages; *Synthetic Data* (1.5) isolates risks unique to model-generated corpora, including model collapse through recursive training [35] and bias amplification through feedback loops; and *Data Provenance and Integrity* (1.6) addresses the metadata infrastructure recording data origins and transformations, which constitutes a bidirectional attack surface: provenance records can be tampered with to disguise poisoned data [2], while overly detailed records may leak sensitive infrastructure information [38].

4.2 Layer 2: Model (Stages 2.1–2.9)

The Model layer spans all activities transforming curated data into a deployable artifact. Its nine-stage decomposition substantially extends prior two- or three-stage treatments [7]. Therefore, we separate acquisition from training (supply-chain vs infrastructure trust), SFT from alignment (different threat actors and poisoning vectors), and introduce dedicated stages for packaging, signing, and adversarial testing, as they involve different security concerns. Stages 2.1–2.3 (Acquisition, Pre-training, SFT), 2.6 (Evaluation), and 2.7 (Packaging) refine existing categories. Four additional stages, introduced here, address gaps: *Alignment* (2.4) is important for model safety, as preference data and reward models can be poisoned to embed backdoors [47], and issues introduced during alignment can weaken safety mechanisms used in later stages. *Optimization* (2.5) addresses post-training transformations (quantization, pruning, merging) where models may appear benign at full precision but behave differently when quantized [9], and compromised models propagate backdoors through weight averaging [48]. *Model Signing* (2.8) addresses cryptographic attestation of artifacts, architecturally distinct from both packaging and distribution, where signing key exposure [37] and the absence of widely adopted standards leave many models distributed without integrity verification. *Red Teaming* (2.9) is separated from general evaluation because it measures robustness under attack rather than capability; red-team findings can also be misused [29], and models can be crafted to evade safety evaluations while remaining harmful in production [49]. Together, these stages make the Model layer the locus of the most consequential and least reversible security decisions: compromises introduced here, whether through poisoned alignment data, backdoored reward models, or absent integrity attestation, propagate through every downstream layer and are seldom remediable by deployment-time controls alone.

4.3 Layer 3: Distribution (Stages 3.1–3.5)

The Distribution layer covers all activities between production of a signed artifact and its instantiation in a running application, which is a major supply-chain attack surface [13]. Stages 3.1–3.3 (Registry, Distribution, Dependencies) refine existing categories. Two additional stages, introduced here, address gaps: *Updates* (3.4) separates post-deployment refresh mechanisms from initial distribution because the trust model differs: updates propagate automatically, often without manual review, and malicious payloads can be delivered through established channels. *AI Bill of Materials (AIBOM) and Model Provenance* (3.5) addresses generation and verification of AIBOMs [30], where AIBOM records may be forged [41] while overly detailed AIBOMs may disclose proprietary details enabling targeted attacks [38].

4.4 Layer 4: Application (Stages 4.1–4.12)

The Application layer spans model instantiation through runtime operation, monitoring, and eventual decommissioning: it is the largest layer reflecting the diverse architectural patterns characterising modern LLM deployments. Stages 4.1–4.8 (Serving, Inference, Orchestration, Vector Store, Retrieval, Monitoring, Output Filtering, Feedback Collection) are present in varying degrees across existing frameworks. Serving (4.1) and Inference (4.2), while sharing end users as a threat actor class, differ in artifact type (infrastructure configurations versus inference requests and outputs) and attack vector space (resource exhaustion and configuration tampering versus prompt injection and output manipulation), justifying their separation. Four additional stages, introduced here, address gaps: *Multi-Model* (4.9) captures interaction effects that are not present in single-model deployments, including cross-tenant information channels through shared KV-cache entries that allow one tenant's context to leak into another's generation [46] and adversarial prompt contagion across multi-agent systems [8]. *Input Validation* (4.10) separates defensive infrastructure, such as prompt guards and classification models, from inference, as encoding manipulation and tokenizer-level tricks bypass detection [50] and probing attacks reverse-engineer filter rules. *Agency and Permission Control* (4.11) governs what autonomous agents are permitted to do [29], encompassing tool-use authorization protocols such as the Model Context Protocol (MCP) and Agent-to-Agent (A2A) that define the interface through which agents invoke external capabilities: agents with overly broad permissions can be manipulated into unauthorized actions [28], privilege escalation exploits inter-agent trust [17], and individually permitted tool invocations can be chained to achieve unauthorized outcomes. *Decommissioning* (4.12) addresses model retirement, which is treated explicitly only by a small number of the frameworks reviewed in Table 1: deprecated weights may contain extractable data, orphaned API keys may remain valid, and namespaces of retired models can be claimed by adversaries.

5 The LLMOps Pillar

LLMOps should not be treated as a single step within the Model layer. Prior work [7,32,36] characterises LLMOps as an end-to-end orchestration concern, and the compromise of LLMOps infrastructure carries cascading consequences that exceed those of any single pipeline stage, since it can simultaneously disable enforcement mechanisms and suppress detection. We therefore elevate LLMOps to a cross-cutting pillar comprising twelve sub-stages[1] derived through the three-phase process described in Sect. 3. We define a sub-stage as *consensus* when it appears as a named function in at least two of the three primary sources, as *elevated* when it is treated implicitly in one or more sources but never named as a distinct operational function, and as *gap-closure* when it is absent from the inventory of all three primary sources. Under this criterion, seven sub-stages are

[1] We use *stage* for core pipeline units and *sub-stage* for LLMOps units throughout.

consensus, two are elevated, and three are gap-closure. Together, these sub-stages capture the main operational functions required to manage LLM systems across the lifecycle, and make explicit several aspects that are treated only implicitly in existing definitions. Table 2 summarises how each sub-stage relates to existing definitions of LLMOps and indicates the synthesis phase from which it was derived.

Table 2. LLMOps Sub-stage Derivation: Source Coverage and Phase

Sub-stage	D[a]	S[b]	P[c]	Phase
L.1 CI/CD & Pipeline Automation	✓	✓	✓	Consensus
L.2 Experiment Tracking & Versioning	✓	✓		Consensus
L.3 Prompt Engineering & Management	✓	✓	✓	Consensus
L.4 Infrastructure & Resource Mgmt	✓		✓	Consensus
L.5 Observability & Drift Detection	✓	✓	✓	Consensus
L.6 Guardrails & Content Safety		∼	∼	Elevation
L.7 Human Feedback Integration	✓	✓		Consensus
L.8 Security & Compliance Automation	∼			Elevation
L.9 Cost Management & Optimization	✓	✓	✓	Consensus
L.10 Foundation Model Selection & Eval.		✓		Gap closure
L.11 Fine-tuning Orchestration		✓		Gap closure
L.12 Evaluation & Testing Automation		✓		Gap closure

[a]Diaz-De-Arcaya [7]; [b]Sinha [36]; [c]Pahune [32]; ✓ = named function; ∼ = implicit treatment.

Every named function in Sinha et al. [36] is represented among the twelve sub-stages. Two additional sub-stages, Infrastructure and Resource Management and Security and Compliance Automation, are present in other primary sources but not in Sinha et al. Together, this suggests that the principal operational functions of LLMOps are accounted for. The relationship between the LLMOps pillar and the core pipeline is bidirectional: in the forward direction, LLMOps orchestrates stage progression, provisions resources, enforces safety constraints, and applies validation checks; in the reverse direction, the pipeline generates the signals, dataset metadata, training metrics, user interactions, and inference costs, on which LLMOps operates. This bidirectional relationship has direct security implications, since controls are applied through LLMOps while security events originate from the pipeline, with the consequence that a single compromise of LLMOps infrastructure can simultaneously degrade enforcement and suppress detection. Consider, for instance, an attacker who compromises CI/CD and Pipeline Automation (L.1): such an attacker may introduce a poisoned model into the deployment workflow, tamper with experiment-tracking and versioning records (L.2) so that the poisoned model appears to pass evaluation, disable the guardrail configurations (L.6) that would otherwise catch anomalous outputs, and suppress the observability alerts (L.5) that would notify defenders. The resulting cascade illustrates how a single entry point can propagate across four LLMOps sub-stages, a pattern that motivates treating LLMOps as a distinct security-analytical layer rather than as a single operational concern.

6 The Governance Pillar

The governance pillar synthesises the NIST AI RMF [25], the EU AI Act [12], and ISO/IEC 42001 [20] into a unified, lifecycle-mapped governance structure. Figure 2 presents the mapping of the governance stack to the LLM lifecycle layers.

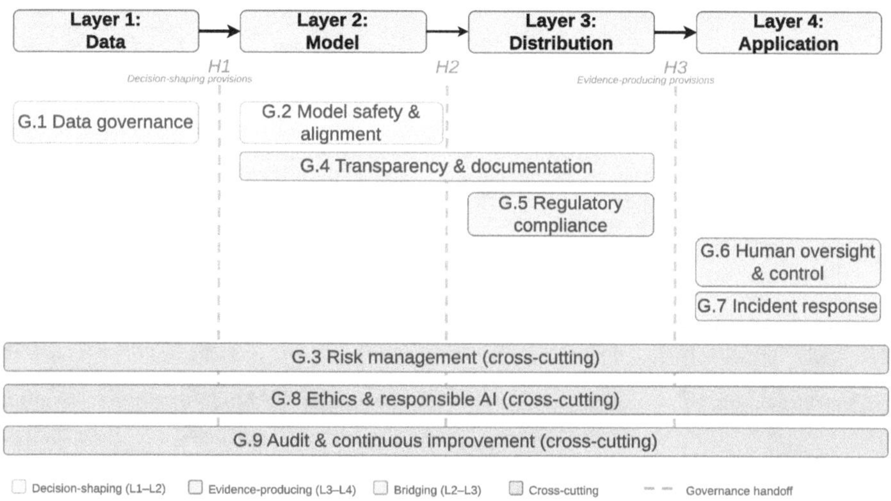

Fig. 2. Governance stack mapped to the LLM lifecycle: nine categories assigned to their primary lifecycle layers.

6.1 Design Rationale and Nine Categories

The three frameworks embody structurally distinct logics: functional (NIST), risk-and-role (EU AI Act), and management-cycle (ISO/IEC 42001), none of which maps directly onto development stages. The governance pillar reframes provisions along a lifecycle axis by assigning each provision to the lifecycle stage at which the activities it regulates actually take place. The EU AI Act, in particular, imposes obligations on providers of *General-Purpose AI (GPAI)* models, that is, foundation models offered for downstream integration; these obligations (Arts. 53–55) are treated here as a distinct sub-class of provisions within the existing categories rather than as a separate governance framework. The nine categories, ordered from data-proximal to cross-cutting, are: Data Governance (G.1), primarily Layer 1; Model Safety and Alignment (G.2), primarily Layer 2; Risk Management (G.3), cross-cutting; Transparency and Documentation (G.4), concentrated at the Layer 2/3 boundary; Regulatory Compliance (G.5), primarily Layer 3, carrying the heaviest enforcement weight (EU AI Act fines up to €15 million or 3% of global turnover); Human Oversight and Control (G.6), primarily Layer 4; Incident Response (G.7), primarily Layer 4; Ethics and Responsible AI (G.8), cross-cutting; and Audit and Continuous Improvement (G.9), cross-cutting. Table 3 presents a representative excerpt of the provision-to-stage mapping.

Table 3. Governance Provision-to-Stage Mapping

Category	Layer	Key Provisions
G.1 Data Gov.	L1	EU AI Act Art. 10: data governance and quality; GPAI Art. 53(1)(d): training data summary; N: MAP 1, MAP 4: data sources and third-party risks; ISO A.4: data resource controls
G.2 Model Safety	L2	EU AI Act Art. 9: risk management; GPAI Art. 55: adversarial testing; N: MEASURE 1–2: evaluation and risk assessment; GenAI 600-1: hallucination and bias; ISO Cl. 6.1: risk and impact assessment
G.4 Transp. & Doc.	L2/L3	EU AI Act Art. 11: technical documentation; GPAI Art. 53: transparency report; N: GOVERN 4: transparency culture; ISO Cl. 7.5: model cards and AIMS records
G.5 Reg. Compl.	L3	EU AI Act Art. 43: conformity assessment; Arts. 16–17: provider QMS; N: MANAGE 1, GOVERN 1.1: risk treatment and legal requirements; ISO Cl. 8.1: release controls; A.10.3: supplier oversight
G.6 Human Oversight	L4	EU AI Act Art. 14: human oversight; Art. 50: AI disclosure; Art. 27: FRIA; N: GOVERN 5: stakeholder engagement; ISO A.9.3: oversight controls
G.7 Incident Resp.	L4	EU AI Act Art. 12: logging; Arts. 72–73: post-market monitoring and incident reporting; N: MANAGE 4, GOVERN 4.2: residual risk and incident protocols; ISO Cl. 9.1, 10: monitoring and corrective actions; A.8: information for interested parties
G.3 Risk Mgmt	Cross	N: GOVERN (all 6): culture, policy, accountability; EU AI Act: AI Office and MSA oversight; ISO: PDCA cycle; Cl. 5: leadership; Cl. 9: audits
G.8 Ethics	Cross	N: GOVERN 4, MAP 5: ethics and societal impact; EU AI Act Art. 10(2)(g), 10(3): bias and representativeness; ISO A.6: AI system lifecycle controls
G.9 Audit & CI	Cross	N: GOVERN 1, MEASURE: accountability and re-assessment; EU AI Act Arts. 16–17, 72: QMS and post-market monitoring; ISO Cl. 5, 9, 10: leadership, audits, improvement

N = NIST AI RMF; ISO = ISO/IEC 42001; GPAI = General-Purpose AI obligations under the EU AI Act (Arts. 53–55); L1–L4 = Data, Model, Distribution, Application; Cross = cross-cutting. Category order matches Fig. 2.

Three features of this distribution are worth noting. The first is that the categories most directly shaping the system, namely Data Governance and Model Safety and Alignment, fall at the upstream end of the lifecycle, where decisions about training corpora, alignment strategy, and capability boundaries are made and where the consequences of those decisions become difficult to reverse. The second is that the categories carrying the heaviest external accountability, namely Transparency and Documentation and Regulatory Compliance, cluster at the boundary between model development and distribution, where evidence produced inside the organisation is handed over to external regulators. The third is that Risk Management, Ethics and Responsible AI, and Audit and Continuous Improvement apply throughout the lifecycle rather than attaching to any one layer; they operate as cross-cutting concerns that interact with every other category.

6.2 Governance Handoffs

Three formal governance handoffs were identified at layer boundaries, with the identification criteria stated in Sect. 3. The *first handoff* (Layer 1→2) transfers data governance responsibility from data engineering to model development. The data team must produce provenance records, bias assessments, consent documentation, and training data summaries (EU AI Act Art. 10, Art. 53(1)(d)); the model development team consumes these as the evidentiary foundation for model governance. No external enforcement mechanism verifies completeness before consumption, with the consequence that if these artifacts are incomplete, model governance begins on uncertain foundations that downstream testing cannot fully remediate.

The *second handoff* (Layer 2→3) is the most consequential of the three, since at this boundary the provider formally releases the model and accountability transitions to the external regulatory chain. The model development team must transmit conformity declarations (EU AI Act Art. 47), technical documentation (Annex IV), model cards, and, where applicable, GPAI transparency reports (Art. 53) to the distribution function. The EU AI Act's role distinctions become legally operative at this boundary, and releasing without complete documentation propagates irrecoverably into the regulatory chain.

The *third handoff* (Layer 3→4) transfers primary accountability from provider to deployer. The provider retains responsibility for post-market monitoring and incident cooperation (EU AI Act Arts. 72–73), while the deployer assumes accountability for human oversight (Art. 14), logging (Art. 12), and user disclosure (Art. 50). The deployer typically lacks visibility into upstream development decisions, creating an information asymmetry between the entity bearing deployment-time accountability and the entity that made the foundational choices on which that accountability rests.

6.3 Structural Asymmetry

The governance mapping surfaces a notable structural property of the current regulatory landscape: governance obligations and evidence-production requirements concentrate at the deployment-facing end of the lifecycle, while the decisions that most fundamentally determine system security are made at the development-facing end, where regulatory visibility is lowest.

The asymmetry operates along two dimensions. At Layers 1–2, provisions are predominantly decision-shaping, governing what data to collect, what alignment strategy to pursue, and what capability boundaries to impose. These choices are difficult or impossible to reverse once training completes. At Layers 3–4, provisions shift to evidence-producing, requiring documentation, conformity processes, logging, incident reporting, and oversight implementation. Quantitatively, the asymmetry is near-monotonic: of the thirty-three governance provisions mapped to lifecycle-bound categories in Table 3, ten of the eleven provisions assigned to Layers 1–2 are decision-shaping, whereas all twenty-two provisions assigned to Layers 2/3 through 4 are evidence-producing.

At the same time, the EU AI Act places its heaviest enforcement at Layers 3–4, with fines up to €15 million or 3% of global turnover, while the most consequential decisions are made at Layers 1–2, where enforcement is absent. The practical consequence is that an organisation can satisfy every downstream requirement while having made unverified foundational decisions upstream. This misalignment has direct security implications, since data poisoning, alignment subversion, and capability-boundary violations originate at Layers 1–2, and by the time systems reach Layers 3–4 these compromises are already embedded in model weights. The GPAI provisions (Arts. 53–55) partially bridge this gap by imposing transparency and adversarial-testing requirements on foundation-model providers, but they do not resolve it: the provisions remain evidence-producing rather than decision-shaping, and they do not subject upstream design choices to external verification.

7 Discussion

The model proposed in this paper defines 32 core lifecycle stages, 12 LLMOps sub-stages, and 9 governance categories. Together, these create 53 points where security and governance questions can be asked. The aim is not to claim that these are the only possible boundaries, but to make important differences visible, for example between packaging and signing, input validation and inference, or alignment and supervised fine-tuning. On *architectural completeness*, the model combines end-to-end coverage from data sourcing through decommissioning with both an operational and a governance pillar as cross-cutting structures, a combination we did not identify among the frameworks surveyed in Table 1. On *security-specific decomposition*, the 13 stages introduced here as distinct lifecycle stages fall into three categories: security-critical activities previously subsumed under broader categories (1.4, 1.5, 2.4, 2.5), lifecycle activities omitted entirely (1.6, 2.8, 2.9, 3.4, 3.5, 4.12), and emerging architectural paradigms (4.9, 4.10, 4.11). The *governance mapping* also points to an important imbalance. Many of the most important security decisions are made early, during data and model development, but much of the formal evidence, documentation, and accountability appears later, around distribution and deployment.

Three incident mappings illustrate this finer decomposition's analytical value. These examples should be read as illustrative mappings, not as empirical validation of the model. First, the 2024 Hugging Face serialization attacks [3] map to Stages 2.7–3.2, a distinction between packaging, signing, and registry that two-phase models collapse into a single category, obscuring where the trust boundary was breached. Second, reward model poisoning attacks [43] target Stage 2.4 (Alignment) specifically; frameworks that merge alignment with SFT cannot distinguish whether the poisoning vector is instruction data or preference labels, yielding different mitigations. Third, agentic exploitation attacks target Stage 4.11 (Agency and Permission Control) through tool-use protocols such as MCP, a stage no framework reviewed in Sect. 2 treats separately.

The model also has several limitations. The most fundamental is complexity: 53 addressable units provide resolution for per-stage analysis but impose cognitive cost. For this reason the model can be adopted gradually using a three-tier adoption model: Tier 1 adopts the four-layer abstraction and three governance handoffs as an organizational orientation tool; Tier 2 adds the 13 additional stages as priority extensions to existing frameworks; Tier 3 adopts the full 32-stage decomposition with LLMOps pillar as organizational security maturity increases. The framework is intentionally detailed: organisations that skip stages inherit the residual risk that the skipped stage was designed to address, and the framework makes this risk explicit at the point of omission.

The continuous feedback loop from Layer 4 to Layer 1 is not assigned its own stage but is governed by three distributed components: Stage 4.8 (Feedback Collection), Stage 1.1 (Data Sourcing, which consumes feedback as retraining data), and LLMOps sub-stage L.7 (Human Feedback Integration, which orchestrates the loop); dedicated security analysis of the loop's properties is distributed across these units. Certain stages are LLM-specific (alignment, prompt engineering, agentic orchestration); extending to other foundation model types would require modifications.

The governance mapping is interpretive. Other analysts may assign some provisions to neighbouring stages, especially broad provisions related to risk management or ethics. However, the main pattern is likely to remain: early lifecycle stages shape the system, while later stages produce much of the evidence used for oversight and accountability. The stage separation criterion is conservative by design and may cause under-decomposition where security-relevant distinctions exist but lack sufficient published research. Internal validity is bounded by the interpretive nature of stage derivation; external validity by focus on the current regulatory landscape; construct validity by the analytical rather than empirical stage derivation, which a companion study is designed to validate through systematic mapping of security concerns to the lifecycle structure.

8 Conclusion

This paper has presented a lifecycle model for LLM systems, designed to support security analysis, comprising 32 stages across four core pipeline layers organised by attack surface exposure, introducing 13 stages first identified here as distinct lifecycle stages, absent from all surveyed frameworks; a 12-stage LLMOps pillar elevated to a cross-cutting layer whose bidirectional relationship with the pipeline ensures dedicated security analysis of operational infrastructure; and a 9-category governance pillar synthesising the NIST AI RMF, the EU AI Act, and ISO/IEC 42001 into a lifecycle-mapped governance structure that identifies three governance handoffs and reveals a structural property of the current regulatory landscape, a misalignment between where governance evidence concentrates (Layers 3–4) and where the most consequential governance decisions are made (Layers 1–2). Future work will focus on a literature review to map known threats, attacks, and security controls to each stage of the proposed lifecycle. This would help validate the usefulness of the stage boundaries and support more practical per-stage security analysis. Additional priorities include practitioner validation, multi-modal extension, and upstream governance attestation mechanisms extending conformity-assessment logic to the development-facing stages where the most foundational security compromises originate.

Acknowledgments. This work received partial funding from the European High-Performance Computing Joint Undertaking (JU) under Grant Agreement No. 101234269 for the Pharos AI Factory project, as well as from the Greek Ministry of Digital Governance and Artificial Intelligence.

Disclosure of Interests. The authors have no competing interests to declare that are relevant to the content of this article.

References

1. Aryal, K., Gupta, M., Abdelsalam, M.: Analysis of label-flip poisoning attack on machine learning based malware detector. In: IEEE/ACM International Conference Automated Software Engineering (ASE) (2022). https://doi.org/10.1109/BigData55660.2022.10020528
2. Baracaldo, N., Chen, B., Ludwig, H., Safavi, J.A.: Mitigating poisoning attacks on machine learning models: a data provenance based approach. In: Proceedings AISec Workshop (2017)
3. Casey, B., Santos, J.C.S., Mirakhorli, M.: A large-scale exploit instrumentation study of AI/ML supply chain attacks in Hugging Face models (2024)
4. Chaudhari, S., et al.: RLHF deciphered: a critical analysis of reinforcement learning from human feedback for LLMs. ACM Comput. Surv. **58**(2) (2026). https://doi.org/10.1145/3743127
5. Chernigovskaya, M., Walia, D.S., Neumann, K., Hardt, A., Nahhas, A., Turowski, K.: Towards a standardized business process model for LLMOps. In: Proceedings of the 27th International Conference Enterprise Information Systems (ICEIS), vol. 1, pp. 856–866. SciTePress (2025)
6. Cinà, A.E., et al.: Wild patterns reloaded: a survey of machine learning security against training data poisoning. ACM Comput. Surv. **55**(13s) (2023). https://doi.org/10.1145/3585385
7. Diaz-De-Arcaya, J., López-De-Armentia, J., Miñón, R., Ojanguren, I.L., Torre-Bastida, A.I.: Large language model operations (LLMOps): definition, challenges, and lifecycle management. In: 2024 9th International Conference Smart and Sustainable Technologies (SpliTech), pp. 1–6. IEEE (2024). https://doi.org/10.23919/SpliTech61897.2024.10612341
8. Ding, R., Xu, T., Shen, X., Ding, A.A., Fei, Y.: MoEcho: exploiting side-channel attacks to compromise user privacy in mixture-of-experts LLMs. In: Proc. 2025 ACM SIGSAC Conference Computer and Communications Security (CCS) (2025)

9. Egashira, K., Vero, M., Staab, R., He, J., Vechev, M.: Exploiting LLM quantization. In: Advances in Neural Information Processing Systems (NeurIPS) (2024)
10. ENISA: multilayer framework for good cybersecurity practices for AI. In: ENISA (2023). Tech. rep
11. ETSI: Securing artificial intelligence (SAI); baseline cyber security requirements for AI models and systems, European Telecommunications Standards Institute (2025). EN 304 223 V2.1.1 Tech. Rep. ETSI
12. European Parliament and Council of the European Union: Regulation (EU) 2024/1689 of the European parliament and of the council laying down harmonised rules on artificial intelligence (2024)
13. Gokkaya, B., Aniello, L., Halak, B.: Software supply chain: a taxonomy of attacks, mitigations and risk assessment strategies. J. Inf. Secur. Appl. **97** (2025). https://doi.org/10.1016/j.jisa.2025.104324
14. Google: Secure AI Framework (SAIF) (2023)
15. Greshake, K., Abdelnabi, S., Mishra, S., Endres, C., Holz, T., Fritz, M.: Not what you've signed up for: compromising real-world LLM-integrated applications with indirect prompt injection. In: Proc. 16th ACM Workshop on Artificial Intelligence and Security (AISec '23), pp. 79–90 (2023). https://doi.org/10.1145/3605764.3623985
16. He, F., Zhu, T., Ye, D., Liu, B., Zhou, W., Yu, P.S.: The emerged security and privacy of LLM agent: a survey with case studies. ACM Comput. Surv. **58**(6) (2026). https://doi.org/10.1145/3773080
17. Hou, X., Zhao, Y., Wang, S., Wang, H.: Model context protocol (MCP): landscape, security threats, and future research directions. ACM Trans. Softw. Eng. Method. (2025). https://doi.org/10.1145/3796519
18. Hu, H., Salcic, Z., Sun, L., Dobbie, G., Yu, P.S., Zhang, X.: Membership inference attacks on machine learning: a survey. ACM Comput. Surv. **54**(11s) (2022). https://doi.org/10.1145/3523273
19. Huang, K., et al.: Lifting the veil on composition, risks, and mitigations of the large language model supply chain (2024)
20. International Organization for Standardization: ISO/IEC 42001:2023 — artificial intelligence management system (2023)
21. Jiang, W., et al.: An empirical study of artifacts and security risks in the pre-trained model supply chain. In: Proceedings 2022 ACM Workshop on Software Supply Chain Offensive Research and Ecosystem Defenses (2022). https://doi.org/10.1145/3560835.3564547
22. Kreuzberger, D., Kühl, N., Hirschl, S.: Machine learning operations (MLOps): overview, definition, and architecture. IEEE Access **11**, 31866–31879 (2023). https://doi.org/10.1109/ACCESS.2023.3262138
23. Kusaka, S., Saito, K., Kudo, M., Tanabe, T., Wachi, A., Akimoto, Y.: Cost-minimized label-flipping poisoning attack to LLM alignment (2025)
24. MITRE Corporation: MITRE ATLAS — adversarial threat landscape for artificial-intelligence systems (2025)
25. National Institute of Standards and Technology: Artificial intelligence risk management framework (AI RMF 1.0). Tech. Rep. NIST AI 100-1, NIST (2023). https://doi.org/10.6028/NIST.AI.100-1
26. National Institute of Standards and Technology: NIST AI 600-1: Artificial intelligence risk management framework: Generative AI profile. Tech. Rep. NIST AI 600-1, NIST (2024). https://doi.org/10.6028/NIST.AI.600-1

27. Nguyen, T.A., Le, T.H.M., Babar, M.A.: Securing the AI supply chain: what can we learn from developer-reported security issues and solutions of AI projects? In: Proceedings 2026 IEEE/ACM 48th International Conference Software Engineering (ICSE), pp. 1–13. ACM (2026). https://doi.org/10.1145/3744916.3787796
28. Operant, A.I.: Shadow escape: Zero-click MCP exploit (2025)
29. OWASP: Top 10 for agentic applications (2025)
30. OWASP Foundation: OWASP AIBOM Project (2025)
31. OWASP Foundation: OWASP top 10 for large language model applications (2025)
32. Pahune, S., Akhtar, Z.: Transitioning from MLOps to LLMOps: navigating the unique challenges of large language models. Information **16**(2), 87 (2025). https://doi.org/10.3390/info16020087
33. Patel, R., et al.: Towards secure MLOps: surveying attacks, mitigation strategies, and research challenges (2025)
34. Saeeda, H., Mohamad, M., Knauss, E., Horkoff, J., Nouri, A.: Re for AI in practice: managing data annotation requirements for AI autonomous driving systems (2025)
35. Shumailov, I., Shumaylov, Z., Zhao, Y., Papernot, N., Anderson, R., Gal, Y.: AI models collapse when trained on recursively generated data. Nature **631**(8022) (2024). https://doi.org/10.1038/s41586-024-07566-y
36. Sinha, M., Menon, S., Sagar, R.: LLMOps: definitions, framework and best practices. In: 2024 International Conference Electrical, Computer and Energy Technologies (ICECET). IEEE (2024). https://doi.org/10.1109/ICECET61485.2024.10698359
37. Sood, A.K., Zeadally, S.: Malicious AI models undermine software supply-chain security. Commun. ACM (2025). https://doi.org/10.1145/3704724
38. Spoczynski, M., Melara, M.S., Szyller, S.: Atlas: a framework for ML lifecycle provenance and transparency (2025). https://doi.org/10.1109/EuroSPW67616.2025.00058
39. Stalnaker, T., et al.: An empirical analysis of machine learning model and dataset documentation, supply chain, and licensing challenges on Hugging Face. ACM Trans. Softw. Eng. Method. (2025). https://doi.org/10.1145/3776739
40. Steidl, M., Felderer, M., Ramler, R.: The pipeline for the continuous development of artificial intelligence models: current state of research and practice. J. Syst. Softw. **199**, 111615 (2023). https://doi.org/10.1016/j.jss.2023.111615
41. Vandendriessche, W.: AiBoMGEN: generating an AI bill of materials for secure, transparent, and compliant model training (2026)
42. Vassilev, A.: Adversarial machine learning: a taxonomy and terminology of attacks and mitigations. Tech. Rep. NIST AI 100-2e2025, National Institute of Standards and Technology (2025). https://doi.org/10.6028/NIST.AI.100-2e2025
43. Wang, J., Wu, J., Chen, M., Vorobeychik, Y., Xiao, C.: RLHFPoison: reward poisoning attack for reinforcement learning with human feedback in large language models. In: Proceedings 62nd Annual Meeting Association Computational Linguistics (ACL), pp. 2551–2570 (2024). https://doi.org/10.18653/v1/2024.acl-long.140
44. Wang, S., Zhao, Y., Hou, X., Wang, H.: Large language model supply chain: a research agenda. ACM Trans. Softw. Eng. Method. **1**(1) (2024). https://doi.org/10.1145/3708531
45. Wang, S., Zhao, Y., Liu, Z., Zou, Q., Wang, H.: SoK: understanding vulnerabilities in the large language model supply chain (2025)
46. Wu, G.: I know what you asked: prompt leakage via KV-cache sharing in multi-tenant LLM serving. In: Network and Distributed System Security Symposium (NDSS) (2025). https://doi.org/10.14722/ndss.2025.241772

47. Wu, J., Wang, J., Xiao, C., Wang, C., Zhang, N., Vorobeychik, Y.: Preference poisoning attacks on reward model learning. In: IEEE Symposium on Security and Privacy (S&P) (2025). https://doi.org/10.1109/SP61157.2025.00094
48. Zhang, J.: BadMerging: backdoor attacks against model merging. In: Proceedings ACM SIGSAC Conference Computer and Communications Security (CCS) (2024)
49. Zhao, W.X.: A survey of large language models (2025)
50. Zhu, W., Xiang, Z., Niu, W., Guan, L.: MetaBreak: jailbreaking online LLM services via special token manipulation (2026)

Proceedings of the Sixth Workshop on Security and Privacy in Intelligent Infrastructures (SP2I 2026)

On the Structural Dependencies of Post-quantum Cryptographic Standards

Sara Ricci[1(✉)], Petr Dzurenda[1], Lucia Hirnerová[1], and Petr Muzikant[2]

[1] Brno University of Technology, Czechia, Czechia
{ricci,dzurenda,257107}@vut.cz
[2] Cybernetica, Estonia, Estonia
petr.muzikant@cyber.ee

Abstract. Post-Quantum Cryptography (PQC) standardization efforts have led to the selection of multiple algorithms across different international organizations. While these schemes appear diverse at the algorithmic level, their security ultimately relies on a limited set of underlying hardness assumptions. In this work, we propose a graph-based representation of PQC standards that explicitly links standardized algorithms to their computational problems and captures structural relationships between these assumptions. Using network analysis techniques, we study the organization of the resulting dependency graph. Modularity analysis reveals a strongly structured ecosystem, with a densely connected algebraic core and distinct peripheral components corresponding to alternative paradigms such as hash-based and MPC-in-the-head constructions. Betweenness centrality further identifies a small number of core problems, in particular, the Shortest Vector Problem (SVP), as critical connectors within the network. Extending the analysis across standardization bodies, we observe a significant convergence toward lattice-based constructions, resulting in a concentration of dependencies on closely related hardness assumptions. This structural concentration suggests potential systemic risks, as advances in cryptanalysis could simultaneously affect multiple schemes and standards. In general, our results highlight the importance of considering structural diversity at the level of underlying assumptions in the design and evaluation of PQC ecosystems.

Keywords: Post-quantum Cryptography · NP-Hardness Assumptions · Dependency Graph · Cryptographic Standards · Lattice-based Cryptography · Code-based Cryptography · Hash-based Cryptography

1 Introduction

Classical cryptographic methods rely on the hardness of mathematical problems such as integer factorization and the discrete logarithm problem, which underpin widely deployed public-key schemes, including RSA and Diffie–Hellman. However, the advent of quantum computing fundamentally challenges these

P. Kieseberg et al. (Eds.): ARES 2026 Workshops, LNCS 16903, pp. 423–438, 2027.
https://doi.org/10.1007/978-3-032-37218-5_25

assumptions. In particular, Shor's algorithm [5] enables efficient solutions to integer factorization and discrete logarithms, thus breaking the most commonly used asymmetric cryptographic schemes. In contrast, symmetric cryptography is less severely affected. Grover's algorithm provides a quadratic speedup for brute-force search, effectively reducing the security level of symmetric primitives. This impact can be mitigated by increasing key and output sizes [13], and therefore does not require fundamentally new cryptographic constructions. As a result, Post-Quantum Cryptography (PQC) focuses primarily on the design of new asymmetric schemes that remain secure in the presence of quantum adversaries [30].

In response, several international standardization bodies have initiated processes to identify and deploy secure PQC algorithms. Notably, the National Institute of Standards and Technology (NIST) [16,35] in the United States, the Korean Post-Quantum Cryptography (KpqC) initiative [26], and European cybersecurity agencies such as ANSSI [34] and BSI [10,18] have selected or recommended schemes for practical use. These efforts provide a representative view of the current PQC landscape in different regions. Other initiatives, including those led by the Institute of Commercial Cryptography Standards (ICCS) in China [22] and state programs in Russia [23], are ongoing, but have not yet produced widely adopted standards and are therefore not included in our structural analysis.

Most PQC schemes are asymmetric constructions whose security is based on the assumed hardness of the underlying computational problems. Importantly, these assumptions are not independent: different schemes may rely on closely related problems, structured variants of common primitives, or assumptions connected through reductions and shared algebraic properties. However, despite the central role of these relationships, there is currently no unified representation that captures how standardized algorithms relate to their underlying hardness assumptions at the structural level. In this work, we address this gap by modeling the PQC ecosystem as a dependency graph that connects cryptographic algorithms, underlying computational problems and primitives, and standardization bodies. This representation enables a systematic analysis of how different constructions relate through their foundational assumptions. This perspective provides insight not only into the structure of current PQC constructions, but also into potential systemic dependencies across standards.

1.1 Contribution.

This work aims to provide a structural understanding of the post-quantum cryptography ecosystem by addressing the following research questions:

RQ1: How are post-quantum cryptographic schemes structurally organized with respect to their underlying hardness assumptions?

RQ2: Which computational problems play a central role in connecting different cryptographic constructions within the PQC ecosystem?

RQ3: To what extent do international PQC standardization efforts provide diversity in terms of underlying hardness assumptions?

To answer *RQ1*, we present a unified structural representation of the relationships between standardized post-quantum cryptographic schemes and their underlying hardness assumptions. We construct a dependency graph linking PQC algorithms selected or recommended by major international bodies to the computational problems and primitives on which their security is based, as well as to known relationships between these assumptions.

Building on this representation, we perform a network-based analysis of the resulting graph using metrics such as modularity and centrality. The modularity analysis reveals a strongly structured organization of the PQC ecosystem, characterized by distinct clusters corresponding to the main cryptographic families (*RQ1*). The centrality analysis identifies a small set of core problems that act as structural bridges between these families (*RQ2*).

We further analyze the relationship between standardization efforts and underlying assumptions, showing that different international standards exhibit significant overlap both at the algorithmic and assumption levels. This provides a quantitative perspective on the diversity of current PQC deployments and highlights potential concentrations of dependencies (*RQ3*).

To the best of our knowledge, this is the first work to provide a unified structural representation and network-based analysis of hardness dependencies across multiple international PQC standardization efforts.

2 Modeling Hardness Dependencies as a Graph

Figure 1 represents the relationships between standardized post-quantum cryptographic algorithms and the computational problems or primitives on which their security is based. In the graph, yellow nodes denote hardness problems, primitives, or paradigms, while colored nodes represent cryptographic algorithms. Colors further indicate the standardization or recommendation body: NIST (green), KpqC (pink), and BSI/ANSSI (blue labels). Gray nodes correspond to additional schemes that were considered in standardization processes but were not ultimately selected. Directed edges represent dependencies between schemes and assumptions, as well as known relationships between hardness problems. These include formal reductions, worst-case to average-case hardness connections, and structural relationships. Each edge is supported by results from the literature, with a detailed mapping provided in Appendix A, Tables 1 and 2.

The graph is organized into three major families of post-quantum cryptography: code-based, lattice-based, and hash-based/MPC-in-the-head constructions. This organization reflects both the underlying mathematical structure and the design paradigms used in current standardized schemes. For clarity, we refer to algorithms using their commonly used names (e.g., Kyber, Dilithium), while noting that some have been standardized under different designations (e.g., ML-KEM, ML-DSA in NIST standards).

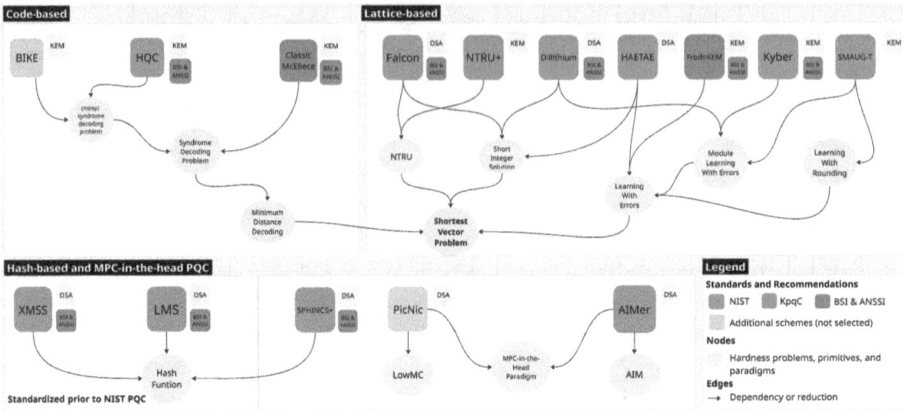

Fig. 1. Dependency graph of post-quantum cryptographic schemes and their underlying hardness assumptions.

Code-Based Constructions. In the code-based portion of the graph, the algorithms BIKE [4], HQC [32], and Classic McEliece [6] rely on variants of the Syndrome Decoding (SD) problem, a well-known NP-hard problem in coding theory. In its standard form, SD consists of recovering a low-weight error vector e from a given syndrome $s = He^T$, where H is a matrix of check for parity. Classic McEliece relies directly on this formulation. More recent constructions such as BIKE and HQC instead rely on noisy variants, in which the syndrome itself is perturbed, i.e., $\tilde{s} = He^T + \epsilon$. Although this increases the apparent decoding complexity, it enables the use of structured code families (e.g., quasi-cyclic constructions), improves efficiency in practice, and contributes to resistance against structural and decoding attacks [27]. This modeling also brings these constructions conceptually closer to assumptions used in lattice-based cryptography, such as Learning With Errors. From a structural perspective, Classic McEliece is based on unstructured binary Goppa codes, leading to conservative and well-understood security guarantees at the cost of large public keys. In contrast, BIKE and HQC exploit structured codes and noisy decoding variants, resulting in smaller key sizes and improved performance, but relying on more recent assumptions. Related formulations, such as Minimum Distance Decoding, capture the intrinsic difficulty of decoding linear codes and appear as intermediate nodes in the graph.

Lattice-Based Constructions. The lattice-based part of the graph includes the schemes Kyber [8] (standardized as ML-KEM in FIPS 203 [37]), Dilithium [17] (standardized as ML-DSA in FIPS 204 [36]), Falcon [20], FrodoKEM [2], and NTRU+ [24]. These algorithms are based on a family of hardness assumptions rooted in lattice problems, including Learning With Errors (LWE) and its variants (Module-LWE and Learning With Rounding), the Short Integer Solution (SIS) problem, and the NTRU problem. These assumptions can be broadly divided into two categories: problems based on noisy linear equations (e.g., LWE and its variants) and structured lattice problems (e.g., Short Integer Solution (SIS) and NTRU), both closely related to the task of finding short vectors in lattices. Schemes such as Kyber and FrodoKEM rely on LWE-type assumptions, with Kyber using the structured Module-LWE variant for efficiency and FrodoKEM relying on standard LWE for more conservative security. Similarly, Dilithium combines Module-LWE and Module-SIS assumptions to construct efficient signatures. On the other hand, Falcon is based on the NTRU problem and leverages structured lattices together with discrete Gaussian sampling, resulting in compact signatures. However, this efficiency requires careful implementation, as precise Gaussian sampling involves delicate numerical considerations and potential side-channel risks. NTRU+ follows a similar design paradigm in a key encapsulation setting. Notably, the KpqC process schemes follow closely related principles: SMAUG-T [15] relies on Module-LWE, while HAETAE [14] is structurally related to Dilithium and combines Module-LWE and Module-SIS assumptions. It is worth mentioning that these modern lattice problems are connected to classical lattice problems, i.e. the Shortest Vector Problem (SVP). In particular, LWE and SIS can be related to SVP worst-case lattice problems, providing theoretical evidence for their hardness. This part of the graph highlights the central role of SVP as a foundational node linking several lattice-based assumptions.

Hash-Based and MPC-in-the-Head Constructions. Hash-based and MPC-in-the-head constructions are grouped as a distinct family. Although these approaches differ in design, they share the property of being grounded in symmetric cryptographic primitives rather than algebraically structured hardness assumptions. As a result, they form a largely disconnected component in the graph. Hash-based schemes such as XMSS [11], LMS [31], and SPHINCS+ [7] (standardized as SLH-DSA in FIPS 205 [38]) derive their security from the properties of cryptographic hash functions, typically combined with Merkle tree constructions. A key distinction is between stateful and stateless designs: XMSS and LMS require careful state management to prevent key reuse, whereas SPHINCS+ is stateless. Specifically, stateful schemes generally achieve smaller signatures and faster operations, making them suitable for constrained environments where state can be reliably maintained. In contrast, SPHINCS+ offers greater robustness in general-purpose settings, at the expense of increased communication overhead. XMSS and LMS, standardized prior to the NIST PQC competition, are included as established quantum-resistant schemes, providing a useful point of comparison. In parallel, schemes such as Picnic [12] and AIMer [25] are based on the MPC-in-the-head paradigm, where security is obtained by simulating secure multiparty computation protocols instantiated with symmetric primitives LowMC and AIM, respectively.

Finally, the graph highlights cross-family relationships between the hardness assumptions. For instance, the Minimum Distance Decoding problem is connected to lattice problems such as SVP through structural relationships, providing a bridge between code-based and lattice-based cryptography. These

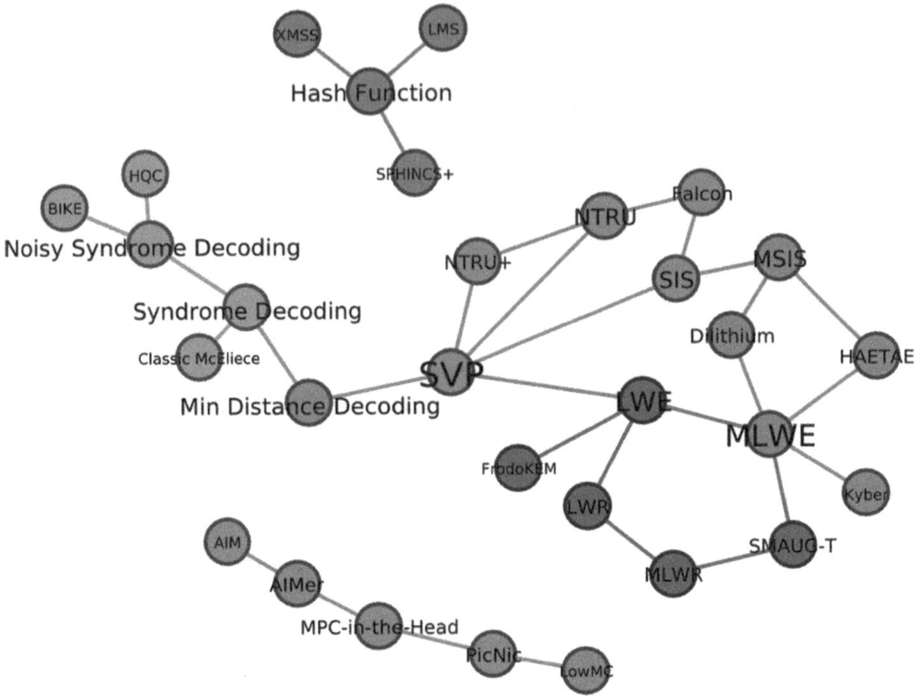

Fig. 2. Modularity-based community structure of the dependency graph. Node colors represent the communities identified by the modularity algorithm (five classes), grouping together nodes that are more densely connected.

connections illustrate that, despite the diversity of cryptographic constructions, different schemes may ultimately rely on related underlying computational principles.

3 Structural Analysis of Hardness Dependencies

In this section, we analyze the structure of the dependency graph using standard network analysis techniques. In particular, we consider modularity to identify clusters of closely related nodes and betweenness centrality to detect nodes that act as structural bridges within the graph. These complementary metrics provide insight into both the global organization of hardness assumptions and the role of individual problems in connecting different cryptographic families.

The modularity analysis (score 0.657) reveals a strongly structured dependency graph, with clearly separated communities corresponding to major classes of cryptographic assumptions. This structure is shown in Figure 2, where the colors of the nodes indicate the communities identified by the modularity algorithm. In total, five distinct communities are detected, capturing the main structural groupings of the PQC landscape. The largest community forms a central

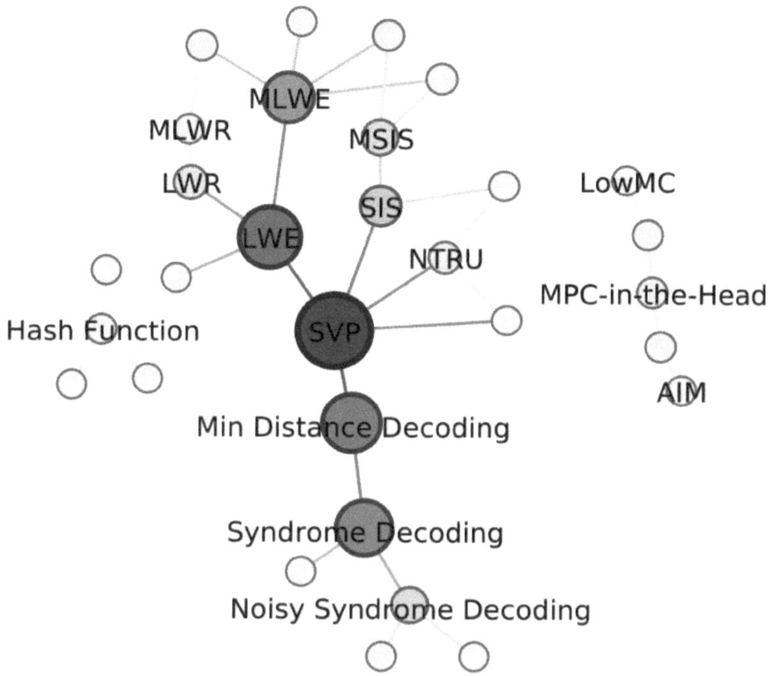

Fig. 3. Betweenness centrality in the dependency graph. Node size is proportional to centrality, highlighting structural bridge nodes; labels are shown only for problems and primitives to improve readability.

algebraic core, in which lattice-based and code-based constructions are interconnected through shared intermediate problems, with the SVP acting as a central hub. Surrounding this core, distinct communities emerge corresponding to alternative design paradigms. In particular, hash-based constructions form a separate cluster centered on cryptographic hash functions, whereas MPC-in-the-head schemes appear as an isolated component based on symmetric primitives. Within the lattice-based region, additional sub-communities reflect structural distinctions between different families of assumptions, such as Module-LWE-based constructions and NTRU/SIS-based approaches. Overall, this decomposition highlights a dual structure in the PQC ecosystem: a densely connected algebraic core linking multiple hardness assumptions and a set of structurally independent peripheral paradigms. The presence of multiple communities within the lattice-based region further indicates that, despite a shared mathematical foundation, different design choices induce meaningful structural separations within this family.

While modularity captures the global organization of the graph in terms of communities, it does not reflect the relative importance of individual nodes. To complement this perspective, we analyze betweenness centrality, which identifies nodes that act as key connectors within the network. Figure 3 illustrates the distribution of betweenness centrality, where the SVP exhibits the highest centrality, confirming its role as the primary structural bridge between different families of hardness assumptions. Intermediate problems such as LWE, SIS, and Minimum Distance Decoding form a layered structure linking concrete cryptographic schemes to more fundamental problems. This organization indicates that many PQC constructions are connected through a relatively small set of intermediate assumptions. Moreover, the relatively small diameter of the network (7) suggests that these dependencies remain shallow, implying that advances in solving or weakening central problems could propagate across multiple cryptographic families. This observation underscores the importance of analyzing hardness assumptions at a global level rather than considering schemes in isolation. A simple count of dependencies further illustrates this concentration: among the considered schemes, 7 rely on lattice-based assumptions, compared to 3 code-based and 5 hash/MPC-based constructions. This imbalance reflects the dominant role of lattice-based approaches within the current PQC ecosystem.

An additional structural asymmetry emerges when considering functionality. Code-based constructions in current standards are used exclusively for key encapsulation mechanisms, while hash-based and MPC-in-the-head constructions are used only for digital signatures. In contrast, lattice-based constructions support both functionalities, further reinforcing their central role within the PQC landscape.

4 Cross-Standard Structural Analysis

In this section, we analyze the relationships between standardization bodies and selected cryptographic schemes to assess the degree of diversity across international PQC efforts. A modularity analysis of the resulting standard–algorithm graph yields a relatively low modularity score (0.269), indicating a weakly separated community structure. This suggests a significant overlap between standards, with multiple organizations selecting largely similar sets of algorithms. Figure 4 represents these relationships, providing a visual representation of the overlap between standards. In particular, NIST, ANSSI, and BSI converge toward a shared subset of lattice-based and hash-based constructions, including Kyber, Dilithium, and SPHINCS+. A similar convergence is observed for stateful hash-based signature schemes such as XMSS and LMS, which are recommended by NIST, ANSSI, and BSI. Despite relying on independent hash-function assumptions, their applicability is typically restricted to specific use cases due to their stateful nature [10,16,34]. These schemes form a dense common core across Western standardization efforts. Although based on independent hash-function assumptions, these schemes are typically limited to specific use cases due to their stateful nature. Although additional recommendations, such as FrodoKEM and Classic McEliece, introduce some diversity, they do not substantially alter the overall structure. Therefore, European agencies such as ANSSI and BSI do not define entirely independent PQC standards but largely

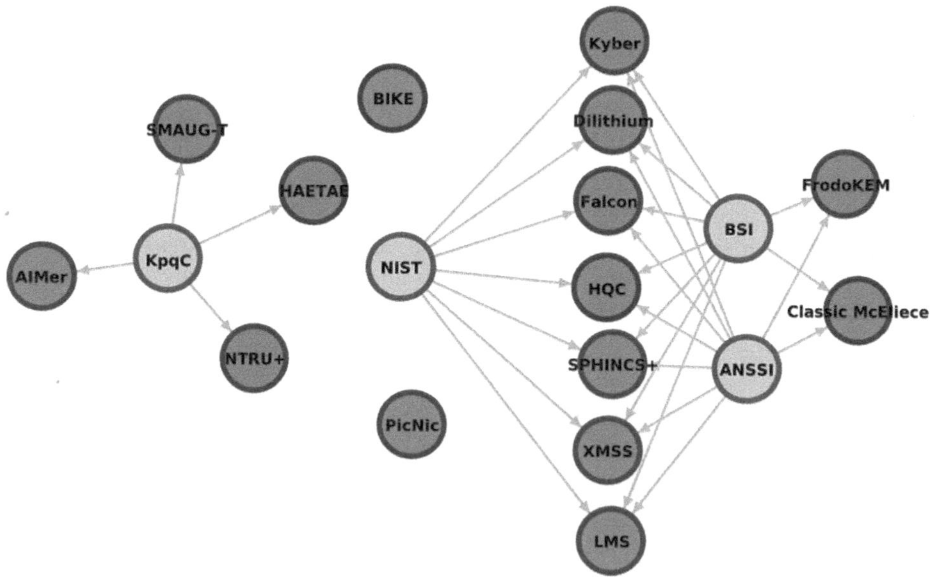

Fig. 4. Relationships between standardization bodies and selected post-quantum cryptographic schemes. Gray nodes represent standardization bodies, colored nodes represent algorithms (colored by cryptographic family), and edges indicate selection or recommendation.

build upon the algorithms selected by NIST, adapting them within their own recommendation frameworks and often requiring hybrid deployments. This results in a high degree of transatlantic alignment, while preserving some degree of strategic and operational autonomy.

In contrast, the Korean KpqC initiative follows an independent standardization process, selecting partially different schemes. However, these constructions remain largely based on the same underlying hardness assumptions (e.g., LWE and its variants), ensuring a degree of conceptual compatibility with NIST standards, even if direct interoperability at the protocol level is not guaranteed. Notably, the main deviation is represented by MPC-in-the-head constructions such as AIMer, which provide an alternative design paradigm based on symmetric primitives.

When mapped to their underlying hardness assumptions, these selections reveal a strong concentration around a limited set of problems, particularly LWE and its variants. As a result, the diversity observed at the level of algorithms does not directly translate into diversity at the level of underlying assumptions. This concentration has important implications for the robustness of the PQC ecosystem. In particular, advances in cryptanalysis targeting central problems such as LWE could affect multiple standardized schemes across different organizations. This observation highlights a potential systemic dependency that arises from the convergence of standardization choices, complementing the structural insights obtained from the dependency graph.

Finally, emerging efforts outside Western standardization frameworks suggest the possibility of alternative trajectories. In particular, recent initiatives in China have expressed interest in exploring less structured lattice constructions and alternative assumptions, motivated by concerns about the long-term robustness of highly structured designs. Although these efforts have not yet resulted in finalized standards, they indicate a potential direction toward increased diversity. In contrast, current Russian initiatives remain focused primarily on quantum computing infrastructure rather than on the standardization of post-quantum cryptographic schemes.

5 Systemic Risk Analysis

The hardness dependency graph provides a natural framework for assessing potential systemic risks in the post-quantum cryptography ecosystem. By linking standardized algorithms to their underlying assumptions, it enables a structural view of how vulnerabilities in core problems could affect multiple constructions simultaneously. A central observation is the concentration of dependencies around lattice-based assumptions, in particular, LWE and its variants. As discussed in Section 4, these assumptions underpin a large fraction of standardized and recommended schemes across different organizations. Consequently, a significant theoretical or algorithmic advance targeting LWE or related problems could have wide-ranging implications across multiple algorithms and standards. This risk is further informed by the structural properties of the dependency graph. The modularity analysis reveals a densely connected algebraic region, while the betweenness centrality analysis identifies the SVP problem as a key bridging node. Together, these results indicate that many hardness assumptions are linked through a layered structure rather than forming independent foundations. This interdependence suggests that advances that affect central problems may propagate across multiple constructions.

Code-based cryptography provides a partially independent alternative, relying on the syndrome decoding problem and related coding-theoretic assumptions. However, the graph indicates that the number of such alternative foundations remains limited compared to the prevalence of lattice-based constructions. In contrast, hash-based and MPC-in-the-head constructions appear to be structurally independent components. Their security is based on symmetric primitives and generic constructions and, therefore, does not depend on algebraic hardness assumptions. This separation introduces an additional layer of diversity in the ecosystem, contributing to resilience against concentration of assumptions, although with different performance characteristics.

Consequently, the analysis highlights a structural asymmetry in the current PQC landscape. Although diversity is achieved at the level of algorithmic constructions, there is a significant convergence at the level of underlying hardness assumptions. This suggests that the long-term resilience of the ecosystem depends not only on the number of schemes deployed, but also on the diversity of the mathematical problems that support them.

6 Conclusion

In this work, we introduced a graph-based representation of post-quantum cryptographic standards, linking standardized algorithms to their underlying hardness assumptions, and capturing the relationships between these assumptions. This representation provides a unified structural view of the PQC ecosystem, enabling the analysis of dependencies that are not immediately apparent when considering schemes in isolation.

The resulting analysis reveals a highly organized structure in which a large fraction of constructions are connected through a common set of algebraic assumptions, alongside alternative paradigms based on symmetric primitives that form structurally independent components. Although standardization efforts exhibit diversity at the algorithm level, this diversity is more limited at the level of the underlying hardness assumptions. These observations have direct implications for the robustness of the PQC ecosystem, suggesting that dependencies between assumptions should be carefully considered when evaluating long-term security. In particular, resilience depends not only on the number of available schemes, but also on the diversity of the mathematical problems on which they rely.

Acknowledgements. This work was supported by the European Union under Grant Agreement No. 101225691 QARC. The project funded under Grant Agreement No. 101225691 is supported by the European Cybersecurity Competence Centre. Funded by the European Union. Views and opinions expressed are however those of the author(s) only and do not necessarily reflect those of the European Union or the European Cybersecurity Competence Centre. Neither the European Union nor the granting authority can be held responsible for them.

Disclosure of Interests. The authors have no competing interests to declare that are relevant to the content of this article.

Appendix A: Hardness Dependency References

This section provides bibliographic sources supporting the dependency relationships represented in the graph. Tables 1 and 2 list the edges between nodes, indicating for each pair the most related corresponding reference in the literature. For clarity, dependencies are separated into algorithm-to-problem mappings and problem-to-problem relationships. Each entry ensures the traceability and reproducibility of the constructed dependency graph. While algorithm-to-problem mappings follow directly from scheme specifications and security analyses, problem-to-problem relationships require more careful interpretation. These connections may correspond to formal reductions, worst-case to average-case hardness results, structural generalizations, or heuristic relationships.

Table 1. Algorithm-to-problem dependencies derived from scheme specifications and security analyses.

Algorithm → Problem / Primitive		
From	To	Reference
AIMer	MPC-in-the-Head	[25]
AIMer	AIM	[25]
BIKE	Noisy Syndrome Decoding	[4]
Dilithium	Module SIS (MSIS)	[17]
Dilithium	Module LWE (MLWE)	[17]
Falcon	NTRU Problem	[20]
Falcon	Short Integer Solution (SIS)	[20]
FrodoKEM	Learning With Errors (LWE)	[2]
HAETAE	Module SIS (MSIS)	[14]
HAETAE	Module LWE (MLWE)	[14]
HQC	Noisy Syndrome Decoding	[32]
Kyber	Module LWE (MLWE)	[8]
LMS	Hash Function	[31]
Classic McEliece	Syndrome Decoding	[6]
NTRU+	NTRU Problem	[24]
PicNic	LowMC	[12]
PicNic	MPC-in-the-Head	[12]
SPHINCS+	Hash Function	[7]
XMSS	Hash Function	[11]
SMAUG-T	Module LWR (MLWR)	[15]
SMAUG-T	Module LWE (MLWE)	[15]

The relationships between lattice-based problems represented in the graph rely on worst-case to average-case reductions. In particular, the hardness of problems such as SIS and LWE is based on the assumed difficulty of approximating classical lattice problems, including the SVP problem. Ajtai [1] established a reduction from approximate SVP to the SIS problem, while Regev [39] introduced a (quantum) reduction from approximate SVP to LWE. Subsequent work has further strengthened the theoretical foundations of LWE. In particular, Brakerski et al. [9] established classical hardness reductions for LWE under certain parameter regimes, showing that solving LWE with polynomial modulus would imply efficient algorithms for worst-case lattice problems. These results provide additional evidence for the hardness of LWE, although the classical reductions are more nuanced than in the case of SIS. Therefore, the edges connecting SIS and LWE to SVP should be interpreted as capturing foundational hardness connections rather than direct reductions to exact SVP.

Furthermore, within the lattice-based family, some relationships correspond to closely related problem variants. In particular, the relationship between LWR and LWE is supported by formal reductions and structural connections, showing that the hardness of LWR is closely related to that of LWE [3]. In the same spirit, Module-LWR can be viewed as a structured variant of LWR defined over module lattices [15], reflecting a parameterized generalization rather than a formal reduction. Finally, other relationships in the graph are of a different nature. For instance, the security of NTRU is traditionally understood as being heuristically related to the hardness of finding short vectors in structured lattices [21]. More recent work has provided additional theoretical insight into this connection. In particular, Felderhoff et al. [19] relate the NTRU problem to a structured variant of the SVP, known as module unique-SVP, and establish reductions connecting worst-case and average-case instances under certain assumptions. These results suggest that NTRU can be viewed as representative of a broader class of structured lattice problems, although the connection remains more nuanced than the classical reductions known for SIS and LWE.

Table 2. Problem-to-problem relationships, including reductions, derivations, and structural connections documented in the literature.

Problem → Problem (Reductions / Relations)		
From	To	Reference
Module LWE (MLWE)	Learning With Errors (LWE)	[28]
Learning With Errors (LWE)	Shortest Vector Problem (SVP)	[9,39]
Module SIS (MSIS)	Short Integer Solution (SIS)	[28]
Short Integer Solution (SIS)	Shortest Vector Problem (SVP)	[1]
NTRU Problem	Shortest Vector Problem (SVP)	[19,21]
Minimum Distance Decoding	Shortest Vector Problem (SVP)	[29,33]
Module LWR (MLWR)	Learning With Rounding (LWR)	[15]
Learning With Rounding (LWR)	Learning With Errors (LWE)	[3]
Noisy Syndrome Decoding	Syndrome Decoding	[4]
Syndrome Decoding	Minimum Distance Decoding	[6]

Similarly, the connection between the Minimum Distance Decoding problem and lattice problems such as SVP can be understood through a sequence of reductions linking decoding problems to lattice problems [33]. In particular, Lyubashevsky and Micciancio [29] establish tight relationships between the Bounded Distance Decoding (BDD) problem and lattice problems such as the unique SVP (uSVP) and GapSVP, showing their equivalence up to polynomial approximation factors. Since decoding problems such as MDD are closely related to BDD, this provides a conceptual bridge between coding-theoretic assumptions and lattice-based hardness. This connection should therefore be interpreted as an indirect reduction chain rather than a direct reduction to SVP.

An analogous situation arises in the code-based setting. Noisy Syndrome Decoding can be viewed as a generalization of the standard Syndrome Decoding problem, in which additional noise affects the syndrome, corresponding to a modeling extension rather than a formal reduction [4]. Moreover, the Minimum Distance Decoding problem is closely related to the Syndrome Decoding formulation commonly used in code-based cryptography. In practice, decoding problems are typically expressed in terms of syndrome decoding, which is equivalent to finding a minimum-weight error vector consistent with a given syndrome [6].

References

1. Ajtai, M.: Generating hard instances of lattice problems. In: Proceedings of the Twenty-Eighth Annual ACM Symposium on Theory of Computing, pp. 99–108 (1996)
2. Alkim, E., et al.: Frodokem learning with errors key encapsulation. NIST PQC Standard.: Round **3**, 10–20 (2020)
3. Alwen, J., Krenn, S., Pietrzak, K., Wichs, D.: Learning with rounding, revisited: new reduction, properties and applications. In: Annual Cryptology Conference, pp. 57–74. Springer (2013)
4. Aragon, N., Barreto, P., Bettaieb, S.: Bike: bit flipping key encapsulation. In: NIST Post-Quantum Cryptography Standardization Project (2022)
5. Bernstein, D.J.: Introduction to post-quantum cryptography. In: Post-Quantum Cryptography, pp. 1–14. Springer (2009)
6. Bernstein, D.J., et al.: Classic McEliece: conservative code-based cryptography. NIST Subm. **1**(1), 1–25 (2017)
7. Bernstein, D.J., Hülsing, A., Kölbl, S., Niederhagen, R., Rijneveld, J., Schwabe, P.: The SPHINCS+ signature framework. In: Proceedings of the 2019 ACM SIGSAC Conference on Computer and Communications Security, pp. 2129–2146 (2019)
8. Bos, J., et al.: Crystals-Kyber: a CCA-secure module-lattice-based KEM. In: 2018 IEEE European Symposium on Security and Privacy (EuroS&P), pp. 353–367. IEEE (2018)
9. Brakerski, Z., Langlois, A., Peikert, C., Regev, O., Stehlé, D.: Classical hardness of learning with errors. In: Proceedings of the Forty-Fifth Annual ACM Symposium on Theory of Computing, pp. 575–584 (2013)
10. BSI: Cryptographic mechanisms: recommendations and key lengths. Tech. Rep. TR-02102-1, Version 2026-01, Bundesamt für Sicherheit in der Informationstechnik (BSI) (2026). https://www.bsi.bund.de (2026). Accessed 22 April 2026
11. Buchmann, J., Dahmen, E., Hülsing, A.: XMSS-a practical forward secure signature scheme based on minimal security assumptions. In: International Workshop on Post-Quantum Cryptography, pp. 117–129. Springer (2011)
12. Chase, M., et al.: Post-quantum zero-knowledge and signatures from symmetric-key primitives. In: Proceedings of the 2017 ACM SIGSAC Conference on Computer and Communications Security, pp. 1825–1842 (2017)
13. Chen, L., et al.: Report on Post-quantum Cryptography, vol. 12. National Institute of Standards and Technology., US Department of Commerce (2016)
14. Cheon, J.H., et al.: HAETAE: shorter lattice-based fiat-Shamir signatures. IACR Trans. Cryptograp. Hardw. Embedded Syst. **2024**(3), 25–75 (2024)
15. Cheon, J.H., Choe, H., Seo, J., Seong, H.: Smaug (-t), revisited: timing-secure, more compact, less failure. IEEE Access **12**, 188386–188397 (2024)

16. Cooper, D., Apon, D., Dang, Q., Davidson, M., Dworkin, M., Miller, C.: NIST special publication 800-208: recommendation for stateful hash-based signature schemes (2020)
17. Ducas, L., et al.: CRYSTALS-Dilithium: a lattice-based digital signature scheme. IACR Trans. Cryptogr. Hardw. Embedd. Syst. **2018**, 238–268 (2018)
18. Federal Office for Information Security (BSI): Quantum-safe cryptography – fundamentals, current developments and recommendations. https://www.bsi.bund.de/SharedDocs/Downloads/EN/BSI/Publications/Brochure/quantum-safe-cryptography.html (2022). published: 2022-05-18; Accessed 09 Mar 2026
19. Felderhoff, J., Pellet-Mary, A., Stehlé, D.: On module unique-SVP and NTRU. In: International Conference on the Theory and Application of Cryptology and Information Security, pp. 709–740. Springer (2022)
20. Fouque, P.A., et al.: Falcon: fast-Fourier lattice-based compact signatures over NTRU. Submission to the NIST's post-quantum cryptography standardization process **36**(5), 1–75 (2018)
21. Hoffstein, J., Pipher, J., Silverman, J.H.: NTRU: a ring-based public key cryptosystem. In: International Algorithmic Number Theory Symposium, pp. 267–288. Springer (1998)
22. Institute of Commercial Cryptography Standards (ICCS): Next-generation commercial cryptographic algorithms program (NGCC). https://www.niccs.org.cn/en/ (2025). published: 2025-02-05. Accessed 03 April 2026
23. Ivezic, M.: Quantum technologies and quantum computing in Russia. https://postquantum.com/quantum-computing/quantum-russia/ (2024). published: 2024-12-26. Accessed: 03 April 2026. Online Article
24. Kim, J., Park, J.H.: NTRU+: compact construction of NTRU using simple encoding method. IEEE Trans. Inf. Forens. Secur. **18**, 4760–4774 (2023)
25. Kim, S., et al.: The aimer signature scheme. Tech. rep., Technical report. NIST (2023)
26. Korean Post-Quantum Cryptography (KPQC): KPQC algorithms. https://www.kpqc.or.kr/contents/03_exhibit/sub_03.html (2026). published: 2026-01-30. Accessed 10 April 2026
27. Kuznetsov, O., Kandiy, S., Frontoni, E., Smirnov, O.: Trade-offs in post-quantum cryptography: a comparative assessment of BIKE, HQC, and classic McEliece. In: CQPC, pp. 1–11 (2023)
28. Langlois, A., Stehlé, D.: Worst-case to average-case reductions for module lattices. Des. Codes Crypt. **75**(3), 565–599 (2015)
29. Lyubashevsky, V., Micciancio, D.: On bounded distance decoding, unique shortest vectors, and the minimum distance problem. In: Annual International Cryptology Conference, pp. 577–594. Springer (2009)
30. Mavroeidis, V., Vishi, K., Zych, M.D., Jøsang, A.: The impact of quantum computing on present cryptography (2018). arXiv:1804.00200 arXiv preprint
31. McGrew, D., Curcio, M., Fluhrer, S.: RFC 8554: Leighton-Micali hash-based signatures (2019)
32. Melchor, C.A., et al.: Hamming quasi-cyclic (HQC). NIST PQC Round **2**(4), 13 (2018)
33. Micciancio, D.: Lattice-based cryptography. In: Encyclopedia of Cryptography, Security and Privacy, pp. 1400–1403. Springer (2025)
34. National Agency for the Security of Information Systems (ANSSI): Anssi views on the post-quantum cryptography transition (2023 follow-up). https://messervices.cyber.gouv.fr/guides/en-follow-position-paper-post-quantum-cryptography (2023). published: 2023-12-21. Accessed 09 Mar 2026

35. National Institute of Standards and Technology (NIST): Post-quantum cryptography project. https://csrc.nist.gov/projects/post-quantum-cryptography (2025). Accessed 09 Mar 2026
36. NIST: Module-lattice-based digital signature standard. Tech. Rep. FIPS 204, National Institute of Standards and Technology (2024). https://doi.org/10.6028/NIST.FIPS.204, https://nvlpubs.nist.gov/nistpubs/FIPS/NIST.FIPS.204.pdf. Accessed 22 April 2026
37. NIST: Module-lattice-based key-encapsulation mechanism standard. Tech. Rep. FIPS 203, National Institute of Standards and Technology (2024). https://doi.org/10.6028/NIST.FIPS.203, https://nvlpubs.nist.gov/nistpubs/FIPS/NIST.FIPS.203.pdf. Accessed 22 April 2026
38. NIST: Stateless hash-based digital signature standard. Tech. Rep. FIPS 205, National Institute of Standards and Technology (2024). https://doi.org/10.6028/NIST.FIPS.205, https://nvlpubs.nist.gov/nistpubs/FIPS/NIST.FIPS.205.pdf. Accessed 22 April 2026
39. Regev, O.: On lattices, learning with errors, random linear codes, and cryptography. J. ACM (JACM) **56**(6), 1–40 (2009)

Market-Analysis-Driven Methodology for Assessing Charging Station Cybersecurity

Jakob Löw(✉), Lukas Eder(✉), Alexander Müller, and Hans-Joachim Hof

Technische Hochschule Ingolstadt, Security in Mobility, Ingolstadt, Germany
{jakob.loew,lukas.eder,hof}@thi.de

Abstract. Modern charging communication standards for electric vehicles include optional security controls such as TLS-based authentication and encryption. However, with tens of thousands of fast charging points deployed in any given country, individually testing each one for security control support is infeasible. This paper proposes a scalable, extrapolation-based methodology for assessing charging station cybersecurity at a national level. A market analysis identifies operator-manufacturer pairs, enabling the targeted selection of charging stations for field testing, whose results can then be extrapolated to all stations sharing the same combination. We demonstrate this methodology for Germany, covering over 40000 CCS charging points as of December 2025. With a manageable number of field tests, our extrapolated data examines 51.9% of german CCS charging stations. It shows that only 27.4% of charging stations in our scope provide TLS-protected communication, despite widespread theoretical support.

Keywords: Security · Charging · ISO 15118 · Electric Vehicles · Plug and Charge · CCS · Fast Charging · Rapid Charging · TLS

1 Introduction

Electric vehicles are becoming increasingly popular in Germany and the rest of the world [3]. While many users charge their vehicles at home or at work, fast charging stations are required on long-distance trips in order to minimize break times. Fast charging stations rely on high-level communication to keep the high-power charging process within safe limits, preventing battery damage and degradation. While this high-level communication enables convenience features such as automatic digital payment handled by the vehicle and the charging station, it also results in a larger attack surface for charging communication. Recent papers have demonstrated the feasibility of man-in-the-middle attacks [11,12,26] as well as payment fraud [4,9] against charging communication. Although current charging communication standards already include security controls that

J. Löw and L. Eder: Both authors contributed equally to this work.

P. Kieseberg et al. (Eds.): ARES 2026 Workshops, LNCS 16903, pp. 439–455, 2027.
https://doi.org/10.1007/978-3-032-37218-5_26

provide session authentication and could prevent such attacks, their use is currently optional. At present, there is no overview of what percentage of charging stations in the field today actually support these optional security controls.

Given the scale and heterogeneity of modern charging infrastructures, exhaustive security testing of all deployed charging stations is impractical. To address this challenge, we introduce an extrapolation-based methodology that leverages market structure and targeted measurements to assess the cybersecurity posture of charging infrastructure at national scale. By performing a market analysis, specific charging stations are selected, allowing extrapolation from a small number of tested stations to an overview of the current cybersecurity posture of charging communication. The methodology is based on two assumptions, which are validated later. Most charging point operators do not manufacture their own charging hardware. While there are thousands of fast charging stations in the field today, operated by hundreds of operators, the vast majority were built by a small number of manufacturers. The first assumption is therefore that charging stations manufactured by the same company support the same set of features, e.g. support for transport layer security (TLS). The second assumption is that two charging stations built by the same manufacturer and operated by the same company use the same configurations and thus support the same set of security controls. Together, these assumptions imply that testing one charging station allows the test results to be extrapolated to all stations built by the same manufacturer and operated by the same company.

We validate these assumptions and demonstrate the methodology for Germany, where it enables a qualified assessment of security control availability for more than half of all charging stations using a manageable number of field tests.

Our analysis reveals a significant gap between the security mechanisms defined in standards and their deployment in practice. While most charging station hardware supports TLS-based secure communication, only a minority of stations in the field actually enable and successfully use these mechanisms. This indicates that the current security posture of charging infrastructure is primarily limited by operational and configuration challenges rather than technical capabilities.

2 Charging Communication Security

In order to charge an electric vehicle, AC power from the grid has to be converted to an adequate DC voltage for charging the vehicle battery. In addition, safety parameters such as maximum current, temperature constraints, and voltage limits need to be followed. For fast charging stations, this AC to DC conversion happens outside of the vehicle, inside the charging station. Therefore, the vehicle needs to be able to communicate with the charging station and exchange safety parameters.

The leading standard for charging communication in Europe is ISO 15118 [17–19]. The standard builds on common communication protocols such as powerline communication, IPv6, and Transport Layer Security. Figure 1 shows the communication technology used in ISO 15118 for each of the open systems interconnect (OSI) model layers. The initialization steps, namely signal level attenuation characterization (SLAC) and the service discovery protocol (SDP), are designed specifically for charging communication. SLAC is used to form a joint powerline network between the vehicle and the charging station. Afterwards, SDP is used to exchange network addresses and to decide on the optional use of TLS for encrypting the main charging communication. Since SLAC messages are transmitted in plain text and SDP messages do not include means of message authentication, the initialization steps of ISO 15118 open up the possibility of misuse scenarios [4,10,11,22,26]. When both the vehicle and the charging station signal support for TLS, the main charging communication can be authenticated and encrypted using state-of-the-art algorithms. When TLS is used, the ISO 15118 standard also enables a special certificate-based automatic payment scheme. The use of TLS prevents potential attackers from impersonating a communication party or eavesdropping on the communication, significantly improving the security posture of a charging communication session.

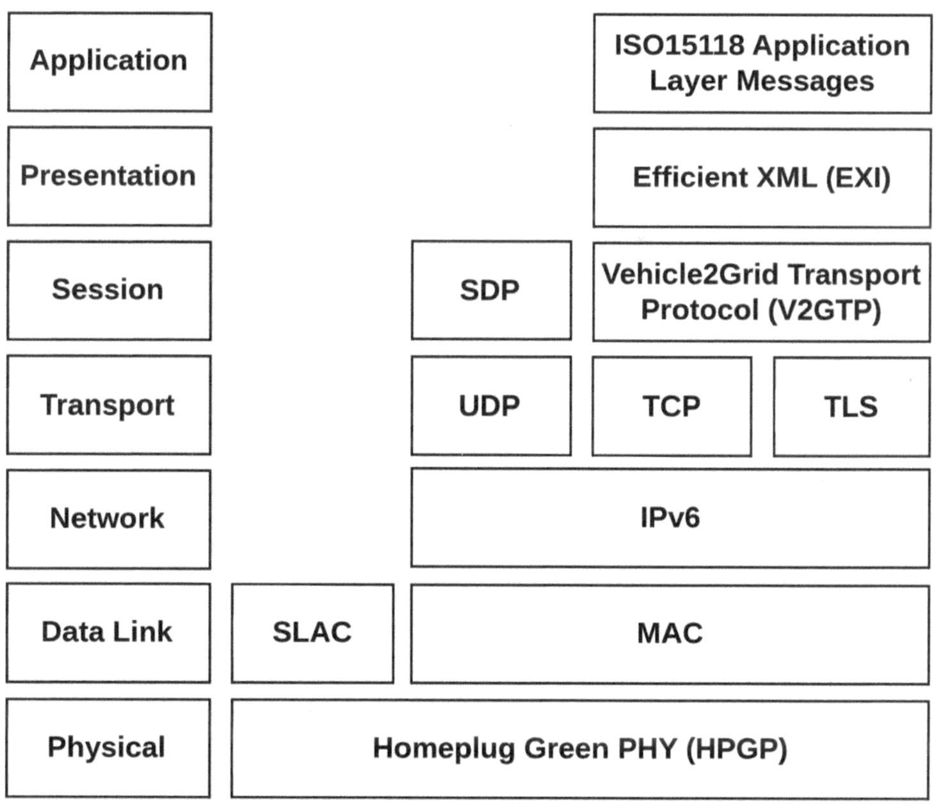

Fig. 1. Charging Communication OSI Layer Overview

For clear terminology throughout the paper, Fig. 2 shows the participants in the charging process relevant to this work. Charging stations can have one or more charging points, i.e., can serve one or more vehicles at the same time. For comparability, we count individual charging points rather than charging stations, since stations can have varying numbers of points depending on manufacturer, model, and hardware version. Charging stations are often part of charging parks, each run by one charge point operator (CPO). Operators run multiple parks, resulting in larger operators operating hundreds or even thousands of charge points. The charging stations operated by a CPO also have a manufacturer, which is generally not the CPO itself. Most CPOs do not manufacture charging stations themselves; instead, they buy off-the-shelf models. Another participant in the charging process is the mobility operator (MO), which handles everything related to billing. Multiple roles (MO, CPO, manufacturer) can be held by the same party or company, but this is not required.

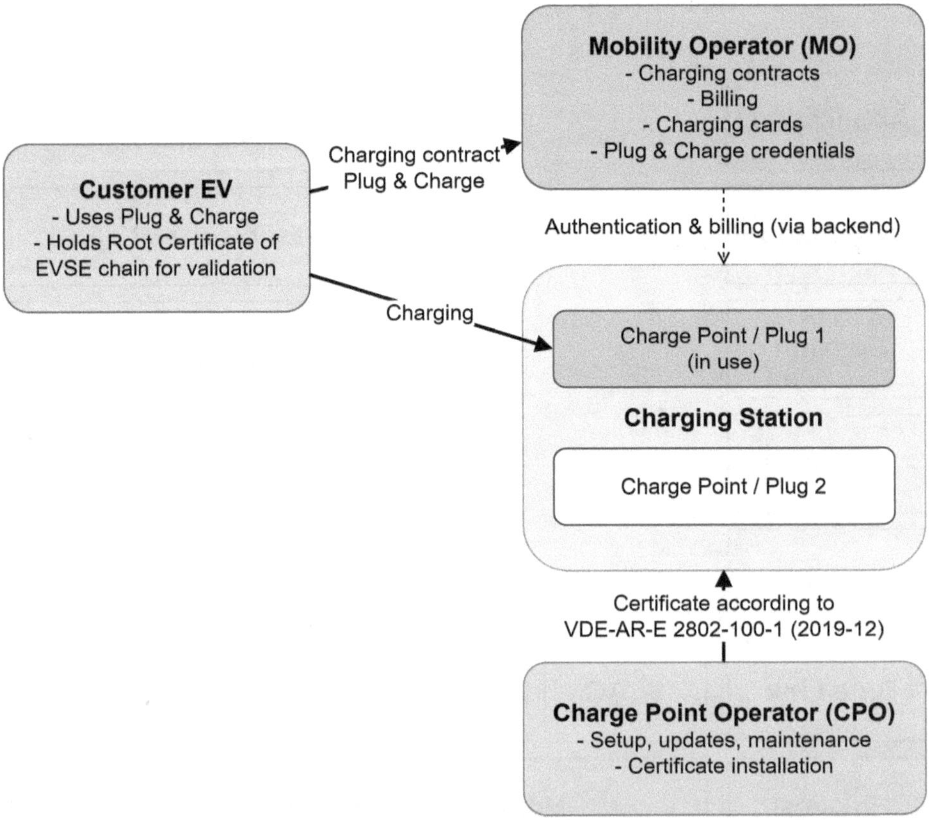

Fig. 2. Simplified overview of EV charging participants

3 Related Work

Prior surveys and threat analyses have examined the attack surface of ISO 15118 and CCS-based fast charging [6,21,22]. At the powerline and physical layer, concrete attacks have been demonstrated, including practical exploitation of HomePlug AV [10], powerline-based command injection against V2G charging [11], passive PHY-layer eavesdropping of CCS sessions [5], wireless denial-of-service via signal interference [20], and wireless SDR-based man-in-the-middle attacks including TLS stripping [26]. A separate line of work targets the powerline modems themselves: these have been shown to expose configuration and data-extraction interfaces over the powerline [25], a primitive that has subsequently been leveraged to install filter and firewall rules enabling sniffing and man-in-the-middle attacks on the charging session [12]. At the application layer, relay attacks against the charging protocol [9] and plug-and-charge payment-authentication relays [4] have been used to commit payment fraud. While most of these works propose new countermeasures alongside the vulnerabilities they identify, the basic security mechanisms already specified in the charging standards – most importantly TLS for authentication and encryption – are themselves only optional and require support from both the vehicle and the charging station to take effect. Whether deployed charging stations actually enable these standardized mechanisms is an empirical question that has so far received only limited attention; this paper argues that closing the deployment gap for these existing controls is at least as pressing as proposing new ones.

Szakály et al. [24] present the closest prior measurement study. The authors tested almost 400 charging stations across the United Kingdom, Switzerland, and Hungary for supported communication protocols and security controls. Their sample is opportunistic rather than stratified: stations were measured as accessible, without targeted selection by charge point operator or hardware manufacturer. As a result, their work establishes that TLS deployment varies significantly between operators and documents concrete configuration shortcomings, but it cannot quantify how prevalent each configuration is within a given country or region. The methodology proposed in this paper is designed for exactly this question: by stratifying field tests along the (CPO, manufacturer) dimensions that, as shown in Sect. 4.4, govern configuration in practice, we extrapolate from a small sample to national-scale deployment estimates. The two approaches are complementary; we in fact incorporate 25 of the charging stations measured by Szakály et al. into our assumption-validation set in Sect. 4.4, where their cross-country measurements of overlapping CPOs strengthen the case that configurations are consistent within a (CPO, manufacturer) pair across borders.

4 Market Analysis Methodology

The proposed methodology combines a market analysis of the target region with targeted field testing and extrapolation to assess the cybersecurity state of charging infrastructure at scale. The goal is to identify all charging stations, their manufacturers, and their operators, in order to select a minimal set of stations for field testing that maximizes extrapolation coverage. We demonstrate this methodology for Germany using openly available data sources, as described in the following subsections.

Extrapolating from a limited number of field-tested charging stations to a larger population requires two assumptions to hold:

- A1: Charging Stations of the same manufacturer support the same set of features, while the CPO controls which features are enabled through configuration and certificate provisioning.
- A2: CPOs use the same configuration on all Charging Stations from the same manufacturer.

The validity of these assumptions is empirically evaluated in Sect. 4.4 based on measurements across multiple manufacturers, models, installation years, and CPOs.

4.1 Extrapolation-Based Assessment Methodology

The methodology consists of the following steps:
Step 1 - Data Acquisition: Publicly available datasets are collected to obtain charging point locations, charge point operators (CPOs), and charging station manufacturers and models. In this work, data from the Bundesnetzagentur [7] and goingelectric.de [2] are used.

Step 2 - Data Preprocessing: The collected data is cleaned and normalized. This includes unifying inconsistent manufacturer labels (e.g., *Tesla* vs. *Supercharger*) and removing incomplete entries. The resulting dataset contains only charging points with known CPO and manufacturer assignments.

Step 3 - Clustering: Charging points are grouped into clusters based on their CPO and manufacturer:

$$\texttt{Cluster} = (\texttt{CPO}, \texttt{Manufacturer})$$

Each cluster is assumed to represent a homogeneous configuration domain.

Step 4 - Sampling Strategy: Clusters were ranked according to the number of charging points represented in the dataset. Starting with the largest clusters, charging stations were selected for testing within a reachable distance from our office. The selection aims to maximize coverage of charging points while minimizing the number of required tests.
Step 5 - Field Testing: Selected charging stations are analyzed using the proposed EV-side testing device. The following properties are evaluated:

- availability of TLS,
- supported communication protocols (DIN SPEC 70121, ISO 15118-2),
- presence of valid certificate chains.

Step 6 - Extrapolation: The results obtained from tested charging stations are extrapolated to all charging points within the same cluster. This is based on the assumption that charging stations within a cluster share identical capabilities and configuration.

Step 7 - Aggregation: The extrapolated results are aggregated across all clusters to estimate the overall security posture of the charging infrastructure, including TLS deployment rates and protocol distribution at national scale.

This structured approach enables scalable assessment of large charging infrastructures while requiring only a limited number of field measurements.

4.2 Data Collection

The proposed extrapolation of charging station tests requires quantified knowledge about charging points, manufacturers, and charge point operators. While official sources such as the charging station list provided by the federal network agency [1] exist, these include only operator and connector information and lack details about the hardware used. Therefore, the official data must be enriched with additional sources in order to obtain a fully featured dataset.

The German website goingelectric.de hosts a community of electric vehicle enthusiasts, including a forum, a wiki, and a curated map of charging stations. In addition to charging locations, users can add pictures and metadata to each charging point, such as supported charging power, manufacturer, and model. While the dataset includes information about some charging points in other countries, its main focus is on charging stations in Germany. As part of this research, we used the official goingelectric API as well as web scraping to download information such as charging station manufacturers and models.

Since the information about charging station manufacturers and models is added manually by individuals, the data required some manual sanitization. For example, some charging stations built and operated by Tesla are labeled as *Tesla*, while others are labeled as *Supercharger*. Out of 114078 CCS charging points present on goingelectric.de in December 2025, 44313 (or 39%) are located in Germany. Of these 44313 charging points, another 3364 (or 7.6%) do not have a charging station manufacturer labeled, leaving 40949 charging points for analysis.

For each of these charging points, the charging station manufacturer, the model, the CPO operating the station, and the corresponding mobility operator were extracted. In most cases, the charge point operator is identical to the mobility operator handling the billing of charging sessions.

4.3 Data Summary

The collected data shows a large number of small and medium-sized charge point operators. Many traditional companies active in the energy sector, such as *EnBW*, *EWE*, *allego*, *innogy*, *Vattenfall*, *E.ON*, and *TEAG*, have invested in the electric vehicle charging market. Automotive players are also among the top charge point operators, including *Tesla*, *Volkswagen* (as *Elli*), and various other carmakers through *IONITY*. Retail chains such as *Lidl*, *Aldi*, *Kaufland*, and *Edeka* have built charging stations at their existing locations. Lastly, players from the fossil energy sector, such as *Aral* with *Aral Pulse* and *Shell* are also among the top CPOs in Germany.

Regarding charging station manufacturers, the collected data shows that nearly 66% of CCS charging points belong to charging stations built by a single manufacturer: *Alpitronic*. Both *ABB* and *Tesla* hold around a 10% market share of installed charge points in Germany. The remaining 14.5% are split among multiple smaller manufacturers. Figure 3 shows an overview of the manufacturer market share among all CCS charging points in Germany.

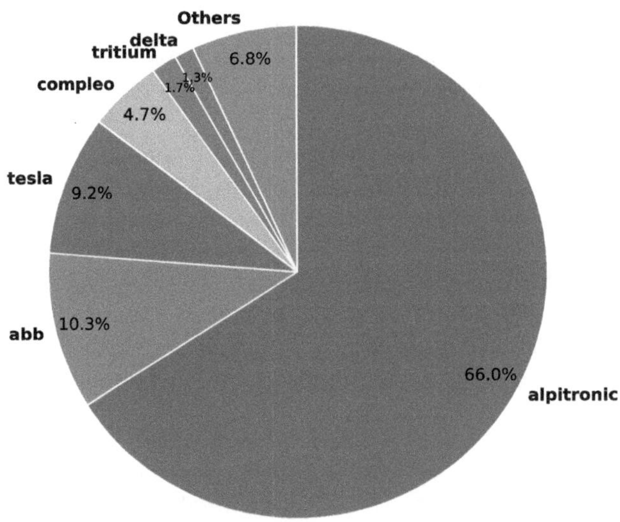

Fig. 3. Charging Station Manufacturers Market Share

Many charge point operators use *Alpitronic* charging stations almost exclusively. As shown in Table 1, four of the five leading CPOs use Alpitronic charging stations for more than 90% of their charging points; the fifth is Tesla, which builds its charging stations itself. This concentration simplifies the planned security analysis of charging stations in Germany.

4.4 Validation of Extrapolation Assumptions

The proposed methodology relies on two assumptions: (A1) charging stations from the same manufacturer provide the same set of communication capabilities, and (A2) charging stations operated by the same CPO are configured consistently within each manufacturer group. For the validation, the extrapolation dataset was expanded with additional charging stations selected to maximize diversity in manufacturers, installation years, and deployment locations in order to identify potential counterexamples to these assumptions. The data used for the validation can be found in the repository linked at the end of Sect. 6. In addition, existing data from [24] was used to verify and extend our validation data with EVSE tests in Hungary, the UK, and Switzerland.

Validation of A1 (Manufacturer Capability Consistency). To evaluate (A1), charging stations from multiple manufacturers (Alpitronic, ABB, Tritium, Compleo, Efacec, EKOenergetyka, ChargePoint) were analyzed across different model generations and installation years (2018–2024). In all observed cases, charging stations from the same manufacturer supported the same set of communication capabilities at the protocol level.

In particular, no case was observed in which two charging stations from the same manufacturer differed in their capability to support TLS. Charging stations manufactured between 2018 and 2024 showed identical TLS capability within each manufacturer, including both older and newer hardware generations. This suggests that hardware revisions do not significantly affect the availability of the communication capabilities considered in this work.

Additionally, analysis of publicly available firmware documentation [14] indicates that different models of a major manufacturer share a common software platform and configuration interface, further supporting this assumption.

Validation of A2 (CPO Configuration Consistency). To evaluate (A2), multiple charging stations from the same CPO–manufacturer combinations were tested across different locations and installation years. In total, 16 charging stations from three major CPOs were analyzed:

- EnBW (Alpitronic): 8 stations across 5 locations
- Aral (Alpitronic, Compleo): 5 stations across 4 locations
- IONITY (Alpitronic, ABB, Tritium): 3 stations across 3 locations

Across all tested stations within each CPO–manufacturer pair, identical behavior regarding TLS support and supported protocols was observed, independent of installation year (2019–2025) and hardware model. This suggests a high degree of configuration standardization within each CPO.

To further support this observation, measurement data from [24] was incorporated. For overlapping CPOs (e.g., IONITY, Allego, Fastned), consistent configurations were observed across different European countries. This adds 25 additional charging stations (ABB and EKOenergetyka, 2018–2022) to the validation set.

Limitations. The validation is based on a finite number of sampled charging stations and may not capture all sources of variation. In particular, the following factors may influence the validity of the assumptions:

- configuration changes over time (e.g. certificate rollouts),
- regional differences within large CPOs,

- temporary misconfigurations or partial deployments,
- underrepresented small CPOs.

Therefore, the extrapolation results should be interpreted as an approximation of the current deployment state rather than an exact measurement. Nevertheless, the high consistency observed across all tested samples suggests that large-scale charging networks are operated with highly standardized configurations, supporting the feasibility of the proposed methodology.

Table 1. Charging Station Manufacturers per Operator

Operator	Points	Points (%)	Manufacturer	Points (%)
enbw	7593	18.5	alpitronic	96.1
			abb	3.0
tesla	3770	9.2	tesla	100.0
aral	2887	7.1	alpitronic	92.8
			volkswagen	6.9
ewe	1999	4.9	alpitronic	99.3
allego	1860	4.5	alpitronic	95.3
			efacec	4.2
pfalzwerke	1662	4.1	alpitronic	82.9
			enercharge	8.1
			abb	6.5
			siemens	2.2
newmotion	1573	3.8	alpitronic	59.8
			abb	35.0
			volkswagen	5.0
be.energised	1454	3.6	alpitronic	67.6
			ads-tec	13.3
			compleo	6.5
			abb	6.1
			ekoenergetyka	1.1
ionity	1363	3.3	tritium	48.3
			abb	32.9
			alpitronic	18.8
ladenetz	1355	3.3	alpitronic	58.2
			compleo	15.9
			abb	8.7
			enercharge	7.7
			ads-tec	4.0
			siemens	2.0
			delta	1.0

5 Charging Station Testing Device

To analyze the supported communication protocols and security mechanisms of CCS charging stations under real-world conditions, a dedicated charging station testing device was developed. The device is designed to emulate the EV-side communication behavior required for standardized high-level charging communication, while deliberately excluding any energy transfer functionality. This enables systematic, reproducible, and safe measurements of protocol support, TLS availability, and certificate deployment across different electric vehicle supply equipments (EVSE) without interacting with high-voltage components. The following subsections describe the hardware and software architecture of the testing device in detail.

5.1 Hardware Setup

We designed our testing device to be portable. It emulates the EV side required for charging communication analysis. The system can be operated in a fully mobile manner, requiring only the test device itself and an external power bank, which enables flexible deployment independent of fixed laboratory infrastructure.

A Raspberry Pi Zero 2 W serves as the central processing unit of the test device. It executes the complete communication logic and is responsible for recording and logging all exchanged data. To enable HomePlug Green PHY (HPGP) power line communication, a Codico RED-BEET-EVAL-BOARD-E 2.0 power line modem is integrated into the system. The modem is electrically connected to the Raspberry Pi via an existing SPI interface and a power connection, providing a compact and efficient communication link between both components.

The physical interface to the EVSE is realized using a modified Type 2 charging cable. Since the test device is exclusively intended for communication analysis, no DC power contacts are required. The communication process is intentionally terminated before the EVSE would enable any power transfer, thereby ensuring that no voltage is applied during operation.

Within the Type 2 connector, a set of resistors combined with switches is implemented to accurately reproduce the different CP-states as specified by the relevant standards. Furthermore, a diode is integrated into the connector to suppress negative voltage components of the PWM signal on the control pilot line. The PP resistor is statically implemented in the connector to represent a fixed cable current rating. The CP and PE conductors are directly connected to the power line communication modem.

Overall, the proposed hardware setup provides a complete emulation of the EV-side communication components required for charging while omitting high-power and high-voltage elements. This approach enables a portable analysis of the communication behavior between EV and EVSE in a controlled manner.

5.2 Software Setup

The charging station testing device implements a vehicle-side simulation of standardized charging communication between an EV and an EVSE for testing purposes. The simulated communication supports DIN SPEC 70121, ISO 15118-2, and ISO 15118-20, thereby enabling a systematic and reproducible assessment of protocol compliance and security-related properties of charging stations.

The software strictly follows the normative communication sequence defined by the standards. This sequence comprises the SLAC coupling procedure, the service discovery protocol, the optional establishment of a secured communication channel using TLS, and the subsequent supported application protocol negotiation. These phases collectively determine the protocol stack, security mechanisms, and application profiles that are supported and selected for a charging session.

To systematically evaluate EVSE behavior under different communication and security configurations, the test process is executed in multiple independent test cycles. In each cycle, the simulated EV advertises a predefined set of communication capabilities and security requirements during the service discovery and protocol negotiation phases. The tested scenarios include:

1. Service discovery requests that require TLS exclusively, allowing the detection of TLS support and the availability of certificates at EVSE-side
2. Protocol negotiation requests for ISO 15118-2 without the use of TLS
3. Protocol negotiation requests without TLS that advertise all supported standards, including DIN SPEC 70121, ISO 15118-2, and ISO 15118-20
4. Protocol negotiation requests without TLS that advertise only DIN SPEC 70121

The first test allows the detection of TLS support and the availability of certificates on the EVSE side. Tests 1, 2, and 4 check for HLC communication protocol availability. Test 3 identifies the specific communication protocol selected by the EVSE when the EV supports all available protocol options.

All information relevant for protocol selection and security evaluation – including the supported and selected communication standards, the availability of secured communication, and the use of digital certificates – is exchanged during these early stages of the communication process. As no additional information required for the intended analysis is negotiated beyond this point, the test process is deliberately terminated after the successful completion of these steps. This controlled termination ensures that the charging session does not proceed to energy transfer, resulting in the desired behavior that the EVSE does not output charging voltage.

6 Test Results

Table 2 summarizes the observed protocol and security feature support across the analyzed CCS charging stations. As expected for CCS EVSEs, all tested charging stations implement DIN SPEC 70121 while most also support ISO 15118-2. In contrast, the practical use of TLS is limited. Although ISO 15118-2 allows TLS for secure communication, only a small fraction of the measured charging stations successfully established TLS-protected sessions. In most cases,

TLS was either disabled or not operational. Our extrapolation covers 51.9% of German charging stations and specifically shows that only 27.4% of them provide TLS-secured charging communication.

The measurement results suggest that the lack of TLS deployment is not caused by technical limitations of the charging hardware, but by challenges in certificate provisioning and trust management. This conclusion is supported by the observation that charging stations from the same product families – and in several cases even newer hardware revisions – exhibited differing TLS behavior. Specifically, EVSE models that did not establish TLS were observed alongside equivalent or older models from the same product line that successfully supported TLS, indicating that hardware capabilities alone do not explain the absence of TLS in practice.

For TLS to be accepted by the vehicle, the EVSE certificate chain must terminate in a root CA trusted by the EV. While on the web, obtaining certificates for encrypted communication is free and easy to automate, in the charging domain PKI providers usually charge a one-time fee as well as recurring fees for each charging station. This effectively hinders the use of TLS for secure charging communication.

At the time of writing, at least four operators of V2G public key infrastructures are known to provide trusted root CAs for ISO 15118 [8,15,16,23]. However, within our dataset, only certificates issued under the Hubject V2G Root CA [15] were observed. All other stations either operated without TLS or failed to present a certificate.

TLS in ISO 15118 is mandatory when using plug and charge. Therefore, all networks that support plug and charge payment also support TLS. IONITY has supported plug and charge since October 2021 and appears to have updated chargers built before that date, providing them with the certificates required for successful TLS communication. Similarly, Aral introduced plug and charge in early 2022. Charging stations built before this introduction also support TLS, indicating updates after initial construction.

In general, support for TLS seems to be mainly driven by the introduction of plug and charge payment rather than security concerns. While in our dataset 27.4% of charging spots support TLS, we assume the real-world number to be even lower. Due to the required effort and upfront cost, plug and charge is currently mainly supported by large charging point operators. While our dataset includes both large and small operators, the distribution is not proportional to the total number of charging points installed. Small CPOs left out of the dataset are expected to have an even lower rate of support for TLS.

This expectation can be substantiated for a part of the remaining 48.1% of charging points not covered by our extrapolation. While in most cases the CPO also acts as the mobility operator handling billing, several mobility operators – *NewMotion*, *be.energised*, *Ladenetz*, and *innogy* – do not operate charging stations themselves, but instead allow third parties, typically small CPOs, to register charging stations within their network. None of these networks advertise support for plug and charge, which makes the availability of security controls such as TLS in those charging stations unlikely. Our field tests of some CPOs that use these networks confirm this assumption. The same reasoning applies to the long tail of small CPOs and networks outside these mobility operator networks: each of them operates only a small number of charging stations, for which the integration effort and the one-time and recurring PKI fees required for plug and charge rarely pay off. We therefore expect the TLS deployment rate among the charging points outside our extrapolation scope to be considerably below the 27.4% observed within it.

As discussed above, this deployment gap is operational rather than technical: the hardware of all major manufacturers supports TLS, but enabling it requires certificate provisioning and trust management that many operators forgo. Regulatory incentives may close this gap in the future. The technical specifications adopted under the European Alternative Fuels Infrastructure Regulation (AFIR) [13] require newly deployed publicly accessible charging points to support ISO 15118-20 starting in 2027. Since ISO 15118-20 mandates the use of TLS, this requirement effectively enforces TLS deployment for new installations, although the existing infrastructure measured in this work remains unaffected.

Apart from the extracted results shown in table 2 we are also publishing all raw data gathered from various charging stations including communication dumps as well as model information on github: https://github.com/M4GNV5/charging-station-tests-germany

7 Conclusion

Our research shows a significant lack of support for security controls in chargers deployed in the field today. While current research continues to identify vulnerabilities and shortcomings in charging communication and to propose new security controls to prevent attacks, in reality most chargers do not support even basic authentication or encryption. While some operators have made the effort to support TLS, this appears to be a prerequisite for introducing plug and charge rather than a proactive step to improve the cybersecurity of the charging infrastructure. The current state of cybersecurity in charging communication appears to resemble that of the web years ago. Making TLS mandatory for all charging sessions could improve the confidentiality and integrity of charging communication.

The proposed market-analysis-driven methodology is not limited to Germany and can be applied to any country or region where charging station data is available, enabling comparable assessments of charging infrastructure cybersecurity elsewhere.

Future research could evaluate current certificate distribution techniques and investigate how a certificate enrollment process similar to the Automatic Certificate Management Environment (ACME) used for web servers could be integrated into the charging ecosystem. Similar to the service provided by Let's Encrypt, an easy, automatic, and free way to obtain certificates could significantly accelerate the adoption of authentication and encryption in charging communication.

Table 2. Test Results for various CPOs

CPO	CPO %	OEM	OEM %	Cluster %	Model	Year	ISO 15118-2	TLS
EnBW	18.5	Alpitronic	95.9	17.7	HYC400	2023	✔	✖
					HYC300	2019, 2025	✔	✖
					HYC200	2024	✔	✖
					HYC150	2021, 2023	✔	✖
Aral	7.1	Alpitronic	92.8	6.6	HYC300	2021, 2023	✔	✔
		Compleo	0.1	0.0	Cito BM 500	2020	✖	✖
EWE	4.9	Alpitronic	99.3	4.9	HYC300	2021, 2022	✔	✖
allego	4.5	Alpitronic	95.2	4.3	HYC300	2022	✔	✔
pfalzwerke	4.1	Alpitronic	82.9	3.4	HYC150	2021	✔	✖
IONITY	3.3	Tritium	48.3	1.6	Veefil PK	2019	✔	✔
		ABB	32.9	1.1	HP CP500	2024	✔	✔
		Alpitronic	18.8	0.6	HYC400	2023	✔	✔
Lidl	2.4	ABB	79.2	1.9	Terra 60	2021	✔	✖
Elli	2.3	Compleo	95.7	2.2	Cito BM 500	2022	✔	✖
Mer	2.0	Alpitronic	90.8	1.8	HYC150	2021	✔	✖
Aldi	2.0	Alpitronic	98.8	2.0	HYC150	2021	✔	✖
Kaufland	1.7	ABB	92.4	1.6	Terra 54	2022	✔	✖
Edeka	1.1	Compleo	84.1	0.9	Cito BM 500	2021	✖	✖
fastned	0.8	Alpitronic	100	0.8	HYC300	2021	✔	✖
Circle K	0.7	ABB	65.0	0.5	HP CP500	2021	✖	✖
% Of All	55.4			51.9			48.7	14.2
% Of Clusters				100			93.8	27.4

Additionally, such an approach could help bring secure-by-default practices to charging communication, rather than requiring network operators to manually obtain and configure certificates for each charging station individually.

Acknowledgments. This work was created in the research project "Elektromobiles Sicheres Laden" (ESiLa) funded by the Bavarian Ministry of Economic Affairs, Regional Development and Energy under grant DIK0512/01.

Disclosure of Interests. The authors have no competing interests to declare that are relevant to the content of this article.

References

1. Bundesnetzagentur - Ladesäulenkarte. https://www.bundesnetzagentur.de/DE/Fachthemen/ElektrizitaetundGas/E-Mobilitaet/Ladesaeulenkarte/start.html
2. Dokumentation der Stromtankstellen API. https://www.goingelectric.de/stromtankstellen/api/docs/, https://www.goingelectric.de/stromtankstellen/api/docs/
3. Open EV Charts. https://open-ev-charts.org/, https://open-ev-charts.org/. Accessed 30 June 2025
4. Iso 15118 security controls, vulnerabilities and possible remedies, pp. 1–2 (2026)
5. Baker, R., Martinovic, I.: Losing the car keys: wireless PHY-layer insecurity in EV charging, pp. 407–424 (2019). https://www.usenix.org/conference/usenixsecurity19/presentation/baker
6. Bao, K., Valev, H., Wagner, M., Schmeck, H.: A threat analysis of the vehicle-to-grid charging protocol ISO 15118. Comput. Sci. Res. Dev. **33**(1), 3–12 (2018). https://doi.org/10.1007/s00450-017-0342-y
7. Bundesnetzagentur: Anzahl der öffentlichen Ladepunkte in Deutschland von Januar 2017 bis Oktober 2023 [Graph], Bundesnetzagentur (2024). https://www.bundesnetzagentur.de/SharedDocs/Downloads/DE/Sachgebiete/Energie/Unternehmen_Institutionen/E_Mobilitaet/Ladesaeuleninfrastruktur.xlsx?__blob=publicationFile&v=5
8. CharIN: CharIN V2G PKI goes live!. https://www.charin.global/news/charin-v2g-pki-goes-live/, https://www.charin.global/news/charin-v2g-pki-goes-live/
9. Conti, M., Donadel, D., Poovendran, R., Turrin, F.: EVExchange: a relay attack on electric vehicle charging system. In: Atluri, V., Di Pietro, R., Jensen, C.D., Meng, W. (eds.) Computer Security – ESORICS 2022, pp. 488–508. Springer International Publishing, Cham (2022). https://doi.org/10.1007/978-3-031-17140-6_24
10. Dudek, S.: HomePlugAV PLC: Practical attacks and backdooring. Netw. Anal. **15** (2015). https://penthertz.com/resources/NSC2014-HomePlugAV_attacks-Sebastien_Dudek.pdf
11. Dudek, S., Delaunay, J.C., Fargues, V.: V2G Injector: whispering to cars and charging units through the power-line. In: Proceedings of the SSTIC (Symposium sur la sécurité des technologies de l'information et des communications), pp. 1–26. SSTIC, Rennes, France (2019), https://www.sstic.org/2019/presentation/v2g_injector_playing_with_electric_cars_and_charging_stations_via_powerline/
12. Eder, L., Löw, J., Hof, H.J.: Charging communication sniffing and man-in-the-middle attacks. In: Proceedings of the 16th ACM International Conference on Future and Sustainable Energy Systems, pp. 799–804. E-Energy '25, Association for Computing Machinery, New York, NY, USA (2025). https://doi.org/10.1145/3679240.3734648

13. European Parliament and Council of the European Union: Regulation (EU) 2023/1804 of the European Parliament and of the Council of 13 September 2023 on the deployment of alternative fuels infrastructure, and repealing Directive 2014/94/EU (2023). https://eur-lex.europa.eu/eli/reg/2023/1804/oj
14. GmbH, A.: hyperdoc — dashboard. https://doc.hypercharger.it/
15. Hubject: Download Public Key Infrastructure (PKI) | Hubject. https://www.hubject.com/download-pki
16. irdeto: Open and secure EV charging. https://irdeto.com/smart-mobility/crosscharge-ev-charging
17. ISO/IEC: ISO/IEC DIS 15118-2: Road vehicles - Vehicle to grid communication interface – Part 2: network and application protocol requirements (2012). http://www.iso.org/iso/iso_catalogue/catalogue_ics/catalogue_detail_ics.htm?ics1=43&ics2=120&ics3=&csnumber=55366
18. ISO/IEC: ISO/IEC DIS 15118-3: Road vehicles - vehicle to grid communication interface – part 3: physical and data link layer requirements (2012). http://www.iso.org/iso/home/store/catalogue_ics/catalogue_detail_ics.htm?ics1=43&ics2=120&ics3=&csnumber=59675
19. ISO/IEC: ISO/IEC DIS 15118-20: Road vehicles - vehicle to grid communication interface – part 20: 2nd generation network layer and application layer requirements (2022). https://www.iso.org/standard/77845.html
20. Köhler, S., Baker, R., Strohmeier, M., Martinovic, I.: Brokenwire: wireless disruption of CCS electric vehicle charging. In: Proceedings 2023 Network and Distributed System Security Symposium. Internet Society, San Diego, CA, USA (2023). https://doi.org/10.14722/ndss.2023.23251, https://www.ndss-symposium.org/wp-content/uploads/2023/02/ndss2023_s251_paper.pdf
21. Lee, S., Park, Y., Lim, H., Shon, T.: Study on analysis of security vulnerabilities and countermeasures in ISO/IEC 15118 based electric vehicle charging technology. In: 2014 International Conference on IT Convergence and Security (ICITCS), pp. 1–4 (2014). https://doi.org/10.1109/ICITCS.2014.7021815, https://ieeexplore.ieee.org/document/7021815
22. Löw, J., Mayer, K., Hof, H.J.: Fast Charging communication and cybersecurity: a technology review (2024)
23. Nexusgroup: identities for plug and charge/vehicle-to-grid - V2G PKI. https://doc.nexusgroup.com/pub/identities-for-vehicle-to-grid-v2g-pki
24. Szakály, M., Köhler, S., Martinovic, I.: Current affairs: a security measurement study of CCS EV charging deployments (2025). https://doi.org/10.48550/arXiv.2404.06635, http://arxiv.org/abs/2404.06635, arXiv:2404.06635 [cs]
25. Szakály, M., Köhler, S., Martinovic, I.: Short: PIBuster: exploiting a common misconfiguration in CCS EV Chargers, pp. 243–249 (2025). https://www.usenix.org/conference/vehiclesec25/presentation/szakaly
26. Szakály, M., Strohmeier, M., Martinovic, I., Köhler, S.: DCeption: real-world wireless man-in-the-middle attacks against CCS EV Charging (2026). https://doi.org/10.48550/arXiv.2601.15515, http://arxiv.org/abs/2601.15515

Private Quantised Neural Network Inference

Hendrik Eerikson[1,2](✉), Sven Laur[1], and Pille Pullonen-Raudvere[2]

[1] Institute of Computer Science, University of Tartu, Tartu, Estonia
[2] Information Security Research Institute, Cybernetica AS, Tallinn, Estonia
hendrik.eerikson@cyber.ee

Abstract. Neural networks based machine learning models are used in many classification problems yet privacy issues in model usage are mostly unresolved. When a model owner provides their model to other parties for inference, either the model owner has to share the parameters of the model or the model user must share their query and result with the model owner. Depending on the usage scenario, the user's query or query result could contain sensitive information that the model provider should not see. And on the other hand, the model parameters themselves could be a valuable business secret or leak private training data. In such cases, neural network inference must be performed in a privacy preserving manner, for example, using secure multi-party computation (MPC).

We propose protocols for the private inference of neural networks and evaluate them within the Sharemind MPC secure computation framework. Our protocols are based on the per-tensor quantisation scheme in PyTorch which maps floating point model parameters to 8-bit integer values. Quantisation improves the efficiency of our protocols and our protocols are interoperable with models trained using PyTorch. We extend constant round integer convolution and matrix multiplication protocols for quantised model weights, propose constant round protocols for re-quantising values and analyse the optimal secret share bit width for efficient re-quantisation. The resulting protocols are used to evaluate the VGG16 image classification network with an amortised throughput of 24.3 s per image classification in a LAN setting.

Keywords: Multi-party computation · privacy-preserving machine learning · neural networks · secure inference

1 Introduction

Privacy-preserving inference of neural networks can enable new data driven applications. Predictive models using neural networks are widely and successfully used for image classification, spam filtering, text translation, speech recognition and in other fields. But for applications where the query and its result are particularly sensitive, neural networks have not made an impact. For example, for CSAM detection in messaging or cloud storage services as well as detection

P. Kieseberg et al. (Eds.): ARES 2026 Workshops, LNCS 16903, pp. 456–474, 2027.
https://doi.org/10.1007/978-3-032-37218-5_27

of rare medical conditions, existing implementations have triggered significant public privacy concerns [2,13,26].

To illustrate the security challenges, consider using neural networks for medical diagnosis as a service. The query and its result are obviously sensitive and should be seen only by the patient and their doctor. The model would be considered a medical device developed by some company at a great cost, meaning the model provider wants to keep it private. The model could also have been trained on sensitive data which could be extracted from the model parameters. Thus, the model parameters and query are secret data that belong to different parties and the goal of secure inference can be achieved with multi-party computation.

Multi-party computation (MPC) enables mutually distrusting parties to jointly compute on joint data without revealing secret information. The landscape of MPC is very diverse in terms of the security guarantees, the complexity of deployment, performance, the supported operations and programmability. All the possible approaches have their own benefits and drawbacks. For example, two-party protocols are the easiest to deploy but they require more complex cryptographic primitives and are generally less performant compared to three-party protocols with two honest parties. Actively secure protocols provide privacy and correctness guarantees against adversaries who can deviate from the protocol, yet they come with a performance penalty compared to similar passively secure protocols where the adversary must follow the protocol.

Although, an actively secure inference protocol can protect the correctness of model evaluation, it can not protect against an attack that is equivalent to one of the parties selecting a different input. Thus, active security is not sufficient to argue that the result is the correct evaluation of the correct model. In the medical diagnosis example, both the query and model provider are incentivised to provide the correct input and follow the protocol. If the secure computation is outsourced, similar incentives and organisational security measures must be in place to ensure correct evaluation of the protocol. However, if deviating from the protocol gives an advantage in leaking some private input, the protocol is not private. Privacy against passive adversaries is not sufficient when the data is as sensitive as, for example, medical records. Our protocol is private against an active adversary.

1.1 Our Contribution

We present honest-majority three-party protocols for evaluating neural networks where all parties are assumed to follow the protocol. Our protocol is private against an active adversary but ensures correctness only for a passive adversary. The privacy of the query, the model weights and the query result are protected. Our protocol does not require a preprocessing phase or correlated random inputs. We use the combination of input-private and secure components to obtain efficient secure protocols as outlined in [3].

We cover the evaluation of fully connected, convolution, ReLU and MaxPool layers. The core of the protocols is a new optimised matrix multiplication protocol and normalisation protocol for quantised values. We implement our protocols in the Sharemind MPC framework using its core three-party additive secret sharing scheme. Using the same secret sharing scheme enables the use of Sharemind MPC's large standard library and falling back on secure floating point computation for other activation functions. The protocols that we have developed form a library for privately evaluating common neural network architectures trained outside of MPC, for example using PyTorch.

We evaluate our implementation on the VGG16 [32] convolutional network for image classification. The VGG16 model has 138 million parameters, of which most are in the linear layers. As a reasonable mid range model, it has been used as a benchmark for many implementations (e.g. Falcon [33], XONN [30], FANNG-MPC [1], Orca [15], Piranha [34], PIGEON [12]).

The main goal in our protocol design is to minimise the communication complexity of the protocol without introducing costly cryptographic primitives such as pairings and homomorphic encryption. In this context, the main bottleneck is the memory footprint of the neural network parameters and its evaluation graph. This problem has been extensively studied in the machine-learning community [25,35]. The resulting quantised neural network models use integer arithmetic that is more efficient and easier to implement as MPC protocols. We establish the optimal bit width of the secret sharing to prevent overflow and enable efficient normalisation of shares while minimising communication in the protocols. Additionally, we precisely profile the execution of our protocol in different network settings to gain a clear view of where performance bottlenecks lie and which optimisation strategies should be further pursued.

2 Preliminaries

2.1 Secure Multi-party Computation

The goal of secure multi-party computation (MPC) is to enable distrusting parties to compute on their joint data while ensuring the privacy of the data. An MPC protocol is said to have active security if it ensures security with respect to any adversarial behaviour. Conversely, the protocol has passive security if security is ensured for participants that follow the protocol. In many cases, a protocol can ensure privacy against an active adversary while only ensuring correctness (and, therefore, security) against a passive adversary [11]. There are various concrete technologies used to build MPC protocols such as secret sharing, function secret sharing, garbled circuits and (fully) homomorphic encryption. In addition to these, secure hardware can be used to give similar guarantees. Each of these approaches has their own strengths and weaknesses, for further discussion see [21,31].

We focus on reducing the amount of communication needed to compute private inference with three parties and additive secret sharing. Often, secure computation protocols are split into a precomputation phase that generates correlated randomness and an online phase that uses the inputs of the parties and the correlated randomness to compute the results. Precomputation can be used to make the online phase very efficient but the combined complexity is often ignored. Efficient precomputation can be devised if the shape of the computation is known whereas optimizing more general protocol execution is difficult. In this work, we consider protocols without precomputation.

2.2 Three-Party Additive Secret Sharing

Our protocols are based on additive secret sharing over rings $\mathbb{Z}_{2^\ell}$. We denote a secret sharing of $x \in \mathbb{Z}_{2^\ell}$ as $[\![x]\!]_\ell = \{x_1, x_2, x_3\}$ where $x_1 + x_2 + x_3 = x \mod 2^\ell$. For brevity, the subscript ℓ is sometimes omitted. The computing parties are denoted as P_1, P_2 and P_3, P_{i+1} and P_{i-1} denote the next and previous parties respectively (the index rolls over). Similarly, we denote the share of $[\![x]\!]$ that belongs to party P_i as $[\![x]\!]^i$. Matrices are written using capital letters, e.g. X, and their elements in the ith row and jth column are denoted with the respective lowercase letter x_{ij}.

To secret share a value $x \in \mathbb{Z}_{2^\ell}$, uniformly sample x_1 and x_2 from $\mathbb{Z}_{2^\ell}$, set $x_3 \leftarrow x - x_1 - x_2 \mod 2^\ell$, give the share x_i to P_i. To reconstruct a secret shared value, receive the shares from the three parties and find the sum modulo 2^ℓ.

This secret sharing scheme is *perfectly private* with a threshold of 3-out-of-3, meaning that any set of two or fewer shares leaks no information about the underlying value and it can be completely reconstructed from three shares. Computing linear combinations of secret shared values requires no communication:

$$[\![x + y]\!] = \{x_1 + y_1, x_2 + y_2, x_3 + y_3\}$$
$$c \cdot [\![x]\!] = \{c \cdot x_1, c \cdot x_2, c \cdot x_3\}$$

Resharing is an operation that re-randomises the shares while keeping the same value. To reshare $[\![x]\!]$, each party P_i samples a random value r_i and sends it to the next party, the new secret sharing of x is then

$$\mathsf{reshare}([\![x]\!]) = \{x_1 + r_1 - r_3, x_2 + r_2 - r_1, x_3 + r_3 - r_2\}$$

As a common optimisation technique, each pair of parties can agree on a pseudorandom number generator seed beforehand so that both parties P_i and P_{i+1} can uniformly sample the same value instead of sending the sampled value, making the resharing protocol non-interactive.

Sometimes it is useful to share a secret value between just two parties such that $[\![x]\!]_\ell = \{x_1, x_2, 0\}$ and $x = x_1 + x_2 \mod 2^\ell$. A single-round interactive protocol for achieving this is denoted as $\mathsf{reshareToTwo}([\![x]\!])$.

Multiplication of shared values arises naturally from the distributive property of multiplication, see Algorithm 1. This protocol is a modification of the multiplication protocol proposed in [5] that also reshares the final output z before returning it as output. Removing the final reshare was discussed in [3]. While the final resharing can be important to ensure that the outputs are simulatable, it is not necessary to ensure privacy. It is possible to omit the final resharing when combining many multiplications, only resharing the final output of the computation. Hence, we can use this reduced multiplication protocol as a component

Algorithm 1. Multiplication Protocol [5]

Require: $[\![x]\!]$ and $[\![y]\!]$ are additively shared over $\mathbb{Z}_{2^\ell}$
Ensure: $[\![z]\!] = [\![x \cdot y]\!]$
  $[\![x']\!] \leftarrow \mathsf{reshare}([\![x]\!])$
  $[\![y']\!] \leftarrow \mathsf{reshare}([\![y]\!])$
  P_i sends $[\![x']\!]^i$ to P_{i+1} and $[\![y']\!]^i$ to P_{i-1}
  $[\![z]\!]^i \leftarrow [\![x']\!]^i [\![y']\!]^i + [\![x']\!]^{i+1} [\![y']\!]^i + [\![x']\!]^{i+1} [\![y']\!]^{i-1}$
  return $[\![z]\!]$

in matrix multiplication. Note that while the protocol preserves security against a passive adversary, it is perfectly private against the active adversary [28]. The latter means that while an active adversary may make the output of the protocol incorrect, it does not learn information about the private inputs from this protocol.

Note that after the communication steps, the final part of the multiplication protocol is local computation. We use this property in the convolution and matrix multiplication protocols (Algorithm 2) to reduce the required communication. The same multiplication protocol can be used for computing the binary AND operation in which case $x \in \mathbb{Z}_2$. The protocol for binary OR can also be constructed similarly.

2.3 Convolutional Neural Networks

Convolutional neural networks are used across a wide range of computer vision application domains, including image classification, medical imaging, and facial recognition. We use the VGG16 image classification model [32] as our motivating example. VGG16 consists of 13 convolution layers, 3 fully connected linear layers, 5 MaxPooling layers and ReLU activation functions. The model has 138 million parameters, most of which are in the linear layers. While VGG16 has been superseded by newer model architectures, models based on the same building blocks of convolution, linear and pooling layers with ReLU activations are still relevant for many computer vision tasks. In plaintext inference of VGG16 [32], convolution layers and fully connected layers form the majority of the computation costs. Thus, it is important that these layers are efficiently evaluated. Similarly, optimising the secure computation of convolution and fully connected layers is critical for efficient secure inference.

2.4 Quantisation

Quantisation reduces the memory footprint of neural network models by reducing the size and precision of model parameters. Generally, neural networks are trained with 32-bit or 16-bit floating point parameters but after training, for precise inference, less precise discretised parameters suffice. Many schemes for discretising the model parameters exist varying in the size of the parameters, accuracy trade-off and quantisation algorithm [10,18,20]. In plaintext inference, quantisation is used to fit very large models into the limited size but high-speed memory of GPUs. In private inference, it reduces the communication required for inference and simplifies the evaluation of the neural network's layers. While the non-quantised model requires floating point arithmetic, which is expensive in MPC, the quantised model requires mostly integer arithmetic. Note that in weight-only quantisation schemes, such as AWQ or GPTQ, quantised weights are converted back to floating point values for computing layer activations, thus these schemes are not viable for secret sharing.

In this work, we use per-tensor post-training 8-bit integer quantisation as is supported by PyTorch[1]. For a real number value x, the quantised value is

$$\bar{x} = \left\lfloor \frac{x}{\Delta} - z \right\rceil$$

where Δ is a scaling factor and z is the quantisation zero point, both of which are determined per each tensor in the computation. For 8-bit quantisation, the scaling factor and zero point are such that for all values x that an element of the tensor can take, the quantised value $\bar{x}$ is in the range $[0, 255]$ for unsigned or in $[-128, 127]$ for signed quantisation. The bit-width of the quantised values could be larger or smaller to either improve inference accuracy or reduce the memory footprint. The 8-bit quantisation was chosen as it has wide support among PyTorch modules, meaning that most neural networks in PyTorch can be automatically quantised to 8 bits.

2.5 Private Inference

In privacy-preserving machine learning (PPML), we are interested in ensuring the privacy of all or some of the following: the training data, the trained model, the input to an inference query and the query result. In private inference, the query of the client is protected and the client should not learn the model parameters. If implemented with MPC, then either the model is also protected or known to the computing parties. In this work, we are implementing a scenario where both the query and the model parameters are secret shared. A recent overview of PPML approaches can be found in [7,14]. For a benchmark, we consider VGG16 image classification model, which is a commonly used large benchmark for PPML. For example, it is supported by Falcon [33], XONN [30], FANNG-MPC [1], Orca [15], Piranha [34], PIGEON [12].

Using floating-point arithmetic in PPML is improving [29], but using fixed-point arithmetic is more common [1,33]. Approaches, such as [9,15,16,22], focus on using quantised models. Whereas, [34] uses approximations of the non-linear computations which reduces the accuracy of the results and [30] uses binary neural networks.

Significant work in PPML has been dedicated to optimizing the matrix multiplication and the inner product protocols. ABY3 [23] uses replicated secret sharing which allows to compute the additive shares of the inner product

[1] https://pytorch.org/docs/stable/quantization.html.

locally, whereas resharing is necessary to get the replicated shares of the output. However, the input privacy idea allows us to reuse the share throughout the matrix multiplication protocol and we do not need to reshare the final output. ASTRA [6], Blaze [27] and Swift [17] design secret sharing schemes to allow efficient operations for machine learning and also extend the ideas of ABY3. Note that these protocols rely on a precomputation phase.

Not all PPML frameworks and protocols consider the model parameters as secret inputs. Opening the model parameters to the computing parties results in protocols with much lower communication. However, if the model is not secret, then the query party could compute inference locally, making PPML unnecessary. If the model is kept secret from the query party but the computing parties are allowed to see it, then the deployment requires finding computing parties that can be trusted with the model but are also trusted to not collude to reveal the query. A PPML framework that ensures the secrecy of both the model and the query against an active adversary is most fitting for real-life deployment.

3 New Protocols for Private Inference

We propose secure computation protocols for evaluating quantised neural network models such that the model parameters, queries and results are secret shared. The model is secret shared among the MPC computing parties. An input party secret shares their query, sends shares to the computing parties and receives shares of the output.

3.1 Fully Connected and Convolution Layers

Given real number matrix X with elements x_{ij}, a matrix consisting of quantised elements $\overline{x_{ij}}$ is such that

$$x_{ij} = \Delta_x \cdot (\overline{x_{ij}} - z_x)$$

where Δ_x is the scaling factor and z_x is the zero-point specific to the matrix X. The scaling factor and zero-point are determined during neural network quantisation for each tensor in the network evaluation and are not considered secret inputs. It is possible to keep them confidential, but it introduces a computational overhead. Moreover, the potential information leakage is minor compared to leakage from the outputs of the neural network itself.

Let the matrix product $P = X \cdot Y$ have elements p_{ij}. The real matrix products can be computed in terms of the quantised matrices as such:

$$\begin{aligned} p_{ij} &= \sum_k x_{ik} \cdot y_{kj} = \sum_k \Delta_x(\overline{x_{ik}} - z_x) \cdot \Delta_y(\overline{y_{kj}} - z_y) = \\ &= \Delta_x \Delta_y \cdot \sum_k (\overline{x_{ik}} - z_x)(\overline{y_{kj}} - z_y) \end{aligned}$$

and the quantised matrix product is computed as such:

$$\overline{p_{ij}} = \left\lfloor \frac{\Delta_x \Delta_y}{\Delta_p} \cdot \left(\sum_k (\overline{x_{ik}} - z_x)(\overline{y_{ki}} - z_y) \right) + z_p \right\rceil . \tag{1}$$

Algorithm 2. Matrix Multiplication Protocol

Require: $[\![X]\!]$ and $[\![Y]\!]$ are matrices of additive shares over $\mathbb{Z}_{2^\ell}$ with dimensions (M, K) and (K, N) respectively.
Ensure: $[\![W]\!] = [\![XY]\!]$
  $[\![X']\!] \leftarrow \mathsf{reshare}([\![X]\!])$
  $[\![Y']\!] \leftarrow \mathsf{reshare}([\![Y]\!])$
  each party P_i sends their share of $[\![X']\!]$ to party P_{i+1}
  each party P_i sends their share of $[\![Y']\!]$ to party P_{i-1}
  for $m \in \{1, \ldots, M\}$ **do**
    for $n \in \{1, \ldots, N\}$ **do**
      for each party P_i:
      $[\![w_{mn}]\!]^i \leftarrow \sum_{k=1}^{K} [\![x'_{mk}]\!]^i \cdot [\![y'_{kn}]\!]^i + [\![x'_{mk}]\!]^{i+1} \cdot [\![y'_{kn}]\!]^i + [\![x'_{mk}]\!]^{i+1} \cdot [\![y'_{kn}]\!]^{i-1}$
    end for
  end for
  return $[\![W]\!] = ([\![w_{mn}]\!])$

In the default PyTorch quantisation scheme, input and activation tensor are quantised to 8-bit unsigned integers, model weight tensors are quantised to 8-bit signed integers, the zero-point is an 8-bit unsigned integer and the scale is a 32-bit floating point value. When evaluating Eq. 1, the quantised matrix element offset by the zero-point $(\overline{x_{ik}} - z_x)$, is stored as a 16-bit integer and the product and sum are stored as 32-bit integers.

Our secure protocol for quantised matrix multiplication must compute Eq. 1. Thus, the protocol steps are integer matrix multiplication, multiplication by a scalar fraction and clamping the result to 8 bits. The integer matrix multiplication uses the secret shared multiplication protocol from Algorithm 1, but since in matrix multiplication each matrix element appears as an operand in many scalar multiplications we can reuse the communication from earlier scalar multiplications. In fact, we can communicate the shares of the input matrices beforehand and the remainder of the integer matrix multiplication is only local operations. The optimised protocol is detailed in Algorithm 2. Note that we optimise the full matrix multiplication not just the inner products within the matrix multiplication.

Suppose our input matrices have sizes (M, K) and (K, N), then the unoptimised matrix multiplication consists of $M \cdot K \cdot N$ multiplications, each requiring sending two shares per party. As a result of reusing the sent shares between the scalar multiplications, only $K(M + N)$ shares must be sent per party for the entire integer matrix multiplication. Note that this is the same as the online communication required by the Beaver triple based multiplication using matrix triples [8,24]. However, Beaver triple based multiplication also requires communication in the precomputation phase and the matrix shapes must be known in advance. We focus on fully-online multiplication to accommodate variable size matrices during runtime.

Intuitively, this optimised matrix multiplication protocol is private as no party sees any more information than they would if the matrix multiplication

Algorithm 3. Secure Quantised Matrix Multiplication Protocol

Require: $[\![X]\!]$ and $[\![Y]\!]$ are matrices of additive shares of $\mathbb{Z}_{2^{32}}$, $\Delta_x, \Delta_y, \Delta_w, z_x, z_y, z_w$ are public constants.
Ensure: $[\![W]\!]$ is the quantised matrix multiplication of X and Y.
  $[\![X']\!] \leftarrow [\![X]\!] - z_x$
  $[\![Y']\!] \leftarrow [\![Y]\!] - z_y$
  $[\![A]\!] \leftarrow \mathsf{matmul}([\![X']\!], [\![Y']\!])$ ▷ Algorithm 2
  $s \leftarrow \frac{\Delta_x \Delta_y}{\Delta_w}$
  for $[\![a_{ij}]\!] \in [\![A]\!]$ **do**
    $[\![a'_{ij}]\!] \leftarrow \mathsf{reshareToTwo}(a_{ij})$
    $[\![c]\!] \leftarrow \mathsf{carry}([\![a'_{ij}]\!])$ ▷ Algorithm 4
    $[\![w'_{ij}]\!] \leftarrow [\![\lfloor s \cdot a'_{ij} \rceil]\!] - \lfloor s \cdot 2^{32} \cdot [\![c]\!] \rceil + z_w$
    $[\![w_{ij}]\!] \leftarrow \mathsf{clamp}([\![w'_{ij}]\!])$ ▷ Algorithm 5
  end for
  return $[\![W]\!] = (w_{ij})$

were performed using the scalar multiplication protocol in Algorithm 1. On the other hand, significant reuse of the shares might introduce strong dependencies between the different shares that we get as an output and introduce a security risk if published [3]. Formally, the multiplication protocol is a composition of input private parts that makes it input private itself [3]. Hence, using the blueprint for secure protocols from [3], we can use this multiplication to build secure protocols if the outputs of the matrix multiplication are consumed by other secure computation protocols that ensure that the low randomness in the outputs is hidden when they are used. This is indeed the case for the full neural network evaluation that uses this multiplication protocol.

Using the integer multiplication as a sub-protocol, we construct the protocol for the quantised matrix multiplication (Eq. 1) as Algorithm 3. The final part of the protocol normalises the result of the integer matrix multiplication to the range of the quantised output. The protocols required for this are described in the following subsection.

The convolution protocol is optimised similarly to matrix multiplication by sending the shares of the image and the kernel before performing the rest of the protocol locally. Thus, the communication pattern of the convolution protocol is the same as the matrix multiplication protocol and the only difference is in the local computation. As with the matrix multiplication protocol, the privacy of the convolution protocol follows from the input-privacy argument.

3.2 Normalisation of Quantised Shares

After the integer matrix multiplication step in Algorithm 3, the elements of the resulting matrix are not in the 8-bit interval of the quantised output. Thus, the result needs to be scaled by the scaling factor and clamped to the range of 8-bit signed integers. The scaling factor $s = \frac{\Delta_x \Delta_y}{\Delta_w}$ is represented as a public 32-bit floating point value.

To scale a secret shared integer by a floating point value, it is not sufficient to simply multiply each share with the float. To simplify the explanation, let $[\![x]\!] = \{x_1, x_2\}$ such that $x_1 + x_2 = x \mod N$, then $x_1 + x_2 = x - c \cdot N$ where $c \in \{0, 1\}$. By multiplying the shares with s we get $sx_1 + sx_2 = sx + scN$, since scN rounded to the nearest integer is not necessarily divisible by N, $sx_1 + sx_2 \neq$ sx mod N. To get the correct scaled value $[\![y]\!] = [\![\lfloor s \cdot x \rceil]\!]$, we have to correct for the carry c by, for example, setting $y_1 = \lfloor sx_1 \rceil - \lfloor scN \rceil \mod N$ and $y_2 = \lfloor sx_1 \rceil \mod N$. Since the carry c leaks information about x, we must compute the carry and perform the correction step under secret sharing.

One option for finding the carry is through bit decomposition using a process similar to Algorithm 6 but such an approach is very costly. Instead, we can take advantage of the fact that we use an integer ring for secret sharing that is much larger than the plaintext values. If we look at the binary representation of the value x and its shares x_1 and x_2, then c is the final carry bit of the addition of x_1 and x_2. The carry c can be computed as such:

$$c = (x_1[-1] \cdot x_2[-1]) + (c_{in} \cdot (x_1[-1] + x_2[-1]))$$

where the suffix $[-1]$ indicates the highest bit of an integer and c_{in} is the carry from adding the second to last bits. But, if $x < N/2$, the highest bit of x is 0 meaning that c does not depend on the incoming carry. This means that we can compute c without having to ripple the carry bits through the entire addition of x_1 and x_2. The resulting protocol is detailed in Algorithm 4.

Algorithm 4. Carry Bit Protocol

Require: $[\![x]\!] = \{0, x_2, x_3\}$, $x \in \mathbb{Z}_N$ and $x < N/2$.
Ensure: $[\![c]\!]$ such that $x_2 + x_3 = x - c \cdot N$
  $[\![a]\!]_2 \leftarrow \{0, \mathsf{highestBit}(x_2), 0\}$
  $[\![b]\!]_2 \leftarrow \{0, 0, \mathsf{highestBit}(x_3)\}$
  $[\![c]\!] \leftarrow \mathsf{shareconv}([\![a]\!]_2 \vee [\![b]\!]_2)$
  return $[\![c]\!]$

The sub-protocol $\mathsf{shareconv}([\![x]\!]_2)$ takes a value secret shared in a smaller ring and returns the same value secret shared in a larger ring [5].

In the clamping protocol (Algorithm 5), we need to decide whether the input is greater than 255, less than 0 or in-between the two and choose the appropriate output. Notice that clamping is not equivalent to taking the bottom 8 bits of the input. In the protocol, we convert secret shares of x over $\mathbb{Z}_{2^\ell}$ to binary shares $[\![x_1]\!]_2, \ldots, [\![x_\ell]\!]_2$ where

$$x = \sum_{i=1}^{\ell} 2^{i-1} x_i.$$

We call this conversion bit extraction (Algorithm 6). In this representation, we can compute whether x is already in the 8-bit range or if it is over or under it.

Algorithm 5. Secure Clamp to Interval [0, 255] Protocol

Require: $[\![x]\!]$ is a two's complement signed integer additively shared over $\mathbb{Z}_{2^{32}}$.

Ensure: $[\![y]\!] = \begin{cases} [\![x]\!] \text{ if } 0 \leq x \leq 255 \\ [\![255]\!] \text{ if } x > 255 \\ [\![0]\!] \text{ if } x < 0 \end{cases}$

$[\![x_1]\!]_2, \ldots, [\![x_{32}]\!]_2 \leftarrow \mathsf{bitExtract}([\![x]\!])$ ▷ Algorithm 6
$[\![c]\!]_2 \leftarrow \mathsf{foldOR}([\![x_9]\!]_2, \ldots, [\![x_{31}]\!]_2)$
$[\![a]\!] \leftarrow \mathsf{choose}([\![c]\!]_2, [\![255]\!], [\![x]\!])$
$[\![y]\!] \leftarrow \mathsf{choose}([\![x_{32}]\!]_2, [\![0]\!], [\![a]\!])$
return $[\![y]\!]$

In Algorithm 5, $[\![c]\!]_2 = \mathsf{foldOR}([\![x_1]\!]_2, \ldots, [\![x_n]\!]_2)$ is a sub-protocol call, which computes

$$c = \bigvee_{i=1}^{n} x_i$$

through a folding algorithm, giving a protocol with $O(\log_2(n))$ communication depth. The sub-protocol $\mathsf{choose}([\![b]\!]_2, [\![x]\!], [\![y]\!])$ outputs the secret sharing of either x or y based on the value of the control bit b. Both of these sub-protocols are introduced in [5].

The bit extraction protocol (Algorithm 6) works by sharing the input between two parties and using those two shares as if they were binary secret shares, which are then added using a binary adder circuit. The binary adder circuit can be implemented using secret shared operations over $\mathbb{Z}_2$. For brevity, we detail a simple binary addition protocol based on the ripple-carry adder in Algorithm 7 but use a more efficient implementation based on the Kogge-Stone adder [19] in the actual protocol. The protocol based on the Kogge-Stone adder trades increased communication for fewer rounds and simpler local computation.

Algorithm 6. Bit Extraction Protocol [19]

Require: $[\![x]\!]$ is additively shared over $\mathbb{Z}_{2^\ell}$
Ensure: $[\![y_1]\!]_2, \ldots, [\![y_\ell]\!]_2$ such that $x = \sum_{i=0}^{\ell} 2^{i-1} \cdot y_i$
$[\![x']\!] \leftarrow \mathsf{reshareToTwo}([\![x]\!])$
Let $[\![x']\!] = \{0, a, b\}$
$[\![a_i]\!]_2 \leftarrow \{0, a[i], 0\}$ for $i \in 1, \ldots, \ell$
$[\![b_i]\!]_2 \leftarrow \{0, 0, b[i]\}$ for $i \in 1, \ldots, \ell$
$([\![y_i]\!]_2)_{i=1}^{\ell} \leftarrow \mathsf{binAdd}([\![a_1]\!], \ldots [\![a_\ell]\!], [\![b_1]\!], \ldots, [\![b_\ell]\!])$
return $[\![y_1]\!], \ldots, [\![y_\ell]\!]$

After scaling and clamping, all but the last layer of VGG16 are followed by the ReLU activation function which simply outputs 0 if the input x is negative and x otherwise. In our quantised scheme, we must compare x against the zero point of

Algorithm 7. Ripple-Carry Adder Protocol

Require: $[\![x_1]\!]_2, \ldots, [\![x_\ell]\!]_2$ and $[\![y_1]\!]_2, \ldots, [\![y_\ell]\!]_2$ such that $x = \sum_{i=1}^{\ell} 2^{i-1} \cdot x_i$ and $y = \sum_{i=1}^{\ell} 2^{i-1} \cdot y_i$
Ensure: $[\![z_1]\!]_2, \ldots, [\![z_\ell]\!]_2$ s.t. $\sum_{i=1}^{\ell} 2^{i-1} \cdot z_i = x + y$
  $[\![c_0]\!] \leftarrow [\![0]\!]_2$
  for $i \in 1, \ldots, \ell$ **do**
    $[\![z_i]\!] \leftarrow [\![x_i]\!] \oplus [\![y_i]\!] \oplus [\![c_{i-1}]\!]$
    $[\![c_i]\!] \leftarrow ([\![x_i]\!] \wedge [\![y_i]\!]) \oplus ([\![c_{i-1}]\!] \wedge ([\![x_i]\!] \oplus [\![y_i]\!]))$
  end for
  return $[\![z_1]\!], \ldots, [\![z_\ell]\!]$

the corresponding tensor instead. Because after clamping, x is necessarily an 8-bit value, we can truncate the shares of x and perform ReLU on $\mathbb{Z}_{2^8}$. Truncation of shares is a local only operation. The protocol for ReLU is given in Algorithm 8, it uses the integer comparison protocol from [4].

Algorithm 8. Quantised ReLU Protocol

Require: $[\![x]\!]$ and zero point z
Ensure: $[\![y]\!] = \begin{cases} [\![z]\!] & \text{if } x < z \\ [\![x]\!] & \text{otherwise} \end{cases}$
  $[\![c]\!] \leftarrow \mathsf{lessThan}([\![x]\!], z)$
  return $\mathsf{choose}([\![c]\!], [\![z]\!], [\![x]\!])$

The protocol for the 2×2 MaxPooling layer in VGG16 is implemented similarly to the ReLU protocol and also performed on shares in $\mathbb{Z}_{2^8}$. After ReLU and MaxPooling, the shares are converted back to $\mathbb{Z}_{2^{32}}$ using the share conversion protocol from [5].

The communication cost in terms of total bits sent between all parties over all rounds and the number of communication rounds are given in Table 1. In low bandwidth network settings, the amount of communicated bits is the constraining factor, in high latency settings, the number of rounds is the constraining factor. Note that for bit extraction and clamp protocols, we give the communication amount for the implementation that has been machine optimised by the PDSL [19] compiler. The compiler's optimisations remove redundant messages between parties, reducing communication slightly.

Table 1. Communication amount and round count of selected protocols.

Protocol	Input	Comm. bits	Rounds
Mult. (Algorithm 1)	$x, y \in \mathbb{Z}_{2^\ell}$	6ℓ	1
Matrix mult.(Algorithm 2)	$X \in \mathbb{Z}_{2^\ell}^{M\times K} Y \in \mathbb{Z}_{2^\ell}^{K\times N}$	$6\ell \cdot K(M+N)$	1
Carry bit (Algorithm 4)	$x \in \mathbb{Z}_{2^\ell}$	$6+\ell$	2
Bin. add (Algorithm 7)	$x, y \in \mathbb{Z}_{2^\ell}$	12ℓ	$\ell - 1$
Bit extract (Algorithm 6)	$x \in \mathbb{Z}_{2^{32}}$	339	32
Bit extract [19]	$x \in \mathbb{Z}_{2^{32}}$	1120	7
Clamp (Algorithm 5)	$x \in \mathbb{Z}_{2^{32}}$	1646	15

3.3 Analysis of Required Share Size

In the implementation of our PPML framework, we use 32-bit shares to store the 8-bit quantised weights and neuron activation values of the network. The larger share size means that the results of arithmetic operations on shared values will not overflow and we can omit an expensive share extension protocol. As a drawback, due to the larger shares, the communication amount and round count of our protocols is larger than it would be with smaller shares.

The analysis to substantiate the choice of 32-bit shares follows the steps of the protocol. The input values and weights of a quantised neural network layer are 8-bit integers. Assuming the zero-point of the input matrices is also an 8-bit value, the result of subtracting the zero-point from a matrix can fit into 9 bits. Note that in the PyTorch plaintext implementation of the quantisation scheme, this intermediate result is 16-bit. Within the matrix multiplication or convolution, the result of a scalar multiplication of 9-bit values is 18-bit. A number of these products is summed together, depending on the matrix dimensions or convolution kernel size. With 32-bit shares, in the worst case, the summation will overflow with 2^{14} addends. In VGG16, the largest number of addends in a single layer is 2^{12}, thus the highest bit of the sum will necessarily be 0, as required for the optimised carry bit protocol in Algorithm 4.

4 Performance Evaluation

We implement our protocols within the Sharemind MPC framework. The carry, clamp, ReLU and MaxPool protocols are implemented using PDSL, a domain specific language for writing MPC protocols [19]. The compilation process of PDSL performs automatic rewrites of the computation graph to optimise arithmetic expressions. The compiler also schedules expression evaluation such that a minimal number of communication rounds is required. A static analyser is used on the optimised computation graph to automatically prove privacy against an active adversary [28]. The code generated from the PDSL protocol implementations is single-threaded LLVM IR.

The rest of the protocols are implemented in C++. The local computation part of matrix multiplication and convolution protocols is deferred to torchlib, the C++ backend library of PyTorch. The torchlib library performs matrix multiplication and convolution on multiple CPU threads. The library is capable of performing the computations on GPUs and other accelerators but we did not have the specialised hardware to utilise this.

4.1 Analysis and Comparison to Related Work

We perform our measurements on a cluster of three servers, each has two Intel Xeon E5-2640 v3 2.6 GHz CPUs, 128 GB of system memory and 10 Gbit/s dedicated network links with each of the other servers. We use traffic shaping to simulate network conditions with lower bandwidth and higher latency. We set bandwidth to 10 Gbit/s and RTT (round-trip time) to 2 ms to simulate a deployment with dedicated network links between computing parties and a network with 1 Gbit/s bandwidth and 10 ms RTT to simulate separate data centres within the same region. Note that RTT includes the network latency in both directions.

In Fig 1, the private inference of three layers of the VGG16 model in a LAN setting is visualised. The coloured areas of the time series indicate phases of the computation and the blue bars indicate communication between the computing parties in Gbit/s. Deeper layers within the network have more parameters but smaller output sizes and thus lower overall computation time. In deeper layers of the network, the integer convolution protocol or integer matrix multiplication protocol take up a larger part of the computation time with low network utilisation, indicating an opportunity for optimisation using parallelisation and hardware acceleration.

Note that in Fig 1, network utilisation is measured in aggregate over all three parties, thus the theoretical maximum utilisation is 30 Gbit/s. In all layers, the protocol execution never reaches this theoretical maximum, indicating that in the LAN setting, the bottleneck lies in the local computation steps.

Table 2. Total inference time of VGG16 in various network conditions.

Setting	Inference time (seconds)			Amortisedinference time
	batch=1	batch=10	batch=20	
10 Gbit/s2 ms RTT	84.0	259.6	485.4	24.3
1 Gbit/s2 ms RTT	103.7	422.7	831.5	41.6
1 Gbit/s10 ms RTT	108.4	431.1	833.2	41.7

The total private inference time of the quantised VGG16 model in three different network conditions is given in Table 2. We measured the inference time

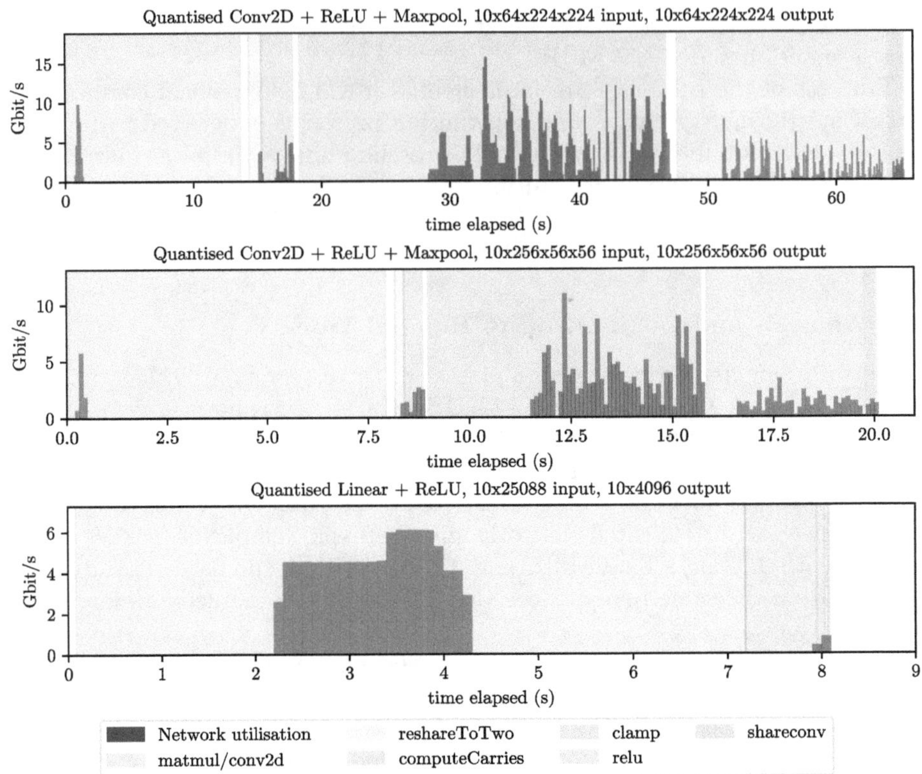

Fig. 1. Performance measurement of private inference of selected layers in the VGG16 model, 10 Gbit/s bandwidth, 2 ms RTT.

for batches of 1, 10 and 20 images, the input image size is $3 \times 224 \times 224$. In the LAN setting, the amortised throughput of inference is 24.3 s per image and the time to first result is 84 s. The total communication between all three parties is 7.1 GB for inferencing one image.

While multiple papers benchmark private inference using the VGG16 model, the results are unfortunately not directly comparable. The FANNG-MPC framework performs VGG16 inference in 534 s [1] but this result does not include preprocessing time. The Piranha platform reports VGG16 inference in 0.469 s with 88.39 GB of communication [34], this result is inconsistent with the reported network setting. The PIGEON framework performs VGG16 inference on a batch of 192 CIFAR-10 images in 0.92 s and on ImageNet images in 25.10 s [12]. It is unclear from the reported results how the different input image sizes affect the model architecture as the VGG16 model takes an input of size $3 \times 224 \times 224$. The PIGEON framework benchmarking results also claim to require 10 MB of total communication for evaluating the linear layers of VGG16 which contain 123 million parameters. The Falcon protocol implementation [33] computes the inference of a 32×32 image with the VGG16 model in 0.79 s (1.4 s reported in [34]). For a direct comparison of protocols, equivalent implementations and testing scenarios are needed.

5 Conclusion

We showed that the amortised running time of private inference of a deep convolutional neural network with private input, weights and output is 24 s in an ideal network setting. In a high bandwidth setting, further optimisation using parallelisation of local computations is substantiated. In low bandwidth settings, only a large reduction in the communication of the underlying protocols would improve performance significantly. While the presented protocols are applied to an image classification model, they are mostly applicable to other neural network architectures as well. Our chosen security setting with three parties, honest majority and privacy against an active adversary is well suited for a real world deployment. Reducing the number of computing parties to two or protecting against a dishonest majority would require much more expensive protocols that are based on asymmetric encryption. Adding a correctness guarantee against active adversaries would increase the communication of the protocols while not making a significant impact in terms of real-world security.

Acknowledgments. The research was supported by the European Union through the European Defence Fund (EDF) under Grant Agreement No. 101121405, the Office of Naval Research Global (ONRG) under grant number N62909-23-1-2046, the Estonian Research Council through PRG1844, and the Estonian Ministry of Education and Research, through the Estonian Centre of Excellence in AI (EXAI), grant number TK213.

Disclosure of Interests. The authors have no competing interests to declare that are relevant to the content of this article.

References

1. Aaraj, N., et al.: FANNG-MPC: framework for artificial neural networks and generic MPC. IACR Trans. Cryptogr. Hardw. Embed. Syst. **2025**(1), 1–36 (2025). https://doi.org/10.46586/TCHES.V2025.I1.1-36
2. Belanger, A.: Apple hit with $1.2b lawsuit after killing controversial CSAM-detecting tool. https://arstechnica.com/tech-policy/2024/12/thousands-of-child-sex-abuse-victims-sue-apple-for-lax-csam-reporting/ (2024), ars Technica. Accessed 24 Oct 2025
3. Bogdanov, D., Laud, P., Laur, S., Pullonen, P.: From input private to universally composable secure multi-party computation primitives. In: IEEE 27th Computer Security Foundations Symposium, CSF 2014, pp. 184–198. IEEE Computer Society (2014). https://doi.org/10.1109/CSF.2014.21
4. Bogdanov, D., Laur, S., Willemson, J.: Sharemind: A framework for fast privacy-preserving computations. In: Jajodia, S., Lopez, J. (eds.) Computer Security - ESORICS 2008, pp. 192–206. Springer, Berlin Heidelberg, Berlin, Heidelberg (2008)

5. Bogdanov, D., Niitsoo, M., Toft, T., Willemson, J.: High-performance secure multiparty computation for data mining applications. Int. J. Inf. Secur. **11**(6), 403–418 (2012). https://doi.org/10.1007/s10207-012-0177-2
6. Chaudhari, H., Choudhury, A., Patra, A., Suresh, A.: ASTRA: high throughput 3PC over rings with application to secure prediction. In: Sion, R., Papamanthou, C. (eds.) ACM SIGSAC Conference on Cloud Computing Security Workshop, CCSW (CCS) 2019, pp. 81–92. ACM (2019). https://doi.org/10.1145/3338466.3358922
7. Chen, C., Wei, L., Xie, J., Shi, Y.: Privacy-preserving machine learning based on cryptography: a survey. ACM Trans. Knowl. Discov. Data **19**(4) (2025). https://doi.org/10.1145/3729234
8. Chen, H., Kim, M., Razenshteyn, I.P., Rotaru, D., Song, Y., Wagh, S.: Maliciously secure matrix multiplication with applications to private deep learning. In: Moriai, S., Wang, H. (eds.) Advances in Cryptology - ASIACRYPT 2020. LNCS, vol. 12493, pp. 31–59. Springer (2020). https://doi.org/10.1007/978-3-030-64840-4_2
9. Dalskov, A.P.K., Escudero, D., Keller, M.: Secure evaluation of quantized neural networks. Proc. Priv. Enhanc. Technol. **2020**(4), 355–375 (2020). https://doi.org/10.2478/POPETS-2020-0077
10. Frantar, E., Ashkboos, S., Hoefler, T., Alistarh, D.: GPTQ: accurate post-training quantization for generative pre-trained transformers (2023). https://arxiv.org/abs/2210.17323
11. Genkin, D., Ishai, Y., Prabhakaran, M., Sahai, A., Tromer, E.: Circuits resilient to additive attacks with applications to secure computation. In: Shmoys, D.B. (ed.) Symposium on Theory of Computing, STOC 2014, pp. 495–504. ACM (2014). https://doi.org/10.1145/2591796.2591861
12. Harth-Kitzerow, C., Wang, Y., Rajat, R., Carle, G., Annavaram, M.: PIGEON: a high throughput framework for private inference of neural networks using secure multiparty computation. Proc. Priv. Enhancing Technol. (2025). https://doi.org/10.56553/POPETS-2025-0090
13. Hern, A.: Royal free breached UK data law in 1.6m patient deal with Google's deepmind. https://www.theguardian.com/technology/2017/jul/03/google-deepmind-16m-patient-royal-free-deal-data-protection-act (2017), the Guardian. Accessed 24 Oct 2025
14. Heydari, G., Mahdavi, M., Mala, H.: A review on secure inference from neural networks. SN Comput. Sci. **6**(6), 668 (2025). https://doi.org/10.1007/S42979-025-04190-Z
15. Jawalkar, N., Gupta, K., Basu, A., Chandran, N., Gupta, D., Sharma, R.: Orca: FSS-based secure training and inference with GPUs. In: IEEE Symposium on Security and Privacy, SP 2024, pp. 597–616. IEEE (2024). https://doi.org/10.1109/SP54263.2024.00063
16. Keller, M., Sun, K.: Secure quantized training for deep learning. In: Chaudhuri, K., Jegelka, S., Song, L., Szepesvári, C., Niu, G., Sabato, S. (eds.) International Conference on Machine Learning, ICML 2022. Proceedings of Machine Learning Research, vol. 162, pp. 10912–10938. PMLR (2022). https://proceedings.mlr.press/v162/keller22a.html
17. Koti, N., Pancholi, M., Patra, A., Suresh, A.: SWIFT: super-fast and robust privacy-preserving machine learning. In: Bailey, M.D., Greenstadt, R. (eds.) 30th USENIX Security Symposium 2021. pp. 2651–2668. USENIX Association (2021). https://www.usenix.org/conference/usenixsecurity21/presentation/koti
18. Krishnamoorthi, R.: Quantizing deep convolutional networks for efficient inference: a whitepaper (2018). https://arxiv.org/abs/1806.08342

19. Laud, P., Randmets, J.: A domain-specific language for low-level secure multi-party computation protocols. In: 22nd ACM SIGSAC Conference on Computer and Communications Security. CCS '15, Association for Computing Machinery (2015). https://doi.org/10.1145/2810103.2813664
20. Lin, J., et al.: AWQ: activation-aware weight quantization for LLM compression and acceleration (2024). https://arxiv.org/abs/2306.00978
21. Lindell, Y.: Secure multiparty computation. Commun. ACM **64**(1), 86–96 (2021). https://doi.org/10.1145/3387108
22. Lu, T., Zhang, B., Zhang, X., Ren, K.: A new PPML paradigm for quantized models. In: 32nd Annual Network and Distributed System Security Symposium, NDSS 2025. The Internet Society (2025). https://www.ndss-symposium.org/ndss-paper/a-new-ppml-paradigm-for-quantized-models/
23. Mohassel, P., Rindal, P.: Aby3: a mixed protocol framework for machine learning. In: Lie, D., Mannan, M., Backes, M., Wang, X. (eds.) PACM SIGSAC Conference on Computer and Communications Security, CCS 2018. pp. 35–52. ACM (2018). https://doi.org/10.1145/3243734.3243760
24. Mohassel, P., Zhang, Y.: SecureML: a system for scalable privacy-preserving machine learning. In: 2017 IEEE Symposium on Security and Privacy, SP 2017, pp. 19–38. IEEE Computer Society (2017). https://doi.org/10.1109/SP.2017.12
25. Nagel, M., Fournarakis, M., Amjad, R.A., Bondarenko, Y., van Baalen, M., Blankevoort, T.: A white paper on neural network quantization (2021). https://arxiv.org/abs/2106.08295
26. Ossowski, Y.: Time is running out for EU member states to decide on chat control. https://www.euronews.com/next/2025/09/05/time-is-running-out-for-eu-member-states-to-decide-on-chat-control (2025). euronews. Accessed 24 Sept 2025
27. Patra, A., Suresh, A.: BLAZE: blazing fast privacy-preserving machine learning. In: 27th Annual Network and Distributed System Security Symposium, NDSS 2020, San Diego, California, USA, February 23-26, 2020. The Internet Society (2020). https://www.ndss-symposium.org/ndss-paper/blaze-blazing-fast-privacy-preserving-machine-learning/
28. Pettai, M., Laud, P.: Automatic proofs of privacy of secure multi-party computation protocols against active adversaries. In: Fournet, C., Hicks, M.W., Viganò, L. (eds.) IEEE 28th Computer Security Foundations Symposium, CSF 2015, pp. 75–89. IEEE Computer Society (2015). https://doi.org/10.1109/CSF.2015.13
29. Rathee, D., Bhattacharya, A., Gupta, D., Sharma, R., Song, D.: Secure floating-point training. In: Calandrino, J.A., Troncoso, C. (eds.) 32nd USENIX Security Symposium 2023, pp. 6329–6346. USENIX Association (2023). https://www.usenix.org/conference/usenixsecurity23/presentation/rathee
30. Riazi, M.S., Samragh, M., Chen, H., Laine, K., Lauter, K.E., Koushanfar, F.: XONN: XNOR-based oblivious deep neural network inference. In: Heninger, N., Traynor, P. (eds.) 28th USENIX Security Symposium 2019, pp. 1501–1518. USENIX Association (2019). https://www.usenix.org/conference/usenixsecurity19/presentation/riazi
31. Ricciato, F., Kubo, B., Pullonen-Raudvere, P., Kisand, A.D., Talviste, R., Tali, K.: JOCONDE D2.1 Technology Survey and Analysis. Tech. rep., European Union (2025). https://cros.ec.europa.eu/joconde
32. Simonyan, K., Zisserman, A.: Very deep convolutional networks for large-scale image recognition (2015). http://arxiv.org/abs/1409.1556

33. Wagh, S., Tople, S., Benhamouda, F., Kushilevitz, E., Mittal, P., Rabin, T.: FALCON: honest-majority maliciously secure framework for private deep learning. Proc. Priv. Enhancing Technol. **2021**(1), 188–208 (2021). https://doi.org/10.2478/POPETS-2021-0011
34. Watson, J., Wagh, S., Popa, R.A.: Piranha: a GPU platform for secure computation. In: Butler, K.R.B., Thomas, K. (eds.) 31st USENIX Security Symposium 2022, pp. 827–844. USENIX Association (2022). https://www.usenix.org/conference/usenixsecurity22/presentation/watson
35. Wei, L., Ma, Z., Yang, C., Yao, Q.: Advances in the neural network quantization: a comprehensive review. Appl. Sci. **14**(17) (2024). https://doi.org/10.3390/app14177445, https://www.mdpi.com/2076-3417/14/17/7445

Threat Modeling for Digital Twin-Driven Agri-Food Supply Chain

Sabah Suhail[1,2(✉)], Mubashar Iqbal[3], George D. O'Mahony[1], and Kieran Mclaughlin[2]

[1] Munster Technological University, Cork, Ireland
{Sabah.Suhail,GeorgeD.OMahony}@mtu.ie
[2] Queens University Belfast, Belfast, UK
kieran.mclaughlin@qub.ac.uk
[3] University of Tartu, Tartu, Estonia
mubashar.iqbal@ut.ee

Abstract. Digital twins (DT) are increasingly deployed across agri-food supply chains to support monitoring, optimization, and decision-making. The bidirectional interactions between DTs and their cyber-physical system (CPS) create complex security risks that span both the digital and physical domains. Compromised physical assets can serve as a springboard for attacks on the DT, while tampering with data, resources, or services in the DT can, in turn, propagate to the CPS, disrupting its operations and decision-making. Consequently, security analysis must consider all three dimensions, including CPS, DT, and their bidirectional interactions. In DT-driven agri-food supply chains, such analyses remain underexplored. To address this gap, we propose a six-step STRIDE-based threat modeling that encompasses DTs and their bidirectional interactions, following a CPS-first approach to DT construction. Using a strawberry greenhouse, which represents the pre-harvest phase of the strawberry supply chain, as a use case, we identify threats and assess their impact on greenhouse operations. We also examine security risks across DT lifecycle phases, design-and-engineering, operation-and-maintenance, and end-of-life, adopting a DT-first perspective to highlight how lifecycle decisions influence system exposure and operational risk. The proposed methodology enables greenhouse operators and agricultural engineers to systematically identify threat origins, determine affected components, and anticipate how security risks evolve across the DT lifecycle.

Keywords: Cyber-Physical System (CPS) · Cybersecurity · Digital Twin (DT) · STRIDE · Threat modeling

1 Introduction

In agri-food supply chains, digital twins (DT) are increasingly adopted across multiple stages, from primary agricultural production to post-harvest handling

P. Kieseberg et al. (Eds.): ARES 2026 Workshops, LNCS 16903, pp. 475–493, 2027.
https://doi.org/10.1007/978-3-032-37218-5_28

and distribution, for monitoring food quality, predicting food spoilage, and supporting optimized shipping solutions [3,18]. For instance, in controlled environment agriculture (CEA), such as greenhouses, DTs support the monitoring of environmental and crop conditions, the simulation of what-if scenarios to evaluate cultivation strategies, and the optimization of irrigation and nutrient recycling processes [3]. To provide these services, DTs rely on the integration of multiple technologies, including cyber-physical systems (CPS), Internet of Things (IoT) devices, AI-driven analytics, computing infrastructures, and networked communication mechanisms [2]. The confluence of these technologies, combined with the continuous synchronization between DTs and their physical counterparts, creates a complex attack surface [2,7], leading to security and cyber–physical risks that remain insufficiently explored in DT-driven agri-food supply chains. For instance, tampering with data, resources, or services in the cyber-physical domain could disrupt DT services [2,16].

Threat modeling has been recognized as a fundamental practice for systematically identifying vulnerabilities and their potential impact on physical processes [11]. However, in DT-driven systems, security analysis is often confined to the underlying CPS, while the DT itself and its continuous interaction with the physical system remain largely unexamined. This separation is increasingly untenable, as DTs directly influence monitoring, decision-making, and control actions in the physical environment. Therefore, threat modeling needs to be extended beyond the CPS to encompass the DT and the CPS–DT interactions. By explicitly analyzing threats across the physical system, the DT, and their bidirectional data and control flows, threat modeling provides a structured means to identify, assess, and mitigate cyber and cyber–physical risks throughout the DT-enabled system. The existing literature lacks a structured framework for applying STRIDE-based threat modeling to DT-driven systems in agri-food supply chains. This represents an important gap because without a systematic approach, potential cyber and cyber-physical threats in DT-enabled operations may go unrecognized, increasing the risk of disruptions to greenhouse processes, decision-making, and ultimately crop quality and yield.

We propose a six-step methodology (Fig. 1) to guide greenhouse operators and agricultural engineers in conducting systematic threat modeling. While the proposed methodology applies to any greenhouse in a CEA system, in this work, we focus on the pre-harvest phase of the strawberry supply chain (Fig. 2). The pre-harvest phase is critical because strawberry quality deterioration begins at the production level, where disruptions, such as imprecise climate control, irrigation, or sensing processes, can reduce fruit quality and yield, producing cascading effects on downstream supply chain performance and economic returns [10]. Consequently, conducting threat modeling at the pre-harvest stage is paramount, as security failures in DT-driven greenhouse operations can propagate into post-harvest stages, increasing risks across the entire strawberry supply chain.

We follow a CPS-first approach [7] where the greenhouse CPS is analyzed before constructing its DT. We also consider threats across DT lifecycle phases and CPS–DT interactions, addressing the DT-first approach [7], where the green-

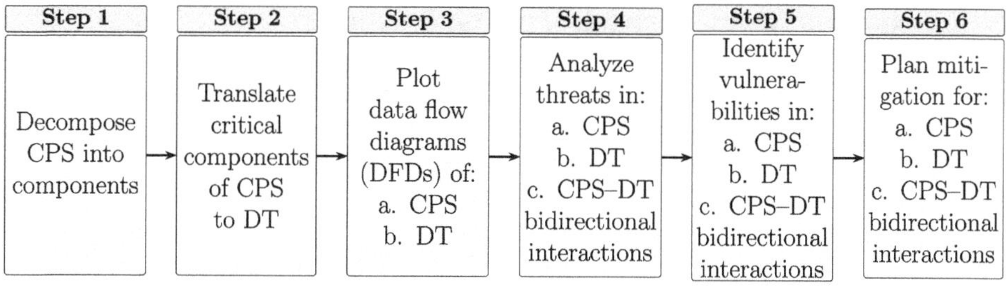

Fig. 1. A six-step methodology: Threat modeling for CPS, DT, and their bidirectional interactions (adapted from [11]) following a *CPS-first* approach to DT construction.

house DT exists before the CPS, and concurrent development, where CPS–DT bidirectional interactions are particularly critical. Our main contributions are as follows.

- To guide greenhouse operators and agricultural engineers, we proposed a six-step threat modeling methodology for DT-driven CPS, following a *CPS-first* approach to DT construction. Using a strawberry greenhouse[1] as a use case, we conduct STRIDE-based threat modeling for the greenhouse CPS and its corresponding DT, and further analyze CPS–DT bidirectional interaction(s) to identify threats, affected components, and their potential impact on greenhouse operations.
- We analyze security threats across the DT lifecycle phases in a strawberry greenhouse (following a *DT-first* approach to DT construction), including design-and-engineering, operation-and-maintenance, and end-of-life, showing how DT lifecycle decisions influence cyber and cyber-physical security risks.

The paper is organized as follows. Section 2 provides an overview of the strawberry greenhouse. Section 3 describes STRIDE-based threat modeling for the CPS, the DT, and their mapping within a strawberry greenhouse. Section 4 presents a discussion of the findings. Section 5 concludes the paper.

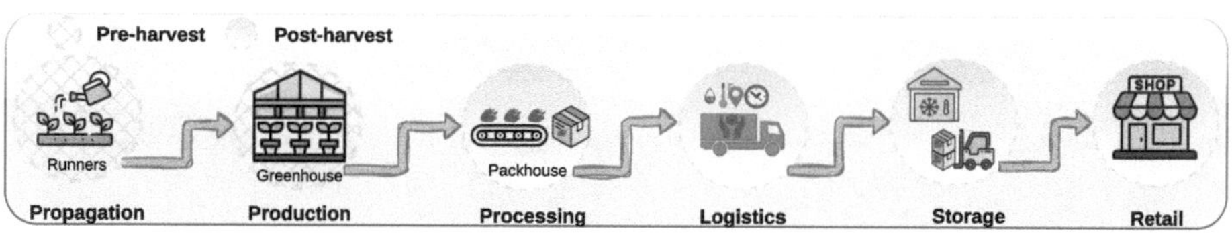

Fig. 2. *Pre-harvest* and *post-harvest* phases of the strawberry supply chain.

[1] In this work, the terms 'greenhouse system' and 'greenhouse CPS' are used interchangeably to refer to a physical greenhouse.

2 Case Study on Strawberry Greenhouse

A greenhouse comprises several components depending on factors such as crop type, size, and automation level. Following prior work such as [4], we focus on the key components that underpin greenhouse operations. Figure 3 shows a high-level representation of a strawberry greenhouse. *Field devices* comprise sensors and actuators deployed within the greenhouse to acquire crop and environmental data and to effect control actions such as irrigation or ventilation. A *gateway* aggregates sensor data, forwards it to local or cloud-based services, and relays control commands and setpoints back to field devices. The *control and monitoring system* forms the local control layer responsible for real-time monitoring, execution of automation rules and control logic, alert generation, and on-premise data storage and logging. *Cloud platform* provides services, including remote computing and storage capabilities, supporting data analytics, decision-support functions, and visualization dashboards used to monitor and optimize greenhouse operations. *Operators*, including greenhouse operators and agricultural engineers, are responsible for daily operations, system configuration, and maintenance. In this work, we assume a human-in-the-loop operating mode, where the DT provides monitoring and decision-support capabilities, while greenhouse operators and agricultural engineers retain final authority over control actions, ensuring human oversight in operational safety and control decisions. *External agricultural data sources* provide contextual information such as weather forecasts, pest and disease alerts, and satellite imagery, which are integrated into analytics and decision-making processes.

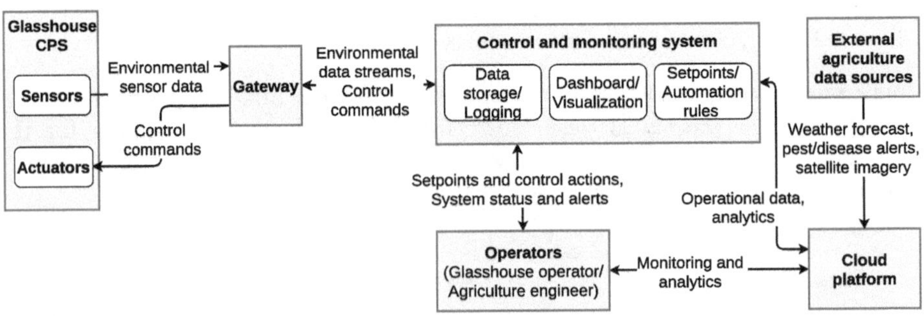

Fig. 3. A high-level overview of a strawberry greenhouse CPS, corresponding to *Step 1* of Fig. 1.

Attack Scenario: Greenhouses, as CPS-driven systems, are inherently exposed to cyber threats [1]. For example, in 2023, hacker attacks disrupted irrigation systems in Israel, highlighting the vulnerability of critical agricultural infrastructure [12]. We illustrate a hypothetical attack scenario in a strawberry greenhouse, where an adversary targets the integrity of environmental data used by the control and monitoring system. By compromising sensors, the gateway, or the data transmission path, manipulated soil moisture readings are injected into the system. These falsified data streams are ingested by the cloud platform and analytics components, including the DT, resulting in an inaccurate digital representation of soil conditions and incorrect irrigation recommendations. The control system translates these distorted insights into inappropriate automation rules and control commands, which can cause over- or under-watering of plants.

Impact on Greenhouse: The attack can have multi-level impacts. At the tactical level, manipulated data can lead to incorrect irrigation actions, resulting in plant stress and soil degradation. At the operational level, monitoring reliability and operator decision-making are undermined. At the strategic level, repeated manipulation erodes trust in automation and degrades system resilience, with adverse effects on cost efficiency, productivity, and financial sustainability. In the presence of corresponding DTs, such an attack further degrades the utility of DTs, as they fail to represent the greenhouse state and generate misleading recommendations accurately.

3 STRIDE-Based Threat Modeling

STRIDE, proposed by Microsoft, is a mnemonic representing six categories of security threats: (i) **S**poofing, (ii) **T**ampering,(iii) **R**epudiation, (iv) **I**nformation disclosure, (v) **D**enial of Service, and (vi) **E**levation of privilege [8]. STRIDE-based threat modeling can be performed using two approaches: (a) STRIDE-per-element, which analyzes each system component individually for security threats, and (b) STRIDE-per-interaction, which enumerates threats against system interactions based on tuples of source, destination, and data flow [14]. We chose STRIDE for its systematic approach, which enables the identification of security threats affecting both the strawberry greenhouse CPS and its corresponding DT. STRIDE further supports the analysis of key security properties, including confidentiality, integrity, availability, authentication, authorization, and non-repudiation [11], and enables the assessment of how vulnerabilities across CPS components, the DT, and their interactions propagate to affect the overall greenhouse CPS. In this work, we adopt the STRIDE-per-interaction approach to identify threats within the strawberry greenhouse CPS and its DT, emphasizing key attack surfaces while capturing vulnerabilities that could propagate through CPS–DT interactions. Note, due to page length restrictions, this paper focuses on the first five steps (Sects. 3.1–3.5) illustrated in Fig. 1.

3.1 Decompose Greenhouse CPS

Step 1 (Fig. 1) involves decomposing the strawberry greenhouse CPS into six components: field devices, gateway, control and monitoring system, cloud platform, operators, and external agriculture data sources (Fig. 3). Further details on greenhouse CPS components are provided in Sect. 2.

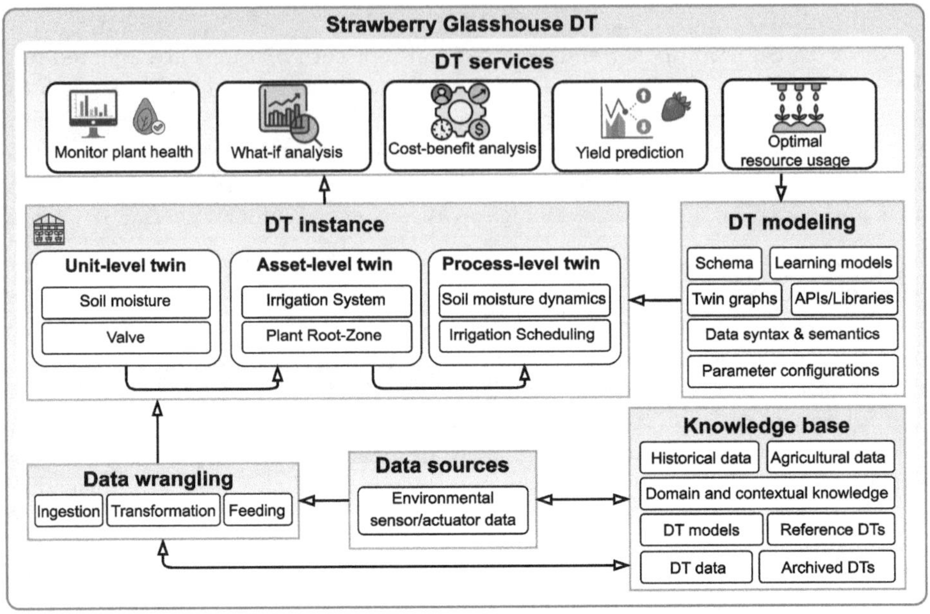

Fig. 4. Building blocks of a strawberry greenhouse DT, corresponding to *Step 2* of Fig. 1.

3.2 Translate Greenhouse CPS Components to DT

Step 2 (Fig. 1) involves translating the critical greenhouse components into DTs. Figure 4 illustrates the building blocks of a strawberry greenhouse DT. Data sources are obtained from asset state data, real-time measurements from field devices, or historical records, which are processed through a data wrangler to ingest, transform, and feed data to the respective DT instances [9]. Given that the underlying DT objectives significantly shape subsequent modeling parameters [17], we include basic features required for DT modeling. For each critical asset, such as sensors or the irrigation system, a schema specifies the asset's data type, format, and associated parameters. The twin graphs are then constructed from the schema and cross-checked against data syntax and semantics to ensure consistency in data type, structure, and format.

Following a composable DT architecture [13], unit-level DTs, including sensors and actuators such as soil moisture sensors and valves, provide foundational state information. These unit-level DTs are aggregated into asset-level DTs, representing subsystems such as the irrigation system and the plant-root zone. Asset-level DTs are further composed into process-level DTs, which model higher-level functions such as irrigation scheduling and soil moisture dynamics. The DT interface provides operators with monitoring, visualization, querying, and analytics capabilities.

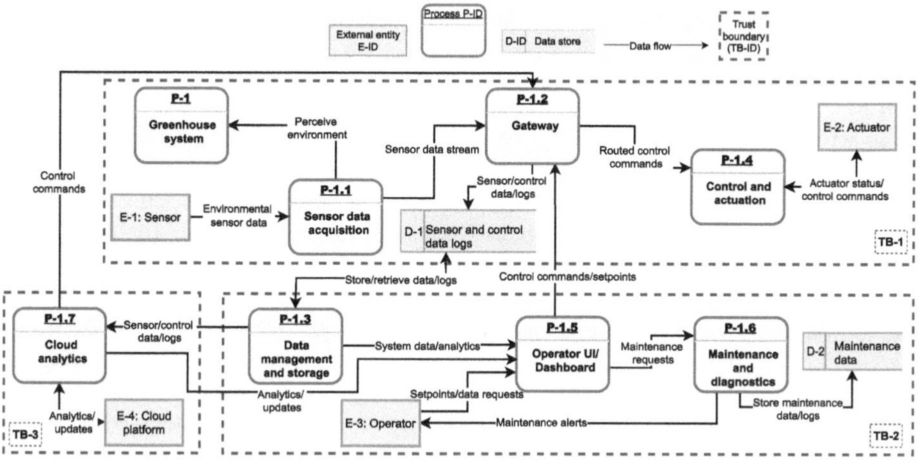

Fig. 5. Level 1 DFD of a greenhouse CPS, corresponding to *Step 3a* of Fig. 1.

3.3 Plot Data Flow Diagrams

Step 3 (Fig. 1) involves plotting data flow diagrams (DFDs) of the greenhouse CPS (Fig. 5) and its DT (Fig. 6) to visualize their functionalities. Both DFDs illustrate the interaction among external entities (E-ID), processes (P-ID), data stores (DS-ID), data flows, and trust boundaries (TB-ID).

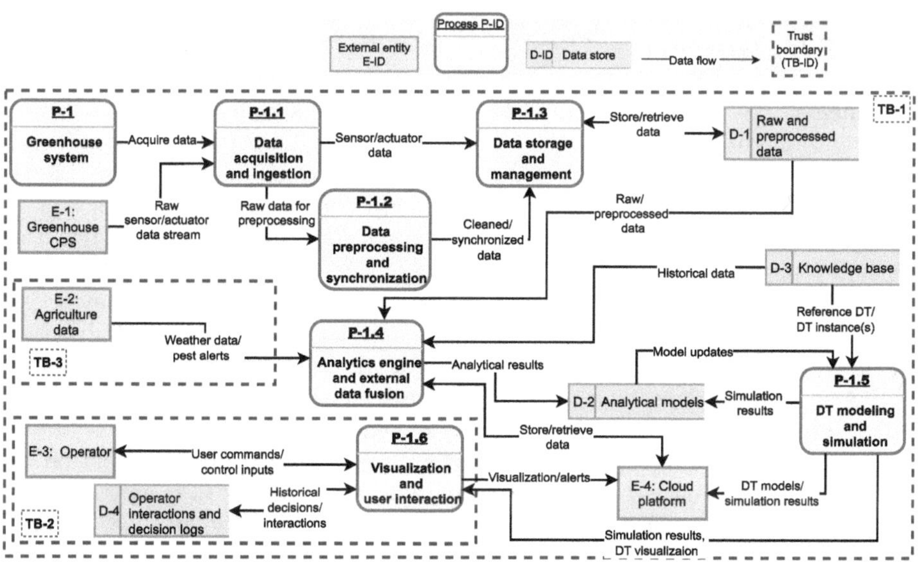

Fig. 6. Level 1 DFD of a greenhouse DT, corresponding to *Step 3b* of Fig. 1.

3.4 Analyze Threats

Step 4 (Fig. 1) involves analyzing threats in the greenhouse CPS and its corresponding DT. Tables 1 and 2 present a STRIDE-per-interaction threat analysis of the strawberry greenhouse CPS and its DT based on the Level 1 DFD (Figs. 5 and 6), respectively. Each row corresponds to a data flow between system components, grouped by trust boundaries (TB-1, TB-2, and TB-3), with marked (×) STRIDE categories indicating threats that can reasonably occur for that interaction. While Repudiation (R) and Elevation of Privilege (E) are not explicitly included in Tables 1 and 2, these threats may arise implicitly in specific interactions. For example, operator-issued setpoints or maintenance requests (e.g., E-3 → P-1.5 and P-1.5 → P-1.6) may be subject to repudiation if commands are not cryptographically signed, time-stamped, or securely logged. Similarly, unauthorized control commands executed by actuators or processed by CPS control logic may constitute elevation-of-privilege risks if access-control mechanisms are bypassed. However, systematically identifying and reasoning about such threats requires a STRIDE-per-element perspective focused on identities, roles, and authorization boundaries. In this work, we adopt a STRIDE-per-interaction approach to explicitly capture data-flow dependencies and Garbage-In Garbage-Out (GIGO) effects across CPS and DT layers. The analysis assumes a hybrid monitoring and decision-support DT that mirrors the greenhouse state and provides predictive analytics and recommendations, while human operators retain final authority over control actions. Consequently, the analysis prioritizes confidentiality, integrity, and availability, which dominate the security risks associated with data propagation and CPS–DT interactions.

STRIDE for Greenhouse CPS (*Step 4a* of Fig. 1): *Spoofing* primarily affects data flows in which identity and trust are assumed between communicating components. The data flow from E-1 → P-1.1, where spoofed sensors can inject false environmental readings, causing the greenhouse CPS to perceive incorrect temperature, humidity, or soil conditions. These incorrect perceptions propagate through P-1.1 → P-1.2 and influence the routed control-command data flow P-1.2 → P-1.4, leading to inappropriate responses such as unnecessary irrigation or insufficient ventilation. Similarly, spoofing of the P-1.4 → E-2 allows attackers to issue unauthorized control commands to actuators. The actuators may accept these commands as legitimate and perform actions without proper validation, i.e., the physical device state may differ from its digital representation. By spoofing E-3 → P-1.5, the attacker may impersonate legitimate operators and submit control setpoints or data requests. These spoofed inputs may then propagate via P-1.5 → P-1.2 and reach P-1.4, resulting in unauthorized physical[2] actuation. Furthermore, spoofing P-1.5 → P-1.6 may allow the attacker to trigger unnecessary diagnostics or consume system resources. Conversely, the attacker may use

[2] The term 'physical' refers to the real-world state of greenhouse devices, as opposed to their digital representations in the control system. Mismatches between physical and digital states can result from malicious actions that override device operations.

Table 1. STRIDE-per-interaction (tuple: ⟨Source→Destination, Data flow⟩, derived from Fig. 5) threat modeling for the greenhouse CPS (corresponding to *Step 4a* of Fig. 1).

TB	Source → Destination	Data flow	S	T	R	I	D	E
TB-1	E-1 → P-1.1	Environmental sensor data	×	×		×	×	
	P-1.1 → P-1.2	Sensor data stream	×	×		×	×	
	P-1.2 → P-1.4	Routed control commands	×	×			×	
	P-1.4 → E-2	Control commands	×	×			×	
	E-2 → P-1.4	Actuator status	×	×		×		
	P-1.2 → D-1	Store sensor/control data/logs		×		×	×	
	D-1 ↔ P-1.3	Store/retrieve sensor/control data/logs		×		×	×	
TB-2	P-1.3 → P-1.5	System data/analytics		×		×		
	E-3 → P-1.5	Setpoints/data requests	×	×			×	
	P-1.5 → P-1.2	Control commands/setpoints	×	×			×	
	P-1.5 → P-1.6	Maintenance requests	×	×			×	
	P-1.6 → D-2	Store maintenance data/logs		×		×		
	P-1.6 → E-3	Maintenance alerts		×		×	×	
TB-3	P-1.3 → P-1.7	Sensor/control data/logs		×		×	×	
	P-1.7 → E-4	Analytics/updates		×		×	×	
	P-1.7 → P-1.5	Analytics/updates		×		×		
	P-1.7 → P-1.2	Control commands	×	×			×	
	P-1.7 ↔ E-4	Analytics/updates	×	×		×	×	

spoofed identities to cancel or override legitimate maintenance actions. Spoofing P-1.7 → P-1.2 may allow the attacker to control physical operations remotely without direct access to field devices.

Tampering threats affect the integrity of data and commands across nearly all trust boundaries. If environmental data is tampered with during E-1 → P-1.1 or P-1.1 → P-1.2, the system operates on altered sensor readings, resulting in incorrect control logic execution in P-1.4. This may result in sustained over-irrigation, overheating, or unsuitable humidity levels, all of which negatively affect strawberry growth. Tampering with control commands in P-1.2 → P-1.4 or P-1.4 → E-2 can force actuators to operate outside safe or optimal ranges. Additionally, tampering with actuator feedback in E-2 → P-1.4 can conceal failures or provide false confirmation of successful actuation, thereby disrupting the control logic. Tampering with data flows such as P-1.2 → D-1, D-1 ↔ P-1.3, and P-1.3 → P-1.7 reduces data integrity. Tampering with P-1.3 → P-1.5 may hide abnormal conditions or falsely indicate normal system behavior, delaying corrective action. Tampering with E-3 → P-1.5 can result in unsafe control objectives being applied to the greenhouse, and tampering with P-1.5 → P-1.2 can lead to inappropriate actuation. For P-1.5 → P-1.6, tampered requests may suppress necessary maintenance actions or trigger unnecessary diagnostics. Tampering with P-1.6 → D-2 compromises the integrity of maintenance records. Tampering on P-1.6 → E-3 can delay, modify, or suppress alerts, preventing operators from responding to emerging faults. Tampering with analytics updates in P-1.7 → P-1.5 or P-1.7 → P-1.2 can further mislead operators or directly influence the behavior of CPS. For the bidirectional flow P-1.7 ↔ E-4, tampering in either direction can corrupt analytics pipelines or configuration updates that can affect downstream services and propagate incorrect system states or predictions.

Information disclosure on E-1 → P-1.1 and P-1.1 → P-1.2 exposes real-time temperature, humidity, CO_2, and soil conditions. This information reveals crop growth patterns, operational schedules, and control sensitivities, which may increase the risk of targeted attacks on critical control periods. Disclosure of E-2 → P-1.4 reveals actuation behavior and system responsiveness, while P-1.2 → D-1 and D-1 ↔ P-1.3 expose aggregated and historical operational data that may not cause immediate disruption; however, they significantly weaken the system, making it more susceptible to precise and effective follow-on attacks. Information disclosure on P-1.3 → P-1.5 exposes decision-making logic and operational priorities, which can enable targeted manipulation. Disclosure of maintenance-related flows such as P-1.6 → D-2 and P-1.6 → E-3 reveals fault histories, maintenance schedules, and system health status, allowing attackers to identify vulnerable components. Information disclosure on P-1.3 → P-1.7 exposes detailed and historical operational data, disclosure on P-1.7 → E-4 and P-1.7 ↔ E-4 reveals optimization results and configuration logic, while leakage on P-1.7 → P-1.5 exposes how outputs influence operator decisions, increasing the risk of targeted manipulation and loss of trust in decision support.

Denial of service (DoS) attacks on E-1 → P-1.1 and P-1.1 → P-1.2 prevent the timely delivery of environmental measurements, causing the system to operate with an incomplete or outdated perception of greenhouse conditions. DoS on P-1.2 → P-1.4 and P-1.4 → E-2 disrupts the execution of actuation decisions, delaying or preventing physical responses such as irrigation or ventilation. Availability loss on P-1.2 → D-1 and D-1 ↔ P-1.3 prevents reliable data storage and retrieval. This degrades operational monitoring and reduces traceability. A DoS affecting E-3 → P-1.5 prevents operators from issuing control inputs during abnormal conditions. Similarly, disruption of P-1.5 → P-1.2 blocks operator-driven adjustments from reaching the CPS. DoS attacks on P-1.5 → P-1.6 and P-1.6 → E-3, delay fault reporting and response. A DoS attack on P-1.3 → P-1.7 disrupts data synchronization between the physical greenhouse and cloud services. Meanwhile, the disruption of P-1.7 → P-1.2, P-1.7 → E-4, and P-1.7 ↔ E-4 renders cloud-based analytics and optimization services unavailable.

STRIDE for Greenhouse DT (*Step 4b* of Fig. 1): *Spoofing* of E-1 → P-1.1 allows falsified CPS data to enter the DT. As the DT relies on this data to reflect the physical state of the greenhouse, spoofed inputs result in an incorrect digital representation of environmental and actuation conditions. These effects propagate further through P-1.1 → P-1.2, where falsified data is treated as legitimate and prepared for downstream analytics and simulation, amplifying the impact across the DT workflow. Spoofing of E-3 ↔ P-1.6 enables unauthorized entities to impersonate legitimate operators. This can lead to false user interactions, misleading visualization requests, or unauthorized control inputs influencing DT simulations and displayed results. Spoofing of E-2 → P-1.4 allows attackers to

Table 2. STRIDE-per-interaction (tuple: ⟨Source→Destination, Data flow⟩, derived from Fig. 6) threat modeling for the DT of the greenhouse (corresponding to *Step 4b* of Fig. 1).

TB	Source → Destination	Data flow	S	T	R	I	D	E
TB-1	E-1 → P-1.1	Raw sensor/actuator data stream	×	×		×	×	
	P-1.1 → P-1.2	Raw data for pre-processing	×	×		×	×	
	P-1.2 → P-1.3	Cleaned/synchronized data		×		×	×	
	D-1 → P-1.3	Store/retrieve data		×		×	×	
	D-1 → P-1.4	Access raw/pre-processed data		×		×	×	
	P-1.4 → D-2	Analytical results		×		×	×	
	P-1.5 → D-2	Simulation results		×		×	×	
	D-2 → P-1.5	Model updates		×		×	×	
	D3 → P-1.4	Historical data		×		×	×	
	D-3 → P-1.5	Reference DT/DT instances		×		×	×	
	P-1.5 → E-4	DT models/simulation results				×	×	
	P-1.4 ↔ E-4	Store/retrieve data				×	×	
	P-1.5 → P-1.6	Simulation results/DT visualization				×		
	P-1.6 → E-4	Visualization/alerts		×		×		
TB-2	E-3 ↔ P-1.6	User commands/control inputs	×	×			×	
	P-1.6 → D-4	Store/retrieve historical decisions/interactions		×		×	×	
TB-3	E-2 → P-1.4	External agricultural data sources	×	×		×	×	

inject falsified weather data, pest alerts, or external environmental information into the analytics engine. Since this data is fused with CPS data to generate analytical results, spoofed external inputs can bias predictions, simulations, and recommendations produced by the DT.

Tampering of E-1 → P-1.1 and P-1.1 → P-1.2 compromises the integrity of CPS data entering the DT, subsequently impacting downstream analytics and simulations. Tampering on P-1.2 → P-1.3 further embeds corrupted data into the DT data pipeline, making inaccuracies persistent rather than transient. Tampering with stored data accessed through D-1 →P-1.3 and D-1 → P-1.4 further propagates incorrect information, reducing DT fidelity. Modification of analytical and simulation outputs in P-1.4 → D-2 and P-1.5 → D-2, as well as model updates in D-2 → P-1.5, directly affects DT behavior by altering model logic and prediction outcomes. Tampering with historical and reference information in D-3 → P-1.4 and D-3 → P-1.5 distorts long-term learning and baseline comparisons. Additionally, tampering of P-1.6 → E-4 results in misleading information being presented to users, undermining trust in DT outputs. Tampering of E-3 ↔ P-1.6 alters operator–DT interactions and can influence simulation results or displayed insights. Tampering with decision logs in P-1.6 → D-4 compromises traceability and weakens confidence in DT-assisted decision-making. Tampering with E-2 → P-1.4 biases analytics and data fusion, resulting in incorrect predictions and recommendations that compromise the reliability of DT.

Information disclosure of CPS data flowing through E-1 → P-1.1, P-1.1 → P-1.2, and P-1.2 → P-1.3 exposes raw and processed sensor and actuator information, revealing greenhouse environmental conditions and system behavior. Leakage of stored and reused data via D-1 → P-1.3 and D-1 → P-1.4 further exposes long-term operational patterns and control sensitivities, increasing the risk of targeted cyber-physical attacks. Disclosure of analytical and simulation outputs in P-1.4 → D-2, P-1.5 → D-2, and D-2 → P-1.5 reveals analytical logic, model parameters, and prediction outcomes used by the DT. Exposure of historical and reference knowledge in D-3 → P-1.4 and D-3 → P-1.5 provides insight into system baselines and expected behavior, reducing the effectiveness of anomaly detection. Information leakage in P-1.5 → E-4, P-1.4 ↔ E-4, P-1.5 → P-1.6, and P-1.6 → E-4 exposes DT models, simulation results, and visualizations, revealing how DT outputs are generated and communicated to users and external platforms. Disclosure of decision records in P-1.6 → D-4 exposes operator behavior, decision rationale, and response patterns. This weakens confidentiality and increases the risk of targeted manipulation or social engineering. Disclosure of E-2 → P-1.4 reveals the types and timing of external data used in analytics and data fusion. While indirect, this information helps attackers infer dependencies and influence points within the DT analytics pipeline.

Denial of service (DoS) affecting E-1 → P-1.1 and P-1.1 → P-1.2 disrupts the continuous ingestion and preprocessing of raw sensor and actuator data, resulting in stale or incomplete digital representations of the greenhouse. DoS on P-1.2 → P-1.3, D-1 → P-1.3, and D-1 → P-1.4 prevents access to stored data, which can degrade analytics and simulation accuracy. Unavailability of analytical and modeling outputs due to DoS on P-1.4 → D-2, P-1.5 → D-2, and D-2 → P-1.5 disrupts model updates and simulation execution, reducing the DT's ability to generate timely predictions. DoS on D-3 → P-1.4 and D-3 → P-1.5 blocks access to historical and reference DT instances, limiting long-term analysis and anomaly detection. Disruption of DT outputs through P-1.5 → E-4 and P-1.4 ↔ E-4 prevents the delivery and storage of DT models in the cloud. DoS on E-3 ↔ P-1.6 prevents operators from interacting with the DT or receiving timely insights. DoS on P-1.6 → D-4 blocks access to historical decisions and interaction logs for weakening traceability and continuity in DT-assisted decision-making. DoS affecting E-2 → P-1.4 disrupts the ingestion of weather and pest information used in analytics and data fusion. As a result, DT predictions and simulations operate with incomplete context, reducing their reliability and usefulness.

Greenhouse CPS and DT Bidirectional Interactions (*Step 4c* of Fig. 1): In this section, we illustrate how a greenhouse CPS-level attack (Sect. 2) propagates to the DT through CPS-DT interactions, as summarized in Table 3. Note, all referenced DT processes and data stores are shown in Fig. 6. With compromised soil moisture data from the greenhouse CPS, the attack first affects DT processes P-1.1 (Data Acquisition and ingestion) and P-1.2 (Data Pre-processing and synchronization), resulting in a GIGO problem. The corrupted input further propagates to P-1.5 (DT Modeling and Simulation), where inaccurate soil and climate representations distort the DT's state and decision logic. Analytical models and the knowledge base (D-2, D-3), which store information for multiple DT instances, including unit-, asset-, and process-level DTs (Fig. 4), become corrupted. This leads to digital thread or knowledge tampering, propagating errors across DT instances and disrupting synchronization between the CPS and the DT. Finally, the attack manifests as representation tampering at P-1.6 (Visualization and user interaction), misleading operators and automated decisions. Note, the threats discussed are not exhaustive; readers are referred to [2] for a comprehensive survey of security threats on DTs.

Table 3. Threats arising from CPS–DT interactions (corresponding to *Step 4c* of Fig. 1) and their impact on the greenhouse, illustrating how a CPS-level attack (Sect. 2) propagates to the DT.

Threat, Attack origin	Affected components: process; data flow; data store (Fig. 6)	Impact on greenhouse CPS
GIGO [16], DT/Greenhouse CPS	P-1.1 (Data Acquisition and ingestion), P-1.2 (Data pre-processing and synchronization); Raw sensor/actuator data stream, raw data for pre-processing, cleaned/synchronized data; D-1 (Raw and preprocessed data)	Compromised or spoofed sensor/actuator data can lead to incorrect irrigation decisions, resulting in soil over- or under-watering and reduced crop yield.
Digital Thread/ Knowledge Tampering [2], DT	P-1.4 (Analytics engine and external data fusion), P-1.5 (DT modeling and simulation); DT models/simulation results, analytical results, reference DT/DT instance(s), model updates; D-2 (Analytical models), D-3 (Knowledge base)	Tampered analytics or DT models compromise the integrity and accuracy of the DT representation, disrupting synchronization between physical and digital spaces (particularly in the case of multiple DT instances, as Fig. 3) shows.
Representation tampering [2], DT	P-1.6 (Visualization and user interaction); D-4 (Operator interactions and decision logs)	Manipulated visualizations or suppressed alerts can mislead operators, leading to incorrect control actions and delayed responses to stress conditions.

3.5 Identify Vulnerabilities

Step 5 (Fig. 1) involves identifying vulnerabilities in the greenhouse CPS, its corresponding DT, and CPS-DT greenhouse interactions. Based on the irrigation attack scenario (Sect. 2), key vulnerabilities include sensor data integrity, manipulation of communication pathways (e.g., gateways), and weaknesses in control logic that can trigger incorrect automation rules. In systems with a DT, vulnerabilities also arise from inaccurate state representation, compromised decision-support outputs, and potential propagation of falsified data through CPS-DT synchronization. Identifying these points highlights how attacks on a single component can cascade through both physical and digital layers, affecting monitoring, control, and predictive capabilities.

4 Discussion

Given the critical role of DTs in controlling and optimizing greenhouse operations, understanding the security risks across both CPS and DT components is essential. However, the contribution of this analysis is not limited to applying

Table 4. Cybersecurity threats across DT lifecycle phases in the strawberry greenhouse CPS arising from CPS–DT bidirectional interactions, following a *DT-first* approach to DT construction.

DT lifecycle phase	Threat	Attack origin	Threat implications on greenhouse
Design-and-engineering (*Phase I*)	DT trilemma [16] (Fig. 7)	DT	High-fidelity DTs increase the risk of model leakage, inference attacks, or poisoning affecting irrigation strategies, climate thresholds, and yield optimization logic.
	DT objective and degree of autonomy	DT,hybrid	DT role (e.g., security or resource optimization) and autonomy level (reactive, predictive, or prescriptive) expose different data and interfaces.
	Confluence of technologies in DT [2]	DT,hybrid	Coupling of IoT sensing, external agricultural data, computing infrastructure, and AI models in strawberry greenhouse DTs increases cross-layer security complexity and vulnerability propagation.
	DT architecture: monolithic vs. composable (Fig. 4)	DT,hybrid	Composable DT architectures introduce multiple DT instances and inter-DT synchronization points, increasing the attack surface and the risk of delayed, inconsistent, or selectively manipulated DT states. In contrast, monolithic DTs reduce synchronization complexity but may introduce single points of failure affecting overall greenhouse operation.
Operation-and-maintenance (*Phase II*)	Sensor data integrity manipulation [2]	CPS,hybrid	Compromised humidity, temperature, or soil moisture data biases irrigation and climate control logic in strawberry greenhouses.
	CPS–DT synchronization lag [15] (Replication mode)	DT–CPS	Stale or replayed environmental states misaligned DT recommendations during critical strawberry growth stages.
	Control logic manipulation	CPS,hybrid	Compromised irrigation thresholds compromise control logic, resulting in prolonged over- or under-watering in strawberry greenhouses.
	Feedback loops (GIGO: Fig. 8)	DT–CPS	Compromised CPS data increased through DT feedback loops reinforces incorrect irrigation and climate control decisions in strawberry greenhouses.
End-of-life (*Phase III*)	Model reuse and residual knowledge exposure	DT	Decommissioned DT models retain sensitive crop and control knowledge, risking unintended reuse or leakage of strawberry greenhouse operational strategies.
	Insecure DT migration or archival [6]	DT,hybrid	Poorly secured storage or transfer of DT artifacts exposes historical strawberry greenhouse operational and agronomic data.

Hybrid indicates that the attacker could be at either DT or CPS, or both. DT-CPS indicates threats that exploit the feedback loop between CPS and DT.

STRIDE as a classification framework. Instead, STRIDE is used as an analytical lens to examine how security threats propagate and transform within tightly coupled CPS–DT interactions and across the DT's lifecycle phases. This allows us to move from component-level threat identification to a system-of-systems understanding of security behavior. In this work, we perform STRIDE-based threat modeling for the strawberry greenhouse CPS (Table 1), its corresponding DT (Table 2), and further analyzed the CPS-DT interactions (Table 3).

Depending on the chronology of DT construction [7], we analyze threats using a CPS-first approach (Sect. 3.3). However, we also consider DT-first and concurrent development scenarios. Framing the analysis around DT chronology is particularly useful for evaluating CPS-DT interactions and understanding how decisions made across lifecycle phases influence security risks. Table 4 summarizes these threats, highlighting that the risks in the strawberry greenhouse CPS are not limited to operational attacks but evolve from design to decommission. During the *design-and-engineering (Phase I)*, decisions such as fidelity level, objective, and degree of autonomy act as design-time security determinants, shaping the initial attack surface by determining which data, models, and interfaces are exposed. Higher-fidelity DTs and more autonomous objectives embed detailed irrigation strategies, climate thresholds, and yield optimization logic into DT models, increasing susceptibility to model leakage, inference attacks, and poisoning. This trade-off between fidelity and information leakage is termed the DT trilemma [16], which illustrates how design choices that enhance operational capability also elevate exposure to sensitive operational knowledge (Fig. 7). The confluence of IoT sensing, external agricultural data, computing infrastructure, and machine learning models further increases security complexity by introducing cross-layer dependencies that can propagate vulnerabilities across the CPS–DT boundary.

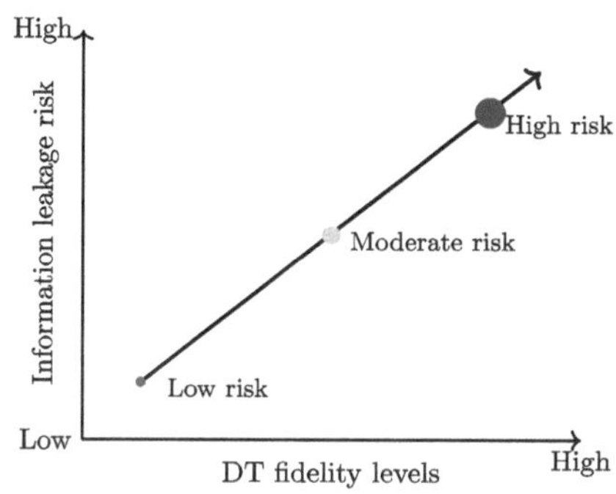

Fig. 7. DT trilemma [16] in a greenhouse CPS, which manifests during DT design-and-engineering (Phase I of Table 4). The trade-off between DT fidelity and information leakage is shown for three scenarios: *(a)* Low risk: coarse-grained sensor data and simplified irrigation rules result in limited exposure of operational knowledge. *(b)* Moderate risk: higher-resolution sensor data, basic predictive analytics, and integration of external agricultural data increase the risk of inferring irrigation schedules and climate thresholds. *(c)* High risk: fine-grained sensor data, detailed crop growth models, and prescriptive control recommendations maximize operational insights but at the risk of leaking irrigation strategies, climate thresholds, and yield optimization logic.

In the *operation-and-maintenance (Phase II)*, threats manifest through the CPS–DT feedback loops and time- or state-based synchronization mechanisms. Manipulated sensor data, delayed CPS–DT state replication, or compromised control logic can bias DT recommendations, reinforcing incorrect irrigation and climate control decisions, which may propagate operational consequences throughout the system. As illustrated in Fig. 8, erroneous sensor interpretations, models, or control recommendations, such as irrigation or climate control decisions, may propagate from a malicious or compromised DT through APIs, interfaces, and shared knowledge bases. These risks are exacerbated in architectures involving multiple interconnected DT instances, such as federated DT networks, where DTs of different greenhouses or subsystems share data, models, or services.

In such settings, corrupted knowledge or representations can cascade across DT threads and reference DTs, leading to system-wide degradation. Finally, the *end-of-life (Phase III)* shows that CPS–DT security risks persist beyond active operation. Decommissioned DT models and archived artifacts may retain sensitive agronomic and operational knowledge, exposing historical greenhouse strategies if migration or disposal is inadequately secured.

Our findings show that STRIDE enables the systematic analysis of core security properties; however, greenhouse CPS and DT systems also involve additional critical attributes, such as resilience and utility, that STRIDE does not explicitly capture. Resilience means the greenhouse CPS maintains operations under disruptions, and the DT continues to provide reliable decision-support functions despite compromised inputs or components. Utility refers to the effectiveness of the greenhouse CPS in achieving desired operational outcomes and the ability of the DT to provide accurate and actionable insights for decision-making. Considering these attributes alongside STRIDE enables a more comprehensive risk assessment across both the DT and greenhouse CPS. Moreover, the significance and impact of STRIDE-identified threats depend on the DT lifecycle phase in which they arise, as design, operation, and end-of-life decisions influence what data, models, and interfaces are exposed and how failures propagate. Interpreting STRIDE results through the DT lifecycle perspective provides a comprehensive understanding of how threats affect CPS–DT systems and supports more informed risk assessment across the CPS–DT lifecycle.

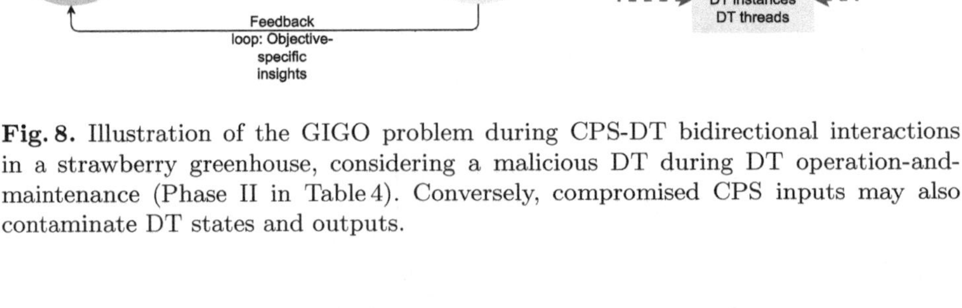

Fig. 8. Illustration of the GIGO problem during CPS-DT bidirectional interactions in a strawberry greenhouse, considering a malicious DT during DT operation-and-maintenance (Phase II in Table 4). Conversely, compromised CPS inputs may also contaminate DT states and outputs.

5 Conclusion and Future Directions

In this work, we present a six-step methodology (Fig. 1) to perform threat modeling for a strawberry greenhouse CPS (Fig. 3) and its corresponding DT (Fig. 4).

We further analyze CPS-DT interactions to assess their potential impact on the greenhouse (Table 3). In agri-food supply chains, existing research has several gaps: *(a)* underexplores cybersecurity aspects in DT-driven solutions, *(b)* often isolates the CPS from its digital counterpart, and *(c)* lacks a structured STRIDE-based methodology for DT-driven systems. These gaps are addressed through our six-step methodology.

Our findings establish that *(a)* CPS and DTs should be considered as a tightly coupled and interdependent socio-technical system rather than isolated entities when performing threat modeling, and *(b)* insufficient consideration of DT lifecycle phases can propagate errors during CPS-DT interactions, affecting irrigation and climate control decisions and potentially impacting crop yield. We anticipate that our work can guide greenhouse operators and agricultural engineers in: *(a)* systematically identifying where security threats emerge across the greenhouse CPS, the DT, and CPS–DT interaction points; *(b)* understanding which system elements are affected by these threats, including data flows, DT models, storage, and visualization components; and *(c)* accounting for how security risks evolve across the DT lifecycle phases.

The proposed methodology can be complemented by established risk management guidance, such as NIST IR 8356 [19], to enhance trust in DT-driven greenhouse CPS and prevent potential cascading failures from DT to CPS. Building on this foundation, the next steps of our research will address the following challenges. *First*, we aim to develop a transferable DT playbook to guide security practitioners in enhancing cyber resilience across multiple strawberry supply chain phases, extending beyond the pre-harvest focus of this work to post-harvest stages (Fig. 2). *Second*, we will investigate methods for benchmarking DTs for end-to-end trustworthiness across both design-time and operational phases, building on security threats and trustworthiness characteristics identified in previous works [2,5]. This includes extending existing evaluation metrics to cover both pre- and post-harvest phases of the strawberry supply chain. *Third*, building on cross-phase DT threat modeling and trustworthiness benchmarking, future work will leverage the TIPSS-PESTEL (trust, identity, privacy, security, and safety-political, economic, social, technological, environmental, and legal) framework to interpret and prioritize STRIDE-based threats within broader regulatory, organizational, and socio-technical contexts, supporting informed governance and design of DT-driven food supply chains.

Acknowledgments. This work is supported under MTU's TU RISE Research to Impact, co-funded by the Government of Ireland and the European Union through the ERDF Southern, Eastern & Midland Regional programme 2021-27.

Disclosure of Interests. The authors have no competing interests to declare that are relevant to the content of this article.

References

1. Alahe, M.A., et al.: Cyber security in smart agriculture: threat types, current status, and future trends. Comput. Electron. Agric. **226**, 109401 (2024). https://doi.org/10.1016/j.compag.2024.109401
2. Alcaraz, C., Lopez, J.: Digital twin: a comprehensive survey of security threats. IEEE Commun. Surv. Tutor. **24**(3), 1475–1503 (2022). https://doi.org/10.1109/COMST.2022.3171465
3. Ariesen-Verschuur, N., Verdouw, C., Tekinerdogan, B.: Digital twins in greenhouse horticulture: a review. Comput. Electron. Agric. **199**, 107183 (2022). https://doi.org/10.1016/j.compag.2022.107183
4. Badji, A., Benseddik, A., Bensaha, H., Boukhelifa, A., Hasrane, I.: Design, technology, and management of greenhouse: a review. J. Clean. Prod. **373**, 133753 (2022). https://doi.org/10.1016/j.jclepro.2022.133753
5. Bicocchi, N., Fogli, M., Giannelli, C., Picone, M., Virdis, A.: Requirements and design architecture for digital twin end-to-end trustworthiness. IEEE Internet Comput. **28**(4), 31–39 (2024). https://doi.org/10.1109/MIC.2024.3376439
6. Eckhart, M., Ekelhart, A.: Digital twins for cyber-physical systems security: state of the art and outlook, pp. 383–412. Springer International Publishing, Cham (2019). https://doi.org/10.1007/978-3-030-25312-7_14
7. Eckhart, M., et al.: Security-enhancing digital twins: characteristics, indicators, and future perspectives. IEEE Secur. Priv. **21**(6), 64–75 (2023). https://doi.org/10.1109/MSEC.2023.3271225
8. Howard, M., Lipner, S.: The Security Development Lifecycle. Microsoft Press, Redmond, WA, USA (2006)
9. Iqbal, M., et al.: IOV-Twinchain: predictive maintenance of vehicles in internet of vehicles through digital twin and blockchain. Int. Things **30**, 101514 (2025). https://doi.org/10.1016/j.iot.2025.101514
10. Kelly, K., et al.: A novel approach to determine the impact level of each step along the supply chain on strawberry quality. Postharvest Biol. Technol. **147**, 78–88 (2019). https://doi.org/10.1016/j.postharvbio.2018.09.012
11. Khan, R., McLaughlin, K., Laverty, D., Sezer, S.: STRIDE-based threat modeling for cyber-physical systems. In: 2017 IEEE PES Innovative Smart Grid Technologies Conference Europe (ISGT-Europe), pp. 1–6. IEEE (2017). https://doi.org/10.1109/ISGTEurope.2017.8260283
12. Kovacs, E.: Irrigation systems in Israel disrupted by hacker attacks on ICS (2023). Available at: https://www.securityweek.com/irrigation-systems-in-israel-disrupted-by-hacker-attacks-on-ics/. Accessed 14 Jan 2026
13. van Schalkwyk, P., Isaacs, D.: Achieving scale through composable and lean digital twins, pp. 153–180. Springer International Publishing, Cham (2023). https://doi.org/10.1007/978-3-031-21343-4_6
14. Shostack, A.: Threat Modeling: Designing for Security. John Wiley & Sons (2014)
15. Suhail, S., Iqbal, M., Hussain, R., Jurdak, R.: ENIGMA: an explainable digital twin security solution for cyber-physical systems. Comput. Ind. **151**, 103961 (2023). https://doi.org/10.1016/j.compind.2023.103961
16. Suhail, S., et al.: The perils of leveraging evil digital twins as security-enhancing enablers. Commun. ACM **67**(1), 39–42 (2023). https://doi.org/10.1145/3631539
17. Suhail, S., et al.: A framework for enhancing cyber incident response with security-enhancing digital twins in cyber-physical systems. In: Internet of Things, p. 101547 (2025). https://doi.org/10.1016/j.iot.2025.101547

18. Tzachor, A., Richards, C.E., Jeen, S.: Transforming agrifood production systems and supply chains with digital twins. NPJ Sci. Food **6**(1), 47 (2022). https://doi.org/10.1038/s41538-022-00162-2
19. Voas, J., Mell, P., Laplante, P., Piroumian, V.: Security and trust considerations for digital twin technology. Tech. rep., National Institute of Standards and Technology (2025). https://doi.org/10.6028/NIST.IR.8356

Privacy-Preserving Distributed Complex Event Processing Using Order-Revealing Encryption

Sehrish Shafeeq(✉) and Mathias Fischer

Universität Hamburg, Germany, Germany
sehrish.shafeeq@uni-hamburg.de mathias.fischer@uni-hamburg.de

Abstract. Complex Event Processing (CEP) enables real-time processing and analysis of large event streams across various Internet of Things (IoT) applications. Despite the deployment of CEP systems in areas that handle sensitive data, privacy protection in CEP systems has remained largely unexplored in the literature. In particular, existing approaches assume a trusted CEP system and focus mainly on pattern-level privacy, often neglecting event-level privacy. Order-revealing encryption enables comparison-based pattern detection over encrypted events without decryption, making it suitable for CEP systems, but it remains vulnerable to inference attacks from order leakage. In this paper, we propose a distributed privacy-preserving CEP framework that applies differential privacy before order-revealing encryption to reduce inference leakage. The proposed scheme achieves both event-level and pattern-level privacy against passive external adversaries and honest-but-curious internal adversaries. We formally analyze the privacy guarantees of our approach under the defined threat model and demonstrate that it achieves high detection accuracy under privacy protection and improves scalability by reducing per-node computational burden compared to a centralized CEP system.

Keywords: Complex event processing · Order revealing encryption · distributed stream processing

1 Introduction

Internet of Things (IoT) environments consist of a large number of autonomous, spatially distributed devices that continuously generate streams of raw events across a wide range of application domains, such as healthcare [19] and environmental monitoring [1]. The large volume and continuous nature of these streams make it difficult to derive meaningful high-level insights directly from raw events. Meaningful high-level events often emerge from the filtering, aggregation and correlation of multiple low-level events.

Complex Event Processing (CEP) [7] enables the analysis of large volumes of event streams through a set of processing rules, such as filtering, correlation,

P. Kieseberg et al. (Eds.): ARES 2026 Workshops, LNCS 16903, pp. 494–511, 2027.
https://doi.org/10.1007/978-3-032-37218-5_29

and aggregation, to infer higher-level complex events from multiple low-level event streams. For example, in a traffic monitoring application, a CEP system continuously processes a stream of vehicle speed and traffic density events to infer a complex event of traffic congestion.

Traditional centralized CEP systems rely on a single CEP engine for all processing, which creates scalability bottlenecks in IoT environments [6,13]. In a distributed CEP system, multiple CEP engines process events closer to their sources, improving scalability and eliminating a single point of failure. However, a distributed CEP system introduces security and privacy challenges because events are transmitted to local CEP engines for processing [5,21]. Since these CEP engines are deployed closer to data sources, they are generally more exposed and thus cannot always be assumed fully trusted [22]. This is particularly concerning because event streams often carry sensitive information, such as user behavior and operational states linked to a particular user. As a result, an honest-but-curious CEP engine may try to infer private information from events it processes, making event privacy an important requirement in a distributed CEP system.

Privacy in CEP systems has not been extensively studied in the literature. Existing works that address privacy in CEP systems [17,18] primarily suffer from the following shortcomings: (1) They assume the CEP system itself is trusted, which may be acceptable in a centralized CEP system operated by a single trusted entity. It becomes problematic in distributed CEP systems, where multiple CEP engines are deployed across different administrative domains. (2) They primarily focus on protecting pattern-level privacy from external consumers, while overlooking event-level privacy from honest-but-curious internal adversaries. Therefore, there is a need for a privacy-preserving distributed CEP system that protects both the privacy of events and the detected patterns.

One approach to protect event privacy while allowing the CEP engine to process encrypted data is homomorphic encryption [25]. However, homomorphic encryption is computationally expensive and primarily supports arithmetic operations, whereas CEP queries often rely on comparison-based predicates and temporal correlations.

Order-preserving encryption schemes allow comparison operations on encrypted data without decryption. Although these schemes do not support general arithmetic computations over ciphertexts, they are well-suited for CEP systems because CEP predicates involving filtering, threshold detection, and order-based correlation rely on comparisons.

Order-revealing encryption (ORE) and Order-preserving encryption (OPE) are two prominent examples of comparison-preserving encryption. We specifically chose ORE over OPE because it provides stronger security guarantees. However, both ORE and OPE remain vulnerable to inference attacks [9]. These attacks exploit order information along with auxiliary information, such as value distributions and rank information, to infer sensitive plaintext values from ciphertexts.

Prior work has shown that applying Distance-based Local Differential Privacy (dLDP) [24] before property preserving encryption reduces inference leakage [20]. To the best of our knowledge, prior work has not integrated dLDP and ORE into distributed CEP systems for privacy.

In our scheme, data providers first encode their events using dLDP, which perturbs event values with controlled random noise. The perturbed event values are then encrypted using ORE [14] before being transmitted to their assigned local CEP node, which hosts the CEP engine responsible for pattern detection. The local CEP nodes analyze patterns over the received encrypted events using comparison-based rules to detect complex local events. Subsequently, the global CEP node performs final aggregation and correlation on the local complex events and forwards the results to the consumer.

This hybrid approach achieves two goals. First, it reduces the effectiveness of inference attacks [20]. Second, it helps achieve pattern-level privacy, as patterns inferred from noisy, encoded events inherently incorporate perturbations in the detected pattern, thereby reducing the risk of sensitive information leakage from detected local complex events.

The key contributions of the paper are as follows: 1) A privacy-preserving distributed CEP system that supports comparison-based pattern detection over the encrypted event streams. 2) Protection of both event-level and pattern-level privacy under a threat model that removes the trusted CEP assumption and considers CEP entities as honest-but-curious adversaries. 3) A formal privacy analysis of the proposed scheme under the defined threat model. 4) An experimental evaluation showing that the proposed scheme achieves up to 96.9% detection accuracy under privacy protection while reducing per-node computational burden through the distributed CEP system.

The remainder of the paper is organized as follows: Sect. 2 describes the threat model and related work. In Sect. 3, we briefly describe the cryptographic algorithms and other building blocks of the proposed scheme. Section 4 describes the proposed CEP framework in detail. Then we formally prove the privacy guarantees under the defined threat model in Sect. 5.1. In Sect. 5.2, we conduct an experimental evaluation to assess performance. Finally, Sect. 6 concludes the paper.

2 Threat Model and Related Work

This section discusses the threat model and then presents the related work in light of it.

2.1 Threat Model

In our threat model, we consider an external adversary $\mathcal{A}_e$ and internal adversaries $\mathcal{A}_p$, $\mathcal{A}_{lc}$, $\mathcal{A}_{gc}$, $\mathcal{A}_c$. An external adversary $\mathcal{A}_e$ is a passive eavesdropper on communication channels. The internal non-colluding adversary $\mathcal{A}_p$, $\mathcal{A}_{lc}$, $\mathcal{A}_{gc}$, and $\mathcal{A}_c$ represent honest-but-curious provider, a local CEP node, a global CEP node, and a consumer, respectively. They are part of the CEP system and follow the CEP protocols, but may try to infer sensitive event information and detected patterns. Each adversary has access to only the information available through its system role. For example, providers have access to their own events; a local CEP node processes encrypted noisy event encodings; a global CEP node receives the local complex events; and consumers receive the final complex event. We do not consider collusion of adversaries.

2.2 Related Work

We organize the related work into two categories: pattern-level privacy-preserving CEP schemes and event-level privacy-preserving data aggregation schemes. Although event-level privacy-preserving techniques for CEP remain limited, we include related work on privacy-preserving data aggregation, as data aggregation is a component of the CEP pipeline.

An early work on privacy-preserving CEP was introduced by [12]. In this work, private and public patterns are formally defined, and it is shown that the utility-optimization problem is NP-hard. That is, finding a modification to event streams that preserves public patterns while avoiding disclosure of private patterns.

Patterns are categorized as private or public patterns by [18]. Their system deploys a pattern access control system on the data provider side, which protects privacy-sensitive patterns by reordering events before sending them to the CEP engine while maximizing quality of service. However, they do not consider event-level privacy and do not discuss how data providers classify events as private or public patterns.

A pattern-level privacy protection mechanism for a distributed CEP system is also proposed by [17]. The proposed framework supports various obfuscation techniques and dynamically selects the one that maximizes quality while preventing adversaries from revealing private patterns. However, since [17] is a preliminary work, further research and discussion are required.

Pattern-level privacy using differential privacy is studied by [10]. This work proposes two mechanisms: one that distributes the privacy budget uniformly, and the second that adapts the noisy budget to improve data quality. The uniform privacy budget mechanism does not achieve optimal performance, and the adaptive mechanism requires access to historical data. In all of the above pattern-level privacy protection mechanisms, the CEP engine is assumed to be a trusted entity, and data providers and consumers are assumed to classify patterns perfectly as private or public. However, in real-world settings, their pattern classification can be inaccurate or intentionally manipulated, thereby raising privacy risks.

While several studies focus on pattern-level privacy in CEP, to the best of our knowledge, no prior work has addressed individual event-level privacy because the CEP engine is assumed trustworthy. Although this assumption may hold in centralized CEP systems, it becomes less realistic in distributed CEP systems.

There is extensive research on distributed data aggregation techniques for protecting privacy of individual data stream. For example, in [26], smart devices encrypt their data using BGN encryption [4] before transmission. Due to homomorphic properties, the receiving node can perform homomorphic aggregation on the data. In [11], data providers split their data values into pieces and send them to different intermediate nodes for aggregation to protect data privacy. A privacy-preserving comparison-based aggregation protocol for mobile sensing applications is proposed by [16]. Although this work achieves event-level privacy, it uses multiparty computation [15] to perform privacy-preserving comparisons, which incurs a high communication cost.

Overall, existing research on privacy-preserving CEP systems has focused primarily on only pattern-level privacy, while privacy-preserving stream data aggregation is typically limited to standard aggregation functions and often relies on computationally expensive cryptographic algorithms. This highlights the need for a privacy-preserving complex event processing system that protects individual event and pattern privacy while efficiently supporting comparison-based operations.

3 Background

In this section, we explain the necessary cryptographic algorithms that form the basis of the proposed framework.

3.1 Symmetric Encryption

Symmetric encryption (SE) [2] conceals the transmitted data from disclosure to any entity other than the intended recipient. The sender and receiver use a single key for both encryption and decryption. There are various SE algorithms, such as AES [8]. A SE scheme consists of three probabilistic polynomial-time algorithms ($\mathsf{SE.Setup}$, $\mathsf{SE.Encrypt}$, $\mathsf{SE.Decrypt}$).

- $\mathsf{SE.Setup}(1^\lambda) \rightarrow \mathsf{sk}^{\mathsf{se}}$: The algorithm takes a security parameter λ as input and outputs a secret encryption key sk^{se}.
- $\mathsf{SE.Encrypt}(\mathsf{sk}^{\mathsf{se}}, \mathsf{m}) \rightarrow \mathsf{c}^{\mathsf{se}}$: It takes a secret key sk^{se} and message m that user wants to encrypt and outputs a ciphertext c^{se}.
- $\mathsf{SE.Decrypt}(\mathsf{sk}^{\mathsf{se}}, \mathsf{c}^{\mathsf{se}}) \rightarrow \mathsf{m}$: It takes a secret key sk^{se} and a ciphertext c^{se} as input and outputs a message m.

3.2 Distance-Based Local Differential Privacy

Local DP [24] guarantees that the output of a randomized mechanism is insensitive to any particular input, meaning that the released output cannot reveal whether a specific individual's input is in the dataset. Under local DP, each individual perturbs their data by adding noise and sends the perturbed data to an aggregator, which then computes aggregate statistics over the noisy data.

The standard local DP offers the same level of privacy protection for all pairs of inputs. However, achieving this uniform protection requires adding substantial noise, resulting in lower utility. Distance-based Local Differential Privacy (dLDP) relaxes this requirement by ensuring only pairs of inputs that are close to each other remain indistinguishable, with the privacy guarantee degrading with the l_1 distance (the sum of absolute differences) between input values. Formally, a randomized function $\mathcal{K} : \mathcal{X} \rightarrow \mathcal{Y}$ gives a ϵ-distance based local differential privacy (ϵ-dLDP), if for any pair of private inputs, $x, x' \in \mathcal{X}$ and any subset of output $\mathcal{S} \subseteq \mathcal{Y}$

$$Pr[\mathcal{K}(x) \in \mathcal{S}] \leq e^{\epsilon|x-x'|}.Pr[\mathcal{K}(x') \in \mathcal{S}] \tag{1}$$

The privacy loss is captured by ϵ, where $\epsilon = 0$ is perfect privacy.

3.3 Order Revealing Encryption

An ORE [14] is a symmetric encryption scheme in which a public comparison function allows for performing comparison operations over the ciphertext without revealing the underlying plaintext. An ORE is a tuple of four probabilistic polynomial time algorithms ($\mathsf{ORE.Setup}$, $\mathsf{ORE.Enc_L}$, $\mathsf{ORE.Enc_R}$, $\mathsf{ORE.Compare}$)

- $\mathsf{ORE.Setup}(1^\lambda) \rightarrow \mathsf{sk^{or}}$: It takes a security parameter λ as input and outputs a secret key sk^{or}.
- $\mathsf{ORE.Enc_L}(\mathsf{sk^{or}}, \mathsf{m}) \rightarrow \mathsf{c_L^{or}}$: It takes a secret key sk^{or} as input, a message $m \in \mathcal{M}$ and outputs a ciphertext $\mathsf{c_L^{or}}$.
- $\mathsf{ORE.Enc_R}(\mathsf{sk^{or}}, \mathsf{m}) \rightarrow \mathsf{c_R^{or}}$: It takes a secret key sk^{or} as input, a message $m \in \mathcal{M}$ and outputs a ciphertext $\mathsf{c_R^{or}}$.
- $\mathsf{ORE.Compare}(\mathsf{c_{1,L}^{or}}, \mathsf{c_{2,R}^{or}}) \rightarrow \mathsf{b}$: It takes a ciphertext $\mathsf{c_{1,L}^{or}}$ (output of $\mathsf{ORE.Enc_L}(\mathsf{sk^{or}}, \mathsf{m_1}) \rightarrow \mathsf{c_{1,L}^{or}}$) and a ciphertext $\mathsf{c_{2,R}^{or}}$ (output of $\mathsf{ORE.Enc_R}(\mathsf{sk^{or}}, \mathsf{m_2}) \rightarrow \mathsf{c_{2,R}^{or}}$) as inputs and outputs $b \in \{-1, 0, 1\}$

Compared to traditional ORE [3], ORE [14] splits the encryption function into left and right parts to strengthen security guarantees. This design makes the right ciphertexts alone semantically secure, that is, they reveal no information about the underlying plaintext, including their order. The left part enables comparison but leaks only the ordering information for small domains, and for large domains, the index of the first differing block.

ORE satisfies the correctness property that is for any messages $m_1, m_2 \in \mathcal{M}$:

$$Pr[ORE.Compare(c_1^{or}, c_2^{or}) = (m_1 < m_2)] = 1 - negl(\lambda)$$

ORE achieves indistinguishability under an ordered chosen plaintext attack (IND-OCPA) for small domains. For large domains, it provides simulation-based security with respect to leakage functions that reveal only the index of the first differing block.

4 Framework for Privacy Preserving Distributed CEP

In this section, we first describe the system model, then explain the proposed framework, starting with the rationale for our approach, an overview of the CEP system, and then a detailed description of the CEP system.

4.1 System Model

The system consists of a trusted third party (TTP) that is fully trusted for key generation and distribution. A consumer is an entity interested in the complex events derived from continuous event streams. There are n providers, each generating and submitting events, which correspond to sensor data values. The providers are divided into disjoint sets, each associated with a local CEP node.

Each local CEP node applies a predefined pattern-detection rule to the events received from its assigned providers and generates a local complex event. A global CEP node executes a global pattern-detection rule to generate events of interest to the consumer.

4.2 System Overview

Our framework for privacy-preserving CEP consists of four phases: (1) system setup and key distribution, (2) Event encoding and encryption, (3) local pattern detection, (4) global aggregation and pattern detection.

During the system setup and key distribution, providers are divided into disjoint subsets, with each subset assigned to a dedicated local CEP node, as shown in Fig. 1. We refer to these subsets as segments. TTP generates an ORE secret key for each segment and securely distributes the corresponding ORE secret key to all providers within that segment. In addition, the TTP encrypts the comparison threshold used in the event predicates under the segment-specific ORE secret key and distributes the resulting ciphertexts to the corresponding local CEP nodes.

In the event encoding and encryption phase, each provider first applies dLDP to its raw events. The perturbed events are then encrypted using the segment-specific ORE secret key and sent to the assigned local CEP node.

During the local pattern-detection phase, each local CEP node evaluates the pattern-detection rules over the received encrypted events to detect local complex events, which are subsequently forwarded to the global CEP node for further processing.

In the global aggregation and pattern-detection phase, the global CEP node aggregates and correlates local complex events from multiple segments to detect a global complex event. The resulting complex event is then transmitted to the consumer.

In the proposed system, the local CEP nodes evaluate comparison-based predicates over encrypted events, while the resulting local complex events can then be processed for additional CEP operations such as aggregation and correlation.

In the following, each phase is described in detail.

4.3 Phase 1: System Setup and Key Distribution

The goal of this phase is to generate and distribute the necessary cryptographic keys. Providers are divided into segments, and each segment is assigned its local

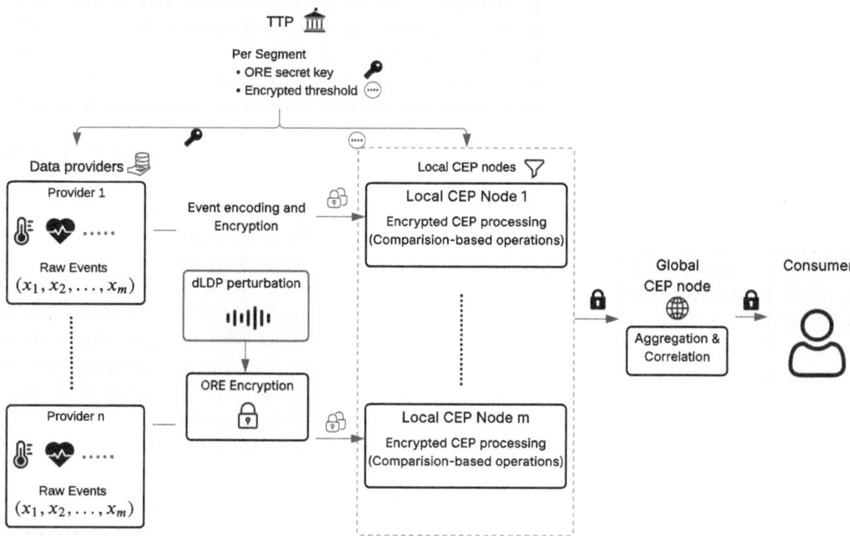

Fig. 1. Architecture of the proposed privacy-preserving distributed CEP framework

CEP node, which processes its events. This design reduces the computational burden on each local CEP node by allowing it to compute only for events from a subset of providers. TTP runs $\mathsf{ORE.Setup}(1^\lambda)$ to generate secret key sk_j^{or} for each $localCEP_j$, as shown in Algorithm 1. It also generates the comparison-threshold ciphertext c_t^{or} using $\mathsf{ORE.Encrypt}(\mathsf{sk_j^{or}}, \mathsf{t})$ that is later used by the local CEP node to detect local complex events. Secret keys and threshold ciphertexts are generated independently for each segment. TTP then distributes to each provider the ORE secret key corresponding to the segment to which the provider belongs and the threshold ciphertexts to the corresponding local CEP node. By employing segment-specific ORE secret keys, the system achieves clear separation of encryption domains by localizing cryptographic access and processing for that segment.

TTP also partitions the input domain (e.g., temperature $[1 - 100]$) into k buckets ($[0 - 10], [11 - 20], ..., [91 - 100]$) and makes this public information because the event encoding mechanism samples noisy bucket encoding from the bucketization domain. Bucketization reduces the effective output domain, thereby limiting excessive perturbations during dLDP encoding. Additionally, it preserves the approximate distance and ordering relationship between values needed for CEP predicate evaluations.

Each data provider and its assigned local CEP node establishes symmetric encryption secret keys for secure communication (Algorithm 5). Symmetric encryption protects the confidentiality of transmitted data against an external adversaries. Similarly, each local CEP node establishes a symmetric encryption key with the global CEP node for the same purpose (Algorithm 9).

Algorithm 1 System setup and key distribution

```
for all LocalCEP_j in system do
    TTP runs sk_j^or ← ORE.Setup(1^λ)
    for all Provider_i assigned to LocalCEP_j do
        TTP → Provider_i: sk_j^or
        Establish symmetric key sk_{i,j}^se between provider_i and LocalCEP_j
    end for
    TTP runs c_{t,j}^or ← ORE.Enc(sk_j^or, t)
    TTP → LocalCEP_j : c_{t,j}^or
    Establish symmetric key sk_{j,G}^se between LocalCEP_j and GlobalCEP
end for
```

4.4 Phase 2: Event Encoding and Encryption

Following the findings [20], applying dLDP before property-preserving encryption significantly mitigates the success of inference attacks. To mitigate inference leakage from ORE, providers first apply dLDP to encode events and then encrypt the resulting encoded event using ORE. Specifically, we adopt the exponential mechanism of dLDP described in [20].

The exponential mechanism probabilistically samples an output bucket index for an input event x, assigning higher probability to closer buckets while still inducing controlled randomness for privacy protection. As shown in Algorithm 2, the probability of outputting a bucket index l is given by $p_{x,l} = \frac{e^{-|x-d_l|.\epsilon/2}}{\sum_{j=1}^{k} e^{-|x-d_j|.\epsilon/2}}$, where d_l is the weighted median of the l-th bucket and ϵ is the privacy budget. For instance, given input 40, and $\epsilon = 1$, the noisy encoding mechanism most likely outputs bucket index 3, starting bucket indexing at 0 (Algorithm 8).

After encoding, the provider encrypts the resulting noisy encoding using the ORE encryption algorithm (Algorithm 9). For notational simplicity, we are showing only the encryption algorithm rather than the separate left- and right-hand encryption algorithms of ORE. In practice, the provider generates both left and right ciphertexts, and the ciphertext sent to the local CEP node depends on the predicate defined in the pattern.

For predicates that compare an event only against an encrypted threshold, providers submit only the right ciphertext, while the corresponding threshold is provided as the left ciphertext. Although the system design allows predicates that compare events generated by different providers, the instantiation used in the paper is primarily threshold-based. In this setting, the comparisons are performed between the provider ciphertext and the threshold ciphertext. Accordingly, the experimental evaluation and security analysis are restricted to threshold predicates. When comparing events from different providers, both ciphertext components may be transmitted to the CEP node, which then selects the appropriate pair for comparison.

Finally, the provider wraps the resulting ORE ciphertext with an outer SE layer (Algorithm 10). Since all providers assigned to the same local CEP node share the same ORE secret key, the outer SE layer protects data confidentiality against other providers, even if they also possess that key.

Algorithm 2 Event encoding and encryption

---

for all LocalCEP_j in system **do**
    for all Provider_i assigned to LocalCEP_j **do**
        for all event x generated by Provider_i **do**
            for $l = 1$ to k **do**
                $p_{x,l} = \frac{e^{-|x-d_l|.\epsilon/2}}{\sum_{r=1}^{k} e^{-|x-d_r|.\epsilon/2}}$
            end for
            $p_x = \{p_{x,1}, \ldots p_{x,k}\}$
            $o \sim p_x$ ▷ noisy encoding drawn at random from the distribution p_x
            $\mathsf{c}_{i,j}^{or} \leftarrow \mathsf{ORE.Enc}(\mathsf{sk}_j^{or}, \mathsf{o})$
            $\mathsf{c}_{i,j}^{se} \leftarrow \mathsf{SE.Enc}(\mathsf{c}_{i,j}^{or}, \mathsf{sk}_{i,j}^{se})$
            $\text{Provider}_i \rightarrow \text{LocalCEP}_j$: $\mathsf{c}_{i,j}^{se}$
        end for
    end for
end for

4.5 Phase 3: Local Pattern Detection

Once the local CEP node has received encrypted data from all providers assigned to it, it begins complex event processing to detect local complex events. The processing starts by decrypting the outer SE layer using the secret key established between the local CEP node and the corresponding provider, as shown in Algorithm 3 (Algorithm 7). The local CEP node then evaluates comparison-based predicates by comparing the ORE-encrypted ciphertext against the corresponding encrypted threshold c_t.

The local CEP node supports comparison-based predicates over encrypted events, conjunction operators, and temporal window constraints. Specifically, local pattern detection involves evaluating threshold-based predicates over multiple encrypted event types within a time window Δt. The set $\mathcal{R}_j$ (Algorithm 10) denotes the comparison-based predicates defined in the local pattern rule.

If all predicates in the local pattern rule evaluate to TRUE within the time window Δt, corresponding to a logical AND over the predicates, the pattern trigger count is incremented (Algorithm 11). The final pattern trigger count represents the number of providers within the segment whose encrypted events satisfy the local pattern. This value is then transmitted to the global CEP node as a local complex event.

4.6 Phase 4: Global Aggregation and Pattern Detection

The global CEP node receives the privacy-protected local complex events from local CEP nodes. Each incoming local complex event includes a detected local pattern trigger and is associated with a specific segment.

Algorithm 3 Privacy preserving local CEP

for all LocalCEP_j in system **do**
  $\mathcal{M}_j \leftarrow \emptyset$ ▷ providers whose local pattern matched
  pattern_trigger ← 0
  for all Provider_i assigned to LocalCEP_j **do**
    $\mathcal{W}_{i,j} \leftarrow \emptyset$ ▷ events in current window Δt
    for all encrypted event $\mathsf{c}^{\mathsf{se}}_{\mathsf{i,j}}$ received from Provider_i **do**
      $\mathsf{c}^{\mathsf{or}}_{\mathsf{i,j}} \leftarrow \mathsf{SE.Dec}(\mathsf{c}^{\mathsf{se}}_{\mathsf{i,j}}, \mathsf{sk}^{\mathsf{se}}_{\mathsf{i,j}})$
      Add $\mathsf{c}^{\mathsf{or}}_{\mathsf{i,j}}$ to $\mathcal{W}_{i,j}$
      Remove events older than Δt from $\mathcal{W}_{i,j}$
      if $\text{Provider}_i \notin \mathcal{M}_j \ \wedge\ \forall r \in \mathcal{R}_j,\ \exists \mathsf{c}^{\mathsf{or}} \in \mathcal{W}_{i,j} : \mathsf{ORE.Compare}(\mathsf{c}^{\mathsf{or}}, \mathsf{c}^{\mathsf{or}}_{\mathsf{t,r}}) = \mathsf{TRUE}$ **then**
        pattern_trigger ← pattern_trigger + 1
        $\mathcal{M}_j \leftarrow \mathcal{M}_j \cup \{\text{Provider}_i\}$
      end if
    end for
  end for
  $\text{LocalCEP}_j \rightarrow$ GlobalCEP: pattern_trigger
end for

The global CEP node performs logical aggregation and correlation over local complex events. Specifically, it maintains a sliding time window of duration Δt and monitors incoming local events from different segments. Within each window, the global CEP node tracks the distinct segments that have reported the pattern trigger. If the number of distinct segments exceeds a threshold κ, the global CEP node emits a global complex event to the consumer.

Algorithm 4 Global aggregation and pattern detection

ActiveSegments ← $\emptyset$
for all LocalComplexEvent e **do**
  remove entries older than Δt time from ActiveSegments
  if $e.pattern\_trigger > 0$ **then**
    Add $e.segmentID$ to ActiveSegments
  end if
  if $|ActiveSegments| \geq \kappa$ **then**
    GlobalCEP → Consumer: $GlobalComplexEvent$
    Clear ActiveSegments
  end if
end for

5 Evaluation

This section evaluates the proposed scheme through security, privacy, and experimental analysis. Section 5.1 presents the formal security and privacy analysis and Sect. 5.2 presents experimental evaluation.

5.1 Security and Privacy Analysis

Theorem 1. *Assuming the underlying SE scheme is IND-CPA secure, the proposed CEP framework preserves the confidentiality of providers' event data against a passive external adversary.*

Proof. Let $\mathcal{A}_e$ be an external probabilistic polynomial time (PPT) adversary eavesdropping on all communication between providers and local CEP nodes, as well as on the communication between local CEP nodes and the global CEP node. $\mathcal{A}_e$ obtains access to ciphertext $\mathsf{c}^{\mathsf{se}}_{\mathsf{i,j}}$ transmitted between provider i and local CEP node j.

Before transmission, the provider i encrypts the data using SE with the shared secret key $\mathsf{sk}^{se}_{i,j}$. Since the underlying SE is IND-CPA secure, any PPT adversary observing $\mathsf{c}^{\mathsf{se}}_{\mathsf{i,j}}$ learns no information about the underlying plaintext event data except with negligible probability.

Similarly, communication between the local and global CEP nodes is protected using the same IND-CPA-secure SE scheme. Therefore, a passive external adversary eavesdropping on these communications cannot distinguish the underlying plaintext except with negligible advantage.

Theorem 2. *The proposed CEP system provides ϵ-dLDP with respect to each provider's event data and, in addition, provides simulation-based security under a leakage function $\mathcal{L}_{BLK}$ for the left ciphertext and IND-CPA security for the right ciphertext, against an honest-but-curious internal adversary.*

Proof. An internal PPT adversary may act as an honest-but-curious provider $\mathcal{A}_p$, a local CEP node $\mathcal{A}_{lc}$, a global CEP node $\mathcal{A}_{gc}$, or a consumer $\mathcal{A}_c$.

First, consider $\mathcal{A}_p$, acting as an honest-but-curious provider. The goal of $\mathcal{A}_p$ is to infer the private data of other providers. Since each provider encrypts its data with a symmetric encryption key $\mathsf{sk}^{se}_{i,j}$ that is shared only between provider i and local CEP node j, $\mathcal{A}_p$ does not have access to it. Therefore, without access to $\mathsf{sk}^{se}_{i,j}$, the advantage of $\mathcal{A}_p$ in distinguishing any two messages is negligible due to the IND-CPA security of SE.

Next, consider $\mathcal{A}_{lc}$, acting as an honest-but-curious local CEP node. $\mathcal{A}_{lc}$ has access to the ORE ciphertext and the comparison results. We adopt the noisy encoding mechanism of [20] to encode events, and the resulting noisy bucket encoding is then encrypted using ORE. As shown in [20], the noisy encoding mechanism satisfies ϵ-dLDP, guaranteeing that for any pair of events x and x', the output distribution differs by at most $e^{\epsilon|x-x'|}$.

The resulting noisy bucket encoding is then encrypted using ORE. ORE provides simulation-based security with a leakage function $\mathcal{L}_{BLK}$ that reveals the index of the first differing block during comparison; in our setting, any leakage pertains only to the dLDP-perturbed bucket encodings. The right ciphertexts in isolation are IND-CPA. As shown in [20], applying property-preserving encryption to an ϵ-dLDP noisy encoding preserves the ϵ-dLDP guarantee by post-processing. Therefore, any inference performed on the encrypted noisy encoding is also post-processing of the dLDP mechanism, which limits the adversary's ability to infer the original event value: $Pr[\mathcal{K}(x) \in \mathcal{S}] \leq e^{\epsilon|x-x'|}.Pr[\mathcal{K}(x) \in \mathcal{S}]$.

Another advantage of ORE is that comparisons require the left ciphertext of one input and the right ciphertext of another. In our system, the evaluation of event predicates is threshold comparison, where the TTP submits the left ciphertext corresponding to the threshold while providers submit the right ciphertext corresponding to their dLDP-encoded event values. Consequently, $\mathcal{A}_{lc}$ can only evaluate comparison outcomes against the threshold and cannot reconstruct the global ordering among providers' raw event values, since it does not obtain providers' left ciphertexts.

Consider $\mathcal{A}_{gc}$, acting as an honest-but-curious global CEP node. $\mathcal{A}_{gc}$ receives local complex events and may attempt to infer more than intended from them. The local complex event received by the global CEP node is derived from comparison-based, temporal, and conjunctive operations over a dLDP-perturbed noisy bucket encoding. Since these operations are post-processing of a dLDP mechanism, and therefore do not weaken the ϵ-dLDP guarantee with respect to the original events.

Finally, consider $\mathcal{A}_c$, an honest-but-curious consumer, who receives global complex events and may try to infer individual event information. Similarly, the global complex event result is obtained by further aggregating and correlating local complex events. These are also post-processing steps applied to the dLDP-protected output, which satisfy the privacy guarantee.

5.2 Experimental Evaluation

To evaluate our proposed distributed CEP framework, we run experiments with a varying number of providers and local CEP nodes. We use synthetic data, where each provider generates events uniformly at random from the range $[0, 100]$. This bounded domain represents normalized real-world metrics (e.g., utilization percentage, scaled temperature, or bounded sensor readings). The use of uniformly distributed synthetic data enables a controlled evaluation of privacy and computational overhead independent of application-specific event distributions. Each provider submits two event types, and the local CEP node detects a local complex event when both encrypted events satisfy their corresponding threshold predicates within a temporal window.

We used the FastORE [23] library to implement ORE encryption. We compare the proposed framework with a baseline CEP system that is a conventional centralized CEP system, and it protects communication channels using symmetric encryption, but does not support privacy-preserving encrypted event processing. Each experiment is repeated 30 times, and the results are averaged. All experiments are run in a Docker container on an Ubuntu machine with QEMU Virtual CPU emulating an Intel processor with 8 cores and 8 GB of RAM.

Based on this setup, we conduct the following experiments to evaluate the proposed scheme. First, we assess accuracy as the proportion of correctly detected complex events compared to the ground-truth results obtained from the non-private CEP execution. Second, we measure the total computational cost to evaluate the overhead introduced by the privacy-preserving CEP scheme. Third,

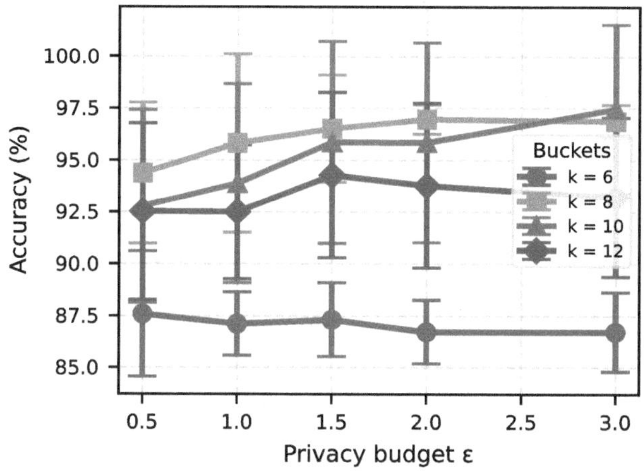

Fig. 2. Accuracy vs Privacy budget ϵ for different number of buckets.

we analyze how the computational burden is distributed across different entities. Lastly, we examine the effect of distributed CEP system on scalability. The evaluation focuses on utility and computational overhead, while inference-attack resilience follows from the formal dLDP guarantees established in [20] and the security analysis in Sect. 5.1.

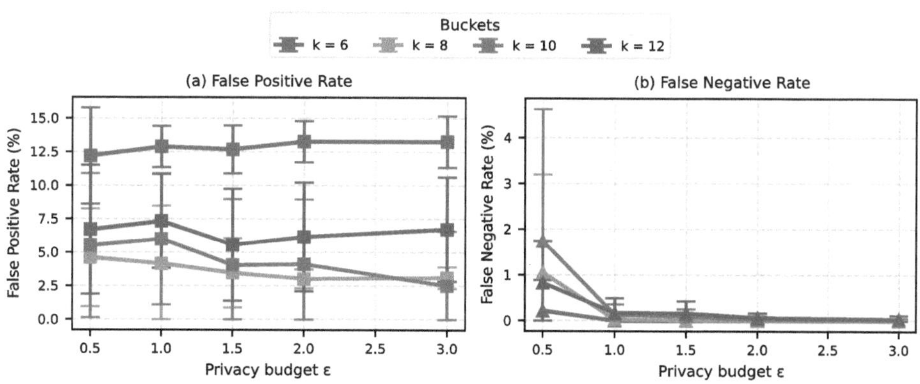

Fig. 3. False positive and false negative rates under different privacy budgets.

Figure 2 shows the accuracy of the proposed scheme for different bucket sizes. The accuracy ranges from 87% to 97.5% across the tested settings, demonstrating that the proposed scheme maintains a high pattern-detection accuracy under privacy protection. The system achieves a peak accuracy of 96.9% at $k = 8$ and $\epsilon = 2.0$, where k is the number of buckets. Even under stronger privacy protection at $\epsilon = 1.5$, the system still achieves comparable accuracy of 96.6%.

The results further show that bucketization significantly affects utility. Specifically, $k = 10$ and $k = 12$ achieve slightly lower accuracy than $k = 8$ because finer granularity increases the likelihood of noise-induced boundary crossings near the threshold. Conversely, $k = 6$ also results in lower accuracy because values that are far apart may fall into the same bucket, leading to false-positive pattern matches. Therefore, $k = 8$ and $\epsilon = 1.5$ were selected for the remaining experiments because they provide a favorable balance between privacy and accuracy.

In addition to detection accuracy, we also measured the false-positive rate (FPR) and false-negative rate (FNR), as shown in Fig. 3. The results indicate that utility degradation is mainly caused by false-positive detections rather than missed detections. In particular, $k = 6$ consistently produces a high FPR due to coarse bucketization, which increases collisions of unrelated values. In contrast, the FNR remains close to zero across most parameter settings, indicating that the proposed CEP system maintains sensitivity to true complex events despite the dLDP perturbation. Overall, increasing the privacy budget decreases the FPR while maintaining a near-zero FNR.

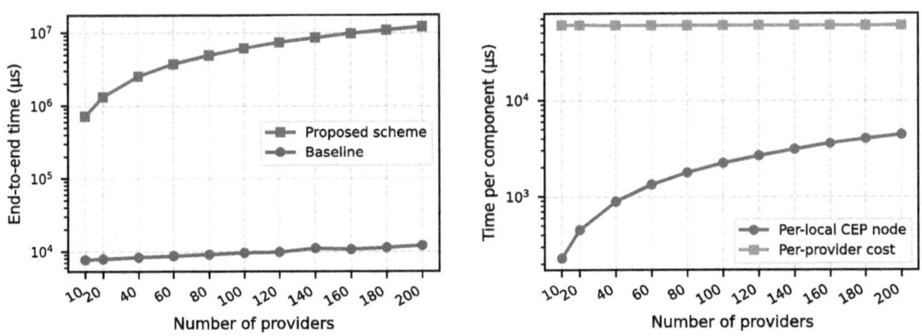

(a) Computational Overhead. (b) Cost Breakdown.

Fig. 4. Computational cost evaluation of the proposed scheme. Both y-axis are shown in logarithmic scale.

Using this configuration ($k = 8$, $\epsilon = 1.5$), we examine the total computational cost of the proposed CEP system. Figure 4a compares the total computational cost of our proposed system with the baseline, keeping the number of local CEP nodes fixed at 4. As expected, the total cost for both systems increases with the number of providers due to the additional per-provider event-processing overhead. However, the proposed privacy-preserving CEP system incurs significantly higher computational cost than the baseline due to the additional overhead of dLDP and ORE encryption.

Figure 4b presents a breakdown of the computational burden in the proposed privacy-preserving CEP system, with 4 local CEP nodes. The computational cost for providers remains independent of network size. In contrast, the cost for local

CEP nodes increases with the number of providers, since the number of events to process grows with each additional provider.

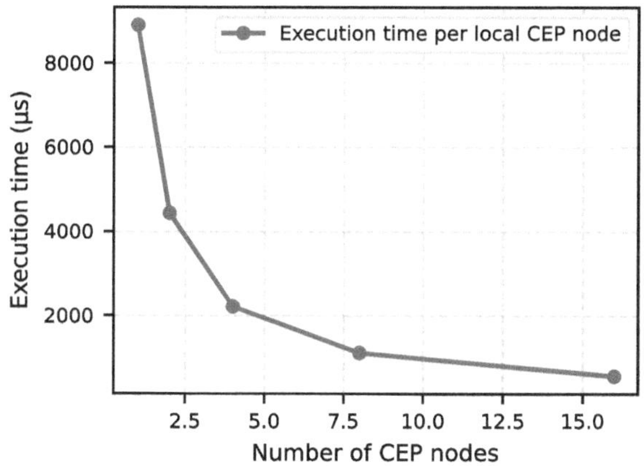

Fig. 5. Effect of scaling the number of local CEP nodes on the execution time per local CEP node.

Figure 5 illustrates the scalability benefits of the proposed distributed CEP system. With a fixed total of 100 providers, the experiment varies the number of local CEP nodes. As shown, the per-node execution time (μs) scales almost linearly with the number of local CEP nodes. For example, increasing the number of local CEP nodes from 1 to 16 reduces per-node execution time from 8904 μs to 558 μs. These results indicate that the proposed privacy-preserving CEP framework reduces the per-node computational burden while preserving privacy.

6 Conclusion

In this paper, we proposed a privacy-preserving distributed CEP framework that combines dLDP and ORE to support comparison-based pattern detection over encrypted event streams. The proposed scheme achieves both event-level and pattern-level privacy. We formally showed that the proposed scheme preserves ϵ-dLDP privacy under the considered honest-but-curious threat model. Experimental results show that the distributed architecture improves scalability by reducing the computational burden on CEP nodes. Furthermore, the proposed scheme achieves high pattern-detection accuracy with low false-negative rates, although privacy preservation introduces additional computational overhead compared to conventional CEP systems. In the future, we plan to extend the work to stronger adversarial settings, including malicious or colluding entities, and to investigate support for more expressive CEP patterns over encrypted streams.

Acknowledgements. The authors acknowledge the assistance of OpenAI's GPT-5 model in editing and improving the clarity and readability of the manuscript. Specifically, this prompt was used: "You are an editor. Improve flow and correct any spelling, grammar, and language mistakes in the following text. Do not add or change any information." The model was solely used for language refinement and did not contribute to the research content or analysis.

Disclosure of Interests. The authors have no competing interests to declare that are relevant to the content of this article.

References

1. Akyildiz, I.F., Su, W., Sankarasubramaniam, Y., Cayirci, E.: Wireless sensor networks: a survey. Comput. Netw. **38**(4), 393–422 (2002)
2. Alenezi, M.N., Alabdulrazzaq, H., Mohammad, N.Q.: Symmetric encryption algorithms: review and evaluation study. Int. J. Commun. Netw. Inform. Security **12**(2), 256–272 (2020)
3. Boldyreva, A., Chenette, N., O'Neill, A.: Order-preserving encryption revisited: Improved security analysis and alternative solutions. In: Annual Cryptology Conference, pp. 578–595. Springer (2011)
4. Boneh, D., Goh, E.J., Nissim, K.: Evaluating 2-DNF formulas on ciphertexts. In: Theory of Cryptography Conference, pp. 325–341. Springer (2005)
5. Chanal, P.M., Kakkasageri, M.S.: Security and privacy in IoT: a survey. Wireless Pers. Commun. **115**(2), 1667–1693 (2020)
6. Chen, C.Y., Fu, J.H., Sung, T., Wang, P.F., Jou, E., Feng, M.W.: Complex event processing for the internet of things and its applications. In: 2014 IEEE International Conference on Automation Science and Engineering (CASE), pp. 1144–1149. IEEE (2014)
7. Cugola, G., Margara, A.: Processing flows of information: from data stream to complex event processing. ACM Comput. Surv. (CSUR) **44**(3), 1–62 (2012)
8. Daemen, J., Rijmen, V.: Aes proposal: Rijndael (1999)
9. Grubbs, P., Sekniqi, K., Bindschaedler, V., Naveed, M., Ristenpart, T.: Leakage-abuse attacks against order-revealing encryption. In: 2017 IEEE Symposium on Security and Privacy (SP), pp. 655–672. IEEE (2017)
10. Gu, H., Plagemann, T., Benndorf, M., Goebel, V., Koldehofe, B.: Differential privacy for protecting private patterns in data streams. In: 2023 IEEE 39th International Conference on Data Engineering Workshops (ICDEW), pp. 118–124. IEEE (2023)
11. He, W., Liu, X., Nguyen, H., Nahrstedt, K., Abdelzaher, T.: PDA: Privacy-preserving data aggregation in wireless sensor networks. In: Proceedings of the IEEE INFOCOM, pp. 2045–2053. IEEE (2007)
12. He, Y., Barman, S., Wang, D., Naughton, J.F.: On the complexity of privacy-preserving complex event processing. In: Proceedings of the thirtieth ACM SIGMOD-SIGACT-SIGART Symposium on Principles of Database Systems, pp. 165–174 (2011)
13. Ku, T., Zhu, Y., Hu, K., Nan, L.: A novel distributed complex event processing for rfid application. In: Third International Conference on Convergence and Hybrid Information Technology, vol. 1, pp. 1113–1117. IEEE (2008)

14. Lewi, K., Wu, D.J.: Order-revealing encryption: New constructions, applications, and lower bounds. In: Proceedings of the 2016 ACM SIGSAC Conference on Computer and Communications Security, pp. 1167–1178 (2016)
15. Lindell, Y.: Secure multiparty computation. Commun. ACM **64**(1), 86–96 (2020)
16. Liu, W.: Privacy-preserving comparison based data aggregation protocols for mobile sensing. Peer-to-Peer Network. Appl. **15**(1), 549–558 (2022)
17. Lotfian Delouee, M., Koldehofe, B., Degeler, V.: Poster: Towards pattern-level privacy protection in distributed complex event processing. In: Proceedings of the 17th ACM International Conference on Distributed and Event-Based Systems, pp. 185–186 (2023)
18. Palanisamy, S.M., Dürr, F., Tariq, M.A., Rothermel, K.: Preserving privacy and quality of service in complex event processing through event reordering, pp. 40–51. ACM DEBS (2018)
19. Rahmani, A.M., et al.: Exploiting smart e-health gateways at the edge of healthcare internet-of-things: a fog computing approach. Futur. Gener. Comput. Syst. **78**, 641–658 (2018)
20. Chowdhury, R., Ding, A., Jha, B., Liu, S., Zhou, W., J.: Strengthening order preserving encryption with differential privacy. In: ACM CCS, pp. 2519–2533 (2022)
21. Saleh, O., Sattler, K.U.: Distributed complex event processing in sensor networks. In: IEEE 14th International Conference on Mobile Data Management, vol. 2, pp. 23–26. IEEE (2013)
22. Tawalbeh, L., Muheidat, F., Tawalbeh, M., Quwaider, M.: IoT privacy and security: challenges and solutions. Appl. Sci. **10**(12), 4102 (2020)
23. Wu, D., Lewi, K.: FastORE: Fast order-revealing encryption (2016). https://github.com/kevinlewi/fastore, gitHub repository
24. Xiong, X., Liu, S., Li, D., Cai, Z., Niu, X.: A comprehensive survey on local differential privacy. Security Commun. Netw. **2020**(1), 8829523 (2020)
25. Yi, X., Paulet, R., Bertino, E.: Homomorphic encryption. In: Homomorphic encryption and applications, pp. 27–46. Springer (2014)
26. Zeng, Z., Liu, Y., Chang, L.: A robust and optional privacy data aggregation scheme for fog-enhanced IoT network. IEEE Syst. J. **17**(1), 1110–1120 (2022)

Proceedings of the Sixth International Workshop on Security Testing and Monitoring (STAM 2026)

Automating Security-by-Design in Microservices via Model-Driven DevSecOps

Ciro Gallucci[1], Felice Moretta[2], Massimiliano Rak[1], and Umberto Villano[3](✉)

[1] DIETI, University of Naples Federico II, Naples, Italy
ciro.gallucci@unina.it, massimiliano.rak@unina.it
[2] Department of Engineering, University of Campania Vanvitelli, Aversa (NA), Italy
felice.moretta@unicampania.it
[3] DING, University of Sannio, Benevento, Italy
villano@unisannio.it

Abstract. Microservices architectures are increasingly adopted for distributed application development, but their dynamic and heterogeneous nature introduces security challenges that are difficult to address with traditional Secure Development Lifecycle methods. This work presents an automated and model-driven methodology for the secure design of microservices-based applications, combining the MetaSEnD metamodel with a DevSecOps-oriented workflow. Starting from declarative specifications (e.g., Docker compose files), the approach generates a Multi-purpose Application Composition Model (MACM) that represents the structure and interactions of the application. Automated graph-based pattern matching is then used to identify architectural vulnerabilities and derive a threat model, which guides the generation of customized DevSecOps pipelines with security tools integrated into the CI/CD cycle. The methodology was validated on a real use case, showing how risk identification and security testing activities can be systematically derived from the application model and embedded into the development lifecycle. By automating these activities and integrating them into CI/CD pipelines, the approach can help reduce release latency associated with manual security assessment, while supporting security-by-design in cloud-native environments through a stronger connection between architectural modeling, threat analysis, and automated security validation.

Keywords: Microservices Security · Secure Software Development Lifecycle · DevSecOps · Model-Driven Security · CI/CD · Threat Modeling · Vulnerability Assessment · Security-by-Design · Pipeline Automation

1 Introduction

Microservice architectures have transformed modern software engineering by enabling modularity, scalability, and rapid delivery. However, their highly dis-

P. Kieseberg et al. (Eds.): ARES 2026 Workshops, LNCS 16903, pp. 515–532, 2027.
https://doi.org/10.1007/978-3-032-37218-5_30

tributed nature significantly increases architectural complexity, making system-wide security a challenging and still largely unresolved problem.

Traditional Secure Development Lifecycles (SDLCs), such as the Microsoft Security Development Lifecycle [25], were designed to provide a structured set of security-focused activities throughout the software development process. While effective in conventional settings, these methodologies tend to be time-consuming, resource-intensive, and difficult to reconcile with the accelerated pace of microservices development. Even agile adaptations of SDLCs [5,29] often introduce significant overhead, thereby reducing cost-effectiveness and slowing down the time-to-market. This tension between the need for robust security guarantees and the demand for rapid delivery highlights the necessity of new approaches to secure software engineering, specifically tailored to the microservices paradigm.

In this work, we propose an innovative methodology for secure microservices development, grounded in the MetaSEnD metamodeling approach described in [11]. The overarching goal is to automate all phases of secure development—ranging from design to deployment—so as to reduce costs, minimize delays and integrate security as a first-class concern rather than a retrofitted control. The methodology builds upon four foundational principles:

1. **Security-by-Design approach**, meaning that security requirements and constraints are considered from the very beginning of the application lifecycle, ensuring that microservices are designed to mitigate vulnerabilities by construction rather than through reactive countermeasures;
2. **Model-Based Development**, whereby a formal model of the application provides the basis for both development and assessment. This enables early and systematic evaluation of security properties, even when some microservice components are incomplete or not yet implemented;
3. **Adoption of the SecDevOps paradigm**, in which development and operational processes are tightly coupled, ensuring that the security implications of both new features and configuration changes are addressed jointly. This guarantees that deployment, monitoring and maintenance activities are consistently integrated into the secure development workflow;
4. **Continuous Integration/Continuous Deployment (CI/CD)**, where development, unit testing, integration testing and deployment are fully automated. This facilitates immediate feedback on the global impact of any modification – whether it involves the implementation of a new microservice, the update of an existing one, or a configuration change.

Based on these principles, the proposed methodology introduces the use of *declarative specifications* as the initial input of the development process. In the current implementation, the approach has been developed and validated on Docker compose files, which are used to describe multi-container microservice applications. However, the methodology is not intrinsically tied to this specific artifact: its model-driven structure makes it potentially extensible to other deployment or infrastructure descriptions, such as Kubernetes manifests, or other infrastructure-as-code templates, by adapting the initial transformation step. Even when some containers are not fully implemented, these specifications serve as high-level descriptions of the application, outlining the technological solutions adopted in development – which influence strongly the system security and the methods used for its assessment and evaluation.

The proposed approach enables two key outcomes: first, it allows the automatic generation of an application model suitable for systematic and automated security assessment; second, it supports the creation of a dedicated CI/CD environment where testing, evaluation and deployment are carried out in both staging and production contexts. Within this environment, a variety of security and testing tools can be integrated seamlessly, ensuring that secure development is achieved without sacrificing agility.

By combining modeling, automation, and security-by-design, this methodology addresses the limitations of traditional secure development lifecycles. It provides a practical pathway toward efficient and secure engineering of microservices-based applications, reducing the trade-off between security and time-to-market. Ultimately, our approach aims to foster a new generation of security-aware, model-driven, and DevOps-integrated development processes capable of supporting the complex demands of distributed, cloud-native software ecosystems.

This paper is structured as follows. Section 2 reviews related work, highlighting existing approaches and their limitations. The proposed methodology is described in Sects. 3, 4, and 5, which introduce the Security-by-Design workflow, the model generation and analysis process and the security-aware pipeline generation, respectively. Section 6 presents a case study demonstrating the applicability and effectiveness of the methodology in a representative scenario. Finally, Sect. 7 concludes the paper and outlines directions for future work.

2 Related Work

This section presents an analysis of existing security assessment practices within DevSecOps for microservice- and container-based systems. The literature outlines a broad range of security practices adopted across different domains. These include general-purpose vulnerability analysis methodologies, such as the orchestration of Static and Dynamic Application Security Testing (SAST/DAST) tools as OWASP ZAP and SonarQube within CI/CD pipelines [1]. Specialized testing includes automated penetration testing architectures leveraging Metasploit and OWASP ZAP for web applications [22]. For container environments, practices emphasize image vulnerability analysis through static and dynamic scanning [3], automated scanning and patching workflows integrated with CVE and OWASP databases [18], and frameworks designed to correlate vulnerabilities across both application and container images (e.g., CAVAS) [26]. Furthermore, security practices extend to domain-specific areas such as privacy-preserving frameworks based on Secure Multi-Party Computation (MPC) protocols for record linkage in health contexts [13]. Practices also cover novel areas like Machine Learning (ML)-based runtime attack detection in microservices using models such as XGBoost, KNN, and SVM [6].

As regards the stage in which these security practices are introduced into the software development lifecycle, there is no dominant solution at the state of the art, even if it is possible to find a tendency towards late integration. **Early-stage (Design/Build)** contributions include efforts to automate threat modeling through techniques such as the automatic extraction of security-enriched Data Flow Diagrams (DFDs) from Java microservice applications [23]. Other design-phase works focus on defining security baselines and secure requirements using manual processes such as the Microsoft Threat Modeling Tool (TMT) and the SQUARE method [8,12,14]. Practices heavily integrated into the **Build and Deploy** phases involve automated scanning and patching of Docker images [18] and the automation of security measures during deployment for multi-cloud applications [24]. Practices addressing the **full lifecycle**, from design through runtime, are often conceptual—such as the MetaSEnD meta-model [11] and the SecCo framework, which proposes modules for hardening and compliance across the DevOps paradigm [28]. **Runtime** assessment is also critical, including continuous security assessments in Cloud Native Applications (CNA) [27], attack detection via ML [6], and serverless component discovery through approximate concrete execution (ACE) [4].

The level of automation provided in existing solutions varies significantly. Several studies demonstrate **high automation** through tool orchestration in CI/CD pipelines, such as the integration of SAST/DAST tools (ZAP and SonarQube) [1], automated binary discovery (ACE) [4], and the use of Python scripts to automate vulnerability scanning and patching for Docker images [18]. Automated penetration testing frameworks also reach a high level of automation by orchestrating tools like Metasploit and OWASP ZAP [22]. Conversely, many early-stage security activities – such as defining security baselines and applying traditional threat modeling [17,19] – remain largely **manual or conceptual guidelines**, lacking concrete automation artifacts. This suggests that automation is generally achieved where tools can be easily integrated into build and operational workflows, often resulting in reactive practices.

Model-driven or model-based approaches used for security assessment are explicitly **rare** [2,4], confirming the existence of a research gap. Only a few studies adopt formal models to drive automation. Key contributions include the use of data flow diagrams (DFDs) [23] as artifacts automatically extracted from code, the application of the meta-model (or planned mapping) within the MetaSEnD framework to integrate security into the SSDLC [11], and the utilization of knowledge graphs (KGs), such as DocSecKG [31], to represent relationships between Docker images and vulnerabilities for holistic visibility and actionable insights. While the SecCo framework suggests model-driven potential through its focus on pipeline modularity for full-lifecycle composition [28], it remains conceptual and lacks full implementation. The vast majority of retained studies rely on *ad hoc* or hybrid methodologies that do not utilize formal model-driven techniques.

Furthermore, the analysis of the literature and of existing frameworks and tools identifies several recurring limitations. Many conceptual proposals –such as frameworks providing only security baselines [12]– lack **empirical validation**

[2,17] or large-scale evaluation [11,16]. Technical limitations include restricted scope, such as the specific focus on Java/Spring in automatic DFD extraction methods, limiting polyglot support [22,23]. Security tools often have limited coverage, failing to include dependencies or containers in their analysis [1]. Furthermore, highly automated systems face challenges in ensuring accuracy (e.g., tuning required for ACE fingerprinting [4]), dealing with scanner inaccuracies [26], and relying on external vulnerability feeds for knowledge-based systems like DocSecKG [31]. Finally, specialized domains face constraints related to performance, network limitations, and the complexity of legal assessments when integrating advanced security solutions as MPC protocols into DevSecOps [13].

In conclusion, an in-depth analysis of the state of the art reveals a **fragmented landscape** characterized by heterogeneous practices, uneven automation, and inconsistent validation depth. The key finding emerging is that the **systematic integration of model-driven reasoning with automated DevSecOps pipelines remains largely unexplored**.

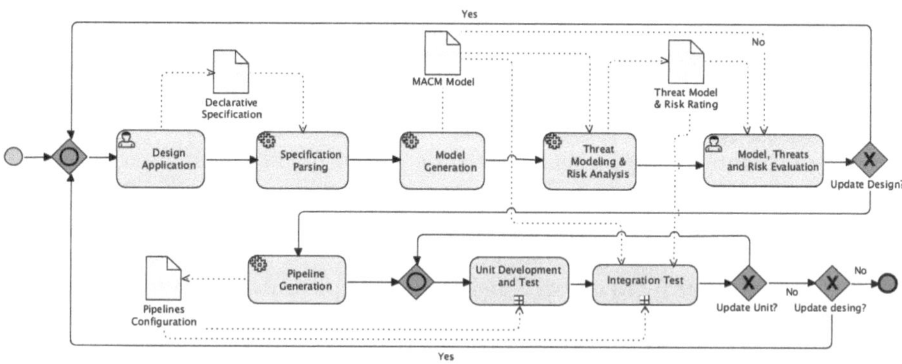

Fig. 1. Security-by-Design Workflow. An expanded version of the diagram is available in the project repository [30].

3 The Security-by-Design Workflow

The proposed approach introduces a model-driven workflow for the secure development of container-based applications, represented in the BPMN diagram reported in Fig. 1. The process begins when the developer initiates the project by creating a *declaration specification* – for example, a `docker-compose` file, that describes the application in terms of microservices (containers) and their interactions.

From the declaration specification, the workflow first derives an **application model**, which acts as the foundation for the subsequent security activities. This intermediate step is necessary because deployment descriptors, such as `docker-compose` files, mainly capture operational configuration details, whereas security analysis requires an explicit representation of services, dependencies, communication paths, exposed interfaces, and trust boundaries. The model therefore provides a normalized and technology-independent abstraction of the application, reducing the complexity of directly processing heterogeneous deployment artifacts and making the following analyses reproducible and automatable.

The application model is then used as a common artefact for multiple activities. It enables the automatic derivation of a detailed threat model of the system – similar to what is produced by threat modeling tools – together with an estimation of the risk associated with each identified threat. The same model also supports the selection of security controls and testing activities that will later be embedded into the pipeline configuration. This choice improves traceability, since each generated threat, risk, control, or pipeline step can be linked back to specific architectural elements in the model. Moreover, decoupling the workflow from the concrete input format makes the approach extensible: while the current implementation starts from a `docker-compose` specification, other descriptors, such as Kubernetes manifests or infrastructure-as-code templates, could be supported by replacing only the initial transformation step.

The design phase then proceeds by iteratively reviewing both the threat model and the application architecture before generating the final pipeline configuration. This allows security experts and developers to identify architectural weaknesses early, refine the model, and introduce additional security-related components before these decisions are propagated to container images, deployment settings, or pipeline definitions. Once the application description and its associated threat model are deemed satisfactory, the process advances to the generation of the complete pipeline configuration.

The **pipeline configuration** consists of multiple automated pipelines. Each container image within the application is assigned a **dedicated pipeline**, customized according to the technologies used in the image. These pipelines incorporate container-specific security testing to ensure that the resulting container images comply with security requirements and are free from common vulnerabilities. In addition, an **integration pipeline** is generated for the application as a whole. This pipeline orchestrates the deployment of the microservice-based system into a testing environment and executes a series of automated assessments, including static configuration analysis, dynamic security testing, and penetration testing. These tests are automatically derived from the application model, ensuring that security validation is consistent with the architecture and threat landscape of the system[1].

Overall, this workflow seamlessly integrates security considerations into the application lifecycle. By coupling automatic model generation, threat modeling, and CI/CD pipelines, it enables a continuous and systematic enforcement of secure development practices in microservice-oriented applications, while preserving an explicit feedback loop between architectural design, risk analysis, and implementation-level security validation.

[1] Due to space constraints, the detailed workflow of the pipelines (BPMN subprocesses) is collapsed and not fully visible in Fig. 1.

4 Model Generation and Analysis

The adopted model-based approach relies on the **Multi-purpose Application Composition Model (MACM)** [15,21], which is a *Property Graph*. In this model, each node represents a system asset (e.g., services, networks, hardware) and each edge represents a relationship between two resources (e.g., uses, hosts, connects). The distinctive feature of property graphs is that both nodes and edges can be annotated with types (labels) and properties, giving MACM the expressive power needed to capture both the architectural structure and the operational semantics of the system under analysis.

Each node in MACM is described by three levels of classification: a *Primary Label* (broad category, e.g., `Service`, `Network`, `HW`), an optional *Secondary Label* (specialization, e.g., `LAN`, `OS`, `VM`), and a mandatory *Asset Type* property, which provides the most fine-grained classification (e.g., `Network.LAN`, `SystemLayer.OS`). In addition, nodes include unique identifiers and descriptive properties. Edges can also have associated properties, particularly useful for describing communication. For instance, a `connects` edge could include `network_protocol` = "IPv4" or `application_protocol` = "HTTP", while a `uses` edge could specify `transport_protocol` = "TCP".

The **MACM schema** defines the rules that any model must follow. A schema specifies the admissible node and edge types, the properties that can be attached to them, and the constraints that govern their use. In MACM, these constraints are divided into *Syntactic Constraints* and *Semantic Constraints*. The former ensure structural validity of the model, such as the uniqueness of identifiers, the cardinality of property values, overall graph connectivity, and the acyclicity of specific relations. The latter ensure domain-specific correctness. For example, one constraint specifies that each service must be hosted or provided by exactly one node.

MACM models are implemented as **Neo4j**[2] graph databases, where structural and semantic constraints are enforced through *Cypher queries* and automated *APOC triggers*[3], ensuring model consistency. In summary, MACM is a formal, extensible, and verifiable modeling framework that captures heterogeneous IT infrastructures at multiple abstraction levels. An existing MACM-based web platform, Pennet[4], already supports threat model and penetration testing plan generation, as well as semi-automatic risk analysis [15,20,21]. This work builds on these capabilities by using MACM as the intermediate representation in the proposed security-by-design workflow.

---

[2] https://neo4j.com.

[3] https://neo4j.com/labs/apoc/2025/background-operations/triggers/.

[4] https://pennet.vseclab.it/.

Algorithm 1: MACM generation from docker-compose (Property-Graph abstraction)

```
Data: Docker Compose YAML dcYAML
Result: Property graph G (MACM instance)
Function DockerComposeToMACM(dcYAML):
    G ← PG_NewGraph()
    vm ← PG_AddNode(G, labels= (Virtual, VM),
      props= {name : "VM", type : "Virtual.VM"})
    vmOS ← PG_AddNode(G, labels= (SystemLayer, OS),
      props= {name : "VM_OS", type : "SystemLayer.OS"})
    PG_AddEdge(G, type= hosts, src= vm, dst= vmOS)
    docker ← PG_AddNode(G, labels= (SystemLayer, ContainerRuntime),
      props= {name : "Docker", type : "SystemLayer.ContainerRuntime"})
    PG_AddEdge(G, type= hosts, src= vmOS, dst= docker)
    dc ← ParseYAML(dcYAML)
    S ← keys(dc.services)
    Nets ← keys(dc.networks) ∪ {default}
    Initialize NetNodes ← {}
    foreach net ∈ Nets do
        netNode ← PG_AddNode(G, labels= (Network, LAN),
          props= {name : net, type : "Network.LAN"})
        PG_AddEdge(G, type= hosts, src= vmOS, dst= netNode)
        NetNodes[net] ← netNode
    end foreach
    Initialize ServiceNode ← {}, Uses ← {}
    foreach (svc, cfg) ∈ dc.services do
        ext_ports ← ExtractHostPorts(cfg.ports)
        c ← PG_AddNode(G, labels= (Virtual, Container),
          props= {name : svc + "_container", type : "Virtual.Container"})
        PG_AddEdge(G, type= hosts, src= docker, dst= c)
        sOS ← PG_AddNode(G, labels= (SystemLayer, OS),
          props= {name : svc + "_OS", type : "SystemLayer.OS"})
        PG_AddEdge(G, type= hosts, src= c, dst= sOS)
        (sN_Labels, sN_AssetType) ← CustomizeAssetType
          (GetSuggestedLabels(ext_ports), GetSuggestedAssetType(ext_ports))
        sN ← PG_AddNode(G, labels=sN_Labels,
          props= {name : svc, type : sN_AssetType, ports : ext_ports})
        PG_AddEdge(G, type= hosts, src= sOS, dst= sN)
        ServiceNode[svc] ← sN
        foreach net ∈ cfg.networks do
            PG_AddEdge(G, type=connects, src=NetNodes[net], dst=c)
        end foreach
        if cfg.depends_on exists then
            Uses[svc] ← cfg.depends_on
        end if
    end foreach
    foreach (s, deps) ∈ Uses do
        foreach d ∈ deps do
            PG_AddEdge(G, type= uses, src= ServiceNode[s], dst= ServiceNode[d])
        end foreach
    end foreach
    return G
```

Algorithm 1 shows the pseudocode of the function that builds a MACM graph from a Docker compose specification. The function receives the Docker Compose file in YAML format and produces a representation of the system as a property graph, encoded as a Cypher query. In the pseudocode, however, the details of Cypher are hidden by abstract functions such as PG_AddNode and PG_AddEdge. The procedure begins by creating a new property graph G and adding a base structure: a virtual machine (*VM*) that hosts an operating system (*VM_OS*), which in turn hosts *Docker*. Next, the Docker Compose file is parsed. Since YAML is a structured format, it makes it easier to extract elements of interest, such as services and networks. Networks are added first. This ensures that when services are created, they can be connected to the correct networks immediately. Each network node is stored in a structure (called *NetNodes*) so that it can be referenced later. For every service defined in the Compose file, three nodes are created in the graph: one for the container, one for the operating system running inside it, and one for the service itself. Moreover, by leveraging the ESSecA (Expert System for Security Assessment) knowledge base that maps well-known ports to service categories and asset types, the auxiliary functions `GetSuggestedLabels` and `GetSuggestedAssetType` can infer suggested node labels and an asset type for each service based on the exposed ports; these suggestions can be overridden or refined during subsequent validation. If a service depends on other services (via the `depends_on` directive), this information is collected in a dedicated structure (*Uses*). Finally, each dependency is translated into an edge of type `uses` between the two service nodes. These edges are added only after all services have been created, because during the first pass the dependent service may not yet exist in the graph.

Once the MACM model is instantiated and enriched, it serves as the basis for automated Threat Modeling and Risk Analysis (TM/RA). Using graph pattern-matching techniques, the system identifies structural motifs corresponding to known vulnerability classes. For instance, a container exposing a database port to a public network may be flagged as a critical misconfiguration. The output of this step is a set of annotated threats and security requirements propagated back into the MACM. These annotations formalize security constraints to be enforced in subsequent stages and provide a machine-readable representation of the system threat landscape. Sufficiently complex systems often exhibit a considerable number of threats that need to be analyzed. For this reason, Risk Analysis is applied to identify the threats with the highest risk, thereby establishing a priority order for their analysis and mitigation. The analysis follows the OWASP Risk Rating Methodology[5], which combines *Likelihood* and *Impact* to classify risks as Low, Medium, or High. Likelihood is derived from threat-agent and vulnerability factors, using the Threat Agent Library taxonomy and the MACM threat catalogue, while Impact combines technical effects on confidentiality, integrity, availability, and accountability with user-customizable business values. Most parameters are computed from the model and catalogues, limiting manual input to context-specific business aspects. A full description of the threat model generation and risk analysis is beyond the scope of this paper. The interested reader is referred to [7–10] for further details.

[5] https://owasp.org/www-community/OWASP_Risk_Rating_Methodology.

5 Security-Aware Pipeline Generation

Guided by the provided Docker compose, the framework automatically synthesizes Jenkins-based DevSecOps pipelines. Pipelines are instantiated both at the level of individual containers (microservices) and at the composite system level. Microservice pipelines, each associated with a single Dockerfile, perform local operations such as repository cloning from GitHub, technology-specific static application security testing (SAST), build and run, Docker image creation, local deployment, and configuration auditing with tools such as Chef InSpec. In contrast, the pipeline at the composite system level orchestrates the deployment of the integrated application using tools such as Terraform, executes remote deployment procedures, and performs system-wide security verification, including dynamic application security testing (DAST) and penetration testing. Unlike manually crafted pipelines, these automatically-generated workflows directly reflect the architectural model, ensuring reproducibility, consistency, and traceability across different application contexts.

Table 1. Selection of SAST tools for different technologies.

Tool	Description	Technology
PMD	Detects code quality issues, best practice violations, and code smells.	Go, Java, JavaScript, Kotlin, PHP, Python, Ruby, Scala, and Swift
Semgrep	Searches for patterns and vulnerabilities using syntax-based rules; highly configurable.	C, C++, Go, Java, JavaScript, PHP, Python, Ruby, and TypeScript
Bandit	Detects security vulnerabilities in Python code	Python
FindSecBugs	Security vulnerability detection for Java code.	Java
Flawfinder	Identifies security issues in C/C++ code.	C and C++
Bearer CLI	API security analysis, identifies misconfigurations and vulnerabilities.	RESTful Web APIs
Betterscan CE	Analyzes vulnerabilities in open-source dependencies.	OSS software dependencies

The framework we propose considers a set of static application security testing (SAST) tools, each targeting the programming languages of application components identified in the MACM model as custom code, and enforcing security rules or coding best practices. Table 1 reports the SAST tools planned for the complete framework, including their descriptions and applicable programming languages. The implementation of the proposed tool is publicly available in the project repository [30] and currently supports Bandit (version 1.8.3) for Python, PMD (version 6.21.0) for Java, and Flawfinder (version 2.0.19) for C/C++.

The function in Algorithm 2 takes as input only the `docker-compose` file, from which it parses and extracts structured information about the target system. The overall algorithm can be divided into two main phases: the first is responsible for generating pipelines for each individual microservice defined within the Docker compose, while the second constructs a pipeline for the entire application as a whole.

Algorithm 2: GeneratePipelines

```
Data: Docker compose YAML dcYAML
Result: Jenkins pipeline XML files for each SaaS component and XML file for the global
        pipeline
Function GeneratePipelines(dcYAML):
    dc ← ParseYAML(dcYAML)
    imageToolList ← GetImageToolList()
    ordServices ← ReorderServices(dc.services)
    pipelinesConfs ← {}
    foreach (svc, cfg) ∈ ordServices do
        /* Create single microservice pipeline                                    */
        svcRepo ← RequestServiceRepository(svc)
        outDir ← InitializeLocalRepo()
        RepositoryClone(svcRepo, outDir)
        technology ← IdentifyTechnology(outDir)
        sastToolList ← GetSastToolList(technology)
        foreach sastTool ∈ sastToolList do
            pipelineConfs[svc].appendStage(Execute, sastTool)
        end foreach
        if NeedCompile(technology) then
            pipelinesConfs[svc].appendStage(BuildRun, outDir, technology)
        end if
        pipelinesConfs[svc].appendStage(BuildRunImage, svc,cfg)
        foreach imageTool ∈ imageToolList do
            pipelinesConfs[svc].appendStage(Execute, imageTool)
        end foreach
    end foreach
    /* Create microservice application pipeline                                   */
    appPipelineConf ← []
    appPipelineConf.appendStage(AcquireResources)
    appPipelineConf.appendStage(DeployApplication)
    dastToolList ← GetDastToolList()
    foreach dastTool ∈ dastToolList do
        appPipelineConf.appendStage(Execute, dastTool)
    end foreach
    appPipelineConf.appendStage(RetrievePentests)
    appPipelineConf.appendStage(ExecutePentest)
    return (pipelinesConfs,appPipelineConf)
End Function
```

For each microservice, after obtaining the repository link and cloning it locally, the process starts by detecting the programming language in use. This information is then leveraged to determine the set of static analysis tools (SAST) that are applicable. Each identified tool is incorporated into the microservice's pipeline, following the formalism *pipeline*.`appendStage`(function, `variables`), where function denotes the operation to be executed within the pipeline, and variables are the parameters provided to that stage. If necessary, an additional stage is inserted to compile and locally execute the service code.

Subsequently, the pipeline includes steps to build and execute the container image for the microservice – an essential prerequisite for the next stage, which involves analyzing the base image using dedicated tools, such as operating system scanners. Since some microservices may depend on others (as indicated by the 'depends-on' relationships), the system first performs a dependency-based sorting, sequencing pipeline builds "from least dependent to most dependent". This ordering prevents cascading pipeline failures at the build and execution stage.

Once the pipelines for individual microservices have been generated, the focus shifts to building a unified pipeline for application-wide analysis. This phase begins by acquiring the resources required for deploying the entire project. At this point, the pipeline is enriched with dynamic analysis tools (DAST), which are incorporated into the process. The final stages involve extracting and executing penetration tests on the target system. These operations utilize the system's MACM model, derived by applying Algorithm 1 to the Docker compose file, and employ the ESSecA framework for security assessment.

6 Case Study: the Bookinfo Application

We developed a proof-of-concept system capable of implementing the workflow, and we tested the proposed methodology using the *Bookinfo* application[6], a widely adopted benchmark provided by the Istio service mesh framework. The application is specifically designed as a representative microservice-based system, offering a realistic yet controlled environment for experimenting with cloud-native deployment, service interaction, and security validation.

The Bookinfo application simulates an online retail scenario in which users can view information about a book, including its description, details, and reviews. It is composed of multiple loosely coupled microservices, each encapsulated in its own container and interconnected through well-defined APIs. This structure reflects typical design patterns of cloud-native applications, making it particularly suitable for research on DevSecOps automation.

At its core, the system includes the following main services:

- `productpage`: the entry point of the application, responsible for dynamically assembling book information by querying other backend services;
- `details` service: provides additional metadata about the book, such as the author, publication year, and other descriptive fields;
- `reviews` service: aggregates user-generated reviews for the book; this service exists in multiple versions, each illustrating incremental complexity and dependency on external components. In our setup, we selected the simplest version to ensure clarity and reproducibility of the experimental results;
- `ratings` service: manages the rating values associated with user reviews, typically relying on a simple data store.

From a DevSecOps perspective, the Bookinfo application provides an effective testbed for analyzing the implications of service exposure, inter-service communication and configuration management. Each microservice exposes interfaces and ports that may represent potential attack vectors if not properly secured. Dependencies between services must also be validated to avoid cascading vulnerabilities, particularly in the presence of third-party libraries or heterogeneous runtime environments. Additionally, the realistic yet bounded scale of the application enables systematic threat modeling, automated pipeline generation, and

[6] https://istio.io/latest/docs/examples/bookinfo/.

iterative validation of security enforcement mechanisms without the overhead of large-scale production systems.

The Bookinfo case study thus serves as a controlled and realistic environment for testing model-driven DevSecOps methodologies. Its combination of modular architecture, version variability and cloud-native deployment context makes it highly representative of the challenges faced in securing modern microservice-based applications.

6.1 Generation of the MACM Model for the Bookinfo Application

As outlined in Sect. 4, the proposed approach involves primarily the generation of an artifact, the MACM model of the system under analysis. By applying Algorithm 1, we obtained the MACM graph shown in Fig. 2. In addition to the basic structure described in Sect. 4, the model highlights the presence of the `bookinfo net` network, which interconnects all services, their corresponding containers and the related operating systems (user space). Moreover, from the `docker-compose` specification it is possible to infer that the `productpage` service relies on the `details` and `reviews` services, with the latter – in turn – depending on the `ratings` service.

The next step of the methodology consists in constructing the Threat Model for the system, followed by a Risk Analysis to prioritize the identified threats. For this purpose, we employed the ESSecA framework [20, 21], which automatically derives results directly from the MACM representation of the system. The analysis produced a total of 179 threats. The excerpt presented in Table 2 includes those threats that were evaluated as highest risk, according to the results of the risk analysis.

Table 2. Selection of highest-risk threats from the automated ESSecA analysis.

ID	Asset	Threat	Description	STRIDE	Likelihood	Impact	Overall Risk
1	productpage, details, ratings, reviews	Sensitive Data Exposure	Sensitive data can be stolen or modified, leading to fraud or identity theft.	I	Medium	High	High
2	productpage, details, ratings, reviews	Broken Authentication	Flaws in authentication let attackers access or impersonate users.	S	Medium	High	High
3	productpage_OS, details_OS, ratings_OS, reviews_OS	Data Breach	Confidential data may be accessed or stolen by unauthorized users.	I	Medium	High	High
4	productpage_OS, details_OS, ratings_OS, reviews_OS	Elevation of privileges	An attacker can obtain higher system privileges.	E	Medium	Medium	Medium
5	bookinfo_net	Topology Disclosure	An attacker can discover the internal network topology.	I	Medium	Medium	Medium
6	bookinfo_net	Eavesdrop-ping	An attacker can intercept transmitted communication data.	I	Medium	Medium	Medium

6.2 Pipeline Generation for the Bookinfo Application

To demonstrate the integration of DevSecOps practices within the proposed methodology, we deliberately focused on a single microservice of the Bookinfo

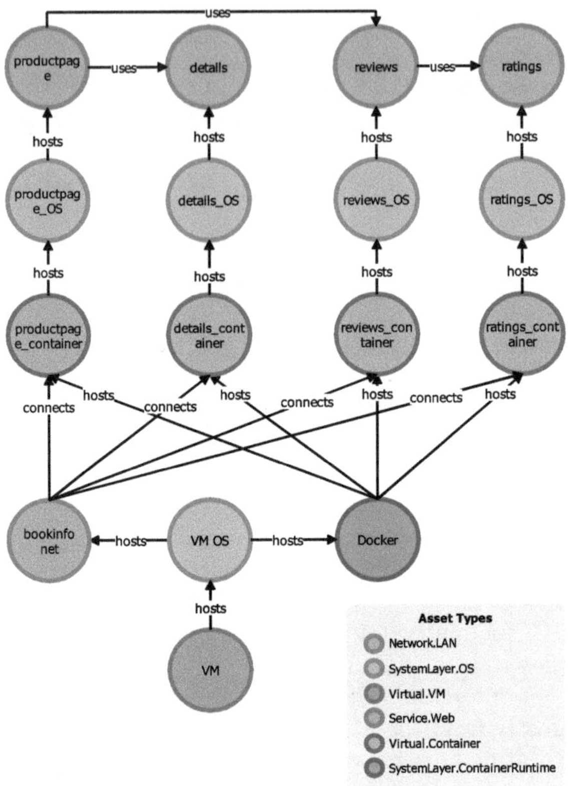

Fig. 2. BookInfo MACM

application. Among the available services, we selected the `productpage` component, as it represents the main entry point of the system and interacts with multiple back-end services. The decision to analyze the pipeline of a single microservice – rather than the comprehensive pipeline of the entire application – was made to provide a clear and manageable example of the proposed approach, while still capturing the essential characteristics of cloud-native DevSecOps workflows.

The corresponding Jenkins pipeline consists of multiple sequential stages, encompassing code retrieval, static analysis, build, containerization, runtime security assessment and final image publication. In particular, the pipeline automatically clones the Istio repository, extracts the code of the `productpage` service, initializes a local Git repository and executes language-aware static code analysis. A detection mechanism was introduced to select the appropriate tool depending on the programming language of the target service: for Python codebases (as in the case of `productpage`), the pipeline executes Bandit; for Java projects, PMD is triggered; and for C/C++ services, Flawfinder is applied.

For the `productpage` service, implemented in Python, Bandit produced reports in different formats. The analysis encompassed the entire codebase and identified a total of 584 issues, distributed across severity levels: 15 high, 36 medium, and 533 low. Among the most relevant findings, Bandit reported the absence of timeouts in HTTP requests, which could expose the service to denial-of-service attacks, and the exposure of the service on all network interfaces (threat ID 5). Another critical issue involved the presence of potentially dangerous Unicode characters that may obfuscate the source code. Additional warnings highlighted the use of assert statements in production code, unsafe command execution patterns, and the use of insecure modules for XML parsing. These results show that, despite being a benchmark application, `productpage` embeds both common and advanced security risks, emphasizing the value of automated code review in cloud-native development.

Following the static analysis, the pipeline proceeds with the build and run phases, generating a container image of the `productpage` service. The container then undergoes an additional security assessment based on Chef InSpec (version 7.0.107), leveraging the Linux baseline that comprised 109 checks, of which 8 failed. The results highlighted several issues, including an insecure configuration of `/etc./login.defs` parameters (UMASK set to 022 instead of the recommended 027; password maximum age set to 99999 days instead of 60; minimum password age set to 0 days instead of 7), world-readable cron configuration directories (`/etc./cron.daily` and `/etc./cron.d`), and a missing `noexec` mount option for `/dev`. These misconfigurations expose the system to unauthorized disclosure of scheduled jobs (threat ID 3), broken authentication due to weak credentials (threat ID 2) and privilege escalation (threat ID 4). The Apache baseline analysis further validated web server security, reporting only minimal findings for this specific setup.

Overall, the pipeline automates the complete build and deployment lifecycle and provides continuous, multi-layered security validation: code-level flaws are identified early via static analysis, while container hardening is verified at runtime through compliance benchmarks. This case study demonstrates the practical feasibility of embedding automated security checks in DevSecOps workflows for microservice-based, cloud-native applications.

7 Conclusions and Future Work

This paper has presented a Security-by-Design methodology for containerized microservices. It systematically links declarative specifications, currently Docker compose files, with automated DevSecOps workflows through the MACM modeling approach. Validation on the Bookinfo case study demonstrated that the model enables the automatic extraction of threats and security requirements, integrating them directly into Jenkins pipelines that manage validation, hardening of code and runtime configurations. This supports continuous and traceable enforcement of security properties throughout the application lifecycle.

The results should be interpreted in light of some limitations. The inference of MACM asset types from deployment descriptors is heuristic and may require manual validation, since the generated threat model can include false positives or redundant threats. Moreover, validation is currently limited to the Bookinfo case study, a realistic but bounded-scale benchmark, so scalability in enterprise, hybrid-cloud, or production-grade environments remains to be demonstrated. Finally, this work does not directly measure time-to-release, robustness, or effort reduction; the reported results therefore show technical feasibility and workflow integration, rather than a quantitative improvement over a baseline.

The current proof-of-concept also has specific platform limitations. It supports Docker Compose as input and generates Jenkins-based pipelines. The implemented security toolchain currently includes Bandit, PMD, Flawfinder, and InSpec, together with the model-based threat and risk analysis components described in this paper. Support for Kubernetes, Helm, Terraform, and broader tool ecosystems is not yet implemented and is considered future work.

As for future developments, the methodology is intended to be extended to other application and infrastructure scenarios. This would make it possible to address security directly at the level of cloud and network resource provisioning, thereby further expanding the scope of automation and control. We also intend to strengthen automated penetration testing before deployment, integrate compliance and monitoring tools in hybrid-cloud and multicluster environments, and quantitatively assess the effectiveness of the approach on larger-scale case studies and real production contexts.

Acknowledgments. This work was partially supported by the ECHO-TWIN project (B69H26001070007), the SUNS project (B69H26000520007), and the SecCo-OC project within the SERICS framework (D33C22001300002), all funded by italian MUR.

Disclosure of Interests. The authors have no competing interests to declare that are relevant to the content of this article.

References

1. Aparo, C., Bernardeschi, C., Lettieri, G., Lucattini, F., Montanarella, S.: An analysis system to test security of software on continuous integration-continuous delivery pipeline. In: 2023 IEEE European Symposium on Security and Privacy Workshops (EuroS&PW), pp. 58–67 (2023)
2. Bali, M.K., Mehdi, A.: Hariharan: AI-driven DevOps transformation: a paradigm shift in software development. In: 2024 3rd International Conference on Sentiment Analysis and Deep Learning (ICSADL), pp. 117–123 (2024)
3. Brady, K., Moon, S., Nguyen, T., Coffman, J.: Docker container security in cloud computing. In: 2020 10th Annual Computing and Communication Workshop and Conference (CCWC), pp. 0975–0980 (2020)
4. Byrne, A., Nadgowda, S., Coskun, A.K.: Ace: Just-in-time serverless software component discovery through approximate concrete execution. In: Proceedings of the 2020 Sixth International Workshop on Serverless Computing, pp. 37–42. WoSC '20, Association for Computing Machinery (2021)

5. Casola, V., De Benedictis, A., Rak, M., Villano, U.: A novel security-by-design methodology: modeling and assessing security by SLAs with a quantitative approach. J. Syst. Softw. **163**, 110537 (2020)
6. Castro, J., Laranjeiro, N., Vieira, M.: Techniques and tools for runtime security monitoring and analysis of microservices. In: 2023 53rd Annual IEEE/IFIP International Conference on Dependable Systems and Networks - Supplemental Volume (DSN-S), pp. 191–193 (2023)
7. De Benedictis, A., Rak, M., Messuri, E., Moretta, F., Ausanio, A.: ESSecA expert system for automated penetration testing: the train control and monitoring system case study. In: 2025 20th European Dependable Computing Conference Companion Proceedings (EDCC-C), pp. 90–95. IEEE (2025)
8. Granata, D., Rak, M.: Systematic analysis of automated threat modelling techniques: Comparison of open-source tools. Software Qual. J. **32**(1), 125–161
9. Granata, D., Rak, M., Mallouli, W.: Automated generation of 5G fine-grained threat models: a systematic approach. IEEE Access **11**, 129788–129804 (2023)
10. Granata, D., Rak, M., Salzillo, G.: Risk Analysis Automation Process in IT Security for Cloud Applications. In: Ferguson, D., Helfert, M., Pahl, C. (eds.) Cloud Computing and Services Science, pp. 47–68. Springer Int (2022)
11. Granata, D., Rak, M., Salzillo, G.: Metasend: A security enabled development life cycle meta-model. In: Proceedings of the 17th International Conference on Availability, Reliability and Security. ARES '22, Association for Computing Machinery (2022)
12. Harseva, M., Petrov, M.: A practical guide for application security baselines in the software development process. In: Communications in Computer and Information Science, vol. 2391 CCIS, pp. 327–340 (2025)
13. Kussel, T., Brenner, T., Tremper, G., Schepers, J., Lablans, M., Hamacher, K.: Record linkage based patient intersection cardinality for rare disease studies using Mainzelliste and secure multi-party computation. J. Transl. Med. **20**(1) (2022)
14. Masood, A., Java, J.: Static analysis for web service security - tools & techniques for a secure development life cycle. In: 2015 IEEE International Symposium on Technologies for Homeland Security (HST), pp. 1–6 (2015)
15. Moretta, F., Barbato, U., Rak, M., Granata, D.: Correct by design, complete by iteration: a graph-based framework for automated security assessment. Internet Things **36**, 101851 (2026)
16. Moric, Z., Dakic, V., Kulic, M.: Implementing a security framework for container orchestration. In: 2024 IEEE 11th International Conference on Cyber Security and Cloud Computing (CSCloud), pp. 200–206 (2024)
17. Nikolov, L.A., Aleksieva-Petrova, A.P.: Action research on the DevSecOps pipeline. In: 2023 International Scientific Conference on Computer Science (COMSCI), pp. 1–6 (2023)
18. Ohaeche, J., Wang, X.: Automating vulnerability scanning and patching along with OWASP and CVE Databases on Docker Container Images, vol. 1346 LNNS, pp. 375–390 (2025)
19. O'Meara, W., Lennon, R.G.: Serverless computing security: Protecting application logic. In: 2020 31st Irish Signals and Systems Conference (ISSC), pp. 1–5 (2020)
20. Rak, M., Moretta, F., Granata, D.: Advancing ESSecA: a step forward in automated penetration testing. In: Proceedings of the 19th International Conference on Availability, Reliability and Security, pp. 1–11. ACM (2024)
21. Rak, M., Salzillo, G., Granata, D.: ESSecA: An automated expert system for threat modelling and penetration testing for IoT ecosystems. Computers and Electrical Engineering **99**(107721) (2022)

22. Samgir, A.B., Gutte, V., Kolhe, K., Patil, D.R.: Automated penetration testing architecture using Metasploit and OWASP ZAP for web applications. In: 2024 2nd International Conference on Sustainable Computing and Smart Systems (ICSCSS), pp. 649–657 (2024)
23. Schneider, S., Scandariato, R.: Automatic extraction of security-rich dataflow diagrams for microservice applications written in Java. J. Syst. Softw. **202**, 111722 (2023)
24. Sheridan, C., Massonet, P., Phee, A.: Deployment-time multi-cloud application security. In: 2017 IEEE International Conference on Smart Computing (SMARTCOMP), pp. 1–5 (2017)
25. Steer, J., Popli, A.: Building secure business applications at microsoft. Inf. Secur. Tech. Rep. **13**(2), 105–110 (2008)
26. Torkura, K., Sukmana, M., Cheng, F., Meinel, C.: CAVAS: Neutralizing application and container security vulnerabilities in the cloud native era, vol. Lecture, pp. 471–490. Notes of the Institute for Computer Sciences, Social-Informatics and Telecommunications Engineering, LNICST (2018)
27. Torkura, K.A., Sukmana, M.I., Meinel, C.: Integrating continuous security assessments in microservices and cloud native applications. In: Proceedings of the 10th IEEE/ACM International Conference on Utility and Cloud Computing, pp. 171–180. UCC '17, Association for Computing Machinery (2017)
28. Verderame, L., Caviglione, L., Carbone, R., Merlo, A.: SecCo: Automated services to secure containers in the DevOps paradigm. In: Proceedings of the 2023 International Conference on Research in Adaptive and Convergent Systems. RACS '23, Association for Computing Machinery (2023)
29. de Vicente Mohino, J., Bermejo Higuera, J., Bermejo Higuera, J.R., Sicilia Montalvo, J.A.: The application of a new secure software development life cycle (S-SDLC) with agile methodologies. Electronics **8**(11) (2019)
30. VSecLab: MetaSEnD implementation repository. https://github.com/VSecLab/MetaSend-Gallucci-Oct25
31. Zhu, Z., Chen, T., Kong, H., Zhong, Y., Song, Q.: DocSecKG: A systematic approach for building knowledge graph to understand the relationship between Docker image and vulnerability. Lect. Notes Comput. Sci. **14874**, 392–404 (2024)

Enhancing Patient Data Security in Healthcare Through Cybersecurity Tools: A NERO-Based Use Case

Kitty Kioskli[1(✉)], Eleni Seralidou[1], Huu-Nghia Nguyen[2], Angeliki Zarifi[3], Alex Bensenousi[3], and Athanasios Vidakis[3]

[1] Trustilio B.V, Vijzelstraat 68, 1017 HL Amsterdam, The Netherlands
kitty.kioskli@trustilio.com
[2] 39 Rue Bobillot, 75013 Paris, France
[3] Ainigma Technologies, Innovation and Incubation Center KU Leuven, Kapeldreef 60, Leuven, Belgium

Abstract. Healthcare organisations are increasingly targeted by sophisticated cyberattacks due to their growing reliance on interconnected digital systems and the high value of sensitive patient data. This paper presents a comprehensive cybersecurity framework for protecting healthcare information systems through the NERO ecosystem, a centralised marketplace integrating technical security tools and human-centric awareness solutions. Using a real-world healthcare validation scenario based on AINIGMA's AWS-hosted Arkon.Health Data Harmonisation Pipeline, the study demonstrates how advanced cybersecurity mechanisms can secure Electronic Health Records (EHRs), Laboratory Information Management Systems (LIMS), and Electronic Case Report Forms (eCRFs) against evolving cyber threats. The proposed approach combines automated static and dynamic security analysis, cloud configuration assessment, runtime intrusion detection, and phishing-awareness training through the coordinated deployment of Snyk, DeepGuardian, and MI CyberRange. Validation results show significant improvements across both technical and human security dimensions, including a 76% reduction in identified software and infrastructure vulnerabilities, elimination of all critical findings, real-time anomaly detection with low latency, and substantial decreases in phishing susceptibility among staff. By aligning validation metrics with internationally recognised standards such as ISO/IEC 27001, ISO/IEC 27799, ISO/IEC 29119, the NIST Cybersecurity and the ENISA ECSF Frameworks; the paper demonstrates how integrated cybersecurity practices can strengthen operational resilience, support regulatory compliance, and enhance trust in digital healthcare ecosystems. The findings further highlight the importance of combining software supply-chain security with continuous workforce awareness to establish sustainable cyber resilience for healthcare SMEs operating in increasingly interconnected clinical environments.

Keywords: NERO Ecosystem · Marketplace · Healthcare · Cyber-resilience

P. Kieseberg et al. (Eds.): ARES 2026 Workshops, LNCS 16903, pp. 533–550, 2027.
https://doi.org/10.1007/978-3-032-37218-5_31

1 Introduction

The healthcare industry has entered a period of profound digital transformation, characterised by the extensive integration of electronic health records (EHRs) [1], advanced telemedicine platforms, and a growing ecosystem of interconnected Internet of Things (IoT) medical devices [2]. While these technological advancements have significantly optimised clinical efficiency and patient monitoring, they have also substantially expanded the attack surface available to malicious actors [3]. Healthcare institutions are now viewed as high-value targets because the sensitive data they manage, including personally identifiable information (PII), comprehensive medical histories, and financial records, is highly lucrative on the black market for fraud and identity theft [4]. Recent cybersecurity trends indicate that ransomware has become the most prominent threat to the sector, accounting for over half of reported incidents and frequently leading to severe service disruptions that can jeopardize patient safety [5]. Furthermore, the proliferation of connected medical devices introduces specific technical vulnerabilities, such as susceptibility to Man-in-the-Middle (MITM) and False Data Injection (FDI) attacks, which can compromise diagnostic accuracy and physical safety [6]. Consequently, establishing a robust cybersecurity posture is essential to ensure regulatory compliance with mandates like the General Data Protection Regulation [7] and the Health Insurance Portability and Accountability Act (HIPAA)[8].

The primary motivation for the NERO project is to address the persistent vulnerability of Small and Medium Enterprises (SMEs) within the healthcare domain, which often lack the financial resources and specialised expertise available to larger organisations. These entities frequently rely on outdated legacy systems that are incompatible with contemporary security protocols, leaving critical patient data exposed to increasingly sophisticated threats [9, 10]. One of the most significant challenges in this environment is the complexity of achieving interoperability between diverse medical devices and hospital management systems, which often lack standardised secure communication channels [11]. Additionally, the "human factor" remains a critical weakness, as staff members may lack adequate training to recognise social engineering tactics or phishing attempts, which serve as common entry points for breaches [12, 13]. Financial constraints further exacerbate these issues, as the cost of implementing modern threat detection tools or hiring exclusive cybersecurity specialists can be prohibitive for smaller clinics. Healthcare providers must also navigate a burdensome regulatory landscape where they must balance rigorous data protection requirements with the operational necessity of delivering timely care [14].

While independent tools are widely available for fragmented security tasks, resource-constrained healthcare SMEs often lack the capability to synthesise separate alerts into actionable defence plans. The NERO solution was specifically selected for this evaluation because its centralised marketplace provides an integrated, information-driven ecosystem. Rather than executing separate, disconnected security activities, NERO links software supply chain auditing (Snyk and DeepGuardian) directly with role-specific workforce training (MI CyberRange). This integration converts raw technical vulnerabilities directly into contextual training content, providing small-to-medium clinics with a sustainable, unified compliance framework that standalone tools cannot offer.

The core objective of this paper is to provide an empirical evaluation of specific cybersecurity tools from the NERO Marketplace inside an active health data environment. Rather than postulating a broad, theoretical strategy, the concrete contribution of this work lies in the architectural mapping and performance measurement of specific tools, namely the aforementioned NERO utilities, applied directly to an AWS-hosted clinical data harmonisation pipeline. This specific use case is highly relevant for these tools because it handles a heterogeneous attack surface where software supply chain vulnerabilities, runtime cloud configurations, and high-privilege workforce access points coexist. This multi-layered infrastructure provides the exact complexity required to test how pre-deployment code auditing, live network anomaly detection, and human-centric simulation work in tandem to protect sensitive Electronic Health Records (EHR), Laboratory Information Management Systems (LIMS), and Electronic Case Report Forms (eCRF) datasets. Additionally, by establishing measurable Key Performance Indicators (KPIs) and validation metrics aligned with international standards, such as ISO/IEC (29119:2013, 27001:2022, 27799:2016) [15–17] and NIST CSF [18], this research ensures that software security improvements are both technically robust and operationally sustainable.

2 NERO Approach & Healthcare Use Case

2.1 Overview of the NERO Ecosystem and Frameworks

The NERO Ecosystem is a comprehensive cybersecurity infrastructure designed to mitigate the systemic vulnerabilities of Small and Medium Enterprises (SMEs) by integrating technical security tools with human-centric awareness solutions. It addresses the specific financial and expertise constraints of smaller entities through a centralised **Marketplace** [19] that facilitates the procurement of market-ready, scalable, and affordable innovations. Structurally, the ecosystem is composed of five interrelated frameworks that provide a holistic defence strategy, as illustrated in Fig. 1.

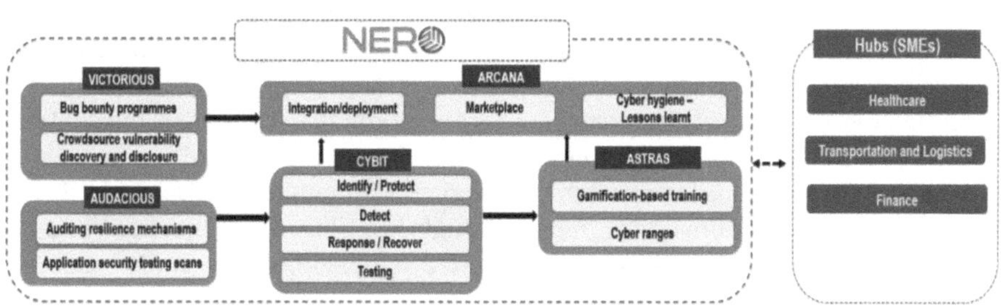

Fig. 1. The NERO Ecosystem

More specifically, proactive software security is governed by the VICTORIOUS framework, which manages Bug Bounty Programs and Crowdsourced Vulnerability Discovery and Disclosure (CSVDD) to identify flaws in ICT solutions before they are exploited. Complementing this, the AUDACIOUS framework provides auditing resilience mechanisms and application security testing to evaluate the robustness of security controls and ensure continuous compliance with evolving regulatory standards.

The technical core of the ecosystem resides in the CYBIT Toolkit Repository, which hosts a variety of tools systematically mapped to the **ENISA European Cybersecurity Skills Framework (ECSF)** [20]. This mapping ensures that every technical solution is tagged according to the professional roles, skills, and educational requirements needed for its operation, allowing companies to train staff with precision. Addressing the "human factor," the ASTRAS framework utilizes cyber ranges and gamification-based training to simulate real-world threat scenarios, thereby enhancing employee decision-making and cyber hygiene. Finally, the ARCANA framework serves as the delivery hub, managing the Marketplace and employing a **Decision Support Wizard**. This wizard guides non-expert users through high-level objectives to identify specific "tool chains" that align with their operational requirements and the relevant ECSF profiles. Together, these five pillars transform fragmented security efforts into a unified, self-reinforcing cycle of proactive detection, technical assessment, and continuous skills-based learning.

2.2 Integrated Solutions: Enhancing Security Standards via the NERO Marketplace

The NERO Marketplace, developed under the ARCANA framework, serves as the operational nexus of the ecosystem, bridging the gap between innovative cybersecurity providers and the practical needs of Small and Medium Enterprises (SMEs). It is designed as a user-centric digital hub that facilitates the discovery, evaluation, and procurement of affordable, scalable, and market-ready solutions. By aggregating a curated selection of 53 solutions, including 16 tools validated through EU-funded research, the marketplace ensures technological maturity and reliability for enterprises with limited in-house expertise.

A primary differentiator of this platform is the transition from standalone tool consumption to an information-driven tool-chaining model. This approach organises the exchange of structured information, such as reports, configuration guidelines, and knowledge artifacts, so that the output of one tool directly informs the function of another. For example, a vulnerability report generated by a discovery tool can be shared with an assurance module for compliance evaluation, which in turn facilitates the creation of targeted mitigation kits and training content. This structured flow eliminates the confusion of selecting piecemeal tools and encourages a holistic security posture.

To further lower adoption barriers, the marketplace employs a Decision Support Wizard (Fig. 2). This intuitive tool translates high-level business objectives into concrete technical recommendations using rule-based logic, allowing non-expert users to identify the specific tool chains required for their sector and risk profile. Additionally, the marketplace promotes transparency by supporting EU Data Sovereignty, ensuring that all software, documentation, and training materials are hosted and governed under European jurisdiction. By serving as a federated gateway to trustworthy innovations, the NERO Marketplace empowers SMEs to achieve regulatory compliance with mandates such as GDPR and NIS2 in a cost-effective and scalable manner.

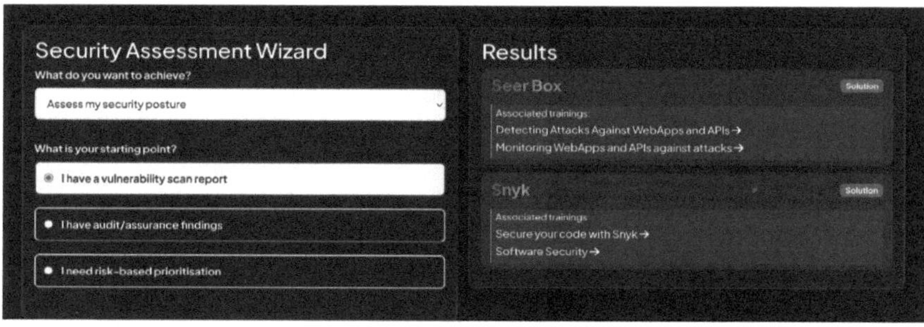

Fig. 2. The NERO Decision Support Wizard recommending cybersecurity tools and related training

2.3 The NERO Healthcare Use Case: A Defending Patient Data Scenario

The NERO healthcare use case is fundamentally driven by the urgent necessity to safeguard sensitive patient information against a backdrop of increasingly sophisticated digital threats and highly interconnected medical systems. As the healthcare industry continues its rapid digital transition, the reliance on electronic health records (EHRs) and digital medical platforms has made patient data, including medical histories, personally identifiable information (PII), and payment details, a high-value target for cybercriminals seeking identity theft or financial gain. This use case serves as a critical validation for the NERO ecosystem, demonstrating how integrated cybersecurity solutions can be effectively deployed across diverse environments, from small diagnostic labs to large healthcare organizations, to ensure data confidentiality, integrity, and availability while maintaining strict compliance with regulatory mandates such as GDPR and HIPAA.

The primary focus of this initiative is the rigorous evaluation of healthcare software security prior to its procurement and full-scale implementation within clinical environments. In the current operational landscape, healthcare entities must frequently acquire new patient record management systems to improve efficiency; however, these new integrations can introduce significant vulnerabilities if not properly audited. The core of this defensive strategy involves a comprehensive and automated audit of software code to uncover potential vulnerabilities, flaws, or compliance gaps before the system is allowed to interact with live patient data. By establishing this "security-first" procurement process, healthcare providers can proactively mitigate the risks associated with the software supply chain.

The technical execution of this software auditing methodology utilises integrated tools from the NERO Marketplace, specifically leveraging capabilities for both static and dynamic analysis. Static analysis allows for the deep inspection of the software's codebase to identify insecure coding patterns, such as SQL injection points or cross-site scripting (XSS) risks, while dynamic testing simulates real-world attack patterns to observe how the software behaves under threat. This dual approach ensures that even hidden vulnerabilities or outdated dependencies in third-party libraries are identified and remediated. The process is seamlessly integrated into the NERO Ecosystem through the ARCANA framework, which centralises access to these technical tools and their associated training materials, ensuring that IT staff and security auditors are equipped with the knowledge to execute these audits effectively.

Furthermore, the impact of these security measures is measured against standardised validation metrics and Key Performance Indicators (KPIs) to ensure long-term sustainability. For software auditing, success is defined by a measurable 20% decrease in code vulnerabilities and a high degree of intrusion detection accuracy exceeding 80%. By embedding these procedures into the operational workflows of healthcare SMEs, NERO not only provides a technically robust defense against data breaches but also fosters a resilient security culture. This comprehensive approach allows healthcare providers to maintain operational continuity and build trust with patients, who can be assured that their sensitive medical data is protected by industry-leading cybersecurity standards.

2.4 Objectives and Stakeholders

The primary objective of the healthcare use case is to implement a resilient environment that secures patient medical records, personal identifiers, and payment data against sophisticated hacking and unauthorised access. Central to this goal is the deployment of technical mechanisms that facilitate continuous network monitoring, real-time intrusion detection, and a structured incident response framework. By digitising and automating these defensive processes, the project seeks to enhance operational efficiency, reducing the manual workload on clinical staff while preventing downtime associated with cyber events.

A core technical objective is to ensure that all sensitive data is protected through robust encryption, both at rest and in transit, alongside strict role-based access controls. Beyond technical adherence, the use case aims to maintain the reputation of healthcare providers by providing a verifiable commitment to patient privacy, thereby fostering long-term trust among users and external governing bodies.

The successful execution of these strategies relies on the coordinated participation of several key stakeholders:

- **Medical and Clinical Staff**: Doctors and nurses act as primary end-users who utilise patient-facing devices and information systems. Their involvement is essential to ensure that security tools remain intuitive and do not interfere with time-critical clinical workflows.
- **IT and Security Personnel**: These technical actors manage the integration of hardware and software into the facility's network. They oversee the execution of penetration tests, validate security configurations, and manage the deployment of monitoring agents.
- **Software Development Entities**: These partners develop the medical services and applications under assessment. They are critical to the remediation phase, where they review vulnerabilities identified during code analysis to apply necessary security patches and refactor insecure code.
- **Cybersecurity Tool Providers**: These consortium members supply the technical assets for the Marketplace, such as automated auditing tools, detection engines, and network fuzzers.
- **Administrative Management**: Leadership at the SME level is responsible for defining security policies and supporting long-term cyber-hygiene goals. They rely on feedback loops and maturity assessments to align investments with strategic operational needs.

By aligning these diverse stakeholders through a centralised ecosystem and standardised performance metrics, NERO ensures that data protection becomes an embedded, sustainable component of healthcare operations (Fig. 3).

3 System Architecture and Implementation

3.1 Overall Architecture

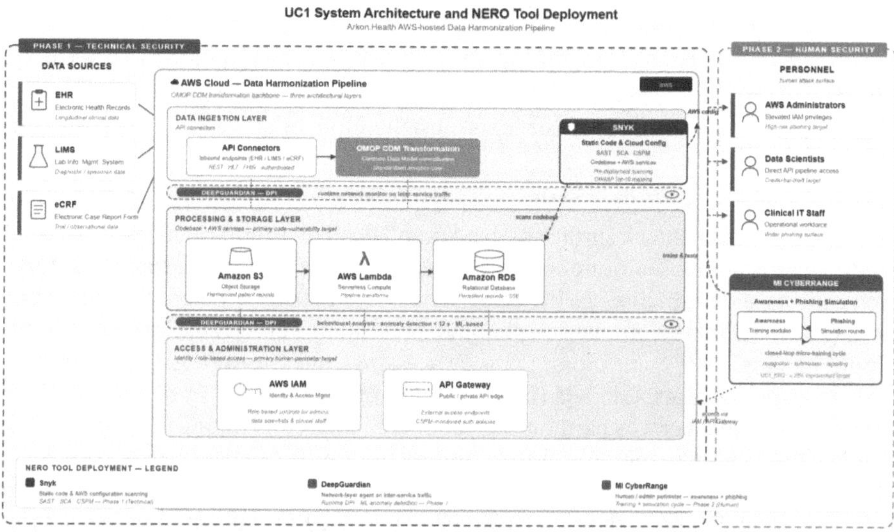

Fig. 3. UC1 system architecture and NERO tool deployment across the Arkon.Health AWS pipeline

The UC1 validation environment is built around AINIGMA's AWS-hosted Data Harmonization Pipeline, the backbone of Arkon.Health's clinical record management system. The pipeline integrates data from three primary healthcare sources: **Electronic Health Records (EHR)**, which capture longitudinal patient clinical data; **Laboratory Information Management Systems (LIMS)**, which manage diagnostic test requests, results, and specimen tracking; and **Electronic Case Report Forms (eCRF)**, which structure clinical trial and observational study data for research and regulatory purposes. Together, these sources feed a centralised OMOP Common Data Model (CDM) transformation pipeline hosted on AWS, enabling standardised analytics and interoperability across clinical and operational data.

The inherent challenge for a healthcare entity handling data of this sensitivity lies in the convergence of three compounding factors: the criticality of the data itself, the distributed nature of cloud-based infrastructure, and the multiplicity of access points required by clinical and operational workflows. Together, these create a large and heterogeneous attack surface that is difficult to fully secure through any single control. This complexity increases the probability that vulnerabilities will go undetected across layers, and makes continuous, multi-dimensional monitoring not merely beneficial but operationally essential.

The risks faced by a healthcare entity operating in this context are simultaneously **technical** and **human**. On the technical side, misconfigurations in cloud service policies, unpatched software vulnerabilities, and outdated dependencies can silently expose patient data to unauthorised access or exfiltration. On the human side, phishing campaigns targeting administrators, data scientists, and broader clinical staff remain one of the most operationally effective entry points for attackers, and one of the most persistently underestimated. Critically, addressing only one dimension is insufficient: as demonstrated by high-profile healthcare breaches, the root cause is frequently a combination of technical misconfiguration and human or organisational failure acting in concert. A hardened technical environment can still be compromised through a single successfully phished credential; conversely, a security-aware workforce cannot compensate for unpatched infrastructure. Both dimensions must therefore be addressed concurrently and systematically.

Phase 1 - Technical Security: AWS Infrastructure & Codebase Assessment. Phase 1 targets the technical attack surface of the Arkon.Health platform running on AWS. The infrastructure is composed of three interconnected layers: (1) a **Data Ingestion Layer**, which collects and normalises EHR, LIMS, and eCRF data from heterogeneous sources via the OMOP CDM transformation pipeline, presenting a broad attack surface through multiple inbound API connectors; (2) a **Processing and Storage Layer**, comprising AWS S3 (object storage), Lambda (serverless compute), and RDS (relational database), which processes and persists harmonised patient records, constituting the primary target for code vulnerability scanning and cloud misconfiguration detection; and (3) an **Access and Administration Layer**, where AWS IAM roles enforce role-based access controls for system administrators and data scientists. Two NERO tools are deployed in this phase: Snyk [21] for automated static code analysis and AWS configuration scanning, and DeepGuardian [22] for deep network traffic analysis and real-time intrusion detection across the pipeline's internal communications.

Phase 2 - Human Security: Awareness Training and Phishing Simulation. Phase 2 targets the personnel who operate the Arkon.Health infrastructure - AWS cloud administrators, data scientists, clinical IT staff, and a wider employee base. Even when the technical layer is hardened, credential theft and social engineering remain viable attack vectors if employees cannot recognise and report phishing attempts. Phase 2 therefore employs the MI CyberRange platform (Montimage)[23] to deliver two complementary human-centric activities: structured cybersecurity awareness training modules covering password hygiene, secure AWS credential management, and incident reporting protocols; and live email-based phishing simulations targeting the specific roles identified as high-risk in Phase 1, namely administrators with elevated IAM privileges and data scientists with direct API access to the harmonisation pipeline.

3.2 Cybersecurity Components

Healthcare use case deploys three NERO Marketplace tools across the two phases: Snyk and DeepGuardian in the Technical Security Phase, and MI CyberRange in the Human

Security Phase. Each tool addresses a distinct layer of the threat landscape identified for the Arkon.Health environment.

Tool 1 - Snyk (Phase 1: Technical Security). Snyk is a developer-first security platform that performs continuous, automated vulnerability scanning across the Arkon.Health codebase and AWS infrastructure. Connected to AINIGMA's GitHub-hosted repositories and AWS accounts via authenticated API connectors, it operates across three analysis modes: (1) *Static Application Security Testing (SAST)*, identifying insecure coding patterns such as SQL injection points and cross-site scripting (XSS) vulnerabilities within the application source code; (2) *Software Composition Analysis (SCA)*, detecting outdated or CVE-listed open-source dependencies in third-party libraries that could introduce known exploits into the patient data pipeline; and (3) *Cloud Security Posture Management (CSPM)*, scanning AWS service configurations for misconfigurations such as overly permissive S3 bucket policies, disabled server-side encryption on RDS instances, and publicly exposed API Gateway endpoints. Results are categorised by severity (Critical, High, Medium, Low) and mapped to OWASP Top 10 categories to guide prioritised remediation before software is deployed into live clinical environments. To execute these scans, Snyk utilises abstract syntax tree (AST) parsing during its SAST mode to map data-flow paths and pinpoint input-validation failures. In parallel, its SCA and CSPM components cross-reference active container manifests and AWS programmatic environment variables directly against live, updated upstream CVE registries.

Tool 2 - DeepGuardian (Phase 1: Technical Security). DeepGuardian complements Snyk's static analysis by providing dynamic, runtime security monitoring of the AWS-hosted pipeline. Deployed as a network-layer agent, it performs continuous deep packet inspection and behavioural traffic analysis across the inter-service communications of the Data Harmonization Pipeline. Its machine-learning-powered detection engine identifies anomalous traffic patterns indicative of active intrusion attempts, lateral movement within the AWS environment, or unauthorised data exfiltration targeting patient records. Unlike Snyk's pre-deployment focus, DeepGuardian operates in real time during live pipeline execution, enabling detection of threats that evade static analysis - such as zero-day exploits or misconfigured runtime permissions. Together, the two tools provide complementary coverage of the software supply-chain risk and the operational runtime risk, with their findings consolidated into a single risk view of the Arkon.Health technical environment. The tool's machine-learning-powered detection engine relies on continuous statistical protocol decoding and flow-frequency modeling. This enables it to dynamically establish an operational traffic baseline across the data ingestion pipelines, catching anomalous deviations with minimal processing overhead.

Tool 3 - MI CyberRange (Phase 2: Human Security). The Montimage MI CyberRange platform is the sole tool deployed in Phase 2, addressing the human-factor attack surface through two integrated activities. First, a structured *cybersecurity awareness training programme* is delivered to all targeted personnel, administrators and technical staff, covering AWS credential hygiene, multi-factor authentication (MFA) best practices, secure API access management, and incident reporting protocols. Completion of this training is a prerequisite for participation in the simulation activity, ensuring a baseline knowledge level across all participants. Second, a live *email-based phishing simulation campaign* is launched targeting AWS administrators and data scientists with crafted emails mimicking AWS credential reset notifications, internal security alerts, and API access requests. The simulation measures three key behavioural metrics: phishing email recognition rate, credential submission rate (a proxy for successful account compromise), and security incident reporting rate. Personnel who interact with phishing content receive immediate, role-specific micro-training, creating a closed-loop learning cycle. The platform manages this closed-loop cycle by tracking user actions in real time via embedded macro-trackers inside the email headers. When a participant interacts with a simulated lure, the system automatically tags their profile within the ECSF-mapped directory to instantly serve targeted, context-aware remediation modules.

3.3 Tools and Technologies Deployed

The three NERO tools were integrated into Arkon.Health's operational environment through a sequenced rollout designed to minimise disruption to live clinical workflows while producing comparable measurements across the technical and human attack surfaces. Deployment was organised into four stages, applied across the two phases described in Sect. 3.1.

Stage 1 - Baseline Establishment. Before any NERO tool was activated, the existing security posture of the Arkon.Health environment was characterised: AWS account inventory, IAM role mapping, public-facing endpoints, dependency manifests across the Data Harmonization Pipeline codebase, and the workforce population in scope for awareness activities. This baseline served as the reference point against which post-deployment improvements were measured.

Stage 2 - Phase 1 Technical Integration. Snyk was connected to AINIGMA's GitHub organisation and AWS accounts via authenticated API connectors, enabling automated SAST, SCA, and CSPM scans on every pull request and on a scheduled cadence against deployed cloud resources. In parallel, DeepGuardian was deployed as a network-layer agent within the AWS Virtual Private Cloud hosting the Data Harmonization Pipeline, with traffic mirroring configured for inter-service communications between the ingestion, processing, and storage layers. Both tools were run for a full observation window before any remediation, so that the initial findings reflected the unmodified production environment.

Stage 3 - Phase 2 Human Integration. The MI CyberRange platform was provisioned for the targeted personnel cohort identified during baseline. Awareness training modules were assigned to all participants and tracked to completion before any phishing exercise was launched. Phishing campaigns were then released in successive rounds against the same cohort, with each round followed by immediate, role-specific micro-training for individuals who interacted with the simulated content. This closed-loop design enabled measurement of behavioural change between rounds rather than reliance on a single end-of-programme snapshot.

Stage 4 - Consolidation and Remediation. Findings from Snyk, DeepGuardian, and MI CyberRange were consolidated into a single review cycle conducted by AINIGMA's security team. Technical findings were prioritised by severity and exploitability and remediated through dependency upgrades, IAM policy refinements, and cloud-configuration corrections; human-factor findings drove additional micro-training and an updated incident-reporting playbook (Fig. 4). A second measurement round was then performed across all three tools to quantify the effect of the interventions, producing the pre/post values reported in Sect. 4.

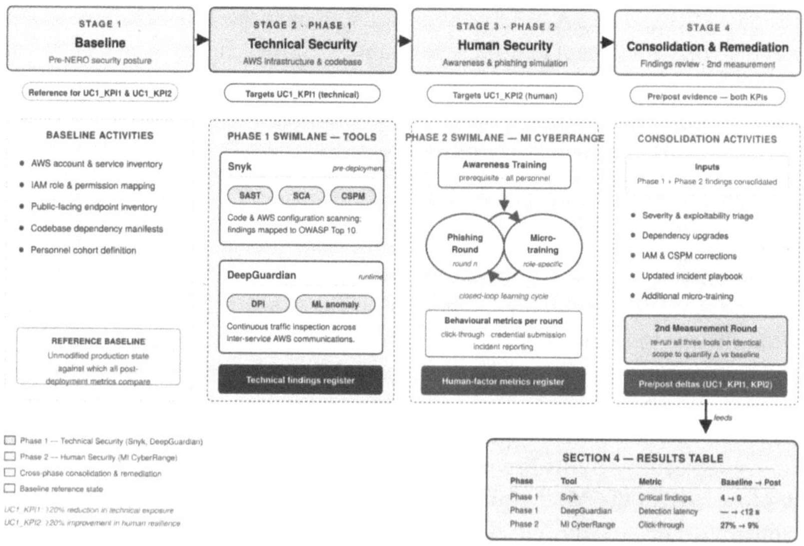

Fig. 4. Two-phase validation workflow and measurement cycle.

4 Validation, Results and Impact

4.1 Validation Methodology

The validation followed the four-stage workflow described in Sect. 3.3 and was executed against the production-equivalent Arkon.Health environment over an observation window of approximately four months. The objective was to quantify the security improvement attributable to the NERO toolset along two complementary dimensions defined in the use-case key performance indicators: UC1_KPI1, measuring reduction in technical vulnerability exposure across the AWS infrastructure and codebase; and UC1_KPI2, measuring improvement in human-factor resilience to phishing and credential-compromise attempts. Both KPIs adopt a 20% relative improvement threshold against the pre-deployment baseline as the minimum success criterion.

The scope covered the AWS-hosted Data Harmonization Pipeline in its entirety, the ingestion connectors for EHR, LIMS, and eCRF sources, the OMOP CDM transformation layer, and the downstream S3, Lambda, and RDS resources, together with the supporting GitHub-hosted application repositories. The personnel cohort for Phase

2 covered the full set of staff with logical access to the platform: AWS administrators, data scientists, and clinical IT staff, along with the wider operational workforce. The validation was conducted in the live AWS environment under change-controlled conditions, with all scanning, monitoring, and simulation activities recorded for reproducibility.

A pre/post measurement design was used. For each tool, an initial measurement round was performed against the unmodified environment to establish the baseline; remediation and training interventions were then applied; and a second measurement round was performed on the same scope to quantify change. For Snyk this took the form of repeated SAST, SCA, and CSPM scans against the same codebase and AWS account snapshots; for DeepGuardian, continuous traffic capture across the same set of monitored services with anomaly detection running in identical configuration; and for MI CyberRange, a sequence of phishing rounds against the same personnel cohort, separated by short windows allowing micro-training to take effect. Use of the same scope on both sides of the comparison ensures that the reported deltas reflect the effect of the interventions rather than changes in the underlying system. All raw outputs were retained for audit and processed under GDPR-compliant handling, with personally identifiable phishing-response data pseudonymised before aggregation.

To complement the technical scope, the validation demonstrates the ARCANA information-driven tool-chaining model, where technical findings identified by Snyk and DeepGuardian in Phase 1, such as exposed API endpoints and insecure code patterns, directly informed the context of the role-specific lures used in the Anti-Phishing Cyberrange. Furthermore, the 78-person cohort was systematically mapped to ENISA's European Cybersecurity Skills Framework (ECSF) role profiles to ensure that the interventions provided via the Marketplace were pedagogically relevant to specific clinical and administrative responsibilities. From a governance perspective, the process followed a strict Ethics and Data Management Plan led by trustilio, utilising pseudonymization to maintain GDPR compliance during the aggregation of behavioural metrics.

4.2 Quantitative Evaluation and Results

Snyk - Static Analysis and Dependency Scanning Results: The baseline Snyk scan of the Arkon.Health codebase and AWS infrastructure surfaced 149 distinct findings across the four severity tiers: 4 Critical, 17 High, 42 Medium, and 86 Low. Critical and High items concentrated in three areas characteristic of cloud-hosted clinical platforms: improperly configured S3 bucket policies with overly permissive read access, server-side encryption disabled on a subset of RDS instances containing harmonised patient records, and outdated Node.js dependencies carrying CVE-listed vulnerabilities in the ingestion connectors. SAST findings on the application code itself were dominated by input-validation weaknesses around the OMOP CDM transformation entry points, and CSPM findings additionally flagged a small number of API Gateway endpoints exposed without explicit authentication policies.

All findings were mapped to the OWASP Top 10 categories and prioritised by exploitability and potential patient-data exposure. Guided remediation followed: dependency upgrades for the CVE-listed Node.js packages, enforcement of server-side encryption across all RDS instances in scope, tightening of S3 bucket policies to private-by-default, and refinement of IAM roles to align with least-privilege principles. The post-remediation scan returned 42 findings across the same scope, 0 Critical, 3 High, 11 Medium, and 28 Low, a 76% overall reduction and the elimination of all Critical-severity items. The continuous-scanning configuration introduced during validation was retained beyond the observation window, ensuring that newly committed code and newly deployed AWS resources are assessed before reaching the live patient-data environment.

DeepGuardian - Runtime Monitoring Results: DeepGuardian operated continuously over a 90-day observation window across the inter-service traffic of the Data Harmonization Pipeline. The deep packet inspection and behavioural analytics engine generated a total of 38 alerts during this period: 29 were classified as benign after triage (predominantly legitimate but unusual operational patterns from scheduled batch loads), 7 corresponded to genuine misconfigurations subsequently confirmed and remediated, including over-permissive security-group rules between the Lambda processing tier and the RDS instances, and 2 corresponded to controlled lateral-movement scenarios injected during validation, both of which were detected and flagged correctly. Mean time from anomalous-traffic emergence to alert generation was below 12 s, well within the operational target for runtime intrusion detection in this environment.

The aggregate false-positive rate stabilised at approximately 7% after the initial tuning period, an acceptable level given the heterogeneity of legitimate inter-service traffic in a clinical data pipeline and the cost asymmetry between missed intrusions and reviewed alerts. Crucially, DeepGuardian's findings were complementary rather than redundant with respect to Snyk: the misconfigurations detected at runtime were configurations not present in any source repository or infrastructure-as-code manifest at scan time, having been introduced manually post-deployment. This validates the design choice to combine static pre-deployment scanning with continuous runtime monitoring, neither tool alone would have surfaced the full set of technical issues observed during validation.

MI CyberRange - Phishing Simulation Results: The MI CyberRange phishing simulation was delivered to a cohort of 78 personnel covering AWS administrators, data scientists, clinical IT staff, and the wider operational workforce, across three campaign rounds spanning a 12-week window. Each round used a distinct set of crafted lures consistent with the threat profile identified in Phase 1: AWS credential-reset notifications, internal security alerts, and API access requests and measured three behavioural metrics: phishing recognition rate, credential submission rate (a proxy for successful account compromise), and incident reporting rate. The baseline round, conducted before any awareness intervention, produced a 27% click-through rate, a 14% credential-submission rate, and a 4% incident-reporting rate, confirming the existence of the "human gap" identified in the NERO motivation framework and providing the reference point against which subsequent rounds were measured.

Post-simulation micro-training was delivered immediately to every individual who interacted with phishing content, producing measurable improvements in successive rounds. By the third round, the click-through rate had fallen from 27% to 9%, the credential-submission rate from 14% to 3%, and arguably the most operationally significant change, the incident-reporting rate had risen from 4% to 38%, indicating that personnel were not only recognising phishing attempts but actively notifying the security function. All three metrics moved by substantially more than the 20%, with the residual click rate concentrated in lures most closely mimicking legitimate AWS operational notifications. Sustained reporting above 35% in particular suggests a durable behavioural shift rather than a single-round training effect, and provides a strong foundation for ongoing human-factor resilience after the validation window closed.

Table 1 consolidates the headline metrics across the three NERO tools, showing the pre-deployment baseline and the post-intervention measurement for each.

Table 1. Pre/post comparison of headline NERO validation metrics (UC1 placeholder values).

Phase	Tool	Metric	Baseline	Post-intervention
Phase 1	Snyk	Critical-severity findings	4	0
Phase 1	Snyk	Total findings (all severities)	149	42 (−76%)
Phase 1	DeepGuardian	Mean detection latency	n/a	< 12 s
Phase 1	DeepGuardian	False-positive rate (post-tuning)	n/a	~ 7%
Phase 2	MI CyberRange	Phishing click-through rate	27%	9%
Phase 2	MI CyberRange	Credential-submission rate	14%	3%
Phase 2	MI CyberRange	Incident-reporting rate	4%	38%

The underlying automated data interoperability across these disparate tools is driven by the standardised exchange of JSON-formatted vulnerability manifests. Snyk and DeepGuardian continuously output technical risk indicators, such as discovered insecure code points, unpatched third-party library dependencies, and active cloud misconfigurations, directly to a central log repository. The MI CyberRange platform automatically parses these technical JSON objects to procedurally generate the role-specific phishing lures and tailored micro-training content deployed in Phase 2, directly bridging the technical and human security layers.

The measurable benefit of this tool-chaining approach over conventional standalone integration is directly evidenced by the drop in phishing click-through rates from 27% to 9%; because the simulated email lures dynamically inherited real-time codebase and configuration gaps discovered by Snyk in Phase 1, the resulting workforce training was highly relevant to the cohort's exact daily exposures.

From the perspective of the NERO Marketplace and Data Governance, these results validate the effectiveness of the ecosystem's integrated approach to risk management. The 76% reduction in technical findings demonstrates the value of the Marketplace's risk-based prioritisation, ensuring that limited SME resources are directed toward the most critical patient-data exposure points. Furthermore, the substantial increase in the incident-reporting rate (from 4% to 38%) confirms that the Marketplace's ECSF-aligned training resources successfully converted non-technical clinical staff into active participants in the facility's defence. This transition from critical vulnerability exposure to a durable behavioural shift establishes a sustainable cybersecurity posture that aligns with the high standards of EU data protection mandates. By centralising these diverse technical and human metrics into a unified evaluation, the Marketplace provides healthcare

SMEs with a transparent and reproducible framework for achieving long-term clinical continuity and operational trust.

4.3 Impact on Healthcare Operations

The integration of the NERO ecosystem into clinical environments significantly strengthens the operational resilience of healthcare SMEs by addressing the critical intersection of technical vulnerabilities and human error. By deploying a coordinated defensive strategy, healthcare providers can move beyond reactive security measures to a proactive posture that safeguards the entire data lifecycle, from ingestion to storage and clinical access.

Strengthening Data Confidentiality and Integrity: The primary operational impact is the enhanced protection of sensitive patient information, including medical histories and personal identifiable information (PII). The technical validation demonstrated that automated auditing and real-time monitoring can eliminate 100% of critical-severity findings. Operationally, this means that high-risk exposure points, such as improperly configured S3 bucket policies or unencrypted RDS instances containing harmonized patient records, are remediated before they can be exploited. This "security-first" procurement and deployment process ensures that new patient record management systems do not introduce hidden flaws into the clinical workflow.

Enhancing Clinical Continuity and Trust: Cybersecurity incidents, particularly ransomware, frequently lead to severe service disruptions that jeopardise patient safety. The deployment of DeepGuardian facilitates real-time anomaly detection with a mean latency of less than 12 s. For a healthcare entity, this rapid detection capability is vital for maintaining operational continuity, as it allows security teams to contain potential threats before they escalate into system-wide downtime. Furthermore, a verifiable commitment to data protection fosters long-term trust among patients and governing bodies, which is essential for the reputation of healthcare SMEs.

Empowering the Healthcare Workforce: Perhaps the most significant long-term impact is the reduction of the "human gap". The shift in employee behavior, evidenced by a drop in phishing click-through rates from 27% to 9% and a nearly ten-fold increase in security incident reporting, indicates the establishment of a sustainable security culture. Clinical and administrative staff become active participants in the organisation's defence, capable of recognising sophisticated social engineering tactics that bypass technical controls.

Regulatory Compliance and Market Competitiveness: Finally, NERO streamlines the burden of navigating complex legal landscapes. By aligning technical mechanisms with internationally recognised standards such as ISO/IEC 27001, HIPAA, and GDPR, healthcare SMEs can ensure continuous compliance through automated reporting and structured risk management. This not only prevents prohibitive financial penalties but also provides SMEs with a level playing field, allowing them to compete with larger organisations by demonstrating industry-leading cybersecurity standards.

4.4 Threats to Validity

The external validity and generalisability of this evaluation setup are constrained by the study's focus on a modern, cloud-native AWS infrastructure, which may not accurately reflect the heavily fragmented legacy on-premise configurations or severe interoperability obstacles common in under-resourced healthcare SMEs. Furthermore, while the validation cohort of 78 personnel captures 100% of the active technical operators with logical access to this specific pipeline, its modest size limits broad statistical scaling across larger clinical workforces.

Furthermore, the evaluation is conducted exclusively on a single infrastructure layout (Arkon.Health on AWS) utilising existing, market-ready technologies. The framework's core value is framed as a practical industrial validation and operational use-case blueprint rather than a novel technological design or detection methodology, and the observed metrics may vary when applied across alternative cloud providers or larger on-premise hospital networks.

5 Conclusion and Future Work

The implementation of the NERO healthcare use case establishes a robust methodological and technical groundwork for securing patient data within the SME clinical landscape. By integrating advanced cybersecurity tools, ranging from AI-powered threat detection to automated software auditing, into a centralised Marketplace, the NERO ecosystem provides a scalable solution to the persistent vulnerabilities of the healthcare sector. The practical application of these frameworks demonstrated that proactive vulnerability discovery and structured software auditing can significantly mitigate risks within the software supply chain before deployment in sensitive clinical environments. Furthermore, the synergy between technical tools and human-centric risk management ensures that staff behaviour and cybersecurity awareness are treated as integral components of organisational resilience.

The planning and integration phases detailed in this paper serve as the baseline for upcoming validation and demonstration activities. Future work will focus on the operational execution of structured test campaigns across representative infrastructures to evaluate the real-world performance and interoperability of the integrated tools. These activities will prioritise refining the feedback loop between end-users and developers to enhance the usability and maturity of the NERO platform. Additionally, long-term research will explore the sustainability of these cybersecurity improvements, aiming to broaden the outreach to a larger number of healthcare SMEs and ensuring that cyber-hygiene practices remain effective against an ever-evolving threat landscape.

Acknowledgments. The authors would like to acknowledge the financial support provided for the following projects: The 'Advanced Cybersecurity Awareness Ecosystem for SMEs' (NERO) project, which has received funding from the European Union's DEP programme under grant agreement No. 101127411; 'the 'Harmonizing People, Processes, and Technology for Robust Cybersecurity' (CYberSynchrony) project, which has received funding by the European Union's Digital Europe programme under Grant Agreement no. 101158555 and supported by the European Cybersecurity Competence Centre (ECCC). The views expressed in this paper represent only the views of the authors and not those of the European Commission or the partners in the above-mentioned projects. Finally, the authors declare that there are no conflicts of interest, including any financial or personal relationships, that could be perceived as potential conflicts.

Disclosure of Interests.. The authors have no competing interests to declare that are relevant to the content of this article.

References

1. Hameed, K., Naha, R., Hameed, F.: Digital transformation for sustainable health and well-being: a review and future research directions. Discov Sustain **5**, 104 (2024). https://doi.org/10.1007/s43621-024-00273-8
2. Ashwini, A., Kavitha, V. and Balasubramaniam, S.: Interconnected Healthcare 5.0 ecosystems: enhancing patient care using sensor networks. In Networked Sensing Systems (eds R.K. Dhanaraj, M. Sathyamoorthy, S. Balasubramaniam and S. Kadry), pp. 225–246. https://doi.org/10.1002/9781394310890.ch9 (2025)
3. Newaz, A.I., Sikder, A.K., Rahman, M.A., Uluagac, A.S.: A survey on security and privacy issues in modern healthcare systems: attacks and defenses. ACM Trans. Comput. Healthcare **2**(3), 1–44 (2021)
4. Toth, D., Erb, D., Petz, E.: The challenges of medical identity theft. In: Collection Papers from International Scientific Conference Organized on the Occasion of the Day of the Faculty of Law, University of Niš (p. 237) (2025)
5. Shahzadi, A., et al.: Safeguarding the healthcare sector from ransomware attacks: insights from a literature review. Peer J. Comput. Sci. **11**, e3073 (2025). https://doi.org/10.7717/peerj-cs.3073
6. Ismail, D.: Securing implantable medical devices against remote attacks by anomaly detection: enhancing IoT security within healthcare. https://www.diva-portal.org/smash/get/diva2:1935815/FULLTEXT01.pdf (2024)
7. GDPR, E. General data protection regulation (gdpr). Cit. on, 4 (2018)
8. Edemekong, P. F., Annamaraju, P., Afzal, M., Haydel, M. J.: Health insurance portability and accountability act (HIPAA) compliance. StatPearls Publishing. https://www.ncbi.nlm.nih.gov/books/NBK500019/ (2024)
9. Qureshi, R., Koo, I.: A comprehensive survey of cybersecurity threats and data privacy issues in healthcare systems. Appl. Sci. **16**(3), 1511 (2026). https://doi.org/10.3390/app16031511
10. Akinsanya, A.: manufacturing cybersecurity for SMEs: implementing zero trust in legacy industrial environments 09 March 2026. (Preprint - Version 1) available at Research Square https://doi.org/10.21203/rs.3.rs-8846670/v1 (2026)
11. Singh, J.: Challenges with medical devices connected to hospital network. Int. J. Res. Appl. Sci. Eng. Technol. **12**(VI) (2024)
12. Kioskli K, Maglaras L, Fotis T, Varouchas E. Human factors and strategic approaches in cybersecurity: threats for critical infrastructures in NIS2 domains.: In: Abbas Moallem and Kitty Kioskli (eds) Human Factors in Cybersecurity. AHFE (2025) International Conference. AHFE Open Access, vol 168. AHFE International, USA. http://bit.ly/46NseqG (2025)
13. Fotis T, Kioskli K, Seralidou E. Charting Trustworthiness: a socio-technical perspective on AI and human factors. : In: Abbas Moallem and Kitty Kioskli (eds) Human Factors in Cybersecurity. AHFE (2025) International Conference. AHFE Open Access, vol 168. AHFE International, USA. http://bit.ly/44ASvHq (2025)
14. Ilieva, J., Todosovski, A.: Navigating legal aspects of health management: a simplified overview. Open Access Int. J. Acad. Res. Univ. **2**(2), 61–69 (2024)

15. ISO/IEC 29119 (Software Testing): International Organization for Standardization.: ISO/IEC/IEEE 29119 Software and systems engineering - Software testing (Parts 1–5) (2013)
16. ISO/IEC 27001 (Security Management): International Organization for Standardization.: ISO/IEC 27001:2022 Information technology - Security techniques - Information security management systems – Requirements (2022)
17. ISO/IEC 27799 (Healthcare Specific): International Organization for Standardization.: ISO 27799:2016 Health informatics - Information security management in health using ISO/IEC 27002 (2016)
18. National Institute of Standards and Technology.: *Framework for Improving Critical Infrastructure Cybersecurity* (Version 1.1). U.S. Department of Commerce. https://doi.org/10.6028/NIST.CSWP.04162018 (2018)
19. NERO Marketplace Homepage. https://nerocybersecurity.eu/marketplace. Accessed 13 May 2026
20. ENISA European Cybersecurity Skills Framework. https://www.enisa.europa.eu/topics/skills-and-competences/skills-development/european-cybersecurity-skills-framework-ecsf. Accessed 13 May 2026
21. Snyk. https://snyk.io/. Accessed 13 May 2026
22. Deepguardian. https://deepguardian.org/en. Accessed 13 May 2026
23. MI CyberRange. https://play.google.com/store/apps/details?id=com.montimage.cyberrange&hl=el. Accessed 13 May 2026

Evaluating a Combined ISTG/BSI Penetration Testing Methodology

Valentino Schwarz(✉), Roland Schmitz, and Joachim Charzinski

Stuttgart Media University, Stuttgart, Germany
contact@valentino-schwarz.com, {schmitz,charzinski}@hdm-stuttgart.de

Abstract. This paper evaluates a combined methodological approach for structured IoT security assessment, integrating the OWASP IoT Security Testing Guide (ISTG), which defines *what* to test across hardware, firmware, network services, and communication interfaces, with the five-phase penetration testing model of the German Federal Office for Information Security (BSI), which defines *how* to proceed. The combination is evaluated through a real-device case study of a commercially available low-cost smart home camera. The assessment produced a verified end-to-end attack chain from physical access to full system compromise and recovery of private video data, demonstrating that the combined methodology can drive a non-trivial real-device assessment to completion. More importantly, the case study exposed integration gaps the combination does not resolve. We describe the adaptations that were necessary to bridge these gaps, present a per-test-case documentation scheme and a consolidated gap-adaptation overview as reusable artifacts, and formulate concrete recommendations for future revisions of IoT-specific test catalogues.

Keywords: IoT security · Penetration testing methodology · Case study

1 Introduction

The Internet of Things (IoT) has fundamentally changed how everyday objects interact with their environment and with each other [12]. Despite this shift, manufacturers and users alike continue to perceive connected devices primarily as consumer products rather than as network-connected computers, contributing to a widespread underestimation of the security risks they introduce [14]. This gap is most pronounced in the low-cost segment, where competitive pressure routinely leads to security being deprioritized in favor of affordability [13], a pattern reflected in recurring technical shortcomings documented across this product category [5,8,16].

Smart home cameras represent a particularly critical target within this landscape, because they continuously capture audio and video data of the residents of a home. A successful attack therefore constitutes a direct intrusion into personal privacy and physical safety. Yet the methodological question of *how* to

P. Kieseberg et al. (Eds.): ARES 2026 Workshops, LNCS 16903, pp. 551–569, 2027.
https://doi.org/10.1007/978-3-032-37218-5_32

systematically assess the security of such devices is not settled by any single established framework. The OWASP IoT Security Testing Guide (ISTG) provides IoT-specific attack-surface coverage but explicitly delegates process structure to external frameworks – and names the penetration testing model of the German Federal Office for Information Security (BSI) as an example [11]. The BSI model provides a mature process structure but is not IoT-specific. The two frameworks therefore appear complementary—the ISTG supplying the IoT specificity the BSI model lacks, the BSI model supplying the process structure the ISTG delegates. This raises a question that, to the best of our knowledge, has not been empirically addressed: does the combination of the two actually produce a coherent methodology when applied to a real device?

The present paper addresses this question: Using the Boykeep 2K Petcam K30 as a representative low-cost smart home camera, we apply the combined ISTG/BSI methodology end-to-end and evaluate where it succeeds, where it fails, and what adaptations are needed to bridge the gaps. More precisely, we aim to answer the following research question:

> *To what extent does the combination of the OWASP ISTG and the BSI penetration testing model provide a suitable basis for a structured IoT penetration test?*

Three sub-questions guide the analysis:

- SQ1 What contribution does the ISTG make to the assessment?
- SQ2 What contribution does the BSI penetration testing model make?
- SQ3 Where do the frameworks reach their limits when applied to an embedded IoT target, and what adaptations are required?

Contributions. This paper makes three contributions. First, we report on the application of the ISTG/BSI combination to a commercial low-cost IoT camera, verified through an exploitable attack chain that serves as empirical basis for the framework evaluation. Second, we derive two reusable methodological artifacts that address the gaps encountered: a per-test-case documentation schema and a consolidated gap-adaptation-recommendation overview. Third, we formulate concrete recommendations for future revisions of IoT-specific test catalogues.

The remainder of the paper is structured as follows. Section 2 covers background and related work. Section 3 describes the combined methodology and introduces the documentation schema. Section 4 summarizes the application of the methodology to the case study device along all five BSI phases. Section 5 evaluates the methodology against the sub-questions, and Sect. 6 concludes the paper.

2 Background and Related Work

2.1 IoT Devices and Security Assessment

IoT devices differ from conventional computing systems in ways that directly affect their security posture. They are resource-constrained, frequently operate unattended in physically accessible environments, and span heterogeneous ecosystems of protocols, operating systems, and cloud back-ends [1,2,10]. These properties make standard security mechanisms difficult to apply and require assessment approaches that go beyond classical IT penetration testing, spanning hardware, firmware, network services, and communication interfaces [17]. Firmware analysis is a particularly relevant technique in this context, because security-relevant implementation details such as credential storage and cryptographic constructions are often only visible at the binary or filesystem level [15,17].

2.2 Testing Models

The procedural reference used in this work is the penetration testing model of the German Federal Office for Information Security (BSI) [7]. The model treats penetration testing as a controlled, goal-directed attempt to detect and verify weaknesses through active exploitation, and structures this work into five sequential phases: **Preparation** fixes objectives, scope, and the legal and technical test conditions; **Reconnaissance** gathers information about the target; **Information Analysis** consolidates and prioritises that information into candidate attack paths; **Active Intrusion** carries out the actual exploitation attempts; and **Consolidation** integrates the results into findings, ratings, and recommendations. The concrete testing activities within these phases are organised into information-gathering and intrusion modules, and the model supplies explicit classification criteria for scope, information basis (black-, gray-, white-box), and aggressiveness. Its emphasis is therefore on *how* a test is conducted and documented. The model provides a mature process scaffold, which the ISTG itself names as a suitable host framework [11], but contributes no IoT-specific content of its own.

The OWASP IoT Security Testing Guide (ISTG) is an open-source reference framework that provides a structured catalogue of security test cases specifically designed for IoT devices [11]. It organises test objectives into eight technical domains reflecting the distinct attack surfaces of IoT hardware and software: Processing Units, Memory, Firmware, Data Exchange Services, Internal Interfaces, Physical Interfaces, Wireless Interfaces, and User Interfaces. Within each domain, test cases are defined at a generic, technology-agnostic level of abstraction, making the guide applicable across a wide range of device types and architectures, and are further organised into categories such as information gathering, authorization, configuration and patch management, secrets, cryptography, business logic, input validation, and side-channel attacks, with the applicable subset varying per component. Test objectives are scoped using two structuring artefacts: an attacker model, which specifies assumed physical and authorisation access levels, and a device model, which maps the target's components to the relevant ISTG domains. A central design principle is the ISTG's explicit positioning as a supplement to existing penetration testing workflows, meaning it should be embedded into a higher-level process framework [11].

2.3 Related Approaches and Research Gap

Several methodologies address IoT security assessment more specifically. Practical and Agile Threat Research for IoT (PatrIoT) combines attack-surface decomposition with a curated weakness catalogue and step-by-step testing guidelines [15]. Penetration and Exploitation Testing for IoT (PETIoT) adapts the cyber kill chain for IoT and adds an explicit remediation step [4]. Yadav et al. propose an end-to-end penetration testing framework for IoT that argues against component-isolated testing and instead targets vulnerabilities arising from the interaction between subsystems, illustrated through a Philips Hue smart-home case study [18]. Building on this concept, IoT-PEN is a network-centric automated framework that pursues end-to-end coverage by mapping device software against the National Vulnerability Database and constructing multi-host attack-path graphs from the preconditions and postconditions of known vulnerabilities [19]. ETSI EN 303 645 provides baseline conformance criteria for consumer IoT but is not designed for offensive, hardware-intensive testing [6].

A recent systematic literature review of 99 IoT penetration testing publications between 2015 and 2021 catalogues a range of protocol-, device-, and framework-specific approaches and identifies IoT penetration testing as an understudied area relative to other aspects of IoT security [9]. The ISTG is content-rich but procedurally incomplete, while process-oriented approaches like PatrIoT and PETIoT are methodologically structured but not broadly validated on real commercial devices. Case studies on specific devices—such as the hardware-level exploitation of a VAVA outdoor IP camera via UART access and firmware manipulation [3]—illustrate the kinds of vulnerabilities that arise in practice but do not themselves constitute a generalisable methodology. It therefore remains open to what extent an IoT-specific catalogue and a classical process model can be combined into a practically feasible real-device methodology. The present paper addresses that question.

3 Combining the Frameworks

The two frameworks are combined here with the ISTG as the technical reference for *what to test* and the BSI five-phase model as the procedural reference for *how to proceed*. The ISTG explicitly positions itself as a supplement to an existing process framework and states that "it will be shown how this methodology can be integrated into other frameworks based on the example of the BSI penetration testing model" [11]. We stress that the combination set out in this section is the *starting point* of the assessment, not its result. Whether it constitutes a coherent methodology, and where it does not, is the object of the evaluation in Sect. 5. On this basis, the section operationalizes both frameworks, introduces the per-test-case documentation schema developed during the study, and defines the evaluation criteria used to answer SQ1–SQ3.

The ISTG is instantiated through an attacker model and a device model. The attacker model specifies physical and authorization access levels following the ISTG's PA/AA classification. The device model describes the relevant internal components, interfaces, trust boundaries, and external dependencies of the target. Together they constrain which ISTG domains are in scope and which are not.

For each in-scope domain, device-specific test cases are derived from the generic ISTG catalogue. In this paper, the resulting instantiated set is referred to as the *CAM catalogue*, where `CAM` identifies the target as a camera. Each identifier follows the structure `CAM-[DOMAIN]-[CATEGORY]-[NUMBER]`, e.g. `CAM-PHY-AUTHZ-001` for the first authorization test case in the Physical Interfaces domain. Within the defined scope, each instantiated test case is evaluated against two exclusion criteria: *R0 (Not Applicable)*—the required functionality, interface, or precondition is not present, and *R1 (Physical Integrity)*—the activity carries a significant risk of permanently damaging the single laboratory device.[1].

The BSI model is primarily intended for commercial engagements [7]. For an academic single-target case study, contractual and engagement-management aspects are excluded, while the process structure, the classification criteria of Chapter 3.4, and the documentation logic of Chapters 6 and 7 are retained in adapted form. The five phases are instantiated for this study as follows. Preparation is used to define the assessment scope, attacker model, device model, and test environment, and to instantiate the CAM catalogue. Reconnaissance is centered on the device itself and is organized around the ISTG's information-gathering and configuration and patch management categories across the in-scope domains. Information Analysis consolidates and interprets the collected evidence with respect to security relevance and prioritizes candidate attack paths. Here the ISTG device model serves as the grid for clustering observations at the component level, whereas the sequencing across paths is driven by the BSI process rather than by the ISTG. Active Intrusion validates the prioritized paths under controlled conditions, drawing on the ISTG's authorization, secrets, cryptography, business logic, and input validation categories. Consolidation integrates all results into verified findings, severity ratings, and recommendations, using the ISTG domain and category taxonomy as the classification grid. This assignment of ISTG categories to phases is the configuration adopted for this study. Whether it follows from the frameworks themselves or must be supplied by the tester is examined in Sect. 5.3.

3.1 Per-Test-Case Documentation Schema

Neither framework provides a sufficiently result-oriented documentation template. The BSI model's documentation template provides expected results, test steps, and a done checkbox, but no field for recording what was actually observed, no artifact references, and no outcome classification beyond binary completion.

[1] Only one unit of the target device was available for this study. Activities classified under R1 were therefore excluded to preserve the device or the remainder of the assessment.

The ISTG defines a structure for its own catalogue entries (Requirements, Summary, Test Objectives, Remediation), but provides no template for documenting what the tester actually *found*. A schema was therefore developed that combines the BSI principle of phase-spanning documentation with the ISTG's per-case granularity, and explicitly separates *observation* from *interpretation*. The resulting fields are shown in Table 1.

Table 1. Per-test-case documentation schema developed during the assessment.

Field	Purpose
CAM identifier and title	Links to ISTG domain and category
Domain / component	Maps to concrete ISTG attack surface
Required PA/AA level	Scope boundary from attacker model
Objective	Concise test goal
Execution steps	Reproducible procedure with tools
Observed result	What was technically observed
Artifact references	Logs, captures, extracted files
Outcome	Verified / Not Verified / Not Pursued Further

The three-valued outcome classification is a deliberate choice. A binary Verified/Not Verified distinction collapses two meaningfully different situations: cases that were executed and failed to reproduce the test objective, and cases that could have been executed but were consciously deprioritized under resource constraints. Preserving this distinction supports the traceability of coverage, which is revisited in Sect. 5.1.

3.2 Evaluation Criteria

Beyond producing a technical assessment, the combined methodology is evaluated qualitatively against SQ1–SQ3. The observations used to answer these questions are drawn from the preparation, reconnaissance, test-case derivation, execution, and documentation steps of the case study. We explicitly note that the evaluation reflects the subset of test cases actually executed under the resources of a single-device academic study. A fully exhaustive coverage may surface additional contributions or limits not visible here (Fig. 1).

4 Case Study: Pentesting the Boykeep 2K Petcam K30

The target is the Boykeep 2K Petcam K30, a commercially available low-cost smart home camera. The assessment was conducted in an isolated laboratory environment comprising a Kali Linux workstation acting as controlled Wi-Fi hotspot, gateway, and analysis host, the target camera, an Android smartphone running the vendor application, and an attacker-controlled host. Hardware-assisted access was supported by an FT232RL USB-to-TTL adapter and a CH341A programmer with SOIC-8 clip. This section summarizes the application of the combined methodology along the five BSI phases in sufficient depth to support the framework evaluation in Sect. 5.

Fig. 1. The Boykeep 2K Petcam K30.

4.1 Phase 1 – Preparation

Attacker Model. Consistent with the ISTG's PA/AA classification [11], we assumed **PA-4 (invasive physical access) with AA-1 (no authorization).** PA-4 is both realistic in the product's intended context (e.g., guests, technicians, previous owners) and methodologically necessary for evaluating hardware-near attack paths. AA-1 captures the starting position of an adversary without legitimate credentials on the target device. Escalation to higher AA levels is therefore treated as a potential *outcome* of the assessment rather than as a starting assumption. *Test classification and scope delimitation.* Following the BSI classification logic (Chap. 3.4), the assessment is best characterized as a *gray-box* test: no manufacturer-internal documentation or source code was available, but physical availability of the device enabled teardown, firmware extraction, and inspection of internal interfaces, which generated partial internal knowledge. Aggressiveness was deliberately kept low because only a single laboratory device was available. The scope was restricted to the device itself and to directly reachable local interfaces, cloud services, the mobile application, and other vendor infrastructure were observed only where necessary to understand device behavior in the lab, but were not treated as direct targets.

Laboratory Setup and Planning Assumptions. Preparation also defined the practical conditions under which the methodology would be applied. The camera was provisioned inside an isolated laboratory environment consisting of a controlled Wi-Fi network, a smartphone running the vendor app, and an attacker-side analysis host. This setup was chosen so that normal user workflows could be reproduced while keeping all locally observable device behavior under control. At the same time, hardware-assisted access was planned from the outset because

the selected attacker model made board-level inspection, serial observation, and offline storage analysis legitimate parts of the assessment.
Device Model and Catalogue Instantiation. The printed circuit board (PCB) was examined manually and the relevant components were identified through teardown and public datasheet correlation (Table 2). This produced a device model that was used to map the target's concrete attack surfaces to ISTG domains. On that basis, 89 device-specific CAM test cases were instantiated. The instantiated catalogue defined the assessment space, made exclusions explicit, and created an auditable baseline against which later coverage decisions could be interpreted. Test cases for absent or unjustified attack surfaces were excluded under *R0*. Activities that posed disproportionate risk to the single device were excluded under *R1*.

Table 2. Security-relevant components identified during teardown.

Component	Function
Anyka AK3918EV300 SoC	Main system-on-chip, ARM926EJ-S core
Puya PY25Q64HA SPI flash	8 MiB non-volatile storage
AltoBeam ATBM6132 module	Wi-Fi and BLE connectivity
UART debug pads	Exposed serial interface, unlabelled
MicroSD card slot	Externally accessible local storage
Image sensor, motors, LEDs	I/O peripherals

4.2 Phase 2 – Reconnaissance

Reconnaissance focused on information-disclosure and configuration-oriented test cases across all in-scope domains. In contrast to a classical infrastructure engagement, it was organized around four device-centric information streams: inspection of exposed interfaces, passive observation of the boot process, offline reconstruction of the firmware, and observation of runtime communication behavior under normal operation.

Physical and Serial Observations. Inspection of the opened device confirmed the presence of several security-relevant interfaces and components, including exposed UART pads, SPI flash storage, a wireless communication module, and an externally reachable MicroSD slot. Passive UART capture then disclosed bootloader, kernel, and flash-related identifiers without requiring authentication. Although the serial interface did not yield an interactive console in the tested configuration, it still provided important orientation for later firmware analysis by exposing platform characteristics and confirming that the device could be observed during boot at a level deeper than the user-facing application behavior.

Offline Firmware Reconstruction. A second reconnaissance stream focused on the non-volatile storage of the device. Repeated acquisition of the SPI flash yielded stable dumps, which were reconstructed into a boot region, two read-only filesystem layers, and a writable area. At a high level, this made it possible to move from black-box observation of the camera's behavior to white-box- like visibility into initialization logic, packaged binaries, persistent configuration, and update-related artifacts. Several later findings originated here: startup scripts, a gated SD-card maintenance path, credential material, and application-layer update logic all became visible only once the firmware had been reconstructed and its filesystem structure interpreted. Within the reconstructed filesystem, the binary `ukey` was identified as a central component of the device's update and maintenance logic, providing the necessary context for the later investigation of the SD-card authorization gate.

Runtime and Network Observations. Reconnaissance further examined how the device behaved when used as intended. Network observation during provisioning and normal operation showed no obvious inbound service surface, but several device-initiated encrypted channels to vendor-controlled infrastructure. Two sustained TLS sessions in particular stood out because their traffic pattern was consistent with media transport. This did not yet establish an attack path, but it indicated that a post-compromise privacy impact might be observable on the wire if the trust relationship of the device could be influenced later in the assessment.

Methodological Role of the Phase. Importantly, the outputs of Phase 2 were not treated as findings in themselves. Rather, they formed the evidence base that allowed the device and attacker models to be refined and candidate attack paths to be compared in the next phase. This distinction between collecting security-relevant evidence and already interpreting it as an exploitable weakness proved important, because several observations looked suspicious during reconnaissance but only became meaningful once they were evaluated in relation to each other in Phase 3.

4.3 Phase 3 – Information Analysis and Prioritization

Information Analysis consolidated the reconnaissance evidence and translated it into candidate attack paths. In practical terms, this was the phase in which the assessment moved from "interesting technical artifacts" to explicit hypotheses about reachability, preconditions, and likely impact. The analysis clustered observations around a small number of plausible paths: local maintenance functionality reachable through removable media, latent remote-administration capability present in system startup logic, credential material stored in the firmware, trust and certificate handling in the application layer, and outbound encrypted communication that could become relevant after a foothold.

Prioritization Logic. Candidate paths were prioritized along four dimensions: consistency with the PA-4/AA-1 profile, expected security impact, practical feasibility in the laboratory setup, and risk to the operational integrity of the single test device. The goal was to choose the path most likely to produce a methodologically informative validation under controlled conditions. This mattered because some technically plausible checks would have consumed substantial effort while adding comparatively little evidence for the framework evaluation.

Selected Priorities. The SD-card maintenance path emerged as the P1 target because it combined a directly reachable local input surface with signs of a vendor-intended authorization gate and a potentially high-impact outcome at system start-up. By contrast, the recovered application credential and root password hash were classified as relevant but less urgent, because their practical exploitability depended on confirming a consuming authentication interface within scope. Observations related to the boot chain and encrypted transport channels were treated as promising follow-up paths, but they required either broader reverse engineering effort or a prior device foothold to become actionable.

Methodologically, Phase 3 was the point at which the BSI process discipline most clearly shaped the study. Without an explicit analysis and prioritization step, the assessment could easily have followed the first visible low-effort lead. Instead, the evidence collected in reconnaissance was compared systematically, weaker hypotheses were contained, and active work was concentrated on the path most likely to explain how independent observations might combine into a larger attack chain. This analytical bridging step later proved essential for the framework evaluation, because it exposed exactly where the ISTG alone provides coverage but not sequencing guidance.

4.4 Phase 4 – Active Intrusion

Active Intrusion validated the prioritized path in three high-level steps: establishing an initial foothold through the SD-card maintenance mechanism, converting that foothold into durable privileged access, and using the compromised device position to influence the trust basis of its outbound encrypted communication.

Initial Foothold. Reverse engineering of the `ukey` binary confirmed the central hypothesis from Phase 3: the SD-card gate did not behave like a cryptographic signature check tied to a device-held secret. Instead, validation was derived deterministically from the file itself. This meant that the authorization value protecting the maintenance script could be reconstructed (Fig. 2).

Privileged Access and Persistence. Once the maintenance path had been validated, it provided boot-time execution with root privileges. This initial foothold was sufficient to reactivate a dormant remote-administration component already present in the device's startup logic and to explore the live system under controlled conditions. That exploration showed that the available runtime environment also supported a reconnecting access path using binaries already present on the device. Persistence was therefore moved from a one-off laboratory foothold to a boot-resident mechanism that re-established access after restart. Importantly, this access survived a factory reset via the device's reset button, showing that the compromise was anchored in a part of the system state that ordinary user recovery actions did not remove.

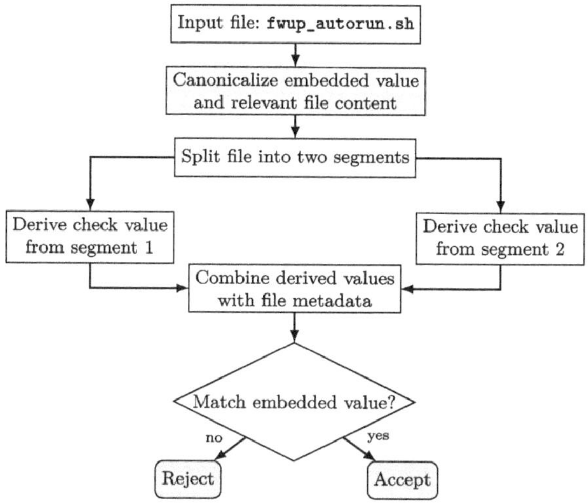

Fig. 2. High-level reconstruction of the `ukey -t` authorization flow.

Post-compromise Privacy Impact. The final step used the combined vantage point of a compromised device and a controlled gateway position to influence how the camera established trust for outbound encrypted communication. This involved manipulating certificate-related material so that previously opaque TLS sessions became observable under the laboratory man-in-the-middle setup. Once this trust relationship had been altered, private H.265 video data transmitted by the device could be recovered from intercepted traffic. This completed the chain from physical access to a concrete privacy violation without requiring direct exploitation of external cloud systems.

Scope and Restraint. Even in this phase, validation remained selective. The assessment did not attempt to exhaust every theoretically plausible post-compromise path. Active work stopped once the chain had produced clear, causally linked evidence of system compromise, persistence, and privacy impact. This restraint was deliberate: it reduced unnecessary risk to the single device while preserving enough technical depth to support a meaningful framework evaluation.

4.5 Phase 5 Consolidated Assessment

The practical assessment confirmed an end-to-end exploitable attack chain from physical access to full system compromise and privacy violation. The consolidated view is important because the individual observations would understate the overall risk if read in isolation: firmware disclosure alone is not yet compromise, a local maintenance weakness alone is not yet durable access, and being able to observe encrypted traffic is not yet a privacy loss. Only when the phases are read together it becomes clear how these independently observed weaknesses formed a coherent progression.

Findings in Context. At a high level, the chain moved through four stages: disclosure of internal implementation details, validation of a local maintenance channel, establishment of privileged and reset-resilient access, and use of that access to undermine the confidentiality of the device's media traffic. This sequence matters analytically because it shows that the most severe privacy impact was not rooted in the network layer alone. It depended on earlier weaknesses in hardware-adjacent and firmware-level attack surfaces. The consolidated perspective therefore links the technical findings back to the device-centric scope of the methodology.

Coverage and Outcome Interpretation. Consolidation also integrated the per-case outcome documentation with the broader assessment narrative. Of the 89 instantiated CAM test cases, 34 were verified, 38 were documented as not pursued further, and 17 were excluded from scope under R0 or R1. This distribution shows which parts of the ISTG catalogue produced actionable evidence under the selected conditions and which remained analytically relevant but practically deferred. In other words, the final assessment captures both what was demonstrated and what remained open under the limits of a single-device academic study.

Severity Characterization. Table 3 summarizes the consolidated severity classification. Qualitative ratings based on confidentiality, integrity, and availability impact in the intended deployment context are used because they provide a more meaningful characterization here. Table 4 shows the coverage of the 89 instantiated test cases per ISTG domain.

Table 3. Severity overview of assessed findings (qualitative, based on CIA impact in the intended deployment context). V = Verified, NPF = Not Pursued Further.

Finding	Status	Severity
SD-card authorization bypass (CRC-16 reconstruction)	V	Critical
Boot-time root code execution via dormant `telnetd`	V	Critical
Reset-resilient persistence (factory-reset bypass)	V	Critical
Recovery of private video data from intercepted traffic	V	Critical
MITM certificate update manipulation	V	High
Post-compromise DNS manipulation	NPF	High
Root password hash disclosure (MD5-crypt)	NPF	High
Default application credential (`admin/closeli`)	NPF	Medium–High
Unauthenticated UART boot log disclosure	V	Low

Residual Limits. Several security-relevant observations remained outside the set of verified findings not because they appeared irrelevant, but because a deeper validation would have required additional tooling, broader scope, or a higher operational risk than was acceptable for the available device. Recording those paths as *Not Pursued Further* (NPF) rather than silently dropping them was therefore part of the final result.

5 Framework Evaluation

This section answers the three sub-questions by drawing on concrete observations from the case study.

Table 4. CAM catalogue: instantiated test cases per ISTG domain. V = Verified, NPF = Not Pursued Further, Out = excluded from scope under R0/R1.

Domain	Total	Out	V	NPF
Processing Unit (PROC)	4	4	–	–
Memory (MEM)	6	0	4	2
Firmware (FW, FW[INST], FW[UPDT])	19	1	10	8
Data Exchange Services (DES)	12	0	6	6
Internal Interfaces (INT)	12	0	3	9
Physical Interfaces (PHY)	12	0	8	4
Wireless Interfaces (WRLS)	12	0	3	9
User Interfaces (UI)	12	12	–	–
Total	**89**	**17**	**34**	**38**

5.1 Contribution of the ISTG (SQ1)

The ISTG turned an unfamiliar physical device into a structured and scoped test catalogue. The device model forced an explicit component-level representation of the target before any testing began, while the attacker model fixed the scope of what was plausible under the selected access conditions. Without this structure, deciding *what* to test would have required ad hoc judgement throughout the assessment. In particular, the ISTG's hierarchical partitioning of the attack surface into domains made it possible to reason about coverage systematically. This is a concrete improvement over a classical network-centric approach that would have largely ignored the hardware and firmware domains.

A second contribution lies in the catalogue's *coverage logic*. Because the ISTG requires an explicit definition of the test scope and supports the identification of applicable test cases through the device and attacker models, it created a structured basis for coverage tracking. This was operationalized by assigning an explicit outcome to each of the 89 instantiated test cases (Table 4). The resulting view made it possible to distinguish deliberate non-pursuit (38 NPF) from accidental omission and from verified findings (34 V), and reduced the risk that relevant test cases would simply be overlooked. The NPF rate is itself informative: it concentrates in the WRLS and INT domains, where executed coverage was limited by missing specialized tooling—a pattern the ISTG surfaces directly rather than leaving implicit.

The ISTG catalogue also served as a *classification tool*. It provided a structured way to map each verified finding back to components and categories, to identify which test objectives were already satisfied by the chain, and to determine which paths remained open.

5.2 Contribution of the BSI Penetration Testing Model (SQ2)

The BSI model's most concrete contribution was the enforced separation between reconnaissance, analysis, active validation, and consolidation. This phase structure prevented premature exploitation conclusions from being drawn on the basis of incomplete observations, and imposed a discipline that the ISTG alone does not provide. In practice, the five-phase model determined *when* information gathering was sufficiently mature to support analysis, *when* analytical observations justified active intrusion attempts, and *when* the results were ready to be consolidated.

This procedural discipline had a direct effect on the structure of the assessment. The Information Analysis phase forced an explicit prioritization step before any exploitation activity began. As a result, the SD-card maintenance channel was identified as the P1 target on the basis of reconstructed logic, not because it was the first interesting-looking path. Without such a prioritization step, the natural failure mode is to exploit the first visible weakness and then retrofit a narrative around it—which would have obscured the causal structure of the chain and understated the severity of the actual root-cause weakness. The BSI model's documentation principles additionally enforced an explicit separation between *observation* and *interpretation*, which the per-case schema (Table 1) operationalizes and which proved valuable for analytically dense findings such as the `ukey` gate and the certificate update mechanism.

Beyond phase discipline, the BSI classification criteria of Chap. 3.4 provided a structured vocabulary for specifying the test conditions (blackbox, whitebox, low aggressiveness, overt, hybrid technique). This vocabulary is not IoT-specific but translated directly to the present assessment without friction and made the test conditions comparable to those of classical engagements.

5.3 Limits and Required Adaptations (SQ3)

The ISTG explicitly presents itself as a supplement to pre-existing penetration testing workflows and, using the BSI model as an example, states that no changes to the overall test workflow should be required [11]. In the present case study, this expectation did not hold. The integration gaps encountered, the adaptations applied, and the resulting recommendations for future framework revisions are summarized in Table 5 and discussed below.

Sequencing and Phase Mapping. The ISTG organizes test cases by component and category, not by assessment phase. Within a single ISTG domain,

Table 5. Integration gaps encountered when combining ISTG and BSI and the adaptations applied in this study.

Gap	Adaptation in this study
No mapping between ISTG test-case categories and BSI phases	Reconnaissance-oriented cases executed first across all domains. Active cases deferred to post-analysis
No cross-domain sequencing guidance for parallel in-scope domains	Ad-hoc ordering based on what was logical for the available device and attacker model
No result-oriented documentation template in either framework	Developed per-case schema (Table 1) with separation of Observed Result and Outcome, artifact references, and three-valued outcome classification
BSI model not designed for IoT-specific reconnaissance	Preparation and Reconnaissance extended to cover PCB teardown, SOIC-8 flash extraction, SquashFS/JFFS2 reconstruction
BSI model's commercial-engagement scope not applicable to academic single-device study	Contractual and engagement-management aspects dropped, phase structure, classification criteria, and documentation logic retained

reconnaissance-oriented cases (information disclosure, configuration checks) appear in the same domain alongside active exploitation-oriented cases (authorization bypass, business-logic circumvention). The BSI model provides prioritization logic, but only after Phase 2 has been completed. The tester therefore first needs to recognize which ISTG test cases constitute reconnaissance in the IoT sense, execute those, and only then apply BSI-style prioritization to the remaining active cases. This mapping is nowhere described. For a tester without prior experience in embedded IoT assessment, the initial catalogue of 89 test cases provides no indication of which cases belong to reconnaissance, which to active intrusion, or how to sequence work across eight domains simultaneously. In the present study, the sequencing problem was resolved implicitly—INFO and CONF cases were executed first based on what seemed most logical for the available device, not because either framework indicated this as the correct starting point. Future revisions of the ISTG could resolve this by annotating each test case with its intended execution stage.

Documentation Schema Gap. The BSI model's module structure provides expected results, test steps, and a done checkbox, but no field for recording what was actually observed, no artifact references, and no outcome classification beyond binary completion. The ISTG defines a structure for its own catalogue entries (Requirements, Summary, Test Objectives, Remediation), but provides no template for documenting what the tester actually *found*. The schema in Table 1 was developed in response to this integration gap and combines BSI-style phase-spanning documentation with ISTG-style per-case granularity. Without

such a schema, test-case outcomes collapse to binary Verified/Not Verified, which obscures the difference between failed execution and conscious deprioritization—a distinction that matters both for interpreting the NPF rate in Table 4 and for reviewer traceability.
Scope of the BSI Model. A substantial portion of the BSI model addresses contractual, legal, and organizational aspects of commercial penetration testing engagements, which are not applicable to an academic single-device case study. The evaluation in this paper therefore applies to the methodological and procedural dimensions of the model only. Conversely, the BSI model was not designed for IoT targets: hardware-level access, firmware analysis, and physical interface testing fell outside the scope of its original network-centric conception and had to be accommodated in Preparation and Reconnaissance.

Practical Constraints. The documentation workload generated by the combined methodology was underestimated. Maintaining per-test-case records across 89 instantiated test cases in parallel with active technical work created a non-trivial overhead that contributed directly to the NPF rate. Some test cases additionally presupposed tooling that was not available in this study. The framework evaluation therefore reflects the combination's performance under constrained conditions. Additional limits or contributions may only become apparent in a more exhaustive assessment.

5.4 Recommendations for Future Framework Revisions

The gaps identified in Sect. 5.3 suggest five concrete directions for future revisions of IoT-specific test catalogues.

Phase Mapping. The ISTG should annotate each test case with its intended execution stage. Without this, the mapping to BSI phases is left to tester judgement and cannot be consistently reproduced across assessors with different levels of embedded IoT experience.

Cross-Domain Sequencing. Future revisions should add explicit orchestration guidance for parallel in-scope domains, specifying how to prioritize across them when reconnaissance produces observations in multiple areas simultaneously.

Per-case Result Template. A standardized template for recording test-case outcomes should be adopted as part of a revised ISTG, providing fields for observed results, artifact references, and a multi-valued outcome classification. The schema in Table 1 provides a concrete starting point.

IoT-Specific Reconnaissance. Hardware-level activities such as PCB teardown, flash acquisition, and filesystem reconstruction should be formalized as IoT-specific reconnaissance sub-steps, either within the BSI model or as part of an ISTG-native process framework, so that they are treated as first-class assessment activities rather than ad-hoc extensions.

Academic Scope Variant. The BSI model should define an explicit research or academic scope variant that omits commercial engagement management while retaining the phase structure, classification criteria, and documentation logic, lowering the adaptation overhead for single-device studies.

5.5 Synthesis and Limitations

The combination is effective because each framework addresses a gap the other leaves open: the ISTG provides the IoT-specific technical content that a general process framework cannot substitute, while the BSI model provides the process discipline that the ISTG explicitly delegates. Together they produced a methodologically traceable assessment with verified findings, severity classification, and remediation recommendations. However, the suitability of this basis is conditional on bridging decisions that the tester must currently supply independently. The two artifacts proposed in this paper (Tables 1 and 5) are intended as a reusable starting point, but a more durable solution would be an ISTG that incorporates a process framework of its own—one that defines assessment phases, provides sequencing guidance, classifies test cases by execution stage, and supplies a documentation template for results.

Threats to Validity. The evaluation is based on a single-device case study and therefore cannot claim generality across device classes. Observations were made by the same researchers who applied the methodology, introducing potential bias in favor of the methodology's perceived strengths. We have tried to mitigate this by anchoring all claims in concrete test-case outcomes. Finally, the NPF rate in Table 4 reflects a pragmatic trade-off between depth and coverage. A more exhaustive assessment may reveal framework behaviors not visible here.

6 Conclusion

This paper evaluated the combination of the OWASP IoT Security Testing Guide and the BSI penetration testing model as a basis for a structured IoT penetration test. Applied to a commercially available low-cost smart home camera, the combined methodology identified and verified a coherent attack chain from physical access to full system compromise and recovery of private video data. Each step of the chain exploits a technically independent weakness, but the steps are causally linked through a common substrate of low-cost IoT design decisions.

The combined methodology is *suitable*, but only conditionally. The ISTG provides the IoT-specific attack-surface coverage and coverage-tracking logic that classical frameworks lack. The BSI model supplies the procedural discipline that the ISTG explicitly delegates. Neither framework alone is sufficient, and their integration currently requires bridging decisions that neither framework supplies. We contribute two reusable artifacts that address these gaps (Tables 1 and 5) and recommend that future revisions of IoT-specific test catalogues incorporate a process framework of their own, annotate test cases with their intended execution stage, and adopt a standardized per-case result template.

Future work includes extending the evaluation across additional device classes, validating the framework evaluation under broader test-case coverage, and exploring whether a tighter integration of ISTG content with a classical process model can be codified into a single, IoT-native penetration testing methodology.

Responsible Disclosure.. The findings of this study were reported to the manufacturer (Boykeep). The manufacturer has acknowledged the receipt of the report. This research was conducted strictly for methodological evaluation purposes in a controlled laboratory environment to ensure no impact on external infrastructure or third-party privacy.

Disclosure of Interests. The authors have no competing interests to declare that are relevant to the content of this article.

References

1. Al Kabir, M., Elmedany, W., Sharif, M.: Securing IoT devices against emerging security threats: challenges and mitigation techniques. J. Cyber Sec. Technol. **7**(1), 1–25 (2023)
2. Alaa, M., Zaidan, A., Zaidan, B., Talal, M., Kiah, M.: A review of smart home applications based on internet of things. J. Netw. Comput. Appl. **97**, 48–65 (2017)
3. Almazrouei, O., Magalingam, P., Hasan, M., Almehrzi, M., Alshamsi, A.: Penetration testing for IoT security: the case study of a wireless IP security CAM. In: 2023 IEEE 2nd International Conference on AI in Cybersecurity (ICAIC) (2023)
4. Bella, G., Biondi, P., Bognanni, S., Esposito, S.: PETIoT: PEnetration testing the internet of things. Int. Things **22**, 100707 (2023)
5. Butun, I., Österberg, P., Song, H.: Security of the internet of things: vulnerabilities, attacks, countermeasures. IEEE Comm. Surv. Tutor. **22**(1), 616–644 (2019)
6. European Telecommunications Standards Institute (ETSI): Cyber security for consumer internet of things: Baseline requirements. https://www.etsi.org/deliver/etsi_en/303600_303699/303645/02.01.01_60/en_303645v020101p.pdf (2020)
7. Federal Office for Information Security (BSI): Implementation concept for penetration tests. https://www.bsi.bund.de/SharedDocs/Downloads/EN/BSI/Publications/Studies/Penetration/penetration_pdf.pdf (2003)
8. Fei, W., Ohno, H., Sampalli, S.: A systematic review of IoT security: research potential, challenges, future directions. ACM Comput. Surv. **56**(5), 111 (2023)
9. Greco, C., Fortino, G., Crispo, B., Choo, K.K.: AI-enabled IoT penetration testing: state-of-the-art and research challenges. Enterprise Info. Syst. **17**(9), 2130014 (2023)
10. Miorandi, D., Sicari, S., De Pellegrini, F., Chlamtac, I.: Internet of things: Vision, applications and research challenges. Ad Hoc Netw. **10**(7), 1497–1516 (2012)
11. OWASP Foundation: OWASP IoT security testing guide (ISTG), version 1.0.0. https://owasp.org/www-project-iot-security-testing-guide/ (2024)
12. Rose, K., Eldridge, S., Chapin, L.: The internet of things (IoT): an overview (2015). https://www.internetsociety.org/resources/doc/2015/iot-overview/
13. Schiller, E., Aidoo, A., Fuhrer, J., Stahl, J., Ziörjen, M., Stiller, B.: Landscape of IoT security. Comput. Sci. Rev. **44**, 100467 (2022)
14. Schneier, B.: Click Here to Kill Everybody: Security and Survival in a Hyperconnected World. W. W. Norton & Company, New York (2018)

15. Süren, E., Heiding, F., Olegård, J., Lagerström, R.: PatrIoT: practical and agile threat research for IoT. Int. J. Info. Sec. **22**(1), 213–233 (2023)
16. Valente, J., Koneru, K., Cardenas, A.: Privacy and security in internet-connected cameras. In: 2019 IEEE International Congress on Internet of Things (ICIOT), pp. 173–180 (2019)
17. Yaacoub, J.P., Noura, H., Salman, O., Chehab, A.: Ethical hacking for IoT: security issues, challenges, solutions and recommendations. Int. Things Cyber-Phys. Syst. **3**, 280–308 (2023)
18. Yadav, G., Allakany, A., Kumar, V., Paul, K., Okamura, K.: Penetration testing framework for IoT. In: 8th International Congress on Advanced Applied Informatics (IIAI-AAI), pp. 477–482. (2019)
19. Yadav, G., Paul, K., Allakany, A., Okamura, K.: IoT-PEN: a penetration testing framework for IoT. In: 2020 International Conference on Information Networking (ICOIN), pp. 196–201 (2020)

Autonomous AI-Driven Pentesting Agent for Healthcare Systems Security

Manh-Dung Nguyen[1(✉)], Manuel Méndez Hurtado[2], Miguel Benito-Parejo[2], Ana Rosa Cavalli[1], and Edgardo Montes de Oca[1]

[1] Montimage EURL, 37 rue Bobillot, 75013 Paris, France
manhdung.nguyen@monKmage.eu

[2] Design and Testing of Reliable Systems Research Group, Universidad Complutense de Madrid, Madrid 28040, Spain

Abstract. DICOM and PACS infrastructures are essential components of modern healthcare systems but remain exposed to protocol-level security and robustness issues. Traditional fuzzing approaches are often not well suited for testing complex and stateful medical communication protocols. In this paper, we present an extension of NetworkFuzzer, a smart network protocol fuzzer, for intelligent security assessment of DICOM-based systems. Our approach combines rule-based replay, GAN-based traffic generation, LLM-assisted rule synthesis, and a reinforcement learning-guided fuzzing engine that adapts mutation strategies according to runtime feedback from the target system. We also develop an autonomous pentesting agent that integrates reconnaissance, analysis, fuzzing, and reporting capabilities to support scalable security assessments of healthcare infrastructures. Experimental evaluation on multiple real-world DICOM server implementations demonstrates the effectiveness of the proposed framework in exploring deep protocol states and identifying robustness and security issues, including hangs, crashes, and abnormal behaviors.

Keywords: Network Fuzzing · Reinforcement Learning · Synthetic Traffic · Pentesting Agent · LLM · DICOM Protocol Testing

1 Introduction

Context. Medical imaging plays a fundamental role in modern healthcare, supporting diagnosis, treatment planning, and patient monitoring. The Digital Imaging and Communications in Medicine (DICOM) standard defines the widely adopted protocol for exchanging, storing, and retrieving medical images and associated clinical data [7], enabling interoperability across heterogeneous imaging devices and hospital systems. Within this ecosystem, the Picture Archiving and Communication System (PACS) serves as the core infrastructure for managing and distributing medical images in healthcare environments. Although PACS deployments are typically confined to internal hospital networks, they remain

P. Kieseberg et al. (Eds.): ARES 2026 Workshops, LNCS 16903, pp. 570–588, 2027.
https://doi.org/10.1007/978-3-032-37218-5_33

vulnerable to insider threats, misconfigurations, unauthorized access, denial-of-service attacks, and data manipulation, all of which may compromise the confidentiality, integrity, and availability of medical imaging data [12,31]. Recent studies and security reports have revealed serious weaknesses in DICOM-based systems, showing that they can be exploited through a wide range of cyberattacks [11]. These incidents highlight the security risks associated with insufficient protection mechanisms in real-world DICOM deployments and motivate the need for systematic and intelligent testing approaches, such as smart fuzzing techniques, to proactively identify and mitigate vulnerabilities in DICOM and PACS systems.

Proposal. This paper extends NetworkFuzzer [3], a smart network protocol fuzzer, to evaluate the robustness of healthcare systems, with a focus on the DICOM protocol. Unlike traditional coverage-driven fuzzers [6,8,19,23], our approach operates at the network level, targeting protocol semantics and real communication behavior rather than code coverage. The original NetworkFuzzer improves rule-based fuzzing [25] by integrating Generative Adversarial Networks (GAN)-based traffic generation and Large Language Model (LLM)-based rule synthesis, reducing the manual effort required to craft attack scenarios and improving contextual awareness.

In this work, we further extend NetworkFuzzer with reinforcement learning (RL) for adaptive fuzzing and introduce an autonomous agent that supports the full security testing workflow. NetworkFuzzer uses feedback from server responses and runtime signals (e.g., errors, state changes, and performance indicators) to continuously refine packet generation in a closed-loop manner, enabling more effective exploration of protocol behaviors and vulnerabilities. We also develop an autonomous pentesting agent built on top of NetworkFuzzer that orchestrates reconnaissance, vulnerability analysis, fuzzing, and reporting, supporting scalable security assessment of PACS and DICOM systems.

Contributions. Our main contributions are summarized as follows.

1. We design and implement an RL-guided fuzzing engine that leverages reinforcement learning algorithms to enable the agent to learn mutation strategies that effectively explore deeper execution paths and destabilize target systems through crashes, hangs, and other abnormal behaviors.
2. We develop an autonomous agentic pentesting framework based on NetworkFuzzer [22], capable of performing key assessment stages, including discovery, analysis, testing, and reporting, while generating structured security assessment reports. The framework supports multiple access interfaces, including an Model Context Protocol (MCP) server for LLM-agent integration and reusable skills, enabling users to assess the robustness of healthcare systems through natural-language prompts.
3. We conduct extensive experiments on real-world healthcare systems, including Orthanc [13], DCMTK and other DICOM implementations, demonstrating effective identification of robustness and security issues.

The remainder of this paper is organized as follows. Section 2 presents background information on the DICOM protocol, while Sect. 3 reviews related work on network fuzzing and agentic AI for pentesting. Section 4 describes the design of NetworkFuzzer, with a particular focus on its RL-guided engine. Section 5 introduces the autonomous pentesting agent for healthcare systems built on top of NetworkFuzzer and external security tools. Section 6 presents the implementation details and experimental evaluation of the framework. Finally, Sect. 7 concludes the paper and outlines future research directions.

2 Background

We provide an overview of the DICOM protocol to describe the connection establishment process, review known attacks against PACS servers and the DICOM protocol, and discuss existing rule-based replay fuzzing approaches.

2.1 DICOM Protocol

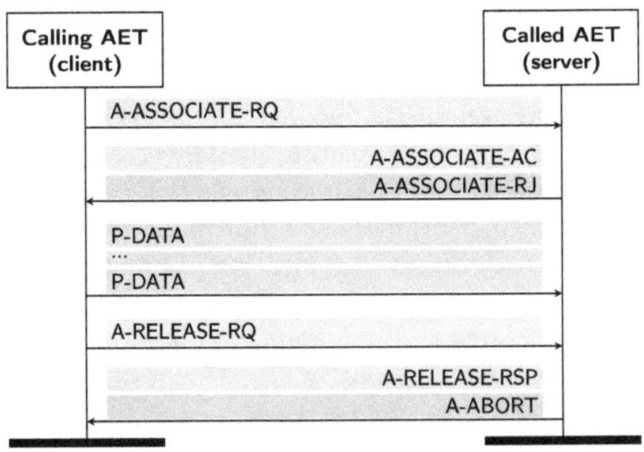

Fig. 1. DICOM communication protocol [3].

The DICOM protocol is an application-layer standard for exchanging, storing, and retrieving medical imaging data over TCP, enabling stateful communication between systems such as PACS and imaging devices. As shown in Fig. 1, communication occurs in three phases: association, data transfer, and release. The association phase establishes a connection via A-ASSOCIATE-RQ, followed by either A-ASSOCIATE-AC or A-ASSOCIATE-RJ. Once established, the data transfer phase exchanges medical content through P-DATA messages, potentially split across multiple packets. The session ends with A-RELEASE-RQ/A-RELEASE-RSP, or A-ABORT for abrupt termination.

On top of this transport layer, the DIMSE protocol defines application services such as storage, query, retrieval, and verification. These operations are encoded as command datasets within P-DATA and enable structured interactions like image transfer, patient queries, and connectivity checks, making them a key target for robustness and security evaluation.

2.2 DICOM Attacks

DICOM and PACS systems are exposed to multiple security threats affecting confidentiality, integrity, and availability. Since many deployments prioritize interoperability and legacy compatibility, they often rely on weak authentication and insufficient validation mechanisms [12].

Several attacks have been reported against DICOM infrastructures. Unauthorized access attacks exploit permissive AET configurations or unauthenticated DIMSE services, enabling attackers to query or retrieve sensitive patient information [11]. Denial-of-service attacks target malformed Protocol Data Unit (PDU) fields, oversized payloads, or association flooding to exhaust server resources or trigger abnormal states. In addition, malformed DICOM attributes may lead to parser inconsistencies, memory corruption, buffer overflows, or path traversal vulnerabilities [30].

Another important attack surface concerns protocol state handling. Attackers may send out-of-order PDUs, duplicated association requests, or traffic after abort conditions to exploit weaknesses in session management and protocol validation logic. Previous work has also shown that compromised PACS infrastructures can be used to manipulate medical images using AI-based techniques, potentially affecting clinical decision-making [15]. These attack categories motivate the use of intelligent fuzzing techniques capable of generating malformed protocol structures, invalid state transitions, and adversarial payloads for robustness testing of DICOM systems.

2.3 Rule-Based Replay Fuzzer

The rule-based replay fuzzers [25] provide a deterministic framework for generating and replaying malicious traffic. Implemented in C and built on top of the MMT-DPI deep packet inspection engine [1], they support both *offline* mode, where attacks are replayed from PCAP traces, and *online* mode, where packets are intercepted and modified in real time from a live network interface. At their core, the fuzzers rely on a *rule-based abstraction*, where each XML-defined rule specifies a packet-matching condition and an associated transformation action. Rules combine boolean expressions over protocol fields with embedded handlers that apply deterministic mutations before forwarding packets. For example, Listing 1.1 illustrates a rule targeting invalid DICOM PDU configurations by modifying the maximum PDU length field.

```
<beginning>
<!-- Property 36: Set Max PDU Length to zero in A-ASSOCIATE-RQ -->
<embedded_functions><![CDATA[
    static void em_invalid_max_pdu_length(
        const rule_info_t *rule, int verdict, uint64_t timestamp,
        uint64_t counter, const mmt_array_t * const trace) {
        uint32_t new_length = 0;
        replace_dicom_attribute(701, 8, &new_length, 0);
        forward_packet();
    }
]]></embedded_functions>

<property property_id="36" type_property="FORWARD"
        description="Set DICOM Max PDU Length to zero in A-ASSOCIATE-RQ"
        if_satisfied="em_invalid_max_pdu_length">
    <event description="Got DICOM A-ASSOCIATE-RQ packet (PDU type 1)"
        boolean_expression="(dicom.pdu_type == 1)"/>
</property>
</beginning>
```

Listing 1.1. Rule 36 - Invalid max-PDU-length injection (CVE-2024-28130 class).

However, this determinism comes with inherent limitations: rule execution is largely static, with no inherent randomness beyond rule selection, and no automatic contextual adaptation to evolving protocol states or server responses. As a result, the rule-based replay fuzzers cannot dynamically adjust mutation strategies based on observed behavior during execution. Overall, this rule-based design supports systematic and explainable traffic mutations, forming a strong foundation for controlled replay-based fuzzing, while complementing more adaptive approaches such as learning-based fuzzing strategies (Table 1).

Table 1. Selected NetworkFuzzer DICOM attack rules [3].

Rule	Name	Target field	CVE/CWE
36	Invalid max-PDU-length	Max PDU Length = 0xFFFFFFFF	CVE-2024-28130
47	Message-ID zero	CommandField/MessageID	CWE-20
56	Association flood	A-ASSOC-RQ burst	CWE-400
59	Format-string injection	CallingAETitle/UID	CWE-134
60	Path-traversal UID	Affected SOP Class UID	CVE-2022-2119
61	Buffer-overflow PDV	PDV item data	CVE-2015-8979 class
65	C-FIND patient enum	C-FIND wildcard query	CWE-862

3 Related Work

DICOM Testing. Wang et al. [30] proposed DICOM-Fuzzer, a fuzzing framework for discovering vulnerabilities in open-source DICOM libraries. Evaluation on DCMTK uncovered a buffer-overflow vulnerability triggered by large inputs, leading to denial-of-service conditions in PACS systems. Mirsky et al. [15] demonstrated GAN-based attacks against PACS servers using conditional GANs to inject or remove medical evidence from CT scans, potentially causing critical misdiagnoses and highlighting the security risks of AI-driven image manipulation in healthcare systems.

RL-Based Fuzzing. RL-based fuzzing has recently emerged as a promising approach for adaptive vulnerability discovery, learning mutation strategies from runtime feedback across diverse applications and environments [9,29]. Previous work has explored stateful and coverage-guided fuzzing techniques to improve exploration of complex execution paths and protocol states [6,8]. Recently, LLM-assisted approaches such as ChatAFL [14] have demonstrated the potential of intelligent guidance for protocol-aware fuzzing. In contrast, our approach applies RL-guided fuzzing to DICOM healthcare infrastructures.

Agentic AI for Security Assessment. Recent advances in LLM models and autonomous agents have enabled the development of AI-assisted security assessment frameworks capable of orchestrating reconnaissance, vulnerability analysis and exploitation workflows [10]. Existing approaches have demonstrated the usefulness of AI-driven automation for cybersecurity operations and incident response [21], while recent LLM-based pentesting assistants have shown promising capabilities for interactive security assessment tasks. However, limited attention has been given to autonomous fuzzing and protocol-aware testing of healthcare infrastructures. Unlike existing approaches, our framework integrate autonomous planning, DICOM discovery, adaptive fuzzing, and structured reporting into a unified workflow for healthcare protocol assessment.

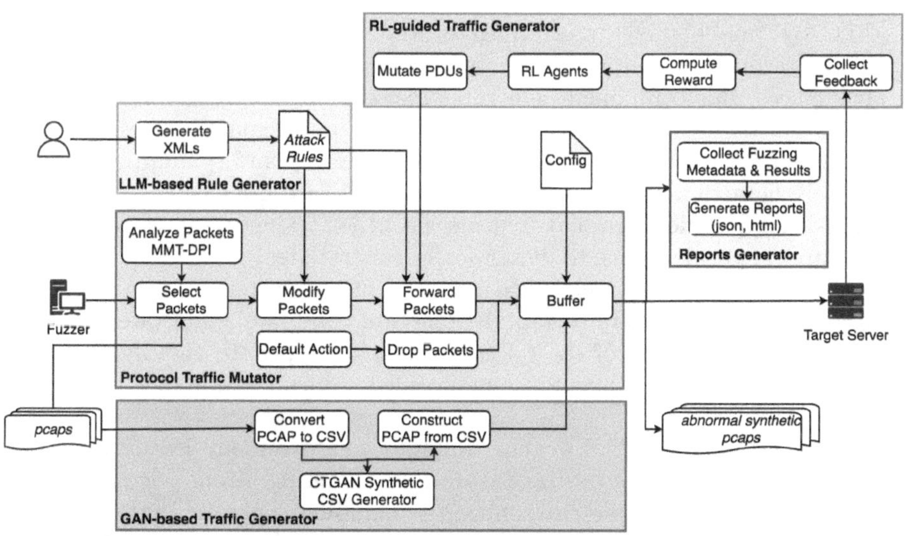

Fig. 2. Architecture of NetworkFuzzer.

4 NetworkFuzzer Design

In this section, we present the architecture of NetworkFuzzer and describe how its main components support the generation of malicious traffic for assessing the robustness of target protocols and systems.

4.1 Architecture

Figure 2 illustrates the overall architecture and fuzzing workflow of NetworkFuzzer. Similar to traditional network traffic fuzzers, NetworkFuzzer takes network traffic as input, either directly from a network interface card (NIC) or from pre-captured traces in PCAP format, and applies a variety of mutations before forwarding the modified traffic through an output NIC. Unlike conventional fuzzing approaches, however, NetworkFuzzer adopts an adaptive *closed-loop* fuzzing paradigm, in which mutation strategies are dynamically adjusted according to real-time feedback collected from the target system. This adaptability is enabled by a Feedback Collector module that monitors multiple runtime signals, including server responses, log error codes, code coverage variations, and system health indicators and system behavior after receiving malformed traffic.

1. **Protocol Traffic Mutator** analyzes legitimate network traffic to extract protocol-specific attributes and applies mutation operators such as deletion, forwarding, duplication, and reordering [3]. It relies on XML-based attack rules to generate diverse test cases covering both realistic and edge-case scenarios, similarly to rule-based replay fuzzers such as 5Greplay [25].
2. **GAN-based Traffic Generator** leverages Conditional Tabular GAN (CTGAN) model [32], to produce synthetic traffic samples that complement deterministic mutations [3]. By learning traffic patterns from real network traces, this component generates realistic yet previously unseen packet sequences, thereby improving traffic diversity and expanding test coverage. It is also useful for generating datasets for training and evaluating AI-based anomaly detection systems, especially in healthcare use cases.
3. **LLM-based Rule Generator** utilizes a LLM, trained on a large collection of protocol specifications, to dynamically generate testing rules based on protocol specifications, extracted features, and historical testing results [3]. This component enables users to rapidly generate compilable and directly usable attack rules, primarily of the *forward* and *drop* types, by modifying specific protocol features with invalid or malformed values for different testing scenarios.
4. **RL-guided Traffic Generator** employs reinforcement learning (RL) to intelligently explore the protocol state space. The RL agent selects mutation strategies across multiple environments, including semantic mutations, payload injection, protocol state manipulation, session-level attacks, and hybrid attack combinations inspired by real-world vulnerabilities. A multi-signal reward function, incorporating various criteria related to the target system,

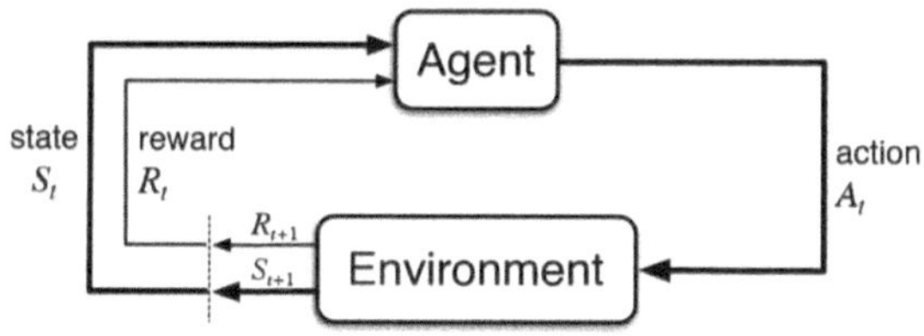

Fig. 3. The agent–environment interaction in reinforcement learning [27].

guides the agent toward inputs that trigger deeper and more complex execution paths within the system under test.

5. **Reports Generator** produces structured security assessment reports (e.g., in HTML and JSON formats) upon completion of the testing process. It consolidates findings from discovery and vulnerability analysis phases, assigns CVSS scores to identified issues, and provides actionable remediation recommendations for each detected vulnerability.

The first three components were introduced in a previous version of NetworkFuzzer [3]. In this work, we extend the framework with the RL-guided Traffic Generator and the Reports Generator, enabling a more autonomous and intelligent security assessment workflow for healthcare systems. The following subsections provide a detailed description of the two new components.

4.2 RL-Guided Traffic Generator

Problem Formulation. We model the fuzzing process as a Markov Decision Process (MDP), where each episode corresponds to a fuzzing session against a live DICOM server. The proposed approach leverages RL algorithms to guide mutation operations toward generating higher-quality malicious traffic with a greater likelihood of reaching deeper execution paths and triggering abnormal behaviors in the target system. At each step, the RL agent selects a mutation strategy, observes the resulting server response, and receives a reward that reflects the effectiveness of the generated input (Fig. 3).

Formally, the MDP is defined as $\mathcal{M} = (\mathcal{S}, \mathcal{A}, \mathcal{T}, \mathcal{R}, \gamma)$, where $\mathcal{S}$ denotes the set of environment states observed during fuzzing, $\mathcal{A}$ represents the set of mutation actions available to the agent, and $\mathcal{T}$ defines the state transition dynamics resulting from applying an action to the target system. The reward function $\mathcal{R}$ evaluates the effectiveness of each action based on the observed system behavior, while the discount factor $\gamma \in [0, 1]$ controls the balance between immediate and long-term rewards during the learning process.

State Representation. The environment state is represented as a fixed-length observation vector capturing: (i) normalized values of protocol-critical fields; (ii) recent server response patterns; (iii) indicators of normal behaviors (e.g., acceptances or rejections) and abnormal behaviors (e.g., hangs or crashes); (iv) mutation context and fuzzing progress; and (v) optional instrumentation signals, such as log-derived features or code coverage metrics. This representation enables the RL agent to learn correlations between mutation strategies and their impact on the target system.

Action Space Design. We provide two action-space configurations. A simplified discrete space enables efficient training by enumerating predefined mutation combinations, while a full hybrid space models mutations across multiple dimensions (e.g., field selection, payload type, and sequence structure), enabling more fine-grained exploration at the cost of increased complexity.

The action space integrates five complementary mutation strategies designed to explore both protocol-compliant and adversarial behaviors:

1. *Semantic mutations* modify protocol-compliant fields using valid or boundary DICOM values, enabling deeper traversal of parsing logic while preserving syntactic correctness. Example targets include *command_field* (all 27 DIMSE commands together with boundary values 0×0000 and 0xFFFF), *message_id* (0, 255, 32767, 65535), the *msg_control* header byte (0×00, 0×80, 0xFF), and *max_pdu_length* values ranging from 0 to 0xFFFFFFFF.
2. *Aggressive payload injection* introduces crafted payloads into string-based DICOM fields (e.g., AET, SOP UIDs, and patient names) to trigger robustness issues such as memory corruption, improper validation, or parser inconsistencies. Payloads include format strings, oversized buffers, null-byte sequences, path traversal patterns, integer-overflow length values, and malicious inputs derived from previously reported security vulnerabilities.
3. *Byte-level structural mutations* apply low-level perturbations, such as bit or byte flips, and corruption of protocol-critical byte offsets within PDUs. These mutations specifically target critical header fields and structural components in order to expose weaknesses in packet parsing and protocol handling logic.
4. *Protocol state-machine attacks* generate abnormal or out-of-order message sequences that violate expected communication flows, aiming to expose flaws in session handling. For instance, out-of-order PDU sequences that exploit server assumptions about session state, covering 70 distinct sequences, for example, *pdata_first* (P-DATA before association), *double_assoc* (duplicate A-ASSOCIATE-RQ), *abort_continue* (PDU after A-ABORT), etc.
5. *Hybrid attacks* simultaneously apply multiple mutation types (e.g., semantic and state-based), creating complex scenarios that forcing the server to handle a semantically ambiguous DIMSE command while receiving unsolicited additional traffic.

Reward Function. The reward function guides the agent toward inputs that trigger meaningful and diverse protocol behaviors. It combines five complementary signals: server response type, response latency, behavioral novelty, mutation relevance to sensitive protocol fields, and overall system health impact. Higher rewards are assigned to behaviors associated with protocol violations, abnormal processing, service degradation, or deeper protocol interaction, while repetitive or low-value responses receive smaller rewards. To monitor operational impact, the framework continuously issues C-ECHO probes before and after each episode to detect crashes, hangs, latency increases, or reduced association capacity. When a crash is detected, the episode terminates and the responsible PDU sequence is preserved for further analysis.

The overall reward is defined as:

$$R = R_{base} + R_{time} + R_{novelty} + R_{field} + R_{health} - 1.0 \tag{1}$$

where the constant -1.0 term penalizes unnecessary exploration steps. The individual components are summarized as follows:

- R_{base} rewards server outcomes according to their security relevance, prioritizing crashes, aborts, hangs, and deeper protocol interactions over expected responses.
- R_{time} provides an additional reward proportional to server response latency, encouraging the agent to prioritize mutations that induce longer processing delays or more resource-intensive execution paths.
- $R_{novelty}$ rewards previously unseen response patterns while progressively reducing rewards for repeated behaviors, promoting protocol-state exploration.
- R_{field} assigns higher rewards to mutations targeting security-sensitive DICOM fields, such as PDU length, AETs, and PDV-related attributes.
- R_{health} rewards measurable degradation of server health, including failed C-ECHO probes, increased latency, reduced association capacity, and connection instability.

Learning and Exploration Algorithms. We support both value-based and policy-based RL methods, including Deep Q-Networks (DQN) [16] and Proximal Policy Optimization (PPO) [26], implemented using Stable-Baselines3 [24]. These algorithms enable efficient exploration of the mutation space and adaptation to complex target behaviors.

To avoid getting stuck during exploration and to improve test coverage diversity, we incorporate a Thompson Sampling-based bandit [28] on top of the RL policy. The bandit dynamically selects different categories of mutation strategies based on their observed effectiveness during fuzzing. This mechanism continuously updates the selection probabilities to promote exploration of under-tested attack surfaces and prevent the agent from relying too heavily on the same mutation strategies during training.

4.3 Reports Generator

This component aggregates results from all fuzzing phases into structured, analysis-ready outputs for both machines and humans. It produces a JSON report containing all findings with metadata (severity, evidence, remediation, CVSS score, and CVE), alongside an HTML report with an executive summary, severity breakdown, and detailed per-finding views. An LLM-generated natural-language summary complements these artifacts with a concise, prioritized assessment, enabling easy integration into downstream tools and automated workflows.

5 Pentesting Agent for Healthcare Systems

The pentesting agent implements a fully automated security assessment workflow for DICOM-based healthcare systems, organized as a sequential pipeline of five subagents: Reconnaissance, Planning, Scanning, Fuzzing, and Reporting, as illustrated in Fig. 4.

Reconnaissance Subagent. This stage establishes the initial network context through TCP reachability checks, optional external reconnaissance tools (e.g., nmap service and port scanning), and C-ECHO validation with latency measurement. It then performs AE title enumeration using a 28-entry wordlist (including default, wildcard, and common titles such as "ORTHANC") to identify valid calling identities. Server fingerprinting is derived from A-ASSOCIATE-AC responses and mapped to known PACS vendors with confidence scoring. Finally, SOP-class probing across Verification, Storage, and Query/Retrieve services determines the set of supported DICOM capabilities and exposed attack surface.

Planning Subagent. The planning stage transforms reconnaissance outputs into an execution scope. A validated AET is selected as the default caller identity, ensuring subsequent results are not biased by authentication failures. Activated checks are conditioned on discovered capabilities (e.g., Query/Retrieve enables `C-FIND`, Storage enables fuzzing, etc.). When high-confidence fingerprinting is available, product-specific rules are enabled (e.g., Orthanc defaults), and contextual metadata (UIDs, versions) is forwarded to downstream modules for tailored analysis.

Scanning Subagent. The scanning stage executes 11 structured checks across four categories: *authentication weaknesses* (invalid, empty, or wildcard AETs), *unauthorised data access* via C-FIND, *denial-of-service conditions* (PDU overflow and association exhaustion), and *information leakage* (TLS absence, verbose errors, and version disclosure). Each finding is recorded with severity, CVSS score, CWE mapping, and protocol-level evidence.

Fuzzing Subagent. An RL-guided fuzzing engine explores deeper protocol states beyond static checks by mutating DICOM messages based on runtime feedback. Interesting behaviors (abort, hang, or valid P-DATA exchanges) are stored in a structured corpus for offline analysis. The fuzzing process is restricted to validated SOP classes to improve efficiency and reduce irrelevant exploration.

Reporting Subagent. The reporting module consolidates all findings into structured outputs. An HTML report provides an executive summary with severity-ranked issues (Critical/High/Medium/Low/Pass), CVSS scores, CWE references, and full protocol traces. A JSON export mirrors the same information for integration with SIEM systems [2,17,20] and CI/CD security pipelines.

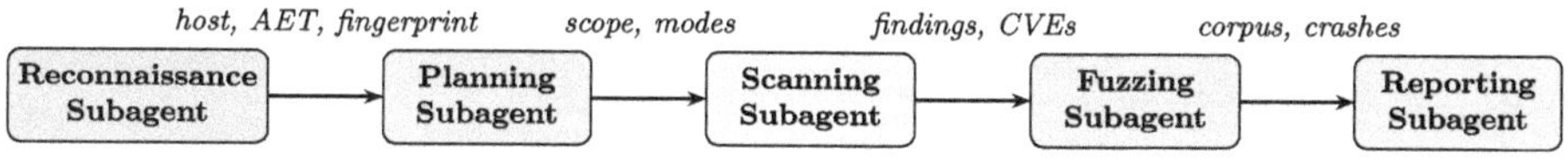

Fig. 4. Overview of the pentesting agent for healthcare systems.

6 Implementation and Evaluation

6.1 Implementation

MMT-DPI Plugin. We develop a new plugin for MMT-DPI [1] to extract 31 attributes, including 21 DICOM-specific attributes and 10 general network flow statistics. The plugin is evaluated using a dataset of PCAP traces captured on a DICOM server while receiving traffic generated by another machine running a Python-based DICOM simulator built with the *Pydicom* and *Pynetdicom* libraries, which replicate standard DICOM communication functionalities.

NetworkFuzzer. NetworkFuzzer extends 5GReplay [25] by integrating new mutation operators, a GAN-based traffic generator, an RL engine, and an LLM-based rule generator. The GAN-based engine generates synthetic traffic using CTGAN (v0.11.0), while the LLM-based module leverages GPT-4 and compatible open-source models (e.g., LLaMA and Mistral) to automatically derive mutation rules from structured protocol prompts. The RL-guided engine implements multiple Gymnasium environments using Stable-Baselines3 [5] with default hyperparameters ($\gamma = 0.99$, ϵ-greedy exploration with linear annealing from 1.0 to 0.05), targeting different layers of the DICOM protocol stack. RL agents are trained using DQN, with PPO available as an alternative backend. Rewards are assigned based on observed server behaviors, prioritizing crashes, aborts, and hangs. The framework is protocol-agnostic and interfaces with target systems through pluggable protocol adapters, enabling reuse across protocols without modifying the RL training loop.

Pentesting Agent. The pentesting agent is implemented as a dual-interface system that exposes identical fuzzing and scanning capabilities through two complementary integration paths. Both interfaces share a common `FuzzerRunner` backend, ensuring consistent behavior across deployments. All components are built on top of *pynetdicom* for low-level DICOM communication.

The first interface is a LangChain/LangGraph ReAct agent that exposes discovery, scanning, fuzzing, and reporting as modular callable components. The agent follows a fixed workflow (i.e., discover → scan → fuzz → report) and can be driven by any LangChain-compatible LLM backend (e.g., GPT-4).

The second interface is a MCP server built with `FastMCP`, which exposes the same capabilities as core NetworkFuzzer operations. Each capability is further exposed as a reusable *skill*, enabling composition of higher-level behaviors from atomic pentesting primitives. Once registered via `.mcp.json`, these skills are automatically exposed to any MCP-compatible client, enabling natural-language instructions such as *"Assess the DICOM server at localhost:4242"* to invoke the full end-to-end assessment pipeline.

6.2 Experimental Setup

Testbed Setup. Figure 5 illustrates the simulated environment used to evaluate the capabilities of NetworkFuzzer and the pentesting agent across different DICOM protocol testing scenarios.

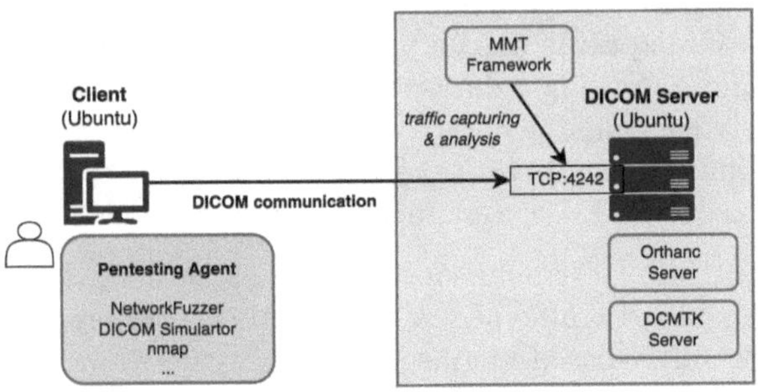

Fig. 5. The DICOM testbed.

The testbed consists of three main components: a client machine, a server machine, and a traffic capture and analysis framework. The client machine is an Ubuntu virtual machine (version 22.04) running NetworkFuzzer, which generates and injects test traffic, including potential attack scenarios. The server machine is another Ubuntu VM (version 22.04) hosting DICOM target servers, such as Orthanc [4], a lightweight open-source DICOM server deployed to process and respond to DICOM requests. In addition, the MMT security monitoring framework [2] is installed on the server machine to support packet sniffing, traffic analysis, and anomaly detection.

Ethics Statement. All experiments were conducted in a fully isolated and controlled testbed using dedicated virtual machines and self-hosted DICOM servers. No real patient data or personally identifiable information was used; all datasets and traffic were synthetically generated. The framework and pentesting agent were evaluated only on systems owned by the authors or in authorized laboratory environments, with no testing performed on production hospital networks, PACS systems, or third-party infrastructures without explicit authorization.

Research Questions. In this section, we conduct experiments to evaluate the effectiveness of NetworkFuzzer and the pentesting agent in testing PACS servers and DICOM systems.

RQ1 (RL-Guided Fuzzing Evaluation)—How effective is RL-guided fuzzing compared to rule-based and GAN-based engines in triggering abnormal behaviors (e.g., hangs or crashes)?

RQ2 (Ablation Study)—Which mutation strategies are the most effective against a target DICOM server under the same experimental configuration?

RQ3 (Autonomous Agent Evaluation)—How usable and effective is the autonomous pentesting agent for identifying security and robustness issues across different DICOM server implementations?

Table 2. Evaluation results for 10,000 timesteps against Orthanc.

Strategy	Abort	Accept	Hang	P-DATA	Reject	sps
Random	83 (0.8%)	1,981 (19.8%)	4,291 (42.9%)	0	2,422 (24.2%)	2.88
Rule-based	995 (10.0%)	**2,774** (27.7%)	1,814 (18.1%)	0	1,309 (13.1%)	6.80
GAN-based	8,824 (88.2%)	988 (9.9%)	174 (1.7%)	0	**0**	1.36
RL-Byte†	5 (1.5%)	82 (24.6%)	35 (10.5%)	0	79 (23.7%)	11.05
RL-Semantic	**8,826** (88.3%)	0	553 (5.5%)	**621** (6.2%)	**0**	8.80
RL-State	8,361 (83.6%)	0	0	0	**0**	**781.34**
RL-Aggressive	7,300 (73.0%)	0	590 (5.9%)	0	**0**	2.43
RL-Hybrid	663 (6.6%)	6 (0.1%)	**6,227** (62.3%)	99 (1.0%)	**0**	0.46

† RL-Byte: percentages computed over 333 valid steps (30 steps/episode by design)

6.3 RQ1: RL-Guided Fuzzing Evaluation

To answer RQ1, we conducted a controlled evaluation of 8 fuzzing strategies against a live Orthanc DICOM server [4] (latest version 1.12.11, default configuration), a widely deployed open-source system in clinical and research environments, making it a representative and practically relevant target. Each strategy was allocated 10000 environment timesteps under identical conditions, without prior knowledge of the target server internals. The primary metrics are Abort count (A-ABORT responses indicating protocol violations), Accept count (A-ASSOCIATE-AC responses), Hang count (no-response timeouts), P-DATA count (successful data-transfer exchanges), Reject count (A-ASSOCIATE-RJ responses), and steps per second (sps), measuring overall throughput and latency.

Fuzzing Strategies. We evaluate a set of baseline and learning-based fuzzing strategies spanning random, rule-based, GAN-driven, and RL-guided approaches.

Random (Baseline). A valid `A-ASSOCIATE-RQ` PDU is generated and mutated using one of 7 randomly selected byte-level operators, including bit flips, substitutions, insertions, deletions, duplication, shuffling, and randomization. This baseline represents a protocol-agnostic fuzzer without structural awareness.

Rule-Based Engine. A corpus of 47 XML mutation rules captures knowledge of the DICOM protocol by targeting critical protocol fields. At each iteration, 1–3 rules are randomly selected and applied to a valid base PDU, representing the current practice in protocol-aware rule-based replay fuzzing [25].

GAN-Based Engine. This strategy generates structured *session plans* specifying attack categories, target DICOM fields, payloads, protocol sequences, and PDU parameters, which are converted into valid DICOM PDUs via a protocol-aware builder. Plan generation combines Thompson Sampling for adaptive selection with CTGAN trained on successful executions, while runtime feedback continuously refines future plans in a closed loop.

RL Variants. We evaluate 5 RL strategies based on mutation categories: *RL-Byte*, which learns byte-level mutations; *RL-Semantic*, which applies field-aware protocol mutations; *RL-Aggressive*, which incorporates exploit-oriented payloads; *RL-State*, which targets invalid protocol state transitions; and *RL-Hybrid*, which combines all strategies with diversity-aware exploration.

Results Analysis. Table 2 compares all strategies using unified fuzzing metrics, where higher Abort/Hang/P-DATA and lower Reject indicate stronger protocol stress and exploration capabilities. Overall, *RL-based* and *GAN-based* approaches substantially outperform *Random* and *Rule-based* fuzzing, demonstrating a stronger ability to trigger abnormal behaviors and explore deeper protocol states. In particular, *RL-Semantic* is the only strategy reaching the DICOM data-transfer layer through successful P-DATA exchanges, while *RL-State* achieves the highest execution throughput. In contrast, *Random* and *RL-Byte* remain largely ineffective, highlighting the limitations of unguided byte-level mutation for DICOM protocol testing.

During the fuzzing evaluation, NetworkFuzzer identified 8 security and robustness issues, summarized in Table 3. The discovered issues mainly affect protocol-state handling, malformed DIMSE processing, denial-of-service conditions, and unauthenticated service interactions, demonstrating the ability of RL-guided fuzzing to expose abnormal behaviors beyond simple protocol rejection. Although several hangs and degradation scenarios were triggered, none of the evaluated strategies caused a full DICOM server crash on the latest Orthanc release, indicating a robust and well-maintained implementation.

Root Cause of Issue I1. The issue arises from Orthanc's handling of the DICOM Command Data Set Type field `(0000,0800)`. Any value other than 0×0101 indicates that additional dataset PDVs will follow, causing Orthanc to enter a blocking receive loop without a timeout. If the dataset is never sent, the handler thread stalls indefinitely. The issue affects multiple DIMSE services, including C-STORE, C-GET, and N-EVENT-REPORT, and repeated triggering can exhaust the thread pool, resulting in a denial-of-service condition (CWE-400).

Table 3. Issues identified on the Orthanc DICOM server.

ID	Category	Trigger	Response	Severity
I1	DIMSE field DoS	Invalid SOP/UID in C-FIND	Abort	Medium
I2	Post-abort hang	Response sent after A-ABORT	Hang	Medium
I3	PDU flood hang	Repeated raw P-DATA-TF	Hang	High
I4	Release-after-abort	A-RELEASE sent after A-ABORT	Hang	Medium
I5	C-STORE DIMSE hang	C-STORE without session cleanup	Hang	High
I6	C-MOVE flood DoS	C-MOVE flood (sub-association exhaustion)	Hang	High
I7	PDU length overflow	`max_pdu_length = 0xFFFFFFFF`	Hang	High
I8	C-GET DIMSE hang	Malformed abstract syntax in C-GET	Hang	Medium

RL and GAN-based approaches consistently outperform traditional fuzzing baselines, demonstrating superior ability to explore abnormal protocol behaviors and stress DICOM processing logic. The GAN-based method achieves performance comparable to the strongest RL variants without requiring online training during execution.

6.4 RQ2: Ablation Study

The ablation study focuses on the behavior of individual RL strategies under the same experimental setup. *RL-Semantic* achieves the deepest protocol interaction, being the only variant capable of consistently reaching the DICOM data-transfer layer through P-DATA exchanges. *RL-State* provides the highest execution efficiency, rapidly exploring protocol-state violations with minimal parsing overhead. *RL-Aggressive* emphasizes payload-oriented mutations, increasing hang behavior through stress on memory- and string-processing paths. In contrast, *RL-Byte* remains largely ineffective due to sparse low-level feedback, showing that byte-level mutation alone is insufficient for complex protocol fuzzing.

RL-Hybrid, despite combining multiple mutation families, shows a clear preference for generating blocking behaviors over protocol-level errors. Figure 6 tracks cumulative hang and abort rates, where the abort rate quickly stabilizes below 10%, while the hang rate steadily rises to 62.3% at convergence. Figure 7 shows the distribution of 534 novel action combinations, where hang-inducing cases dominate (469/534, 87.8%) and yield higher median reward (74.2) than aborts (44/534, 8.2%, median 53.0). This indicates a shift toward inputs that stall execution rather than trigger explicit errors, highlighting how the learned policy concentrates on resource-exhaustion-style behaviors. Overall, aborts capture protocol failure handling, while hangs reveal robustness issues tied to service availability in real-world systems.

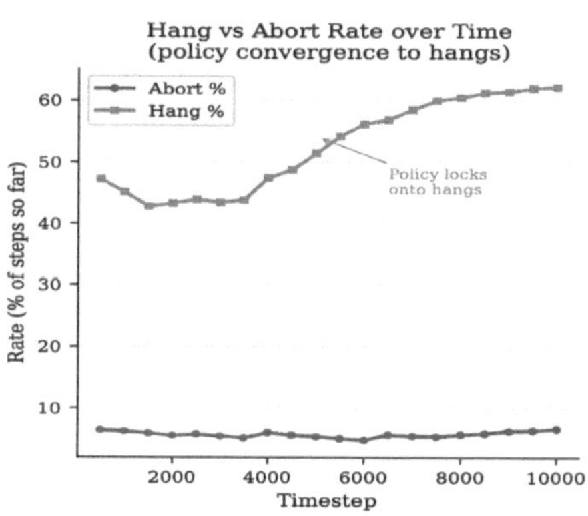

Fig. 6. Hang and abort rate over time for the *RL-Hybrid* run.

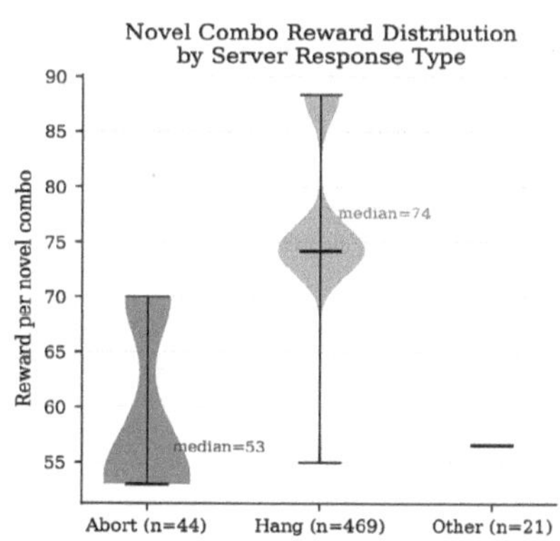

Fig. 7. Novel combo reward distribution for the *RL-Hybrid* run.

Overall, the results indicate that the effectiveness of RL-guided fuzzing depends primarily on semantic protocol awareness and the quality of the action space, rather than on the RL algorithm alone. Strategies integrating protocol semantics, state modeling, or structured mutation logic consistently outperform purely low-level mutation approaches.

6.5 RQ3: Autonomous Agent Evaluation

Table 4 reports the seven findings produced by the automated pipeline against the default Orthanc deployment. In a default Orthanc configuration, it identifies 1 Critical, 3 High, 1 Medium, and 1 Low severity findings and generates a CVSS-scored HTML report in under 5 min, with no false positives observed in our experiments. For instance, the most critical finding is the combination of absent AET access control with unauthenticated C-FIND services: any network-adjacent attacker can enumerate patient names, study dates, and Study Instance UIDs without any credentials, enabling bulk patient record extraction. The PDU max-length overflow finding (accepting `MaxPDU=0xFFFFFFFF`) is confirmed by the RL campaign below. Furthermore, we can apply the pentesting agent to evaluates multiple DICOM server implementations across different programming languages, including Orthanc, DCMTK-based systems, and implementations built with *pynetdicom* (Python) and *go-netdicom* (Go). The security operator can quickly verify security and robustness issues of healthcare system, before going with more extensive and comprehensive with fuzzing engines.

Table 4. Automated pentest findings for the latest version of Orthanc with default configuration.

Finding	Severity (CVSS)	Evidence
Unauthenticated C-FIND (Patient)	Critical (9.0)	Patient records returned without credentials
Wildcard AE title accepted	High (7.5)	* and "" return A-ASSOC-AC
Unauthenticated C-FIND (Study)	High (7.5)	Study UIDs exposed anonymously
Max PDU overflow (DoS)	High (7.5)	Accepts `MaxPDU = 0xFFFFFFFF`
No TLS encryption	High (7.5)	Plaintext DICOM on port 4242
No AE title validation	Medium (5.0)	Accepts arbitrary unregistered AE titles
Version disclosure	Low (2.5)	Product and version leaked in A-ASSOCIATE-AC

The automated pipeline successfully evaluates multiple DICOM server implementations across different programming languages, demonstrating its general applicability across heterogeneous PACS deployments.

7 Conclusion and Future Work

We present an extension of NetworkFuzzer, a smart network protocol fuzzer, for evaluating the robustness and security of DICOM-based healthcare systems.

The proposed framework integrates rule-based replay, GAN-driven traffic synthesis, LLM-assisted rule generation, and a new RL engine to enable adaptive and diverse test case generation for protocol security analysis. We further introduce an autonomous pentesting agent built on top of NetworkFuzzer, which orchestrates the full security assessment pipeline, including reconnaissance, analysis, fuzzing, and reporting, and effectively identifies robustness and security issues across diverse DICOM system implementations.

Future work will focus on extending the framework to additional network protocols and critical infrastructures, particularly in 5G/6G environments. We aim to enhance automation through improved LLM-driven protocol reasoning [18] and to integrate defensive mechanisms [21] and complementary AI agents to support comprehensive and continuous security evaluation and mitigation.

Acknowledgement. The research is supported by the H2020 project AIAGENT4CYBER N° 101249698, INTACT N° 10126241, NERO N° 101127411 and CYBERSUITE N° 101145861. The research is also the result of a three-month research stay by the second and third authors at Montimage EURL. This work was partially supported by the State Research Agency (AEI) of the Spanish Ministry of Science and Innovation under grant PID2021-122215NB-C31 (AwESOMe), and by the Comunidad de Madrid under grant TEC-2024/COM-235 (DESAFÍO-CM).

Disclosure of Interests. The authors have no competing interests to declare that are relevant to the content of this article.

References

1. Mmt-dpi (2026). https://github.com/Montimage/mmt-dpi
2. Mmt-probe (2026). https://github.com/Montimage/mmt-probe
3. Networkfuzzer (2026). https://github.com/Montimage/NetworkFuzzer
4. Orthanc, open-source, lightweight dicom server (2026). https://www.orthanc-server.com/index.php
5. Stable baselines3 (2026). https://github.com/DLR-RM/stable-baselines3
6. Ba, J., Böhme, M., Mirzamomen, Z., Roychoudhury, A.: Stateful greybox fuzzing. In: 31st USENIX Security Symposium (USENIX Security 22) (2022)
7. Bidgood Jr, W.D., Horii, S.C., Prior, F.W., Van Syckle, D.E.: Understanding and using dicom, the data interchange standard for biomedical imaging. J. Am. Med. Inform. Assoc. (1997)
8. Böhme, M., Pham, V.T., Nguyen, M.D., Roychoudhury, A.: Directed greybox fuzzing. In: CCS '17 (2017)
9. Böttinger, K., Godefroid, P., Singh, R.: Deep reinforcement fuzzing. In: IEEE Security and Privacy Workshops (2018) SPW
10. Deng, G., et al.: {PentestGPT}: Evaluating and harnessing large language models for automated penetration testing. In: 33rd USENIX Security Symposium (USENIX Security 24), pp. 847–864 (2024)
11. Desjardins, B., et al.: Dicom images have been hacked! now what? Am. J. Roentgenol (2020)
12. Eichelberg, M., Kleber, K., Kämmerer, M.: Cybersecurity challenges for pacs and medical imaging. Acad. Radiol. (2020)

13. Jodogne, S.: The Orthanc ecosystem for medical imaging. J. Digit. Imaging (2018)
14. Meng, R., Mirchev, M., Böhme, M., Roychoudhury, A.: Large language model guided protocol fuzzing. In: Proceedings of the 31st Annual Network and Distributed System Security Symposium (NDSS) (2024)
15. Mirsky, Y., Mahler, T., Shelef, I., Elovici, Y.: {CT-GAN}: Malicious tampering of 3d medical imagery using deep learning. In: 28th USENIX Security Symposium (USENIX Security 19) (2019)
16. Mnih, V., Kavukcuoglu, K., Silver, D.: Human-level control through deep reinforcement learning (2015)
17. Nguyen, H.N., Nguyen, M.D., Montes de Oca, E.: A framework for in-network inference using p4. In: ARES '24
18. Nguyen, L., Nguyen, M.D., Bui, A.H., Cavalli, A.R., de Oca, E.M.: LLMs in security testing and monitoring: an initial study. In: International Conference on Availability, Reliability and Security
19. Nguyen, M.D., Bardin, S., Bonichon, R., Groz, R., Lemerre, M.: Binary-level directed fuzzing for Use-After-Free vulnerabilities. In: 23rd International Symposium on Research in Attacks, Intrusions and Defenses (RAID 2020)
20. Nguyen, M.D., Bouaziz, A., Valdes, V., Rosa Cavalli, A., Mallouli, W., Montes De Oca, E.: A deep learning anomaly detection framework with explainability and robustness. In: ARES '23 (2023)
21. Nguyen, M.D., Mallouli, W., Cavalli, A.R., Montes de Oca, E.: Ai4soar: a security intelligence tool for automated incident response. In: ARES '24 (2024)
22. Nguyen, M.D., Nguyen, H.N., de Souza, L.M., Karagiannis, S., Cavalli, A.R., de Oca, E.M.: An intelligent network fuzzer for protocol testing in healthcare systems. In: Availability, Reliability and Security (2025)
23. Pham, V.T., Böhme, M., Roychoudhury, A.: Aflnet: A greybox fuzzer for network protocols. In: 2020 IEEE 13th International Conference on Software Testing, Validation and Verification. In: ICST (2020)
24. Raffin, A., Hill, A., Gleave, A., Kanervisto, A., Ernestus, M., Dormann, N.: Stable-baselines3: Reliable reinforcement learning implementations (2021)
25. Salazar, Z., Nguyen, H.N., Mallouli, W., Cavalli, A.R., Montes de Oca, E.: 5greplay: A 5g network traffic fuzzer-application to attack injection. In: Proceedings of the 16th International Conference on Availability, Reliability and Security (2021)
26. Schulman, J., Wolski, F., Dhariwal, P., Radford, A., Klimov, O.: Proximal policy optimization algorithms (2017)
27. Sutton, R.S., Barto, A.G.: Reinforcement learning: An introduction (1998)
28. Thompson, W.R.: On the likelihood that one unknown probability exceeds another in view of the evidence of two samples. Biometrika (1933)
29. Wang, J., Song, C., Yin, H.: Reinforcement learning-based hierarchical seed scheduling for greybox fuzzing. In: 2021 Network and Distributed System Security Symposium (2021)
30. Wang, Z., Li, Q., Wang, Y., Liu, B., Zhang, J., Liu, Q.: Medical protocol security: Dicom vulnerability mining based on fuzzing technology. In: Proceedings of the 2019 ACM SIGSAC Conference on Computer and Communications Security (2019)
31. Widup, S., Bassett, G., Hylender, D., Rudis, B., Spitler, M.: Verizon protected health information data breach report (2015)
32. Xu, L., Skoularidou, M., Cuesta-Infante, A., Veeramachaneni, K.: Modeling tabular data using conditional GAN (2019)

Security Auditing for RISC-V SoCs via Process Mining

Salvatore Bramante[1(✉)], Matteo Busi[2], Alessandro Cilardo[3], Riccardo Focardi[2], Flaminia Luccio[2], Nicola Mazzocca[3], and Francesco Vitale[3]

[1] IMT School for Advanced Studies Lucca, Lucca, Italy
salvatore.bramante@imtlucca.it
[2] Ca'Foscari University of Venice, Venice, Italy
{matteo.busi,focardi,luccio}@unive.it
[3] University of Naples Federico II, Naples, Italy
{acilardo,nicola.mazzocca,francesco.vitale}@unina.it

Abstract. The rapid adoption of open-hardware RISC-V System-on-Chip (SoC) designs in security-sensitive embedded and edge scenarios is raising the bar on observability and assurance requirements for such platforms. In fact, unforeseen runtime misbehaviors due to incompatible third-party IPs, hardware trojans in peripherals, and compromised drivers can cause misbehaviors that core-level monitors, such as RISC-V Formal Interface (RVFI), cannot see. We introduce the Peripheral Formal Interface (PFI), a passive AXI-aware observation interface that extends the RVFI philosophy from the core to the peripherals. The PFI emits a structured event stream that off-chip auditors can consume without touching the functional path. On top of it, we define an auditing architecture that merges the peripheral-bus stream and the RVFI retirement stream into a single event log, and a process mining pipeline that turns this log into a Contract: a behavioral model with allowlist, count, and timing constraints. We validate the framework on Simply-V, an open-source reconfigurable soft-SoC, auditing representative workloads to localize injected firmware defects event by event.

Keywords: RISC-V · System-on-Chip · Security Auditing · Hardware Monitoring · Formal Interfaces · Process Mining

1 Introduction

The RISC-V Instruction Set Architecture (ISA) has accelerated the adoption of open-hardware SoC in real-world deployments, spanning IoT end-nodes, automotive electronic control units, and critical infrastructure gateways [4,7]. These SoCs are networked, exposed, and frequently built by integrating third-party Intellectual Property (IP) blocks whose internal behavior is only partially trusted. The attack surface now extends well beyond the core, reaching memory controllers, DMA engines, cryptographic accelerators, and communication peripherals on the on-chip bus.

P. Kieseberg et al. (Eds.): ARES 2026 Workshops, LNCS 16903, pp. 589–604, 2027.
https://doi.org/10.1007/978-3-032-37218-5_34

The RVFI [25] allows auditing the system behavior, exposing retired instructions, register writebacks, and memory accesses through a well-defined, non-intrusive port; it enables formal verification, instruction tracing, and runtime monitoring of the core itself. However, a similar mechanism at the *peripheral* level is missing. As a result, bus-level interactions, where many realistic attack primitives manifests (malicious DMA transfers, unauthorized control-register accesses, or Trojan-induced covert channels), are either invisible or observable only through ad hoc probes that are hardly reusable across platforms [8,9].

We aim to enhance the existing RVFI-based auditing mechanism through systematic security auditing of bus-level transactions. We introduce the PFI, an AXI-aware observation port that captures the relevant fields of each peripheral transaction and streams them towards an external auditor without perturbing the functional path. Advanced eXtensible Interface (AXI) is the state-of-the-art on-chip interconnect protocol for the ARM AMBA family, widely adopted in RISC-V SoCs to connect the core to memories and peripherals via separate address, data, and response channels. Attaching the PFI to existing peripherals requires only thin wrapper logic and does not alter the semantics of the underlying IP. We integrate the PFI into Simply-V [13], an open-source FPGA-based reconfigurable soft-SoC, and use the resulting platform as a reproducible playground. We then treat the PFI event stream as the log of a concurrent process and feed it to a *process mining* pipeline, which reconstructs behavioral models from time-stamped events. The resulting models provide a compact, human-readable view of the SoC runtime and support anomaly detection.

In summary, this paper sets forth a **security auditing framework** with three core components:

- The *Peripheral Formal Interface (PFI)*, a passive bus-level observation interface for peripherals in RISC-V SoCs, with an AXI-oriented signal set and well-defined semantics.
- An auditing architecture that integrates the PFI into the Simply-V, instrumenting peripherals with low overhead and without disrupting the interconnect.
- A process mining-based log analysis methodology that consumes PFI traces to derive behavioral models, evaluated on a proof-of-concept with representative peripherals.

The remainder of the paper is organized as follows. Section 2 reviews background on hardware monitoring, RISC-V SoCs, and process mining. Section 3 presents the proposed security auditing framework and the related contributions. Section 4 reports on the proof-of-concept evaluation. Section 5 concludes and outlines future work.

2 Background and Related Work

In this section, we first explore the landscape of current hardware monitoring techniques, followed by an architectural overview of RISC-V-based SoCs. We conclude by detailing the fundamentals of process mining and its specific utility in monitoring computer systems.

2.1 Hardware Monitoring

Runtime hardware monitoring complements static verification and software defenses by observing system execution and flagging deviations that may indicate faults, malwares, or hardware Trojans. We classify existing techniques by their observation points.

The first and widely adopted class exploits hardware performance counters exposed by the processor's Performance Monitoring Unit. Branch, cache, and instruction-retirement events are sampled at runtime and fed to machine-learning classifiers to detect control-flow hijacking, rootkits, ransomware, and other malware families [6,10,19,24].

The second class observes the retired instruction stream of the core. Hardware-assisted runtime monitors check the dynamic execution trace against properties from the program or from a reference model, detecting illegal jumps, out-of-spec control flow, and injected Trojan payloads [3,17,21]. The RVFI [25] takes this idea one step further by standardizing the observation port: a passive, formally specified interface that exposes retired instructions, register writebacks, memory accesses, and trap information through a fixed signal set. The broader RVFI-V Verification Interface (RVVI) [16] generalizes RVFI to out-of-order and multi-hart designs.

The third class targets the bus and inter-module communication layer, and is the closest to our work. Early work showed that on-chip traffic carries a signature that changes when a Trojan hides in a peripheral, and proposed statistical or property-based detectors on top of bus traffic from open SoCs [9]. More recent work treats AXI-level protocol misuse as an attack surface in its own right: information-flow tracking identifies compliant controllers that still cause bus stalls or fairness violations [14,18], while IMSs embed a neural-network detector as a memory-mapped IP that observes AXI transactions on FPGA, reporting denial-of-service attempts with a small footprint [8].

Compared to these classes, the PFI—our hardware monitoring solution—differs from this line of work on two axes. First, existing bus monitors are detector-coupled: the observation and decision logic are baked into a single IP, limiting reuse. Second, they do not expose a formal, standardized observation interface like RVFI: each design defines its own probes, which prevents composition and cross-platform experimentation. The PFI addresses both points by defining a passive, AXI-aware event port whose semantics are independent from any specific auditing back-end.

2.2 RISC-V-Based SoCs

The RISC-V ISA has produced a wide ecosystem of cores and SoC designs, from microcontrollers to Linux-capable processors.

Several open-source SoCs are mature enough to serve research and prototyping, each with a distinct design focus. *OpenTitan* [5] targets a silicon root-of-trust profile with a fixed, security-hardened architecture. *Chipyard* [2] uses Chisel HDL and the Rocket Chip generator to support agile development with RTL simulation, FPGA-accelerated emulation (FireSim), and VLSI flows. The *PULP* family [20] offers a collection of ultra-low-power microcontrollers and multi-core platforms (PULPino, PULPissimo, Cheshire, Carfield) built on PULP cores and an AXI-based interconnect. *X-HEEP* [12] proposes a configurable RISC-V microcontroller for edge accelerators. Each platform pairs a specific CPU family with a largely fixed interconnect and peripheral set.

In this paper, we build on *Simply-V* [13], an FPGA-based, reconfigurable soft-SoC that explicitly targets fast prototyping and open hardware research. Simply-V has three AXI interconnects, namely a main bus (MBUS), a peripheral bus (PBUS), and a high-performance bus (HBUS), and encapsulates the CPU within a vendor-agnostic *RV Socket* that hosts the core and its debug module. A configuration-driven flow supports multiple RISC-V CPUs (including CV32E40P, Ibex, CVA6, and MicroBlaze-V), automatic clock-domain crossing, and packaging of third-party IPs from RTL or HLS. Three features make Simply-V a good fit for integration with the PFI. First, its interconnect is entirely AXI-based, which matches the transaction-level semantics of our observation port. Second, the custom-IP packaging flow lets us attach PFI wrappers to existing peripherals, a lightweight, repeatable step that does not modify the host SoC. Third, reconfigurability lets us to run the PFI-equipped SoC across different CPU and peripheral combinations, which supports experiments presented in Sect. 4.

2.3 Process Mining

Process mining is a hybrid discipline that bridges data-driven insights with model-based analyses through process discovery, which extracts normative behavioral models from event data, and conformance checking, which verifies the adherence of new event data with such models [1]. Process mining mainly deals with two types of objects: event logs and process models.

An event log groups events into traces, where each trace represents a specific execution of a process (a process instance). While the definition of an event is context-dependent, ranging from high-level healthcare tasks to bus-level RISC-V transactions, this paper focuses on simple events defined strictly by three core attributes: a unique ID, a timestamp, and an activity. Formally, we denote an event log as $L \in \mathcal{B}(\mathcal{A}^*)$, where $\mathcal{A}$ is the set of activities, $\mathcal{A}^*$ represents all possible traces built from $\mathcal{A}$, and $\mathcal{B}(\mathcal{A}^*)$ is the universe of possible trace multisets. A trace $\sigma \in \mathcal{A}^*$ is an ordered sequence of k activities, defined as $\sigma = \langle a_1, a_2, \ldots, a_k \rangle$, where $a_i \in \mathcal{A}$.

A process model describes the control flow of a process, including sequencing, concurrency, choice, and loops. We use Petri nets, a formalism for concurrent systems, defined as $N = (P, T, F)$ where P is a set of places, T a set of transitions with $P \cap T = \emptyset$, and $F \subseteq (P \times T) \cup (T \times P)$ the flow relation. A marking $M \in \mathcal{B}(P)$ represents the distribution of tokens over places. A transition is enabled if all its input places contain a token; firing consumes tokens from inputs and produces tokens in outputs. In process mining, transitions correspond to activities in $\mathcal{A}$ (including possible silent ones), while places and tokens represent dependencies and the current state.

Process mining presents itself as a particularly strong candidate for hardware monitoring, as it can leverage system event logs to discover normative Petri nets and formally verify the correctness of newly observed behaviors. More recently, its scope has successfully expanded to technical domains; for instance, it has been actively used for anomaly detection and monitoring in industrial control systems [15] and, notably, in complex cyber-physical systems [22,23]. Yet, existing research has not leveraged process mining for analyzing pure hardware execution logs, let alone for monitoring fine-grained, bus-level transactions within a processor. This paper addresses this gap by introducing process mining as a formalized methodology for low-level hardware monitoring from traces collected through our proposed security auditing framework.

3 The Proposed Security Auditing Framework

This section presents our proposed security auditing framework, decomposed into the PFI, an auditing architecture, and the process mining-based log analysis.

3.1 The PFI

RVFI works as a monitoring interface because it is *passive*, *formally specified*, and *orthogonal* to functional design: a core implementer can expose it without changing the pipeline, and a verification engineer can use it without knowing the micro-architecture. We apply the same three principles one level below, on the on-chip bus. The *PFI* is a passive observation port that exposes, in a structured and vendor-neutral form, every register-level transaction that crosses the peripheral interconnect of a RISC-V SoC.

Design Principles. Three properties guide the PFI definition.

- **Passivity:** The PFI sits outside the functional path. It taps existing AXI wires via an observer that has no master or slave ports on the interconnect, applies no back-pressure to the monitored peripherals, and can be removed with a one-line edit to the parent bus. This is the main difference from AXI-level firewalls or arbiter replacements [14,18], which break the native data path.
- **Formality:** The PFI is a schema, not RTL. Each event is a tuple over a fixed set of fields with well-defined semantics. Downstream formal techniques (formal checkers, anomaly detectors, process mining) can be written against the schema alone, without knowing the peripheral set. Just as an RVFI trace is meaningful whether it comes from Ibex, CV32E40P, or CVA6, a PFI trace is meaningful whether the tap sits on AXI-Lite, AXI4, or any other register-transfer bus that fits the schema.

- **Orthogonality:** The PFI complements RVFI, it does not replace it. RVFI reports *what the core executed*; PFI reports *what the bus observed.* The two streams share a cycle-level timebase and are joined offline, so that for every bus transaction we recover the instruction that caused it, and for every retired instruction we recover its bus effect.

Table 1. PFI event schema. Each emitted event is a tuple whose fields describe one AXI handshake observed on the peripheral interconnect.

Field	Domain	Meaning
`ts`	N	Cycle-count timestamp (shared timebase with RVFI)
`op`	$\{0, 1\}$	0 = write request, 1 = read request
`addr`	32-bit word	Bus-relative transaction address
`data`	32-bit word	Write or read data, as applicable
`resp`	3-bit code	Request / response discriminator and AXI response
`strb`	byte-mask	Write-strobe bundle
`irq`	bit-vector	Snapshot of peripheral IRQ lines at event time

Event Schema. A PFI event records one AXI handshake on the peripheral interconnect. The event is a tuple (`ts`, `op`, `addr`, `data`, `resp`, `strb`, `irq`) whose fields are summarized in Table 1: `ts` is a monotonic cycle counter sampled on the bus clock and shared with the RVFI stream, so offline joining is a lexicographic merge; `op` distinguishes reads from writes; `addr` carries the bus-relative address, which the analysis pipeline resolves against the SoC address map to produce a decoded *`device.register`* label; `data` carries the payload (write data on write requests, read data on read responses); `resp` discriminates request from response rows. This distinction is crucial at the bus level because AXI handshakes separate address and data phases. `strb` is the write-strobe bundle; `irq` is a snapshot of the peripheral-interrupt bundle at event time, which makes interrupt-handler boundaries visible without any software instrumentation. The schema is minimal by design. Anything that is not a property of the *transaction on the wire* (the calling function, the owning task, the memory region semantics) is left to offline enrichment, where the event stream is correlated with the RVFI trace and an ELF symbol table to recover function-level context. Keeping the on-chip interface thin makes it cheap to instantiate per-peripheral buses and keeps it independent of any software stack or operating system.

Scope of Observability. A PFI connection on a single bus sees only the transactions that cross that bus. In SoCs with multiple buses of different protocols, like Simply-V, one tap is not enough to observe Platform-Level Interrupt Controller (PLIC) `CLAIM`/`COMPLETE` sequences. We treat this as a design dimension, not a limitation: the schema is protocol-agnostic, so the same observer pattern can be instantiated on any relevant bus. The auditing architecture of Sect. 3.2 uses this strategy, combining the PFI stream on the peripheral bus with a dedicated trace on the memory bus covering the PLIC, and with the RVFI retirement stream of the core into a single enriched event log (Fig. 1).

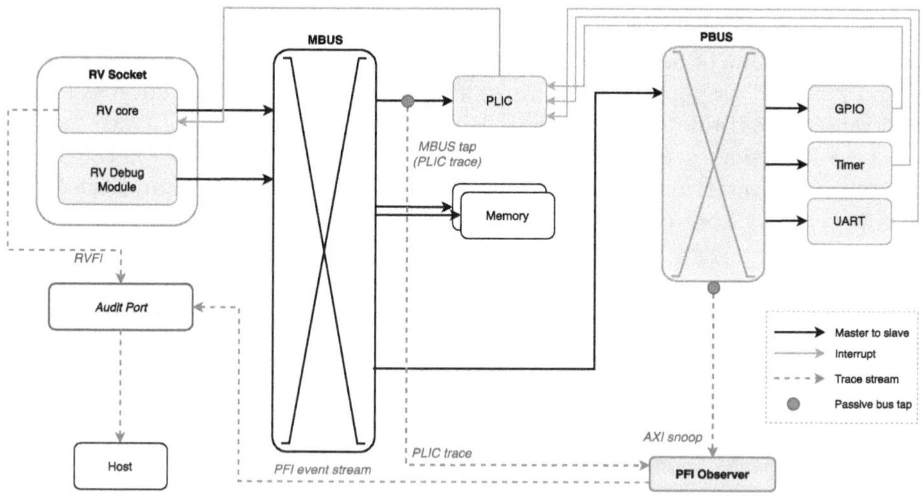

Fig. 1. Auditing architecture for a Simply-V SoC extended with the PFI.

3.2 Auditing Architecture

The audit infrastructure has three observation points, one per protocol:

- The *PFI Observer* sits on the AXI-Lite peripheral bus (PBUS) and produces the PFI event stream of Sect. 3.1;
- The *MBUS tap* sits on the AXI4 main bus (MBUS) at the PLIC address window and produces a PLIC register-access trace;
- The core's RVFI port produces a CPU retirement trace.

Table 2. The three trace sources. PFI and PLIC share the same schema; RVFI is core-centric.

Source	Bus / Port	Recorded fields
PFI (PBUS)	AXI-Lite	`ts, op, addr, data, resp, strb, irq` (one row per handshake)
PLIC (MBUS)	AXI4	Same schema as PFI; `irq` carries PLIC source bundle
RVFI	Core port	PC, instr., dest. reg/value, mem. addr/mask, data, trap flag/cause

All three taps are passive: they observe existing wires, do not interpose in the functional path, apply no back-pressure, and share a single cycle-count timebase that supports offline merging. Streams are forwarded to the *Audit Port*, an off-SoC interface (the simulation testbench in our prototype) that writes one CSV file per source. A *trace* is a finite sequence of timestamped, structured records produced by one observation point during one firmware execution. Each record is a tuple over source-specific fields and includes a `ts` field comparable across sources. A trace is not yet a process-mining event log: it is the raw input that the offline pipeline of Sect. 3.3 turns into a log through enrichment, source merging, and case-id assignment. The three traces differ in protocol, address space, and granularity. Table 2 summarizes their schemas, where the PFI trace records AXI-Lite handshakes to capture peripheral accesses on the PBUS, the PLIC trace monitors interrupt controller transactions on the main bus, and the RVFI trace provides a core-centric view of the architectural effects of every retired instruction.

The three sources are complementary. The RVFI stream is rich on the core side but blind to bus-level detail. The PFI and PLIC streams are bus-rich but software-blind. Joining them by cycle timestamp recovers, for every bus event, the function and instruction that caused it. The resulting unified log is what the pipeline of Sect. 3.3 consumes.

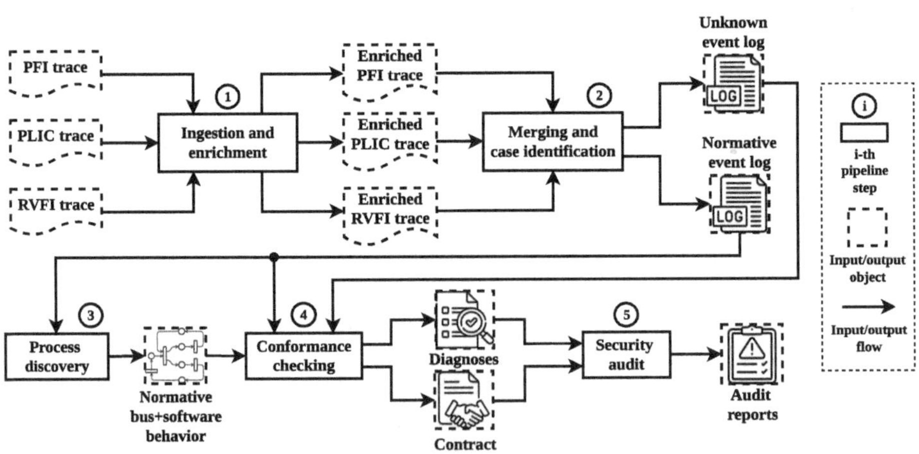

Fig. 2. The process mining-based processing pipeline for log analysis. The PFI, PLIC and RVFI traces are ingested and enriched with meaningful event names; the enriched traces are merged to produce an event log; the normative behavior is characterized through process discovery; the unknown behavior is verified through conformance checking; the resulting diagnoses are parsed by a dedicated security audit.

3.3 Process Mining-Based Log Analysis

Figure 2 shows the process mining-based processing pipeline for log analysis. First, the raw PFI, PLIC and RVFI traces are ingested and enriched to abstract the events and make them more meaningful and interpretable. In particular the PFI trace, which captures PBUS events, is enriched by converting raw hexadecimal signals into integers and appending device, register, and access_kind (read, write request, or response) classifications based on a predefined address map. Similarly, the PLIC trace monitors MBUS-side register accesses, uniformly resolving the device to "PLIC" while decoding specific interrupt-related addresses. Concurrently, the RVFI trace, which logs cycle-by-cycle CPU state, is enriched by classifying each row's kind as either a standard instruction or a CPU trap. Crucially, this RVFI enrichment accurately translates raw Program Counter addresses into human-readable function names.

Next, the three enriched traces are merged to create a comprehensive trace. By interleaving the PFI, CPU retirement (RVFI), and PLIC traces based on their shared cycle-count timestamps, a single chronological event log is built. During this merging process, RVFI rows are collapsed so that consecutive CPU instructions within the same function are reduced to a single event. Conversely, every individual PFI and PLIC register access is preserved without collapsing. Each merged event is annotated with an explicit source tag (pfi, rvfi, or plic) and a standardized activity label, such as func:<name> for RVFI or plic_r:PLIC.CLAIM_CTX0 for a PLIC claim read. The set of all uniquely labeled events derived from PBUS peripheral accesses, MBUS-side PLIC register transactions, and collapsed CPU function executions makes up the set of activities $\mathcal{A}_{PPR}$. Table 3 shows some events from an example event log obtained from the enriched traces.

Table 3. Excerpt of interleaved events from the enriched normative event log.

Case ID	Timestamp	Source	Activity
irq1	2275	pfi	reg_r:TIM0.TCSR0
irq1	2285	rvfi	func:xlnx_tim_clear_int
irq1	2294	rvfi	func:iowrite32
irq1	2310	pfi	reg_w:TIM0.TCSR0
irq1	2311	pfi	resp:TIM0.TCSR0
idle	2322	rvfi	func:xlnx_tim_clear_int
idle	2330	rvfi	func:_ext_handler
idle	2333	rvfi	func:plic_complete
idle	2343	rvfi	func:iowrite32
idle	2352	plic	plic_w:PLIC.CLAIM_CTX0
idle	2354	plic	plic_resp:PLIC.CLAIM_CTX0

Based on the log analysis phase, either a normative ($L_{Norm} \in \mathcal{B}(\mathcal{A}^*_{PPR})$) or unknown ($L_{Unk} \in \mathcal{B}(\mathcal{A}^*_{PPR})$) event log is generated. In the former case, a process discovery algorithm γ, such as the inductive miner [11], is used to generate the normative bus+software behavior, i.e., $\gamma(L_{Norm}) = N$. L_{Norm} is also used to generate a *contract* through conformance checking, reporting the exact constraints the system must abide by during runtime. Specifically, the contract encodes an allowlist of permitted activities, explicitly denied activities, required per-case activity counts, cycle-accurate timing bands for case duration and inter-activity transitions, and process-mining sequence constraints bounded by strict fitness and precision thresholds.

Conversely, the unknown log L_{Unk} represents a trace from a system under audit; rather than being used for discovery, it is subsequently replayed against the reference model N via conformance checking to detect structural and timing deviations. These deviations are collected in a comprehensive diagnoses file, which is compared against the contract to generate audit reports. Each finding in the reports explicitly details the violated detector (e.g., activity allowlist, required counts, sequence fitness, trace duration, or inter-activity timing), assigns a severity level ranging from MEDIUM to CRITICAL, and provides the offending activity along with the expected versus observed parameters. Specifically, a MEDIUM severity denotes timing anomalies—such as case durations or inter-activity transitions falling outside the prescribed cycle bands—while a CRITICAL severity flags outright violations of the activity allowlist, such as the execution of explicitly forbidden or unknown operations, representing a severe security breach.

4 Proof-of-Concept

We evaluate the framework on an end-to-end setup. The PFI-equipped SoC runs a representative workload; the three observability streams are collected; the log construction and analysis pipelines run on the resulting traces; and a set of injected firmware defects is audited against the baseline Contract. The proof-of-concept demonstrates three points:

- **Monitoring System Integration**: the PFI and its auditing architecture integrate cleanly into an open, non-trivial RISC-V SoC;
- **SoC Characterization**: describing the SoC's behavior under the selected workload using the Contract described in Sect. 3.2;
- **Faulty Behavior Evaluation**: evaluating whether the proposed security auditing highlights any faulty behaviors.

4.1 Monitoring System Integration

The platform is Simply-V configured with the Ibex RISC-V core, three AXI interconnects (main, peripheral, and high-performance), SRAM-based instruction and data memories, and a standard peripheral complement: two timers, a

UART, and two General Purpose Input/Output (GPIO) banks on the peripheral bus, and the PLIC on the main bus. The PFI observer of Sect. 3.1 is instantiated on the peripheral bus, where it captures every register access to the on-SoC peripherals. Because the PLIC sits on the main bus, it is outside the scope of this single PFI connection; we recover its visibility through a dedicated memory-bus trace at the testbench level, as described in Sect. 3.2. The RVFI port of Ibex is exposed at the testbench level as the third stream.

Simulation runs under a cycle-accurate RTL simulator using vendor netlists for the peripheral Intellectual Propertys (IPs) and the RTL of the PLIC from OpenTitan [5].

The firmware initializes the PLIC and the interrupt-controlling timer, then waits for a configurable number of timer ticks, handling each in an external interrupt handler that claims the interrupt, clears the timer, and completes. Termination is signaled by storing a sentinel value at an address served, which the testbench detects to end the simulation deterministically. Every simulation run emits three csv files, one for each observer, that feed the log construction and analysis pipelines described in Sect. 3.2.

4.2 SoC Characterization

We characterize the SoC's behavior with two workloads of complementary complexity. The simpler one, `timer_tick`, exercises only the timer-interrupt path: the firmware programs TIM0 in auto-reload count-down mode with a fixed reload value and waits for a fixed number $N = 4$ of ticks; each tick raises an external interrupt routed through the PLIC to the core, whose ISR claims the source, clears the timer's interrupt-status bit through a write-1-to-clear of `TIM0.TCSR0`, and completes the claim at the PLIC. The richer one, `multi_periph_tick`, has the same skeleton and the same number of interrupts. However, its ISR additionally touches a second peripheral chosen on the parity of the tick counter: even ticks write to the UART (`UART.TX` payload and a dummy `UART.CONTROL` write), odd ticks write to the output GPIO bank (`GPIO_OUT.DATA` and `GPIO_OUT.TRI`). The W1C clear of `TIM0.TCSR0` remains the last PFI write of every handler in both workloads, which keeps it usable as a handler-exit marker for the bus-driven case-id strategy.

Running the two workloads through the analysis pipeline, explained in Sect. 3.3, yields the Petri nets shown in Fig. 3 and Fig. 4, respectively.

- The `timer_tick` net (Fig. 3) is a sequential block of three transitions and reflects exactly the per-handler footprint of the firmware on the bus: a read-modify-write of `TIM0.TCSR0` to clear T0INT, followed by the corresponding AXI write-response. The model is therefore a tight sequence of permitted bus behavior for this workload: anything that deviates from those three transitions, in either set or sequence, is a candidate defect.
- The `multi_periph_tick` net (Fig. 4) is structurally richer: it contains the same final `TIM0.TCSR0` clear shared by both parity paths, and an exclusive choice between the UART branch and the GPIO branch. The Inductive Miner

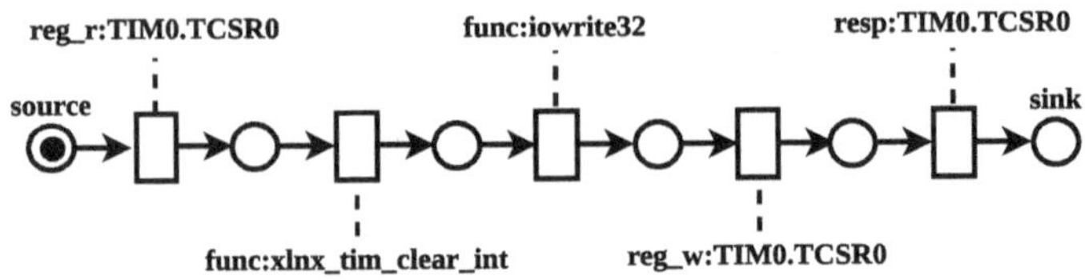

Fig. 3. Petri net discovered by the Inductive Miner from the `timer_tick` unified event log (handler cases only). Three transitions capture the entire PFI-side footprint of the ISR body: `reg_r:TIM0.TCSR0`, `reg_w:TIM0.TCSR0` (the W1C clear), and the corresponding write-response `resp:TIM0.TCSR0`.

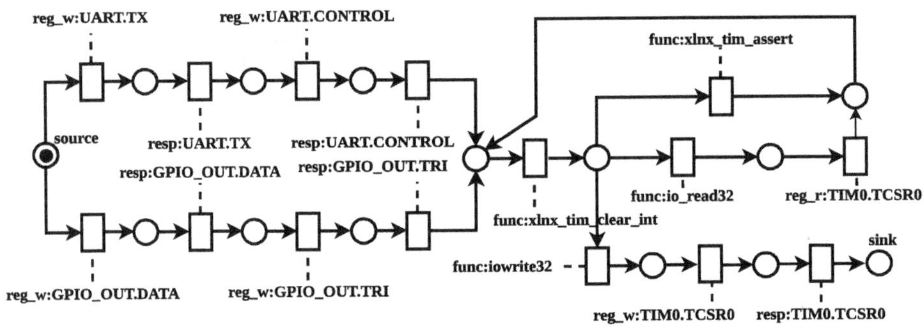

Fig. 4. Petri net discovered by the Inductive Miner from the `multi_periph_tick` unified event log (handler cases only). The model exposes the two-way exclusive choice between the UART path and the GPIO path that the firmware selects on tick parity, and rejoins on the common `TIM0.TCSR0` clear shared by both branches.

discovers the choice block from the data alone; the two variants observed in the log correspond exactly to the even-tick and odd-tick cases.

4.3 Faulty Behavior Evaluation

To probe the auditing architecture, we craft three variants of the baseline firmware. Each injects a realistic defect that is small in code but distinct on the bus:

- *Defect A (unauthorized read).* The Interrupt Service Routine (ISR) reads a timer status register that the clean firmware never accesses. The read has no functional effect, but adds an activity outside the allowlist: the simplest information-leak primitive.
- *Defect B (missing acknowledgment).* The W1C of the timer status register is removed from the ISR. The timer stays armed and keeps raising its interrupt, causing an interrupt storm. The activity alphabet is unchanged, but the per-case count of handler entries explodes.

- *Defect C (cross-peripheral access).* The ISR reads a GPIO input register without authorization. Like Defect A this is an allowlist violation, but the new symbol now touches a peripheral the clean handler never uses.

Running the audit pipeline of Sect. 3.3 on the three buggy traces against the `timer_tick` Contract returns a *FAIL* verdict in every case. As a reference, the Petri net of Fig. 3 shows that every clean ISR is three transitions in the same order, `reg_r:TIM0.TCSR0`, the W1C `reg_w:TIM0.TCSR0`, and its write-response, packed into 36 cycles and repeated identically across the four interrupts.

Defect A: Extra Read of an Unused Register. The buggy ISR reads `TIM0.TCSR1`, adding a fourth symbol to each handler and stretching its window from 36 to 96 cycles. The allowlist detector raises a CRITICAL finding for each of the four handler invocations and points the analyst at the nearest legitimate neighbor, `reg_r:TIM0.TCSR0`, one register away. The sequence-fitness detector confirms the divergence with an alignment fitness of 0.86 and a precision of 0, both below the contract's thresholds of 1.0 and 0.95. It also identifies `log_insert:reg_r:TIM0.TCSR1` as the first non-synchronous move in every case. The two timing detectors record the 36 $\rightarrow$ 96-cycle stretching as a MEDIUM violation once per handler. Four of the five detectors converge on the same root cause.

Defect B: Missing Acknowledgment. The buggy ISR drops the W1C of `TIM0.TCSR0`. The interrupt line never releases: the PLIC re-fires immediately after every `COMPLETE`, and the core stays in a tight claim/complete loop until the tick counter reaches its terminating value. Since the W1C was the only PBUS event of the clean handler, removing it strips every interrupt from the PFI stream.

This empty body breaks the case-id machinery of Sect. 3.3, which relies on the W1C as its handler-exit marker. The FSM never advances out of the initial `setup` phase, and the entire suspect trace lands in a single, never-closing `setup` window with zero $\texttt{irq}_n$ cases. The four per-case detectors have nothing to evaluate; the allowlist detector fires only on boot-time `TIM0.TLR0` programming, but raises the same finding when self-auditing the clean baseline, so the verdict cannot tell the two runs apart. The structural difference is plain in the raw counts (four $\texttt{irq}_n$ cases and twenty-five PFI rows for the clean run, zero cases and ten rows for the buggy one).

Defect C: Cross-Peripheral Access. The buggy ISR reads `GPIO_IN.DATA` between the W1C and the PLIC completion. The alphabet grows *across* a device boundary instead of within `TIM0`, and the nearest legitimate neighbor of `reg_r:GPIO_IN.DATA` is `reg_r:TIM0.TCSR0` at edit distance *nine*, an order of magnitude beyond Defect A. The distance alone signals a lateral-movement primitive rather than a near-miss within the same peripheral, and the surrounding-events window flanks the unauthorized GPIO read with the otherwise-legitimate `TIM0.TCSR0` sequence. Timing detectors corroborate the finding on the single

$\texttt{irq}_1$ case that the case-id machinery still recognizes before the cross-peripheral read perturbs it; sequence fitness and required-counts pass cleanly on the surviving handler.

Discussion. The results fall into two patterns. When a defect enlarges the bus alphabet (A and C), the allowlist detector localizes every event, and timing detectors agree wherever the case-id partition still admits them: on all four handlers for Defect A, and on the single surviving handler for Defect C, where the cross-peripheral read absorbs the others into the `stop` phase. When a defect erases the handler body (B), the bus signal is qualitatively different: there is nothing to flag at the alphabet level, and the deviation surfaces only as the absence of $\texttt{irq}_n$ cases. The proof-of-concept thus validates the methodology against alphabet-level deviations and, on the same set of three defects, identifies the smallest contract extension needed to close the gap.

5 Conclusions

The growing adoption of open-hardware RISC-V SoCs in security-sensitive embedded and edge scenarios has outpaced the observability infrastructure available for systematic auditing. While the RVFI provides a passive, formally-specified interface for the core's retired instruction stream, no analogous mechanism exists at the peripheral side of the on-chip bus, where many realistic attack primitives manifest. Bus-level deviations are today either invisible to core-centric monitors or observable only through ad hoc, non-reusable probes.

To address this gap, we proposed a three-pronged approach. First, the *PFI*: a passive, formally-specified, AXI-aware observation port that emits a structured event stream of every register-level access to the peripheral interconnect, without interfering with the functional path. Second, an auditing architecture that integrates the PFI into the open-source Simply-V SoC alongside an MBUS-side PLIC tap and the RVFI retirement stream. Third, a process mining-based log analysis pipeline that fuses the three traces into a unified event log, mines a behavioral model of the firmware as an Inductive Miner Petri net, and derives a serializable Contract that pairs the discovered model with allowlist, count, and timing constraints; the Contract drives an audit step that is suitable both for human triage and for CI gating.

The proof-of-concept on Simply-V validates the three contributions in turn. The PFI integrates cleanly to the peripheral bus through a thin, non-intrusive wrapper, demonstrating that the observation port is a lightweight extension to an existing SoC. The Petri-net models inferred from the `timer_tick` and `multi_periph_tick` workloads provide compact, human-readable characterizations of the firmware's bus-level behavior, with the more complex workload exposing the data-driven exclusive-choice structure that the firmware uses to dispatch on tick parity. Finally, the audit pipeline flags two of the three injected firmware defects against the clean baseline Contract: an unauthorized intra-peripheral read and an unauthorized cross-peripheral read.

Future work spans three directions. On the hardware side, a hardened on-SoC sink (e.g. AXI-Stream DMA to DDR or to a UART streaming endpoint) would make the PFI usable on a real FPGA target rather than only in simulation. It would also enable on-chip filtering and compression of the event stream to mitigate FIFO overflow under bursty traffic. On the analysis side, a richer Contract with state-dependent activity allowlists, anomaly-detection-driven timing interrupt, and cross-correlation with the core's privilege mode would tighten the execution and reduce false positives on workloads with legitimate behavioral variability.

Disclosure of Interests. The authors have no competing interests to declare that are relevant to the content of this article.

References

1. van der Aalst, W.M.P., Carmona, J.: Process Mining Handbook. Springer, Cham, Switzerland (2022)
2. Amid, A., et al.: Chipyard: integrated design, simulation, and implementation framework for custom SoCs. IEEE Micro **40**(4), 10–21 (2020)
3. Arora, D., Ravi, S., Raghunathan, A., Jha, N.K.: Secure embedded processing through hardware-assisted run-time monitoring. In: Proceedings of the Conference on Design, Automation and Test in Europe (DATE), pp. 178–183. IEEE (2005)
4. Asanović, K., Patterson, D.A.: Instruction sets should be free: the case for RISC-V. Tech. Rep. UCB/EECS-2014-146 (2014). http://www2.eecs.berkeley.edu/Pubs/TechRpts/2014/EECS-2014-146.html
5. Ciani, M., Bertuletti, M., Scherer, M., Pullini, A., Rossi, D., Benini, L.: Unleashing OpenTitan's potential: a silicon-ready embedded secure element for root of trust and cryptographic offloading. ACM Trans. Embed. Comput. Syst. (2025)
6. Demme, J., et al.: On the feasibility of online malware detection with performance counters. In: Proceedings of the 40th Annual International Symposium on Computer Architecture (ISCA), pp. 559–570. ACM (2013)
7. Dörflinger, A., et al.: A comparative survey of open-source application-class RISC-V processor implementations. In: Proceedings of the 18th ACM International Conference on Computing Frontiers, pp. 12–20. CF '21, Association for Computing Machinery, New York, NY, USA (2021)
8. Foudhaili, W., et al.: IMS: intelligent hardware monitoring system for secure SoCs. In: 2026 Design, Automation & Test in Europe Conference (DATE), pp. 1–7 (2026)
9. Khalid, F., Hasan, S.R., Hasan, O., Shafique, M.: SIMCom: statistical sniffing of inter-module communications for run-time hardware trojan detection. Microprocess. Microsyst. **77**, 103122 (2020)
10. Khalid, F., Hasan, S.R., Zia, S., Hasan, O., Awwad, F., Shafique, M.: MacLeR: machine learning-based runtime hardware trojan detection in resource-constrained IoT edge devices. IEEE Trans. Comput. Aided Des. Integr. Circuits Syst. **39**(11), 3748–3761 (2020)
11. Leemans, S.J.J., Fahland, D., van der Aalst, W.M.P.: Discovering block-structured process models from event logs - a constructive approach. In: Application and Theory of Petri Nets and Concurrency, pp. 311–329 (2013)

12. Machetti, S., Schiavone, P.D., Müller, T.C., Peón-Quirós, M., Atienza, D.: X-HEEP: an open-source, configurable and extendible RISC-V microcontroller for the exploration of ultra-low-power edge accelerators (2024). arXiv:2401.05548 arXiv preprint
13. Maisto, V., Mercogliano, S., Maddaluno, M., Cilardo, A.: The Simply-V Framework: an extensible RISC-V reconfigurable soft-SoC for open research and fast prototyping. ACM Trans. Design Autom. Electron. Syst. **31**(3) (2026)
14. Meza, A., Restuccia, F., Kastner, R., Oberg, J.: Safety verification of third-party hardware modules via information flow tracking. In: Proceedings 1st Workshop on Real-Time and Intelligent EdgemComputing (RAGE), co-located with the 59th ACM/IEEE Design Automation Conference (DAC), pp. 1–4 (2022)
15. Myers, D., Suriadi, S., Radke, K., Foo, E.: Anomaly detection for industrial control systems using process mining. Comput. Sec. **78**, 103–125 (2018)
16. OpenHW Group and Imperas: RVVI: RISC-V Verification Interface. https://github.com/riscv-verification/RVVI (2023). draft open standard. Accessed April 2026
17. Rahmanikia, A., Jahanirad, H.: Runtime hardware trojan detection by reconfigurable monitoring circuits. J. Supercomput. **78**, 14095–14126 (2022)
18. Restuccia, F., Pagani, M., Biondi, A., Marinoni, M., Buttazzo, G.: Is your bus arbiter really fair? Restoring fairness in AXI interconnects for FPGA SoCs. ACM Transactions on Embedded Computing Systems **18**(5s), 51:1–51:22 (2019)
19. Sayadi, H., Aliasgari, M., Homayoun, H.: Intelligent malware detection based on hardware performance counters: a comprehensive survey (2024). arXiv:2404.05891 arXiv preprint
20. Schiavone, P.D., Rossi, D., Pullini, A., Di Mauro, A., Conti, F., Benini, L.: Quentin: an ultra-low-power PULPissimo SoC in 22NM FDX. In: Proceedings IEEE SOI-3D-Subthreshold Microelectronics Technology Unified Conference (S3S), pp. 1–3 (2018)
21. Vijayan, A., Tahoori, M.B., Chakrabarty, K.: Runtime identification of hardware trojans by feature analysis on gate-level unstructured data and anomaly detection. ACM Trans. Design Autom. Electron. Syst. **25**(4), 33:1–33:23 (2020)
22. Vitale, F., Dall'Ora, N., Gaiardelli, S., Fraccaroli, E., Mazzocca, N., Fummi, F.: Process mining-driven modeling and simulation to enhance fault diagnosis in cyber–physical systems. J. Manuf. Syst. **84**, 189–206 (2026)
23. Vitale, F., Guarino, S., Flammini, F., Faramondi, L., Mazzocca, N., Setola, R.: Process mining for digital twin development of industrial cyber-physical systems. IEEE Trans. Industr. Inf. **21**(1), 866–875 (2025)
24. Wang, X., Karri, R.: NumChecker: detecting kernel control-flow modifying rootkits by using hardware performance counters. In: Proceedings of the 50th Annual Design Automation Conference (DAC), pp. 79:1–79:7. ACM (2013)
25. YosysHQ: RISC-V Formal Interface (RVFI) Specification. https://github.com/YosysHQ/riscv-formal/blob/main/docs/source/rvfi.rst (2024). Accessed April 2026

A Knowledge-Grounded LLM Agent for Critical Infrastructure Cybersecurity: Toward a Smart Digital Twin

Quoc-Viet Pham[1], Fatiha Zaidi[1], and Ana Rosa Cavalli[2](✉)

[1] Paris-Saclay University, Orsay, France
viet.pham@universite-paris-saclay.fr,
fatiha.zaidi@universite-paris-saclay.fr
[2] Montimage, Paris, France
arosa.cavalli@montimage.eu
https://montimage.eu

Abstract. Operators of critical infrastructure increasingly rely on heterogeneous catalogs of cybersecurity services (probes, intrusion detection systems, monitoring tools), yet selecting and reasoning about these services remains a manual, expert-driven task. Digital Twins (DTs) have emerged as virtual replicas of physical systems for monitoring and simulation, and platforms have been built to manage the catalogs of cybersecurity services that can be deployed into such twins; however, the interaction layer of these platforms typically does not provide a reasoning interface above the catalog. To address this, we propose a *smart digital twin* augmented with cooperating LLM-based agents that perform knowledge-grounded reasoning, automated deployment, and incident response. As a first step, we present a *Boss Agent* embedded in an existing DT management platform. This conversational assistant uses Retrieval-Augmented Generation (RAG) to ground responses in the platform's service catalog. To preserve data government in regulated sectors, the agent runs entirely on local infrastructure using open-source models. We detail the system architecture and a lightweight, embedding-margin-based intent classifier that eliminates retrieval overhead during conversational turns. Additionally, we provide an empirical evaluation on commodity hardware that measures factual accuracy, hallucination rate, and latency against a no-retrieval baseline. We conclude with limitations and a research agenda to extend the agent's grounding to live DT states and introduce additional specialized agents.

Keywords: Digital Twin · Cybersecurity · Critical Infrastructure · Large Language Model · Multi-Agent System · Retrieval-Augmented Generation

1 Introduction

The protection of critical infrastructures (CI), such as transportation, healthcare, telecommunications and energy, has become an urgent priority. These systems

P. Kieseberg et al. (Eds.): ARES 2026 Workshops, LNCS 16903, pp. 605–623, 2027.
https://doi.org/10.1007/978-3-032-37218-5_35

are characterized by large-scale sensor networks, remote control and monitoring, edge and cloud connectivity, and the merging of Information Technology (IT) and Operational Technology (OT) domains [7]. Traditional perimeter-based cyber-defense strategies are proving insufficient against sophisticated adversaries who target not only network connectivity but also physical processes, supply chains, and digital-physical convergence.

Two technological currents are reshaping how this challenge is addressed. The first is the advancement of the *Digital Twin* (DT), a virtual replica of a physical system that enables monitoring, simulation, and optimization [14,23,32]. By gathering real-time data and updating the virtual model accordingly, a DT can reflect the states of physical systems and enable what-if analysis. The second is the rapid evolution of *Large Language Models* (LLMs) and Generative AI, which has been shown to support cyber-threat intelligence by synthesizing network traffic, malware behavior, and adversarial attack campaigns [4,13,18].

The convergence of these two currents introduces a new promise: by embedding LLM-based agents within DTs of critical infrastructures, one can complement existing automated defenses, such as machine learning-based intrusion detection and reinforcement-learning agents embedded in the twin [1,30], with knowledge-grounded *natural-language reasoning* that operators can supervise directly. Even where DTs already host active ML-based detection, operators still face the task of interpreting events and taking actions. Conversely, LLM-based cybersecurity assistants typically operate as standalone systems, independent of any structured representation of the infrastructure they advise on, and consequently prone to hallucinating domain-specific facts.

The long-term goal of our work is a *smart digital twin*. By this we mean a DT augmented with a coordinated set of LLM-based agents that, between them, (i) reason over the twin's service catalog and runtime state to answer operator questions, (ii) deploy and configure cybersecurity services into the twin under controlled experimentation, and (iii) propose and execute incident-response actions under human supervision. A smart digital twin in this sense is therefore neither a richer simulation model nor a stand-alone chatbot, but the combination of a digital-twin management platform with a multi-agent layer that grounds every action in the platform's structured state.

The long-term goal of our work is a *smart digital twin*. By this we mean a DT augmented with a coordinated set of LLM-based agents that, between them, (i) reason over the twin's service catalog and runtime state to answer operator questions, (ii) deploy and configure cybersecurity services into the twin under controlled experimentation, and (iii) propose and execute incident-response actions under human supervision. A smart digital twin in this sense is therefore neither a richer simulation model nor a stand-alone chatbot, but the combination of a digital-twin management platform with a multi-agent layer that grounds every action in the platform's structured state. The contribution of an LLM layer above the DT is therefore complementary to other ML-based and RL-based active defenses already studied in the literature: it provides an interface where operators can understand the rationale behind detections and the reasoning underlying mitigation decisions.

This paper presents a first step in a broader research proposition aimed at the smart digital twin defined above. We focus here on its entry point: a *Boss Agent* embedded in an existing digital-twin management platform that serves as a centralized hub for a catalog of cybersecurity services and for the design, deployment, and evaluation of digital-twin scenarios in virtualized environments. The Boss Agent grounds its conversational answers in the platform's service catalog via Retrieval-Augmented Generation (RAG). The agent runs entirely on local infrastructure (open-source LLMs served via Ollama), a design choice motivated by the data government and regulatory constraints that characterize the critical infrastructure. Our contributions are:

- **System design.** We describe an architecture in which an open-source LLM, deployed locally, queries a vector index built from the digital-twin management platform's service catalog. The agent treats the DT as its primary knowledge source rather than relying on the LLM's parametric memory.
- **Lightweight intent classification.** To avoid retrieval overhead on conversational "casual" turns, we introduce a fast embedding-based classifier that re-uses the already-loaded embedding model. The classifier does not require an additional model footprint and applies a configurable similarity margin that defaults to RAG.
- **Initial empirical evaluation.** We report on the factual accuracy, hallucination rate, and end-to-end latency on commodity hardware, comparing the grounded agent against a no-retrieval baseline using the same model. We also report latency expectations on server-grade GPU hardware.

The remainder of the paper is organized as follows. Section 2 reviews the necessary background on DTs, LLMs, and Retrieval-Augmented Generation. Section 3 discusses related work on DT-AI integration for cybersecurity. Section 4 presents the system architecture and design decisions. Section 5 describes the implementation. Section 6 reports the initial empirical evaluation. Section 7 discusses limitations. Section 8 concludes and outlines future work.

2 Background

2.1 Digital Twin

A DT is a virtual representation of a physical system, process or asset that is continuously synchronized with its real-world counterpart via data and models. According to the Digital Twin Consortium [5], it comprises a physical system, a digital counterpart that mirrors the physics and operational logic of the system, and an information-processing layer linking the two [6]. The literature distinguishes three levels of integration [14,19]: a digital model (static, offline), a digital shadow (one-way data flow from the physical system, enabling passive monitoring), and a digital twin proper, characterized by bidirectional, real-time synchronization with closed-loop control.

In this paper, we work with an existing digital-twin management platform that maintains a structured representation of the cybersecurity services that can be deployed into a DT of a critical infrastructure. Our Boss Agent is grounded in this catalog, and extending the architecture with additional specialized agents is left for future work.

2.2 Large Language Models

Large Language Models (LLMs) are autoregressive transformer architectures trained via self-supervised next-token prediction over very large corpora [18,31]. In digital-twin contexts, LLMs have been proposed as a natural-language interface, as automated code generators for simulation parameters, and as translators from unstructured threat-intelligence reports into simulation scenarios [4,18]. A central limitation is *hallucination*: because the model is bounded by patterns seen in training, it can produce plausible-sounding but factually incorrect content in specialized domains [13]. This is a critical concern in cybersecurity, where a fabricated configuration or a non-existent tool name in a generated answer could mislead an operator.

2.3 Retrieval-Augmented Generation

Retrieval-Augmented Generation (RAG) [20] addresses hallucination by augmenting the LLM's input with passages retrieved from an external corpus. A query is embedded into a dense vector, the top-k most similar passages are retrieved from a vector index, and the retrieved text is concatenated with the user's question in the prompt sent to the LLM. RAG has become a widely-used approach for grounding LLM outputs in domain-specific knowledge.

2.4 Local Open-Source LLMs

All LLMs are locally deployed via the Ollama runtime [22]: an instruction-tuned chat model (`qwen3:14b`, a variant of Qwen3 [33]) and a sentence-embedding model (`mxbai-embed-large`, 1024 dimensions) [21]. Local deployment is motivated by data-governance constraints in critical infrastructure: catalogs, deployment configurations, and operational queries are commercially sensitive and cannot be transmitted to third-party cloud LLM providers without regulatory complications, particularly under regimes such as the EU NIS2 Directive [12].

3 Related Work

3.1 Digital Twins for Cybersecurity

DTs have been studied as monitoring and resilience tools for cyber-physical systems (CPS) for several years [7], and several recent surveys compare architectures, techniques, and open challenges in the area [8,15,23,28,32].

Several studies illustrate industrial application. Salvi et al. [26] model physical and cyber links in the electric power sector to enable proactive defense. Varghese et al. [30] present a DT-based intrusion-detection system for industrial control networks, using the twin as a reference behavioral model against which deviations are flagged. Epiphaniou et al. [10] use a DT for the port of Southampton, integrated with cyber modeling and simulation, to test resilience metrics under attack scenarios, with deep learning to support understanding of vulnerabilities, threats, and risk. Ali et al. [1] explicitly use the term *smart digital twin* for a vehicle-to-grid cyber-physical security framework, embedding ML-based attack detection and a coordinated response loop directly within the twin. Homaei et al. [16] propose a Causal Digital Twin (CDT) framework that integrates causal inference with DT modelling, reporting high root-cause accuracy and a low false-positive rate on standard industrial security datasets (SWaT, WADI, HAI). In smart-grid systems, Boi and Esposito [3] propose TwinSec-IDS, which uses a DT to verify the physical consistency of network commands. Sayghe [27] reports a DT-driven IDS for SCADA systems with an F1 score of 96.3% and an average detection latency below 500 ms. Somma et al. [29] propose a multi-layer cyber DT framework specifically tailored to cybersecurity for CPS, integrating bidirectional data flows and adaptive service layers. Across this group, the common pattern is the use of the DT as a host for ML-based or RL-based detection system, with strong quantitative results on detection accuracy but no interactive reasoning interface above the detector itself.

3.2 Generative AI in Cybersecurity

Recent surveys cover the rise of Generative AI in cybersecurity [4,13,25]. Beyond synthetic-data generation, LLMs are being developed as assistants for security operations centers and SOC analyst support [13,18]. Application-level studies include Barletta et al. [2], who explore DTs and Generative AI for cybersecurity education, and Ray [24], who combines on-device edge agents with a centralized DT and generative scenario training (EdgeAgentX-DT), using diffusion models and transformers to generate adversarial scenarios within the DT. The cited study reports improved learning convergence and resilience under simultaneous jamming and node failure compared to baseline methods. A complementary line of work studies the safety of LLM-based agents themselves: Kale et al. [17] study the reliable monitoring of LLM agents under adversarial conditions.

3.3 Comparative Synthesis

Related-Work Synthesis. Table 1 summarizes representative DT-based cybersecurity studies across five dimensions: target domain, primary technique, DT integration, validation setting, and reported metrics. Three patterns emerge. First, DT-based ML and RL defenses [1,3,16,27,30] report strong detection performance but provide limited interpretability and remain tied to predefined threat models and labeled training data. Second, LLM-based cybersecurity assistants [13,18] are typically deployed as standalone systems and grounded in generic corpora rather than structured representations of the target infrastructure, making them susceptible to domain-specific hallucinations. Third, when LLMs and DTs are combined [2,24], the LLM is generally used to generate attack scenarios or training data rather than interact with and support operators. The system presented in Sect. 4 occupies this under-explored intersection: an interactive LLM agent grounded in a DT-managed service catalog, currently serving as a decision-support layer and designed for future extension toward autonomous cybersecurity-service orchestration.

4 System Architecture

4.1 Overview

Figure 1 shows the high-level architecture. The Boss Agent sits at the center and coordinates four backend components and a web frontend. The four backend components are: (i) the *LLM Gateway*, which connects to the Ollama runtime and exposes streaming chat and synchronous embed operations; (ii) the *Vector Store*, which holds dense embeddings of service descriptions together with their metadata; (iii) the *RAG Retriever*, which indexes new or updated services and retrieves the top-k most similar entries for a given user query; and (iv) the *Conversation Manager*, which persists multi-turn conversation history. The frontend is the chat interface, which communicates with the Boss Agent. On the data side, service-related write operations issued through the platform trigger an asynchronous re-indexing call so that the vector store reflects the current state of the catalog. The Ollama runtime and the MongoDB/Atlas instance that hosts both the application database and the vector index are external dependencies of the agent.

4.2 Indexing the Platform's Service Catalog

Each service in the platform's catalog is serialized into two distinct text representations, motivated by the differing requirements of retrieval and generation. A *full* representation concatenates all important attributes (short name, title, provider, category, sector, description, type, TRL, license, supported standards, inputs, outputs, and interactions with other services) and is stored alongside the vector as the raw text that is later fed to the LLM as RAG context. A separate *embedding-oriented* representation, used to compute the dense vector, focuses on the service's identity and excludes cross-reference fields, which we found to degrade retrieval quality while remaining valuable as generation context (Sect. 5). The embedding-oriented text is sent to the embedding model with a task prefix where applicable, and retrieval-time metadata is stored alongside both texts.

4.3 Intent Classification

Sending every user message through the RAG pipeline wastes compute and latency on conversational turns that do not require catalog knowledge, while

Table 1. Comparative synthesis of representative DT and AI studies in cybersecurity.

Study	Domain	Technique	DT role	Validation	Reported metrics
Epiphaniou et al. [10]	Port / IoT-CPS	DT + deep learning	Simulation substrate	Case study (Southampton)	Qualitative resilience
Varghese et al. [30]	ICS	DT + behavioural IDS	Reference behaviour model	Simulated ICS attacks	Detection accuracy
Ali et al. [1]	V2G CPS	"Smart DT" + ML detection + response loop	Active defence host	Simulated V2G attacks	Detection accuracy, response time
Homaei et al. [16]	ICS	Causal DT (SCM)	Reasoning model	Public datasets (SWaT, WADI, HAI)	Root-cause accuracy, FPR
Boi & Esposito [3]	Smart grid / SDN	DT + LSTM/CNN	Physical-consistency check	Simulated FDI attacks	Detection accuracy
Sayghe [27]	SCADA	DT + IDS, GenAI for adv. injection	Training environment	Cyber-physical case study	F1, FPR, latency
Ray [24]	Tactical edge networks	DT + diffusion + transformer + RL agents	Training environment	Simulation (jamming, node failure)	Convergence, resilience
Barletta et al. [2]	Cyber education	DT + GenAI	Sandbox environment	Educational scenarios	Qualitative
This work	CI	**Local LLM + RAG over DT-management platform catalog**	**Knowledge source**	**Local prototype + initial evaluation**	**Accuracy, hallucination, latency**

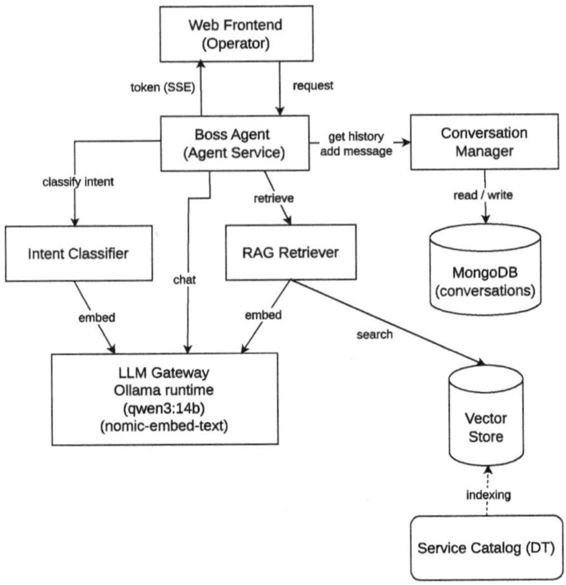

Fig. 1. High-level architecture of the Boss Agent. The agent coordinates four backend components (LLM Gateway, Vector Store, RAG Retriever, Conversation Manager) and exposes a streaming chat interface to the interactive web frontend. The LLM Gateway talks to the local Ollama runtime. The Vector Store and Conversation Manager are backed by MongoDB.

common alternatives such as fine-tuned classifiers or separate small LLMs require labeled data or add model-loading overhead. We instead exploit the embedding model already loaded for retrieval, using two small reference clusters of typical operator and casual exchanges that are embedded once at startup and cached in memory:

- **Service-query cluster**: twelve representative queries drawn from typical operator language about catalog services (e.g. "Tell me about cybersecurity tools for network monitoring.").
- **Casual cluster**: ten conversational exchanges (greetings, farewells).

For each incoming user message, we compute its embedding (a single forward pass through the embedding model, and the same embedding is reused for retrieval if the query is classified as service-related) and obtain the maximum cosine similarity to each cluster. RAG is invoked unless casual similarity exceeds service similarity by a configurable margin δ:

$$\text{useRAG}(q) = \mathbb{1}[\, s_c(q) < s_s(q) + \delta \,], \tag{1}$$

where $s_s(q) = \max_{r \in R_s} \cos(\mathbf{e}(q), \mathbf{e}(r))$ and $s_c(q)$ is defined analogously for the casual cluster R_c, and $\mathbf{e}(\cdot)$ is the embedding function.

Setting $\delta > 0$ biases the classifier toward retrieval, so that borderline queries default to running RAG. We selected $\delta = 0.08$ by inspection during development as the smallest margin that recovered a near-tie pilot query: a service question whose casual-cluster similarity narrowly exceeded its service-cluster similarity, without causing greetings to be misclassified. Unlike absolute similarity thresholds, the margin-based rule depends on the relative proximity of the query to the two clusters, and the same procedure applies unchanged when the embedding model is replaced, although the appropriate value of δ depends on the score distribution of the chosen model (Sect. 5).

4.4 Streaming Response and Source Attribution

Responses are streamed token-by-token from the LLM gateway to the frontend over Server-Sent Events. Once generation begins, the frontend also receives a `sources` event listing the services whose embeddings were retrieved for this turn (with similarity scores), enabling the operator to inspect the origin of the answer and click through to detailed service descriptions.

5 Implementation

The system is implemented in TypeScript with a Node.js/Express backend and a React/Vite frontend. The backend exposes a JWT-authenticated REST API and uses MongoDB both as the application database and, through Atlas's `$vectorSearch` aggregation pipeline, as the vector index. A co-located vector store keeps the deployment footprint minimal, with an alternative Qdrant backend provided for users who prefer it. The Ollama runtime is invoked over its local HTTP API; the chat model (`qwen3:14b`, $\approx$ 9 GB) and the embedding model (`mxbai-embed-large`, $\approx$ 670 MB) must both be pulled to the host, and the agent's `healthCheck` endpoint exposes per-model availability. Table 2 summarizes selected configuration parameters.

Choice of Embedding Model. During evaluation, the retrieval pipeline exhibited noticeable failures with `nomic-embed-text`, a 137M-parameter asymmetric embedding model. Queries directly naming services often failed to retrieve the target service within the top-k results, and similarity scores remained tightly clustered. Several refinements, including the addition of the recommended `search_document` and `search_query` prefixes and the separation of indexed text from LLM-context text (Sect. 4.2), produced only minor improvements. We therefore switched to `mxbai-embed-large`, a 335M-parameter model with a 1024-dimensional embedding space, which consistently ranked the target service first with a clear score gap. These observations suggest that embedding-model selection is a critical design choice in catalog-based RAG systems.

Multi-turn Context Handling. In the early stage, we observed that multi-turn conversations could exhibit a stale-context behavior: when an earlier turn is a casual message and a subsequent turn required fresh retrieval, the LLM occasionally keeps the earlier "no relevant services" phrasing rather than takes the freshly retrieved context. We propose two complementary modifications as solution: (a) the retrieval-context prompt explicitly states that the new context "supersedes any earlier context from the conversation", and (b) the context is injected as a system message immediately before the most recent user turn. This solution was introduced with the choice of embedding model described above. In the evaluation (Sect. 6), we did not observe instances of this failure, so we cannot conclude from the present results which of the three changes is responsible. We therefore keep both modifications in the design of the system.

Prompt Design. The agent is guided by two prompts. The *system prompt* defines its role as a cybersecurity-catalog assistant and instructs it to ground factual claims in retrieved context, refuse unsupported answers, and cite services by their catalog identifiers. The *retrieval-context prompt*, injected immediately before the latest user turn, contains the top-k retrieved service entries together with an instruction that this context supersedes earlier conversation context. Entries are serialized as structured records with explicit field names to facilitate grounding. The complete prompts and retrieval template are available in the public source repository.

6 Evaluation

This first phase prioritizes a complete, working pipeline together with an initial empirical evaluation that quantifies the contribution of grounding and the its cost.

6.1 Test Set

We constructed a small evaluation test set of 30 questions over the platform's cybersecurity service catalog. The set is divided into four categories:

- **Factual** (10 questions): queries with a single ground-truth answer derivable from a service field, e.g., "What license does service X use?".
- **Comparative** (8 questions): queries that require summarizing information across multiple services, e.g., "Which services from provider Y support anomaly detection?".
- **Adversarial** (6 questions): queries about services or attributes that do not exist in the catalog, used to test hallucination resistance.
- **Casual** (6 questions): conversational exchanges used to evaluate the intent classifier.

Table 2. Selected configuration parameters of the Boss Agent.

Parameter	Value	Rationale
Chat model	`qwen3:14b`	Largest instruction-tuned open-source model that fits on a 32 GB Apple-silicon laptop while still leaving headroom for the embedding model and the application stack.
Embedding model	`mxbai-embed-large` (1024-d)	Open-source sentence embedder; preliminary tests showed it ranked the target service first with a clear similarity score gap, unlike the smaller `nomic-embed-text` that we initially used (see paragraph "Choice of embedding model").
`NUM_PREDICT`	768	Empirically chosen to avoid mid-sentence truncation on comparative answers while balancing with latency.
`NUM_CTX`	4096	Fits the system prompt, retrieved RAG context for $k=4$, and several turns of conversation history.
`TEMPERATURE`	0.2	Low but non-zero, biasing the model toward deterministic factual outputs while still allowing some natural language variation.
Top-k retrieval	4	Sufficient to cover most single service and small comparative queries; higher values increase context window pressure and answer latency without improving accuracy in our tests.
Casual margin δ	0.08	Selected by inspection during development as the smallest margin that prevented a target service from a direct query from being routed away from retrieval. Section 4.3 discusses how this value depends on the embedding model.

Ground-truth answers were derived directly from the service catalog, which is the authentic source of record for the platform: factual and comparative questions were answered from one or more service fields, and adversarial questions were designed to refer to services or attributes that do not appear in the catalog. The author manually constructed and curated each question-answer pair, cross-checking the expected answer against the corresponding catalog entries. We acknowledge that an independent multi-annotator review would strengthen the reliability of the test set, particularly for the comparative subset where multiple correct phrasings are possible, and we identify this as future work as the test set scales.

6.2 Baselines and Metrics

We compare the full grounded system (**RAG**) against a no-retrieval baseline (**Cold-LLM**) that uses the same chat model with the same system prompt but no retrieved context. Both configurations were executed on the same machine, on the same day, with identical parameters.

We report the following metrics. *Factual accuracy* is the percentage of factual and comparative questions for which the answer matches the ground truth, graded manually by the authors against a checklist. *Hallucination rate* is the percentage of answers that contain at least one claim not supported by the catalog, including any answer to an adversarial question that fails to refuse. *Latency* is end-to-end time from query submission to the last generated token. *Intent classifier* performance is summarized by accuracy on the casual/service split and by a confusion matrix.

6.3 Setup

Measurements were obtained on an Apple Silicon laptop with an M-series chip and 32 GB of unified memory. Both Ollama and the application ran locally on the same machine and no external services were used. To control for run-to-run variance in token streaming, every question was issued $r = 3$ times, separated into three independent runs over the full test set and both configurations, and median latencies are reported. A pair of warm-up queries (one with RAG, one without) was run before timing began to ensure that the chat and embedding models were loaded.

6.4 Factual Accuracy and Hallucination

Table 3 reports the accuracy and hallucination of the agent on the factual, comparative, and adversarial subsets.

The grounded RAG configuration answers every factual question correctly (30 of 30 across three runs) and refuses every adversarial query, while the Cold-LLM baseline using the same chat model with no retrieved context refuses every factual and comparative query. The 100-point gap on factual accuracy is the

Table 3. Answer quality (%) on the 24 quality-graded questions (10 factual + 8 comparative + 6 adversarial), averaged over three independent runs.

Metric	Cold-LLM	RAG
Factual accuracy	0.0%	**100.0%**
Comparative accuracy	0.0%	**62.5%**
Adversarial refusal rate	100.0%	100.0%
Hallucination rate	0.0%	0.0%

strongest evidence of the grounding contribution and is consistent with the design hypothesis that the digital-twin management platform's service catalog can serve as a knowledge-grounded reasoning substrate.

Two observations are worth highlighting. First, both configurations achieved a hallucination rate of 0% in our evaluation. The Cold-LLM baseline declined to answer questions outside its knowledge, while the RAG configuration answered them correctly when relevant context was retrieved. This suggests that, in our setting, the primary contribution of RAG is improved accuracy rather than reduced hallucination, as it converts refusals into correct answers. However, this observation is based on a small test set (30 questions) and may not generalize to larger or adversarial evaluations (Sect. 7).

Second, comparative accuracy (62.5%) was substantially lower than factual accuracy. Most errors occurred when the ground-truth answer contained more services than the retrieval limit k could return (e.g., seven services with $k = 4$). In these cases, answers were generally correct but incomplete and were graded as partial. Addressing this limitation will require a category-aware retrieval policy, as discussed in Sect. 7.

6.5 Intent Classifier Performance

Table 4 reports the confusion matrix of the embedding-margin classifier on the union of the casual and service-query subsets, with $\delta = 0.08$. False positives mean casual queries need retrieval and false negatives mean service queries bypass retrieval.

Table 4. Intent classifier confusion matrix at $\delta = 0.08$ in three runs ($n = 90$ RAG rows: 72 service, 18 casual).

	Predicted: casual	Predicted: service
Actual: casual	18	0
Actual: service	0	72

The classifier achieved 100% accuracy on this test set. We attribute this result to the wider similarity-score margins produced by `mxbai-embed-large`, which were not observed with the smaller `nomic-embed-text` model. This outcome is consistent with the margin-based decision rule, which defaults borderline cases to retrieval to favor correctness over latency savings. However, the test set is small and does not contain borderline cases, so a larger-scale evaluation can reveal misclassifications. Therefore, a δ -sweep is planned as part of future quality retrieval evaluation to assess the sensitivity of the classifier.

6.6 Latency

Table 5 reports end-to-end latency in seconds by question category and configuration. Each cell reports the median and the 95th-percentile in three independent runs of the full test set.

Table 5. End-to-end latency in seconds on the laptop setup, median (p95), over three runs.

Category	RAG		Cold-LLM	
	median	p95	median	p95
Factual ($n = 30$)	39.7	61.8	36.1	69.1
Comparative ($n = 24$)	59.6	108.7	42.7	71.6
Adversarial ($n = 18$)	51.0	85.2	38.6	52.1
Casual ($n = 18$)	32.0	64.7	32.3	62.2

The LLM inference speed accounts for most of the latency of each turn. This is supported by the Cold-LLM baseline, which has no retrieval pipeline: on factual queries it still takes a median $\approx$ 36 s end-to-end (Table 5), of which most of the time can be attributed to LLM inference speed. The full RAG pipeline adds an additional median $\approx$ 3.6 s on the same category, a roughly one-tenth of LLM generation. RAG turns are systematically slower than Cold-LLM turns on the categories where answers with RAG are longer (factual, comparative, adversarial), while on casual questions the two configurations have almost the same answer time. This is consistent with the intent classifier correctly skipping retrieval on those queries. We anticipate that on a server-grade GPU, the same workload would complete considerably faster. Measuring this reduction is part of the planned deployment on the GPU server.

7 Discussion and Limitations

The Initial Evaluation is Promising; Open Questions Remain. The evaluation reported in Sect. 6 is an encouraging first step: in our test set, the agent correctly answered all factual queries using RAG, and the intent classifier perfectly separated casual and service queries. However, these results remain preliminary, as the test set is small (30 questions over a 45-service catalog) and was constructed and labeled by the first author. Several questions remain open, including comparison against a stronger commercial LLM baseline, systematic evaluation of `mxbai-embed-large` against other open-source embedding models, a larger-scale δ-sweep for the intent classifier (Sect. 4.3), independent multi-annotator review of the test set, and adoption of a standardized RAG evaluation framework such as RAGAS [11]. These directions are left for future work.

The Agent is Grounded in the Catalog, not Yet in the Live DT. At this stage, the agent relies on the structured service catalog maintained by the digital-twin management platform and does not yet exploit dynamic DT dimensions such as topology, traffic, runtime state, or physics-based system models. Future work will extend the agent from catalog grounding to full DT grounding and use the DT as a sandbox in which proposed actions can be validated before deployment to production infrastructure. Bridging the reality gap between physical systems and their digital counterparts, including effects such as thermal behavior and component degradation, will likely require complementing data-driven models with physics-informed approaches such as physics-informed neural networks [9].

The Absence of Observed Hallucination is not a General Claim. Our evaluation reports a hallucination rate of 0% on 30 questions in a 45-service catalog. We do not claim that the system is hallucination-free in general, rather, the Cold-LLM baseline's tendency to refuse rather than fabricate, combined with the small test-set size and the narrow operator-assistant role, plausibly explains the absence of observed errors. A larger and adversarial test set is required before any stronger claim can be made.

Dense Retrieval Over Short Identifiers is Prone to Error. The choice of embedding models (Sect. 5) revealed that smaller embedding models can fail to discriminate between catalog entries when queries refer to services by short hyphenated identifiers in the catalog, because such identifiers are fragmented by the tokenizer into low semantic subtokens. Changing to a stronger embedding model resolved this in our deployment, although further evaluation is required to determine whether the model robustly handles such identifier-based queries.

Top- k Retrieval Bounds Comparative-Query Coverage. As discussed in the qualitative observations of Sect. 6, a fixed retrieval k limits the system's ability to enumerate exhaustive lists. A category-aware retrieval policy, such as a higher k for queries detected as "list all ..." patterns, would address this without increasing costs on simple look-ups.

Latency on Local Hardware is High. Median end-to-end response times of approximately 32 s on casual turns and 40–60 s on RAG-grounded turns (Table 5) on a laptop are acceptable for the present use case but will not scale to multi-agent incident response, where several agents may be invoked sequentially per event. Potential mitigations explored in the multi-agent phase (Sect. 8) include hierarchical model sizing, parallel fast and slow agents, and human-in-the-loop validation as a deliberate safety feature.

The Intent Classifier's Reference Clusters are Manually Selected. While the margin-based decision rule is robust to small embedding variations, the choice of reference exchanges is a manual design decision that may not be generalized across deployments. We plan to investigate clustering-based or supervised alternatives.

Failure Modes a Larger Test Set is Likely to Expose. The current test set covers questions whose surface form closely tracks the catalog fields, but several failure modes are likely to appear once the set is broadened. (i) *Negation queries*: questions of the form "which services do *not* support X" are difficult both for the retriever, as it still retrieves the services that support X, and for the LLM, which must reason over the complement of the retrieved set. (ii) *Comparative queries targeting multiple services* that exceed k services (Sect. 6). We plan to construct subsets targeting each of these modes for the next round of evaluation.

Evaluation of the Benefits for Security. The metrics reported in Sect. 6 (factual accuracy, hallucination rate, latency) are metrics for RAG quality: they measure that the agent answers correctly and on time, but not that it provides a noticeable *security* benefit. The more security-oriented evaluation would measure, for example: operator's time to select a tool correctly compared with a manual catalog search, or the rate at which the agent's insight leads operators to consult the correct catalog entries. Defining these metrics and running an operator-in-the-loop study against them is necessary for next steps.

Security of the Digital Twin Itself. As several authors have noted [7,15,28], the DT itself or the platform managing it is a high-value target: it contains the configurations and defense logic of the protected infrastructure, and a compromised twin could be used by an attacker to optimize attacks against the real system. Thus, in our deployment the platform is behind authenticated endpoints and the LLM never has write access to physical infrastructure.

8 Conclusion and Future Work

We have presented the initial step of a multi-agent LLM system in a DT for cybersecurity: a knowledge-grounded *Boss Agent* embedded in a digital-twin management platform, which retrieves information from the platform's service catalog to answer operator queries, runs entirely on local infrastructure for data privacy, and incorporates a lightweight embedding-based intent classifier that avoids retrieval overhead on conversational turns. Initial empirical results show that the grounded configuration answers all factual queries correctly while a no-retrieval baseline using the same chat model refuses uniformly. Both configurations achieved a zero hallucination rate on our test set, at the cost of a modest latency overhead that is dominated by LLM generation rather than retrieval.

The future work is organized around three research questions that are produced directly on the present system. **RQ1.** *Can a digital twin serve as* *a knowledge-grounded reasoning environment for cybersecurity agents?* Subsequent work will scale the test set, run additional evaluation (with a stronger commercial LLM, a keyword-retrieval baseline, alternative embedding models), and extend the agent's knowledge source from the platform's catalog to the runtime telemetry of a deployed DT. **RQ2.** *Can LLM-driven agents perform automated deployment and configuration of cybersecurity services within a digital twin, and how does their reliability compare to manual deployment?* The next phase introduces an *Installer Agent* that uses the platform's deployment pipeline to deploy and configure services in a DT sandbox before any change is applied to the real infrastructure. **RQ3.** *How does a multi-agent architecture with human-in-the-loop control perform for incident response in critical infrastructure?* The final phase combines specialized agents (monitor, mitigator, installer) under the Boss Agent's coordination, with human supervisor, and evaluates the trade-off between response speed and decision quality against fully manual and fully automated baselines.

By answering these three research questions, we plan to build a *smart digital twin*: a system in which the digital twin plays three complementary roles, which are knowledge base, deployment sandbox, and experimentation platform; as well as a coordinated multi-agent LLM layer provides knowledge-grounded reasoning, sandboxed deployment, and human-supervised incident response within a coherent environment. The Boss Agent presented in this paper is the initial step toward that goal.

Acknowledgments. This research was supported by the European Union through the Horizon Europe projects INTACT (No. 101168438) and SECASSURED (No. 101225858). Views and opinions expressed are however those of the authors only and do not necessarily reflect those of the European Union or the granting authority. Neither the European Union nor the granting authority can be held responsible for them.

Disclosure of Interests. This work was carried out in the context of a CIFRE doctoral program in partnership with Montimage, which develops the digital-twin management platform studied in this article. The authors have no other competing interests to declare relevant to the content of this article.

References

1. Ali, M., Kaddoum, G., Li, W.T., Yuen, C., Tariq, M., Poor, H.V.: A smart digital twin enabled security framework for vehicle-to-grid cyber-physical systems. IEEE Trans. Inf. Foren. Secur. **18**, 5258–5271 (2023). https://doi.org/10.1109/TIFS.2023.3305916
2. Barletta, V.S., Bavaro, V., Calvano, M., Curci, A., Piccinno, A., Posa, D.P.: Enabling cyber security education through digital twins and generative AI (2025). arXiv:2507.17518 arXiv preprint
3. Boi, B., Esposito, C.: A digital twin network for proactive security: the smart grid use-case. In: 2025 55th Annual IEEE/IFIP International Conference on Dependable Systems and Networks Workshops (DSN-W), pp. 152–159. IEEE (2025)

4. Coppolino, L., D'Antonio, S., Mazzeo, G., Uccello, F.: The good, the bad, and the algorithm: the impact of generative ai on cybersecurity. Neurocomputing **623**, 129406 (2025)
5. Digital Twin Consortium: Digital twin consortium defines digital twin (2020). https://www.digitaltwinconsortium.org/2020/12/digital-twin-consortium-defines-digital-twin/
6. Dihan, M.S., Akash, A.I., Tasneem, Z., et al.: Digital twin: data exploration, architecture, implementation and future. Heliyon **10**(5), e26503 (2024)
7. Eckhart, M., Ekelhart, A.: Digital twins for cyber-physical systems security: state of the art and outlook. In: Security and Privacy in Cyber-Physical Systems, pp. 383–412. Springer (2019)
8. El-Hajj, M., Itäpelto, T., Gebremariam, T.: Systematic literature review: Digital twins' role in enhancing security for industry 4.0 applications. Secur. Priv. **7**(5), e396 (2024)
9. Emmert-Streib, F., Tripathi, S., Farea, A., Holzinger, A.: Implementing physics-informed neural networks with deep learning for differential equations. Front. Artif. Intell. **9** (2026). https://doi.org/10.3389/frai.2026.1717117
10. Epiphaniou, G., Hammoudeh, M., Yuan, H., Maple, C., Ani, U.: Digital twins in cyber effects modelling of IoT/CPS points of low resilience. Simul. Model. Pract. Theory **125**, 102744 (2023)
11. Es, S., James, J., Espinosa-Anke, L., Schockaert, S.: Ragas: automated evaluation of retrieval-augmented generation (2025). https://arxiv.org/abs/2309.15217
12. European Commission: The NIS2 directive. https://digital-strategy.ec.europa.eu/en/policies/nis2-directive (2023). Accessed 14 May 2026
13. Ferrag, M.A., et al.: Generative ai in cybersecurity: a comprehensive review of LLM applications and vulnerabilities. Int. Things Cyber-Phy. Syst. **5** (2025)
14. Fuller, A., Fan, Z., Day, C., Barlow, C.: Digital twin: enabling technologies, challenges and open research. IEEE Access **8**, 108952–108971 (2020)
15. Homaei, M., Mogollón-Gutiérrez, Ó., Sancho, J., et al.: A review of digital twins and their application in cybersecurity based on artificial intelligence. Artif. Intell. Rev. **57**, 201 (2024)
16. Homaei, M., Tarif, M., Rodriguez, P.G., Caro, A., Avila, M.: Causal digital twins for cyber-physical security: a framework for robust anomaly detection in industrial control systems (2025). arXiv:2510.09616 arXiv preprint
17. Kale, N., Zhang, C.B.C., Zhu, K., Aich, A., Rodriguez, P., Team, S.R.: Reliable weak-to-strong monitoring of LLM agents (2025). arXiv:2508.19461 arXiv preprint
18. Karras, A., Theodorakopoulos, L., Karras, C., Theodoropoulou, A., Kalliampakou, I., Kalogeratos, G.: LLMs for cybersecurity in the big data era: a comprehensive review of applications, challenges, and future directions. Information **16**(11), 957 (2025)
19. Kritzinger, W., Karner, M., Traar, G., Henjes, J., Sihn, W.: Digital twin in manufacturing: a categorical literature review and classification. IFAC-PapersOnLine **51**(11), 1016–1022 (2018)
20. Lewis, P., et al.: Retrieval-augmented generation for knowledge-intensive NLP tasks. In: Advances in Neural Information Processing Systems, vol. 33, pp. 9459–9474. Curran Associates, Inc. (2020)
21. Mixedbread ai: mxbai-embed-large-v1. https://huggingface.co/mixedbread-ai/mxbai-embed-large-v1 (2024). embedding model
22. Ollama: Ollama. https://ollama.com (2025). Accessed 14 May 2026

23. Patel, H., Akbarfam, A.J., Maleki, H.: A survey on digital twin: from industrial applications to cybersecurity. In: 2024 IEEE Smart World Congress (SWC), pp. 2111–2118. IEEE (2024)
24. Ray, A.: EdgeAgentX-DT: integrating digital twins and generative AI for resilient edge intelligence in tactical networks (2025). arXiv:2507.21196 arXiv preprint
25. Sai, S., Yashvardhan, U., Chamola, V., Sikdar, B.: Generative AI for cyber security: analyzing the potential of ChatGPT, DALL-e and other models for enhancing the security space. IEEE Access, p. 1 (2024)
26. Salvi, A., Spagnoletti, P., Noori, N.S.: Cyber-resilience of critical cyber infrastructures: integrating digital twins in the electric power ecosystem. Comput. Sec. **112**, 102507 (2022)
27. Sayghe, A.: Digital twin-driven intrusion detection for industrial Scada: a cyber-physical case study. Sensors **25**(16), 4963 (2025)
28. Sekione, R.J., El Azzaoui, A., Xiong, N.N., Park, J.H.: A comprehensive survey of digital twins: Applications, technologies and security challenges. J. Syst. Architect. **151**, 103120 (2024)
29. Somma, A., Casola, V., Cavalli, A.R., De Benedictis, A., Mallouli, W., Valdés, V.E.: A cyber digital twin framework to support cyber-physical systems security. In: 2023 IEEE Smart World Congress (SWC), pp. 1–10. IEEE (2023)
30. Varghese, S.A., Dehlaghi-Ghadim, A., Balador, A., Alimadadi, Z., Papadimitratos, P.: Digital twin-based intrusion detection for industrial control systems. In: 2022 IEEE International Conference on Pervasive Computing and Communications Workshops and Other Affiliated Events (PerCom Workshops). pp. 611–617. IEEE (2022). https://doi.org/10.1109/PerComWorkshops53856.2022.9767492
31. Vaswani, A., et al.: Attention is all you need. In: Advances in Neural Information Processing Systems, vol. 30, Curran Associates, Inc (2017)
32. Wang, Y., Su, Z., Guo, S., Dai, M., Luan, T.H., Liu, Y.: A survey on digital twins: architecture, enabling technologies, security and privacy, and future prospects. IEEE Int. Things J. **10**(17), 14965–14987 (2023)
33. Yang, A., et al.: Qwen3 technical report (2025). https://arxiv.org/abs/2505.09388

AMTD-EC: An Adaptive Moving Target Defense Framework for Edge-Cloud Systems

Daniele Iorio[1,2](✉) and Alessandra De Benedictis[1]

[1] Department of Electrical Engineering and Information Technologies, University of Naples Federico II, Naples, Italy
{daniele.iorio2,alessandra.debenedictis}@unina.it

[2] Department of Management, Information, and Production Engineering, University of Bergamo, Bergamo, Italy
daniele.iorio@unibg.it

Abstract. Distributed Edge-Cloud systems offer scalable, flexible, and modular infrastructure but introduce significant security challenges due to heterogeneity, decentralized data processing, expanded attack surfaces, and the difficulty of enforcing consistent protections across dynamic and resource-constrained environments. Traditional security mechanisms are not well suited to cope with these systems as they assume stable infrastructures and predictable threat models. On the other hand, Moving Target Defense (MTD) offers a proactive approach by continuously reconfiguring system parameters, reducing the attack surface and increasing uncertainty and complexity for adversaries. Nonetheless, the existing techniques for distributed environments have limited practical integration into real systems due to the complexity of systems and mechanisms. In addition, they target specific technologies or isolated mechanisms, lacking modularity and unified orchestration strategies. In this paper we present AMTD-EC, a novel adaptive MTD framework tailored to distributed infrastructures built upon container-based technologies following a threat modeling methodology. The framework leverages specific monitoring rules to enable automated detection of attacks, and includes automated selection and enforcement of adaptive response to ongoing attacks by the activation of suitable MTD mechanisms from a pool. By abstracting and orchestrating heterogeneous defense mechanisms within a unified architecture, AMTD-EC enables the scalable deployment and streamlined management of security measures across distributed Edge-Cloud environments. The experimental evaluation conducted on a Kubernetes-based testbed shows low mitigation latency and negligible system overhead when simulating realistic attack scenarios, enhancing system resiliency against dynamic threats.

Keywords: Moving Target Defense · Edge-Cloud Computing · Kubernetes · Intrusion Detection · Adaptive Security · Cyber Resiliency

P. Kieseberg et al. (Eds.): ARES 2026 Workshops, LNCS 16903, pp. 624–643, 2027.
https://doi.org/10.1007/978-3-032-37218-5_36

1 Introduction

Distributed Edge-Cloud systems are increasingly being adopted to provide scalable and robust infrastructure that dynamically adapts to environments, granting flexibility and modularity to the system. The heterogeneity of the components and data sources are the first challenges to be addressed.

These characteristics also have the drawback of enlarging the attack surface and introducing complex security issues. In fact, the distribution of computation and data across a wide range of heterogeneous, resource-constrained, and often physically exposed devices often leads to inconsistent security controls and patching, while the decentralized and sensitive nature of edge data increases exposure during processing and transmission. Additionally, deployment in uncontrolled environments and complex, dynamic orchestration make it harder to enforce uniform security policies, creating more entry points and opportunities for compromise. Due to limited computational power and storage capacity, these systems are susceptible to several threats [12], not only at the physical (e.g., HW and firmware), network and application levels, but also at the data level, where data leakage and breaches are more frequent since highly sensitive and contextual data (e.g., location, video, health, industrial signals) are processed locally and can be accessed or inferred directly at the source. Moreover, cloud integration in Edge-Cloud systems introduces additional threats because it extends trust boundaries and creates new interfaces between distributed components.

Traditional security solutions struggle to cope with the dynamic and large-scale nature of these systems as they assume relatively stable infrastructures and predictable threat models. Innovative approaches such as the **Moving Target Defense (MTD)** paradigm introduce proactive and dynamic reconfiguration strategies aimed at increasing uncertainty for attackers [17]. The activation is subject to a trigger (time or event-based), enhancing *security* and *resilience* of such systems, granting anticipation, withstand, and recovery from, and adapt to adverse events [7,10]. Crucial challenges are determining *what*, *how* and *when* a specific technique (or a combination of) should be enforced to thwart an attack [15].

In the literature, several studies propose different MTD techniques to cope with different types of threats. Their main classification depends on *how* the movement is realized and entails Shuffling, Diversity, and Redundancy [15]: i) *Shuffling* dynamically alters configurations (e.g., IPs, ports) to hinder scanning and enumeration, with relatively low cost and overhead. ii) *Diversity* uses different components to perform the same function, increasing resilience but requiring additional resources. iii) *Redundancy* replicates components to ensure continuity in case of failure, improving availability at the cost of higher resource usage. The choice of *what* to change depends on the system layer involved (e.g., network, OS, architecture), while *when* to apply changes is context-dependent and driven by system requirements and security needs, with no universal rule.

Common strategies include event-driven responses to attacks, risk-adaptive decisions based on real-time threats, and context-aware approaches that consider workload and system state. These are often combined with periodic mechanisms, and modern systems use hybrid, adaptive methods to adjust actions based on attacker behaviour and past data.

In practice, although there are several MTD strategies and techniques for distributed systems [9,16], their integration into real systems is still limited due to the specificity of each proposal and the variety of technologies addressed by existing implementations, hindering the full exploitation of the MTD [5].

In order to cope with this issue, our main contribution is the proposal of an adaptive rule-based MTD framework namely **AMTD-EC** targeted at Edge-Cloud systems, able to trigger reconfigurations upon the detection of anomalies by a real-time monitoring system. The novelty of our proposal lies in the *tailoring* of the framework following a threat modeling methodology that enables us to fine-tune both the monitoring rules and the enforced MTD techniques. Furthermore, we propose 4 evaluation metrics to validate the performance of the framework.

To demonstrate our approach, we discuss an implementation that leverages on the *Falco* ecosystem[1] of tools and components for anomaly detection and mitigation enforcement automation. We conducted an experimental evaluation on a Kubernetes-based simple Cloud application, for which a set of customized monitoring rules and MTD-oriented enforcement actions were implemented. Our evaluation proved the effectiveness of the framework and its concrete feasibility thanks to its low mitigation latency and negligible system overhead under simulated attack scenarios.

This work is structured as follows: Sect. 2 will provide an overview of the related work on the topic exploring the existing proposed technologies in the literature. Section 3 describes the methodology used in the definition of the framework, while Sect. 4 describes the test case environment and the framework implementation. Section 5 will provide the evaluation and results of the study while Sect. 6 will discuss their relevance. Section 7 will draw some conclusions and provide direction about future works.

2 Related Work

In this section, the investigation of the existing frameworks proposed in the literature is presented, to determine the state-of-the-art and define the research gap that needs to be filled. The currently available studies propose a few different solutions for MTD frameworks, ranging from IoT to cloud systems and showing how different architectures are affected by different challenges.

Von der Assen et al. [1] focus the analysis on IoT devices, proposing an autonomous framework composed of four MTD mechanisms changing their network, data, and runtime environment to mitigate multi-purpose malware. Since the goal is to enhance the security of the single device, due to its limited resource capabilities (memory, CPU, RAM), the main issue is to define the framework as lightweight as possible to be installed on the device itself. The novelty relies

[1] https://falco.org/about/ecosystem/.

on the use of two modules supporting the decisions about "*when*" the techniques must be enforced. The first one relies on the introduction of a lightweight Machine Learning algorithm that analyses the data and behaviour of the device, while the second one relies on the generation of alarms based on action or time rules. The main drawback of this framework is its limited applicability outside the IoT environment but, as the data show, it is quite efficient and effective in mitigating various malware like backdoor C&C, rootkit and ransomware encryption.

Another framework proposal implemented in JAVA and applicable in a cloud environment based on Kubernetes is proposed by Casola et al. [4]. Within the framework, four different techniques were implemented: *IP Shuffling* (continuously updates the IP address of a pod), *Node Migration* (migrating pods to different nodes), *Dynamic Replica* (changes the number of pod clones), and *Service Account Shuffling*. These techniques are quite simple and are connected to the network and application architectural level but, despite their simplicity and as shown in the results section, they contribute to improving the overall system's security without adding a relevant overhead. The main drawback of this work is that MTD technique activation is manual, and does not fully comply with the dynamism required for MTD purposes.

Kashkoush et al. [6] focus on the analysis of Linux containers since they offer lightweight virtualization and isolated execution. This work presents a resilient intrusion detection and resolution system for cloud-based containers. It relies on a real-time smart behaviour monitoring mechanism to detect malicious containers, and a moving target defence approach that applies runtime container migration to quarantine malicious ones. Furthermore, it also induces random live migrations between running containers to obfuscate their execution behaviour. The system was tested by a big-data application based on an Apache Hadoop cluster. The innovation of this approach relies on the introduction of live migration or roll back of the malicious container to a safe and secure state.

Soussi et al. [13,14] describe a novel framework (namely MERLINS) applied on a 5G testbed. It performs both reactive and proactive detection and mitigation by avoiding reconnaissance and attack or planning and modifying the network as a counterattack or to restore infected parts. It collects monitoring data and risk values and uses them to support an AI-aided decision module (using Multi-Objective Markov Decision Process) connected to a decision optimizer (OptSFC). The novelty of this work relies on the use of AI to make optimal decisions about the MTD techniques (hard/soft depending on the architectural level involved) to enforce when an attack occurs.

Finally, Bagheri et al. [2,3] focus on the analysis of container clusters orchestrated by Kubernetes. In these works, the use of a real-time cloud-oriented security monitoring system, namely Falco, is discussed. The authors argue that automatically reacting to every alert can cause service interruptions due to false positives leading to manual validation. Hence, they propose the use of a proactive and non-disruptive incident response mechanism (ACEWARP) activating mitigation based on predicted (rather than confirmed) attacks. It is non-disruptive because it uses live container migration as a mitigation strategy, avoiding service interruptions even in the presence of false positives. The novelty of this approach relies in the use of a cloud monitoring system that allows fast detection, integrated analysis, and low overhead in threat response.

In this paper, we extend the work done in [4] by adding a mechanism to automatically select and activate suitable MTD techniques based on the alerts generated by a monitoring system. We adopt a lightweight monitoring system and an integrated and non-disruptive mechanism to automate the enforcement of MTD, both based on the Falco ecosystem. The main difference between our work and [2,3] is that we propose a framework based on open source technologies that are cloud-oriented, highly modular and accessible to security engineers, not just researchers.

3 Proposed Methodology and Framework

In this section, we describe the methodology proposed for configuring the AMTD-EC framework, designed to be *tailored* to the specific requirements of the system under analysis. In particular, the framework is intended to autonomously activate the most appropriate MTD techniques according to the alerts produced by a monitoring system that has been properly configured through a tailored threat-monitoring process.

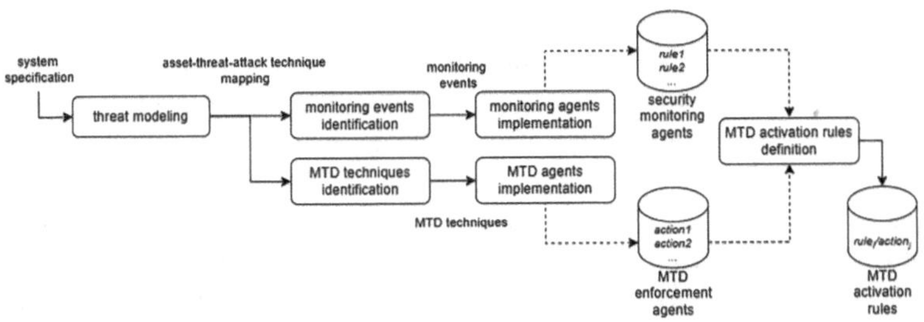

Fig. 1. Proposed methodology: set-up of the AMTD-EC framework.

Figure 1 sketches the methodology followed for the set-up/tailoring of the AMTD-EC framework. Let us assume we have a system under analysis to secure. Our methodology is devised to conduct a first step of **threat modeling** based on the system specification; this activity can be carried out either by hand or with the support of a plenty of automated or semi-automated tools such as Microsoft Threat Modeling Tool, Irius Risk, OWASP Threat Dragon, and so on. In our approach, the threat modeling step not only requires the identification of high-level threats, but also the extraction of associated information that can help concretely characterize the threat realization scenario, such as vulnerabilities, weaknesses or attack techniques associated with the high-level threats that can be derived from existing frameworks such as the popular

Mitre CWE and ATT&CK projects. This information, represented by a mapping $< asset - threat - attack\_technique >$, helps us identify, in the following steps, both the specific **monitoring events** to detect in order to flag ongoing attacks and the actual **MTD techniques** to enforce in order to counteract these attacks. Based on these high-level information, suitable agents can be designed and implemented both for monitoring and security enforcement in the two subsequent steps. Clearly, **agents implementation** steps depend on the actual technologies adopted to develop the AMTD-EC framework; later on we will show an example based on Falco. Independently of the adopted technology, the goal is to build, on the one hand, ad-hoc monitoring rules to detect possible ongoing attacks realizing identified threats and, on the other hand, suitable rules/actions to mitigate the same threats. After this process, the **MTD activation rules definition** step is responsible for establishing a mapping between monitoring rules $rule_i$ and MTD techniques mtd_j, in order to enable the automated activation based on the current conditions.

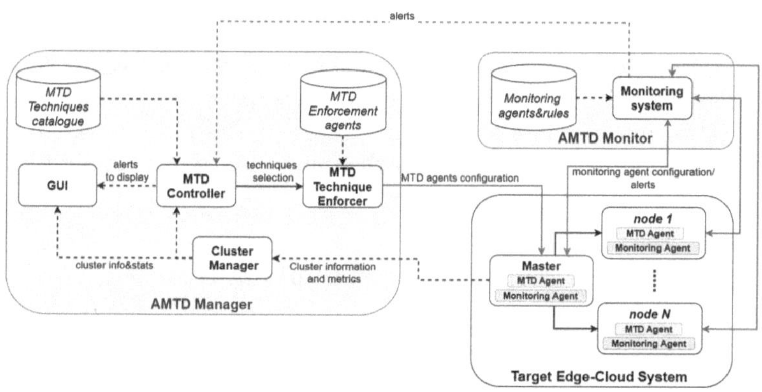

Fig. 2. High-Level AMTD-EC Framework architecture.

Figure 2 provides a high-level view of the proposed AMTD-EC framework. As shown, the framework includes two main subsystems plus some specific agents deployed within the target application under analysis. The latter, in particular, is assumed to be composed of different software modules that are deployed onto several nodes forming a **cluster**; the cluster, as usually happens in common distributed deployments, includes one master node and N worker or edge nodes where the actual target application modules are deployed. As shown, the target distributed system nodes are instrumented with suitable **monitoring agents** that collect and process data both locally (on the worker nodes) and globally (on the master node). Monitoring rules are defined and enforced within the **AMTD Monitor** sub-system, which configures the agents and collects the alerts generated, forwarding them to the **AMTD Manager**.

As shown in Fig. 2, the application nodes also host specific **MTD agents**, which enable them to perform different reconfiguration actions based on the instructions provided by the **MTD Technique Enforcer** component belonging to the AMTD Manager. As discussed, monitoring rules and agent configuration directly depend on the output of a threat modeling process during the framework set-up. Within the AMTD-EC framework Manager, the **MTD Controller** is responsible for identifying and activating suitable MTD techniques from the **MTD Catalogue** based on the actual security monitoring events coming from the monitoring system deployed in the target application and based on the knowledge of the target system.

Finally, generated alerts and other information on the target cluster status (provided by e **Cluster Information Provider**) can be made available to external users by means of a **GUI** (for example to enable the manual configuration and activation of specific agents).

4 Case Study Application and Framework Implementation

In this section we discuss the implementation of the proposed AMTD-EC framework by first introducing the target *case study application* used to demonstrate the framework operation. Then, we discuss the software and tools leveraged for the instantiation of the high-level components of the framework described in Fig. 2. Finally, we illustrate the steps of the methodology provided in Fig. 1 with respect to the case study target application.

4.1 The Case Study Application: A Banking App

As anticipated, the **target application** considered in our implementation is a microservice-based application made of several software modules deployed onto the nodes of a Kubernetes cluster. Kubernetes is a containerized orchestration platform commonly used to manage distributed systems granting security, scalability, resilience, and modularity. Our target application is deployed onto a cluster of 3 nodes: one master in charge of managing the whole infrastructure and two workers on which applications can be deployed[2]. In particular, we considered a simple banking application (**banking app** in the following) allowing user registration and authentication, balance view, payments, and transaction chronology report generation. The *frontend* (network and connection security management, logging, rate limiting, and URI rewriting) and *database* (stores user access and balance information) are deployed on worker 1, while the *backend* (manages the access to the database) is deployed on worker 2[3].

In order to carry out a realistic design of the banking app, we adopted the taxonomy proposed in the Kubernetes OWASP Top 10[4] and NIST SP 800-53

[2] https://anonymous.4open.science/r/MTD-Framework-6068/Setups/How_to_kubernetes.md.

[3] https://anonymous.4open.science/r/MTD-Framework-6068/Setups/Bank_setup.md.

[4] https://owasp.org/www-project-kubernetes-top-ten/.

Rev.5 [8] to identify some baseline security controls to integrate within the application, such as input validation & sanitization, secure password management, and network segmentation[5].

4.2 AMTD-EC Framework Implementation

The **AMTD Monitor** and the main components of the **AMTD Manager** (i.e., the *MTD Controller* and *MTD technique Enforcer* of Fig. 2) were implemented by relying upon the components and tools available in the Falco ecosystem[6]. Falco is a Cloud Native Foundation incubating an open-source project that provides real-time security for cloud-native environments by detecting anomalous system and container behaviour using kernel event monitoring and rules. It is composed of three main parts: i) **Falco**, a rule-based probe installed on each node of a cluster providing alerts when anomalies occur, ii) **Falco Sidekick**, an optional proxy that receives HTTP messages from the probes, provides an informative web UI to visualize them, and allows the forwarding of the alerts to different subsystems, and iii) **Falco Talon**, a response engine for threat management in Kubernetes clusters. In our implementation[7] , *Falco probes* were installed on each node of the target application's deployment cluster, while *Falco Sidekick* was used to implement the functionalities of the devised GUI and MTD Controller components. Finally, *Falco Talon* was used to build the MTD Technique Enforcer.

The strength of this ecosystem is that both Falco and Falco Talon are rule-based. Rules are the conditions under which an alert should be generated or reconfiguration actions are performed and are defined using YAML files, making the management and extension guided and user-friendly even without specific knowledge.

4.3 AMTD-EC Framework Set-up for the Banking App

As discussed in Sect. 3, the framework set-up devises an initial step of threat modeling. To conduct this step, we adopt Irius Risk[8], a powerful automation tool that has a large number of stencils helping the analyst to model the system in a more accurate way compared, for example, to the Microsoft Threat Modeling Tool[9], and that generates a report in which threats can be classified on the basis of the desired security standard.

Figure 3 shows the system model (Data Flow Diagram - DFD) developed for the considered application, for which, after proper configuration of the model and

[5] https://anonymous.4open.science/r/MTD-Framework-6068/Setups/Bank_req_sec.md.
[6] https://falco.org/about/ecosystem/.
[7] https://anonymous.4open.science/r/MTD-Framework-6068/Setups/Falco_setup.md.
[8] https://www.iriusrisk.com/.
[9] https://www.microsoft.com/en-us/securityengineering/sdl/threatmodeling.

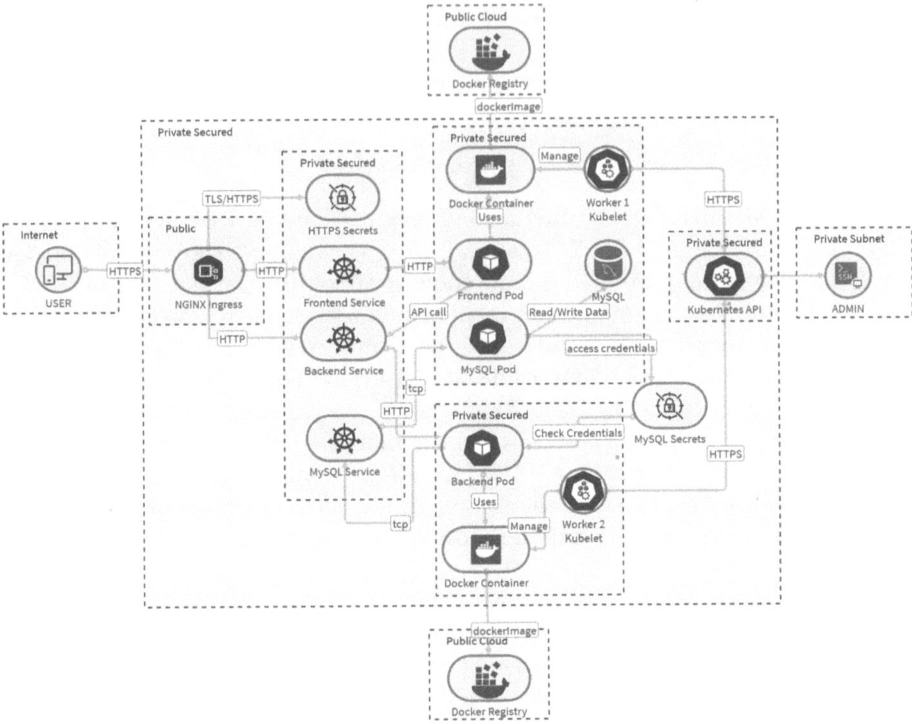

Fig. 3. Banking app DFD.

considering Kubernetes built-in features, 82 high-level remaining threats were identified and grouped by impacted assets. Moreover, IriusRisk automatically helps organize threats based on the STRIDE Category and associates them with CWE[10] weaknesses, providing also a risk score for each threat. To further enrich the analysis, we extended this mapping by linking threats also to specific Mitre ATT&CK techniques tailored with Caldera framework[11]. To derive the mapping, the *red-team engagement* was leveraged to simulate attacks according to the descriptions of the associated ATT&CK techniques, allowing the related CWE to be identified. Table 1 shows an extract of the threat list related to a subset of system assets. As a proof of concept, 5 threats were selected among the ones with a high-critical risk level.

The identification of attack techniques linked to existing threats was useful to configure the monitoring rules needed to detect them. We implemented 9 rules[12] of which the following 5 were directly connected to the identified attacks:

---

[10] https://cwe.mitre.org/.

[11] https://attack.mitre.org/.

[12] https://anonymous.4open.science/r/MTD-Framework-6068/miscConfig/falco/falco-rules.yaml.

Table 1. Analysed Threats

Asset	Threat	CWE	MITRE ATT&CK
Backend Pod	Pod Security Misconfiguration	CWE-200,CWE-250,CWE-284,CWE-285,CWE-668	T1609 - Container Administration Command
Kubernetes API	Improper Control Plane node configuration	CWE-200,CWE-276,CWE-284,CWE-73,CWE-732	T1070 - Clear Network Connection History and Configurations
MySQL	Unencrypted database traffic interception	CWE-326	T1040 - Network Sniffing
MySQL Service	Denial of service via exposed services	CWE-400	T1498 - Network Denial of Service
Docker Container	Runtime access elevation of privilege	CWE-921	T1611 - Escape To Host

1. T1609: *Write below root* detecting when a file is opened for writing below the root directory ("/") or the root user's home directory ("/root");
2. T1070: combining *Clear log Activities* (detecting when a log file is truncated), *delete or rename shell history*, *Modified shell configuration file* (monitoring write operations on files that are commonly used for shell configuration), and *Remove Bulk Data from Disk*;
3. T1040: combining *Launch of Suspicious Network Tool in Container* (like netcat, and nmap indicating a lateral movement of the attacker), and *Packet socket created in a container* (detecting the creation of a packet socket, i.e., a kernel feature that allows a process to capture raw network traffic, bypassing the standard TCP/IP stack);
4. T1498: *Unexpected UDP Traffic* detecting an abuse of UDP connections leading to possible DoS;
5. T1611: *Mount Launched in Privileged Container* intercepts a privilege escalation attempt from a container to the host by mounting sensitive file systems from the host node.

Beside the monitoring rules, we also identified a set of MTD techniques useful to thwart attacks linked with the threats resulting from the threat modeling step. In particular, we identified three techniques, namely *IP shuffling*, *node migration*, and *network topology shuffling*, and implemented several *Falco Talon actionners* representing the current MTD agents. Implemented actionners, performing actions like logging, pod termination, outbound pod connection management, and node draining were suitably mapped onto specific Talon monitoring rules, in order to enable the automated activation whenever the corresponding rule is triggered by the related Falco alert[13].

Among the implemented rules, the following six (summarized in Table 2) can be directly mapped to MTD countermeasures.

Table 2. Mapping Talon Rule - MTD technique

Talon Rule	Description	MTD Technique
Label IP Shuffling Logs	Labels the misbehaving pod as suspicious, saving its logs for analysis purposes and then terminating it.	IP Shuffling
IP Shuffling Logs MTD	Counters evasion of an attacker trying to cover its prints by capturing the logs and immediately terminating the pod.	IP Shuffling
Cordon Drain MTD	Isolate an infected node (cordon), preventing workloads from being scheduled on it and then safely empty it (drain), migrating legitimate pods elsewhere.	Migration
Launch Suspicious Network Tool in Container	Blocks the pod's outbound communications by applying a network policy.	Network Topology Shuffling
Packet socket created in container	Reacts to the creation of a raw socket by closing pods' outbound connections.	Network Topology Shuffling
Unexpected UDP Traffic	Reacts to the abuse of UDP connections by closing pods' outbound connections.	Network Topology Shuffling

[13] https://anonymous.4open.science/r/MTD-Framework-6068/miscConfig/falco/falco-talon-rules.yaml.

5 Evaluation and Results

In this section, we present an evaluation of the proposed framework from the security and the performance points of view. With regard to security, we performed a threat modeling of the system that integrates the target banking app and the AMTD-EC framework as an additional security layer, collecting node info and reacting to threats accordingly. Figure 4 shows how AMTD-EC is modelled in the system.

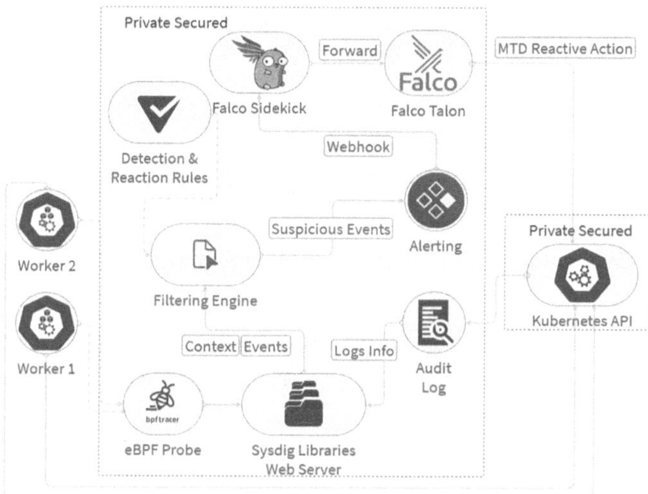

Fig. 4. AMTD-EC framework DFD.

Table 3 summarizes the outputs of the threat modeling process conducted with Irius Risk before and after the MTD framework integration. Given the cluster configuration, the test case application, and the simulated attacks, results clearly show that this framework enhances detection and mitigation capabilities.

Table 3. Threats summary with and without AMTD-EC framework

Threats	Without	With
Not applicable	10	10
Not detectable	72	34
Detectable	0	14
Detectable and Mitigable	0	24
Total	82	82

Threats classified as "Not applicable" are false positives introduced by the modeling tool after its configuration and do not apply to the system. In addition to the threat modeling, we also carried out an estimation of the risk by adopting the OWASP Risk Calculator[14], which can be used for the semi-quantitative assessment of the risks associated with threats. This tool allows the level of risk associated with specific threats to be estimated by combining factors such as the probability of exploitation and the potential impact on the organization, assigning each factor a score from 0 to 9. Once identified, the risk is estimated as: $Risk = Likelihood \cdot Impact$ by obtaining a corresponding value in the Risk Severity Matrix (Low, Medium, High, Critical), calculated for each possible threat identified both before and after applying the framework. The computation is based on estimates provided by experts: the likelihood is estimated by considering the complexity of the attack pattern and the detection capabilities of the framework, while the impact is estimated considering the efficacy of Talon's actions triggered and how fast they intervene.

Table 4 reports the risk computation for the system with and without the framework for the five example threats of the extract in Table 1.

Table 4. Risk variation for MITRE ATT&CK Techniques before and after AMTD-EC deployment

MITRE Technique	Metric	Without AMTD-EC		With AMTD-EC	
		Value	Level	Value	Level
T1609	Likelihood	5.750	High	4.000	Medium
	Impact	8.500	High	1.500	Low
	Risk	**48.875**	**High**	**6.000**	**Low**
T1070	Likelihood	7.000	High	4.750	Medium
	Impact	6.125	High	1.500	Low
	Risk	**42.875**	**Critical**	**7.125**	**Low**
T1040	Likelihood	8.000	High	6.000	Medium
	Impact	6.500	High	1.500	Low
	Risk	**52.000**	**Critical**	**9.000**	**Medium**
T1498	Likelihood	8.000	High	4.500	Medium
	Impact	8.625	High	1.500	Low
	Risk	**69.000**	**Critical**	**6.750**	**Low**
T1611	Likelihood	7.125	High	5.875	Medium
	Impact	8.500	High	2.000	Low
	Risk	**60.562**	**Critical**	**11.750**	**Low**

As for the performance analysis, the literature study led us to the selection of the following metrics:

[14] https://javierolmedo.github.io/OWASP-Calculator/.

- **Configuration Diversity (CD)** identifies the number of non-empty combinations of atomic reactive actions (α) that a system can enforce. Since not all of them are valid due to rule precedence or redundancy, CD is defined as follows.
$$\begin{aligned} CD_{max} &= 2^{\alpha} - 1 \\ CD_{useful} &= CD_{max} - CD_{invalid} \end{aligned} \tag{1}$$
- **Attack Surface Coverage (ASC)** measures the portion of the attack surface that is effectively covered by mitigation techniques.
$$ASC = \frac{|Numerator|}{|Total\_Threats - Not\_Applicable\_Threats|} \tag{2}$$
Where $Numerator$ can be each of the values of the "With AMTD-EC" column in Table 3.
- **Alert to Action Convergence (AAC)** measures the degree of variability in the system's responses to generated alerts. If the value is low, the mapping between alert and action is strict and easy to predict, while if the value is high, it implies greater diversification in responses, increasing unpredictability and therefore the system's resilience to automated tactics. A system with the same response for each alert is: i)*predictable* as the attackers can test a behaviour to bypass it, ii)*stable but strict* as it does not adapt the behaviour to different contexts, iii)*deterministic* as it behaves as a traditional IPS/IDS. This metric is computed as follows:
$$AAC = \frac{\sum |action(alert_i)|}{alerts} \tag{3}$$
Where the $Numerator$ counts the number of different actions related to the $alert_i$ while the *Denominator* is the total number of active Falco rules in the whole system.
- **Mean Time to Mitigation (MTTM)** (equivalent to Mean Time to Compromise [11] but in the defense perspective) measures the time between the start of the attack and the end of the recovery action of the target's operations; the goal is its minimization. This interval includes both the detection time and the time required to complete the associated response action.

Configuration Diversity CD. In such a context, a high CD value is desirable, as it increases the unpredictability of defensive responses and makes it more difficult for an attacker to automate their operations.

For the calculation, we consider each unique combination of actions and its significant parameters. Specifically, 12 distinct atomic actions and 3 composite configurations (combinations of actions) have been implemented. Therefore, the **total number of actions** implemented is 15.

We can now compute the theoretical *maximum CD* as follows:
$$CD_{max} = 2^{12} - 1 = 4095 \tag{4}$$

This number represents all possible non-empty combinations of atomic actions, but not all of them are valid or useful in an operational context. Some configurations may be semantically inconsistent (combining *Terminate Pod* and *Exec command* is illogical, it is impossible to execute a command in a terminated pod), may act on unrelated entities (combining *Cordon Node* -action on the node- with *Get logs of Pod* -action on a pod-), may be redundant (combining *Label Pod as Suspicious* with another diagnostic action may not add value if already logged), and have critical temporal order (*Download file* or *Sysdig* must occur before Terminate, not after).

We estimate that approximately 65% of configurations are inconsistent, redundant, or not usable in a real-world automated response context. Therefore, the computation results in the following:

$$\begin{aligned} CD_{invalid} &\approx 0.65 \cdot 4095 \approx 2661 \\ CD_{useful} = CD_{max} - CD_{invalid} &\approx 4095 - 2661 \approx 1434 \end{aligned} \tag{5}$$

The theoretical number of usable combination configurations is approximately 1434. This level of diversification in the monitoring represents a break with the static and deterministic approach typical of traditional IDS systems, which tend to always perform the same action for each specific type of alarm, without the possibility of dynamic adaptation to the operating context.

Attack Surface Coverage – ASC. For this computation, only the threats that are detectable and mitigable were considered in order to evaluate the efficacy of the framework. The computation is performed as follows using threat values shown in Table 3:

$$ASC_{Detect\&Mitigate} = \frac{24}{82 - 10} \approx 0.333 \rightarrow 33.3\% \tag{6}$$

Iterating this computation for each value (excluding the "Not applicable"), we built Table 5 as a summary of the threats distribution.

Table 5. Threats distribution summary

Threat type	Quantity	Percentage
Detectable and Mitigable	24	33.3%
Detectable	14	19.4%
Not Detectable	34	47.2%
Total	72	100%

The system is therefore able to detect over half of the threats, but only 24 of these can be mitigated. A value of $ASC = 33.3\%$ indicates that one third of the attack surface is actively covered by the framework, suggesting a good level of runtime visibility.

Alert to Action Convergence - AAC. This metric evaluates the mean number of different action connected to each alert. In the system, there are 9 active Falco rules, each with one or more associated actions, while the total number of Talon actions is 12 and the computed value is:

$$AAC = \frac{12}{9} \approx 1.33 \tag{7}$$

This result tells us that, on average, each Falco alert triggers two different Talon actions. This is better than a 1 : 1 mapping, but there is still room for improvement in terms of unpredictability.

Mean Time to Mitigation - MTTM. For each Falco rule implemented, the time elapsed from the start of the attack to the complete restoration of the target's operability was estimated. This interval includes both the detection time by Falco and the time required for Falco Talon to perform the associated response action.

In the analysis, the most significant and useful delta times for system performance testing are:

- **Detection time**: time between the start of the attack and its detection by Falco measuring the **speed** with which the attack is identified.
- **Response time**: time between Falco detection and the Talon reactionmeasuring the **latency** in implementing mitigation after detection.
- **Recovery time**: time between Falco Talon's action and the target being back online; measures how long it takes for the system to become fully **operational** again after the mitigation action.
- **Total handling time**: total time between the start of the attack and when the target is back online, and computes the total time required to detect, mitigate and recover from the attack.

Table 6 shows a summary of the metrics evaluated for 5 Falco rules (*Clear Log Activities - CLA, Remove Bulk from Data - RBD, Mount Launched in Privileged Container - MLPC, Launch Suspicious Network Tool - LSNT, Packet Socket Created in Container - PSCC*). The attacks were performed on a single run and the values were obtained by analysing the timestamp of the attack framework, the Falco logs, and Kubernetes logs themselves.

Table 6. MTTM summary

Time	CLA	RBD	MLPC	LSNT	PSCC
Detection	3 s	66 s	15 s	3 s	3 s
Response	0 s	0 s	N/A*	0 s	0 s
Recovery	2 s	5 s	5 s	2 s	2 s
MTTM	5 s	71 s	20 s	5 s	5 s

The response time of the MLPC is marked with * as it is not possible to estimate directly the time of the Falco Talon action since it isolates the pod and migrates it to another node and it strictly depends on the system architecture. The total is computed considering Kubernetes logs when the pod is migrated, up and running on the new node. Moreover, the delay in RDB detection is likely traceable to the nature of the simulated attack, which requires more time to perform the actions that trigger the rule. It is worth noticing that the response time is always reported as 0 s, since the interaction between Falco and Falco Talon occurs in terms of milliseconds, hence negligible due to the efficiency of the webhook communication channel.

6 Discussion

In this section, obtained results are discussed and the pros and cons of the use of the proposed framework are analysed. With the introduction of **AMTD-EC**, referring to the *threat analysis*, we obtained an enhancement of the system detection and reaction capabilities to incoming threats (Table 3). Moreover, the risk-based analysis highlighted the high capability of risk mitigation (Table 4).

With **Configuration Diversity**, we were able to assess the framework's ability to introduce unpredictability into the system's behaviour in response to threats. The **Attack Surface Coverage** showed that the Falco Talon-based system can activate reactive actions in real time, enabling automatic and dynamic mitigation of detected events, demonstrating that AMTD-EC has great potential effectiveness in protecting the entire application stack. The **Alert to Action Convergence** showed that, although each rule can activate more than one Falco actionners, the combination is fixed. Attackers observing the system can still understand the expected response for each alert. Therefore, we can conclude that the number of actions is different from the runtime variability and that the metric measures the structural complexity of the policies, not their dynamism. **Mean Time to Mitigation** measures how fast Falco Talon reacts to a Falco alert and recovery times, showing that this framework reduces the attack window and minimizes the disruption of the service.

Resource consumption for maintaining the agents in the system can be monitored via the Grafana dashboard installed[15] and typically it is assessed around 100-200MB of RAM depending on the node CPU count. Finally, framework scalability is achieved through Falco's decentralized, edge-native architecture that analyses events locally within the Linux kernel using low-impact eBPF technology. Moreover, the Falco ecosystem implements the fundamental principles of SOAR platforms (receives an alert, enriches data, runs automated actions, and resolves the incident) but while SOARs are typically enterprise platforms, Falco is open source and highly modular.

[15] https://anonymous.4open.science/r/MTD-Framework-6068/Setups/Grafana_setup.md.

6.1 Limitations

The Falco ecosystem introduces numerous benefits in terms of modularity, automation, observability, and responsiveness. However, it also has structural limitations and operational risks that impact the proposed implementation. In particular, Falco offers limited context awareness due to kernel-level operations, requiring a *trade-off between granularity and semantic understanding.* Rules are linked to human expertise in their writing: there is the risk of false positives or false negatives. Furthermore, the absence of *semantic validation* makes it possible to unintentionally implement redundant, inconsistent or poorly performing rules. Falco Sidekick is susceptible to risk of event loss due to network congestion. Its reliability can be improved by integrating external asynchronous buffering systems (such as FIFO, queues, Redis, or messaging brokers). Another issue is its centralized configuration file shared among all agents, thus preventing defining specific outputs for individual rules. As an automated response engine, Falco Talon is very powerful, but this power comes with a potential operational risk, as a *misconfigured policy* can lead to the termination of critical pods, the interruption of essential services, or the application of destructive actions. Finally, unintentionally repeated actions can cause unexpected or harmful behaviour.

7 Conclusion and Future Works

In this work it was proposed an automated rule-based framework with MTD capabilities (AMTD-EC) demonstrating its seamless integration within cloud-based environments. Experimental results indicate that it provides a more effective defense mechanism by enabling fast, reliable, and accurate responses to detected threats, without significant overhead. The framework operates by executing a set of configurable actions (*HOW*) triggered whenever a specific Falco alert is matched (*WHEN*). While this approach ensures reactive protection, it also highlights a limitation in terms of adaptability to emerging and unforeseen threats. To address rule scalability, we are currently working on the introduction of AI models for dynamic and automated rule management, generation, and optimization. Furthermore, edge device integration is currently under analysis since Falco operates with a minimal resource footprint and uses eBPF technology to evaluate Linux syscalls, suitable for resource-constrained environments.

Acknowledgments. This work was partly funded by the ECHO-TWIN project, an initiative of the Italian National Center on HPC, Big Data and Quantum Computing. PN RIC 2021-2027. CUP: B69H26001070007, B62F26000630005, B69J26002770005, and by the European Union - NextGenerationEU - National Recovery and Resilience Plan (NRRP) - MISSION 4 COMPONENT 2, INVESTMENT N.1.1, CALL PRIN 2022 D.D.1409 14-09-2022 - (Threat-driven security testing and proactive defence identification for edge-cloud systems). PROJECT CODE: P2022TT7A7. CUP: E53D23016380001.

Disclosure of Interests. The authors have no competing interests to declare that are relevant to the content of this article.

References

1. Assen, J.V.D., et al.: A lightweight moving target defense framework for multi-purpose malware affecting IoT devices. In: IEEE International Conference on Communications, vol. 2023-May, pp. 6010–6015. Institute of Electrical and Electronics Engineers Inc. (2023). https://doi.org/10.1109/ICC45041.2023.10278951
2. Bagheri, S., et al.: Ace-Warp: a cost-effective approach to proactive and non-disruptive incident response in Kubernetes clusters. IEEE Trans. Inf. Forensics Secur. **19**, 8204–8219 (2024). https://doi.org/10.1109/TIFS.2024.3449038
3. Bagheri, S., Kermabon-Bobinnec, H., Majumdar, S., Jarraya, Y., Wang, L., Pourzandi, M.: Warping the defence timeline: non-disruptive proactive attack mitigation for Kubernetes clusters. In: ICC 2023-IEEE International Conference on Communications, pp. 777–782. IEEE (2023)
4. Casola, V., De Benedictis, A., Iorio, D., Migliaccio, S.: A moving target defense framework to improve resilience of cloud-edge systems. In: Barolli, L. (ed.) Advanced Information Networking and Applications, pp. 243–252. Springer Nature Switzerland, Cham (2025)
5. Hamed Okhravi: Moving target defense - article for encyclopedia of cryptography, security and privacy - springer. https://web.mit.edu/ha22286/www/papers/Encyclopedia23.pdf
6. Kashkoush, M.S., Clancy, C., Abed, A.S., Azab, M.: Resilient intrusion detection system for cloud containers. Int. J. Commun. Netw. Distrib. Syst. **24**, 1 (2020). https://doi.org/10.1504/ijcnds.2020.10025197
7. National Institute for Standards and Technology: NIST special publication 800-160, volume 2 revision 1. developing cyber-resilient systems: A systems security engineering approach. https://nvlpubs.nist.gov/nistpubs/SpecialPublications/NIST.SP.800-160v2r1.pdf
8. National Institute for Standards and Technology: NIST special publication 800-53 revision 5. security and privacy controls for information systems and organizations. https://nvlpubs.nist.gov/nistpubs/SpecialPublications/NIST.SP.800-53r5.pdf
9. Navas, R., Cuppens, F., Cuppens-Boulahia, N., Toutain, L., Papadopoulos, G.Z.: MTD, where art thou? A systematic review of moving target defense techniques for IoT. IEEE Int. Things J. **PP**, 1–1 (2020). https://doi.org/10.1109/JIOT.2020.3040358
10. Ross, R., Pillitteri, V., Graubart, R., Bodeau, D., McQuaid, R.: Developing cyber resilient systems: a systems security engineering approach. Tech. rep, National Institute of Standards and Technology (2019)
11. Sharma, D.P.: Evaluating moving target defense methods using time to compromise and security risk metrics in IoT networks. Electronics **14**(11) (2025). https://doi.org/10.3390/electronics14112205, https://www.mdpi.com/2079-9292/14/11/2205
12. Sheikh, A.M., Islam, M.R., Habaebi, M.H., Zabidi, S.A., Bin Najeeb, A.R., Kabbani, A.: A survey on edge computing (EC) security challenges: classification, threats, and mitigation strategies. Fut. Int. **17**(4) (2025). https://doi.org/10.3390/fi17040175, https://www.mdpi.com/1999-5903/17/4/175
13. Soussi, W., Christopoulou, M., Gur, G., Stiller, B.: Merlins - moving target defense enhanced with deep-RL for NFV in-depth security. In: 2023 IEEE Conference on Network Function Virtualization and Software Defined Networks, NFV-SDN 2023 - Proceedings, pp. 65–71. Institute of Electrical and Electronics Engineers Inc. (2023). https://doi.org/10.1109/NFV-SDN59219.2023.10329594

14. Soussi, W., et al.: Demo: closed-loop security orchestration in the telco cloud for moving target defense. In: Proceedings of IEEE/IFIP Network Operations and Management Symposium 2023, NOMS 2023. Institute of Electrical and Electronics Engineers Inc. (2023). https://doi.org/10.1109/NOMS56928.2023.10154420
15. Sun, R., Zhu, Y., Fei, J., Chen, X.: A survey on moving target defense: intelligently affordable, optimized and self-adaptive (2023). https://doi.org/10.3390/app13095367
16. Torquato, M., Vieira, M.: Moving target defense in cloud computing: a systematic mapping study. Comput. Sec. **92**, 101742 (2020). https://doi.org/10.1016/j.cose.2020.101742
17. Zhuang, R., DeLoach, S.A., Ou, X.: Towards a theory of moving target defense. In: Proceedings of the First ACM Workshop on Moving Target Defense, pp. 31–40. Association for Computing Machinery, New York, NY, USA (2014). https://doi.org/10.1145/2663474.2663479

DREAMER: Domain-oriented Realistic Emulation for Attack Monitoring and Evaluation Research

Vincenzo Carletti, Pasquale Foggia, Speranza Ranieri(✉), and Mario Vento

University of Salerno, Fisciano, SA 84084, Italy
{vcarletti,pfoggia,sranieri,mvento}@unisa.it

Abstract. The growing complexity of modern IT infrastructures, combined with the proliferation of stealthy and persistent attack techniques, has made the validation of security monitoring systems a major challenge for both industry and academia. Evaluating such systems requires experimental environments that combine realism, controllability, observability, and reproducibility. However, production networks cannot safely support repeatable adversarial experimentation, and existing evaluation approaches often provide limited support for distributed attack scenarios and benchmarking. Motivated by this limitation, this paper introduces DREAMER, a domain-oriented network emulation and virtualization environment designed to support advanced security testing, monitoring, and reproducible evaluation. The proposed network integrates multiple hosts and security components, enabling the creation of a high-fidelity experimental testbed. Within this environment, attack scenarios were executed to validate the feasibility of collecting distributed telemetry from heterogeneous monitoring sources. The results indicate that the proposed environments can support realistic security testing, systematic telemetry acquisition, and reproducible evaluation, thereby helping to bridge the gap between academic research and industrial practice.

Keywords: Corporate Testbed · Network Emulation · Threat Emulation · Security Monitoring

1 Introduction

Organizations are increasingly exposed to a broad spectrum of cyber threats, ranging from malicious insiders [18] to organized criminal groups conducting persistent and covert campaigns [5], all sharing the common objective of stealing sensitive and valuable data. Rather than manifesting as isolated events, such threats often unfold through multi-stage behaviors involving different assets, services, and components across the infrastructure. This challenges traditional evaluation methodologies for security systems, as defensive mechanisms can no longer be assessed only against isolated signatures or individual events, but must be evaluated with respect to coordinated attack behaviors.

P. Kieseberg et al. (Eds.): ARES 2026 Workshops, LNCS 16903, pp. 644–661, 2027.
https://doi.org/10.1007/978-3-032-37218-5_37

Within this context, cyber ranges and security testbeds have emerged as practical instruments for security research across different domains, including Internet of Things (IoT) [17,21], Industrial Control Systems (ICS) [12] and security posture testing [20], especially when experiments on production systems would be unsafe, costly, or legally infeasible. To be effective, these environments must replicate not only the target infrastructure, but also the structural, functional, and information layers required to support realistic attack and defense experiments, together with the workflows involved in security assessment.

The need for realistic evaluation extends beyond industrial applications and is equally evident in academic research. Public datasets play a pivotal role in developing and benchmarking Machine Learning (ML) and Deep Learning (DL)-driven systems for detecting evolving cyber threats. However, dataset-centric evaluations are often hindered by limited realism, class imbalance, biased train–test split methodologies, and restricted scope [15,23]. These limitations undermine the operational validity of proposed approaches, creating a substantial gap between benchmark performance and real-world effectiveness. Although several studies report promising results from evaluations conducted in operational environments [13,35,36], the proprietary data on which they rely are typically unavailable to the research community due to confidentiality constraints and regulatory compliance requirements. Consequently, replicating realistic enterprise infrastructures represents a viable strategy to bridge this gap, enabling the testing of defensive assets, the collection of high-fidelity data, and the assessment of custom-built security solutions under controlled yet operationally plausible conditions.

Contributions. In this paper we introduce DREAMER, a realistic corporate testbed for controlled yet operationally plausible security evaluations. It supports the execution of multi-stage attack scenarios and the collection of network- and host-level telemetry during both benign and malicious activities.

To this end, we make the following contributions:

- **Testbed Design and Implementation.** We design and implement a realistic corporate testbed that reproduces endpoints, services, and core network components commonly found in corporate infrastructures.
- **Multi-stage Attack Scenarios.** We systematically design and carry out multi-stage attack campaigns against internal hosts to assess the effectiveness of the deployed defensive mechanisms.
- **Feasibility of Data Acquisition.** We evaluate the feasibility of collecting security-relevant data within the emulated environment, showing that both raw network traffic and host-based telemetry can be collected to produce a domain-specific and realistic dataset.

Organization. The remainder of this paper is organized as follows. Section 2 reviews related work on testbeds for security testing and domain-specific solutions. Section 3 describes the proposed testbed and the core elements of the implemented corporate network. Section 4 presents the methodology adopted to evaluate the testbed, while Sect. 5 discusses practical implications and limitations. Finally, Sect. 6 concludes the paper and outlines directions for future work.

2 Related Work

This section reviews prior works on security testbeds and the related dataset generation for network and host security. It covers the main experimental environments used in cybersecurity research, with attention to domain-specific security proposals.

2.1 Security Testbeds and Emulated Environments

Experimental platforms play a central role in cybersecurity research, enabling controlled and repeatable studies in settings where experiments on operational systems would be unsafe, costly, or difficult to reproduce [11]. Prior work commonly distinguishes among simulators, emulators, and testbeds, each offering different trade-offs in terms of realism, scalability, cost, and reproducibility [16].

Simulators reproduce the behavior of networked systems through abstract models of nodes, links, protocols, and traffic patterns. Rather than deploying full operating systems and applications, they typically approximate system behavior using software abstractions and event-driven execution models. This makes simulation highly controllable and scalable, enabling researchers to study large-scale networks and protocol interactions with limited computational resources. Representative examples include Network Simulator 3 (ns-3) [26], Objective Modular Network Testbed in C++ (OMNeT++) [33], and COOJA [27]. However, the reliance on abstraction can limit fidelity, as simulators may omit implementation-specific protocol-stack behavior, system calls, timing effects, and host-side artifacts that are often relevant in cybersecurity experiments.

Emulators provide a higher degree of realism than pure simulation by executing real software components, services, applications, and protocol implementations within controlled virtualized or containerized environments. Rather than relying solely on abstract models of nodes and protocol behavior, emulation instantiates virtual hosts and network devices through virtual machines, containers, or lightweight network name-spaces, while reproducing the target topology and link conditions through software-based network emulation. This enables researchers to run real applications, generate traffic from actual protocol implementations, and collect concrete host- and network-level traces, while retaining a significant degree of control and repeatability. Mininet [22], for instance, is widely used for Software-Defined Networking experimentation, whereas CORE [4] and IMUNES [28] provide virtualization-based capabilities for constructing and executing emulated network topologies. Emulation offers a practical compromise between realism and reproducibility, although it generally incurs higher computational overhead and may be affected by resource contention and timing artifacts.

Physical and hybrid testbeds can further increase experimental fidelity by relying on real hardware, real network devices, or combinations of physical and virtual components. In physical testbeds, experiments are conducted on dedicated machines, sensors, controllers, switches, or routers, whereas hybrid testbeds integrate such components with emulated or simulated elements to improve flexibility and scalability. Platforms such as Emulab [34] and GENI [9] provide configurable experimental infrastructures that allow to deploy and evaluate systems under more realistic conditions. In the cybersecurity domain, DETERLab [8] represents a notable example of a security-oriented testbed derived from Emulab and designed to support controlled and repeatable cyber-defense experiments. The main advantage of physical and hybrid testbeds is their ability to capture hardware-specific behavior, timing constraints, and operational characteristics that are difficult to reproduce through simulation or emulation alone. Nevertheless, these environments generally entail higher deployment and maintenance costs, reduced flexibility, limited scalability, and more complex reconfiguration procedures [16]. Finally, *Cyber Ranges* build upon testbed infrastructures to provide controlled and configurable environments for reproducing realistic cybersecurity scenarios, supporting the development and evaluation of security tools, defense mechanisms, attack techniques, and assessment methodologies [20].

2.2 Domain-Specific Security Testbeds

Several domain-specific security testbeds have been proposed to capture the characteristics of particular operational environments. In the ICS domain, LICSTER [31] provides a low-cost physical testbed for industrial security education and research, aiming to support hands-on experimentation while reducing the cost and complexity of physical ICS infrastructures. ICSSIM [12], instead, follows a virtualized approach to building customized ICS security testbeds, combining container-based deployment with network emulation through Graphical Network Simulator-3 (GNS3) [14] and supporting software- and hardware-in-the-loop process modeling. In the IoT domain, Gotham [10] provides a reproducible GNS3-based security testbed that integrates emulated IoT devices, services, and threat actors, supporting security experiments and network security dataset generation.

However, IoT and ICS testbeds are typically designed around constrained devices, industrial protocols, or cyber-physical processes. Corporate environments, by contrast, are characterized by user-centric activity, identity-driven access, general-purpose endpoints, and complex service interactions. These differences limit the direct applicability of IoT- and ICS-oriented approaches to corporate security testing.

3 Testbed Design and Architecture

DREAMER is a testbed designed to emulate a realistic corporate network, ensuring reproducibility, isolation, and experimental control. To this end, its architecture provides a configurable environment for executing benign activities, adversarial behaviors, and security monitoring workflows under controlled conditions.

Emulation Layer. Emulation is based on GNS3 [14], a free and open-source network software emulator that enables the execution of real network software within a controlled virtual environment. Its client–server architecture separates the execution backend from the graphical management interface: the server hosts and manages the emulated nodes, links, and virtualization backends, while the client is used to design, inspect, and control the topology. In the proposed deployment, the entire testbed runs on the GNS3 server, including all virtualized and containerized components of the emulated corporate network. The client is used only for topology design, node inspection, link configuration, and experiment supervision.

To balance fidelity and resource consumption, the testbed relies on a hybrid virtualization strategy. Docker containers [24] are used for lightweight services, whereas QEMU-based virtual machines [7] are used for full-stack operating systems, attacker workstation, and security appliances.

3.1 Scenario Overview

To evaluate the capabilities of the testbed in an enterprise-like setting, we set up a realistic corporate scenario organized into three high-level zones: an *Internet Zone*, a *Threat Actor Zone*, and a *Target Corporate Network*. These zones define the main trust boundaries of the experimental environment, separating external connectivity and adversarial infrastructure from the target corporate network. Figure 1 shows the complete topology.

Network Connectivity Appliances. The network infrastructure is built around four main classes of appliances: a perimeter router (R1), a perimeter firewall, multiple Layer-2 switches and a mirroring hub.

R1 provides perimeter connectivity between the corporate environment and the external network. The firewall centralizes Domain Name System (DNS), Dynamic Host Configuration Protocol (DHCP), Network Address Translation (NAT), port forwarding, and inter-segment traffic filtering. It mediates external access to selected exposed services through HTTPS port forwarding and enforces restrictive inter-segment communication policies, allowing only predefined and authorized traffic flows. Internal connectivity is provided through Layer-2 switches. Each switch is configured with a single bridge and supports both trunk and access ports, enabling logical separation between internal corporate segments and monitoring components. Finally, the mirroring hub is integrated within the security area to support passive traffic inspection by forwarding network traffic to the monitoring sensors. All devices are interconnected through virtual links.

Details about network connectivity components used in the testbed is summarized Table 1.

Internet Zone. This zone provides controlled external connectivity for the emulated environment. Connectivity between internal devices and external resources

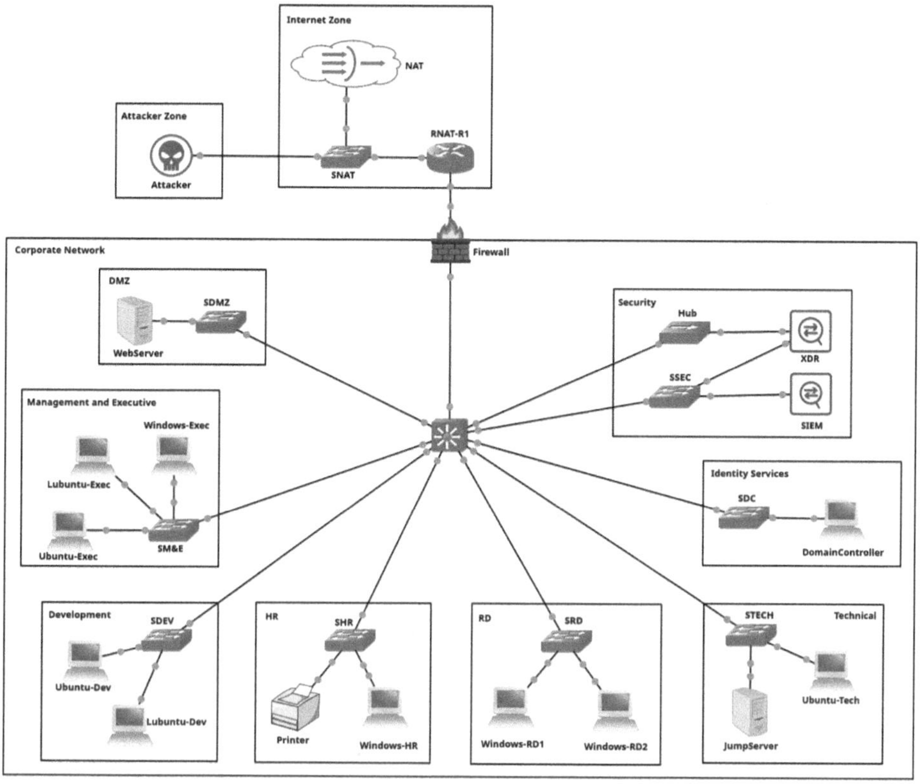

Fig. 1. Corporate Scenario implemented in GNS3.

is mediated by a dedicated NAT node, which enables outbound communication and supports the generation of background traffic. At the same time, unsolicited inbound connections are blocked. This design isolates the emulated nodes from the underlying host system and physical network, confining potentially harmful traffic to the emulated environment. The zone also includes the R1 router and a switch, which provide connectivity to the remaining of the topology.

Target Corporate Network. It represents the main environment under analysis and is subdivided into multiple functional segments that reflect common enterprise operational roles. These include a Demilitarized Zone (DMZ), a security monitoring segment, an identity services segment, a management segment, and several user-oriented office segments. This segmentation avoids a flat network structure and allows the testbed to reproduce trust boundaries typically found in enterprise environments.

The DMZ segment represents the portion of the infrastructure intended to expose services while keeping them separated from the internal corporate LAN. It hosts a public web server and enforces network isolation by preventing direct communication with the internal corporate segment. A dedicated security seg-

Table 1. Network layer node templates and corresponding implementations.

Node Template	Implementation
Switches	Docker image with Open vSwitch [2] version 3.3.7.
R1 router	Alpine Docker Container with IPtables.
Perimeter Firewall	QEMU VM with OPNsense [3] version 24.7.
Mirroring hub	built-in GNS3 Ethernet Hub node.

ment hosts the monitoring infrastructure. This area includes a Suricata-based Network Intrusion Detection System (NIDS) and a Wazuh-based XDR server, used for log collection, endpoint telemetry aggregation, and event correlation. The Identity Services segment contains a Windows Server Domain Controller. This node provides the core identity and trust services for the emulated enterprise environment, including centralized authentication, domain management, and policy enforcement. Its placement in a dedicated segment reflects the critical role of identity infrastructure in enterprise networks and enables the testbed to reproduce domain-based authentication workflows involving workstations, users, and internal services. The Technical segment includes a system administrator workstation and a jump server. This segment models the administrative infrastructure used to operate and maintain the environment. The jump server acts as an intermediate access point for privileged operations, preventing direct access from general-purpose user segments to sensitive backend systems and security appliances. This configuration supports a controlled privileged-access model and limits the potential impact of a compromised workstation. The user environment is distributed across several departmental segments, whose devices are associated with specific corporate roles and joined to the Active Directory domain. The Management and Executive (M&E) segment includes three employee workstations with heterogeneous operating systems, including Linux and Windows endpoints. The Research and Development (R&D) segment contains two additional employee workstations, running Windows operating system. The Human Resources (HR) segment includes a Windows employee workstation and a network printer, allowing the testbed to also reproduce common office activities such as document handling and printing operations. The Development segment includes two Ubuntu workstations.

Details about hosts and services included in the testbed is summarized Table 2.

Threat Actor Zone. This zone contains the resources used to execute adversarial activities. It includes an attacker-controlled workstation implemented as a QEMU-based Virtual Machine running Kali Linux. From this zone, adversarial activities are launched against exposed services and reachable assets in the Target Corporate Network. Details about implemented attacks are provided in next section.

Table 2. Target Corporate Network node templates and corresponding implementations.

Node Template	Implementation
WebServer	Debian-based QEMU VM running Apache2 and MariaDB and hosting a portal.
Domain Controller	Windows Server 2022 QEMU VM providing Active Directory Domain Services, DNS, and internal certification services.
Suricata NIDS	QEMU VM running Suricata.
Wazuh Server	Ubuntu-based QEMU VM running the Wazuh manager.
JumpServer	Ubuntu Server-based QEMU VM running OpenSSH.
Windows 11 Workstations	Windows 11-based QEMU VM with graphical interface, joined to the Active Directory domain.
Ubuntu/Lubuntu Workstations	Ubuntu/Lubuntu-based QEMU VM with graphical interface.
Printer	Debian-based QEMU VM running CUPS.

4 Methodology

This section describes the methodology used to evaluate the effectiveness of the proposed testbed. First, we present the experimental setup, including the generation of user behavior and the design of attack scenarios defined according to the Cyber Kill Chain [19]. Next, we define the evaluation metrics adopted for the analysis. Finally, we assess the capability of our testbed to support the collection of host-level and network-level data within the proposed scenario.

4.1 Employee Behavioral Modeling

Taking inspiration from previous work [25], Ansible [6] is adopted as the automation framework for the distributed execution of user-like activities. The implemented workflow consists of three main stages: an *Activity Orchestrator*, a *Remote Dispatch Layer*, and a set of *Endpoint Interaction Agents*.

The Ubuntu Workstation, named `Ubuntu-Tech` and located in the Technical segment, acts as Control Node and hosts the *Activity Orchestrator*, from which automation tasks are distributed to the target hosts.

During execution, the orchestrator dynamically creates a list of active nodes and assigns random tasks to the machines, including web browsing, document management, email access, and printing. For each internal segment, the implemented selection policy assigns a different probability for the execution of each task. Each selected task is launched as an independent process. This design allows a new activity to be dispatched while previously started sessions are still running, thereby enabling potentially overlapping user-like behaviors. The scheduler assigns a nominal execution window randomly selected between five and seven minutes. For email and document-printing related tasks, this nominal interval is halved.

Interactive automation on Windows endpoints requires an additional mechanism due to session isolation, which prevents SSH-launched commands from displaying GUI applications in the active user session. To overcome this limitation, a Task Wrapper mechanism is implemented: Ansible transfers the configuration payload to the target host and subsequently triggers a preconfigured scheduled task, enabling tasks to be performed automatically within the interactive desktop session.

It should be noted that this activity modeling is limited to active machines not directly involved in the attack execution. During the Kill-Chain execution, both the attacker and the target node are manually controlled to ensure consistent triggering of the attack workflow.

4.2 Threat Model and Attack Scenarios

We consider an external attacker whose objective is to gain unauthorized access to the corporate network and exfiltrate sensitive information from internal hosts. The attacker may rely on different initial access vectors, including the exploitation of vulnerabilities in exposed or widely used software and social-engineering techniques, such as phishing, to induce users to execute malicious payloads. Once an initial foothold is obtained, the attacker may establish persistence, escalate privileges, move laterally across the network, execute commands, and exfiltrate data. The purpose of this threat model is not to exhaustively cover all possible enterprise attack paths, but to define realistic adversarial behaviors that involve multiple components of the testbed. In particular, these adversarial activities are expected to generate observable traces in network traffic, host-level logs, authentication events, and security alerts.

Based on this threat model, the analysis considers two attack scenarios. These scenarios are designed to assess both the ability of the proposed environment to reproduce realistic attack workflows and the capability of the deployed detection systems to identify malicious activities that abuse legitimate protocols or communication channels. Specifically, the scenarios include *(i)* a Command-and-Control (C2) scenario that abuses legitimate application-layer services and *(ii)* a DNS tunneling scenario that exploits the widespread use of DNS traffic in enterprise networks.

To simulate more realistic compromise scenarios, the attack workflow is aligned with a hypothetical employee routine. The execution of the attack is scheduled during selected phases of the working day in which, according to the assumptions of the scenario, the user may be more susceptible to social-engineering attempts or less likely to notice anomalous behavior. In addition, workstation restart events provide opportunities for triggering or reactivating the infection process.

Telegram Bot C2 Tunneling Attack. This scenario models an attacker-controlled C2 channel that leverages Telegram's legitimate API services for command exchange and data exfiltration. The scenario abuses an existing application-layer service as an intermediary for malicious communications. This configuration allows the analysis to examine the challenges associated with detecting adversarial activities that rely on legitimate communication services.

The experimental setup involves the external attacker and an internal target machine, specifically, the Windows 11 workstation, named `Windows-HR`, located in the HR segment. The workflow combines social engineering with the exploitation of a malicious archive and establishes persistence on the target workstation before activating the Telegram-based C2 channel.

Figure 2 summarizes the Cyber Kill Chain phases and maps the corresponding attacker activities to the related MITRE ATT&CK techniques.

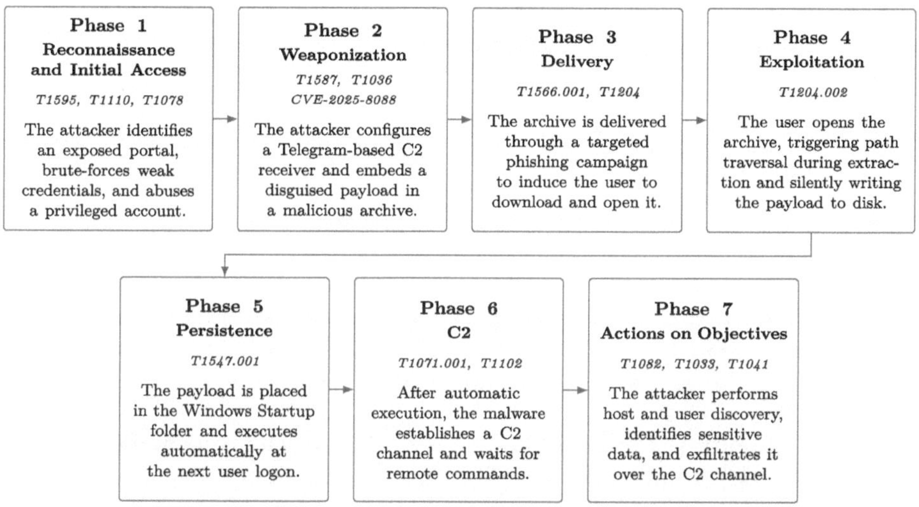

Fig. 2. Cyber Kill Chain phases, MITRE ATT&CK techniques, and attacker activities for the Telegram-based C2 scenario.

DNS Tunneling. This scenario models a covert C2 channel that abuses DNS traffic for command exchange and data exfiltration. Whereas the previous scenario relies on a legitimate external application-layer service as an intermediary for malicious communications, this scenario embeds adversarial exchanges within DNS queries and responses. The experimental setup involves the same external attacker, a compromised organizational web portal hosted on the DMZ Web Server, and an internal target host, specifically the Ubuntu workstation named `Ubuntu-Dev`, located in the Development segment. During the attack workflow, the attacker compromises the web portal and uses it as a staging point for the malicious archive. The attacker-controlled infrastructure acts both as the C2 endpoint and as the authoritative name server for the malicious domain.

Figure 3 summarizes the Cyber Kill Chain phases maps the corresponding attacker activities to the related MITRE ATT&CK techniques.

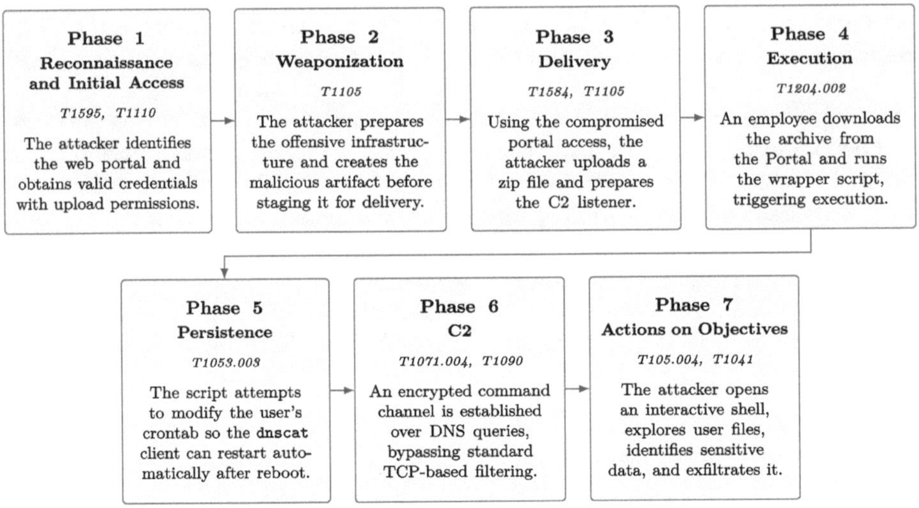

Fig. 3. Cyber Kill Chain phases, MITRE ATT&CK techniques, and attacker activities for the DNS-tunneling scenario.

4.3 Evaluation

This section evaluates the testbed performance and effectiveness, specifically analyzing resource consumption and scalability. Furthermore, it presents the preliminary results derived from the integrated collection of host- and network-level telemetry.

Resource Consumption and Scalability. The backend is deployed on a dedicated workstation running the GNS3 server. The machine is equipped with an Intel Core i7-4770 CPU operating at 3.40 GHz, 32 GB of RAM, an NVIDIA TITAN Xp GPU, and hardware-assisted virtualization support. All nodes are executed on this server, while the GNS3 graphical management interface is provided as a separate containerized service used to access the server, inspect node states, and design the network topology.

The single-server deployment is selected to evaluate the feasibility of the proposed implementation and the integrated collection of host- and network-level telemetry. In particular, the evaluation focuses on verifying whether the configuration can support the execution of the corporate scenario under controlled conditions. For this purpose, we analyze CPU and memory usage during the incremental startup of the different zones and segments that compose the testbed.

The monitoring campaign is organized into five runs, each corresponding to the activation of a specific subset of the infrastructure. Run 1 includes the startup of the Attacker Zone, the Internet Zone, and the OPNsense firewall. Run 2 includes the DMZ, the Open vSwitch and the M&E segment. Run 3 includes the HR and R&D segments, while Run 4 includes the Technical segment and the Domain Controller. Finally, Run 5 includes the Development and the

Security segments. Each run is monitored for a three-minute observation window after nodes startup. This duration is selected empirically based on preliminary experiments, which indicate the time required for CPU and memory utilization to stabilize after the nodes are launched. The resulting measurements allows us to characterize the resource impact of each functional area and to observe how overall resource consumption evolves as the testbed is progressively instantiated.

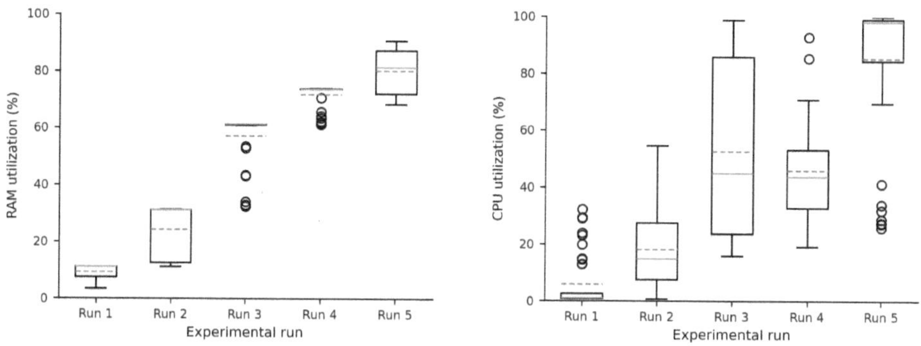

(a) RAM utilization distribution. (b) CPU utilization distribution.

Fig. 4. RAM (a) and CPU (b) utilization (%) distributions during the five incremental startup runs. Each run corresponds to the activation of an additional subset of testbed zones. The orange line indicates the median values, whereas the dashed green line indicates the mean values. (Color figure online)

As expected, RAM usage increases consistently across the five runs (Fig. 4a), reflecting the cumulative memory footprint of the progressively activated nodes. CPU utilization (Fig. 4b), by contrast, exhibits a more variable behavior: while the overall load increases as more components are introduced, the distributions are affected by transient startup operations, service initialization, and background processes, especially in Runs 3–5. Run 5 exhibits the highest overall utilization, corresponding to the activation of the complete testbed.

The analysis is then repeated with the nodes in an active state and operating under the workloads associated with their roles. This second measurement captures the resource demand generated by user activity, services, monitoring components, and background traffic generation. The results of this active-state evaluation, which lasts 15 min, are reported in Fig. 5.

The figure highlights two different trends in CPU and RAM utilization. CPU usage exhibits substantial variability, as concurrent activities performed by different nodes may introduce transient peaks in resource consumption during testbed operation. In contrast, RAM utilization shows a more stable trend, although it reaches approximately 95%. The absence of sharp fluctuations suggests that, despite the high memory footprint, the testbed operates without evident memory-related instability during the observation window and supports the reproduction of the considered scenario.

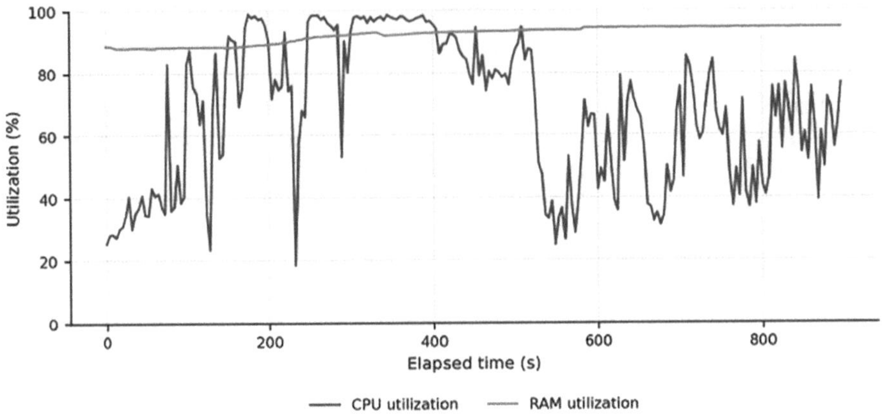

Fig. 5. CPU and RAM utilization during full testbed operation. Measurements are collected over a 15-minute interval while all nodes are active and performing different tasks.

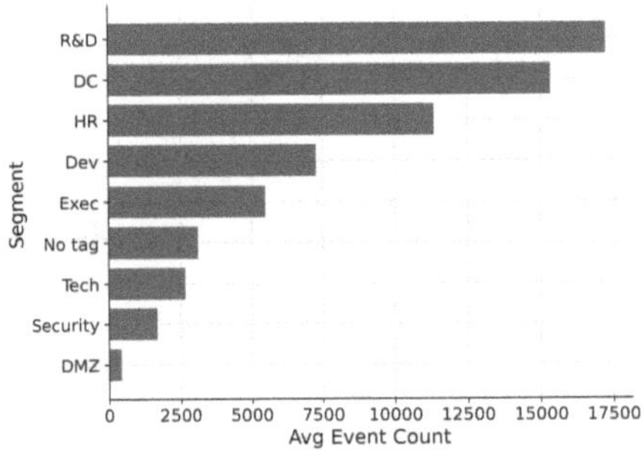

(a) Segment – avg. number of events.

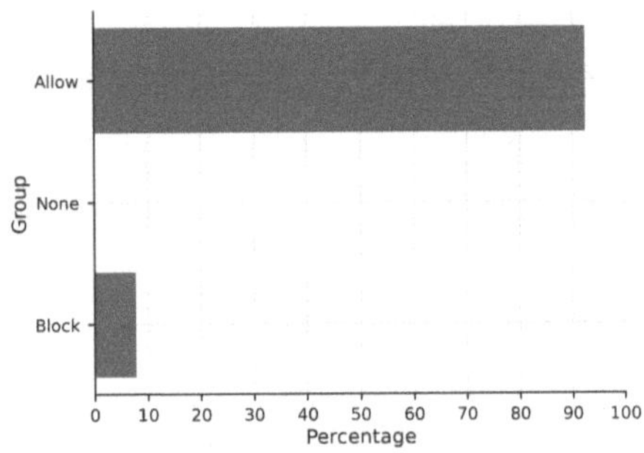

(b) Process creation – reputation.

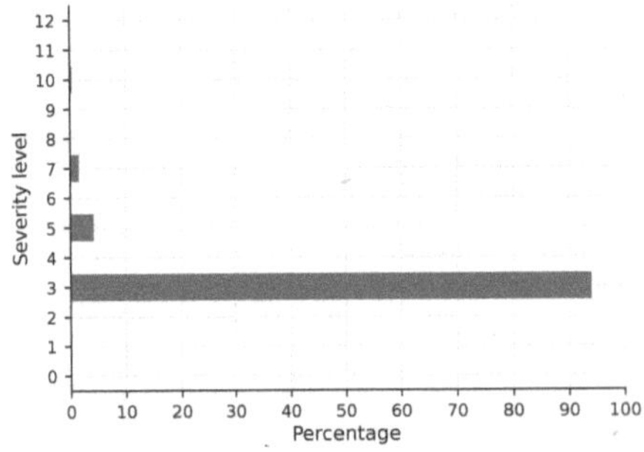

(c) Severity level – alert distribution.

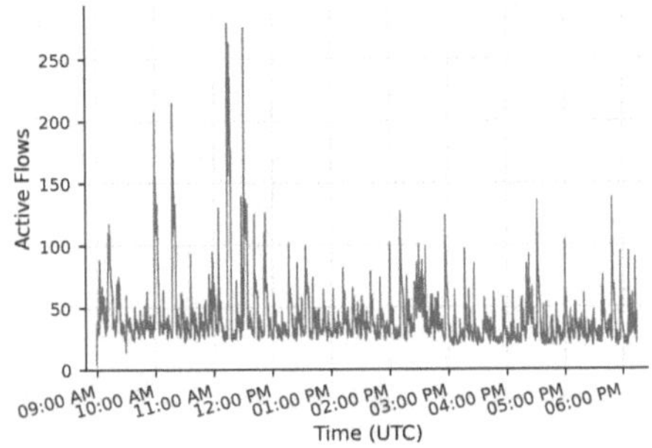

(d) Network – avg. Active Flows.

Fig. 6. High-level overview of the telemetry collected during testbed operation: (a) average (Avg.) event count by network segment, (b) distribution of policy actions, (c) alert distribution by severity level, and (d) Avg. number of active network flows over time.

Security Monitoring Setup. The testbed incorporates security components across both network and host layers. In particular, Wazuh agents are deployed on the main endpoints of the testbed, integrated with host-native telemetry sources. On Windows hosts, events are collected with Sysmon [30], whereas auditd [1] is used on Linux hosts. The resulting observations includes system logs, authentication events, file changes, and security-relevant events, while noisy or low-informative events are excluded from the collection. At the network level, full packet capture in PCAP format is performed with Wireshark on the virtual bridge. Network-level observations also includes firewall logs and alerts generated by Suricata.

The monitoring campaign lasted three days, with approximately eight hours of activity collected per day to emulate a typical corporate working schedule. The first day was reserved for benign activity, whereas adversarial activities were carried out during the second and third days. This organization made it possible to observe how normal operations and adversarial actions were reflected across multiple monitoring points. At the end of the acquisition campaign, the testbed produced around 13 GB of raw network traffic and 245,625 collected events.

Figure 6 provides a high-level quantitative characterization of the collected telemetry. Figure 6a reports the average number of events generated by each network segment. The distribution reflects the infrastructure layout and the modeled activities: segments with enabled logging agents produce higher event volumes, whereas the Security and Technical segments generate fewer events, consistently with the absence of agents in the former and the presence of a single agent in the latter. Approximately 5% of the events are not associated with a VLAN tag, which is consistent with the expected presence of untagged traffic, such as ARP, DHCP, and broadcast traffic. As shown in Fig. 6b, most created processes are included in an allow list, while a smaller fraction is classified as blocked by the EDR policy. Figure 6c reports the distribution of SIEM alerts. Most alerts are associated with severity level 3, whereas higher-severity alerts occur less frequently. In particular, the proportion of alerts progressively decreases for severity levels 5, 7, 10, and 12. This skewed distribution indicates that routine monitoring primarily generates low-severity notifications, while potentially critical conditions account for a limited fraction of the observed alerts. Finally, Fig. 6d depicts the number of active network flows over time. The most pronounced peaks occur around midday and exceed 250 active flows, while additional fluctuations are observed throughout the monitoring window. This behavior is consistent with the concurrent execution of user-like activities, background traffic generation, and service-related operations across the emulated infrastructure.

5 Discussion

The findings outlined in the previous section suggest that GNS3-based emulation can support the design and execution of reproducible cybersecurity scenarios in corporate networks. Nevertheless, the testbed remains an approximation of an enterprise infrastructure, and some operational, scalability, and behavioral aspects cannot be fully captured. This section discusses the main insights derived from the implementation and evaluation of the testbed, as well as the limitations identified during its development and use.

Scalability. The resource analysis presented in Sect. 4.3 shows that DREAMER testbed can be executed on a single GNS3 server for the considered corporate scenario. Nevertheless, scalability remains bounded by the computational resources of the host machine. Increasing the number of endpoints and services would progressively increase resource consumption. This limitation could be addressed through a distributed GNS3 deployment, in which multiple interconnected servers share the workload, enabling larger and more complex scenarios [10].

Behavioral Modeling. During the attack workflow, both attacker and target nodes actions are manually orchestrated to preserve control over the execution of each attack step. Although automated attack-orchestration frameworks are available (e.g., [29,32]), offensive operations are performed manually to validate each phase and assess the network impact of attacker-generated activity. Background benign activity, by contrast, is automated through Ansible. This approach provides a practical trade-off between experimental control and behavioral variability. The automated workloads generates consistent background traffic and host-level events suitable for controlled evaluation and data generation.

Telemetry Acquisition. The experiments conducted on DREAMER demonstrate the practical applicability of the proposed testbed for reproducing corporate-like attack scenarios in a controlled and reproducible setting. The environment supports the collection of network traffic, alerts, and host-level telemetry, allowing attack activities to be observed at different levels of abstraction. The data collected in this preliminary phase, and analyzed in Sect. 4.3, provide initial evidence of the testbed potential for dataset construction, representing a starting point for the future generation of datasets combining network-level and host-level telemetry.

Reproducibility. The experimental process can be replicated by following the device configurations described in Sect. 3. The testbed relies on publicly available appliances and open-source tools, which facilitates reproducibility and reuse. The scenario includes both Linux-based and Windows-based hosts to better reflect a representative corporate environment. For nodes equipped with Windows OS, the activation state was reset to maintain the system within its evaluation period, without affecting the functional behavior of the testbed.

6 Conclusion and Future Work

In this paper we presented DREAMER, a reproducible and open-source testbed for the emulation of corporate-like cybersecurity scenarios. The proposed environment combines GNS3-based network emulation with a hybrid virtualization strategy, enabling the deployment of heterogeneous hosts, segmented corporate services, attacker infrastructure, and integrated monitoring components within a controlled setting. The resource evaluation indicates that the complete scenario can be executed on a single server under controlled conditions, although memory usage increases with the number of active components and CPU load is affected by transient workload and service initialization phases.

Future work will focus on improving the scalability, heterogeneity, and behavioral realism of the proposed testbed. From a scalability perspective, we plan to adopt more powerful hardware and distribute the infrastructure across multiple GNS3 servers, enabling larger topologies, more endpoints, and additional domain-oriented services. This will allow the current corporate scenario to evolve toward a more complex enterprise-scale infrastructure.

A second direction concerns device and network heterogeneity. Future versions could include Wi-Fi interfaces for wireless traffic generation, as well as a dedicated Bring Your Own Device (BYOD) segment composed of mobile and personal devices governed by security policies different from those of the existing segments. This would enable the reproduction of additional attack surfaces.

With regard to adversarial activities, we plan to adopt red-team automation frameworks [29,32], for the systematic execution of well-defined attack techniques. Finally, future research will investigate autonomous AI agents for emulating adaptive, context-aware, and diverse user behaviors, enabling more realistic benign activity patterns and more challenging detection scenarios.

Acknowledgments.. The authors have no competing interests to declare that are relevant to the content of this article. We sincerely appreciate the constructive feedback provided by the reviewers for our paper.

References

1. The Linux audit daemon. https://linux.die.net/man/8/auditd. Accessed 10 May 2026
2. Open vSwitch (2009). https://www.openvswitch.org/. Accessed 10 May 2026
3. OPNsense (2026). https://opnsense.org/. Accessed 10 May 2026
4. Ahrenholz, J., Danilov, C., Henderson, T.R., Kim, J.H.: CORE: a real-time network emulator. In: MILCOM 2008-2008 IEEE Military Communications Conference, pp. 1–7. IEEE (2008)
5. Alshamrani, A., Myneni, S., Chowdhary, A., Huang, D.: A survey on advanced persistent threats: techniques, solutions, challenges, and research opportunities. IEEE Commun. Surv. Tutor. **21**(2), 1851–1877 (2019)
6. Ansible Project Contributors: Ansible. https://docs.ansible.com/. Accessed 10 May 2026
7. Bellard, F.: QEMU, a fast and portable dynamic translator. In: Usenix ATC, Freenix Track, pp. 41–46 (2005)
8. Benzel, T., Wroclawski, J.: The deter project: towards structural advances in experimental cybersecurity research and evaluation. Info. Media Technol. **7**(4), 1615–1625 (2012)
9. Berman, M., et al.: GENI: a federated testbed for innovative network experiments. Comput. Netw. **61**, 5–23 (2014)

10. Sáez-de Cámara, X., Flores, J.L., Arellano, C., Urbieta, A., Zurutuza, U.: Gotham testbed: a reproducible IoT testbed for security experiments and dataset generation. IEEE Trans. Depend. Secure Comput. **21**(1), 186–203 (2023)
11. Conti, M., Donadel, D., Turrin, F.: A survey on industrial control system testbeds and datasets for security research. IEEE Commun. Surv. Tutor. **23**(4), 2248–2294 (2021)
12. Dehlaghi-Ghadim, A., Balador, A., Moghadam, M.H., Hansson, H., Conti, M.: ICSSIM–a framework for building industrial control systems security testbeds. Comput. Ind. **148**, 103906 (2023)
13. Dong, F., et al.: DISTDET: a cost-effective distributed cyber threat detection system. In: 32nd USENIX Security Symposium (USENIX Security 23), pp. 6575–6592 (2023)
14. GNS3 Technologies: Graphical Network Simulator-3 (GNS3) (2026). https://www.gns3.com/. Accessed 10 May 2026
15. Goldschmidt, P., Chudá, D.: Network intrusion datasets: a survey, limitations, and recommendations. Comput. Sec. **156**, 104510 (2025)
16. Gomez, J., Kfoury, E.F., Crichigno, J., Srivastava, G.: A survey on network simulators, emulators, and testbeds used for research and education. Comput. Netw. **237**, 110054 (2023)
17. Hindy, H., Bayne, E., Bures, M., Atkinson, R., Tachtatzis, C., Bellekens, X.: Machine learning based IoT intrusion detection system: an MQTT case study (MQTT-IoT-IDS2020 dataset). In: International networking conference, pp. 73–84. Springer (2020)
18. Homoliak, I., Toffalini, F., Guarnizo, J., Elovici, Y., Ochoa, M.: Insight Into Insiders and IT: a survey of insider threat taxonomies, analysis, modeling, and countermeasures. ACM Comput. Surv. (CSUR) **52**(2), 1–40 (2019)
19. Hutchins, E.M., Cloppert, M.J., Amin, R.M., et al.: Intelligence-driven computer network defense informed by analysis of adversary campaigns and intrusion kill chains. Leading Issues Info. Warfare Sec. Res. **1**(1), 80 (2011)
20. Kampourakis, V., Gkioulos, V., Katsikas, S.: A step-by-step definition of a reference architecture for cyber ranges. J. Info. Secur. Appl. **88**, 103917 (2025)
21. Koroniotis, N., Moustafa, N., Sitnikova, E., Turnbull, B.: Towards the development of realistic botnet dataset in the internet of things for network forensic analytics: bot-IoT dataset. Futur. Gener. Comput. Syst. **100**, 779–796 (2019)
22. Lantz, B., Heller, B., McKeown, N.: A network in a laptop: rapid prototyping for software-defined networks. In: Proceedings of the 9th ACM SIGCOMM Workshop on Hot Topics in Networks, pp. 1–6 (2010)
23. Liu, J., Inam, M.A., Goyal, A., Riddle, A., Westfall, K., Bates, A.: What we talk about when we talk about logs: understanding the effects of dataset quality on endpoint threat detection research. In: 2025 IEEE Symposium on Security and Privacy (SP), pp. 112–129. IEEE (2025)
24. Merkel, D.: Docker: lightweight Linux containers for consistent development and deployment. Linux J. **2014**(239) (2014)
25. Myneni, S., et al.: Unraveled–a semi-synthetic dataset for advanced persistent threats. Comput. Netw. **227**, 109688 (2023)
26. NS-3 Consortium: NS-3: Network simulator (2022). https://www.nsnam.org/. Accessed 10 May 2026
27. Österlind, F.: A sensor network simulator for the Contiki OS, Swedish Institute of Computer Science (2006)

28. Puljiz, Z., Mikuc, M.: IMUNES based distributed network emulator. In: International Conference on Software in Telecommunications and Computer Networks, pp. 198–203. IEEE (2006)
29. Red Canary, a Zscaler company: Atomic Red Team. https://github.com/redcanaryco/atomic-red-team. Accessed 10 May 2026
30. Russinovich, Mark and Garnier, Thomas: Sysmon. https://learn.microsoft.com/en-us/sysinternals/downloads/sysmon. Accessed 10 May 2026
31. Sauer, F., Niedermaier, M., Kießling, S., Merli, D.: LICSTER-a low-cost ICS security testbed for education and research (2019). arXiv:1910.00303 arXiv preprint
32. The MITRE Corporation: MITRE Caldera. https://github.com/apache/caldera. Accessed 11 June 2026
33. Varga, A., Hornig, R.: An overview of the OMNeT++ simulation environment. In: Proceedings of the 1st International Conference on Simulation Tools and Techniques for Communications, Networks and Systems & Workshops, pp. 1–10 (2008)
34. White, B., et al.: An integrated experimental environment for distributed systems and networks. ACM SIGOPS Operat. Syst. Re. **36**(SI), 255–270 (2002)
35. Yang, F., Xu, J., Xiong, C., Li, Z., Zhang, K.: PROGRAPHER: an anomaly detection system based on provenance graph embedding. In: 32nd USENIX Security Symposium (USENIX Security 23), pp. 4355–4372 (2023)
36. Zhang, X., et al.: Robust log-based anomaly detection on unstable log data. In: Proceedings of the 2019 27th ACM Joint Meeting on European Software Engineering Conference and Symposium on the Foundations of Software Engineering, pp. 807–817 (2019)

Memory Sanitization for Bare-Metal Firmware Fuzzing via Static Analysis and Memory Access Observation

Luca Jungnickel, Karsten Isakovic(✉), Ramon Barakat, and Martin A. Schneider

Fraunhofer Institute for Open Communication Systems (FOKUS), Berlin, Germany
{Luca.Jungnickel,Karsten.Isakovic,Ramon.Barakat,
Martin.Schneider}@fokus.fraunhofer.de

Abstract. Memory sanitization is a key technique for detecting memory corruption bugs during fuzzing. While tools such as AddressSanitizer are widely used in OS-hosted environments, they cannot be applied to bare-metal firmware due to the absence of operating system abstractions. We propose a sanitization architecture for bare-metal firmware fuzzing that combines static analysis of the firmware binary with runtime memory access observation inside an emulator. Built on top of the Hoedur firmware fuzzer, our approach tracks accesses to global, stack, and heap memory regions without requiring source-code instrumentation. Evaluation on 22 real-world firmware targets demonstrates that the architecture correctly reconstructs program flow and intercepts memory accesses that remain invisible to conventional crash- and hang-based fuzzing. The program flow reconstruction correctly handles diverse control-flow patterns including tail calls, loop functions, and multi-threaded execution across all targets. We trace the remaining inaccuracies to incomplete pointer resolution and unhandled bulk memory operations in the static analysis, both of which represent solvable engineering challenges. We systematically analyze the sources of imprecision encountered and identify concrete directions for achieving practical detection accuracy in future work.

Keywords: firmware fuzzing · bare-metal fuzzing · memory sanitization · IoT devices · embedded security · static analysis

1 Introduction

Software designed for Internet of Things (IoT) and embedded devices typically operates as self-contained firmware running directly on hardware without an operating system, commonly referred to as "bare-metal". The limited observability and debugging capabilities of such devices can pose significant challenges during the testing phase (including fuzzing). Consider an application that writes beyond the boundaries of a local buffer. In an OS-hosted environment, a binary instrumented with AddressSanitizer (ASan) [12] could be used to detect this

P. Kieseberg et al. (Eds.): ARES 2026 Workshops, LNCS 16903, pp. 662–676, 2027.
https://doi.org/10.1007/978-3-032-37218-5_38

overflow. In the context of bare-metal firmware, the overflow silently corrupts adjacent stack variables. Unless the corruption results in a crash or hang, the vulnerability cannot be detected.

This example illustrates a fundamental gap in existing fuzzing approaches for bare-metal firmware: the lack of memory sanitization. While this challenge has been well-addressed in operating system contexts, effective sanitization for bare-metal firmware remains an open problem.

Sanitizers such as ASan rely on compiler instrumentation and OS-level runtime support: intercepting memory allocation functions, maintaining shadow memory, and reporting violations via standard library hooks. Bare-metal firmware lacks these abstractions entirely. There is no standard C library to intercept, no OS to manage shadow memory, and no error reporting infrastructure. Applying ASan to bare-metal firmware is therefore not feasible.

We address this gap by proposing a sanitization architecture specifically designed for bare-metal firmware fuzzing. Our approach combines static analysis of the firmware binary with runtime observation of memory accesses within the emulator, enabling the detection of previously undetectable memory bugs without requiring source code or recompilation. We cover all three memory regions present in bare-metal firmware: global, stack, and heap. Our contribution is threefold. First, we propose an architecture for memory sanitization in the context of bare-metal firmware fuzzing that requires only the firmware binary with debug symbols. Second, we describe the design of a sanitization engine that tracks memory accesses by combining static analysis via Ghidra [7] with runtime observation of QEMU [2] basic block execution, built on top of the Hoedur firmware fuzzer [10]. Third, we evaluate the approach on 22 real-world firmware targets, analyzing the challenges encountered including false-positive sources, their root causes, and runtime overhead, thereby providing a roadmap for achieving practical sanitization accuracy.

The remainder of this paper is organized as follows. Section 2 provides background information on grey-box firmware fuzzing and memory sanitization. Section 3 discusses related work. Section 4 presents our sanitization architecture, covering static firmware analysis, the sanitization engine, program flow reconstruction and heap handling. Section 5 evaluates the approach on 22 real-world firmware targets and discusses the results. Section 6 concludes the paper and outlines directions for future work.

2 Background

2.1 Grey-Box Firmware Fuzzing

Fuzzing bare-metal firmware is challenging due to the close interactions between the software and the hardware peripherals. There is no operating system that provides an abstraction layer and input interfaces vary across devices.

One approach to fuzz bare-metal firmware is to emulate it in a virtual environment, which provides better determinism, observability, and scalability compared to testing on physical hardware. Firmware fuzzers such as Fuzzware [9] and Hoedur [10] exploit the observation that memory-mapped I/O (MMIO) accesses are a natural input interface for bare-metal firmware: by intercepting MMIO reads and supplying fuzzer-generated data, they can systematically explore firmware behavior. Both tools adopt coverage-guided grey-box fuzzing, using basic block coverage information from the emulator to guide input mutation, following the approach pioneered by AFL [16].

2.2 Memory Sanitization

Fuzzing detects vulnerabilities primarily through two signals: crashes and hangs of the System Under Test (SUT). However, many memory corruption vulnerabilities do not cause either. For example, a buffer overflow that silently overwrites an adjacent variable corrupts the program state but does not necessarily crash the system. Such vulnerabilities remain invisible to the fuzzer unless additional mechanisms are in place.

Sanitization tools address this gap by instrumenting the SUT so that a wider range of memory errors produces observable signals. The most widely used sanitizer is AddressSanitizer [12]. At compile time, ASan inserts *redzones*, regions of inaccessible memory, around heap, stack, and global objects. Additionally, it maintains a *shadow memory* that tracks which addresses are accessible. On each memory access, ASan checks the shadow memory and reports violations such as out-of-bounds accesses and use-after-free errors. Figure 1 illustrates this principle for stack frames: redzones inserted between local variables enable detection of invalid memory accesses that would otherwise silently corrupt neighboring variables.

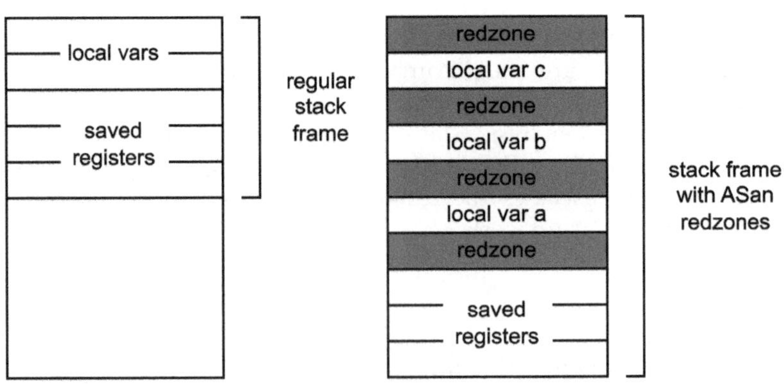

Fig. 1. Stack frames compiled without (left) and with ASan (right). ASan inserts redzone regions between local variables and at the boundaries of the local variable area to detect out-of-bounds memory accesses at runtime.

2.3 Bare-Metal Firmware Memory Layout

Figure 2 shows the typical memory layout found in bare-metal ARM firmware. The lowest addresses contain read-only memory (ROM), which stores the firmware code and constant data. The random-access memory (RAM) region is divided into three areas: globals, heap and stack. Global variables occupy fixed addresses determined at link time, the stack grows downward from a defined starting address, and the heap, managed by an allocator linked into the firmware, occupies the upper portion of RAM. Memory-mapped I/O (MMIO) registers are mapped at fixed, device-specific addresses above the RAM region.

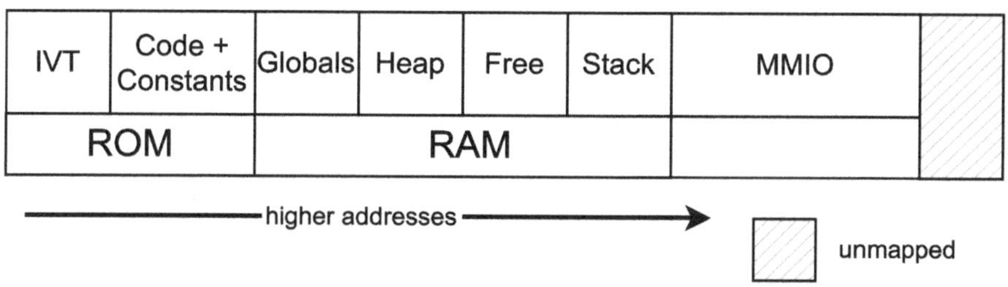

Fig. 2. Typical memory layout of bare-metal ARMv7 firmware. ROM starts with the Interrupt Vector Table (IVT) at the lowest addresses, followed by code and constants. In RAM, global variables occupy fixed addresses at the base, followed by the heap growing upward toward higher addresses. The stack is placed at the top of RAM and grows downward, leaving a shared free region between heap and stack. MMIO registers are mapped at higher, device-specific addresses.

3 Related Work

3.1 Emulation-Based Firmware Fuzzing

Several emulation-based approaches have been proposed for fuzzing bare-metal firmware, progressively improving peripheral modeling and fuzzing performance. P^2IM [5] introduces automated peripheral interface modeling, and HALucinator [3] enables firmware re-hosting through abstraction layer emulation. Fuzzware [9] uses automated MMIO modeling to increase fuzzing effectiveness and Hoedur [10] improves fuzzing performance by using multi-stream inputs. None of these approaches incorporate memory sanitization into the fuzzing loop.

3.2 Compiler-Based Sanitization

In the OS-hosted domain, several sanitizers have been developed that rely on compiler instrumentation. AddressSanitizer (ASan) [12] detects out-of-bounds accesses and different heap violations, such as use-after-frees by inserting redzones and maintaining shadow memory. MemorySanitizer (MSan) [14] detects reads of uninitialized memory by tracking the initialization state of accessed memory. ThreadSanitizer (TSan) [13] identifies data races by instrumenting memory accesses and synchronization operations while maintaining a shadow memory. All three depend on OS-level runtime libraries for shadow memory management, which are unavailable in bare-metal environments.

3.3 Binary-Level Sanitization

RetroWrite [4] performs static binary rewriting on position-independent Linux executables to insert ASan instrumentation without source code, achieving comparable detection to compiler-based ASan. However, it relies on position-independent code, relocation information, and standard OS abstractions such as dynamic linking, none of which are available in bare-metal firmware.

3.4 Firmware-Specific Sanitization

EmbSan [6] performs sanitization for embedded OS firmware by intercepting relevant instructions within the emulator and checking on the host side for access violations. DFirmSan [15] targets Linux-based firmware by monitoring memory boundaries at sensitive function call sites during runtime to detect silent memory corruptions. Both approaches rely on OS-level abstractions, making neither directly applicable to bare-metal firmware.

4 Design

We implement our approach on top of Hoedur [10], which demonstrated strong fuzzing performance on bare-metal ARM firmware and is available as open-source software[1]. Hoedur uses QEMU as its emulation backend, providing the necessary observability into the firmware's runtime behavior to intercept basic block execution, inspect register state, and trace all memory accesses performed by the firmware.

The following classes of memory errors are targeted: stack buffer overflows and underflows between local variables, heap buffer overflows and underflows beyond allocated boundaries, use-after-free accesses to deallocated heap memory, and unauthorized access to global variables from unexpected code locations. Intra-object overflows and underflows (e.g., within a single array) and non-address-related undefined behavior are out of scope.

Our approach determines the validity of each memory access by combining two information sources. First, static analysis of the firmware binary extracts the expected memory layout: the positions and sizes of global variables, stack frame layouts of all functions, and the locations of heap management functions. Second, at runtime, we intercept QEMU basic block execution to reconstruct the program flow by tracking function calls and returns via the program counter

[1] Under the GNU Affero General Public License Version 3.

and stack pointer. The two sources are combined and memory *access control lists* are created, which keep track of which memory accesses are allowed and prohibited. When a memory read or write occurs, the sanitization engine checks these access control lists and reports violations. Figure 3 depicts the complete pipeline.

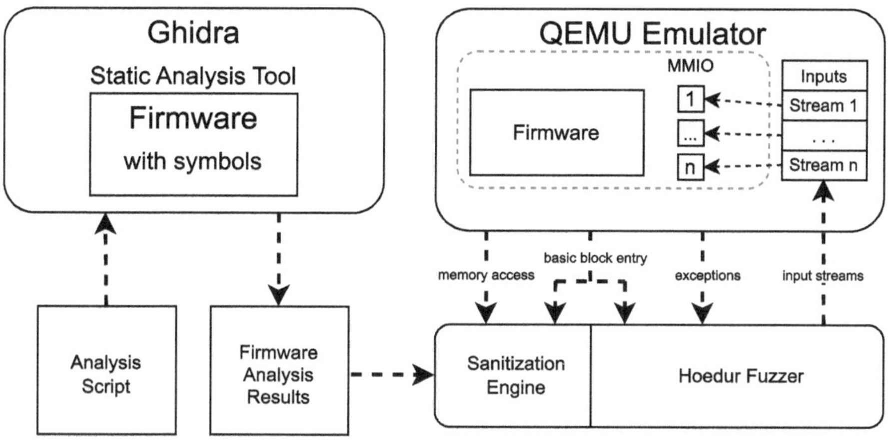

Fig. 3. Architectural overview. Before fuzzing, the firmware binary is statically analyzed by Ghidra to extract memory layout information. During fuzzing, QEMU executes the firmware and reports memory accesses and basic block entries to the sanitization engine, while basic block entries and exceptions are forwarded to the Hoedur fuzzer. The sanitization engine combines these runtime observations with static analysis results to determine whether each memory access is valid. Fuzzer inputs are supplied to the firmware via n independent MMIO input streams.

4.1 Static Analysis

Before running the fuzzing campaign, the firmware binary is analyzed statically to extract information about the expected memory layout. The analysis is divided into three parts, corresponding to the three memory regions of interest.

For *global variable sanitization*, the analysis extracts the absolute memory address and size of each global variable. Additionally, for each function in the firmware, the analysis records which global variables the function accesses and whether the access is a read or write. This produces per-variable *allow-lists* that specify which functions may legitimately access each global variable.

For *stack sanitization*, the analysis collects the following information about every function: its address range, stack frame size, and the position and size of each local variable and structure within the frame, as well as function parameters.

For *heap sanitization*, the analysis identifies heap management functions (e.g., `malloc`, `free`, `calloc`, `realloc`) by name. Their addresses are recorded so that the sanitization engine can intercept calls to these functions at runtime.

We perform static analysis using Ghidra [7] via its Java API. The analysis requires a firmware binary with debug symbols. The requirement is a limitation; however, firmware research corpora such as the Hoedur-Experiments suite provide debug builds [11], and many vendor SDKs ship debug-enabled binaries during development. Extending the approach to stripped binaries, for instance by leveraging Ghidra's heuristic type recovery or partial DWARF information, is left to future work.

4.2 Emulation Interface

Hoedur invokes custom hook functions on each QEMU basic block entry and on each memory access. On a basic block entry, the hook provides the program counter (PC), stack pointer (SP), and a callback function to read and modify registers R0–R3. On a memory access, it provides the target address, width, and type (read or write). These two callbacks are the sole interface between the emulator and the sanitization engine.

4.3 Sanitization Engine

The sanitization engine evaluates whether each memory access during emulation is allowed or prohibited. It reconstructs the program flow using call stacks and manages separate access control lists for global variables, stack variables, heap in-use redzones, and freed heap memory. The engine hooks into QEMU at two points: at each basic block entry and at each memory read or write. At each basic block entry, the sanitization engine receives information about all registers. Inspecting the program counter and stack pointer, together with the information about functions acquired during static analysis, allows the engine to reconstruct the program flow. The sanitization strategy is as follows: entering a function adds all addresses of the caller's stack frame to the stack redzones; returning from the function removes them. For heap memory, the engine intercepts calls to heap management functions such as `malloc` and `free`. On allocation, it modifies the return value to insert redzones around the allocated block and records their addresses in the heap in-use redzone list. On deallocation, the corresponding addresses are moved from the in-use list to the freed heap redzone list. Global variable sanitization operates on an allow-list basis, permitting only accesses from expected code locations. Stack and heap sanitization, in contrast, operate on a deny-list basis: any access to a restricted address is flagged, regardless of where in the program it originates.

When the QEMU emulation encounters a memory read or write, the access control lists are inspected:

If the accessed address

- refers to a global variable, it is checked whether the current program counter is in its allow-list. If not, a forbidden global variable access is reported.
- is contained in the stack redzones, a forbidden stack access is reported.
- is contained in the heap in-use redzones, a heap buffer overflow is reported.
- is contained in the freed heap redzones, a use-after-free is reported.

4.4 Program Flow Reconstruction

The sanitization engine receives a callback from QEMU at each basic block entry. Each callback provides the current program counter (PC), stack pointer (SP), and registers R0–R3. Based on these values, the engine classifies each transition as a function call, a function return, or continued execution within the current function, thereby reconstructing the firmware's program flow.

A naïve approach would rely solely on SP changes, since function calls conventionally grow the stack. However, in our dataset of 22 SUTs, 70% of functions do not allocate a stack frame: they operate entirely in registers or access only global variables. The ARMv7-M architecture [1] adds further complexity to SP-based tracking through its link register (LR) mechanism, which enables tail calls and leaf-function returns without modifying the stack. Consequently, changes to the PC are more reliable indicators of control-flow transitions than SP changes alone.

The sanitization engine maintains a *call stack*, an ordered sequence of *frame records*. Each frame record stores the SP value at function entry, the function's statically determined frame size, and its start address. We refer to the most recently pushed frame record as the *top of call stack* (TOC).

On each basic block entry, the sanitization engine classifies the transition by inspecting the PC and SP relative to the call stack state. If the PC is at the start address of a known function and the SP has not increased (i.e., the stack has not shrunk), the engine registers a *function call*: a new frame record is pushed onto the call stack and becomes the new TOC. If, instead, the PC lies inside a function that already appears on the call stack but is not the TOC, and the current SP falls within the range recorded in that function's frame record, the engine registers a *function return*: all frame records above the matching entry, including the TOC, are popped. This reflects one or more completed returns. If neither of these conditions applies, it is assumed that execution will continue within the current function.

Stack Variable Access Control Each modification to the call stack triggers a corresponding update of the stack redzones, as illustrated in Fig. 4. When a function call pushes a new frame record to the call stack, the addresses of all local variables in the *caller's* frame, except for variables passed as pointers to the callee, are added to the deny-list. The static analysis provides both the layout of each stack frame and the locations where variable pointers are passed to callees. When a frame record is popped upon function return, the corresponding locked addresses are removed from the stack redzones, restoring access within the returning function.

This mechanism ensures that a callee can only access the caller's stack variables through explicitly passed pointers. Any other access to a locked variable is flagged as a stack access violation.

Edge Cases Applying the classification described above to the 22 SUTs of the Hoedur-Experiments suite [11] reveals several recurring edge cases that require special handling.

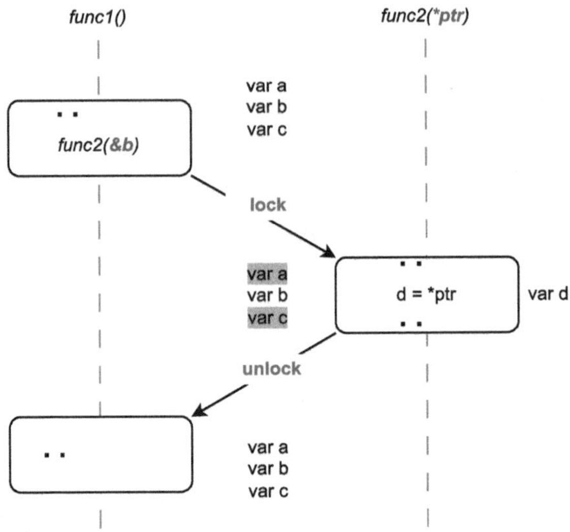

Fig. 4. Stack variable locking during a function call. Function `func1` has three local stack variables `a`, `b`, and `c`. When `func1` calls `func2`, the engine locks all of `func1`'s local variables except `b`, which is passed as a pointer. Inside `func2`, the variable `d` refers to `func1`'s variable `b`, allowing legitimate access inside another stack frame. Accessing variables `a` or `c` (highlighted in red) would trigger an access violation. When `func2` returns, the locked variables are unlocked, restoring full access within `func1`.

Frame-Size Adjustment. The callee's entry SP may overlap with the caller's statically determined frame region. The engine handles this by computing the *effective* frame region as the intersection of the static frame and the region above the callee's entry SP; only variables within this region are locked. Every target in our dataset required at least one such adjustment.

Direct Branches into Function Bodies. In 11 of 22 SUTs, the PC enters the body of a function not present on the call stack, without passing through its entry point, while the SP remains unchanged. This pattern corresponds to compiler-generated tail jumps, where one function branches directly into the middle of another to reduce code size or latency. The engine handles this case by replacing the TOC with a new frame record for the target function, since the original function has been left without a conventional return.

Loop Functions. Some functions have their entry point located inside a loop body. Without special handling, each iteration of the loop's back-edge would be misclassified as a new function call, since the program counter repeatedly reaches the function's start address. The key observation is that the SP remains constant across iterations: unlike a genuine function call, no stack frame is allocated or deallocated.

When this pattern is observed, the engine adds the function to a list of recognized loop functions. Subsequent entries into a registered loop function with an unchanged SP are treated as continued execution rather than new function calls. This list also ensures that interrupt returns into a loop context are handled correctly.

In our dataset, 10 of 22 SUTs featured at least one loop function.

Threading. Some firmware targets execute multiple threads, each with its own stack region. A thread switch causes the SP to jump into a different region, which would corrupt the call stack state if not handled explicitly. Thread creation is dynamic and cannot be derived reliably from static analysis alone.

The engine addresses this by maintaining multiple call stack instances. On each basic block entry, it selects the call stack whose SP range contains the current SP value. If no existing call stack matches, a new instance is created as follows. The upper bound of the new call stack is initialized from the current SP. Bare-metal firmware commonly allocates thread stacks as global arrays of fixed size. If the current SP falls within such an array, the array's base address is used as the lower bound of the new call stack. Otherwise, the lower bound is estimated and adjusted downward as deeper function calls are observed on that call stack.

In our dataset, 5 of 22 SUTs used more than one thread.

4.5 Heap Memory Management Functions

In OS-hosted environments, ASan intercepts heap management functions such as `malloc` and `free` by replacing them with instrumented versions provided by the ASan runtime library. In bare-metal firmware, this approach is not applicable: the ASan runtime library cannot be ported, as it depends on OS interfaces (e.g., `mmap`) that do not exist on the target.

Our approach overcomes this limitation by identifying heap management functions by name during static analysis and recording their entry addresses. At runtime, the sanitization engine detects when the program counter enters or leaves these functions and updates the heap access control lists accordingly.

Upon detecting a call to an allocation function (e.g., `malloc`, `calloc`), the engine modifies the size parameter to request additional space for leading and trailing redzones. When the function returns, the engine adjusts the returned pointer to account for the leading redzone. The addresses occupied by both redzones are added to the heap in-use redzone list. Any subsequent read or write to a redzone address is flagged as a heap boundary violation.

Upon detecting a call to `free`, the engine records the entire freed block, excluding its redzones, in the freed heap redzone list. Any subsequent access to an address in this list is reported as a use-after-free violation.

When a new allocation returns an address range that overlaps with previously freed blocks, the engine removes the affected entries from the freed heap redzone list and updates the in-use redzone list for the new allocation.

Finally, heap memory violation detection is disabled while execution is inside a heap management function. This is required because allocators routinely read and write freed memory as part of their internal bookkeeping.

4.6 Access Violation Suppression via Permits

Static analysis of the firmware binary has inherent limitations that cause false positives during sanitization. Two cases are particularly common. First, for global variables, accesses performed through pointers or structure offsets may not be attributable to a specific function during static analysis. As a result, the global variable allow-list may be missing legitimate access entries, causing valid accesses to be flagged as violations. Second, for stack variables, when a function receives a pointer to a structure, the static analysis may not resolve all fields accessed through that pointer, leading to legitimate accesses being flagged as violations.

Unaddressed, false positives result in the premature termination of the respective fuzzing run, preventing deeper exploration of the firmware's behavior. To mitigate this without discarding sanitization entirely, the engine implements an automated *permit* mechanism.

The engine counts how often each unique access pattern is flagged as a violation. For global variables, a pattern is identified by the accessed variable and the accessing function. When a pattern has been flagged more than n times across fuzzing runs (in our experiments, $n = 10$), the engine creates a *permit* that silently allows this access in subsequent executions.

For stack access violations, the same mechanism is applied, with patterns identified by the owning function, the stack offset, and the accessing function.

To preserve the reproducibility of individual fuzzing runs, the current set of permits is stored within each fuzzing input file and inherited during mutation. When a fuzzing input from the corpus is replayed, it carries exactly the permits that were active during its initial execution. This design ensures that a given input always produces the same sanitization outcome.

5 Results and Discussion

5.1 Evaluation Goals and Experimental Setup

The evaluation addresses three questions:

(1) Does the sanitization architecture run stably on diverse real-world firmware, correctly reconstructing program flow across all targets?

(2) Does it produce reports beyond conventional crash- and hang-based detection?

(3) What are the sources of imprecision, and how do they inform future improvements?

We evaluated the sanitization engine on 22 real-world firmware targets from the Hoedur-Experiments suite [11]. Each target was fuzzed for 10 min in 10 independent runs. This duration was chosen because findings stabilize rapidly: as Table 1 shows, nearly all targets exhibit a standard deviation of zero or near-zero, indicating that the set of reported violations converges within the first minutes of execution. Since the primary evaluation goal at this stage is to characterize the types and sources of reports rather than to maximize code coverage, extending the campaign duration would not change the qualitative results. Table 1 reports the number of distinct findings per target, averaged over the 10 runs, with standard deviation reported. The *Slowdown* column shows the slowdown factor, defined as the baseline throughput divided by the sanitized throughput (e.g., 17x means fuzzing with sanitization is 17 times slower).

The *Hoedur* column lists bugs detected through the existing crash- and hang-based mechanisms of the baseline fuzzer, which remain functional with the sanitization engine active. The *Global* and *Stack* columns list additional reports produced exclusively by our sanitization engine. These are memory access violations not detectable by conventional crash- and hang-based fuzzing. No heap-related memory violations were detected across any target; we therefore omit the heap column from the table. An empty cell indicates zero findings for that category.

Table 1. Average number of findings (± std. dev.) over 10 runs of 10 min each. *Hoedur*: bugs detected by baseline fuzzer. *Global* / *Stack*: additional reports from the sanitization engine. *Slowdown*: slowdown factor (baseline throughput / sanitized throughput). No heap violations were observed.

SUT	Hoedur	Global	Stack	Slowdown
3Dprinter	1.0 ± 0.0		2.4 ± 0.7	17×
6LoWPAN_Receiver	2.0 ± 0.0		2.0 ± 0.0	25×
CNC		2.0 ± 0.0	6.0 ± 0.0	64×
Console			8.0 ± 0.0	22×
contiki_ng_41873			4.0 ± 0.0	29×
Drone			20.4 ± 1.0	18×
Gateway	1.0 ± 0.0			62×
Heatpress				28×
LiteOS_IoT		17.0 ± 0.0	1.0 ± 0.0	68×
PLC			2.0 ± 0.0	81×
Reflow_Oven	1.0 ± 0.0		19.0 ± 0.0	53×
RF_Door_Lock		70.6 ± 2.1	15.0 ± 0.0	154×
riot_24823			23.3 ± 1.7	8×
Robot	1.0 ± 0.0		21.1 ± 0.7	63×
Soldering_Iron			5.2 ± 1.2	89×
Steering_Control			5.0 ± 0.0	12×
Thermostat		64.2 ± 2.5	128.9 ± 0.3	125×
uemu_gpstracker	1.0 ± 0.0	0.1 ± 0.3		23×
utasker_MODBUS			38.9 ± 0.7	62×
utasker_USB			73.0 ± 5.1	48×
XML_Parser		16.0 ± 0.0	37.4 ± 1.1	27×
Zephyr_SocketCan		43.0 ± 0.0	41.9 ± 1.6	11×

5.2 Architectural Stability

The sanitization engine ran successfully on all 22 targets without crashes or call stack corruption. The program flow reconstruction correctly handled all identified edge cases, including tail jumps (11 targets), loop functions (10 targets), and multi-threaded execution (5 targets). The low standard deviations across runs confirm that the engine produces deterministic, reproducible results. The sanitization engine produced additional reports for 20 of 22 targets: 7 targets triggered global variable violations and 19 triggered stack violations.

5.3 False-Positive Analysis

Manual inspection revealed that none of the sanitizer reports could be confirmed as true positives at this stage. We systematically traced the false positives to two identifiable root causes, both of which stem from limitations of the static analysis input rather than from flaws in the sanitization architecture itself. The first root cause is inaccuracies in the static analysis that lead to incomplete or incorrect variable boundary information. When Ghidra does not fully resolve pointer-based accesses, structure field offsets, or indirect references, the resulting allow-lists and variable layouts are incomplete, causing legitimate accesses to be flagged as violations. This affects both global variable allow-lists and stack frame layouts. The second root cause is that bulk memory operations such as `memcpy`, `memset`, and formatted output functions (e.g., `printf` variants) access memory regions that span multiple variable boundaries. Because these functions operate on raw address ranges rather than individual variables, they are systematically flagged by the sanitization engine. These operations occur both during firmware initialization and during normal execution, making simple whitelisting of startup routines insufficient.

Targets with high report counts, such as Thermostat (128.9 stack, 64.2 global) and RF_Door_Lock (70.6 global), are dominated by such false positives. The absence of heap findings stems from the limited prevalence of dynamic allocation in firmware binaries, with only 5 of the 22 SUTs utilizing heap management functions. Among these five targets, heap usage is limited to allocation during initialization, with no dynamic allocation patterns during the fuzzed execution paths. Longer fuzzing campaigns reaching deeper program states may be necessary to trigger heap-related violations.

5.4 Runtime Overhead

As shown in the *Slowdown* column of Table 1, the sanitization engine introduces substantial runtime overhead, ranging from 8× (riot_24823) to 154× (RF_Door_Lock). Three factors contribute to this overhead. First, QEMU's memory-access tracing mechanism, which is disabled during normal fuzzing, intercepts every load and store instruction executed by the firmware. Second, at each basic block entry, the sanitization engine must classify the control-flow transition, maintain the call stacks, and update the stack deny-lists accordingly.

Third, on each intercepted memory access, the engine performs lookups against multiple access control lists.

This overhead is comparable to other heavyweight dynamic analyses that operate without compiler support: Valgrind's Memcheck, for instance, incurs 30× slowdown on native Linux binaries despite having access to OS abstractions [8]. In our setting, the analysis is more demanding because every memory access must be checked externally through the emulator interface.

Nonetheless, reducing the overhead is important for practical deployment. Promising directions include improving the precision of static variable boundary analysis, extending allow-lists to account for bulk memory functions such as `memcpy` and `memset`, augmenting the static analysis with type and access information gathered at runtime, and adopting more efficient data structures for the access control lookups.

6 Conclusion

We presented a memory sanitization architecture for bare-metal firmware fuzzing that operates without source code or recompilation. By combining static analysis of the firmware binary with runtime memory access observation inside QEMU, the approach extends the Hoedur firmware fuzzer with sanitization capabilities for global, stack, and heap memory regions. Evaluation on 22 real-world firmware images demonstrated that the architecture is stable across diverse firmware targets, correctly reconstructing program flow in the presence of tail calls, loop functions, and multi-threaded execution. The sanitization engine intercepts memory accesses that are invisible to conventional crash- and hang-based fuzzing. However, the current false-positive rate prevents practical deployment. Our analysis traces these false positives to two concrete, identifiable limitations of the static analysis input: incomplete pointer resolution and unhandled bulk memory operations. The runtime overhead further limits scalability. Reducing the false-positive rate represents the most critical next step. Since both root causes are attributable to the static analysis quality rather than to the sanitization architecture, targeted improvements are feasible: improving the precision of static variable boundary analysis, extending allow-lists to account for bulk memory operations and formatted output functions, and combining static analysis with runtime type information gathered during emulation. Reducing the runtime overhead through more efficient access control list data structures is a further prerequisite for practical deployment.

Acknowledgments. This work was supported by the DOSS project, funded by the European Union's Horizon Europe research and innovation program under grant agreement No 101120270 – DOSS.

Disclosure of Interests. The authors have no competing interests to declare that are relevant to the content of this article.

References

1. ARM Limited: ARMv7-M Architecture Reference Manual (2021). document DDI 0403E.e
2. Bellard, F.: QEMU, a fast and portable dynamic translator. In: Usenix ATC, Freenix Track, pp. 41–46 (2005)
3. Clements, A.A., et al.: HALucinator: firmware re-hosting through abstraction layer emulation. In: USENIX Security (2020)
4. Dinesh, S., Burow, N., Xu, D., Payer, M.: RetroWrite: statically instrumenting cots binaries for fuzzing and sanitization. In: IEEE S&P (2020)
5. Feng, B., Mera, A., Lu, L.: P2IM: scalable and hardware-independent firmware testing via automatic peripheral interface modeling. In: 29th USENIX Security Symposium (USENIX Security 20), pp. 1237–1254 (2020)
6. Liu, J., Shen, Y., Xu, Y., Sun, H., Shi, H., Jiang, Y.: Effectively sanitizing embedded operating systems. In: Proceedings of the 61st ACM/IEEE Design Automation Conference, pp. 1–6 (2024)
7. National Security Agency: Ghidra software reverse engineering framework. https://ghidra-sre.org/ (2019). Accessed 12 June 2026
8. Nethercote, N., Seward, J.: Valgrind: a framework for heavyweight dynamic binary instrumentation. ACM Sigplan Not. **42**(6), 89–100 (2007)
9. Scharnowski, T., et al.: FuzzWare: using precise MMIO modeling for effective firmware fuzzing. In: 31st USENIX Security Symposium (USENIX Security 22), pp. 1239–1256 (2022)
10. Scharnowski, T., Wörner, S., Buchmann, F., Bars, N., Schloegel, M., Holz, T.: HOEDUR: Embedded firmware fuzzing using multi-stream inputs. In: Proceedings of the 32nd USENIX Conference on Security Symposium. p. articleno. 162. SEC '23, USENIX Association (2023)
11. Scharnowski, T., Wörner, S., Lu, R.: Hoedur experiments. https://github.com/fuzzware-fuzzer/hoedur-experiments (2023). Accessed 12 June 2026
12. Serebryany, K., Bruening, D., Potapenko, A., Vyukov, D.: AddressSanitizer: a fast address sanity checker. In: 2012 USENIX Annual Technical Conference (USENIX ATC 12), pp. 309–318 (2012)
13. Serebryany, K., Iskhodzhanov, T.: Threadsanitizer: data race detection in practice. In: Proceedings of the Workshop on Binary Instrumentation and Applications, WBIA (2009)
14. Stepanov, E., Serebryany, K.: MemorySanitizer: Fast detector of uninitialized memory use in C. In: IEEE/ACM International Symposium on Code Generation and Optimization (CGO), pp. 46–55 (2015)
15. Yang, S., Gao, Y., Kuang, B., Yang, Y., Fu, A.: DFirmSan: a lightweight dynamic memory sanitizer for Linux-based firmware. Comput. Sec. **155**, 104467 (2025)
16. Zalewski, M.: American Fuzzy Lop. http://lcamtuf.coredump.cx/afl/ (2017). Accessed 12 June 2026

Author Index

P. Kieseberg et al. (Eds.): ARES 2026 Workshops, LNCS 16903, pp. 677–679, 2027.
https://doi.org/10.1007/978-3-032-37218-5

Kolibri 360 GmbH
Ferdinand-Jühlke-Straße 7
99095 Erfurt, Deutschland
produktsicherheit@kolibri360.de